SEVENTEENTH-CENTURY
ECONOMIC DOCUMENTS

Seventeenth-Century Economic Documents

EDITED BY

JOAN THIRSK

Reader in Economic History in the University
of Oxford

and

J. P. COOPER

Fellow and Lecturer in Modern History,
Trinity College, Oxford

CLARENDON PRESS · OXFORD

1972

Oxford University Press, Ely House, London W.1

GLASGOW   NEW YORK   TORONTO   MELBOURNE   WELLINGTON
CAPE TOWN   IBADAN   NAIROBI   DAR ES SALAAM   LUSAKA   ADDIS ABABA
DELHI   BOMBAY   CALCUTTA   MADRAS   KARACHI   LAHORE   DACCA
KUALA LUMPUR   SINGAPORE   HONG KONG   TOKYO

PRINTED IN GREAT BRITAIN
BY WILLIAM CLOWES & SONS, LIMITED
LONDON, BECCLES AND COLCHESTER

PREFACE

THE remarkable growth of studies in the economic history of Tudor England owes much of its stimulus, directly or indirectly, to the publication in three volumes of *Tudor Economic Documents* by R. H. Tawney and Eileen Power in 1924. In many universities other than London for which they were originally designed, the sixteenth century became the subject of special study for undergraduates interested in economic history, and their work was centred upon these three wide-ranging volumes of original sources. These undergraduate courses inspired an interest in the period which led on later to postgraduate research in the same field.

By comparison the seventeenth century has been neglected. The documentary sources in print are scattered and unevenly distributed over the subject. Moreover, because of the paramount influence of political events on the century, economic historians have been persuaded to divide its economic history along the same lines, whereby the documents are still further fragmented and dispersed. The first period from 1600 to 1640 has become merged with the sixteenth century; the third period from 1660 to 1700 has been merged with the eighteenth century; and the economic developments of the twenty years between 1640 and 1660 have been allowed to lie for the most part shrouded in the dark shadows cast by political instability. Yet strong and continuous themes are woven into the fabric of economic developments and debates in the seventeenth century, which cannot be properly assessed and appreciated until we abandon the conventional tripartite division of these hundred years.

This volume of economic documents, therefore, spans the hundred years of the seventeenth century, and attempts to view it as a unified whole. It owes its existence to discussions in Oxford for improving the selection of sources used in one paper of the Final Honour School in Modern History on English economic history, 1485–1730. When the decision was taken to gather a new collection of seventeenth-century documents it soon became clear that we could not 'make do' with multiple sets of photocopies and typed transcripts. The selection needed, and, indeed, deserved, a longer life. And since it had a secondary propagandist purpose to encourage more research on seventeenth-century economic history, the collection required to be put in print. This the Clarendon Press willingly agreed to. It is to be hoped that this volume will serve generations of students as valiantly as *Tudor Economic Documents* have done for the last fifty years.

The selection of documents on economic history is notoriously difficult. Since generalizations depend upon the quantity as much as the quality of the evidence, no single document ever seems to be an adequate illustration: one wishes to print at least three documents saying much the same thing. More-over, the subject matter of economic history is large and its frontiers vague. The editor of a selection of sources could fill a dozen volumes far more easily than one. So the choice made here is unlikely wholly to satisfy anyone, but its aims have been those that would doubtless motivate all editors of a similar collection: to illustrate as many aspects of economic life as possible, and to indicate new paths for exploration as well as traversing old ones.

I have incurred many debts in the preparation of this volume. Colleagues and students have helped in the choice of documents, in transcribing some of them, and in commenting on the final selection. For their good counsel and ready assistance I would particularly like to thank Adrienne Batchelor, Dennis Baker, John Bennell, John Broad, John Chartres, Clyde Chitty, C. S. L. Davies, Peter Dickson, Richard Grassby, David Kiernan, David Palliser, Elizabeth Rainey, G. D. Ramsay, Roger Richardson, and Keith Thomas. I would also like to thank the many keepers of archives, who sent me photocopies of documents, answered other questions, and gave per-mission to print from their collections. My principal debt, however, is to John Cooper who has been my closest adviser throughout. He has been untiringly generous in his suggestions, comments, advice, and practical help. This choice of documents is as much his as mine.

JOAN THIRSK

January, 1971

CONTENTS

II. AGRICULTURE

CONTENTS ix

IV. INLAND AND COASTAL TRADE AND COMMUNICATIONS

VII. ALIENS

VIII. WEALTH, POPULATION, AND LAND: SOME CONTEMPORARY STATISTICS

ACKNOWLEDGEMENTS

THANKS are due to the following owners and keepers of manuscripts for permission to print documents: The Warden and Fellows of All Souls College, Oxford; the National Library of Australia, Canberra; the Bodleian Library, Oxford; the Trustees of the British Museum; Cambridge University Library; the Trustees of the Chatsworth Settlement; Cheshire Record Office; Exeter City Library; the Company of Weavers, Fullers, and Shearmen of Exeter; Mr. A. T. Foley, and the Herefordshire Record Office; City of Gloucester Public Library; Mr. J. Horridge; Kent Archives Office; Lancashire Record Office; London University Library; House of Lords Record Office; Messrs. Nevill, Druce, & Co. Ltd.; City of Plymouth Public Libraries; the Royal Society, London; His Grace the Duke of Rutland; the William Salt Library and Staffordshire Record Office; the Controller of H.M.S.O.; Ipswich and East Suffolk Record Office; and to the following authors and publishers for permission to reproduce printed material: Mr. W. J. Cameron and the University of Auckland; Dr. Patrick McGrath and the Bristol Record Society; Cambridge University Press; Miss Elizabeth Donnan and the Carnegie Institution of Washington; Mr. J. D. Marshall, Professor T. S. Willan, and the Chetham Society; Mr. J. P. Cooper and the Economic History Society; Prof. E. E. Rich and the Hudson's Bay Record Society; Mr. R. M. Lees and Messrs. Longman; the Johns Hopkins Press; Munksgaard of Copenhagen; Dr. J. Robey and the Peak District Mines Historical Society; Dr. G. D. Ramsay; Mr. John S. Roper; Prof. G. N. Clark, Prof. F. J. Fisher, Dr. G. E. Fussell and the Royal Historical Society; the John Rylands Library, Manchester; Mr. G. H. Kenyon and the Sussex Archaeological Society; Yale University Press; York City Library.

RULES OF TRANSCRIPTION

Some spelling has been modernized, but proper names have generally been left in the form in which they appear in the document.

Punctuation, capitalization, and italicization have been modernized.

Abbreviations in the original documents have been expanded where there is no doubt of their meaning.

—— signifies a blank in the original manuscript.

——[?] signifies an illegible word in the original manuscript.

[?] signifies that the preceding word in the original manuscript is illegible, and this is the suggested reading.

[??] signifies extreme doubt about the correct reading.

[   ] Words enclosed in square brackets consist of matter that is not in the original text but has been inserted by the editors to make grammatical sense or to elucidate the text.

... denotes the omission of passages that are in the original text.

Dates in the documents are set out as they appear in the original manuscript. The heading of each document, however, gives the date according to modern reckoning, starting the year 1 January.

Dates in the headings to documents which are given in brackets with a question mark are tentative dates suggested either by editors who have printed these documents before, or by the present editors.

B.M.   British Museum.
P.R.O.   Public Record Office.

I. ECONOMIC CRISES

1. A COMMONS DEBATE ON THE TRADE DEPRESSION, RECORDED BY JOHN PYM, 26 FEBRUARY, 1621

[W. Notestein, F. H. Relf, and H. Simpson, *Commons Debates, 1621*, New Haven, 1935, IV, pp. 104–6]

26 February 1621

SIR EDWIN SANDYS. The King commended to the consideration of this House the consideration of the scarcity of money. The causes and the remedy: The causes are matters of grief, the remedy matter of ease. There is besides great and pressing necessity of our entering into this business. The poor man's inheritance is his hands. Looms are laid down. Every loom maintains forty persons. To seek another inheritance is difficult. *Bellum Rusticorum* in Germany proceeded from this, that the poor wanted work. The farmer is not able to pay his rent, not for want of cattle or corn but money. The fairs and markets stand still. What then will be the case of the gentleman and nobleman? And if these be not able to support themselves, by whom will the merchant and tradesman be satisfied? No distemper is so pressing as the distemper of want. Therefore for a select committee, and he would contribute somewhat both to the discovery of the causes and the remedies.

The causes now alleged, besides those which were propounded the 6th of February, as before, were: (1) The loss by exchange because our money is better than theirs beyond sea. (2) Importation of Irish cattle, beef, and butter, which carrieth away 10,000*li.* per annum. (3) The excessive use of Spanish tobacco. The commodities we sent thither were wont to bring in bullion 100,000*li.* per annum, for which now there is no other return but in smoke. (4) The importation of foreign grain, which carrieth away our money and makes the price too low for the husbandman to live, it being against all policy of state that foreign commodities should be brought in till our own be spent. (5) The great expense in French wines, the impost is no more than it was in Queen Elizabeth's time, and it came then but to 15,000 and now it comes to 42,000. (6) The melting of coin. (7) The inequality in value betwixt gold and silver. (8) The increase of the gold-beater's trade by expense of gold foliat. (9) Transportation into Poland of 60,000*li.* per annum.

Other observations concerning this business were these: a computation was made of the plate wrought in the seven last years of the Queen and the

seven last years of the King. And less now than then. That twenty goldsmiths' shops in Cheapside are now to be let at one-third of the rents they
were wont to be let at, which is a sign that trade is decayed. Betwixt the
1 Eliz. and 16 Jacob. was coined in gold nine millions and one half. That
twelve millions were brought out of the Indies in the Queen's time. That
100,000*li.* hath been brought out of France in cobweb lawn and tiffanies.

All the reasons were reduced to three heads: (1) Impediment of importation. (2) Occasions of exportation. (3) Consumption within the kingdom.
And it was ordered to be handled weekly in a Committee of the whole house
upon Tuesday, that the merchants should attend and the Custom Books be
perused.

2. THE SAME COMMONS DEBATE RECORDED BY
SIR THOMAS WENTWORTH, 26 FEBRUARY, 1621

[Notestein, Relf, and Simpson, *Commons Debates, 1621*, V, pp. 490–3]

26 February 1621

THERE was a motion made, that the House should enter into debate according to his Majesty's pleasure, both of the causes and the remedies of the
want of money; that there was great necessity to enter into the consideration
thereof, looking into the estates and several possessions of persons in the
kingdom. First the case of the lowest, we should find, that they had the
inheritance of their hands taken from them through monopolies and restraint
of commerce, insomuch that in one place there were 200 looms laid down,
and each loom would have set on work 40 persons; these men by these means
turned out of their inheritance, which is their trades, and to seek new, which
is not only pitiful but fearful, lest, as in Germany, it should cause *Bellum
Rusticum.* The state of the husbandman likewise, that labours for other men,
is as lamentable, not that there is a want of corn or cattle, but that they
yielded no price, and that the fairs stood still. The gentlemen and noblemen
that could not maintain their estates but by their rents were not paid. The
merchant and tradesmen could get no ready money for their commodities,
but were forced to sell them of trust, which was occasion of a great mischief
in those professions.

It was further said, that whereas formerly there had been 23,000*l.* coined
yearly in silver, there was now not a penny. That there was more silver
melted into plate in the last seven years of Queen Elizabeth than in these last
seven years of his Majesty; that every third shop of goldsmiths in Cheapside
was shut up, that money was the measure of trade, that the want thereof
causeth cheapness of commodities.

The reasons assigned of the scarcity, were these; first, the standing of the
mint for eleven years now past, whereas in Queen Elizabeth's time there were

eight millions and an half coined from *primo* to *tricesimo nono* of her reign; the second, the loss of the exchange of Spanish Rials of eight, not being of equal worth as they are in other places, and therefore the low valuation of silver at the mint, by reason our standard was better than that of foreign parts, was the reason silver was not imported so as it was in other places; and that there was an agreement in Henry the Seventh's time with all the Princes in Christendom to make the standard equal. The third, melting of silver against the law. The fourth, the patent of gold foil, whereby a great deal of bullion was wasted. The fifth, the East India Company, which had licence to carry out 11,000*l.* by year. The sixth, the unequal balance of trade, the goods imported exceeding those that were exported, which would appear, and means to satisfy the House, not by discourse but by record, which was by examining the Custom Book, and to see what the merchants carried out and what they brought in. If that which they bring in be of more value than what they carry out, then the balance must needs be unequal, which would appear by demonstration. That in Queen Elizabeth's time, the Customs upon wines came but to 15,000*l.*, now they are 42,000*l.* and yet we do not export into those parts from whence we fetch our wines a third part so much as formerly we did. And here it was concluded, that the French Company was judged a seventh cause, in regard that all that trade was altogether driven with money and carried forth fourscore thousand pounds a year; yet it was urged, that it was not to be known by the values we set upon foreign commodities when they come hither, by reason the merchant buyeth them much cheaper than they make us pay. An eighth cause was the patent of gold and silver thread, which did waste 20,000*l.* of our coin, and stayed the importation of 20,000*l.* more in bullion brought in from Venice in that commodity; which patent to stop importation was against an Act of Parliament. A ninth reason was assigned to be the bringing in of Irish cattle, for which they transported money, and did not turn it into commodities, and it was affirmed the number of Irish cattle so brought into the kingdom were yearly 100,000 which were some of them worth twenty shillings, some worth forty shillings, and some worth three pounds. A tenth reason was the bringing in of Scottish cattle in like manner as out of Ireland, and carrying away nothing but money, it being said, the victual always takes away money. An eleventh reason was transportation of money into Polonia for corn. A twelfth, consumption of coin within the kingdom. A thirteenth, that those commodities which came into the kingdom formerly for cloth, now comes for money. A fourteenth, the great quantities of Spanish tobacco, which the merchant bringeth out of Spain, where formerly he used to bring money. For a fifteenth, some were of opinion, that the withdrawing of the Dutch merchants was the cause of this sudden damp.

3. COMMONS DEBATE ON THE DEPRESSION, RECORDED BY JOHN PYM, 17 MAY 1621

[Notestein, Relf, and Simpson, *Commons Debates, 1621*, IV, pp. 357–9]

17 May 1621

SIR GEORGE MANNORS reported the Bill against importation of foreign grain, etc., which upon the first commitment endured much debate and was therefore recommitted, and could not yet be so cleared but that occasion was left for divers objections for the rejection and propositions for the amendment of the Bill. All which, with the answers, though propounded at several times, are here together inserted.

The reasons upon which that law was grounded were these: (1) The increase of coin [=corn] exportation brings in money, restraint of importation stays money. It was affirmed by Mr. Alphard that in his county 30,000*l.* was received yearly for corn exported. (2) The low price of corn, causing a decay of rent and discouragement of husbandry. (3) The drift and scope of law agreeable to the wisdom of the Parliament 3 Ed. 4, [i.e. c. 2] wherein the like restraint was made, but that the limitation of prizes suitable to that time are not fit for this.

Objections against the Bill: (1) That it seems to be against free trade, and if we forbid the commodities of other countries we must expect the prohibition of ours with them. (2) It argues unthankfulness to God to be discontented at the cheapness of that which is one of the greatest blessings. (3) Will hurt the poor two ways, (*1*) by increasing their charge, rye is the food of the poor and there are forty buyers to one seller, (*2*) by diminishing their relief, it cannot choose but hinder charity when that is made worth a penny which would not be worth a half penny. (4) That native commodities should be cheap within the realm and dear in the exportation is never good for the State. (5) The disability of some parts of the kingdom to supply themselves with corn; Devonshire hath disbursed 120,000*l.* in a year for foreign grain, 10,000 quarters in a week are spent in London only. (6) That it will overthrow a third part of the trade into Poland and other eastern countries, where 30,000 cloths are yearly vented, and the return most in white rye, for money is there so base that a merchant cannot transport from thence without 40 in the 100*l.* loss. (7) It will monopolize the trade to the Low Countries, who have ever great provision in their granaries, and if corn should chance to rise here will furnish us much sooner than we can send into the East Country, and thereby will drain away all our money. (8) If wool and cloth be nine-tenths of the trade of the kingdom, the setting the poor awork doth not depend so much upon tillage as upon other manufactures. We that sit here do few of us buy our own corn, but we serve most of us for towns who may think that we have made this Bill for our own profit and to their undoing. (9) It is not so much the plenty of corn which causeth this cheapness as the want of money.

Some things were spoken by way of reply to these objections: the husbandman beareth the greatest burthen of the commonwealth, and yet the present state of things are nothing indifferent betwixt them and other tradesmen, for the commodities of the country yield very little and other manufactures hold the same rate or greater. By this course London is like to swell and the greatest part of the kingdom to decay. As for the northern and western parts, which oppose this Bill, they have coals and tin and other means to make money. But the middle countries, which are the greatest part, have nothing but corn wherewith to furnish themselves with such things as they want.

The propositions for the amendment of the Bill were these: (1) That there may be inserted a clause of repeal of the statute 39 Eliz. [i.e. c. 2] for the conversion of pasture grounds into tillage, which is now of no use but for promoters. (2) The penalty to be moderated because the price may alter betwixt the time the merchant sends for corn and the time of bringing it into the port. (3) To provide for the abuse of customers who use to stay the exportation of corn, though it be within price limited by the law. (4) That such ships may not be within the penalty of the law as by foul weather are driven into English ports and cannot relieve themselves without selling of corn. (5) It was moved by some that the restraint of importation should be limited only to strangers, because the inconveniencies grew from them. Others would not have strangers barred, but limited by a greater price. A third sort would have the first part of the Bill wholly taken away, which concerned importation, and the second part touching storehouse and granary to be left, and that every man may buy when corn is under a certain price without danger of the laws against engrossing.

But because out of so many differences no good resolution could be composed, the bill was again recommitted.

4. LIONEL CRANFIELD'S NOTES FOR A SPEECH TO PARLIAMENT, NOVEMBER 1621

[Notestein, Relf, and Simpson, *Commons Debates, 1621*, VII, pp. 617–19]

Notes for Parliament, 20 November 1621

WHETHER ever the people of England lived eighteen years together in such peace and plenty and with so little charge to their King as they have done since his Majesty's reign.

The staple commodities of the kingdom, viz. wool, corn, yea, and even land itself hath been improved one third part at the least since his Majesty's reign and hath so continued all his Highness's reign until this last two years.

The trade of the kingdom increased one third at the least if not doubled since his Majesty's reign until this last two years.

The people notwithstanding all this improvement to their estates never since the Conquest gave so little to their King in eighteen years as they have done to his Majesty.

But that which his Majesty is most sensible of these benefits of his Highness's reign are so far from being thankfully acknowledged as some make use of them to his prejudice. For wool and corn by reason of plenty and some foreign accidents being within these two years fallen in price, and trade by like foreign occasions of late being somewhat decline and yet all of them in more flourishing estate than when his Majesty came to the Crown, the murmuring and grudging of some ill affected against the present government is such as would grieve any honest man to hear.

The general cry is of the poverty of the people. If eighteen years with a flourishing trade and one third part improvement of all the staple commodities of the kingdom for so long time together will not make the people rich, they have strangely abused God's blessing under his Majesty's government . . .

Whether the seminaries of learning, viz. the two universities and all other public schools and all houses of charity were ever more countenanced or better protected. Whether the navy of the kingdom was ever in that glory, strength, and readiness as at present. Whether Scotland heretofore a doubtful friend and often a mighty and fearful enemy be not now secured to us by being made one with us and that in his Majesty's person only.

Whether Ireland which his Majesty found all in combustion, the place that exhausted the treasure of the kingdom, the stage upon which many brave English spirits spent their blood, be not by his Majesty not only settled in peace and civilized, but reduced unto that flourishing estate as we begin to fear and complain it will prove an undermining neighbour, it being now not only able to sustain itself by reason of the peace that it enjoys but to afford to us such plenty of corn, cattle, and wool that we propound to make laws to prevent the inconvenience which this kingdom may suffer.

O happy exchange! And which may not be forgotten that land which was not worth 400*l.* when his Majesty came to the Crown is now worth 4,000*l.* so that it may be truly said the land in Ireland is improved not one in ten, but ten in one and the land in England one third part since his Majesty's reign.

5. SIR THOMAS CULPEPPER'S *TRACT AGAINST USURY*, 1621

[Sir Thomas Culpepper, *A Tract against Usurie, presented to the High Court of Parliament*, London, 1621]

TO LEAVE the proofs of the unlawfulness of usury to divines, wherein a number, as well Protestants as Papists, have learnedly written; here is only set down some arguments to show how great the hurt is it doth to this kingdom which hath no gold nor silver mines, but plenty of commodities, and many and great advantages of trade to which the high rate of usury is a great prejudice and decay.

For proof, how much the high rate of usury decays trade: we see that generally all merchants, when they have gotten any great wealth, leave trading and fall to usury, the gain thereof being so easy, certain, and great; whereas in other countries, where usury is at a lower rate, and thereby lands dearer to purchase, they continue merchants from generation to generation to enrich themselves and the State.

Neither are they rich tradesmen only that give over trading, but a number of beginners are undone or discouraged by the high rate of usury, their industry serving but to enrich others, and beggar themselves.

We also see many trades themselves much decayed, because they will not afford so great a gain as ten in the hundred; whereas if the rate of usury were not higher here than in other countries, they had still subsisted and flourished, and perhaps with as much advantage to the public, as those that do bring more to the private adventurers.

Yet are not those the greatest hindrances the high rate of money brings to trade; our greatest disadvantage is that other nations, especially our industrious neighbours the Dutch, are therein wiser than we; for with them, and so in most countries with whom we hold commerce, there is not any use for money tolerated above the rate of six in the hundred. Whereby it must of necessity come to pass, though they have no other advantages of industry and frugality, that they must out-trade us; for if they make return of ten *per centum*, they almost double the use allowed, and so make a very gainful trade. But with us, where ten in the hundred is so current, it is otherwise; for if we make not above ten, we are losers, and consequently the same trade being with them and us equally good for the public, is to the private adventurers loss-full with us, with them very gainful. And where the good of the public and private men's go not together, the public is seldom greatly advanced.

And as they out-trade, so they may afford to undersell us in the fruits of the earth, which are equally natural to our and their lands, as to our great shame we see our neighbours the Dutch do, even in our own country; for in most commodities the earth brings forth, the stock employed in planting and managing of them makes a great (in many the greatest) part of their price; and consequently, their stock with them being rated at six in the hundred, they may with great gain undersell us, our stock with us being rated at ten.

And as they may out-trade us and undersell us, so are all contributions to the war, works of piety, and glory of the state, cheaper to them than to us; for the use for money going with us near double the rate it doth in other countries, the giving the same sum must needs be double the charge to us, it is to them. Amongst other things which the King with so much wisdom delivered to the House of Parliament, he committed to their consideration the balancing of trade and commerce, wherein there is nothing of greater consequence than the rate of usury, which holds no proportion with us and other nations, to our disadvantage, as by experience we see and feel.

Neither is the high rate of usury less hurtful to commerce within the land, the gain by usury being so easy, certain, and extreme great, as they are not only merchants and tradesmen, but landed men, farmers, and men of profession that grow lazy in their professions, and become usurers; for the rate of usury is the measure by which all men trade, purchase, build, plant, or any other ways bargain.

It hath been the wisdom and care of former Parliaments to provide for the preservation of wood and timber; for which there is nothing more available than the calling down of the high rate of usury; for as the rate of money now goeth, no man can let his timber stand, nor his wood grow to such year's growth as is best for the commonwealth, but it will be very loss-full to him, the stock of the woods, after they are worth forty or fifty shillings the acre, growing faster at ten in the hundred than the woods themselves do. And for shipping, which is the strength and safety of this land, I have heard divers merchants of good credit say, that if they would build a ship, and let it to any other to employ, they cannot make of their money that way, counting all charges, tear and wear, above ten or twelve in the hundred, which can be no gainful trade, money itself going at ten in the hundred. But in the Low Countries, where money goeth at six, the building of ships, and hiring them to others is a gainful trade; and so the stock of rich men and the industry of beginners are well joined for the public.

And yet that which is above all the rest the greatest sin against the land is that it makes the land itself of small value, nearer the rate of new-found lands, than of any other country, where laws, government, and peace, have so long flourished. For the high rate of usury makes land sell so cheap; and the cheap sale of land is the cause men seek no more by industry and cost to improve them; and this is plain both by example and demonstration, for we see in other countries, where the use of money is of a low rate, lands are generally sold for 30, 40, in some for 50 years' purchase. And we know by the rule of bargaining that if the rate of use were not greater here than in other countries, lands were then as good a pennyworth, at twenty years' purchase, as they are now at sixteen. For lands being the best assurance and securest inheritance will still bear a rate above money. Now if lands were at thirty years' purchase, or near it, there were no so cheap purchase as the amendment of our own lands, for it would be much cheaper to make one acre of land, now worth five shillings by the year, to be worth ten shillings, or being worth ten to be worth twenty shillings, and so in proportion, than to purchase another acre worth five or ten shillings. And in every acre thus purchased to the owner, by the amendment of his own, there were another purchased to the commonwealth . . . Then would all the wet lands in this kingdom soon be drained, the barren lands mended by marl, sleech, lime, chalk, sea-sand, and other means, which for their profit, men's industry would find out. We see with how great industry and charge our neighbours, the Dutch, do drain and maintain their lands against the sea which floweth higher above them, than it doth above the lowest parts of our drowned lands. I will admit a great deal to their industry, but I should very unwillingly grant that they are so much more ingenious and industrious than we, as that all the odds were therein. Certainly, the main cause of it is that with us money is dear, and land cheap, with them lands dear, and money cheap; and consequently the improvement of their lands at so great a charge with them is gainful to the owners, which with us would be loss-full; for usury going at ten in the hundred, if a man borrow five pounds, and bestow it on an acre of ground, the amendment stands him in ten shillings the year; and being amended, the land is not worth above fifteen years' purchase. But if the use of money went at no more with us than in other places, then five pound bestowed upon an acre of ground would stand a man but in five or six shillings a year, and the acre of land so amended would be worth, as hath been shewed, six and twenty or thirty years' purchase. Whereby it appeareth that as the rate of use now goeth, no man (but where the land lieth extraordinarily happily for it) can amend his land, but to his own loss; whereas if money were let as it is in other countries, he might bestow more than double so much as now he may, and yet be a great gainer thereby; and consequently, as was before remembered, should to his own benefit purchase land to the common-wealth.

Neither would such purchase of land to the commonwealth be the benefit to the landed men only; the benefit would be as much to the poor labourers of the land. For now when corn and other fruits of the land which grow by labour are cheap, the plough and mattock are cast into the hedge, there is little work for poor men, and that at a low rate, whereas if the mendment of their own lands were the cheapest purchase to the owner, if there were many more people than there are, they should readily set awork, at better rates than they now are, and none that had their health and limbs could be poor, but by their extremest laziness.

And as the high rate of usury doth imbase land, so it is as great a hindrance to discoveries, plantations, and all good undertakings, making it near double as chargeable to the adventurers (money being at ten in the hundred), as it is in other countries, where the use of money is so much lower . . .

The objections likely to be made against the calling down of money are first, that general objection of ignorance against all changes, be they never so necessary and apparently good, that it hath been so a long time, and been well enough; what will become of the alteration, we cannot tell, why then should we make any change?

Secondly, that as in bodies natural, so in politic, great and sudden changes are most commonly dangerous.

Thirdly, that money will be suddenly called in, and so all borrowers greatly prejudiced.

Fourthly, that money will be harder to come by, and thereby commerce greatly hindered.

Lastly, that much money of foreigners, by reason of the high rate of usury, is brought over here to be managed at interest, which would be carried away again, if the rate of usury should be called down.

To the first, that money hath long gone at ten, and things been well enough.

It is answered, that it is not long that the practice of usury hath been so generally used, without any sense or scruple of the unlawfulness of it; for men's consciences were hardened to it, with example and custom, by degrees, and not upon the sudden. And as the beginning of many dangerous diseases in healthful bodies, so the beginning of many inconveniences in a state, are not presently felt. With us, after that with long civil wars the land was half unpeopled, so as till of late years, it came not to his full stock of people again, there being the same quantity of land to half the number of people, the surplusage of our inland commodities must needs be so great, that though trade were not equally balanced with us and other nations, we could not but grow rich. Beside, France and the Low Countries were for many years half laid waste with wars, and so did trade but little, nor manage their own lands to their best advantage, whereby they did not only not take the trade and market from us, which now they do, but they themselves were fed and clothed by us, and took our commodities from us at great high rates. Whereas now we see the Dutch do everywhere out-trade us, and the French feed us with their corn, even in plentiful years. So as now our land being full stocked with people, our neighbours industrious and subtle in trade, if we do not more equally balance trade and bring to pass, that we may afford the fruits of our land as cheap as other countries afford the same of the same kind, we must (though we leave a number of our superfluities) as (God forbid but we should) in a short time grow poor and beggarly...

And this we see and feel too well by experience at this present; for having a great surplusage of corn, we can find no vent for it; the French with their own, the Dutch with the corn of Poland, everywhere supplying the markets at cheaper rates than we can afford it. And even our clothes which have hitherto been the golden mine in England, I have heard many merchants say, that (except it be in some few of the finest sort of them, which is a riches peculiar to this nation) other countries begin to make them of their own wool, and by affording them cheaper than we may, so to take our markets from us.

And this I hope may in part serve for answer to the next objection that all great and sudden changes are commonly dangerous; for that rule holds true, where the body natural or politic is in perfect state of health, but where there is a declining (as I have some cause to fear there is or may soon be with us) there to make no alteration is a certain way to ruin.

To the third that money will be suddenly called in, and so all borrowers greatly prejudiced; for that there may be a clause in the end of the statute whensoever it shall be made that it shall be lawful for all that have lent money at ten in the hundred, which is now forborne and owing, to take for such money so lent and owing, during two years after this Session of Parliament, such use as they might have done if this Act had not been made. Whereby borrowers shall be in less danger of sudden calling in of their money than now they are; for where the lenders upon continuance of their old security may take ten in the hundred; upon new security they must be content with less, so the calling in of their money will be to their own prejudice.

And if there be any borrower to whom this giveth not sufficient satisfaction, if such borrower have lands of value to pay his debt, the worst condition he can fear is to have at the least twenty years' purchase for his land, wherewith to clear his debts; for, as I said before, land being the best security, and securest inheritance, will still bear a rate above money. And so there being no use allowed for money above the rate tolerated in other countries, land will as readily sell at twenty years' purchase, as it doth now at twelve. And I think there is no borrower that hath land of value to pay his debts doth doubt if he will now sell his land at ten years' purchase, he might soon be out of debt.

To the fourth objection, that money will be hard to be borrowed, and so commerce hindered: I answer, that it were true, if the high rate of usury did increase money within this land; but the high rate of usury doth enrich only the usurer, and impoverish the kingdom, as hath been shewed; and it is the plenty of money within the land that maketh money easy to be borrowed, as we see by the examples of other countries, where money is easier to be borrowed than it is with us, and yet the rate tolerated; for use is little more then half so much. It is the high rate of use that undoeth so many of the gentry of the land, which maketh the number of borrowers so great, and the number of borrowers must of necessity make money the harder to be borrowed, whereas if use for money were at a lower rate, land, as hath been shewed, would be much quicker to be sold, and at dearer rates, and so the nobility and gentry would soon be out of debt, and consequently the fewer borrowers, and so to tradesmen and merchants money easy to be had . . .

To the last and weakest of objections that there is now much money of foreigners in the land to be managed at ten in the hundred, which, if money should be called down, would be carried out of the land, there is no doubt it is true. But I desire to know whether any man think it better for the state that they should now carry out one hundred pounds, or seven years hence, two; or fourteen years hence, four, or one and twenty years hence, eight; for so in effect upon the multiplying of interest, they do . . .

Besides, we must not conceive that the money of foreigners, which is here managed at usury, is brought into the land in ready coin or bullion; the course is that merchants send over bills of exchange to their factors, for which they receive our money here; and this is the money they manage at interest, and so they eat us out with our own monies. The old comparison, which compares usury to the butler's box, deserves to be remembered. Whilst men are at play, they feel not what they give to the box, but at the end of Christmas it makes all or near all gamesters losers; and I fear the comparison holds thus much farther that there is as few escape that continue in usury, as that continue gamesters; a man may play once or twice and leave a winner, but the use of it is seldom without ruin.

Now because I know men's private interests doth many times blind their judgements, and lest any may be tempted for their own, against the public good, I will desire them to remember that, if they have lands as well as money, that what they lose in their money they shall get it in their land; for land and money are ever in balance one against the other, and where money is dear, land is cheap; and where money is cheap, land is dear.

And if there be any yet so hearty a well-wisher to ten in the hundred as that he still think it fit to be continued, my wish is that he and his posterity may have the privilege to borrow, but not to lend at that rate . . .

6. THE CAUSES OF WANT OF MONEY IN ENGLAND AND WALES, 1621

[B.M., Add. MS. 34, 324, f. 181]

Causes of Want of Money in England and Wales, 3 Junii, 1621 [Endorsement]

1. High rate of the mint here.
2. Not executing the Statute of Employment.
3. Return of tobacco from Spain, which wont to be 100,000*li*. in money.
4. The proclamation that no foreign coin shall be current here.
5. The exportation of money to Ireland, Scotland, foreign parts, to France for wines, to the East Indies for spices, and to Germany and the Low Countries for corn, by tricks of exchange and through the over weight or over fineness of our monies, to Ireland for cattle.
6. The restraint of free trade.
7. The inequality of our gold and silver.
8. The pretermitted customs.
9. The want of importation of silver and gold from Spain and Indies, of gold from Barbary and of silver from Germany all which came within these twenty years past and less in great abundance.
10. The consumption of gold and silver in England in gilding and silvering of beds, houses, swords, stools, chairs, etc.
11. The turning of money into plate.
12. The charges of Merchant Adventurers upon English cloth at home and abroad.
13. The want of vent of English cloths at home and abroad, at home for want of wearing cloth, abroad both in respect of our cloths not well made as in former times or not well dyed, and in regard of the great clothing in foreign parts at this present which maketh our cloths less needed or much now undersold.

14. The importation of foreign commodities surmounting the exportation of our home and native commodities by many thousands yearly causeth the want of so much money at the least as that surplusage and excess amounteth unto, which hath been reported by some officers of trust to be of late about 300,000*li.* sterling in one year.

7. SUGGESTIONS FOR THE RELIEF OF THE CLOTH TRADE, *c.* 1621

[B.M. Add. MS. 34, 324, f. 25]

The Helps and Means of Relief in the Trade of Clothing

1. That there may be more merchants both to buy and to transport cloth beyond the seas.

2. That the patents for dyeing stuff may be called in.

3. That the wool and fullers earth of this kingdom be carried by land carriage only, saving that the clothiers of Suffolk and Essex may have licence to transport 100 tun of fullers earth apiece yearly from Maidstone into their shires, the said clothiers coming themselves to buy it and giving security safely to deliver it into their said counties, and the mayor of Maidstone at their charges appointing a man to see the same shipped in such barks as the clothiers themselves shall hire, and in none other.

4. That the Staplers may not buy any wool in these shires where the clothiers dwell and make cloth.

5. That the Staplers may fetch in the wool out of Scotland, and Ireland, and of the Isle of Man, and of the Isle of Wight, and that it may be delivered at the water's side by weight and the weight thereof set upon their sacks and there to take their cocket into what part of this kingdom they will have it brought.

6. That there may be not only searchers but researchers appointed in all parts of this kingdom along the water's side to see that no wool or fullers earth be carried any way by sea, for that considering the small quantity of cloth which hath been made this seven years in respect of the former times, there should be three years' wool in this kingdom, and it is supposed that there is not sufficient to set the poor on work for six months if cloth should be made as it hath been in times past when there was 100,000 cloths vented in one year, and now there is vented but only 36,000 and there is now more people than was heretofore.

7. That if any man have sold his wool or fullers earth and it be suspected that it be carried away by sea, that he may be called before an officer to certify to whom he hath sold it.

8. And that every country cloth may be known by a several list for that Northern cloth having Kentish list is often times sold for Kentish cloth to the great discredit of the said Kentish cloth and the buyer thereby deceived.

9. That some speedy order may be taken for the relief of the poor who are like to perish for lack of work, having no other means to maintain themselves and their families.

All these being duly reformed, there is great hope that clothing will flourish again which hath maintained more (when clothing was good and commodities cheap) than all the trades in this kingdom besides.

8. THE CLOTHIERS' PLAN FOR THE IMPROVEMENT OF TRADE, MAY 1622

[Belvoir MSS. Letters, vol. XVI, f. 194]

THE remedies which we suppose will prove effectual for the quickening and repairing of our trade, and which we in all humble manner do desire to obtain are these that follow:

1. We desire that there may be liberty of trade granted to all his Majesty's loving subjects to buy and vent any woollen cloth into any foreign parts beyond the seas, or that the ancient and hereditary right of shipping cloth may be restored unto the merchants of the Staple, and that it may be lawful for any man to come into their company upon such rates as have been anciently allowed.

2. That his Majesty with the advice of the right honourable the Lords of his Majesty's Privy Council would be pleased to sweep away all unnecessary charges imposed upon our cloth, after it is made, whether by his Majesty by pretermitted customs, piracy, licence money, etc., or by the States of Holland and the Archduke beyond the seas for consumption money, excise, and other payments so far forth as by treaty or other means better known to their lordships it may be brought to pass.

3. That under the severest punishment his Majesty will be pleased to forbid the exportation of wools, wool fells, fulling earth, and wood ashes out of England, Scotland, Wales, and Ireland into any foreign parts beyond the seas, and the wools of Scotland, Ireland, and Wales to be shipped but over into England, and that no wools, wool fells, yarn, fulling earth, and oad ashes may be shipped from one port to another, except out of the Isle of Wight and the Isle of Man into the mainland, and that the wools which are laden out of Ireland, Wales, and Scotland into England should be entered and received by weight.

4. That the patent of Guinea wood alias red wood lately granted with all other patents granted upon dyeing stuffs, whereby the price of that commodity is raised to an excessive rate, may be called in, which only enricheth the patentees and is a general hindrance to the commonwealth.

5. For the preservation of the coin and bullion of the kingdom, which by reason of the shipping of Spanish ryals by the East India Company is exhausted and consumed, his Majesty would be pleased to dissolve that company which hath occasioned (in manner) a suspension of his mint.

6. Lastly, we desire that his Majesty would be pleased to enjoin the solemnities of funerals to be performed in cloth and stuffs made of wool within the kingdom.

It is not unknown to this honourable table, and we remember that we received it from your own mouths, that of so many thousands of cloths which in Queen Elizabeth's days have been shipped out of this kingdom two-third parts through the kingdom are now wholly lost. Now we desire your honours to understand that there is no one cloth but doth employ a great number of poor people in their labour, by which labour of theirs not only themselves but their children, some of them perchance being young or sick (and so unable to sustain themselves) so that the livelihood of so many thousands being taken from them, we leave it to your honourable discretions to consider how difficult a thing will be like to be to contain them from mutiny and rebellion. True it is that we have long laboured against the stream and some have strained themselves to the height of their estates, perchance so far as their credit and reputation can extend, so that if they fail to go further it is for want of breath, which we thought good to signify unto your honours, and thereby to express our utter disability to proceed without speedy reformation. The desire both to relieve our poor and preserve our country's peace have pricked us on, though more slackly than before we have done, to continue trading, which hath in some measure contained the poor, though in some want, from greater insolency, but now being come to the pinch of extremity and want we fear that bare words will scarce prevail to afford them satisfaction. Wherefore we do in all humble manner implore your honourable favour to intercede to his Majesty in their behalfs that he would vouchsafe to take the consideration of their miseries into his royal thoughts and out of princely compassion to commiserate their calamities by affording (if it may be) some timely reformation, and especially considering that the necessities of the poor [have] been so great and have already enforced them to be so insolent that they have presumed (though we have done our best endeavours to repress them) to seize upon men's corn from the market, to commit many robberies both by day and night, and yet protesting their unwillingness thereunto, but that extremities of miseries did enforce them and that they would gladly content themselves to work for bread were it never so coarse, although they had no other sustenance allowed them, and we believe that this truly proceeding from his Majesty's gracious care for the preservation of his people hath restrained them from many mischiefs, which if in some measure it answer not their expectations (will be we fear) out of the compass of our power to prevent, which makes us afraid to return into our own countries without hopes of sudden reformation.

[Endorsed:] April and May 1622. Remedies proposed by the clothiers for their grievances unto the Commissioners.

9. THE CLOTHIERS GRANTED FREEDOM OF TRADE IN NORTH-EAST EUROPE, MAY 1622

[R. W. K. Hinton, *The Eastland Trade and the Commonweal in the Seventeenth Century*, Cambridge, 1959, p. 174]

ACT OF THE PRIVY COUNCIL, 17 May 1622

WHEREAS upon a petition lately presented to the Board by the clothiers of the county of Suffolk and Essex complaining that they were disabled from going forward in their trade by reason of the great quantity of cloths lying upon their hands for which they could find no utterance or vent, it was thought meet that if the Eastland merchants did not forthwith buy off their cloths, the clothiers themselves should have free liberty, as was then desired, to ship forth their cloths into foreign parts, so as they carry them to the said markets and places of residence used by the said merchants; it was accordingly this day ordered that in case the Eastland merchants have not bought up the cloths, but that the market is still clogged therewithal to the prejudice and decay of trade, the Lord High Treasurer of England do give order to the officers of the ports to permit the said clothiers to ship and transport their cloth into foreign parts, as aforesaid, without let or interruption.

10. INSTRUCTIONS TO THE COMMISSION ON TRADE, OCTOBER 1622

[*Rymer's Foedera*, XVII, pp. 410–15]

JAMES, by the Grace of God, etc., to our right trusty and right well-beloved Cousin and Counsellor, Henry Viscount Mandeville, Lord President of our Privy Council, our right trusty and right well beloved cousin, William Earl of Northampton, Lord President of our Council within the Principality and Marches of Wales, etc.

Gentlemen, greeting.

Whereas we have understood, by the general complaints of our loving subjects from all the parts of this our realm of England, as also by information from our ministers employed in parts beyond the seas, that the cloth of this kingdom hath of late years wanted that estimation and vent in foreign parts which formerly it had, and that the wools of this kingdom have and are fallen much from their wonted values, and trade in general to be so far out of frame, that the merchants and clothiers of this kingdom are greatly discouraged, so that great numbers of people employed by them, and depending on them, want work, the best means of their livelihood, the landlords fail in their rents and revenues wherewith to maintain their ordinary charges, and the farmers have not so good means whereby to raise their rents as heretofore they had, and ourself also find the defects thereof by the decay of our customs and other duties, and generally the whole commonwealth suffereth, so as it is high time to look into the cause of this great decay of trade and the commodities of this our kingdom, as also how to have fit remedies applied for the restoring the same to their former flourishing estate.

And whereas we, out of princely care by all good means to encourage our people in their honest and industrious courses, and to advance the welfare and wealth of our kingdoms and dominions, have often and seriously considered with ourself, and advised with our Privy Council, of the best means how to redress the many inconveniences which these things draw upon our state, for which purpose, by the advice of our Privy Council, we first made choice of twelve persons, to whose care we especially recommended these things by way of preparation for after remedies to be thought of and resolved upon; which committee having spent many days in this important service, and having had many conferences, according to our directions given unto them, with many knights and gentlemen of quality of divers counties of this realm, with merchants of several companies and societies, with the clothiers of several clothing shires, and divers others of understanding and experience, at last returned unto us and our Privy Council a certificate in writing of their opinions touching the premises.

Whereupon we, by the advice of our Privy Council, did presently by our royal proclamation enter into a way of reformation of some things which for the present we could do; but because we found that the matters worthy of deliberate consideration in this so great and weighty a work are very many, and that the occurrents of trade are variable, and must be directed and governed as times and occasions shall serve or do vary, and that it is impossible to foresee what may be the future event of these things, or to set down such constant rules for trade as shall not require an addition or alteration upon just reasons and grounds.

We have, therefore, by the like advice of our Privy Council, thought fit and resolved to have a standing commission for these causes, and to make choice of a convenient number of persons of quality, understanding, experience, and judgement, to be our commissioners, to whose judgement, industry, and care we might commit the further searching out and better discerning of the true causes of the decay of trade, and the finding out of fit and convenient remedies to be applied for the same; and that after they shall have with mature deliberation prepared the same, they might from time to time certify us and the body of our Privy Council of their opinion, to the end that thereupon we might give such order for remedies herein as may be for our own honour and the wealth and prosperity of our people.

Know ye, therefore, that we, reposing great trust and confidence in your wisdoms, integrities, and good discretions, have authorized and appointed, and by these presents do authorize and appoint you to be our Commissioners, and by these presents do give unto you, or any six or more of you (the said Henry Viscount Mandeville Lord President of our Privy Council,

Fulk Lord Broke, Sir John Suckling, Sir George Calvert, our Principal Secretary, and Sir Julius Caesar, Master of the Rolls, we will always to be one) full power and authority, from time to time, to take into your considerations and cares the causes aforesaid, with these particular articles following.

First, what are the true causes why the wools of this our kingdom of England are so much fallen from their wonted values? And to consider what are the most probable means to raise them again to their former price and estimation?

Secondly, to advise of the best means how to prevent the transportation of wools, wool fells, woollen yarn, fullers earth, and wood ashes of this our kingdom of England, into foreign parts, into our kingdoms of Scotland or Ireland, and how the offenders, contrary to our royal proclamation lately made in that behalf, may be discovered and punished? how the wools of our kingdom of Ireland, not draped there for the necessary use of the inhabitants of that our kingdom, or for merchandize, if they shall hereafter so employ the same, may most commodiously be transported or brought into this realm of England, and here from time to time be bought up at reasonable and fit prices, and be here employed? how the wools of our kingdom of Scotland not there draped, may also be brought into England, and here usually sold and converted into the draperies of this kingdom, that so all parts of our dominions may mutually be helpful one to another, and further each others' common good?

And lest the drawing of so great quantities of wool from all parts of our dominions into this our realm of England, and the great quantities of wools of the proper growth of this realm, might bring so great a glut of woollen to this our realm, as that our people shall not be able profitably to convert the same into cloth and other manufactures, and so our plenty of so royal a commodity might vilify the same; we would have you to consider advisedly whether there will be in truth any such excess of quantity, and if there be, or by this means shall be, how the inconvenience which may grow thereby may be best prevented or avoided? That ye take into your special care how and by what means the wools of these kingdoms and dominions may be converted and better employed unto the making of cloth and stuffs and other manufactures to the best profit and advantage? And the ways and means how the cloth and stuff made of wool may be well and truly made, dyed, and dressed, that so they may recover that ancient estimation in foreign parts which by ill and deceitful making, dyeing, and dressing they have of late years lost.

And because there are now many laws in force concerning the making of cloth, which for their number and contradiction do perplex and entangle the makers of cloth, and makes it hard to be discerned what the law is in many particulars; we would have you to collect and observe those laws which are most convenient and fit for the present times, to the end that those may be specially commanded to be observed, and that such laws which are less fit for the times may be spared from execution, that they entangle not our people, and this to be observed until, at a convenient opportunity, one clear and fit law may be made in this case, and all former laws which admit contradiction or doubtful interpretation may be repealed.

And whereas there is yet no Statute Law made directing the true making and dressing of the stuffs known by the names of the New Draperies, our will and pleasure is, that until by law they may likewise be regulated, that ye conceive and set down some fit and convenient rules and orders, whereby the true and substantial making and dressing of them may be enjoined to all the makers and workers thereof, because it is found by experience that the sleight and deceitful making of those stuffs hath brought them out of request, and exceedingly hindered their sales in foreign parts where they were in good estimation, and would have increased much more if the false making of them had not brought them into discredit.

And that when good rules and orders shall be conceived and set down for the making, dyeing, and dressing of cloth and stuffs made of wool, that you foresee also the best and most probable ways how those rules and orders may be put into a due and constant execution, and that those which shall be trusted therewith be of such abilities and skill, as that they can, and of such integrity and honesty, as that they will, diligently and faithfully perform that which shall be committed in trust to them.

And whereas the broggers and jobbers of wools are in some places complained of, as a means to raise the prices of wool, and to falsify the same by unhonest mixtures, by their interposing before it come to the hands of the clothier and weaver who converteth the same, and in some other places they are desired to be continued as necessary instruments to convey wools by smaller quantities to such weavers or clothiers as cannot conveniently furnish themselves immediately from the grower, so as they do not falsify their wools before they sell them again, we would have you to take into your considerations, whether there be any good use at all to be made of those jobbers or broggers of wool; and if there be, then to consider in what places and under what conditions they are to be continued?

And because the prices of dyed cloths may be much enhanced by the dearness of the dyes, although the values of wools be not raised, we will you to enquire into the causes how dyeing stuffs become dear, either upon patents of privilege obtained upon untrue or unfit suggestions for the sole importation of any sort or kind of dyeing stuff, or by engrossing of dyeing stuffs into a few hands, whereby they become overdear to the dyer or clothier, or by what other means or practice the dyeing stuffs are anyway endeared, and to foresee the best means you can for remedy and prevention thereof?

And whereas a suspicion hath been raised upon the societies and companies of the Merchant Adventurers and other merchants, and of some companies of handicraftsmen, that for their private grain and particular advantage they make and put in execution divers ordinances amongst themselves for ordering their trades and mysteries, which tend to the hurt of the public, we will and command you, and hereby give you power and authority, upon any complaint to be made unto you thereof, to inform yourselves of the ordinances, orders, and constitutions of such companies and societies of merchants and others for the ordering of their trade, to the end that if it shall appear that anything therein contained be unfit to be continued, as tending to the general hurt of others, either in making the cloth, or other merchandize and wares of this kingdom over dear or otherwise, that the same may be laid down, and that no new orders or ordinances be hereafter made and executed by the said companies or any of them, before they be first perused and allowed by us and our Privy Council, or so many of them as we shall thereunto especially appoint.

And because it is conceived by many that by reason of the discouragements happened to trade, the number of merchants now applying themselves in course of merchandize are of too small a number to manage the same and that if the number of traders were enlarged, trade itself would be enlarged, which is now said by some to be imprisoned, being for the most part confined to companies and societies of merchants, and others excluded which are not members of those companies, we will and require you to take into your considerations, whether it be necessary to give way to a more open and free trade or not? And if it be, then in what manner it is fittest to be done? Wherein we would always have you take care that government and order in trade may be preserved, and confusion avoided, and that to be done which may be best for us and our people; and, amongst other things which we conceive to be hindrances of a fair and free trade, we will and require you to consider how far it shall be fit to admit of a joint stock in companies or societies of merchants?

And also whether it be at all fit to allow any merchant to be also a retailer, at least of those sorts of merchandize which himself returneth from beyond the seas?

And because the life of commerce and trade is money, whereof a greater scarcity is now found in this our kingdom than hath been in former times, we will and require you with all diligence and care to take into your considerations, what are the principal causes and occasions thereof; and by what means coin or bullion may be hereafter more plentifully brought into this kingdom; and how the same may be here kept and preserved from exportation unless it be only in cases necessary and profitable for the state?

That to prevent an apparent consumption and confusion, which cannot otherwise be avoided, ye diligently observe the true balance of the trade of this kingdom, lest the importation of merchandize from foreign parts exceed the exportation of our own native commodities, and consider of some fitting courses to reduce the same to more equality, and to think upon the gain or loss that comes to our kingdom by the course of exchange now used by our merchants.

And we require you likewise to take into your considerations the ways for the improvement of the native commodities of the kingdom to the best advantage.

And the avoiding of vain and unprofitable returns of the commodities of foreign kingdoms in superfluities and the wasteful consumption thereof, which must needs exhaust the wealth and treasure of the kingdom.

And for the better increase of the wealth of the kingdom, and the importation of coin and bullion from foreign parts, where we have traffic and commerce, we would have you consider what native commodities of this kingdom are of that necessary usefulness to our neighbour nations, that they may fitly return home a proportion of coin or bullion for a supply of treasure, and to advise in what manner that may be best done?

And because the maintenance of our navy and the shipping of our kingdom is a principal means to advance the honour, strength, safety, and profit thereof, we will and require you, chiefly and above other things, seriously and carefully to consider by what good ways and means our navy and the shipping of this kingdom may be best maintained and enlarged, and mariners bred up and increased to furnish the same, and to this end we require you to take into your best and most mature considerations and judgments these things following, which ourself conceive to be very good means to attain unto that end we especially aim at as aforesaid.

First and principally that the herring fishing upon the seas and coasts appertaining to our own realms and dominions may be undertaken by our people for the common good, for the encouragement whereof we shall be always ready to yield our best assistance and protection; the work in itself being apparently profitable for the undertakers of the same, and the consequences thereof for the good of us and our people, being by God's blessing such and so many as no one achievement can equalize.

And to the end that the shipping of other nations may not be employed for the bringing in of foreign commodities, whilst our own shipping shall want employment, we will and require you to take into your considerations how our laws do now stand in force for the prohibiting of merchandize to be imported in foreign bottoms, and to advise what is fit to be done therein?

And further to advise if it be not behooffull to put in execution our laws and statutes established and continuing in force, which enjoin the merchant strangers, as well denizens as not denizens, to employ and bestow the proceed of their merchandize imported hither on the native commodities of this realm, to be exported by them and by what means they may most fitly be done?

And to the end our merchants may be encouraged and enabled to export the cloth of our kingdom, which they would doubtless perform more amply if they had better advantages to make their returns upon, we would have you to take into your consideration, by what means to enlarge their returns, and with what sorts of merchandize, which may be most profitable for our kingdom and to avoid those things by which they are now stopped and prevented?

And because our merchants' trading into the Eastland countries were wont to make good returns by corn, which they have neglected of late to their own hurt and the hurt of the kingdom, we would have you to consider how to give them encouragement in that trade, and to do it so as our own dominions may be supplied in time of want, and yet in time of plenty the husbandry and tillage of this realm not to be discouraged.

Further, whereas our Eastland merchants in former times did lade their ships with hemp and flax, rough dressed, in great quantities, which did not only help them much in their returns, but did also set great numbers of our people on work with dressing the same, and converting the same into linen cloth, which kind of trade we understand is of late almost given over, by bringing in of hemp and flax ready dressed, and that for the most part by strangers, we commend unto your care by what means this hurtful error in trade may be reformed, to the help of our merchants and the relief of our poor subjects.

And because the Company of Merchants trading for the East Indies have been much taxed by many for transporting the coin and treasure of this realm to furnish their trade withal, or that which would otherwise have come in hither for the use of our subjects, and that they do not return such merchandize from thence as doth recompense that loss unto our kingdom; we will and command, and by these presents do authorize you, to enquire and search whether that company do justly and truly perform their contract with us concerning the carrying out of money; and to consider by what means that trade, which is specious in show, may really and truly be made profitable to the public, without exhausting the treasure of our kingdom.

And because we understand that a great mass of treasure is yearly spent upon linen cloth, brought and bought from beyond the seas at dear rates, and for that it is conceived, if the fishing so much desired by us be thoroughly undertaken, and our shipping increased, it will require much greater proportion of hemp for cordage and other uses in the craft or mystery of fishing, which would set an infinite number of our people on work in preparing and making the same; we commend unto your considerations the best ways how the sowing of hemp and flax may be encouraged and undertaken within this kingdom, whereby so much good would redound unto us and our people?

And for that it is very fit to commend the wearing of the cloth of our kingdoms to other nations by our own example at home, we would have you to consider by what means the cloth and stuffs made of the wools of these our kingdoms may be more frequently worn by our own subjects; to what sorts of people; to what purposes; and in what manner it were fit the wearing thereof were enjoined.

And generally our will and command is that with all care and diligence ye apply yourselves to inform us and our Privy Council, from time to time, of these and all other things which in your experiences, or out of your judgements, ye find or conceive may be a means to advance and quicken trade, raise again the native commodities of our kingdom, encourage traders, clothiers, and the woolgrowers and manufactors, or to remove the impediments or discouragements thereof, and to that purpose we hereby give you power and authority, to send for such persons to attend you, and to have view of all records and writings, as you shall find needful for your better information in anything concerning this our service.

In which your travails, or in the execution of this our commission, if any complaints shall be presented or offered unto you which concern the interest or particular grievance of any particular persons in points of trades or commerce, we will and require you to endeavour, by all good means, so to mediate and persuade with the parties, as that ye may set a final end thereunto if ye can; or, if ye shall find any wilfully stubborn or refractory, that you send both them and their causes unto our Council Board, there to be further ordered, that such of our subjects as should intend their trades be not delayed or diverted therefrom by unnecessary suits and unjust vexations.

And our pleasure and command is that when, and as soon as, ye shall maturely have considered and resolved upon any material parts or points of these our instructions, that ye certify the body of our Privy Council thereof from time to time, that by their advices we may proceed to a present reformation of the same as occasion shall require, without the expectation of a total and absolute reformation of every part of these our instructions all at once, for that of necessity must be the work and labour of a long time, when timely redress may happily be given to some while others are in handling. And this our Commission to stand and be in force until our pleasure be signified, under our Privy Seal or Great Seal, to determine and declare the same to be void.

In witness whereof, etc.

Witness ourself at Westminster the one and twentieth day of October.

Per Breve de Privato Sigillo.

11. THE STATE OF THE EAST ANGLIAN CLOTH TRADE, 1622

[B.M., Add. MS. 34, 324, f. 211]

Touching the New Draperies in Essex and Suffolk and Norfolk,
19 December 1622

BAYS, says, perpetuanas and New Draperies are for the most part vented into Spain which market is likely not to last by reason of a pragmatical sanction there to forbid the bringing in of manufactures made of any foreign wool and forbidding his subjects to buy them.

Spain hath three times as much wool as England.

These New Draperies come not into Guildhall, but to Leadenhall, Lombard Street, etc.

Mr. Geo. Strowde is a great dealer in those commodities for Spain.

It is feared this Spanish prohibition will turn to a toleration by licence, the procuring whereof will be very chargeable to the merchants, or by an imposition to be laid by them upon the stuffs.

There is weekly above 2,000*li.* paid in those countries for those commodities and stuffs, and yet by reason of the great quantities of those stuffs made of late and at this time, than heretofore, viz. for 70,000*li.* of late time, but heretofore 8 or 10 thousand *li.* at the most. For the trade of bays of late time is equal to the trade of the white cloths.

A letter or message to the Spanish ambassador touching the stay or revoking of that pragmatic.

Venice receiveth from Spain so much wool yearly as maketh between 40 and 50 thousands cloths larger than ours.

Much wool likewise sold into France and the Low Countries from Spain.

Spanish wool excellent good, without dust or sand, but pure and clean and dear in shew by reason of tucking, but cheap in truth.

12. A LINCOLNSHIRE LANDLORD DESCRIBES THE DEPRESSION, APRIL 1623

[Lincolnshire Notes and Queries, I, i, 1888, pp. 15–16]

RIGHT honourable brother, the best news I can send you is that we are all in good health God be praised. I am now here with my son to settle some country affair, and my own private, which were never so burdensome unto me as now. For many insufficient tenants have given up their farms and sheepwalks, so as I am forced to take them into my own hands and borrow money upon use to stock them. It draweth me wholly from a contemplative life, which I most affected, and could be most willing to pass over my whole estate to the benefit of my children so as I were freed of the trouble. Our country was never in that want that now it is, and more of money than corn, for there are many thousands in these parts who have sold all they have even to their bed straw and cannot get work to earn any money. Dog's flesh is a dainty dish and found upon search in many houses, also such horse flesh as hath lain long in a deke for hounds. And the other day one stole a sheep who for mere hunger tore a leg out, and did eat it raw. All that is most certain true and yet the great time of scarcity not yet come. I shall rejoice to have a better subject to write of, and expect it with patience. In the mean time and ever

> I will remain
> Your honour's most loving brother to serve you
> William Pelham

Brocklesby this 21 of April
To the Right Honourable my very loving brother, Sir Edward Conway,

knight, Principal Secretary to His Majesty and one of his Most Honourable Privy Council

[Endorsed:] April 21, 1623. Sir William Pelham. Concerning the great want and scarcity in Lincolnshire.

13. SIR RALPH MADDISON ON THE HELP OF TRADE, JULY 1623

[B.M., Add. MS. 34, 324, f. 179]

Sir Ralph Maddison's Note touching the Help of Trade, 2 July, 1623 [Endorsement]

IN THE pricing of all the commodities of this kingdom, money doth bear his part or one half of the sway, and to approve the same I have seen in my time a dearth of corn without need and a famine without dearth, for if it fall out that the least doubt of want of corn shall possess the opinion of men when all things else do bear price, and there be ready vent or sale and general employment by reason of plenty of monies in the kingdom, then corn will bear a round price although there be store enough and to spare, and this year, although the scarcity and famine be great in the north parts especially, where many do perish for food, yet the prices of corn are not great but such prices as have been in the time of indifferent plenty, and this happeneth because of want of monies and want of employment and labour for the poor, which always hath happened when monies have been exported and failed, so that plenty of money and plenty of corn maketh the price indifferent, scarcity of money and scarcity of corn the price indifferent, plenty of money and scarcity of corn maketh exceeding great price, plenty of corn and scarcity of money bringeth corn to a contemptible low price and maketh promise or shew of more plenty than there is.

Thus it is manifest that of two causes proceeds three different effects, high, mean, and low prices; even so it is in all commodities: plenty of money enforceth a mediocrity of price even in the plenty of our own commodities, and if the quantity or plenty fail within us, yet plenty of monies do keep up the balance, as when there is much money and little corn, and if monies be scarce and plenty of commodities, the commodities will be vilified in price and then the balance becometh too light, which going on in traffic exporteth the money to balance the said trade. Now our monies being exported and our wares vilified, how should these evils be remedied, or how shall money be regained ever as the case now standeth, when no silver can be imported but to the merchants' hindrance that bring it, because it will give more in another place, and how should our plate or money be kept when it will give profit beyond the seas to be delivered there to merchants, that for the substance of eighteen received there, will pay twenty here? That this disproportion of eight in the hundred is true upon trial was approved, and so long as this proportion continueth foreign silver will never come again to the mint, and that which is minted will be exported for gain as lately hath been proved.

Now the disease is plain, the remedy is to be sought, of which there be four, the first is to advance it as in times past, secondly to imbase the alloy, thirdly or otherwise to divide our monies so much less by the sheares as to make 60–66 pieces in the pound troy, these or one of these being once fixed, there will rest no certainty for foreign nations may immediately exceed us therein and so frustrate us, and our remedies therefore, seeing there is no certainty in any of the former three, we must of force be driven to the fourth remedy or else suffer a downfall of commodities and consequently a fall of rents, an undoing of lease occupants, a general impoverishing of farmers, and desolation of habitations, which exceedingly doth press upon the kingdom, and will yet more until money return, for that the landowners, not under-standing or not willing to make abatements according to the proportion of the absence or scarcity of money, will have their lands cast up tenantless, and none to be found by reason of the general poverty of the kingdom to occupy them, and as you have heard of great wants among the clothing people crying out for hunger, so will the landowners, husbandmen, and labourers be distressed, each one in their degree, and beggary and thievery abound. When was it seen a land so distressed without war? Wherefore, necessity will enforce the fourth remedy, which is to foresee by politic providence that money be imported and not for gain exported again, and to prevent the exporting where gain is, there is no law will stand in force. Therefore, of necessity the gain must be taken away—I mean the deceitful gain which receiveth less than he giveth or receiveth more than he giveth in quantity in respect of change and to order it so in respect of loan there be always gain to the lender and that more or less according to the scarcity of monies.

And hereof, as of all their doings in gross or general there should be a politic watch or eye over all complots or combinations, lest under colour of exchange, which is one thing used and first tolerated for necessity, it be turned to a biting trade of usury, which worketh upon necessity, becometh a grievous oppression wherefore no positive law can be set, but the crafty wit of the merchant will find a starting hole or some just, temporary, or local exception may be found against any law, which temporary or local exception may be for the time allowed, and revert to the pristinate use again, the time of necessity being passed over, which pressed the exception, as, for example, this year the want of corn in England did enforce a great price of the exchange in the Eastlands from whence it was brought, because there was much employment for monies and less than was used to be had there, that is, the commodities of that country did exceed the wares exported, which enforced the exporta-tions of our monies in specie, which when the dearth ceaseth may be reduced to a moderate gain to the deliverer. And if we shall have no more scarcity or famine of corn in England we shall no more send out our monies for the same, which, by the providence of magazines may be prevented. So likewise on the other side there must be special regard that the commodities of the earth be not vilified nor the earth labourers discouraged because many set on labour do cast up their labours thereby, so in all things the price of our home commodities must be maintained lest the general overbalance of trade happening by decay of prices enforce a general want and poverty in the kingdom by means aforesaid, the efficient cause whereof is the want of money.

14. AN ENQUIRY INTO THE DECAY OF THE CLOTH TRADE, 1623-5 [?]

[P.R.O., SP 16/155, no. 52]

The Answer of the Commissioners to the several Articles of the Commission as they lie in order.

1. The cause why wools are fallen from their wonted values is in general the want of vent for our cloth and stuff beyond the seas; and this want of vent proceedeth from these causes:
   1. The wars abroad where our cloth was wont to be vented.
   2. The scarcity of money.
   3. The false making, dyeing, and dressing which discrediteth them.
   4. The burden upon cloth which maketh them over dear.
   5. The few Adventurers to drive the trade.
   6. The few mart towns where they are sold.
   7. The making of cloth beyond the seas.
   8. The not wearing of cloth plentifully at home.

And the most probable means to raise them again to their former price and estimation, applied to these several causes, we conceive to be these.

1. For the first to have patience, and to pray for the peace of Christendom.
2. To quicken trade which will beget money, and to use the means to bring coin in and to preserve it here. And for a present help herein to have the Spanish rials to be current in payment, holding their weight at 4s. 8d. the rials of viii which will doubtless bring in store of money.
3. To make the stuff and cloths good and workmanlike, and to that purpose to prescribe apt orders and to see to the due execution thereof by fit persons to be appointed in every city, corporate town, and county.
4. To take off unnecessary burdens that cloth may be sold the cheaper, and yet our wools will rise in value.
5. For the number of Adventurers, to admit more fit persons being merchants into the companies and societies at 20 nobles fine, and they all to trade under government.
6. To make choice of a mart town more in the Archduke's country as at Antwerp, if it may be fitly procured.

7. To stop the wools of our kingdom that they be not transported to enable strangers to make cloth with our wools.

8. To make the wearing of cloth frequent at home, by example in the greater and by command to the meaner sort.

2. To the second article, the best means we can think upon to prevent the transportation of wools and wool fells, etc. and fullers earth are:

1. For wool fells, to permit none to be exported by any licence or toleration, for it will be but an evasion to transport wools on the fell which is as bad as in the fleece.

2. For wools of England, to have none at all got by land into Scotland, for that would be but a cloak for transportation.

3. To have an eye to the barns and houses near the sea coast where wools are used to be secretly stowed, and from thence on the sudden slipped away.

4. To lay a strict charge on the officers of the ports and a severe hand if they connive at it.

5. To punish the exporters without favour when they be discovered.

6. At the next opportunity to make a sharp law to punish those offences as was intended at the last meeting in Parliament.

7. For fullers earth, that the grounds whence it is digged being not many, and these notorious and well known, may be put into the charge of some gent. of quality near adjoining, to whom the owners of the earth (upon good bond) shall give an exact account to whom and what quantity they sell and deliver. And as much as may be, that care be had that fullers earth be not water borne, or if it be at all, that it be only to cross some rivers for easing of land carriage, and that at certain places only, and that by the oversight of the principal magistrates of those places.

[3.] *Article.* For the wools of Ireland, beside the former conditions, to provide that some certain and few ports be appointed as Staples, both in Ireland and England, from whence and whither these wools shall be brought; and being brought hither, we conceive there will be little doubt but if these cloths and stuffs recover their former reputation and vent they will be bought up at reasonable prices to the contentment of the merchant.

4. To the fourth article for the wools of Scotland we think it fit that such of them as may be there spared be brought to certain Staples in England, but the means and the conditions thereof to be referred to the conference intended between the Commissioners of both kingdoms.

5. To the fifth we are of opinion that all the wools of these three kingdoms may be profitably converted into cloth and stuffs, without making any glut at all to hinder our markets, if the cloth and stuffs made of our wools be well and substantially made, for all the wools which are not now draped here are draped in those parts whither they are now carried, and prevent the sales of so much of our cloth there. And if our wools be carried over, the stealing of them from hence without [customs?]; the mingling of them with the wools of their own country; the putting of no charge upon their own cloth, but rather the encouraging the makers out of their common treasury and the putting

of licence and consumption money and other charges upon ours may daily enable them to undersell our cloth, which is charged with all these burdens. But if experience shall shew that we shall have a greater quantity of wools than we can well convert and vent, there is no other way to prevent that inconvenience than to moderate the excess of converting grounds fit for dairy or tillage into sheep pastures, that so by proportioning them indifferently we may be well stored with all, and not superabound in any; and so a less quantity of wool may yield to the owners as great a profit when the price shall recompense it.

15. A FURTHER EXPLANATION, 1623–5[?]
[P.R.O., SP 16/155, no. 53]

Answers conceived to the first Articles of the Commission

THESE articles which are immediately directed to the consideration of the wools and cloth of this kingdom and whose scope is to advance the reputation and values of them and to remove the impediments thereof are so linked together that it will be very hard to resolve what is fit to be concluded upon in any of these articles severally and apart, but that withal they be considered and determined of together that so *quasi uno intuitu* a man may discern the causes and the effects of this disease of trade, and the cures and remedy to be applied thereunto, we then answer them together thus:

To the first that the true cause of the decay of the prices of the wools of this kingdom is conceived to be this in general which was so formerly certified by the committees.

The want of the vent for our cloth and stuff made of wool at good prices which in former years it hath had.

This within the general: but then to enter more particularly into it there is *causa causæ*.

The want of vent is occasioned by these means:

1. The falsity of our cloth and stuff in making, dyeing, and dressing which hath discredited it in foreign parts.

2. The dearness of our cloth and stuff by the burdens which lie upon it.

3. The making of cloth in more abundance in foreign parts than in former times; being thereto enabled by the wools of our kingdoms, and being thereunto driven by occasion of the two former.

4. The disturbance of trade by the troubles in Germany and other parts where much of our cloth was vented.

5. The universal stop of trade by scarcity of money, which driveth the wheel of trade about.

The fourth of these hath no other cure but patience and prayers for the peace of Christendom.

The fifth will gather life again by the quickening of trade and by some preservations and restorations which may be used in the handling of other branches of the Commission.

The three first may be, if not wholly, yet in a great measure, cured by the remedy which the next articles will produce.

3rd and 4th[1]

2. For the 2nd we find the necessity to be great of keeping the wools of these kingdoms from being transported into foreign parts, for our wools are so useful to them that by their mixture with their own wools they are enabled to make cloth in great abundance, especially the middling or sorting cloths which are the greatest number which cloths hinder the vent of ours. And we are so well informed of the usefulness of our fulling earth that we find it also to be fit to be restrained from exportation with all possible care, which to effect we conceive these courses fit to be held.

For the wools of England that there be no barns or other houses of receipt suffered near the sea cliffs or sea shores, where they secretly stow their wools intended to be transported.

That the officers of all ports be secretly enjoined to take care hereof.

That some be appointed to watch and observe the ports of Amsterdam, Delph, Hamborough, etc. whither the greatest store of wools are carried, to give true information thereof, for more is carried from hence by stealth out of creeks than in the great ports, and yet too much thence also.

That the delinquents be severely punished for example to others when they shall be discovered, without any connivance.

That at the next opportunity the punishment be made so heavy by a statute law both to the exporters and shippers, as will be too hard to be adventured.

For the wools of Ireland, besides the former, that none be brought from thence into England but to a few certain ports, to be made Staples for their wools.

For the borders that none be carried into Scotland which would be merely to colour transportation thence.

For the wools of Scotland (which may be spared) to have them brought to certain Staples in England but the manner and the conditions thereof to be referred to the conference intended between the Commissioners of both kingdoms.

For fullers earth that the grounds or pits whence it is digged which are not many and in places notorious and well known, be put into the charge of some gentlemen of quality near adjoining, to whom the owners of the earth (upon good bond) shall give exact account to whom and what quantity they sell or deliver the same.

And that as much as may be there be care that no fullers earth be water borne or, if it be at all, that it be but only to cross the river of Thames,

---

[1] Thus in MS. The numbering evidently relates to the original set of questions.

and that at a certain place and by the oversight of the principal magistrates of that place.

For the 5th we are of opinion that all the wools of these kingdoms may be converted into cloth and stuff and make no glut at all to hinder our markets nor so much as if they be suffered to be transported for all those wools not now draped here are draped in those parts whither they are carried, and prevent the sale of so much as the half of our cloth.

And they prevent them also not only in their number but in their prices for stealing the wools from hence without custom, and mingling it with their own, and putting no charge upon their own cloth, but rather encouraging the makers out their common treasury; they may easily undersell our cloth which is charged with all these burdens.

But withal we should advise that there should be a moderation used in converting ground to sheep pastures according to the ancient wisdom of this kingdom seen in many laws, lest the dairy and the plough be neglected, which are as necessary for the maintenance of the state, and so by an equal and indifferent proportion we might be well stored with all these provisions which are of necessity and neither want in one nor superabound in any.

For the 6th, we are of opinion that the best profit to the kingdom will be to make them all well and truly and substantially in their several kinds, for the falsifying of them in their length, breadth, and goodness out of a present desire of gain doth utterly discredit them and make them not vendible at all. And therefore we are of opinion that all licences and toleration for the stretching and straining of cloth be recalled.

Item. We especially recommend the converting of as much as may be into stuff and the new drapery, for we find that a pound of wool made into cloth will be worth to the kingdom at least thrice the value thereof in wool by the workmanship thereof, and the same quantity thereof turned into perpetuanas, says, and other stuffs will yield at least six times as much. So that 50,000*li.* worth of wools thus employed will produce to the kingdom at least 300,000*li.* in value.

For the 7th we have recommended the consideration of the laws in force for clothing to Mr. Attorney, Mr. Solicitor, and Mr. Recorder, who this time of vacation will peruse them and make report thereof unto us of their pains and opinions therein.

For the 8th because there are no laws already made till these can be regulated by a binding law, we intend to conceive and prescribe some general orders and rules to the makers, and for the particulars which must of necessity be subject to much variation according to the occurments of times and as divers shall be discovered, they must be left to the discretion of those to whom it shall be recommended to have the oversight thereof; and to give us the better information herein, we have already directed letters to the mayors and other principal officers of the cities and towns of Norwich, Colchester, Canterbury, Sandwich, etc. where most store of the new drapery are made, who out of their experience shall send us instructions herein before Twelvetide next and in the mean time ourselves have had conference with some merchants and mercers of London, skilful in that trade; and our advice is that such orders as shall be taken for making of cloth shall be likewise used for the dyeing and dressing thereof well and workmanlike. And because most sorts of the new draperies are not vendible unless they be pressed with the hot presses, which for cloth and kerseys is not sufferable, and we have received a petition recommended unto us from his Majesty proffered by the hot pressers of London, wherein is mention of some former directions given unto them by his Majesty, we have made choice of a special committee to consider of these former orders and directions, and to report unto us their opinions in what sort it is fit to govern them, that the stuffs may be pressed well and workmanlike and the prices for doing thereof be moderate and not enhanced.

And for the persons to whom the charge of the oversight of these things shall be committed, we conceive they must be able and fit persons thought up in every county, city, and town corporate where clothing of any kind is used, and where it may conveniently be set up, whereof some must be persons of skill and experience and some others of worth and quality to give account of the trade and of the orders to be made.

16. DEPRESSION IN THE ESSEX CLOTH INDUSTRY, 1629[1]

[Bodleian Library, Oxford, MS. Firth c. 4, pp. 486–7]

To the King's most excellent Majesty,
the humble petition of the clothiers and workmasters in
the manufactures of wool in the county of Essex.

SHEWETH that your poor petitioners have for a long time employed many thousands of poor people, whose livelihood wholly depend upon the manufactures of bays and says, and some proportion of cloth within the county. That this trade of bays and says, since they were prohibited in Spain about two years before the breach of the peace, hath been much decayed. That yet notwithstanding there are not less within that county than forty or fifty thousand who live by those manufactures, not being able to subsist unless they be continually set on work, and weekly paid. And many of them cannot support themselves and their miserable families unless they receive their

---

[1] For more of this correspondence between Essex and Whitehall on the cloth depression, see Section III on Industries, pp. 224–32.

wages every night, which, without a weekly sale, very few of the work-masters are able without great difficulty to perform. That for this five or six weeks past which was wont to be the best season of the year for sale, there hath been little or rather no sale at all, so that their warehouses both in London and the country are full and no markets to put them off. That hereby a very great number of workmasters who have heretofore set thousands of those poor people awork are now utterly undone, and enforced to give over trade. That the stock and credit of all the rest are so spent that it is utterly impossible for them long to subsist, and many of them are afraid to repair to their own dwellings lest they should be oppressed with multitudes of those poor people whose necessity make[s] them very unruly.

Upon bended knees your petitioners do therefore humbly pray your most excellent Majesty to commiserate this their lamentable condition, and in tender compassion of their distressed and almost desperate estate by your princely wisdom to give some order and direction by which many thousand of your poor and faithful subjects may be preserved from utter perishing.

And your petitioners shall ever pray for your Majesty's long and happy reign.
[undated. April 1629]

17. REPORT ON THE ILLEGAL EXPORT OF VICTUALS, 1629[?]
[P.R.O., SP 16/155, no. 54]

Some Few Instances of the General and Great Abuse by the Transportion of Victuals and Other the Prohibited and Staple Goods of this Kingdom from All or Most of the Outports.

1. It appears that in the several years since the beginning of his now Majesty's reign very great quantities of the several prohibited commodities of this realm (and which are specified in this margin) have been, and daily are, conveyed into Holland, France and elsewhere in parts beyond the seas, whereby aliens and foreigners have been and are daily plentifully supplied with those kinds of victuals and staple commodities to the great disadvantage of this state and public weal, and hath thereby occasioned a dearth and scarcity of butter and sundry other the said victuals and staple goods of this kingdom.

2. It further appears that the said illegal transportations are for the most part accomplished through the connivance and wilful neglect of the searchers, wayters, and sundry other the officers of the outports whose several places and duties are expressly to hinder and restrain the transportation of the said prohibited goods; as by several good laws, proclamations, and acts of state, hath heretofore and of late years been signified.

3. It appears, moreover, that very many of the said transporters and delinquents of that kind are men of great estates having made an exorbitant gain

and profit by the transportation of butter, all kinds of victuals, and other the said prohibited goods, and are well able to pay good fines unto his Majesty for their said offences if effectually prosecuted.

And it is humbly conceived that the best means to discover and reform the great abuses of that kind as also to prevent the French and Dutch from being supplied with such great quantities of victuals and other the staple commodities of the kingdom as heretofore and of late years they have been, will be by executing one or more commissions of enquiry to be executed throughout all the ports in such sort as the like commission of enquiry hath lately been executed at the port of Kingston upon Hull, and some other ports thereabouts, by which commission many great abuses of that kind are already discovered, as in part is known to his Majesty's Attorney General, who hath exhibited two several informations against sundry of the principal transporters, the one in the Court of Star Chamber, and the other in the Exchequer Chamber, for which commissions are to be issued to examine witnesses this long vacation as by the said informations upon the file, and the proceedings sithence had thereupon, will appear.

[The list of commodities in the margin runs as follows:] Wools, wool fells, corn and grain, fullers earth, butter, leather, lead, biscuit and ship-bread, meal, beef, pork, bacon, cheese, beer, tallow, money, pewter, ship-timber, barrel boards, barrel staves, brass and shruff metals, brass and iron ordnance, powder and shot.

18. THE EFFECTS ON FOOD SUPPLIES OF THE DUNKIRK PRIVATEERS, 1630
[P.R.O., SP 16/162, no. 41]

To the Right Honourable the Lords and other Commissioners for His Majesty's Highness Admiralty,
the humble petition of the cheesemongers and fishmongers of the City of London.

HUMBLY shewing that by reason of the many sails of Dunkirk that lie on the Norfolk, Suffolk, and Essex coasts insomuch that no barque can without great danger of taking pass between Yarmouth Roads and the river of Thames, the City of London cannot be served with provision to serve his Majesty's Navy Royal or merchants' occasions so that these provisions of butter, cheese, and fish which have long lain at sea and greatly wanted in the markets of this city will decay and not be fit for his Majesty's service or for sale unless your honours be pleased to give speedy order and command for good convoys to guard these coasts.

The premises considered the petitioners in all humility pray your Honours to be pleased to consider seriously and favourably of their cases and to send and appoint one or more of the Lyons whelps or the King's catch or some other safe convoys that these provisions so greatly wanted may come in safely to this city. And they according to their bounden duties shall pray etc. [Endorsed:] R[eceived] 6 Martii 1629. Petition of the cheesemongers and fishmongers of London.

19. GRAIN SHORTAGES IN 1630–31 AND THE MEASURES TAKEN IN SOMERSET, DERBYSHIRE, NOTTINGHAMSHIRE, AND NORWICH

[P.R.O. SP 16/183, no. 50; 185, no. 93; 187, no. 28; 186, no. 26]

Sir,

According to his Majesty's directions these are to certify you that we have done and do our best endeavours for the well furnishing of our markets with corn, and to that end have suppressed all superfluous maltsters and ale-houses in the several hundreds within our division. And yet notwithstanding in regard of the populousness of our country, corn holds in our market of Bridgwater at a very dear rate, viz. wheat at 8s. per bushel, rye at 8s. per bushel, barley 6s., beans 6s., oats 3s. 4d. And thus for the present we heartily take our leaves and rest

Your loving friends,

G. Poulett, Robert Cuffe, William Bassett, Wm. Bull.

* * *

To Francis Bradshaw, esq., High Sheriff for the County of Derby.
Sir,

According to his Majesty's commandment, in his proclamation and book of orders for the bringing down of the price of corn, our doing in which we are directed monthly to certify yourself, we have thought fitting to make known unto you. That upon our former survey of every man's store more than will relieve their several families and make their present seednes [sic], we do observe that the inhabitants of the Hundred of High Peak wherein we inhabit upon our admonishment do bring into the markets of Bakewell and Tideswell all the overplus of their corn and grain, which we have caused to be sold at reasonable rates, being chiefly oats and oatmeal, little other grain growing in the said Hundred. And in our monthly meetings we do also take order for the punishment of rogues and vagabonds, relief of the poor, binding of children to be apprentices, suppressing the third part of the alehouses as superfluous, and the condign punishment of negligent comers to the church according to the statute in that behalf made and provided, being always ready to our utmost power and endeavours to see the same performed, and all other branches of the said book of orders and other statutes which shall concern us in our places to execute.

JOHN MANNERS   RAND. ASHENHURST

*   *   *

Most Honourable,

May it please your lordships to be advertized that we have, according to orders appointed by his Majesty to be observed for the preventing the dearth of grain and other victual, done our best endeavours therein, and have caused the petty constables and other honest and substantial inhabitants to make true search and trial what store of corn every householder then had, either in barns, stacks, or other where, as near as they could within the several parishes, with other circumstances expressed in the book of orders.

And it hath appeared by the presentment of the juries that the greatest number of people have a great want of corn. And we also find that those that have the greatest store have very willingly brought their corn to the markets, it giving so great a price thereof as it hath done; and have been likewise willing to help their poor neighbours at home upon reasonable prices and upon trust, who otherwise would have tasted of want in greater measure than they have done; and many husbandmen would have wanted corn to have sown again if they had not been so trusted. And we do now find that the price of barley is at a less rate than it was about Christmas last for then it was at about 6s. a strike, and now it is sold for about 5s. or 16 groats and some less, according as it was dry or wet gotten.

And we conceive that the reason that the prices at this time do somewhat abate in our markets is for that a good quantity of corn hath been brought into our country by the river of Trent from remote places where corn was not at so great a price as with us, and we hope that in summer time, when coal carriages do come into our country for coals, that they will bring corn with them as formerly divers countries have done. We will do our best endeavours that there be no engrossers of corn and that those that have corn to spare shall bring it to the markets in such a measure as it may continue until new corn come. We have already and will still do our endeavours to keep alehouses and tippling houses from disorder, and cause them to sell their beer and ale according to the assize which (as we conceive) will prove the most prevalent means to keep corn at reasonable prices.

And now if it may stand with your lordships' good pleasure to approve of it, we hold it not so needful to have any further general search for corn, for that we perceive that most men's barns are emptied and that those few who have some proportion to spare will willingly sell the same at the prices it is now at. And seeing the seed time hath been good and seasonable, the next year's increase is like to be the more plentiful and therefore those that can now spare corn cannot expect to be gainers by keeping it in.

All which we humbly submit to your lorships' good pleasures and will ever rest at your Honours' service to be commanded

Fra. Morley   Ro. Sutton, vic.

Hardolph Wasteneys, Geo. Lassells, Fran. Thornhaugh, W. Cooper, Jo. Woods, Ro. Williamson, Gilbert Millington, Tho. Hutchinson, Math. Palmer, Gervas Teverey, Will. Coke.

Nottingham this 24th of March, 1630

[Endorsed] To the Rt Honourable Lords and others of his Majesty's Most Honourable Privy Council present these.

*   *   *

Our duties most humbly remembered,

We crave leave humbly to inform your lordships that the want of trading, want of work for the poor, and scarcity and dearth of corn and other victuals have so increased the number and misery of the poor of this city as albeit for many years we have taxed ourselves and the citizens and inhabitants in this city for the poor relief at exceeding high weekly rates, yet are we now enforced to put upon ourselves and the better rank of citizens in this city treble so much as we did formerly pay. And all other citizens and inhabitants are rated to pay weekly twice so much as they formerly paid. And although we have for divers months past continued to pay the same, and shall still be enforced to continue those our extraordinary payments, yet all we can do is not sufficient to find them bread. Our corn stock being little less than CCC*li*. is wholly disbursed in provision of corn which we do weekly deliver unto them at much less rates than the market do afford. We have borrowed three hundred pounds to disburse in corn to continue that course. Our markets are sparingly served by the country adjoining as we cannot there make any provision for them without such enhancing the prices of corn as would be dangerous. We have caused a collection to be made of such monies as every able citizen charitably disposed would willingly give to buy corn in this extremity to the end we might still be the better enabled to mitigate the price to the poor. We have been careful by all due means to regulate the market of this city, appointing every market day one justice of peace and one alderman to be present to persuade the sellers of corn to moderation in their prices, and the poor buyers to contentation, and hold them from tumult. We have commanded all our maltsters by direction of the judges of Assizes to forebear malting to the end there may be a greater quantity of barley preserved for bread.

All this notwithstanding we find that we shall not be able to procure corn for our poor at any rates unless exportation of corn may by your honourable order be timely prevented, for we have been credibly informed that since his Majesty's orders and your honourable directions promulg[at]ed by his Highness's proclamation, great quantities of corn have been exported from out the county of Norfolk at divers ports in the said county especially at

Wells and Cley and that there is now a licence obtained from your lordships for exportation of divers lasts of corn from those ports, since the rumour whereof we have used the best means we can to provide corn at excessive prices and cannot get it for our money, even in those places of the country where there is thought to be greatest plenty.

We most humbly beseech your lordships that if any such licence be gone forth, it may be presently recalled, and a strict commandment given for preventing that inconvenience, otherwise neither our payment of excessive taxes for the poor's weekly relief or borrowing of monies for their provision or charitable contribution for that purpose will serve to procure corn to sustain life, which lamentable case we humbly leave to your honourable consideration, and will ever remain at your lordship's service and command,

Willm. Browne, mayor, Peter Gleane, Alexr. Anguish, Ric. Rose, Robert Craske, Robt. Debney, Thomas Blosse, Tho. Cory, Francis Smallpeice.

Norwich, the 4th of March, 1630.

20. DEPRESSION IN THE HAMPSHIRE CLOTH INDUSTRY, 1631

[P.R.O., SP 16/182, no. 45, I]

To the Rt. Honourable Sir Nicholas Hide, Kt.,
Lord Chief Justice of England and other his Majesty's Justices of the Peace for the county of Southampton, the humble petition of the clothiers of the town of Basingstoke.

SHEWETH unto your good lordship and the rest of his Majesty's justices now assembled. Whereas there were heretofore made within the said town of Basingstoke weekly 30 broadcloths and a hundred kersies whereby not only the greatest number of the poor in the said town but the poor of four score parishes were employed and set on work, and thereby they and their families relieved and maintained. Now so it is that there are not above 6 or 7 broad cloths and above some 20 kersies made in the said town weekly by reason our whole stocks of money are in cloth that lieth upon our hands for want of sale, the merchants refusing to buy at such reasonable rates as we may afford. For some of them having gotten the trade into their hands do exact upon us that in those few cloths that we have lately sold, we have lost 20 or 30s. in a broad cloth and 6s. 8d. in a kersey of the price they stood us in. So that we are discouraged to proceed in our trade of clothing and disabled to continue the poor in work in the said town and the other parishes that depended on us, and thereby do now for want of works and for that the prices of corn, being now more than ordinary, the said poor do daily increase, for there are in the said town 60 householders, whose families do amount to 300 persons and upwards being weavers, spinners, and clothworkers, the most of them being heretofore rated towards the relief of the poor, do now many of them depend upon the alms of the parish, for by the space of 12 months past they have earned but little. By reason whereof they intended to have preferred their complaint unto your lordship and the rest of His Majesty's justices now assembled, but that we thought fit by this course to prevent it.

May it therefore please your good lordship and the rest of his Majesty's justices that you will vouchsafe to take this our humble petition into your considerations, and that by your good means we may find relief. And we shall according to our bounden duty daily pray for your prosperities.

John Hall, Richard Bradley, William Blunden, Thomas Hall, John Blunden, John Smyth, Richard Spier, Tho. South, Robert Stocker, Henry Cater, John Spier, John Cooper, Richard Spier, vic., William Blunden junior, Edward Scayes, Richard Woodrofe, John Warner, Thomas West, Robert Newman, Jo. Clarke.

[12 January 1630/1]

21. THE LONDON MERCHANTS COMPLAIN OF A TRADE DEPRESSION, 1641

[House of Lords Record Office, Main Papers H.L., Addenda 1641, no. 3560]

To the Right Honourable the Lords assembled in Parliament, the humble petition of the merchants in London.

SHEWETH that the trade and more especially the navigation of this kingdom is of late years very much decayed and fallen into the hands of our neighbour nations and that not because they have either a greater capacity or good will for the honour and welfare of their countries or are more industrious or that their advantages as to trade and navigation are greater or, indeed, as great as those which God hath bestowed on England, but by reason of the great burdens which have been laid upon them and for want of such due encouragement and regulation by law as is necessary for the maintenance and support of them, which, until given, they will and must certainly fail every day more and more, and the whole kingdom, having lost its shipping and seamen (which under God are its walls and bulwarks) become a scorn and a prey to everyone that shall have an evil eye towards it. Your petitioners do therefore humbly pray that it may please this Right Honourable House of Parliament to take the premises into their most serious, speedy, and thorough consideration, and to provide such necessary, wholesome, and suitable remedies as to them in their great wisdom shall seem mete.

And your petitioners shall ever pray etc.

[One page of signatures]

22. LONDON CITIZENS ON THE CAUSES OF THE DECAY OF TRADE, 1641

[P.R.O., SP 16/478, no. 86]
[March] 1641

The humble petition of divers citizens of London.

SHEWETH that whereas there hath been a great decay of trade in this kingdom and great scarcity of money thereby ever since the first motions in the kingdom of Scotland, but more especially since the most unhappy breach of the Pacification, whereby this State, being looked upon by foreign nations as in an unsettled condition, it hath been a cause that such strangers who were wont to furnish great sums of money at use have called in and remitted those monies by exchange into foreign parts. And such of our own nation as were wont to be lenders have called in their monies and stand in expectation of what the issue of things may be. Commodities also brought in find no usual vent but at great loss, which, if it shall continue still, will hinder exportation also by reason of the high exchange abroad, whereby there is as great loss as by goods imported. Such among us as have monies owing in Scotland cannot yet receive them by reason of their great disability through their troubles since the last breach. Ireland is so impoverished by the great oppressions that lately exercised there that such debts as have been owing there are still for the most part detained; and by our general fears and distractions the inland trade of this kingdom is so far decayed that country tradesmen cannot pay their debts in London as formerly and many of them have been ruined. The stopping of 130,000*l.* in July last and taking forth a third thereof for the King's use hath caused great scarcity of money for that now the merchants and strangers forbear to bring in bullion to the Mint which till then was accounted the safest place and surest staple in these parts of the world.

And whereas at the first sitting of this present Parliament we hoped that we should soon have our grievances removed and the incendiaries of the kingdoms and oppressors of our liberties speedily, condignly, and exemplarily punished and all things so perfectly settled that security might appear and a free and full trade return as before; yet after five months' sitting of the Parliament we see no man's person condignly punished, no man's estate confiscate, the Earl of Strafford himself used with unusual favour, though a man charged by all the three kingdoms, and whose life and our safety are, as we conceive, incompatible, which cannot but be a great encouragement to the rest of the great incendiaries, and other offenders highly guilty. Subsidies are granted, monies still required, but our grievances remain; the laws continue still unexecuted; Papists still armed, some of the most active of them still resident at Court; the Irish Popish army not yet disbanded, though all these often humbly and earnestly by both Houses of Parliament desired; the great affairs of the Church sticking in debate and not yet determined.

Merchant strangers hereupon more and more remit their money by exchange, and all our former straits are much increased, and such practices we fear there are to put off all agitations that tend to reformation by them that (perhaps) desire to confound and mingle all things together; with so much time spent in the business of the Earl of Strafford, with his often and earnest desire to obtain yet more, and his slighting carriage in this time of his trial at that bar where in reason he can expect no less than a heavy sentence according to the nature of his high crimes; as also the guilt and activity of some ministers of State now fled, which together with some of the premises, makes us fear we may now lie under a deeper and more dangerous plot than we can yet discover.

Which considerations we present to this most honourable Assembly as the true grounds of the decay of trade, the scarcity of money, and the increase of our fears, not expecting that the Scottish army should be willing to depart, or if they should depart, that we shall be in any better condition, till justice be executed upon the notorious offenders, a perfect peace concluded by Parliament between the kingdoms, and thereby security given to our fears. All which we most humbly pray and hope we shall in the end receive no less from this most honourable Assembly as those from whom under God we expect our peace; and for His blessings upon you and presence with you in this great work shall ever humbly pray.

23. SIR THOMAS ROE'S SPEECH ON THE DECAY OF TRADE, 1641

[Harleian Miscellany, IV, pp. 412–6]

Sir Thomas Roe's Speech in Parliament,
wherein he sheweth the cause of the decay of coin and trade
in this land, especially of merchants' trade. And also
propoundeth a way to the House, how they may be increased.
Printed in the year, 1641.

I T is a general opinion, that the trade of England was never greater, and it may be true, that if it be so, yet it will not absolutely conclude, that the kingdom doth increase in riches, for the trade may be very abundant, and yet, by consumption and importance [= importing] of more than is expected [= exported], the stock may waste.

The balance would be a true solution of the question, if it could be rightly had; but, by reason it must be made up by a medium of the Books of Rates, it will be very uncertain.

Therefore we must seek another rule that is more sensible, upon which we may all judge, and that may be by the plenty or scarcity of money; for it is a true rule, if money increase, the kingdom doth gain by trade; if it be scarce, it loseth.

Let us therefore consider: first, whether our gold and silver be not decreased, and then by what means it is drained; and lastly, how it may be prevented, and what remedies are applicable to effect it.

It is out of doubt our gold is gone to travel without licence, that is visible beyond seas, and every receiver of sums of money must find it privately; and I fear the same of silver, for observing the species of late coining, many half-crowns were stamped which are no more to be seen, and by this measure, I conclude the kingdom grows poor.

The causes of this decay of money may be many: it may be stolen out for profit, going much higher beyond seas, especially in France and Holland.

Much hath been drawn away by the stranger upon fears of our troubles, of which I have experience by exchanges, and exchanges are the great mystery, especially such as are used as a trade, and governed by bankers who make many returns in a year, and gain by every one, more than the interest of a year; and the greatest danger to a state is when money is made merchandise, which should be but the measure thereof.

And here I will propose a problem, whether it were profitable to a kingdom or not that the stranger for many years had a great stock here at interest, and still hath some; I confess it hath supplied the necessities of merchants, and helped to drive trade. But my query is this: suppose the first principal were truly brought in by the stranger, yet doubling every ten years, what becomes of the increase? Have they not lived by our trade and the merchant adventurers, and soaked the kingdom of as many times principal, as they have practised this usury many times ten years, and in the end drawn or carried all away? This is a point to a state very considerable.

Much coin hath been drawn away, without doubt, by the French, who have brought in wares of little bulk, perhaps without custom, but of dear price, and, having turned it into gold, have returned without investing any part thereof; and such petty merchants cannot be reached by the Statute of Employments.

Another cause of scarcity of coin may be the over-strict rule of the uncurrentness of any good coin, and that it must be sold here as bullion; in that case, what stranger will bring in money? Whereas, if every good species be current, according to this assay and weight in proportion to our coin, or rather a little higher, it will draw, namely, money by degrees into England, as lower grounds do water from higher, though they see not the channels; and we see France, Holland, and Germany admit all good coins, though foreign, far and above their intrinsic value.

But I will end this search by proposing some general remedies; for I do now but make essays, and give occasion to more subtle and particular disquisitions:

1. To the first leak of stealing away coin, I would make it felony by an act; for, if a man may justly suffer death for robbing of a private man, I see no

injustice nor cruelty to inflict the same punishment upon him that robs a kingdom.

2. That the neighbour princes and states do cry up our money, and so entice it from us. This, in my judgement, ought to be provided for by our treaties, which was the old way, especially of commerce, by agreeing and publishing of placarts, according to a true par; for that prince, that will make a treaty of commerce, doth it for the use of the commodity; which, certainly, I would deny any prince, that would not consent to keep monies even, by their true values; at least, that would set a higher price upon our money than the King hath done; and if our coin did either keep beyond the seas the English value, or were bullion and uncurrent, the stranger should have as little of our money as we have of theirs.

How to recover the stranger's money, drawn away since our troubles, is a hard endeavour, and can no ways be brought to pass, but by peace and trade; and the resolution of this will fall into the general remedy, which I shall propose.

The peddling French trade must be met with by diligent search, at the landing of these creamers [sic], what they bring in, and by suffering none of them to pass any goods by private warrants; but that, according as they shall be valued, they give bond to invest it in English commodities, natural or naturalized, and that with surety; nay, in this case, not to allow them exchange by bills; for it will not hurt the Commonwealth, if, by any rigour, they were beaten out of their private toyish traffic.

I shall not doubt to offend any but the Mint, which may be recompensed to his Majesty, in his Customs, if money be plentiful; for all goods will follow money. If I did propose the currentness of all goods, and great species of foreign coins, for their true intrinsic value, according to the par with ours; and if I say a little higher, according to occasions, keeping our own coin pure and constant to be cried down as much under according to occasions, I think it will be a policy both reasonable and profitable, by experience tried in other states.

But, leaving these empirical practices, I come now to the great and infallible rule and remedy, which is, in plain English, to settle and assure the ground of trade upon staple commodities; which like the *Lady of Whitsuntide* to her pipe-money, will dance after that; for, as merchandise doth follow money, so doth money, commodity.

I said at first, it was a general opinion, that trade never flourished more than now, and it may be so; but we must consider this be not accidental, and changeable and depending more upon the iniquity or misery of the times, than upon our own foundation and industry; and, if that be so, then it is no sure ground for a state to rely upon; for if the causes change, the effects will follow.

Now it is true that our great trade depends upon the troubles of our neighbours, and we enjoy almost the trade of Christendom; but, if a peace happen betwixt France, Spain, and the United Provinces, all these will share what we now possess alone; and therefore we must provide for that day, for nothing stands secure but upon its own foundation.

To make, then, our own trade secure, we must consider our own staple commodities, whereof wool is the chiefest, and seek the way to both, to keep up the price at home, and the estimation of all commodities made of that, and to be vented abroad.

Some other helps we have, as tin, lead, and such like; but I dare confidently affirm that nothing exported, of our own growth, hath balanced our riotous consumption at home, but those foreign commodities, which I call naturalized, that is, that surplus of our East India trade, which being brought home in greater quantities than are spent within the kingdom, are exported again, and become in value and use as natural commodities; and therefore, by the way, I hold it absolutely necessary to maintain that trade by a regulation with the Dutch, of which more reason shall be given when that particular shall be taken into consideration.

We have yet another great help which is our own, and wants only our industry, to gather the harvest; which is our fishing and erecting of busses, both for the enriching of our kingdom, and the breeding of mariners; and this by private industry, though to private loss, is beaten out already, and shall be offered to the Commonwealth, if they please to accept of it; and to give you one only encouragement, I do avow that before the Dutch were lately interrupted by the Dunkirkers, by their industry and our fish, they made as great returns between Danzig and Naples, as the value of all our cloth, which is one million yearly; and this, in a due place, I desire should have its due weight and consideration.

We have one help more, if we knew how to use it, that is, by the new drained lands in the fens, most fit for flax and hemp, to make all sorts of linen for the body, for the house, and sails for ships. That is a Dutch and French trade: but, in Holland, one acre of ground is rented at three pounds, which if the Hollanders may have in the fens for ten or twelve shillings, it will be easy to draw the manufacture into England, which will set infinite people at work, and we may be able to serve other nations with that, which we buy dear from them; and then the state and kingdom will be happy and rich, when the King's Customs shall depend upon commodities exported, and those able to return all things which we want, and then our money must stay within our kingdom, and all the trade return in money; to encourage you to this, I give you one example:

That if the several sorts of calicoes made of cotton wools, in the Mogul's and Dan's dominions, doth clothe from head to foot all Asia, a part of Europe, Egypt, much of Africa, and the Eastern Islands, as far as Sumatra; which makes that prince, without mines, the richest prince in the world; and, by his Majesty's grace and privileges granted to the Dutch, I am confident we may make and undersell, in all linen cloth, all the nations in Europe.

But I have now wandered far from my theme, which was the decay of trade, and of the woollen commodity.

I must first, therefore, present to your consideration the causes thereof, in my observations, whereof some are internal, and some external.

The internal have proceeded from our own false making, and stretching, and such like practices, whereby, indeed, our cloth is discredited; I speak by experience, from Danzig and Holland, northward to Constantinople, as I will instance in due time.

This false lucre of our own, and the interruption in the dyeing and dressing projected and not overcome, gave the first wound, though, could it have been compassed, it had doubled the value of our commodity.

This hath caused the Dutch, Silesians, and Venetians to attempt the making of cloth, and now, by experience, as I am informed, the half is not vented, that was in the latter age.

Another internal cause hath risen from such impositions as have made our cloth too dear abroad, and, consequently, taught others to provide for themselves.

Another internal cause hath sprung from pressures upon tender consciences, in that many of our clothiers and others have forsaken the kingdom, and carried their arts with them, to the inexpressible detriment of the Commonwealth.

The external causes have been the want of perfection, and countenance to our merchants, established abroad in factories by the state, and by the treaties; whereby the capitulations have not been kept, nor assured to them, neither in Prussia, nor in the Sound, nor Hamburg, nor Holland, nor in the East; and this I dare say, that Laban never changed Jacob's wages so often, as the Hollanders have forced our merchants to change their residences, and the very course of this trade, by laws and tricks, for their own advantage, of which the Merchant Adventurers will more fully inform you.

Another external cause is lamentable, a report of the increase of pirates, and the insecurity of the Mediterranean seas; whereby Bristol and the Western ports, that cannot have so great shipping as London, are beaten out of trade and fishing; and, if once those thieves shall find the way to [the] Bank[s] and Newfoundland, they will undo the west parts of England.

I will trouble you with a consideration, very considerable in our government, whether, indeed, London doth not monopolize all trade. In my opinion, it is no good state of a body to have a fat head, thin guts, and lean members.

But, to bring something before you of remedy, I say thus, for my first ground, that, if our cloth be not vented, as in former years, let us embrace some other way, to spend and vent our wools. Cloth is a heavy and hot wearing, and serves but one cold corner of the world. But if we embrace the New Draperies, and encourage the Walloons and others, by privileges and naturalizations, we shall employ all the wool we have, set more people to work, than by cloth, and a pound of wool, in those stuffs, true made, will outsell two pounds in cloth; and thus we may supply France, Italy, Spain, Barbary, and some parts of Asia, by such light and fine stuffs as will fit those warmer regions, and yet have sufficient for the cold climates, to be spent and adventured in true made cloth, by the reputation both of our nation and commodity.

But, in this course, I must observe that these strangers, so fit to be nourished, and being Protestants, may have privileges to use their own rights in religion, so as they be not scandalous, as the Dutch and French had granted to them by Queen Elizabeth; and certainly, the settling of religion secure in England, the fear whereof made many weak minds to waver and abandon this country, is, and will be, a great means to resettle both the great and lesser manufactures of woollen commodities.

For the external causes, we must fly to the sanctuary of his Majesty's gracious goodness and protection, who, I am confident, when the whole business shall be prepared for him, and that we have shewed him our duty and love, and settled his Customs, in such a bountiful way as he may reap his part of the fruit of trade, I am confident, I say, that he will vouchsafe you all favour, fit to be conferred upon good subjects; and not only to protect you abroad, by his forces and authority, and by treaties with his neighbours, but by increasing the privileges of merchants at home, and confirming all their charters; the breach whereof hath been a great discouragement unto them; and, without which duly observed, they cannot regulate their trade.

There are some particulars in the Spanish trade perhaps worthy of animadversion, as underselling a good commodity to make money, or barter for tobacco, to the imbasement of our own staple for smoke, which, in a due place, ought to be taken into regulation.

Another consideration for a ground of trade ought to be the nature of it, with whom, and for what we trade, and which trade is most principally to be nourished; which, out of doubt, are the northern trades, which are the root of all others, because the materials, brought from those parts, as from Sweden, Muscovy, Norway, Prussia, and Livonia, are fundamental, and of absolute necessity; for, from these trades, get we the materials of shipping, as pitch, tar, cordage, masts, and such like, which enables us to make all the southern trades themselves of less use, being only wine, fruit, oranges, and curiosities for sauces, or effeminacy; but, by these, we sail to the East Indies, and may erect a Company of the West Indies, for the golden fleece which shall be prepared for you, whensoever you are ready for so great a consultation.

The right way to nourish these northern trades is, by his Majesty's favour, to press the King of Denmark to justice, not to insist on his intolerable taxes, newly imposed upon trade, in the passage of the Sound; in example whereof, the Elector of Brandenburg, joined with the King of Poland, hath likewise more than trebled the ancient and capitulated duties; which, if that they shall continue, I pronounce all the commerce of the Baltic Sea so over-burthened, that the Eastland Company cannot subsist, nor, without them, and the Muscovy Company, the navigation; but that the materials for shipping will be doubled, which will eat out all trades. I have given you but essays, and struck little sparks of fire before you; my intention is but to provoke the wit and ability of others; I have drawn you a map, wherein you cannot see things clearly and distinctly; only I introduce matter before you, and now I have done, when I have shewed you the way how to enlarge and bring every particular thing into debate.

To which end, my motion and desire is this, that we may send to every several company of merchants, trading in companies, and under government and privileges; and to ask of them, what are their grievances in their general trade (not to take in private complaints); what are the causes of decay, or abuses in their trades, and of the want of money, which is visible; and of the great losses, both to the kingdom, and to every particular, by the late high exchanges; and to desire every one of these companies, to set down their judgement, in writing to the committee, by a day appointed. And having from them all the general state of the complaints severally, we shall make some judgements of these relations one to another. This done, I desire to require all the same several companies, upon their own papers, to propose to us, in writing, the remedies applicable in their judgement; which materials having all together, and comparing one with another, we shall discover that truth which we seek; that is, whether trade and money decay or not? And how to remedy it.

But I have one request more, and so I will ease you of my loss of your time. That when, from all these merchants, we shall have before us so much matter, and without such variety, and, perhaps, not without private and particular ends, that then you will give me leave to represent to you the names of some general, and others disinterested and well experienced in many particulars, who may assist our judgements in all the premises, particularly in money and exchanges, and give us great light to prepare our result and resolution, to be, by the whole House of Commons, represented to his Majesty; and, for expedition, that a sub-committee may be named, to direct this information from the merchants.

24. A PETITION FROM LONDON ARTIFICERS IS REFERRED TO THE HOUSE OF LORDS, 1642[1]

[*House of Lords MSS.*, N.S., XI, Addenda, 1514-1714, p. 307]

1 February 1641/2

THAT this petition was delivered by a few in the name of many thousands poor and mean petitioners, but a strong and high petition and being extraordinary both for the matter and manner of it the House of Commons thought fit to present it to your Lordships.

Read the petition.

---

[1] This is the calendared version of the document, the original being barely legible.

The cries of the poor pierce the heavens.
Make impression in the hearts of the Commons and hope in their Lordships.
Want makes them cry and hunger which breaks through walls.
They have not bread to put in their mouths.
Relief they must have, which must be by setting them on work.
That cannot be but by settling of trade and restoring it.
Trade will not settle till these fears and distractions be taken away.
Fears will not remove till we see a change, that the great affairs of the
kingdom be carried in another channel, that those evil counsellors be re-
moved who have discomposed the frame of this com.
That we may secure ourselves, be in a posture of defence; now exposed to
dangers; no man sure of anything but what he carries about him.
Till this be we cannot expect, trade should run in such a way as that the poor
may be set on work
Some things extraordinary in the petition.
At another time should be very tender of this, as a breach of privilege, but
now consider the necessity of a multitude, a sleeping lion, not good to awaken.
It would but pull on the mischief sooner, show *quibus vitijs impares sumus.*
Our distractions have weakened us.
The manner extraordinary.
Come in twice or thrice, say they wanted bread, they must not starve.
We told them we were sensible of their wants, our endeavours had been and
should be to remove the causes, and we were now about it, and did hope we
should give them satisfaction.
They answered they knew we were not in fault, did what we could.
Knew some of the Lords were the cause that stopped all, the disturbers of
our peace desired to know who they were.
This but the beginning of evils like a small cloud, soon cover the sky.
A pattern out of a great piece, these say what all the rest think.
Wisdom to prevent it in the beginning, in the end break out, and past cure.
Concerns their Lordships. It will come to them: like a flame goes upwards.
. . . will come to them by degrees, rents not paid.
Therefore wisdom and will had need concur.
House of Commons not in fault, done what they could, therefore protest not
guilty of the mischief.
For their own safety must declare it, least involved.

25. AN ESSEX PARSON'S[1] RECORD OF
THE DISASTROUS YEARS, 1646–51

[*The Diary of the Rev. Ralph Josselin, 1616–1683,*
ed. E. Hockliffe, Camden Soc., Third Series, XV, 1908, *passim*]

September 15, 1646. A marvellous wet season, winter coming on very early.
A great hop year; wheat this year was exceedingly smitten and dwindled and

[1] Ralph Josselin, vicar of Earls Colne, Essex.

lank, especially on strong grounds. All manner of meats excessive dear, beef at cheapest 2½d. per lb., butter and cheese very dear, and yet it was a very rich grass year . . .

October 24, 1646. A wonderful sad, wet season, much corn in many places abroad rotted and spoiled in the fields; grass exceedingly trodden under foot and spoiled by cattle through the wet which hath continued almost since the Assizes. Work very dead, wool risen to 16d. in the pound and upwards; butter and cheese and meat very dear, and corn rising. Little corn sown and a very sad season still continued. Great divisions and fears of our utter ruin in the kingdom . . .

November 1, 1646. This week the wetness of the season continued with little or no intermission and so it hath continued for above two months . . .

May 23, 1647. This spring was forward. Yet all things continued excessive dear; if grass had not come on our wants would have been very great . . .

August 15, 1647. Times of great sickness and illness, agues abounding more than in all my remembrance last year and this year also. Fevers spotted rise in the country. Whether it arise from a distempered and infected air I know not, but fruit rots on the trees as last year, though more, and many cattle die of the murrain. This portends something . . .

August 16, 1647. A fair day. Land is through mercy in a good case, and the seed time good. The Lord send us plenty; all provisions are excessive dear and scarce to be gotten for our money . . .

September 26, 1647. The Lord good in the season which was very fair, and as fit a good time as ever came. Things are at that rate as never was in our days: wheat 8s., malt 4s., beef 3d., butter 6½d., cheese 4d., candle 7d., currants 9d., sugar 18d., and every other thing whatsoever dear. The soldiers also returning to quarter again with us, and that in a great proportion, viz. 25.

October 17, 1647. The season was very fair, and wholesome. The plague abated in London and Chester, blessed be God. The kingdom in a strange, unsettled frame . . .

February 6, 1648. This time was a sad, dear time for poor people, only their work beyond expectation continued plentiful and cheap. Money almost out of the country . . .

May 9, 1648. Among all the several judgements on this nation, God this spring, in the latter end of April, when rye was earing and eared, sent such terrible frosts that the ear was frozen and so died, and cometh unto nothing. Young ashes also that leaved were nipped and blacked, and those shoots died, as if the Lord would continue our want and penury, we continuing our sins . . .

June 28, 1648. The Lord goeth out against us in the season, which was wonderful wet, floods every week, hay rotted abroad. Much was carried away with the floods, much inned but very dirty and dangerous for cattle. Corn laid, pulled down with weeds. We never had the like in my memory and that for the greatest part of the summer. It continued to August 14 when it rained that it made a little flood, and commonly we had one or two floods weekly, or indeed in the meadows there was as it were a continual flood . . .

August 16, 1648. A very great flood with the great rains last day and night. The season sad and threatening.

The nation's sins are many and sad. Lord let public ones be pardoned. The nation's judgements are: 1. continual rain to the spoiling of much grass, and threatening of the harvest; 2. the sad charge by war to the undoing of the country. The sad decay of trade in reference to our poor, to our undoing except God find out some other way of subsistence.

The war in the nation, the divisions among ourselves, our cryings out after peace on any terms to save our skins and estate, whatsoever become of others, Lord remove these judgements from us for thy name sake . . .

August 24, 1648. Daily rains, but especially this morning, we found it exceeding wet. It caused a very great flood, abundance of hay rotten, much corn cut and not cut groweth, and yet men repent not, to give glory unto God . . .

January 7, 1649. This week the Lord good and merciful to me and mine in our health, peace in providing for us, notwithstanding the great dearness of every thing, beef at 3½*d.* per pound, wheat 7*s.* 6*d.*, rye 6*s.* 4*d.*, cheese 4*d.*, butter 6½*d.* per pound, and men expect it will be dearer and dearer . . .

February 18, 1649. Great dearth and want of all things. I gave 4*d.* per pound for pork . . .

March 18, 1649. Cheese now at 4¾*d.* per pound, butter sold by some at 8*d.*; pork 4¼*d.* or 4½*d.*, beef 3¾*d.* Great fear of the decay of trade.

April 15, 1649. This week the Lord was good and merciful to me and mine in all outward mercies, when as there is a great scarcity of all things, beef ordinarily 4*d.* per lb., butter 7*d.* or 8*d.*, cheese 5*d.*, wheat 7*s.* 6*d.*, rye 6*s.* 8*d.*, yet we wanted nothing needful or fitting for us . . .

May 20, 1649. This week the Lord was good to us in our peace, in health, and providing for us, notwithstanding the great scarcity of all things; rye at 6*s.* 8*d.* bushel, butter at 7*d.* pound, cheese 6*d.*, beef 5*d.*, lamb 7*d.* . . . .

July 8, 1649. Made a collection for Lancashire which is much afflicted with famine and pestilence . . .

August 6, 1649. This week I went about to gather up some tithes. I find money scarce . . .

August 19, 1649. A week of harvest, corn abated in price a little . . .

September 11, 1649. This day I went to visit Mr. Jacob. Heard of some stir at Oxford by the regiment there upon the levelling score.

September 16, 1649. The disturbances at Oxford over in a good season, and by a very finger of God. The rate of things continueth dearer and is likely to increase.

October 7, 1649. This week all things very dear: wheat 8*s.* 6*d.*, rye 6*s.*, barley 5*s.* a bushel, cheese 4½*d.*, butter 7½*d.* the pound.

November 25, 1649. The times were wonderful hard, wheat at above 9*s.* and rye about 7*s.* a bushel . . . We began this week to fast ourselves a meal or two in a week, and give away a meal's provision in meat broth, or money to the poor. The times were very sad in England so that men durst not travel and, indeed, rich men were afraid to lie in their houses, robbers were so many and bold. Men knew not how to carry monies and many gentlemen's houses were set upon and pilfered . . .

December 1 to 16, 1649. This time all things were wonderful dear: wheat 9*s.*, malt 4*s.* 8*d.*, rye 7*s.* 6*d.*, oatmeal 8*s.* per bushel, and cheese 4½*d.* All things dear, yet the season was indifferent warm and dry; beggars many, givers few. Lord of thy bounty, provide for the poor. I constrained myself to do more than ordinary for our poor. It is better to give than to receive; and yet poor people were never more regardless of God than nowadays . . .

April 25, 1650. Hay was very scarce and dear at 3*s.* and 3*s.* 4*d.* per hundred-weight . . .

September 22, 1650. The season is very sad in wet, hinders seed time, raiseth corn already, rotteth our muttons . . .

March 1, 1651. The season cold and very sad, work scarce, the poor in a sad condition, and it's feared it will be far worse with the spinner[1] . . .

March 2, 1651. The season cold and things hard, price of corn and commodities rise and little or no work . . .

April 20, 1651. Many suppose our Commonwealth lost. Spain and France and Holland against us. Ireland and Scotland heavy work, and not to be effected; the English divided and worn out with taxes and burthens; the merchants' trade even ruined, and so all tending to poverty . . .

June 9, 1651. The state of England, although worn with civil wars and scarcity and ill trading for many years, being but in bad terms with Holland, and not altogether sure of Spain, proclaimed open war with Portugal, and is in open war with France, our fleets being in the Midland Sea. We at the same time are endeavouring to conquer Scotland and Ireland; attempt Sicily with a fleet and yet send a fleet also to reduce the islands of Barbados in America. And yet the nation is much discontent and divided, yet feareth not the attempts of any foreigner against them.

December 1, 1651. This day we killed a good hog. Through mercy the price of things and cattle abateth very much . . .

26. FAMINE IN THE NORTHERN COUNTIES, 1649

[*The Moderate*, no. 42, 24 April–1 May, 1649, pp. 473–4]

Newcastle, April 26

Sir,

The necessities of these parts are very great especially Cumberland and Westmorland; the poorer sort are almost famished and some really so, the

---

[1] i.e. the clothworkers in Colchester and the neighbourhood.

number whereof are too many and more than I shall now mention that have died in the highways for want of bread. Most of the meaner sort in Cumberland have left their habitations and travel with their wives and children into all these parts to get relief, but few are able to help them, their own conditions being so sad and miserable. A certificate came to this town, signed with the committees and justices of peace of the county of Cumberland that there were at this time no less than 30,000 families in that county that had neither seed nor bread corn, nor monies to buy either, desiring a speedy collection amongst them for their present subsistence, else most of them will unavoidably famish. A collection was made as desired and something given but nothing considerable to feed so great a multitude. The anger of the Lord begins to be kindled and the flame thereof will consume all before it, especially those that provoke him to it . . .

April 24 [sic]

A petition from Kendal and other parts of Westmorland complaining of their sad condition for want of bread, desiring relief: the House thereupon referred it to the Council of State to consider of convoys for all parts of the Commonwealth and that the merchants may send to Hamburg for importation of corn and to take a speedy and effectual course therein. Alas, they have no seed corn to sow their grounds and what bread corn is imported they have no monies to buy it, and before any corn can come from Hamburg they are like to be famished.

27. HENRY ROBINSON ON THE STATE OF TRADE, 1649

[Henry Robinson, Briefe Considerations concerning the Advancement of Trade and Navigation, 1649]

I Conceive it will appear upon inquiry,

1. That in whatsoever country the greatest stock of money and credit shall be raised, there will the greatest trade of the world be established.

2. That the greatest trade of one country hath a capacity of undermining and eating out the lesser trades of any other countries.

3. That the greatest trade will be able to make the greatest number of shipping. And,

4. That what nation soever can attain to and continue the greatest trade, and number of shipping, will get and keep the sovereignty of the seas, and, consequently, the greatest dominion of the world.

If this be true, it will a little concern especially all well-willers to the Commonwealth of England, whom all neighbouring states look upon with an envious malignant aspect, timely to consider in what posture and condition our trade is, as well within ourselves, as in relation to other countries.

'Tis well known that, even till within these ten years, our trade was famous amongst all known nations, and at the same time, our ships at sea as dreadful to whomsoever became our enemies; but as neither our trade, nor consequently our shipping, were improved to one quarter of what they might have been, even so, some other nations had then advantage, and did get ground upon us, in such manner, that if but for some few years longer they continue proportionably to gain upon us in trade, riches, mariners, and shipping, it will be impossible we should defend ourselves from their puissance; and so much the rather, in that our trade at present, as touching exportation, is not one fourth part of what it was ten years ago, as will appear by the receipt of Custom.

If then we desire to be long free from the yoke of foreign dominion, and to enjoy that liberty, which we have so dearly purchased, it concerns us seriously to inquire into all the ways and means, whereby trade and navigation may be increased and multiplied unto the utmost.

The trade of England may briefly be divided into inland and maritime.

Inland trade is that which is driven in every city, or from one town or place unto another within the land, according to the increase whereof, both exceedingly the whole nation, in their respective stations and callings, is not only accommodated and enriched, either by what they deal in, or with what they stand in need of, but the maritime trade is likewise thereby advanced, by exportation of the overplus of all such commodities as the inland trade hath produced more than are sufficient for service of the nation.

This inland trade is chiefly to be improved by increasing, and continually employing all manner of artificers, and especially of manufactors, not only of our old and New Draperies, the product of our native staple, the wool of England, but even of foreign unwrought materials, as raw silk, cotton wool, grograin yarn, hemp, flax, etc. which by politic ordering might be so managed, as that though the materials come from abroad, yet so much cordage, silks, linens, or other stuffs, as are required and brought in from abroad, for the use of England, might be made amongst us, to the setting awork many thousands more of poor people.

In order whereunto, it is necessary either that those unwrought materials be carried to and fro upon the cheapest terms where these people live that must work them up into their full manufacture; or else that the people set up their habitations in such places where these unwrought materials are to be had cheapest; for that which makes any commodity dearer in one place than another is chiefly the carriage, according to the nearness or distance from one place where it is made or grows, unto another where it is to be spent; particularly of wool, it may be observed, that great store thereof is brought to London to be sold, and the same wool carried again into the country to and fro, perhaps to different places, to be carded, spun, and weaved into stuffs, and these stuffs brought up again to London to be sold, through so often carriage by land must needs come to cost so much dearer; the redressing whereof, and to make all things alike plentiful with all people throughout the land, it is necessary to reduce, as much as maybe, all straggling tenements, villages, and towns together into so many cities, nearer to one another, that there may be people enough of each trade, calling, and occupation, for supplying one another's occasions within themselves with whatsoever shall be commodious and necessary both for their own sustentation, and in order to advancing the inland trade of the nation.

And in regard all parts of the earth do not produce all fruits alike, neither in plentifulness nor goodness, it is necessary these cities should be situated near unto navigable rivers, or where artificial ditches may be made for conveying all things to and fro by water from one city to another; though this be a great work and of great charge, since it is feasible, it must be done, otherwise such nations, who in this respect either have got the start of us already, or shall begin to practise it before us, will have such advantage of us, as that we must necessarily become subservient to them, and continue at their mercy.

Another way for increasing inland trade is to make all materials, not only sheep's wool, but silk, hemp, flax, goat's hair, cotton wool, and the like, free from excise, customs, and all manner of taxes, whereby the people of this land may be enabled to work them up into their full manufactures, and vent them abroad as cheap as other nations.

And because neighbouring nations have not only, through our want of foresight, bereft us of our peculiar prerogative of furnishing all foreign parts with iron ordnance, gained the grand fishing employment from us, made new discoveries of tin and lead mines, in prejudice of ours, but for these twenty years together have been stealing away our woollen manufactures, which through continuance of this war, and rot of sheep, are reduced to about $\frac{1}{4}$ of what they were, it is more than necessary.

First, that there should be a severe prohibition against killing sheep for some few years, that may in some measure recover our stock of wool again. And secondly, there is as great a necessity of engrossing all or the greatest part of the wools of Ireland, Scotland, and Spain, into our own hands for some few years together before these nations be aware thereof, as the only course for getting our native workmen home again, and hindering the progress and establishing these manufactures in other countries; and if monies shall be wanting to compass so great a work, the propounder hereof will undertake to discover how it may be furnished.

The other branch of trade called maritime consists in exportation of our native commodities, importation, and transportation of foreign.

The advantage to be made of maritime trade is to procure the exporting of as great a quantity of native commodities as possible, whereby so many more of our people may be set awork, and find money for their wares. And as this will be very much furthered by ordering matters in such manner as that they may be furnished with materials in all parts of the land upon the easiest terms, so likewise by suffering our native commodities in their full manufacture and artifice to be exported with little or no customs or other charges.

As touching importation, that ought to be managed in such manner, as that all foreign necessary commodities, as victuals of all sorts, ammunition, pitch, tar, timber, sheep's wool, goat's hair, raw silk, hemp, flax, and other unwrought materials, might be encouraged to be brought in in greater abundance, and superfluities, as wrought silks, wines, fruits, and sugars, (which three last we may shortly be sufficiently furnished with, from some of our own plantations) by taking off the greatest part of customs from the former, and charging it on the latter.

And transportation, I term the bringing in of foreign commodities into any part of England, to be carried out again into any other country; and this doubtless would be much enlarged if all or most part of the outports were made free ports; that is, that whatsoever foreign commodities were brought into any of the said outports, and the customs paid, whensoever they were again extracted, the said customs should be forthwith returned to him that extracted the said goods.

By this course, England would become a warehouse or storehouse of all manner of foreign commodities, from whence not only Ireland and Scotland, but even France, the Low Countries, and nether parts of Germany, Muscovia, Norway, Denmark, Swedeland, and Dantzick, with all those parts adjoining (besides Italy and Spain) might most commodiously be furnished, not without large employment to our shipping, and great benefit to our merchants.

This is that trade whereby our neighbours, the Hollanders and Zealanders, so much increase both their navigation and their wealth, their own territories are so straight and barren as would neither feed nor set the twentieth man awork, in which respect, they are necessitated to be industrious, and get themselves a living, by becoming purveyors to other nations.

Whereby they have this advantage into the bargain that such nations as are thus provided for, by them, of all necessaries must continually live at their mercy, be contented to be fed with a bit and a knock, and always be forced to stand in awe of them, lest they should pick a quarrel, and set the dice on them, or starve them outright, before they could be relieved from other hands.

And unto the people of our own nation, would redound another advantage of no small concernment, in that when all the outports were thus stored with all manner of foreign commodities, the countries which lie near those outports would first furnish themselves therewith at far easier rates than now they can from London, in regard of the charge of bringing them from London to such respective ports, besides the loss of time, for which interest is likewise reckoned and charged upon account thereof.

But if it be objected that this course will lessen the present customs and revenue of the Commonwealth, it is answered that a little custom on a great trade is equivalent to a great custom on a little trade, besides the multiplying of shipping, mariners, manufactors, and artificers of all sorts, and settling the public revenue and trade upon a sure foundation.

Another way of advancing both our importation and transportation is by requiring restitution of such plantations as the Hollanders most subtly bereft us of, both at and since the exercising their cruelties upon our merchants at Amboyna, by which stratagem of theirs they have almost worried us out of the East India trade, which, if we apply ourselves to again, as also in the West Indies, Persia, China, Guinea, we may not only be enabled to furnish ourselves and other foreign nations with all sorts of their commodities, which we stand in need of, but even plant colonies there, and employ as many of our ships and mariners as we can make (an unknown trade, and therefore gainsome) by transportation of their commodities from one port unto another within those countries, whereby we shall not only advance great sums of monies yearly for freight thereof, but make discovery both of their weaknesses and necessities, as well as of their strength and riches, to be much more improved upon all occasions unto our great advantage.

And last of all, or most of all, the grand fishing employment, that which is predominant over all others, as having in itself a capacity of drawing all other trades after it, not only serving as a nursery for breeding mariners, and completely victualling us for three days a week, but also supplying us with such store of all sorts of fish to be transported to other nations, as may bring us home in return commodities of all sorts, more than were needful, both for our own occasions, and supplying of our neighbours.

This fishing employment is of greater concernment and benefit unto the Hollanders and Zealanders at present than all the trade of England ever was to us in its most flourishing condition, which, if they still go on enjoying to themselves, they will daily get so much more advantage over us; for this fish, which costs them nothing but a little toil, except nets to catch them with; besides all things else they purchase masts, timber, pitch, tar, cordage, and all other materials, although they have none of them of their own growth, they can build shipping cheaper, and in greater quantity, than we can do, which is worth the taking notice of in time.

By reason of our situation, we have the advantage of them for setting upon this fishing work; we have the fry come home to our very doors in shoals, even all along the northern and western coasts, whereas others must make a journey to seek them out, which imports expense of time and charges.

And if formerly the plenty of flesh-meat made us neglect such opportunities, the scarcity and dearness thereof at present should so much the more move us to embrace it, and the Parliament out of pure necessity engage us to it, by enjoining us to forbear all manner of flesh-meats three days a week.

Now as government and order is necessary in all affairs, so that there might be good order and rule observed in trading, it hath been thought requisite by our ancestors to reduce almost all traders into so many several companies, according to the respective places they traded to; but whereas this course was intended for multiplying and advancing trade, for enhancing the price of our native commodities, and bringing down that of foreign, it is now become the great obstruction, through the private interests and over swaying of particular men. I wish therefore that both the setting open and at liberty all trade free alike to all men, and the enclosing of it, by charters and corporations, may be seriously debated and agreed on, that it may neither be quite ruined, for want of good government, nor yet obstructed, no less than if monopolized, by colour of a corporation.

And for conclusion to what I have said, I will only add this, that unless an Act be speedily passed against cutting down timber or wood, whether for firing or building of ships or houses, save in such places as sea coals cannot be had for firing; and withal for putting all former statutes in execution, for securing us unto all generations with continual supplies of timber for shipping, and that in the mean time, whilst they are to be had, we may be forced upon fetching all masts and timber from abroad, free of all custom, and all manner of charges, as the Hollanders have done continually; our navigation first or last must necessarily be endangered through the excessive dearness and decay of shipping, and whatsoever course be taken for advancing trade, it will never succeed currently and with equal success to other countries, unless bills of debt may most compendiously and securely be assigned over from one man unto another, by authority of Parliament, and that there be a particular court of merchants, and others well versed in merchandizing, erected, for speedy determining all differences about trade and navigation. Concerning other matters incident hereunto, I shall desire the reader to be referred to a more large discourse entitled, *England's Safety in Trade's Increase*, printed by Mr. Nicholas Borne, at the south entrance of the Royal Exchange 1641.

28. THOMAS VIOLET'S REPORT ON THE DECAY OF TRADE, 1650

[P.R.O., SP 18/9, no. 61]

IN OBEDIENCE to the commands of this honourable Committee of Parliament, having seriously considered of the debates had before you on Wednesday last the 22 of May 1650 concerning the importation and exportation of coin and bullion in relation to the Mint and the trades and commerce of this nation, I do humbly present such reasons of the decay of trade and the causes that so small quantities of coin and bullion have been brought in of late, and so much of ours carried out, as in the short time limited I could call to mind; which I desire they may be accepted as they are by me intended for the best advantage of our Commonwealth as followeth.

The first and principal reason of the decay of trade hath been the late intestine and unhappy wars of this nation; before the breaking out thereof, the trade of England was both free and flourishing at home and abroad. But immediately after by reasons of obstructions both at home and abroad it began to fall into a consumption, under which it hath languished ever since. Our golden fleece (which is our Indies) was with their supporters destroyed and devoured by the rapine of the soldiers, and great quantities of the remainder by the exorbitant liberty taken on both sides, was transported to our industrious neighbours the Netherlanders, the most active improvers of such advantages, and the best fishers in troubled waters. Our clothiers and workmen in all sorts of manufactures in most parts of this Commonwealth were by continual losses discouraged or destroyed and many of them enforced to take up arms, or to forsake their dwellings and not only so but to forsake their native country and to set up their trades and gain their bread in foreign parts.

The merchants were much discouraged and many of them undone by seizures and confiscations of their ships and goods in foreign parts by some princes and states that favoured the late King's designs; and many more were robbed and spoiled at sea under pretence of the late King's commissions without hope of reparation for want of sufficient and constant convoy, which, being never wanting to the Hollanders and Zealanders, they carried the trade from the English merchants and seamen but more especially since they have concluded a peace with Spain, so much to their honour and advantage.

It is well said by a late writer that 'commerce is the life of a State, manufactures are the sinews of trade, and money is the soul of both'. When the soul is separated from the body, it is without life or motion. Our money employed in trade was either belonging to strangers or to our own nation; that of strangers which was employed by exchange or let out at interest was soon drawn in and returned from whence it came upon the first breaking out of the war where they thought it more secure, whereof our merchants had upon their credits made use for the enlarging of their trade which they were not able to carry on with their own stocks, and many of our nation as well merchants as others did visibly dispose of a great part of their estates into foreign parts and some also transported their persons and families as well as their estates, fearing what the issue might be of the sad distractions and divisions which the sins of our nation had justly drawn upon themselves, which, by the blessing of God upon the Council and endeavours of the supreme authority of our nation, I hope and pray may be happily and timely composed, now the enemies of our peace are suppressed.

For the monies belonging to our nation it hath been very much exhausted in the time of the late war, not only by the losses aforementioned and diminution of trade but by the excessive charge the Commonwealth hath been necessarily put to upon maintaining so long the war itself in the just defence of those things which are most dear and precious to them; but most of all in relation to the auxiliary forces out of Scotland, which our Parliament were necessitated to make use of both here and in Ireland for the preservation of the whole, for not only their pay, which amounted to a very considerable sum of money, but what was indirectly gotten, both here and in Ireland, was carried away into Scotland, whereas by the pay of our own army the stock of England is not diminished but remaineth amongst us, except the treasure and materials of war that hath been transported into Ireland which is hoped may in time be returned with advantage; the materials of war for the furnishing of our armies by land and our navy at sea which have been bought in foreign parts hath also much diminished the stock of the nation.

And lastly by reason of the great dearth and scarcity of corn of late years a considerable sum of money hath been expended in corn which hath been imported to supply the necessities of this nation whereby the small quantities of the native commodities of this commonwealth of late years exported in comparison of what hath been in former times hath been so overbalanced by the surplusage of commodities imported that the public stock hath thereby been much impaired; for it is a maxim that when the exportation of native commodities exceeds the importation of foreign, the stock of the Commonwealth is so much increased and money brought in, and the contrary hath contrary effects, and then our money goeth away, and for the same reason little or no money cometh in.

I may add that when retailers and shopkeepers take liberty to become merchants, as many have done of late years under pretence of liberty and free trade, the Commonwealth suffereth great damage; for either they carry out some of the native commodities which, for want of experience therein, they have neither skill to buy or sell; besides their end being to make their gain upon the commodities they intend to import for the furnishing of their retailing trades in their shops and not upon the commodities exported, which they have neither the skill nor patience to improve to the best advantage of the market, for their returns must be speedy or else their shops are unfurnished, which is not only prejudicial to the Commonwealth in beating down the prices of native commodities to strangers and by enhancing the prices of foreign commodities to our nation, but also to such merchants who labour to advance our native commodities abroad, and to keep down the price of foreign commodities, which are necessarily expended in this nation.

And such as have or do sit at the receipts of customs can tell you that these shopkeepers and another sort of disorderly and unskilful traders, commonly called interlopers, made up of factors, clothworkers, packers, and drawers, which follow trade to the like disadvantage to the state, and frequently to the ruin of themselves and families for want of experience, are the importers of fine spices, silks, both wrought and unwrought, fine linens, and other fine commodities made up in small parcels on purpose to be stolen ashore without paying custom or excise.

And by the same means they are dexterous and active to transport money also, to furnish themselves with commodities for their purpose to bring in as aforesaid, which is a great discouragement and detriment to merchants that follow an orderly trade, wherein they have been bred, and honestly paid to the state both custom and excise.

And for the transportation of the money of our nation, I have reason to believe that the said interlopers and shopkeepers, having most of them the opportunity of making and packing up of their goods, and opening of them themselves privately in their own houses (which merchants have not) they may be instrumental in packing up and conveying away our money in their goods, not only for themselves but for strangers who do employ them to colour their indirect dealing.

I hold it my duty also to discover unto this honourable committee that I have been often advised by some lovers of the Commonwealth who live beyond seas that very much money both gold and silver hath ordinarily been carried over in the Dutch men of war because they thought themselves free from search.

Now having to the best of my understanding discovered the obstructions of trade and the inconveniences accompanying the same, and the causes thereof, I shall crave leave to cast in my mite into your treasury by proposing some remedies for the removal and prevention thereof for the future, which I humbly conceive to be within the latitude of the commands you were pleased to impose upon me.

First, seeing it hath pleased God to direct the Parliament to change the form of government of this nation, in order to a settlement of peace and happiness both in church and commonwealth, I humbly offer to your grave considerations whether the particulars ensuing may be conducible to that end. First to settle able, godly, and peaceable ministers in all churches through-out the nation, that will with care and conscience endeavour to teach the people to fear God, to obey their superiors, and to live peaceably with each other, together with a competent and comfortable subsistence for all such ministers where it is wanting. Secondly, to sweeten your new government to the people and to allay the bitterness of the late years past, wholly to take off free quarter, being taken to be the greatest mark of slavery in the nation. Thirdly, that the Parliament would pass an act of oblivion with exceptions of all such as have made themselves incapable of that favour.

For the recovery of the decayed and almost lost trade and commerce of this nation, the merchants have need of encouragement and protection from the State and their trade and government cherished at home, and counten-anced abroad according to the laudable practice of the Lords, the States of the United Provinces, who are so vigilant over their traffic that upon the least complaint of any obstruction either at home or abroad, they use all means either by treaty or by force to remove it. By which means they have gone beyond all nations in all manner of trade which they have undertaken, and have made their country the magazine of the native commodities of all other countries, wherein our own nation had not many years past a considerable share; also their country is a granary for all Christendom and yet they have not corn of their own growth to feed the hundredth man in their dominions. They also outstrip all nations in number of ships and seamen, and yet they have not wood of their own growth to warm them in winter. They abound in quality and quantity of all manufactures and yet they fetch the materials thereof from all other parts of the world which are so much improved by their policy and industry that they eat out other nations that trade with them in the same manufactures made of their own materials. Their fishing trade upon our coast bringeth them not only food but infinite advantage by way of trade in furnishing other nations therewith and employeth abundance of their ships and men.

I am of an opinion that for the encouragement of bringing in coin and bullion the importer must be at liberty to make his best advantage thereof and not be limited to the price of the mint; and that the goldsmiths may be at liberty to buy that or any other money not current here, to use in their trade; which is a mystery beyond my understanding.[1]

But I conceive it not necessary nor essential to the trade of a goldsmith nor for the advantage of the Commonwealth to give liberty to the goldsmiths to sell any coin of this nation either current or not current for by that means monies are in a readiness for the transporters whereby they can make more advantage with least trouble, noise, or hazard than can be procured any other way.

I have observed that in other countries very strict laws have been made against the exportation of their money and bullion; the penalties have been not only the forfeiture of the money and bullion but three and four times the value thereof, sometimes whipping, sometimes banishment, and sometimes loss of life and goods, and of the forfeiture of all the ships wherein it shall be found, if it be taken in by the master's consent.

Now if out of zeal to the good of the Commonwealth I have said anything that is impertinent or besides the text, or have been too tedious, I humbly crave pardon and submit all I have said to the grave wisdom of this honourable committee. This proposition is presented to the Parliament with all humility as a sure and speedy way for the bringing in of treasure into the mint and to restrain the goldsmiths from giving for gold or silver above the price of the mint, for such a liberty will destroy your mint, and the regulation of the goldsmiths' trade according to the Act now presented from the Council of State to the Parliament is agreeable to the old statute laws of this nation and to the daily practice of all our neighbour nations, as I have lately presented to the Parliament. And I humbly desire this proposition to be seriously considered of by this honourable committee.

1. That for the encouragement of bringing in gold and silver which usually cometh from Spain, being the fountain thereof, that there be an Act made that the importers shall have liberty to transport the two-thirds of what they shall bring in to the harbour without paying any composition whatsoever for any foreign bullion either in coin or in bars; and a free declaration in the Act to all merchants that they shall have constant convoy in the Downs for the transportation of the full two-thirds, as heretofore when the composition

---

[1] This sentence is accompanied by a marginal comment in another hand: 'No other man gives advice for the managing of a trade and yet confesseth it is a mystery beyond his understanding. I pray mark it.'

trade flourished at Dover; which within these twenty years that little port paid above forty thousand pounds yearly for the composition trade.

2. The merchants strangers or others to deliver in the other third part into the mint and they are there to have liberty to enter it in what names they please, and they are to do the like at Dover if they conceive any damage may come by their registering of it either at Dover or in the mint.

3. The State to declare in their Act that all the said gold or silver to be imported shall be coined with all expedition and just advantage to the owners.

4. The Act to declare that any such gold or silver so brought into the Tower to be coined shall not be subject to any arrest, embargo, claim, sequestration, attachments, or any other demands whatsoever, either by the State or any merchant or any other person whatsoever upon any demand, pretence, or suggestion in any manner whatsoever either by the State or any other person or persons whomsoever; nor by any order or orders shall infringe and break this Act. But that the same person or persons either merchants, seamen, or of any other condition whatsoever that did bring in the said gold or silver shall receive their monies out of the mint according to the just standard and fineness; and the master, warden, and controller and all other officers of the mint are to make all expedition possible may be for the coining thereof (deducting out the usual fees to the State which is 2s. the pound for the pound weight troy and 15s. the pound weight troy for gold) and they are to be required upon the strictest penalties not to make any stop of any merchant's gold or silver upon any warrant whatsoever, but to pay it with all expedition to the party or parties or their assigns that did bring it into the mint; and the Act to warrant them against any pretence or demands whatsoever for the doing thereof.

5. That all gold and silver imported by merchants strangers from Spain, every such merchant or merchants or other persons upon certificate of the officers of the mint of the value of the money either in gold or silver coined in the mint, shall have liberty and free leave to transport the full value of all gold or silver either in bays, serges, perpetuany, cloth, or any other commodity of the growth of England; every such person or persons, having a certificate as aforesaid of the officers of the mint, shall pay only English customs for so much as they shall prove coined either in gold or silver in the mint. And for all foreign commodities bought up here by merchant strangers they shall pay strangers' customs as formerly.

And the farmers and officers of the mint are to be required the last day of every term to certify up to the barons of the Exchequer the several sums so brought into the mint and allowed by the farmers of the Custom House that so the State may see there are no more warrants for any greater value than only for the gold and silver coined in the Tower of London, and all other goods whatsoever that are bought and exported out of this nation over and above the value of the gold and silver brought into the mint every merchant stranger shall pay the full rate and custom for it as hath formerly been accustomed, notwithstanding this Act desired or any clause therein contained.

Motives and Reasons—humbly presented to you why you should with all expedition pass this Act.

In imitation of the Council of Spain who hath ever given leave to all merchants, nay, his enemies for the transportation of silver and gold for the returns of all corn or ammunition imported into Spain without paying any custom; and when the Hollanders were in hostility, yet they had free liberty to bring in corn and ammunition and to return money without paying the State licence money which is always two and a half per cent.

It is well known to all merchants that trade for Spain that one-third part of their gold and silver at the least is never registered; which silver and gold is consigned to particular merchants for the avoiding the king's duty before it come within the Bar at St. Lucas (and generally now it is sent for Holland). Now if you were pleased to use them so cheap in their customs and to give them the like privileges and encouragements as the Hollanders do, and to see to give them a constant convoy as hath been heretofore used within these twenty years at Dover, then I humbly conceive the Spaniards and other traders from foreign parts would make our English ports their scale of trade which would be a great improvement to the composition trade which within these twenty years made this Commonwealth some score of thousand pounds yearly and now maketh little or nothing by reason the merchants strangers have not those encouragements as they find in other countries. Gold and silver is a precious thing in this Commonwealth and as you make a law for to punish the transporters, so in all humility the importers, I humbly conceive, ought to have all encouragement and protection. Plymouth lying for the west, and Dover for the east, more advantageous than any town in Holland or Flanders, we might here have the same bars of silver and pieces of eight which they have in Holland, which monies are for the most part invested in our commodities there, because they can buy them there cheaper (by reason of the great customs here laid on the merchants strangers), and beyond seas there is no difference between the merchants strangers and the natives. And those that bring in gold and silver beyond seas have all encouragement and privileges that any of the natives have for the returning of commodities for their money imported, never paying more custom than the natives.

The benefit you have already received whilst the Act is but in dispute against transportation of gold and silver, I shall humbly offer it to you: that whereas gold was the 20s. piece, 22s. about a month ago, now no man will give 21s. nay not 20s. and 6d. And the like for silver, it was at 5s. and 2d. the ounce, it is now 5s. and 1d. If you please to pass the Act, I am confident, having vigilant men to look after it as you must have, this mischief will quickly be stopped. All what I have said I humbly submit to your grave wisdoms.

London this 30 of May   T.V.

29. A LIST OF ITEMS ON THE AGENDA OF THE COUNCIL FOR TRADE, 1651[?]
[P.R.O., SP 18/16, no. 138]

Narrative of what things have been reported from the Council for Trade

Report to the Council of State for the settling a convoy for the southward, October 9th, 1650.

Report to the Council of State for the establishing of a constant convoy for Holland, Zealand, and Flanders, October 9th, 1650.

Report to the Council of State for the settling the Guinea trade for fourteen years, November 6th, 1650.

Report to the Parliament about the cutting of the river of Wey in Surrey, December 4th, 1650.

Report to the Parliament concerning a licence for exportation of monies to the East India Company, December 6th, 1650.

Report to the Parliament about enlarging the number of meal markets for the ease of the inhabitants about London, December 16th, 1650.

Report to the Parliament concerning encouragement to be given for importation of bullion, December 20th, 1650.

Report to the Parliament about an expedient for the carrying on the Greenland fishing for the last year, March 24th, 1650.

Two reports to the Council of State concerning restraint of goods of foreign growth to be imported in foreign bottoms; one dated April 4th, 1651, and another dated July the last, 1651, with some alterations and amendments.

Report to the Parliament about a clause to be explained in the late Act touching the encouragement of bringing in bullion and coin, April 28th, 1651.

Report to the Council of State concerning the settling and regulating of the trade of dornix weaving in the counties of Norfolk and Suffolk, September 3rd, 1651.

Report to the Parliament about the complaint of several mariners and masters of ships trading to Newcastle, September 26th, 1651.

General Report of the Council to the Council of State concerning their opinion of the necessity and benefit that would be of reforming and settling all the inland trade and manufactures of the nation under a certain way of government and superinspection, September 22, 1651.

Report to the Council of State concerning several petitions in reference to indulgence to be given to some persons concerned in the late Act for increase of shipping, November 20th, 1651.

Narrative of things concluded on and ready to be reported

Opinion about free ports; their necessity and way of settlement.

Opinion about the settling and reforming of heavy dyed silk with the manner of it and laws to be established about it.

Opinion about settling and regulating the manufacture of Colchester bays; with the manner of it; and laws to be established about it.

Opinion about the settling and regulating the dyeing of cloths, stuffs, and linen of all sorts throughout the whole nation; with the manner of it; and laws to be established about it; together with a determination about the import and use of logwood.

Opinion about the settling and regulating the great commodity of tin, with several particulars concerning it.

Opinion about settling the regulation and manufacture of gold and silver thread.

Narrative of such other businesses wherein a great progress hath been already made by the Council

The settling and regulating the Greenland fishing for the future.

The settling and regulating the Bilbao or Spanish trade.

The settling and reforming some differences among, and several abuses incident both to, the companies of trades in general, and in particular to the companies of clothworkers, skinners, woolwinders, upholsterers, horners, combmakers, and others.

The assignation of bills and court merchant.

The encouragements for the cutting of the river of Derwent in Derbyshire.

The several encouragements fit to be given to promote our fishery.

The drawing of a yearly balance of the general export and import of this nation.

The settling and reforming of our clothing; with some expedients about that great dispute between the clothier, grower, stapler, and brogger and jobber in the buying of wool.

A further progress also in most of which businesses hath been for some months suspended; and the many suitors quieted in expectation of the issue or resolutions of the Parliament to the general report of the Council about our manufactures before mentioned, and dated September last the 22nd.

[Endorsed:] Narrative of what things have been reported by the Council for Trade.

30. A COMPLAINT OF TRADE DEPRESSION, 1659

[A Collection of the State Papers of John Thurloe, Esq. . . . , London, 1742, VII, p. 616]

[Part of a letter from Mr. John Barwick to Sir Edward Hyde, 16 February 1658/9]

. . . There was never greater complaints in the city for want both of trading and money, and that they are real appears by the falling of house rent in the city 10 per cent. The Spanish merchants especially go down the wind; not one in ten but finds himself a loser upon his audit this last year. What is got by commodities of Spanish growth in England is pocketed by the Dutch, insomuch as some suggest to have a law made to lower (or otherwise destroy) all commodities of Spanish growth that shall be brought into England. No marvel then the city should be so desirous (for so they are always) to have peace with Spain, and war with the Dutch. The former, I hear, has been endeavoured underhand; and Whitelocke is made one of the Keepers of the Great Seal to give him a title with a greater noise for an ambassador (as is thought) in order to such a treaty. And yet in this tottering condition they foresee none will treat with them, however otherwise inclinable. But whether the Spaniard be inclinable or no, I know not. It should rather seem not, by some endeavours there are now on foot to settle an intelligencer for Spain here in England, wherein they desire the assistance of some of the English nation; and this I am well assured of, if it signify anything.

Great preparations are making for sea. It is said, they will have 40 sail at sea by the middle of the next month; and 30 more as fast as they can after. It seems they are in good forwardness, for there is a press out for 1,500 seamen, and a good many are pressed already. The Sound in likelihood will be the chief cause of this expedition; and yet I believe they have one eye upon their own security at home, in case there should be any intestine division. Febr. 16, 1658, late at night.

31. ROYALIST PROPAGANDA ON THE DECAY OF TRADE, 1660

[*Awake O England: or the People's Invitation to King Charles, being a Recital of the Ruins overrunning the People and their Trades, with an Opportune Advice to return to Obedience of their Kings, under whom they ever flourished*, 1660, *Harleian Miscellany*, I, London, 1744, pp. 269–70]

. . . We remember that in the beginning of our late transcendent Parliament (which none before it could reach in comparison of dangerous issues, and deadly fruits) how high the cries went against ship money, patents, monopolies, illegal imprisonments, and such other breaches into our free-born interests, as appeared by the then condemning complaints, which searched our sores, to the worth of a sin; and yet amongst all those lamentations, which hooded our eyes, and deafened our ears, whilst our pockets were picked, and our wives' fingers stripped) we never heard of excises, fifth and twentieth parts, sequestrations, taxes and contributions and amongst all these oppressions, gifts to maintain foreign rebellions; but well we remember that, whilst we honestly paid our tithes, we and our ministers enjoyed such a double blessing, as our souls fed upon the food, which now they want; and our ministers rested contented with their dues, for which they returned grateful hospitalities, without the new ungodly encumbrances of augmentations whereby, robbing Peter to pay Paul, many of our church doors have so lost their keys, as none have entered into them for many years.

When we paid ship money, which amounted not to so much as one of our Friday-night suppers, in the whole year, by the pole, we had safeguard to our seas, our wool went to the workmen, our clothing passed by the merchants to all parts of the world; returns were made of all things we wanted at easy rates, even to richness, glory, and plenty; our navigation was as sure as our travel from one market to another; our meanest seamen, who took charge, had noble receptions at home and abroad; we enjoyed our houses and lands in peace, and had no complaining in our streets; our woods were guarded by laws, and supplied by plantation; our fleets were formidable upon all seas, and our people of all conditions, as well civil as soldiery, brought honour and dignity to our kingdoms.

Instead of these rejoicings, we are filled with howlings; our trades are generally lost, and there is none to give us work; our wool and leather, and corn, and butter, and cheese, are daily transported, and whilst we are lessened in our manufactures and vocations and industries, we are raised in rents, and food, and taxes, and all things belonging to our livelihood; the mysteries of our crafts, and the materials of our manufactures, do find such acceptable receipt in foreign parts, as unconscionable men have brought the ruins of their own country into a trade; and those laws, which for the chief benefit of the people, and the very life of trade, are made, are so boldly affronted, as the good patriots, who for the benefit of themselves and country endeavour to prevent the great damages which come by such bold attempts, are by cunning practices of clerks, and the remissness of superior officers, so discouraged, as that law, which was made to defend and encourage them, is carried fully against them, and the plaintiffs are sued at law, till they have neither cloak, nor coat, nor bed, nor board, nor house, but a prison to receive them; widows wring their hands, and orphans lament, whilst there is none to deliver them; every man oppresseth his neighbour, for it seems good in his own eyes so to do, because, alas, we have no King.

If we look into our neighbour nations, we are the subjects of their mirth, and the song of the scornful; we (as if we were all guilty) are styled murtherers, king-killers, and the very abjects among them trample upon us, for the blasphemous people among us have committed so horrible treasons, as ought not once to be named among us; if we turn our eyes and ears from these dismal spectacles and groans, we presently encounter another object of our sorrows, the body of our trades is anatomized, dissected, and, from the most intrinsic secrets thereof, is discovered to foreigners; all workings in wool, which together with that material have, by the providence of our ancestors, been, with all their wisdom, restrained from other nations, are now so much at liberty, and, by false-hearted Englishmen, made so familiar to strangers, as not only our mysteries are laid open, but our materials are made theirs, and that trade of clothing, which, in one valuable kind or other, maintained eleven or twelve parts of our kingdoms, is almost totally lost to England, which, for many hundreds of years, hath made them be both loved and feared of all other nations.

As for our fleets, which were formidable, and our navigation, which was honourable throughout the world, our ships are now daily brought into captivity, insomuch as, through our short and improvident war made with Spain, above two thousand English vessels have been carried into their ports, and all the goods in them are made prizes; many, who have been very able merchants, who have not only kept hospitality at home to the great relief of the needy, but have built and maintained tall ships abroad, to the honour and strength of our kingdom, and to the increase of mariners and trade, have in these times been and still are brought to compound their debts, not with more disrepute to their credit than grief to their hearts, and ruin to their families . . .

32. NOTES OF THE LORDS' COMMITTEE ON THE DECAY OF RENTS AND TRADE, 1669

[House of Lords Record Office, Main Papers, H.L., 28 October 1669]

Committee concerning [Rents] and Trade, 1669[1]

Die Jovis, 28 October 1669

Bridgewater

The power of the committee is read.

It's offered as a cause of decay of rents in Shropshire the prohibiting the bringing in of Irish cattle.

The bankers engrossing money.

The living of gentry generally in this town.

The grazing of great quantities of land managed by one man, viz. a shepherd or the like to the depopulation of the country.

The gentry and generality of people living beyond their fortunes by which the consumptive trade is greater than that of the manufacture exported.

Want of people a cause of decay of trade.

It proposed that the cause may be without the land, of the decay of trade within the land.

Qu. whether it be within the power given to the committee.

It's offered that the want of a fleet at sea is a cause.

Qu. whether the words of the power of the committee be not large enough to admit of considering causes without the kingdom for the decay of the trade within.

---

[1] The Lords Committee was appointed on 25 October 1669 'to consider of the causes and grounds of the fall of rents and decay of trade within this kingdom and to make report thereof to the House'. The Earl of Bridgewater was in the chair.

No power at present to propose remedies without further direction of the House.

Ques. whether the Council by virtue of this order may consider of the trade without this kingdom in order to the finding out of the cause of the fall of rents and decay of trade within the kingdom.

The order for the committee is read and the question read again and being put was received in affirmative. Content: 11; Not content: 3.

The causes proposed are repeated.

The not bringing in of bullion is offered.

It's proposed that some members of the Council of Trade be desired to attend this committee to inform their lordships of what they find to be the cause of the decay of trade within this kingdom.

It's proposed to examine the officers' books of the mint to compare the quantity of money lately coined with those of former times.

Ordered etc. that

1. Sir Henry Blunt,	2. Doctor Worsley,	members of the
3. Capt. Titus,	4. Mr. Tho. Papillon,	Council of Trade
5. Mr. Childe		

be desired to attend this committee on Thursday, the 4th day of November next at 3 oc. in the afternoon in the Prince's Lodgings near the House of Peers to inform their lordships of what they find to be the cause of the decay of trade within this kingdom.

Adjourned to Thursday next 3 oc.

Die Jovis, 4th November 1669

E[arl of] Dorset

The gentlemen members of the committee of trade being summoned to appear.

Dr. Worsley. As to the decay of rents not properly cognizable by them. The way of enriching of kingdom by manufactures and by exporting and importing. It impoverisheth a kingdom. Whether the import exceeds the export. The negligence of manufacture whereby the nation have lost their repute abroad.

Mr. Childe. The trade of England not decayed in gross but increased. To consider how the Dutch have advanced their trade. The Dutch are very faithful in the seal. Aulnage was intended an advantage but now the tickets are to be bought. There wants a regulation upon our fish. None will give credit to the packing of them. They give encouragement to all inventors. Here a patent is granted, there the party rewarded, and the design made public. Their ships are of small burden and useful. Their thrifty way of living. The education of their children. The lowness of their custom. The well-providing for their poor and employing of them. He conceives the laws not good because the parishes provide for themselves only. Their banks and Lombards. Their law merchant very useful. The way to promote trade is to increase the stock of the nation. To make returns of commodities by bills of exchange. To upon [sic] which traffic is now current. Registers useful. The frugality in all their public affairs. Their easy admission of burghers. Their multitude of navigable rivers. The lowness of their interest. The increase of the fishing trade. The freedom makes the nation valiant. All men are led by ease or profit. They have gotten all trade from us but what is ours by fortification natural or artificial. They can have no trade of our pilchards because they might be saved of our shore. Newfoundland fish. New plantations. In cloth if they could the 3 per cent would root us out of all. Liberty of religion. Trading people are musing people. The persecution of other places brought us our divers trades, Milan fustians and jean fustians. Comfit making brought in by one that escaped the Inquisition. Trade of Maidstone thread carried all the world over. Silk-throwing and silk dyeing maintains 20,000 people in this city. Post office by Burlamachi. Statute bankrupt prejudicial to trade. All taxes that lay impositions upon our own commodities prejudicial to trade. Advantage of trade would have all freedom laid open. The statute of 5 Eliz. against exercising a trade without serving apprenticeship prejudicial. The exportation of coin hurtful. Bylaws among artificers very destructive. The want of hands is one cause of decay of trade. The fire in London and the plague. The great land taxes not preceded these judgements. The usual plenty of corn. The racking up of rents '51 and '52. The great improvement of Ireland. The Irish Act well intended but hath not taken the effect. They now send the beef into the plantations. An Englishman can hardly put in a ship into any Irish port being stopped up by the Dutch. The late innovated trade by the bankers in London. While interest goes up, land must go down. Anticipation of his Majesty's revenue. Our fishing trade in Newfoundland very small. Our cloth trade hath not increased here by the great increase of it in Germany and in other countries. New tax upon cloth in France. The Eastland and Norway trade much impaired. All Easterlings have liberty of bringing any trade hither. There is in the charges nothing to balance the account but a small impost to balance the profit. Nothing to remedy this but to lay a considerable tax upon the ships. If the French king take exception, he hath laid the like upon us. Another cause of the decay of the Eastland trade the straitness of the trade, they admit none unless they give 20*li*. The Russia Greenland Company. They have lost the Greenland trade and now call for help. We had but one ship this year and the Dutch 3 or 400. Two ways only appear for the cure of the Irish trade: that they bring what they can of the native commodity but no foreign. The Scotch trade quite lost to the English by laying high duties on both sides. Whatever tends to the increase of hands and stocks doth increase the trade of a nation. Taking off burdens makes trades easy. The way to make it necessary. Usurers must let the money lie dead or purchase lands. Industry more profitable than idleness. All trade a kind of warfare.

Dr. Worsley. To the fall of rents. The fall of rents ariseth from corn, cattle, or wool. It must be as these months to confirm it. This lies as the increase of the manufacture in the country. The wool must of necessity be manufactured and where that is, there must be the more to consume it. Where it is not manufactured, it increaseth the number of poor. It concerns the import of this nation. We have lost much of our trade of cloth. We do not now send forth a third, scarce a fifth of the cloth we did forty years since. To give encouragement to all that set up trade. Though we have lost our woollen manufacture to the value of 900,000*li*. yet we take no care to bring in the manufacture of linen and cordage. If it be the interest of the Dutch as a small nation, it is ours as an island. The French have set up a Council of Trade and the king hath given a very large bounty and largesses to encourage trade.

Mr. Papillon. Three essentials to the carrying on of trade: stock, people, and carrying on of trade. Stock much impaired by the fire so that the stock is employed in building which should carry on trade. Some 100,000 people wasted by the plague. Some things divert trade. Abundance of money spent in suits of law, both common and civil, which might be employed in trade. Freedom in religion necessary to the increase of trade, the doubt of which disheartens and take[s] of[f] trade. Foreigners that would incorporate into the nation would much advantage the nation. The weavers not suffered to use the trade by the weavers of London but clapt in prison. More land improved in England than ever, so trade. Every nation sets upon trade, and if we will carry on trade we must make it easy. We had the whole trade of Ireland in our own hands but now gotten by the Dutch.

Mr. Titus. No more to offer than what hath been.

Sir H. Blunt. The chief thing is matter of interest being so high. The countryman harps much upon the interest of their portion, the land tax, and the slow taking of the commodities. Ireland takes many away, some the fens, and some the plantations. The lowness of interest the *unum magnum* to help the business. Trade cannot be carried on without lending or borrowing. Money may be borrowed at 4 per cent.

Mr. Childe. If interest were reduced to 4 per cent after a little sullenness the usurer will let it; they would not be able to sleep without disposing it. If reduced to 4 per cent land must be 24 or 25 years purchase.

Dr. Worsley. The stock of the nation much to be considered. The way to bring down interest. If we take the course to be the greatest monarchy in the world we should have the best shipping and stock enough.

The consideration of these heads to be referred to Monday.

Customers. Ordered that the farmers of the customs be appointed to wait upon their lordships upon Monday and to bring with them the best information they can give concerning the balance of trade inward and outward for these seven years past: 1. Interest. 2. Negligence and deceit in our manufactures. 3. Great troubles and charge in suits of law both common and civil. 4. The want of registers. 5. The ease from pressures upon people's consciences.

Ad[journed] Monday etc.

Die Lunae, 8 November 1669
E[arl of] Essex

The Customers appear and say it is a weighty business and for a long time they understand not what is meant by the balance of trade. There was a possibility heretofore of making a balance of trade when the goods rated at 1s. per pound. But now uncertain. If their lordships desire to know whether trade doth increase and decrease, they may do it.

Home goods may come to 70,000*li.* and foreign at 400,000*li.* Dutch commodities imported from our own plantations.

The Customers withdraw and after some debate they are called in again.

They are desired to bring in account of all commodities in the several species. To begin at the furthest year. Nobody able to guess at the time. Being asked what cloth exported in such a year, they say it is very easy.

Mr. Millington. Great store of fish go out of the nation which pay no custom. Gaining of freight abroad. The pocket commodities and laces that come from France and Flanders do undo us. There is no discouraging of them but by great persons not wearing or using them.

The years '69 and '63 to be accounted for and to be brought in.

Ordered etc. that the farmers of the customs being assisted by his Majesty's patent officers do, with what expedition they can, bring unto Mr. Browne, clerk of the Parliament, an account of the importation and exportation of all commodities with the several species, quantities, and measures distinguished as much as may be by the several countries and places from whence they are carried. And this to be for seven years ending at Michaelmas last past. And that they begin this account with the dispatch of the years '63 and '69 in the first place. And the said patent officers are required to give their assistance accordingly . . .

Die Mercurii, 10 November 1669
E. Essex

The order read for the Council of Trade to attend.

L[ord] Lucas. To take away interest is unjust, because therein no gain to recompense. It will hinder the building of London. It will hinder the bringing money into this kingdom. It will discourage industrious men and encourage prodigality. It will be most hurtful to widows and orphans.

The Council of Trade called in as also Mr. Grey and Mr. Love.

Mr. Childe. The abatement of interest for the advance etc. 1. It advanceth the value in land. 2. It increaseth trade. The experience and what hath been may be. Testimony of old Sir Tho. Culpeper printed '61. Land at 12 years' purchase and since advanced to 16 or 17. Pressures upon land, the great land taxes. The great plague. The fire in London. Dry summers for 4 or 5 years together, corn plentiful. Racking up of rents '51 and '52. The great improvement of Ireland. The banking of the goldsmiths. It improves the rents of farms, stocks growing cheaper. The abatement of interest preceded the raising of lands. It advanceth trade. The reason of all laws of interest expressed in the preamble the benefit of lowering interest.

Sir Tho. Culpeper. By consequence it must be so for the usurer, if he lends not, his money must trade or buy land. By reason no man trades but he promiseth himself a greater benefit than 6 per cent. All trade lost to the Dutch. They have the white herring trade, we the red because we have charcoal, and nearest to be brought on shore. Whereas we had four or five Eastland ships for one Dutch, they have now the great advantage of us in having above 20 for one of ours. If interest were at 8 per cent, it would abate a third; if at four, it would increase it. It multiplies artificers. It inclines a nation to thrift. Where interest is high, they are unthrifty. When interest is low, the merchant must trade for little profit. Since the abatement we are grown more frugal in hospitality and housekeeping. The other expense of cloths and coaches is profitable. It increaseth the number of people, affords more subsistence for maintenance. If we want people of our own, we shall have them from other places. A country improved gives more employment and feeds more fruitful.

Ob[jection]. If a low interest would do all this, it were easy to be rich.

A[nswer]. This cannot be done *per saltum*. An old custom is not easily changed.

Ob. If a law would do it in England, what is the reason it is so in Holland without a law?

A. The law or some effects of a law have done it in Italy and other provinces. P[ope] Paul 6th did dispense with usury upon condition the borrower did gain so much money.

Ob. Low interest not a cause but an effect of great riches. A fruitful land causeth multitude of people, but a multitude of people increaseth a fruitful land. More elder brothers good husbands than younger; the one hath encouragement, the other despair.

The Dutch master us in trade. We always begin young men here; there it holds from generation to generation. A little money will make a great trader, but a small gentleman. The abatement of interest is the greatest sumptuary law in the world. This will quicken our invention. It will advance land and increase trade. Mr. Manley's book saith it is luxury and buying foreign commodities. Not one half of the wine imported as was when money at 8 per cent. The wages of a labourer the certainest pulse of a nation's poverty or riches. In Scotland, poorer than this, labour is cheap. The height of wages proceedeth not from paucity of people but lives[? ?] of them, saith Manley.

M. Make a shilling 10*d.*, you will avoid weighing, clipping, and exporting.

A. If the King should raise money from 10*d.* to 1*s.*, no foreigner would take it at more than 10*d.*

Mr. Grey. In Holland interest is very low. Because they have great store of money and little land. In Ireland and Scotland it is high because money is scarce.

Mr. Titus. The consequences. The usurer will call in for his money. All the nobility and gentry that have mortgaged their land must sell it at the usurer's rate. The trade must be broke. The setting a rate upon other commodities have not made them cheaper. When money called in, it shall be very scarce and the law for lowering of it will be evaded or eluded. Land was 20 years' purchase and now at 16 years. The racking of the rents make the purchase low. When noblemen and gentry come to trade they shall not put money to interest. When there is gain, gentry shall have no more than is due, and when there is loss, he shall be sure to bear his part. In all monarchical and aristo-cratical governments the first pulling down thereof hath been lowering of interest.

Mr. Love. He agrees with Mr. Childe that Holland is a rich country and interest low, whereas because Holland is a rich country therefore interest is low. Holland is a trading country and have freedom of religion. They have more money than land to buy, and the father entails it to his posterity. It is produced there by a law of prudence because they do not know how to dispose of a better. In Italy there is little difference between interest and exchange of money which costs them at least 10 per cent. In Turkey money at 40 per cent, never under 12. Turkey full of money as a sum[??] of money passing through Barnet to pay an army at York, which makes not a country rich. Whether weak security can borrow money on weak security. What shall become of orphans' money and gentlemen's monies? What argument is there to bring money to 4 per cent which may not be used to bring to 3–2–02. No man will bring twice a commodity from foreign parts where there is not hope of profit. He is of opinion with Mr. Childe that money may be brought lower, but not by a law. No way to make it lower but by making England flourish with money.

Dr. Worsley. Interest of money so necessary an appendix to all civil affairs as any can be. In undertaking anything that is to be considered. When in-terest is low, if a man builds a house and interest low, he cannot set it at a rate as when it is high. In Ireland great scarcity of money and cannot be remedied. That lowness of interest may make people rich 'tis probable, but not without other things to accompany it. He that persuades[?] the lowness of interest must show that there is sufficient for trade, for the rebuilding of London, for the nobility and gentry's use, and for his Majesty's occasion. And if it should be brought down there will be our[?] brokers and the scri-veners which will cozen all. Holland trade with an overbalance but they gain much by freight and by the East India Company. They let out money by exchange and interest. Where seed is made choice of and the land not manured and fitted for the seed, the crop must fail.

Mr. Childe. Generally confessed that a low interest increaseth trade. One argument of the increase of wealth is that 3,000*li.* is no more than 2,000*li.* 20 years ago. The wages of labourers. The building of City. All the trade of London was carried on at vast time and now pay ready money. The Act of Navigation have improved our trade. There were not half the cranes in London for landing of goods which now are.

Q. Whether a law will do it.

A. It will do what it hath done thrice already.

Those [that] are in want shall pay more than those that are in credit. Usurers are a sly, cunning, and timorous people and will not disobey the laws. To keep their money they must bar meat and sheep. In Holland they have in effect a law. They are masters of the cash of the nation and if they [own the banks?] they are masters of the money. So in Italy they have Pontifical laws and auricular confession. Wherever money is high, were difficult to take up. Here you take up money at real security for 100*li*. per annum whereas in Ireland you cannot under 400*li*. Young men trading with a Dutchman must needs fail.

Mr. Titus. When usurers call for their money (*ut supra*). A great part of the money used in trade and for the building of London is Dutch money.

Mr. Childe. Whether the lowness of interest be the cause or effect of the plenty of money. Were it possible to do things as to think of them, were somewhat possible but not all *per saltum*. If we lower interest, the Dutch must do it.

Dr. Worsley. No connection between plenty of money and bringing down interest.

Q. What store of foreign money here?

A. Mr. Childe believes there is not 10,000*li*.

Love. Ald. Love thinks it an advantage to have the Dutch take away their money, if there be 10,000*li*. Dutch money here. If there be money enough in the kingdom, it were well the interest were low[?]. It would discourage merchants to bring in money. More money given in portions than formerly because the trade greater. The more money spent in building the less in trading. Most of the trade driven for ready money because the most of them are young men and must trade for ready money, but if he could take up money at interest it were better to sell at 10 or 12 months time. There is more trade but a tumultuous trade which will certainly undo us. Much money sent away beyond sea as to the Indies which is extremely advantageous. It cannot be carried on without money.

Mr. Childe. What merchant will bring home money if he can get but 4 per cent, if he can [get] 10 per cent in goods? A merchant abroad hath no respect to the interest of England.

Ald. Love. If a man hath 100*li*. in money and 100*li*. in goods, it is all one.

Mr. Hobland. In bringing goods they consider the profit with the commodity which will be most advantageous. Upon the fall of gold they were feign to change their gold into pieces of eight. They never let money to interest when they can buy goods. When they intend any voyages, if they cannot advance at 6 per cent they are disgusted. Interest is a custom and charge upon their trade.

Dr. Worsley. The lowering of interest is a general good, but the time is to be respected. It is not now seasonable. Though we make a great show in trade yet 'tis questioned whether there be money enough in England.

Q. Whether we shall get more money by keeping up interest.
A. If there be an occasion of money, the calling in of money if you desire it. The straits and necessities of men will be put to a plunge.
Mr. Papillon. The commodities must be cheap at home which must be by lowness of interest.
Dr. Worsley. The lowering of interest will mend trade (but not by a law). But our money being carried out, we shall have none brought in.
Q. Why money scarce in Ireland?
A. Little manufacture in Ireland.
Mr. Childe. More exported than imported yet the country poor because of the height of the interest and because the profit of the country goes to persons absent.

They all withdraw. Their lordships debate the business. The question put: whether it be the opinion of this committee that it is advisable that the interest of money be reduced to 4 per cent and that a bill be prepared to that purpose.

C[ontent]   12
                          carried in the affirmative
N[ot]C[ontent]   1

To report this to the House that they have called the Council of Trade and do add what reason he sees fit.
Adjourned to Saturday 3 o'clock.

Die Sabbati, 13 Nov. 1669

E. Essex
The order of Monday read. Sir Robert Murray called in, delivered to their lordships a paper concerning the use of registers in Scotland. He believes the land in Scotland sells better in Scotland by reason of these registers. Land near Edinburgh will give 20 or 22 years' purchase and money rents will give 25. And the land in Scotland gives a better value to be sold than the land in England. The land in the highlands worth 20 years' purchase.
Sir Walter Walker. A notary made by royal authority and shall have a testimony which shall give him a protocol according to which every man that hath business; in England we pass by seisin or enrolment in the four courts at Westminster, or before the justices, by lease and release, and by record. Beyond the sea he gives an attorney or procurator power to. A public testimony at least charge is a notarial contract. A protocol particularizeth and boundeth the land, out of which is made an instrument for passing the land. The notary of every town and country is such that what passeth before him is good surety[?] against the voucher.
Sir Walker to attend their lordships with the customs of France and Holland on Thursday next 3 o'clock.
Sir Robert Murray to be desired to give further information out of Scotland.
1. To report that it is the opinion of this committee that one cause of the decay of rents and value of lands is the uncertainty of titles of estates. And

as a principal remedy for this their lordships offer it as their opinion to the House that there be a bill of registers for the future.

2. Touching naturalization. After a long and serious debate touching the admitting of strangers to be very useful to this nation, especially such as fit[?] for managing the lands in the country rather than artificers, that the want of people in England is one of the causes of the decay of rents. And one chief remedy for this is to have a bill of naturalization.

Order. Alderman Bucknell to be heard to the decay of rents.

Col. Worsley, Mr. Titus, Mr. Childe. Order to be sent to the Council of Trade to attend their lordships on Wednesday 3 o'clock and bring such papers as they have in their hands touching the ill making of the manufactures of England.

An intimation to be given to Col. Birch.

Adjourned to Wednesday 3 o'clock . . .

Die Mercurii, 1 December 1669

E. Essex

Those gentlemen members of the Council of Trade that were ordered to be here are called. Being asked for their papers, they say that Alderman Love hath them in his hands.

Mr. Childe. A law cannot be made too strict for staple commodities. Colchester bays were sold by the credit of the seal, but since the siege of Exeter [= Colchester?] those bays are not so good by 15 or 20 per cent.

Mr. Titus. Transportation of wool is the destruction of the manufactures. The law against it cannot be too strict. The law made against it already is not sufficient. The proof for bringing wool to the seaside should be easy. There should be a benefit to the informer. It should be easy to come by.

Mr. Papillon. Where any seal of the staple is put, it is for the credit of it. But he is of opinion that for every man to put his own particular seal would be more advantageous. If wool be proved to be carried to the seaside it should be confiscated.

There should be care taken for bringing in the main part of Irish wool; then the endeavouring to get hands for working it. That upon all treaties with foreign princes and states care be taken. There is no care taken for Irish wool. And if we should stop up all the avenues in England against exporting wool, and leave Ireland free, it will be ineffectual. A patent in Ireland for transporting wool. A licence for transportation from Guernsey and Jersey. If the Irish are left at liberty to ship the wool from what ports they please, it is impossible not to be cozened. Any vessel carrying over wool should be burnt, and then few men would adventure to carry over any.

Ordered that Mr. Du Moulyn, secretary to the Council of Trade, do attend their lordships upon Saturday next 3 o'clock in the Prince's Lodgings etc., and bring with him such papers as he hath in his hands whereby their lordships may be the better informed concerning the ill-making of the manufactures of this kingdom.

Adjourned to Saturday 3 o'clock . . .

Die Mercurii, 8 December 1669

E. Essex

Mr. Du Moulyn, secretary of the Council of Trade, called in and delivers in such papers as are in his hands touching Colchester bays and ill making of cloths in Somerset and Wiltshire and the remedy thereof. The first of them, called Mr. Brewers paper, read and all of them delivered to him back again and referred to a further time.

Order. The Council of Trade to attend their lordships.

Touching indulgence, to know the commands of the House whether the committee shall proceed further therein.

The opinion of the Committee whether some ease and relaxation in ecclesiastical matters will be a means of improving the trade of this kingdom.

C[ontent] 8
N[ot] C[ontent] 1   carried in the affirmative

Adjourned to Saturday 3 o'clock.

Die Mercurii, 23 February 1669

E. Dorset

Trade: their lordships fall upon some debate about the lowering of interest and respited it till a further time. The order of 7 November to the Customers to be renewed . . . Next their lordships fall into debate of naturalization and of registers. The taking off of customs will increase trade. The debate deferred . . .

33. THE LORDS CONSIDER THE REPORT ON THE DECAY OF RENTS AND TRADE, 1669

[Lords Journals, XII, pp. 273–4, 280]

Die Mercurii, 24 die Novembris 1669

THE Earl of Essex reported that he was appointed by the committee for considering of the reasons and grounds of the fall of rents and decay of trade within this kingdom to acquaint this House that the committee have often met and made some progress in the business and have had before them several persons of the Committee for Trade and merchants to give their lordships the best information they could concerning the fall of rents and decay of trade within this kingdom. And after a serious debate of the matter for the present the Lords Committees do think fit to offer to the consideration of this House three things as in their opinions most conducible to those ends: as that it is advisable:

1. That the interest of money be reduced to £4 *per centum* and that a bill be prepared for that purpose.

2. That one cause of the decay of rents and value of lands is the uncertainty of titles of estates and as a principal remedy for this their Lordships offer it as their opinion to this House that there be a bill of registers for the future.

3. That the want of people in England is one of the causes of the decay of rents and one chief remedy for this is to have a bill of naturalization . . .

Die Veneris, 3 die Decembris 1669

The Earl of Essex reported that the committee of the whole House have considered of the matter concerning the reducing of interest money and the opinion of the committee is that the lowering of interest money from £6 to £4 *per cent*. will increase the value of land.

The question being put whether to agree to this report from the committee, it was resolved in the negative.[1]

34. SIR WILLIAM COVENTRY ON THE DECAY OF RENTS, 1670

[B.M., Sloane MS. 3828, ff. 205–10]

An Essay concerning the Decay of Rents and their Remedies, written by Sir William Coventry about the year 1670

THAT rents decay every landlord feels, the reasons and remedies are not so well understood. Those which accrue to me as the most probable ground of the fall of rents are: 1. Plenty of product. 2. Want of vent for our product. 3. Want of tenants. 4. Want of money to stock grounds and keep the country markets.

1. That our product is greater than formerly cannot be denied by any who considers not only the draining the fens, grubbing up woods, enclosing common fields and commons, parks, chases, etc. but also the great improvements made upon the lands of private men by watering, marling, liming, clover, grass, sainfoin, etc. so that offering proof to this head would be time mis-spent.

2. As our own product is more so our vent is less, whether we consider our foreign vent or domestic.

For the foreign, that the vent of woollen manufactures into foreign parts is decayed is evident to all, which proceeds not all from the adulterating our manufactures, which makes them less esteemed than formerly, but also from the growth of woollen manufactures in foreign parts, especially Holland and France. Holland supplyeth their want of our finer wool with the Spanish, which makes a finer cloth and more pleasing to the gentry than

---

[1] The House was prorogued on 11 December, but the committee was appointed on 17 February in the following session, and revived on 28 February. However, no further report was made.

ours, and for the coarser sort of cloth Germany and Silesia being now in peace (which in the time of our greatest prosperity in clothing they were not) furnish a wool capable enough of it—and what they will not do, Ireland or by stealth England supplies them. I shall leave this head not being willing to enter into a copious discourse on that subject, but shall only add that the late discomposure in our trade with Scotland and Ireland takes from us much vent and gives it to foreigners which whether it be recompensed by their keeping out their cattle is by some disputed.

That our domestic vent is likewise diminished must be granted by any that considers: 1. That we have fewer people than heretofore. 2. That those we have consume less than heretofore.

That we have fewer people than formerly is imputable not only by the hand of God on the late visitation, but more especially to the long continued diverting of the young and prolific people to the plantations, and to the re-peopling of Ireland besides those whom the late civil wars devoured in England, or as a consequence of it drove into foreign parts, either as soldiers or otherwise, to seek bread and find a grave instead of contributing to the peopling of their own country.

That those we have consume less may be made evident not only from the practice introduced in the late civil war for saving charge of eating but one meal a day but also by the observation of the increase of the use of fruits, herbs, and roots, especially near all great towns, whereby an acre of garden will maintain more than many acres of pasture would have done.

Hence it is demonstrable that this evil of abundance is not likely to receive a cure but either by increasing our exportation or our domestic consumption, which cannot be but by increasing our people or by diverting some of the ground (now employed to corn and cattle) to other uses.

For that of our exportation an attempt towards it is now made by an Act entitled An Act for Encouraging of Tillage, etc. by which corn, cattle, and horses are permitted to be carried out, which, though good, yet are no way sufficient for the entire cure.

To mend our domestic vent by the increasing our people there are two ways, either by naturalization of strangers with such restriction as shall be judged fit, or by encouraging our own people to marry and taking away those restraints which now hinder it, as the laws against cottages, inmates, etc. and the method of obliging poor people to give security to save the parish from charge before they are permitted to inhabit, which I believe it will be hard to persuade, till the erection of workhouses (where such as will not work for themselves may be compelled to work for others) being encouraged shall have shewed another method of easing the parish, which would also produce another effect beneficial to the farmer, viz. by banishing laziness in the poor would make wages cheaper than now, that the poor, relying on the main-tenance of the parish, work but when they will and at what rates they please.

For the changing the use of our land two things occur to me most rea-sonable and most desirable. The one to encourage the planting of wood and severely to punish (either by laws in force or by new if needful) the destruction of it. This besides the employing the ground is very necessary for posterity in order for shipping. The other is to encourage the sowing of hemp and flax, which, besides the diverting the ground from corn and cattle, would employ all the poor that can be found, and almost of all ages and conditions scarce any so impotent but might do somewhat in the linen trade. This would also keep a very great sum of money in the land which is now sent out for linen, and would make in time of war less dependence upon foreign supplies either for cordage or sail cloth. Of the latter (by experience it is found) we can make as good as any abroad and the former might doubtless be improved, though perhaps it might not arrive to the perfection of some foreign hemp.

There is one particular more to be mentioned relating to our domestic consumption, which is that the consumption is not well distributed, the constant residence of the court at London (which was heretofore a little remedied by progresses), the sole administration of the law being likewise there (except a little at Ludlow which is now much eclipsed, that at York being wholly taken away), and the frequent and long sessions of Parliament draw so much to London that it hath decayed the hospitality formerly used in the country, which gave a great help to the consumption of that country whence the revenue arose to maintain it.

The remedies of this part are so much above a private hand, and have such a connection with the greatest interest of state that I shall not venture to propose any.

3. The third reason which occurs to me for the fall of rents and the want of tenants. Here again it is necessary to touch the general want of people, for we considered it in order to the consumption only. Now may be considered again as a means to multiply tenants: if there were a general naturalization, doubtless many men would come furnished with stock, skill, and industry, capable to make them good tenants as experience shows in the fens, where the best tenants are said to be the foreigners.

Besides the want of people there is a misapplication of them at least as to the present end of raising rents, and that misapplication is not caused more by any one thing than by the nobility and gentry's living so much in London which produces these effects.

1. That it discourages people from being tenants in the country, because the remote parts want vent for their corn and cattle, and more for their poultry, butter, eggs, etc., and if any be so industrious as to employ their spare time in fishing, fowling, etc., it yields nothing unless to those who are within a little distance of London, whereas if the master lived in the country, not only what he now spends in lodgings and equipage would be spent in the country hospitality, but even what his servants spend in clothes would be laid out in the market towns, and what they now spend in the London tavern would be spent in the country alehouse, and both alehouse keepers and traders would be farmers also.

2. It withdraws men from being tenants who otherwise would apply themselves to it, e.g. if a gentleman live in the country and his servant, having gotten a little money in his master's service, marry, his great ambition is to get a farm, where his and his wife's industry is employed with the little stock they had gotten in service. On the other hand, if a gentleman living in town, his servant marry, he thinks not of a farm in the country, but if it be a groom, coachman, or footman, he contrives to set up an alehouse, perhaps a hackney coach into the bargain. If it be the *valet de chambre* a barber's shop, and letting lodgings completes his hopes, and the truth is as the masters so many servants are by living in London grown so expensive that the profit of a farm cannot satisfy their expense so that luxury cannot live but upon luxury which must be met with in London.

Another occasion for the want of tenants arising from the gentry's living in London is that when the nobility and gentry lived in the country they kept a considerable demesne in their hands, which, since they have lived much in London, they have strove to let even to the very door of their mansion house. By this means added to others there are more farms than tenants, which the country fellows perceiving have not so little wit as to make use of the advantage, and therefore unless their old landlords will let them fall in their rent they will leave them and go to a better pennyworth to be had of another who, whilst he is busy in spending his estate in London, cannot have leisure to manage it in the country, and this is so certainly true that I have been told that some tenants, being about to leave their landlords, being discoursed with, and the landlord demonstrating to them that even according to the lowest value of corn and cattle their farms must produce them considerable profit, they could not deny it, but answered the landlord with what he could as little deny, that though the land was worth the money, yet if he could have a better pennyworth from another who lived remote from his land, he had no reason to stick to a worse.

It is not impossible but that for the present the great conflux of artificers for the Building may make tenants more scarce, since hardly any of that sort of men in the country rely so entirely on their trade as not to have a small farm, the rent of which they are the more able to pay by the gains of their trade, but this will remedy itself when the city is built by the return of many of them into the country more wealthy than they came, though probably many of them may never return.

It is useless to mention those who by the employment in the excise, chimney money, and other branches of the revenue, as also by military employments, are diverted from seeking their livelihood by farming of land, since those employments must be performed.

As there is a want of tenants, so there is another want which partly occasions that want of tenants, and cripples many of those tenants which are, and that is want of money in the country to stock the grounds and keep the markets quick, and this want, besides the ill husbandry amongst that sort of people by the increase of alehouses, and from the expense they and their wives learn from gentlemen's servants who bring it from London, I conceive to rise from several occasions which draw the money to London, and upon this occasion the resort of the nobility and gentry will come in for a great share. In London they spend all their revenue. In London they borrow what money they spend above their revenue. The lender scarce thinks he can have a security well drawn (for the money he lends) but in London, and the gentry had rather borrow in London than in the country where his borrowing will be known to his discredit. So that both borrower and lender agree in bringing the money to London where the borrower (by spending it) takes the best care he can it shall return no more into the country.

A temporary occasion for the want of money in the country arises from the building in London where men make more profit of their money than by letting it out in the country, and if they did not, yet many are concerned in reputation to build their houses, lest they should be thought unable to build, which to trading men would be an utter undoing. Therefore, if they have not money of their own, they must borrow at any rate to carry on their building.

But the great reason for want of money in the country is the banker in London, who by receiving ten per cent of the King is enabled to give to another man 6 per cent with such conveniences attending it as neither the trader nor the usurer can meet with anywhere else. They shall have interest from the very day they pay it to the day they receive it back, whereas if a man will let out his money in the country or even in London by a lawyer or scrivener he shall keep it many months perhaps before he put it out to his satisfaction and perhaps give somewhat to the broker too.

They shall have it always at command. The trader, if he have customs or a bill of exchange to pay, the usurer, if he have a daughter to marry or a purchase to buy, or a young spendthrift to devour by a mortgage, a builder shall command it to pay his workmen and that by such proportions only as they need, the rest still going on at interest, whereas by the scrivener or lawyer you must receive all or none, and then you are at a loss again how to dispose of it.

A banker receives it either much or little, whereas the scrivener cannot dispose of it but by sums fitted to the occasion of the borrower. A banker will receive and pay money gratis, the usurer or trader shall not need to trouble himself or keep a servant for the reserving or paying out the money, nor shall he run hazard by false money or mis-telling, to which either himself or servant might be subject, or by accidents attending a servant debauched to play or expense, or by robbery which sometimes befalls the most wary.

These and other advantages are tempting enough to draw all the money (which is to be lent) out of the country, and to persuade perhaps the very grazier, having sold in Smithfield, to leave his money in London in the bankers' hands, and to buy upon credit in the country, to which the farmer is forced to submit or else, when pressed by a rent day, to sell under the price for ready money, and the price, being once fallen, is not easily raised, whilst our product being more plentiful than our consumption keep the market glutted.

I cannot believe any so incredulous upon this point as to need further arguments to prove that the bankers (as now used) are an inconvenience. I am rather apt to fear men will be too eager upon the remedy, and so mistake it and cry down with the banks, which if well used, have a great convenience in them both to private and public. To private, it will easily be collected from what was said before that they will be a convenience though the interest they give should be less, viz. 3, 4, or 5 per cent till men can otherwise dispose of their money. To the public they are of great convenience because if there be a want of the species of money, as many think there is, by banks it is supplied, paper many times supplying the place of money. They are a convenience in regard of trade, since a young merchant not known in many places abroad, when he hath occasion to trade, having credit with any of the known bankers with whom he is used to deposit his money is enabled to drive on his trade when his goods come home. Here he borrows to pay his customs, and by it saves his credit as well as prevents damage to his goods. Here he repays his debt by such proportions as he can sell his goods without being necessitated to sell at an under rate, or if he sell part, his money lies not dead till he be able to sell the rest and pay the whole. Many other conveniences might be instanced. But some may say what are we the nearer for concluding that the banks draw up the money out of the country and by it destroy the trade of the country markets unless we remedy it, and how shall it be remedied but by destroying the banks? The remedy is plain. Let the King's debts be paid and for the future either let the King not borrow, which is the best of all, or if he must upon urgent necessity borrow some little, or for some short time, let him not give above 6 per cent. Then I am sure the bankers will not give others above three or at most four per cent, and then it is certain that none but the traders' money, and some little which lies ready to redeem or mortgage or pay a marriage portion or such like occasion, will be lodged in the banks, so that the country usurer will either buy land or stock land or at least lend his money to those that will.

I will not deny but that the lowering of interest in general might contribute to the raising the value of land both in rent and purchase. That is a matter of great moment which hath great consequences, and upon which there hath been much argument of late both in print and discourse, and therefore it is needless to enter further into it; the rather till I see the King cease to give 10 per cent, I have no hope to see the generality of the subject borrow at less than 6. I wish that even from private men's exceeding 6, there were not reason to subscribe to the truth of the old saying: *Regis ad exemplum totius componitur orbis.*

35. SIR EDWARD DERING ON THE
DECAY OF RENTS IN KENT, c.1670

[Bodleian Library, Oxford, MS. Top. Kent, a1, f. 26]

HE that considers the great decay of rents in this kingdom and particularly in this county of Kent as much or more than in any other part of England will doubtless think it a very good service to the king and his country to propose any remedy to this grievous and still increasing mischief.

The cure of this as of all other diseases, being to be obtained by enquiring into the causes, there first occur the general decay of trade, especially of exportation, the neglect and disesteem of our native commodities and fondness of foreign, the extraordinary resort to London, the general decay of hospitality, the draining of the fens, the ploughing up of parks by the nobility and gentry, the want of people by resort to the plantations, the goodness of our coin in comparison to the standard of some foreign states, the great consumption of French wine and brandy, the dissolving the Canary company, and some other things which do without doubt contribute to the present decay, yet, being general and common to other countries as well as ours, are not to be here insisted on.

Those which more immediately concern this county I conceive are:

1. The loss of the cloth trade which lieth much heavier upon our county than upon other parts of England, for the trade of fine cloth at Worcester and in the west holdeth up still reasonably well. And Essex hath vent for all its wool at Colchester, as Norfolk, Cambridge, and Lincolnshire have at Norwich, whereas the Kentish cloth being a coarse rough cloth, the great vent thereof was formerly into Germany, increased very much during the wars of the Palatinate, our cloth furnishing both the armies there and the inhabitants, but since the peace of Münster, 1648, our trade hath visibly declined, and is now in a manner totally lost, not likely ever to be recovered, that country now making a coarse cloth sufficient for their own use.

2. The extreme and disproportionable weight of taxes which hath lain upon us beyond any part of the kingdom ever since 1646, and what the consequence of that hath been may be seen in Essex, Norfolk, and part of Suffolk, who were nearest to us in their proportion of taxes and do yet smart of that wound.

3. The Irish act prohibiting the importing of their cattle, so that we are forced to buy at dear rates and sometimes cannot get wherewith to stock our land unless we will buy lean cattle as dear as we can sell them when fat.

4. The vast and almost incredible increase of sheep in Ireland occasioned by the aforesaid act prohibiting their importing of great cattle hither, whereby their stock of wool is become so great as either they must transport it or sell it into England at low rates, both which are destructive to us and of necessity pull down the price of our wool.

5. The want of convenient fairs and markets, there being but few and they very ill frequented and as ill furnished.

6. The great plantation of hops in Herefordshire and in some parts of the west, which hath even dried up one of the main springs that fed our country with money, the hop trade being formerly, next to the clothing trade, the greatest and quickest returns we had.

7. The insolence and carelessness of servants requiring more wages and doing less work here than any county of England.

8. The neglect of breeding and rearing cattle, though our country, being enclosed and generally well watered, is exceeding fit for that employment, whereby the Welsh carry out every year in ready money many thousand pounds, whereas, if we bred of our own, the money for buying would not go out and the cattle would be of a size and weight fit for London market or for the navy and so would bring in money to us.

9. The drinking of brandy grown of a sudden to a very great mischief, it being now sold generally in every village, and the sellers despising the authority of the justice of peace, as thinking themselves not within the statutes for selling ale and beer.

10. The improvement made of the barren and dry parts of some other counties by clover, sainfoin, and trefoil, which is not yet and probably can never be so advantageous to this country where the lands are generally not so fit for it.

11. The being situate so near to London, which may seem a paradox, but I apply it only to this particular, that by that occasion all our taxes, subsidies, poll money, and the standing payments of excise and hearth money are still carried up to London in specie from whence it never returns, whereas from the remoter parts of the kingdom it is returned by bills of exchange, which I conceive to be one reason why Devonshire, Lancashire, Yorkshire, and Northumberland hold up at this day much better than the counties nearer London.

12. The neglect of that part of the statute for the poor, whereby the justices of peace are empowered to put apprentices to husbandry; instead whereof they bind them generally to small trades, whereby the whole race of farmers is almost utterly lost.

13. And lastly the combination as we have great cause to believe of all the brewers in London for malt and hops and of the bakers for wheat, who are said to have united themselves so as to allow but some few factors to buy for them all, who set what price they please upon the commodities they want when they are brought to market, it being evident that of late years it hath not been the great crop of wheat, barley, or hops that hath made the price so low, and it being a mystery why the excise should make the brewer rich and the maltman and hopmaster poor.

But many of these things being not to be remedied at all, and some others not without special acts of Parliament, I see very little hopes of recovering the former flourishing condition of this county. Yet to invite others to communicate their more useful reflexions which I shall much more willingly comply with than any conceptions of my own, I shall adventure to propose: That a general stock may be raised to be laid out every year in the commodities of this country.

That this stock be the sum of ten thousand pounds supposing there may be fifty gentlemen in the county able and willing for the public good to advance each 200*l*.

This stock to be put in for five years and then to be divided, for a less time will hardly try the experiment sufficiently and to a longer time men will not be willing to be tried. And during that time to be managed by a small number not above seven to be chosen by the interested and to account to them once a year at the summer assizes at Maidstone and there to take directions from them for their proceeding the year following.

This money to be laid out in wool, hops, corn, fat cattle, and what else the country affords, with this regulation never to buy when the commodity in the market bears a reasonable price, as wheat 36[*s.*] the seame, barley 18[*s.*], oats 10*s.*, wool ten pounds the pack, etc. And with part of it we may endeavour to bring into our country some of the new woollen manufactures, either bays from Colchester or serges from Exeter, or stuffs from Norwich by advancing of money to them and taking it back in work, or hiring houses to them at very small rents or letting them rent free for some years till they are settled among us and have taken prentices and get families here when there will be no fear of their removal. And in all probability next winter many Dutch will be removing into England who would stop at Sandwich, Canterbury, or Maidstone, if they found any encouragement so to do.

And a great part of this stock I conceive may be returned three times a year, as, for example, it may be laid out in August in wool, in November in hops, and in the spring in corn.

And it seems to me that this is no prejudice to any person and will be a great encouragement to the farmer and grazier when they know where to have a reasonable price for their commodity, and yet may take the freedom of the market whenever it is for their advantage.

As for the particular rules how the money shall be managed, by what authority laid out, where kept, where it is in cash, and all other things of that nature, it will not be hard to settle them if the substance of the proposal be agreed to be reasonable and feasible.

One objection is obvious that those who do not deposit any money will find as much benefit by it if it produce any good effect as those who do, which is very true, but the end of this proposal being chiefly the common good of the country, not any particular advantage, this is no discouragement to him that proposeth it, nor ought to be to them that engage in it. Though it may always be reasonable in case of equal goodness and equal price of any commodity rather to buy from one of the adventurers than from a stranger.

And if the stock were larger and the participants fewer probably it might produce better effect, but considering the present poverty of the county, I do not think a greater sum can well be raised nor by greater proportions.

As for the money which shall at any time lie in hand unemployed, it may be left in London to be paid upon demand and that, as I have heard, at 4 per cent interest, so that there may probably be no considerable loss for that time in which it would otherwise lie dead.

After all the adventure is not very great it being in the whole but 200*l.* and that under the probability that they who have a great stock and ready money to pay and buy at the best hand, when and where they please, may make at least the interest of their money, that being the lowest gains that any trader doth propose to himself.

36. SIR RICHARD HAINES ON THE DECAY OF TRADE, 1674

[Richard Haines, *The Prevention of Poverty, or a Discourse of the Causes of the Decay of Trade, Fall of Lands, and Want of Money throughout the Nation; with certain Expedients for remedying the Same and bringing this Kingdom to an eminent Degree of Riches and Prosperity*, London, 1674, pp. 1-9, 12-16]

The prevention of Poverty

So general and loud, for divers years past, have been the complaints for want of trade and money throughout this nation, and so pressing are the necessities of most men, that there is scarce any person can be insensible of it. And this is not only in time of war (though then more especially), but also in time of peace, when the seas were open, and we might promise ourselves the largest share of prosperity. Whence 'tis evident that the causes are not wholly outward or accidental, but rather internal, and as it were in our own bowels, which consume us, and have reduced us to such a low ebb, that a general poverty seems to have invaded the whole nation, leases being continually thrown up in the country, and tradesmen daily breaking in the City. In brief, all conditions of men seem to have changed their stations, and sunk below themselves: the gentry, by reason of the fall of their lands, and uncertainty of rents, being brought to live at the rate of a yeoman; the yeoman can scarce maintain himself so well as an ordinary farmer heretofore; the farmer is forced to live as hard as a poor labourer anciently; and labourers generally, if they have families, are ready to run a begging, the poverty of most parishes being such that they can hardly supply or relieve them.

The consideration whereof, and that no man is born for himself, but ought to do what in him lies to promote the public good and general welfare of his country, has invited me (though uncapable, and not sufficiently qualified to do any considerable service, yet however) to testify my well-wishes, and throw in my mite into the public treasury, by endeavouring some expedients for raising the trade of the nation, and advancing the temporal prosperity of all its inhabitants.

In order whereunto I first applied myself to find out the causes of such national poverty, which like an armed enemy hath threatened to invade the whole kingdom.

Secondly, to discover a remedy, if possible, that might not only subdue this potent adversary, but also introduce and maintain a constant stock of trade and plenty of money, and so consequently riches and honour both to King and kingdom, and prosperity to all estates whatsoever.

I do humbly conceive, that the general causes of poverty (unless it be purposed by the Lord by reason of iniquity) are:

First the daily decrease of goods and commodities of our own growth fit for exportation.

Secondly, the double increase of foreign costly goods and commodities, brought over more and more from beyond the seas, viz. iron, timber, brandy, French wines, linen cloth, and other French commodities; and also mum, coffee, chocolate, salt, and saltpetre, with many more. All which expensive commodities have been brought into general use and imported in this nation within the space of forty years last past or little more (linen cloth and wine only excepted).

The value of these commodities imported cannot but amount to a vast sum, we may modestly (though at rovers) guess it twenty or thirty hundred thousand pounds every year; which mighty sums of money, thirty or forty years ago, were for the greatest part kept at home.

Now easily observable it is that, ever since such prodigious increase of new imported goods, our own most great and richest manufactories have decreased, and the manufactors become impoverished, especially in those of woollen cloth and iron; and forasmuch as no commodities answerable have been raised in their stead, equally to balance what we have therein lost of our own growth and production.

It remains, then, that of necessity those vast sums of money aforesaid must every year go out of the nation to make the balance of trade even, and this for the greatest part in ready coin, as may, I conceive, evidently be demonstrated. Thus, if money were not transported, then our own manufactories, which are much diminished, and become far less than what they were thirty or forty years ago, would now find quick markets and yield good prices, to the great encouragement of the manufactors; but the contrary is notorious; wherefore I conclude that, according to the present course, money every year must unavoidably decrease amongst us, to the great impoverishing of the whole nation.

Obj.   If it be alleged that I mistake the cause of this national consumption, and that the great taxes and many impositions laid upon the nation, obliging us to part with so much money for his Majesty's uses, ought to be assigned as the grand cause of this great scarcity of money.

Sol.   I humbly answer that this cannot be the cause for this reason: because what monies are given by the representatives of the nation to his Majesty are but like the moistures drawn up by the beams of the sun from the earth, which soon return down again in showers to refresh the ground, or like the blood in its circulation; for what is carried out of the country goes but into the city, and is there expended again; and forasmuch as it goes not beyond the seas, soon returns again. So that in the nation there is not one groat the less to be bestowed on what the farmer or any others have to spare; wherefore, and for that the public coffers do not hoard or keep up any extraordinary sums, I humbly hope I may conclude that this is not the proper cause why the nation is so empty of money, and that general want of this necessary thing (which beneath grace, and glory, and what is conducing thereunto) is most to be desired.

But doubtless it is the many hundred thousand pounds, which our bad husbandry and ill conduct sends every year beyond the seas, which we see again no more; this is the grand cause of our miseries, wasting thus our noblest spirits, that hath brought the body politic into this pining consumption, and makes us so loudly complain of bad trade and empty pockets, and that the nation is become thus indigent and discontented. But alas! what advantage is it only to complain? Diseases are not cured with outcries, but rather increased; let us then wipe our eyes, and make use of our heads and our hands to get out of this quagmire of necessity, wherein we are unhappily plunged.

Too true it is that we are very poor, and, as I conceive, 'tis no less plain that the reason of it is the necessity of parting every year with vast sums of money, to make the balance of trade even, because we import much more than we export, and therefore I humbly apprehend the best means to prevent this growing evil, must be:

First, to raise new manufactures, whereby to improve what doth or may arise of our own English growth: by which means our lands may some other way be employed, besides that of corn and cattle.

And secondly, to shut the door of importation against those new imported goods, especially such as are superfluous and injurious to the well-being of the kingdom.

Thus the first manufacture to be prohibited that may be made of our own growth, and most advantageous to the general good and profit of persons of all estates, is linen cloth; for it is most certain that our English ground will produce hemp and flax in such abundance, as may make linen cloth sufficient for all occasions; whence several great conveniences, of much advantage to the public, will arise. As:

First, it will improve the lands which are proper for hemp and flax to that degree that what before was worth but twenty shillings per acre for corn or pasture, by this means, will be worth forty or fifty shillings the acre per annum.

Secondly, great numbers of poor families, who have little to do from the beginning of the year to the end thereof, unless some few of them in the country, in time of harvest, might hereby most profitably be set to work constantly, by raising a continual stock of employment, not only for men, but also women, boys, and girls, that can do little thing besides it; whereas for want thereof most of them now are trained up in idleness, and live by the labours of others, whose number by computation, after the rate of threescore in each parish throughout the kingdom, doth amount unto five hundred and eighty thousand people and upwards.

Thirdly, by this means every parish, which by reason of poverty is not able to set up a manufactory for the employment of their poor, in making of woollen cloth, according to the statute in that case made and provided, may easily provide employment for them in making of linen, whereby many thousands that now wholly rely on the parish wherein they live for maintenance might very well support themselves.

Fourthly, some thousands of wandering persons that go from door to door, to the great dishonour and disadvantage of the nation, might by this means become instruments for the enriching of the same . . .

Lastly, besides all these advantages, several hundred thousand pounds, which are now expended and sent out of the nation for linen, might hereby be kept at home, or better improved, to the great advantage of his Majesty's subjects. Besides, a farther advantage by this planting of hemp, etc., will accrue towards making of sails, cables, and other cordage necessary for shipping, of which sufficient may be made at home, without being beholden to our neighbours for a commodity so important for navigation, parting with our money to strangers for it, as we usually do to a very great yearly value.

Obj. If any allege that this planting of hemp and flax, employing a great part of the best lands, will create an inconvenience by causing both corn and cattle to be less plenty.

Ans. I answer, that I apprehend no grounds for such fear. For as for corn, great quantities of rich lands being broken up to be planted with flax may after flax be most properly sown with corn, and that to great advantage; so that on the contrary, corn will be hereby the more plenty. Then as for the decrease of cattle, it is easily cured; for land, kind for corn, when by long sowing 'tis impoverished, so that 'twill bear corn no longer, may be sown with trefoil or clover, and then one acre shall produce as much hay or pasture as two or three acres did before; and as soon as that is decayed, the land will bear corn more kindly than before (provided it be ploughed up before the couch-grass gets in it); for clover and trefoil, I know by experience, prepares the ground for wheat, as much as a good crop of tares or French wheat, otherwise called buck wheat, can do. Besides, if cattle should fail, the remedy is easy and cheap; for when the King and Parliament please, Ireland is ready, and will be glad to supply us speedily.

A second thing to be prohibited coming over is the growing trade of that outlandish, robbing, and (by reason of its abuse) man-killing liquor, called brandy, which will promote the consumption of our own commodities, as beer and ale; or if such a liquor be thought necessary for seamen or the like, then to raise some commodity of the like nature and strength at home; for (as I am credibly informed by persons well experienced that way) as good and as strong liquor may be made with what doth abound at home. Which if so, the profit will not be inconsiderable, since three hundred thousand pounds that brandy now costs us every year will be kept at home.

A third thing to be prohibited may be bay salt from beyond the seas: for it is well known that salt for all occasions, and as good for all intents and purposes, may be made at home; and that not only to the great improvement of much land on the sea coast, which now lieth waste, and is of no profit either to king or subject; but will also preserve in the nation fifty thousand pounds per annum, to the great enriching of the kingdom, and may be done with very much ease, and as little difficulty.

A fourth commodity to be prohibited may be saltpetre, of which we might make and raise in our nation sufficient for all occasions.

A fifth improvement, which I conceive may be made, is in iron, which most certainly might, as well now as heretofore, be raised at home, the benefit whereof would be very great; because some hundred thousand pounds might hereby every year be saved or otherwise improved (and many thousands of his Majesty's subjects employed), which now is expended in that commodity. *Obj.* But if it should be supposed that such ironworks would too much consume our woods, I must so far beg leave to think otherwise; that I conceive, and many well skilled in those works are of opinion, that the neglect of ironwork has been a main cause that our woods are so much decayed, and so many coppices grubbed up and converted into tillage. For when ironworks were carried on, both wood and coals would yield ready monies, which encouraged the owners not only to preserve the coppices and woods from destruction, but also to plant and promote more; whereas now without doubt in a few years, our oak timber (deservedly accounted the best in the world, and a great strength and ornament to the kingdom) will be so far destroyed, that little will be to be had; and the reason is, because the only nurse that maketh the oak and other timber to flourish is underwoods, and where underwoods are not, there cannot (or very rarely is) any good timber; so that although great quantities of wood may be consumed by ironworks, yet woods becoming thereby more carefully preserved, they grow again, and consequently there is no less plenty, but for want of ironworks they are destroyed, both wood and timber, root and branch, and that more and more every year.

And this the rather, and more to the destruction of timber, because people in divers countries have got a mischievous trick to elude and avoid that wholesome statute, whereby it is enacted that on every fall of underwoods they should leave so many standels, tellows, or young trees to grow for timber; which indeed they will do, but then at the next fall of the same wood, viz. about nine or ten years after, they will cut those very standels or tellows left before (so that they never become timber), and then they leave new ones, and this successively, whereby the intention of the statute is unworthily defeated . . .

What the nation hath now to spare, and fit for exportation, is much less than was forty or fifty years ago, as aforesaid; and yet then, when none of these things, with many more, did come into the kingdom, there was a better trade by far than what is now; for commodities then went for commodities of greater worth, without parting with any monies, and in those days our commodities went farther from home, and instead of brandy, iron, and the like, produced far better returns. So that then, both silver and gold, not originally produced in England, was very plenty, but now our monies and commodities are carried forth, and in conclusion turn to little or no account.

And unless our commodities for exportation did increase answerable to the increase of commodities imported, as it is most certainly true that they do not, then of necessity out goes money, and in comes poverty; the truth whereof doth appear by sad experience. For all that our goods and money bring in is soon consumed, and comes as it were to the dunghill, whilst our wealth becomes a prey to other nations. Whereas if the door of importation for those unnecessary and injurious commodities were shut, money would be prevented from going out, and people unavoidably would apply themselves to the making them at home, whereby there would be a far better and quick trade, and all people would have sufficient employment to gain a comfortable livelihood, and the said commodities in a little time become as good and as cheap of our own manufacture, as now we have them from beyond the seas, and the importation of bullion no way hindered, but greatly promoted hereby, and the exportation thereof prevented, and consequently money much more plenty than ever it was.

To these several commodities, which I humbly conceive fit to be prohibited to be imported, might be added commodities which necessarily should on greater penalties be forbidden to be exported, and some better means used for that end than what hath yet been appointed. Such are fullers earth and wool, the one of excellent use, the other being a very plentiful commodity of this kingdom, which to be converted into cloth would employ great numbers of our people, and bring in much wealth to the nation; but by reason of the exportation thereof privately from hence, or growth of wool in other nations, those vast advantages formerly arising hereby are now greatly diminished, others furnishing those markets where formerly our commodities found quick trade and good prices. And since 'tis well known that woollen cloth cannot be made without fullers earth, and that fullers earth is nowhere to be had but in our nation; then to prevent fullers earth from going beyond the seas must infallibly revive the former flourishing trade of woollen cloth, without which many nations cannot subsist, and by which we may become very rich; which if so, what care ought not to be taken to secure this one thing, so useful that silver ore by way of exchange is not to be accepted for it.

We might likewise add the conveniency, though not of a total prohibition, yet of some restraint of the extraordinary importation of French wines, for the encouragement of the manufactories of this kingdom, which abounds with excellent liquors, as beer, ale, etc., the consumption of which ought to be promoted, and foreign drinks discouraged. Besides, the want of French wines might be easily supplied (in some measure by wines made at home, for some gentlemen have experienced it with very good success, or however) by excellent ciders, which being produced in our own climate, may be more agreeable and wholesome for our bodies than those foreign liquors, especially when adulterated. But I dare not launch out too far into this ocean, for me thinks I see a powerful objection arising, that like a tempest seems to threaten no less than the blasting of all our projects, viz.

Obj.   If linen cloth, iron, brandy, salt, etc. shall be wholly prohibited from being imported, his Majesty's revenue arising out of the Customs will be much impaired and diminished.

Ans.   To which most important objection I humbly answer that, having by the expedients before mentioned settled a constant and sure method of trading, commodities for commodities, his Majesty's revenue may for the future stand upon a firmer basis, and our own commodities fit for exportation being hereby increased, will doubtless bring home greater returns than formerly in other commodities, and those of a richer nature, and such as our industry at home cannot supply us with. For instead of things before mentioned to be prohibited from being imported, out of which Customs now arise, we may have spices, and other Indian commodities brought in, and afterwards again exported from hence to other nations; as is practised in Holland, which thereby is become the common spicery for the northern nations, and most part of Europe, which way of trade may, as 'tis conceived, supply his Majesty's Customs, so as in some measure to balance the loss in the Customs of brandy, linen, iron, etc., especially if that ancient staple trade of this nation, the making and exporting of woollen cloth, were but encouraged and promoted as in former ages, and fullers earth secured, as possibly it may.

Secondly, that since such prohibition tends to the great advantage of the whole nation, and that his Majesty in kindness to his people shall part with such part of his revenue, his subjects will be obliged not only in duty but gratitude to supply his Majesty; and the wisdom of their representatives may find out some other way by taxes, impositions, or the like, to compensate such his Majesty's loss, which now may with great advantage and more easily and cheerfully be borne and paid, seeing all people by this means only may enjoy a quick trade and plenty of money, nor may it be given upon a better consideration.

Furthermore, if it were not too much a presumption, I would willingly (though still with all humble submission to those in authority, in whose power alone it lies to make the alteration) propose a way and means more advantageous, which in my apprehension, if it may be approved of by better judgments, may serve considerably towards his Majesty's supply, and also be a means to raise and preserve plenty of money, and also tend much to the wealth and prosperity of the whole nation, which is thus: if all his Majesty's coin were called into the Tower, and three-pence taken out of every twelve-pence, and then new coined for a shilling, then might his Majesty have five shillings out of every pound; and so suppose that in the whole nation there be eightscore hundred thousand pounds, a fourth part being taken out of it, will amount to forty hundred thousand pounds, or four millions of money for his Majesty's use, charges of coinage only deducted. And for as much as 9*d.* in weight is made 12*d.* in value, no subject may complain that he is hereby a penny the worse.

But if threepence be thought too much, instead thereof suppose it but three-halfpence, there will arise for his Majesty's use thereby, two millions of money, coinage deducted as aforesaid.

What inconveniences may hereby arise I confess I cannot foresee, but to me it seems that these conveniences and advantages will not fail to be the consequents of it.

1. It will enrich the whole nation, since there will be near a fourth part as much money more than was before.

2. After all money's new coined, it will invite persons who have stocks of plate to melt it down, and have it put into coin.

3. As it increases money, so it will secure it from going beyond the seas; for by its being made more in value, and less in weight, all nations will cease to rob us of it, as in some measure they have done of our Guinea gold, which by reason of its being lighter than others keeps at home the better.

4. Whereas before his Majesty's coin, being more in weight and less in value than that of his neighbours, the profit thereby to be made gave great encouragement to them to covet our money, and refuse to take our goods for their commodities, those very ill effects will now cease.

5. By this means those very merchants, who carried away money from us, will now rather bring money to us; because that as before it was for their advantage to carry our money, being heaviest and least in value, so now on the contrary it may be their advantage to bring their money, being now the heaviest, to us, where it may suffer the same improvement.

6. As by this means only money will increase and continue, so all commodities, that we have to spare and fit for transportation, will unavoidably find quick and good markets, so as to encourage all people cheerfully to manage their affairs.

7. By means of this variation of coin, a considerable advance will arise to his Majesty's revenue; for if bullion be brought into the Tower at the rates as heretofore, then so much as money is made less than formerly, so much profit and advantage will arise to the Crown . . .

37. JOHN LOCKE'S NOTES ON TRADE, *c.* 1674[1]
[Bodleian Library, Oxford, MS. Locke c 30, f. 18]

THE chief end of trade is riches and power which beget each other. Riches consists in plenty of moveables that will yield a price to foreigner and are not like to be consumed at home, but especially in plenty of gold and silver. Power consists in numbers of men and ability to maintain them. Trade conduces to both these by increasing your stock and your people and they each other.

Trade is twofold: 1. domestic manufacture whereby is to be understood all labour employed by your people in preparing commodities for your consumption, either of your own people (where it will exclude foreign importation) or of foreigners. 2. carriage i.e. navigation and merchandise.

People also are twofold: 1. Those that contribute any way to your trade, especially in commodities for exportation, the chief whereof are men employed in husbandry, drapery, mines, and navigation. 2. Such as are either idle and so do not help, as retainers to gentry and beggars, or, which is worse, hinder trade, as retailers in some degree, multitudes of lawyers, but above all soldiers in pay.

Promoters of traders: freedom of trade; naturalization easy; freedom of religion; register or certainty of property; small customs; public workhouses; coin good certain, hard to be counterfeited; transferring of bills; increase and encouragement of seamen in an island, not seamen nor navigation in a continent that wants not supplies but can subsist of itself; cheap labour; fashions suited to your own manufacture; suitable manufactures to the markets whose commodities we want; low customs on exportation; new manufactures at home.

Hindrances of trade: intricacy of law; arrests; imprisonments; arbitrary power.

Vices tending to prodigality.

[Endorsed:] TAE I   Trade Essay.

---

[1] Dr. Patrick Kelly of Peterhouse, Cambridge, points out that the endorsements of f. 19v. suggest that these are notes for an essay on trade which Locke abandoned after 1674. The endorsements include five page references to Carew Reynell's *True English Interest* (1674, licensed 5 September 1673) [see extracts on pp. 386, 683], but the notes contain propositions which are not in Reynell and their general emphasis is on foreign trade, where Reynell's is on domestic manufactures. In my view the section 'Hindrances of Trade' derives from Reynell, as do the points under 'Promoters of Trades', except for land registers and transferring of bills. Reynell's criticism of the Navigation Act (p. 15) is ignored.—J. P. C.

38. MORE ADVICE FOR REMEDYING THE DECAY OF TRADE, 1675

[*Harleian Miscellany*, I, London, 1744, pp. 376–8]

The Art of Good Husbandry, or the Improvement of Time:
Being a sure Way to get and keep Money.
In a Letter to Mr. *R.A.* by *R.T.*

In this tract are prescribed several rules for merchants, shopkeepers, and mechanical tradesmen (as well servants as masters) how they may husband their time to the best advantage; the loss whereof is the sole cause of poverty in this city and nation. Likewise, the loss of a man's time spent in a tavern, coffeehouse, or ale-house, computed. Also instructions to all sorts of people, how to order their business for the future, both to the enriching of themselves and their families.

Sir,

In compliance to your late requests, obliging me to write to you, as soon as I came to London, I have sent you the result of a few serious minutes concerning the great Decay of Trade and Want of Money; which is now the general cry of all people both in city and country; the grounds and reasons of which many have attempted to find out, by curious enquiries into the several laws and statutes made for the promoting of trade, supposing the non-execution of those laws to be the occasion of it. To this end large discourses have been made concerning the decay of the fishing trade; several proposals offered by ingenious persons for the restoration of it; and the great advantages that would ensue thereupon; with the many damages destructive to trade in general that arise from the enquiries into the wool trade, alleging the exportation of wool, the importation of foreign manufactures, and the permission of foreigners to work here, to be the chief cause of that decay of trade, and want of money, which every person complains of.

Now though the grounds and reasons before mentioned are guarded with so many probabilities, and seeming rational demonstrations, that every understanding person will be ready, at the first view, to hold up his finger and give his assent to them; yet upon critical inspection, or more curious survey, we shall find them to be only circumstantial.

There is something more material which is near us, that we overlook by looking so far off; that is, the little value or price we set upon that inestimable jewel, time, which most people slight, like the cock in the fable, if they cannot make use of it, to satisfy their lascivious appetites. It is the industrious hand that enricheth the land, and not the contriving pate. The wasps and hornets, by their rapine, bring to their nests more honey at once than the industrious bees can at many times; and yet, for all this, they usually die for want in the winter; whilst the industrious bees, by continual labour and improvement of time, gather sufficient to serve themselves in the winter, and can afford their masters a liberal share out of their plentiful stock.

I shall first begin with the inferior rank of people, for those are the persons most concerned in this general complaint, and shew them, how they may remedy what they complain of.

First, let them be diligent and industrious in their several trades and callings.

Secondly, let them avoid all such idle societies that squander away a great deal of time at a cheap rate.

I shall instance in those sober and civil conventions, as at coffee houses, and clubs, where little money is pretended to be spent, but a great deal of precious time lost, which the person never thinks of; but measures his expenses by what goes out of his pocket; nor considers what he might put in by his labour, and what he might have saved, being employed in his shop. As for example:

A mechanic tradesman, it may be, goes to the coffee house or ale house in the morning, to drink his morning's draught, where he spends twopence, and in smoking and talking consumes at least an hour. In the evening, about six o'clock, he goes to his Twopenny Club, and there stays for his twopence till nine or ten; here is fourpence spent, and four hours at least lost, which in most mechanic trades cannot be reckoned less than a shilling; and, if he keep servants, they may lose him near as much by idling, or spoiling his goods, which his presence might have prevented. So that, upon these considerations, for this his supposed groat (a day's expense) he cannot reckon less than seven groats; which comes to fourteen shillings a week (Sundays excepted) which is thirty-six pounds ten shillings a year. A great deal of money in a poor tradesman's pocket!

Now the same may be applied to the higher trades and professions, whose loss of time is according to the degree or spheres they move in; and yet this is the least thing thought of. We are apt to favour and excuse ourselves, and impute a general calamity to things afar off, when we ourselves are the occasion of it at home.

It will be necessary, before I proceed, to take notice of one objection, which seems to be most material, viz. that some men's business lies abroad, and cannot be so well managed at home, and that these meetings or societies are advantageous to them. As first, merchants, by these clubs or meetings, have intelligence of ships'going out, and coming in; and also of the rates and prices of commodities, and meet with customers by accident, which possibly might never make enquiry at their houses or warehouses. The like excuses all men of business and trade pretend.

To this I answer: that indulging this custom hath made it seemingly necessary; but yet there is no absolute necessity for it; for the Exchange is appointed for the merchant's intelligence, and his warehouse is his shop. And, to other tradesmen, their shops are their markets; to which, if they would be reserved, they might better themselves, and improve that time they spend in taverns and coffee houses, to a greater advantage. For, by these idle meetings, they lose not only what they spend, but what might be improved by the overseeing their goods, and examining their accounts, which they now wholly trust to the fidelity of a servant or servants; who, being led by their masters' examples, grow idle and extravagant; and, knowing their masters sure, make sure for themselves; furnishing themselves for their debauched assignations, they now plot and invent the means and ways for their extravagant meetings, which are the occasion of the ruin of many masters and hopeful servants; all which might be prevented by the diligent eye of the master; the want of which is the occasion of all the debauchery, poverty, and misery, which every place cries out of. From this negligence and loss of time come many more inconveniencies, that heap on poverty, and entail it upon themselves and generations.

From these clubs and societies (how civil soever they appear to be) it is impossible in any such meeting, but some of them are given to vice; and it is probable, the greatest part. By this means are introduced gaming, foolish wagers, wenching, swearing, and other debaucheries. And usually at parting, or breaking up of these clubs, they divide themselves according to their several inclinations or dispositions; some go to a tavern, some to a convenient place for gaming, others to a bawdy-house, by which means the family is neglected, and not governed as it ought to be; the wife (though possibly a very virtuous and careful housewife) exasperated by the extravagancies of her husband, and foreseeing poverty and want attending her and her children, grows desperate; and, it may be, yields to some temptations that are too common in these days; by which means oftentimes an estate, that was gathered by grains, is scattered abroad by bushels.

The servants too, by these examples, fall into the same vices, and many times ruin both themselves and their friends, who have strained their estates to the utmost, to get them into those places, and engaged their friends for their fidelity, hoping that their industry might afterwards make them some retaliation; all which is frustrated, and they become vagrants and extravagants, by which means city and country are filled with so many idle persons that live only by spoil and rapine; or like drones, feeding upon others' labours; the greatest part of their business being to undo what others do, and to devise or contrive ways to cozen, supplant, or cheat each other; accounting it as lawful to get twenty shillings by cheating or playing, as by the most honest and industrious labour; so that, by this means, our commodities, which might be employed by industrious manufacturers, lie waste; and no wonder that we complain for want of trade, when the hands that should be employed about it are idle; for, if a strict enquiry were made into the city and suburbs of all the persons that are capable of work, either in the wool or fishing trade, as men, women, and children from seven years upwards, that are now all together idle, or not employed to any purpose in trade, there would not be found less than an hundred and fifty-thousand, that live like drones, feeding upon the stock of others' labours.

Now, it is our own negligence and idleness that brings poverty upon us; for, if these idle persons were employed, we need not cry out of the exportation of wool, neither would industrious foreigners have that encouragement to work here, if we would mind it ourselves; but, if we will not improve our manufactures, we cannot blame others for doing of it . . .

39. THE EFFECTS OF WAR ON ENGLISH TRADE, 1689, 1691-2

[*The Autobiography of William Stout of Lancaster,
1665–1752*, ed. J. D. Marshall, 1967, pp. 94–5, 106]

1689. Before this war with France [i.e. 1689–97], it was computed that we paid to [that] nation at least one million of money sterling for their fashions, product, and manufactories over and above what they took from us of our product and manufactories; and although it was evident during the first year of this war they took from us at least five hundred of our ships, which was computed at half a million in value more than we took of their ships—which losses were great to particular persons or merchants—yet the nation got or saved yearly one million of money this year to carry on the war with France, by being prohibited trade with them, and put us upon the silk, linen, paper, and many other of their manufactories, to the enriching this nation; and particularly in the south of this county, in making canvas in imitation[1] and as good as their Normandy canvas and Brittany linen. As to wine and salt, we now had them from Portugal and Spain, who took from us the double value in goods of what we had from them. Also, at this time, the salt rock was found in Cheshire,[2] from the brine of which they formerly made fine salt. But now they digged out the rock and carried it by sea to all parts of England and Ireland, and melted it in sea water and boiled it up into a strong salt as good French [and] Spanish salt.

Also abundance of stills[3] were set up for extracting good and strong spirits from malt, molasses, fruit, and other materials, instead of French brandy. Some thousand tons of prunes used to be brought yearly from France to England, and commonly sold three pounds for fourpence—and now not to be had at 40*s.* a hundred, which now turned to the butcher's profit. Resin from France, usually sold for ten shillings a hundred, now advanced to 6 or 8*d.* a pound till got from New England, where it was in few years extracted in as great plenty as cheap and fine as French.

We had now no carriage from London but by land, and the cheese of Lancashire and Cheshire, which used to employ at least twenty ships yearly

---

[1] The largest manufacturing industry of Warrington in the eighteenth century was that of sailcloth. See G. A. Carter, *Warrington Hundred*, 1947, p. 49.

[2] Rock salt was first discovered in Cheshire at Marbury in 1670.

[3] Doubt arose whether such distilling could be legally carried on, and in 1690 a declaratory clause was inserted in an act declaring it permissible.—2 W & M, Sess. 2, cap. 9, sec. 11.

to carry cheese from Liverpool and Chester to London, were now no more employed, but all the cheese sent by wagon to London.[1] And for back carriage brought groceries and other merchandise into the country, by whom we got our goods to Standish at the rate of 3s. to 5s. a hundred in summer, they choosing to bring them thither in order to [carry] coals or cannel back into Cheshire. And we usually gave 1s. 6d. a hundred bringing them from Standish to Lancaster. But all our goods from 20s. a hundred and under, we got them elsewhere; iron from the bloomeries in Cartmel and Furness, there being then no furnaces erected there for refining it, and what Swede iron we got, it was from York or Leeds by land. Tobacco, we had always one or more ships yearly hither from Virginia importing it, where we had opportunity to buy small bundles[2] of the sailors at moderate prices; but at the beginning of the war it was high, most ships being taken. Our neighbour John Hodgson sent a ship with a cargo about two hundred pounds value, which purchased about 200 hogsheads, [and] got well home, by which he gained at least one thousand five hundred pounds, tobacco being then near 12d. a pound. And in Virginia then 20s. worth of English goods here would purchase one hogshead of good tobacco there. It was then permitted to be imported in bulk or small parcels to stow close. The said John Hodgson had then, and some years before, a sugar house in Lancaster for refining sugar, which supplied us with refined sugar and molasses. But as no natural sugar was then imported here, he got his from Bristol or Liverpool, from whom we got ours. There was then no copperas works erected at Liverpool[3] to supply this country, and alum works in Yorkshire, and many other manufactories to answer what we formerly had from London and foreign parts to the ease and benefit of this country. . . .

1691 and 1692. And although at that time the ships taken by the French seemed to be a great loss to this nation, yet the great loss was to the inhabitants of our plantations, who sold their sugars and tobacco at half price and paid three pounds a barrel for their beef, and other necessaries proportionally, which much reduced them.

But, on the contrary, the merchants here bought provisions and our manufactures low, and not above half the value of a cargo as in times of peace—and had their returns at a low price, but sold them here at a double price. So that it was computed that if a merchant made an equal adventure in three ships, if but one came but in safe, he was in the main no loser; and if two came safe, a good gainer; and if all, much more. And in the main it could not be computed that above one in five miscarried, for by this time there was convoys appointed to most parts, and ships went in fleets together.

---

[1] Stout seems to be in error here. According to T. S. Willan cheese and coal were still the most important cargoes being shipped along the coast from Chester in 1689.—*The English Coasting Trade, 1600–1750* (Manchester, 1938), p. 181.

[2] The right to import tobacco in small bundles was removed in 1699 when, to prevent smuggling, it had to be imported in casks, chests, or cases, and not otherwise.

[3] Copperas is proto-sulphate of iron and was used in the manufacture of sulphuric acid. A copperas works is shown in Buck's *View of Liverpool*, 1728.

And it was observable that the quantity of burthen of shipping rather increased at Liverpool, and the town increased in buildings and merchants during all the war in King William's reign.

40. SIR RICHARD COCKS'S VIEWS ON PRICES AND THE ECONOMY, 1698[?]

[Bodleian Library, Oxford, MS. Eng. Hist. b 209, ff. 90–89.[1]
Manuscript of speeches and views on public affairs by Sir Richard Cocks, knight of the shire for Gloucestershire, early 1698(?).]

Of wool [and] of wool manufactured

THERE is no dispute but we ought to encourage the wool of all parts to be brought in here and to work it here into the several manufactures . . . some gentlemen have a notion that wool would be dearer could we have liberty to export it. It is possible it may be so for a season but I can't see the advantage even the landed man (I mean the proprietor, not the tenant) can have . . . by having the product of the land at such great rates. Indeed, it would be of great advantage to the owner of the land to have fixed rates for the product of land, for according to the rates of things do we set our land; if corn bears a great price and so for cattle, cheese, and butter, when we set land, we shall have many tenants offer themselves, but very few that will offer any advance of rent. For these commodities having been of late of lower value, the tenant says to himself, I will venture to give no more rent than I can make if commodities were of the lowest price I have known them, so that if that should happen I am safe; if the present price continues, I am then a gainer. Now in this case if the prices of things continue, these tenants grow vastly rich and the landlord poor: the poor is reduced to extremities, the usurer is enriched, and trade not encouraged. No man in the kingdom but the occupier of land advan-[taged] . . . To explain this every man that sets land considers with himself that my land will probably produce so many quarter of corn, so many tod of wool, so many hundred of cheese, will fat so many beefs, so many muttons, and at such a rate the bushel and . . . the pound, my tenant may live by his labour and pay me so much rent and live. Now in case these commodities rise or fall by plenty or scarcity then there is no great damage or advantage to me or my tenant: if they sink and continue so to do lower than we expected when we made the bargain, then he is broke. If they rise and continue to do so, then I am at a loss; for though men have their rent paid in silver and gold, it is in effect but wool, beef, mutton, butter, and cheese; and when commodities are very low my tenant pays me more wool, etc., than he could raise of my land, which must ruin him. When corn, wool, beef, etc., rise without any visible cause, as scarcity or the unseasonableness of the year, then my tenant does pay me, it is true in law, so many bushel, pounds, etc. as we agreed to, but

---

[1] This volume is written from back to front as well as from front to back.

this advance of price is a cheat that is come between us and has taken one half away. For as the landlord really believed his rent would bring him such and such things which he knew his tenant might pay him, now he finds he is mistaken and he has not half and yet his tenant from the goodness of the bargain well able to have paid the whole. The poor that thinks the parish is obliged in old age, extremities, and necessities to provide for him, who in plenty and cheap times will either work little, or live without saving, in hard times, viz. when the prices of every thing rises except his work, is reduced to extreme necessities. The usurer is in a worse case than the landlord; the landlord may either advance or occupy his land himself, but the usurer, if he keeps his money idle, gets nothing; if he sets it out, if the prices of things run low he is the only true gainer, as in the other case he is the only true loser of necessity. In a quick trade where money circulates, all commodities will bear a tolerable good rate, but for men to endeavour ... to make necessaries extremely dear is rather a danger than an advantage to the public. For as I have showed before the poor are made poorer, the landlord in effect [has] not half his rent and in short no gainer, but the tenant gets all. So when commodities bear such high rates not only the gentlemen that set their estates, but all mechanics, retailers, merchants, and all traders are at great expenses more than usually, which they must of necessity raise out of the advance of the commodity they trade in, or live less profusely or more saving (which we shall hardly persuade them to). Then if the commodities are advanced, suppose 4s. in the pound; suppose I advance my land 4s. in the pound, am I a gainer? No, certainly I am in a manner, if I spend my yearly income, just where I was ... So much for home trade, now as for our English manufactures that are exported. If our manufacturers themselves are forced by reason of the dearness of necessaries to live at an higher and more expensive rate, and if on the same reason our merchants are forced to do the same, then of necessity our manufactures exported must be sold at foreign markets dearer by so much as well as the retailer at home to sell commodities imported or manufactured at home. It may be for the interest as before of the occupier of land to have the product advanced in price, but it is prejudicial to all the nation besides and very hurtful to trade itself. As for trade it must flourish best undoubtedly where there is the most encouragement. I speak chiefly as to manufactures, and people have the most encouragement to settle work there where they can subsist comfortably by their work and worked goods do bear a proportionable rate to the provisions of the country where they are manufactured. 'Tis this makes the Yorkshire stockings, the Welsh flannings so reasonable and so for many more. But had we no trade but with and amongst ourselves, it would be hardly worth our time to provide for these matters, but to let chance take place and to let necessity give rules and law, but since we are an island and our very subsistence and mere being does in a manner depend upon trade, it is our interest and, therefore, our duty to encourage trade which must be first by making such laws as are wanting, repealing such as are inconvenient, and in short to take care that speedy and cheap justice be done upon all occasions. The next thing is if practical to make sumptuary laws if possible to hinder the expensive and vain way of living of our merchants and traders, by which profuseness if any losses happen by land or sea, by fire or water, they are feign to turn bankrupts, to cheat their creditors, and to give of[f] trading to the ruin of their own and other families and the great damage of the public. Next to this we ought to take care that our provisions may bear such rates that our working people and those that buy from them may be able to subsist, and at foreign markets to sell as cheap as good as any other nation that use that market with the same goods; there must therefore be no duty on any commodity or relating to any commodity prepared hence . . . Now for the high prices of our wools, if the price did proceed from the quickness of the manufactured trade used amongst us, and if our nation had monopolized the trade of the world so that they could afford to give what prices they would for unwrought wools, because they could sell their manufactured woollen goods at what rate they would abroad; in that case, if the price of wool did proceed from such causes if they did not get to [set][1] a price upon their manufactured goods so high as to force other nations to set up for themselves, this would undoubtedly be good from us. But if the high price of our wools does proceed from this reason, because foreigners buy our unwrought wools to manufacture them at home with them and if that makes a quick trade by forcing our clothiers to advance price in order to keep our wools at home and to have them manufactured here, it is no good to the nation. If there was a rent established between landlord and tenant a[ccording] to the rates of goods, I mean the product of the land; if money was settled at a low and proportionable r[ate] and if the price of all the products of the earth was very moderate from our good husbandry and pl[enty not] from want of trade and people, it would be no damage to us at home and an advantage to us [. . .][1] onto a foreign trade. As for example, if I set my land for a low rent and everybody does so, this low rent brings me as much of everything I want as the bigger rent did. Gentlemen may fancy what they please: by examination and a wise enquiry it will be found that the same estate will keep the master in the same condition, [as] many horses, as many servants, as good a table and everything as plentifully, if commodities are as cheap, nay, I dare affirm better than if at a great price. As for example if all things are cheap, if this is not from a decay of trade, but plenty, certainly I am at no damage; no, though this plenty should proceed from the good husbandry of improvements, if my own land is not worsted, I shall mow as much hay, thresh as much corn, fat as many cattle and, let the prices of your product sink or fall, I can live the same as ever I could, so it is the same thing to me! But in relation to trade, if provisions are very dear, the artificer must either starve, or work at a great rate, so that when we come to a foreign market the merchants, for example, that live and trade in Ireland, if it was permitted them to manufacture cloth, would undersell, undo, and ruin our English woollen merchants. Upon which reasons it seems to me probable that if the Irish corn,

[1] MS. damaged.

cattle, and all their provisions came in hither, if they should make ours cheaper that would by no means hurt us, but would vastly advance and encourage our trade. I have heard many tradesmen have left England and went and settled in other more remote countries merely for the more conveniency of provision. Now if by any means provisions by a greater plenty became cheaper, I have made it appear the occupier of land would by no means suffer, and it is rather more than probable that such conveniencies would keep our own natives at home and invite foreigners from abroad to come and settle amongst us and that by the cheapness of our victuals, by the conveniency of our situation we might be masters of the woollen manufacture and of all handicraft trades outdo and excel and undersell all Europe, which would do the nation more good than to sell her commodities unwrought at a vast expensive rate.

II. AGRICULTURE

1. EXEMPLARY ARABLE FARMING IN THE VALE OF TAUNTON DEAN, 1607

[J. Norden, *The Surveyor's Dialogue*, 1607, pp. 230–3]

Bayly. I was once in Somersetshire, about a place near Taunton, called Tandeane. I did like their land and their husbandry well.

Surveyor. You speak of the Paradise of England; and indeed the husbandry is good, if it be not decayed since my being in those parts . . . Now I say, if this sweet country of Tandeane, and the western part of Somersetshire be not degenerated, surely, as their land is fruitful by nature, so do they their best by art and industry. And that makes poor men to live as well by a matter of twenty pounds per annum, as he that hath an hundred pounds.

Bay. I pray you, Sir, what do they more than other men upon their grounds?

Sur. They take extraordinary pains in soiling, ploughing, and dressing their lands. After the plough there goeth some three or four with mattocks to break the clods, and to draw up the earth out of the furrows, that the lands may lie round, that the water annoy not the seed: and to that end they most carefully cut gutters and trenches in all places, where the water is likeliest to annoy. And for the better enriching of their ploughing grounds, they cut up, cast, and carry in the unploughed headlands, and places of no use. Their hearts, hands, eyes, and all their powers concur in one, to force the earth to yield her utmost fruit.

Bay. And what have these men in quantity upon an acre, more than the ordinary rate of wheat, which is the principal grain?

Sur. They have sometimes, and in some places four, five, six, eight, yea, ten quarters in an ordinary acre.

Bay. I would think it impossible.

Sur. The earth, I say, is good, and their cost and pains great, and there followeth a blessing, though these great proportions always hold not. And the land about Ilchester, Long Sutton, Somerton, Andrey, Middlezoy, Weston, and those parts, are also rich, and there are good husbands.

Bay. Do they not help their land much by the fold?

Sur. Not much in those parts: but in Dorset, Wiltshire, Hampshire, Berkshire, and other places champion, the farmers do much enrich their land indeed with the sheepfold. A most easy, and a most profitable course: and who so neglecteth it, having means, may be condemned for an ill husband; nay, I know it is good husbandry to drive a flock of sheep over a field of wheat, rye, or barley newly sown, especially if the ground be light and dry, for the trampling of the sheep and their treading doth settle the earth about the corn, keeping it the more moist and warm, and causeth it to stand the faster, that the wind shake it not so easily, as it will do when the root lieth too hollow.

2. A DEBATE ON ENCLOSURE, 1607

[W. Cunningham, *The Growth of English Industry and Commerce in Modern Times*, Part II, Cambridge, 1903, pp. 898–9]

A Consideration of the Cause in Question before the Lords touching Depopulation

5 July 1607

IN REDRESS of these offences, enclosures, converting of arable, depopulation made the pretended cause of this last tumult. Two things may fall into consideration: 1. Whether the time be fit to give remedy when such encouragement may move the people to seek redress by the like outrage, and therefore in Edward the sixth his time the remedy was not pursued until two years after the rebellion of Kett. 2. Whether these pretended be truly inconvenient and therefore fit to consider what just reason may be alleged for
I. Enclosures, which are

    1. Security of state from (i) foreign invaders who cannot so easily march, spoil, and foray in an enclosed country, as a champion; (ii) domestic commotions which will be prevented when their false pretences (enclosures which they use *ad faciendum populum*) are taken away.

    2. Increase of wealth and people, proved (i) *a contrario*: the nurseries of beggars are commons as appeareth by fens and forests, of wealthy people the enclosed countries as Essex, Somerset, Devon, etc.; fuel, which they want in the champion, is supplied by enclosures. And labourers increased as are their employments by hedging and ditching; (ii) *a comparatis*: as Northamptonshire and Somerset, the one most champion, more ground, little waste, the other all enclosed but inferior in quantity and quality, yet by advantage of severalty, and choice of employment exceeding far in:

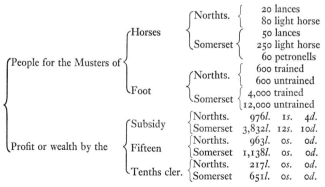

People for the Musters of	Horses	Northts.	20 lances			
			80 light horse			
		Somerset	50 lances			
			250 light horse			
			60 petronells			
	Foot	Northts.	600 trained			
			600 untrained			
		Somerset	4,000 trained			
			12,000 untrained			
Profit or wealth by the	Subsidy	Northts.	976*l.*	1*s.*	4*d.*	
		Somerset	3,832*l.*	12*s.*	10*d.*	
	Fifteen	Northts.	963*l.*	0*s.*	0*d.*	
		Somerset	1,138*l.*	0*s.*	0*d.*	
	Tenths cler.	Northts.	217*l.*	0*s.*	0*d.*	
		Somerset	651*l.*	0*s.*	0*d.*	

II. Leaving the employment of the ground to discretion of the occupants; so all the houses and land may be maintained in several tenantries, engrossing being truly the disease and not converting which may be justified for

1. Equality, for the law of tillage having left Essex and many other shires to their choice, and thereby no inconvenience in the state found, and that all arguments alleged for those counties will infer as much for the inland shires of Northampton, Leicester, etc. and because their situation so remote from any port or navigable river (whereby the charge of carriage far exceeding the full worth of the corn they sell) leaveth to them a disadvantage only; it were more just to give the free employing of their ground to such husbandry as will reduce them to an equality of benefit with the navigable shires, (which is by grazing to which their soil is more fit than other counties) whereby the vent of such their commodities shall be more easy being by drift and not by carriage.

2. For the true balancing of our best commodities, wool and corn (wherein the overweight will appear in the last), for in Henry VIII his time wool was the tod vij$^{d.}$ and viij$^{d.}$, barley (the greatest grain of the inland shires) vi$^{d.}$ and vii$^{d.}$ the bushel; the one is now usually xxiiij$^{d.}$ the tod, the other xviij$^{d.}$ and xx$^{d.}$ the strike. So wool risen above 2 thirds holdeth almost a proportion with all other commodities treble improved by the increase of monies. And corn, little more than double, is the reason of converting arable to reduce the profits equal to the husbandman, for keeping the land in divided tenantry. The good individual is the good general; for corn being dearer than cloth or meat comparatively, the husbandman will plough, since his only end is profit. If equal or under no reason to constrain him for that law which divideth labour from profit (as the art of tillage) is that which causeth the great difference of the wealths and abilities of several shires as they are oppressed with that statute.

III. Depopulation which (as all other engrossment) admitteth no defence doth justly move a course of remedy which must be for

1. Redress of what is already done either by (i) a new law (for the old is defective and will hardly support an information). And to reach to all is most just, since by no reason antiquity ought to turn mischief into conveniency, when it were more fit that he, that by longest offending hath done the most prejudice and received the best benefit, should in the punishment undergo the greatest censure. And therefore it were convenient to tie by statute all men to hold as their demesne not above the 4th part of any manor, the other 3 to be divided into tenements and no one to exceed 100 acres. And that no man in the same parish should keep two such tenements in his occupation. Or, (ii) by authority of Council, as about the 9 of Henry VII; 22 of Henry VIII; and 4 or 5 of Edward VI when the offenders were called up, and were by order enjoined to reedify half as many in every manor as they had decayed, and became bound by recognisance as appeareth in the Exchequer in the case of Andrews of Winwick and others, from time to time

to maintain so many and so much land to them as they were ordered by the Lords to do.

2. Prevention of that to come. And that may best be to cause through the champion countries or the whole kingdom such a survey to be made by commission as was 7° of Edward the first, returned into the Chancery and at this day called the Hundred Rolls, expressing what land is the lords demesne, and the particular number of all the houses and quantity of land belonging to them in every parish in the kingdom. That done to enjoin in every parish by a new law that number to be maintained; and the judges in their circuits usually to enquire of all defaults therein. And that upon every decay or unpeopling of any of those houses recorded and no other, within the space of one year builded within the same manor or near thereunto with a like quantity of ground annexed to it, it shall be lawful for the Lord Treasurer and Barons of the Exchequer to lease it for 21 years only as a mortmain, and demise it for that term to the King's use, and return it in charge into the Exchequer.

By redressing the fault of depopulation and leaving enclosing and converting arbitrable as in other shires the poor man shall be satisfied in his end: habitation; and the gentleman not hindered in his desire: improvement. But as there is now a labour to suit our dwellings for as much stock of people as the commonwealth will bear, it must likewise be fit, as good husbands do with their grounds, to provide that you do not overburthen it. But as they do with their increase remove them to other places, so must the State, either by transferring to the wars or deducing of colonies, vent the daily increase that else will surcharge the State; for if in London, a place more contagious than the country, the number of christenings doth weekly by 40 exceed the burials, and that the countries proportionally doth equal if not outgo that rate, it cannot be but that in this State, as in a full body, there must break out yearly tumours and impostumes as did of late.

3. HOW TO USE ALL LAND PROFITABLY, 1607

[J. Norden, *The Surveyor's Dialogue*, 1607, pp. 206–9]

FOR the first, namely, your low and spongy grounds trenched is good for hops, as Suffolk, Essex, and Surrey, and other places do find to their profit. The hot and sandy, (omitting grain) is good for carrot roots, a beneficial fruit, as Orford, Ipswich, and many sea towns in Suffolk: as also inland towns, Bury, Framlingham, and others in some measure, in the same shire, Norwich, and many places in Norfolk, Colchester in Essex, Fulham, and other places near London. And it begins to increase in all places of this realm, where discretion and industry sway the minds of the inhabitants. And I do not a little marvel that husbandmen and farmers do not imitate this for their own families, and to sell to their poor neighbours, as in some places they begin to their great profit. I have also observed in many places, where I have had occasion to travail, that many crofts, tofts, pightles, pingles, and other small quillets of land, about farm houses and tenements, are suffered to lie together idle, some overgrown with nettles, mallows, thistles, wild teasels, and divers other unprofitable weeds, which are fat and fertile, where, if the farmer would use the means, would grow sundry commodities, as hemp, and mustard seed, both which are so strong enemies to all other superfluous, and unprofitable weeds, as they will not suffer any of them to grow, where they are sown. The hemp is of great use in a farmer's house, as is found in Suffolk, Norfolk, Sussex, Dorset, and in many places in Somerset, especially about Burport and Lyme, where the people do find by it great advantage, not only for cordage for shipping, but also for linen, and other necessaries about a house. So is also the flax, which is also sown in many places, where good housewives endeavour their wits, wills, and hands to that commodious and profitable course, and the flax will like well enough in a more light and gentle, and leaner soil, than the hemp. And indeed there is not a place so rude and unlikely, but diligence and discretion may convert it to some profitable end. And among many other commodities, I marvel, men are no more forward in planting of apple trees, pear trees, crab-stocks, and such like in their hedges between their fields, as well as in orchards—a matter praiseworthy and profitable to the planter, and to the commonwealth very beneficial.

Bayly. Indeed, I have thought upon this kind of husbandry, but I have been prevented of mine own desires by a prejudicial conceit, that these fruits would redound little to my benefit, for that I think they will be stolen, the hedges trodden down, and the trees broken for the fruit's sake.

Surveyor. Negligence may easily find excuse, but this objection is frivolous, for I know in Kent, Worcestershire, Shropshire, Gloucestershire, Somerset, and Devon, and many parts in Wales, full of this commodity, even in their remote hedgerows. And although some few be lost, sith the rest come so easily, so fully, and so freely, a good mind will not grudge at a wayfaring passenger taking for his refection, and to qualify the heat of his travel, an apple or a pear, for the remnant will content the well conditioned owner. For I have known, that (all the stolen allowed) the fruit thus dispersedly planted have made in some little farms, or (as they call them in those parts) burgaines, a tun, two, three, four, of cider and perry, which kind of drink, resembling white wine, hath, without any further supply of ale or beer, sufficed a good householder and his family the whole year following, and sometimes hath made of the overplus twenty nobles, or ten pounds, more or less.

Bay. This surely cannot be but confessed to be very beneficial, both for private and public weal. And I myself have noted, that Mid[dlesex ?], in former times, hath had regard to this kind of commodity. For many apple trees, pear trees, service trees, and such like, have been planted in the fields and hedgerows, especially in the north and east part of the shire, as also in the south part of Hertfordshire, which are at this day very beneficial to the inhabitants, both for their own use and relief, as also to vent divers ways at London. But the trees are now for the most past very ancient, and I do not see such a continual inclination in the time present to continue or increase this benefit for the use of posterity. Neither did I ever know much cider or perry made in these parts, neither do I think they have sufficient skill or means.

Sur. I think, indeed, little cider is made there; some perry there is here and there; but more in the west country and in Kent, a place very fructiferous of that kind of fruit.

Bay. Yet is there not so much cider made, for all the great abundance of fruit, as there might be but in the inland.

Sur. The reason is because that near London and the Thames side, the fruit is vented in kind, not only to the fruiterers in gross, but by the country wives, in the nearest part of Kent, Middlesex, Essex, and Surrey, who utter them in the markets, as they do all other vendible things else.

Bay. But above all others, I think, the Kentishmen be most apt and industrious in planting orchards with pippins and cherries, especially near the Thames, about Faversham, Sittingbourne.

4. THE BENEFITS OF MANURE, 1607

[J. Norden, *The Surveyor's Dialogue*, 1607, pp. 226-30]

Bayly. We have, indeed, a kind of plodding and common course of husbandry hereabouts, a kind of peevish imitation of the most, who (as wise men note) are the worst husbands, who only try what the earth will do of itself, and seek not to help it with such means, as nature hath provided; whereas if men were careful and industrious, they should find that the earth would yield in recompense for a good husband's travail and charge, *centum pro cento* without corrupt usury.

Surveyor. I am glad you can now approve it so in reason; for I think experience doth not yet so fully teach you. I have known where land hath been very base and barren, and so continued many generations, as ground in manner forsaken and forlorn, abandoned of the plough, which after hath come into the hands of a discreet and industrious husband, that knew how and would take the pains, and bestow the cost to manure it in kind, hath much enriched himself by it, and where before it would not bear a crop of requite-full increase, by marling and good usage, hath borne crop after crop, 12, 16, or 20 years without intermission. The benefit of marling, Lancashire, Cheshire Shropshire, Somerset, Middlesex, Sussex, Surrey, among many other places, can witness, though not all by one kind of soiling and marling. For neither is all kind of marl in one place; neither any one kind in all places. But few places are so defective, but it yieldeth of itself, or is near unto some place of help. And men that will have profit must use the means. They must not sit and give aim, and wish and repine at others' increase. There must be observation to mark how others thrive, inclination and imitation to do the like endeavour and charge. And if one experiment fail, try a second, a third, and many. Look into places and persons, note the qualities of the land of other men, and confer it with thine own. And where there is a resemblance, mark what the best husband doth upon his land like unto thine. If it prosper, practise it, and follow the example of him that is commonly reported a thrifty husband. And by this means, will experience grow, and of one principle of reason, many conclusions will proceed. If a man look into Cornwall, there shall he find that in divers places, especially upon the north coast about Padstow, that the inhabitant farmers do soil their lands with sea sand, which because the country affordeth not in all places pass for cart-carriage, men fetch this kind of sand 3, 4, 6 miles in sacks on horseback. And poor men live by fetching and selling it to the more wealthy. In Devon and Somerset, and in some places of Cornwall, Sussex, and in the south part of Surrey, besides their other commendable courses of husbandry, they burn their land, and call it in the west parts, burning of beat, and in the south-east parts, Devonshiring, and by that means in barren earth have excellent rye, and in abundance. In Shropshire, Denbighshire, Flintshire, and now lately in some part of Sussex, the industrious people are at a more extraordinary charge and toil, for the poor husbandmen and farmers do buy, dig, and fetch limestones, 2, 3, 4, miles off, and in their fields build lime kilns, burn it, and cast it on their fields, to their great advantage, which kind of lime is of the nature of hot chalk, great helps to cold and moist grounds.

Bay. But this kind of stone is not to be had in all places.

Sur. That kind or some other is to be found in or near most places, and there is no kind of stone, but being burned, will work the like effect. So will also and especially the beach or pebble stones burned, that frequent the sea shore in many places, as upon the Camber shore near Rye, and at Eastbourne in Sussex, near Pevensey about Folkestone, and upon the coast of Kent, upon Orford Ness, and about Aldburgh, Hollesley, and that coast in Suffolk, and sundry other places upon the sea shore, in some places in so great abundance, as if there were wood in competent measure, would make good and great store of lime for building.

Bay. It is far to fetch it; for I do not think but every load fetched 5 miles is worth 5 shillings the carriage, and four pence at the pit; this is very chargeable.

Sur. Yet it quitteth the cost well enough; he that is able doth find it profitable. But you are in the mind of some that I have heard when they have been moved to entertain a help for their land, either it is too dear, or too far to fetch, or too deep in the earth, or some difficulty they pretend in it, that few undertake the right way to good husbandry ... Many fetch moor-earth or murgion from the river between Colebrooke and Uxbridge, and carry it to their barren grounds in Buckinghamshire, Hertfordshire, and Middlesex, eight or ten miles off. And the grounds whereupon this kind of soil is employed, will endure tilth above a dozen years after, without further supply, if it be thoroughly bestowed. In part of Hampshire they have another kind of earth for their dry and sandy grounds, especially between Fordingbridge and Ringwood, and that is the slub of the river of Avon, which they call mawme, which they dig in the shallow parts of the river; and the pits where they dig it will in few years fill again. And this mawme is very beneficial for their hot and sandy grounds, arable and pasture. And about Christchurch, Twineham, and up the river of Stour, they cut and dig their low and best meadows, to help their upland hot and heathy grounds. And now of late the farmers near London have found a benefit by bringing the scavengers' street soil, which being mixed as it is with the stone coal dust, is very helpful to their clay ground; for the coal dust being hot and dry by nature, qualifieth the stiffness and cold of the soil thereabouts. The soil of the stables of London, especially near the Thames side, is carried westward by water to Chelsea, Fulham, Battersea, Putney, and those parts for their sandy grounds.

5. THE MANAGEMENT OF MEADOWS, 1607

[J. Norden, *The Surveyor's Dialogue*, 1607, pp. 192–3, 195–6]

Surveyor. It is most necessary for a surveyor to remember what he hath observed, and to consider well the natures and qualities of all kinds of grounds, and to inform the lord of the means how to better his estate by lawful means, especially in bettering his own demesnes. So shall he the less need to surcharge his tenants by uncharitable exactions. And forasmuch as of all other grounds, none are (of their own nature) so profitable and less chargeable as meadow grounds, which are always ready to benefit the owner, summer and winter, they especially are to be regarded.

Bayly. That is true, indeed, and peradventure it takes the name of the readiness; for we call it in Latin *pratum*, as if it were *semper paratum*, either with the fleece for hay, as with the pasture to feed; and this meadow wherein now we are, is the best meadow that I know, and I think, for sweetness and burden, there is not a better in England.

Sur. You do well to advance the credit of the lord's land, and you speak, I think, as you conceive, because you are not acquainted with the meadows, upon Dove-bank in Tandeane, upon Severn-side, Allermoor, the lord's meadow in Crediton, and the meadows about the Welsh-pool, and many other places, too tedious to recite now.

Bay. These belike are made to good by art, but naturally, I think, this may match the best of them.

Sur. Indeed, meadows very mean by nature may be made excellent by charge; but they will decay, unless they be always relieved. But these that I speak of require little or no help at the owner's hand, only the aid of these rivers overflowing do feed them fat, gives great burden, and very sweet . . .

Sur. All overflowing waters do bring a slimy and fat substance with them, and leave it behind them; which together with the working of the water, through the spongy ground you speak of, worketh that effect in all grounds where it comes.

Bay. But water cannot be brought into all kinds of boggy grounds, nor into all kinds of meadows.

Sur. No, for there are two sorts of meadows, low and moist, and upland and dry meadows. Of these kinds the low is commonly the best, because they are aptest to receive these falling and swelling waters, which for the most part brings fatness with it; and besides, it moisteneth the ground, and makes the grass to grow cheerful; yet howsoever fat and fruitful they be, continual mowing yearly without intermission may weaken them and impair their goodness, and will require some help, unless they be such meadows as I recommended unto you yet while, that are so fed with fat overflowing waters, as do still maintain them in strength.

Bay. Then must the upland meadow, by often and continual shearing, needs decay.

Sur. The upland meadows have but the name of meadows; for, indeed, they are but the best pasture grounds, laid for hay. And to distinguish between that kind of meadow and pasture ground, or between pasture and arable, is frivolous; for that kind of meadow is most properly pasture, and all pasture grounds may be tilled. For when we say arable, it is as much as if we said, it is subject to the plough, or land which may be ploughed; and why then may not a man say that which is now pasture is arable, that is, convenient to be tilled? And on the contrary, that which is now tilled, may be pasturable; namely, apt to graze, and to feed cattle.

6. FISHPONDS, 1607

[J. Norden, *The Surveyor's Dialogue*, 1607, pp. 218–20]

Surveyor. If my memory fail not, there is a deep bottom in this field, and a little rill of water rising out of the hill runs through it.

Bayly. If you look but over this hill, you shall see it.

Sur. I see it, and I marvel that there hath been no respect had of this place, for it is a desert bottom, full of bushes and shrubs, yielding now little or no benefit.

Bay. What can you advise to be done with it, to make it more profitable?

Sur. I could wish some cost to be bestowed herein, making a fish pond, nay, it would make at the least two or three, one below the other.

Bay. Alas, that were to little purpose, as I take it, considering the charge of making the ponds, the clearing of the water course, the cleansing of the bodies, the making of the dams or heads of the ponds will be more chargeable than the fish will be profitable.

Sur. As you conceive it, for where reason or experience teach not, there the will follows to be untoward in all actions; and seldom men practise doubtful things, howsoever probable, for experience sake. But in this there is no doubt at all, the benefit is certain by approved experience, and it payeth the charge to the founder in short time, and afterward the benefit comes without much labour or cost. He that hath travailed, and is acquainted with Sussex and Surrey, and hath observed this commodity, may find that gentlemen and others able in those parts will not suffer such a convenient place as this for the purpose to lie unprepared for this use; and the sweetness of the gain they yearly make of it, hath bred such an increase of ponds for fish, as I think these two shires have more of them than any twenty other shires in England. *Bay.* That were very much, but I take it, the making of them is very charge-able, for the cleansing and digging, the ridding of the stuff, and making the head, I think will consume a greater charge, than many years will pay or redeem again, as I said before.

Sur. That which commonly cometh out of these kind of places is good soil for other lands, and will of itself quit the cost of cleansing and carrying. As for the head wherein the greatest charge consisteth, may be done for a mark or a pound a pole at the most, but where there is good fast earth, as is here, I think less will do it. This pond may be 20 pole at the head, few so much; and after 2 or 3 years being well stored, it will yield requital, not only for domestical use, but to be vented very beneficially. For the fishmongers of London do use to buy the fish by the score or hundred, of a competent scantling, when the ponds in the country be sewed, and bring them to London in cask, 20, 30, 40, 50 miles, and vent them by retail. And if the ponds be so remote from the main mart London as the fish cannot be con-veniently transferred, other confining cities, towns, and inhabitants, besides the owner's private families will find good use of them. And many times also these kinds of ponds may have sufficient fall of water for corn mills, fulling, or wake mills, scythe mills, and mills of other kinds, as the country where such convenient places are, may require.

7. A BERKSHIRE FARMER CASTS UP HIS CORN ACCOUNT, 1611

[*Robert Loder's Farm Accounts, 1610–20*, ed. G. E. Fussell, Camden Soc., 3rd Ser., LIII, 1936, pp. 19–20]

I MADE all manner of ways in Anno 1611 upon my farm is as followeth:

Imprimis the whole profits of my land was (as is aforesaid), I mean the crop thereof of corn, amounted to the value of lxxxxij*l*. iij*s*.; and the straw and chaff of the said corn amounted to the value of (as is aforesaid)—xj*l*. xj*s*. vij*d*.; the layings out being deducted as followeth; for allowances towards the tilling of my land to halves—vij*l*. xx*d*.; for threshing and winnowing of the corn iij*l*. xiij*s*. viij*d*.; for all charges at harvest—iiij*l*. ij*s*. ob.; for thistling lands—ij*s*. vj*d*.; for hayward's wages—iij*s*. iiij*d*. ob.; these layings out (I say) deducted, being xv*l*. ij*s*. iij*d*.; out of the aforesaid profits being ciij*l*. xiiij*s*.

vij*d*., there remains of the clear profits of my land and crop the sum of lxxxviij*l*. xj*s*. iiij*d*.

Item my hay came to (as is aforesaid) xliij*l*. xvi*s*.; deducting of it for the mowing and making—v*l*. vij*s*.; and for wanting and watering—v*s*. x*d*.; there remains then I say of clear profits, the Lord be thanked, the whole sum of—xxxviij*l*. iij*s*. ij*d*.

Item the whole sum of all other my profits is as aforesaid 27*l*. 16*s*. viij*d*.; and the whole sum of all other my charges and layings out for them (as aforesaid) vij*l*. xiij*s*. vj*d*. ob.; which being deducted there remains *de claro* unto me xx*l*. ij*s*. v*d*. ob.

But of these profits particularly I may read in my notes before. So that the sum of the clear profits (given unto me, unworthy thereof, by the most merciful God) is as abovesaid, cxlvj*l*. xvj*s*. xi*d*. ob.

Which of my lands yielded me most profit, of those sowed with wheat or of those sowed with barley and pulse?

Imprimis my wheat lands, being xxvj (as I may see in my notes aforesaid) the profits of them came to (as aforesaid) xxxj*l*. vij*s*. ij*d*. (and but very little if any jot bigger than ordinary) And my barley lands, being lxxv, which was iij times so many (lacking but iij lands) the profits of them came to (as aforesaid) liij*l*. vij*s*., which is not twice so much profit (as my wheat lands) by and above viij*l*., which is very much, the lands being dunged alike as far as I now can remember; wherefore I think it were good sowing more store of wheat, if the profit rise thus in other years hereafter following.

Memorandum that the wheat lands being xxvj (as abovesaid) bore me xx qtrs. vij b. i p.; and the lxxv barley lands xlvj qtrs. iij b. ij p. (being let to halves), so that the barley lands did not bear so much upon a land one with another as the wheat by about vj qtrs.; and yet the wheat was worth xxx*s*. the quarter; and the barley but xxiij*s*. the quarter (as afore is said) wherefore here is to [be] seen great reason for sowing more wheat and less barley.

8. THE KING'S SURVEYOR ON THE IMPROVEMENT OF THE FORESTS, 1612

[B.M., Add. MS. 38444, ff. 4–6]

Reasons to prove that the enclosing of Wastes and Common Forest Grounds and Chases are lawful, profitable, necessary to the King and People

THAT it is lawful is proved by the Statute of Merton 20 H. 3, cap. 4 thus: that the lords of wastes, woods, and pastures may approve the same notwithstanding the contradiction of their tenants, so that the tenants may have sufficient pasture to their tenements, which sufficient pasture is by the law expounded to be for so many beasts as the tenants' several pasture will maintain summer and winter. Westminster 2, 13 Ed. I enlargeth this law and maketh it to take place betwixt such lords and their neighbours also. By this statute this improvement shall be a bar in an assise of common, and so is it by the former statute. Certain augmentations of enclosures are by this statute of 13 Edw. I made good against the commoners. By the same statute of 13 Edw. I, if the enclosures be thrown down by persons unknown, the towns next adjoining shall be distrained to make the same hedge or ditch and to render damages to the owner of such enclosures.

Many statutes are made for improvement of unprofitable lands, as wastes and commons are. Sundry statutes are made against converting of tillage into pasture. Thus then it is manifest that the wisdom of all ages did not only allow but provide and make it lawful to enclose common and waste grounds. And so doth the forest laws for forest grounds and chases.

That it is profitable to the King and subjects is proved thus: first to his Majesty insomuch as it will advance the revenue of the crown exceedingly. To the subjects that it will enable them to live in a far better manner than now they do, and make them more able to serve his Majesty as well in time of war as peace, and minister them better means to provide for their posterity. And whereas his Majesty's annual charge is wonderful great in regard of the fees of officers in forests, parks, and chases, which lie remote and such as neither the King nor his progeny have or are like to have any pleasure thereby. It is out of question that his Majesty, if so he please, might by enclosing the same both save this needless charge and much augment his revenue. It will lessen the multiplicity of beggars which are begotten daily by reason there is not placing sufficient for them considering that the wastes and commons are not inhabited and the number of people do mightily increase, the burden whereof is grown almost insupportable.

Commons, which lie open undivided, every man may furnish with what sort of cattle he liketh *sans* number, which is an occasion that the richer sort of people by surcharging the commons do eat up both their own part and their poor neighbours', which commons, if they were divided and made into severals, then every man might know his own, and dispose thereof as he should think good for his best profit which otherwise they cannot do. It is likewise found by daily experience for *experiencia est magistra artium* that commons undivided are never so commodious as when they be divided in severalties, for when they be so, they become much more fertile, and in a short time the grass in it[s] own nature will become quite changed and the compost that cattle yearly breed therein (together with a little good husbandry) will so fatten the ground and make it fit either for meadow or pasture and in many places, where the soil is good, for corn, as that which will not yield 12*d.* an acre will then be worth 10*s.* an acre.

Furthermore, the commons that be open are much subject to ill weather so as their goods are not able to continue upon the moors above 4 months in the year. But if once they be made into severalties, they then become warm, and the walls and hedges which do environ them do mightily preserve and defend their cattle both from wind and weather, and by means thereof they may continue the most part of the year to the great good of the owners. And this is approved to be so by the daily improvements that are made of commons in sundry places of this kingdom by the people of their own accord, without any manner of persuasion or enforcement thereunto, nay, without any warrant at all in many places so to do, for it is not to be doubted they would undergo that labour and charge of enclosing if they found not both great ease and profit thereby, and hereof ourselves are eye witnesses and know it to be true in our own particular.

That it is necessary first for his Majesty is proved thus: that forasmuch as God hath blessed his Majesty with hopeful issue, who, as they grow up in years, so will they grow in charge; and it may so please the Almighty as that they may have children who must have maintenance fitting their princely calling; all which cannot be unless some speedy course be taken to enlarge his Highness's revenue in the nature of a support, that from out the same a competent allowance may be extracted for this purpose. And what course can be thought of more beseeming the King himself than out of his own means to do this without burdening his subjects (with our duty and reverence be it spoken)? Therefore in our poor opinion there is no such project to be put in practice as for his Majesty to improve his wastes, commons, forest grounds, and chases, leaving sufficient common as is formerly expressed.

We could lay down many more reasons to prove the necessity hereof, but we fear to give offence in taking upon us. Only thus much we will presume to deliver that, if his Majesty by the advice of the lords of his Highness's most honourable Privy Council shall hold this course fit to be entertained, that it would be set on foot in time, for it will require long time to finish so good and great a work, and the business would be settled whilst his royal issue are but young, and then will follow that, when they shall be fit to take the benefit, it will be ready for them. And in the mean time his Majesty may take to himself whatsoever shall arise thereby.

That it is necessary for the subject is proved thus: the rate of corn and victuals of all kind, cloths, leather, and whatsoever else that the farmer standeth in need of, being grown to so high a pitch, it standeth them upon to make their best benefit of their tenements so far as lawfully they may, and so consequently they must embrace this as a special means to enable them to live the better. Moreover, the King's Majesty may haply have occasion to call on his subjects for such contributions as commonly great princes have use for many ways, as well in time of peace as war. And if the subject be unprovided the King cannot be furnished. And therefore it is necessary that this course be holden for the good of both. The subjects also shall hereby be more enabled to bring up their children in some good fashion to make them more able to live in future times, and so abolish in time the multiplicity of beggars as hath been formerly said.

And to conclude, though the benefit that may come unto them hereby in the judgment of an understanding man cannot be so little as treble, to the former may be added these considerations following, viz. 1. The manner how to proceed in this important service. 2. The place where to begin. 3.

And lastly what course is to be holden with such as have already encroached upon the King's wastes and commons without leave and not yielding any rent for the same to his Majesty.

For the manner how to proceed in this great affair, with our duty and under reformation be it spoken, it would be thus: a commission would be awarded from his Majesty to certain honest, discreet, and serviceable gentlemen, but not unto many, for that will beget but dispute and fruitless discourses, and consume and idly spend both his Majesty's allowance and time without any effect at all, and with them would be joined and [=men] learned in the laws and an exquisite surveyor. These commissioners would be such as are well acquainted with business of this kind, and are able out of their own experience and judgment to yield sufficient reasons for their doings and be able to answer every objection and to meet with every opposition.

There must likewise be such as will carry themselves wisely, mildly, and with much patience, for the well managing of this business is to him *in toto*. They must be very circumspect that the least distrust that may be given to the people be avoided either by word or deed, for the vulgar sort are not to be drawn by violence but *pian piano*. And the best motive is to draw them by examples, for *vivimus exemplis*.

The place where to begin his Majesty may do well, as we think, to set this practicable business on foot within his Highness's county of York for there the commons, moors, forest grounds, and chases be spacious and large, for when it shall be known abroad that this his Majesty's intention is there embraced, and that the country taketh good liking thereof (which is not to be doubted), then will other countries follow very readily, and so the service may be performed with much more facility, for *omnia principia sunt difficilia* and *dimidium est plus toto*. And for the encroachments which are daily made upon the King's wastes without his Highness privity, permission, or benefit (without innumerable), it is thought fit *salvo semper meliori judicio* that his Majesty should award another commission to the forenamed commissioners, thereby giving them power to enquire by jury who have transgressed in this kind, to survey the same by the foresaid surveyors, and to give unto them full power to impose a moderate rent (as to their discretions shall think fit) to be yearly paid in his Majesty's Receipt for the same, and in all the premises, the commissioners must carry themselves very respectfully that his Majesty may have no cause of offence, nor the county of clamour, and they must be very circumspect that both themselves and their followers be free from bribery and corruption, which, when the people shall find to be so, it will find a better passage to the business, and God will give a blessing to their endeavours. And in running this course all fear of discontent will be laid away, and the business will go on with much better success. And when the people shall be made to perceive that nothing is done but what is warranted by the law, because it is our protection, nor anything intended but a future benefit to the King and his subjects, which will be our preservation, then will they give way readily to the intended purpose, and God will be pleased with the work, the King's Majesty well pleased with their labour, and the commonwealth exceeding well satisfied, and all parties wonderfully well contented. But in all this we submit to your lordships in all humble manner this our poor comments of this business, humbly craving pardon for our errors.

Thos. Lascelles, Anth. Dyot, Ro. Church

9. THE LESSONS OF SHEEPKEEPING IN A BAD YEAR, 1613

[Robert Loder's Farm Accounts, 1610–20, ed. G. E. Fussell, Camden Soc., 3rd Ser., LIII, 1936, pp. 68–9]

In anno 1613

OF THE sheep which I rotted in this year.

Imprimis memorandum that my shepherd rotted me iiijC; but Cxx I sold; C of them at x*l.* the XX; the other at v*l.* xiij*s.* iiij*d.* against winter.

Memorandum of the other cclxxx, not sold so well; I had lost of the rot this xjth of January *in anno* 1614 (for now even at this time do they die although they were rotted in *anno supradicto* afore Michaelmas, and all the winter too;) abouts some (as I think) lxxx or upwards.

Memorandum that I sold some at beginning of winter *in anno* 1613 for v*s.* the piece, even xxx; and many more I might have so sold; which had been my best course certainly, or else to have sold them afore this winter *in anno* 1614, I mean in the summer, and then to have put them to grass and feeding.

Memorandum also that I lost not above xxxvij of ccxxxj the vth of May after the other xlix I sold and killed, the which I would I had done to many more; for I have lost this xjth of January *in anno* 1614 lxxx or upwards (as is said) and divers and many more I am like to lose.

Memorandum also that I had lost of sheep which I bought at spring *in anno hoc* 1614 afore this day, some xix.

Memorandum therefore that it is good to take heed of buying sheep (and to buy none after so great a rot year) except a man do certainly know what they are. *Cave caveto,* I say, of buying and always in keeping thy sheep.

Memorandum that this was the greatest rot year that hath been known in many years before.

Memorandum that for the seething of their livers, they broke all to pieces which were so in the last of November and beginning of December, and these had in their bellies water or jelly places, great galls, and livers some; except one which had none of these signs but looked a little whiteish at top, yet broke as the rest. But some which were killed after Christmas whenas they had eaten fodder (but what was the cause I know not) so hard and sound and yet had all the aforesaid ill signs.[1]

---

[1] These are the symptoms of liver fluke.

Memorandum ever hereafter that I sell away my sheep afore winter if I know them to be rotten; or else if I know it after winter, that I put them off in that summer to —— grass and feeding, and sell them afore winter come again. And that I take heed in buying sheep after such great rot years especially. I say, *cave*, beware, be wise (which the Lord grant if it be his will) in buying always and in keeping continually.

10. SERVANTS' WAGES ON A BERKSHIRE FARM, 1613

[*Robert Loder's Farm Accounts, 1610–20*, ed. G. E. Fussell, Camden Soc., 3rd Ser., LIII, 1936, p. 72]

In anno 1613

MONEY I paid servants for their wages at Faith Tide

Imprimis to Robert Earnold for his year's wages	iij*l*.
Item to Jak Andrews, my boy	xvs. vj*d*.
Item to Dick, my shepherd	xl*s*.
Item to Johan Colle[?] my maid	xlvij*s*. vj*d*.
Item to Alce Keates my other for part of the year	xxx*s*.
Summa totalis est—	ix*l*. xiiis.

Memorandum that these spent me in meat and drink every of them for a year (as I may see in my notes *in anno* 1612) x*l*. vs.

Memorandum then that thus I have written; for th'end that I might see the great charges in keeping servants; and therefore I think it were best course to keep none; to effect which there is no other means, but either to put forth my land to tillage by the land, or else to keep my servants at board wages.

11. RELAXING THE POLICY TOWARDS ENCLOSURES AND THE DECAY OF TILLAGE, 1621

[Notestein, Relf, and Simpson, *Commons Debates, 1621*, VII, pp. 512–3]

The Motives and Reasons of the Commissioners for Pardons for Decay of Tillage[1]

THE owners and purchasers of lands improved by decay of tillage are by this means free from informers, and the great penalty of 20*s*. an acre yearly due thereby, who if they should be compelled to plough it up by rigour of the law, would ruin the estates of many of them.

[1] The original document is British Museum, Harleian MS. 7616, f. 6 (Alford papers). It may be an example of information which came to Alford as a member of the subcommittee for grievances which prepared work for the Grand Committee. The subcommittee had been appointed on 2 March 1621.

It hath relation to pardon the offence past only, and not to future. These sort of offenders were at the mercy of the informer before without end, and now are to be relieved with his Majesty's pardon. Some great offenders were spared by connivance of the informer and others that were innocent were vexed without end.

There were near 2,000 informations in and depending in the several courts before this Commission without benefit to his Majesty which sithence have been taken away, and they have ceased to proceed thereon, lest pardon make it fruitless to them.

There is no want of corn land at this time, but want of pastures and cattle for much woodlands and barren grounds are become fruitful cornlands instead of pasture.

That by occasion of this suit upon his Majesty's reference, it was certified by the Lord Chancellor, Lord Chief Justice, and his Majesty's Council that this pardon was not only lawful for his Majesty to do but necessary and convenient, for it is no prosecution of a law, but a pardon of an offence past. That it meddles not to pardon any depopulations nor crying offence. That it hath not been executed to the grievance of any nor any one petition or clamour against the Commissioners. That this kind of pardon hath been granted in the late Queen's time in the same manner to Jenkinson, Dormer, and others. That the late Lord Chancellor for conveniency settled by decree much pasture land of this nature to the lessor, which the lessee (by the law notwithstanding the covenant) might have ploughed up.

[Endorsed:] Mr. Ramsey.

12. REASONS IN FAVOUR OF ENCLOSURE AT SLIMBRIDGE, GLOUCESTERSHIRE, 1639

[*The Berkeley Manuscripts. A Description of the Hundred of Berkeley in the County of Gloucester and of its Inhabitants by John Smyth of Nibley*, III, ed. Sir John Maclean, 1885, p. 328]

Slimbridge

A PARISH that is great and rich in soil, yet few of the inhabitants wealthy, most very poor. The warth and other waste grounds of this manor and parish, if enclosed, would yield above 1,500*l.* per annum, wherein is verified the observation of many wise men, that the more large the waste grounds of a manor are, the poorer are the inhabitants. Such common grounds, commons, or waste grounds, used as commonly they are, and as here I know they are, yield not the fifth part of their true value, draw many poor people from other places, burden the township with beggarly cottages, inmates, and alehouses, and idle people; where the great part spend most of their days in a lazy idleness and petite thieveries and few or none in profitable labour. And I am persuaded that amongst other motives, this hath been one and yet is, and none of the least, why King James and the king that now is have reduced into severalty, and into smaller parcels let to private men's uses and farmers thereof, so many of their forests, chases, and wild and waste grounds in most shires of the kingdom, as they have done, to the private benefit of themselves and the general good of the commonwealth, both in the breed of serviceable men and subjects, and of answerable estates and abilities. Whereas now, not one of these beggars, lazy and idle people, thus living and bred, are any ways useful or serviceable in any kind. And what you, my son John, do now in this present month and year of August 1639 observe in the Forest of Dean, now in disafforesting and in converting to better private profits, wherein as a Commissioner I understand you are employed, in the very hour and day wherein I write this page, your afteryears and riper observations will more pregnantly appear and inform you.

13. PRUDENT SHEEP MANAGEMENT ON THE YORKSHIRE WOLDS, 1641

[Henry Best, *Rural Economy in Yorkshire in 1641, being the Farming and Account Books of Henry Best of Elmeswell in the East Riding*, ed. C. B. Robinson, Surtees Soc., XXXIII, 1857, pp. 3–4, 72–4]

THE best way (for those that have enclosed and warm grounds and good succour for lambs) is to keep their tups and ewes together all the year long, and to strive and endeavour by all means possible for timely lambs; and that for these reasons:—

1. For their better succour: for grounds that are to be laid up for hay are not to be eaten above a fortnight after Ladyday at the most, and therefore these lambs which come about the middle of February will have two months' time or thereabouts; whereas these that come about the middle of March shall not have above a month's time; and the longer and better succour that lambs have before they go to field the better able will they be to shift when they come there, and the loftier sheep will they make afterwards.

2. For the owner's profit; for he that hath lambs within a week or fortnight of Candlemas will oftentimes have fat lambs to sell about St. Helenmas, at which time they are rare, and very hard to come by; wherefore good, fat, and well-quartered lambs will usually (at that time of the year) give nobles and seven shillings a piece.

3. To ease the shepherd that hath a great keeping of ewes; for the tups going always with them, some of the ewes will tup sooner, and some later, so that the lambs falling not over thick together, he will have the more time to suckle and provide for one lamb after another.

4. To make them harder sheep; for being once nipped (about Candlemas) with frosts and cold weather, it will be a means to make them like better when God sends better weather; for as the saying is, *Sheep that will live in*

*winter, will live and thrive in summer; and sheep that grow fleshy with four
teeth, will grow fat with eight.*

It is usual, in pasture grounds where they take not up their tups for them
to ride about a fortnight or three weeks before Michaelmas; and these lambs
that are gotten then will fall about Candlemas, and sometimes a week afore;
but the ewes will begin to tup wholly about Michaelmas, and their lambs most
of them come about the middle of February; but those that take up their
tups, put them not to the ewes till St. Luke day, and then their forwardest
lambs will fall about the middle of March. The reason why they take up
their tups is want of succour for their lambs, and therefore they would not
have them to come till the Spring begin to shew itself on the ground.

A tup, if he be kept loftily and in lust, is said to be sufficient for forty, or
fifty ewes, yet the usual and best course is to allow four tups to an hundred
ewes, i.e. to every thirty ewes, a tup. The most judicious sheep-men endeavour by all means possible to provide good tups for their ewes; for they
say, *a bad ewe may bring a bad lamb, yet she spoils but one, but an ill tup is
likely to spoil many. . . .*

For foddering of sheep

If there chance to fall a light thin snow, which be not above two or three
inches thick, you need not begin to fodder for the space of three or four days,
till you see further alteration in the weather, for they will scrape away the
snow with their feet, and get to the grass; and you are also to have a care
that you begin not to fodder in wet weather; for they will not fall freshly to
their fodder at the first, but tread it under foot and waste it; but rather, if
you doubt a storm, bring them out of the dale-bottoms and lay them in the
Spellowe, or some such like close, where they have shelter against the storm,
and also some victuals for scraping for; then, if the weather break not up,
or if more snow come, you are to bring them home, and begin to fodder, if
the weather be so that it take them quite off the ground; otherwise, you
are not to begin to fodder if you see that they can come to the ground, or be
likely to come to the ground.

Sheep will make a shift for a long time in a thin snow to scrape for their
living. . . . Shepherds are to have an especial eye to their hogs, and always
to give them the shortest, learyest, and best hay; and if they see any that
forbear and do not work on their meat, they are to take them from the
company, and put them into some close where some banks are bare that lie
against the sun, till it recover some strength, and then to put it to them
again, and they will fall to. We always put three or four of the eldest ewes to
the hogs to show them the way, and teach them to eat hard-meat; if there be
any of the hogs that be sturdy, lame, weak, give over, and be not able to keep
company with the rest, we put them into the closes to the fat sheep, where
there is grass sufficient, whereby they may get flesh and be made worthy
their death, or otherwise recover heart and strength to help them over winter.
It doth hogs a world of good to be put to an hay stack where they may serve

themselves, and beside if the hay stack stand in such a place where there is good beeld and shelter against a storm, many will put them to it as much for the beeld as the fodder; and if they do chance to pull out more than they eat, and tread it under foot, if you but rake it together, and lay it in some place where the wind may blow in it a while, it will dry and sweeten it again, for that it will make good fodder for the oxen that are in the house; or otherwise you may bottle it up, and carry it, and put it in one of the stand-hecks, as you do your staddle-hay.

There fell (this year) a thin snow on Monday, the 22nd of November, at which time our hogs were in the Carr; the snow continuing still, the towns-folks brought all their field sheep and put them into the Carr on Thursday morning, the 25th of the same month; wherefore we fetched away our hogs, and put them into the Wandill closes, and went and brought down all our field sheep from the Spellowe, and laid them in the Brick close the first night, and then the next morning we put them into the Carr, because the townsfolks would not fetch theirs out, and if it had then been open weather, the Carr would not have lasted them three days to an end; or if they had been there all the waygate of the snow, they would have trodden it all to muck; but the weather continuing at a certain without either increasing or decreasing, they remained there, and made a shift to scrape for their living till Sunday morning; for on Saturday night there came more snow, and a frost with it, wherefore on Sunday morning our shepherd carried a bottle of hay into the Carr, as much as we thought they would eat readily, and shilled ours out from amongst the town sheep, and foddered them on our own lands, and stood by them till they had eaten it. The townsfolks desired that every one might bring hay proportionable to the number of their sheep, and then they brought a little of their steer hay, and by this means our hay should have been spent in foddering of other men's goods; wherefore on Sunday night we brought them into the West-Hall East close, and there foddered them so long as the snow lasted.

14. FEASTING AFTER PEAS HARVEST, 1641

[Henry Best, *Rural Economy in Yorkshire in 1641, being the Farming and Account Books of Henry Best of Elmeswell in the East Riding*, ed. C. B. Robinson, Surtees Soc., XXXIII, 1857, p. 93]

For pulling and working amongst peas

WE USE means always to get either 18 or else 24 peas pullers, which we set always six on a land, viz.: a woman and a man, a woman and a man, a woman or boy and a man, etc.; the weakest couple in the fore furre, the next weakest in the hinder furre, and the strongest on the rigg, which should always come hindermost; we furnish all or most of them with pease hooks, excepting one or two, and these we call for and see carried to the place

where they used to lie so soon as that labour is done that our workfolks be
come home. It is usual in most places after they get all peas pulled or the
last grain down, to invite all the workfolks and their wives (that helped them
that harvest) to supper, and then have they puddings, bacon, or boiled beef,
flesh or apple pies, and then cream brought in platters, and everyone a
spoon; then after all they have hot cakes and ale; for they bake cakes and
send for ale against that time; some will cut their cake and put into the cream,
and this feast is called the cream-pot or cream kitte; for on the morning that
they get all done the workfolks will ask their dames if they have good store of
cream, and say that they must have the cream kitte anon.

15. PARLIAMENTARY SURVEYORS DESCRIBE LAND IN ALTERNATE HUSBANDRY, 1649

[P.R.O., E 317, Warws., 12, ff. 6, 20, 21; survey of
Hampton-in-Arden, Warwickshire, 1649]

ONE close of pasture ground called the Hill Field, now divided into four
several parts, whereof some part thereof is at the present ploughed, and the
rest of it unploughed, it being a usual course with the inhabitants to plough
their ground which they do call pasture for two or three years together, and
then to let it lie for pasture fifteen or twenty years and then plough it again,
and this they do with a great part of their pasture ground. And therefore we
thought good to give it as pasture ground, it being so called by them, for the
ground that is this year pasture is sometimes the next year ploughed, and the
ground that is this year ploughed is the next sometimes laid for pasture, it
being counted with them at an equal estimate when either ploughed or not
ploughed . . .
   One close of pasture ground called the Castle Hills being now divided into
seven parts whereof some part thereof is at the present ploughed, it being a
usual course thereabouts so to do as is before expressed . . .
   All that parcel of pasture ground called the Old Park, there being some
small part thereof ploughed as aforesaid abutting upon the said ground called
the Castle Hills.

16. LIME AND OTHER MANURES; AND THE MERITS OF PIG KEEPING, 1652

[Walter Blith, *The English Improver Improved*, 1652, pp. 132–3,
144–7]

AND in thy tillage are these special opportunities to improve it, either by
liming, marling, sanding, earthing, mudding, snail-codding, mucking,
chalking, pigeons' dung, hens' dung, hogs' dung, or by any other means, as
some by rags, some by coarse wool, by pitch marks, and tarry stuff, any oily

stuff, salt, and many things more, yea, indeed, anything almost that hath any liquidness, foulness, saltness, or good moisture in it, is very natural enrichment to almost any sort of land, all which as to all sorts of land, they are of an exceeding meliorating nature, and of most of these more particularly.

And first for liming, it is of most excellent use, yea, so great that whole countries, and many counties that were naturally as barren as any in this nation, and had formerly (within less than half an age) supply with corn out of the fielden corn country, and now is and long hath been ready to supply them, and doth and hath brought their land into such a posture, for bearing all sorts of corn, that upon land not worth above one or two shillings an acre, they will raise (well husbanded with lime) as good wheat, barley, and white and grey peas, as England yields, yea, they will take a parcel of land from off a lingy heath or common, not worth the having; nay, many will not have it to husbandry it, and will raise most gallant corn, that naturally is so barren, worth five or six pound an acre.

And though some object it is good for the father, but bad for the son, I answer, so are all extremes whatsoever, that is, to plough it after liming so long as is either any spirit left in the lime, or heart in the land, or it will bear any sort of corn or grain, it will ruin it for posterity. But if that after liming men would but study moderation in their tillage, and not (because the land yields such abundance of corn) plough or till it so long as it will carry corn, no, nor so long as it will carry good corn; but if men would, after good liming, take three, four, or five crops, and then lay down their lands to graze, it would not be the least prejudice. Or if upon the laying of it down, men would but indifferently manure it, or else upon the last crop you intend to sow, dung it well before sowing, and lay it down upon the rye, or wheat stubble, it would produce a sweet turf, and I am confident prove excellent pasture, as good again as it was before; but if after it is laid down you would manure it once again, a little manure now will produce more fruit than as much more upon the old sward, it would be warrished for ever. Many men have had ten crops of gallant corn after one substantial liming, some more, upon very reasonable land of about six shillings eight pence an acre, some land worth a little more, but more land less worth, and some upon land not worth above one or two shillings an acre, have got many gallant crops upon a liming as aforesaid. Some men have had and received so much profit upon their lands upon once liming, as hath paid the purchase of their lands; I myself had great advance thereby, yet I lived twenty miles from lime, and fetched it so far by wagon to lay upon my lands, and so not capable to make like advantage as other borderers. The land natural and suitable for lime is your light and sandy land, and mixed sound earth, so also is your gravel, but not so good, and your wet and cold gravel is the worst, except your cold hungry clay, which is worst of all, but all mixed lands whatever are very good . . .

As for chalk, Sir Francis Bacon affirms it to be of an over-heating nature to the land, and is best for cold and moist land, but as it appears to me in Hertfordshire and other parts thereabout, there are great improvements to be made upon barren, gravelly, flinty lands, and it hath great fruitfulness in it, but not having fallen under my own experience I dare affirm little therein, only advise any that have opportunity therein to be well resolved of the fruitfulness of the said chalk, or of the nature of the said lands, for there is some chalk, though not very much thereof, that is of so churlish a binding nature, that it will so fodder and bind, and hold the water upon the top of the earth so long till it destroy the corn, nor work a sterility in the earth, that neither corn or ground shall yield but little fruit; but there is a chalk in thousand places of great fruitfulness for improvement.

And I also conceive that chalk, earth, and manure, mixed together, makes an admirable, sure, and natural fruitful composition for almost any sort of lands, and is a very excellent, unfallible remedy against barrenness, and raiseth corn in abundance, and enricheth it also for grazing when you lay it down; many great countries in this nation are under this capacity.

Also the mud of old standing pools and ditches, the shovelling of streets and yards and highways, the overswarths of common lanes, or of commons near hedges, is very good both of itself, and compounded with other soil, manure, mud, or straw; and very much account made thereof in some countries; nay more than this of manure that is made of horse or cow, for some sorts of land, and some sorts of corn, which I conceive is for lands very flinty, stony, and gravelly, or a little mixed with clay amongst them; as also for wheat and barley it is very natural, and is of constant use and great esteem in Hertfordshire, Essex, Sussex, and divers other countries thereabout, and also to great advantage being put in execution in most of the countries in this nation, if ingenuity was of as good esteem among us all as is a base outlandish fashion, for no sooner can that be brought into any part of the country, but it will be dispersed presently into all the parts thereof; but such as these, that are advantage to all, and vastly profitable to the practitioner and commonwealth, are slighted and little practised.

Earth of a saltish nature is fruitful, especially all such earth as lies dry, covered with hovels or houses, of which you make saltpetre, is rich for land, so is old floors under any buildings.

There are many other gallant soils or manure, as your pigeons' dung, a load whereof is more worth than twenty shillings in many parts, your hens' and poultry dung, that live of corn, is very excellent. These being of a very hot or warm and brackish nature are a very excellent soil for a cold moist-natured land; two load hereof will very richly manure an acre; so is all dung, the more it is raised from corn or richer matter, the richer itself is usually by far; as where horses are highly corned, the richer is the dung than those only kept with hay.

There is another sort of soil, and that is swine's dung, by most men accounted the worst of all, nay, not worth preserving, out of an old received tradition taken up by most men, upon what ground I know not, and so generally disliked of almost every one. And therefore they will not experiment it, and much an end no use at all is made thereof. Possibly it came from Scotland, who knew they but the excellency thereof, they would love the flesh the better for the dung's sake.

Which to me is very irrational, that an English man who loves swine's flesh so well, that more account and use is made of all the parts of him, rather than of the beef or sheep, yea, his very blood and guts are highly prized, and yet the soil of him so much undervalued.

This dung is very rich for corn, or grass, or any land; yea, of such accompt to many ingenious husbands that they prefer it above any ordinary manure whatsoever; therefore they make their hogs' yards most complete with an high pale, paved well with pebble or gravel in the bottom, where they set their troughs partly in, and some part without the pale, into which they put their meat. But the most neat husbands indeed, plant their trough without the pale or hog-yard, all along by the side of it, and for every hog they have a hole cut, the just proportion of his head and neck, and cannot get in his feet to soil his meat, and out thence he eats his meat forth of the trough very cleanly and sweet. They keep the trough also very clean; they have their house for lodging by itself with dry straw always for them to lie in, and their cornish muskings they cast into the yard for that purpose, and all garbage and all leaves out of gardens, and all muskings forth of their barns, and of their courts and yards, and great store of straw or weeds and fern, or anything for the swine to root amongst, to make all the dung they can into the yard for raising dung. And here they keep their swine the year round, never suffering them to go one day abroad; and here your dairy husbands or housewives will feed them as fat as peas or beans, and are of opinion that they feed better and fatter and with less meat, than when they are abroad with all their grass they spoil; which I did more than three-quarters believe, but now know it to be true of my own knowledge. Some hog-yards will yield you forty, fifty, some sixty, some eighty load, and some more, of excellent manure of ten or twelve swine, which they value every load worth about two shillings sixpence a load in their very yards, and prize it above any other. This is practised much about King's Norton, both in the counties of Worcester and Warwick, and in many other parts, as in Cheshire, Stafford-shire, Derbyshire, also, I believe, an excellent piece of husbandry. I speak experimentally hereof, having made great advantage myself hereby, and do far more prize it than suffering swine to run and course abroad, knowing that rest, quiet, and sleep, with drink, and lesser meat will sooner feed any creature than your meat with liberty to run and strayle and course about into harms and wash off what they get with their meat, with their vexing and running up and down, and do advise as thou valuest thy own advantage, some good dairies will make the soil of their hogyard produce them twenty or thirty pounds worth of profit in a year.

As for rags of all sorts, there is good virtue in them, they are carried far and laid upon the lands, and have in them a warming, improving temper;

one good load will go as far as half a dozen or more of the best cow dung. Coarse wool, nippings, and tarry pitchmarks, a little whereof will do an acre of land; there is great virtue in them. I believe one load thereof will exceedingly well manure half an acre, marrow-bones, or fish-bones, horn, or shavings of horn, or broths made of beef, meat, or fish, or any other thing whatsoever that hath any liquidness, oiliness, or fatness, have a wonderful virtue in them. Let all be precious to thee and preserved, for every little adds too, and helps in the common stock, and he that will not be faithful in a little, will not be faithful in a greater quantity, as is alway seen by constant experience.

As for sheep dung, cow dung, and horse dung, such old ordinary soil I intend to say little in regard the common use thereof, which hath extracted the virtue and excellency to the Commonwealth's great advantage. . . .

17. CLOVER: THE CHOICE OF SEED AND THE ANNUAL PROFIT, 1652

[Walter Blith, *The English Improver Improved*, 1652, pp. 177–9, 184–5]

The best way of planting the trefoil or great claver grass, which is the highest advantage our English lands will produce

And herein I will discover the best seed, and the best means to gain it, how to sow and husbandry it for food and seed, with the most suitable land thereto, and the profit that may accrue thereby; and for brevity's sake shall speak little to what other public spirits have discovered, but enlarge a little from later experience in relation to our English lands and husbandry.

THERE are so many sorts of claver as would fill a volume, I shall only speak of the great claver, or trefoil we fetch from Flanders, called by Clusius *Trifolliummajus tertium*, which bares the great red honeysuckle, whose leaf and branches far exceeds our natural meadow claver; it bears a very small seed as mustard seed, not so round but longer, like a bean; the best is of a greenish, yellow colour, some a little reddish, but the black I fear will not do well. The choice whereof is the only piece in the whole work.

Your Dutch, Holland, or Low Country seed, or from the lower parts of Germany, is very much of it very hazardous that comes over hither, but being well chose there, the transporting of it by sea is no considerable prejudice unto it, but much that is sold in the seedmen's shops in London was either corrupted by the Dutch before it came thence, or else parched by over-drying, or else by the shopkeepers, either mingling old and new, or keeping it another year, and then selling it for new. I myself within this four year sowed divers acres with seed bought in London, which cost me about two shillings a pound, and lost it all; I am not able to say any one seed came up at all. And I have heard that the Dutch out of an evil spirit, lest we should find the same benefit they have, have kiln-dried it. Therefore my advice is, to send over a knowing man that hath had experience of it, and knows the right coloured seed to buy, and search all the country and buy the best and choicest seed he can possibly buy for silver, and take care of the bringing of it over too; and as for the sale of it, if you bring over more than you shall use, you need not, nor shall not, want customers to take it off of hand; for I had rather give a double price for such, than run the hazard of common merchants' experience.

But if you desire me to speak my mind from the experience myself hath made, I do affirm that our own seed, that is, seed of our own claver, after the first sowing of the Dutch seed, called the great claver, is the best and most certain seed to grow, and so successively from time to time, if you can ripen it kindly, get it dry, and preserve it. And this will bring me to my second particular.

Which is how to get good seed, or recover it out of our own crop to sow again, if you could get it kindly out of the husk, which to us as yet is a mystery, and we cannot do it artificially and feasibly, as they do in Flanders. The best means we do use is to thrash it out of the straw; and then chave it or cleanse it from the straw, as you do corn, and then polt it, or faulter it as some call it, that is, beat it over again in the husk, and then get out as much of the refuse by chaving of it with a narrow toothed rake as possibly you can get; which done, if you would bestow sunning of it in a hot dry season, and then rubbing of it, will get very much of it, for this is all the means that hitherto I have ever heard of in England, but I am confident that it may be very feasibly got forth of the husk, being very thoroughly dried in the sun, upon a corn-mill, oatmeal, or malt-mill, and shelled as they do oats by a skilful miller, and no seed hurt as they will oats, and not break the kernel, having his mill-stones exceeding level hung, neither too sharp nor too dull, and very curiously set that it cut not the seed, nor yet leave too much seed behind; which if it prove, as I am confident it will, it will be a very great advantage to the nation. . . .

And as to the annual profit that may accrue thereby, I shall little differ from the Flanders husbandry, but shall affirm that one acre after the corn is cut, the very next year if it be well husbandried, and kind thick claver, may be worth twenty marks, or twelve pound, and so downward as it degenerates weaker, less worth. In Brabant they speak of keeping four cows winter and summer, some cut and laid up for fodder, others cut and eaten green; but I have credibly heard of some in England that upon about one acre have kept four coach horses and more all summer long, but if it keep but two cows, it is advantage enough upon such lands as never kept one. But I conceive best for us, until we be come into a stock of seed, to mow the first crop in the middest or end of May, and lay that up for hay, although it will go very near together, yet, if it grow not too strong, it will be exceeding good and rich, and feed anything, and reserve the next for seed. And if we can bring it up to perfect seed, and it will but yield four bushels upon an acre, it will amount to more than I speak of by far, every bushel being worth three or four pound a bushel. And then the aftermath or eddish that year may put up three middling runts upon an acre, and feed them up; all which laid together will make up an improvement sufficient; and yet this property it hath also, that after the three or four first years of clovering, it will so frame the earth that it will be very fit to corn again, which will be a very great advantage: first to corn your land, which usually yields a far better profit than grazing, and sometimes a double profit, and sometimes more, near a treble profit, and then to clover it again, which will afford a treble, fourfold, yea 10 or 12 fold advance, if not more. And so if you consider one acre of land with the claver and husbandry thereof may stand you the first year in twenty five shillings, the three other years not above ten shillings, the land being worth no more, which may produce you yearly easily five, six, or eight pound per annum per acre; nay some will affirm ten, or twelve pound or more, then most of my improvements promised are made good . . .

18. COLESEED: ITS CULTIVATION AND USE, 1652

[Walter Blith, *The English Improver Improved*, 1652, pp. 249, 248]

The Discovery of Rape and Coleseeds Husbandry

THE planting of coleseed or rape-seed is another excellent good means for the improving land; the coleseed is of late days best esteemed. And it is most especially useful upon your marshland, fenland, or upon your new recovered sea-land, or any lands very rank and fat, whether arable or pasture. The best seed is the biggest, fairest seed that you can get, it being dry, and of a pure clear colour, of the colour of the best onion seed. It is to be had in many parts of this nation, but Holland is the centre of it; from thence comes your good seed usually.

The season of sowing is at or about Midsummer, you must have your land ploughed very well, and laid even and fine, whether upon the ley, turf or arable, and both may do well, but your arable must be very rich and fat, and having made your land fine, then you may sow it, and about a gallon of seed will sow an acre, the which seed must be mingled, as afore was directed about the claver, with something, that you may sow it even, and not upon heaps; the even sowing of it is very difficult, it grows up exceedingly to great leaves, but the benefit is made out of the seed especially.

The time to cut it is when one half of the seed begins to look brown; you must reap it as you do wheat, and lay it upon little yelms, or two or three handfuls together till it be dry, and that very dry too; about a fortnight will dry it; it must not be turned nor touched, if it were possible, for fear of shedding the seed, that being the chief profit of it. About a fortnight the seed will be dry, it must be gathered in sheets, or rather a great ship sail-cloth, as big as four or six sheets, and carried into the barn, erected on purpose, or to that place designed on purpose to thrash it that day; you must have sixteen or eighteen men at a floor, four men will thrash abundance of a day. I have heard that four men have threshed thirty comb of a day.

The seed is usually worth sixteen shillings a comb, that is four shillings a bushel, sometimes more and sometimes less.

It will, if exceeding good, bear ten comb upon an acre, or five quarter, if it be but indifferent, and will not bear above seven or eight comb of an acre. It will raise a good advance upon your lands.

It is a commodity you will not want sale of; the greater the parcel is, the better price you will have. It is used to make the rape oil, as we call it. The turnip seed will grow among it, and it will make good oil also; you may sell a thousand pound together to one chapman; it is best to be planted by the water, or near it.

It cannot be too rank; the eddish or stubble will exceedingly nourish sheep in winter.

It hath another excellent property: it will fit the land so for corning, for wheat; it may produce a crop as good or better than itself; and for barley after that.

The charge of the whole crop, I conceive, may come to betwixt twenty and thirty shillings an acre, and a good crop may be worth four, five, six, seven, or eight pound an acre; the least is a very good improvement, because it will do excellent well, if well ordered, and a kind season upon land the very first year after recovery, when it will do nothing else, if it can be but ploughed, when other things, as corn or grain may be hazarded; and so have you this discourse, though in much brevity; your experience will teach you whatever here is wanting, and my weighty business will not suffer me to supply.

19. THE INIQUITY OF TITHES, 1652

[D. Lupton, *The Tythe-Takers Cart Overthrown or the Downfall of Tythes*, London, 1652, pp. 5, 46–8]

MANIFOLD have been the petitions (and not without just cause) for the putting down and taking away of tithes . . . The gross abuses, inconveniences, troubles, lawsuits, quarrellings, contentions, strifes, debates, hatred, heart-burnings, suspicions, wrongs, vexations, murmurings, grudgings, and mischiefs, which have and do daily arise betwixt the tithe-takers and the tithe-payers, as they are not be numbered, so 'tis pity they should not be extinguished, the one think they take too much, the other think they have not enough. What parish, hamlet, town, or city in all England, which either is not, or hath not been quarrelled withal by their wrangling tithing ministers? What term hath not been filled with complaints one against another? What courts have not, and yet do not even swarm with suits one with another, to the

great charges, loss, and vexation of the good people of this land in travelling
and journeying to London about lawsuits for setting out and paying tithes?
How are the justices and committees toiled and wearied at their meetings and
sittings in hearing causes, one party against the other, even with bitterness
of spirit, and all for tithes? We could weary the readers, and relate such
stories of quarrels in this kind as are not indeed worth the naming, and yet
have been prosecuted with all vehemency and virulency of spirit. How can
such ministers teach the word of God in meekness, who are filled with
rancour and ill will for want of their due in tithes, merely conceiving so to
themselves, not being so in truth? What base informations and suggestions,
with indirect intelligence too, are brought to their ears, of men's stealing,
pilfering, and carrying away more than they should, which inflames their
spirits so high and so deeply against their neighbours and parishioners, that
they are not fully and truly reconciled to them during their whole lives?

20. IN PRAISE OF ALTERNATE HUSBANDRY, 1652

[Walter Blith, *The English Improver Improved*, 1652, pp. 100–1]

THERE is a parcel of land in Warwickshire, near Stratford upon Avon, that
is oaded [= woaded] every fourteen years, and corned divers years after that.
And so there may be many more parcels also besides this I speak of, and so
I know there is, and after that fourteen years' rest and grazing, oaded again,
and corned also. So there are some in Northamptonshire, Buckinghamshire,
and many other parts will do the like. And so runs round, grazing fits for
ploughing and corning, and corning fits for grazing; a most gallant opportunity; doubles the grazing rent while under corning and more under
oading. And grazeth again immediately at a very considerable rent, and
might do the first year at old rent, and so forward, would they plough but
three or four years according to my direction, but they plough five, six, or
seven. Such a method would please me gallantly, advance the Commonwealth
exceedingly, and prejudice whom, I fain would know? Abundance of poor
set on work; abundance of corn raised; abundance of straw which spent and
fed upon the land shall make that up again whatever the ploughing fetched
out. Doubles rent and more, four or five years in one and twenty. And so
every age near fetcheth in the purchase.

21. PROPOSALS FOR THE IMPROVEMENT OF
WASTE GROUND, 1653
[B.M., Thomason Tract, E715 (18)]

WASTE LAND'S IMPROVEMENT[1]

Or certain

PROPOSALS

Made and tendered to the Consideration of the Honourable
Committee appointed by Parliament for the Advance of
Trade, and general Profits of the Commonwealth.

*Wherein are some hints touching the best and most commodious way of improving
the forests, fenny grounds and waste lands throughout England, tending very
much to the enriching of the Commonwealth in general, the prevention of robbery
and beggary, the raising and maintaining of a public stock for the perpetual
supply of armies and navies without taxations and excise, and also a way for
satisfaction for part of the nation's debts and obligations.*

IT IS well known to all what vast quantities and what great circumferences of
grounds do at this day lie waste and desolate (in forests, and fenny grounds,
and other commons), almost in all the countries of this nation, but although so
well known (together with the multitudes of inconveniences and disprofits
depending thereupon), yet either sluggishness or worse drowns the sense of
those discommodities, so that little or no consideration is had (at least not
effectually) for their improvement; which as it is a shame and reproach unto
Irish, and other like lazy people, so much more is it a shame to us English,
because we bear the name and reputation of an ingenious and industrious
people; but now our hopes are that such as are now set in the throne of
authority will not only be the repairers of some breaches, but also will convert the desolate wastes into fruitful fields, and our wide howling wildernesses
into comfortable habitations, that in this (as well as in other things) we
may enjoy at last some benefit by all our revolutions, transplantings, and over-
turnings in authorities.

In a word, that which we have to offer to serious deliberation is that those
many and wild vacant waste lands, scattered up and down this nation, be not
suffered to lie longer (like a deformed chaos) to our discredit and disprofit, but
that some way be effectually thought upon (either agreeable with what is
touched herein or otherwise) for their best employment and improvement by
enclosing, tilling, planting, and all other ways of manuring, necessary unto
increase, and proportionable unto the goodness of the several soils of the said
lands, to provoke unto which, weigh these brief subsequent proposals.

---

[1] The handwritten date on this pamphlet is 31 October 1653.

Prop. 1. That much of the said ground (for nature and kind) is most generally very rich and good, and much of it very fat soil, the reason and cause of it present barrenness and infertility being not from the nature of the soil, but from the defect of manuring and improving, by reason of which much of it is overgrown and encumbered with bushes, briars, and other combustibles that do now render it scarce worth sixpence per acre, which being removed and the land enclosed and manured, would bring forth plenty of flax, hemp, hops, corn, also increase cattle of all kinds, and many other things, by which means the State would be sufficiently supplied with hemp for cordage for their shipping, and the poor more richly replenished with bread corn (the staff of sustenance) and many other necessary and profitable fruits.

Prop. 2. Such enclosing, manuring, etc. aforesaid, will tend very much both to the preservation and augmentation of timber, for the building and re-pairing of shipping for the Commonwealth, whereas many persons now taking too much liberty to fell and lop the wood of every respective forest doth occasion the embezzling of much sound good oaken timber and other wood, which might be so ordered and disposed in letting, with such pro-hibitions and penalties of forfeitures of leases and otherwise, as would effectually prevent such spoils and misspendings as aforesaid.

Furthermore, in order to the said timber's increase, there may be such indentments in letting that for every tree the State shall have occasion to sell the tenant may be obliged to plant two or three in the stead of it, which as they will freely engage to perform, so may such plantings be ordered in such selected vacant places as would be no impediment to the growth of corn, hemp, and other fruits, etc. as aforesaid.

Prop. 3. Such letting, enclosing, etc. the said lands would be of an effectual tendency to the anticipation and suppression of many robberies, thefts, burglaries, rapes, and murders, which do much annoy this Commonwealth and do receive their nourishment and encouragement from those vast, wild wide forests, which (by reason of their vastness and largeness, their distance from towns and houses, the paucity of passengers, etc.) do administer liberty and opportunity unto villainous minds to perpetrate and commit their wicked and vicious actions, according to the common proverb and acknow-ledgement of many rogues, 'that opportunity makes a thief', etc. which occasion robberies of passengers and travellers on the one hand, and of sheep, horses, and other cattle grazing on the said commons on the other which goods so stolen cannot suddenly be missed, and therefore the thieves not easily be discovered, to the utter undoing of many persons and families.

All which inconveniencies of this kind may be preoccupated by such an improvement as is propounded; especially considering that it's far more facile to prevent than to remove annoyances. Moreover, better it is to lay the axe to the root, than (by employing soldiers to thief-catching) to be always lopping the branches; which if the root remain, will upon every occasion grow again notwithstanding, and may in time make England's wastes a receptacle and harbour for troops of assassinating rogues like the Tories in

Ireland, and the Moss-troopers in Scotland; and what more discommendable than that which might be so profitable, should through neglect be made not only unprofitable but disprofitable, and that which would breed and produce plenty of cattle and other excellent fruits, now breeds and cherisheth plenty of idle, vagrant, pilfering, and pernicious persons?

Prop. 4. Such letting and improving, etc. would directly tend to the employing and setting to work many thousands of persons that are now idle, and such as some of whom by reason of poverty cannot (others for want of due encouragement) will not work; and a third sort are old men and youths, which men will not employ in their lands, because they cannot perform a man's labour in a day; now the proverb is well known and too much experienced, viz. that of idleness cometh no goodness, but commonly much evil and wickedness, both which are too much indulged; whereas if the said lands were let to such and other men at reasonable rates, poor men would take and rent there small proportions, and employ themselves upon their own, although not able satisfyingly to serve other men; insomuch that leases distributed of ninety or one hundred years would set multitude of hands to digging, manuring, and planting (both in hedging and ditching for inclosure, and in founding and building cottages for habitation), which would be like unto, and instead of, a manufacture to set awork multitudes in all the corners of the nation; and more effectually yield a comfortable maintenance and supply to the said country poor than the erected houses do unto the poor of the City; and truly to conclude this proposition, the time past may suffice for wording, it's now high time to be working and doing of something for removing and preventing of poverties, vagrancies, etc. which through permissive allowances of idleness (both heretofore and hitherto, to the shame and reproach of this nation) hath abundantly been multiplied.

Prop. 5. Such improvements, etc. before specified will not only benefit and advantage particular persons and interests (as hath been minded, and shall more amply be evidenced) but also it will very much enrich and replenish the public purse, i.e. being let at half the ordinary value, it would bring in to the State's Treasury near one hundred thousand pounds *per mensem*, which upon calculation will amount unto near twelve hundred thousands pounds per annum. As for instance in that one county of Essex, there is as much of the said waste land as (if let at the aforesaid rate) will (upon like calculation) levy near eighty thousand pounds per annum, which the inhabitants professedly would rather give in rent for enclosure, than to enjoy the present privilege and immunity of commoners upon the said land, and more utility and benefit would redound unto them by it, which sum and sums of money coming in as an annual revenue aforesaid, would (together with the custom) near answer the necessary disbursements of the Commonwealth, and would so defray the charge of armies and navies, as to banish excise and assessments out of the nation as a superfluous overplus, thereby discharging the malcontented people from those ponderous and discontentful impositions.

The premises well considered and rightly construed will sufficiently persuade the general benefit and public advantage that will accrue to the State, and redound to all sorts of men, by employing the said waste lands, and putting them in a way of improvement by enclosing, etc. But then in the next place it will be necessary in the disposure of the said lands to make use of the utmost prudence, if possible, to bring forth the utmost improvement, and to do what may be done in the most commodious and beneficial way; taking for granted, as a matter altogether indisputable, that the just right of possessing and disposing of them do belong unto the supreme authority of the nation (in exercise), which is the Parliament, as formerly it was assumed by the late King, upon which therefore I shall not insist.

But the next thing necessary to be made a question and answered will be, whether selling or letting the lands aforesaid by the Parliament will be most convenient and commodious, to which I offer that the said lands be taken, possessed, and retained by the Parliament, and not in any wise put to sale, nor any way so disposed as to enervate the right and interest of Parliament in them, for these three following reasons.

Reas. 1. Because if they should be so sold and disposed, they would bring in but one single sum of money into the State's Treasury; and it's well known that a stock not increased is commonly soon spent, and the greater the sum the more liable unto embezzling, and expended, will occasion greater impositions upon the people, and they will appear more irksome, and with the greater face of burden, and prove consequently more discontentful than before, by reason of no constant revenue.

Reas. 2. Such selling would sow the seed of discontent and lay a foundation of disaffection in the minds of the people against this representative, because the Parliament *pro tempore*, by such sales, collecting great sums of money, it would during their authority much supply their necessary occasions, and excuse the people for the time being from the burdens of many disbursements, by taxes and otherwise; and then the next Parliament (having no such incomes) must be necessitated to renew the old impositions, which cannot but occasion the harder thoughts, and the more censorious heart-risings against them, as judging them either worse taskmasters, or greater spendthrifts than the former, their predecessors.

Reas. 3. The sale as aforesaid would (in necessary effect) prove an act of unrighteousness because all persons poor and others whose habitations being adjacent to the said commons have a right to the benefit as commoners, would be robbed of their right; whereas in letting there might be such consideration had, and such allowances made unto the said persons, as might be proportionable and answerable unto that their right and interest, and would give them full (yea, better) satisfaction than their lying waste (notwithstanding their common benefit) as now they do.

To proceed therefore, the best and most utilious way of improving the said wastes will be (in few words) for the Parliament in being to take them into their hands and custody, ascribing to them, and stamping on them the name of State's lands; that the State may stand as the public landlord, employing faithful and judicious overseers and surveyors to measure longitudes and latitudes, determine the fatness of the soils, divide it into tenures, and let them out at reasonable rates; by all which we mean not that they should divide it into proportions among themselves, and call the lands after their own personal names, and so resolve it into particular interests and properties, but that it be employed wholly in the name and behalf of the public, for the sole use and service of the Commonwealth; by which way such conveniencies would be effected, and such inconveniences removed and prevented, as have been before hinted, to which I shall add briefly some encouragements.

1. Such letting would not only be the profit but the glory of the nation, that a military force at land and a naval force at sea should be perpetually maintained, and yet the inhabitants freed from the impositions of taxes and excise.

2. It would much oblige all sorts of men to the present government, partly out of respect to the governors their landlords, and partly out of respect to their own interests as tenants, that in case of domestic insurrections against authority, or foreign invasions against the nation, the State would doubtless have a considerable army out of the numbers of their own tenants to defend the Parliament's authority, and to preserve therein their own properties.

3. By such letting, such persons whose habitations being near unto the said lands, and by law have right of commoners, would not be robbed nor dispossessed of their right, but might be first and best considered in the letting, and also have it at such underrates, as may not only be proportionable with, but somewhat more beneficial unto them than, their right of commoners, as before minded; provided that in letting there be such orders and rules observed and due proportions kept that the benefit of one redound not to the detriment of many, and that rich men be not left boundless and unlimited, so as to trample upon (and to make furrows in the back of) the poor; to prevent which, it's further offered.

Prop. 1: That the poor that have now right and benefit of common may have that which is called the pre-emption, or first offer in the letting, before the rich; for the truth is they have suffered already too much face-grinding from them. Amongst many other things even in this, viz. in paying great rents for cottages adjacent to the forest, in order to the profit of the common; and by reason of the multitudes of sheep and other cattle the said rich men have clogged the said commons withal, they have eaten out and deprived the poor of their just expected benefit; which now therefore deserves such due consideration as that effectual provision be made in the first place for them, that they be not left to the mercy of the rich.

Prop. 2. That in the letting the said lands, as aforesaid, there be due indulgence shewn unto, and respectful consideration had of three sorts of persons, whose suffering conditions loudly require it at the State's hands, and such as by former authority have been too much neglected.

1. Such who have lent and spent voluntarily great part of their estates in the

service of the honest interest of this nation in the late wars; some upon public faith, and some otherwise yet unpaid, and unrecompensed.

2. Such soldiers who have lost their particular trades and callings, and with hazard of their blood and lives have purchased instrumentally the nation's peace, freedom, and tranquillity, many of whom lame and maimed.

3. Such whose estates are embezzled and wasted, and they impoverished by plunderings, free-quarterings of soldiers, and other such like providential accidents in the late wars, many of them reduced to a state both of very much poverty and misery, and therefore are, and should be, objects of pity and charity.

All which offering their conditions upon good evidence may be considered in the said lands' letting next unto them who have the right of commoners. *Prop.* 3. That if the State have extraordinary occasion of a present sum of money, such persons as rent above 8 acres may pay one year's rent beforehand, to be deducted about the seventh year of their lease, or when the State upon consideration shall think most fit; and for the wood upon the ground in their divisions, the State's timber excepted, which will amount to near 100,000*li*.

As touching a way of security of the tenants' rents needs not much to be offered; nevertheless considering hedging and ditching, the labour and cost of enclosures will be a sufficient security and engagement to the performance of such conditions, to which may be added such forfeitures of leases (with twenty or thirty days of favour after the time prefixed in the indenture) as will effectually persuade the due and punctual payment of the rents of all such tenants respectively as aforesaid.

In fine, we leave and submit the premised proposals to consideration hoping (although they are but a little mite) that they will not altogether be unacceptable nor unprofitable, and also desiring that some better judgement will amplify and illustrate both provocations and encouragements unto, and directions and instructions in, this desirable (and in event may prove if rightly managed), profitable undertaking.

E.G.

22. THE OWNER AND TENANTS OF A FORFEITED ROYALIST ESTATE IN DISPUTE, 1654

[P.R.O., SP 18/67, no. 76; 18/69, no. 28]

To his Highness the Lord Protector of England, Scotland, and Ireland, and the Right Honorable his Council, the humble petition of divers the inhabitants of Hambleton in the county of Rutland.

SHEWETH that through the oppression of Colonel Thomas Waite by enclosing the town of Hambleton and taking away the best of their lands contrary to his many promises made to your petitioners upon their signing of a petition to the trustees appointed for the sale of delinquents' estates that he might become purchaser of the said town of Hambleton, your petitioners were constrained, to their very great expense, to come up to London to petition the then Council of State, who were pleased to commend the same to the late Parliament. And the Parliament, taking into consideration your petitioners' sad, oppressive condition did order a committee to examine the same and upon examination the said Colonel offered an agreement to your petitioners before the committee in order to satisfaction, which for peace sake was accepted, since which the Parliament dissolving, the said Colonel taking advantage thereof refuseth to make good the same merely (as your petitioners have just cause to conceive in regard of his former carriages in the business) to put such an utter impossibility upon them (by reason of their poverty he hath already reduced them to) to help themselves as that, if not relieved by your honours, they, their wives, and children must speedily be ruined and the town in a great measure depopulated.

Now for as much as the said Thomas Waite (before your petitioners would give him their hands to become purchaser of the said town) promised not to enclose it, nor to take anything from them but that they should hold the same lands they formerly held and have leases for 21 years or three lives at the rent he bought it of the State, the breach of which promises was the substance of their first complaint to the honourable Council, and for that the said agreement before the committee of Parliament was made by him in point of satisfaction to your petitioners for the breach of his said promises.

Therefore, they humbly pray that your honours will please either to appoint some commissioners to examine the truth of the said agreement and upon proof thereof compel the said Colonel speedily to make it good or that your poor petitioners may re-enter upon their lands and commons which they formerly held, and also that your petitioners may have satisfaction for their unsupportable costs and damages sustained by reason of this unjust enclosure.

And they shall ever pray, etc.

[Endorsed:] A true copy of the petition of divers the inhabitants of Hambleton in the county of Rutland presented to the honourable Council, March the 13th, 1653. Presented and read 13 March 1653. Col. Waite to be summoned.

* * *

In the difference between Colonel Waite and the tenants of Hambleton: to be reported that it is agreed that whereas there were chosen formerly Sir Thomas Hartopp and Major Horsman as arbitrators to compose and settle things according to the articles already agreed in writing between them, that in regard that they two as arbitrators may not agree, that therefore Mr. William Sheild of Preston in the county of Rutland be umpire and that he do fully determine when the said arbitrators do not agree. And that eighteen days is allotted to finish the whole business by the arbitrators and umpire. [Endorsed:] Report in the case of Col. Waite and the tenants of Hambleton made by Col. Mackworth, 6 April 1654.

23. TENANTS' COMPLAINTS AGAINST OPPRESSIVE LANDLORDS IN LANCASHIRE AND CHESHIRE, 1654

[P.R.O., SP 18/74, no. 33]

To his Highness the Lord Protector of England, Scotland, and Ireland, the humble petition of divers well affected persons in Lancashire and Cheshire, tenants to oppressing landlords.

SHEWETH that your petitioners, having from the beginning of these wars faithfully served the Parliament freely hazarding their lives and all that was dear unto them to maintain the interest of the Commonwealth against the bloody Papists and cavaliers, hoping that when the Lord should have subdued their enemies, your petitioners and many others should have been set free from future bondage. But so it is that, to their great grief, the yokes of their oppressors are not yet broken, but when your petitioners had, by their opposition to them, heated them in wrath and malice seven times hotter than they were before, were given up to their mercy, who have already begun to express their cruelty by turning some of your petitioners out of doors and threatening the like to the rest, and that expressly for their services done to the Parliament, which will not only weaken the nation by depopulation of the northern counties of many of your faithful and cordial friends, but gradually dishearten many thousands of such under your happy government, the redress of which great grievance now through the providence of God lieth in the power of your Highness to effect. Wherefore your petitioners most humbly pray that your Highness will be pleased to take their sad condition under consideration, and that the act intended and drawn up for the relief of tenants against oppressing landlords, and read twice in the late Parliament but never brought to a period by reason of their dissolution, may again be revived and established by your Highness. Or that your Highness would please by your order to empower the persons, whose names are expressed in the draft of an order hereunto annexed, being gent[lemen] of known integrity, and most of them having very many tenants of their own, as commissioners to hear the grievances of oppressed tenants, and to examine upon oath matter of fact between them and their landlords in the said counties respectively, and to certify to your Highness the true state of your petitioners' complaint. And that in the mean time all proceedings at law for ejection of such tenants may be suspended until certificate be made from your said commissioners, provided such certificate be returned before the 31st day of January, 1654.

And not only your petitioners but many thousand others shall (as in duty bound) daily pray, etc.

John Jollie in the behalf of the petitioners.

24. SIR GEORGE SONDES OF FAVERSHAM, KENT, REBUTS THE CHARGE OF BEING A HARSH LANDLORD, 1655

[Sir George Sondes, his Plaine Narrative to the World of all Passages upon the Death of his two Sonnes, London, 1655. Harleian Miscellany, X, p. 50]

To the Charge of being a hard Landlord

It is said I am a hard landlord, and raise my rents. I confess as tenants' leases expired, I took no fines to renew, as my ancestors used to do, but let out my farms at improved rents, both the tenants and myself better liking of it. But I do not know that I let a farm to any tenant for more than I thought (and I had some little skill) it was really and honestly worth, nor for more than (had I been to have taken a farm) I would have given for it myself. Nor have I any tenant (though the times be now very bad) who shall say, sir, my farm is too dear, I cannot live upon it at the rent; if he leave it to me but as good as it was when he took it, I will take it again. Nay, notwithstanding corn is so cheap, I give any tenant I have liberty to leave his farm, and I will take it. I never did, or ever will, force any tenant to keep his farm. Neither in all this time hath any tenant come to me to take his farm again. Some indeed I would have ousted of their farms (being none of the best tenants), but could not persuade them. I never arrested or imprisoned any tenant for his rent, nor willingly used any severe course, if I could indifferently be satisfied any other way. I have scarce demanded my rents of late because of the cheapness of corn, but have made all the shifts I could to get money to serve my occasions, and spared my tenants, that they might not be forced to put off their corn at too mean rates. If these be the signs of an hard landlord, then I am one. There is one Ellen, of Stausfield, I hear, hath complained of me for being so. I will tell you the case, and then you shall judge whether I deserve it or not. Last Michaelmas was two years, I let a farm there to him of forty pounds a year. At the end of the year I sent to him for his rent; his answer was, that it went hard with him the first year, being to buy all his stock and seasons, therefore he desired me to have a little patience till he could make money of his corn; upon his desire I did forbear him. About half a year after I sent to him again, and then he said corn was so low that he could make but little money of it. Upon this I forbore him till the other year was up, and he indebted to me two years' rent, and went myself to him, and wished him to leave the farm if he found he could do no good upon it. He desired to keep it, hoping the times would mend, and offered to make over his stock to me for my security; this he did, and continued in his farm, and at Lady Day next promised to clear all. About a month after the time I sent to him to fulfil his promise, and was informed that he had sold all his corn, driven away his stock, and carried all his goods, and was gone himself, and had left me about twenty pounds worth of corn on the ground, to satisfy for three years rent, which was six score pounds; so I was to be a loser one hundred pounds by him. This is the truth, and who now do you think did the wrong? Many of these hardnesses have I used to my tenants, and have been so served by them.

25. ARGUMENTS AGAINST COMMON FIELDS, 1656

[Pseudonismus, *A Vindication of the Considerations concerning Common Fields*, 1656, pp. 42–7]

GOD is the God of order, and order is the soul of things, the life of a Commonwealth; but common fields are the seat of disorder, the seed plot of contention, the nursery of beggary; as will appear by these following considerations:

1. Disorder appears there by the intermixed and dispersed lands, lying here one and there another, as 4, 6, 8, or 10 parcels of ground to an acre of land, to the great hindrance and damage of the owners, both in tilling the land, and inning the fruits of the same. For example, if one day's work in 20, 30, 40 lands' tilling be wholly lost, how many days' work must necessarily be lost in 1, 10, or 20 fields? How many more in 1, 10, or 20 counties? So likewise in carriage of manure and harvest stuff, and also other carriages, the labour is lost, which might be saved, if each man's land lay together.

2. The Statute of Tillage hath excited some, and affrighted others, that the land in each field is not, neither can be, husbanded as it ought; and hereupon the tithes are the fifth of the value of the whole lordship, and sometimes the fourth.

3. Tillage lands in common fields have no rest at all, wherewith to be rich and fertile; and so the husbandmen are necessitated to plough the same land each year, though it be barren, to the utter undoing of the weak or unstocked husbandman.

4. Every 800 acres of tillage in the common fields takes 4,000 strikes of seed, both of barley and peas, at 5 strikes an acre, and some sow more; and so 2,000 strikes in a year in a great field containing so many acres of land are utterly lost and cast away; which might be saved by order, and more corn might be gotten of one third part of so much land being in strength.

5. The fallow field to the weak or unstocked husbandman is a great charge, and no profit. 1. The ordure or dung of sheep is in many places of more worth to be let than the grass on which they feed. 2. This field often rots the sheep, to as much damage as the whole lordship is valued at per annum.

6. The peas crop is not for man's food, and (one year taken with another) of little value, the labour and seed and value of the ground being counted.

7. The white corn, as wheat and barley, hath 4 or 5 tilths yearly where it is sown, and the owner or husbandman loseth the profit of that land 18 or 20

months together for one crop; and the crop of so much resty land, with one tilth, in 5 months' time, will double the increase of that of 4 or 5 tilths.

8. This intermixed situation of the lands causeth disorder of herding of cattle; as of cows, 200, 300, or 400 are kept on a ruck, or herd, driven to and fro by day, and fasting by night, and in wet seasons their feet do more hurt than their mouths; and in winter time they spoil the highways for traffic and commerce. Also men use to dog their sheep into heaps, compelling both sheep and cows to rest against nature, when they would feed, and to feed when they would rest; and the poor creatures must not feed but when their keepers stand by and look on, all the day time being under check. They also tether great cattle chargeable with keepers; and many times they are without stint.

Secondly, common fields are the seedplots of contention.

1. There is much unrighteous dealing, and catch as catch can is upheld, they being glad of one another's overthrow, unchristianly accustoming themselves to ruin, and eat up one another's grass, doing to others what they would not have others do to them.

2. Every man being for himself, he that thrives on his farm thriveth commonly by hurting his neighbour, and by his loss; and so they clash one another in their cattle, and the weakest suffers. For he which wanteth sheep (as many husbandmen either want or owe for them) wanteth half the stock of his farm; yet in taxes and payments his land pays equally with the land of other husbandmen, which eat him up. And in the heat of the war past, the poor unstocked husbandman's loss of his horses was greater than his neighbour's; for those lost what was their own, but the poor husbandman that which he borrowed or owed for.

3. Trespasses are very frequent, so that if a man walk or ride to see his land in several kinds he shall trespass on 10 or 20 neighbours' land, and from trespasses by men and cattle, grudges, debates, and great suits in law do arise.

4. No man can be just there in taking his own grass and no more, though with a tether; he must either take more, or leave some; for a circle cannot fill a square, nor a square a circle; and so dissensions follow.

5. The tax of land is after the yard land, a name very deceitful by the disproportion and inequality thereof, the quantity of some one yard land being as much as one and a half or two in the same field, and yet there is an equality of taxes; but if the taxes be paid by the pound rent, then the rich man saith, shall my yard lands bear out or pay for another's barren land? So they are at variance.

6. Herdsmen and shepherds fall out and stain the ground by striving, and by driving their cattle to and fro; so commonness and uncleanness twinlike go together; and whatsoever is unclean who will not avoid?

Thirdly, common fields are the nurseries of beggary; for disorder and contention brings in poverty.

1. Poor husbandmen and herdsmen are necessitated to keep men the summer

for work, and put them off against winter; and many beg by reason of their master's poverty.

2. Where the labour exceeds the benefit or profit of the work done, there poverty must needs follow, but this happens often to the unstocked husbandman. Again, let a farm be hired to be dressed by servants, and it is usually seen that the servants' diet and wages surpass the annual rent of the farm.

3. The unstocked husbandman is consuming every year like one in a consumption, and cannot help himself; he hath the name of lands, others have the nature and profit; he hath the burden, others the bit and herbage; he leanness, labour, and sweat; others the rest and fatness. A sheep's grass in the common fields is not worth more than 2*d*., 4*d*., 6*d*., or at most 12*d*. per annum.

4. There is no plantation of wood or trees, but wasting the same because the land is common.

5. The eating up the grass very bare before winter maketh long and hard winters, lean and hungry cattle, and poor husbandmen.

6. An husbandman unstocked and unfurnished with sheep loseth every year $\frac{2}{3}$ of his herbage, viz. $\frac{1}{3}$ in the fallow field, and the other fields lying open $\frac{1}{2}$ of the year, in another $\frac{1}{3}$ of the whole.

7. 100*l*. or 200*l*. being lost per annum in some one field, how many hundreds are lost in a county or many counties?

8. Husbandry is the fundamental prop and nutriment of the Commonwealth; therefore this calling being in decay many ways (as is said before) all other trades depending thereon suffer and are impoverished.

9. No example of common fields in all the divine word, nor in any skilful author writing of husbandry, as Virgil, Tully, etc.; therefore not prosperous.

10. If all unrighteousness be sin, how great then is the common fields? And sin often brings a curse.

11. Also the many poor families thrust out of depopulated towns are necessitated to get harbour there; and others likewise having little land, but stocks of money, live upon the poor man's rights; and those for the most part are glad of the clashing or breaking of the husbandman.

Obj. 1. It may be objected that he which is not able to stock his farm may set the same for rent.

Answ. Grant that, then half the husbandmen in a town must set, and where will they dwell? For the pasture grounds have not houses, and the common field towns are full. Besides, that will not remedy the lying of lands dispersed, nor give help to the continual tilling the same land being barren, nor to 5 strikes sown in an acre, nor to the loss of ground 18 months together for the crop of corn, nor to the herding and driving of cattle, and clashing one another as they do with their flocks and herds, nor to trespassing one upon another, nor to other evil customs, etc.

Obj. 2. Depopulation usually followeth enclosure.

Answ. It is true, but the fault is in the men, not the ground; and if it be evil in the beginning thereof, then is it likewise evil in the continuance of the same.

Yet a man may drink strong beer without drunkenness, and eat fat meat without gluttony, and enclose land without depopulation.

The covetous gripe is against enclosure many times and saith he eats but his own; but this is sure, that the commoners all eat his part of grass, which wants stock and hath a right there; and if he have a right he ought to have something for it, otherwise where is charity, doing to others as you would that others should do to you?

To conclude, if each man have his land belonging to his house lying together, as he ought to have, then he may till his best land, and let the other lie to rest, etc., he may keep his cattle in order, the lesser from the greater, etc. and the Commonwealth much bettered.

There is a golden mean to be kept by husbandmen betwixt the extremes of depopulating enclosure and disordered common fields, of which the latter like Charybdis hath split many passengers husbandmen, and the other like Scylla swallows down and sends away men, women, and children. Yet by land it is not so as by sea: *Incidit in Scyllam, qui vult vitare Charybdim*, the examples of many countries and neighbour towns shewing the contrary.

26. A MIDLAND SPOKESMAN AGAINST ENCLOSURE, 1656

[John Moore, *A Scripture word against Enclosure*, 1656, pp. A4, 7–11]

An Advertisement of three Things, to such Reader who, as he loves God, loves his Neighbour also

FIRST, if thou chance to meet with a book, called *A Vindication of Regulated Inclosure* thou hast very little reason to believe much in it. The man speaks of what may be, and not of what usually is. He hath fancies, notions, and dreams of innocent enclosure both from depopulation and decay of tillage. And for the towns he names to be free, they are grossly guilty either of the one, or of the other, or of both.

Secondly, whereas that book tells thee that such desolations are *vitia personarum non rei*, it is the fault of the persons and not of the thing, I must confess with him they are vicious persons indeed that produce such enclosure. What better issue can we look for from such parents? Enclosure, making of hedges and ditches, is not a sin, but such enclosure that is destructive to public and poor is a crying sin. Lastly, I complain not of enclosure in Kent or Essex, where they have other callings and trades to maintain their country by, or of places near the sea or city, but of enclosure in the inland countries, which takes away tillage, the only trade general they have to live on; and whereby they are so beneficial to the rest of the nation in time of scarcity. Pray with me, *God speed the Plough*.

Thy Friend, if thou be so to the Public and the Poor,

John Moore

... First, on the ruin of the public, thou takest away tillage, which is the general trade we live on in Leicestershire, and the counties adjacent; by which trade or tillage and husbandry we have been as beneficial to the rest of the Commonwealth of England as any counties whatsoever. We have fed them not only with our wheat, corn, and malt, not only in plentiful years, but also in times of famine and dearth, we being the only magazine for corn in the middle of the nation. But also we have fed them with fat mutton, and swines' flesh, yea also, with victualling our ships by our peas and beans that come by the plough. As our open fields breed abundance of sheep, so the plough provides abundance of the aforesaid provisions to feed them fat; yea, at such times when no fat flesh is to be had elsewhere in the nation. If the tillage of these inland counties be turned into grazing, the rest of the nation must be in a starving condition whensoever the Lord shall slack his hand of this abundance of corn, he seems of late years to have rained from heaven amongst us. Thus are we as beneficial by our trade of tillage to other counties, as they to us by other manufactures which are so commodious, they lying near to the sea and city which we are so far from.

Yea, to shew the intolerableness of such enclosure: behold it takes away the general trade that all the inhabitants of these counties live on, except some great ones and tradesmen in market towns, etc. Can any deny but that the farmer lives of the plough, the cottagers live of the plough, and the children of both brought up to the trade of the plough, and do not the children of the poor become men servants and maid servants to the plough-man? Doth not that ancient, honest, venerable, and profitable trade of husbandry maintain all these? Yea, and all these lived as happily, plentifully, and richly of this trade of tillage in these counties before so much enclosure, as any in other counties whatsoever, or of what other trade soever they were of. What must become of these thousands and ten thousands if such enclosure be not speedily stopped? As every honest heart prays God speed the plough, so every good minister will have a word to uphold it, and every good magistrate make use of his power to save it from ruin. What now, mayest thou do what thou listest with thine own, and advance thine own nest on high thus upon the ruin of the public? Why art thou not content with thine own, since especially thy lands in common are worth as much and more than ever thy forefathers purchased them at, or thou of late hast purchased thine at? If they that sold thy lands in common had had thy evil conscience to have improved them upon the ruins of the public and poor, thou and thy forefathers must have paid twice as much, if not thrice as much more for them. But now these covetous wretches have got the trick of it to buy lands in common, and presently improve them, and so double if not treble their money upon a public account. These cruel ones care not how many they ruin so they may be rich, nor how many they make beggars so they may be gentlemen. Let them answer me this one question, viz: how so many thousand families can subsist, when their livelihood is taken away, to wit, their trade of tillage? And how shall so many thousands of children be disposed of from starving, vagrancy, or thieving, since so much enclosure hath caused so many tradesmen already they cannot live one by another?

But, it will be objected, some books have been printed of late that prove enclosure both lawful and laudable. Surely my heart bleeds within me to see some hands at such books of whom I hoped better things, that they should daub o'er this black sin with such untempered mortar. Oh how men will scrabble for gain! They would not have a spade called a spade. They would not (though they are such) be called oppressers, unjust, unconscionable, uncharitable, unmerciful. And surely such books are stuffed so full of levity and untruths, that the authors of them deserve rather to be pitied than answered. Ay, but these books say there may be an innocent enclosure. What then? The petitioners to Parliament formerly, and the petitioners now to his Highness and Council seek a redress against such enclosure that doth depopulate towns and decay tillage. And such the authors of these books hold to be hateful to God and man. Yes, but they say there may be an enclosure without decay of tillage or depopulation. Surely they may make men as soon believe there is no sun in the firmament as that usually depopulation and decay of tillage will not follow enclosure in our inland counties. We see it with our eyes. It is so. . . . Yea, but the books tell of some towns free from both depopulation and decay of tillage. They scrabble up a few towns that are innocent (as they say) which are just none at all in comparison of those many hundreds are guilty of both. And these few they are forced to fish out of the county of Leicester, Warwick, Northampton, etc. Let's see what truth is in this. For I know two or three of these places, because they are near unto me. They brag of the innocency of Ashby Magna, which hath been enclosed above fifty years. The truth of this business stands thus: the lord of that place gave most of his tenants leases for three lives, and one and twenty years after, which are not yet expired. And therefore the time of depopulation of that town is not yet come. But they name Misterton and Poultney as innocent also. I wonder they dare do so, since in regard of depopulation there is no house at all left in either of them but the minister's. And the closes now are called by the town's name that were anciently there. And as for decay of tillage in those places they have not been ploughed in the memory of man, except some part of them of late; and the tenants that rent them must plough them now but for four years only. How dare they print such falsehoods? And as little credit I hear and believe is to be given to the innocency of the rest of the towns named.

I have one word to speak to men that have not put off humanity, natural compassion towards their own flesh, and to Christians that love much, because God hath forgiven them much, which is this. If you did but hear what complaining and lamentation is made of farmers that rented land turned out of those enclosed places, and of poor cottagers together with them, that the one cannot get, no, not at any excessive rate, a little land to plough, whereby he might keep his team and cattle, that himself and family might be employed in husbandry, to get a poor living by, but is constrained to sell all these to all their utter undoings; that the other cannot get a house anywhere to harbour himself and his poor babes.

Surely, it would make all ministers and others, yea ministers above others, to ride and run, spend their pains and estate to petition, entreat, beg, wait, and never cease to be importunate for relief for these oppressed fellow creatures, and many of them fellow citizens of heaven together with us.

Behold now the oppressions of towns in open fields and market towns. For when these enclosures have made farmers cottagers, and cottagers beggars, no way of livelihood being left them, these poor with their families are forced into market towns and open fielded towns, hoping they may find some employment there to preserve them and theirs from perishing. Whereupon, these open fielded places are so loaden with poor, that the inhabitants are not able to relieve them. Ay, but these bookmen for enclosure say they pay more taxes. And truly well they may, when they lay such burthens upon open fields that they are not able to bear them; not only all those poor the enclosure have beggared, but all carriages the State hath need of, free quarter, attendance at the assizes and sessions, etc. The enclosures get the gain, and have the ease; and poor open fields pay the shot, and endure all the drudgery.

27. THE GEORGICAL COMMITTEE OF THE ROYAL SOCIETY AT WORK, 1664

[Royal Society, Domestic MSS., vol. V, no. 65]

An Account given to the Society of the Performances of the Georgical Committee

THIS committee having met the first time June 23, 1664 at Mr. Charles Howard's lodgings in Arundel House, they began to consider the end of their meeting, which being the composing of a good history of agriculture and gardening in order to improve the practise thereof; and resolved that for this end lists of Georgical authors should be brought in out of which inquiries should be collected and digested; and then sent by the Fellows of the Society into all the counties and shires of England, Scotland, and Ireland, where they have a special interest to procure by this means from their acquaintances experienced in husbandry good answers to such inquiries, whereby it may be known what is practised already and every place be enriched with the aids that are found in any place.

This list of inquiries was accordingly drawn up as to arable and meadows and many copies of them were made and distributed among the Fellows of the Society at several meetings thereof. Some returns have since been made by Mr. Howard, Dr. Smith, Mr. Beale, both the Secretaries; and 'tis hoped if others will awaken their friends in the country to send in theirs also.

Moreover, Dr. Merret having brought in a list of what is cultivated in

England, and the Committee thereupon thinking fit if such as had opportunity should procure the history of the culture of several of the vegetables
mentioned in the said list, as that of woad, hops, flax, hemp, madder, buckwheat, liquorice, rapeseed, it was ordered that these particulars should be
recommended to Mr. Beale by H. Oldenburg.

Further Mr. Howard brought in a list of materials for kitchen garden and of
winter greens together with inquiries concerning their culture and use, of
both which it was ordered that several copies should be made and those
recommended to such Fellows of the Society (Dr. Wilkins, Mr. Henshaw,
Dr. Holder) as had acquaintance with skilful gardeners to procure from them
answers thereunto, which is begun to be done accordingly.

Mr. Boyle having recommended to this committee some proposals of
Mr. Austin touching the planting both of timber and fruit trees it was
ordered that Mr. Parker, Mr. Waterhouse, and Mr. Hoskins should be
desired to consider what the law had already provided in this matter, and also
to bring in their advice how these proposals may be best ordered to make them
effectual.

Mr. Howard moving if it might be considered by this committee how
waste lands, heathy grounds, and bogs might be well employed and improved,
he was desired to bring in what himself knows of the ways of such improvements; who promised to contribute his part therein, but desired withal that
others might give their assistance to it of which he is in expectation of.

28. AN ANSWER TO THE GEORGICAL ENQUIRIES
FROM WHARFEDALE, WEST RIDING OF
YORKSHIRE, 1664

[Royal Society, Classified Papers, vol. X (3), no. 22]

IN THE parts of Wharfedale (to which Airedale adjoins, the rivers running
for some space at equal distance) the soil by the rivers is most part sandy, some
more sharp and stony. Both these are dry. In the declining or hanging part
more clayish and wet. On the hills a hard kind of grass we call bent; on the
highest part grows that stalky flowering shrub we call ling; all which by
industry are made arable. The general tillage: lime washed out of the banks
of the River Wharfe by floods, the stones are gathered and burnt in kilns with
coal—a whiter and sharper kind of lime than that which in our parts is digged
out of a soft quarry and which is more fat and unctuous. The two higher sort
[sic] of land (when enclosed) are ploughed commonly in winter and lie fallow
sometimes two years before it can be mellowed. The oftener ploughed the
better. The tillage: lime, the heat and sharpness whereof burns and mellows
this coarse land, working best on the driest land. The quantity laid on
an acre is as the owner can, perhaps 40 horse loads of lime unfallen; at the
first breaking up requires more than after. If the ground lie not very high,

sometime sown with wheat or maslin at Michaelmas or before, otherwise sown in March with black oats, and will yield four crops of that grain with one tillage, and after will bear a sweet but short grass for pasture.

The clay land is mostly tilled with lime; being fallowed one summer will bear good wheat after barley, beans, or oats; often liming this ground makes it become better grass, unless manured with dung or ashes. The lowest and best land fallowed one summer, sown first with wheat, then barley, then beans, it may be tilled once with lime but usually with dung. It is observed that lime makes all ground more stiff or fat so that land which at first was proper for rye or maslin grows more proper for wheat.

Our ploughs are strong and plain with crooked beams and this for all sorts of land. Only wheat is by some men prepared by steeping in brine or salt water; others wet their wheat in water and throw new fallen lime amongst it and stir it, which will clean to every single corn and dry on. This is thought to preserve from smut which we call slain corn, but doth surely at first preserve it from crows, the chief enemy of new sown corn in these woody dales. When the blade is new sprung up they scratch it out of the earth and eat the corn whence the blade comes, leaving the tender blade on the surface of the ground. But what we find to be best against smut or slain corn is to buy the purest wheat growing in the more champion country about twelve miles off near Wetherby, as those who there have the best seed do yearly buy theirs at like distance of about York.

The quantity of wheat or barley sown on a statute acre I conceive to be near three bushels of Winchester measure, our oats and barley being sown beginning of March in the valleys of Craven which lie low and on a hot limestone ground. They sow barley the latter end of May, yet reap betimes, being often but eight or nine weeks betwixt their sowing and reaping.

For the diseases of corn, the smut or slain we think to come from ill seed; for the mildew, when the straw is blackened and the corn pinched and doth not feed, we cannot well judge whence the cause is whether from mists (which are more frequent from our hills) as the name may import, or from the nature or hidden quality in the ground. I have observed in the same field divers parts as it were cheryndred[?], some mildewed and blackish, others pure and white, the mildewed a sandy land, the pure a sharp and stony land.

We cut all our corn with sickles, mow none with scythes. When shorn we set it in stooks and sheaves, upright one against other, hood it with two. I have observed our harvests not so late as in former years, whether the summers more hot and dry, or better tillage and sowing betimes have been the cause thereof. We bind and set up our corn when we reap, the only enemies of corn ——[?] in the barns and granaries are rats and mice, which we have no ways to destroy but those usual ones of cats, ratsbane; and we have no ways to better our meadows but by dung or ashes, our wet meadows by ditches to take off the water. I have seen those grounds which were covered with ling being first tilled with lime and after with dung become fine meadow full of honeysuckle.

Joseph Wilkinson

29. AN ANSWER TO THE GEORGICAL ENQUIRIES FROM EAST AND NORTH YORKSHIRE, 1664

[Royal Society, Classified Papers, vol. X (3), no. 23]

Answer to these Enquiries concerning Agriculture from Holme Beacon, Ouse and Derwent, and Holdenshire

To the first.[1] These three above mentioned wapentakes consists [sic] generally of warp clay and several sorts of sand ground which several sands works [sic] most to our effect when employed for arable. And as for warp which is our chiefest soil the best sort of it with once ploughing will bring barley without any additional help, and is then fit for barley again being thrice ploughed, or otherwise after the first crop, being but once ploughed, 'twill bring wheat without any sort of manure also, and so will continue for nigh twenty years, fallowing once every seventh year, bearing good oats in any of the first years from the first crop but no beans until after the first seven years.

Our clay ground being more stiff and of an hungrier nature must be five times ploughed beginning at Michaelmas, ploughing it thin and upwards, lying all winter until Lady Day, and then ploughing with a deep hold downwards. Then do we lie upon every statute acre two chalder and a half of lime or else about 25 coupe loads of beast manure and all the other ploughings taken it upwards, and so 'tis prepared to sow wheat upon at Michaelmas, or otherwise at the spring following (with one more ploughing) it may be sown with barley. And after either of them 'twill bring a crop of beans, and after beans upon once ploughing at Michaelmas following 'twill bring wheat again, or with thrice ploughing barley, and then either beans, oats, or fallow, and, so long as continued ploughing, fallowed every fourth year.

Our sand ground we begin to plough putting down thin about Lady Day,

---

[1] A revised list of questions issued by the Royal Society in 1665 is printed in R. V. Lennard, 'English Agriculture under Charles II: the Evidence of the Royal Society's "Enquiries"', *Econ. Hist. Rev.*, IV, 1932–4, pp. 25–6. The numbering of the questions in this Yorkshire return shows that it was a reply to the questionnaire *before* revision. Most of the answers make the substance of the questions clear. However, question 9 asked for remedies for diseases of grain; question 10 for remedies for weeds, worms, flies, birds, mice, and moles; question 12 for the seasons and ways of reaping grain; question 15 for methods of storing grain. On meadows, question 2 asked for remedies for weeds, moss, fern, briars, sedge, etc; question 3 asked for ways of draining marshes, bogs, and fens; question 4 (here ignored) asked about varieties of grasses and which were the best; question 5 asked about local practices when cutting grass and making hay; question 6 asked what grasses were best for winter feeding of which animals.

and ploughing thrice more, being limed or manured according to the proportions above mentioned. After the second ploughing 'tis prepared to sow rye upon at Michaelmas following which is the hopefullest crop, and then with three ploughings more after the rye crop be taken off, prepares it for barley against the spring following, which afterwards will bring one crop of oats.

The second. Answered in the first.

The third. Answered *ut supra* save that our ploughs for all the above mentioned grounds are alike, which is a small going plough drawn in warp and clay with four oxen and two horses, and in sand with less force.

The fourth. Answered in the first.

Fifth. We steep none, only we mix lime being wet and beast blood with wheat when we sow it, which preserves it from vermin and from being slain. We sow much hemp upon land made very fat, beginning to plough it about Candlemas and twice afterwards, choosing the largest, sound, and brightest seed. We also sow much flax upon the fullest and driest swarth we have, ploughing but once, and that a little after Lady Day, and then sowing about St. George's Day in April, harrowing the ground (with iron harrows) very well both before and after the seed be sown. We likewise sow rape or coleseed, sometimes upon fallow, ordered only as for corn, only made much fatter, but more generally upon burnt ground and getting as many ashes as we can, lying it very dry and beginning to plough for burning soon after May Day and sows at or soon after midsummer, the ashes being spread and ploughed once again, which we so let lie and never harrowed at all. We choose the brightest coloured seed and sows about a peck upon a statute acre.

Sixth. We take our seed wheat which grows northward of us and from a hungrier soil; and rye from a weeping sand to sow upon a dry; and barley from a warp to sow upon sand or clay.

Seventh. We sow 8 pecks of wheat upon a statute acre and somewhat less quantity of rye; and of barley 12 pecks; and of beans and oats 16 pecks.

Eighth. We use iron harrows for clay and warp, and wood harrows for light sand. We clod and roll only barley and that immediately after it be sown.

Ninth. This answered in the fifth as to wheat and for remedies of other grain we use none.

Tenth. We use no prevention.

Eleventh. When wheat or rye is too proud at Candlemas before it be bladed we eat it with sheep or cut it with a scythe.

Twelfth. The common way of scythes and sickles.

Thirteenth. We throw water sand amongst all white corn, which preserves it from vermin especially from mice, and to prevent heating we draw up by degrees a leape in the middle of the stack or roomstead.

Fourteenth. We thrash with flails generally but some lasheth over on board or door which preserves the colour of wheat if slain be amongst it. When the wind serveth not to dress the corn from the chaff, we do it with a fan and thereby preserves the chaff clean and dry for horses.

Fifteenth. We only turn it well in the garners at first for two months time.

Second for Meadows

First. We lie our warp and clay ground upon beans or peas stubble, and sand sometimes upon rye and sometimes upon oat stubble, being all left in good plight.

Second. The lying ground upon peas stubble, and well goaling to lie it dry, and shacking hay, and feeding cattle, whereby they may tread the ground, is the best prevention we have.

Third. We are not experienced.

Fifth and sixth. We are guided by the season of the year.

Seventh. We use a large ditch setting thorns and upon a less ditch we set stakes and thorns and under both we set quickset and willow plants which, if well weeded and carefully preserved from all annoyance, are of very great advantage.

30. AN ACT PROHIBITING THE IMPORT OF IRISH CATTLE, 1666

[*Statutes of the Realm*, V, p. 597. 18 & 19 Car. II. c. 2]

An Act against importing Cattle from Ireland and other Parts beyond the Seas and Fish taken by Foreigners

Rot. Parl.
18 & 19 C.II.
nu. 2.

WHEREAS by an act of this present Parliament entitled *An Act for the Encouragement of Trade* amongst other things some provision was made for the preventing of coming in of vast numbers of cattle whereby the rents and values of the land of this kingdom were much fallen, and like daily to fall more, to the great prejudice, detriment, and impoverishment of this kingdom, which nevertheless hath by experience been found to be ineffectual, and the continuance of any importation either of the lean or fat cattle dead or alive hereinafter specified not only unnecessary but very destructive to the welfare of this kingdom; be it therefore enacted by the King's most excellent Majesty by and with the advice and consent of the Lords Spiritual and Temporal and Commons in this present Parliament assembled; that such importation from and after the second day of February in this present year one thousand six hundred sixty and six is a public and common nuisance and shall be so adjudged, deemed, and taken to be to all intents and purposes whatsoever. And that if any great cattle, sheep, or swine, or any beef, pork, or bacon (except for the necessary provision of the respective ships or vessels in which the same shall be brought, not exposing the same or any part thereof to sale) shall from and after the said second day of February by any wise whatsoever be imported or brought from beyond seas into this kingdom of England, dominion of Wales, or town of Berwick upon Tweed, that then it shall and may be lawful for any constable, tithingman, headborough, churchwardens, or overseers of the poor, or any of them within their respective liberties, parishes, or places, to take and seize the same and keep the

Recital of
15 C. II. c. 7.
§ 13.

Importation of
cattle declared
a common
nuisance.

Importing
cattle (excep-
tion)

Cattle to be
seized.

How seizure to
be proceeded
with.

same during the space of eight and forty hours in some public and convenient place where such seizure shall be made; within which time if the
owner or owners or any for them or him shall make it appear unto some
Justice of the same county where the same shall be so seized by the oath of
two credible witnesses, which oath the said Justice of Peace is hereby empowered and required to administer, that the same were not imported from
Ireland or from any other place beyond the seas not hereinafter excepted
after the said second day of February; then the same upon the warrant of
In what case to
be forfeited. such Justice of Peace shall be delivered without delay, but in default of such
proof and warrant, then the same to be forfeited, one half thereof to be dis-
posed to the use of the poor of the parish where the same shall be so found
or seized, the other half to be to his or their own use that shall so seize the
same.

III.
Proviso for
importation of
cattle from the
Isle of Man.

Continuance of
Act.

. . . Provided always that nothing in this Act shall be construed to hinder
the importation of cattle from the Isle of Man in this kingdom of England
so as the number of the said cattle do not exceed six hundred head yearly.
And that they be not of any other breed than of the breed of the Isle of Man.
And that they be landed at the Port of Chester or some of the members
thereof and not elsewhere. This Act to continue until the end of seven years
and from thence to the end of the first session of the next Parliament.

31. ARGUMENTS FOR THE REPEAL OF THE IRISH
CATTLE ACT, 1666[1]
[P.R.O., SP 29/176, no. 130]

**Reasons humbly offered to the consideration of Parliament;
for taking off the prohibition, and giving leave to the importation
of Irish cattle**

[October?]

THE prohibition hath proved,
Very prejudicial to his Majesty's revenue of customs, his Majesty now losing
not only the duty imposed formerly upon great cattle, sheep, and other goods
imported from Ireland, but also the custom that used to be paid for the goods
imported from beyond the seas into England, and which were wont to be
sent into Ireland in return for their cattle, which goods paid a custom upon
the importation, and another upon the exportation, and a third in Ireland.
2. This prohibition hath greatly prejudiced all or most of the landowners in
England:
1. Because the breeding lands in England are not able to raise a stock for the
feeding.
2. It makes breeders impose a greater rate upon their lean beasts than they
can be sold for when fatted, which makes all feeding lands worth little or
nothing.

[1] A more convincing date for this document would be 1675.

3. It hath by reason thereof transferred most of the victualling both for home consumption, foreign trade, and naval provisions out of England into Ireland, and to such places where Ireland sends them; so that lean cattle though they be dearer than they were before the prohibition, yet are fatted cattle cheaper by reason we have lost the consumption we formerly had, so that feeding lands must and do fall for want of a cheap stock, and breeding lands through the decay of trade that this prohibition hath brought upon us.

Thirdly, This prohibition is destructive to our navigation and trade.

1. To navigation: for when Irish cattle were imported, at least 3 or 400 sail of ships were kept in constant employ for carrying on that trade, whereby great number of seamen were bred and maintained; but since the prohibition the whole trade is managed in foreign bottoms, and the breeding of seamen and building of ships for that service wholly neglected.

Secondly, To the trade of the kingdom:

1. Because foreigners, who formerly victualled here, do now victual in Ireland, where they have beef at 12s. per barrel, which is two hundred and a half; in England his Majesty's subjects pay 23 and 24s. a hundred.

2. This is so great a truth, as that it will not be difficult to prove, that Holland hath during this war been supplied with their naval provisions out of the King of England's own dominions for the fourth part of the price his Majesty hath been forced to pay for his. Let every man then judge at what a disadvantage his Majesty hath gone to war with his enemies. Having provisions so much cheaper than we, they can sail for less freight and wages, and so have great advantage of us in point of trade, and may undersell us in all markets. And to prevent as much as possible can be this mischief, the English now, when they sail long voyages, only take a month's or six weeks' provision here, because in Ireland, Spain, or other parts they can touch in and be supplied with Irish provisions at far cheaper rates than in England.

3. The Irish took no money out of England for the cattle imported, but took of our manufactures and goods of our growth in return thereof, which kept our poor at work whereby they earned money, the which they spent upon the provisions and manufactures of the kingdom, which was a help to consumption and kept up the price.

But now their cattle are sent beyond seas, and from thence they fetch the goods they want, which formerly they had from us, so that the traders in Lancashire and Cheshire and other parts, where breeding land lies, lose more for want of the consumption of the manufactures of those parts, which formerly they had when they were sent into Ireland, than the advantage the breeders of cattle do get by the price of lean cattle.

4. This prohibition hath made Ireland lessen their breed of great cattle and increase their flocks of sheep, so that they have prodigious quantities of wool, which together with their hides and tallow proves mischievous to England three ways:

1. By sending vast quantities of wool beyond seas unmanufactured, by

manufacturing whereof foreigners grow rich, whilst our poor in England starve for want of the work they had for foreign consumptions when Ireland did not send their wool thither.

2. By vast quantities of wool and hides sent into England, where we have more than we can consume ourselves or will supply the —— trade they have left us, or which we had before they transported those wools, so that what they now send to us, brings down the price of our own, we having more than we can use.

The like mischiefs attend their importation of their hides and tallow, for they sending such vast quantities beyond sea, and selling so much cheaper than we, who will buy of us? And we having more in England than we can spend among ourselves, consequently it must follow that whatever is imported from Ireland must, by glutting the market, bring down the price of our own commodity.

3. They prejudice England by setting up the woollen manufactures in Ireland, where having wool, hides, and tallow cheaper than we, and all sorts of provisions at a far less rate, necessarily they must have workmen for half the price. If then the commodity to be wrought and the working of that commodity be cheaper there than here, what shall hinder but that they may not only make of woollen and leathern manufactures for their own, but for to supply foreign markets also, and then what will become of the staple trade and commodities of England? It will of necessity be undermined, and the many hundred thousands of his Majesty's subjects, whose livelihoods depend upon the manufactures of the said commodities will be reduced to beggary, and their families inevitably fall upon the parishes wherein they dwell for maintenance, and England want the consumption of those vast quantities of provisions and manufactures they spent when they had employ, which must bring down the price of them and consequently of land.

This prohibition hath put Ireland out of a capacity of trading with us in England, though they desire the same, because they cannot pay us for what they buy unless they send over money in specie, which being of late much practised tends to ruin that kingdom, or return it by bills of exchange, which costs 15 or 16 *lib.* per cent. and that is double the advantage the trader gets here by the sale of their commodity; which high return also enforceth those noblemen and gentry who live in England, and whose estates lie in Ireland, to retrench a 6th part of their expenses, which is a further hindrance to the consumption of the provisions and commodities of the growth and manufacturing of this kingdom.

This prohibition hath undone many eminent tradesmen in London, as drapers, mercers, milliners, haberdashers, etc. For besides the staple commodities sent thither, when fashions were out here, they went into Ireland in return for their cattle, and were as good as new, for want of which utterance by reason of the often changing of fashions here, many able tradesmen have been undone.

But lastly, this prohibition is likely to prove fatal to England in its fishery, for Ireland thereby is put upon industry, and some part of it laying nearer to France, Spain, and Italy than England doth, they having salt from France, and cask in Ireland cheaper than we have in England, and men's provisions and wages being cheaper there than here, they have set up the fishery trade there, from whence they need but one wind to carry them to the foreign market, and lying so many leagues nearer the market, and catching their fish six weeks before we take any in England, what hinders but that they may be at market with them sooner and cheaper than we can afford to do, which in time will destroy the fishery of this kingdom.

By reason of the loss of our manufactures, our people, not being able to live here, are removed and removing thither, as combers, weavers, and other artists; which will in the consequence, if not remedied, prove a great advantage to them, and a greater disadvantage to England than the bringing over their cattle.

There being for custom, freights, and charges at the least 20s. surcharge on Irish cattle per head to bring them to our markets; if that be not thought sufficient to continue the commerce between both nations, 'tis humbly submitted to the wisdom of the Parliament to settle it, so as may be least prejudicial to England.

The riches of a nation arising from the labourer, artificer, and manufacturer, from their labour money is first raised to pay the tenant, and by his hands to the landlord; now to check the labourer is to stifle the riches of the nation in embryo, and how much the prohibition of Irish cattle hath either in reality or pretence done this, is to be considered; manufactures, and consequently manufacturers, are much lessened thereby, the exportation from England to Ireland before this prohibition being, as appears by examining the books to be, 204,000 *li.* per annum, which now will scarce be found above a tenth part, if so much, which results in a double prejudice.

1. The manufactures and things of the growth of this nation are much lessened.

2. The consumption of the nation lessened, and the labourers left cannot now feed so well, since provisions are dearer and the most minute addition on that amounts to a vast bulk in the total; for supposing the people of England to be 8 millions, and, one with another, to expend 20s. worth of flesh meat, which if reckoned one with another but at 2*d.* per p. the adding but one farthing per p. in the price of the meat amounts to one million of money spent more than was before; and so proportionably; whereas the cattle brought out of Ireland did not amount to above 80, or 90 thousand pounds per annum or thereabouts; and since such as do labour are for number the body of the kingdom, and generally of beef and mutton-eaters, the dearer that is the more money they consume in meat, and the more they consume the less they have to pay to the tenants, and they the less to the landlords. Further, if riches do consist chiefly in the work of hands, and no kingdom be the richer for what it doth consume within itself, but in what it furnisheth abroad, then breeding of cattle in England, which requireth but a few hands, doth tend to the

dispeopling of the land, and so to the abatement of the riches thereof, and to encourage that with a preference to our manufactures will be a course quite contrary to the policy of former times, which did provide laws principally enjoining tillage and manufacture as the best means to increase the yeomanry, which were deemed to be the strength and riches of the kingdom, and 'tis most certain that the lessening of tillage and increase of breeding doth abate the tithes thereof.

32. AN ACT ENCOURAGING THE EXPORT OF CORN AND CATTLE, 1670

[*Statutes of the Realm*, V, pp. 685–6. 22 Car. II, c. 13]

An Act for Improvement of Tillage and the Breed of Cattle

FOR the further encouragement of tillage for the common good and welfare of this kingdom, be it enacted by the King's most excellent Majesty, by and with the advice and consent of the Lords Spiritual and Temporal and the Commons in this present Parliament assembled and by authority of the same, that from and after the twenty fourth day of June which shall be in the year of our Lord one thousand six hundred and seventy and from thence forward, it shall be lawful for all and every person or persons, native or foreign at any time or times to ship, lade, carry, and transport as merchandise all sorts of corn and grain although the prices thereof shall exceed the rates set down in one act of this present Parliament, made in the fifteenth year of his Majesty's reign entitled An Act for the Encouragement of Trade: the said act or any other law, statute, usage, or other prohibition to the contrary thereof in any wise notwithstanding; paying for the same such rates as are to be paid when the same might have been transported by one act of this present Parliament entitled A Subsidy granted to the King of Tonnage and Poundage, and none other.

Corn and grain may be exported at certain times, although the prices exceed the rates of 15 Car. II. c. 7.

Paying duty as by 12 Car. II. c. 4.

II.

When corn does not exceed the rates herein certain duties as herein mentioned to be paid.

And it is hereby further enacted by the authority aforesaid that when the prices of corn and grain at the times, havens, and places when and where the said corn or grain shall be imported into this kingdom exceed not the rates hereafter following, there shall be answered and paid for the custom and poundage thereof these rates, that is to say: for every quarter of wheat when the same shall not exceed the price of three and fifty shillings and four pence the quarter, there shall be paid for the custom and poundage thereof the sum of sixteen shillings. And when the same shall exceed the sum of three and fifty shillings and four pence the quarter, and yet not above four pounds the quarter, that then there shall be answered and paid for the custom and poundage of every quarter of wheat the sum of eight shillings; for every quarter of rye when the same doth not exceed the price of forty shillings the quarter, there shall be answered and paid for the custom and poundage thereof the sum of sixteen shillings the quarter; for every quarter of barley or malt, when the same doth not exceed the price of two and thirty shillings the quarter, there shall be answered and paid for the custom and poundage thereof the sum of sixteen shillings the quarter; for every quarter of buckwheat, when the same doth not exceed the price of two and thirty shillings the quarter, there shall be answered and paid for the custom and poundage thereof the sum of sixteen shillings the quarter; for every quarter of oats, when the same doth not exceed the sum of sixteen shillings the quarter, there shall be answered and paid for the custom and poundage thereof the sum of five shillings and four pence the quarter; for every quarter of peas or beans, when the same doth not exceed the sum of forty shillings the quarter, there shall be answered and paid for the custom and poundage thereof the sum of sixteen shillings the quarter, each quarter to contain eight bushels, and each bushel to contain eight gallons and no more.

But when the prices of the several sorts of corn and grain above mentioned shall exceed the respective rates above said at the time and places of importation, that then and in every such case there be answered and paid for the same the duties payable in such case before the making of this Act. *But when corn exceeds those rates then the old duties to be paid.*

And for the further encouragement of French or pearl barley in this kingdom, that there shall be paid for the custom of every hundredweight of French or pearl barley the sum of five shillings. *III. Duty of French or pearl barley.*

And for the further encouragement of breeding and feeding of cattle of all sorts, be it enacted by the authority aforesaid that from and after the twenty-fourth day of June which shall be in the year of our Lord God one thousand six hundred and seventy and from thence forward, it shall be lawful for every person or persons, native or foreigner at any time or times to ship, lade, and transport by way of merchandise these sorts of goods following, that is to say, beef, pork, bacon, butter, cheese, and candles, though the same do exceed in price at the ports from whence they are laden, and at the time of their lading the prices set down and limited in the aforesaid act of this present Parliament entitled A Subsidy granted to the King of Tonnage and Poundage; the said act or any other law, statute, usage, or other prohibition to the contrary thereof in any wise notwithstanding, paying for the same the respective rates appointed by the said act and no more. *IV. Beef, pork, etc. may be exported, though the same exceed the prices in 12 Car. II. c. 4.*

Except and always provided that for the custom and poundage of every barrel of butter there shall be paid one shilling, and for every hundredweight of cheese four pence and no more, the aforesaid Act of Tonnage and Poundage or any other law or statute to the contrary notwithstanding. *V. Proviso for poundage on butter and cheese.*

And it is hereby further enacted by the authority aforesaid that from and after the twenty fourth day of June which shall be in the year of our Lord one thousand six hundred seventy and one there shall be paid for every ox or steer that shall be transported into the parts beyond the seas by any person or persons native or foreigner the sum of twelve pence and no more, the aforesaid Act of Tonnage and Poundage or any other law, statute, usage, or other prohibition to the contrary hereof in any wise notwithstanding. *VI. Duty of 12d. on every ox or steer exported.*

VII.
Duty of 12*d.*
on exportation
of cows or
heifers;

and of 2*d.* on
swine or hogs.

VIII.
Duty of 5*s.* on
exportation of
horses, mares,
and geldings.

And it is hereby further enacted by the authority aforesaid that from and after the said twenty fourth day of June in the year aforesaid, it shall be lawful for any person or persons, native or foreigner, to ship, lade, or transport cows or heifers, paying for each cow or heifer the sum of twelve pence and no more. And also to ship, lade, or transport all sorts of swine or hogs paying for each swine or hog twopence and no more; any statute, law, usage, or other prohibition to the contrary thereof in any wise notwithstanding.

And for the further encouragement of the breed of horses, be it enacted by the authority aforesaid that from and after the twenty-fourth day of June in the year of our Lord one thousand six hundred and seventy, and from thence forward it shall be lawful for any person or persons, native or foreigner, at any time or times to ship, lade, and transport by way of merchandise, horses or mares into any parts beyond the seas in amity with his Majesty paying for each horse or mare the sum of five shillings, and for each gelding the sum of five shillings and no more; the aforesaid Act of Tonnage and Poundage, or any other law, statute, usage, or any other prohibition to the contrary hereof in any wise notwithstanding.

33. THE FIRST CORN BOUNTY ACT, 1672

[*Statutes of the Realm*, V, pp. 780–2. 25 Car. II. c. 1]

An Act for Raising the Sum of £1,238,750 for Supply of His Majesty's Extraordinary Occasions

Reasons for
passing this
Act.

Grant of
£1,238,750.

To be raised
within 18
months, at the
times, in man-
ner, and on the
counties, etc.
herein men-
tioned.

WE your Majesty's most dutiful and loyal subjects the Commons assembled in Parliament, acknowledging with all humility and thankfulness your Majesty's abundant care for our preservation, and being deeply sensible of that extraordinary charge and expense with which your Majesty's present occasions are to be supported, have cheerfully and unanimously given and granted, and do hereby give and grant unto your most excellent Majesty, the sum of twelve hundred thirty eight thousand seven hundred and fifty pounds, to be raised and levied in manner following. And do humbly beseech your Majesty that it may be enacted and be it enacted by the King's most excellent Majesty, by and with the advice and consent of the Lords Spiritual and Temporal and of the Commons in this present Parliament assembled and by the authority of the same, that the sum of twelve hundred thirty eight thousand seven hundred and fifty pounds shall be raised, levied, and paid unto your Majesty within the space of eighteen months in manner following, that is to say, the sum of threescore and eight thousand eight hundred and nineteen pounds and nine shillings by the month for eighteen months beginning from the fourth day of February one thousand six hundred seventy and two shall be assessed, taxed, collected, levied, and paid by six quarterly payments in the several counties, cities, boroughs, towns, and places within England and Wales, and the town of Berwick upon Tweed, according to the several rates and proportions and in such manner as is hereafter expressed, that is to say, for every month of the said eighteen months.

For the County of Bedford the sum of eight hundred ninety six pounds seventeen shillings and nine pence.

For the County of Berks. the sum of one thousand one hundred thirty two pounds six shillings and seven pence.

For the County of Bucks. the sum of one thousand three hundred and fifteen pounds six shillings and five pence. [etc.] . . .

And to the end that all owners of land whereupon this tax principally lieth may be the better enabled to pay the same by rendering the labours of the husbandman in raising corn and grain more valuable by exportation of the same into foreign parts which now is already at a very low rate, and that the nation in general may have her stock increased by the returns thereof, be it further enacted that for the space of three years from the first day of this session of Parliament and from thenceforward to the end of the next session of Parliament, when malt or barley (Winchester measure) is or shall be at twenty four shillings a quarter, rye thirty two shillings a quarter, and wheat forty eight shillings a quarter or under in any port or ports of this kingdom or dominion of Wales every merchant or other person who shall put on shipboard in English shipping (the master and two thirds of the mariners at least being his Majesty's subjects) any sorts of the corn aforesaid from any such ports where the rates shall not then be higher than as aforesaid with intent to export the said corn to parts beyond the seas, every such merchant or other person shall bring a certificate in writing under his or their hands containing the quantity and quality of corn so shipped to the farmers, commissioners, collectors, or other persons appointed or to be appointed by his Majesty, his heirs, or successors to collect the duties and rates arising by customs within any such port and upon proof made of any such certificate by one or more credible persons upon their oaths, which oaths the said commissioners or other persons are hereby authorized and required to administer, and upon bond given by every such merchant or other person in the sum of two hundred pounds at the least for every hundred tons of corn so shipped and so proportionably, that the said corn (danger of the seas excepted) shall be exported into parts beyond the seas and not be again landed in the kingdom of England, dominion of Wales, the islands of Guernsey or Jersey, or town of Berwick upon Tweed, every such merchant so shipping off any of the aforesaid corn and giving certificate and bond as aforesaid shall have and receive from such farmers, commissioners, collectors, or other persons in any port respectively where the same corn shall be so shipped, for every quarter of barley or malt, ground or unground, two shillings and six pence, for every quarter of rye, ground or unground, three shillings and six pence, for every quarter of wheat, ground or unground, five shillings, which sum or sums every such commissioner, farmer, or other persons are hereby authorized and required upon demand by such exporter to make present payment of accordingly, without taking or requiring any

XXXI. For three years, etc. when corn herein mentioned persons shipping for exportation to bring a certificate of quantity and quality of corn is at the price on oath to the commissioners, etc.

And thereupon, and upon bond given not to Ireland the same corn, etc.

To receive the bounties herein mentioned without fee;

thing for custom or any fee or reward for corn so laden to be exported, or
for so much grain as shall be exported in any ship wherein any other goods
shall be shipped; any law, statute, or usage in any wise to the contrary notwithstanding. And upon certificate returned under the common seal of the
chief magistrate in any place or places beyond the seas, or under the hands
and seals of two known English merchants upon the place that such corn was
there landed, or upon proof by credible persons that such corn was taken by
enemies or perished in the seas, the examination and proof thereof being left
to the judgement of such commissioners, farmers, or other persons; which
proof being made or certificate delivered to such person or persons respectively as took bond as aforesaid, the said bond shall be delivered up to such
importer or his order to be cancelled without any fee for the same; and the
moneys by any such commissioners, farmers, collector, or other person so
paid in obedience to this act shall be accepted of in his or their accompts as
so much paid to his Majesty, and he and they is and shall be discharged
thereof accordingly . . .

and upon certificate of corn being duly landed, bond to be delivered up to exporter to be cancelled without fee;

and commissioners, etc. discharged.

34. LAND IMPROVEMENT AND A CONSEQUENT TITHE DISPUTE, 1673

[P.R.O., E 134, 25 Chas. II, Mich. 12. Depositions by Commission]

[Some of the evidence of witnesses in a dispute between George Rivers, esq.,
complainant, and William Norman, defendant, taken at Tonbridge on
Wednesday, October 8, 25 Chas. II [1673], relating to the payment of tithe.
George Rivers was the owner of the tithe of all corn and grain arising and
increasing in Stairward in Hadlow, Kent]

WILLIAM BRATTLE of Hadlow in the county of Kent, husbandman, aged
about three score years, being sworn and examined [on behalf of the defend-
ant] deposeth as followeth:

To the second interrogatory, this deponent saith that he doth know the
enclosed grounds of Little Park and North Frith in the defendant's possession
lying in Hadlow in Kent and being within the precinct of Stairward, but as
to the certain number of acres lying in the said precinct of Stairward he this
deponent knoweth not.

To the third interrogatory, this deponent saith that he doth know that all
the land in the defendant's possession lying in the precinct of Stairward to
be very barren, poor, heathy ground, and that the same is not fitting to be
ploughed to sow any corn upon without amendment.

To the fourth interrogatory, this deponent saith that he doth know the
four parcels of land in the interrogatory mentioned, which were lately
broken up by the defendant, one field containing by estimation 9 acres,
another about 2 acres, another about 10 acres, and another about 3 acres,
being the four parcels first mentioned in this interrogatory and that the said

four parcels are very poor, barren, heathy ground, and hath heard the defendant offer any of the said four pieces aforesaid to several persons for a groat an acre to convert it to tillage without improvement, but the defendant doth believe that no person would give that rate for the same and further saith not to this interrogatory.

To the fifth interrogatory, this deponent saith that to his knowledge the defendant hath been at improving, manuring, and making the said four parcels of land fitting for tillage for every acre thereof £8 or near thereabouts before such time as the defendant received any profit to himself thereby.

Robert Webb of Hadlow in the county of Kent, tanner, aged 50 years or thereabouts, sworn and examined deposeth as followth . . .

To the fourth interrogatory, this deponent saith that he hath known one piece of land of 10 acres to have had five crops, three whereof wheat, one of peas, and one of oats, out of which said 10 acres tithe hath been paid by the defendant for half an acre or thereabouts; one other piece of four acres called the hop garden to have had two crops, one of wheat and the other of beans; one other field 10 acres with three crops, two whereof were wheat and the other peas; 3 acres more seven crops, three with wheat, two with oats, and two with peas; one other field of about 3 acres five crops, the first with wheat, second and third oats, fourth peas, the fifth sowed but he knoweth not with what grain. This deponent further saith that the defendant for several years aforesaid hath mowed, cut, and carried away the several crops, denying to pay tithe for the same or any part thereof, and that the tithe due in the whole for the several years amounts to £14 or thereabouts. And further he deposeth not.

35. ANIMALS AND POULTRY ON THE FARM, 1675

[John Worlidge, *Systema Agriculturae: the Mystery of Husbandry Discovered*: . . . , 1675, pp. 160–1, 163–4]

Of several Sorts of Beasts, Fowls, and Insects, usually kept for the Advantage and Use of the Husbandman

OUR country farm is of little use and benefit to us, notwithstanding all our care, pains, and cost in fencing, planting, or otherwise ordering the same, unless it be well stocked and provided with beasts and other animals, as well for labour and strength in tilling and manuring the ground, and facilitating other labours and exercises, as for the furnishing the market and kitchen.

Of the Horse

The Horse hath the preeminence above all others, being the noblest, strongest, swiftest, and most necessary of all the beasts used in this country for the saddle, for the plough and cart, and for the pack.

Where you have good store of pasture, either in several, or in common, or in woods or groves, it is no small advantage to keep a team of mares for the breed; but where there is most of arable, and little of pasture land, horses or geldings are more necessary; which difference we may observe between the great breeding places for horses in the pastures and woodlands, and the naked corn countries; the one full of gallant lusty mares, the other of horses and geldings.

As to the shape and proportion, colours, age, ordering, breeding, feeding, and curing the several diseases of horses, I shall here be silent, and refer you to the several authors who have copiously treated of that subject, it being too large for this place . . .

Of Cows and Oxen

These worthy sort of beasts are in great request with the husbandman, the ox being useful at his cart and plough, the cow yielding great store of provision both for the family and the market, and both a very great advantage to the support of the trade of the kingdom.

Concerning their form, nature, and choice, I need say little, every countryman almost understanding how to deal for them.

The best sort is the large Dutch cow that brings two calves at one birth, and gives ordinarily two gallons of milk at one meal.

As for their breeding, rearing, breaking, curing of their diseases, and other ordering of them; and of milk, butter, and cheese, etc. I refer you to such authors that do more largely handle that subject than this place will admit of.

Of Sheep

Next unto these, the sheep deserves the chiefest place, and is by some preferred before any other, for the great profit and advantage they bring to mankind, both for food and apparel.

Whereof there are divers sorts, some bearing much finer wool than others: as the Herefordshire sheep about Leominster bear the fairest fleeces of any in England. Also they are of several kinds, as to their proportion; some are very small, others larger. But the Dutch sheep are the largest of all, being much bigger than any I have seen in England, and yearly bear two or three lambs at a time. It is also reported that they sometimes bear lambs twice in the year. It may doubtless be of very good advantage to obtain of those kinds; and also of Spanish sheep that bear such fine fleeces.

As for their breeding, curing, and ordering, I refer you (as before) to such authors that have largely treated of them.

Of Swine

This beast is also of a very considerable advantage to the husbandman, the flesh being a principal support to his family, yielding more dainty dishes and variety of meat than any other beast whatsoever, considering them as pig, pork, bacon, brawn, with the different sorts of offal belonging to them.

Also they are of the coarsest feed of any creature whatsoever; being content with anything that's edible, so they have their fill, for they are impatient of hunger.

It is a great neglect that they are no more bred and kept than they are, their food being obtained at so easy a rate . . .

Of Fowl

The countryman's farm or habitation cannot be said to be completely stored or stocked without fowl, as well as beasts, yielding a considerable advantage by their eggs, brood, bodies, and feathers, amongst which the poultry seems to have the preeminence, being more universally kept than any other sort whatsoever; insomuch that any poor cottager that lives by the highway-side may keep of them, being able to shift for themselves the most part of the year, feeding on insects, and on anything almost that's edible by any other sort of animal.

Profit of Poultry

They are also kept to a very great advantage in the back-sides, and at the barns-doors of great farms; and as I have been certainly informed, a good farm hath been wholly stocked with poultry, spending the whole crop upon them, and keeping several to attend them; and that it hath redounded to a very considerable improvement. It seems also consonant to reason, especially if within a day's journey of London, that they might have a quick return, and a good market, being in a capacity to furnish the market, throughout the year, either with eggs, chickens, pullets, capons, or cocks and hens. Also the feathers must needs yield a considerable advantage; and the dung of poultry being of great use on the land, much exceeding the dung of any cattle whatsoever.

Therefore, if convenient places or houses were made for them, as dark as may be, which doth much expedite their fattening, and the poultry there fed, and their dung reserved, and before it hath taken wet, let it be mixed with earth, it will undoubtedly answer the expense of a great part of the corn you feed them withal.

If they are fed with buck, or French wheat, or with hemp seed, they will lay more eggs than with any other sort of grain.

Buckwheat either ground and made in paste, or whole (the former way is the better), is the best single fattener of fowl; hemp seed, as they say, giving an ill favour to the flesh of the bird that feeds on it: but this only upon report; if it prove otherwise, it would be one great encouragement to the planting or sowing of hemp, that the seed should be of so great use . . .

Of Geese

They are a fowl very profitable in many places where there are commons to feed them on, being a creature that requires little care and attendance, and little charge in feeding them.

They multiply extraordinary in some places, breeding twice a year; and in all places yielding a considerable price.

Also their feathers are no small advantage, especially if you shear them as they do sheep, as in some places is usual.

36. THE USES OF CORN AND PULSES AND METHODS OF STORAGE, 1675

[John Worlidge, *Systema Agriculturae : the Mystery of Husbandry Discovered :* . . . , 1675, pp. 51–3]

Of the General Uses of Corn, Grain, Pulse, and other Seeds propagated by the Plough

Use of Wheat

THIS is the most general grain used here in England for bread, although it be not unfit for most of the uses the other grains are fit for. As for beer, the best beer to keep hath usually a proportion of wheat added to the malt; and the bran also of wheat, a little thereof boiled in our ordinary beer, maketh it mantle or flower in the cup when it is poured out, which sheweth with what a rich spirit wheat is endowed withal, that so much remains in the very bran. Also starch is made of musty and unwholesome wheat, and of the bran thereof, than which there are few things whiter.

Of Barley

Its principal use is for the making of beer, being the sweetest and most pleasant grain for that purpose. It is also one of the best grains for fatting of swine, especially being either boiled till it be ready to break, with no more water than it drinks up; or ground in a mill, and wet into a paste, or made into a mash; either way it produces most excellent sweet bacon.

Of Rye

Its general use is for bread, either of itself or mixed with wheat; it makes bread moist, and gives it a very pleasant taste to most appetites. I know no other particular use thereof (it being not universally propagated), only it's reported that it yields great store of spirit or *aqua vitæ*.

Of Oats

This is the only grain for a horse, and best agrees with that beast of any other, and in which the horse most delighteth; and is a constant food either for bread, cakes, or oatmeal to the Scots and several northern places in England, and in some part of Wales. Oats also will make indifferent good malt, and a little thereof in strong beer to be kept, is usual. They are a grain that poultry also love to feed on, and it makes them lay store of eggs above what other grain doth.

Of Pulses

The common use of pulses are generally known, as well for men as beasts; but there are several that pretend to extract from them excellent liquors, and distil very good spirits or *aqua vitæ*, without malting, as one (in a certain tract, published by Mr. Hartlib) pretends, that rye, oats, peas, and the like inferior sort of grains, handled as barley until it sprout, needing not for this work to be dried, but beaten and moistened with its own liquor, and soundly fermented, will yield a monstrous increase. He also affirms that out of one bushel of good peas will come of spirit at the least two gallons or more, which will be as strong as the strongest aniseed water usually sold in London: this he affirms to be of the least . . .

The Uses of Hemp seed, Flax seed, Rape and Coleseed

Hemp seed is much commended for the feeding of poultry and other fowl, so that where plenty thereof may be had, and a good return for fowl, the use thereof must needs be advantageous, ordered as you shall find hereafter when we treat of poultry.

Flax seed or linseed, rape and coleseed are generally made use of for the making of oil.

Of the Preservation of Corn

The preservation of corn, when it is plenty and good, is of very great advantage to the husbandman and the kingdom in general, for in scarce and dear years the husbandman hath little to sell to advance his stock, and the buyers are usually furnished with musty and bad corn from foreign parts, or from such that were ignorant of the ways to preserve it.

Therefore, in cheap years it will be very necessary to make use of some of these ways for the storing up your plenty of corn, against a time of scarcity.

The way of making of it up in reeks, on reek-stavals, set on stones that the mice may not come at it, is usual and common.

But corn thrashed and clean winnowed is apt to be musty; therefore some advise that you lay up your corn in the chaff in large granaries made for that purpose secure from the mice; and when you use or sell it, then to winnow it.

Also it is advised to mix beans with corn, and that it will preserve it from heating and mustiness. It is probable that if the beans be well dried on a kiln it may succeed, for then will they attract all superfluous moisture unto them, which is the only cause of the injury to the corn; for in Egypt where it is so dry, corn will keep in open granaries many years, as in Pharaoh's time. The beans are easily separated afterwards from the corn.

It is also reported, that pieces of iron, flints, pebbles, etc. mixed with corn, preserves it from heating, which may be true, for it is usual to set a stick on

end in corn, only to give passage for the air to prevent heating. A large
granary also full of square wooden pipes, full of small holes, may keep long
from heating, though not so well as the chaff, beans, etc.

Also some have had two granaries, the one over the other, and filled the
upper, which had a small hole in the bottom, that the corn by degrees, like
sand in an hourglass, hath fallen into the lower; and when it was all in the
lower, they removed it into the upper, and so kept it in continual motion,
which is a good way also to preserve it.

37. TURNIPS, 1675

[John Worlidge, *Systema Agriculturae: the Mystery of
Husbandry Discovered: ...*, 1675, p. 42]

Turnips

ALTHOUGH this be a plant usually nourished in gardens, and be properly a
garden plant, yet it is to the very great advantage of the husbandman sown
in his fields in several foreign places, and also in some parts of England, not
only for culinary uses, as about London and other great towns and cities, but
also for food for cattle, as cows, swine, etc. They delight in a warm, mellow,
and light land, rather sandy than otherwise, not coveting a rich mould. The
ground must be finely ploughed and harrowed, and then the seed sown, and
raked in with a bush or such like. They are sown at two seasons of the year,
in the spring with other the like kitchen tillage, and also about Midsummer,
or after, in the fields for the use of cattle, or any other use. In Holland they
slice their turnips with their tops, and rapeseed cakes, and grains, etc. and
therewith make mashes for the cows, and give it them warm, which the cows
will eat like hogs.

Cows and swine also will eat them raw, if they are introduced into the diet
by giving the turnips first boiled unto them, and then only scalded, and afterwards they will eat them raw.

38. UNCOMMON VARIETIES OF GRAIN, PULSES, AND GRASSES GROWN IN OXFORDSHIRE, 1676

[Robert Plot, *The Natural History of Oxfordshire*, 1676, pp. 150–4]

OF unusual plants now cultivated in the fields, to pass by the ordinary red
and white Lammas wheats, black and white ryes, the common barley, peas,
beans, and oats, there are several worthy notice now sown in this county that
have been scarce ever heard of, much less used, in some others; where by
the way let it be noted that the word *unusual* is not so much to be applied to
this, as other counties, and that in these matters of husbandry, I rather write

for the information of strangers than the inhabitants of Oxfordshire, as I must hereafter in other counties for the information of this, there being many things in each county thought common there and unworthy notice, that perhaps in some others will appear so strange, that they will scarcely be believed. And such are

Triticum spicâ muticâ rubrum, caule item rubro : red stalked wheat (mistaken by many for red Lammas) so commonly called from the redness of its straw, especially near the joints when the corn begins to turn; which redness yet will vanish for the most part away, when it is full ripe. This corn, as I was informed, was first propagated from some few ears of it, picked out of many acres, by one Pepart near Dunstable about fifty years ago, which sowed by itself till it amounted to a quantity, and then proving mercatable, is now become one of the commonest grains of this county, especially about Oxford; which yet, because not known in many other places, I thought fit at least to mention it, and the rather because of its seldom or never smutting, a conveniency that pleases the baker and husbandman both; and yet it seems 'tis not now sown about Thame and Watlington so much as formerly, because it brings not so certain, nor so good a burthen as:

Triticum spicâ muticâ albicante, granis rufescentibus : white eared red wheat, white corn, or mixed Lammas, which latter name I take to be as agreeable as any, because of its participating both of the white and red Lammas, having a white ear and red grain; whereas the white Lammas has both ears and grain white, and the red Lammas both red. Nor has this, as I was told, been long in Oxfordshire, it being first advanced like the former from some few ears, and at last being found to yield considerably better than most other wheat, viz. sometimes twenty for one, it is now become the most eligible corn all along the Vale under the Chiltern Hills, and in far better esteem than the red stalked wheat, or,

Triticum spicâ aristatâ glumis hirsutis : the long cone wheat, which yet is the best of any to be sown in rank clay land, its stalks being reedy and not subject to lodging; and by hedges sides, because the birds cannot eat it; for which reason also it must be good in enclosures, besides its being the least subject of any corn yet known to the inconveniency of mildews. This sort also yields extremely well, but its flour, being coarse and not pleasing the bakers, it is seldom sown but under the mentioned circumstances, except sometimes mixed amongst the other wheats . . .

All which, 'tis true, in Oxfordshire are so commonly sown, that they cannot indeed in this respect be styled unusual; but because scarce ever heard of in the south-east parts of England, I thought it convenient at least to hint them. And so likewise our

Hordeum distichum præcox, or rathe ripe barley, deservedly so called from its early ripening, it having been sometimes sown and returned to the barn again in two months' time, and often in nine or ten weeks. This barley, 'tis true, is no native of Oxfordshire, only much sown here, it being all had either immediately or mediately from Patney in Wiltshire, whence by some 'tis also called Patney Barley; where the soil (as I am told) is of so peculiar a quality, that whatever other barley is sown there, it is turned forthwith into this we call rathe ripe; a feat, which they say, no other land will perform. But we are told by Dr. Childrey that in the western parts of Cornwall they sow a sort of barley near the seaside, which they carry to mill in eight or nine weeks time after they have sowed it. However, what we have here comes all from Patney, but is not so agreeable to our Oxfordshire soil immediately from thence as when it has been sown elsewhere twice or thrice; after which, it endures not above three or four years, but degenerates again into common barley. Its conveniency notwithstanding is very considerable in wet and backward springs and moist autumns, when many other countries lose their seasons, and some of the more northern ones perhaps their crop, the common barley there never coming to be ripe, whereas this may be sown at the latter end of May, and will come to be ripe in the worst of summers. This I heard of first at Gaunt House (the paternal estate of the Right Reverend Father in God, John Lord Bishop of Oxon, one of the noblest encouragers of this design), but met with it after all over the county, it being generally approved of by all sorts of husbandmen. And this is the only barley sown in this county unknown in some others.

But of peas there are many sorts little thought of southward, that possibly were they known, might prove as agreeable to the soils there, as here, and as advantageous to the husbandman. Such are the peas called Henley-gray, and another sort called Red-shanks, for fresh new broken land; the Vale-gray for strong; and Hampshire kids for new chalked land; the small rathe ripes, for poor and gravelly; and the Cotswold pea for sour ground. And of vetches: in deep clay lands they sow the gore and pebble-vetch; in cold moist grounds the rathe ripe vetch; and dills or lentils in poor stone-brash land, which are a good podware for cattle, and sown in many parts of the county.

As for beans and oats, they sow only the common that are everywhere else; but for grasses, the usual name for any herbage sown for cattle, especially if perennial (to pass by the *trifolium purpureum majus sive sativum*, clover-grass; and *Onobrychis spicata flore purpureo, semine echinato*, commonly called sainfoin, or everlasting-grass; but according to Dr. Morison, the true lucerne, now everywhere known, and therefore nothing concerning the qualities and advantages of it.) They have lately sown ray grass, or the *Gramen Loliaceum*, by which they improve any cold, sour, clay-weeping ground, for which it is best, but good also for drier upland grounds, especially light stony, or sandy land, which is unfit for sainfoin.

It was first sown (as I was told) in the Chiltern parts of Oxfordshire, and since brought nearer Oxford by one Mr. Eustace, an ingenious husbandman of Islip who, though at first laughed at, has been since followed even by those very persons that scorned his experiment, it having precedence of all other grasses in that it takes almost in all sorts of poor land, endures the drought of summer best, and in the spring is the earliest grass of any, and cannot at that time be overstocked; its being kept down making it sweeter and better beloved by cattle than any other grass: nay, sometimes they have been known to leave meadow hay to feed on this; but of all other cattle, it is best for horses, it being hard hay; and for sheep, if unsound, it having been known by experience to have worked good cures on them, and in other respects the best winter grass that grows.

39. METHODS OF TILLING THE SOILS OF OXFORDSHIRE, 1676

[Robert Plot, *The Natural History of Oxfordshire*, 1676, pp. 239–40]

HOW many sorts of soils I met with in Oxfordshire, viz. clay, chalk, and others from their different mixtures called maum, redland, sour-ground, stone-brash, stony, sandy, and gravelly, were enumerated amongst earths, Chap. 3. It remains that we here give a particular account, by what arts they are tilled to the best advantage. And first of clay,

Which, if kind for wheat, as most of it is, hath its first tillage about the beginning of May; or as soon as barley season is over, and is called the fallow, which they sometimes make by a casting tilth, i.e. beginning at the outsides of the lands, and laying the earths from the ridge at the top. After this, some short time before the second tilth, which they call stirring, which is usually performed about the latter end of June, or beginning of July, they give this land its manure; which if horse dung or sheep's dung, or any other from the home stall, or from the mixen in the field, is brought and spread on the land just before this second ploughing. But if it be folded (which is an excellent manure for this land, and seldom fails sending a crop accordingly if the land be in tillage) they do it either in winter before the fallow, or in summer after it is fallowed. And these are the manures of clay land in the greatest part of Oxfordshire, only in and near the Chiltern; where beside these, it is much enriched by a soft mellow chalk that they dig from underneath it; when it is stirred, it lies again till the time of sowing wheat, except in a moist dripping year, when running to thistles and other weeds, they sometimes give it a second stirring, before the last for sowing.

All which tillages they are very careful to give it as dry as may be, ridging it up twice or thrice for every casting tilth (i.e. in their stirring, and for sowing, beginning at the top of the land and laying the earth still upwards to the ridge) by which means both land and corn lie drier, warmer, and healthier, and the succeeding crop becomes more free from weeds. After it is thus prepared, they sow it with wheat, which is its proper grain; and if it be a strong stiff clay, with that they call cone wheat; and the next year after (it being accounted advantageous in all tillage to change the grain) with beans; and then ploughing in the bean brush at All Saints, the next year with barley; and amongst the several sorts of that grain, if the land be rank, with that they call sprat barley; and then the fourth year it lies fallow, when they give it summer tilth again, and sow it with winter corn as before. But at most places where their land is cast into three fields, it lies fallow in course every third year, and is sown but two; the first with wheat, if the land be good, but if mean with miscellan [=maslin], and the other with barley and pulse promiscuously. And at some places where it lies out of their hitching, i.e. their land for pulse, they sow it but every second year, and there usually two crops wheat, and the third barley, always being careful to lay it up by ridging against winter; clay lands requiring to be kept high, and to lie warm and dry, still allowing for wheat and barley three ploughings, and sometimes four, but for other grains seldom more than one. When at any time they sow peas on this land, the best husbandmen will choose the Vale-gray as most proper for it; and if vetches, the gore or pebble-vetch; but if so cold a weeping clay that unfit for these, then they improve it with ray grass.

As for the chalk lands of the Chiltern hills, though it requires not to be laid in ridges in respect of dryness, yet of warmth it doth; when designed for wheat, which is but seldom, they give it the same tillage with clay, only laying it in four or six furrowed lands, and soiling it with the best mould or dung, but half rotten to keep it from binding, which are its most proper manures; and so for common barley and winter vetches, with which it is much more frequently sown, these being found the more suitable grains. But if it be of that poorest sort they call white land, nothing is so proper as ray grass mixed with Nonsuch, or melilot trefoil.

40. ARGUMENTS IN FAVOUR OF A LAND REGISTER, 1677

[Andrew Yarranton, *England's Improvement by Sea and Land*,
London, 1677, pp. 26–7]

ALL Scotland is under a register and worth 24 years' purchase; and on the other side in the north of Ireland, although but three hours' sail, is worth but 8 years' purchase; and in England on this side Tweed, it is worth but 16 years' purchase: the register is the cause. The manor of Taunton Dean in Somersetshire is under a register, and there the land is worth three and twenty years' purchase, although but a copyhold manor and at any time he that hath £100 a year in the manor of Taunton may go to the castle and take up £2,000 upon his lands and buy stuffs with the money, and go to London and sell his stuffs, and return down his monies and pay but five in the hundred for his monies and discharge his lands. This is the cause of the great trade and riches in and about Taunton Dean. (O happy Taunton Dean!) What gentleman can do thus with free lands? No, it is not worth 16 years' purchase all England over, one place with another; and if not timely put under a register, it will come to 12 years' purchase before long. Now you see a register is practicable in Scotland and also in England. And if it were so by Act of Parliament in these particular places I have formerly mentioned in this treatise, there would be no complaint for want of people or trade in England.

41. FATTENING YOUNG STOCK IN HERTFORDSHIRE, 1681

[John Houghton, *A Collection of Letters for the Improvement of Husbandry and Trade*, 1681, pp. 162–6]

The Way they fat Calves at Tring, in Hertfordshire

WHEN we would make an excellent fat calf, we choose a large cow-calf, and as soon as 'tis calved and clean, if it hath not strength enough to stand up and suck, we help it; and if it be a hard milched cow, we milk out some milk before the calf sucks; and while the calf sucks on one side, we always milk on the other, and so often the first day, as the calf sucks, and sometimes oftener, if the udder be apt to core, or the cow does not well give down her milk; and also, what the calf can't suck, we draw out even to the last drop . . .

The second day, and so forward, we milk twice a day all we can get out, and then let the calf suck, and she, for a while, will thus get enough; but as she grows bigger, we abate in our milking.

We keep the calf in a pen, such an one as described about rearing of milch cows; only this we tie, and give her just room to lie down, and hang by her a chalk stone to lick on, that it may be white, and a wisp of fine short hay, which the calf will now and then eat a little of.

When the calf is a week old we let it blood, by cutting off an inch of the tail, and let it bleed as long as it will, which never does hurt, and every week or ten days we cut another piece of the tail off, and always two or three days before it be killed; for we find that this bleeding both fattens and whitens the calf. Till this way of bleeding was brought in fashion into our town by one John Geree, a yeoman, we never could have so good calves as we have had since.

All the while we keep it very dry, and with clean wheat straw, some use bean straw, thinking it better, because it will lie hollow.

About nine weeks old we sell our calves, sometimes for 3*l.* 10*s.* apiece, seldom or never for less than 40*s.* although we are thirty mile from London. If the cow hath not milk enough, we let the calf suck two cows.

This is the method we use, and I like best; but I have known at Leyton in Essex, they cob their calves morning and evening with cobs made of boiled rice, and let the calves suck only what they can get after the cows are milked, and by this means, save so much milk; or buy their neighbours' calves, and fat with a few cows so many more calves. Some, with their rice prepared as afore, mix malt, flour, a little cream, and some powder of chalk. And I have heard of some that mix a little brandy with it, thinking it makes the calves sleep, and they fatten the faster.

Sometimes the calves are subject to a scouring, which we always cure by giving them two or three spoonfuls of rennet, or rubbing their mouths with a handful of salt.

The Way they fat Lambs for the London Market at Hadley, near Barnet in Hertfordshire

We take the lambs as soon as they are yeaned, and put them in a close, warm pen, and in a trough by them we put white peas and bran mixed together, and hang by it a handful of good fine hay, tied in a cord, as also a chalk stone for them to lick on. So let the ewes go in good grass, but bring them to the lambs four times a day, viz. at eight, twelve, four, and eight of the clock, that they may suck as much as they will, and let the youngest lamb suck first a little of every ewe, which the ewes will permit, after the lambs have been held to them, and they have been used to it a while. Then we let the next in course suck, and be sure the eldest at last, for we find that the last milk nourishes most.

Thus, if we can have early lambs, we can, after they are three weeks, or a month old, sell them for fifteen or sixteen shillings apiece.

When we sell any lambs off, we still let the rest suck all the ewes, as long as we have a lamb left. And some with us use much the same method in fatting of calves.

Notes on the 'Account of Fatting Calves and Lambs'[1]

The chalk stone to lick on, mentioned in page 163 [above, p. 175], I am afraid the country people think, because it is white, it makes the calf so, but I believe it is a great mistake. But I know that chalk is a great alkali, that is, a destroyer of acid or sharp matter, as may be seen by scraping a little into vinegar, juice of lemons, or any other sharp matter, for it will make a great effervescency or working, and after a while, take away the sharpness of the acid liquor. Now, if it be true that it is sharp or acid matter that hinders thriving, and often causes laskes or fluxes, then 'tis very reasonable that chalk may hinder leanness, and much help the colour of the veal. And whether this may not be a proper thing to give in milk to such as are in consumptions, and other pining leanness, I submit to the judgement of the learned . . .

The bigness and great consumption of London doth not only encourage the breeders of provisions and higglers thirty miles off, but even to four score miles; wherefore I think it will necessary follow, that if London by its bigness, or any other way, should consume as much again, the country within these four score miles would have a greater employment; or else, those that are further off will get some with them.

---

[1] These comments on the foregoing articles were added by the editor of the *Collections* John Houghton.

42. JOHN AUBREY ON WILTSHIRE AND HEREFORDSHIRE AGRICULTURE, 1684–5

[Bodleian Library, Oxford, MS. Aubrey 2,[1] ff. 83–9, 100–1, 123, 152–3]

Of Agriculture

CONSIDERING the distance of place where I now write, and the distance of time that I lived in this country, I am not able to give a satisfactory account of the husbandry thereof. I will only say of our husbandmen, as Sir Thomas Overbury does of the Oxford scholars, that they go after the fashion, that is, when the fashion is almost out, they take it up. So our countrymen are very late and very unwilling to learn or be brought to new improvements. The Devonshiremen were the earliest improvers. I heard Oliver Cromwell, Protector, tell the Lord Arundel of Wardour and the Lord Fitzwilliam that he had been in all the counties of England and that the Devonshire husbandry was the best. The Civil Wars did mightily refine our language, husbandry, and agriculture, and at length we have obtained a good deal of it which is now well known and need not be rehearsed. But William Scott of Heddington (a very understanding man in these things—country affairs) told me that since 1630 the fashion of husbandry in this country had been altered three times over: still refining. I wish I had taken the account of him but he is now lately dead.

Mr. —— Bishop of Merton first brought into the south of Wiltshire the improvement by burnbaking (Denshiring) about 1639. He learnt it in Flanders; it is very much used in this parish and their neighbours do imitate them. But they say *'tis good for the father, but naught for the son*! by reason it does so wear out the heart of the land. The way to restore it is by muck, but best of all by the fold. But for burnbaked land worn out that lies upon chalk, the best way is to sow it with cinquefoil. About 1674 my countrymen of North Wiltshire took up this way of burning; I think it began first about Lyneham.

From the River Avon in North Wiltshire to Cotswold the country is generally a stonebrash, and very natural to bear good barley. I do remember very well that before the Civil Wars wheat was rarely sowed in these parts. There were baked then twenty bushels of barley to one bushel of wheat. So that in those days the poor people and the hinds did eat only barley bread (which nowadays they would think a very hard fare). Since the aforesaid time, they have changed that course of husbandry (how rationally I know not. I something doubt—*Quippe solo natura subest*) and now they spend twenty bushels of wheat to one of barley.

At Patney (a manor of the Earl of Craven) they sow not their barley till about Whitsuntide and yet it is ripe as soon as barley in other places, which is

---

[1] This is John Aubrey's MS. of *The Natural History of Wiltshire*.

sown according to the course of husbandry in April. This barley is much bought for seed . . .

The improvement by cinquefoil (clover grass) (which now spreads much in the stone brash lands) was first used at North Wraxhall by Nicholas Hall, who came from Dundry in Somersetshire, about the year 1650. It turned to great profit to him, which hath made his neighbours to imitate him.

Two loads of turf will make above a load of ashes, and about ten loads of ashes will make any rushy, coarse, and mossy ground good for fine clover naturally for seven years, and good for ever. It is observed that ashes kill moss, and breed good grass, and amongst others the tare vetch. Quicklime kills furzes by liming the ground after the furzes are felled. . . .

The improvement of watering meadows began at Wylye about 1635 about which time I remember we began to use them at Chalke. Watering of meadows about Marlborough and so to Hungerford was (I remember) about 1646; and Mr. John Bayly of Bishopsdown (near Salisbury) about the same time made his great improvements by watering there, by Sir Thomas Bridges much about the same time. St. Nicholas Mead at Salisbury (14 acres) was let for 15*li.* per annum; now 'tis improved to £60 per annum.

In the street at Biddestone are several springs which do afford a constant stream and runs into the highway wherein is to be seen rich blue marl. Mr. —— Mountjoy about 1662 did turn this fat water that runs in the street as aforesaid by a gutter into a pasture ground of his, which by this means is improved from 5*li.* per annum to (at least) 25*li.* per annum so by the nitrous water and filth of the highway; and I hear he is farther continuing it.

But in the main those improvements do settle into a kind of equilibration, for as the values of lands are raised in one part of the country, they fall as much in another. For those excellent pastures at and about Wootton Bassett etc. where before was but little tillage, of late they break up and sow those rich pastures with corn.

Anciently in the Hundreds of Malmesbury and Chippenham were but few enclosures and those near houses. The north part of Wiltshire was in those days admirable for field sports, all vast champion fields as (yet) about Sherston and Marshfield. King Henry 7th brought in depopulations and that enclosures; and after the dissolution of the abbeys in Henry 8's time, more enclosing. About 1595 all between Easton Piers [= Easton Percy] and Castle Combe was a *campania* like Cotswold upon which it borders; and then Yatton and Castle Combe did intercommon together. Between these two parishes much hath been enclosed in my remembrance, and every day more and more. I do remember about 1633 but one enclosure in Chippenham field, which was at the north end; and by this time I think it is all enclosed. So all between Kington St. Michael and Draycot Cerne was common field; and the West Field of Kington St. Michael between Easton Piers and Heywood was enclosed in 1664. Then were a world of laborious people maintained by the plough, as they were then likewise in Northamptonshire. 'Tis observed that the enclosures of Northamptonshire have been unfortunate since and not one of them have prospered.

Carrots were first sown at Beckington in Somersetshire. Some very old men there (in 1668) did remember their first bringing thither (from Jo. Ash of Teffont Ewyas, esq.). Now there is plenty of them at Redehill especially, etc.

Mr. Alexander James, Alderman of Bristol, when he was a boy, all the turnips that they had there did come from Wales, and now they have great plenty of them about Bristol and better than those of Wales.

The mother of Mr. John Ash (the great clothier) was born at Weymouth in Dorsetshire, who remembered when all the cabbages were brought from Holland. She was eighty years old and upward when she died. This I had from her son, Mr. Samuel Ash of Langley Burrell.

Sir Anthony Ashley of Wimborne St. Johns in the county of Dorset had great plantations of cabbages. He was the first . . .

When did wheel ploughs come into use? I think but about 1630. They serve best in stony land. Foot ploughs are somewhat later. In north Wiltshire they plough with oxen. In south Wiltshire with horses.

Wagons not used (commonly) in south Wiltshire till about 1655. Before that they altogether did use carts which are now grown quite out of fashion. In 1632 Mr. Canent of Woodyates had the first from Amesbury. They at Amesbury saw the use of them by the professed wagon drivers to London . . .

But Jo. Shakespeare's wife of Worplesdon in Surrey, a North Wiltshire woman and an excellent housewife, does assure me that she makes as good cheese there as ever she did at Wraxhall or Biddestone; and that it is merely for want of art that her neighbours do not make as good. They send their butter to London. So it appears that some time or other, when [in] the Vale of Sussex and Surrey they have the North Wiltshire skill, that half the cheese trade of the markets of Tedbury and Marlborough will be lost . . .

Grounds that do yield excellent butter, do not yield good cheese *et vice versa*, e.g. at Pertwood and about Lydiard as good butter is made as any in England but the cheese is not so good. At and about Lydiard in those fat grounds in May etc. in hot weather the best housewives cannot keep the cheese from heaving. Sour woodsere grounds do yield the best cheese, and such are Cheshire. Bromefield (in the parish of Yatton) is so sour and wet and where I had better cheese made than anywhere in all the neighbourhood . . .

Falling of Rents

The falling of rents is a consequence of the decay of the Turkey trade, which is the principal cause of the falling of the price of wool. Another reason that conduces to the falling of the prices of wool is our women's wearing so much silk and Indian ware,[1] as they do. By these means my farm at Chalke is worse by £60 per annum than it was before the Civil Wars.

[1] The Indians do work for a penny a day, so their silks are exceeding cheap and rice is sold in India for 4*d.* per bushel.

The gentry living in London, the daily concourse of servants out of the country to London makes servants' wages dear in the country and makes scarcity of labourers.

The great quantity of corn that is brought into England from Scotland and Ireland and Danzig and other places beyond sea besides the improvement in Wales.

Memorandum: the increase of sainfoin now in most places fit for it. Improvements of meadows by watering, ploughing up of the King's forests and parks. But as to all these as 10,000*li.* is gained in the hill barren country, so the Vale does lose as much, which brings it to an equation.

A Digression

Remarks taken from Henry Milbourne, esq., concerning husbandry, trade, etc. in Herefordshire.

Irchenfield (sandy soil) about 1647 was the barrenest part of Herefordshire before the use of liming their land was known. Since it is grown very considerable for rye and barley, and now by the long use of lime the Leer. The nature of the ground is so much bound up that it far exceeds Monmouthshire (which is a clay ground) for wheat, which before furnished this part of the country with wheat. Now they buy their seed wheat and the rate of the land is so advanced by it that what before was not worth ten groats per acre for rye, now is worth eighteen shillings per acre for wheat, and so is let in several places; so where the lime does so well agree is in the sandy part of the country.

About 1661 they used to send their kine to Letton (rich pasturage which lies upon the side of the River Wye) and then generally paid a mark a cow for their pasture. Sent them at May and took them away at St. Andrew's Tide. And the owner of the land did provide people of the neighbourhood to milk the kine and make the butter and cheese; and they did proportionate (though they milked altogether) everyone's share so equally that they found as good advantage of their kine they sent thither as of those they kept at home; and the reason of the justness was because that the landlord had the more kine into his pasture, the more careful he was of it; and therefore, when he found any of the poor milkers faulty, that party should have no more kine the next year. And their whole being depending upon this way made them the more exact in it, for fear of being deprived.

Now they are fallen into the vein of clover, all their fashion is altered, and those which kept no kine before, now keep some 12, some 20, and they take care that they have two or three pieces of clover one under another, for it holds but three years at most. And that that makes it the more generally used is that they have lately learned to get out the seed, which before they bought from beyond the sea.

They thrash it on a hurdle, through which the seed falls. It is very small, as mustard seed. Before they thrash it, they grind it in a cider mill, and then thrash it four or five times. Ground that before was not worth ten groats per acre is worth (while clover holds) xxs. per acre, and nothing better to feed pigs than that. (The reason why liming is now left off is because clover supplies it.)

Note that as Irchenfield hath advantaged itself by crops of wheat, so they have a disadvantage in not having so good crops of barley as formerly they had after rye. 'Tis a proverb among them, I will pay you when I sell my barley and when I sell my wool, which were then the two commodities that brought in the money, both which are now decayed, viz. the barley by liming and the wool by the importation of Spanish wool, and also by making cloth so fine thin, that it doth not spend one half of the wool that formerly it did.

Formerly about 1637 or 1643 wool 35s. or 36s. per stone (= 12lbs.) and since sc. about 1666 or 1667 it hath been at xxs. or xxiis. per stone, whereby it is thought we go out of the fine Lemster [=Leominster] wool called the Lemster Ore and fall upon coarse wool and the body carcase of the Lemster sheep are not worth above ten groats or two shillings, whereas the body of the coarse-wool sheep is worth a crown or a noble, and twice as much wool; and were it not for the compost that is made of the fine-wool sheep, they would not keep any fine-wool sheep.

At Canon Pyon, they do affirm that liming of their lands hath made their wool coarse. About Lemster in regard that lime is very scarce, they sow it out of a seed lip as they do corn and thereby do make very good manure for their ground as in any other part of the country they do by heaps. Liming of ground began about 1590s or some time after the bringing in of tobacco by Sir Walter Raleigh ...

43. THE CONDITION OF POOR FARM TENANTS, 1691

['The Reverend Richard Baxter's Last Treatise', ed. F. J. Powicke, *Bulletin of the John Rylands Library*, X, no. 1, 1926, pp. 21–2, 25–8, 37–9]

The Husbandman's and the Nation's Advocate and Petition to Racking Landlords

Gentlemen,

Though these lines must expect to meet with much prejudice, I beseech you let them not be rejected with so much contempt as to be denied your perusal and sober consideration. They are short and you find time for work of less importance. Because they that live in ease and fulness do seldom truly know the case of the laborious and poor, I will first describe the matter of fact and tell you truly the poor husbandman's case, and consequently, the case of England, and then I will tell you the importance of this case, and next the causes of it, and lastly the cure so far as it is curable.

Chap. 1
The matter of fact described

The body of this kingdom consisteth of land-proprietors, of hand-labourers, of tradesmen and merchants, and of the literate professions of divers sorts. The land-proprietors are such as use their land by themselves and servants, or by tenants. These tenants are they whose case I am now to open and plead. The husbandmen are the stamen[1] of the commonwealth. All the rest do live by them. It is the fruits of the earth and of their labours (with a little addition of fishing) that maintaineth all. And yet whose case is so hard as theirs? Gentlemen say, our land is our own and therefore we may make the best of it for our own commodity, and he that will give most for it shall be our tenant.

The old custom was to let lands by lease for lives or for a long term of years, and to take a fine at first and a small yearly rent afterward, and so, when a man, with his marriage portion, had taken a lease he lived comfortably afterward and got somewhat for his children. But now in most countries the custom is changed into yearly rack-rents:[2] or, if a man takes a lease for many years it is yearly to pay as much as the tenement is worth and that is as much as any man will give for it, and in all counties the small livings are the far greatest number: where there is one of £80 or £70 or £60, yea or £50 value, there are many of £30 or £20 or £10 or £5. And what will one of £10 or £20 do towards the charge of stocking and manuring it, and the maintaining of himself, wife, and children with food and clothing, and paying them for their labour. And how hard will it be after all this, to pay for it £20 rent? And greater livings must have a greater stock and more servants and labourers to manage them. But usually such have the better advantage, having much to sell besides what maintaineth them. But few have so good a bargain as to lay up anything considerable for their children. It's well if all their care and toil will serve to pay their rent . . .

The case of their servants, could they but continue so and contain themselves from marriage, is far easier than of the poor tenants that are their masters. For they know their work and wages, and are troubled with no cares for paying rents, or making good markets, or for the loss of corn or cattle, the rotting of sheep, or the unfavourable weather, nor for providing for wife and children and paying labourers' and servants' wages.

But the condition of their landlords' household servants is as far above these poor tenants as a gentleman is above a day labourer. They live in fullness to the satisfying of the flesh and comparatively in idleness. They feed on the variety of flesh and fish that cometh from their masters' tables, when the poor tenants are glad of a piece of hanged bacon once a week, and some few that can kill a bull eat now and then a bit of hanged beef, enough to try the stomach of an ostrich. He is a rich man that can afford to eat a joint of

---

[1] The stamen is the warp in an upright loom.
[2] A rent equal or nearly equal to the value of the land.

fresh meat (beef, mutton, or veal) once in a month or fortnight. If their sow pig or their hens breed chickens, they cannot afford to eat them, but must sell them to make their rent. They cannot afford to eat the eggs that their hens lay, nor the apples or pears that grow on their trees (save some that are not vendible) but must make money of all. All the best of their butter and cheese they must sell, and feed themselves, and children, and servants with skimmed cheese and skimmed milk and whey curds. And through God's mercy all this doth them no harm. But how great is the difference between their diet and labour and case and that of the poorest household servants of lords, knights, and gentlemen; the poor tenant taketh every foot boy or groom or porter of his landlord to be a gentleman whose favour seemeth a preferment to him: but if a butler, or a chamberlain, or a clerk, or steward do but smile on him he thinks he is blest.

It is much easier with the handicrafts labourer that hath a good trade. A joiner or a turner can work in the dry house with tolerable or pleasant work and knoweth his price and wages. A weaver or a shoemaker or a tailor can work without the wetting or tiring of his body, and can think and talk of the concerns of his soul without impediment to his labour. I have known many [at Kidderminster] that weave in the long loom that can set their sermon notes or a good book before them and read and discourse together for mutual edification while they work. But so the poor husbandman can seldom do. And though the labour of a smith be hard, it is in a dry house and but by short fits; and little, in comparison of threshing and reaping, but as nothing in comparison of mowing, which constantly pulls forth a man's whole strength. And though a poor carrier hath a toilsome life, going through all weathers and all roads, yet he knoweth his work and wages, and is free from abundance of the husbandman's losses and cares. The same I may say of others that work in iron: the nailers and spurriers and scythesmiths and swordmakers and all the rest about Dudley and Stourbridge and Brumicham [= Birmingham] and Walsall and Wedgbury [= Wednesbury] and Wolverhampton and all that country. They live in poverty, but not in the husbandman's case. They know their work and pay; and have but little further care. The same I may say of fishermen at sea. Labour is tolerable and knoweth its time and bounds, and their care is but to catch their fish and sell it. As to seamen and soldiers, if they be such as only make a trade of serving the covetousness of merchants, or of killing men for their military gain or honour or a licentious tyrannical life, rather than for the good or safety of the Commonwealth, I shall not bring them into comparison, but acknowledge them more miserable than the husbandman and than a highway robber is than any honest labourer, or the wolf than the sheep that shall not escape the pastor's revenge, though he tear the lambs. . . Among merchants, mercers, drapers, and other corporation-tradesmen, and among weavers, tailors, and such like labourers, yea among poor nailers, and such like, there is usually found more knowledge and religion than among the poor enslaved husbandmen.

I may well say enslaved: for none are so servilely dependent (save household servants and ambitious expectants) as they are on their landlords. They dare not displease them lest they turn them out of their houses; or increase their rents. I believe that their great landlords have more command of them than the king hath. If a landlord be but malignant, an enemy to piety or sobriety or peace, his enslaved tenants are at his beck to serve him, in matters of any public consequence. And of old time it was worse than it is now; when every earl or baron or bishop could do much towards raising of an army, and all their dependents would follow them. And in Scotland it was worse, and in Ireland, and in other lands where the lord could raise war against their king upon discontents, till kings were fain to take them down, as they now are. And all this cometh from the enslaving of husbandmen.

In all this the reader must know that I speak not the case of all husbandmen, but of the racked poor. I doubt not but some that live about London, or that know not the common case, will say that I misreport it, and it is not so bad, and that husbandmen live as plentifully and contentedly as others. But (1) I speak not of freeholders that pay no rent; (2) I speak not of the richer sort (who are few) that have lands of their own, besides their farms; there are near London some husbandmen that have per annum £200, £300, £400, yea £500 lands of their own, that in remote parts would pass for gentlemen of great rank; (3) nor do I speak of Middlesex and the parts near it, especially near London; for though they pay double for their grounds, they have treble opportunity to improve them and to make their rents so. They have all the dung of the city, cow dung, horse dung, and cold ashes for the carriage; and when their horse teams bring hay or other vendibles to London to be sold, it is small trouble to carry back a load of dung, which they do at ten or twelve miles distance at least. And there they make a great dung hill, of one row of the superficies of the green earth, and another row of weeds, and another of lime, and so again and again, till it be near two yards high; and this they leave many months to rot, and then carry it to their ground. And they come near 20 miles for waggon loads of old rotten rags, which some make great gain by selling, hiring abundance of poor people to rake them out of dunghills. And though they give a great price for them, it so much furthereth their grass and corn as fully recompenseth their cost and labour. And, above all, London is a market which will take up all that they bring, so that nothing vendible need to stick on their hands; and, by garden stuffs and by peas and beans and turnips, they can make more gain of their grounds, than poor country tenants can do of ten times the same quantity.

And they that live but 30 or 40 miles off, that have rich pasture grounds, will never want a market at London for their lambs and fat sheep, and their fat cattle, and pigs, and geese, and whatever they can spare: when even the countries an hundred miles off think it worth the great cost of sending droves of swine and cattle in the London markets; yea, even from Ireland by sea and land. And Gloucestershire, Suffolk, Warwickshire, etc., send their charge to this all devouring market. And I suppose those that live near other great cities, as York, Norwich, Bristol, etc., have some good degree of the same advantage. (4) Nor do I speak of those tenants that have some small tenement of £5 or £10 per annum, and have besides a trade which doth maintain them. A weaver, a butcher, a tailor, a joiner, a carpenter may afford to pay his landlord's rent, which another cannot that hath nothing but the ground to live upon. These exceptions premised, it is the ordinary case of racked poor tenants that have no other trade to live on, that I am speaking of. . .

*   *   *

Chap. 4

The Remedies of the poor Husbandman's Case proposed to Rich Landlords

I am not, after so long experience, so ignorant of the pravity of corrupted nature as to expect any universal or general success of anything that I, or any wiser man, can say. . .

Gentlemen (mistake me not) the sum of my request to you is but this that you will regard the public welfare of the nation above any few particular cases, and the interest of Christian religion in the souls of men above all your worldly interest and fleshly pleasure, and that you will on such accounts set your lands to the poorer sort of your tenants at such rates as by their labour and frugality they may comfortably live on, so as not to be necessitated by care for their rents, and by tiresome excess of labour, to be strangers to God's word, and to forbear family religion, and to be prayerless or sleep when they should pray, and to live in ignorance for want of good books or time to read them, and think of what they hear at church; and that poverty constrain them not to educate their children like themselves. This [is] all that I have now to request of you.

In order to this, I think it would be a blessed example to the nation, if to such poor tenants you would abate a third part of your rack rents. (Some great ones that know where I was born, may know what I instance in.)[1] When most tenants fifty years ago sat on the old rents, perhaps some one landlord set his land on the rack rent from year to year, and was hardly spoken of for it by all the country. If another come and buy his land and then raise it higher and set that at £50 or £60 which he set at £40, and that at £40 which he set at £30, and that at £4 which he set at £2 or £3, may not I justly petition that the poor people may have the clemency of their former rack which they called *cruelty*? This is no rare case. Few scruple raising rents to as much as they can get, when poor men, rather than beg and have no dwelling, will promise more than they can pay; and then, with care and toil, make shift as long as they can; and then run away and do so in another country. And so the gentlemen lose more by their racking then they get, whereas if they would abate a third part, and let their tenants live a comfortable life, they might have their rents constantly paid, and have the

---

[1] Crossed through in the MS.

people's love, and partake of the comforts of those that are benefited or comforted by them.

To this end I humbly entreat you, Gentlemen, to retrench your needless and sinful charges for superfluities, prodigality, and fleshly lust. That you may not need so much to feed your sin as will not leave you enough to discharge your duty to God and to the poor. Cannot you live as healthfully and decently with fewer dishes, and less variety, and less cost and curiosity, and less ostentation, attendance, and pomp? Do not your tables and your furniture speak unbelief and contempt of Christ?

44. THE ADVANTAGES OF ENCLOSURE, 1697

[Leonard Meager, *The Mystery of Husbandry: or Arable, Pasture, and Woodland Improved*, 1697]

Wonderful Improvement of Land, by planting Trees, and by Enclosures; shewing the Advantage of it over those Lands that lie in Common

WOOD may be greatly improved by enclosing ground with it for corn and pasture; yielding a great many advantages to the painful husbandman, whose good industry well deserves a good recompense.

First, for that well-grown trees, and good hedgerows, shelters his tender corn, etc. from bleak winds; and keep off the blastings that would much annoy it, even when grown.

Secondly, it is a great advantage to pasture lands, in sheltering cattle, both in the heat of summer, and in the the extreme of winter; as also from violent storms of rain, hail, or snow, etc.

Thirdly, it secures corn from high roads being made into it by idle persons and cattle; which, if it lay in common, or open, could not be avoided, since those that know not the toil and cost the husbandman is at to bring his crop to a harvest, little regard what havoc they make through laziness, for wanton disportment, or the nearest way; which, if there were a barrier of good fence, they could not do: and then for cattle, it saves the trouble of pounding, and many frivolous suits, that frequently arise on trespasses of these kinds; and therefore is advantageous both to the owner of the one and the other.

Fourthly, trees growing up, their lops afford much fuel and fencing, perpetually supplying the owner with both, as occasion requires; and indeed few know the scarcity of the first so well as those that live distant from enclosures, in open champion countries, where coals cannot at all, or at least, without great charge and labour, be had; not only the pinching winters afflict these, but even their necessary occasions of brewing, baking, and dressing their provision, make them sensible to their great cost and loss of time, that the planting of trees is extremely beneficial, for that, being at hand, they may keep it in a readiness, by getting it in, and laying it up to dry at leisure times,

to their great comfort and advantages; and be profited in selling the overplus
to the rich, and charitably bestowing some on their poor neighbours; and,
for their Christian compassion towards them, be loaded with their blessings
and prayers; and of this, one Mr. Tusser, one very much experienced in
rural affairs, in his old fashioned rhyme thus speaks:

> The woodland above all I praise,
> The champion delighteth not me . . .

There is, indeed, a great difference in the advantage arising between
enclosures or woodlands, and such as lie open; and though some may be apt
to grudge at the enclosing of commons, yet, were there a good measure taken
therein, it would greatly turn to the advantage of the poor, and much improve the riches of the nation; there being so much good land, lying as it were
waste, might be enclosed and let to the benefit of the poor; to the great easing
of the parishes, and advantaging those that claim a right therein, three or four
times more than what now it can; for the poor having little stock to put there,
the rich make their advantage, who have much; which, if it was enclosed, and
let out for the general benefit, they could not do; and so thereby the stock of
corn would be greatly advanced; and, in some years, a good improvement of
timber might be made, many commons and moors, that now lie in a manner
waste and are of little profit, being capable with a little industry of producing
equal with lands of a good value; so that things thus rightly stated, everyone
concerned might have a right understanding, and be highly satisfied in so
good a work.

Consider, in this case, where the grounds are enclosed, how happily
people live: as in Hertfordshire, Essex, Kent, Berkshire, Surrey, Wiltshire,
Somersetshire, Hampshire, and others; all which not only raise corn for themselves, but supply other open countries, and even the great City of London,
which consumes a vast quantity thereof; and yet no parts of England set a
greater rate, or make a greater advantage by grazing.

Therefore, I must say that all interests upon commons, or rights of common
pasture upon any of these lands, may, without prejudice to any particular
interest, be advantaged, and much improvement made to the public, considering what vast quantities of land lie, as I may term it, waste, some overrun
with molehills, anthills, gorse, fern, briars, twitch-grass, and the like; others
under water, for the want of opening the currents, and passages for brooks,
or water descending from hills, for, whilst it lies thus, everyone concludes it
not his business, and so it lies neglected; and many, however, claim their part
in it that will bestow neither cost nor labour in making it fit for good pasture,
or corn land; though, if it was so ordered, it might prove in a little time the
enriching of them, and be a means to disburden the parish, by the rents
arising therefrom, of the chargeable poor, and be a means to employ labouring
men; so that every one would live at ease from encumbrances, or suffering
wants.

III. INDUSTRIES

1. A PETITION FROM WEST MIDLAND METAL WORKERS AGAINST THE ENGROSSING OF IRON, 1603

[The Staffordshire Quarter Sessions Rolls, V, 1603–6, ed. S. A. H. Burne, Collections for a History of Staffordshire, 1940, pp. 19–22]

[Petition, undated, addressed to the King's justices from 'A multitude of his poor and oppressed subjects']

WHEREAS diverse and sundry persons in the counties of Stafford, Warwick, Worcester, and Salop which were brought up in the mysteries or manual occupations of nailers, buckle-making, spurriers, locksmiths, lorimers, stirrup-makers, and such like sciences and certain other persons of other trades being all now grown into wealth and having given over their said trades of making the said wares and other trades wherein they were brought up, have used of late to buy the said wares of others that do make them and to sell the same in other countries. Who do now engross or get into their hands the most part of all the iron made in those woodland countries and then do sell the same by retail, some in bars and some slit, or in other manner at excessive and very great prices, whereby the poorer sort can have no iron to work or very little but at their hands and that at a very unreasonable rate. And do also now altogether refuse to buy any nails, buckles, spurs, locks, bridlebits, stirrups, arrowheads, or any such like wares of any the makers thereof for ready money, but constrain them to depart with and sell unto them their said wares by way of exchange for iron, corn, malt, leather, tin, brass, and divers such like things (as mercery wares and grocery wares and drapery) at such excessive dear and unreasonable rates that they cannot any longer live by their said sciences by means whereof some twenty or thirty persons using the said oppressive kind of trading are exceedingly of late enriched and many thousands of the said poor artificers of the said trades, together with many blacksmiths, whitesmiths, stringers of iron, and other the workers thereof are all ready to beg their bread not only to the great ruin, hurts, and miseries of themselves and their families, but also to the hindrance, impoverishing, and utter decay of all of the inhabitants there by the daily increasing of many beggars. Wherefore they pray that it may be ordered as followeth:

1. That no person or persons whatsoever (except blacksmiths, stringers of iron, and free and lawful ironmongers shall or may buy any iron either in bars, lumps, or billets to sell the same again to any person or persons either slit, unslit, or otherwise howsoever until it shall be wrought and made into such ware as the buyer thereof shall use to make and may lawfully make.

2. That no chapman, buyer, carrier, or driver of nails, buckles, locks, spurs, stirrups, bridlebits, and such like wares whatsoever shall buy any iron in bars, lumps, billets, or otherwise howsoever either slit or unslit to sell, exchange, or put away again to any person or persons unless they shall have the same made and converted into wares in their own shops according as hath been heretofore used and most usually accustomed.

3. That no chapman, driver, carrier, or buyer of nails, buckles, spurs, locks, stirrups, bridlebits, arrowheads, or any such like wares whatsoever or any other person or persons whatsoever shall constrain, compel, enforce, or bind (either directly or indirectly) any the makers of any the said wares to buy, receive, or take iron of any person or persons whatsoever or to exchange their wares with any person or persons for iron, corn, malt, leather, tin, brass, or any other thing whatsoever. But that every such artificer shall and may buy his iron where he will without restraint, let, interruption, or hindrance.

4. That no nailer which may lawfully keep or set others on work shall at any time hereafter keep ma——[1] to work on his trade any more persons at once than shall dwell, inhabit, and lodge within his own —— or shall have, keep, or take at any one time as —— whereof the one shall have served four years at the least before he shall take the other, saving [that it shall be] lawful for any nailer to bring up his own children in his said trade as apprentices to him at [. . .]

*   *   *

[Petition of the chapmen of Walsall, 20 June 1603,
addressed to the justices]

Whereas we understand that complaint is made to your wor[ships] against our chapmen dwelling in and about Walsall for buying, selling, and ——, craftsmen thereabouts, with pretence that the same will tend to a general spoil and undoing of a great number of artificers —— for that the same our chapmen, being carriers to London and elsewhere, do buy wares of the same craftsmen and carry —— whereby (as is suggested) they greatly enrich themselves and do not a little impoverish the other. And because we —— wor: know the truth and ground of this complaint, we are bold to certify thus much: that we and divers and —— men do not only buy of them iron at as reasonable a rate as others in our parts, being no carriers, do usually sell —— dealing with them for the same have the better utterance of our wares at their hands, there for ready money or iron or —— for our wares readily wrought and resting upon us which hath been and is a very great supply and

[1] MS. damaged.

help unto us and our —— specially at such times of the year as in the winter season when our wares rest most upon us not uttered. And besides if —— our chapmen should be restrained in this course, the poorer sort, not having ready money to pay for iron, would be —— the exercising of their said craft and put to other labours, and so in fine grow thereby to extreme —— at home with us hath sufficiently proved. And a few of the better and richer sort of craftsmen about us (—— ready money for the iron they buy) shall thereby reap the greater benefit, which would turn to a greater and more —— now it is. And therefore we humbly pray your worships to have due consideration of the premises, and so crave —— from Walsall this xxth of June, 1603.

Your worship's poor Craftsmen,

Mr. Greene, lorimer, Robt. Ball, [and 24 other signatures].

[Note added.] It is agreed by the motion of the justices at these Sessions that Henry Stone, John Hall, and John Turtons, three of the parties supposed engrossers —— petition of the common petitioners for the hardware men shall upon —— (to pay ready money for any wares they buy of the petitioners —— own offers cease to buy and engross any more iron for three months next —— nsides whereof in case all others likewise complained on shall not so —— cease to buy and engross iron and other wares within the said three months that after the said three months the said Hall, Stone, and Turton shall be at liberty as now they —— for that the said justices have found them very reasonable in their answers to the said petition.

Robert Stanford, William Crompton

2. THE PERSONAL GOODS OF A WORCESTERSHIRE SCYTHESMITH, 1605

[John S. Roper, Belbroughton Wills and Probate Inventories, 1539–1647, Dudley, 1967–8, p. 51]

A TRUE inventory of all the goods and chattels of one Richard Prin, late of the parish of Belbroughton in the county of Worcester, scythesmith, deceased; taken and indifferently praised [=appraised] by Nicholas Badger, Thomas Cox, ... Thomas Badger, and John Cox, the 7th day of May, *anno Domini* 1605, in the third year of the reign of our sovereign Lord James by the grace of God of England, France, and Ireland, King, Defender of the Faith, etc., and of Scotland the 38th.

	£	s.	d.
Imprimis his purse, girdle, dagger, and all his other apparel, praised at		3	6	8
In the Hall:			
Item, one table board, one form, two chairs, one cupboard, and benches, etc.			10	0

In the Chambers:

Item, four bedsteads, one feather bed, flock beds, bolsters, and other furniture to them belonging, praised at		10	0	0
Item, sheets and all manner of apry [=napery] ware, praised at		3	6	8
Item, one press and coffers, praised at		1	0	0
Item, all manner of brass and pewter, etc.		3	6	8
Item, all manner of treen and coupery ware, praised at			13	4
Item, cupboards, broches, pothooks, links, hatchet axe, and other iron implements of husbandry			8	0

In the Smithy:

Item, two anvils, bellows, and all other working tools, praised at		5	0	0
Item, all iron and steel unwrought, praised at		9	0	0
Item, all scythes ready wrought, price		100	0	0
Item, corn and malt within the house and corn unthreshed		5	0	0
Item, corn on the ground, praised		7	0	0
Item, 7 kine and one weaning calf, price		14	0	0
Item, sheep praised at		12	0	0
Item, one mare and a colt, praised at		3	6	8
Item, store swine		1	0	0
Item, poultry praised at				18
Item, one cart and one pair of harrows with all things praised and unnamed, etc.		2	0	0

Summa £180 19s. 6d.

3. THE DORSET CLOTH INDUSTRY, 1608

[P.R.O., E 134, 6 Jas. I, Easter 30]

[Depositions of witnesses taken at Lyme Regis, Dorset, April 8, 6 Jas. I, in the course of an enquiry concerning the making and export of Dorset, Devonshire, and Cornish dozens]

RICHARD BLACHEFORD, the elder, of Dorchester in the said county of Dorset, merchant, aged three score years or thereabouts, sworn and examined . . .

To the second interrogatory this deponent saith that . . . he did cause to be made many a thousand of the said cloths [i.e. Dorset dozens] forty years past and sithence, and yet doth continue the making of them, and saith that at his first making of the said cloths he made them in Devonshire with yarn which he bought in Dorsetshire, and did likewise make Devonshire kersies at that time with yarn spun and bought in Devonshire . . .

To the fourth interrogatory he saith that he knoweth that the said cloths called Dorsetshire dozens are transported into some parts of Normandy and most of all into Base Brittaine, and the cause why those countries do buy of the said cloths sooner than of the better woollen cloths made within this kingdom is for that the people of the country are poor and of a base disposition and will not go to the price of good cloth.

To the fifth interrogatory he saith that the said Dorsetshire dozens are made of the coarsest of the wools grown within the county of Dorset, which coarse wools whereof the said Dorsetshire dozens are now made were about forty years past employed in making of pinned whites and coarse linens.[1]

To the sixth interrogatory he saith that the said Dorsetshire dozens are made of the coarsest sort of the wool growth within the said county of Dorset for such as buy the wools to spin up in yarn do make two sorts, whereof the best is spun and sold into Wiltshire and Somerset to make fine broad cloths and fine Reading kersies and the coarsest is bought to be employed into Dorsetshire dozens. And this deponent further saith that there is usually paid for spinning of every pound of the better sort of the said yarn converted into broad cloths and Readings as aforesaid 4d., whereas is usually paid for every pound of the worser sort of the said yarn converted to make Dorsetshire dozens 2d., 2½d., and not above 3d. . . .

And this deponent further saith that a Dorsetshire dozen containeth in length some 9, some 10, and none above 12 yards, and in breadth with hard racking them . . . about a yard, and in weight about 9 or 10 lbs., and so hath continued from the time of his first knowledge of them. And saith that about forty years past there was little cloth or none at all made within the county of Dorset except coarse linens and pinned whites and that he this deponent was one of the first that brought the trade of making of Dorsetshire dozens into the said county of Dorset.

To the seventh interrogatory he saith that the Devonshire dozens are made of the best wool that can be gotten in the county of Devon and most hand washed, and that every Devonshire dozen doth contain 12 yards and upwards in length and in breadth one yard and quarter or thereabouts and doth weigh 12 lbs and better. And this deponent further saith that the Devonshire dozens are accompted generally beyond the seas the truest made cloth within this realm . . .

To the eighth interrogatory he saith that the said Dorsetshire dozens are usually bought from the weaver's beam, some at 12s., some 14s., and so upwards to 22s. the best or thereabouts. And that the said Devonshire and Cornish dozens are usually sold for £4, £3, 40s. the dozen and the worst at 30s., and further thinketh in his conscience 6 Dorsetshire dozens one with the other as they are usually transported are worth £5 8s. and no more.

To the ninth interrogatory he saith that in such places within the dominions of France where this deponent hath by the space of these thirty years past traded, the usual custom hath been to pay 6 sous for every Dorsetshire dozen which is about 7d. sterling and for every Devonshire dozen 12

---

[1] Another deponent says pinned whites, plain whites, and coarse cottons.

sous, which is about 14*d.* sterling, and knoweth the same to be true by the
several accompts of his factors.

4. LEASE AND AGREEMENT FOR HOATHLY IRON FORGE IN THE KENTISH WEALD, 1614

[*Kentish Sources III. Aspects of Agriculture and Industry*,
ed. E. Melling, 1961, pp. 96–7]

[Agreement for leasing Hoathly Forge, 1614]

31th day of March, 1614

I T I S agreed betwixt Sir Edward Filmer, knight, and Thomas Saunders of
Wadhurst in the county of Sussex, gentleman, in form following:

That whereas the said Thomas hath had in use the occupation of a forge
called Hothleige forge of the said Sir Edward to work out iron by the ton at a
certain price agreed between them and for that the time of agreement was
ended at the Annunciation of our Blessed Lady the Virgin Mary last past it
is now further agreed by these presents.

That the said Thomas Saunders and Thomas Ballard of the said parish of
Wadhurst, gentlemen, shall have the free use and occupation of the foresaid
forge together with the cottages and other easements as they have had to
work out iron, yielding and paying to the said Sir Edward and his assigns
the sum of thirteen shillings and four pence for every ton of iron they have or
shall work out in the said forge from the said feast of the Annunciation till
the feast of St. Michael next ensuing.

And for every ton of iron they shall work from the said feast of St. Michael
next ensuing till the Annunciation of the Virgin Mary one thousand six
hundred and fifteen, ten shillings for every ton; quarterly to be paid.

That the said Thomas Saunders doth covenant and promise for the said
Thomas Ballard, that they shall bring into the said forge over and above the
coals which now are at the said forge, four hundred load of coals at the least
to be wrought out and shall work the same betwixt this and our Lady Day
1615, if the season and time will give leave, and if it shall become any of the
said coals to be left at the said Lady Day not wrought out, the workmen
doing their best endeavours.

That then it shall be lawful for them to work out the rest of coals so left
unwrought out forthwith at the said price of thirteen shillings four pence to
be paid to the said Sir Edward, his heirs or assigns.

That the said Sir Edward is to find all reparations of timber work, accept
helves[1] and arms, so that the workmen do not wilfully or negligently spoil
the same.

And that the said Thomas is to leave up the said forge with all the tools,

---

[1] A handle of a hammer.

bellows, and other implements sufficient and fit to work with, at the end of the working out of the said coals.

Provided and it is agreed betwixt the said parties that if the said Sir Edward be determined otherwise to dispose of the said forge for this present year, that then if the said Sir Edward shall give notice of such intention within fourteen days after the date hereof, that then the said Thomas having liberty to work out the coals now lying at the said forge at the price of 13s. 4d. aforesaid that then it shall be free for the said Sir Edward otherwise to dispose of the said forge, after such coals wrought out as aforesaid, anything to the contrary notwithstanding.

In witness whereof to the one part of these articles remaining in the custody of the said Sir Edward Filmer, knight, the said Thomas Saunders have put to his hand and seal and to the other part remaining in the custody of the said Thomas Saunders the said Sir Edward Filmer have put to his hand and seal the day and year first above written.

5. ALDERMAN COCKAYNE'S PROJECT FOR DYEING ENGLISH CLOTH, 1614

[Astrid Friis, *Alderman Cockayne's Project and the Cloth Trade*, Copenhagen and London, 1927, pp. 459–63, 468–9, 472–3]

[Notes made by Julius Caesar at Privy Council meetings relating to Alderman Cockayne's Project]

Sir George Coppin

The Answer of the Merchants of the East Countries, that the country shall receive more benefit by dressing of cloths at home, than sending them unwrought abroad: 1,500 cloths broad sold weekly in London which costeth 12,000*li*. Merchants will not presently buy them. Dyeing stuff will not be presently provided. No wools to be sent overseas. The Merchants Adventurers of all companies excepted out of the consultation for the certificates. Stay the transportation of wool and of the transportation of bucks and sheep and of fullers earth. 5 E. 6. cap. 6[7] forfeiture upon transportation of wool. *Salus reipublicae suprema lex est.* Much wool carried to Scotland, and from thence to Camphire in the Low Countries, where there is a staple of wool. The French certificate that if it would not hinder the trade, whereof we doubt, it would be better to have our cloths dressed and dyed in England. A certificate from the Turkey merchants to like purpose. A certificate from the Spanish company to the like purpose. The Eastland merchants certificate, 2° to like purpose. The grounds of particular licences are always private; the statute of 8 Eliz. which gave licence to transport white cloths, would that of ten to be transported, but 9 might be transported white, and the tenth dressed. 3 H. 7. cloths of 4 marks. 5 H. 8. cloths of 5 marks. Queen Elizabeth granted to the merchants the carriage of 30,000 white cloths yearly.

Three questions.
1. Whether they will transport the dressed cloths, if all dressed.
2. Whether they will buy up 50,000 cloths yearly.
3. Whether they will pacify foreign princes upon their refusal of such cloths.
   Fishing and trading the upholders of this State.
   Fishing translated over to the Hollanders and if trading too, then all is gone.
1. To the 1. They will venture to the said places where the goods are sold.
2. To the 2. They would buy all the cloths as before and so are able.
3. To the 3. The merchants are no plenipotentiaries, but they will do the like
   endeavours.

*   *   *

4 Julii 1614
The business of the dyeing all the cloth to be transported over sea

Of 80 thousand cloths yearly transported, 50,000 cloths are offered to be dyed
by some few. Middelburg, Hamburg, and Stade offer to take all our
dyed and dressed cloths. Our cloth dyed in England better than any foreign
cloth whatsoever. The Low Countries make 20,000 cloths a year, and Germany as many. The new company offered to join with the Merchants
Adventurers, and to adventure with them in their white cloths, or to take
their cloths from them, giving for every cloth 6s. for gain. That there are
now 700,000*li.* worth of cloth transported, whereof 300,000*li.* in credit, the
rest in money. But now the new company will be provided of 1,100,000*li.*
in stock.

Reasons against our English dyeing.
1. They will not buy dressed and dyed cloth, because they will have their
inhabitants employed.
2. The English cannot dye so well as the strangers.
3. The want of the materials in England.
4. The stand of trade in England by this new invention.
5. To change a settled estate into an hope was never held good policy.
6. It is not feasible to send so many cloths dyed, as are now vented undyed;
and then better to set one 1,000 men on work in making cloth, than 100 men
on work in dyeing.

Points concluded

1. That this new company is profitable to the State, and can maintain the
trade, if the Merchants Adventurers will join with them.
2. The Merchants Adventurers refuse to join with them, because they fear,
by experience, that they shall not have vent for the dyed cloths, unless they
shall carry away dyed cloths.
3. If the Low Countries can make 15,000 cloths and Germany the like, the
loss of that will hurt England more, than the dyeing of cloths will profit the
land.

4. A cloth dyed and dressed may be strained, viz. after the first shearing, but cannot be strained after the workmanship is perfected.

If we keep from the Low Countries our wool and fullers earth, they cannot live without our cloth, albeit dyed and dressed in England. There shall be strangers fetched over, who shall dye and dress the cloths here, as well as the cloths dyed and dressed beyond the seas. The strangers beyond sea dye and dress the cloths more truly and more cheaply, than the English do. The cloths dyed and dressed in England may come to the mart beyond the seas, being dyed at any time of the year. At Artevelde[?] and Delft the water reasonable there to dye, but not in other places there; neither can they dye for 3 months of the year, as we may in England. A certificate *in ann.* 8 Elizab. from the Lord Mayor to the Lords of the Council, testifying the good and sufficient dyeing and dressing of cloths in England.

[At the top of a separate column.]

Ante tempus meritum, in tempore debitum, post tempus peccatum. My Lord Cooke.

*   *   *

9 Julii 1614
Dyeing and dressing of cloth in England. At the Council table

The benefit of this kingdom will be improved to 300,000*li.* by dyeing and dressing of cloths in England. 2 things considerable: materials, workmanship. Materials are oade, alum, brasil, cochenilo, indico, anele, fullers earth, either growing plentifully here, as oade, alum, and fullers earth, the rest easily brought hither. 80,000 white cloths carried over sea yearly which cost 140,000*li.* the dyeing there. Here one —[?] offereth the dyeing and perfect dressing of 50,000 cloths, and strangers Dutchmen offered to come over hither and teach our men here the perfect workmanship.

Obj. And since the stock of providing the said 80,000 cloths must be 700,000*li.*

Resp. It is provided by the new company that there shall be a stock of 1,100,000*li.* to serve that turn. Or if the Merchants Adventurers will join with them their stocks will perform all very liberally.

Obj. But the Merchants Adventurers hold this project very unfeasible for three things considerable: 1. Firstly, the stock to buy cloths. 2. Secondly, the materials and workmanship to dye and dress the said cloths. 3. Thirdly, to vent the same abroad to gain.

The King's Questions

1. If this thing be profitable to the Commonwealth if feasible.
   Confessed by the Merchant Adventurers.
   Merchant Adventurers.
2. Whether it be feasible or no?
   Denied to be feasible because

1. Our workmanship is not so good as theirs in the dyeing and dressing.

2. They buy the dressed cloths, because of the white, whereby they set their people on work.

3. They employ their merchants, whereby they maintain their navigation, and increase their customs.

4. They gain exceedingly in their stretching out of our cloths, which they cannot do but in white cloths, which made them recall an edict which they had made for the banishing of our coloured cloths.

5. Our merchants find by experience, yet were it not for our white cloths, the coloured cloths would presently be banished from there.

6. This project hath been often on foot in King Edward's time, and in the late Queen's time, but after long and deliberate dispute, the State and Councillors then refused to meddle with it.

7. The trade is now settled in the hands of the Merchants Adventurers which trade maintaineth many thousands of people. If this be stayed or interrupted but for a month, the poor of England will perish by many thousands.

8. Then most humbly left to the Councillors of State, whether for the hope of 300,000*li.* a year in gain, so great a calamity, as this cause ill succeeding may bring, shall be ventured upon at this time.

9. Add to this that since the news of this project, they of that side do settle themselves to make cloths themselves, whereby they may be sufficiently furnished without us, as France, Noremberk, Pomerland, Lübeck; and they do already make as good cloth as we do here. *Licentia summus omnes deteriores.*

10. The customs of his Majesty for cloths transported over sea amount to 60,000*li* every year ... There is not carried over sea above 25,000 cloths yearly dressed and dyed.

11. The western counties of England, that furnish out the white cloths, cannot dye and dress as the other eastern counties do; and whilst they learn to dye and dress them, the trade will impair. Ten to one of the poor people will be undone, and we cannot foresee the great inconveniences which may ensue and follow. *In libro judicum*, consider, consult, and then judge the matter. Leave not to tread in the steps of thy predecessors, unless there do appear unto thee great and evident profit to the contrary.

12. This project is not fit for this time, for that the Dutch countries are already provided for a year; so that they will rather now than hereafter take an occasion to forbear buying any more cloth for a year, and so trade will stop to the inestimable evil of this State. There is not vented above the fourth part of all the cloths made, dyed, and dressed in England.

*   *   *

11 September 1616
The new Merchants Adventurers at the Council table at
Whitehall in the King's presence. Their 14 petitions

Observations

1. Twice as many people needing work as 14 years since.
2. Cloths sold for 10 in the hundred better cheap than 2 years sithence.
3. Wool sold dearer than 2 years sithence by 10 in the hundred.
4. New drapery consumes a third part at least of the wools of England and Wales.
5. Great quantities of wools carried out of England, Wales, Scotland, and Ireland and unto Middelburg.
6. In most parts of England broggers and staplers buy up the wools so fast, that the clothiers cannot buy but at the second hand, and so enforced to sell more dear.
7. In Gloucestershire, Worcestershire, and Wiltshire either one half or a third part of the looms are abated.
8. There are not made and brought to London from Gloucester, Wiltshire, and Worcestershire, above 52,000 cloths yearly.
9. The medium of the king's custom for broad cloths *communibus annis* is 40,000*li.* or 42,000*li.* but this year not like to be 30,000*li.* or 26,000*li.*, which sheweth a decrease of cloths transported.

No cloths wrought beyond the seas shall be brought into England 11 E. 3. cap. 3 *et* 4, nor Wales, Ireland, nor, Scotland *ibidem*. The same for England 4 E. 4. 1. No ribbands, laces, girdles, cauler, points made of silk, and the like to be brought into this realm if it be wrought out of the realm 19 H. 7. cap. 21 . . .

Offered by them to the Lords to buy up all the cloths till Christmas next, viz. all cloths brought to the Guildhall in London. Affirmed by Mr. Wolstenholme that the same quantity of wool spent in the new drapery doth yield more custom to the King than so much quantity of wool spent in broad cloth. *Vide* the difference of the *anno* 1599. 15,000 cloths likely to come up to Blackwell Hall before Christmas next, which may be the value of 150,000*li.* 200 of Worcester, 300 of Gloucester, 500 of Wiltshire weekly to remain unbought without imputation of a stand.

*   *   *

25 September 1616
The new Merchants Adventurers
At Hampton Court

Report of Sir Lionel Cranfield kt. of the coloured cloths searched by him by the King's commandment.

	The whole	831	Green	48
	Narrow	746	Feds [sic]	50
	Broad	85	Violets	20
D. A. [sic]	Black	528	Orange Colour	2
D. A. [sic]	Blues	139	Russets	6
	Purples	5	Stamells	8
	Tawnies	25		

Nota: that blacks were seldom or never carried before.

All likely to be transported at this shipping —— 1,400 cloths dyed.

There being but 2 shippings this year; and yet by contract 12,000 dyed cloths were to be sent this year, viz. from midsummer 1616 till midsummer 1617.

Then the merchants to dye their cloths, and dress them fully and sufficiently for sale.

In the old Merchants Adventurers' time there was never any stand of cloth before and at the shipping as now it is.

Sir Thomas Heyes wont to buy 2,000 white cloths yearly.

There is now equal proportion in the carriage of dyed cloths, but the younger men are overcharged, and the abler men undercharged.

Reported of Sir Lionel Cranfield from the —— of 600,000 wool fells carried out of Ireland the last year to the Low Countries.

Sir William Cokain, Withers, Grenewell, and two others at Hampton Court, being asked by the Lords what security their Lordships should have that the cloths should receive no stand till Christmas, they have promised to take the private men's bonds for their proportions till Christmas eve. Being demanded the said assurance till twelve day market, they have directly refused it, unless they may find vent in the same time.

Misselden and divers other false brethren of the company have stolen out divers white cloths without coloured cloths, contrary to the orders of this company. Being further questioned by the Lords touching the half dyeing and dressing of cloths to the bereaving of the English people of dyeing and dressing of cloths, they answer that there were six stalls or depths in dyeing, viz. six steepings, whereof the merchants take sometimes one, sometimes two or more, after which the said cloths may receive a further dyeing and dressing beyond the seas, and into other colours. Being again pressed by the Lords that if they deal well in their number of cloths dyed and not in their value, in dealing in cloths of less value and not in the better and richer cloths, then they break their contract with the King. And confessed by Sir William Cokain that want of vent of the richer cloths in the Low Countries forceth them to vent cloths of lesser value.

The merchants, farmers, and clothiers questioned whether the new drapery be not the occasion of hindrance of the making of broad cloths, and how far and what else may be the occasion of broad cloth [sic]. They answered that the new draperies do make up the value of the broad cloths for the custom;

and yet the new draperies were two years since as many as now, and yet the broad cloths yielded for custom 40,000*li.*

For the 15,000*li.* loss in broad cloth, there is but 1,000*li.* increase in new draperies touching the customs. The reason of the decay of cloth is said to be the want of vent of the cloth. The cloth cheap because the clothier must utter it; the wool dear and therefore the clothiers enforced to decay their looms because they buy dear wool and sell cloths cheap, and therefore it of needs be that wools are transported oversea. And it is constantly reported that in Middelburg very lately wool by reason of the plenty thereof there was abated in the sale by 10 in the 100.

16,000 cloths yearly spent in the whole countries.

The new Merchants Adventurers have lying cloth at the mart town at Middelburg 400,000*li.* worth of cloth, so they cannot go further in their stock; and therefore must have vent there, or help here.

6. THE COCKAYNE EXPERIMENT GETS UNDER WAY, 1615

[Acts of the Privy Council, 1615–16, pp. 217–21]

At Suffolk House, the 19th of June, being Monday, in the afternoon.

Present: The Lord Archbishop of Canterbury, Lord Chancellor, etc.

The new Company of Merchant Adventurers, being this day by his Majesty's special commandment called before their lordships[1] for the settling of that trade, and setting forward the work for dyeing and dressing of cloth within the kingdom, Mr. Secretary Winwood delivered a paper which was formerly exhibited by the said merchants, containing the resolution and purpose of that Company for the advancing of the dyeing and dressing of cloth, together also with such points of privilege as was desired might be granted unto them in favour and assistance thereof, and was *in haec verba.*

Whereas it pleased the King's most excellent Majesty, by relation from the right honourable the Lord High Treasurer of England, to express his gracious favour for the encouragement of the new Company in setting forward the worthy intended work of dressing and dyeing cloths, formerly used to be shipped out by the late Merchants Adventurers undressed and undyed, the said Company (to manifest their willing minds to further his Majesty's princely desire, tending so much to his Highness's honour and the good of the commonwealth), have at a general court, holden the 18th of this present June, 1615, enacted and fully agreed that thirty-six thousand cloths shall be dressed and dyed out of such cloths white as were formerly used to be shipped out by the old company undressed and undyed, the said thirty-six thousand cloths to be exported by the said Company as followeth, that is to say, from the 24th day of this month of June, 1615, to the 24th of

---

[1] Of the Privy Council.

June, 1616, six thousand cloths; from the 24th of June, 1616, to the 24th of June, 1617, twelve thousand cloths; and from the 24th of June, 1617, to the 24th of June, 1618, eighteen thousand cloths. And do purpose, after the said three years, with all cheerfulness to proceed, as it shall please God to give ability and the trade encouragement, humbly desiring (for the better performance of the premises) his Majesty's favour and assistance in the particulars following:

First, that we may have forthwith a Charter granted to this Company in as large, ample, and beneficial manner, as any company of merchants formerly had or now have, with such further privileges as may be reasonably required as well for the government of the Company as for the settling orders amongst ourselves for the rating of the dyed and dressed cloths upon the several trades, according to the quantity of each man's annual exportation.

Secondly, for preventing of interloping, which will tend to the overthrow of this Company, we humbly pray his Majesty to give strict order presently to all his officers, in all and every of his ports, creeks, and members, within all his Majesty's dominions of England, Wales, and Ireland, and the town of Berwick, that they and every of them, upon pain of loss of their place and offices, and such further punishment as his Majesty or honourable Council shall think fit to be inflicted upon them, shall not suffer any his Majesty's subjects to ship out any of the native commodities of this kingdom for any of the territories formerly granted to the late Merchants Adventurers, and now granted to this new Company, but such whose entries shall be subscribed by the governor of this Company for the time being, or such other as the governor and Company shall appoint for that purpose. And that none whatsoever shall ship any goods in any ship or vessel but by due and direct warrant made upon such bills as aforesaid, and to be shipped in such ship or ships as are named in those bills, subscribed by the governor for the time being, or some other by him and the Company to be thereto appointed, and not in any other ship by certificate without the hand of the said governor or such other as shall be thereunto appointed as aforesaid.

Thirdly, we further humbly pray his Majesty that there may be at the Company's charges, an office[r] or officers appointed by this Company to sit in the Custom House in the port of London, or in any other port, creek, or member within his Majesty's said dominions, where this Company shall think fit, fully authorized by all ways and means to search for the preventing of any indirect course of interloping in prejudice of this Company, as well for the native commodities of this kingdom to be exported for any place whatsoever, as also for all commodities to be imported from the territories where this Company shall be privileged . . .

Fourthly, this Company are humble suitors to his Majesty to be pleased to be a means, the better to further the sale of their dressed and dyed cloths, that the placate set forth by the States of the United Provinces, prohibiting the importation of dressed and dyed cloth into their Provinces may be revoked, or that his Majesty will be pleased to give this Company leave to make choice of such place or places for their residence in the parts where this Company shall be privileged, and with them to parley, confer, and agree, as may give us best hope for the vent of our cloth dressed and dyed here in England, with expectation of encouragement and benefit by our trade.

Fifthly, we also humbly pray for the better perfecting of this great business of dressing and dyeing the cloth in England, and for the preventing the malice and opposition by foreign nations intended, his Majesty would be pleased to forbid all his subjects and others, upon pain of confiscation of their goods and further punishment at his Majesty's pleasure, the exportation or carrying out by sea or land (out of any his Majesty's foresaid dominions) of wool, wool fells, woollen yarn, and fullers earth, and the confiscation of the ship or vessel that shall carry out any of the same, with the loss of the goods of the master and mariners of the said ship or vessel that shall know and not reveal the same to some of his Majesty's officers, whereby stay thereof may be made.

Which being read, and duly considered of, their lordships desired to be satisfied in these three points:

First, whether if any of the principal members of the Company should fail, either by death or otherwise, the rest of the Company would bind themselves jointly by an order of court, to make good the parts of such as failed, and pass an Act to that purpose.

To which answer was made that they would bind themselves by a joint order of court, to perform that which they had undertaken, notwithstanding any of their members should fail.

Secondly, whether their meaning was to pass those cloths for dyed and dressed that were only wadded or dipped in a light blue, or slightly rowed, and had but one cut of four, and so left to be perfected by the stranger.

Answer was made that their purpose and meaning was fully to dye and dress the cloth, and to make it ready for sale and present wearing.

The third was concerning such Suffolk blues as have been heretofore, and are usually, sent into Germany, that the said blues may be no part of the number of dyed and dressed cloths undertaken as aforesaid.

Wherein after they had given their lordships satisfaction, it was by a general consent and agreement of the Board ordered, that the offer made by the said merchants for dyeing and dressing the white cloths of this kingdom should be accepted, with such favour and encouragement as a work so much tending to the public weal of this kingdom and the honour of the State, may any way deserve; and that a charter be granted unto them in as large, ample, and beneficial manner as was formerly granted to the Merchant Adventurers: whereof Mr. Attorney General is hereby to take notice, and to make the same ready for his Majesty's signature. And for such further privileges as they require for their furtherance and assistance in their course of trade, it is ordered that his Majesty's Attorney and Solicitor General shall consider thereof, and acquaint their lordships with their opinion of the same, and what they think fit to be offered to this Board as meet to be added to the

former grant that thereupon such further order may be taken as shall be
expedient.

7. WOOL BROGGERS AND SMALL CLOTHWORKERS IN WARWICKSHIRE PETITION AGAINST THE STAPLERS, 1615[1]

[P.R.O., SP 14/80, no. 14]

To the Rt. Hon. the Lords of His Majesty's Privy Council
the humble petition of the broggers of wool in the county
of Warwick [January?] 1615.

HUMBLY shewing unto your lordships that whereas the petitioners used to
buy of the husbandmen and other poor people small quantities of wool and
did use to sell the same oftentimes upon credit to the combers, spinners, and
poor clothiers from 3 or 4*li.* to a tod in divers towns which are not staple
towns for the ease of such poor people who, buying such small quantities,
cannot repair to the staple towns without more expense than their gains can
countervail.

And whereas the staplers of wools do enforce your petitioners either to
give great sums of money to be of their company or by continual arresting of
them compel them to be bound not to deal for wools. And the staplers using
to buy and sell by wholesale only will not buy such small quantities unless
they have them at their own prices. Neither will they sell the like small
quantities to the combers, spinners, or poor clothiers upon credit nor for
ready money but at their own rates, they seeming to neglect such small
quantities and knowing none can deal for wool but themselves.

By means whereof your petitioners and their families, being many in
number, not being permitted to use their trades, are utterly undone. Those
that sell small quantities of wool suffer great loss and the commissioners and
poor clothiers are like to perish.

The petitioners' humble prayer is that your lordships would be pleased
to be a means to his Majesty that the petitioners may have their former
liberties of exercising their trades of brogging without molestation by informers or staplers.

We whose names are hereunder subscribed do conceive that your ho.
petitioners have just cause of complaint in this behalf.

[101 signatures.]

---

[1] This document is one of a group on the cloth industry. The first, entitled 'Reasons to
prove the convenience of buying and selling wool within the kingdom', is printed in Bland,
Brown, and Tawney, *English Economic History, Select Documents*, pp. 354–5. This is the
second. The fourth is printed below, p. 204.

8. OLD AND NEW DRAPERIES COMPARED, 1615
[P.R.O., SP 14/80, no 16]

THE manner of disposing the ordinary sorts of wools in the old drapery, as
those of North Bucks. etc., is, with the benefit that comes thereby to the
commonweal, instanced by the wool of one cloth which is 3 tods [January ?]
1615.

Three tods, that is four score and four pounds, being draped by the
clothier into a sorting pack cloth:

	li.	s.	d.
The spinners have for spinning at 3*d*. the pound	1	1	0
The weavers for weaving	0	10	0
The tucker for his work	0	2	6
Summa	1	13	6

The custom thereof to his Majesty.   0   6   8
The number of people kept by the work thereof xiiii.
These are all servants and work to the clothier for small wages so that they
live very poorly.

The same quantity of wool being converted in the new drapery (viz.) into
stuff and stockings as is now abundantly used.

	li.	s.	d.
The combers have for combing it	0	10	0
The spinning and draping the noils and coarse wools	0	6	0
The spinning and twisting of the tire[?] wool	3	4	0
The working of it, two parts thereof into stuff and one third part into stockings			
The poor weavers, tuckers, and knitters have for the working thereof	3	0	0
Totalis	7	0	0

The custom thereof to his Majesty   1   4   0
The number of people kept in work thereby   40 or 50.

There is more people supposed to be employed in this new manufacture
than by all the clothiers of the kingdom. All sorts of these people are masters
in their trade and work for themselves. They buy and sell their materials that
they work upon so that by their merchandise and honest labour they live
very well. These are served of their wools weekly by the wool buyer, either
merchant or other. So that 200 tods of wool which is the proportion weekly
spent in one market is improved over and above that which it would be in
cloth weekly to his Majesty in custom 40*li*. and to the poor in their wage
300*li*.

9. A PETITION AGAINST A GLASS MONOPOLY, 1616

[*Staffordshire and the Great Rebellion*, ed. D. A. Johnson and D. G. Vaisey, Staffs. Co. Council County Records Committee, n.d., p. 16]

[The Petition of Sir Walter Bagot to Sir Robert Mansell, who, through his glass monopoly, has driven Bagot out of business, 1616]

WORTHY knight, I have long been silent but now, enforced thereto, must challenge a loser's privilege to speak ... When it was his Majesty's pleasure by proclamation to forbid the making glass in this kingdom, being now a year and more past, I had a work in my grounds which before had continued and been maintained with underwoods and crop wood the space of eight years; the like was in my father's time and other my ancestors the space of two hundred years which I can prove by good records. The proclamation was published here in this county of Stafford the 16th of June, and the third day after a messenger took away Jacob Henze, my chief workman, who hath sithence been and still is employed in your works at Wollerton. By this means my wood to the value of three hundred pounds, ... cut, corded, and a great part brought and cleaned at the glass house door [has been lost]. And their materials provided by one Mr. Gillot of Leicester, unto whom they are engaged for great sums of money, and had the glass made at a certain rate, out of which he had some hope to recover the most part of their debt (being at least two hundred pounds). We are now in despair to recover our loss, having first been in hope it would please you to have given consideration for them; which, if shortly we receive not, both materials and wood will be unprofitable for anything. I protest unto you upon the faith of a gentleman I have made offer unto the masters of iron works, who I confess are near unto it. They refuse absolutely to deal for it. I have made proclamation in the next market towns adjoining for the sale of it, and have not nor know not how to sell to the value of 40s. Sir, my request unto you is not to grant us liberty to work up this wood and materials, for I know it to be expressly against the proclamation; yet if it may please you to give way unto us that we may work, and that you will either signify by writing or give your word to this bearer that neither by yourself or any other you will molest, trouble, or inform against us, we will adventure by force of that liberty given unto others at the Council table to work that wood already fallen. If we be questioned by others I doubt not but, freeing ourselves from doing anything prejudicial to the estate (for the prevention whereof the proclamation was published), that most honourable table will grant the same to us [as] hath been given to others ...

10. BENEDICT WEBB'S ACCOUNT OF HIS CAREER
AS A CLOTHIER, *temp.* JAMES I

[Gloucester Public Library, Smyth of Nibley MSS., SZ 23.2(4)]

A Narration of my Employments sithence I came to discretion

1. I was brought up under my father in the trade of clothmaking until I came to sixteen years of age, and then bound apprentice in London to a linen draper and French merchant, who, after I had been with him in London some three months, sent me to Rouen where I remained certain years. And being prettily well entered in the clothing trade before my service, I spent all my vacant time to see the manner of the drapery they made there and in the parts near adjoining, which much delighted me, being in the workmanship far more curious and better than ours. And after two years' observation I contracted with a western merchant near Exeter to procure me two looms to be made there and gave full direction how the clothers [sic] should be made I desired, which accordingly was done and so continued some four or five years, spending my time partly at Rouen partly at Paris, and still held my old course to visit all the bordering towns where any cloth was made, and took notice of all things that I might make use of them as occasion served, and so did resolve as soon as I was quit of my service to quit London and betake myself to be a clothier again, in all this time not thinking but they had used Spanish oil because to that time I never saw other used in this kingdom.

2. Being matched in the western parts in Taunton in Somersetshire, I began to examine all my particulars with many that I had procured out of Italy, out of all which I resolved to make two sorts of drapery as the most fitting for many respects for this commonwealth, both for our use in the kingdom and for transportation. The one sort being thin and light I called it perpetuanis, of which sort there hath been sithence many thousands made yearly and exported, and is in truth for his uses the best stuff that ever was made in this kingdom, and for this 35 years hath held his reputation, unless by the default of the makers sometimes it hath an eclipse.

The second sort was a sort of medley cloth which Sir William Stone, a mercer in Cheapside, dealt with me for, and called them Spanish cloths, which are now known through the kingdom and in foreign parts by the name of Webbs cloth, and by that name are entered in the custom houses, which sort of cloth hath been and is the most useful of any other (in the general). The imitation whereof hath added more perfection to the drapery of mixed colour cloth than all the statutes made sithence Edward III's time, and finding that the colours then in use in this kingdom were very unfitting for the nobility and gentry of the kingdom, as also of foreign parts, I devised divers and sundry colours which at this day is made common to all, and by which more cloth has been worn than in former ages, and with much more pleasure and content; which manner of drapery is now exceedingly increased in many parts of the kingdom and in which I continue to this day.

Thus much for my general employments, now follows my particular.

In the last Parliament of our famous Queen Elizabeth, the white clothiers of Wiltshire, Gloucestershire, Somerset, Oxfordshire, and Worcestershire, having been sorely pinched by the merchants returning certificates on them of great value to the hazard of the undoing of many of them, made choice of two of every county the most able men to procure a repeal of that statute, who having spent half the time of the Parliament returned without effect, not finding any ground whereon to lay a good foundation. At their return, it pleased the shires near adjoining to send to me who appointed a meeting not far from my house when they acquainted me with their grievances and prayed my advice and assistance, which I readily afford them, but in conclusion importuned me to undertake the managing of the business myself, the which I did. And it pleased God to give such a blessing to my endeavours that I repealed that statute, and eased them of some other grievances all which was chargeable to their counties 5,000*li.* sterling per annum. In which service I spent 40*li.* of my own money more than I received of the clothiers, my masters.

In this year aforesaid there was an edict made by the French by which they might at all times confiscate all our English cloth found in that kingdom, and for proof in the same year they seized at one time all the cloth [that] was found in the hall at Rouen to the value of 8,600 crowns, never searching or receipting which was faulty but seizing all. Whereupon suit was made by the merchants to her Majesty, and Sir Thomas Edmonds sent over with divers clothiers but could effect no more but the release of the goods, but no revocation of the edict, by virtue whereof in the first year of his late Majesty's reign they made another seizure of a great value at Rouen. The Duke of Lennox being then in France, the merchants were petitioners for his assistance, who obtained of the king a release of the goods, but the edict to stand still in force, which so terrified the merchants that they were continual petitioners at the Council table for remedy, but could show no ground to work upon. During this their clamour the Lord Chief Justice Popham, who had often used me in matters about and concerning drapery (and had received good satisfaction), writ me a letter to come forth to him, which accordingly I did, who acquainted me with the cause and showed me the edict, and appointed a meeting at a merchant's house where I might have a full view of all passages, which when I had well considered of, I perceived well on sound grounds how to revoke the edict, and by the next morning went to my lord Popham and acquainted him with it, who seemed to be very joyful of the news, willed me to attend him to the court at Whitehall, and there calling certain of the lords, acquainted them with it and called me before them to deliver my reasons, which they all approved of. Yet on farther consideration they thought needful that I should be sent over to effect it, lest the French by some tricks and devices shift off the matter. In fine, it was so resolved and through God's assistance I overthrew the edict grounded on false suggestions to their great disgrace and honour of this kingdom, for which service I never received recompense to the value of the damage I sustained in my particulars by being absent so long from home.

[Endorsed:] The progress of the whole life of Mr. Ben. Webb written by himself [no date, but either 1619 or 1624].

11. CLOTHWORKERS TESTIFY IN SUPPORT OF BENEDICT WEBB, 1618

[P.R.O., SP 14/98, no. 242]

MAY it please your honours to admit us to this testimony of our well deserving neighbour, Mr. Benedict Webb, induced thereto upon the advertisement of certain controversies arisen between him and George Mynne of London, draper, which as he informeth us, stands referred to your honours. That for the time of twenty years and more, wherein we have taken notice of his life and behaviour, we can upon certainty of each of our knowledges, assure your honours that it hath been reputed very honest and commendable, and that such hath been his industry and singular discerning in all points concerning the mystery of drapery of woollen cloth, that we have not known him equalled by any, under whose labours many more poor people are and have been set on work and maintained than by any other of that profession in all this our county of Wiltshire; not presuming to speak of his employment by the State into France and otherwise in the late question of drapery because his service therein standeth (as we conceive) well approved to his Majesty. In whose behalf our humble requests are that your honours would vouchsafe to give speedy ending to his cause lest through the violence of an adversary, as we have heard both of wealth and will, he should want leisure and means for the support of that great number of poor people, who now live and are maintained under him. And so we humbly take our leaves this xiiith of August, 1618.

N. Poole, Nevill Poole, Geo. Eye, Henry Mady, Jo. Warneford, John Ayliffe, Tho. Gore.

12. A BILL TO REGULATE ABUSES IN THE METAL-WORKING INDUSTRIES, 1621

[Notestein, Relf, and Simpson, *Commons Debates, 1621*, VII, pp. 141–3]

An Act for Reformation of Sundry Abuses committed by divers evil disposed persons that engross and get into their Hands great Store of Victuals and other Commodities and exchange the same at unreasonable Rates with poor Handicraftsmen that work in Iron and Steel within the several Counties of

Stafford, Salop, Wigorn, and Warwick; and also for the better Government
of the said Craftsmen in that none of them hereafter shall keep above two
Prentices at one time, and the one to serve three Years before the taking of
the second, and they to serve Seven Years before they shall be free to work
of Themselves in the said Handicraft

FORASMUCH as many thousands of the subjects of this realm inhabiting
within the counties of Stafford, Worcester, Salop, and Warwick have usually
been employed in the manual occupation, crafts, and mysteries of framing,
fashioning, and making of iron into nails, locks, spurs, bridlebits, buckles,
stirrups, arrowheads, and other like things. By means whereof not only the
greatest part of the people of this realm are and have been to their benefit and
ease (at reasonable prices) furnished with the said wares. But also the said
artificers and handicraftsmen have by such their labour and industry gained
their own livelihood and sustenance for their families and set on work great
numbers of men, which otherwise must have been destitute of any honest
vocation or course of life. And whereas of late certain rich but evil disposed
persons of these parts too greedily intending their own private commodities
without regard of their poor neighbours or the true meaning of sundry good
laws and statutes of this kingdom have and do engross, forestall, and get into
their hands most part of the iron made or brought into the said several
counties and great store of other wares, merchandizes, and commodities
which appertain and belong to many several trades, arts, occupations, and
mysteries (other than their own) together with corn, grain, and other
victuals, and exchange the same at excessive and unreasonable rates with the
said iron workers and artificers to their utter impoverishment and the ruin of
their wives, children, and families and destruction of their trade and course
of life. Be it therefore enacted . . . that no person or persons whatsoever shall
from henceforth sell or exchange or cause to be sold or exchanged any iron,
metal, victuals, or commodities whatsoever (except for money) with the
said artificers or handicraftsmen aforementioned, or any of them, for any
nails or any other the aforesaid wares that they or any of them have, do, or
shall usually make of iron. And for the better government and order of the
said artificers and their trades, in regard that some of them being idle and
lewd persons (to maintain themselves therein) do take so many apprentices
as they can procure for their own private benefit, and do turn them off at
their pleasure before they have served half their time; by means whereof
there groweth a great number of unskilful persons in the said handicrafts
that make bad wares whereby ariseth great prejudice to the commonwealth of
this realm. Be it therefore further enacted by the authority aforesaid that all
and every person and persons whatsoever that hereafter shall use the said
trades, handicrafts, or mysteries according to the provision aforesaid, or any
of them do not henceforth keep above the number of two apprentices at one
time, the one whereof shall have served three years before the taking of the
second, and they to serve seven years before they be made free or allowed to
work of themselves in any the said trades, mysteries, or handicrafts upon pain

to forfeit, for every such offence committed against all or any branch or member of the articles or provisions in this Act contained, ten pounds of lawful money of England, the one half to the king, his heirs, and successors, and the other half to such person or persons as shall sue for the same in any the Courts of Record of the king's Majesty, his heirs, and successors by action of debt, bill, plaint, or by information, wherein no protection, essoin, or wager in law shall be allowed, any act, statute, or law of this realm to the contrary in any wise notwithstanding.

13. THE REPORT OF THE CLOTHING COMMITTEE OF THE PRIVY COUNCIL, JUNE 1622

[G. D. Ramsay, *The Wiltshire Woollen Industry in the Sixteenth and Seventeenth Centuries*, 2nd edn., 1965, pp. 147–53]

MAY it please your Lordships,

Having received directions by your honourable Letters dated the xiiijth day of April last, to take into our considerations, what are the true grounds and motives of the great decay of the sale and vent of our English cloth in foreign parts and what are likely to be the fittest remedies for the same, and thereof to make report to your lordships in writing, we have with the best of our endeavours applied ourselves to observe your lordships' commandments; and upon many conferences had with the Merchants Adventurers, and the merchants of other societies and companies, with the gentlemen of quality of several counties of this realm, with the clothiers of the several clothing shires, with the officers of his Majesty's Custom House in the port of London, and the drapers and dyers of London, and after many days spent in this weighty service; for those two principal points which were recommended by your lordships to our care we humbly offer these things following in answer:

The causes of this decay of the vent of our cloth

1. The making of cloth and other draperies in foreign parts in more abundance than in former times, being thereunto chiefly enabled by the wools and other materials transported from the kingdoms of England, Scotland, and Ireland, we conceive to be the chief cause that less quantity of ours are vented there.

2. The false and deceitful making, dyeing, and dressing of our cloth and stuffs which disgraceth and discrediteth it in foreign parts.

3. The heavy burden upon our cloth, whereby it is made so dear to the buyer that those who were wont to furnish themselves therewith in foreign parts either buy cloth of other countries, or clothe themselves otherwise in cheaper manner than our cloth can be afforded. And the clothiers apprehend that the staplers, jobbers, and broggers of wool are also a cause of the endearing of wool by deceitful mingling and often selling it from hand to hand before it come to the clothier.

4. The present state of the times, by reason of the wars in Germany, is

conceived by many to be some present impediment to the vent of our cloth, partly by reason of the interruption of the passages, partly by want of money occasioned by foraging of the countries.

5. The policies of the Merchant Adventurers, which draw upon them a suspicion of combination in trading; and the smallness of their number, which now do usually buy and vent cloth, and the like policies of other merchants who are not able or willing to extend themselves in this time of extremity to take of the cloth from the hand of the clothier.

6. The scarcity of coin at home, and the baseness of foreign coins compared with ours.

7. The want of means of returns for our merchants especially out of the Eastland countries, which discourageth them to carry out cloth thither, because they can neither sell for ready money, nor in barter for vendible commodities.

8. The too little use and wearing of cloth at home, and the too much of silks and foreign stuffs which overbalance our trade.

The remedies humbly propounded:

1. That for preventing of the making of cloth beyond the seas; there be a strict course taken under the severest penalties both against the transporters, and against all officers belonging to the Custom House which shall connive thereat, to prohibit the exportation of wools, woolfells, yarn, Cornish hair, fullers earth, and wood ashes out of England at all, and out of Scotland and Ireland to be carried out of the king's dominions. For it is generally conceived that in those parts where cloth is now made beyond the seas, they cannot possibly furnish themselves otherwise so commodiously and so cheap to undersell us.

Also to prohibit the bringing of any wools into the Low Countries or Germany from Spain, Turkey, etc. in any English bottoms or by any Englishmen in any foreign bottoms.

And that all licences already granted for transportation of wool be revoked (so much excepted as is fit for Jersey and Guernsey, for their own employment only in point of manufacture), and for a present help herein (as far as it may) that his Majesty by his royal proclamation may forthwith prohibit these things.

2. That for the preventing of the false and deceitful making and dyeing of cloths and stuffs, these things may be observed: that whereas the laws now in force concerning the making and dressing of cloth are so many, and by the multitude of them so intricate that it is very hard to resolve what the law is herein; that those former laws (when opportunity shall serve) might be repealed, and one clear law made for a direction herein. And in the mean time, till these can be done, that some committee may be chosen to peruse the laws now in force, that those which are fit for the present times may be quickened, and those which are less fit, may be tolerated.

That where there is yet no law made concerning the New Draperies, that some plain rules, and easy to be observed, may be prescribed, for the true making, dyeing, dressing, and pressing of those stuffs which being observed may bring them into request again.

That a corporation in every county be made of the most able and sufficient men of the same, whereby they may be authorized to look carefully to the true making, dyeing, and dressing of cloth and stuff in every shire, and not to trust to mean and mercenary men by whose connivancy too many faults are committed to the great disgrace of our drapery. And the committee to be appointed may also take into their consideration the manner of putting this into execution.

That the aulnagers' seal may not be set to any cloth or stuff until it have been searched, tried and approved by such as shall be thereunto appointed, and that none who for that time doth themselves use clothing be made deputy aulnager.

That the use of all false dyeing stuff be strictly forbidden for cloth and the New Draperies.

3. That for the ease of the heavy burthen upon cloth, his Majesty is humbly desired by the aforesaid gentlemen, merchants, clothiers, and others to interpose his power with the Archduchess and States to take of their consumption and licence money. And it is also by them desired that the Merchant Adventurers would take off their private impositions which they term imprest money (care being had) for the repayment of such monies as bona fide they have disbursed for his Majesty's service, and which they have not yet reimbursed again.

And that neither that, nor any other company of merchants, be hereafter suffered to impose upon their own members to the endearing of the cloth exported without the allowance of the State.

And it is the general opinion of the gentlemen, merchant officers of the Custom House, and clothiers with whom we have had conference that the pretermitted customs, and the Earl of Cumberland's licence are so great a burthen upon cloth, that it much hindereth the vent.

And although they hope that the increase of trade will recompense these losses to the King in his customs, yet because this is so weighty a point to the King's revenue, we will not presume to give our opinion therein, because we cannot secure the event.

That dyeing stuffs be not made dear by patents of privilege, as that of the sole importation of Gynnywood, or by engrossing of dyeing commodities at home, before it come to the dyer or clothier; else the dyed cloths will continue dear, although wools be over cheap.

And the clothiers desire that the wool jobbers, which are but engrossers and forestallers of their markets may be forbidden except in Yorkshire and Devonshire, where the manner of clothing differing from other countries maketh them useful; but in those places where they shall be allowed, it will be fit to tie them to these conditions:

That they sell immediately to the converter and not to come to him at the second or third hand.

That they mingle not their wools deceitfully before they sell.

That they sell not again in the same market they buy.

And the clothiers also complain that the woolgrower doth not clip off his pitchmark before he wind his fleece, which we think fit were reformed.

4. For the wars in Germany, we can only pray to God to stay the effusion of Christian blood. But we conceive that the wasting of several parts of these countries by the wars, the consumption of their flocks, the disturbance of their trade in making, are probable means to open the way for our better vent, when it shall please God to send peace, or but to settle the wars, so as that there may be a free and safe intercourse for the merchants, and that they dare trust their wares for reasonable time.

5. For the policies of the Company of Merchant Adventurers and other societies of merchants spoken against by many, we conceive that such ordinances as tend to government of trade must necessarily be continued. But such as draw with them a suspicion of combination, either in buying at home or selling abroad, should be forbidden.

And to increase and encourage the number of merchants, and so enlarge trade which is said to be imprisoned as it is now carried, we humbly propound: that into the Merchant Adventurers' Company, and all other companies of merchants, such others as shall be desirous of it may be received for the fine of five marks and no more, thereby to increase the number of buyers and adventurers.

And that none may be discouraged to come into their companies, for fear of private impositions or unequal charges to be put upon them, we think it fit that the orders and constitutions of the companies of merchants (in whom the public hath so great an interest) either already or hereafter to be made, be surveyed and approved by a committee to be appointed by his Majesty for that purpose, to the end they may put no such ordinances in execution, which shall tend more to their private than to the public good.

That because the Merchant Adventurers have disbursed great sums of money which they affirm come to the King's purse, it will be but just (that they laying down their impositions) those monies be repaid unto them by such a way as your lordships in your wisdoms shall think fittest.

That in no society of merchants there be a joint stock (except in the East India Company as long as it shall continue which cannot be avoided) for in that course it is as if one man alone were the adventurer and buyer.

That such be not admitted to trade as merchants, who shall not submit themselves to government in some company or other. Nor that any being admitted as merchants to trade, shall sell by retail the same commodities they return.

6. For the scarcity of money at home, we conceive this rather to be a general hindrance of all sorts of trade than of cloth in particular.

Some remedies whereof we conceive may be these:

That a careful eye be had that our coin be not stolen or carried away and that it be severally punished in the offenders.

That some course may be taken, that money (which is *communis mensura*

rerum) may bear some equality with us and with our neighbour nations
with whom we trade; or else if ours hold still so great a disproportion o:
value, as now it doth, to that it is esteemed abroad, greediness of gain wil
entice the stealing over of our money though the kingdom smart for it.

But the most important remedy as we conceive is to provide against the
overbalance of trade; for if the vanity and superfluity of our importatior
be a greater than the exportation of our home commodities will bear, the
stock of this kingdom must need be wasted, for money must necessarily turr
the scale.

The help of this consisteth in these two things:

To improve our native commodities in their use and vent, as time will give
leave, whereunto our manufactures do chiefly conduce; and of these above
others our New Draperies. And amongst these improvements of our kingdom we heartily wish that the fishing upon our coasts as a matter of great
and important consequence may not only be cherished, but that the subjects
of this kingdom in all the several countries, cities, and port towns be drawn
to undertake the building, furnishing, and maintaining of fishing busses at
their public charge, and for their public benefit, whereas now that trade is
in a manner wholly possessed by strangers. This being well managed would
enable the King to maintain his absolute right to the narrow seas, by maintaining a fit number of able ships there, as well for defence as offence upon al
occasions; and that without extraordinary charge or noise, it would increase
navigation in general, set many people on work, beget money, and revive the
outports, who now do and long have languished, and hardly will find any othe*
means than this to restore them to trade.

And generally we wish that such commodities of our kingdoms as oun
neighbour nations cannot well spare as corn, tin, seacoals, etc. might return a
proportion of bullion. And out of this consideration we humbly recommenc
to your lordships' wisdoms that a staple for seacoals might be appointed.
whence all strangers should fetch their coals for ready money brought from
foreign parts. And our own shipping only to be employed in carrying on
coals to the Staple; or if your lordships shall think fit that the seacoal be
still fetched from Newcastle, yet we wish that the stranger should pay ready
money for them there and not barter for commodities; or if the English shal.
merchandise them beyond the seas, that they may be bound to return at the
least the one half of their value in bullion or money.

That whereas the East India Company stand accused by many for carrying
away of money to furnish their trade, and return only commodities again, we
humbly offer this to redeem them from this complaint:

1. That according to their covenant with his Majesty it be looked unto that
they do truly and really bring in that money from foreign parts, wherewith to
furnish themselves, and not to expend our own money or bullion, or buy
their foreign money from other merchants that else would have brought the
same hither to the King's Mint.

2. That, when they have returned hither their East Indian wares, care be had

that a reasonable proportion being taken for the use of the kingdom, the surplusage be exported from hence as a merchandise of our kingdom, and of the proceed of that return, at least so much in bullion or money be returned to the Mint as shall equal that sum they first carried out to furnish their trade withal. And that like care be taken for the Turkey trade and other trades, that they use the best husbandry they may in buying as little of foreign commodities with money as they can.

The other help is to restrain our over much vanity in importing foreign commodities, especially those which are superfluous and needless, and which cost ready money. And whereas a mass of money is yearly bestowed upon lawns, cambrics, Hollands, Silesia, and other linen cloth brought from beyond the seas, we wish that to ease that expense, and to set our poor on work, flax and hemp might be enjoined (according to the laws) to be sown and converted into linen cloth; and that the vanity of ruffs and laces brought from beyond the seas be restrained.

That merchant strangers and denizens who drive a great trade with us, as also the masters of ships of foreign bottoms for their freight may be held to observe the Statutes of Employments in some good measure.

That strangers naturalized take their oaths in their own persons in the Custom House, that they carry out and bring in their own proper commodities and merchandise only, and colour not the goods of strangers.

That no English assure or underwrite any policy of assurance for any ship or goods for any stranger or denizen fraught from or for any port beyond the seas.

7. To help the return of our merchants, that some course be taken according to the laws for bringing in our merchandises in English and not in strangers' bottoms, which are not of the proper growth of that country.

That the Eastland merchants may have allowance to make their returns in corn; and have free liberty to transport again that corn into foreign parts with this restriction: that what corn they bring in shall not be vented in our kingdom to the hindrance of our husbandry at home, when corn is under such rates, as the corn of the growth of our country may by the same be exported.

8. To help the expense of cloth within our kingdom, that there may be the less left to vent abroad, and the less vanity in the expense of silks and foreign stuffs. That the nobility and gentry of the kingdom might be persuaded to the wearing of cloth in the winter season by example rather than commandment.

That the meaner sort of people as apprentices, servants, and mechanics be enjoined by proclamation to the wear of cloth and stuff of wool made in this kingdom, which would be more durable and less chargeable.

That when blacks are given at funerals, that they be of cloth or woollen stuff made in this kingdom.

And yet that housewives may not make cloth to sell again but for the provision of themselves and their families, that the clothiers and drapers be not discouraged.

And lastly because many questions may arise from time to time between the woolgrower, clothier, and merchants, we humbly propound to your lordships, that a commission may be granted by his Majesty to some selected persons who may thereby have authority.

To hear and determine all such differences.

To look unto the Statutes of Employments by strangers and denizens.

The licences and privileges for wool and dyeing wood.

And generally for all other things which may conduce to those ends before propounded, whereby trade may be orderly governed and duly balanced.

And although matters of greater difficulty may be ever brought to this honourable Board, by your lordships to be determined or directed, yet thus may your lordships be eased of much trouble and loss of time, which these kinds of grievances have often caused heretofore. And the suitors be despatched more speedily which shall have occasion to attend thereabout.

Jo. Suckling, Thomas Coventrye, R. Heath, Paul Pinder, Geo. Paule, Ri. Sutton, Heneage Finche, Wm. Richardson, William Turnor, Thomas Man, H. Stafford, Abraham Dawes.

22th June 1622

14. A MEETING OF THE COURT OF THE MINERAL AND BATTERY WORKS, 1622

[B.M., Loan MS. 16. Court Minute Book of the Mineral and Battery Works, 1620–1713]

A COURT for the Mineral and Battery Works holden at Mr. Mynne's chamber in Lincoln's Inn, the 7th day of February, 1621 [= 1622] at which were present: George Mynne, esq. one of the deputy governors, Mr. Thomas Morgan, Mr. Chute, Mr. Tamworthe, Mr. Wrighte, Mr. Martyn, Mr. Palmer, Mr. Danford, Mr. Camden, Mr. Downer, Mr. Lee, Mr. Hynd, Mr. Thomas Combe.

At this court Mr. Edward Palmer having satisfied the company as touching his right to the quarter part by him claimed as well by being heir at the common law to his uncle, Thomas Palmer, deceased, as also by a grant thereof from his said uncle by his last will and testament (a copy whereof was here produced under the register's hand) he was thereupon admitted and took the oath of an assistant of this society.

The state of the treasurer's account, having been examined by the auditors, was here certified to be as followeth:

	£	s.	d.
The charge thereof from 15 Decembris 1620 to 6 Decemb. 1621 was	365	8	5
The payments in that time were	176	9	0
There remaineth in the treasurer's hands undisbursed	188	19	5

which accompt subscribed by the said auditors was here shewed and allowed of by the said company, and was ordered to be delivered to the clerk to be entered into the company's book of accompts.

The said treasurer did here inform the company that he had already received their Christmas rents from their farmer of the wire works. And that the pensions and other charges being deducted, he had of the money remaining now also in his hands the sum of £55.

Whereupon it was agreed and ordered by the company that out of all the foresaid monies remaining in stock as aforesaid a dividend should be made after the rate of £10 a part to be paid according to the usual manner to such persons as are wont to receive dividend. And a warrant to the treasurer was here signed for that purpose.

But forasmuch as the said treasurer had before this day received from Sir John Bourchier and Mr. Tourner the sum of £200, part of the joint stock first raised for setting up the latin battery works near Maidstone in Kent, whereof part had been already divided, it was now ordered that the residue thereof remaining in his hands should also be divided with the company's monies that are now in stock. And further that before the 20th of this month Mr. Danford, Mr. Martyn, Mr. Camden, Mr. Downer, and the clerk should meet together to examine Sir William Rider's lease, which is to be taken out of the chest for that purpose, and the latin battery accompt, thereby to find out what is further due to the company either by arrearages of rent or otherwise.

It is also ordered that the right honourable the Lord Chamberlain, the Earl of Dorset, and the Earl of Leicester shall have their last year's dividends whereof they are yet unpaid, together with the money now due to them upon this present dividend. And that Mr. Mynne, Mr. Morgan, and the treasurer shall present the same unto them from the company. And that for the payment thereof as aforesaid this order shall be their warrant.

Mr. Edmond Nicholson of Edmonton in the county of Middlesex, esquire, did here desire a lease of the company's mines at Stamford in the county of Lincoln and within ten miles of the said town extending any way in the said county of Lincoln. And also within three miles of the said town extending any way within the county of Northampton, which was granted by the company to hold to him, his executors, administrators, and assigns, from the day of the date hereof unto the end and term of ten years, paying for the first year at Christmas next the rent of 50s. and for the two next years yearly £5; and for seven years residue of the said term yearly the sum of £10 half yearly at Midsummer and Christmas or within forty days after by even portions. And the said lease to be made with such covenants as other of the company's leases are wont to be made and a bond for payment of the said rent . . .

15. AN ACT TO REDUCE LITIGATION BY INFORMERS, 1623

[*Statutes of the Realm*, IV, part 2, pp. 1214–15]

21 Jas. c. 4

An Act for the Ease of the Subject concerning the Informations upon Penal Statute

WHEREAS the offences against divers and sundry penal laws and statutes of this realm may better and with more ease and less charge to the subject be commenced, sued, informed against, prosecuted, and tried in the counties where such offences shall be committed. And whereas the poor commons of this realm are grievously charged, troubled, vexed, molested, and disturbed by divers troublesome persons commonly called relators, informers, and promoters, by prosecuting and enforcing them to appear in his Majesty's Courts at Westminster, and to answer offences supposed by them to be committed against the said penal laws and statutes, or else to compound with them for the same. For remedy whereof be it enacted by the authority of this present Parliament, that all offences hereafter to be committed against any penal statute, for which any common informer or promoter may lawfully ground any popular action, bill, plaint, suit, or information before justices of assize, justices of nisi prius or gaol delivery, justices of oyer and terminer, or justices of the peace in their General or Quarter Sessions, shall after the end of this present session of Parliament be commenced, sued, prosecuted, tried, recovered, and determined by way of action, plaint, bill, information, or indictment before the justices of assize, justices of nisi prius, justices of oyer and terminer, and justices of gaol delivery, or before the justices of peace of every county, city, borough, or town corporate, and liberty, having power to enquire of, hear, and determine the same within this realm of England or dominion of Wales, wherein such offences shall be committed in any of the courts, places of judicature, or liberties aforesaid respectively, only at the choice of the parties which shall or will commence suit or prosecute for the same, and not elsewhere, save only in the said counties or places usual for those counties or any of them. And that like process upon every popular action, bill, plaint, information, or suit to be commenced or sued, or prosecuted after the end of this present session of Parliament by force of, or according to the purport of this act, be had and awarded to all intents and purposes as in an action of trespass *vi et armis* at the common law. And that all and all manner of informations, actions, bills, plaints, and suits whatsoever, hereafter to be commenced, sued, prosecuted, or awarded, either by the Attorney General of his Majesty, his heirs or successors for the time being, or by any officer or officers whatsoever for the time being, or by any common informer or other person whatsoever in any of his Majesty's Courts at Westminster, for or concerning any of the offences, penalties, or forfeitures aforesaid, shall be void and of none effect, any law, custom, or usage to the contrary thereof notwithstanding.

And be it further enacted by the authority aforesaid that in all informations to be exhibited and in all bills, counts, plaints, and declarations in any action or suit to be commenced against any person or persons either by or on the behalf of the king, or any other for or concerning any offence committed or to be committed against any penal statute, the offence shall be laid and alleged to have been committed in the said county where such offence was in truth committed, and not elsewhere. And if the defendant to any such information, action, or suit pleadeth that he oweth nothing, or that he is not guilty; and the plaintiff or informer in such information, action, or suit upon evidence to the jury that shall try such issue, shall not both prove the offence laid in the said information, action, or suit, and that the same offence was committed in that county, then the defendant and defendants shall be found not guilty.

And be it further enacted by the authority aforesaid that no officer, or minister in any court of record shall receive, file, or enter of record any information, bill, or plaint, count, or declaration grounded upon the said penal statutes or any of them which before by this Act are appointed to be heard and determined in their proper counties until the informer or relator hath first taken a corporal oath before some of the judges of that court that the offence or offences laid in such information, action, suit, or plaint, was or were not committed in any other county than where by the said information, bill, plaint, count, or declaration the same is or are supposed to have been committed, and that he believeth in his conscience the offence was committed within a year before the information or suit within the same county where the said information or suit was commenced; the same oath to be there entered of record.

And be it also enacted by the authority aforesaid that if any information, suit, or action shall be brought or exhibited against any person or persons for any offence committed or to be committed against the form of any penal law, either by or on the behalf of the king, or by any other, or on the behalf of the king and any other, it shall be lawful for such defendants to plead the general issue that they are not guilty, or that they owe nothing, and to give such special matter in evidence to the jury that shall try the same; which matter being pleaded had been good and sufficient matter in law to have discharged the said defendant or defendants against the information, suit, or action, and the said matters shall be then as available to him or them to all intents and purposes as if he or they had sufficiently pleaded, set forth, or alleged the same matter in bar or discharge of such information, suit, or action.

Provided always that this act or any clause contained therein shall not extend to any information, suit, or action grounded upon any law or statute made against Popish recusants or for or concerning Popish recusancy, or against those that shall not frequent the church and hear divine service;

nor to any information, suit, or action for maintenance, champerty, or buying
of titles; nor to any suit or information grounded upon the statute made in the
first year of the reign of our sovereign lord the king of a subsidy granted to
the king of tonnage, poundage, wool, etc.; nor for or concerning the concealing or defrauding the king, his heirs, or successors of any custom,
tonnage, poundage, subsidy, impost, or prisage; or for transporting of gold,
silver, ordinance, powder, shot, munition of all sorts, wool, wool fells, or
leather. But that such offence may be laid or alleged to be in any county
at the pleasure of any informer, anything in this act to the contrary
notwithstanding.

16. BENEDICT WEBB ASKS FOR A PATENT TO MAKE RAPESEED OIL FOR THE CLOTH INDUSTRY
1624

[Gloucester Public Library, Smyth of Nibley MS. 8.102; SZ 23.2
(2 and 3)]

To the King's most excellent Majesty,
the humble petition of Benedict Webb of Kingswood in the county
of Wiltshire, clothier

WHEREAS your petitioner *was employed by your Majesty and the State
into France in the 2nd year of your Majesty's reign for the revoking of an
edict whereby the English drapery was confiscated, which was effected to the
honour of your Majesty's kingdom and of that manufacture. At what time by
your petitioner's long continuance in France he there* observed a kind of oil
to be made of rape seed and other small round seeds for the use of clothiers,
part whereof your petitioner then bought and brought home into England,
and having to his great charge almost ever since endeavoured to bring the
same to perfection, hath now attained to the perfect making and mystery
thereof as experience and trial made by most of the clothiers in the counties
of Wiltshire and Gloucestershire and Somerset hath fully declared who find
the said oil far better for the use of clothing than that which is yearly brought
out of the Low Countries, and as useful as the Spanish oil yearly imported
into this kingdom, used for the best sort of cloths. By which mystery and
intention thus found out and brought to perfection by the charge and industry
of your petitioner, the price will be more easy to the clothier than in times
past and this kingdom able to support itself for all the drapery thereof
without the help of the Spanish oil or of that from the Low Countries,
besides the great enriching of much barren land in this kingdom by sowing
of this oil seed which is thereby made fruitful for corn, otherwise of small

* * This passage is struck out and the shorter phrase 'in his travels beyond seas about
20 years past' substituted. This is the phrase used in the Letter Patent.

use or profit, for that the same oil seed best prospers upon dry sandy ground which affordeth small comfort to the husbandman and besides setteth many thousands of poor people on work.

In consideration whereof may it please your Majesty to grant to your petitioner, according to the late statute, your Highness's Letters Patent for the sole making of such oil for the term of 14 years in recompense of his great charge, invention, and bringing to perfection so useful and rich a commodity to your kingdom as the like hath seldom been really effected, your petitioner not intending to impeach any importation by any merchant whatsoever nor of any other subject of this realm who have used the same by the space of three years past and your petitioner shall be encouraged to draw to perfection out of his experience and long labour other matters, which will turn to the honour of your Majesty and benefit of your kingdom many ways. And daily pray for your Majesty's happy and prosperous reign long to continue.

At the Court at Newmarket, 28 November 1624.

His Majesty considering this suit to tend to the good of the commonwealth is graciously pleased at the humble suit of Wm. Smithesbie, his Majesty's servant, and for his benefit that his Highness's Attorney General prepare a bill (ready for his Majesty's signature) containing a grant thereof to the petitioner for 14 years according as is desired.

Sidney Montague.

Q. If not fit to reserve a rent of 5*l.* or 10*l.* per ann. to his Majesty.
A. Proclamation to notify the Letters Patent.

*   *   *

Benedict Webb of Kingswood in the county of Wiltshire, clothier, aged 61 years, maketh oath that he thinketh in his conscience and is verily persuaded that he hath expended and laid out of his own private estate above the sum of two thousand pounds in and about the trial and experiments by him made concerning the true making of oil fit and useful for the clothiers of this kingdom, and what manner of grounds and other husbandries best sorted thereunto, which after many years' labour and pains he hath now attained unto.

Ro. Riche. 26 November 1624.

[Endorsed by Smyth:] Ben. Webb, his affidavit for the charges in trials about oil.

*   *   *

[Draft certificate, unsigned.]

These are to testify his most excellent Majesty that we, whose names are hereunder subscribed, professing the art of clothmaking in his Highness's counties of Wiltshire, Gloucestershire, and Somerset have found by often trial and experience that the oil now made by Benedict Webb of Kingswood in the county of Wiltshire of rapeseeds and other small seeds is as good and useful in our art and mystery of cloth making as the Spanish oil and more useful for the making of fine cloths than the oil brought yearly into this realm out of the Low Countries.

[Endorsed by Smyth:] Clothiers' certificate about oil not subscribed.

17. A PROPOSAL TO REGULATE THE RURAL CLOTH INDUSTRY, 1625[1]

[P.R.O., SP 16/1, no. 24]

THE Letters Patents of incorporation to the several counties where the New Draperies are or shall be set up to contain these clauses: a preamble setting forth the great benefit which doth redound to the kingdom by the manufactory of our wools; the decay thereof by the neglect of the true making of the New Draperies; the great care of his Majesty to restore the New Draperies to their perfected [state] and to encourage the frequent and true making of them; the advice of his Lords that it cannot fitly be done but by trusting the principal men of quality in every county with the oversight and government thereof and giving them power and authority thereunto; and that it is resolved that to incorporate them is the best and safest course.

Therefore the body of the book to contain these parts:

That the justices of peace by name of the county be all incorporated by the name of the Governors for the New Drapery of that county, to them and their successors, justices of the peace of that county.

That these Governors be enabled with power to make laws and ordinances for the advancing of this trade and to choose officers.[2]

To raise stocks.

To inflict punishment upon offenders.

To take account and dispose of all things for the public utility of the county.

That the body of the corporation to be all the inhabitants of or within the county.

All ordinary clauses for corporations to be added.

A special clause to follow the directions of his Majesty and his Lords.

Directions to the Governors to be expressed for the present in a schedule to be annexed to the Letters Patents.

These to be varied from time to time as there shall be occasion by the advice of the Lords of the Council signified under the seal of the Council, and to be registered by the clerk of the company in their register or repertory.

The present directions to be: for the length of every piece to be constant 27 yards; for the breadth to be for broad stuff ——; for narrow ——; for the

---

[1] An earlier version of this proposal (B.M., Add. MS. 34, 324, f. 201) is thought to be by Walter Morell of Hertfordshire, and is dated December 1622.

[2] A marginal note says: The Governors and commonalty to be the name of incorporation.

weight ——. For the searches and trials every piece shall pass[1] from the weaver, from the fuller, from the rower or clothworker, from the dyer, from the presser for the several seals. No fees to any officers but out of the forfeitures.

[Endorsed:] *Gubernatores et Comitat.* The seal of the corporation for trade in the county of Hertford [March, 1625].

18. LEEDS CLOTHIERS RESIST INCORPORATION IN A GILD, 1629

[J. J. Cartwright, *Chapters in the History of Yorkshire*, Wakefield, 1872, pp. 304–7]

To the King's most excellent Majesty,
the humble petition of Robert Sympson and Christopher Jackson and many thousands of poor clothiers of the parish of Leeds in the county of York.

SHEWETH, that whereas it pleased your most excellent Majesty by your Letters Patents dated the 12 day of July in the second year of your Majesty's most happy reign to incorporate the said town and parish for the better increase of the trade of clothing. And your Highness's said Letters Patents did give liberty and power to all the said parishioners and inhabitants to distinguish and divide themselves into gilds and fraternities, not giving authority to the aldermen and assistants there to enforce or compel any to be companies unless they willingly submitted thereunto. So it is, may it please your most excellent Majesty, that the present Alderman[2] (being an Attorney at the Common Law) and a few of the chief burgesses for the increase of their own authority and for their own gain (as the petitioners conceive) and not for the good of clothing contrary to the goodwill and liking of most and of the best of the parish (there being not the fortieth part of the clothiers that do consent thereunto as the petitioners hope to make it appear) endeavour to enforce the petitioners to be a company and to submit themselves to such rules and constitutions as they shall please to make, to be fined, imprisoned, and called from their labour at their wills.

Your petitioners shew that many of them daily setting on work above forty poor people in their trade, and that compelling them to come hither, dwelling 150 miles hence, tendeth much to their impoverishing and overthrow of their trade.

And therefore your petitioners humbly pray that your Majesty would be

---

[1] A marginal note says: Ponnie, draught work, linsy wolsey.
[2] Leeds was incorporated by Charles I in 1626. Sir John Savile, of Howley, was the first 'Alderman', an office equivalent to that of Mayor, and the Savile arms were adopted as the arms of the town.

graciously pleased to refer the examination as well of the consent and allowance of those whom this business doth concern as the consideration of the inconveniency of the thing that is desired by the said Alderman and a few burgesses unto such lords, knights, and gentlemen of the county of York as shall seem best to your Majesty and who best understand the nature of clothing.

And your petitioners etc.

At the Court of Whitehall, 21 March 1628–9.

His Majesty is graciously pleased to refer this petition to the Lord President of the North and the Council there together with Sir Henry Savile and Sir Richard Beaumont, knights and baronets, Sir John Ramsden, knight, Christopher Wainsford, and John Keyes, esquires, or to any six, five, or four of them, whereof the Lord President to be one; who are to call the said Alderman and such of the burgesses together with so many of the poor petitioners as they shall think meet in this cause before them, and upon due consideration of the petition and the reasons annexed, to settle some good course if they can for the remedying of such inconveniences as they shall find cause for, or otherwise, to certify his Majesty of the truth of the matter together with their opinions touching the same that such further order may be taken as to justice shall appertain.

Ra. Freeman

19. THE ESSEX CLOTH INDUSTRY IN DEPRESSION, 1629[1]

[Bodleian Library, Oxford, MS. Firth c.4, pp. 488–94, 504–5, 508–11]

A Brief Declaration concerning the State of the Manufacture of Wools in the County of Essex, 1629

THERE are within this county about twelve or fourteen towns wherein is exercised the manufactures upon wools, in all which there are not fewer that receive the livelihood and dependence thereon by that means than fifty thousand persons. The principal of the clothing is Colchester, Coggeshall, Witham, Bocking, Braintree, Dedham, of which towns upon examination we find the condition at this time to be as followeth.

COLCHESTER

In and by this town of Colchester there are above 20,000 persons maintained and have dependence by the manufactures of wools into bays and says.

---

[1] See also Section I, pp. 32–3.

For the trade of bays, it hath much declined since the time they were prohibited in Spain, which was about two years before the breach of the peace, at which time they made in that town 400 pieces of bays in a week, and as many says, which were then sold for vi*li.* per piece but since that time they had not made above 100 pieces a week, one week with another, and the price fallen to little above iiii*li.* and for this five or six weeks last past they have not made above 50 bays a week. Of which very few are sold unless by some very poor men, who of necessity have been enforced to pawn or sell with very great loss, so as there remains of that poor quantity above 6,000*li.* worth yet unsold.

But the chief manufacture of that town being says whereof they make about 400 pieces a week, the rates and prices whereof are divers from 50*s.* piece to viii*li.* piece. These says within this five or six weeks were bought off as fast as they could make them, but since that time the merchant buyeth none at all, so as there remains upon their hands above 6,000*li.* worth in money unsold. They brought up this week and the last above viii C. and their warehouses now in town are now so full as they are scarce capable of any more. Their chiefest vent was wont to be about the Spring unto the merchant trading into France, Leghorn, and other places. Their course in sale hath not been to tie themselves to any certain persons, but to sell indifferently to such merchants as would give the best price. Their stock and credit being now spent, they are ready generally to give over trade as many already have done.

COGGESHALL

The persons employed in and by this town by the manufacture of bays are at least 5,000. The proportion which they usually made for some years last past hath been a hundred pieces a week but for this last year they have not made above 80 pieces a week. They have remaining upon their hands above 1,500 pieces of which they cannot make sale. As this being a very poor town and unruly, as certain the multitudes of the poorer sort must starve or use unlawful means to support themselves if present relief be not afforded.

WITHAM

In and by this town are above 2,000 maintained about manufactures of bays. The weekly proportion which they were wont to make was some 40 or 50 a week, but within this six weeks they have not been able to make above ten pieces a week, during which time they have had no sale at all, nor can get the merchants so much as to look upon them or take them in panne [= pawn ?]. So as they profess they be afraid to go home being not able to pay their workmen or to set them any more at work.

BRAINTREE

In and by this town by the manufacture of bays is maintained and have dependence between 3,000 or 4,000 persons heretofore. The proportion which they were wont to make was about 100 pieces a week, but within this five or six weeks last past there have not been made above forty pieces a week of which few or none can be sold, so as there remains upon their hands 500 pieces unsold or above whereof above 600 pieces be in this town. The rest they do not bring up because they have no sale for them in town, the town having many poor and those of the better sort are not able long to maintain them. It is doubted many of them will forsake their dwellings suddenly and give over their trade.

BOCKING

In and by this town by the manufacture of bays are set on work 7,000 persons within this seven years. They were wont to make 400 pieces a week. Since they fell by little and little to 300, and lately they have not been able to make above 100 a week, and within this five or six weeks not above forty a week, for having had little or no sale a great number have been undone and forced to give over their trade quite. There remain upon their hands unsold above 2,000 pieces whereof 700 are in this town and their warehouses being full, they forbear to bring up any more. That town abound[s] with poor whereof many are very unruly and having no employment will make the place very hazardous for men of better rank to live amongst them.

DEDHAM AND LANGHAM

This town subsists by making of the cloths called Suffolk[?] cloths by which they set awork above 3,000 people, they having now upon their hands above 3,000 cloths worth at the least 10*li.* a cloth which amount to the sum of 30,000*li.* or above. They have not sold above 100 cloths this eighteen months for that their usual sale and chief time of sale is about the spring of the year, at what time they were wont to have their cloth wholly taken off by the Turkey and East Country merchants who now refusing to buy any these ease [=as?] many other adjoining towns in Suffolk, who subsist by this kind of clothing to the number of above 100,000 persons, are like to be utterly undone and ruinated if some speedy course be not taken therein.

The state of the towns in Essex besides, which are subsisted by these manufactures, is as the former, save that only their numbers are far less, but their poverty is exceeding great, and lamentable is the being of all this multitude of people which live by these manufactures. Few or none that can subsist unless they be paid their wages once a week, and many of them that cannot live unless they be paid every night, many hundreds of them having no beds to lie in nor food, but from hand to mouth to maintain themselves, their wives, and children.

*   *   *

Letters of the Council to the Deputy Lieutenant and Justices
of Peace in the County of Essex

5 May 1629

After our hearty commendations, his Majesty having received several advertisements whereby he understandeth that upon some stop of the accustomed vent of cloth and other woollen commodities made within that county, divers poor people who gain their living by working and making the said commodities are at this present shortened of their wonted employment, you shall hereby understand that his Majesty is very sensible thereof, and careful to remove and take away that stop, and to restore the vent of cloth to the wonted course, for which purpose his Majesty in his own royal person and divers have seriously treated with the principal merchants who were wont to take those manufactures from the clothiers' hands and his Majesty resolved not to desist until the business be brought to some good effect, which we confidently hope will be done within a short time. And because his Majesty is likewise informed that not only the poor workmen themselves, formerly employed in clothing, but also divers others (being lewd and dissolute persons) upon this pretence do take occasion to associate themselves in a disorderly and tumultuous manner, and so unlawfully wander abroad in great and unusual numbers, which may prove of ill consequence and example if speedy redress be not taken therein, we do therefore by his Majesty's special commandment charge and require you to take especial care to prevent the spreading of such a growing evil and as well by your own industry and endeavour as by your strict order and directions to the high constables, petty constables, and other subordinate ministers under you to proceed effectually by the best means you and they can devise to maintain the peace and quiet of the country in preventing and repressing of such tumults as may ensue upon these beginnings. And for the better effecting thereof we do likewise in his Majesty's and by his royal command expressly require and charge you to make diligent search, and enquire to discover and find out such lewd persons as aforesaid that belong not to the trade of clothing and do join themselves with the poor workmen to increase their disorders, and having found them, to take order that either they do betake themselves to some lawful course of life to get their living, or else to see them severely punished according to law and justice. But for such as are poor and do indeed want work in their lawful trades depending upon clothing, that ye take care they be set on work, if not in their own trades in some other good and honest labour, fit for them until they may again be employed in the works belonging to their own vocation. And if any such shall be found that cannot be provided of work in one kind or other, then you are to think of some fit course for their relief according to law, wherein you are to be very careful that if any poor clothing town or the places thereunto adjoining be not able to maintain their own poor, in such a case you are to procure them some necessary and competent contribution from other parts of that county that are best able to bear it. And if any shall notwithstanding presume to wander abroad or gather themselves together in unlawful and disordered manner, you are to cause them both to be repressed, and punished as afore-said ... And so we bid you heartily farewell from Whitehall, the 5 May, 1629.

Your loving friends

Tho. Coventry, Rich. Weston, Manchester, Pembroke, Salisbury, Conway, Willmot, Dorchester, Grandison, John Cooke, Humphrey May, Fra. Cottington.

*   *   *

Justices of the Peace from Braintree to the Lords of the Council

May it please your lordships, upon the receipt of your lordships' letters of the last month, we have met together to consider of the means of putting those your lordships' directions in execution. But when we fell into the examina-tion of the abilities of those parishes within the hundreds where the cloth-workers dwell, we find all so equally interested in that trade as that we know not any one parish within those hundreds which are able to set their own poor on work, and if we should now go about to force the neighbouring parishes to contribute to those towns, instead of appeasing the disorders now on foot in some few of the great clothing towns we should thereby infinitely increase the complaints in all the parishes within those hundreds which by the statute (whereto your lordships are pleased to refer us) are only liable to any taxation which we have power to make out of the general quarter sessions. And whereas your lordships are pleased to require us to make diligent enquiry to find out such disorderly persons as sort themselves amongst the clothiers though they be not of the trade, nor would apply themselves to labour if they should be set on work, and severely to punish all their misdemeanours, we are very careful to inform ourselves of them, and as we shall find them out, and have just proof of the ―― which as yet do not fully appear unto us, we shall be ready to punish them according to their demerits. And upon all occasions to observe your lordships' directions ever resting

At your lordships' command
most humbly

Ro. Warwick, W. Maynard, Thomas Wyseman, W. Maxey, Dru. Deane, Henry Gent., Tho. Higham.

*   *   *

The Petition of the Weavers to the Justices of Peace at their Quarter Sessions

To the Right Honourable and worshipful the justices of these sessions assembled, the humble petition of the poor weavers of the towns of Bocking and Braintree.

SHEWETH that our miseries do still remain upon us though some little refreshment we have had of comfortable answers from his Majesty and some work since our complaint, but nothing in regard that our necessities require. But what with little work and little wages our burden still remaineth heavy, our rents run, and now the time of year to provide our wood, and the greatest number no way able to do it without using unlawful means to serve our necessities in the winter time, which we are very unwilling to do. But yet we see little hope, for in that little work that we have, our bays some of them are half so long again as they were wont to be, and yet never the more wages. We desire that all sorts of bays may be of one equal length, and desire to be eased of this burden which lieth heavy on us. Now for that little they do, and many other burdens that we have lie heavy upon us, and will lie heavier upon us although they had sale more than they have yet, many men take apprentices having their work, some from their kindred, some from their landlords, as most of our principal clothiers are landlords, and many clothiers themselves take many apprentices which is still against us to breed workmen, and when trading serves not, they set them to husbandry, being men able to hold land as well as their trade. Thus we desire to make our miseries known by a regal and honest course, though many of our poor brethren have run beyond compass by violating his Majesty's laws and have suffered therefore, which we the wardens are much grieved for that they fell to such a course, for we always persuaded the contrary, and that they would take a legal course in all humble and obedient manner, the which we are persuaded that they will for they are very sorrowful for that which is done. If we be blamed for complaining more than other towns have done, we know that our misery is the misery of other towns. For witness the poor of Coggeshall themselves, there came seven score together to Braintree thinking to find the magistrates there, and made a petition to lay forth their grievances, condition that lay upon them a long time, therefore being in the quagmire ready to perish, and say Lord help, and use no lawful means to come out, do not they justly perish? Therefore we desire this honourable bench that you commiserate the cause of us poor miserable men, and that, as you have been our friends, we do humbly entreat you that you would be so still to the King's Majesty and to the honourable Council, for we most humbly entreat that we may have an order from His Majesty for the restraining the taking so many apprentices, and some other the like evils that are upon us, until such time as it shall please God and his Majesty that there be a Parliament, that we may have the benefit of poor subjects to have a law for the reformation of those things. And so we leave you to the Almighty entreating him to give you understanding in all things as his blessing here and hereafter.

*   *   *

Order of Sessions touching Weavers, 1 October 1629

It is ordered by the court that William Lane of Bocking, clothier, doth forthwith put away Joseph Neale, his apprentice, who was by him entertained contrary to the law, and deliver him to the churchwardens and overseers of the poor of Bocking aforesaid to be by them provided for. And this court doth further order that all others of the said town of Bocking and of the towns of Braintree and Coggeshall and all other clothing towns of this county who have entertained apprentices contrary to the law do forthwith put them away. And that all weavers do from henceforth forebear to rangell and rone hereafter any bays contrary to the law in that case provided. And that no weaver do hereafter employ for making of bays more than three narrow looms together, or set on work more than three workmen at any one time together, to, for, and about the weaving of such bays. And if any shall refuse to observe and perform this order in all things herein contained respectively according to the true intent and meaning thereof, the next justices of peace of this county are desired by this court to call all such reflectory [= refractory] persons before them and bind them over to appear at the next quarter sessions to answer their contempt in disobeying of this order.

*   *   *

Justices of Assizes to Sir Thomas Wyseman, etc.
20 November 1629

After our hearty commendations, whereas we have formerly written a letter unto you for the staying of certain apprentices in the service of their masters who are clothiers and weavers, which letter whether it be come unto your hands as yet we know not, and because sithence there have been before us Henry Enner and Thomas Layen of Coggeshall, clothiers, and have complained unto us that some of you have made your warrant to send them unto the gaol because the[y] refused to put away their apprentices, which were poor men's children born in the same town, and received by them into their service, who have served a great part of their apprenticeship. And for that we desire all parties interested herein, and the rather because we have taken recognisances of the parties above named for their appearance at the next assizes to be holden for the county of Essex, we do therefore desire you to stay all further proceedings, as well against them in particular as all others in general who have taken apprentices of the children in the same town, and of all other clothing towns until the next assizes or sooner if necessity require, and we will be ready to hear of some fitting course, not disagreeing to law, for the placing and removing of apprentices. So hoping that you will perform this our request, we bid you farewell.

Your loving friends
Geo. Croke, Geo. Vernon.

Serjeant's Inn, the 20th of November, 1629.

*   *   *

A Copy of a Letter from the Justices concerning the Weavers
2nd December 1629

May it please you to understand that since the receipt of your letters dated the 20th of November last whereby you desire us to stay all further proceedings as well against Henry Enewe and Thomas Guyon of Coggeshall, clothiers, in particular, as all others in general, who have taken apprentices of the children of the same town and of all other clothing towns until the next assizes. There hath been many complaints made unto us by divers poor people of the trades of clothing and weaving that they are in great distress for want of work, which hath been the complaint of many of them a long time, as the lords of his Majesty's Privy Council do well know and yourselves do well remember. We doubt not the flocking up of divers of them to the Court this last summer to make their case known to his Majesty which was ill taken. For the preventing the like disorder in time to come . . . the said Earl [Earl of Warwick, Lord Lieutenant of Essex] and we whose names are under written met at Braintree and called before us as well the clothiers as weavers.

And first we propounded that the clothiers should have their bays woven of one length to the end the weavers' wages might be proportioned accordingly, but the clothiers objected many things, that it was not fit that they should be tied to one certain length, and one reason above the rest did much move us not to press them any further in that point, which was that they were to serve the merchant with bays of such lengths as the foreign parts unto which they traded did require, which was of divers lengths and therefore if they should be tied to one certain length it would greatly hinder trading. From that we fell to treat about the assessing of the weavers' wages according to the length and breadth of the bays but therein we found as great a difficulty as in the other, for the clothier alleged that there was great difference of bays which they made, they paying for the weaving of some vi$d$. the string, some vii$d$., some viii$d$., some ix$d$., and some xd., and so to xviii$d$., which diversity made the matter so difficult to assess wages for every several sorts of bays as we knew not how to do it with any certainty, so that in these two points we could effect nothing for the help of the poor weavers, which gave them much discontent.

At last we found there was no way to do them good but to restrain the multitude of apprentices not only for the future, but to discharge such as had been unlawfully taken, and therefore at the next quarter sessions the matter being moved in open court, an order was made accordingly which, being by us put in execution, many turned away their apprentices which had come from remote places and whose parents could dispend no land, and some being taken out of neighbour parishes poor men's children, and some out of the clothing towns themselves, bound by the churchwardens and overseers with the allowance of two justices of peace, which were suffered to remain with their masters. But such poor children as were bound by the overseers, etc., without any allowance of the justices, we did not think fit to give any approbation of them, for that there were more already of the weaver's trade than could live one by the other, for when trading is anything dead, as often in the year it is, there is not work to be had for a number of them, and being used to no other labour, they immediately fall into a miserable estate, as that in one clothing town, which is Bocking, as hath been certified us by the minister and chief inhabitants, there is fifty or sixty families which have not so much as a poor flock bed to lie upon, but are forced to lie only upon straw and can hardly get that.

This being the state and condition of these poor men much charged with wives and children, we held it very necessary to lessen the number of apprentices unlawfully taken or not approved of by the justices, which gave good satisfaction, and many [a] poor householder was taken to work in their places until your letters came. After which their masters took their apprentices again and turned the householder out of his work. And where it is said that their apprentices thus turned from their masters would become rogues, we took a course to place them in other services which the law doth appoint poor men's children to be bound unto, and had as we supposed ere this time effected the same, had we not been interrupted by the clothiers' complaints to you, who indeed care not how many workmen there be of weavers and combers, etc., for by that means they can have their work done better cheap, having of late abridged the weaver some vii*d.* or viii*d.* in a bay of that which formerly they had, so that the best workman of them all cannot earn in a week, although the work be very good, not above iiii*d.* and some iii*d.* and some not above ii*d.* which is small wages to maintain a family, pay house rent, and buy firewood. But the truth is they are made now so poor, they are neither able to pay rent nor buy any wood, but are forced to break hedges, lop trees, and sometimes fell them by the ground, and to do many other unlawful things to the great damage of all their neighbours about them. Now having certified to you the true state of this cause, we desire you to take some speedy course for the settling of this business or otherwise to suffer us to go on in ours, which we hope shall be no way disagreeing to the law, nor to the peaceable government of these parts of our country, and we beseech you be pleased to give us leave to tell you that if somewhat be not presently done, we shall not be able to keep these poor people in quiet, which we assure ourselves will be very displeasing to his Majesty and the lords if as they tell us they should repair unto them. And so recommending this to your grave considerations, we rest

Ever ready to do your service,

W. Maynard, Tho. Wyseman, William Maxey, Dru. Deane, James Heron.

Braintree, the xith of December, 1629. To our much honoured friends, Sir Geo. Croke, knight, one of the justices of the King's Bench and Sir Geo. Vernon, knight, one of the Barons of his Majesty's Exchequer or to either of them.

20. SUGGESTIONS FOR THE REFORM OF ABUSES IN CLOTH MAKING, 1630

[Acts of the Privy Council of England, June 1630–June 1631, no. 262]

At Whitehall, 29th of October, 1630

An Abstract of a Commission for Reformation of the Abuses in Cloth Making

THE preamble reciteth the statutes for true clothing, the disorders against the same, the inconveniences thereupon following and his Majesty's intention for reformation.

1. Charge given to Anthony Wither and Samuell Lively, the Commissioners, to repair with the Commission unto the counties of Gloucester, Wiltshire, Oxford, and Somerset, and the several places therein where white cloth is usually made, and there to notify the Commission.

2. To enquire in the places aforesaid how the statutes for true clothmaking are executed and of what quality, skill, and experience the searchers and overseers of cloth there are, and whether they have taken oath and entered recognisance for the true execution of their offices and do execute the same according to the said statutes. And, if they find any of them not qualified or not doing according to the said statutes, then to acquaint the justices and other head officers therewith.

3. To enquire where there is defect as aforesaid of fit persons to be searchers and overseers and them to present to the justices, and other head officers to be chosen, into the places of others insufficient and removed.

4. Charge to the said justices and chief officers to give oath to the searchers and overseers and to take recognisance of them according to the statutes in the presence of the Commissioners, or one of them if they or one of them may be conveniently present.

5. Charge given to the searchers and overseers to present from time to time to the churchwardens and overseers for the poor the defects found in the cloths with the names of the delinquents, to the end that the same churchwardens may levy the penalties due to the poor according to the statute.

6. Charge to the said churchwardens and overseers to keep a book and therein to enter the said defects together with the names of the delinquents, and to levy the penalties according to the statute. And to shew the same book to the Commissioners requiring it, to the end his Majesty may have account how they the said churchwardens and overseers perform the statute and recover the poor's part.

7. Charge to the justices of peace and other chief officers to execute the statute for abolishing the lower bar in the taintors and other like instruments tending to the concealing of faults in the cloth.

8. Charge to the Commissioners to enquire of such lower bars and other deceitful engines and finding them to acquaint the justices and other chief officers therewith.

9. Charge to the justices and other chief officers forthwith to publish their Commission in their several precincts, to the end all whom it may concern may take notice of his Majesty's pleasure herein, and that they give good respect and countenance to the Commissioners.

10. Power and charge to the Commissioners to do all other good and lawful acts tending to the performance of his Majesty's intention in this Commission, and to inform the Lords of his Majesty's Privy Council of such persons as they find obstinate, remiss, or refractory against the execution of this Commission.

11. Charge to the justices and other head officers and all others whom it concerneth to perform their several duties in all other points also touching the true cloth making according to the statutes. To this article to be added such clauses as Mr Attorney shall find requisite, directing the justices of the peace to give all fit countenance and assistance as well to the Commissioners as the Commission.

Signed: Lord Keeper, Lord Treasurer, Lord Privy Seal, Earl of Suffolk, Lord Viscount Dorchester, Lord Viscount Falkland, Lord Newburgh, Mr. Treasurer.

21. THE APPRENTICESHIP OF GIRLS IN THE BONE LACE INDUSTRY, 1634

[Lancs. Record Office, QSB 1/138/65: 1634]

To the right worshipful the King's Majesty's justices of peace and quorum assembled at this present sessions at Ormskirk, 21 July 1634, the humble petition of Jane Lowe, widow, and Elizabeth Massy, widow.

SHEWETH that whereas your petitioners did compound and agree to and with one Katherin Gerard, spinster, and Margaret, the wife of Gawther Taylor that they the said Katherin and Margaret should have two daughters of your petitioners to work and serve with them the said Katherin and Margaret for the space of one whole year and for that term to make and weave bone lace only and that she the said Katherin or the said Margaret should give and pay to the said children the hire or payment of the several sums following, that is to say to the daughter of the said Jane Lowe xxx*s.* per annum, and to the daughter of the said Elizabeth Massy xlviii*s.* per annum. And further that the said Katherin or Margaret should chastise the said children in due and moderate sort and not otherwise.

But now so it is, if it may please your good worships, that the said Katherin Gerard and Margaret Taylor, being both of them convicted and obstinate recusants, have not only enforced the said children to work upon the Sundays and other holy days, but also in most violent and outrageous manner beaten and abused the said children to the hazard of their lives. In so much as your petitioners for the fear of the loss of their children and to avoid the most wicked and execrable curses of the said Katherin and Margaret and likewise for fear their said children should be seduced from the true religion now established were glad to take their said children from the said Katherin and Margaret and to keep them at home with them, the said children still affirming that they would rather kill or drown themselves than suffer themselves to be maimed by beating and abusing as they have formerly been.

Your petitioners therefore most humbly beseech your good worships to take due consideration of the premises and to take and receive such testimony concerning the same as also touching the carriage and demeanour of the said Katherin and Margaret and also of one Margaret Lightfoote as your petitioners can produce. And your petitioners will daily pray to God for your good worships in all health and happiness long to continue.

Discharged by the quorum.

22. SALTWORKS IN NORTH-EAST ENGLAND, 1634

[Travels in Holland, the United Provinces, England, Scotland, and Ireland, 1634–5, by Sir William Brereton, bart., ed. E. Hawkins, Chetham Soc., I, 1844, pp. 86–9]

RESTING here 23 Jun. I took boat about twelve clock, and went to Tynemouth and to the Shields, and returned about seven clock; it is about seven miles. Here I viewed the salt works, wherein is more salt works and more salt made than in any part of England that I know, and all the salt here made is made of salt-water. These pans, which are not to be numbered, placed in the river mouth, and wrought with coals brought by water from Newcastle pits. A most dainty new salt work lately here erected, which is absolutely the most complete work that I ever saw; in the breadth whereof is placed six rank of pans, four pans in a rank; at either outside the furnaces are placed in the same manner as are my brother Booth's,[1] under the grate of which furnaces the ashes fall, and there is a lid or cover for both; and by the heat of these ashes, there being a pan made in the floor betwixt every furnace, which is made of brick, for which also there is a cover, there is boiled, and made into lumps of hard and black salt, which is made of the brine which drops from the new-made salt, which is placed over a cistern of lead, which cistern is under the floor of the store-house, which is in the end of the building. These great lumps of hard black salt are sent to Colchester to make salt upon salt, which are sold for a greater price than the rest, because without these at Colchester they cannot make any salt. . .

Here at the Shields are the vastest salt works I have seen, and by reason of

---

[1] Sir William Brereton married, for his first wife, Susan, daughter of Sir George Booth, of Dunham. 'Brother Booth' was probably William, the eldest son and heir of Sir George, and father of the first Lord Delamere. He died the following year, 1636.

the conveniency of coal, and cheapness thereof, being at 7s. a chaldron, which is three wain load. Here is such a cloud of smoke as amongst these works you cannot see to walk; there are, as I was informed, about two hundred and fifty houses, poor ones and low built, but all covered with boards. Here in every house is erected one fair great iron pan, five yards long, three yards and a half broad; the bottom of them made of thin plates nailed together, and strong square rivets upon the nail heads, about the breadth of the batt of your hand: these pans are three quarters of a yard deep; ten great bars there are placed on the inner side of the pan, three square, two inches thick; every of these great pans, as Dobson informed me, cost about 100*l*. and cannot be taken down to be repaired with less than 10*l*. charge. Every pan yields four draughts of salt in a week, and every draught is worth about 1*l*. 10*s*. Spent in coal: ten chaldron of coal at 7*s*. a chaldron, which amounts to 3*l*. 10*s*. in coals; deduct out of 6*l*. there remains 2*l*. 10*s*. besides one man's wages. So as in these 250 pans there is weekly spent in coals 775*l*., every pan yielding 6*l*. weekly, being 250. Total of the worth of the salt made in them amounts to 1,500*l*.; gained 735*l*.; deduct of this 120*l*. workmen's wages for making it, 120*l*.; clear gain about 600*l*.[1] a year. A wain load of salt is here worth about 3*l*. 10*s*., and a chaldron of coals, which is worth 7*s*. is three wain load.

23. THE BRICK AND TILEMAKERS OF LONDON PETITION FOR A GILD, *c.* 1634

[Bodleian Library, Oxford, MS. Bankes Papers 12/34]

To the King's most excellent Majesty the humble petition of the brick and tilemakers.

HUMBLY sheweth that whereas your Majesty hath divers times been petitioned unto concerning the granting to the brick and tilemakers a corporation to which your Majesty hath given diverse references without any effect either to the relief and weal of the subject in general or to your Majesty and your rents and revenues.

For the making of bricks and tiles being a matter of great consequence and the commonwealth much suffering by reason of the badness of stuffs now usually made which causeth men to build houses upon leases in slight and dangerous manner. And raiseth much the rents of houses and breedeth many other enormities. For remedy whereof and for prevention of the daily destruction of timber which will cause the decay of shipping within your Majesty's kingdoms, your Majesty's first petitioners offering to your Majesty 4*d*. for every thousand of bricks and tiles which shall be made and sold; and we your now petitioners do willingly offer 6*d*. for every thousand shall be

---

[1] There is an error in this calculation. 775 ought to be 875, and 735 ought to be 625; then the clear gain would be £505 a year.

made and sold, as said is, which truly may be given without wronging the subject or damaging the makers.

May it therefore please your gracious Majesty to prevent further delay and other dangers that may arise in redressing of the abuses for the weal and relief of the subject. And for the speedy furtherance of a good yearly revenue to your Majesty (seeing that there is neither law nor reason to the contrary) that your Majesty would be graciously pleased to cause [to] give order to your Attorney-General for the drawing up of a corporation about the City of London and 20 miles compass thereof for the brick and tilemakers for your Majesty's hand.[1] And that the said corporation may continue such orders and privileges as others the like hath.

And we (as by duty bound) shall ever pray for your Majesty's long life and most happy reign.

[Undated. *c.* 1634.]

24. INFORMERS PROSECUTED IN THE COURTS, 1635

[Bodleian Library, Oxford, MS. Bankes Papers, 44/56, 57, 7]

[Bankes's Notes on Precedents for prosecuting Informers.]

24 Novembris, 30 Eliz. John Crapnall brought *ore tenus* for exhibiting several informations in the King's Bench to the number of seventy for supposed offences against several penal statutes, and yet it was to be presumed the defendant had for money compounded, for Mr. Attorney could not find upon search Crapnall had brought any to trial but one, and received of Lingwood, a defendant, for felling timber £4 8s.

Crapnall committed to the Fleet, fined £10 to make restitution, and never to be informer again and to submit at the Assizes.

*   *   *

[Notes for the Prosecution. n.d. but 1635]

To be a common informer and accuser of others is a thing which hears ill from the common voice of men . . .

Now the only good thing which information has in it, this defendant has omitted and wrought wholly for the contrary; for he has taken a course to cherish offenders in sheltering them from the sentence of law, and has set up as it were a court of protection for them if they will but pay him his fees, making this honourable court and the laws of the land only as a stalking horse for his own game.

*   *   *

[Notes in Bankes's hand for the Prosecution *ore tenus* in Star Chamber of John Sutton.]

---

[1] A warrant to draw up a grant of incorporation was ordered by Charles I in 1635.

I have brought to judgment before your lordships John Sutton, a common informer, who has taken it up for a trade, having been practised in it above seven years as he confesses. He intrudes himself into all public business, intermeddles in matters of state, informs in all courts for all manner of offences against the common law, statute laws, and proclamations, and pretends himself to be a public minister to put the laws and edicts in execution, and that in public business which no way concerns himself, not in zeal to the public but for private ends. How he hath behaved himself in this employment, your lordships have heard by his examinations. He confesseth that in divers suits, when he served process, he never put in a bill; in others he hath put in bills but took out no process of contempt to bring them to answer.[1] He hath replied in some few since he was questioned. He never examined witnesses in any cause but one against Fuller for engrossing of corn and forestalling the market, and in seven years' time never brought any cause to hearing or trial. In some causes he confesseth ingenuously that that [sic] he received compositions having no licence to compound, viz.: Michaelmas, 8 Car. [1632] he exhibited a bill in Star Chamber against Henry Sandford for transporting wool which was dismissed by consent, and had £14 of the defendant for a composition; Sandford afterwards was brought *ore tenus* in the Star Chamber and fined £3,000 for the same offence; £20 composition of Roger Wright and others whom he sued there for transporting of butter; £20 of Bickerley and others whom he sued in another bill for transporting butter.

These undue proceedings are directly against the law. All coven, collusion, and deceit is against the law and inquirable in eyre. 4 Hen. VII, cap. 20: an act made against informers who prosecute informations and popular actions by fraud, collusion, and for private ends; 18 Elizabeth, cap. 5: if an informer shall willingly delay his suit or shall discontinue the same, or make any composition or take any money, reward, or promise of reward for himself, or to the use of any other without order or consent of the king's courts, he shall be adjudged to the pillory, and from henceforth shall be disabled to be an informer to stand in any action popular.[2]

The consequences of these offences and undue proceedings in a well governed state are very ill:

1. By exhibiting bills and informations, he debars the king's ministers and others, who intend to proceed, really from preferring informations and suits for the same offences, for they will plead a former suit depending by Sutton for the same offences, as he hath informations depending for transporting of gold, wool, fullers earth. Though the plaintiff in the second information may reply that the former information was by coven, yet that is a thing

---

[1] Marginal note reads: It appears by the certificate of the officers of this court that he hath issued out process against 100 persons and hath exhibited 21 bills.

[2] Marginal note reads: Precedents in the Court of Star Chamber: 3 May, 37 Eliz. [1595], Sweat v. Yeo; 24 November, 30 Eliz. [1587], Jo. Crapnall sentenced *ore tenus*; 70 informations and brought none to trial but one, and the court presumed he had taken compositions.

secret which can hardly be proved. There is so much art and cunning amongst these common informers who are masters of their art that they prefer yearly informations and receive an annual revenue by it; every great offender hath commonly an informer belonging to him.

2. It encourageth offenders when they see that for a small sum of money paid to an informer they may escape the danger of the law.

3. It perverts the meaning of good laws; nay, it silences and frustrates all Acts of Parliament, which are made by the king and the advice of the whole state for the public good, when they are made use of to shroud and protect offenders and for private lucre.

4. It is a scandal to public justice to have so many suits exhibited and no proceedings to judgement, when under colour of a legal proceeding offenders shall be sheltered and protected from the sentence of law.

If any man shall really and truly inform for the king and for himself, the law allows him so to do and the king's courts of justice are open for him.[1] But these perverters of justice, these prevaricators, the vermin and caterpillars of a republic, who inform merely for themselves and for their private ends and not for the king nor for the commonwealth, I wish that by your lordships' sentence, not only this delinquent at the bar but by his example all other common traders in this kind might be rooted out of this kingdom. So I leave him to your lordships' judgement.

[Written by Bankes at the head of this document:] Sutton fined £1,000 to the king. To stand upon the pillory with papers. To be disabled to inform by himself or any other. To be bound to the [sic] good behaviour and to stand committed.

[Endorsed by Bankes:] Not brought hither because he is an informer but for his abuse. *Ore tenus* John Sutton, the informer, fined in the Star Chamber, Mich. ter. 11 Car.

25. THE HISTORY OF THE KING'S ALUM WORKS, *c.* 1637

[Bodleian Library, Oxford, MS. Bankes Papers 6/4]

To the right worshipful Sir John Bancks, knight, his Majesty's Attorney-General

JOHN FITZ, surveyor of his Majesty's alum works, in discharge of his duty declareth: that three-fourth parts of the charge to the making of alum is expended in coals and other materials and labours in the boilings, and by errors of ignorance (especially in that part of the work) great losses came upon that business during seven or eight years after the beginning to make alum in Yorkshire.

In 1611 the said Fitz then having had practice and experience above 15

---

[1] Space left in the MS. with an asterisk.

years before in works of like nature, upon the instance and agreement of
William Turnor, esquire, and the other patentees, he at his own charges, did
alter the fire chases and vents in the alum furnaces into a better form,
whereby they now boil swifter with less expense of fuel, yielding a greater
return of alum than those furnaces then in use that before were set by the
Germans; which, with other his inventions and directions there, are continued in all his Majesty's alum works, whereby the like losses as formerly
are avoided, his Majesty's revenue in them advanced with many thousand
pounds profit to the undertakers of alum making; and by his time spent in
those works and the great charges for performance thereof he was constrained
to sell £100 per annum land of inheritance, for which he never yet had any
recompense.

The patentees then failing in 1612, Sir Walter Cope, Sir Arthur Ingram,
knight, and Alderman Johnson of London were appointed commissioners for
his Majesty in the alum business. And then upon proof of the said Fitz, his
knowledge and performance in those works, the right honourable the lords
and others of his Majesty's most honourable Privy Council sent for him and
at the board with great trust did entertain him to be surveyor for his Majesty
in the alum works, and to assist the commissioners in that business, with
promise of reward for his extraordinary expenses and performances aforesaid,
and £100 yearly fee and his riding charges to be paid him by the undertakers
upon his Majesty's account beginning the first of May, 1613.

The said Fitz so entertained in discharge of this service upon his surveys
then taken, did certify great damages done unto his Majesty in those alum
works which before his coming thither and then were in hand to be planted in
the Isle of Purbeck. And therein discovered the particulars of that fraud or
ignorant proceeding. Whereupon after many thousand pounds disbursed by
his Majesty and lost in and about that work, that fruitless labour and expense
was ended and his Majesty's further loss thereby prevented. For which his
just performance (that then could not be corrupted by offered bribes or
gratuities) he had great displeasure of the commissioners and Sir William
Cavell, knight (upon whose land those works were planted), whose private
ends then powerful, besides other his discouragements by daily wrongs done
to his Majesty, and to weary him from that service, they kept his fee from
him.

And also upon his surveys then taken of the alum works in Yorkshire, he
discovered the ignorance and gross abuses in those works. And withal to
make it the more apparent that his Majesty (upon the square) might then
have had great profits yearly by them, he discovered and set forth the several
charges concerning the making of alum; and there in presence of the commissioners did prove the same in the particulars unto the principal alum
makers there, which being so apparently proved made them the more yielding
to reasonable agreement. For whereas before the use of the said new invented
furnaces and other his directions, the charge by the former accounts had been
above £20 upon the ton, he with the commissioners by way of contract in the

year 1613 did first settle the making of alum at a rate with them then there employed in those works for £10 per ton. And having since continued that way hath begotten provident husbandry therein, so as now with good gain to the alum makers it is made for £8 per ton.

Although the service of the said Fitz could not be brooked by the alum makers, yet upon special occasions in the alum works he has since been often requested to assist those employed therein. And of late in the years 1634, 1635, and 1636 (so far as he could be suffered) did take three several surveys of all the alum works then remaining in use, which, howsoever the alum makers with others employed therein have contrived their certificates, the said Fitz upon those surveys did then justly certify and will be ready to prove that the said works and his Majesty's stock in them are in a most ruinous condition.

For although to cover the gross abuses in those works it is cunningly given out and passeth current to be good service that the alum works are sufficiently ordered for that there is 1,800 tons of alum made yearly, and his Majesty secured for the performance thereof. But that is not sufficient security for his Majesty except with condition how and in what manner the alum rocks and works should be proceeded upon for that performance, for the same quantity may be made (as now it is done) to the alum makers' private profits and destroying of the alum rocks and works, and in that destroying way may be so continued and left at the expiration of the patent, but in the interim and afterwards will prove to be many thousand pounds damage to his Majesty's stock and revenue in them.

The common providence of landlords in this kingdom, if but of small farms, do limit their tenants how to proceed upon their pasture and arable lands and for repairs so as the state may be maintained or improved for posterity, and to that purpose have yearly surveys taken (not as in the alum works by the farmers thereof) but by themselves or those of judgement and discretion directly on the behalf of the landlord, whereupon the tenants are by warning enjoined to proceed and perform as shall be found to be fit upon those surveys.

Then much more is that providence needful to have an understanding survey of the alum works yearly for his Majesty and so to advise with the alum makers how best to proceed every year for preserving of the alum rocks and works and his Majesty's stock in them, they consisting of so many parts as well of movable goods of great value, as of buildings and works. And to that service is especially required art and judgement for the well ordering of the yearly proceedings upon the different ascents and descents of those mountainous places for baring those rocks, getting and calcining mine, and making alum liquors and alum, a work impossible to be well ordered on the behalf of his Majesty for preserving those alum rocks and works without experience in all parts of them and full knowledge in sciences and rules of advantage and disadvantage to that purpose. But the alum makers and farmers have always opposed his Majesty's having a sufficient surveyor constantly to survey their proceedings for then they could not possibly have compassed their ends upon his Majesty's purse and stock in those works as hath been done and in [= is] doing.

... For howsoever the alum makers to prevent the provident surveys needful to be taken for his Majesty doth cunningly give out that there is alum mine sufficient at those works now in use for the making of 1,800 tons of alum yearly for ever, which fallacy upon the foresaid effectual survey would be disproved as partly by this example.

For when there were 6 alum works all well furnished with mine, alum houses, furnaces, pans, cisterns, and all necessaries for making alum liquors and alum, and those six works in constant use for making but little more than half the quantity that now is made yearly, yet the mines at 3 of those works were worn out in 24 years, one of them in 15 years; and now the fourth, a very large rock of good mine at Newgate Bank also worn out; and the fifth at Asholme, one of the best and greatest alum rocks of mine and of great value, by the neglect of the alum maker is destroyed to increase his private gain during his 7 years' term.

So that now upon the matter there are but two alum rocks in complete use for making of almost double the quantity of alum yearly that formerly was made at those six great alum works, whereby almost double the quantity of mine is now spent at those two rocks that formerly was at six; what then can be expected but a ruin and decay of those alum works except some speedy course be taken for the better ordering of them and planting more works instead of those worn out? As by the said effectual survey with better conveniency would be sufficiently directed.

... Therefore for avoiding the like uncertainties and damages hereafter (which now are too foul to be suffered by the meanest subject), the said Fitz, for discharging his duty in that great trust reposed in him . . ., doth most humbly request that he may have warrant to take that his long intended survey of all the alum rocks and works on the behalf of his Majesty, which to be done shall no ways interrupt the work nor hinder the making of one pound of alum, but the furtherance of many tons hereafter . . .

John Fitz

[Endorsed by Sir John Bankes:] Mr. Fitz in Ould Street at Mr. Dashwood's, a brewer.

26. THE KING'S ALUM WORKS IN 1638

[Bodleian Library, Oxford, MS. Bankes Papers 6/15]

A brief relation shewing the state his Majesty's alum works are now in and how they are situated

FIRST, they were begun at Gisbrugh [= Guisborough, N. Riding, Yorks.] and there were two good alum rocks, one called Bellman Bank and the other Newgate Bank, which did hold 10 or 12d. weight by the assay glass.

But being wrought like necessitated works as that the farmer was always leaving the works, they are now lost and slighted though there hath been more alum made there than in any other.

Yet there may be opened there another alum rock more advantageous to work than any yet hath been there by reason it is close by a beck that will carry away the spent mine and the rubbidge which is a great matter.

Gisbrugh is four miles from the sea so that the carriage of alum to the ships is chargeable. And likewise so is the bringing of coals from the sea to the works.

Next there is another alum work at Slapwath which is close by Gisbrugh so that their carriages are all one. But Slapwath alum rock giveth but 6*d.* weight now at the best and will not long endure.

The principal works now are at Mougrave [= Mulgrave], there being two: the one is called Asholme, which is very good work and holdeth a 10*d.* weight. And the other is called Sands-end, but it is fallen and three or four acres of grounds with it and never to be recovered. But at either end there is a necessitated work which cannot long endure. Mougrave is close by the sea yet they carry all their alum to Whitby to be shipped and likwise fetch from thence all their coals which is about three miles.

Coal and carriage of the alum on shipboard is more than half the charge of making of the alum, and the farmer for the making part of the alum hath 8*li.* per ton and is to make 1,800 tons yearly; at which rate amounteth to 14,400*li.* But that proportion was never made till Mr. Burlamachi was farmer. They made but 1,300 tons before so that he did advance the works very much. But the aforesaid works are exceedingly wasted and not like to endure long to make the full proportion aforesaid . . . [There follows 'A brief reason shewing how the alum works may be erected in Wales'.] Endorsed by Sir John Bankes:] Sept. 1638.

27. LEAD MINING IN DERBYSHIRE,
temp. Charles I

[P.R.O., Duchy of Lancaster Miscellanea, DL 41/17/19]

OBSERVATIONS collected as I passed amongst the miners and others in Derbyshire concerning the working in lead mines and ordering the same at Wirksworth and elsewhere.

Concerning grove work: the mine downwards in sundry places 40 fathoms, some 30, some 20, some 10, etc. According to the depth of the work, more or less workmen are employed, as if it be 40 fathoms, one pickman or hewer will require one carrier from him to the next pit or eye; there one winds or draws it up to another carrier, then to a second pit or eye, then another winder, then another carrier, to him that winds to day, etc. But if the pit be not so deep, fewer according to the depth will serve. Note that where it is 30, 40, or 50 fathoms deep it is not sunk right downwards from the first eye or shaft, but about 8 or 10 fathoms, and then wrought about 6 or 7 yards sideway, and then 8 or 10 fathoms downwards again, and so by several storeys to the depth.

Wages viz.: of a miner or pickman according to the goodness of the workman, some for 4s., some 4s. 6d., some 5s. a week, and if extraordinary workmen 5s. 6d., 6s., or 6s. 6d., but few of those. Winders (which they call drawers) some 18d., some 20d., and, if extraordinary draught, 2s. per week, most of which are women or lads; but if a man draw commonly he hath 2s. or 2s. 2d., and if one cannot draw it, then being two, they have 18d. apiece per week. Bearers who are within ground, which do commonly wind one storey and then carries or bears it to the next pit or eye, have usually 2s. the week, but commonly he that bears it from the workman or miner hath but 12d. or 18d. at the most. And generally none under ground except the miner have above 2s. or 2s. 2d. the week. The miner ever timbers the work as he goes at the same wages, and none are ever accounted workmen, viz. miners, unless they can do the whole work as well timber as mine. When the[y] meet with water they leave the work for the most part as not to be done good with, but at greater charge than any profit can be expected.

To prevent damps (which is want of air that candles will not burn) they have ever a wind shaft about 6, 8, or 10 yards from that they work at, which sometimes at a depth of 30 fathoms is but 6, 8, 10, or 12 fathoms *et sic pro rata* as occasion falls out, which wind shaft is strucken into the other and by small piece of wood which the[y] call fauge with clods of earth, etc. This fauge I imagine is not unlike a lattice or wooden grate.

There is not often above one workman in one grove and seldom above one grove in a meare of ground yet sometimes there be 2 or 3 groves and so many miners and those that serve them. A meare of ground in the Low Peak is 29 yards and in the High Peak 32 yards. Sinking shafts is of several prices as there is stone or no stone, and so a man by probability or common reason may know what wages are fit to give. There be seldom any master of a meare of ground but that the workman, viz. the miner, hath a 3rd, 4th, or 6th part else the work is commonly ill done and much loitering. All hired workmen are to work a set every day which is 8 hours winter and summer.

The Berghmaister his Office

To punish all misdemeanours amongst the workmen and see right measures, to keep Berghmote court, to receive the king's and his own duties, and generally to do all things as their judge, as well things done against the king's peace as against the orders of the mines, there is a Book of Orders made and found by several ancient inquisitions first 16 Edw. I and divers since wherein all their laws are contained, but the most pregnant and modern laws, constitutions, and pains are contained in 33 articles set down and agreed on (*Virtute Commisionis* etc.) by a jury in Queen Mary's time all which articles and inquisitions I have since gotten copies of.

The King's duty throughout all Derbyshire is to have every xiiith dish of ore which is called the lott, and at every load which is nine dishes 6*d*. at Wirksworth, and in the High Peak but 4*d*., which is paid by the buyer of the ore, and this is taken up and collected by the Berghmaister.

The Berghmaister doth measure every man's ore between buyer and seller, and hath a kind of fee (but rather gratuity) which is called gifter ore, which gift is usually about a dish at 8 loads but some more and sometimes less as their affections be to the Berghmaister.

He is to set out every meare of ground for which he hath a dish of ore.

The first finder of a new rake, not formerly wrought in, the finder hath the two first meares, viz. of either side one, and next the king half so much, which the Berghmaister usually disposeth of.

There be divers other profits to the king and Berghmaister respectively by way of forfeitures, profits of courts, fines, etc.

They never weigh ore at all but only go by the dish. And for that purpose there is an ancient brazen measure in the town hall in Wirksworth containing a long square, viz. in length ——, in breadth ——, in depth ——. And by this all their measures are made and examined by or by the appointment of the Berghmaister and jury of the Berghmote court.

All the miners and masters of meares or groves in Wirksworth parish besides the duties before mentioned) pay to the vicar there every tenth dish or tithe which by pretext of an ancient custom (but of long time discontinued) he hath of late time recovered against them.

For Smelting and Smelting Houses their Charge and Ordering

Four men are usually employed for smelting, two of skill at the hearth, the one with the shovel, the other with long iron rod or gavelock, one other to vent the fire and cast in metal, which lesser judgement and pains may perform, yet he must be still in action. And the fourth an old man or lad to take up the lead in a scoop of iron ladle and put it into the stone or iron where the pig is made, and after take it out thence, having first marked it with the mark of the smelting house, and also to make the ore ready for the hearth and as he hath leisure to knock and bruise ore and to mingle it as their manner is fit for smelting.

These seldom or never work by day wages but by the fowder, and usually have 5*s*. for smelting a fowder, having their ore and chop-wood laid in the smelting house at the charge of the owner. The owner of the smelting house payeth for the smelting of a fowder *et sic pro rata*, viz. to the smelter and his three helpers—5*s*., for chop-wood brought ready dried and fit for smelting —9*s*., beside the house rent, bellows, dams, etc. But if any stranger (not owner of the mill) bring ore to be smelted (as is usual) they usually pay 18*s*. or 18*s*. 4*d*. the fowder and sometimes more.

The time of smelting a fowder is commonly 10 hours and every house doth usually smelt one fowder a day, but if the ore be hard or forward then lesser. To the smelting of a fowder there usually goeth 4 horse loads of

dried chop-wood which to be delivered in the smelting house will (as
aforesaid) lie in 9*s.* but in some places it will require 6 or 7 loads to smelt a
fowder, yet if a man have wood of himself it is cheaper, for he may have so
much chopped and dried as will smelt a fowder for 2*s.*, 2*s.* 6*d.*, and sometimes
3*s.* as *the place is wooded and*[1] the ore gentle and apt for smelting. These
horse loads are not so much as a horse will carry but easy loads put in great
paniers which they call banesters.

Many other things I noted as the manner of building their smelting houses
the fashion of their water wheels, their dams, erection of their bellows, their
manner of hearths, storehouses, etc. and divers other things which were too
long here to describe.

R[oger] K[enyon]

28. THE ROYAL COMMISSION ON THE CLOTH INDUSTRY SUGGESTS REMEDIES, 1640

[G. D. Ramsay, 'The Report of the Royal Commission on the Clothing
Industry, 1640', *English Historical Review*, LVII, 1942, pp. 485,
488–93]

M A Y it please your most excellent Majesty

Your Majesty by your royal commissions under the Great Seal of England
the one bearing date the one and twentieth day of September in the fourteenth
year of your reign, and the other the third day of February then next following, hath been pleased to declare unto us that you have taken into your
princely consideration the great decay of the trade of cloths and stuffs, and
other like manufactures of this kingdom, to the impoverishing of many
thousands of your poor subjects whose livelihood and maintenance doth
rely on the same, and that in your great care for the general and public good
you are pleased to provide for timely reformation when the true causes of
these evils shall be discovered, and that we should duly examine and consider
of the best ways and means for the redressing of the great deceits and abuse
used in English manufactures, and how the same may be restored and maintained in their ancient credit and reputation, and so settled in a constant and
continued course for the future, and to represent the same with our opinion
unto your most sacred Majesty as by the said commissions more at large
appeareth[2] . . .

We have therefore to the uttermost of our endeavours considered of the
remedies which we conceive to be most available and effectual, which notwithstanding we submit to better judgements, and do hereby humbly offer
unto your princely consideration the particulars following.

---

[1] These italicized words are crossed through in the MS.
[2] The passages omitted contain the causes of the decay in the sales of cloth. They are
similar to those listed in the report of the clothing committee of 1622. See above pp. 216–
11.

Remedies

1. And first for the abatement of the making of cloths and stuffs beyond the seas, that it be strictly prohibited to transport wools, wool fells, yarn, and worsted, etc., of the growth of your Majesty's kingdoms, not only of England but also of Scotland and Ireland, as also fullers earth and such like, tobacco pipe clay, wood ashes, and the like (which are great helps in dressing of cloth) upon pain of the forfeiture of all the said goods so laden or transported and treble the value thereof to be forfeited by the owner or owners, and also the owners of the ships or vessels wherein any such goods shall be laden to be transported (knowing thereof) to forfeit the said ships or vessels with all their apparel and furniture to them and every of them belonging, every one his part respectively. And the master and mariners of such ship or vessel that shall not give information thereof within one month next after their return into England to forfeit all their goods and chattels and to have imprisonment by the space of one whole year without bail or main-prise, the one moiety of all which forfeitures to be unto your Majesty and the other to him or them that will sue for the same.

2. Secondly, for the high prices of wools and yarn, etc., which are enhanced by staplers, jobbers, broggers, and engrossers, and by them falsified, mingled, and corrupted, and often sold from hand to hand before it comes to the clothier, that the statute be strictly put in execution, and that it be the care of the governors of each corporation (which we do hereafter mention) to punish and suppress them in all parts of your Majesty's kingdoms (excepting Yorkshire and Devon, which the law permits) and, where they shall be allowed, to be enjoined to these conditions: namely, to sell immediately to the converter and not to come to give at the second or third hand, that they do not falsify or mingle their wools deceitfully before they sell them, and not to be suffered to sell at the market where they buy the same.

3. Thirdly, concerning the taxes of our English cloth in the Low Countries, that your Majesty will be pleased to give order to your ambassadors and agents to treat with the archdukes and states for the taking off that heavy burden which doth daily more and more increase and is contrary to the treaty of peace and book of commerce, or at least to impose as much upon their own and also upon the cloth of other countries, which (as we are informed) do pay little or nothing at all, to the advantage of other nations, and to the great hindrance and loss of the English merchants that trade there. And concerning the charges here at home arising upon the custom, pretermitted custom, the Earl of Cumberland's licence, and the company's imposition, we conceive it to be a great burden and if there should be some abatement thereof, we believe the great increase of the transportation of these commodities and the returns thereof would recompense the loss upon that abatement, and prove a good enlargement of trade, for we may not omit to let your Majesty understand that whereas for about twenty years last past the merchants of England did export into the Eastland certain thousand

of low priced cloths yearly, now by reason of the charge the said cloths are subject unto, the vent of them in the East country is wholly lost, and the cloths by these country people made of their own wools, being free from the charge we are subject unto, hath eaten us wholly out of that trade, and the like by the same occasion is fallen out in our trade for France.

4. Fourthly, concerning the gigmills or mozing mills before mentioned, we humbly conceive it necessary that the statute be put in execution for the suppressing of them. But because we find many clothiers do for the present make use of them, it is to be doubted that the sudden inhibition of them will be the cause of stop and interruption of the manufactures about Stroudwater where they are used, and therefore we think it fit that there be twelve months' space given for their suppression, to the end the clothiers there may have time sufficient to provide themselves of workmen to supply what these engines performed.

5. Fifthly, touching the diverse and manifold abuses practised in and about all sorts of English manufactures, as well by the clothier, weaver, fuller, tucker, dyer, and market spinner, as also by the aulnagers, searchers, and sealers, which are the chief and principal cause of the decay of our draperies, we humbly conceive there can be no other way for an absolute and general reformation, but by the granting of several incorporations to all the chief clothing towns of this kingdom, the names whereof, together with the chief heads and most material things that we hold necessary to be observed, are hereunto annexed, and to the end that all the laws and statutes concerning drapery now in force and necessary to be used, and that all other good rules and orders which shall be thought fit as well for the regulation of new as old drapery be duly put in execution and observed by the said several corporations, we humbly conceive it to be most requisite that your Majesty will be pleased to appoint a selected number of able men of gentlemen, merchants, and tradesmen of or near the City of London that may be commissioners from year to year or otherwise, for the well ordering and government of these manufactures, that may always be careful to see that the conditions and undertakings of each corporation may be punctually performed, and that they may have power to depute such able and sufficient officers as they shall make choice of for the better and more exact performance of the work, and that they may also have authority to convent before them such as shall be found remiss or delinquent in the charge and trust committed to them, and to set fines for any manner of fraud or abuse that shall be discovered, and to compose differences which may often happen between the buyers, sellers, and makers of the said manufactures, with power and faculty to apply the said fines as your Majesty in your great wisdom shall please to direct, and that they may have power to settle and provide as occasion offereth, that the poor workmen depending on the said trade of clothing or drapery may have competent wages for their work, and that there may be a commission house appointed, where they may once a week constantly sit or as often as shall be

needful, that when any complaint of wrong or abuses shall be brought, they may hear and determine the same.

Lastly, we conceive it necessary for the reputation and credit of all English commodities that there be a fair and large seal, well cut by your Majesty's engraver that graves to the mint, which may be called the Crown Seal, and used all over England and Wales for all kind of draperies, and that the lead that is to be fixed to every piece may be double, having two rounds for two seals to be stamped thereon, the one whereof to be stamped with the aforesaid Crown Seal, which is to be choicely kept by some person of trust, which shall duly keep an exact account of the number of seals which shall be from time to time delivered out for the use of each corporation. And that when any piece of cloth or stuff shall be viewed, measured, and approved of, the aforesaid piece of lead to be set on, and the seal of the corporation to be fixed upon the other round thereof by such sealer or officer as shall be authorized for the same corporation. Also that there may be yearly, or half yearly, a general account kept and delivered to the Lord Treasurer for the time being, or to the said commissioners, who may give up unto your Majesty when they shall be thereunto required, the number of all the commodities made within the limits of each corporation, whereby it may be certainly known how much shall be the yearly increase of the clothing of the whole kingdom. And if in case there shall happen any decay or abatement thereof your Majesty may also be informed of the original cause, that speedy redress may be had before it be past remedy. And finally when your Majesty in your great wisdom shall have taken order for the best way of setting and well ordering of these manufactures, that you will be graciously pleased to declare your royal will and pleasure by proclamation, to the end that all your loyal subjects may take notice of your great care in so worthy a work, and conform themselves accordingly.

[Annexed] As touching the corporations before mentioned (whereon a great part of the work will principally depend) we humbly conceive it necessary to be settled upon the chief towns which at this present do use the trade of clothing and making of stuffs, which (being for the great advancement of drapery) we believe will be most willingly embraced by all the clothiers of this kingdom, divers of them having already declared their approbation thereof. But by reason we were uncertain how this way would be accepted of, we thought it not expedient to spend much time in entering too far in the particulars until we should receive your Majesty's further commands and directions.

The names of the clothing towns to which we have given intimation of our opinions herein, and which we conceive to be considerable for this work, are these following, viz. *in comitatu* Berks., Reading and Newbury; *in comitatu* Devon, Exeter, Totnes, Tiverton, Kirton, Barnstaple, and Tavistock; in Dorset, Dorchester and Lyme Regis; *in Eboraco*, Halifax, Leeds, Wakefield, Keighley, Bradford, and Kendal; in Essex, Colchester, Coggeshall, and Dedham; in Gloucester, Gloucester and Stroudwater; in Kent, Canterbury,

Sandwich, and Tenterden; in Lancashire, Manchester, Rochdale, Colne, Bolton, Blackburn, and Bury; in Norfolk, Norwich; in Oxford, Burford and Witney; in Salop, Shrewsbury and Oswestry; in Somerset, Taunton, Shepton Mallet, Wincanton, Chard, Beckington, and Wellington; in Suffolk, Ipswich, Hadleigh, St. Edmonds Bury, Sudbury, and Barford; in Stafford, Tamworth, Burton upon Trent, Groton, and Nayland[1]; in Surrey, Guildford; in Southampton, Southampton, Andover, and Basingstoke; in Warwick, Coventry; *in Wigornense*, Worcester, and Kidderminster; and in Wilts., Salisbury, Warminster, Devizes, Chippenham, and Calne. These we conceive necessary to have corporations, if any be granted, and such others as shall be hereafter found convenient and necessary.

For the rules and government of these corporations we hold it not fit to trouble your Majesty with many particulars, there being already a very good model for this work, namely Colchester for the making of bays there, divers of which ordinance (although only for the making of bays) will be very pertinent and agreeable to other places where cloths and stuffs are made. For by the constant rule of their true making they have long continued, and still are in good repute and esteem in all places beyond the seas. And as for the said town of Colchester that hath Letters Patents of incorporation granted for the making of bays, we conceive it requisite the same should be enlarged to all the clothiers thereabouts for the making of all sorts of drapery as your Majesty shall be pleased to grant unto the towns. And for other corporations, we hold it expedient that the limits and bounds of each of them should extend to six, ten, or fourteen miles every way more or less according to their distances from the next clothing towns. And that the members of every corporation should be clothiers, weavers, fullers, clothworkers, and dyers, and that all such as do use any of the said trades may be reduced into some one of the said corporations, and to be a brother or member of some or one of them, and that none may be exempt or freed from the rules and government thereof, and also for the future that none may be admitted into any of the said corporations but such as shall have served their seven years' apprenticeship to one of the said trades, and that all cardsters, combers, spinsters, and such others as have any kind of dependence upon the said manufactures may also be regulated by the said corporations. Also that every corporation that shall use the making of new draperies shall agree of the lengths, breadths, and weights of each kind of stuff which they shall make, which they shall for ever hereafter be obliged to observe without alteration, unless the same be allowed by the commissioners aforesaid. And also that a certain number of threads for the warp of every sort of stuff be prescribed and agreed upon at the setting of this business, that the officers for the searching and sealing be well skilled in the manufactures, and to be made choice of by the Master, Wardens, and Assistants of each corporation, and that these officers before they are admitted may give good security and be sworn for the due performance of their office. And that they may be duly

[1] Groton and Nayland, in fact, are in Suffolk.

and severely punished for any faulty cloth or stuff they shall seal or let pass contrary to their orders. And for their pains and care herein they may be allowed a sufficient competency by each corporation and not suffered to keep deputies but in cases of necessity, of sickness, or otherwise. And for the Master, Wardens, and other the governors of each corporation, that they may have power to levy means for the maintenance of necessary officers, and to hear complaints and impose penalties for punishing offenders as in other corporations of less importance is usual, and that there be a several seal allowed to each corporation for the expressing of the true making or defects of the said manufacture, and when any piece of cloth or stuff shall be measured and approved of, the said double piece of lead, having thereon the Crown Seal before mentioned, shall be fixed unto it, and the said corporation seal shall be stamped on the other part thereof. And if any faulty cloth shall happen to pass that seal (not having the defect expressed) the corporation whose seal it bears to be liable to make good the penalty in the highest degree. And whereas we have found very great abuses to have been practised in and about dyeing, and in particular by the dyers of London, which cannot be discovered here at home until the goods are exported and set to sale beyond sea, we conceive it necessary that whatsoever frauds shall be there found to have been committed in the dyeing of the said manufactures, upon credible and authentic certificate sent over into England of the said frauds and what the damages thereof amount unto, the corporation as well of the said dyers of London as of all other places shall be responsible for the said damages to the party grieved, and the said corporation to right itself upon the party that committed the fault. Also that all men be enjoined to sell their commodity in open markets or halls and other places allowed for that purpose and not privately in —— nor in private houses. By which means all faulty and deceitful cloths and stuffs may the sooner be discovered, and the offenders punished, that likewise no strained cloths be suffered to be made or sold in any part of this kingdom, but all to be made at first perfect and good, and to contain their full weight, length, and breadth, and if any shall desire and procure a toleration for strained cloths, then they to strain no other but true and well wrought cloths which are so sealed, and then to have them strained here in London and nowhere else. And that another seal may be fixed thereon, expressing how much they have been strained and a due account to be kept thereof accordingly. And that another duty may be paid for the straining of every such cloth. And whereas we have before humbly expressed our opinions that every corporation should be liable to make good the losses, damages, and penalties of all faulty cloths or stuffs that are suffered to pass their seal, we conceive it very expedient that there be sufficient power and authority granted unto them to enable them for the performance thereof and that the crown or aulnage seal may be let unto each corporation by farm, yearly rent, or otherwise as your Majesty in your great wisdom shall think most convenient.

Lastly, we humbly crave leave to represent to your Majesty our opinions of the necessity of a court of merchants for the speedy determining of all suits and differences that happen between merchants, factors, clothiers, tradesmen, and shopkeepers concerning account bills of exchange, bargains, and other differences proceeding or depending for wares and all sorts of merchandises or debts arising thereupon, which are seldom or never determined by any of your Majesty's courts of justice without the report and opinion of merchants which will be agreeable to that brief and summary way now used by the commissioners for the policies of assurance. And this we humbly conceive would be a comfort and encouragement to the merchants and an increase of trade and general wealth of the realm.

All which we most humbly submit to your Majesty's great wisdom.

Thomas Jeninges, Ant. Wither, John Howe, George Clerke, George Langham, Richard Bogan, Mathew Cradock, Nathan Wright, John Kendrick, Law. Squibb, Roger Kilbert, John Barker, Hugh Morrell, Richard Middelton.

9 June 1640.

[Endorsed:] Mr. Cradock. Report from the Commissioners for Trade, 9 March 1640.

29. TYPES OF LINEN CLOTH KNOWN TO A YORKSHIRE FARMER, 1641

[Henry Best, *Rural Economy in Yorkshire in 1641, being the Farming and Account Books of Henry Best of Elmeswell in the East Riding*, ed. C. B. Robinson, Surtees Soc., XXXIII, 1857, pp. 105–6]

Short Remembrances for Buying of all Sorts of Linen Cloths

SUCH linen cloth as is here made in England, and commonly called huswife-cloth, is of divers prices, divers breadths, and serveth for divers uses; as some there is of 14*d*. or 15*d*. the yard, being in breadth yard and half quarter, which our maid servants usually buy for holyday aprons, cross cloths, and neck cloths. Some there is again of 16*d*. or 17*d*. the yard, which is ell-wide, or (as some improperly speak) five quarters, *i.e.* a yard and a quarter; this is exceeding good, and much used for table cloths. Some there is again which is yard broad, or yard and nayle, *i.e.* half of the half quarter, which, being of the finest and best sort, is sold for 2*s*. and seven groats a yard, and much used of gentle folks for shirts. The kinds of linen or huswife-cloth are brought about of pedlars, who furnish themselves thereof in Cleveland and Blackamore where they buy very much of this sort; and at New Malton live many at whose houses one may at all times furnish themselves with this kind of cloth. It is to be noted that there is little cloth of what sort soever but either is, or (at least) should be, yard-broad; for when one buyeth a yard of cloth, it is presupposed that it be a yard square, *i.e.* a yard in breadth as well as in length; and furthermore that the buyer is to have yard and inch; and that the truly-dealing-seller desireth no more profit but penny at yard at coarse cloth, and penny at shilling in the sale of fine cloth. The worst sort of Scotch cloth is 18*d.* a yard, and the best sort of all 2*s.* 6*d.* and eight groats a yard; it is spun by their lairds' wives, and brought into England by the poor Scotch merchants, and much used here for women's handkerchers and pocket handkerchers. There is holland from 2*s.* 6*d.* an ell to 6*s.* 8*d.* an ell, for holland is (most commonly) sold by the ell; whereof one sort is called flezy-holland; it is said to be spun by the nuns in the Low Countries, brought over by our merchants, and sold to our linen drapers, at whose shops our country pedlars furnish themselves; it is a strong cloth, and much used for men's bands, gentlewomen's handkerchers, and cross cloths and half shirts, etc. One may buy coarse lawn for 4*s.* 6*d.* a yard, and the finest for 6*s.* and 6*s.* 8*d.* a yard: it is much used for fine neck-kerchers, and fine shadows, and dressings. Cambric is about 8*s.* the yard, and much used for women's ruffs. Cambric lawn, which is the finest of them all, and most used for gentlewomen's and ladies' ruffs, is 10*s.* a yard, or thereabouts. Cock-web-lawn, or tiffeny, is the sheerest and cheapest lawn of all, and may be bought for ten groats and 4*s.* a yard; it is used of gentlewomen for handkerchers for the neck, and is worn over another holland handkercher, in starching of which is some cunning; they are very much used now of late.

30. PLYMOUTH SHOEMAKERS COMBINE TO CHECK JOURNEYMEN'S WAGES, 1643

[Plymouth Corporation Records, W360/36]

1643

18 Chas. I. We whose names are underwritten, master shoemakers and inhabitants of this borough of Plymouth, upon a general meeting, and knowing the extraordinary charges that journeymen of our trade have put us unto, by a general consent, do between us absolutely conclude and agree that neither of us shall henceforth entertain or receive any journeyman to work, unless it be upon the same conditions and usual prizes which heretofore they were accustomed to have. And further we do also conclude and agree that if any journeyman shall upon any pretended matter leave needlessly his said master, then none of us shall or will entertain him into any of our works or services without the privity of his said master, and by his consent from whom he so departed; which said journeymen were formerly to have according to these prizes following: viz.

First for French heel boots xii*d.*; for wooden heel boots x*d.*; for French heel shoes vi*d.*; for footing of French heel boots viii*d.*; for wooden heel shoes and fale [sic] shoes iiii*d.*; for plain shoes iii*d.*

For the true performance of which said conditions and orders we do each of us bind ourselves, our executors, administrators, and assigns unto the

other, their executors, and administrators in the full sum of five pounds of
lawful money of England.

In witness whereof we have each of us hereunder severally set our hands
this 17th day of April 1643.

[16 signatures]

I, Francis Pavey of Plymouth, notary and tabellion publique, do certify
that the orders above written, concluded on as abovesaid, were so done really
in the presence of me, the said notary, witness both hand and seal, being
requested so to do.

Per me   Franciscum Pavey
notarium publicum et tabellionem

31. THE LONDON HEMPDRESSERS COMPLAIN OF DUTCH COMPETITION, *temp*. CHARLES I

[P.R.O., SP 16/520, no. 123]

THE humble petition of the poor hemp dressers in the city of London and
the out liberties thereof, most humbly sheweth that the dressing of hemp hath
been used in this kingdom time out of mind, and that many thousands have
been set on work and have lived thereby very well with their hard labour, as
also it hath been a means to set to work many thousands of idle and vagrant
people that are by authority sent into the hospitals and houses of correction
in this kingdom according to the statute in that case provided.

Now so it is that within these five or six years last past the Netherlanders
and some others have imported into this kingdom hemp ready dressed and
tow, such as is converted into cloth, which daily increaseth their trading and
decreaseth ours. And for a lamentable precedent, as they have already dealt
with the flax dressers which are by their means utterly decayed and brought to
beggary. At first they undersold them both in flax and tow, and so continued
for a time until they had decayed them and quite beggared them, so as at the
last they had gotten the whole trading into their hands and now do sell it at
unreasonable rates well near double the prices as they sold it at the first.

In like manner they begin to deal with your petitioners. They bring into
this kingdom their dressed hemp and tow, which payeth small custom in
respect as it would amount unto if the hemp came over rough and undressed
as it was always wont to do, and do undersell us insomuch that some of your
petitioners that have kept some twenty or thirty men on work and divers of
those workmen have kept families and have maintained them by their hard
labour, they are not able now to keep two or three men on work, whereby
many hundreds are already brought to extreme misery and beggary, and in
short time many thousands more will be if it be not prevented.

Now forasmuch as the Netherlanders and others that bringeth in this
dressed hemp and tow are no Commonwealth men for this kingdom but altogether aiming at their own ends, and when they have quite decayed us, as

they have done the flax dressers, they will advance their prices at their pleasure to the lessening of the King's custom, the hurt of the Commonwealth, and the overthrow and beggaring of thousands that live now by dressing and other working of rough hemp, and that in regard of the employment of so many young and idle people in work, which otherwise would be mere vagrants, and inclined to do evil, that your most honourable assembly would be pleased to enact some good act for them that they may be of a society, and that none may use the said mystery or trade except they serve seven years apprentice to the same and under some government or fellowship as other the like mysteries are. So that ancient housekeepers, who have served their apprentice-hood for the said mystery, may be well able to live and hereafter to guide others in the same as to the said order or statute made shall occur. And for proof of this petition and the ancient making of it within this realm of England to the great good and employment of many his Majesty's poor subjects, we whose names are hereunder subscribed are always ready and will attend upon oath to prove the contents of the same.

In pitiful consideration whereof, whereas many houses of correction in divers shires are constrained to set on work vagrant persons together with other people to beat and dress hemp, and after to spin it into twine, by reason of the Netherlanders which bring it in great quantities in twine, the said houses of correction cannot set people on work as they were ordained for. Your petitioners humbly desire this most honourable assembly that you will be pleased that the importation of dressed hemp, tow, and twine may be prohibited, restrained, and forbidden by some such wholesome laws, cautions, and provisions as to your grave and judicious censures shall be thought most meet and convenient, whereunto they humbly submit them-selves and their suit. And shall daily pray for your long healths and everlasting happiness.

32. THE PROBLEM OF MAINTAINING STANDARDS IN INDUSTRY, 1651

[Margaret James, *Social Problems and Policy during the Puritan Revolution, 1640–60*, London, 1930, pp. 392–3]

22 Sept. 1651. At the Council for Trade at Whitehall

THIS Council having received sundry other petitions complaining ... of many abuses and deceits, namely in the heavy and corrupt dyeing of silk, and adding thereby in the weight thereof a 3rd or 4th part; in the mixing of copper with gold and silver thread; in the selling of gold and silver lace and thread by an uncertain weight, and not that which all bullion and plate is usually bought and sold by; likewise in mixing silk with thread in ribands, points, and other commodities.

With the like frauds and adulterations in upholstery wares, in dressing, dyeing, weaving, and making up of cloth bays, and most other manufactures and handicraft trades; to the great detriment and cozenage of the Commonwealth; some of them as hath been alleged happening for want of their being incorporated; others for want of sufficient power in their respective corporations, to search and punish the abuses known to them; or to lay such a small and moderate assess upon their members or upon the several commodities, as shall defray the charge of the said search; others through the taking in men of several trades under one company, through the undue choice of their officers out of those men; proving oft times unskilful and negligent in the managing of the affairs of their government; others through the want of restraining ill and bad wares appertaining to their several arts to be brought from beyond sea to their great discouragement, and to the prejudice oft times of the nation.

Lastly, some by other corporations entrenching upon or thrusting into their privileges.

All which in former times had usually an application and redress by the late King's Council Table, or were referred to the Lord Keeper, Lord Treasurer, Lord Privy Seal, to the President of the King's Council, the Attorney General, Chief Justices, or to Justices of the Peace in the county, or to some two or more of any of these at the King's pleasure, to hear and to determine or to do therein as should seem good to them upon the grounds of the laws of this nation. Forasmuch therefore as very many thousands of the good people of this nation are greatly concerned in cases of this nature; and that the differences and complaints have been already very numerous.

The Council for these reasons do offer it as their humble opinion that it will be very commodious and advantageous to trade, and will much conduce to the ease and benefit of the people and nation in general, if some way for the viewing, confirming, or rectifying of the byelaws and ordinances constituted and now in use by the several societies of merchants and manufacturers; and for the hearing, examining, and determining of all the cases abovesaid in the several handicraft trades and others, and for the dispatch of the same, be settled and authorized by Parliament; and to such persons or in such manner entrusted as to the wisdom of the Parliament shall be thought fit.

33. FURTHER REFLECTIONS ON THE MAINTENANCE OF STANDARDS IN INDUSTRY, 1651

[P.R.O., SP 18/16, no. 139]

Reasons that have at several times been offered to urge the reforming and settling of our inland trade and manufactures under some certain way of super-spection and regulation.

FIRST, it hath been represented that the trade and manufactures of this nation will unavoidably be hazarded, otherwise to be lost and our people thereby to be more and more reduced into want and poverty; for if some men be, without punishment, permitted to make bad, ill, and unmerchant-like wares, they by reason of this deceit will be able to sell off their commodities cheaper and so for a long time faster than all those other men who make constantly good, which honester sort of persons, being by this means deprived of their livelihoods and trade, it proves in the end a temptation to them also to take up the like false makings and deceit, whereby (besides the abuse and cozenage used here one to another (which seems fit to be redressed).

The generality also of what commodities are exported beyond sea comes at length to be all bad as we have already had experience in every particular manufacture we have yet had, which badness, being once discovered by other nations, causeth the disrepute of our commodities abroad, and that they become of no certain value to us; having no longer a vent with them, then either necessity compels them or other places forbear to make them.

Secondly, it hath been represented that the grief and complaints of all the meaner sort of people cannot without a reforming and regulating our inland trade possibly be eased. For as $\frac{2}{3}$ parts of this nation do depend immediately upon the manufactures of it of one kind or another, so the complaints of the people answerably is for the most part grounded upon the deadness and want of employment and trade: which want of trade notwithstanding (as it hath been probably alleged) hath chiefly proceeded through our neglect and want of care in the making of our manufactures to their due goodness; of which an instance or two hath been given that whereas in one port of Spain alone we used within these few years to vent about 12,000 pieces of says, serges, and the like woollen stuffs, we now scarce vent 2,000; and so rateably in other parts, the Dutch having taken up a way of truer making them. Whereas also formerly we sent into all places great store of dornix draftwork and the like works, it is now, through the badness and falseness of it, become totally disused and lost, which also may be said of several other commodities, as well that of our cloth as others, that through a want of care and inspection of their goodness and trueness come first into a disrepute, and so into an abatement of their value and price, and are at length refused to be bought at all, when either another commodity may serve instead, or men of other countries make it honester than we. The mischief being not without a care and reformation to be prevented; and so whole trades and multitudes of men depending upon them comes at once to be ruined and beggared, and our stock to be more and more lessened. The wealth or main stock of the nation having been ever rated according to the quantity of manufacture made in it and exported.

Thirdly, it hath been represented that without reforming our inland trade in some constant way of regulation, it is impossible to regulate or settle a foreign trade or to exact the performance of such articles as shall be agreed with other nations for the encouragement of our commerce; it being presumed other nations cannot be obliged to entertain our people or a traffic with them, if we will take a liberty to cozen them with our commodities. Nor can we expect a currenty of price in other countries for our manufactures if they be not of any certain and current goodness.

All which is nevertheless humbly submitted.

[Endorsed:] Reasons for reforming our inland trade, December 1651.

34. PETITION FOR FREE IMPORTS OF COTTON WOOL INTO LANCASHIRE, 1654
[P.R.O., SP 18/69, no. 7]

A FEW reasons humbly presented to the Rt. Honourable his Highness's Privy Council by Thomas Waring and the rest of the humble petitioners in behalf of the poor of Lancashire for Liberty for them or any that will adventure to bring in cotton wools from France, Holland, etc.

1st. Be pleased to take notice that the dearth of wools this present year is worser undergone by the poor in Lancashire than the famine of bread was (though that was great) three years past, and there is not only a dearth but now

2ly. There is a great scarcity also for there is not five bags of wool in all the merchants' hands in London to keep at work 20,000 poor, for no less a number are employed in Lancashire by the great manufacture of fustians. And

3ly. Mr. Seed and Mr. Winstanley (that engrossed the last parcels) have by their own confessions disposed of almost, if not, all they had and that report they made to the Hon. Committee of 150 or 200 sacks of prize wool proved but 20 or 30 bags and the sale of it prohibited so that that report of theirs we conceive was but to respite our grant that they might gain the more time to sell theirs at their price which is done.

4. But more especially be pleased to consider that unless cotton wool be brought down to a much lower rate than now sold at, the manufacture of fustians (that keeps at work so many thousands) will revert to Hamburg from whence by our cheaper making than they we gained it, but now they have the commodity at 6*d*. and 7*d*. per lb. bought and we pay 15*d*., 20*d*., and more which will inevitably destroy the trade in England.

5. Whilst we can have no supply but from the Straits (Barbados being not worth naming of late years for cotton) and none but the Turkey merchants have liberty or privilege to bring it in from thence, we have no hope from them only to be supplied (viz.) at such rates as to preserve our great manufacture from ruin, it being not capable as are other commodities of a rise for that aforesaid reason touching Hamburg, for at this day Ozenbrigg fustians are sold at Hamburg for 16*s*. per piece, which now we cannot afford under 20*s*. and formerly sold them at 12*s*. and 13*s*. per piece, and questionless all other sorts will be at the same pass between us, and then if not speedily prevented by your honours, by granting our desires expressed in our late petition presented to your honours.

Be pleased therefore to dispense (so far at least as to cotton wools) with the act that tends so apparently to the enriching of strangers and destruction of the people of this nation, and let your Honours bear with us in saying better such laws were buried in oblivion than by a rigid observing them to bury alive and irrecoverably crush the poor and needy.' All which in all humility we submit to your Honours' wise and serious consideration. And shall beg of God who only is wise to give you wisdom in all things, etc.

Signed in the behalf and by the appointment of the rest of the petitioners

Thos. Waring

Endorsed:] Reasons for free importing of cotton wool into Lancashire. 4 April 1654

35. A CONCESSION TO SOLDIERS ON APPRENTICESHIP, 1654

[P.R.O., SP 18/74, no. 37, II[1]]

WE have considered the petition of several officers of his Highness's army, the same setting forth that divers persons having been officers and soldiers of the army in their youth and desiring now (being reduced) to betake themselves to honest callings find themselves interrupted therein by privileges granted to corporations for debarring persons from exercising any art, etc., there without seven years' apprenticeship.

And are humbly of opinion that every person who shall make it appear he hath served in the late wars in England, Scotland, or Ireland by the space of three years at any time since the year 1642 and before the —— day of —— in the year 1653, though not bound apprentice or not serving up his time, be at liberty to set up and exercise any art, mystery, trade, or manual occupation he shall think fit and be capable of in any city, town, or place in this Commonwealth, notwithstanding any law, custom, or privilege to the contrary. And if any such person shall be sued or molested for the same by any information, action of debt, or other popular action, and shall prove that he hath been a soldier for the space of three years, and the jury shall find him not guilty and the plaintiff shall in that case pay him double costs. And that an ordinance be brought in to that purpose.

[Endorsed:] Report about soldiers' liberty to set up trades.

36. THE FRAMEWORK KNITTERS APPEAL FOR INCORPORATION, 1655

[B.M., Thomason Tract E 863 (4), pp. 1-11]

To his Highness the Lord Protector of the Commonwealth of England, Scotland, and Ireland, &c.

THE humble representation of the promoters, contrivers, and inventors of

---

[1] A rough draft of this document is dated 4 July 1654 and headed Col. Mackworth, Col. Sydenham.

the art, mystery, or trade of framework knitting, or making of silk stockings, and other work in a frame, or engine, petitioners to your Highness, that they may be united, and incorporated by charter under the Great Seal of England; whereby their just right to the invention may be preserved from foreigners, the trade advanced, abuses therein suppressed, the benefit of the Commonwealth by importation, exportation, and otherwise increased; and hundreds of poor families comfortably relieved by their several employments about the same, who will otherwise be exposed to ruin, having no other callings or trades to live off.

May it please your Highness, amongst all the civil ways of improvement of a Commonwealth (next after agriculture) merchandise and manufactory (where, and whensoever orderly regulated) in all ages and times, have been, and are most securely beneficial and prosperous, during their cherishment and retention. But they are very apt to become volant, as soon as sleighted or disordered into neighbouring[1] places and regions, always hospitable to so welcome guests, as bring with them not only their own entertainments, but also profitable advantages to their protectors, leaving behind them unto the place of their former residence, an over-late and remedyless repentance of such improvidence, and most commonly an irrevocable consumption.

The experience whereof hath anciently and generally made it a principle and maxim in state, to encourage by all favourable means requisite, the erectors and practisers of trading; and hath notified for one of the greatest errors in state government the discountenancing and disordering thereof . . .

Whereby the petitioners are emboldened (now at length) to offer to your Highness's consideration and grave judgement the fulness of capacity they humbly conceive themselves to have long been in, to receive the like grant of favour, trust, and protection, which many other companies have (upon fewer and less weighty inducements) obtained; and whereof there is apparent necessity, their trade being no longer manageable by them nor securable unto the profit of this Commonwealth without it.

Which trade is properly styled framework knitting, because it is direct and absolute knitwork in the stitches thereof; nothing different therein from the common way of knitting (not much more anciently for public use, practised in this nation, than this) but only in the numbers of needles, at an instant working in this, more than in the other, by an hundred for one, set into an engine or frame, composed of above two thousand pieces of smiths', joiners', and turners' work, after so artificial and exact a manner, that (by the judgement of all beholders) it far excelleth in the ingenuity, curiosity, and subtilty of the invention, and contexture, all other frames or instruments for manufacture in use in any known part of the world. And for the skill requisite to

---

[1] A marginal note reads as follows:
Many places have had their vicissitude of prosperity and decay, occasioned by access and receding of trade: as witnesseth (amongst many others) Gaunt in Flanders, and those towns from whence the English staple hath removed.

e use and manage thereof, it well deserveth (without usurpation, as some
hers impertinently have) the titles of mystery and art, by reason of the great
fficulty of learning, and length of time necessary to attain a dextrous habit
right, true, and exquisite workmanship therein, which hath preserved it
therto (from the hands of foreigners) peculiar only to the English nation,
om whence it had extraction, growth, and breeding unto that perfection it
now arrived at . . .

Now so it is, may it please your Highness, that this trade of framework
iitting was never known nor practised either here in England, or in any
her place of the world, before it was (above fifty years past) invented and
und out by one William Lee of Calverton, in the county of Nottingham,
intleman; who by himself, and such of his kindred and countrymen, as he
ok unto him for servants, practised the same many years; somewhat
iperfectly, in comparison of the exactness it is sithence brought unto, by the
ideavours of some of these petitioners. Yet even in the infancy thereof, it
ithered sufficient estimation of a business of so extraordinary a national
:ofit and advantage as to be invited over into France, upon allurements of
eat rewards, privilege, and honour, not long before the sudden murther of
ie late French King Henry the fourth, unsuccessfully accepted by the said
Ir. Lee, at that time wanting due encouragement at home. And transposing
imself with nine workmen, his servants (with some frames) unto Roan
=Rouen], there wrought to so great applause of the French that the trade
as in all likelihood to have been settled in the country for ever, had not the
:cease of the said king disappointed Mr. Lee of his expected grant of
:ivilege, and the succeeding troubles of that kingdom delayed his renewed
iit to that purpose into discontentment and death at Paris, leaving his
orkmen at Roan to provide for themselves. Seven of which returned back
gain into England (with their frames) and here practised and improved
ieir trade, under whom (or the master-workmen since risen under them)
iost of these petitioners had their breeding, and served their apprenticeships.
f the other two which remained in France, only one is yet surviving, but
i far short of the perfection of his trade (as it is used here) that of him, or
hat can be done by him, or his means, these petitioners are in no apprehen-
on of fear; nor have not been (since then) endangered in foreign countries
y any that have served out their full times of apprenticeship here.

But near about that time a Venetian ambassador gave five hundred pounds
ir a remnant of time of one Henry Mead, then an apprentice to this trade,
id conveyed him (with his frame) from London unto Venice, where although
is work and manner of it was (for a while) admired, and endeavoured to be
iitated; yet as soon as necessity of reparation of his frame and instruments
appened, for want of artificers experienced in such work there, and of
iility in him to direct them, the work prospered not in his managing; so that
iis bought time of service being expired) affection to his native country
rought him home again into England. And after his departure, the Venetians
rew disheartened in the trade, and impatient of making vain trials, they sent

his disordered frame (and some of their own imitations) to be sold in London at very low valuations.

And within few years afterwards, the trade was greatly endangered by one Abraham Jones, who having (by underhand courses and insinuation, and not by service as an apprentice) gotten both the mystery and skilful practice thereof, did (contrary to his articles with the rest of the company, that had taken some jealous notice of him) pass himself with one more unto Amsterdam; and there (taking some Dutch unto him as servants) erected frames and wrought for the space of two or three years, until the infection of the plague seized on him and his whole family, and carried them all to the grave. His frames also (as things unprofitable to them that could not find out their right use, without an able teacher) were sent to London for sale at slight rates.

These preservations and escapes of this trade from transplantation into foreign countries, these petitioners do with thankfulness acknowledge, and ascribe to have been brought to pass by the divine providence, limiting his bounties and administrations whither he hath been pleased to direct them. For it may well seem marvellous in human judgements, how otherwise this trade should remain (notwithstanding all the covetous and envious attempts to the contrary, practised both at home and abroad, for the space of forty years past) an art peculiar only to this our nation; and to the nimble spirits of the French, the fertile wits of the Italians, and the industrious inclination of the Dutch, a concealed mystery unto this day.

Yet a continued negligence in presumption thereupon would ill beseem the receivers of so many damageless warnings, and may soon prove of hard consequence unto these petitioners, who are, without intermission, environed with the like or greater dangers. For there are by other means than the way of apprenticeship so many intruders crept into this trade that ill work and ill ware is everywhere offered to sale; and the ignominy and disparagement thereof, commonly imputed to the whole manufacture, not without much loss, hindrance, and interruption to the true and allowable artisans, and tending to their utter impoverishment, who (in continual workmanship) produce the best, finest, and most approvedly merchandable and useful ware ever sold or bought in the memory of man. Otherwise the petitioners could not have driven their trade (through many oppositions and difficulties) up unto that height it is now brought, and into fair expectation and open way of large increase, if intrusion were barred, and transportation (and teaching of the mystery unto foreigners) restrained. And none of this our nation (either artisan, apprentice, or intruder) be permitted so mischievously to seek for gain as one here in London maketh his profession and custom to do; exposing himself a teacher of this art and trade, for any inconsiderable parcel of money, unto all manner of people (without distinction, whether native or not) hitherto uncontrollably; nor to inveigle and corrupt apprentices from their masters, to discover and teach unto them the whole trade; and (having gotten it) pretend upon scruple of conscience (in matter of religion) or some

other occasion, to depart your Highness's dominions, and set it up in practice
in a foreign country; as one not long since hath done, whom these petitioners
are labouring all they may to reduce, and are not hopeless to find prevalent
means to recover him back again timely enough, if they receive encouragement in this their humble suit. Wherein they further shew.

That although this manufacture may be wrought in any other materials
that are usually (or can possibly be) made into the form of knitwork; yet
hath it chosen to be practised in silk, the best and richest of all other in use
and wearing, and most crediting the artisans, and of greatest advantage unto
his State and Commonwealth, yielding several payments to the use of the
State before it pass out of the hands of the traders therein, and increasing
merchandise by both the ways of importation and exportation of the self
same material, imported raw at cheap rates, exported ready wrought at the
utmost extent of value; so that the distance of those valuations is totally clear
gain to this Commonwealth, and esteemed upwards of six parts in seven of
the whole quantity of this material in the highest value thereof, wrought up
by this manufacture; which hath vindicated that old proverbial aspersion,
cast upon this nation by foreigners: the stranger buyeth of the Englishman
the case of a fox for a groat, and selleth him the tail again for a shilling; and
may now invert and retort on them: the Englishman buyeth silk of the
stranger for twenty marks, and selleth him the same again for an hundred
pounds.

That this trade encourageth and setteth on work other artificers also, as
smiths, joiners, and turners, for the making, erecting, and repairing of the
frames, and other necessary instruments thereunto belonging; and hath bred
up many excellent workmen among them for further public service.

That the artisans of this trade, do, moreover, employ a multitude of hands
(besides their own) about the preparation and finishing of the material and
ware they work; on which do competently subsist and thrive the winders,
throwsters, sizers, seamers, and trimmers thereof; and also their needle-
makers totally depend thereon.

That although these petitioners seem in the eyes of the world to be (at
present) under a cloud, and every moment ready to be undone by intruders
and foreigners, so that many people fear and forbear to bind their children
apprentices unto a trade of such instant hazard and irregularity, until a
settlement thereof under a corporation, to the great retarding an increase of
able artisans, who are therefore but few in comparison of the number of
knitters, the way common to other nations. Yet do they subsist by their labours
in a more substantial and serviceable degree in the Commonwealth, disbur-
dening it of many poor of both sexes; whereas that common tedious way
multiplyeth needy persons here, rather because the people of other nations
outwork those of this therein, than by any hindrance they receive from the
best artisans of this manufacture, that bend their endeavours (all they can) to
the foreign vent in general (as well as in their own particulars) most profitable
to this nation, leaving the homesale (in great part) unto the common knitters

uninterrupted, unless by the intruders into this art, whose multiplication (i
not restrained) will be equally as pernicious and destructive unto them as
unto these petitioners; who only (and not the common knitters) have shewec
unto this Commonwealth that it is able abundantly to serve itself, *et ultra*
with all commodities of knitwork, as stockings, calceoons, waistcoats, and
many other things, without the help (or rather inconvenience) it formerly
had of importation of the same in quantity, ready wrought from foreign
parts. . . .

That the petitioners have made a large and competent probation of the
worth of this manufacture in itself, and merit thereof to the Commonwealth
. . . have voluntarily amongst themselves kept order in their trading, according to the duty of probationers (hitherto) without making any reques
unto the State for particular countenance and protection, until they found
themselves now risen into a number not uncapable of an incorporation; and
their trade into foreign parts of so great a growing increase (were the
momentary dangers of utter ruin, for want of regulating power, diverted
that it may well be esteemed the most improveable way of benefit and
advantage of this kind apparent to this present age, and (within some late
hundreds of years past) offered unto this nation, and presented unto the
State (as this now is to your Highness) for an enclosure within the boundary
of its native soil, where it may receive its proper husbandry.

That if these petitioners had no other inducements to offer but what
every other trade, which is (common also to foreigners) in fear to be over
wrought and outsold by them, hath heretofore presented as motives and
means to obtain charters and privileges, and consequent provisions by statute
upon reasons drawn from conveniences accruing by civil education of some
youth of the land, employment of idle persons; serving this Commonwealth
with commodities better wrought here than those transported hither from
beyond the seas, and maintaining many of our people at home with the
same money which foreigners did get from hence for maintenance of theirs
Yet might the petitioners (in confidence of the mere right of subjects) sue fo
(at least) the like grant of privilege and power, subordinately (according to
the laws and constitutions of this land) to regulate their own endeavours in
a company and fraternity among themselves. . . .

37. MEETINGS OF THE COURT OF THE MINES ROYAL, 1656-7

[B.M., Loan MS. 16. Court Minute Book of the Mines Royal,
1654–1709]

12 Decembris, 1656

MINES ROYAL. A court was this day holden for the said society at Mr
Kemp's house in Sheere Lane where were present: Michael Oldisworth

sq. deputy governor; Thomas Foley, esq.; Edward Darell, esq.; Mr. Roger Norton; Mr. Knightbridge; Mr. Kemp; Mr. Bolton now admitted *de bene esse*.

At this court came Stephen Bolton, esq., who hath married the late wife and executrix of Mr. John Hawe, late a member of this society, and claimed to be admitted in the right of his said wife to such part and portion in the privileges of this company as did belong to the said Mr. Hawe, which interest of Mr. Hawe being now not clearly understood, Mr. Foley and himself are desired to enquire into the said interest and clear the same to this company that he may be admitted accordingly.

The sergeant having according to the order of the last court summoned certain persons, namely Mr. Miller, Mr. Norman, and Mr. Mills to attend this day to shew by what authority they work a certain mine royal at Downham in or near Whalley in the county of Lancashire, which summons he doth now certify. But they not appearing, and the company being informed by the said sergeant that they pretend to work the said mine at present as assigns of David Ramsey and others by virtue of some grant made about 4 Caroli from the late King; and that they are likewise agents for Mr. Bushell who hath lately obtained some grant from the Lord Protector to search for mines royal); it is ordered that search be made for those grants made to the said Mr. Ramsey and his partners and to the said Mr. Bushell that the company may see what authority they pretend to; and may take order for suppressing of their works.

It is likewise ordered that Mr. Oldisworth and Mr. Foley be desired to speak with the Lord Whitelocke, one of the Lords Commissioners of the Treasury and one of the governors of this company that his lordship will be pleased to give this company a meeting where his lordship shall appoint to consult and advise with them about their powers and privileges, and in the meantime that abstracts be made of the company's grants and of the grants made to Bushell and Ramsey and others and that the case between them be stated.

xvii Februarii, 1656 [= 1657]

Mines Royal. A court was this day holden for the said society at Mr. Kemp's house in Sheere Lane where were present: Michael Oldisworth, esq., William Stephens, esq., deputy governors; Thomas Foley, esq., treasurer; Mr. Knightbridge; Mr. Kemp.

Consideration being this day had about a mine royal at Downham in or near Whalley in the county of Lancaster now wrought by certain persons without any authority derived from this company. It is ordered that a commission be prepared with instructions for the sergeant of this company to go to the said mine, and if he find any there working, to take notice of their names and by what authority they work and to forbid their further working, to enquire into the goodness of the ore, whether it be wrought as a mine royal or not, and how far the mine and vein extendeth itself, to bring

some of the ore to London for a trial to be made whether it be a mine royal
or not . . .

38. THE GARDENERS SEEK CONFIRMATION OF
THEIR COMPANY'S CHARTERS, 1656
[P.R.O., SP 18/127, no. 43]

To his Highness, Oliver Lord Protector of the Commonwealth
of England, Scotland, and Ireland

The humble petition of the Master, Wardens, Assistants, and
Commonalty of the Company of Gardeners, London.

SHEWETH that the late King James by his Letters Patent under the Great
Seal of England in the third year of the reign did incorporate the gardeners
in London and within six miles thereof into a body politic with divers
liberties and privileges; and afterwards in the 14th year of his reign by other
his Letters Patent did both confirm and enlarge the same and caused the
defects of the former to be amended and the doubts that did and might arise
thereon to be taken away. According whereunto and by virtue whereof the
master, wardens, and assistants of the said company for their more orderly
government did contrive amongst themselves fit and necessary laws and
ordinances to be executed and observed, which were approved of by the
Lord Chancellor, Lord Treasurer, and Lord Chief Justice. And that the late
King Charles also upon consideration had of the former charters and of the
benefit which might redound to the Commonwealth by the said trade or
mystery and the well ordering of the same did by his proclamation in the
tenth year of his reign inhibit several abuses which were crept into the said
trade and commanded the due observation of the said former patents, laws,
and ordinances so had and made in that behalf.

Nevertheless, may it please your Highness, so it is that the said charters
and the good laws and ordinances made for the better government of the
said trade have long been and daily are neglected, slighted, and contemned
by many persons who never served apprentices to the same nor were ever
admitted into the said company; who do use the said trade contrary to the
tenor of the said charters, yet never attain the knowledge thereof. By which
means many dead, unuseful, unwholesome, and corrupt plants, trees,
stocks, roots, sets, slips, herbs and seeds are daily by them put to sale and
vended to the great deceit and abuse of the Commonwealth. And whereby
also the freemen of the said company and many persons that have served
their apprenticeships to the said trade are without a livelihood. And those
that would otherwise put their children or others apprentices to the said
trade are utterly discouraged thereunto.

May it therefore please your Highness to take the premises into your pious
consideration, and in regard the said trade and mystery hath been found and

approved (if well ordered) to be very useful and beneficial to the Commonwealth, not only in the improving of land and the product of much wholesome food and physic necessary for men's bodies, but also for setting of thousands of poor at work, which otherwise would be very burthensome to the parishes where they live. And in the breeding up of great number of youth apprentices which may not only be serviceable to the Commonwealth in the way of their trade but otherwise, if occasion shall require, being bred up to hard labour; that your petitioners may obtain your Highness's grace and favour in the confirmation of their said charters and in the approbation of the aforesaid laws and ordinances conceived necessary for the well ordering of the said trade. And that your Highness would vouchsafe to manifest your pleasure concerning such as shall oppose them in enjoying the privileges or exercising the authority granted unto them. That so they and such as they shall breed up may have a livelihood by their calling and with comfort and alacrity proceed therein which otherwise they cannot do.

And the petitioners (as in duty bound) shall daily pray, etc.

Endorsed:] Coy. of Gardeners. Rec. 22 May 1656

39. THE FRAMEWORK KNITTERS FIGHT FOREIGN COMPETITION, 1658

[P.R.O., SP 18/184, no. 34,I]

JOHN CROSON, citizen and merchant tailor of London, and Jonathan Grammar, citizen and clothworker of London,[1] do severally make oath that they are credibly informed and do believe the same to be true, that one Mr. Burdina, an Italian merchant, hath bespoke thirty or forty frames, belonging to the art and mystery of framework knitters with an intention to transport the same beyond the seas, and because he would have the same speedily done, gives, as these deponents have likewise been credibly informed, very great rates for the same, as namely, four score pounds a frame, and hath several already delivered to him and will, as these deponents verily believe, speedily transport the same unless timely prevented. The which will tend very much to the prejudice of the people of this Commonwealth in regard the art will be transported and this nation in a manner lose the same as these deponents do assuredly believe.

John Croson, Jonathan Grammar.

Both sworn the third day of December, 1658, before me, one of the Masters of the Chancery in ordinary.

W. Glascock.

Endorsed:] Framework knitters. Received from Latham, 3 Dec. 1658. Referred 14 December 1658.

[1] This document accompanied a petition from the newly incorporated Framework Knitters' Company to Richard Cromwell to prevent the export of knitting frames, whereby other nations 'will by that means get the chief trade into their hands by making the commodities worse and so to sell them at under rates'.

40. THE NAVY BUILDS A VESSEL, 1658
[P.R.O., SP 18/184, no. 32]

Right worshipful,

After my service presented, these are humbly to give your worships an
account of the going on of the work here in the Forest of Dean, which,
accounting the season of the year and the hands therein employed, I have
made as much improvement thereof as I could, having at present some 14
shipwrights upon the work, being as few as I can possibly employ. The keel
of the ship is laid, the post and stem up, the knee of the post bolted, most
part of the flower timbers cross the keel and bolted, some frame bends of
timber up and most of the naval timbers for the midships ready to get up.
And if your worships would be pleased that a convenient supply of money
might be allowed for the payment of poor workmen, I am confident the work
would come off a great deal better, for although I do what I can in following
them hard to their work from morning to night, being never from them a
quarter of an hour except now and then to ride into the Forest to look after
business there and down to the yard again, although at present I have not
any place in the yard for shelter but now by the Major's advice I am making
a house over the saw pit, which will also serve overhead for a convenient
storehouse for the laying of the provisions in. I humbly desire that your
worships will be pleased to take into consideration the necessity of poor men
that I am confident have neither money nor credit to buy them provision
and for my own part it is almost as bad with me. I have with great patience
waited for a change, but I know not when it will be; for this twenty week
time I have received but 40l. for all business whatsoever which is not above
2l. a week for the payment of some 15l. a week which is the least that we are
at. I thought it not safe by a longer delay in a fruitless expectation to be silent
in giving your worships this account lest I should become guilty of breach
of trust imposed in me in not giving your worships notice of what I find
prejudicial to the work in hand. I humbly leave the premises to your worships' consideration, not doubting but you will be pleased [to find] some way
or other to remove this present obstruction. And do rest your worships'
humble and faithful servant,

Daniel Furzer.

Lidney, this 13 December 1658.
[Endorsed:] For the service of the State. For the rt. worshipful the Commissioners of the Navy at the Navy Office in Seething Lane, London, these
present. To Major Wade.

41. AN ACT TO REGULATE BAYMAKING
AT COLCHESTER, 1660

[*Statutes of the Realm, V*, pp. 253–4]

12, Car. II, *Chapter* XXII

An Act for the regulating of the trade of baymaking in the Dutchy [=Dutch] Bay Hall in Colchester

Rot. Parl. 12
C.II. p. 3. *nu.* 1.

WHEREAS by the special favour of Queen Elizabeth there was a congregation of Dutch people tolerated to practise the art and trade of bay and say making in the town of Colchester in the county of Essex, and for the upholding the credit of the said trade, and for the avoiding and punishing all unjust and fraudulent dealings therein, there have been diverse good and laudable orders and constitutions made, which were confirmed by Letters Patents under the Great Seal of England in the tenth year of King James, and by several orders made by the late King's Privy Council, the strict and exact execution of which said orders and constitutions by the governors of the Dutchy Bay Hall, there hath brought that kind of drapery into high credit not only at home but also in foreign parts, and that by reason of the said trade many thousands of poor people both within the said town of Colchester and places thereabout are daily employed and set to work. Notwithstanding which said orders, and the care of the governors of the said Dutchy Bay Hall many fraudulent and deceitful commodities and slight and naughty bays have been and daily are by the secret and crafty practices of some men made in the said town, and are weekly brought and conveyed to London by certain persons using the trade of buying and selling of Colchester bays before such time as the said bays have been viewed, searched, measured, and sealed by the sworn officers of the said Dutchy Bay Hall, which said bays so deceitfully and fraudulently made are transported beyond the seas under the name and oftentimes with the seal of Colchester bays, whereby the bays there made are not of that credit and esteem as formerly, for the preventing [of[1]] which said practices and deceits be it enacted by the King's most excellent Majesty with the assent of the Lords and Commons in this present Parliament assembled and by authority of the same that the governors of the said Dutchy Bay Hall in Colchester, and the Dutch people there living shall and may from henceforth peaceably and quietly use and exercise the free trade of making bays, says, and other foreign draperies within the said town of Colchester, and be permitted to govern the said trade in their assemblies and congregations with all such liberties, privileges, immunities, and in as full and ample manner as they have at any time heretofore enjoyed the same by virtue of any order, grant, or toleration to them made by Queen Elizabeth, King James, or the late King Charles of blessed memory or any of them.

Recital that under Queen Eliz., Dutch bay and say makers at Colchester were tolerated, and confirmed by Letters Patent.

10 Jac. I.

Benefits resulting from the constitutions of the Dutch Bay Hall there;

and that grievances had arisen by false commodities.

Confirmation of the privileges of the Dutch Bay Hall.

---

[1] Interlined on the Roll.

And be it further enacted by the authority aforesaid that if any person or persons whatsoever from and after the twentieth day of September in the year of our Lord one thousand six hundred and sixty shall weave or cause to be woven within the said town of Colchester or the liberties thereof any bay known by the name of four and fifties, sixties, sixty-eights, eighties, and hundred bays, and shall not within two days after such weaving carry or cause such bay to be carried to the Dutchy Bay Hall called the Raw Hall there to be viewed and searched, to the intent it may appear whether the same bay be well and substantially wrought before as the said bay shall be carried to be stowed and thicked, or if any fuller or thicker or other person using the art or trade of fulling or thicking of bays shall receive any such bay to be fulled and thicked before such time as the said bay hath been carried to the said Raw Hall, and there stamped and marked as by the orders of the said Hall it ought to be; that every such weaver that shall so convey the said bay, and every such fuller or thicker that shall receive such bay before the same be stamped and marked as aforesaid shall forfeit for the first offence the sum of forty shillings to be levied by distress and sale of the offender's goods, returning the overplus, the necessary charges of distraining being first deducted, and such forfeitures, in case such bay be made by an English master maker, then the same to be accounted for to the mayor and commonalty of the said town for the benefit of the poor of the said town, and in case such bay be the bay of a Dutch master maker then the same to be disposed by the governors of the said Dutch Bay Hall for the use and benefit of the poor of the said Dutch congregation, and for the second offence shall forfeit the sum of five pounds to be levied and disposed in manner abovesaid and for the third offence not to be permitted to work any more within the town of Colchester or liberties thereof.

And be it further enacted by the authority aforesaid that if any person or persons shall buy any of the aforesaid bays or convey or carry or cause such bay to be conveyed or carried out of the said town of Colchester before such time as the said bay hath been viewed, searched, stamped, sealed, and measured as aforesaid by the sworn officers of the said Dutchy Bay Hall thereunto appointed, that in such case the said bay so bought or carried, or offered to be carried or conveyed away as aforesaid shall be confiscated, the one moiety to him or them that shall seize the same, and the other moiety to the poor of the parish where the said bay shall be taken and seized.

And be it further enacted by the authority aforesaid that if any person or persons whatsoever shall from and after the said twentieth day of September counterfeit or cause to be counterfeited any of the seals used by the Corporation or Congregation of the Dutch Bay Hall in Colchester, or shall, not being the officer thereunto by the said Corporation appointed, and in the place by them thereunto appointed, affix any such seal or seals to any Colchester bay whether counterfeited or not counterfeited, that every person so offending being thereof lawfully convicted shall for his first offence forfeit and pay to the use of the said governors of the said Dutch Bay Hall the sum of twenty

---

Marginal notes:

II.
All bays made at Colchester must be carried to the Bay Hall and searched.

Fuller etc., working any bays not stamped;

Penalty 40s.

How applied where bay made by English maker;

where by Dutch maker.

Second offence, £5.

Third offence, disabled.

III.
No bays to be carried out of the town until searched and stamped.

Penalty.

IV.
Counterfeiting Corporation seal;

or unduly affixing seal to bays.

First offence, Penalty £20.

pounds to be recovered in any of his Majesty's courts of record or in the town court of Colchester by any action of debt, bill, plaint, information, or otherwise, wherein no essoin, protection, or wager of the law shall be allowed, and for the second offence, being convicted as aforesaid, shall stand Second offence in the pillory in the market or most public place where such offence shall be pillory. committed for the space of one hour, and for the third offence, being as Third offence, aforesaid convicted, shall suffer as a felon, and if any bays shall be taken, felony and forfeiture of carrying or carried out of Colchester without the mark of the maker that all bays. such bays shall be forfeit.

And for the better discovering, finding out, and punishing of the frauds V. and deceits aforesaid, be it further enacted by the authority aforesaid that it Power to shall and may be lawful for the governors of the said Dutch Bay Hall or their governors to search carts and officers, or any of them from time to time in the day time to search any cart, packs; wagon, or pack wherein they shall have notice, or suspect any such deceitful bays to be, and also from time to time with a constable, who are hereby to search houses, required to be aiding and assisting to them to make search in any house, shop, etc. with a constable and or warehouse where they are informed any such deceitful bays to be, and to seize. secure and seize the same, and carry the same to the said Dutch Bay Hall, and that such bay so seized and carried to the said Hall shall be confiscate Deceitful bays and forfeit to be disposed in such manner as the forfeitures herein before forfeited. mentioned to be paid by the weavers and fullers are herein before limited and appointed.

And be it further enacted by the authority aforesaid that for the better VI. managing and regulating of the said art or trade of making the bays aforesaid Power to make by-laws. that it shall and may be lawful to and for the governors of the said Dutchy Bay Hall from time to time to make, constitute, and appoint such orders, by-laws, and constitutions as to them shall seem meet and reasonable.

Provided that no such order, bylaw, or constitution to be made either in VII. diminution of the king's prerogative or the laws of this kingdom be used or Who are to approve of executed until the same orders, bylaws, and constitutions have been examined them. and approved by the Lord Chancellor, Lord Treasurer of England, or Chief Justices of either Bench or any three of them, or before both the Justices of Assize in their circuit or progress in the said county of Essex, upon pain of forfeiture of twenty pounds for every time they shall do the contrary. This Act to begin and take effect from the twentieth day of September, one thousand six hundred and sixty.

42. COPPER MINING AT ECTON, STAFFS., 1660-5

[J. A. Robey, 'The Ecton Copper Mines in the Seventeenth Century', *Bulletin Peak Dist. Mines Hist. Soc.*, IV, part 2, 1969, pp. 152-4]

An Abstract of the Charge of the Copper Mill and Mines at Wetton[1]

In 1660

	£ s. d.
For getting copper ore in Ecton Hill (rent in 27 pages) it seems there was 180 kibbles or horse loads got	96-19- 7
For getting stone and sand, and for lime, and carriage of all, for the mill and mill dam at Eliston	20-11-10
Timber, boards, horse and carriage	17-10- 6
Masons and wallers 14-17-6; carpenters 27-1-6	41-19- 0
Labourers 10-6-5; thatch and thatchers 1-5-0; nails 2-6-11	13-18- 4
Leather and hides for bellows 8-2-0, carriage of 100 ho. load of ore 5	13- 2- 0
Peats 5-11-9; coals 1-7-0; cordwood 15-10; besides 22 yds of lead pipe and a pig of lead from Chatsworth	7-14- 7
	211-15-10

In 1661

For stone, brick, timber, and iron work, etc. for the mill	39- 2- 4
Masons, wallers, carpenters, labourers, etc.	31-16- 5
Leather, oil, tallow, tubs, pails, etc.	5- 7-10
Cordwood, coals, roots, poles, coules and carriage	95-13- 7
85 dishes of copper ore bought at Tissington, etc.	4- 3- 0
Copper workers and their helpers' wages	87- 5- 1
Getting copper ore, to groovers and miners	65-11- 6
Soaps, ——[?], candles, etc.	15-14- 9
Rent of the copper mill	25- 0- 0
	369-14- 6

In 1662

Carriage of 260 horse load to the mill	13- 0- 0
,, ,, 112 ,, ,, ,, ,, ,,	5-12- 0
Jeremy Rhodes wages in 1660 20-0-0 ⎫	
in 1661 30-0-0 ⎬	80- 0- 0
in 1662 30-0-0 ⎭	
Smith and carpenter about the mill	3- 0- 4
——[?] and carriage etc.	29-17- 5
Necessaries as candles, leather, ashes, etc.	3-18- 6
Copper workers' wages	62- 6- 6

[1] Reproduced by permission of the Trustees of the Chatsworth Settlement. Ecton is a hamlet in the parish of Wetton, Staffs. The Ecton Hill mine, which was one of a very small number being worked in the mid-seventeenth century, infringed the monopoly of the Mineral and Battery Works. Robey, *op. cit.*, pp. 145, 150.

	£ s. d.
Miners getting ore	64-13- 1
Necessaries for the mines	12- 6- 8
Carriage of 2 tun and 4C weight of copper to London	16-11- 0
The accountant's riding charges	2-16- 0
A year's rent for the mill	25- 0- 0
	319- 1- 6

In 1663

Carriage of 2 tun and 2 C weight of copper to London at £5	10-10- 0
For 40 cord of wood at 5s. 6d.	10-15- 0
Carriage of 30 cord from Birchall park at 3s. 4d.	5- 0- 0
Cutting 36 cords ¾ at 22d.	3- 7- 4
Repairs about the mill dam	0- 8- 6
Piling up cordwood	0- 7- 6
A year's rent for the mill	25- 0- 0
Miners getting ore	45-13- 8
Candles, coals, leather for pumps, ropes, corves, nails and sharpening picks	8-17-11
	109-19-11

In 1664

For repairing the mill	4- 9- 0
For getting copper ore	27-16- 0
Jeremy Rhodes' wages	20- 0- 0
	52- 5- 0

Before the war laid out about the copper mines	
Before the war laid out about the copper mines	200- 0- 0
the whole charge is	1262-16- 9

Towards the charges mentioned

Sent to London } 2 tun and 4 C weight of copper
                 } 2 tun and 2 C weight of copper

In August 1665, the mill and mine was let to Mr. Mumma who is to pay for the mill	150- 0- 0
For ore already gotten	110- 2- 6
For copper stone	22-10- 0
For cord wood	24- 6-10
For tools	1-12- 0
	308-11- 4

Copper ore before the war cost 10s. a kibble getting, which is a horse load.
Copper ore is worth about 12d. a dish.
In 1668 there is a memorandum, that my lord was to have 1/6 part of the ore measured out upon the spot before it goes to the mill for his duty.

43. MINING CUSTOMS IN DERBYSHIRE, 1665

[Thomas Houghton, *The Compleat Miner or a Collection of the Laws, Liberties, Ancient Custom, Rules, Orders . . . of the several Mines and Miners in the Counties of Derby, Gloucester, and Somerset . . .* , London, 1688, pp. 1, 7–9, 13–15, 28–33, 52–5]

AT THE Great Court Barmoot for the lead mines, held at Wirksworth, for the soke and wapentake of Wirksworth in the county of Derby the 10th of October in the year of our Lord, 1665, the inquisition of the great late inquest, taken upon . . . [oath] . . .

Art. VII

We say that everyone ought to keep his ground in good and lawful possession, with stows and timber in men's sight; and that crosses and holes, without stows and timber, can keep possession but three days.

Art. VIII

We say that all men ought to work their ground truly, and, chase their stoo to their ground's end; and so each one from mere to mere, according to the custom, unless they be justly hindered by water, or for want of wind; and in such cases diligence ought to be used to gain wind, and to get out the water.

Art. IX

We say that the Bar master, or his deputy, ought to walk the mine once a week at least, and where he sees a mere of ground, which to his knowledge is lawfully possessed, to stand unwrought three weeks together, and might be wrought, not being hindered by water, or for want of wind, then he ought if he can conveniently, to give notice to the parties that neglect to work according to custom; then he shall nick the spindle, each week a nick, for three weeks together; and if it be not wrought within that time, nor borrowed of the Bar master or his deputy, then within two days after the last day of the said three weeks, the Bar master or his deputy may lawfully set on another man on such mere or meres of ground, to work according to custom; and if the Bar master neglect to do his duty herein, he shall forfeit five shillings to the lord of the field, or farmer.

Art. X

We say that if two several parties or more set possessions for one and the same thing, claiming for one and the same mere of ground, thereupon the party grieved shall complain to the Bar master, or his deputy, who shall forthwith bring with him four or more of the grand jury, or four and twenty

o view the possessions, and inform themselves the best way they can, who
hath the most ancient and lawful possession for that mere of ground, and
shall settle the same, casting off the other . . .

Art. XIV

We say that the Bar master, or his deputy, ought to lay forth the miners the
next way to the highway, for going and coming to and from their work, and
also for carrying to and from their work the running water to wash their
ore withal.

Art. XV

We say (by the custom of the mine) that all miners and their servants may
wash their ore with vat and sieve upon their works, so that they keep their
vats close covered, and empty their sludge into some convenient place within
their length or quarter cord, as the bar master, or his deputy, shall appoint,
so that the cattle of the owners or occupiers of the land where such washing
is, may have no harm.

Art. XVI

We say (by the custom of the mine within the wapentake of Wirksworth)
tis lawful for all the liege people of this nation to dig, delve, subvert, mine,
and turn up all manner of grounds, lands, meadows, closes, pastures, moors,
or marshes for lead ore, within the said wapentake, of whose inheritance
soever it is, dwelling houses, highways, orchards, or gardens excepted; but
if any arable grounds, lands, or meadows be digged, delved, subverted, or
mined, and not wrought lawfully according to the custom of the mine, then
it may and shall be lawful for the inheritors of the ground so digged, subverted, and mined, the same to fill up, at their will and pleasure.

Art. XVII

We say that no person or persons ought to keep any counterfeit dish or
measure in their houses, coes, or any other place, to measure ore withal, but
everyone ought to buy and sell by the Bar master's lawful dish, and no
other to be used or had; and every buyer offending herein shall forfeit for
every such offence forty shillings to the lord of the field or farmer; and the
sellers thereof shall forfeit their ore, if it be taken at such time . . .

Art. XXXIV

We say that when a mere or meres of ground are wrought under water, and
by reason thereof hath stood many years unwrought, and the owner or
owners of such mere or meres of ground do not use some effectual means to
set forth the water, to recover the same; and that the same might be wrought
by the means of a sough, or engine, and that for the public good, but is yet

neglected; thereupon any person or persons, who are minded to disburse and lay forth money, to recover such works from water, may, at a great Barmoo Court held at Wirksworth, declare such their intentions, in writing, to the grand jury, or twenty four, and they shall take the same into serious con sideration; and if they know such works to have stood long by reason o water and no effectual means used to win the same; and that the person o persons who desire to undertake to win the same by soughs, or otherwise, to be able men, and like to perfect such a work; thereupon the grand jury, o twenty four, shall appoint a day (a month after at least) for themselves, and the party that undertakes, and all the owners of such works, to meet at the place where such works are, and this time of meeting shall be published b the cryer in the great Barmoot Court, that all men may take notice thereof At such meeting the undertakers shall give the grand jury, or twenty four, to understand by what means they intend to lay dry all such works, and to ge out the water, for recovering the same; and if the grand jury, or twenty four thereupon conceive the way and means they propose is like and effectual t recover such works from water so that the public may have advantage there by, the grand jury, or twenty four, shall acquaint the owners of such work with the intentions of the undertakers concerning the recovery of such work from water, and the way and means they propose for the doing of it. And an of the owners of such works (if they please) may join with the undertakers paying their proportionable parts of the charge of such soughs or engines a shall be made to recover the same, according to their parts, and enjoy th benefit thereof. And such of the owners of such works as shall not (by them selves, or others by their authority) appear at such meeting, or then neglec or refuse to join, and pay their proportionable part or parts of charges of suc soughs or engines as shall be made and used for the recovery of such work from water, as aforesaid; thereupon the grand jury, or twenty four, and Ba master, or his deputy, shall have power to dispossess such owner or owner from their part or parts, and to assign and deliver possession of such part c parts to the undertakers thereof, as aforesaid; withal, ordering that the under takers of such works shall give to the owners that refuse and neglect a aforesaid such reasonable satisfaction as the grand jury, or twenty four, sha then think fit . . .

Art. XXXV

We say that when any man is possessed of a groove or mere of ground, an hath found the vein, and works therein, he ought to suffer his neighbour who is the next taker, and shew him the best light and direction he car which way, and upon what point, the vein goeth. But in case any man be s refractory as to deny his neighbour such a courtesy then he may procur three or more of the grand jury, or twenty four, to be summoned, and th Bar master, or his deputy, may put them into his groove who hath the vei in work, where they may (by using of a dial, or some other skill) shew hir that is the next taker, which way, and upon what point the vein goes, so tha

e may know thereby where to sink his shaft to find the vein; that the field
nay be set forwards for the public good; provided always that such of the
rand jury, or twenty four, as go into the groove aforesaid, shall not do any
ther act or thing, or make any other discovery of such groove, save only to
ee which way, and upon what point the vein goes . . .

Art. LVI

Ve do order and say that if any person that works for wages at any groove or
rooves, shaft or shafts, mere or meres of ground, within the said soke and
vapentake, and shall have his or their wages wrongfully detained or withheld
rom him or them, by the owner or owner's servant or agents at any of the
aid grooves, shaft or shafts, mere or meres of ground; that then, if such
erson or persons, from whom such wages shall be due, or from his or their
ervants or agents employed to manage their mines, do not well and truly
ay such wages as shall be due to any workman or servant, within ten days
fter an account given and demand made of such person or person's servant
r agents; that then in such case, the workman or servant who shall be
ehind in arrear and unpaid, as aforesaid, may arrest, where such work was
one, or elsewhere within the said soke and wapentake, his or their part or
arts of ore, or other materials, where such person or person's servant or
gent (doth not pay as aforesaid) are concerned, or have any part or parts
hereof, and so bring it to trial at the next Barmoot Court. And if such person
r persons, servants, or agents, defendant, or defendants shall be cast and
ondemned by the verdict of 12 men; then such defendant or defendants
hall pay all such wages forthwith, which shall be given in damage, and 10s.
ver and besides, for and towards the costs of such workmen or servants,
laintiff or plaintiffs, in the recovery of such just wages, if their ore be
ufficient under arrest to defray the said charge; but if not, and such defend-
nt or defendants refuse and neglect still to pay such wages and charges as
foresaid, then the Bar master of the liberty where the said defendants have
ny grooves, shall have power to levy the same by distress and sale of the
efendant or defendants' ore, or mineral materials, if any; or otherwise, he
hall deliver all his or their grooves, or parts thereof, to the plaintiff, to work
ntil the cost and damages be fully paid, with all charges in working the
ame. . . .

44. DUD DUDLEY ON THE HISTORY OF IRON MANUFACTURE WITH COAL SINCE JAMES I's REIGN, 1666

[Dud Dudley's Metallum Martis: or Iron made with Pit-Coal, Sea-Coal, etc., London, 1666, pp. 1–30]

. . King James, his sacred Majesty's grandfather, and Prince Henry for
le preservation of wood and timber in this island, did in the 9th year of his

reign, grant his Letters Patents of privilege unto Simon Sturtevant, esq., fo
31 years, for the making of iron with pit coal and sea coal for the preservatio
of wood and timber of Great Britain so greatly then consumed by ironwork
This invention was by King James's command to be at large put in prin
which book did contain near a quire of paper in quarto, called *Sim*
Sturtevant, His Metallica. Anno 1612. May 22. Printed by George El
Cum Privilegio.

After Simon Sturtevant could not perform his making of iron with pit co
or sea coal, according unto his engagement, King James and Prince Hen
caused him to render up his patent, and a new patent was granted unto Joh
Rovenson, esq. who also was enjoined to write a book of his invention
called, *Rovenson's Metallica.* Printed for Thomas Thorp, *Cum Privilegi*
May 15. *An.* 1613.

After John Rovenson, esq. had often failed with his inventions, and gre
undertaking, —— Gombleton, esq., a servant of Queen Ann's, undertook (b
patent) to perform the invention of making of iron with pit coal, and s
coal; but he being as confident of his invention as others, did erect his wor
at Lambeth, which the author viewed; and Gumbleton failing, the learne
and ingenious Doctor Jorden of Bath, the author's acquaintance, and sund
others obtained patents for the making of iron, and melting of mines wi
pit coal and sea coal, for the preservation of wood and timber, all whic
inventions and endeavours to effect and perfect the said works have be
by many heretofore well known to have worthily attempted the said inve
tion, though with fruitless success.

Having seen many of their failings, I held it my duty to endeavour, if
were possible, to effect and perfect so laudable, and beneficial, and also s
much desired inventions, as the making of iron into cast works and bar
and also the melting, extracting, refining, and reducing all sorts of mine
minerals, and metals, with pit coal, sea coal, peat, and turf, for the preserv
tion of wood and timber, so much exhausted by iron works of late.

Having former knowledge and delight in iron works of my father's, when
was but a youth; afterward at 20 years old, was I fetched from Oxford, the
of Balliol College, *anno* 1619, to look and manage 3 iron works of m
father's, 1 furnace, and 2 forges, in the Chase of Pensnet, in Worcestershir
but wood and charcoal growing then scant, and pit coals in great quantiti
abounding near the furnace, did induce me to alter my furnace, and 1
attempt by my new invention the making of iron with pit coal, assuring m
self in my invention, the loss to me could not be greater than others, nor s
great, although my success should prove fruitless. But I found such succe
at first trial animated me, for at my trial or blast I made iron to profit wi
pit coal, and found *facere est addere inventioni.*

After I had made a second blast and trial the feasibility of making iro
with pit coal and sea coal, I found by my new invention the quality to b
good and profitable, but the quantity did not exceed above 3 tons per wee
After I had brought my invention unto some perfection and profitabl

doubted not in the future to have advanced my invention to make quantity also.

Immediately after my second trial, I wrote unto my father what I had done, and withal desired him to obtain a patent for it from King James of blessed memory; the answer to which letter I shall insert, only to shew the forwardness of King James in this his much animating the inventor, as he did both Simon Sturtevant, John Rovenson, Doctor Jordanie, and others. The letter follows:

Son Dudley,

The King's Majesty being at Newmarket, I sent Parkes thither on Saturday to some friends of mine, to move the King's Majesty for my patent, which he coming on Sunday morning, in the afternoon his Majesty sent a warrant to Master Attorney to dispatch my patent, for the which I am infinitely bound unto his Majesty that it pleased him of his great grace and favour to dispatch it so soon. I have been this night with Master Attorney, who will make haste for me; God bless you, and commend me unto all my friends.

Your loving father,
Edward Dudley.

March 10, 1619.

This Richard Parkes, à Parkshouse esq., in the letter before mentioned, was the author's brother-in-law, which did about 1 year after the patent was granted, carry for the author much good merchantable iron unto the Tower, by King James's command to be tried by all artists, and they did very well approve of the iron, and the said Parkshouse had a fowling gun there made of pit coal iron, with his name gilt upon the gun, which gun was taken from him by Colonel Levison, governor of Dudley Castle, and never restored.

The said Richard Parkshouse's son, my nephew, Edward Parkshouse, the 5th of January 1664, pressed me much to put pen unto paper, to shew what I have done in the invention of making of iron with pit coal and sea coal, not unknown unto this country, and to my brother Folliott, esq.; and my nephew Parkshouse esq.; and to my kinsman, Master Francis Dingley, to whom I intend to leave the secrets of my inventions, notwithstanding all my sad sufferings from time to time this forty years in the invention, my sufferings in the war, and my estate sold for my loyalty; and also my sad sufferings and obstructions since his sacred Majesty's happy restoration many ways; and also upon sundry and many references, at the author's very great charge, pains, and time spent of four years in his aged days for the general good, by his inventions for the preservation of Great Britain's wood and timber.

Now let me shew some reasons that induced me to undertake these inventions, after the many failings of others, well knowing that within ten miles of Dudley Castle there to be near 20,000 smiths of all sorts, and many iron works at that time, within that circle decayed for want of wood (yet formerly a mighty woodland country).

Secondly, the Lord Dudley's woods and works decayed, but pit coal and iron, stone, or mines abounding upon his lands, but of little use.

Thirdly, because most of the coal mines in these parts, as well as upon the Lord Dudley's lands, are coals, ten, eleven, and twelve yards thick; the top or the uppermost coal or vein gotten upon the superficies of this globe or earth in open works.

Fourthly, under this great thickness of coal is very many sorts of iron, stone, mines, in the earth clay or stone earth, like bats in all four yards thick; also under these iron mines is several yards thick of coals, but of these in another place more convenient.

Fifthly, knowing that when the colliers are forced to sink pits for getting of ten yards thick of coal, one third part of the coals or more that be gotten under the ground, being small, are of little or of no use in that inland country nor is it worth the drawing out of the pits, unless it might be made use of by making of iron therewith into cast works or bars.

Sixthly, then knowing that if there could be any use made of the small coal that are of little use, then would they be drawn out of the pits . . .

The first patent being granted by King James for 31 years in the 19th year of his reign upon just and true information that the author had the year before made many tons of iron with pit coal at a furnace or ironwork in the Chase of Pensnet, in the county of Worcester, besides cast iron works of sundry sorts with pit coals; and also at two forges or iron mills, called Cradly Forges, fined the said iron into merchantable good bar iron. But the year following the grant or patent for making of iron with pit coal or sea coal, there was so great a flood by rain, to this day called the great May-day flood, that it not only ruinated the author's iron works and inventions, but also many other men's iron works; and at a market town called Stourbridge in *Comitate Wigorniæ*, although the author sent with speed to preserve the people from drowning, one resolute man was carried from the bridge there in the day time, and the nether part of the town was so deep in water that the people had much ado to preserve their lives in the uppermost rooms in their houses.

My iron works and inventions thus demolished, to the joy of many iron masters, whose works scaped the flood and who had often disparaged the author's inventions, because the author sold good iron cheaper than they could afford it, and which induced many of the iron masters to complain unto King James, averring that the iron was not merchantable; as soon as the author had repaired his works and inventions (to his no small charge) they so far prevailed with King James, that the author was commanded with all speed possible to send all sorts of bar iron up to the Tower of London, fit for making of muskets, carbines, and iron for great bolts fit for shipping which iron being so tried by artists and smiths that the iron masters and ironmongers were all silenced until 21th of King James. At the then Parliament all monopolies were made null, and diverse of the iron masters endeavouring to bring the invention of making iron with pit coal, sea coal, peat, and turf within the compass of a monopoly, but the Lord Dudley and the author did prevail. Yet the patent was limited to continue but fourteen years, after which Act the author went on with his invention cheerfully, and made annually great store of iron, good and merchantable, and sold it unto diverse men yet living at twelve pounds per ton. I also made all sorts of cast iron wares, as brewing cisterns, pots, mortars, and better and cheaper than any yet were made in these nations, with charcoals, some of which are extant to be seen by any man (at the author's house in the city of Worcester) that desire to be satisfied of the truth in the invention.

Afterwards, the author was outed of his works and inventions before mentioned by the iron masters and others wrongfully, over long to relate; yet being unwilling his inventions (having undergone much charge and pains therein) should fall to the ground, and be buried in him, made him to set forward his invention again at a furnace called Himley furnace in the county of Stafford, where he made much iron with pit coal, but wanting a forge to make it into bars, was constrained for want of stock to sell the pig iron unto the charcoal iron masters, who did him much prejudice, not only in detaining his stock, but also disparaging the iron, Himley furnace being rented out unto charcoal iron masters.

The author erected a new large furnace on purpose, 27 foot square, all of stone for his new invention, at a place called Hasco Bridge, in the parish of Sedgley, and county of Stafford; the bellows of which furnace were larger than ordinary bellows are, in which work he made 7 tons of iron per week, the greatest quantity of pit coal iron that ever yet was made in Great Britain; near which furnace the author discovered many new coal mines 10 yards thick, and iron mine under it, according to other coal works; which coal works, being brought unto perfection, the author was by force thrown out of them, and the bellows of his new furnace and invention by riotous persons cut in pieces, to his no small prejudice, and loss of his invention of making of iron with pit coal, sea coal, etc. So that being with law suits and riots wearied and disabled to prosecute his art and invention at present, even until the first patent was extinct; notwithstanding the author his sad sufferings, imprisonments wrongfully for several thousand pound in the Counter in London, yet did obtain a new patent, dated the 2d of May, *anno* 14. Caroli Primi of ever blessed memory, not only for the making of iron into castworks and bars, but also for the melting, extracting, refining, and reducing of all mines, minerals, and metals with pit coal, sea coal, peat, and turf, for the preservation of wood and timber of this island; into which patent, the author, for the better support and management of his invention, so much opposed formerly at the Court, at the Parliament, and at the law, took in David Ramsey, esquire, resident at the Court; Sir George Horsey, at the Parliament; Roger Foulke, esquire, a Counsellor of the Temple, and an ingenious man; and also an iron master, my neighbour, and one who did well know my former sufferings, and what I had done in the invention of making of iron with pit coal, etc.

All which said patentees, articled the 11th of June following, the grant not only to pay the author all the charges of passing the patent laid down by him, but also to lay in for a common and joint-stock each man of the four, one hundred pounds, and so from time to time, what more stock any three of the patentees should think fit to be laid in for the making of iron into cast works and bars, and likewise for the melting, extracting, refining, and reducing of all mines, minerals, and metals, with pit coal, sea coal, peat, and turf, which articles are yet extant. . . .

Not long after the wars came on, and caused my partners to desist, since which they are all dead, but the author, and his estate (for his loyalty unto his late sacred Majesty) and master (as by the additional Act of Parliament may appear) was totally sold.

Yet, nevertheless, I still endeavoured not to bury my talent, took in two partners into my inventions, Walter Stevens of Bristow, linen draper, and John Ston of the same city, merchant, after the author had begun to erect a new work for the inventions aforesaid, near Bristow, *anno* 51, and there we three partners had in stock near 700*l*. but they not only cunningly drew me into bond, entered upon my stock and work, unto this day detained it, but also did unjustly enter staple actions in Bristow of great value against me, because I was of the King's party; unto the great prejudice of my inventions and proceedings, my patent being then almost extinct; for which, and my stock, am I forced to sue them in Chancery.

In the interim of my proceedings, Cromwell and the then Parliament granted a patent and an Act of Parliament unto Captain Buck of Hampton Road, for the making of iron with pit coal and sea coal. Cromwell, and many of his officers were partners, as Major Wildman and others, many doctors of physic and merchants, who set up diverse and sundry works and furnaces at a vast charge in the Forest of Dean. And after they had spent much in their invention and experiments, which was done in spacious wind-furnaces, and also in pots of glass-house clay; and failing afterwards, got unto them an ingenious glass-maker, Master Edward Dagney, an Italian then living in Bristow, who after he had made many pots for that purpose, went with them into the Forest of Dean, and built for the said Captain Buck and his partners a new furnace, and made therein many and sundry experiments and trials for the making of iron with pit coal and sea coal, etc. But he failing, and his pots being all broken, he did return to Bristow frustrate of his expectation, but further promising to come again, and make more experiments. At which time Master John Williams, Master Dagneys, master of the glass-house, was then drawn in to be a partner for 300*l*. deposited, and most of it spent, the said Williams and Dagney hearing that the author had knowledge in the making of iron with pit coal, sea coal, etc. they from Cap. Buck and the other partners, importuned the author, who was at that time in great danger by the Parliament (being a Colonel of the King's party), to go along with them into the Forest of Dean, which at that time durst not deny; coming thither, I observed their manner of working, and found it impossible that the said Edward Dagney by his invention should make any iron with pit coal or sea coal in pots to profit. I continued with them till all their pots and inventions failed; at every dinner and supper, Captain Buck, Captain Robins, Doctor Ivie, Doctor Fowler, and others would ask the author why he was so confident that iron in quantity could not be made by their new inventions. I found it a difficult thing to dissuade the partners from their way, so confident were they to perform the making of iron with pit coal or sea coal to profit; that they desired me to come again a second time into the forest to see it effected. But at that time, I saw their failings also.

Yet nevertheless Captain Buck and his partners erected new works at the city of Bristow, in which they did fail as much as in their former inventions, but Major Wildman, more barbarous to me than a wild man (although a minister), bought the author's estate, near 200*l.* per annum, intending to compel from the author his inventions of making of iron with pit coal; but afterwards passed my estate unto two barbarous brokers of London, that pulled down the author's two mansion houses, sold 500 timber trees off his land, and to this day are his houses unrepaired.

Anno 1655. Captain Buck and his partners wearied of their invention, desisting, *an.* 1656. Captain John Copley from Cromwell obtained another patent for the making of iron with pit coal and sea coal. He and his partners set up their works, at the coal works near Bristow, and endeavoured by engineers' assistance to get his bellows to be blown at, or near, the pits of coal, with which engines the work could not be performed. But the author coming to see the said works, and after many discourses with Captain Copley, his former acquaintance, told him plainly, if his bellows could have been blown by those engines, yet I feared he could not make iron with pit coal or sea coal; he seemed discontented; whereupon, and without those engines I made his bellows to be blown feasibly . . .

Captain John Copley thus failing in his inventions, *an.* 1657, he went into Ireland, and all men now desisting from the inventions of making of iron with pit coal and sea coal, the author, *anno* 1660 being 61 years of age, and moved with pity, and seeing no man able to perform the mastery of making of iron with pit coal or sea coal, immediately upon his sacred Majesty's happy restoration, the same day he landed, petitioned that he might be restored to his place, and his patent obstructed revived for the making of iron with pit coal, sea coal, peat, and turf, into cast works and bars, and for the melting, extracting, refining, and reducing of all mines, metals, and minerals, with pit coal, sea coal, peat, and turf; . . .

The author, during the Lords Commissioners their time, could get no order upon his reference. But his petition was left with the now Right Honourable the Lord Treasurer to take or grant further order therein, but the author hath gotten hitherto no order.

Therefore compelling necessity doth constrain (having prosecuted his petition hitherto) him to desist from his inventions, in which he hath taken more pains, care, and charge, than any man to perfect his new invention in these kingdoms.

Although the author hath not as yet so fully perfected or raised his invention to the quantity of charcoal iron furnaces, yet the author's quantity being
but seven tons per week at the most, together with the quality of his iron
made with pit coal and sea coal, hath the most eminent triplicity of iron of all
that can be desired in any new invention.

1. More sufficient. 2. More cheap. 3. More excellent.

45. A DESCRIPTION OF LEAD MINING IN SOMERSET, 1667

[*The Philosophical Transactions and Collections to the End of the Year
1700 Abridg'd* . . . , ed. John Lowthorp, vol. II, 1716, pp. 573–6]

Lead Mines in Somersetshire,
by Mr. Joseph Glanvill and others

1. I am well informed that all Mendip in Somersetshire is mountainous. Yet
the hills not equal in height. It is barren and cold, and rocky in some places.
The ridges thereof run confusedly, but most east and west, and not in any
parallel one with another. Upon the surface thereof, it is heathy, ferny, and
furzy; and the cattle it feeds, for the most part, are sheep, which go there all
the year; and young beasts, horses, and colts, at spring and fall. The sheep are
not fair but big-bellied, and will grow to no bigness after they have been
there fed, but will grow fat if they are removed into better soil; and so their
beasts and horses.

The inhabitants live wealthy, saving such as are employed about melting
of the lead at the mines, who, if they work in the smoke, are subject to a
disease that will kill them, and the cattle likewise that feed thereabout. The
smoke that rests upon the ground, will bane them. And therefore the inhabitants have keepers to keep them from it, for fear of the infection. At the foot
of the hills there are many springs which are very wholesome; and produce
rivers, after they have run to some distance from thence. The air is moist,
cold, foggy, thick, and heavy . . .

When they have got the ore, they beat it small, then wash it clean in a
running stream; then sift it in iron rudders, then they make of clay or
fire stone an hearth or furnace which they set in the ground, and upon it
build their fire, which is lighted with charcoal, and continued with young
oaken gadds, blown with bellows by men's treading on them. And after the
fire is lighted, and the fireplace hot, they throw their lead ore upon the wood,
which melts down into the furnace; and then with an iron ladle they take it
out, and upon sand cast it into what form they please.

2. I am farther informed by experienced mine men, that they have sometimes
known the vein to run up into the roots of trees, and yet they have observed
no difference at the top, with respect to the other trees there, into whose roots
no such veins run. The snow and frost near the grooves melt quickly, but

continue long at further distance. Sometimes when a mine hath been very near the surface, the grass hath been yellow and discoloured. They have no value for the *Virgula Divinatoria*; yet they say when the mine is open, they may guess by it, how far the vein leads. White, yellow, and mixed earth are leaders to the country (as they call it); changeable colours always encourage their hopes. For stones, they are sometimes 12 fathom deep, before they meet any. Other while, when a stony reak at top, they meet ore just under the sward (superficies) of the grass, which ore hath gone down about 40 fathom. A black stone is of bad signification, and leads to a jam (a black thick stone, that hinders their work) a grey, clear, dry one, they account best. They seldom encounter damps. If in sinking they come to wet, moorish earth, they expect a jam, and to be closed up with rocks. The nearness they guess by short brittle clay; for the tough is not leading.

The ore sometimes is shole, and again it is 14 or 20 fathom, more or less before they hit it. They follow a vein inclining to some depth, when it runs away in flat bins.

When the stones part it, then they find a vein again. Their draughts are 14 or 16 fathom, till they come to a stone, where they cast aside a draught called a cut. Then they sink plumb again 4 or 5 cuts, one under another. They find ore at 50 fathom. Their best reaks are north and south; east and west are good, though not so deep. The groove is 4 foot long, 2½ foot broad, till they meet a stone, when they carry it as they can. The groove is supported by timber. A piece of an arm's bigness will support 10 ton of earth. It lasts long; that which was put in beyond the memory of man (nay, which by the difference in the manner of working their mines, they know to have lain above 200 years) will serve in new works. It is tough and black, and being exposed to the sun and wind for 2 or 3 days, will scarce yield to an axe.

For the supply of air they have boxes of elm exactly closed, of about 6 inches in the clear, by which they carry it down above 20 fathom. But when they come at ore and need an airshaft, they sink it 4 or 5 fathom distant, of the same fashion with a groove, to draw as well ore as air.

They make use of leathern bags, of 8 or 9 gallons apiece, drawn up by ropes to free the water. If they find a swallet, they drive an adit upon a level, till 'tis dry.

If they cannot cut the rock, they use fire to anneal it, laying on wood and coal, and the fire so contrived, that they leave the mine before operation begins, and find it dangerous to enter again, before it be quite cleared of the smoke, which hath killed some.

Their beetles, axes, wedges, etc., unless so hardened as to make a deep impression upon the head of an anvil, are not fit for their use; and yet they sometimes break them in an hour; others last 3 or 4 days, as it happens. They work clothed in frocks and waistcoats, by candlelight of tallow, 14 or 15 to the pound, each whereof lasts 3 hours, if they have air enough; which if they want to keep in the candles, the workmen cannot stay there. A vein being lost, they drive 2 or 3 fathoms in the breast, as the nature of the earth directs them. They convey out their materials in elm buckets drawn by ropes. The buckets hold about a gallon. Their ladders are of ropes . . .

The clearest and heaviest ore is the best; 36 hundred of ore may yield a ton of lead.

The hearth for melting the ore is about 5 foot high, set upon timber, to be turned as a windmill, to avoid the inconveniences of smoke upon a shifting wind. It contains half a bushel of ore and coal. There is a sink upon the sides of the hearth, into which the lead runs, that holds about 1½ hundred. They have a bar to stir the fire; a shovel to throw it up; and a ladle heated red hot to cast out the melted metal. Once melting is enough; and the best (which is distinguished by its weight) melts first.

There is a flight in the smoke, which falling upon the grass, poisons those cattle that eat of it. They find the taste of it upon their lips to be sweet and when the smoke chances to fly in their faces. Brought home and laid in their houses, it kills rats and mice. If this flight mix with the water, in which the ore is washed, and be carried away into a stream, it hath poisoned such cattle as have drunk of it after a current of three miles. What of this flight falls upon the sand, they gather up to melt upon a flag hearth, and make shot and sheet lead of it.

They sometimes find slags, 3, 4, or 5 foot under ground; but such as they judge were cast aside heretofore.

They have sometimes heard knockings beyond their own works, which when followed by them, have afforded plenty of ore. And one King, of Wells, about 2 years since found in his groove a piece of ore, in which they fancied the shape of a man, eyes, arms, legs, full breast, etc. The whole was about 4 inches in length; the mine proved rich. . .

Those who live near where lead ore is washed cannot keep either dog or cat, or any sort of fowl, but they all die in a short time. And I have known of a little house wherein lead ore was kept some time, though afterward made very clean and well bedded with fern, yet when calves were put into it, they all died shortly after. And children sometimes in these houses have died suddenly. If any sort of cattle eat often of that grass, on which the steam, which rises from the smelting of lead, falls, they all die in a while after. . .

46. THE VALUATION OF LANDS FOR AGRICULTURAL AND INDUSTRIAL PURPOSES, 1667[?]

[Stephen Primatt, *The City and Country Purchaser and Builder*, London, 1667[?], pp. 1–9, 14–16, 26–30]

A General treatise how to compute the value of lands in England and what makes them of that value; with advice to a purchaser, and rules prescribed to purchase

IT is not my intended purpose to make any long treatise on this point, only so much as may somewhat conduce to the information of the purchaser and seller of lands or houses as to their respective values and what makes them of that value in any part of England, the purchaser being sometimes over-reached by the seller; and the seller sometimes selling his lands or houses for less than they are worth, both which proceed either for want of reason and judgement to know the nature of the thing, or for want of skill in arithmetic to find out the true value. Of both which in the ensuing discourse I shall give you some account. And shall therefore commend to you these few observations following, to which the ingenious reader's judgement may make a great addition.

First, to consider the quantity and quality of the thing you are about to purchase, and what casualties it may in probability be subject unto; as if it be land that is near the sea coasts, or any great river, the banks may be subject either to be beaten down by the ebbing and flowing of the sea, or to be overflowed; which banks may require great cost in repairing, and the lands more in draining; lands being often after such overflows of little or no use for three or four years together, there coming in with such overflows very great quantities of sand. But lands lying near great rivers are not altogether so very perilous, but that sometimes it tends to the owners' and purchasers' profit to have their meadows overflowed. Another casualty is that of poor tenants, not able to pay their rents, who are disabled sometimes by a season that is too sicced or dry; or a season that is too moist, so that the earth is not of that due temperature of heat and moisture as to produce its wonted increase; and at other times when there is a good increase, they bear little or no price at the market. Another casualty or accident is that of fire, which comes by lightning or through negligence of neighbours or servants which many times consumes a farmer's house, corn, and barns, and doth undo him; all which are damages that many time light very hard on the landlords.

Secondly, to consider if there be any edifices, as houses, barns, stables, and such like upon the same, and whether they be in good and sufficient repair, or well thatched or tiled; and if not, what will repair them?

Note, that farm houses, and barns upon lands generally in England, are of little or no value, and are not usually valued in the purchase, but are cast in with the lands to the purchase, except it be of decent houses made for the dwelling of gentry or citizens of accompt within twenty miles of London, and of other houses which are situate in some principal cities, and market towns of trade, and such which are not peculiar for a farmer's family and use.

Thirdly, consider whether the land be barren or not, whether it be oc-casioned by the heat or constitution of the climate, situation on a hill, or in a dale, or what the mould or earth is under the superficies thereof; as if it be a clay, whether it be more subject to be dry or moist, or whether in a medium, which is very good ground for grass or beans, and other things which are of a gross and rank nature and quality; or if it be upon an indifferent dry clay, having a convenient degree of moisture, then it may be good for most sorts of corn. Or if it be on a moist, with some degree of drought, then for meadow or pasture; if it be on a rock that is near the surface, then it is very often barren, and good for little or nothing, but to feed sheep and such like uses.

. . . Fourthly, to consider whether the lands to be purchased be enclosed. Enclosed lands in many places doth yield half as much, or as much more, as lands in common fields, and if they be enclosed, whether the enclosures be decayed for want of good husbandry, and if they be, to deduct the charge of repairing them; and to consider what quantity of trees be in the enclosures; whether the same be timber trees or not, and what value they might yield if they were to be felled. And if there be any wood ground, what quantity of acres, and the quality of it; whether the same be coppice, underwoods, or timber trees?

Fifthly, to consider if there be any veins or seams of coal in the bowels of the earth, and if there be, whether valuable or not; many brave collieries being worth little or nothing, either by reason there is no shell stone for a roof to support the ground, or by reason of the great quantities of water which are usually in the caverns of the earth, which are very chargeable in the draining of them; so that many men by such undertakings are often undone. And it may not be valuable upon another account, that is, if it be in a place where there is great plenty of collieries, and although the same have a good roof stone and free from water, yet if it have not the conveniency to convey the same at a small charge to some river to have the coals exported, they will not be worth the trouble and charge in obtaining them; or if there be any rakes or pipes of lead or tin ore, which commonly lie in the caverns of the earth, in a gelf open between two rocks, there being for the most part where there is lead ore above the same great quantities of limestone. These mines are very subject to have great quantities of water in them, but they for the most part lie in mountainous hills; so that in most places they have the conveniency of driving a drift or sough from the bottom of the hills to the sole of the rake; so that the water runs away from the rake upon a descent. But the charge of driving such soughs or trenches is very great, they being sometimes forced to drive through divers hard rocks, so that the same at such places is very chargeable, and costs about forty or fifty shillings or more every fathom, being forced to mollify the rock by fire; so that their tools may make way through the same; and this many times they do for half a mile, or a mile together, or more or less, as it may require. And sometimes after great expense and trouble, they miss the rake or vein, which if they chance to light on, it doth often prove to be of little or no value, having but a small body of lead ore. These mines likewise are very casual, and many an ingenious man often undone by the venturing his certainty, for the uncertainty of the same. Or if there be any tin mines or quarries of iron, stone, limestone, or marl, or what ere it be that the earth doth produce, I refer it to the purchaser's judgement to set his valuation on the same: only this, that mines of what nature or kind soever in England are for the most part very great casualties, and the profit of them very uncertain.

Sixthly, to consider if there be any small or great rivers running through the ground to be purchased; which if there be, let the purchaser make diligent inquiry whether the same be of any considerable value as to the fishing thereof; or what other benefit may arise thereby, whether by overflowing the meadows there adjoining, or if there be corn mills, paper mills, powder mills, smelting mills, fulling mills, forges, or furnaces upon the same. And what the same be, that may produce profit. As suppose them to be corn mills, paper mills, or powder mills, and such like: you may consider whether they be not decayed for want of repairing; which if they be, consider what will be the charge of such repairs, or whether the same be in lease; and whether the miller is not bound thereby to repair the same at his own charge during the said term, and to pay a certain rent for the same, which particular thing may make the same very valuable, the usual bills brought in by millers for their repairs being sometimes a moiety of the rent, or a very considerable part thereof, mills being very subject (although made very strong) to decay. Or if there be any smelting mills or furnaces upon the same, you may in particular take these and such like observations. First, as to the smelting mills, which is properly for refining tin or lead out of their particular ores, you may inform yourself what quantities of woods there be about the same, there being very much consumed by these mills; another thing to be considered is whether the works in mines of lead or tin ore are like to be of any continuance, and not to be drowned or impeded by the great quantities of water which usually attend such works; or whether the body of ore in the mines, which doth employ the smelting mills, be of any considerable wideness or length, and are not likely to be worn out or exhausted suddenly. And to consider the richness or poorness of the mine, some ore in time of peace yielding thirty-six shillings, or thirty-seven shillings a horse load (which is nine dishes, as they compute weighing about four hundred and fifty pound), when as other lead ore in other mines will yield not above thirty shillings, five and twenty shillings, twenty shillings, or it may be not above eighteen shillings. All which are valuations as to the quality and quantity of lead as they respectively yield when they are smelted or cast into sows or pigs of lead. As to furnaces and forges you may take these and such like observations. As to furnaces which are properly for the smelting of ironstone and making metal thereof and sometimes casting the same into iron guns, bullets, and iron backs for chimneys or such like uses, you may consider what charge the digging or procuring of such stone may be; it being in most countries where such furnaces are very plentiful, and procured, and gotten out of the earth for a very small charge; for if it should cost much, the procuring it would not be worth the obtaining, and to be at fifteen hundred or two thousand pounds charge in building such furnaces, laying their hearths, and providing great stocks and quantities of charcoal for the same. As to the forges they being particular for the forming of iron metal into bars of iron, for conveniency of carriage, or into what other form they please, the force of the water lifting a great hammer of about three hundredweight or more, which strikes when they make use of the same upon an anvil for that purpose: these likewise

costs great sums of money, the building and fitting, and they are at great
charges daily for repairs, and consume great quantities of charcoal.

There is another mill employed about iron works which they term a
slitting mill, which is for the forming of iron into some fashion, as into iron
rods, nails, and such like things for common and ordinary occasions. In the
purchasing or dealing for things of this nature, you must have a particular
regard to what quantities of wood there be about your forges or furnaces,
and to have a special care lest when you have the same you be not to seek for
such materials, and be forced to buy them at excessive dear rates. Works of
this kind consume the greatest part of the woods in the countries where they
be; and do require great stocks and a good ingenious contrivancer in the
managing the same. It behooves the purchaser to consider whether his mill
be an undershot mill, which is the water driving the same under the wheel,
or whether it be an overshot mill, which is the water brought to the top of
the wheel, in landers or troughs, which cast the same into buckets made in
the wheel for the receipt of the same, the force and weight of which water
drives the same; or whether the same be both an undershot and an overshot
mill; or whether there be a continual current, so that the mill may be always
moving, if they please; or whether the water be kept up by art, in sluices for
the better managing that little water as they have; if the same be an overshot
mill, it is many times very uncertain as to its water. But suppose it be certain,
as to that it requires for the most part more money for the making of dams
and landers for the conveying of the same upon the wheel than the undershot mill doth, which for the most part runs at a greater certainty. I shall not
need to give you any further account as to these mills, only that you may
observe that there be a continual supply of water for the driving the same;
and to consider if the water you make use of do not come from any spring
near the place, and whether the same be not usually dry in the summer,
although you may have a good supply of water in the winter, the springs in
most places of England increase from the latter end of September until the
latter end of March, and from thence they decrease, and become in many
places either dry or very low . . .

*A particular computation of lands; and how many years purchase, and what
may be given for land in fee simple, for term of life or years, for copyhold estates,
advowsons appendant to manors, or in gross, mines, mills, with other things.*

Having given you some general rules to be observed in buying and selling of
lands, I shall proceed to speak of lands in particular. First, as to lands in fee
simple, they being in many places worth twenty years' purchase, in others
nineteen, in others but eighteen or seventeen, or it may be not above fifteen
or sixteen. Let the purchaser take notice that the rates allowed for money at
interest is for the most part a rule for the valuation of any purchase. And this
not only so in England, but in most places of the world, as in Holland, Venice,
and other places; their moiety [= money] yielding not above three pounds in

the hundred, makes them value their lands at thirty-five or thirty-six years' purchase, and their houses at twenty-eight or thirty years. It may be objected that this rule doth not in this particular hold true, for that lands at the rate of twenty years' purchase doth yield but five pound in the hundred, whereas money at interest yields six per cent; five per cent being an indifferent competency, considering the certainty of the same; and how uncertain money at interest often proves by death of sureties, loss of bonds, and sometimes having to do with knaves, they produce forged releases. And that men are often put to trouble about the same, sometimes being (through prudence) forced to call their money in, either upon the death or supposing failing of one or more of the sureties; or for that they are not willing to be longer obliged, and so are willing to return the money, and divers other casualties do attend the same.

There be many reasons why lands are better than money, although the same do yield less at present, yet if the purchaser have an indifferent pennyworth, his lands are oftentimes upon an improvement, it having been observed that lands let at old rents are sometimes improvable twenty in the hundred per annum, which very thing may make lands more considerable at five pounds per cent than money at interest at six. Another reason is for that lands by the course of the common law of England doth descend to the heirs of the possessor, it being many men's delight to have the same continue to their posterity, and in their own names; whereas money goes to their executors or administrators, and is often embezzled by them, and turns to no such account.

Lands in fee simple in and about London, as in Middlesex, Hertfordshire, in most places of Surrey, Kent, Essex, and Sussex, Buckinghamshire, and other places adjacent to London; and in other places of England, where they lie near any city or market town, or any river for the conveying of their commodities to proper markets for the vending the same, are for the most part valuable at twenty years' purchase, the reason being for that in such places there be choice of tenants, so that the owner of the land is for the most part at a certainty either for a good tenant, or for a good market for the fruits thereof; or if the owner have occasion to borrow money on the same, it is soon inquired after, and he need not seek a chapman for the same; whereas some lands in remote places, as in Yorkshire, Lincolnshire, in the counties of Norfolk, and in Suffolk, and in many other places distant from cities and market towns and rivers, are nothing near the value, and will not yield above fifteen, sixteen, or seventeen years' purchase at the most, the cause being the scarcity of industrious and sufficient tenants in such places, being but poor men for the most part; so that their necessity doth force them to accept of farms upon rack rents, and more than they are worth, let the landlords come by their rents how they can; whereas tenants that live near places of trade are many times more sufficient and more industrious to improve the landlord's ground; so that they may honestly pay their landlords their rents, and are very wary and cautious in making their bargains, and will not accept of any propositions but such as they may have some reasonable profit for their industrious labour in culturing the same, and the enabling them to pay their landlord's rent . . .

Coal Mines

Having considered all those things which are before mentioned as to the coal mines; and that you find by your boring rods that you have a good seam of coals; and either a good inland market, or else the conveniency of some river for the exporting them. The next thing to be considered is whether the same be a colliery that hath been formerly wrought, or whether it were never wrought before, so that all materials working the same are to be new bought and made.

If it be a new colliery that is either on the River Tyne which runs by Newcastle, or on the River Wear which runs by Sunderland, although it hath been formerly wrought, and there doth yet remain great quantities of coals in the earth, you may consider what staithes or wharves there be upon the river, for the loading the coals unto, and whether they be in repair; and to consider what quantities of pits there be sunk ready for use, how many horse engines for drawing up the coals out of the pits, and what engines they use to draw their water with for the conveniency of their working; whether they make use of water in any river, and so draw water with water, or whether they draw water with buckets, or hand pumps, or chain pumps, or whether they make use of tread wheels, or horse wheels, or what other device they have, there being very many devices for that purpose, but very few good for anything. In most collieries in the North they make use of chain pumps, and do force the same either by horse wheels, tread wheels, or by water wheels; and this they find the surest way for the drawing their water, although the charge of such wheels for timber, leathers, chains, pumps, and other materials about the same are very great, and often requires repairing, besides the great charge of men and horses they are daily at; and are forced sometimes to repeat their work. Let the charge be what it will, it is not much matter, so that the profit do exceed the same. All the materials before mentioned are valued by themselves; and if the colliery be likely to be of twenty years' work, you may value the same at three or four years' purchase. If the same hath been formerly wrought, you may find how many chaldron of coals there hath been in any particular year wrought out of the same, by the staithesmen's accompts, or by Newcastle or Sunderland Custom House books, they taking every tide the number of chaldron of coals which comes from every colliery; so by computing the charge of procuring the same, you may find what quantity of coals there hath been wrought out of the same in any year, and so be able to estimate the profit of the same. The purchasing the fee of collieries is very rare, unless it be with the land where the same is. But the most usual way is either to give a fine, and so pay a certain rent, or a certain rent out of every chaldron without any fine. The purchaser may give more or less for the same, according as he may see his advantage. They commonly reckon that two or three years' purchase may be a competent allowance either for the fee, or for a long lease, rendering a small rent, or one shilling for every chaldron, or more or less, as the charge of working the said colliery may be, and as the profit may arise thereby.

It hath been often observed that South country men do very seldom get anything but trouble by undertakings in collieries, it being the nature of many North country men to have a kind of antipathy against the thriving of any but themselves. As to a colliery that hath never been wrought, it is very hard to set a valuation upon the same, the generality of collieries being worth little or nothing.

There are divers other sorts of collieries in inland countries in England, whose profit consists in an inland market, and they do produce in many places great profit to the undertakers, but are as uncertain as others, and subject to the casualties of water and of fire, which many times proceeds from their not making a convenient shaft for the air in their working the same.

There are many projectors (who have more of fancy and imagination in their designs, than of any real operation) that do undertake even impossibilities in the draining these and other sort of mines; being many times such as the owners value at little or nothing, either because of the small body of coal, or by reason of the depth and charge of sinking such pits, and in timbering of them; or by reason that the mines are either fed with some river, or great springs, so that the working of them will not quit their cost: such pits or mines as these they very much applaud and commend to the projectors by informing them what great years' profit would arise if such obstacles as they are troubled with were removed; which prompts the projectors to go forward with their designs, not questioning but to remove all obstacles that hinder the same, until at length by sad experience they find that instead of draining the water, their pockets are drained.

Lead Mines

Lead mines by the custom of the Peak in Derbyshire, a particular part doth belong to any man that doth first find out the same; and after he hath taken his possession which is by driving a cross stake in the earth, he having made election of so much as he may by the custom, whether the same be a mere of ground, which is about 29 yards, or half a mere, or what he pleases, and may lawfully be demanded by the custom, they term him the first founder; then such others who will have any part undisposed (as they may by the custom demand), they likewise take possession by a cross stake, every person concerned having taken their respective possessions, and their respective shares being known to the Bar master, they then proceed to sink their shafts and so to get the ore, which the Bar master doth observe that they do equally divide the same according to their respective shares; the King having every thirteenth dish of ore for his lot and cope; and the minister, it may be, every twentieth for tithes. There be divers peculiar customs that belong to these mines, which doth require a diligent search into by such as do deal with the same, so that he may take care that he lose not his share or part upon any nicety; as if he doth let the same be unwrought fourteen days together, and may well work the same without the impediment of water, or any other lawful impediment, he hath forfeited the same to such person that will come and take possession thereof. There be divers other customs which must be observed, or else the proprietor may forfeit his estate . . .

In many places of England and Wales, where there are these sorts of mines, they do not altogether depend upon such customs, but in many places they do belong to the proprietors of the ground, which makes them more valuable, if they be rich veins or seams of ore, and free from great quantities of water.

47. RIBBON WEAVERS DEFEND THE ENGINE LOOMS, 1675

[P.R.O., SP 29/376, no. 143]

THAT engine looms or looms called broad looms have been in England above seventy years and always found and approved to be of great use and advantage to the City of London and his Majesty's customs and the whole kingdom in general. And the suppressing them from working silk or cotton ribbon will be the ruin or undoing of several hundred families, and be of great prejudice to his Majesty's customs and the trade of the City and the whole nation, and tend to the discouragement of ingenuity in England and the great advantage and encouragements of other nations especially the Dutch and French.

That the Company of Weavers of London about thirteen years since exhibited their bill to the honourable House of Parliament for suppressing and demolishing of engine looms and another bill about five years since to the same effect which was then by the great wisdom of that honourable House and for the reasons then given thought fit to be laid aside and no further prosecution thereupon had since.

But on the 9th, 10th, and 11th of August 1675 a rude multitude of weavers assembled in a riotous and rebellious manner and broke open our houses and burnt and destroyed our looms and robbed some of their goods and money, frighted our wives, children, and servants and had deprived us of our lives had not his Majesty's gracious proclamation interposed, which riotous actions are confessed by the Company of Weavers and all good subjects to be very unjust and unwarrantable proceedings. Yet there is good reason to believe the Company were fomenters of this riot for they did rather encourage than prevent it.

That engine looms make full as good work as the single looms do or can, which hath been proved and confessed by many of the Company that do now oppose them, and will again at any time be made evident; and if engine looms be encouraged, more poor men, women, and children will be employed by them than the single looms do or can employ, and if these looms be encouraged it will prevent the great importation that is now daily of Dutch and French ribbon.

That great quantities of yarn brought from the Indies may by these looms be wrought into manufacture by the King's own subjects in England and sold at as cheap a rate as the French and Dutch do, but the single looms cannot work it at so low a rate, so if engine looms be put down the very trade in a short time would be quite lost here. And the Dutch and French will engross it and undersell us at home and abroad.

The Dutch and French with these looms can with one man in two days make twelve pieces of ribbon of 432 yards of as good work as three or four men can do in two days upon narrow looms.

That great quantities of silk and yarn, if not spent by these looms, will be again exported, and so be of great damage to trade and his Majesty's customs.

If engine looms be suppressed it will force the engine loom weavers, being all natural born subjects, to go to remote cities and nations to the great prejudice of the trade of this kingdom and his Majesty's customs and discouragement of ingenuity.

If these looms be suppressed here the English cannot go to any foreign market by reason the Dutch and French using them will much undersell us and serve our markets at home and abroad, so the suppressing them here will only enrich the Dutch and French and ruin ourselves and trade.

That several people of good fashion have put their children to this trade only, and are since out of their time and have no other way of getting a livelihood.

That if we cannot make our commodities as good and as cheap as our neighbour nations, we cannot expect a trade, for where they are made best and cheapest there will be the greatest trade.

That by the same reason the single loom weavers complain of the engine looms, many self interest and envious people will complain of the engines for water mills, saw mills, and engines for splitting of iron, and ploughs, and printing presses, and cranes for wharves, and many other ingenious, useful, and profitable inventions now in England, but we doubt not but ingenuity will find encouragement in England.

48. THE INDUSTRIES OF OXFORDSHIRE, 1676

[Robert Plot, *The Natural History of Oxfordshire*,
Oxford, 1676, pp. 278–81]

AND 'tis confidently vouched that the engine for cutting of handles of knives, we commonly buy cut into those various figures, was first invented

and practised here in Oxford by Thomas Pierce, a cutler, whose apprentice
now practises the same art in London; but not with so much accuracy as
Robert Alder, another cutler of Oxford, who, only by observance of the
other's work and long study, at last found it out also, and hath improved it
much: which two last, as I am informed, are the only two persons that can
do this in England, perhaps I may say ith' world. Nor can I pass by the
invention in the cooper's trade of making barrels without hoops, whereof I
found a specimen in St. Ebbes parish, Oxon. though I know the invention
belongs to another place, of which more when I come thither.

For improvements, 'tis certain that the blanketing trade of Witney is
advanced to that height that no place comes near it. Some I know attribute
a great part of the excellency of these blankets to the abstersive nitrous
water of the River Windrush wherewith they are scoured, as was mentioned
before, cap. 2, §. 12, but others there are again that rather think they owe it to
a peculiar way of loose spinning the people have hereabout, perhaps they
may both concur to it. However it be, 'tis plain they are esteemed so far
beyond all others, that this place has engrossed the whole trade of the nation
for this commodity; in so much that the wool fit for their use, which is
chiefly fell wool (off from sheep skins) centres here from some of the further-
most parts of the kingdom, viz. from Romney Marsh, Canterbury, Colchester, Norwich, Exeter, Leicester, Northampton, Coventry, Huntingdon
etc., of which the blanketers, whereof there are at least threescore in this
town, that amongst them have at least 150 looms, employing near 3,000 poor
people, from children of eight years old to decrepit old age, do work out
above a hundred packs of wool per week.

This fell wool they separate into five or six sorts, viz. long fell wool, head
wool, bay wool, ordinary, middle, and tail wool. Long fell wool they send to
Wells, Taunton, Tiverton, etc. for making worsted stockings; of head wool
and bay wool, they make the blankets of 12, 11, and 10 quarters broad, and
sometimes send it, if it bear a good price, to Kidderminster for making their
stuffs, and to Evesham, Pershore, etc. for making yarn stockings; or into
Essex for making bays, whence one sort of them I suppose is called bay wool.
Of the ordinary and middle they make blankets of 8 and 7 quarters broad;
and of these mixed with the coarser locks of fleece wool, a sort of stuff they
call Duffields (which if finer than ordinary, they make too of fleece wool) of
which Duffields and blankets consists the chief trade of Witney.

These Duffields, so called from a town in Brabant, where the trade of them
first began (whence it came to Colchester, Braintree, etc. and so to Witney)
otherwise called shags, and by the merchants, trucking cloth, they make in
pieces of about 30 yards long, and one yard $\frac{3}{4}$ broad, and dye them red or
blue, which are the colours best please the Indians of Virginia and New
England, with whom the merchants truck them for beaver, and other furs of
several beasts, etc. The use they have for them is to apparel themselves with
them, their manner being to tear them into gowns of about two yards long,
thrusting their arms through two holes made for that purpose, and so

wrapping the rest about them as we our loose coats. Our merchants have abused them for many years with so false colours, that they will not hold their gloss above a month's wear; but there is an ingenious person of Witney that has improved them much of late, by fixing upon them a true blue dye, having an eye of red, whereof as soon as the Indians shall be made sensible, and the disturbances now amongst them over, no doubt the trade in those will be much advanced again.

Of their best tail wool they make the blankets of 6 quarters broad, commonly called cuts, which serve seamen for their hammocks, and of their worst they make wednel for collarmakers, wrappers to pack their blankets in, and tiltcloths for barge men. They send all the sorts of Duffields and blankets weekly in wagons up to London, which return laden with fell wool from Leadenhall, and Barnaby Street in Southwark, whither 'tis brought for this purpose from most places above mentioned; Oxfordshire and the adjacent counties being not able to supply them.

There are also in this town a great many fellmongers, out of whom at the neighbouring town of Bampton there arises another considerable trade, the fellmongers' sheep skins, after dressed and strained, being here made into wares, viz. jackets, breeches, leather linings, etc., which they chiefly vent into Berkshire, Wiltshire, and Dorsetshire, no town in England having a trade like it in that sort of ware.

Which two trades of the towns of Witney and Bampton are the most eminent, that are too the most peculiar of this county. The malting trade of Oxford and Henley on Thames, 'tis true are considerable, and Burford has been famous time out of mind for the making of saddles; and so has Oxford had the reputation of the best gloves and knives of any place in England; but these trades being not peculiar to the places where they are practised, I therefore pass them by without further notice.

But the starch trade of Oxford, though indeed it be not great, yet being practised in few places, and the method known to fewer how it is made, its discovery perhaps may be acceptable to some. I shall not therefore stick to give a short account of it. Let them know, therefore, that the substance we commonly call starch, notwithstanding its pure whiteness, is made of the shortest and worst bran that they make in the meal shops, worse than that they sell to carriers to feed their horses. This they steep in a water prepared for that purpose (by a solution at first of Roch-alum, about a pound to a hogshead, which will last for ever after) for ten or fourteen days in great tubs; then 'tis taken and washed through a large osier basket over three other tubs, the sour water of the second tub washing it into the first; and the sour water of the third, into the second; and clear water from the pump washing it into the third . . .

What remains in the basket at last after the three washings is thrown upon the dung hill, which, as they have found of late, becomes a very good manure for meadow land . . . And the fine flour thus washed from the bran is let stand again in its own water for about a week, then being all settled at the bottom, it is stirred up again and fresh pump water added, and strained from its smallest bran through a lawn sieve; which done, they permit it to settle again, which it does in one day, and then they draw off the water from it all to a small matter; then standing two days more, it at last becomes so fixed, that with a birchen broom they sweep the water left at the top (which is a slimy kind of matter), up and down upon it to cleanse it from filth, and then pouring it off, they wash its surface yet cleaner, by dashing upon it a bucket of fair pump water.

Which done, they then cut it out of the tubs in great pieces with sharp trowels, and box it up in troughs, having holes in the bottom to drain the water from it, always putting wet cloths between the wood and it, for the more commodious taking it out of the troughs again to dry, which they do within a day; laying it first on cold bricks for about two days, which suck away a great deal of moisture from it, and after over a baker's oven four or five days together, which will dry it sufficiently, if intended only to be ground to powder for hair, as it is chiefly here; but if intended to be sold as starch, they then use a stove to give it the starch-grain, which the oven will not do.

49. TYPES OF IRON AND STEEL, 1677

[Joseph Moxon, *Mechanick Exercises*, London, 1677, pp. 13–14, 54–6]

Of several sorts of Iron, and their proper uses

IT is not my purpose in this place to tell you how iron is made. I shall defer that till I come to treat of metals and their refinings. Let it at present satisfy those that know it not, that iron is by a violent fire melted out of hard stones called ironstones. Of these ironstones many countries have great plenty. But because it wastes such great quantities of wood to draw the iron from them, it will not in many places quit cost to use them. In most parts of England we have abundance of these ironstones. But our English iron is generally a coarse sort of iron, hard and brittle, fit for firebars and other such coarse uses, unless it be about the Forest of Dean, and some few places more, where the iron proves very good.

Swedish iron is of all sorts the best we use in England. It is a fine tough sort of iron, will best endure the hammer, and is softest to file, and therefore most coveted by workmen to work upon.

Spanish iron would be as good as Swedish iron were it not subject to red sear (as workmen phrase it), that is to crack betwixt hot and cold. Therefore when it falls under your hands you must tend it more earnestly at the forge. But though it be a good tough soft iron, yet for many uses workmen will refuse it, because it is so ill, and unevenly wrought in the bars that it costs them a great deal of labour to smooth it. But it is good for all great works that require welding, as the bodies of anvils, sledges, large bell-clappers, large pestles for mortars, and all thick strong bars, etc. But it is particularly chosen by anchor smiths, because it abides the heat better than other iron, and when it is well wrought is toughest.

There is some iron comes from Holland (though in no great quantity) but is made in Germany. This iron is called Dort Squares, only because it comes to us from thence, and is wrought into square bars, three quarters of an inch square. It is a bad coarse iron and only fit for slight uses, as window bars, brewers' bars, fire bars, etc.

There is another sort of iron used for making of wire, which of all other sorts is the softest and toughest. But this sort is not peculiar to any country, but is indifferently made where any iron is made, though of the worst sort, for it is the first iron that runs from the stone when it is melting, and is only preserved for the making of wire . . .

Of several sorts of Steel in common use among Smiths

The difficulty of getting good steel makes many workmen (when by good hap they light on it) commend that country steel for best from whence that steel came. Thus I have found some cry up Flemish steel, others Swedish steel, others English, Spanish, Venice, etc. But according to my observation and the common consent of the most ingenious workmen, each country produces almost indifferently good and bad; yet each country doth not equally produce such steel as is fit for every particular purpose, as I shall shew you by and by. But the several sorts of steel that are in general use here in England, are the English steel, the Flemish, the Swedish, the Spanish, and the Venice steel.

The English steel is made in several places in England, as in Yorkshire, Gloucestershire, Sussex, the Wilde [= Weald] of Kent, etc. But the best is made about the Forest of Dean; it breaks firy with somewhat a coarse grain. But if it be well wrought and proves sound, it makes good edge tools, files, and punches. It will work well at the forge, and take a good heat.

The Flemish steel is made in Germany in the country of Stiermark, and in the Land of Luyck. From thence brought to Colen [= Cologne], and is therefore sometimes called Colen steel. From Colen it is brought down the River Rhine to Dort and other parts of Holland and Flanders, some in bars and some in gads, and is therefore by us called Flemish steel, and sometimes gad steel. It is a tough sort of steel, and the only steel used for watch springs. It is also good for punches; file cutters also use it to make their chisels of, with which they cut their files. It breaks with a fine grain, works well at the forge, and will take a welding heat.

I cannot learn that any steel comes from Sweden, but from Danzig comes some which is called Swedish steel; it is much of the same quality and fineness with Flemish steel.

The Spanish steel is made about Biscany. It is a fine sort of steel, but some of it very difficult to work at the forge, because it will not take a good heat; and it sometimes proves very unsound, as not being well curried, that is well wrought. It is too quick (as workmen call it), that is, too brittle for springs or punches, but makes good edge tools.

Venice steel is much like Spanish steel, but more fine, and works somewhat better at the forge. It is used for razors, chirurgeons' instruments, gravers, etc., because it will come to a fine and thin edge. Razor makers generally clap a small bar of Venice steel between two small bars of Flemish steel, and so work or weld them together, to strengthen the back of the razor, and keep it from cracking.

There is another sort of steel of higher commendations than any of the foregoing sorts. It is called Damascus steel. It is very rare that any comes into England unwrought, but the Turkish scimitars are generally made of it. It is the most difficult of any steel to work at the forge, for you shall scarce be able to strike upon a blood heat, but it will red sear; in so much that these scimitars are by many workmen thought to be cast steel; but when it is wrought it takes the finest and keeps the strongest edge of any other steel. Workmen set almost an inestimable value upon it, to make punches, cold-punches, etc. of. We cannot learn where it is made, and yet as I am informed, the honourable Mr. Boyle hath been very careful and industrious in that inquiry; giving it in particular charge to some travellers to Damascus to bring home an account of it. But when they came thither they heard of none made there, but were sent about fifty miles further into the country, and then they were told of about fifty miles further than that. So that no certain account could be gained where it is made.

50. THE COST OF MANUFACTURING A TON OF BAR IRON, *TEMP*. CHARLES II [?]

[P.R.O., SP 29/443, no. 29]

A True and Perfect Account of the Total Charges in making a Ton of Bar Iron

	£	s.	d.
In primis 27 cwt. of raw iron from the Forest of Dean will make 20 cwt. of bar iron which at 6s. a ton amounts to	8	2	0
Two ½ cords of wood will make a load of charcoal and 3 loads of charcoal will make a ton of bar iron			
7½ cords of wood at 5s. per cord amounts to	1	17	6
The collier will have 2s. per load		6	0
For carriage of 27 cwt. of iron	1	0	0
For carriage of 3 loads of coals	1	5	0
Workmen's wages per ton	1	0	0
For the clerk and carpenters per ton		10	0
For repair of hammers per ton		8	4
	14	8	10

	£	s.	d.
A single work will make 3 tons per week			
A ton of iron made into bars is worth	18	0	0
The charges will amount to	14	8	10
	3	11	2
	3	11	2
	3	11	2
A week's gains	10	13	6
A year's profit if not prevented by floods or other accidents may amount to	555	2	0

51. HOW TO PROMOTE THE LINEN INDUSTRY, 1682

[John Houghton, *A Collection for the Improvement of Husbandry and Trade*, revised and re-issued by Richard Bradley, London, 1727, IV, pp. 114–20, 123]

Thursday, Dec. 14, 1682. Num. XI

An account of some proposals that have not, and what in likelihood will, gain us the linen manufacture; published in hopes of success the ensuing Parliament.

Sir,

Many have been the attempts for gaining the linen manufacture, and as many hitherto the disappointments. Some are for obliging by Act of Parliament a certain proportion of every man's land to be sown with flax or hemp, whereby we should have (as they think) a very great plenty of such flax and hemp, and by consequence a cheapness, whereby we may come so much nearer to the making of cloth, by how much cheaper this flax and hemp will be, than what is imported. But how this will please those whose land is not fit for it, or who think they can put it to a better use, I won't say; but most men love to do what they will with their own, and as yet it is not done.

Others are for raising stocks in all countries, for the erecting public workhouses and engines for dispatch in several places, where the poor shall be compelled to come and learn a trade, by which, when expert, a great many think (as things now stand) they would hardly get their bread by, and so when the public stock was spent, they would knock off to some other trade, or follow the lazy art of begging, by which, with a freedom to walk where they list, they hope to make double wages; and this project hitherto don't take.

A third sort are for public schools almost everywhere, as they do abroad in Germany, where children with some good orders shall be taught to spin, as here they are to read or knit, hoping that by an inurement of their hands to the distaff, almost from their mother's breast, they will learn to be so expert and quick, that thereby they may live most bravely; but the teachers are not yet found, and for want of faith that it shall succeed, and good markets, it is not begun; neither do our poor think it good for their children to work hard in their youth.

A fourth sort think the Irish way of giving a reward to her that yearly should make the best piece of cloth, but I do not hear of any great feats this hath done in Ireland, only they never fear to have one or two to come for the prize.

Fifthly, Bristol hath made a great attempt, and Mr. Firmin here at London hath done mighty things; he hath built a workhouse, bought wheels, reels, etc., taught the children and others gratis; brings them to rules, and for their encouragement, besides better wages than the thing will bear, gives them a good part of their manufacture back, when wove and whited, to make them sheets and shifts, besides money, coals, victuals, and other good things ... Yet for all this and a great deal more it won't do; and I have often told him it never shall, unless he can make it profitable, which he is unlike to do with English yarn, so long as foreign yarn is so cheaply imported. I have heard him say he can buy as much of some sorts of foreign yarn for a shilling, as here he must pay for the spinning, although the flax ready dressed were given him.

Highly to be praised are all these attempters, and much to be encouraged; who can tell, but that time may make a little of everyone's project useful? ...

I wish we may drive that nail which will go easiest, which I think will be by striving to make that sort of cloth first that may be made cheaper than it can be brought in, which I humbly conceive may be coarse linens; and I would have it made of foreign yarn, which yarn I would have brought in as plentifully and cheap as possible; and to make it so, I would have all the duty taken off, which duty in the Book of Rates I find thus, viz.

	l.	*s.*	*d.*
Irish yarn the pack cont. four hundredweight, at six score pound the hundred	5	0	0
Raw linen yarn, Dutch or French the pound		1	0
Sail yarn the pound		0	6
Spruce or Muscovia yarn the hundredweight, cont. a hundred and twelve pound	2	13	4
Scotch yarn the pound		1	0

... I would also have the duty upon coarse linen be doubled, which duty also in the Book of Rates I find thus, viz.

	l.	*s.*	*d.*
Canvas voc.			
Dutch barras and Hessen's canvas the hundred ells cont. six score	3	10	0
Packing canvas, Guttings, and Spruce canvas, the hundred ells cont. six score	2	10	0
Poledavies, the bolt cont. twenty-eight ells	1	00	0
Spruce, Elbing, or Queensborough canvas, the bolt cont. twenty-eight ells	0	15	0
Working canvas for cushions, narrow, the hundred ells, cont. six score	3	00	0
Working canvas broad, the hundred ells cont. six score	5	00	0
Working canvas of the broadest sort, the hundred ells cont. six score	6	00	0
Linen cloth, or Lockerams voc.			
Drilling and packduck, the hundred ells cont. six score	2	00	0
Hinderlands, Middlegood, Headlake, and Muscovia linen, narrow, the hundred ells cont. six score	2	13	4
Irish cloth, the hundred ells cont. six score	2	00	0
Treager, grest and narrow, or common dowlas, the piece cont. one hundred and six ells; broad dowlas, the piece cont. an hundred and six ells	5	00	0
Minsters, the roll cont. 1,500 ells five score to the hundred	56	13	0
Ozenbriggs, the roll cont. 1,500 ells, at five score to the hundred	60	00	0
Soulthwich, the hundred ells cont. six score	4	00	0
Polonias, Ulsters, Hanovers, Lubeck, narrow Silesia, narrow Westphalia, narrow Harford, plain napkening, and all other narrow cloth of High Dutch land, and the East country, white or brown, not otherwise rated, the hundred ells cont. six score	4	00	0
Linen voc.			
Twill and ticking of Scotland, the hundred ells cont. six score...[1]	3	00	0

This is the effect of my thoughts; but supposing my argument undeniable, yet one thing is still wanting, which is an Act for putting it in execution, which for my country's good, I must beg you to desire everybody, whom you shall discourse with about this affair, to further as much as they can; and I hope, if material objections cannot be made against it, it will find in due time some Parliament man that will prefer a bill for it, till when we must have patience.

[1] The list of varieties of linen cloth ends here, but the details of proposals for a duty continue.

52. TROUBLES OF THE CLOTH INDUSTRY, 1684

[George Clark, *A Treatise of Wool* . . ., 1685, pp. 25–30,
in Bodleian Library, Oxford, MS. Aubrey 2, ff. 136–8[1]]

[Presentment of the Grand Jury at the General Quarter Sessions
at Brereton, Somerset, 13 Jan., 36 Car. II]

HEARING the daily sad and lamentable complaint of the greatest part of the
clothiers of this county, concerning the great decay of their trade whereby
many of them within few years last past have been ruined and undone; and
finding by sad experience the great fall that is happened of late on the price
of English wool, that commodity now yielding but little more than one half
the value of what it was wont to be sold for at the beginning of the late
unhappy rebellion in this kingdom; and having seriously considered these
things, do humbly conceive the causes of these great evils to be the importation of Spanish and other foreign wools, without paying any custom or impost
for the same; and the great abuses that have been put upon the clothiers at
the principal mart for cloth in this kingdom by a sort of people called factors,
men first set up in the late times of distraction, and increasing ever since in
number and power, till now at length they have gotten the sole command
and sale of most men's cloth brought thither to be sold, and have thereby
advanced themselves from little or nothing to be men of great estates, and as
much impoverished their masters, who sadly complain of these abuses and
are left without prospect of a remedy; the consideration of which mischiefs
growing more and more upon us, and, if not timely prevented, being likely
in the end to prove the ruin of this ancient staple commodity and manufacture of our kingdom, hath caused us at this time to make this following
presentment.

First, that the wool of this county in particular, as well as of the whole
kingdom in general, is the greatest staple we have, and that which adds more
to the rents and improvement of the real value of the lands and revenues
thereof than any one commodity whatsoever; and that it is as much our
interest (if not more) to improve the rents and revenues of the lands and
estates of this kingdom as to maintain the trade, without which improvement
we shall in no case be able to raise any considerable sum of money by a land
tax if any sudden or extraordinary occasion should require it.

We present therefore that the importation of Spanish and other foreign
wools, without paying any duty or custom for the same, is a very great
prejudice to the price of English wool, and so consequently contributes much
to the abatements of the rents and profits issuing from lands.

We present that the making of woollen cloth is the greatest manufacture
of this kingdom and that wherein many thousands of poor people are employed and set to work, and thereby relieved and maintained; and that since

---

[1] The name of the author is not printed on the pamphlet but is taken from the inscription
by John Aubrey, that it was '*ex dono autoris* Geo Clark, arm.'

the time that the art of clothing was first known amongst us it has continued free, until the beginning of the late rebellion there sprung up a sort of
people who under the name of factors of Blackwell Hall have gotten into
their power the management and disposal of most of the cloth that is sold
there; and besides are grown to be the greatest merchants of oil and dyeing
stuffs, but chiefly of Spanish wool; all goods belonging to the clothing trade,
of whom the clothier is forced to buy, the factor having his stock both of
cloth and money in his own hands; and therefore we present that these
factors of Blackwell Hall are a public nuisance and prejudice to the clothing
trade, and to have been the ruin of many poor clothiers, and the causes of
many other mischiefs and inconveniences that now lie heavy upon us.

Item, we farther present that this honourable bench will be pleased to
implore the royal power and prerogative of his sacred Majesty for convenient
remedies to these great abuses, and that this presentment may be with all
submission presented to his Majesty as the grievance and complaint of the
whole county.

[17 signatures.]

53. A MISCELLANY OF NOTES BY JOHN AUBREY ON WILTSHIRE INDUSTRY AND INVENTIONS, 1684-5

[Bodleian MS. Library, Oxford, Aubrey 2,[1] ff. 64-7, 122, 141, 144]

MEMORANDUM. The art of spinning[2] is so much improved within these
last forty years that one pound of wool makes twice as much cloth (as to
extent) as it did before the civil wars.

In King James's the first time coarse paper commonly called white brown
paper was first made in England especially in Surrey and about Windsor.[3]
At Bemerton near Salisbury is a paper mill which is now (1684) about 130
years standing and the first that was erected in this county; and the workmen
there told me (1669) that it was the second paper mill in England. I remember
the paper mill at Long Deane in the parish of Yatton Keynell was built by
Mr. —— Wyld, a Bristow merchant, 1635. It serves Bristow with brown
paper. Memorandum. There is no white paper made in Wiltshire.

A hint to the invention of paper: memorandum. I have seen a kind of
brown paper which after great rains have been left upon the surface of
floated meadows. I suppose it to be the silt of the water which the wind and
the water brought together. About the time the water goes off weaves and
works it into a close brown thin substance, much like brown paper. I have
taken several pieces of it from the grass which I have seen borne up by the

---

[1] This is John Aubrey's MS. of *The Natural History of Wiltshire.*
[2] Marginal note says 'from Mr. Sam. Ash'.
[3] Marginal note says 'Sir Richard Baker's Chron.'

spires of grass, and have wrote upon it, and it hath (when dry) borne ink. This was in a meadow of the Thames towards Cricklade, 1674. But I have seen it since in other places.

Inventions and Engines

At Warminster is one —— who weaves sacks whole which are of great use to farmers. Invented by him about 1659 . . .

It ought never to be forgot what our ingenious countryman, Sir Christopher Wren, proposed to the silk-stocking weavers of London, A.D. 16— viz. a way to weave seven pair or nine pair of stockings at once (it must be an odd number). He demanded four hundred pounds for his invention, but the weavers refused it, because they were poor; and besides, they said it would spoil their trade. Perhaps they did not consider the proverb that light gains with quick returns make heavy purses. Sir Christopher was so noble, seeing they would not adventure so much money, he breaks the model of the engine all to pieces before their faces . . .

Mr. Rob. Hook, R.S.S., hath contrived a little windmill (which stands on a stem no bigger than a pick stall) of great use for draining of grounds. The model is in the gallery (library) of the Royal Society at Gresham College.

John Snow of East Lavington was a blacksmith at Winterbourne ——. He had a mathematical and mechanical head, and he was in his time sc. between 1630 and 1650 the best watchmaker and clockmaker in our country or the west. He made an organ and virginal together and chimes; all to go with the same movement. Above was a clock which shewed not only the hour of the day, but the sign ascending.

—— Spunley of Lacock hath invented an engine to weave tape turned with a windlace. He makes the shuttles do their office. He is a poor fellow and drives this engine about the country (as they do that grind knives at London) to gentlemen's houses to see it and see it work.

Query if it would not be the better way to send our wool beyond sea again as in the time of the Staple? For the Dutch and French do spin finer, work cheaper, and dye better. Our clothiers combine against the wool masters and keep the spinners but just alive. They steal hedges, spoil coppices, and are trained up as nurseries of sedition and rebellion.

Stroudwater in Gloucestershire is a little commonwealth of clothiers and clothworkers; not the like in the nation. The water here is found by experience to be very proper for the red or scarlet dye, as also for black, in both which kinds they do drive a mighty trade. The water here is run through an iron mine which is the reason that it dyes red the better . . .

A Digression

Benedict Webb[1] of —— in Somersetshire was the first that made medley cloths (before they were blue, green, etc. coloured cloths). Mr. John Ash of

---

[1] See above pp. 206–8, 220–2.

Freshford in Somersetshire was the second[1] that made medleys who improved the art and got a great estate by it *tempore Caroli primi* (his great grandmother was sister to Whiting, the last lord abbot of Glastonbury). He was the greatest clothier in his time, *scilicet tempore Caroli primi*.

Mr. Scott tells me that there are not now, 1685, so many clothiers or so much clothing as heretofore.

54. TIMBER SUPPLIES FROM STAFFORDSHIRE, 1685

[Herefordshire County Record Office, Foley Collection, F/VI/MAc. John Foley's Accounts, Personal and Estate]

April 13, 1685

THEN agreed with Mrs. Nevill for all her cordwood she shall think fit to fall within the township of Croxton[2] at the rate of 6*s.* and 5*d.* by cord; all that shall be stocked to be at the charge of the said Mrs. Nevill. If there happen to be any timber in any of the said wood, Mrs. Nevill to allow the workmen 6*d.* for every log of timber that shall be turned out. All the coppy wood to be cut into 4 fo. and the tree wood to be cut into 3 fo. wood; all the said wood to be stocked at or before Christmas and to begin to stock at or before the 20th of October, 1686, Mrs. Nevill to allow cabbern [=cabin?] and all other conveniences for coaling the said wood and carrying it away, the said wood to be paid for the 5th of May and the 1st of October, 1686.

55. SOME STAFFORDSHIRE INDUSTRIES, 1686

[Robert Plot, *The Natural History of Staffordshire*, 1686, pp. 121–8, 161–4, 335–6, 375–7]

AS FOR tobacco pipe clays they are found all over the county, near Wrottesley House, and Stile Cop in Cannock Wood, whereof they make pipes at Armitage and Lichfield, both which though they are greyish clays, yet burn very white. There is tobacco pipe clay also found at Darlaston near Wednesbury, but of late disused, because of better and cheaper found in Monway field betwixt Wednesbury and Willingsworth, which is of a whitish colour, and makes excellent pipes; as doth also another of the same colour dug near the salt water pool in Pensnet Chase, about a mile and ½ south of Dudley. And Charles Riggs of Newcastle makes very good pipes of three sorts of clay, a white and a blue, which he has from between Shelton and Hanley Green, whereof the blue clay burns the whitest, but not so full as the white, i.e. it shrinks more; but the best sort he has from Grubbers Ash,

---

[1] Marginal note says 'From Samuel Ash of Langley Burrell, esq., and James Ash the son and heir of John Ash'.

[2] In Eccleshall parish.

being whitish mixed with yellow, it is a short brittle sort of clay, but burns full and white. Yet he sometimes mixes it with the blue before mentioned. But the clay that surpasses all others of this county is that at Amblecot, on the bank of Stour, in the parish of Old Swinford yet in Staffordshire, in the lands of that judicious and obliging gent. the worshipful Harry Gray of Enfield esq. . . . I say the most preferable clay of any is that of Amblecot, of a dark blueish colour, whereof they make the best pots for the glasshouses of any in England. Nay, so very good is it for this purpose that it is sold on the place for sevenpence the bushel, whereof Mr. Gray has sixpence, and the workman one penny, and so very necessary to be had, that it is sent as far as London, sometimes by wagon, and sometimes by land to Bewdley, and so down the Severn to Bristol, and thence to London; the goodness of which clay, and cheapness of coal hereabout, no doubt, has drawn the glass-houses, both for vessels and broad glass, into these parts; there being divers set up in different forms here at Amblecote, Old Swinford, Holloways End and Cobourn Brook.

Other potters' clays for the more common wares there are at many other places, particularly at Horsley Heath in the parish of Tipton; in Monway field above mentioned, where there are two sorts gotten, one of a yellowish colour mixed with white, the other blueish; the former stiff and weighty, the other more friable and light; which, mixed together, work better than apart. Of these they make divers sorts of vessels at Wednesbury, which they paint with slip, made of a reddish sort of earth gotten at Tipton. But the greatest pottery they have in this county is carried on at Burslem near Newcastle under Lyme, where for making their several sorts of pots they have as many different sorts of clay, which they dig round about the town, all within half a mile's distance, the best being found nearest the coal, and are distinguished by their colours and uses as followeth:

1. Bottle clay, of a bright, whitish, streaked, yellow colour.

2. Hard fire clay of a duller whitish colour, and fuller interspersed with a dark yellow, which they use for their black wares, being mixed with the

3. Red blending clay, which is of a dirty red colour.

4. White clay, so called it seems though of a blueish colour, and used for making yellow coloured ware, because yellow is the lightest colour they make any ware of.

All of which they call throwing clays, because they are of a closer texture, and will work on the wheel;

Which none of the three other clays, they call slips, will any of them do, being of looser and more friable natures; these mixed with water they make into a consistence thinner than a syrup, so that being put into a bucket it will run out through a quill; this they call slip, and is the substance where-with they paint their wares; whereof the

1. Sort is called the orange slip, which, before it is worked, is of a greyish colour mixed which orange balls, and gives the ware (when annealed) an orange colour.

2. The white slip, this, before it is worked, is of a dark blueish colour, yet makes the ware yellow, which being the lightest colour they make any of, they call it (as they did the clay above) the white slip.

3. The red slip, made of a dirty reddish clay, which gives wares a black colour . . .

When the potter has wrought the clay either into hollow or flat ware, they are set abroad to dry in fair weather, but by the fire in foul, turning them as they see occasion, which they call whaving; when they are dry they stouk them, i.e. put ears and handles to such vessels as require them. These also being dry, they then slip or paint them with their several sorts of slip, according as they design their work . . .

After this is done, they are carried to the oven, which is ordinarily above 8 foot high, and about 6 foot wide, of a round topped form, where they are placed one upon another from the bottom to the top . . . In 24 hours an oven of pots will be burnt, then they let the fire go out by degrees which in 10 hours more will be perfectly done, and then they draw them for sale, which is chiefly to the poor crate men, who carry them at their backs all over the country, to whom they reckon them by the piece, i.e. quart, in hollow ware, so that 6 pottle, or 3 gallon bottles make a dozen, and so more or less to a dozen, as they are of greater or lesser content. The flat wares are also reckoned by pieces and dozens, but not (as the hollow) according to their content, but their different breadths . . .

The history of pit coal, otherwise called sea coal (though in this island country, and seldom carried by water, much less by sea) belongs to this place . . . But first of the several species or rather sorts of coal; which, though they differ somewhat in all pits, nay, in the several measures of the same pit, yet none of them so signally as to obtain a distinct name, except the cannel coal and the peacock coal, from the common pit coal of Wednesbury and other parts; which yet all come under the common genus of Lithanthrax or stone coal, they being all of a competent hardness, and seem to be nothing else but bitumen indurated by subterraneal heats, though not equally; the cannel coal being the hardest, and of so close a texture that it will take a passable polish; as may be seen in the choir of the cathedral church of Lichfield, which in great part is paved lozengy, black and white (as other churches with marble) with cannel coal for the black, and alabaster for the white, both plentifully found in this country; which when kept clean, so well represent black and white marble, that to an incurious heedless eye they seem to be the same. It turns like ivory into many pretty knacks, such as ink boxes, candlesticks, etc. They cut it also into salts, standishes, and carve coats of arms in it, witness that of the right honourable William Lord Paget, in the gallery of his stately seat at Beaudesert . . .

Notwithstanding which, the chiefest use they make of this coal is for firing, wherein they much observe the grain of the coal, for if they would have it burn slow (as the poorer and thriftier sort of people are best pleased it should) they lay it flat ways upon the fire, as it lay before in the bed or measure; but if they would have it burn quick and flame clear (as the gentry commonly will) they surbed it, i.e. set it edgeways, the cleaving way next the fire, by which means it so easily admits it that it presently flames as bright as a candle ... The peacock coal dug at Hanley Green near Newcastle under Lyme is much softer than the cannel ... [and] of an open texture whence 'tis like it comes to pass that it burns so swift, and is therefore better for smithies than kitchen fires.

Which are much better supplied by the common coal of the country, especially that of Wednesbury, Dudley, and Sedgley; which some stick not to prefer even to the cannel itself; the texture and other qualities thereof being such, viz. that it is a fat shining coal, having a pretty open grain, lying seldom in a level with the plane of the horizon but most times somewhat inclining to it (according to which it cleaves into blocks at the discretion of the workman) that it burns away with a sweet bright flame, and into white ashes, leaving no such cinder as that from Newcastle upon Tyne. Of which sort there is so great plenty in all parts of the county (especially about the three above mentioned places) that most commonly there are 12 or 14 collieries in work, and twice as many out of work, within 10 miles round; some of which afford 2,000 tons of coal yearly, others three, four, or five thousand tons, the upper or topmost beds above the ironstone lying sometimes ten, eleven, or twelve yards thick; nay, I was told by Mr. Persehouse of Nether Gournall, that in his grounds at Ettingshall in the parish of Sedgley, in a place called Moorefields, the bed of coal lies 14 yards thick; insomuch that some acres of ground have been sold hereabout for a 100 pound per acre; I was informed of one acre, sold for 150 pound, and well indeed it might be so, since out of one single shaft there have sometimes been drawn 500 pounds worth of coal. Nor indeed could the country well subsist without such vast supplies, the wood being most of it spent upon the ironworks, for it is here (as well as other countries that fetch their winter stores from hence) thought not only fit for the kitchen, but all other offices; even to the parlour and bedchamber.

And not only in private families, but now too in most, if not all the mechanic professions (except the ironworks) that require the greatest expense of fuel; witness the glass houses, and saltworks, brickmaking, and malting; all which were heretofore performed with wood or charcoal, especially the last, which one would think should hardly admit of the unpleasant fumes of such firing: nor indeed does it, no more than of wood; for they have a way of charring it (if I may so speak without a solecism) in all particulars the same as they do wood, whence the coal is freed from these noxious steams, that would otherwise give the malt an ill odour. The coal thus prepared they call cokes, which conceives as strong a heat almost as charcoal itself, and is as fit for most other uses, but for melting, fining, and refining of iron, which it cannot be brought to do, though attempted by the most skilful and curious artists. In the glasshouses, saltworks, and brickclamps, they use the raw coal as brought from the pit; in the former whereof, as to the proportion, I am not so certain; but in the Staffordshire saltworks they spend two tons to a drawing; and for burning a clamp of 16,000 bricks, they use about 7 tons of coal. The last effort that was made in this country for making iron with pit coal was also with raw coal, by one Mr. Blewstone, a high German, who built his furnace at Wednesbury, so ingeniously contrived (that only the flame of the coal should come to the ore, with several other conveniencies) that many were of opinion he would succeed in it. But experience, that great baffler of speculation, shewed it would not be. The sulphurous vitriolic steams that issue from the pyrites, which frequently, if not always, accompanies pit coal, ascending with the flame, and poisoning the ore, sufficiently to make it render much worse iron than that made with charcoal, though not perhaps so much worse as the body of coal itself would possibly do . . .

. . . When they have gotten their ore before 'tis fit for the furnace, they would burn or calcine it upon the open ground, with small charcoal, wood, or sea coal, to make it break into small pieces, which will be done in 3 days, and this they call annealing it, or fitting it for the furnace. In the meanwhile they also heat their furnace for a week's time with charcoal without blowing it, which they call seasoning it, and then they bring the ore to the furnace thus prepared, and throw it in with the charcoal in baskets *vicissim* i.e., a basket of ore, and then a basket of coal S.SS. whereby two vast pair of bellows placed behind the furnace, and compressed alternately by a large wheel turned by water, the fire is made so intense, that after 3 days' time the metal will begin to run, still after increasing, till at length in fourteen nights' time they can run a sow and pigs once in 12 hours, which they do in a bed of sand before the mouth of the furnace, wherein they make one larger furrow than the rest, next the timp (where the metal comes forth) which is for the sow, from whence they draw two or three and twenty others (like the labels of a file in heraldry) for the pigs, all which too they make greater or lesser according to the quantity of their metal. Into these when their receivers are full they let it forth, which is made so very fluid by the violence of the fire, that it not only runs to the utmost distance of the furrows but stands boiling in them for a considerable time; before it is cold, that is, when it begins to blacken at top, and the red to go off, they break the sow and the pigs off from one another, and the sow into the same length with the pigs, though in the running it is longer and bigger much, which is now done with ease; whereas if let alone till they are quite cold, they will either not break at all, or not without difficulty . . .

From the furnaces they bring their sows and pigs of iron when broken asunder and into lengths to the forges; which are of two sorts, but commonly (as at Cunsall) standing together under the same roof; one whereof they call the finery, the other the chafery. They are both of them open hearths, upon which they place great heaps of coal [= charcoal], which are blown by bellows like to those of the furnaces, and compressed the same way, but nothing near so large. In these two forges they give the sow and pigs 5 several heats, before they are perfectly wrought into bars. First, in the finery they are melted down as thin as lead, where the metal in an hour thickens by degrees into a lump or mass, which they call a loop; this they bring to the great hammer raised by the motion of a water-wheel, and first beat it into a thick square, which they call a half bloom. Then 2ly they put it into the finery again for an hour, and then bring it again to the same hammer, where they work it into a bloom, which is a square bar in the middle and two square knobs at the ends, one much less than the other, the smaller being called the ancony end, and the greater the mocket head. And this is all they do at the finery. Then 3. the ancony end is brought to the chafery, where after it has been heated for a quarter of an hour, it is also brought to the hammer, and there beat quite out to a bar, first at that end; and after that, the mocket head is brought also 4. to the chafery, which being thick, requires two heats before it can be wrought under the hammer into bars of such shapes and sizes as they think fittest for sale.

Whereof, those they intend to be cut into rods, are carried to the slitting mills, where they first break or cut them cold with the force of one of the wheels into short lengths; then they are put into a furnace to be heated red hot to a good height, and then brought singly to the rollers, by which they are drawn even, and to a greater length; after this another workman takes them whilst hot and puts them through the cutters, which are of divers sizes, and may be put on and off, according to pleasure; then another lays them straight also whilst hot, and when cold binds them into faggots, and then they are fitting for sale ...

Thus I say the ironworks are exercised in their perfection and all their principal iron undergoes all the forementioned preparations; not but that for several purposes, as for the backs of chimneys, garden rolls, and such like, they use a sort of cast iron which they take out of the receivers of the furnaces, as soon as it is melted, in great ladles, and pour it into moulds of fine sand, in like manner as they cast the other softer metals. Thus the ingenious Will. Chetwynd of Rugeley, esq. at Madeley furnace cast iron rolls for gardens, hollow like the mills for sugar canes, of 5, 6, 7 or 800 weight apiece ... For such purposes as these, this serves well enough, but for others it will not, for it is so brittle that, being heated, with one blow of a hammer it will break all to pieces ... The art of making frying pans may also be referred hither, the secret in great measure consisting in the regulating the heat that is given the plates whereof they are made, before they are brought to the anvil ...

Now that which renders this art of making frying pans so difficult is not only the bringing them to a just heat, which shall hold a sufficient time and yet not make them liable to stick in the hammering; but the number of hammers used in this work, which are not less than twenty of several sorts, which so few know how to manage, or are capable of learning, that there are but two master frying pan makers (as I am credibly informed) in the whole of the kingdom: one, here at Newcastle, and another at Wandsworth in Surrey ...

The iron thus prepared is used both by the white and blacksmiths of this county according as the condition of their wares require; it being forged by the former into scythes, reaping hooks, axes, hatchets, bills, etc. (for each whereof they give their iron a different heat and temper), which being ground at the blade mills to a bright edge (whereof there is one at Himley, another near Swindon, and others on all the little waters thereabout), they have given this sort of artisans that make them the name of whitesmiths. And by the latter it is wrought into plough, cart, and fire irons, into horse locks and shoes, bolts and hinges for doors, bars for windows, squares for trunks and coffins, staffheads, buckles, and nails; for making the last of which there are so prodigious numbers here that in the parish of Sedgley alone there are thought to be no less than 2,000 of the trade reckoning boys as well as men.

But the greatest excellency of the blacksmith's profession that I could hear of in this county lies in their making locks for doors wherein the artisans of Wolverhampton seem to be preferred to all others, where they make them in *sutes*, six, eight, or more in a *sute* according as the chapman bespeaks them, whereof the keys shall neither of them open each other's lock, yet one master key shall open them all . . .

Nor are they less curious in their ironworks as the town of Walsall which chiefly relate to somewhat of horsemanship such as spurs, bridles, stirrups, etc. . . . They make also great variety of bridles, both snaffles and bits . . . Of stirrups they also make these several sorts, the *swivel*, *barr'd*, *Rippon*, and plain stirrup, and these either with broad or narrow bottoms. They make also all the ironwork belonging to a saddle, viz. *sivels*, *barrs*, *plates*, the two former being made by one workman, the latter by another; also the great variety of buckles that belong to the pack and hackney saddles . . . in perfecting of which wares as also of their spurs, bridles, stirrups, etc. they use a great deal of tin, which they superinduce over them to give a better lustre and preserve some of them from rusting; and prevent others from giving a taste of the metals to things boiled in them.

56. LANCASHIRE LINEN WORKERS APPEAL AGAINST A FOREIGN FRIEZING MILL, 1689

[Lancs. County Record Office, QSP 670/28: 1689]

To the Worshipful the justices of peace for the county Palatine of Lancaster at their Quarter Sessions held at Manchester for the said county, the humble petition of the clothworkers friezedressers both masters and journeymen within the town of Manchester and Salford and the places adjacent

HUMBLY sheweth that your petitioners have duly and truly served their several apprenticeships to their respective callings and through God's blessing and their industry have hitherto supported comfortably themselves and their families and have been helpful in relieving others according to their

several powers and abilities and have hitherto borne their share of all burdens
and charges in the places where they live. But so it is, may it please your good
worships, that one Joseph Bacon of Manchester, linen draper, conspiring
with a foreigner, a Frenchman, and several others unknown to your petitioners to undermine and ruin your petitioners and their families in their several
callings have contrived an instrument of new invention called a friezing mill
totally to destroy their callings and that under pretence and colour of some
authority, power, and patent given by the late King James or their now
sacred Majesties which they deny to produce, which said engine, if it shall
take effect, will cast your petitioners and their families upon the places they
live in for support and maintenance.

In consideration therefore of the premises and for the preventing the
inconvenience which may fall upon your petitioners, may it please your worships hereby to call before you the said Joseph Bacon and examine by what
authority he doth attempt this new and strange thing, and to give your
petitioners such further relief and directions herein as to your good worships
shall seem meet and your petitioners shall always pray, etc.

Joseph Bacon to shew his pretended patent or not make use of his friezing
mill to the annoyance and detriment of the petitioners. To go on with your
work for a fortnight and produce the patent to some justice of peace in the
meantime or have no further benefit by it.

57. LOBBYING BY THE WHITE PAPER MAKERS, 1690

[W. J. Cameron, *The Company of White-Paper-Makers of
England*, *1686–1696*, University of Auckland, Bulletin 68,
Economic History Series 1, 1964, pp. 34–6, 38–9]

An Addition to the Case of the Paper Sellers humbly offered
to this present Parliament against the Paper Bill [April, 1690]

WHEREAS the paper sellers of London being very sensible that the bill
offered to this honourable House by the New Company of White-Paper
Makers would not answer the name and pretended design of it, but on the
contrary be very destructive to the general trade of paper making, and the
ruin of many hundreds of families now maintained by the making, selling,
and working of all sorts of paper, did therefore petition, as the ancient
paper makers had before done, that the said bill might not pass, and in a true
state of the case and circumstances of paper making, have, as they humbly
conceive, made it appear that the said bill was contrived for sinister ends and
purposes of private men, and to carry on a monopoly against the common
and statute laws of this realm, and expressly against a statute, 21 Jac. 1,
cap. 3, against monopolies and dispensations with penal laws, and that the
same doth no way tend to any public good, but would be very grievous to

many of their Majesty's subjects, which the said New Company being not able to give a sufficient answer to, by several untrue and reflecting papers, and other disingenuous practices have endeavoured to insinuate, that they the said paper sellers have combined with divers persons to discourage and oppose the increasing of white writing and printing paper in this kingdom.

It is therefore humbly offered, that the said paper sellers are, and will be, ready when they shall have leave to be heard by their counsel, to make it appear, as they now humbly aver, that they have not in any of their proceedings discouraged, and do not desire to obstruct the making of greater quantities of white writing and printing paper in England, which is evident, in that the said paper sellers or the ancient paper makers, though they have suffered for fifteen years past very much by the patentees interloping into their trade and livelihoods, have not endeavoured as they might have done to stop or hinder the said patentees in their prosecuting to make any sort of white or brown paper, as they do at this present day, though they endeavour to conceal that they make brown paper; of all which sorts the said paper sellers have from time to time bought of them, and frequently advised and instructed them what sorts of paper were best for the markets.

That the said paper sellers can make it appear the late patents and grant for a corporation to monopolize the sole making of white writing and printing paper were not only against law, but have greatly hindered the making of that manufacture in England, the ancient paper makers having been thereby threatened and overawed from making thereof.

The said paper sellers do also most humbly offer that there is a considerable number of the ancient paper makers now working in mills very proper for making of writing and printing paper, and have workmen who by their experience well know the best way of sorting white rags to make fine writing and printing paper, and, by reason of the present hindrances from abroad, all the artists in England are few enough to make a sufficient supply of paper for the necessary use of this kingdom.

And whereas the said Company's last paper doth insinuate that by their bill is reserved to the ancient paper makers the freedom of making any sort of paper of the value by them formerly made, the same is untrue, for that it will, if it should pass, confine them not to make any white writing or printing paper above the value of four shillings per ream, when as they have made many sorts of a much greater value; besides if the said New Company were as they have pretended to be the sole inventors and artists of making such sorts, they need not desire to confine others at all.

There are many more contradictions and false insinuations contained in the said New Company's papers, which the said paper sellers to avoid prolixity forbear to take notice of.

The whole considered, it appears unnecessary both in respect of the skilfulness of the ancient paper makers in the said manufacture, and that they want no stock nor mills to manage the same, and that this kingdom will be supplied better by allowing a free and open trade to all persons that are brought up to, or understand, the making of all sorts of paper, and the New Company's bill being in the opinion of learned counsel to confirm a notorious monopoly, and as such will be attended with destructive and mischievous consequences to the public, the said paper sellers most humbly pray the said bill may not pass into an Act.

This is printed upon paper (without the letter W) made in England, and not by the New Company nor Mr. Watkins which the said Company have unadvisedly challenged the paper sellers to produce.

* * *

Reasons humbly offered to this honourable House against the receiving any more petitions against the Paper Bill, or affixing an intended rider thereunto [May, 1690]

The company have formerly set forth to this honourable House the design of the paper sellers to procure petitions from time to time against them, to obstruct the passing the company's bill this present sessions of Parliament; and several of them have made their brags, within these few days, that they shall be able to effect it; and lest the intended petitions should be rejected, they have got a rider engrossed, to be added to the bill, under pretence of inspecting the company's stock; their design being only to hinder the passing the company's bill by delays; some of them having (as the company can prove) declared, that after they have done with the company in the House of Commons, they will begin all over again in the House of Lords.

The intended petitions being of the same purport with those the company have already answered, the company humbly submit it to this honourable House, whether they will think it reasonable to receive petitions *ad infinitum*, which are designed only for delay, the company having already answered five or six petitions that have been dropped in one after another against them.

As to the intended rider, the company do humbly answer that they have, with all candour and faithfulness, discovered their stock before the honourable committee, and do acknowledge that they have not to the value of 20,000*l.* in quick stock, which 400 shares, at 50*l.* per share amounts to. And they humbly hope it will not be expected that they should, at their own charge and expense, contend so long against all the great opposition that they have met with from the French ambassador and others, and be at those great charges of patents, a charter, a proclamation, and expensive suits at law, with those that designed to ruin the manufacture, by drawing away the company's servants to send them into France, besides the charge of passing this bill the last Parliament, and this present sessions, for others to reap the benefit and advantage of the same, and of all other their chargeable experiments; and it is well known to some of the members of this honourable House, that a former pretender was offered 10,000*l.* for his art, if he had had one, which the company neither expect nor desire anything for.

It is well known the company's bill obliges no man to come into the said company, but leaves it *ad libitum* to any of the subjects to come in if they please, any time before next Michaelmas; and if any person think the stock is too high valued, he is at liberty whether he will subscribe or no. But the company do humbly offer that in all companies the actions or shares are not valued according to the intrinsic value of the stock, but according to the prospect of the advantages that accrue thereby. For it cannot be supposed that the East India or African companies' real stocks do increase or impair in proportion to the rise or fall of their actions, but the said actions have been higher or lower, according to the number or disposition of the buyers to offer a greater or lesser price for the same.

The company coming therefore before this honourable House for an encouragement to establish the manufacture in all parts of the kingdom, they humbly hope that this honourable House will not think it reasonable, after the company have been at so great charge and pains, to lessen their interest, and to put them in a worse condition than now they are in.

*   *   *

The Case of the Company of White Paper Makers, most humbly represented to the right honourable the Lords Spiritual and Temporal in Parliament assembled [May, 1690]

His late Majesty, King James, grants the company Letters Patents for the sole making, writing, and printing paper for fourteen years.

Within less than three months after the said grant, the French ambassador (by order of the king his master) with great sums of money gets away several of their servants, whom he first entertained in his own house, to prevent discovery, and sent them over to France by the first conveniency.

Some of the ambassador's confederates were detected, and upon a fair trial at the King's Bench bar were convicted, and fined 500*l.*

About seven or eight of the wholesale paper sellers (who now oppose the bill) were bail for the said ambassador's confederates, and personally appeared for them at the several trials, and have ever since industriously opposed the company in their setting up the manufacture.

At the latter end of March last, the company brought a bill into the honourable House of Commons, for the better establishing the said manufacture, which bill recites the said Letters Patents granted them by King James, and enacts that the Letters Patents be confirmed, except some clauses. That the company have the sole power of making writing and printing paper for fourteen years, to commence from the end of this present sessions of Parliament. That the company lay open their books till the 29th day of September next, for any person to subscribe. That no rags be exported.

No sooner was this bill brought in but the said paper sellers sent to the brown paper makers in the several counties to oppose it, and procured five or six petitions to be delivered against them, which were brought one after another for the space of five weeks, on purpose to delay the bill, and were all heard by the committee.

One of the petitioners was proved to be a bankrupt ever since 1677, and that he had cheated several of great sums of money by his pretended art.

The brown paper makers had several hearings upon two petitions, and could produce no paper worth more than three shillings six pence per ream, unless lumber paper; whereupon the committee ordered that the brown paper makers should make all white paper to the value of four shillings per ream or under, exclusive from the company; and lumber paper, and all blue or coarse paper of any price; and the company to make writing and printing paper only above the price of four shillings per ream.

The brown paper makers at first seemed satisfied therewith; but the said paper sellers (who were resolved to hinder the passing the bill) persuaded them still to oppose it, and prevailed with a worthy member of the said House to move to be heard by counsel at the bar of the House; which was accordingly granted, and where appeared the said brown paper makers and the said paper sellers as witnesses, and three counsel.

The said paper sellers pretended to show paper of a greater value than four shillings per ream, made by the brown paper makers; but upon a strict examination before that honourable House, the paper produced by them was made by one Burnaby, about twelve or fourteen years ago, as a specimen only.

The House of Commons thereupon passed the said bill, and sent it up to this most honourable House: whereupon the paper sellers threatened the company to bring the said petitions all over again, and to procure others to be delivered, they making their boasts that they will prevent the passing of the bill this sessions, hoping thereby to ruin the manufacture, and to enrich themselves; the said seven or eight paper sellers having more paper than is in all England besides, which they hope to sell at extravagant prices, if not prevented by the establishment of the manufacture here.

The said company having been already delayed so long before the House of Commons by the said paper sellers and brown paper makers, where have been so many hearings, wherein the said paper sellers always appeared as witnesses and their design being only to delay the bill by petitions; the company do most humbly offer the same to the consideration of this most honourable House.

58. CHANGES IN THE LAW OF MINES, 1693

[Sir William Waller, *Some Account of Mines and the Advantages of them to this Kingdom*, London, 1707, pp. 25–34]

Chapter III Shewing what the Law is at this Day concerning Royal Mines

THE subjects of the crown of England have in the last century put restraints upon the prerogative in many things, or rather the crown has thought fit to make concessions and limit itself in many particulars relating to the liberties and properties of the subject; an instance whereof we have in the case of mines, which anciently belonged to the crown, whether they were of gold, copper, silver, lead, alum, etc. But now the common law of England fixes and settles the right and title of all mines of baser metals, as copper, lead, iron, etc. in the owner of the soil where they grow, and the crown claims only gold and silver mines, those only at this time being properly called royal mines; concerning which the law was lately this, viz. 'Where the ore digged from any mine doth yield according to the rules of art so much gold or silver as that the value thereof exceed the charges of refining and loss of the baser metal in which it is contained, and from whence it is extracted, then it is called a mine royal and appertains and belongs to the crown by virtue of the prerogative . . .'

But notwithstanding this plain definition of a mine royal, which one would think to be sufficient to prevent all controversies and disputes about that matter, yet there has hardly been anything more contested. One reason hereof was that this matter depended very much on the skill and honesty of the refiners, some having made very great products from that very ore from which less skilful assayers could extract nothing. A fresh instance hereof we have in the famous mines of Sir Carberry Price at Est-kyr-kyr in Cardiganshire which were discovered in the year 1690. A considerable quantity of silver being found mixed with the lead, the King or the patentees of royal mines laid claim to them. Hereupon there ensued several great and solemn trials at Bar in Westminster Hall, which were chiefly occasioned by the different reports that were made concerning the value of the silver extracted from the lead which was taken out of the said mines . . .

After Sir Carberry Price had recovered his right by virtue of several verdicts given for him against the crown in Westminster Hall (the last of them by a jury of Hertfordshire gentlemen, after a very long and solemn trial) or rather after King William had granted a *noli prosequi* which put a stop to any further proceedings against Sir Carberry Price, and left him in the quiet possession of his mines, the Parliament took this matter into consideration, and passed the following Act for the quiet of the subject. For they had observed with what warmth and vigour the prosecution was driven on against that gentleman by the court, many of the nobility and great officers of the crown being present in the Exchequer Court all the time of the last trial, which held twenty-four hours at the Bar, it being commonly reported that Henry Lord Capel had a promise of the grant of those mines if they proved royal. However that was, this is certain that Sir Carberry Price's concern and title to those mines was the first occasion of this Act of Parliament concerning royal mines, which in all probability will redound to the great advantage, not only of private proprietors and owners of mines, but also of the crown and these kingdoms, by promoting the discovery of more mines, and thereby advancing the trade, customs, manufactures, wealth, and strength of them.

[There follows the Act, 5 William and Mary, c. 6. An Act to prevent Disputes and Controversies concerning Royal Mines]

This Act, 'tis hoped, will not only prevent disputes and lawsuits for the future concerning royal mines, but also as was said before be of great advantage both to the crown and the subject. For 'tis plain the crown had little or no benefit from royal mines before this Act was made. No, they were generally granted away under a small duty to the King which was seldom or never paid, and the patentees of them could never agree to raise any great stock or to carry on the works and were always opposed by all the proprietors of the lands where the mines lay in every county, so that they could make no considerable matter of them. But now when every proprietor will make a very considerable advantage by any mines found on his soil, everyone will be industrious to discover them; and there is no doubt but from this encouragement there will in a few years be so many and so good ones discovered that the Queen will get more by the very customs of base metals than all the kings and queens of England have got by royal mines before. So that this Act of Royal Mines has quite altered the scene of the mineral world; for before, everyone that had an estate or interest in his country endeavoured to conceal his mines, but now they all labour to find them out. And formerly if they found a vein of ore that did contain so much silver as would make it a mine royal, they would not let it be known, or else they would presently beat it and mix it with their softer and baser ore, pretending the one would not melt without the other, this being with them a common trick lest their work should be taken from them. But the case now being altered, it is not unlikely but some time or other one of these concealed mines or some other may be found out, and prove so rich in silver as may be worth her Majesty's acceptance at the price proposed in the Act aforesaid.

59. BRASS MANUFACTURE IN SOMERSET, 1693–1700

[The Philosophical Transactions and Collections to the End of the Year 1700 Abridg'd . . . , ed. John Lowthorp, vol. II, 1716, p. 565]

To make brass

by Mr. Thomas Porez[1]

CALAMINE is digged out of several mines in the west of England (as about Mendip, etc.) about 20 foot deep. It is burned or calcined in a kiln or oven made red hot, then ground to powder, and sifted into the fineness of flour, then mixed with ground charcoal, because the calamine is apt to be clammy, to clod, and not so apt or capable of incorporating. Then they put about

---

[1] This description is an abridged account taken from two issues of the *Philosophical Transactions* for May 1693 and January 1700.

7 pound of calamine into a melting pot, of about a gallon content, and about 5 pound of copper uppermost; the calamine must be mixed with as many coals as will fill the pot. This is let down with tongs into a wind furnace, 8 foot deep, and remains 11 hours therein; they cast off not above twice in 24 hours. One furnace holds 8 pots. After melting, it is cast into plates or lumps.

45 pound of raw calamine produces 30 pound burnt or calcined.

Brass shruff serves instead of so much copper, but this cannot always be produced in quantities, because it is a collection of pieces of old brass, which is usually procured in small parcels.

The best guns are not made of malleable metal, and cannot be made of pure copper or brass, but it is necessary to put in coarser metals to make it run closer and sounder, as lead and pot metal; bell metal being copper and tin; and pot metal copper and lead. About 20 pound of lead is usually put into a 100 pound of pot metal; but about 6 pound is sufficient to put into 100 pound of gunmetal.

The calamine stones were heretofore fetched from Poland, but since fetched from hence by the Dutch.

The manufacture of brass was privately kept in Germany for many hundred years; wherein many thousands were employed, and all were maintained; some having thereby raised themselves to great estates.

60. A BRISTOL MERCHANT DISCOURSES ON THE MERITS OF HIGH WAGES, 1695

[John Cary, *An Essay on the State of England in relation to its Trade, its Poor, and its Taxes for carrying on the present War against France*, Bristol, 1695, pp. 143–50]

... THE question was put by an ingenious and worthy gentleman (a true lover of his country) whether the labour of our poor in England being so high does not hinder the improvement of our product and manufactures. Which having some relation to the subject matter of this discourse, I humbly make bold to offer my thoughts thereon, viz. that both our product and manufactures may be carried on to advantage without running down the labour of the poor.

As for the first, our product, I am of opinion that the running down the labour of the poor is no advantage to it, nor is it the interest of England to do it, nor can the people of England live on such low wages as they do in other countries, for we must consider that wages must bear a rate in all nations according to the prices of provisions; where wheat is sold for one shilling per bushel, and all things suitably, a labouring man may work for threepence *per diem*, as well as he can for twelve pence where it is sold for four shillings; and this price of wheat must arise from the rates of land. It cannot be imagined that the farmer whose annual rent is twenty shillings per acre can afford it as low as he who pays but half-a-crown and hath the same crop, nor can he then expect labour so cheap as the other. This is the case of England, whose lands yielding great rents require good prices for their product; and this is the freeholder's advantage, for suppose necessaries were the current payment for labour, in such case whether we call a bushel of wheat one shilling or four shillings, it is all one to him for so much as he pays, but not for the overplus of his crop, which makes a great difference into his pocket. You cannot fall wages unless you fall product, and if you fall product you must necessarily fall land.

And as for the second, our manufactures, I am [of] opinion that they may be carried on to advantage without running down the labour of the poor; for which I offer:

Observation, or experience of what hath been done, we have and daily do see that it is so. The refiners of sugars lately sold for sixpence per pound what yielded twenty years since twelve pence; the distillers sell their spirits for one third part of what they formerly did; glass bottles, silk stockings, and other manufactures (too many to be enumerated) are sold for half the prices they were a few years since, without falling the labour of the poor, or so little as not to stand in competition with the other.

But then the question will be, how this is done? I answer, it proceeds from the ingenuity of the manufacturer, and the improvements he makes in his ways of working: thus the refiner of sugars goes through that operation in a month, which our forefathers required four months to effect; thus the distillers draw more spirits, and in less time from the simples they work on than those formerly did who taught them the art. The glass maker hath found a quicker way of making it out of things which cost him little or nothing. Silk stockings are wove instead of knit. Tobacco is cut by engines instead of knives. Books are printed instead of written. Deal boards are sawn with a mill instead of men's labour. Lead is smelted by wind furnaces, instead of blowing with bellows; all which save the labour of many hands, so the wages of those employed need not be lessened.

Besides this, there is a cunning crept into trades: the clockmaker hath improved his art so high, that labour and materials are the least part the buyer pays for. The variety of our woollen manufactures is so pretty that fashion makes a thing worth both at home and abroad twice the price it is sold for after, the humour of the buyer carrying a great sway in the value of a commodity. Artificers by tools and laves fitted for different uses make such things as would puzzle a stander by to set a price on according to the worth of men's labour. The plumber by new inventions casts a ton of shot for ten shillings, which an indifferent person could not guess worth less than fifty.

The same art is crept into navigation. A ton of sugars, which cost a few years since from six to eight pounds freight from the plantations, was commonly brought home before the war for four pounds ten shillings, and whereas it then weighed but twenty-five hundred, 'twas increased to forty-five, and yet sailors' wages were still the same. Ships are built more for stowage, and made strong enough to carry between decks. Wool is steeved into them by skrews, so that three or four bags are put where formerly one would scarce lie. Cranes and blocks draw up more for one shilling than men's labour could do for five.

New projections are every day set on foot to render the making our manufactures easy, which are made cheap by the heads of the manufacturers, not by falling the price of poor people's labour; cheapness creates expense, and expense gives fresh employments, so the poor need not stand idle if they could be persuaded to work.

The same for our product. Pits are drained and land made healthy by engines and aqueducts instead of hands; the husbandman turns up his soil with the sullow, not digs it with his spade; sows his grain, not plants it; covers it with the harrow, not with the rake; brings home his harvest with carts, not on horsebacks; and many other easy methods are used both for improving of land, and raising its product, which are obvious to the eyes of men versed therein, though do not come within the compass of my present thoughts; all which lessen the number of labourers, and make room for better wages to be given those who are employed.

Nor am I of opinion with those people who think the running down the prices of our growth and product (that so they may buy provisions cheap) is an advantage to the inland trade of this kingdom, but on the contrary I think 'twould be better for it if they were sold higher than they are, which may seem a paradox at first, till the thing be rightly stated. Suppose then the common and usual price of beef to be twopence halfpenny per pound, and wheat three shillings and sixpence per bushel, and all flesh and grain suitable, 'twould be better for our inland trade if the former yielded fourpence, and the latter five shillings, and other things in proportion.

To prove this, let us begin with the shopkeeper or buyer and seller, who is the wheel whereon the inland trade turns, as he buys of the importer and manufacturer, and sells again to the country; suppose such a man spends two hundred pounds per annum in all things necessary for his family, both provisions, clothes, house rent, and other expenses, the question will be what proportion of this is laid out in flesh, corn, butter, cheese, etc. barely considered according to their first cost in the market. I presume we shall find fifty or sixty pounds per annum to be the most, and suitably the advance thereon will be about twenty-five to thirty pounds per annum, but the consequence thereof in the profits of his trade will be much more; for by this means the farmer may give a better rent to his landlord, who will be enabled to keep a more plentiful table, spend more wines, fruit, sugars, spices, and other things wherewith he is furnished from the City, wear better clothes, suit himself and his family oftener, and carry on a greater splendour in everything. The farmer according to his condition may do the same, and give higher wages to the labourers employed in husbandry, who might then live more plentifully, and buy new clothes oftener, instead of patching up old.

By this means the manufacturer would be encouraged to give a better price for wool, when he should find a vent as fast as he could make; and a flux of wealth causing variety of fashions would add wings to men's inventions, when they shall see their manufactures advanced in their values by the buyer's fancy. This likewise would encourage the merchant to increase his exports, when he shall have a quick vent for his imports; by which regular circulation payments would be short, and all would grow rich. But when trade stops in the fountain, when the gentleman and farmer are kept poor, everyone in his order partakes of the same fate. And this hath been a certain rule grounded on the observation of all men who have spent time to look into it, that in those countries where provisions are low the people are generally poor, both proceeding from the want of trade. So that he who would give a right judgement must not always consider things *prima facie*, as they offer themselves to us at first sight, but as they appear to be in their consequences.

61. SUGGESTIONS FOR THE HELP OF THE CLOTH INDUSTRY, 1698[?]

[Bodleian Library, Oxford, MS. Eng. Hist. b. 209, f. 87v.
Manuscript of speeches and news on public affairs by Sir
Richard Cocks, knight of the shire for Gloucestershire, early 1698(?)]

Of Blackwell Hall

OUR chief care ought to be of the clothier and first seller for if they are damaged and suffer loss it affects the very trade itself, for it is impossible for him to maintain the workers under him and support the manufacturers if he shall not have good payment of the money he sells these goods for; if therefore the clothier has not ready money, he ought to have notes which he may transfer or endorse for another, the said notes to go as bills of exchange and subject to the same law and rules as bills of exchange are; this note would save all delays and serve the clothier instead of money, for with this note can he supply himself with oil, Spanish wool, and what he wants, and it will prevent all reckoning, lawsuits, and controversies which [are] the bane and ruin of trade; and further the woollen trade being the trade of most advantage to the nation both for the poor it employs at home and from the riches it brings from abroad, one above all things to be considered and to have all the advantages; no discouragement, no duty upon it at home nor abroad, but that no regard in comparison of the trade should be had of Christchurch Hospital or the privileges of the city: but that the first seller may sell where he will, and the buyer, be he stranger, or free of the city, or alien, may buy in Blackwell Hall or where he pleases. It would also be of great advantage to trade to have some persons appointed, or care taken to have our cloths made well, and that if any cheat should appear that every clothier should set his own mark as well as the seal of the office, that there may be satisfaction given in our courts for cloth sold beyond the seas, and all unwrought wools ought to have no duty in Ireland before they are shipped, nor no custom here, but we ought to give all encouragement imaginable to bring wool unwrought hither from all parts.

62. AN ACT TO ALLOW SOLDIERS TO EXERCISE A TRADE, 1698

[*Statutes of the Realm*, VII, pp. 528–9]

10 Gul. III, *Chapter* XVII[1]

An Act to enable such officers and soldiers as have been in His Majesty's service during the late war to exercise trades and for officers to account with their soldiers

WHEREAS there hath been and are divers officers and soldiers who have served his Majesty in the late wars and were instrumental by the blessing of Almighty God in obtaining an advantageous peace for these kingdoms, some of which are men that used trades, others that were apprentices to trades who had not served out their times, and others who by their own industry have made themselves apt and fit for trades, many of which (the wars being now ended) would willingly employ themselves in those trades which they were formerly accustomed to, or which they are apt or able to follow and make use of for the getting their living by their own labour but are or may be hindered from exercising those trades in certain cities and corporations and other places within this kingdom because of certain bylaws and customs of those places and of the statute made in the fifth year of Queen Elizabeth prohibiting the use of certain trades by any person who hath not served as an apprentice to such trade for the space of seven years. For remedy whereof, be it enacted by the king's most excellent Majesty, by and with the advice and consent of the Lords Spiritual and Temporal and Commons in this present Parliament assembled, and by the authority of the same, that all such officers and soldiers who have been at any time employed in his Majesty's service since his happy accession to the crown and have not since deserted the said service, and that have heretofore used or exercised any trade or that were apprentices to any trade, though they did not serve out the time of their apprenticeship, or any other officer or soldier employed as aforesaid that is apt and able to practice any trade, may set up and exercise such several and respective trades, mysteries, or occupations whereunto he or they have been bound apprentices and served any part of his or their time, or any handicraft or other trade exercised about manufactures, though he was never bound apprentice to the same in manner following (that is to say), such of them as have been apprentices as aforesaid may set up and exercise such several and respective trades

Side notes:
Reasons for passing this Act.

5 Eliz. c. 4. § 31.

Officers and soldiers who have not deserted, and who have heretofore exercised trades, or were apprentices, or are able to practise trades, may set up the same.

---

[1] This is Chap. XI in the common printed editions.

whereunto he or they have been so bound apprentices as fully as if they had served out their respective terms or times for which they have been bound, and shall have and enjoy the same immunities as they should have had and enjoyed if they had served out their said terms or times. And all others of the said officers and soldiers may set up and exercise such trades as they are apt and able for in any town or place within the several and respective counties wherein they were born without any let, suit, or molestation of any person or persons whatsoever for or by reason of the using of such trade.

If any officer or soldier be sued, etc., and making it appear he has served his Majesty, shall, upon the general issue, be found not guilty;

And if any such officer or officers, soldier or soldiers, shall be sued, impleaded, or indicted in any court whatsoever within this kingdom for using or exercising any such trades as aforesaid, then the said officer or officers, soldier or soldiers, making it appear to the same court where they are so sued, impleaded, or indicted, that they have served the king's Majesty as aforesaid shall upon the general issue pleaded be found not guilty in any plaint, bill, information, or indictment exhibited against them. And such persons who notwithstanding this Act shall prosecute their said suit by bill, plaint, information, or indictment, and shall have a verdict pass against them or become

or plaintiff discontinue, etc. Treble costs.

nonsuit therein or discontinue their said suit, such person or persons shall pay unto such officer or officers, soldier or soldiers, treble costs of suit to be recovered as any other costs at common law may be recovered. And all judges

Judges, etc. to conform to this Act.

and jurors before whom any such suit, information, or indictment, shall be brought and all other persons whatsoever are to take notice of this present Act and shall conform themselves thereunto, any statute, law, ordinance, custom, or provision, to the contrary in anywise notwithstanding.

II.
No officer or soldier to have the benefit of this Act, who shall not prove his service.

Provided that no officer or soldier shall have the benefit of this Act that shall not prove his service as aforesaid either by a certificate under the hand and seal of some field officer or two commission officers of the regiment wherein he served or some general officer of the army certifying his knowledge of the service aforesaid, and the same certificate to be proved by one witness at least to be a true certificate or for default of such certificate by the oath of two credible witnesses at least.

III.
Persons pretending to be officers, etc. producing a false certificate, punishment.

Provided also that if any person or persons, pretending themselves to have been officers or soldiers within the qualifications aforesaid, shall produce a false certificate to the intent to have the benefit of this Act, and thereof be convicted by confession or due proof of law, shall suffer imprisonment not exceeding three months and to lose the benefit of this Act, anything therein contained to the contrary notwithstanding . . .[1]

VI.

And for the better enabling and encouraging the said disbanded soldiers (other than commission officers) to set up [and exercise[2]] their trades in such manner as aforesaid, it is hereby further enacted and declared by the authority

Disbanded soldiers setting up their trades,

aforesaid that such of the said disbanded soldiers (other than commission officers) as shall so set up and exercise their trades as aforesaid with their

---

[1] The clauses omitted here relate to the arrangements for officers to settle accounts of pay with the soldiers of their regiments.

[2] Interlined on the Roll.

stock and tools used in or about the exercising their said trades shall be and are hereby freed for the space of three years to be accounted from the first day of May one thousand six hundred ninety nine from having their persons arrested or imprisoned or their said stock or tools seized, distrained, or taken in execution for any debt or monies which was or were owing by them either or any of them at the time when they respectively were first listed into his Majesty's service, anything to the contrary notwithstanding.

freed from arrest, and their goods from seizure, in respect of debts due at the time of their first enlisting.

IV. INLAND AND COASTAL TRADE AND COMMUNICATIONS

1. THE YORK MERCERS LEGISLATE AGAINST CHAPMEN, 1603

[Maud Sellers, ed., *The York Mercers and Merchant Adventurers, 1356–1917*, Surtees Soc., CXXIX, 1918, p. 277]

ACTS and Ordinances made by and for the good Government of the Society of Merchants and Mercers within the City of York, hereafter to be observed and kept, newly corrected and emended, 10 October, 1603.

... no. 36. Whereas of late some brethren of this fellowship have by themselves and their apprentices heretofore used not only to stand at the corners of the streets and in other men's shops, but also have gone to the common inns where the chapmen, buyers of flax, and other merchandise have lodged, and there have often solicited them to their own shops, warehouses, or cellars, for the venting of their own flax, iron, and other merchandise, the said chapmen many of them being deeply indebted to divers brethren of this fellowship, who by means thereof have not only lost their chapmen and ordinary customers, but also have been long times driven of their payments, yea, and sometimes thereby have lost their debts to the great damage of many brethren of this fellowship, and for avoiding of the same, it is by authority of this court established and enacted that from henceforth it shall not be lawful for any brother of this fellowship, nor his servant or apprentice, to lodge or keep table in any common inn where any chapmen, buyers of flax or other merchandise, or their carriers do commonly frequent, eat, or use to lodge, upon pain of every one herein offending to forfeit and pay for every offence, xv*s*.

2. YORK CITY COUNCIL ORDERS THE RETURN OF MERCHANTS AFTER PLAGUE, 1605

[York City Muniments, House Book, B32, p. 346]

[Council minutes] xxi die Februarii 1604 [= 1605]

To OUR very loving friends Mr. George Rosse, Mr. Laurence Ward, Mr. Wm. Breazey, Mr. Michael Hartford, Mr. Ellis Micklethwate, Mr. Mathewe

Topham, Mr. Christopher Dickenson, and to all other merchants and citizens of the City of York, now remaining at the towns of Tadcaster or Selby.

After our hearty commendations, etc., whereas you and divers other merchants, traders, freemen, and citizens of this city have of long time remained at Tadcaster, Selby, and other market towns with merchandises and goods by reason of the great contagious sickness which hath been of late in this city, thereby drawing chapmen and others unto you for the buying of merchandises and other commodities, and forasmuch as it hath pleased Almighty God of his great mercy to appease and mitigate the same great infection to our great comfort, and yet notwithstanding you do still remain at the towns foresaid, thereby drawing chapmen and others unto the same towns, which is not only to the impoverishing of your fellow citizens, tradesmen of this city which have remained in this city during all this time of visitation, but is a means to withdraw gentlemen and others from this city by reason of your remaining in the country. It is therefore agreed by us in our Council Chamber upon Ousebridge that all merchants, citizens, and others of this city using trading abroad in any towns in the country shall make their present repair unto this city, with their servants, merchandises, and goods, and here to remain with the same upon pain, loss, and forfeiture of every merchant or citizen that shall stay or continue in any towns or other place other than in this city with their servants, merchandises, or goods one week after notice thereof given unto them for every week v*li.* that they or any of them shall so continue with their servants or goods, which they are to pay without favour, mitigation, or pardon, which is to [be] employed for the relieving of the poor in this city wherefore we have thought good hereby to give you notice of the same to the end you may provide yourselves to come to this city with your servants, merchandises, and goods, assuring such of you as shall remain in the country with their servants or goods contrary to the meaning of the same order shall pay the payment without any favour or mitigation; and we do hereby also require you to whom this letter shall first be delivered to show the same to the others to whom the same is directed to the end the same may be made known to all that do remain either at Tadcaster or Selby. In haste we bid you farewell from York, this xxth of February, 1604.

Your loving friends

Wm. Greneburie, mayor; Wm. Robinson, alderman; John Burkby, alderman; Henry Hall; Robert Paycock; Tho. Herbert; Robt. Harrison.

3. A COMPLAINT OF DECAYING TRADE
AT CHESTER, 1608

[Hist. MSS. Commission, *Salisbury MSS.*, XX, pp. 27–8]

John Savage, Mayor, and the Aldermen of Chester
to the Earl of Salisbury

25 January 1607–8

HAVING received letters from the Lord High Treasurer of England o
December 9 last touching the impost of wines demanded of the merchant
of this city, and for the taking of such of them bounden to appear before hi
Lordship as should refuse payment thereof, I, the Mayor, with the assistance
of my brethren, did call them before us, and upon their refusal, grounded
upon divers instances and reasons, did take them all bounden for their
appearances according to his commandment. But because the time thereunt
prefixed was with so small a limitation (being the first day of this term), th
days yet being very short, we presumed to take them bound for their appearance the first of February next. Of which our proceedings we pray you
allowance, and in respect some of the parties are so aged and infirm as no
able to travel one day's journey, the snow in these parts very deep, the wa
bad, and the weather inclined to a very sharp and dangerous frost for trave
and some of the parties having not past 6, 4, or 3 tons of wine upon thei
adventure, you would allow of the coming up of these bearers, William
Gamull, William Aldersey, and Robert Berrie, who will attend your pleasure
in the premises. And for that this city is seated in one of the remotest countie
of this kingdom, in effect destitute of trade and traffic both at home an
abroad, where in former times we had trade to Spain for iron (being then
profitable commodity), the benefit whereof is utterly taken away by th
abundance of iron made in the countries here adjoining, sold here at cheape
rates than can be bought in Spain; and that shipping in this port is so decaye
that there are not belonging to it any barks but some few of very small bur
den, which only traffic for Ireland, and the merchants cannot freight an
ship beyond the seas to arrive in this port but at extraordinary rates b
reason of the danger of the river; we embolden ourselves upon your accustomed favour to this poor city and the trade within the same, which (as i
others) is one of the greatest ornaments of this commonwealth, that yo
would be a means to his Highness for renewing her late Majesty's grant t
the merchants of this city for their discharge of the impost of their Frencl
wines arriving in this port, which her Majesty for divers weighty considerations approved by you to bestow upon them.
Chester. 25 Jan., 1607.

[Seven signatures including William Aldersey's.]

4. HORSE TRADING IN THE WEST MIDLANDS, 1609

[Staffordshire Quarter Sessions Rolls, Collections for a History of Staffs., 1948–9, pp. 27–9]

[Letter dated at Eccleshall Castle 9 January 1608/9 from William, Bishop of Coventry and Lichfield, addressed to Sir Walter Chetwynd, bart.]

Sir Walter,

Our late sheriff Mr. Thomas Peshall a little before he died came unto me at my Castle of Eccleshall and informed me that two men out of Derbyshire, under the name and colour of horse coursers, had taken of him some pasture ground to put in such horses as they brought to sell at the fairs and market hereabouts, as namely at Drayton, Newport, and Bridgnorth, and withal told me that he had some intelligence given him from his bailiff in Derbyshire that they had an ill name in that country, and were suspected to be horse stealers, and therefore prayed me to send for them and to examine them about the number of horses which they had in his pasture which I presently did; and upon their examination (which I have sent here to the Bench to be seen) I found that they could give no reckoning how, or where, or of whom they bought them, being indeed riff-raff horses not fit for horse coursers to traffic withal in my fair or market, and therefore being not able to put in any sufficient sureties for their forthcoming, I delivered them to the Constables of Eccleshall with my *mittimus* to carry them to the gaol, but one of them in the night broke from the constables, and so fled and made an escape, and can nowhere be heard of, neither at his own house in Derbyshire nor anywhere else whereby by law he hath made himself guilty of the felony. But his companion was carried to the gaol, and there remains. Now because they were partners together in all their traffic, as by their examinations it doth appear, the one I think is as guilty as the other. And because they do not confess, or rather cannot confess of whom they bought the horses, nor that they paid any toll at the buying of them as by the Statute is required, I take it that they are both guilty. Besides this, having brought hither divers horses at divers times, they have not sold them in any fair or market openly, but in the pastures and fields where they go, and have had divers chapmen secretly to receive them at their hands, who almost are as ill as the horse stealers themselves, whom I have likewise bound over to appear at the next general Assizes, which because they know not to be tomorrow (being an extraordinary gaol delivery) peradventure they will fail of. But upon some further monition may be bound to appear hereafter at the judges' coming down. Surely if the matter shall be lightly passed over, it will confirm them in their trade begun and give boldness to others to follow their steps. It should seem they have stolen the horses they have here out of some commons or forests far off, for though one or two be somewhat reasonably to be liked of, yet the rest, as I said before, are but riff-raff horse flesh, such as they might easily come by without money, and therefore they are likelier to be sold without any great gain because they cost them nothing. To this may be added that they lodged themselves in a blind corner out of the way in a shepherd's house, whereas, if they had been true men, they would have resorted openly to some inn or other honest place the better to justify their merchandise, but they durst not do it which makes them the more to be suspected. And whereas the one of them which is now in the gaol hath written or sent unto you to be a means to have some relief from me, pretending that I have some money of his, it is known well enough that he denied when he was examined that he had any money at all, but his fellow before he fled confessed he had nine or ten pounds in a chest at the shepherd's house, which I likewise confess myself to have, and out of the money which I have, I have sent the knave in gaol as good as a groat a day during his abode there, which were enough to sustain in mean sort one in that place and of his desert. But he wrote unto me that he paid seven shillings a week for his board in the gaoler's house and two shillings and sixpence a week for his bed, which were enough for an honest gentleman if he were there for some light trespass and had some good living of his own, but for such a false knave to be so maintained it is more than he should look for, specially having nothing of his own but only of the alms and charity of other men. And yet it should seem he hath some store of money to employ at his pleasure for he hath offered two or three times to one of my men five pounds to help to get him bailed, and therefore, if he have it, let him relieve himself whilst he is there and not look to live like a gentleman at other men's charges. I give mine own husbandmen and millers and other servants when I am away but iis. iiiid. a week, and such a knave as he might content himself with so much if he might have it, and not think to live like a gentleman amongst his fellow thieves except he have some privy stock that no man knows of but himself or his fellow horse stealers, which peradventure will not see him want for fear of disclosing the brotherhood and fraternity that is amongst them. The surnames of these two felons are Meacocke and Millington. Meacocke is fled and Millington is there forthcoming. I have sent both their examinations, and my servant Ralphe Pickin with others to prosecute the matter against them according to law. I pray you and the other Justices help to cut off such counterfeit horse coursers, or, by their righter name, cunning horse stealers, and the rather because he in the gaol hath been already arraigned before this time for the like, whether the other or no I know not, but it is very likely. And thus I make an end of my long letters and commend you to God.

5. CARRIERS' CHARGES AT IPSWICH, 1613
[Ipswich and East Suffolk Record Office, C1/1(4)]

[Order made at a General Court, 11 November, 11 Jas. I, of the Borough of Ipswich]

IT IS ordered and decreed by the full and whole consent of the bailiff, burgesses, and commonalty now assembled that no wagoner nor common carrier of this town shall after the xvth day of November next exact of any person or persons whatsoever above the sums of money hereafter set down for the carrying of goods, merchandises, letters, and things hereafter mentioned from this town to the city of London and from the said city to this town, that is to say: for the carrying of every trunk not exceeding the length of ¾ of a yard and half, nor weighing above ¾ of a hundredweight—   vs.
For every trunk not exceeding the length of a yard, nor weighing above five score and twelve pounds weight—   vis. viiid.
For every trunk not exceeding the length of a yard and half a quarter, not weighing above a hundred and a quarter weight—   viiis.
For every trunk not exceeding an ell, nor weighing above one hundred and a half—   xs.
For the carriage of every Suffolk cloth—   iis. vid.
For every fivescore and twelve pounds weight from Ipswich to London— vs.
For every fivescore and twelve pounds weight from London to Ipswich—   iiis. iiiid.
And so after that rate for a greater or lesser quantity, unless they be things of great bulk and little weight, as chests, trunks, boxes, and such like things not filled with wares and commodities. For goods not exceeding xiili. to have doubles.
For every letter not exceeding one sheet of paper id., and being paid at the receipt thereof, they shall take nothing at the delivery thereof.
For every passenger—   vs.
And for money, plate, jewels, silks, and other wares of small weight and great worth at their discretions.
Upon pain to forfeit for every letter they shall take more than according to the rate aforesaid or refuse to carry any letter at that rate—   viid.
And for every time they shall take more than according to the rates set upon the other goods or refuse to carry the same—iiis. iiiid. to the use of the poor people of this town to be levied by the chamberlains of this town for the time being by distress or action of debts.
And after that, that is to say, at a great court there holden the fourth day of July *anno regni domini nostri Jacobi etc. Anglie, Franc' et Hibernie* xix *et Scocie* liii, it was likewise ordered as followeth, viz. It is agreed that forasmuch as there appear unto this house many inconveniences to the inhabitants of this town by the weekly going of two carriers to London, that from henceforth there shall go only one. And that the now carriers, Thomas Lane and

Thomas Lucas, shall take their turns; and Thomas Lane to choose whether he will go the first week. And if the said Thomas Lane refuse this order, then the freemen of this town have agreed that the said Thomas Lucas shall have the sole carriage of such things as they have to carry. And the said Lane and Lucas are to be bound with sureties in 100 marks apiece to perform the carriages at such rates as [have] been heretofore taxed and rated by the former constitutions of this town.

6. THE MARKETING OF NORTH-COUNTRY WOOL, 1617

[BM, Additional MS. 34324, ff. 14, 15]

TO THE Rt. Honourable the Lords and others of his Majesty's most honourable Privy Council, the humble petition of the inhabitants of the counties of Cumberland, Westmorland, and Northumberland, whose wool being their chiefest commodity, yet so base as unfit for staple wool and only fit for friezes, cottons, and coarsest cloths, so as, notwithstanding the general restraint by the statute of King Edward the 6th ordaining that none shall buy wool but wool workers and Staplers, with proviso that the wools of the said three counties of Cumberland, Westmorland, and Northumberland might be bought by the merchants of Newcastle and others, with intent to ship and carry them beyond the seas, the which in respect of the meanness of the wool of these counties was never sithence put in use or effected. Yet these counties have ever since been thereby enforced and used to sell their wools wheresoever without impeachment of the same statute, whereupon it pleased your Honours in the time of the late Queen Elizabeth by your honourable letters in May 1585 directed to the Lord President of York to give allowance that the said inhabitants should be freed from the informers of the said statute, and since that time seldom or never any wool workers or Staplers repaired to the said counties to buy wools in regard of the exceeding coarseness thereof and the remoteness of places, some parts of the said counties being 100 miles distant from any clothing town except Kendal which doth not nor is able to retain or employ the fortieth part of the wools of those counties. And in June was twelvemonth it pleased your Honours upon notice of the inconvenience thereof, testified under the hand of the noblemen and others of the said shires, to exempt the said counties from the order therein taken touching the other counties of England, which leave to the inhabitants of the same three counties to continue buying and selling of their wools as in former years they have used, that order notwithstanding, as by an order hereunto annexed appeareth. And whereas by his Highness's late proclamation of the 24th of March in this present 15th year of his Highness's reign, the Staple of wools is removed from parts beyond the seas unto certain places and towns within this realm and namely amongst other towns unto Kendal which is no way able to receive a fortieth part of the wool of the said three counties, nor have many thousand of the wool growers of those three counties (in respect of their great distance) any means to bring their wools to Kendal aforesaid nor to any other of the said staple towns now appointed, by means whereof they are utterly disabled to make their necessary profit in sale of their wools and nevertheless are in danger of the said statute of Edward the 6th if they should keep their wools unsold above the space of one year with intent to sell the same afterward. And the wool buyers, being very poor men, rather choose to give over their trade than to become Staplers by paying a fine to be admitted, the wools being so coarse as their gain is very small. And they far distant from markets cannot come to buy it, for that they are exceedingly troubled with informers who do it rather to make a gain of poor men than for the good of the commonwealth.

May it therefore please your honourable Lordships that in favour of the said counties who otherwise will be exceedingly impoverished hereby to take such order as they may be permitted to sell their wools as usually they have done heretofore. And they shall ever pray, etc.

[Folio 15 of this MS. consists of notes on the foregoing petition, endorsed 'Touching the Wools of Cumberland', summarizing some of the same points and adding the following:]

Few or no clothiers come to buy any [wools], Kendal being in the county of Westmorland converteth not into cottons the fortieth part and that only the refuse.

Halifax, Leeds, and Wakefield in the county of York, Rochdale, and Manchester in the county of Lancaster convert the rest.

In those parts forty thousand families of clothiers, whereof every fortieth man is not able to buy ten stone of wool beforehand nor to fetch it from the growers.

The Staplers being in number a few combine together and buy only at their own rates and make one purse.

The wool buyers are so poor that they are not able to become Staplers.

7. HOP MARKETING IN SUFFOLK, 1618

[*Suffolk in the Seventeenth Century. The Breviary of Suffolk by Robert Reyce, 1618, with notes by Lord Francis Hervey*, London, 1902, pp. 31–3]

Hops

I MAY not here next to the corn omit to speak of our hops, which when they were first perceived to delight in our soil, well was he that could entertain this plant, and of many, even in the best meadow ground which they had, they set it, where in short time it mightily increased, others draining unprofitable marshes and moors proved to plant there, which likewise brought great profit and abundance, othersome being desirous to be partakers of that fruit, which they saw so many enriched withal, as also for the supply of their own expense, planted not in good ground, but in the best which they had or could spare, which was somewhat dry or hard, and so oftentimes met with a sufficient crop and gain. Thus whilst this kind of commodity thrived excellently well, and brought forth such profit to the owners, that many in short time proved wealthy thereby, many leaving their wonted trade betook themselves only to be hop masters, as the title was then given them, in which new found mystery of planting, setting, drying, and trimming they employed themselves wholly; supposing thereby to extract more than an Indian quintessence, for whilst in those times the markets and fairs proved quick, and Stourbridge, London, and the western parts vented whatsoever this or any other country could bring forth, there sprung up a new company, some from London, some from other parts, called hop merchants; these prying into the last year's store then remaining, diligently harkening from beyond the sea what likelihood there was from those parts, and carefully looking into every garden and hop yard here at home, in what towardness they stood, comparing the former year's experience with the time present, at length with themselves resolved and concluded of a price, who travelling into the country where these hops were, they offered to the owners at their own doors, either for those remaining or for new at the next gathering to come. The great desire of this commodity at home by the merchants made the inhabitants every way as desirous for their supply, and thus whilst everyone sought to be enriched with this commodity, see how they were contraried in their excessive desires. First such grounds as were any ways fit for this purpose were raised and let at most exceeding high rates; both roots and poles double increased their wonted prices, workmanship proved more chargeable than formerly. And yet when the owner looked to have all these richly recompensed with a plentiful crop, behold such was the influence of the heavens, and the unkindness of the seasons these sundry years past, that in the best grounds hops failed; the prices fell and the market abated, which when the owner perceived, reckoning therewithal his great charge, with most uncertain gain (if not certain loss), gave up this new trade, by reason whereof this kind of commodity is now come to decay in these parts. I know not what this last year's price 1602 of hops at £10 (the like never before heard) may allure some to renew[?] their former experiments. But the decay of woods for poles, with the usual charge, and the uncertainty of the profit, especially other countries being now replenished with hops, hath made the general care here to be only for the home expense, and that upon waste grounds otherwise not to be employed.

8. A DISPUTE BETWEEN CHAPMEN IN PARTNERSHIP, 1619

[P.R.O., C2, Jas. I, C 24/4]

xxii die Novembris, 1619

To the Right Honourable Francis Lord Verulam, Lord Chancellor of England

HUMBLY complaining sheweth unto your good lordship your daily orator, William Cutts of Wolverhampton in the county of Staffordshire, that whereas your said orator and one Francis Burton and William Tarte of Wolverhampton aforesaid at or about the Feast of Easter in the year of our Lord God 1618 did promise and conclude together and condescend and agree each with other to become chapmen partners, copartners, or parting fellows of divers and sundry wares, merchandises, and other commodities, but especially of divers great quantities of hops amounting to the value of £2,000 or thereabouts. And likewise then concluded and agreed that they with their several stocks as partners and parting fellows would jointly occupy for some time then agreed upon in all manner of buying and selling, bartering, or bargaining of great quantities of hops which they intended shortly to buy together; as likewise of divers other commodities, and of the increase and gains from time to time arising and growing by reason of their said joint occupying by factorship and exchange, alienation, or otherwise; and that during the said joint occupying or partnership every of the said parties should be faithful and true to each other in buying and selling, receiving and accounting, and satisfying one to the other all such true profits and gain, advantage, benefit, and increase as should come, grow, or arise by buying, selling, or other bargaining ... and that, charges deducted, all the profit, lucre, gain, or commodities growing or arising by their joint buying, selling, or other occupying should be equally divided ...

By reason of which agreement your said orator and the said Francis Burton and William Tarte in or about the months of August, September, and October in the year of our Lord 1618 and before and after the said months did jointly buy of several persons divers great quantities of hops and some other commodities amounting to the value of £2,000: that is to say of one Mr. Wynsmore and Mrs. Wynsmore, his daughter, 20cwt. of hops at the price of £3 6s. 8d. the cwt.; of one

			£	s.	d.		
John Turner[1]	10	cwt.	at 3	13	4	a cwt.	
young Collye	1	,,	,, 4	0	0	,,	,,
Geoffrey Norgrosse	8	,,	,, 3	6	8	,,	,,
Thomas Daie	4	,,	,, 4	0	0	,,	,,

[1] The details of hop purchases are tabulated to save excessive repetition in the text. All purchases are included.

			£	s.	d.	
Mr. Creswell	4 cwt.		at 4	0	0	a cwt.
James Fidy	4 ,,		,, 4	0	0	,, ,,
Morgan Dives' men some 20	,,	[some]	,, 3	6	8	,, ,,
		[some]	,, 3	13	4	,, ,,
		[some]	,, 4	0	0	,, ,,
Mr. Colly		600 qtrs.	,, 5	0	0	,, ,,
Mr. Collies' son	2 ,,		,, 5	0	0	,, ,,
Mr. Smalle	2 ,,		,, 5	0	0	,, ,,
Mr. Wickes	4½ ,,		,, 4	0	0	,, ,,
Mr. Hill	2 ,,		,, 4	0	0	,, ,,
the widow Hayes	3 ,,		,, 4	0	0	,, ,,
Hugh Cooke	2 ,,		,, 4	10	0	,, ,,
Roger Beedell	2 ,,		,, 4	2	6	,, ,,
John Panner	1½ ,,		,, 4	6	8	,, ,,
Mr. Debitatt	1 ,,		,, 4	0	0	,, ,,
one — Gooffe	1 ,,		,, 4	7	8	,, ,,
Thomas Hillman	1 ,,		,, 4	10	0	,, ,,
Mr. Barnaby	9 ,,		,, 5	0	0	,, ,,
Mr. Arden	4 ,,		,, 5	12	0	,, ,,
John Cockins	4 ,,		,, 5	0	0	,, ,,
Leonard Monoperocke	3½ ,,		,, 3	5	0	,, ,,
Henry Elke	6 ,,		,, 4	0	0	,, ,,
		and other some	,, 4	6	8	,, ,,
Mr. Reeding	4 ,,		,, 6	13	4	,, ,,

... And most part of the several sums of money for which the hops were so sold away was received by the aforesaid Francis Burton or William Tarte or some one of them in manner and form following, viz. Sold by some of them to the use of the aforesaid parties being partners the 10th day of October 1618 to Mr. Thomas Alldersee and Thomas Knowles of Chester 22 cwt. of hops at £6 10s. a cwt., for which William Tarte received all the money. Likewise sold to the same use at Bridgnorth Fair the 18th day of October 10 cwt. of hops at £7 a cwt., for which Francis Burton and William Tarte received all the money. Sold by some of the aforesaid parties to the use aforesaid at Bristol at £6 10s. a cwt., 10 cwts. of hops for which Francis Burton and William Tarte received all the monies. Sold at another time in Wales to the use aforesaid 4 cwt. of hops at £6 10s. a cwt., for which William Tarte received all the monies. Sold at another time to the use aforesaid at Utsaster [= Uttoxeter?] 2 cwt. of hops at £7 a cwt., for which Francis Burton received all the monies. Sold at another time to the use aforesaid at Birmingham of Medgbury 3 cwt. of hops at £7 a cwt., for which Francis Burton received the money. Sold at another time at Newport 4 cwt. of hops at £6 10s. a cwt., which money Francis Burton or William Tarte received. Sold to Mr. Knowles his man 7½ cwt. of hops at £6 15s. a cwt., which money the said William Tarte wholly received to himself. Sold to John Hannby at Wolverhampton 1 cwt. of hops at £6 10s. a cwt., which money the said William Tarte wholly received. Sold to Thomas Sawer at Stafford 4 cwt. at

£7 a cwt., which money Francis Burton wholly received . . . Notwith-standing your said orator did disburse a full third part and more of the money that bought the aforesaid hops and other commodities . . . they the said Francis Burton and William Tarte or either of them do not only refuse to pay or satisfy unto your said orator such sums as are due unto him, but also deny to reckon account or make even with your said orator which is contrary to all right and equity and good conscience and in manifest breach of their aforesaid promises and agreements, and tending to the loss of your said orator at the least to the sum of £500 . . .

9. TOWN AND MARKET DUES AT SHAFTESBURY DISPUTED, 1620

[P.R.O., E 134, 18 Jas. I, Easter 1]

[A miscellany of the evidence offered in a dispute of Mary Countess Dowager of Pembroke, and William, Earl of Pembroke v. William Grove, John Nicholls, etc., concerning fair and markets, chief rents, and the election of officers in Shafton, alias Shaftesbury, Dorset]

JOHN MOORE formerly examined in the behalf of the defendants now re-examined on the behalf of the complainants. To the fourteenth interrogatory saith that he hath heard that for every signpost of the inns in Shaftesbury 4*d.* is paid to the use of the Countess of Pembroke. And saith that all the inns are in the High Street in Salisbury Way. And this deponent saith that the house called the Sign of the Lamb is the town land and this deponent saith he knoweth of nothing that the Lamb payeth but hath heard of 4*d.* for his signpost as is said before.

John Lush of Shaftesbury in the county of Dorset, labourer, aged 80 years or near thereabouts, sworn and examined. To the twelfth interrogatory saith the courts were kept in the old Guildhall before the new was built which this deponent thinketh was about fifty years since.

Robert Combe formerly deposed and examined on the part of the com-plainants and now produced on the part of the defendants. To the thirty-seventh interrogatory saith that he knoweth that one Gore whom he conceiveth to be Nicholas Gore in the interrogatory did on Midsummer Eve last was twelve months or two years, which of them he now remembereth not, require this deponent to proclaim in the town of Shafton that none should pitch any sheep pens or pen any sheep the day following being Midsummer day in the street at Shafton where usually sheep pens had been formerly placed, which street this deponent conceiveth to be called Bleke Street, on pain and pill should fall thereon, but should pen their sheep in a close between the Angel and St. Rombles upon which proclamation there was no blow given to his knowledge but some little brawling. The which proclamation this deponent (being then the Countess of Pembroke's bailiff, servant, or deputy), did openly make in the said town on Midsummer Eve aforesaid accordingly at three several places where the pens were setting up. And this deponent doth not in all the time of his remembrance know of any sheep fair to be kept in the said close but he hath heard it reported that there have been formerly a sheep fair kept there.

Nicholas Cooper formerly examined *ex parte querentis* and now produced *ex parte defendentis*. To the eleventh interrogatory he saith that he knoweth the new Guildhall within the said borough and hath known the same by the space of twenty-eight years last past or thereabouts, the which hall as he hath credibly heard was built at the charge of the town about fifty years since. And the mayor and commonalty have had the rents and profits thereof and have used to repair the same during all the time aforesaid.

To the twelfth interrogatory he saith that he knoweth certain shops called Chapman's standings, and a plot of void ground where four tanners use to stand the market days and knoweth also the burgage wherein William Warmington now dwelleth, all which are the inheritance of the said mayor and burgesses who received the rents thereof, and they or their assigns use to repair the same all the time of this deponent's remembrance.

To the thirteenth interrogatory he saith that he knoweth the corn market within the said borough . . . and further saith that there is a fair building made with timber and covered with lead over some part of the said corn market, repaired also at the charge of the said mayor and burgesses. And there is also at the top of the said building a bell to ring when the market beginneth which hath been by all the time of this deponent's remembrance reputed to be the inheritance of the said mayor and burgesses.

John Moores of Shafton in the county of Dorset, shoemaker, aged three score and seven years or thereabouts sworn and examined. To the twenty-eighth interrogatory he saith there is usually brought into the market place there on market days sometimes forty carts of corn, sometimes more, sometimes less, besides divers horse loads of corn brought thither also to be sold. And he never knew any toll to be paid for any corn sold there. And he further saith that there is usually brought to every market there more corn to be sold than will land within the compass of the said corn market house and the circuit of the channel of the market place there.

To the twenty-ninth interrogatory he saith that he knoweth a place within the said borough called Goldhill and that there is used to be sold weekly on Saturdays rother cattle, sheep, and swine.

To the thirty-first, thirty-second, and thirty-third interrogatory he saith that one Nicholas Gore or his assigns hath of late time set up on the market days divers stalls and standings in sundry places within the said borough where none have used to be set up before the said Gore's intermeddling with the profit of the said market, that is to say, four standings on the east side of the new Guildhall in the corn market place, and four more on the west side of the said Guildhall, and two standings more by the Fish Cross to sell salt in, and three or four glovers' standings against the Guildhall, the which stalls and standings so erected by the said Gore are a great annoyance to the corn market there and to buyers and sellers of corn and victual there and a straitening unto the usual travelling way through the said market and dangerous for travellers and a hindrance to the market men there. And saith also that complaint hath been made to the mayor for erecting the same by those that were grieved therewith and that thereupon the said mayor hath caused some of them to be taken down.

Thomas Longman of Shafton aforesaid, petty chapman, aged fifty years and upwards, sworn and examined. To the thirty-sixth interrogatory he saith that Nicholas Gore in the interrogatory named and one Hopkins, his deputy or assign, took from this deponent at several times by force six knives and a pair of playing cards because this deponent did refuse to pay him rent for his standing in the market under the pentice of one Weare to whom he this deponent paid rent for the same, and hath heard that the said Nicholas Gore, his deputies or assigns, have exacted toll for corn and toll for cheese and butter and of such as sell candles, roots, besoms, ironwares, and other goods to the great clamour and grudge of the country. And this deponent hath seen the said Gore himself take away by force upon a market day certain ironwares from a smith which stood in the said market to sell the same.

10. A PETITION FOR A NEW ALEHOUSE IN STAFFORDSHIRE, 1623

[Staffordshire County Record Office, Quarter Sessions Rolls, Jas. I, Roll 73; nos. 45 and 46]

11 August 1623

FORASMUCH as the port way leading from Newport, as also from Stafford to Coventry, is a great travelled way from the county of Chester to London and especially for wains, carts, carriages, and droves, and that there is no convenient victualling house in the said way between Hednesford the one way and Norton the other way in the county of Stafford to Minworth in the county of Warwick by reason of the suppression of Henry Hanson, who for his lewd and ill behaviour hath been suppressed, and that a victualling house, in or near that place, is very needful for such travellers; and whereas also one Thomas Stanley of Nether Stonnal, within the parish of Shenstone, yeoman, being a freeholder, and having a convenient dwelling house adjoining to the said port way near Thornes, and closes and grounds to the same very necessary for such receipt; and he being descended of good parentage, and he and his family having always been of honest life and conversation is now willing (if by your worships' favour he may be thereunto licensed) to keep victualling; we whose names are underwritten knowing the premises to be true do make bold to commend the same to your worships' consideration.
[Five signatures and three marks.]

Thos. Stanley admitted to victual for a whole year; the said Thos. (£10), Henry Stanley of Thornes, husbandman, Edward Norris of Stonnal, husbandman (£5 each).

11. AULNAGE PAYMENTS FOR KNITTED STOCKINGS, 1626

[P.R.O., E134, 2 Chas. I, Mich. 38. Exchequer Depositions by Commission]

[A selection of the depositions made in the Court of Exchequer in a suit between Frances, Duchess of Richmond and Lennox, complainant, and Thomas Dawson and Ambrose Appleby, defendants]

RICHARD WALKER of Warmfield, Yorkshire, yeoman, aged 44 years or thereabouts . . . deposeth as followeth. To the first interrogatory he saith that he doth and did know divers and sundry persons that do trade and deal for woollen stockings within the county of York, viz. Mr. William Power of Richmond, Mr. John Metcalfe of the same, Mr. Matthew Bellamy of the same, Henry Atkinson of the same, Cuthbert Cowling, younger, of the same, Ambrose Appleby of Barnard Castle within the county of Durham, William Noffe and Christopher Man of Doncaster, and divers others, and this examinate saith that the said persons or the most of them do send their said stockings to the City of London and to divers other places to be sold, and further saith that the said persons have heretofore to his knowledge paid subsidy for the same, and that he this deponent hath been a collector of the said subsidy for about six years together before these two years last past expired. And this examinate saith that the duties of the said subsidy for the said stockings, when he this deponent was collector thereof, was letten for Richmond to Mr. William Power of the same for three years together at £21 by year and had been formerly letten to him at £22, by year, and that after those three years or thereabout the said traders for stockings did pay after the rate of 20d. the pack.

To the second he saith that in Northampton and Norwich about eight years ago the traders for knit hose and stockings have made composition for aulnage of stockings with Captain Carpenter and the aulnager of the counties, but for what rates he doth not know.

Charles Sanderson of Barnard Castle within the county of Durham, yeoman, aged 52 years or thereabouts, sworn and examined, deposeth as followeth. To the second he saith that the defendants are dealers and traders for woollen stockings, but do not knit or make the same but buyeth them to sell again. And saith further that he was by and privy when the said Thomas Dawson and Ambrose Appleby, the defendants, did agree together that the said Ambrose should buy stockings for the said Thomas Dawson upon an allowance made from the said Thomas Dawson to the said Ambrose of 6d.

for buying of every dozen of stockings, at which agreement making the said Ambrose became servant to the said Thomas by covenant in writing whereof this deponent was witness.

Thomas Raine of Barnard Castle within the county of Durham, yeoman, aged 44 years or thereabouts, sworn and examined, deposeth as followeth. To the tenth he saith that he never knew any allowance given by any knitters or makers of stockings to the buyers thereof, but saith that sometimes he himself hath paid to William Power, gent., subsidy and allowance of aulnage for such stockings as his wife, servants, or other workers for him have knitted or wrought when he sold the same to the said Mr. Power.

12. THE MARKETING OF CORN IN NORFOLK, 1631 [?]

[Walter Rye, *State Papers relating to Musters, Beacons, Shipmoney, etc. in Norfolk*, Norwich, 1907, pp. 180–7]

Reasons against general Sending of Corn to the Markets in the Champion Parts of Norfolk.

1. The county of Norfolk is an island enclosed on the south side towards Suffolk with the river of Waveney running to Yarmouth, and the lesser Ouse passing by Lynn, on the north side with the main sea; and aboundeth by these means with havens and hithes, places of exportation and importation.
2. That part of it towards the sea, and much of the rest westward is champion, the other part towards Suffolk woodland and pasture ground.
3. The woodland and pasture part is sustained chiefly by grazing, by dairies and rearing of cattle, yet it is able both to maintain itself with corn and to afford an overplus to their neighbours of Suffolk.
4. But the inhabitants of that part being many of them graziers, and a great many handicraftsmen, which live by dressing and combing of wool, carding, spinning, and weaving, etc., and the towns there commonly very great, consisting of such like people, and other artificers, with many poor, and none of them all ordinarily having any corn but from the market, it is of necessity that the markets there be furnished with corn to supply them, and the tilth masters do it diligently, as having no other ordinary means of venting their corn, the outlades being far from them, and their quantities of corn so small, as the merchant never seeks unto them for it.
5. The champion part is of another nature, consisting wholly in effect of corn and sheep, which by particular course of husbandry there used, do maintain each other, and this part thereby affordeth such plenty of corn as every town is able generally to feed itself and divers others.
6. For there is commonly about 12, 16, or 20 ploughs in one town, and by estimation about 2,000, 3,000, and 5,000 coombs of corn growing every year

in one of them, and the corn of many several men in one year is much more than the markets adjoining can carry away in one whole year.

7. The inhabitants of the towns in these parts are generally but of three sorts. 1. Tilth masters that have corn of their own growing and sell to others. 2. Labourers that buy it at an under price of them with whom they work. 3. Poor people that are relieved by good orders in every town.

8. If the labourer and poor man should be drawn to market, it would be the loss of his day's work, an occasion of spending somewhat that that his wife and children should want at least 12d. a week loss to him, for being poor he can take but little at once, and must go the oftener and a means to season him with drinking, disorder, and idleness, which vices are already too common and unsuppressable, and where he hath now corn at home upon trust, or by agreement for work, he must then carry ready money in hand, which he commonly wants, and pay dearer for it, than he might have had it at home.

9. On the other side, if the owner or tilth master be compelled to bring any notable quantity of corn to the markets of this part, he is like to find no buyer, and so loseth the labour of himself, his horses and cart, and his servants, and the opportunity of his tillage and husbandry at home; he is in hazard to pay dear for a place to chamber it till the next market day; then he brings it forth as unprofitably, and in all likelihood many days after, not without a continual attendance for selling it, and some or other expense, all which in reason must raise the price.

10. Nor are there granaries in any market, save Lynn and Burnham, sufficient to keep the corn that shall be brought and unsold.

11. If there be any buyers, they are commonly but such as dwell in the market town, shopkeepers, poor handicraftsmen, and poor people that scarcely carry away four coombs in a market day; for the bakers of the town rather choose to buy their provision aforehand in the villages, as they have credit for payment.

12. The maltsters dwell for the most part in the villages, and buy their corn of their neighbours about them, saving thereby the charge of carrying it to and from the market, which is at a middle rate esteemed, about 12d. the coomb, and may therefore afford the malt so much the cheaper.

13. If, therefore, the market by likelihood cannot utter one man's corn, all the rest of that part shall want means of utterance, and though some small sums of money were to be had at the market, yet would it undo the husbandman and farmer, who cannot attend to make his market by delay and retailing, but must sell so in gross, as he may have his rent against the day, or forfeit his lease, and other greater sums for his continual occasions. And so also must the owners themselves.

14. If corn be brought to market (former experience has already so satisfied us), that it cannot almost be prevented but deceit may be committed in the buying thereof by some that need not, or others that need and buy for others, whereas every town knows their own poor and their wants.

15. These and other inconveniences being long ago foreseen, it hath been the

custom of these parts for many hundreds of years past, to utter their corn at the havens, hithes, and landing places upon the sea and rivers' sides, as the proper market there; and this custom is to this day testified by another notorious custom of this country.

16. That because the venting of the corn is by sea and water carriage, whereby it suffers hurt and diminution; therefore according to the censure of St. Gregory Epist. lib. 1, cap. 42. *Nantae iuxta consuetudinem super accipiunt quod minui ipsi in navibus attestantur.* The seller is tied to deliver 21 coomb for the 20 coomb and vi coombs for every six score to recompense the hurt and diminution.

17. If corn be sold at the market, the custom holdeth not for there is no detriment by the carriage or delivery thereof.

18. It were very inconvenient that they which dwell within four or five miles of the seaside, and have used to deliver their corn there, should be constrained to convey it 6, 7, or 8 miles to a market up into the country, when perhaps the buyer must have it brought ten or 12 miles back to the coast to be transmitted to some other part of the kingdom that needs it.

19. It is in a manner impossible that the market town in the champion part should carry away the corn there growing, for there are about 200 towns in that part and scarce a dozen markets, whereof many of them are not able (as is said before) to carry away the corn that some one man in most of those towns may spare; many corn masters and of great tilths having of their own growing some 500, some 600, some 800, some 1,000, some 1,200, some more.

20. To constrain the tilthmen of the champion to carry their corn to the markets of the woodland parts were very grievous, their horses being ordinarily very weak (for that their tilth is easy), the distance great, and the ways commonly bad. Besides it makes a breach and distraction into the policy of former times, that appointed every hundred a market to supply it with common necessaries.

21. If they of the woodland will (as the patriarchs did) fetch it constantly where it is to be had at the market of the champion, it will no doubt be brought thither abundantly; but they shall find the carriage of it so chargeable from thence (if the quantity be much) as that they will rather fetch it 40 or 50 miles by water, than 12 or 15 by land.

22. Those parts of the coast of Norfolk having divers ports and havens use much trade and commerce with Newcastle for salt and coals both summer and winter, and sail about 60 or 70 ships yearly to Iceland, and provide their salt from Newcastle for that voyage, and usually carry great quantities of barley and malt to Newcastle about 500 coomb every spring tide, viz. every fortnight, and should lose much by sailing empty and without freight. And if that transporting to Newcastle were hindered, both the duties and customs to his Majesty would diminish, by disabling the fishing voyage to Iceland, and the county also receive much prejudice for want of wonted supply of salt and coals, and the kingdom suffer in the decrease of shipping and mariners.

23. If the markets of the city of Norwich, or of some of the woodland parts

have at any time been unfurnished (towards whom the hundred of Flegg afford very great supply, seated betwixt Yarmouth and Norwich) the magistrates and justices there might send their badgers (as out of Essex, Suffolk, Northamptonshire, the Isle of Ely, Cambridge, and Peterborough, many come into these parts in a time of dearth) to the principal corn masters of the champion, or as the city of London do their factors to the coasts, then every man's barn and granary would upon the sound thereof be open, and the carriage thence by sea is neither far nor uneasy. Besides in former times when the parts about Norwich and others have complained of their want of corn, and would sue for a stop and stay of corn in the plentiful parts from exportation to other parts within the kingdom, the justices have accordingly (to the charge of others that came to buy, and loss of their time and travail) stayed and restrained the passing away of corn for a fortnight or more and yet in the end never received any answer or heard any more from the parts pretending want.

24. About 12 years since there was about 30,000*li*. by estimation of outlandish gold brought over and taken for corn transported that winter between Lynn and Wells inclusively, when corn was within the price limited by the statute, and yet the country and kingdom sufficiently served, and if that had been carried to markets thereabouts the hundred part thereof would not have been sold, and the rest in likelihood much impaired.

25. It appeareth by the Black Book of the Exchequer that the king's tenants (as other men's did) anciently paid their rents in corn and victuals till Henry I (having occasion to use a great sum of money for his wars in France) constrained them to render it in money, which at that time was so grievous unto them (not knowing how to get it for their corn) as they brought their plough shares to the court, and there did offer them up, complaining that the course of tillage was overthrown; it is to be doubted that now the alteration of the manner of sale of the corn may cause much of the arable ground in those parts to be converted to pasture for sheep or other cattle (for the county of Norfolk is excepted out of the Stat. 39 Eliz. and so doubtless would it have been from carrying much corn to the market of the champion part, if there had been a statute touching that matter).

26. Moreover, it is conceived there is no statute to enforce the tilth masters to bring their corn to the markets, more than the sheep masters their wool, muttons, and lambs, or the grazier his oxen and bullocks, or those that keep dairies their butter and cheese. And although there was a book of orders set forth by Queen Elizabeth, 2nd of January, 1586, commanding generally that corn should be brought to market, yet because the chiefest scope thereof appeared to be but provision for the poor, the Justices of Peace of this county of Norfolk assembled themselves and took such course that (according to her Majesty's pleasure) the poor were provided for at home, without such general carrying of corn to the market (as appeareth by the articles then agreed upon) and that course was never questioned nor reproved; for it appears by Fogusses Case in Plodens Comment, fol. 88b, that if a man

perform the intent of the law, though he follow not the words, yet the law is satisfied.

27. Notwithstanding therefore these general orders, this particular part of the kingdom never changed their ancient use in this behalf; nor is it known that any market town ever complained to any justices of these parts of being unserved with corn.

28. So that all things prudently considered, and the practices of fraudulent and lewd persons duly punished or prevented, the ancient way that hath been in use to this day for every man to sell his corn and deliver it at the places most convenient for him, is so necessary both for this part of the country and of the kingdom itself, as it cannot be altered without great inconveniency.

29. For the alteration may bring a great extremity upon the maritime parts of Lincolnshire, Yorkshire, and towards the north, and upon the fenland parts, which have much (if not most) of their corn from the coasts of Norfolk, as the breast that nourisheth them, and so also the woodland part of Suffolk bordering upon Norfolk, nor will the city of London be pleased to seek and take their provisions at the market towns in the champion.

30. In the year 1622, being a time of great scarcity, the justices essayed and tried (by the causing of corn to be brought to the markets) how profitable and good effect it would produce, but they have found that course too toilsome to the corn master, and fruitless to the poor, as they wholly abandoned the same, and appointed every town to provide for itself at home.

31. So in the last dearth, 1630, the Justices appointed some markets (seated between the grazing and corn parts) to be served, but the corn masters could not there sell, but were enforced to hire room and chambering for their corn to their great charge, and after to recarry the same to their own houses by the appointment of the justices, who then considered, concluded, and ordered, that every town should provide for itself and their own poor at home.

32. And in the said dearth, 1630, the Lord Mayor of London appointed every ward to provide for itself and their own poor, so those that wanted were furnished from the market, at others' cares. In Norfolk where corn abounds the inhabitants of the better and abler sort provide in a dearth for the poor in the market of their own town. Thus the course of the government of the chief city of the kingdom and of the justices of this county agree in one and the same good for the poor.

33. All that hath been said, being duly considered, it is humbly prayed that the corn parts of Norfolk may be left to their wonted use and liberties for selling of their corn: and in time of scarcity and dearth the justices there will not fail to provide corn for the poor at home in their own town, and thereby not only prevent their insurrection or affamishment, but supply them with corn at a very easy and under-rate.

13. ALEHOUSES, 1632

[Donald Lupton, *London and the Country Carbonadoed and Quartred into Severall Characters*, London, 1632, pp. 127–31]

Alehouses

IF these houses have a box bush, or an old post, it is enough to show their profession. But if they be graced with a sign complete, it's a sign of good custom. In these houses you shall see the history of Judith, Susanna, Daniel in the lions' den, or Dives and Lazarus painted upon the wall. It may be reckoned a wonder to see or find the house empty, for either the parson, churchwarden, or clerk, or all, are doing some church or court business usually in this place. They thrive best where there are fewest. It is the host's chiefest pride to be speaking of such a gentleman or such a gallant that was here, and will be again ere long. Hot weather and thunder and want of company are the hostess's grief, for then her ale sours. Your drink usually is very young, two days old. Her chiefest wealth is seen if she can have one brewing under another. If either the hostess, or her daughter, or maid will kiss handsomely at parting, it is a good shoeing-horn or birdlime to draw the company thither again the sooner. She must be courteous to all, though not by nature, yet by her profession; for she must entertain all, good and bad, tag, and rag, cut, and long tail. She suspects tinkers and poor soldiers most, not that they will not drink soundly, but that they will not pay lustily. She must keep touch with three sorts of men, that is: the malt man, the baker, and the justice's clerks. She is merry, and half made upon Shrove Tuesday, May days, feast days, and Morris dances. A good ring of bells in the parish helps her to many a tester. She prays the parson may not be a puritan. A bagpiper and a puppet play brings her in birds that are flush. She defies a wine tavern as an upstart, outlandish fellow, and suspects the wine to be poisoned. Her ale, if new, looks like a misty morning, all thick. Well, if her ale be strong, her reckoning right, her house clean, her fire good, her face fair, and the town great or rich, she shall seldom or never sit without chirping birds to bear her company, and at the next churching or christening, she is sure to be rid of two or three dozen of cakes and ale by gossiping neighbours.

14. RISKS IN THE WHOLESALE TOBACCO TRADE, 1634

[P.R.O., HCA 13/51, f. 178. High Court of Admiralty Examinations]

[Deposition of Barnabas Cutts of the parish of St. Andrew's, Holborn, merchant tailor, aged 42 years, testifying on behalf of the defendant in the case of Cantrell versus Smalwood]

24 *Octobris*, 1634

... *deponit* that *in annis Domini* 1631 and 1632 the best sort of Virginia tobacco in leaf did yield and was sold for a very low rate and price, viz. for 5¾*d.* and 6*d.* per pound clear of all charges; and the freight of that kind of tobacco came to 2*d.* per pound, and the custom at 4*d.* per pound, which made many merchants and others that had Virginia tobaccos brought to this port of London in those years for their accompt to leave the same in the custom house and never fetch it away, because it would not yield so much as would pay for the freight, custom, and other charges due to be paid for the same. The premises he knoweth to be true for that in the said years this deponent, being a broker employed by merchants and others to sell tobaccos and other goods for them, did sell Virginia tobacco for the rates aforesaid for divers merchants and others, and namely in the year 1631 he sold for one Reginald Parker, a linen draper in Tower Street, 5 hogsheads of Virginia tobacco in leaf unto one Gabriel Bonner, a grocer over against St. Sepulchre's church, for 6*d.* per pound clear of all charges, and for Mr. Michael Herring, a merchant dwelling in Walbrook, 4 or 5 hogsheads of Virginia tobacco in leaf unto Mr. Robert Tickner, a grocer dwelling in Redcross Street, for 5*d.* per pound, and *in anno* 1632 he sold for Captain John Preene 48 hogsheads of Virginia tobacco in leaf unto the foresaid Robert Tickner for 5¾*d.* per pound. But how that sort of tobacco was sold *in anno domini* 1630 he remembereth not . . .

15. A SCHEME TO MAKE THE RIVER SOAR NAVIGABLE FROM LEICESTER TO THE TRENT, 1634

[*Rymer's Foedera*, XIX, London, 1732, pp. 597–9]

A Grant enabling Thomas Skipwith to make the River Soar portable for boats and barges to the Town of Leicester.

CHARLES, etc. To all to whom these presents shall come, greeting.

Whereas our well beloved subject Thomas Skipwith, gentleman, by his humble petition hath shewed unto us, that our county of Leicester, being a champion country and destitute of such supplies for fuel, as are abundant in other places, is constrained to fetch their coals into the most parts thereof, at a distance of eighteen or twenty miles, and that the town of Leicester, which is the centre of that county, hath a river dischannelling itself into the great river of Trent, which with some good cost and charges, and without inconvenience to any, might be made fit for carrying of boats and vessels, which would be of good use and much ease and advantage to that county and other adjoining counties, as well for the furnishing thereof with such necessary commodities as they stood in need of, as for the supplying the wants of other adjoining counties with such provisions and commodities which they might well spare, which said petition, and the suggestions and matters therein contained, we were pleased to refer to the consideration of our right trusty and right well beloved cousins, Henry, Earl of Huntingdon and Henry, Earl of Stamford, who calling unto them some of the town of Leicester and others of the county, they might understand what could be alleged either for or against the said design of the petitioner, that such proceedings might be held therein, as might conduce to the common good of that and other adjoining counties, whereupon the said Earls of Huntingdon and Stamford, having duly considered of the premises, and having called and had conference with some of the inhabitants of the town of Leicester and others concerning the same, did find them inclinable and willing to have the said work effected, and did thereupon certify us, that they conceived that the purpose of the said petitioner, if it might be brought to pass, would be of good consequence both to the town and county of Leicester. We, therefore, being willing to promote and advance the good designs and endeavours of our loving subjects, and especially of such as shall tend to a public good, and finding that the said work is to be undertaken and done at the proper costs and charges of the petitioner, and such as shall voluntarily adjoin and assist him therein, and being graciously inclined, as well to favour and further the said work, as to provide for the petitioner that he may receive a meet and just recompense for his labour, disbursements, and expenses to be undergone therein.

Know ye, therefore, that we for the reasons and considerations aforesaid, of our especial grace, certain knowledge, and mere motion, have given and granted and for us, our heirs, and successors, do give and grant unto the said Thomas Skipwith, his heirs, and assigns, full and free licence, power, privilege, and authority by these presents, that he the said Thomas Skipwith, his heirs, and assigns, at his and their own proper costs and charges, shall or may make the said river of Soar portable for boats and other vessels from the river of Trent to the town of Leicester as aforesaid. And, for that end and purpose, shall or may make, erect, and set up such and so many locks, engines, structures, and devices in the said river of Soar, and on the banks thereof, as he or they shall think fit, and shall or may use, employ, and set on work such and so many artificers, workmen, and labourers, as he or they shall find meet for the digging, cleansing, scouring, and making the said river portable and passable for boats and other vessels, and bottoms of competent bulk and burthen, for the carrying and conveying of coals, fuel, and other commodities, as well from the said river of Trent unto the said town of Leicester, as from the said town of Leicester to the said river of Trent, as occasion shall from time to time require, he the said Thomas Skipwith, his heirs, and assigns, first compounding and agreeing with the several lords, owners, or occupiers of the said river, or of any mill or mills thereupon being, or of any the land or soil on either side of the same river, upon reasonable recompense and satisfaction to be in that behalf made and given, according to the loss or damage they do or shall sustain by the premises.

And further, of our especial grace, certain knowledge, and mere motion, we do for us, our heirs, and successors, give and grant unto the said Thomas Skipwith, his heirs, and assigns, that when and so soon as the said work shall be at his and their proper costs and charges effected and brought to pass in such sort as the said river of Soar shall be made capable and portable of boats, vessels, and other bottoms for the carrying and recarrying of coals, fuel, and other commodities as aforesaid, that then it shall and may be lawful to and for the said Thomas Skipwith, his heirs, and assigns, to require, demand, and receive, have, and take to his and their own proper use, of, for, and upon every boat, vessel, or bottom that shall be used or employed upon the said river, for such carriage and recarriage as aforesaid of the owner, user, or occupier thereof, a reasonable recompense, sum, or allowance of and for the same, according to the bulk and burthen of the said boats, vessels, or bottoms, or otherwise as the said Thomas Skipwith, his heirs, and assigns shall compound and agree in that behalf, without any accompt, rent, recompense, or other thing to be answered, made, paid, or done to us, our heirs, or successors for the same, other than as hereafter in these presents is reserved . . .

Rendering and paying, and the said Thomas Skipwith, for himself, his heirs, and assigns, doth covenant, promise, and grant, to and with us, our heirs, and successors by these presents, to yield and pay unto us, our heirs, and successors yearly and every year, one full and just tenth part of all such clear gain, profit, and advantage, as he or they shall yearly raise, receive, have, or make of or by the said river, or of or by means of the passage of any boats, vessels, or bottoms thereupon, over and above his and their yearly costs and charges necessarily to be from time to time disbursed and expended, in and about the making, keeping, repairing, and maintaining of the said work, and other premises . . .

Witness ourself at
Westminster, the tenth day of March
Per Breve de Privato Sigillo.

16. DEPARTURE POINTS OF COASTAL VESSELS, 1637

[*Works of John Taylor, the Water Poet*, 2nd collection, Spenser Society, XIV, 1873, pp. 23–4]

The Carriers Cosmographie, 1637

. . . Here followeth certain directions for to find out ships, barks, hoys, and passage boats that do come to London from the most parts and places by sea within the King's dominions, either of England, Scotland, or Ireland

A HOY doth come from Colchester in Essex, to Smarts quay, near Billingsgate, by which goods may be carried from London to Colchester weekly. He that will send to Ipswich in Suffolk, or Lynn in Norfolk, let him go to Dice quay, and there his turn may be served.

The ships from Kingston upon Hull (or Hull) in Yorkshire do come to Raphs quay, and to Porters quay.

At Galley quay, passage for men, and carriage for goods may be had from London to Berwick.

At Chesters quay, shipping may be had from Ireland, from Poole, from Plymouth, from Dartmouth and Weymouth.

At Sabbs Dock, a hoy or bark is to be had from Sandwich or Dover in Kent. A hoy from Rochester, Margate in Kent, or Faversham and Maidstone doth come to St. Katherines Dock.

Shipping from Scotland are to be found at the Armitage or Hermitage below St. Katherines.

From Dunkirk at the custom house quay.

From most parts of Holland or Zealand, pinks or shipping may be had at the Brewhouses in St. Katherines.

At Lion quay twice almost in every 24 hours, or continually, are tideboats or wherries that pass to and from betwixt London and the towns of Deptford, Greenwich, Woolwich, Erith, and Greenhithe in Kent, and also boats are to be had that every tide do carry goods and passengers betwixt London and Rainham, Purfleet, and Grays in Essex.

At Billingsgate are every tide to be had barges, lighthorsmen, tiltboats, and wherries, from London to the towns of Gravesend and Milton in Kent, or to any other place within the said bounds, and (as weather and occasions may serve) beyond, or further.

Passage Boats and Wherries that do carry Passengers and Goods from London, and back again thither East or West above London Bridge

To Bull Wharf (near Queenhithe) there doth come and go great boats twice or thrice every week, which boats do carry goods betwixt London and Kingston upon Thames, also thither doth often come a boat from Colebrooke, which serveth those parts for such purposes.

Great boats that do carry and recarry passengers and goods to and fro betwixt London and the towns of Maidenhead, Windsor, Staines, Chertsey, with other parts in the counties of Surrey, Berkshire, Middlesex, and Buckinghamshire, do come every Monday and Thursday to Queenhithe, and they do go away upon Tuesdays and Thursdays.

The Reading boat is to be had at Queenhithe weekly.

All those that will send letters to the most parts of the habitable world, or to any parts of our King of Great Britain's dominions, let them repair to the general postmaster, Thomas Withering, at his house in Sherburne Lane, near Abchurch.

17. A CHECK ON LOCAL FOOD STOCKS, 1638
[P.R.O., CO 1/9, no. 101, I]

Southampton.

Whereas there hath been a warrant directed from the High Sheriff of this county unto me, one of the constables of the hundred of Mansbridge, bearing date the 24th day of this instant April, 1638, with express command to make a diligent search for, and a stay of, all such provision of victual (viz. wheat, peas, butter, beer, cheese, bacon, and the like) that is to be transported unto New England, and also, being required to make return what hath been done in the premises unto one of his Majesty's justices of the peace, next unto the place where any such provision shall be found, upon which search being diligently made the provision that I have found is as followeth, dated the 25th of April, *anno* 1638.

By me James Alexander, Constable.

In primis I found in the house of John Dummer of Swathling six bushels of oaten meal or thereabouts with one brewlock of beer containing 5 bushels of malt or thereabouts, the which was (as the wife of the aforesaid John Dummer said) for the provision of her son, Thomas Dummer, his going to New England.

Secondly, I found in the house of Thomas Dummer of Chickenwell one hogshead of beef containing one ox, the which was for the provision of his brother, Richard Dummer, who was to go for New England.

Moreover, I found in the house of Stephen Dummer of Townehill two hogsheads of beef, five hogsheads of meal, four hogsheads of bacon and malt together [with] two firkins of beer and six cheeses which was for the provision of the aforesaid Stephen, his wife, and children in their voyage for New England.

These goods have been by me stayed till Sir John Oglander, High Sheriff of this county, may be farther informed of their honours' pleasure therein.

(By me James Alexander, constable.)

18. THE FAIRS OF EAST YORKSHIRE, 1641

[Henry Best, *Rural Economy in Yorkshire in 1641, being the Farming and Account Books of Henry Best of Elmeswell in the East Riding*, ed. C. B. Robinson, Surtees Soc., XXXIII, 1857, pp. 112–14]

Of the Chief Fairs hereabouts and their Several Customs, as also what Goods and Commodities have the best Vent or may be the cheapest bought at each of these ensuing Fairs.

THE first fair of note hereabouts is Little Driffield fair on Easter Monday. On St. Helen day, the 3rd of May, there is a fair at Weeton. On St. Helen day, the 3rd of May, there is also a fair at Brands Burton in Holderness. At these three fairs handsome lean beasts, lean wethers, old ewes, and the most timely sort of lambs have very good vent, because that Holderness men come in and buy up such for stocking of their feeding grounds. Fat horses, and especially geldings, go also well of.

On Wednesday in Easter week there is a little fair at Beverley. Beverley great fair, called the Cross fair, is said to begin about the 7th of May. But look in your calendar for John Beverley, and it beginneth always on that day. Thither the Londoners send their wares by water, and thither come the York grocers and others, about the day of John Beverley or day afore, to furnish themselves with such commodities as they want. The week before Holy Thursday week is called wholesale week, and Ascension Day, or Holy Thursday, is the great fair day, on which day the Londoners go most of them away. Yet will not this fair be fully ended till the Saturday night after. The first horse fair is the Wednesday fortnight before Ascension day; there is always a little show and horses bought on Tuesday night about watering time; there is another horse fair the Wednesday sennight afore Holy Thursday, but that is of little or no account. Then there is a great horse fair again on Holy Thursday eve, and they that bought horses at the first fair will have carried them up, and be down again to buy more at this fair. There are many horses sold also on Holy Thursday, but mares are in no request at these fairs, and geldings go the best of when they are very fat.

On Monday in Whitsun week there is a fair at Little Driffield, to which Nafferton and Lowthorpe men come with clubs to keep good order and rule the fair. They have a piper to play before them, and the like doings is at the latter Lady Day in harvest.

On Trinity Monday there is a fair at South Cave, at which are many sheep bought and sold. Horses also go well of there, and especially mares, because it is near to Walling fen, the great common. And if a mare chance to fall lame, they can put her to the common and breed of her.

On St. John Baptist or Midsummer day there is a great fair at Beverley; at this fair horses and fat beasts go of indifferent well; this day is also a rule for all this countryside concerning the price of wool.

On St. Peter's day there is a fair at Frodingham, at which fat beasts go of indifferent well, and also fat young calves and horses.

On Mary Magdalen's day, the 22nd of July, there is a fair at Whitgift, and another on Maudlen Hill in Holderness.

On St. James's day there is a fair at Doncaster, and another at Pocklington. Most of this side do use to drape out the worst of their lambs and send to Pocklington fair. I have known four lambs bought for 11d., and the seller gave the buyer one penny again. I have heard of lambs bought there for 2d. apiece, and few lambs are brought hither which exceed the rate of two shillings.

Little Driffield two latter fairs, called Lady Day fairs, are the one upon *Assump[tio] Mar[iæ]* about the 15th of August, and the other *super Nativ-*

[*itatem*] *Mar*[*iæ*] about the 8th of September, where one may be furnished with dishes, earthen vessels, scythes, and hardware, harvest gloves, and all sorts of pedlar wares. Horses do sometimes go indifferent well of here, and fat kine, and calves, with other fat goods. There are but just three weeks and three days betwixt these two fairs.

Malton horse fair begins now of late three days before St. Matthew day. The chief shows are the day before St. Matthew's Eve, and on St. Matthew's Eve. The shows begin about nine of the clock in the mornings, and about three of the clock in the afternoon. They ride the horses upon the lands on the north-west side of the town. On St. Matthew day, which is the 21st of September, most of the horses go away after three of the clock. The beast fair is not till Michael Arch[angel] day, the 29th of September.

On St. Matthew Day, the 21st of September, there is also a fair at Frodingham in Holderness. On St. Lawrence, the 10th of August, there is a fair at Kilham. On the 10th of October there is a fair at Bridlington. On St. Luke day there is a fair at Hunmanby. On St. John day, the 25th of October, being the same day sennight after St. Luke, there is a fair at Beverley, at which fat beasts used to go well of.

On All Saints' day, the first of November, there is a fair at Kilham, to which great store of sucking foals and other young foals are brought to be sold. Here also do we sell all our old horses, after that they are past doing us service. All sorts of sheep go well of here, and especially old ewes and hogs. So that it is a rule for the country till the next spring.

19. THE MARKETING OF PRODUCE FROM A FARM ON THE YORKSHIRE WOLDS, 1641

[Henry Best, *Rural Economy in Yorkshire in 1641, being the Farming and Account Books of Henry Best of Elmeswell in the East Riding*, ed. C. B. Robinson, Surtees Soc., XXXIII, 1857, pp. 26–7, 99–103]

For Tending or Tithing of Lambs

WE usually sell our wool at home, unless it be by chance that we carry some to Beverley on Midsummer day. Those that buy it carry it into the west, towards Leeds, Halifax, and Wakefield. They bring (with them) pack horses, and carry it away in great packs. These wool men come and go continually from clipping time till Michaelmas. Those that have pasture wool sell usually for 10s. and 11s. a stone; and oftentimes, when wool is very dear, for 12s. a stone; but our faugh sheep do not afford so fine a wool, wherefore we seldom sell for above 8s. or 9s. a stone, unless it be by chance when wool is very dear that we reach to 10s. a stone, or very near. Wool men dislike and find great fault with wool that hath much salve or tar in it, and likewise with that which is either black for want of good washing, or else not thoroughly dry; they also find fault with wool that is hairy, and with such fleeces as have many locks thrust into them. . .

For Marketing and Selling of Corn

Barley will usually outsell oats 8*s*. a quarter. Rye will outsell barley hereabouts 7*s*. in a quarter; dodd red massledine (if the wheat be a pubble, proud, and well-skinned corn) will outsell clean rye 12*d*. in a quarter; white wheat massledine will outsell dodd red massledine 6*d*. in a quarter; dodd red wheat and white wheat massledine are oftentimes both at a rate; yet sometimes the wheat will outsell it 6*d*. or 8*d*. in a quarter; grey wheat and long red will outsell dodd red oftentimes 3*s*. and ten groats in a quarter; of which two grey wheat is the more accounted of; white wheat will outsell grey wheat (constantly) half-a-crown or eight groats in a quarter. We sold (this year about a fortnight afore Christmas) oats for 14*s*. a quarter; our best barley for 22*s*. the quarter; clean rye for 27*s*. 6*d*. the quarter; dodd red massledine for 29*s*. 6*d*. the quarter; clean dodd red wheat for 30*s*. the quarter; and the best white wheat was then at 1*l*. 15*s*. a quarter.

Beverley bakers will seldom buy any dodd red wheat for white bread, unless they chance to buy it for mixing with rye and making of rye bread, for it is usually a blea, flinty, wheat; that is, if you bite a corn asunder with your teeth, you shall see that the meal of it is of a darkish, blue, and flinty colour, and maketh nothing so fair and pure bread as doth the white, grey, and long red wheat. Beverley men are altogether for grey wheat and long red, and say that the meal of these is a far whiter and fairer meal than the meal of dodd red; and indeed, grey wheat is a very pure wheat if it be not infected with slain; and so is long red if it be not infected with a wheat called driven wheat; which wheat hath no awns like unto long red, yet oftentimes cometh up amongst it, and hindereth the sale thereof, for it is a very coarse and flinty wheat. White wheat is most in request at Malton, and white wheat massledine is (there) far more desired than dodd red massledine.

Dodd red wheat goeth oftentimes well of at Bridlington, betwixt Martinmas and Christmas, and then do we send a sample of our wheat to the shipmasters (by the salters that go thither), and also the price of our corn, and then, if we can agree, they set down a day; and we send our corn to that quay, or other place assigned; this wheat is carried by shipping to Newcastle and Sunderland. After that we are begun to market, which is about Martinmas or soon after, we send constantly twice a week, viz. always our oats to Beverley on the Wednesday, and oftentimes on the Saturday also. We send our dodd red wheat and massledine usually to Malton market; our barley to Beverley and Pocklington in winter time, and to Malton in summer. We seldom send fewer than eight horseloads to the market at a time, and with them two men, for one man cannot guide the pokes of above four horses. When we send oats to the market, we sack them up in three bushel pokes, and lay six bushels on an horse; when we send wheat, rye, or massledine to market, and also when we send barley, we put it into mette pokes; we are forced to put part of our corn into half quarter sacks, and these we lay on horses that are short coupled and well backed.

Our servants are (in winter time) to be stirring so long afore day that they may be at market before eleven of the clock, or howsoever by eleven at the furthest. On Wednesday, when they go with oats to Beverley, they put their horses into stables that are hard by the market place, where there is hay ready for them against they go in; and there do they pay halfpennies apiece for their horses for their hay and stable room. But in the Saturday market, they have host houses where they dine, and therefore stable room for nothing; unless they call for hay for their horses, and then do they pay for that they call for. Those that buy their corn will sometimes force them to spend a penny or twopence for being beneficial to the house wherein they lodge, and that we willingly allow them again. We allow them also fourpence apiece for their dinners. Norfolk is a great corn soil, and a champion country like unto Yorkshire; there was one man in York that bought 3,000 quarters of barley (this year) all at a time, and brought it hither by shipping; most of it he malted himself, and the rest he sold in the markets; he bought it for 14s. a quarter, whereas we sold ours at the same time for 21s. and 22s. a quarter.

In winter time, when our folks go to Beverley, they are never stirring above two hours before day, because they are soon enough if they get but thither by eleven of the clock. Oats go always well of on Wednesdays and Saturdays in this place, if so be that the Tuesdays and Fridays be calm days, for then do the Lincolnshire men come over to Hull; and to these do Beverley oatmeal men vent and sell a great part of their oatmeal, which they carry and sell again in Brigg market, and other markets thereabouts. When our folks go to Malton, they are usually stirring four hours before day, which is about three of the clock, and then will they be about Grimston by the spring of the day, and at Malton by nine of the clock at the furthest; for in winter time that market is the quickest about nine of the clock, or betwixt nine and ten, because the badgers come far, many of them, wherefore their desire is to buy soon, that they may be going betimes, for fear of being nighted. Good beans are dearer than peas by 12d. or 18d. in a quarter; for when barley is about 20s. and 21s. a quarter, then are peas about 12s. and 12s. 6d. a quarter, and beans about a mark and 14s. a quarter. We oftentimes buy our seed peas at Great Driffield, for change for the Middle and West fields; they are usually dear at Kilham about Candlemas and a week afore, or a fortnight. At St. Helenmass, and so all summer long, when our folks are to go to Beverley market, they go out of our own yard about half an hour after four of the clock; in summer time also they go (most commonly) with each of them six horses, so that when they carry oats, two of them going with twelve horses, they carry nine quarters at a time, for they lay six bushels on an horse, so that four horse load of oats is three quarters. On market days our folks do as on other days, for so soon as they rise they make and give to every two horses a bottle of hay, and that serveth them till their pannells be set on, and what is left is there ready for them against the time they come home. Then, so soon as their pannells are on, and everything fitted, they lead them forth, and look how many each man goeth with, and so many are tied together, each in other's tail; then do they carry one company after another to the garner door, and turning them about with their head towards the gates, all the fellows that are able to carry pokes fall to loading, and in loading they give every horse half his load before that any one be wholly laden. Then one of the boys setteth open the broad gates, and so soon as they are gotten out, shutteth them again; the other folks go usually with them to the Brick wall nook or lane end, till their pokes begin to settle and lie well; then when they come back, they fall to mucking of the stables, and after that to filling of the standhecks, serving and watering of the young calves, if there be any unput forth, serving and watering of their plough horses, and other goods about the yard. The first time that wains were seen (this year) to go to Malton with corn was Saturday, the 30th of April. On Saturday the 21st of May, there were six that came from Agnes Burton, Lowthorpe, and Harpham; they went all night, set down their corn, and took in such things as were bought the Saturday before and left for them, and were met out of Malton before seven of the clock. It is ill going to Malton with draughts, when the fields adjoining to the highway are most of them fough; when our draughts went either to Malton or Hiddisley quarry, look how many went, and they had each of them victuals put up for three meals; for they went forth usually on Friday about four or five of the clock, and went usually as far as Duggleby field, and there loosed and tethered their cattle; and when the pinder had come, they would have given him victuals, and he would have been well pleased. On Saturday the 14th of May, and on Saturday the 21st of May, clean rye was as dear as good dodd red wheat, and dearer than massledine; for clean wheat and clean rye were sold for four nobles a quarter, and massledine somewhat abating of 26s. a quarter: barley was (at the same time) so down at Malton that it would not sell for above 20s. a quarter, and went off the same time at Pocklington at 21s. a quarter; and we had barley (this year) which would not off at Malton at 19s. a quarter, and we carried a sample to Beverley, and sold a score to three Beverley men for twenty pounds. The reason was because barley used to go so well of at Malton that there was seldom any carried to Beverley market from this side of the country. On Wednesday the 1st of June we sold twenty quarters of wheat to a baker in York, and twenty quarters of massledine to other two; for, the king[1] being there, the markets were very quick. In winter also we sold twenty quarters of barley to a York maltster, which was delivered at Cout landing at a day appointed.

[1] Charles arrived at York on 19 March. On 23 April 1642 he went to Hull, to be refused admittance by Sir John Hotham.

20. A CHESHIRE TOWN CONTROLS THE NUMBER OF ITS GROCERS, 1642

[R. Head, *Congleton Past and Present*, Congleton, 1887, p. 61]

[Extract from the Congleton Borough Court Records, 1642.]

WHEREAS Hugh Orratt of Warrington, grocer, threatened to exercise his trade within this borough, though he is no freeman or burgess, and insists on his being admitted a burgess on his own terms; which being taken into consideration at this Hall, and finding there is a sufficient number of grocers in the Corporation already, and that an increase of the number would tend to the hurt rather than improvement of trade, and looking upon the said Hugh Orratt's usage of the Corporation to be a great indignity offered to the body politic, and an attempt to break into and invade our ancient rights and privileges; therefore, it is ordered that the said Hugh Orratt shall not be admitted either burgess or freeman for this borough, neither shall he exercise the trade of a grocer within the said borough, under the pain and penalty of five pounds for each and every day he shall exercise such his trade in the said borough.

*　　*　　*

It is also unanimously ordered by this assembly that all Scotchmen and other persons carrying packs that shall hereafter hawk or expose any goods [for] sale within this borough shall forfeit and pay the sum of one shilling daily and every day they shall so hawk or expose goods [for] sale as aforesaid.

21. ALEHOUSES PUT DOWN IN CHESHIRE, 1645

[Cheshire County Record Office, Quarter Sessions File, Q JF 73/3/110]

Sir,

Among all the means whereby the kingdom of Satan is advanced and sin promoted, one of the chiefest is the toleration of a needless multitude and vain superfluity of alehouses. Sir, we cannot but grieve to see the Sabbath so profaned, the good creatures of God so abused, and the Lord so provoked to a just occasion of further judgements. We, therefore, in conscience of our duty, do humbly appeal to your worship for remedy by the suppression of these houses which are so needless. I have consulted with Raphe Ratcliffe and Raphe Holbrooke, and those that they think fit to be suppressed are these: John Cooke, William Maddock, Andrew Barker, George Holland, Thomas Allet, Raphe Maddock, Richard Darlinton in the wood, Galliard Acton. They do conceive all these to be needless, for beside these there are three more, which we think to be a number sufficient for such a town. We doubt not of your care herein and we remain,

Yours to entreat the Lord for your protection,

John Ford, Raphe Ratcliffe, Raphe Holbrooke.

[Marginal note:] October 6, 1645. All these alehouses put down, and likewise John Maddock and Thomas Hatton.

[Endorsed:] To the worshipful his much honoured friend, Mr. Jonathan Bruen, esq.

22. THE UNPOPULARITY OF FREE QUARTER IN AND ABOUT LONDON, 1647

[*Lords' Journals*, IX, pp. 89–90]

9 March 1646

Gentlemen,

The Lords have received a petition from the Lord Mayor, Aldermen, and Commons of the City of London; wherein as they do seasonably and fully declare their good affections to the Parliament, together with their fixed resolutions carefully to intend the honour, security, and advantage thereof, so they do likewise express a great sense of their present pressures, by reason of the quartering of the forces commanded by Sir Thomas Fairfax in those parts adjoining near to the city. Neither is this resented by them alone, but the county of Essex did some few days since, by petition, make known unto their lordships the burthens and other mischiefs that was likely to fall upon that county, for the quartering of great numbers of the army upon them and the rest of the associated counties.

The Lords, having seriously considered these petitions, do find it to be of very ill consequence to have the army quartered either in the associated counties or any parts adjacent to the City of London; being the place where the Parliament and all the Courts of Justice are kept, must of necessity have a very great concourse of people, as an addition to that numerous body of their own settled inhabitants. If, therefore, this city shall, by the near quartering of the army, be deprived of their usual provisions and necessary accommodations, it may give an occasion to some to break that good orders, and interrupt that government, which in all these times of our great distractions hath been kept in a settled quietness, which hath not only been a security, but an advantage to the Parliament.

And at this conjuncture of time, it may probably increase such jealousies and suspicions as may not suddenly be removed; most men looking upon such actions as these, which prove inconvenient to them, as designs rather than matters of necessity. And their lordships express their fears in this particular the rather, because they have received divers informations that some persons of the army, in all places where they come, do endeavour to disaffect the people to the present established resolutions of the Parliament. They do likewise consider the great assistance and advantage that the Parliament hath had from the Eastern Association; they having been faithful unto the Parliament from the first to the last, when divers other, either in whole or in part, have deserted and opposed the Parliament in this cause. These counties have been, during these troubles, the magazine of provisions to the City; and other parts of the kingdom do now expect to be furnished from them with those necessaries which are not to be had in that plenty in other counties, they being much wasted in their stores of corn and cattle. It will therefore prove a mischief in general to the whole kingdom, if these counties shall have their stores exhausted by the quartering of an army, which, by a provident and orderly management and use, might support themselves and furnish others.

Upon the whole matter thus before them, their lordships do think it necessary that the forces commanded by Sir Thomas Fairfax should not quarter within the associated counties, or any parts near adjoining to the City of London.

And seeing likewise that, by the great blessing of God upon the endeavours of the Parliament, and the successes of their armies, they now enjoy a freedom from any force maintained against them, they do hold it their duty to do what in them lies towards the freeing the kingdom from these burthens that lie upon them. And therefore they press this as the most necessary means, tending to the ease and satisfaction of the kingdom, that a provision of money be made, for the speedy paying and disbanding of our armies; the way of raising this they leave to you to consider; that so we may give a real and speedy relief to the distressed kingdom of Ireland, and keep such a competent force within ourselves as may secure our garrisons, and prevent the designs of such as, out of their ill affections, should at any time attempt to disturb the peace and happiness of the Parliament and kingdom.

23. TRADE AT NEWCASTLE UPON TYNE, 1649

[*Chorographia: or a Survey of Newcastle-upon-Tyne*, Newcastle, 1649, *Harleian Miscellany*, III, pp. 265–6, 268–9]

The Sand Hill

NOW let us describe unto you the other streets and markets in this town. First of the Sand Hill, a market for fish, and other commodities; very convenient for Merchant Adventurers, merchants of coals, and all those that have their living by shipping. There is a navigable river, and a long quay or wharf, where ships may lie safe from danger of storms, and may unload their commodities and wares upon the quay. In it are two cranes for heavy commodities very convenient for carrying of corn, wine, deals, etc. from the quay into the water gates, which are along the quayside, or into any quarter of the town.

In this market place are many shops and stately houses for merchants, with great conveniencies of water, bridge, garners, lofts, cellars, and houses of both sides of them. Westward they have a street called the Close. East, the benefit of the houses of the quay side.

In this Sand Hill standeth the town court, or Guildhall, where are held the guilds every year by the mayor and burgesses, to offer up their grievances, where the mayor keepeth his court every Monday, and the sheriff hath his county court upon Wednesday and Friday.

In it is kept a Court of Admiralty, or river Court, every Monday in the afternoon. This is a Court of Record for enrolling of deeds and evidences.

There is a court of pie powder, during the said two fairs, Lammas and St. Luke; all the privileges and power, that a court leet can have, are granted to this court.

Under the town court is a common weighhouse for all sorts of commodities. King Henry the Sixth sent to this town, as to other cities and towns, brass weights according to the standard.

Near this is the townhouse, where the clerk of the Chamber and Chamberlains are to receive the revenues of the town for coal, ballast, salt, grindstones, etc.

Next adjoining is an almshouse, called the Maison de Dieu, built by that noble benefactor, Roger de Thornton.

Above which is the stately Court of the Merchant Adventurers, of the old staple, resident at that flourishing city of Antwerp in Brabant, since removed to the more northern provinces under the States. Their charters are ancient, their privileges and immunities great; they have no dependence upon London, having a governor, twelve assistants, two wardens, and a secretary.

There is an old chapel upon the bridge.

Next west is a street called the Close where are many stately houses of merchants and others. The Earl of Northumberland had his house in this street.

Near the Sand Hill east, is Allhallows Bank, or Butchers Bank, where most butchers dwell, the way to Allhallows Church; on the south side of which are many chairs or lanes that go down to the quayside.

The Middle Parts of the Town

Next up street is the street called the Side. In the lower part of it standeth a fair cross, with columns of stones hewn, covered with lead, where are sold milk, eggs, butter, etc.

In the Side are shops for merchants, drapers, and other trades. In the middle of the Side is an ancient stone house, an appendix to the castle, which in former times belonged to the Lord Lumley, before the castle was built, or at least coetany[1] with the castle.

Next up the town north is Middle street, where all sorts of artificers have shops and houses.

The west side of this street is the oatmeal market.

On the east side of it is the flesh market, I think the greatest market[2] in England for all sorts of flesh and poultry that are sold there every Saturday; the reason is not the populousness of the town that makes it, it is the people in the country, within ten miles of the town, who make their provision there; as likewise all that live by the coal trade, for working and conveying coals to the water; as also the shipping which comes into this river for coals, there being sometimes three-hundred sail of ships. In this market are kept two fairs in the year, for nine days together; one of them at that remarkable time of the year, the first of August; the other is held the eighteenth of October, upon St. Luke's day.

Next above north, is the bigg[3] and oat market every Tuesday and Saturday in the week. In which street is an ancient house, with a large gate, called the Scots Inn, where the kings, nobility, and lairds of Scots lodged, in time of truce or league with England.

Pilgrim Street

East again is Pilgrim street, the longest and fairest street in the town. In it is a market for wheat and rye every Tuesday and Saturday.

Likewise an house called the Pilgrims Inn, where pilgrims lodged that came to visit the shrine in Gesmond, or Jesu de Munde, which occasioned to call this street Pilgrim Street . . .

Of the River Tyne and the Commodities

The port or haven of this river is able to receive ships of four-hundred tuns, having rocks on the north side of the haven, and sands upon the south, dangerous in a north-east wind: . . .

The south side of the river is Warwickshire [sic], in the county of Durham, where are many salt pans, which make white salt out of salt water, boiled with coal.

Another commodity that this river bringeth forth is coal in great abundance; most of the people that live in these parts live by the benefit of coals, that are carried out of this river into most parts of England southward, into Germany, and other transmarine countries.

Many thousand people are employed in this trade of coals; many live by working of them in the pits; many live by conveying them in wagons and wains to the river Tyne; many men are employed in conveying the coals in

---

[1] Of the same age.   [2] Except Leadenhall Market in London.   [3] i.e. Barley.

keels, from the staithes,[1] aboard the ships: one coal merchant employeth five hundred, or a thousand, in his works of coal, yet, for all his labour, care, and cost, can scarce live of his trade; nay, many of them have consumed and spent great estates, and died beggars. I can remember one of many that raised his estate by the coal trade; many I remember that have wasted great estates . . .

Our coal miners, they labour and are at a great charge to maintain men to work their collieries; they waste their own bodies with care, and their collieries with working; the kernel being eaten out of the nut, there remaineth nothing but the shell; their collieries are wasted, and their monies are consumed. This is the uncertainty of mines; a great charge, the profit uncertain.

Some South gentlemen have, upon great hope of benefit, come into this country to hazard their monies in coal pits. Mr. Beaumont, a gentleman of great ingenuity and rare parts, adventured into our mines, with his thirty-thousand pounds, who brought with him many rare engines, not known then in these parts; as, the art to bore with iron rods, to try the deepness and thickness of the coal; rare engines to draw water out of the pits; wagons, with one horse, to carry down coals from the pits to the staithes, to the river, etc. Within a few years, he consumed all his money, and rode home upon his light horse.

Some Londoners of late have disbursed their monies for the reversion of a lease of colliery, about thirty years to come of the lease. When they come to crack their nuts, they find nothing but the shells; nuts will not keep thirty years; there is a swarm of worms underground that will eat up all before their time; they may find some meteors, *Ignis fatuus*, instead of a mine.

A third commodity that this river bringeth forth is grindstones, which are conveyed into most parts of the world, according to the proverb: a Scot, a rat, and a Newcastle grindstone you may find all the world over.

The fourth commodity of this river is the great plenty of salmon taken in this water, which serveth this town and other parts.

24. THE OBSTRUCTION OF A RIVER BY BALLAST, 1654

[P.R.O., SP 18/72, no. 15, I]

WE are informed that the water of Wyre [= Wear] is like to be utterly spoiled by the shipmasters that use that port for coals by casting of their ballast within the full sea mark and stopping up the river. If there be not timely care taken it will be great prejudice to Sunderland and the adjacent country. Therefore, we order Michael Crake, the water bailiff of the said river, to take the best care he can of it, and that the customers and collectors of the said port of Sunderland shall clear no ship nor give out any cockets till such time as they shall receive the water bailiff's bill of the shipmaster, that they may know where the

---

[1] Or coal-wharves.

ballast is laid as they do at Newcastle, always providing that the said water bailiff take no greater fees but what have been usually paid.

Northumberland, Walter Earle, Gyles Green.

Endorsed:] Inhabitants of Sunderland in the Bishopric of Durham, May the 12, 1654.

25. BROMYARD IN HEREFORDSHIRE PETITIONS FOR THREE EXTRA FAIRS, 1655

[P.R.O., SP 18/100, no. 146, I]

We have, in pursuance of the Council's order of reference to this committee, considered of the humble petition of the inhabitants of the market town of Bromyard in the county of Hereford and of the neighbouring inhabitants adjoining, they thereby praying that in respect of their impoverishment through their entertaining of marching armies and their present charges for maintenance of their poor and other public taxations, as also of the smallness of their trade, they may have an establishment of three fair days to be added to their one fair day within the said town. And we are humbly of opinion that it may be offered to his Highness as the advice of the Council that in case upon return of a writ of *ad quod damnum* it shall appear not to be prejudicial to the Commonwealth, his Highness will please by his charter under the Great Seal to establish the addition of three fair days to be held within that town at the time desired, viz. the Thursday next before the Annunciation of the Virgin Mary, the Thursday next before the Feast of St. James, and the Thursday next before St. Luke's Day. On which days it is alleged no fairs are kept within xx miles of the said town. And that according to the further prayer of the said petition the accustomed tolls to be gathered on any of the said three days may be distributed as need shall require to the use of the poor of the said town and parish, the vicar thereof for the time being keeping a due registry thereof by him or his deputies; the same to be distributed to the said poor by the said vicar with the advice and assistance of the overseers of the said poor yearly, which nevertheless we do humbly submit to the further consideration of the Council.

Th. Wolseley, Wal. Strickland.

Endorsed:] Report on the petition of Bromyard, read 25 September, 1655 and referred.

26. PETITION TO SUPPRESS A FAIR IN WEST YORKSHIRE, 1656

[P.R.O., SP 18/127, no. 20]

To the right worshipful the justices of the peace for the West Riding of the county of York, the humble petition of divers of the inhabitants of, in, and about the parish of West Ardsley, alias Woodkirk, to the justices of the peace for the West Riding of county York.

SHEWETH that there is a certain fair commonly called Lee Fair yearly kept at Baghill in the said parish upon two several days within less than a month of each other in the time of harvest, which fair formerly stood in woollen cloth. But since a cloth market hath been settled at Wakefield there hath not for these many years been any cloth brought to the said fair. So that it is now utterly decayed and become a tumultuous meeting of the idle and loose persons of the country where there is much revelling and drunkenness. And hath been noted these many years to be a meeting where there is usually more or less bloodshed and some lives lost. And also most labourers and servants hereabouts take occasion thereby to neglect the harvest. And as for the commodities brought thither they are (except some few poor horses) only a few peddling trifles of which the country may much better and with as much conveniency be supplied every market day at Leeds or Wakefield.

The consideration of the premises and chiefly of the great dishonour done to God at that meeting hath moved us to entreat this worshipful bench that the said fair (being now become a burden to the country) may be for the future utterly suppressed.

And your petitioners shall pray etc.

John Heathcastle [and 27 other signatures, 4 of which are by mark].

Mr. Tempest. These subscribers are inordinately[?] desirous to have Lee Fair suppressed and do conceive that the justices of peace may do it if you shall find cause for it. Though it hath been ancient and is by charter mine, yet I would not have any interest or profit of mine stand against the good of the country.

Your assured friend,
Suss. Saville[1]

[1] Earl of Sussex, Thomas, Lord Savile.

[Endorsed:] Petition about Lee Fair in Yorkshire, received 9 May, 1656.

27. ACT SETTING UP THE POSTAL SERVICE, 1657

[C. H. Firth and R. S. Rait, *Acts and Ordinances of the Interregnum, 1642–1660*, II, pp. 1110–13]

An Act for settling the Postage of England, Scotland, and Ireland
[9 June 1657]

VHEREAS it hath been found by experience, that the erecting and settling of ne General Post Office, for the speedy conveying, carrying, and recarrying f letters by post, to and from all places within England, Scotland, and Ireand, and into several parts beyond the seas, hath been, and is the best means, ot only to maintain a certain and constant intercourse of trade and comnerce betwixt all the said places, to the great benefit of the people of these ations, but also to convey the public dispatches, and to discover and prevent nany dangerous, and wicked designs, which have been, and are daily conrived against the peace and welfare of this Commonwealth, the intelligence vhereof cannot well be communicated, but by letter of escript.

Be it enacted by his Highness the Lord Protector and the Parliament, nd it is enacted and ordained by authority thereof, that from henceforth here be one General Office, to be called, and known by the name of the ost Office of England. And one officer from time to time to be nominated nd appointed by his Highness the Lord Protector, and his successors, and ɔ be constituted by Letters Patents under the Great Seal of England, under he name and style of Postmaster General of England, and Comptroller of the ost Office; which said officer, and his deputies by him thereunto sufficiently uthorized, and no other, shall have the receiving, taking up, ordering, ending forward, and delivering of all letters and packets, which shall from ime to time come and go to and from all parts and places of England, Scotnd, and Ireland, where he shall settle posts, and from all the said parts and laces of England, Scotland, and Ireland, unto any the parts and places eyond the seas excepting such letters as shall be sent by common known arriers, and by them conveyed along with their carts, wagons, and packorses, and letters of advice of merchants, which shall be sent by masters of ny ship, barque, or other vessel of merchandize, or any of their company or assengers therein, immediately from any port town of England, Scotland, nd Ireland, by them to be conveyed along with such ship, barque, or other essel to any other port town within any of the same, or into the parts beyond he seas, or from the parts beyond the seas to any port town of England, cotland, and Ireland, or members thereof, and no further. And excepting a etter or more sent by a messenger on purpose for his or their own affairs, vho is, or are, the sender or senders thereof, or by any friend to any place or laces within the said nations of England, Scotland, or Ireland.

And also that the said Postmaster General of England, and Comptroller f the Post Office, and his said deputies only, and no other, shall have the

[marginal notes:]
There shall be one General Post Office.

One Officer styled Postmaster General of England and Comptroller of the Post Office

He shall have the sending of all letters and packets.

Exception.

This officer shall have the horsing of all

through posts and persons riding in post. horsing of all through posts, and persons riding in post by commission o without, to and from all places, upon any of the post roads within England Scotland, and Ireland.

And be it further ordained by authority aforesaid, that the said officer, b himself, or his deputy or deputies, by him thereunto sufficiently authorized Prices for letters and horses. shall, or may demand, have, receive, and take for the postage and conveyanc of all or any letters, which he shall so convey, carry, and recarry as aforesaid, o for the horsing of any through post, or person riding in post as aforesaid, th several rates of portage hereafter mentioned, and no other, viz. for ever letter to or from any place within fourscore miles distance from London, if single letter, twopence, and if a double letter, fourpence, and so propor tionably for every packet of letters, and for every packet of a greater bulk eightpence the ounce; and for every letter at a farther distance than four score miles, if a single letter, threepence, and if a double letter, sixpenc and so proportionably; and for every packet of a greater bulk, one shilling th ounce. And for every letter to or from Scotland, if a single letter, fourpence, i a double letter, eightpence, and so proportionably; and if a packet of a greate bulk, one shilling sixpence the ounce. And to or from Ireland, for ever single letter, sixpence, for every double letter, one shilling, and so propor tionably, and for every packet of greater bulk, two shillings the ounce. An for such letters or packets as shall be conveyed or carried within Ireland the rates thereof to be as followeth, viz. for every letter to or from any plac within forty miles distance from Dublin, if a single letter, twopence, if double letter, fourpence, and so proportionably, and if a packet of greate bulk, eightpence the ounce. And for every letter at a farther distance tha forty miles, if a single letter, fourpence, if a double letter, eightpence, and s proportionably, and if a packet of greater bulk, one shilling the ounce. Fo every letter that shall be directed to Legorno, Genoa, Florence, Lyon: Marseilles, Smyrna, Aleppo, and Constantinople, one shilling the singl letter, two shillings the double letter, and three shillings ninepence the ounc weight. For every letter to Bordeaux, Rochelle, Nantes, Bayonne, Cadiz, an Madrid, ninepence the single letter, one shilling sixpence the double, an two shillings the ounce weight. For every letter to Saint Malo, Morlaix, an Newhaven, sixpence the single letter, one shilling the double, and one shillin sixpence the ounce weight. For every letter to Hamburg, Frankfurt, an Cologne, eightpence the single letter, one shilling fourpence the double, an two shillings the ounce weight. And for every letter to Danzig, Lipswic Lübeck, Stockholm, Copenhagen, Elsinore, and Queenesbrough, twelve pence the single letter, two shillings the double, and four shillings the ounc weight. And of every through post, or persons riding in post as aforesai twopence halfpenny the mile for each horse, besides the guide groat fo every stage.

And whereas upon the arrival of ships from parts beyond the seas, to th outports here, letters directed to several merchants in London have bee heretofore frequently delivered by the bringers thereof to loose and uncertai hands, to be conveyed forwards, whereby great prejudice hath accrued to their affairs, as well by the miscarrying of many of the said letters, as oftentimes by the opening of the same, to the discovery of the correspondence and secrets of the said merchants.

Be it further ordained and enacted by authority aforesaid, that all letters and packets, that by any master of any ship or vessel, or any of his company, or any passengers therein, shall be brought to any port town of England, or members thereof, and there delivered to be sent forwards to the City of London, or any other place in any of the post roads, from thence towards the said City (other than such letters as are before excepted, and may be sent by common known carriers as aforesaid, or by a friend as aforesaid), shall by such master, passenger, or other person be delivered to the deputy, or deputies only of the said officer above ordained, by him appointed for the said port towns, and to none other, by him to be sent forward according to the direction hereof. *Letters brought by ships shall be delivered to the Deputy Postmaster.*

And that no person or persons whatsoever, other than such officer as shall be so nominated and appointed by his Highness the Lord Protector or his successors, and constituted by Letters Patents under the Great Seal of England as aforesaid, and his deputies, shall presume to set up, or employ any foot posts, horse posts, or packet boats for the common conveying, carrying, and recarrying of any letters or packets by land within England, Scotland, and Ireland, or from, or to, any the ports of the same by sea, or for the horsing of any through post or persons riding in post as aforesaid, upon pain of forfeiting the sum of one thousand pounds for every month that he or they shall so employ and continue the same, or any of them, the said forfeiture to be sued for, and recovered by action of debt, plaint, or information in any of his Highness's Courts of Record, wherein no essoin, privilege, protection, or wager of law to be admitted, and the said forfeiture so recovered to be the one moiety thereof to his Highness the Lord Protector and his successors, and the other moiety to such person or persons who shall or will inform and sue for the same. *No other person shall set up or employ any footposts, horse posts, or packet boats.* *Forfeiture.*

And for the better management of the said office . . . Be it further enacted and ordained by authority aforesaid . . . that his said Highness the Lord Protector and his successors may grant the said office, together with the several rates of portage above mentioned, and all profits, privileges, fees, perquisites, and emoluments thereunto belonging, or to belong, either for life, or for any term of years, not exceeding eleven years, to such person or persons, and under such covenants, conditions, and yearly rent to his said Highness and his successors reserved, as his said Highness and his successors, with advice of the Council shall from time to time think fit, for the best advantage and benefit of the Commonwealth . . . *His Highness and successors may grant the said office for life or any term of years not exceeding eleven.*

28. THE TRANSPORT OF FRUIT ON THE
RIVER SEVERN, 1659

[P.R.O., E 134, 1659, Mich. 13]

[Deposition of a witness taken in a dispute concerning a contract
for the sale of apples, October, 1659]

SAMUEL HALE of the town of Shrewsbury in the county of Salop., trowman,
aged 26 years or thereabouts, sworn and examined on the defendant's behalf,
deposeth as followeth:

To the 2nd interrogatory he saith that he, this deponent, was present at
and heard a communication touching an agreement in that interrogatory
mentioned between the plaintiff and defendant Hodskins about a certain
quantity of apples; and afterwards he this deponent did go with the defendant
to the house of the plaintiff at the parish of Huntley in the county of Gloucester, where the plaintiff and the defendant had conference and did agree
concerning the sale of the said apples which the plaintiff said he had to sell,
which apples the plaintiff said were at a place called Hope in the said county
of Gloucester; and did then and there agree for all the apples the plaintiff
then had in the house at Hope aforesaid at the rate of 2s. 3d. by the bushel
water measure, which apples are usually sold by, the which measure contains
2 bushels and more of the ordinary Winchester measure by which corn is
usually sold by in market; and further saith that 20 bushels and a half of the
said apples of the said water measure were, according to the said agreement,
delivered to the defendant or to his use at the river of Severn in or near to a
place called Dynny in the parish of Minsterworth in the county of Gloucester, and placed in a barge or trow of the said defendant's there staying to
receive the said apples, and that about 10 or 12 bushels of apples were left
in the plaintiff's house and not brought thither for that the plaintiff's wife
said that she could not get any to carry the same to the place aforesaid.

29. BULK ORDERS FOR ARMY CLOTHING, 1659

[P.R.O., SP 25/I, 115, pp. 4-5. Council of State Order Book]

WHEREAS the officers of the ordnance have represented unto us that they
have contracted with William Saul of London, shoemaker, for 4,600 pairs of
neats' leather shoes for the present service of the forces of this Commonwealth
in Flanders at the rate of 2s. 8d. a pair to be paid within three months next
after delivery, the said shoes to be well and sufficiently tanned and dressed,
both soles and upper leathers with neats' leather rands, and well sewed and
to be of the assize of thirteens and so downwards to nines by equal proportions according to the several patterns left in the hands of the officers of the
ordnance. And that the same shall be in readiness on or before the 16th of this

instant January. All which the Council taking into consideration do allow thereof, and do order that the officers of the ordnance do receive in the said shoes, taking care that they be according to contract and pattern, and do make out debentures for the same according to the custom of that office. And for so doing this shall be their warrant. Given at the Council of State at Whitehall the 9th day of January, 1659.

To the officers of the Ordnance   Signed etc. Tho. Scot, President.

Whereas the officers of the ordnance have represented unto us that they have contracted with John Harvy for 2,300 pair of stockings for the present service of the forces of this Commonwealth in Flanders to be made of good Welsh cottons to be double sewed and of assize and goodness answerable to the pattern left in the office of ordnance at the rate of 12*d*. a pair to be paid in present money. All which the Council doth allow of, and do order the said officers to receive in the same and to take care that they be answerable in goodness and assize to the said pattern delivered. And do make out debentures for the same according to the contract. And for so doing this shall be unto them a sufficient warrant. Given etc. 9th January, 1659.

To the officers of the ordnance   Signed etc. Tho. Scot, President.

Whereas officers of the ordnance have represented unto us that they have contracted with Joshua Woolnough of London, draper, for 2,300 shirts for the service of the forces of this Commonwealth in Flanders to be of good whited Ozenbriggs well sewed and made and answerable in length and assize to a pattern delivered by him to the said officers of the ordnance at the rate of 2*s*. 8*d*. the shirt, to be paid three months after delivery. All which the Council do approve of ... [etc. formula as above] 9th January, 1659.

Whereas the officers of the ordnance have represented unto us that they have contracted with Richard Downes, esq., for 2,300 coats and breeches and for 2,500 yards of broad cloth for the present service of the forces of this Commonwealth in Flanders to be by him provided and sent into the stores of war within the Tower of London according to two contracts made with him by the said officers, copies whereof are hereunto annexed. All which the Council doth approve of and confirm and do order ... [etc. as above] 9th January, 1659.

30. AN ARGUMENT AGAINST RUNNING THE LETTER POST AS A PRIVATE CONCERN, 1659

[P.R.O., SP 18/203, no. 39, I and III]

REASONS humbly presented to the consideration of the honourable Committee of the Council appointed in the behalf of the Postmaster and others concerned why the passage of letters ought not to be farmed [June 11, 1659].

1. That which is of a public interest by farming becomes private, which private interest, as experience tells us, is so usually managed as it becomes a public grievance.

2. The present juncture of affairs bespeaks the Parliament caution not to give the people cause to fear that they shall still be bought and sold but that all things may run in the clear channel of a Commonwealth wherein the common good of all (not the profit of a few) may be taken care for and secured.

3. The service of the Commonwealth, the care of their letters, the hasting of their despatches, is much to be considered. The results of their private counsels, wherein depend the safety of the nations, passing through the hands of the postmasters and one unfaithful hand may do much disservice. How many public letters may be opened, stayed, yea, communicated to our enemy, and no way to find it out by whom or where it was done, when honest and discreet men will not only perform their trust but be as your eyes to discover the intercourses and correspondencies of disaffected persons?

4. As farmers come in that will give most, so will they employ such as will take least, by means whereof unfit and disaffected persons will come into places of trust while honest men are laid aside who cannot comply nor further their oppressions.

5. The office being let to farmers, there is no way to get relief for abuses. If they will not take or deliver a letter of 6*d.* under 9*d.* or 12*d.* where's your remedy, or who will trouble himself for such a trifle to make complaint, or how can the State regulate such abuses if not under their inspection?

6. The multiplied abuses of farmers in all public revenues, their failures to the State, their severe exactions and oppressions of the people, renders the way of farming as unsafe to the Commonwealth as it is hateful to the people and injurious to all commerce and trade.

7. If the Commonwealth expect no more than what the letters afford at present rates, then is not farming best, for you may be sure no farmer will give you his own estate but must either rack the people, oppress the postmasters, seek for a reprise, or break in your debt.

8. As farming is so many ways dangerous, so is it also scandalous, tyrannous, and insecure. The Commonwealth only knows what they should have every quarter or half-year, but in the hands of some honest men who will give as good security as farmers can, it may be answered every month or as often as it shall seem fit. And the whole office and officers be under the continual inspection and ordering of the Council of State.

9. The office though it be a considerable receipt and of no less trust, yet it may be settled in one hand and a check in another so that the Commonwealth need not be wronged of a letter.

10. That most of the postmasters have done the work for the State in times of war trouble and charge with the hazards of their lives and estates when neither undertaker nor farmer durst appear. And now to be turned out and have others put over their heads will not only be a prejudice to them but an ill requital for their past service and unbecoming the honour of the State.

11. If the officers of postage be put out of the management of the State and the old postmasters laid aside who were the instruments in contriving and settling upon the conveyance of letters at their own charge, it will make way, as it did a few years since, for others to take up the same, which may be done and the Commonwealth cannot justly hinder it. By which means the office of postage will be broken and dissolved, private persons in several roads set up, the public letters or expresses laid upon, the charge of the State as it was in the late king's time, and the revenues now brought in, altogether lost. [Endorsed:] The Postmasters. Reasons against Farming

*   *   *

Note of seven deputy postmasters employed by Withers, an attorney, between Ware and York

Ware: Edward Raffs at The Crown;
Royston: John Trippe at The George;
Stamford: Henry Horsley at The Angel;
Grantham: John Watson at The George, William Wilkenson, William Holmes, victualler[s], John Osburne, glover, John Still, tanner, Cordiall Holyday, the guide;
Bawtry: Jeremiah Phillips;
Ferrybridge: Michael Harforth;
York: Chamberlaine; at Christopher Browne's at The Helmet in Coney Street.
[Endorsed:] Withers, deputy postmasters. The Post. Withers an attorney.

31. THE DECAY OF TRADE IN THE CITY OF YORK, 1660[?]

[Analecta Eboracensia, or some Remains of the Ancient City of York, collected by . . . Sir Thomas Widdrington, ed. C. Caine, London, 1897, pp. x–xi]

SIR,[1] – You have told us by the former discourse what the city was, and what our predecessors have been. We know not what this may have of honour in it: sure we are, it hath but little of comfort. The shoes of our predecessors are too big for our feet, and the ornaments which they had will not serve now

---

[1] Sir Thomas Widdrington, to whom this letter is addressed, was recorder of York *temp.* Charles I and the Interregnum, and Speaker of the House of Commons, sitting as M.P. in 1654, 1656, and 1660. He collected records for a history of York and offered to dedicate it to the mayor, council, and citizens of York. The proposal was coldly received; the City Council thought it more urgent to revive the city's economy. The above document is the city's reply to the author, *c.* 1660 [certainly between 1659 and 1661] a copy of which is bound up with his manuscript and entitled, 'A Sad Complaint by the City of York to the author'. Sir Thomas Widdrington was so disgusted that he prohibited publication of the manuscript.

to cover our nakedness, nor will their wealth feed us, who are not able to tell you what we are, unless it be this, that we are poor and miserable. Our predecessors, if they could see us, would either disclaim us, or be ashamed of us. You have told us that this city was some time the metropolis of the Britons; the Royal Court of the Roman Emperors, and a seat of justice anciently, and also in later times; how is it now become unlike itself? The inhabitants have many of them forsaken it, and those who have not, she cannot maintain, whilst some cities are become so big with buildings, and numerous with inhabitants, as they can be hardly fed or governed. York is left alone, situate in a country plentiful for provisions, and stored, if the people had money to buy them. Trade is decayed, the river become unnavigable by reason of shelves. Leeds is nearer the manufactures, and Hull more commodious for the vending of them; so York is, in each respect, furthest from the profit. The body of York is so dismembered, that no person cares for the being the head of it; the suburbs, which were the legs of the city, are cut off; the late Court of Justice, which, indeed, was built upon the sand only, is sunk, and with it many considerable persons are swallowed up; you cannot now see any confluence of suitors and people; he that looks upon the city may see her paps dry, and her eyes bedewed with tears, refusing to be comforted, because all these are gone. Now, sir, for the Britons you mention; we can neither derive pedigree nor wealth from them; nor can we hear of any of their descendants, unless in Wales and Cornwall, or upon some mountain or hill in Cumberland; and when we have found them, we fear that they will not own us for their kindred or relations; we have lost our genealogy, and forgot the British dialect; they tell us that our blood is not British, but Roman, Saxon, and Norman, which, or some of which, did expel these ancient Britons, and we might expect the same reception from the Roman, Norman, or Saxon, if we should appeal to any of them; and we find by experience that it is not a long series, or beadroll of ancestors and predecessors, but wealth and estate which set a value upon men and places. As for our wealth, it is reduced to a narrow scantling; if we look upon the fabric and materials of the city, we have lost the suburbs which were our skirts, our whole body is in weakness and distemper, our merchandise and trade, our nerves and sinews, are weakened and become very mean and inconsiderable: for the earls, dukes, archbishops, deans, prebends, and abbots of York, they are no homogeneal parts of our body, but only our garnishments, embroideries, and ornaments, and sometimes pricks and goads; our present misery is that we can hardly keep together our homogeneal and essential members, some of them using us, as Absalom's mule did him, either leaving of us, or refusing to act as magistrates amongst us, when our very government seems to hang by a weak, or upon some slender twig. Now for all the monuments of our former state and glory, we find no warmth or comfort from them; but it seems to add to our unhappiness that our predecessors were so happy. Give us leave for conclusion to tell you that a good purse is more useful to us than a long story, which might enable us:—
(1) To make our river more navigable; (2) To re-edify the decayed parts of

the city; (3) To raise a stock to set up some manufacture in the city; (4) To relieve our poor, into which number we may all of us fall if some timely course be not taken by which, through God's blessing, this tottering and wasted city may be upheld.

32. REASONS AGAINST CREATING A POSTAL SORTING OFFICE AT OXFORD, *TEMP.* CHARLES II

[P.R.O. SP 29/444, no. 59]

REASONS why there ought to be no cross posts between Oxford and any part of the country without coming first direct for London [unknown date between 1660 and 1685].

1. That it will be a great charge and but to little purpose the difference of time for the conveyance of letters being only one day.

2. If this be we must have as many officers and as many several bags to convey the letters into the respective stages as we have in our office at London which is not practicable, it being impossible for us to spare from this office any one officer more than the two already sent to Oxford.

3. It will break all our methods of accounts and put them all into confusion and cause us to keep doubly the number of books and accomptants that we now have, if it were possible to find men able to perform that sort of business for which nothing can fit them but long practice.

4. Lastly, there would be so many errors committed by the mis-sending of letters through ignorance that the mischief done to some would never be countervailed by the advantage others propose to themselves by it.

33. AN INVENTORY OF THE WHITE HART INN AT PETWORTH, 1670

[G. H. Kenyon, 'Petworth Town and Trades, 1610–1760, Part III. Appendices', *Sussex Arch. Coll.*, 99, 1961, pp. 126–32]

The White Hart in 1670

Henry Goble's inventory.

	£	s.	d.
In the Cock			
2 little tables, 5 joined stools, 1 form, 1 old sideboard, 2 bullrush chairs, 15*s.*, 1 small featherbed, blanket, coverlet, 2 bolsters, 1 pillow, and an old bedstead.	3	5	0
In the Falcon			
A bedstead with curtains and valances, 1 featherbed, 1 bolster, 2 pillows, 2 blankets, 1 jug, 1 coverlet, £3. A little table and form, 3*s.*	3	3	0

£ s. d.

In the Griffin
2 tables, 5 joined stools, 3 bullrush chairs, 1 pr. of iron dogs,
1 pewter still, curtain and rod, a laten sconce.   1   10   0

In the Gun room
1 little table, 1 joined stool, 1 andiron, 1 curtain and rod.   5   0

In the Buttery
A hanging cupboard, a box, trenchers, white ware, glass bottles,
2 little rundletts of strong waters, a flour tub and some lumber.   1   10   0

In the Bar
Cans, glasses, tin candlesticks, pint, half pint, and quarter pint
pewter pots, a dozen jugs, 1 bullrush chair, a cellar of hot waters,
a case of knives, 8lbs. of tobacco.   1   5   0

In the Hall
1 long table, 1 round table, 6 joined stools, 3 bullrush chairs,
1 joined chair, a little carpet, 2 cushions, 2 pr. of playing tables,
1 pr. of cast andirons, a brass sconce, a little curtain and rod. 2   10   0

In the Parlour
2 tables, 3 forms, and a curtain.   15   0

In the kitchen
1 joined cupboard, 1 little table, 1 stone table with a wooden
frame, 6 old bullrush chairs, 3 joined stools and a block, £1 5s.,
1 jack with weights and chains and spits, 4 pr. of pothooks, 2
iron potleads, 1 iron skivell, 1 flesh fork, 3 smoothing irons, 1
toasting iron, 4 pr. of pothangers, 2 fire pans, 2 pr. of tongs,
2 pr. of gridirons, 2 fenders, 2 iron racks, 2 small iron dogs, 2 iron
slices, a pr. of iron andirons, 5 iron pots, £4 9s., 2 brass pots,
1 little brass pot, 3 brass kettles, 5 brass skillets, 4 brass chafing
dishes, 2 little brass mortars and pestles, 2 brass candlesticks,
2 warming pans, 2 brass skimmers, 1 little brass ladle, 1 brass
stewpan, £2 17s. Pewter: 25 flagons, 7 candlesticks, 2 basins, 13
chamberpots, 2 tankards, 14 winepots of several measures, 1
dozen porringers, 1 candlecup, 7 salts, 18 saucers, 2 pint pots,
14 trencher plates, 1 pasty plate, 3 pie plates, 12 sallett dishes,
38 dishes. (Total pewter) £18 6s. 4d. 2 latten colanders, 2s.   26 19   4

In the Bakehouse
1 brass kettle, 1 iron kettle, 3 iron pots, 1 iron grate, 1 iron
skillet, 2 iron frying pans, 1 iron dripping pan, 6 latten dripping
pans, 1 iron candlestick, a baking kiver, a meal tub, 1 bushel,
1 half bushel, 1 half hogshead with a cover, a dresser, trugs, and
other wooden ware, a brass ladle, a little brass skimmer.   2   11   0

In the Brewhouse
1 mash vat, 1 tun, 1 kiver, 1 shoot, 2 jutts, 1 sweetwort tub.   7   0   0

In the Washhouse
2 bucking tubs, 3 rinsing tubs, 2 wash kivers, 3 old tubs.   1   0   0

	£	s.	d.

In the Ostler's chamber over the Washhouse
1 old flock bed and some lumber. — 5 0

In the Cellars
The stock of beer with the butts, pipes, hogsheads, and other beer vessels and stands. — 50 0 0
7 dozen stone and glass bottles. — 1 1 0

In the Bell chamber
1 table, 1 form, 2 bedsteads with curtains and valances, 2 feather beds, 4 blankets, 2 rugs, 2 feather bolsters, 2 flock bolsters, 3 feather pillows. — 6 0 0

In the Dolphin chamber
1 table, 4 joined stools, an old chair, a livery cupboard, 1 pr. of andirons, firepan and tongs, 1 bedstead with curtain and valances, 1 feather bed, 2 blankets, 1 rug, 2 feather pillows, 1 feather bolster. — 5 0 0

In the Hart chamber
1 curtain and rod, 1 table with an old carpet, 1 livery cupboard with a carpet, 2 leather chairs, 2 old turkey wrought chairs, 5 turkey wrought stools, 1 bedstead with curtain and valances, a down bed, 1 down bolster, 2 pillows, 2 blankets, a rug, 1 pr. of andirons, firepan and tongs. — 10 0 0

In the Luce chamber
1 small table, a side cupboard, an old form, 2 leather stools, 1 joined stool, a bedsteddle with curtains and valances, 1 feather bed, 2 blankets and a coverlet, 2 feather bolsters, 1 trundle bed with a feather bed, feather bolster, 1 rug and 2 blankets. — 7 0 0

At the Stairs' head
A little narrow table, a sideboard, a form, and a pr. of bellows. — — 5 0

In the Angel chamber
2 tables, 5 leather chairs, 6 turkey wrought cushions, a pr. of andirons with brass heads, a pr. of small iron andirons, a firepan and tongs, a looking glass, a curtain and rod, a bedstead with curtains and valances, a feather bed, a bolster, 1 feather pillow, 2 blankets and 1 rug. — 10 0 0

In the Star chamber
2 tables, 5 joined stools, 9 Russia leather chairs, 6 cushions, 1 carpet, a side cupboard, 1 pr. of bellows, a brass snuffer, a greater pr. of brass andirons, firepan and tongs, little iron dogs, 2 window curtains and rod, a wickett voyder basket, a bedsteddle with curtains and valances, 1 feather bed, 2 feather bolsters, 1 feather pillow, 2 blankets, 1 rug. — 12 0 0

In the Marigold chamber
2 tables and a carpet, 10 leather chairs, 3 green chairs, 1 old joined stool, a pr. of snuffers, a pr. of bellows, a pr. of iron

	£	s.	d.

andirons with brass knobs, firepan and tongs, 2 window curtains and rods, a down bed with a quilt, 2 blankets and a rug, 1 feather bolster, 1 feather pillow. — 11 10 0

In the Maidservants' chamber

2 feather beds, 2 millpuss beds, 5 blankets, 2 coverlets and a rug, 3 trundle bedsteads, 3 feather bolsters, 3 flock bolsters, and one chest. — 7 0 0

In the Children's chamber

A chest of drawers, a great trunk, 2 chests, a little leather stool, 2 trundle bedsteads, 1 feather bed, 1 flock bed, 2 feather bolsters, 3 blankets, and 1 coverlet. — 5 0 0

In his own Lodging chamber

His wearing apparel and money in his purse. — 30 0 0

A bedstead with curtain and valances, a down bed, 1 feather bolster, 2 feather pillows, 2 blankets, 1 coverlet, 1 sheet, 1 little table and carpet, 1 trunk, 1 great chair, 2 joined stools, a box and a small trunk, a looking glass, a window curtain and rod, 2 hanging shelves, 1 pr. of andirons, firepan and tongs. — 6 0 0

Plate. — 25 0 0

Two pieces of embroidered linen for cushions. — 10 0

Upon the Garret stand

A box and a desk. — 5 0

In the Sun chamber

A high bedstead with curtains and valances, 1 low bedstead, 2 feather beds, 2 feather bolsters, 4 down pillows, 5 feather pillows, 4 blankets, 1 rug, 1 coverlet, 1 press to hang clothes in, a window curtain and rod, 4 joined chests, 1 little table, 1 pr. of iron andirons, firepan and tongs, a close stool, a basket chair, a joined chair, 1 great chair, 4 little green stools, and a pr. of bellows. — 10 0 0

63 pr. of sheets. — 31 10 0
40 Pillowberes. — 3 0 0
10 Large table cloths. — 5 0 0
18 Small table cloths, £2. 14s., 17 dozen napkins, £6 16s., 2 dozen hand towels, 12s. — 10 2 0
A remnant of new cloth. — 8 0
Sperate debts. — 180 0 0
Desperate debts. — 40 0 0
11 Hogs and shutts, £5. 10s., 500 faggots and 2 cord of wood, £6. — 11 10 0
A water cart with wheels and a hogshead. — 1 0 0
A load of hay and hops. — 9 0 0
Lumber about the house. — 1 0 0

Sum total   £540 19 4

Appraisers: John Payne, William Westbrook, John Scutt, John Levett

34. THE DAMAGING ECONOMIC EFFECTS
OF STAGE COACHES, 1673

[*The Grand Concern of England explained, in several Proposals offered to the Consideration of Parliament . . . by a Lover of his Country and Well-Wisher to the Prosperity both of the King and Kingdoms*, London, 1673, *Harleian Miscellany*, VIII, London, 1746, pp. 538–46]

THE seventh proposal, that the multitude of stage coaches and caravans, now travelling upon the roads, may all, or most of them, be suppressed; especially these within forty, fifty, or sixty miles of London, where they are no way necessary. And that a due regulation be made of such as shall be thought fit to be continued.

These coaches and caravans are one of the greatest mischiefs that hath happened of late years to the kingdom, mischievous to the public, destructive to trade, and prejudicial to lands.

First, by destroying the breed of good horses, the strength of the nation, and making men careless of attaining to good horsemanship, a thing so useful and commendable in a gentleman.

Secondly, by hindering the breed of watermen, who are the nursery for seamen, and they the bulwark of the kingdom.

Thirdly, by lessening of his Majesty's revenues.

For the first of these: stage coaches prevent the breed of good horses, destroy those that are bred, and effeminate his Majesty's subjects, who, having used themselves to travel in them, have neither attained skill themselves, nor bred up their children to good horsemanship, whereby they are rendered incapable of serving their country on horseback if occasion should require and call for the same; for, hereby, they become weary and listless when they ride a few miles, and unwilling to get on horseback; not able to endure frost, snow, or rain, or to lodge in the fields. And what reason, save only their using themselves so tenderly, and their riding in these stage coaches, can be given for this their inability?

What encouragement hath any man to breed horses, whilst these coaches are continued? There is such a lazy habit of body upon men, that they, to indulge themselves, save their fine clothes, and keep themselves clean and dry, will ride lolling in one of them, and endure all the inconveniences of that manner of travelling, rather than ride on horseback; so that, if any man should continue his breed, he must be one that is a great lover of them, and resolve to keep and please his own fancy with them; otherwise, most certainly, he (as most breeders already have done) will give over his breeding.

There is not the fourth part of saddle horses, either bred, or kept, now in England, that was before these coaches were set up, and would be again, if they were suppressed; nor is there any occasion for breeding, or keeping such horses, whilst the coaches are continued.

For, will any man keep a horse for himself, and another for his man, all
the year, for to ride one or two journeys, that at pleasure, when he hath
occasion, can slip to any place where his business lies, for two, three, or four
shillings, if within twenty miles of London, and so proportionably into any
part of England ? . . . Neither are there near so many coach horses either bred
or kept in England now, as there were saddle horses formerly, there being no
occasion for them, the kingdom being supplied with a far less number. For
formerly, every man that had occasion to travel many journeys yearly, or to
ride up and down, kept horses for himself and servants, and seldom rid without one or two men; but now, since every man can have a passage into every
place he is to travel unto, or to some place within a few miles of that part he
designs to go unto, they have left keeping of horses, and travel without
servants; and York, Chester, and Exeter stagecoaches, each of them with
forty horses apiece, carry eighteen passengers a week from London to either
of these places, and, in like manner, as many in return from these places to
London; which come, in the whole, to eighteen-hundred seventy-two in the
year. Now take it for granted that all that are carried from London to those
places are the same that are brought back, yet are there nine-hundred thirty-
six passengers carried by forty horses; whereas, were it not for these coaches,
at least five hundred horses would be required to perform this work . . .

There are stage coaches that go to almost every town within twenty or
twenty-five miles of London, wherein passengers are carried at so low rates,
that most persons in and about London, and in Middlesex, Essex, Kent, and
Surrey, gentlemen, merchants, and other traders that have occasion to ride,
do make use of; some to keep fairs and markets; others to visit friends, and
to go to and from their country houses, or about other business, who, before
these coaches did set up, kept a horse or two of their own, but now have
given over keeping the same; so that, by computation, there are not so many
horses by ten thousand kept now in these parts as there were before stage
coaches set up. By which means breeding of good padnags is discouraged,
and coach horses that are bred, by cruelty and ill usage of stagers, are
destroyed.

Secondly, those coaches hinder the breeding of watermen, and much
discourage those that are bred; for, there being stage coaches set up unto
every little town upon the river of Thames, on both sides the water, from
London, as high as Windsor and Maidenhead, etc. and so, from London
bridge to and below Gravesend, and also to every little town within a mile
or two of the water side, these are they who carry all the letters, little bundles,
and passengers, which, before they set up, were carried by water, and kept
watermen in a full employment, and occasioned their increase (whereof
there never was more need than now) and yet, by these coaches, they of all
others are most discouraged and dejected, especially our western and below
bridge watermen, they having little or nothing to do, sometimes not a fare in
a week; so that they dare not take apprentices, the work they have not
answering the charge they are at in keeping themselves and families. The

consequence whereof is like to prove sad in a short time, unless speedily prevented; especially if these wars continue, and we happen to lose so many yearly of those that are bred, as of late years we have done. But, if these coaches were down, watermen, as formerly, would have work, and be encouraged to take apprentices, whereby their number would every year greatly increase.

Thirdly, it prejudiceth his Majesty in his revenue of excise; for now four or five travel in a coach together, and twenty or thirty in a caravan, gentlemen and ladies, without any servants, consume little drink on the road, yet pay as much at every inn, as if their servants were with them; which is the tapster's gain, and his Majesty's loss. But, if travellers would, as formerly they did, travel on horseback, then no persons of quality would ride without their servants; and it is they that occasion the consumption of beer and ale on the roads, and so would advance his Majesty's revenue. I know it will be objected, there are as many people now, as will be when coaches are down, and they drink wherever they are; therefore no matter whether they drink at home, or on the road, since the consumption will be the same. How can the King's revenue, then, be advanced by servants travelling with their masters or mistresses, more than it is already? The answer is plain: at home they drink small or strong drink brewed by their masters, that pay no excise, but whatever they drink at inns pays the King's duties; and all innkeepers do declare, that they sell not half the drink, nor pay the King half the excise, they did, before these coaches set up.

Secondly [sic], these coaches and caravans are destructive to the trade and manufactures of the kingdom, and have impoverished and ruined many thousands of families, whose subsistence depended upon the manufacturing of wool and leather, two of the staple commodities of the kingdom. For before these coaches were set up, travellers rode on horseback, and men had boots, spurs, saddles, bridles, saddlecloths, and good riding suits, coats and cloaks, stockings, and hats; whereby the wool and leather of the kingdom was consumed, and the poor people set at work by carding, combing, spinning, knitting, weaving, and fulling. And your cloth workers, drapers, tailors, saddlers, tanners, curriers, shoemakers, spurriers, lorimers, and feltmakers had a good employ, were full of work, got money, lived handsomely, and helped, with their families, to consume the provisions and manufactures of the kingdoms. But, by means of these coaches, these trades, besides many others depending upon them, are become almost useless, and they, with their families, reduced to great necessity, insomuch that many thousands of them are cast upon the parishes wherein they dwell for a maintenance. Besides, it is a great hurt to the girdlers, sword cutlers, gunsmiths, and trunk makers, most gentlemen, before they travelled in their coaches, using to ride with swords, belts, pistols, holsters, portmanteaus, and hat cases, which, in these coaches, they have little or no occasion for. For, when they rode on horseback, they rode in one suit, and carried another to wear when they came to their journey's end, or lay by the way. But, in coaches, a silk suit, and an

Indian gown, with a sash, silk stockings, and beaver hats men ride in, and carry no other with them, because they escape the wet and dirt, which on horseback they cannot avoid; whereas, in two or three journeys on horseback, these clothes and hats were wont to be spoiled. Which done, they were forced to have new very often, and that increased the consumption of the manufactures, and the employment of the manufacturers, which travelling in coaches doth no way do. And, if they were women that travelled, they used to have safeguards and hoods, side saddles, and pillions, with strappings, saddle or pillion cloths, which, for the most part, were either laced, or embroidered, to the making of which there went many several trades, seeing there is not one side saddle with the furniture made, but, before it is furnished, there are at least thirty several trades have a share in the making thereof; most of which are either destroyed, or greatly prejudiced by the abatement of their trade; which being bred unto, and having served seven years' apprenticeship to learn, they know not what other course to take for a livelihood. And, besides all these inferior handicraftsmen, there are the mercers, silkmen, lacemen, milliners, linen and woollen drapers, haberdashers, and divers other eminent trades, that receive great prejudice by this way of travelling. For the mercers sold silk and stuff in great quantities, for safeguards, hoods, and riding clothes for women; by which means the silk twisters, winders, throwsters, weavers, and dyers had a fuller employment; the silkmen sold more lace and embroidery, which kept the silver wire drawers, lace makers, and embroiderers; and at least ten trades more were employed. The linen draper sold more linen, not only to saddlers, to make up saddles, but to travellers for their own use, nothing wearing out linen more than riding. Woollen drapers sold more cloth than now; saddlers used, before these coaches were set up, to buy three or four hundred pounds' worth of cloth apiece in a year; nay, some five hundred and a thousand pounds' worth, which they cut out into saddles and pillion cloths; though now there is no saddler can dispose of one hundred pounds' worth of cloth in a year in his trade. The milliners and haberdashers, they also sold more ribbons, gloves, hoods, scarves, and other things belonging to their trade; the dust, dirt, and rain, and riding on horseback spoiling and wearing them out much more than travelling in a coach; and, on horseback, these things were apter to be lost than in a coach.

Trade is a great mystery, and one trade depends upon another. Were it not too tedious, I could shew you how many several trades there are that go to the making of every one of the things aforementioned, and demonstrate that there is scarcely a trade in England but what is one way or other concerned and prejudiced by these stage coaches, especially the country trade all over England. For, passage to London being so easy, gentlemen come to London oftener than they need, and their ladies either with them, or, having the conveniencies of these coaches, quickly follow them. And, when they are there, they must be in the mode, have all the new fashions, buy all their clothes there, and go to plays, balls, and treats, where they get such a habit of jollity, and a love to gaiety and pleasure, that nothing afterwards in the country will serve them, if ever they should fix their minds to live there again; but they must have all from London, whatever it costs.

And there is one grand mischief happens to the country thereby; for gentlemen drain the country of all the money they can get, bring it to London, and spend it there. Whereas, if they stayed at home, bought their clothes and other commodities of their neighbours, money would be kept circulating amongst them; and chapmen that have served apprenticeships, and set up near them, would have a good trade, pay their rents, and live handsomely; the trade betwixt them and the City of London would be renewed, country ladies would be as well pleased, provided they be kept from London, as if they had all the rich clothes, modes, and fashions, vainly and extravagantly invented and worn in the City, as soon as they have them there; and gentlemen would not only save the money they spend in journeys to buy clothes, but have as good as need to be worn in the country, at easier rates than they must pay at London, if they buy when the fashion comes first up.

Thirdly [sic], these coaches and caravans hinder the consumption of all sorts of provisions for man and beast, thereby bringing down the rents of lands. For instance: a coach with four horses carries six passengers, a caravan, with four or five horses, carries twenty, or five and twenty. These, when they come to their inn, club together for a dish or two of meat, and, having no servants with them, spend not above twelve pence or sixteen pence apiece at a place; yet, perhaps, foul four, five, or six pair of sheets. Horses they have none, but what draw them; and, for those, the coachmen agree with the innkeeper beforehand to have their hay and oats at so low a rate, that he loseth by them, and is forced to beat down the price of them in the market, yet must let the coachman have them for what he pleaseth, otherwise he carries his passengers to other inns; by which means the innholders get little or nothing, cannot pay their rent, nor hold their inns, without great abatements; two third parts of what they formerly paid is, in some places, abated. Upon such accounts as these, innholders, where these coaches do come, are undone. And, if so, since most travellers travel in coaches, what must become of all the rest of the inns on the roads where these coaches stay not? Believe it, they are a considerable number, take all the grand roads in England, as York, Exeter, Chester, etc. There are about five hundred inns on each road, and these coaches do not call at fifteen or sixteen of them; then what can follow, but that the rest be undone, and their landlords lose their rents? . . .

Most horses go to grass in the summer time, which would raise the rents of pasture lands about cities and corporations, and other towns upon the roads, above what formerly they were; which of late years, by means of those coaches, have fallen half in half, even in Middlesex, and other places adjoining to London itself. And no other reason for it can be given but this, that citizens and gentlemen about the City do not keep horses as formerly they did . . . It is very observable that, before these coaches were set up,

what with the horses kept by merchants, and other tradesmen, and gentlemen in or near London, and the travellers' horses that came to London, that
city spent all the hay, straw, beans, peas, and oats, that could be spared
within twenty or thirty miles thereof. And for a further supply, had vast
quantities from Henley, and other western parts, and from below Gravesend
by water; besides many ships lading of beans from Hull, and of oats from
Lynn and Boston; and then oats, and hay, and other horsemeat, would bear
a good price in that market, which was the standard for all the markets in
England. But now, since these coaches set up, especially in such multitudes,
and those so nigh London, London cannot consume what grows within
twenty miles of it. But, if they were down, the consumption in London would
quickly be as great as ever, and that would raise the price of the commodities, advance the price of lands, and cause rents to be well paid
again . . .

The graziers, they complain for want of a vent for their cattle, which they had
before these coaches were erected; not that I do imagine coaches to be the
only reason of the want of that consumption, though it be evident, they go
far in the promoting that mischief; for the want of people in England, the
loss of many thousands from amongst us of late years, and the leaving off
eating of suppers by those that are left alive, go a great way therein. But these
two may be easily remedied; the former by the general Act of Naturalization,
and liberty of conscience, proposed before, which would bring all foreigners
in amongst us; the latter, by men's spending less in taverns, plays, and balls,
and keeping up in lieu thereof the ancient laudable customs of England, of
good housekeeping, and thereby relieving the poor. Half the money that
gentlemen idly spend in taverns upon French wines, for which the coin of
the kingdom is exhausted, or upon plays, balls, treating mistresses, fine
clothes, toys from France, or other foreign parts, would defray the charges
of having good suppers every night; whereby the product of our own lands
would be consumed, and that would raise rents. Nay, I am verily persuaded,
if it were duly considered, and that all men, as formerly, would fall to eating
of suppers, at least to dressing of them; and when dressed, if they eat not
themselves, would give them to the poor, the increase of the consumption
would raise the rents of lands, as much above what now they do go at, at
least in most places of England, as would defray the charges of those suppers;
if so, would it not then be of great advantage to men in their estates, and to
the kingdom in general? . . .

Men do not travel in these coaches with less expense of money or time
than on horseback. For, on horseback, they may travel faster; and, if they
please, all things duly considered, with as little, if not less charges. For instance, from London to Exeter, Chester, or York, you pay forty shillings
apiece in summer time, forty-five shillings in winter, for your passage;
and as much from those places back to London. Besides, in the journey
they change coachmen four times; and there are few passengers but give
twelve pence to each coachman at the end of his stage, which comes to

eight shillings in the journey backward and forward, and at least three shillings comes to each passenger's share to pay for the coachmen's drink on the road; so that in summer time the passage backward and forward to any of these places costs four pounds eleven shillings, in the winter five pounds one shilling, and this only for eight days' riding in the summer, and twelve in the winter. Then, when the passengers come to London, they must have lodgings, which, perhaps, may cost them five or six shillings a week, and that in fourteen days amounts unto ten or twelve shillings, which makes the four pounds eleven shillings, either five pounds one shilling, or five pounds three shillings; or the five pounds one shilling five pounds eleven shillings, or five pounds thirteen shillings, besides the inconveniency of having meat from the cooks, at double the price they might have it for in inns. But, if stage coaches were down, and men travelled again, as formerly, on horseback, then when they came into their inns they would pay nothing for lodgings; and, as there would excellent horses be bred and kept by gentlemen for their own use, so would there be by others that would keep them on purpose to let; which would, as formerly, be let at ten or twelve shillings per week, and in many places for six, eight, or nine shillings per week. But, admitting the lowest price to be twelve shillings, if a man comes from York, Exeter, or Chester to London, be five days coming, five days going, and stay twelve days in London to dispatch his business (which is the most that country chapmen usually do stay) all this would be but three weeks. So that his horse hire would come but to one pound sixteen shillings, his horse meat at fourteen pence a day, one with another, which is the highest that can be reckoned upon, and will come but to one pound five shillings, in all three pounds one shilling, so that there would be, at least, forty or fifty shillings saved of what coach hire and lodgings will cost him . . . From Northampton men pay for passage in coach to London sixteen shillings, and so much back; from Bristol twenty five shillings, from Bath twenty shillings, from Salisbury twenty shillings or twenty-five shillings, from Reading seven shillings, the like sums back; and so in proportion for longer or shorter stages. Judge then whether men may not hire horses cheaper than five shillings a day. I am sure they may for half the money . . .

Travelling in these coaches can neither prove advantageous to men's health or business. For, what advantage is it to men's health, to be called out of their beds into these coaches an hour before day in the morning, to be hurried in them from place to place, till one hour, two, or three within night; insomuch that, after sitting all day in the summer time stifled with heat, and choked with dust; or, in the winter time, starving and freezing with cold, or choked with filthy fogs, they are often brought into their inns by torchlight, when it is too late to sit up to get a supper; and next morning they are forced into the coach so early, that they can get no breakfast. What addition is this to men's health or business, to ride all day with strangers, oftentimes sick, ancient, diseased persons, or young children crying; to whose humours they are obliged to be subject, forced to bear with, and many times are poisoned with, their nasty scents, and crippled by the crowd of the boxes and bundles.

Is it for a man's health to travel with tired jades, to be laid fast in the foul ways, and forced to wade up to the knees in mire; afterwards sit in the cold, till teams of horses can be sent to pull the coach out? Is it for their health to travel in rotten coaches, and to have their tackle, or perch, or axle-tree broken, and then to wait three or four hours, sometimes half a day to have them mended, and then to travel all night to make good their stage? Is it for a man's pleasure, or advantageous to his health and business, to travel with a mixed company that he knows not how to converse with; to be affronted by the rudeness of a surly, dogged, cursing, ill natured coachman, necessitated to lodge or bait at the worst inns on the road, where there is no accommodation fit for gentlemen; and this merely because the owners of the inns and the coachmen are agreed together to cheat the guests?

Is it for the advantage of business that a man, when he sets out on a journey, must come just at their hour, or be left behind; so that often he is forced, when one hour's staying would finish his business, to go out of town, leave it undone, and make a new journey about it? Is it for advantage of a man's business that, though he have a concern of great weight or moment to transact upon the road as he goes along, yet if it lie but at a stone's cast out of the coach way, the coachmen will not drive thither, nor stay for him at any place, except the baiting or lodging places where he calls, where they change horses; and there stay no longer than he pleases neither? To be forced, whatever accident of sickness or illness happens, to ride these coachmen's stages, though never so late in the night, or else to be left in the middle of a journey in a strange place? Is this for the conveniency or advantage of a man's health or business? Rather the quite contrary: yet this hath been many persons of good quality's case, though they have offered to pay the whole coach hire, and all the passengers' charges, to have put into an inn (late at night on this side the set stage) yet have they been denied, forced to ride, though in peril of their lives, till midnight; and it is not hard to instance in many that have lost their lives by such usage . . .

35. A PROPOSAL FOR RIVER IMPROVEMENTS, 1674

[Carew Reynel, *The True English Interest*, 1674, pp. 42–3]

Cutting of Rivers

THIS nation might be greatly advantaged by cutting of rivers and making them navigable from one town to another and so breed a good commerce where was none before as from London to Bristol, which is very feasible to be done; from Farnham to Guildford, Southampton to Winchester, and from Maidstone higher into the country; and from Lincoln; and in the north and west to many places. In the north of England about Carlisle it may be cut quite across and have course from sea to sea as they have done lately in France where they have cut a river across the nation from Bordeaux in our British seas to Narbonne, and Aude in the Mediterranean Sea, that they may now trade quite through the country about 200 miles.

Mr. Lee of the north, his engine, and Mr. Balye's engine, both lately invented, will cut rivers now at an easy rate. Were they but employed enough, this would also set on work the poor extremely.

36. TOLLS OF FAIRS AND MARKETS AT SPALDING, 1677

[P.R.O., E 134, 29 Chas. II, Easter 6. Exchequer Depositions by Commission]

[Part of the deposition of Thomas Dawson of Spalding, Lincolnshire, yeoman, aged 62 years and upwards, in a dispute between Daniel Wigmore, esq., complainant and William Earle and sixteen others, defendants. This deposition is on behalf of the complainant.]

To THE third interrogatory this deponent saith that he doth know that there hath been usually two fairs in every year held and kept within the said manor, the one upon the 14th of September and the other upon the 6th day of December commonly called by the name of St. Nicholas' Fair. And he knows that there hath been one market kept upon Tuesday in every week within the said manor . . .

To the fifth interrogatory this deponent saith that he doth know that there hath been monies usually paid and taken for pickage and stallage and exposing goods to sale within the said manor of Spalding, but cannot certainly set forth the sums of money that have been paid or taken for the same, for that sometimes more and sometimes less have been paid and taken for the same according to the quantity of goods taken up for their stalls standing to expose their goods and wares to sale in the said fairs and markets of the said manor, and for every wagon going through or coming to the town of Spalding or Cowhurne within the parish of the said town 6*d*., and for every cart so coming to or passing through the said town and parish 4*d*., and for every score of beasts passing through the said parish of Spalding 4*d*., and for every score of sheep for the like passage 2*d*., and that he hath known toll paid for neat beasts that have been sold in the market of Spalding for each of them 1*d*., and for each calf that hath been sold there a halfpenny, and for each beast sold in the fairs of Spalding 2*d*., and for sheep sold within the said markets 4*d*. a score, and for every horse sold in the fair of Spalding 4*d*., and for each score of horses passing through the said parish 10*d*., and for each horse with a pack passing through the said parish 1*d*., and for each score of swine passing through the said parish 10*d*., for each swine sold in the market of Spalding 1*d*., and for every chalder of coals 4*d*., and every last of corn or seed coming to or passing through the said parish by water brought, or passing by any person not inhabiting within the said town 4*d*., and generally for every load of goods so passing by water in barges, boats, or other vessels 4*d*. And that he hath known a toll of corn taken and paid within the fairs or markets of Spalding to the farmers of the said tolls or their collectors or agents, and that he hath known the said tolls and duties paid to the said farmers and their agents by the space of forty years or upwards.

To the sixth interrogatory this deponent saith that he hath heard and believeth that the said manor of Spalding and the fairs and markets kept within the same belong to the Queen's Majesty that now is, and that he hath known and doth know that the fairs for horses and markets for beasts and sheep within the said manor have been usually kept in a place called the Gore within the said manor, and the fairs for the beasts have been usually kept in the highway betwixt Spalding and Pinchbeck, and that he hath known toll taken upon a bridge called The Little Graft Bridge within the town of Spalding upon fair days only; and that the markets for hemp have been usually kept in a place betwixt Mr. Dales his corner and the town hall and no further into the market place of Spalding; and that the usual markets for the sale of bread, meal, and malt have been kept from the Abbey Gates to the High Bridge and so towards the house late Sir Anthony Oldfield's; and that the markets for butchers were usually kept in their shops and shambles and not elsewhere within the said manor.

To the ninth interrogatory this deponent saith that he knoweth that the defendants, William Earle, William Procter, and John Robinson have exposed to sale within the fairs of Spalding divers parcels of hemp, butter, and cheese since the 14th day of February, 1672, for which they ought to have paid as he conceives tolls and duties to the relator for that the inhabitants of Pinchbeck have paid such tolls for the space of forty years to the farmers of the said manor, and further this deponent cannot depose.

Thomas Dawson.

37. A LIST OF HIGHWAYMEN, *TEMP.* CHARLES II
[P.R.O., SP 29/443, nos. 65 and 66]

WILLIAM DOWSING of Shotley Hall in Suffolk two mile from Harwich liveth in a farm seven score pound a year of Sir Henery Felltons. He is a great horse stealer and a harbourer of rogues in his house and a great highwayman himself.

Nathaniel Mayhew of Shalford in Essex there liveth his wife, if not there, at Blythburgh in Suffolk with his brother. He is a highwayman.

Andrew Edwards of St. Edmunds Bury in Suffolk there liveth his wife and children and his father and mother. He is a butcher by his trade and is now a highwayman.

John July of Holkham in Norfolk. He was formerly a servant to Richard Cocke of Holkham and now liveth in the same town with his wife and children. He is a highwayman.

Thomas Satifwhait of Braintree in Essex. His mother keepeth the *Sign of the Boars Head*, a house that entertaineth thieves and pickpockets and such kind of persons and he himself a highwayman.

Thomas King in Essex. His father liveth near Epping and he liveth with his father. He is an upholsterer by trade. His father liveth in a farm of his own, but his son a highwayman.

Isack Bellsham of White Toune in Essex. He is a farmer and liveth among the woods. He harbours a great many thieves and selleth there stolen goods for them, horses, and other things.

Thomas Wheler of Islington near London. He keepeth the *Sign of the Two Wraslers* [=Wrestlers]. He is a bricklayer by his trade and now a highwayman.

Walter Fowler of London. He used to lodge at the *Sign of the Two Blacksmiths* in Turnball Street, a highwayman.

Samuel Webb of London. He used to lodge about Charing Cross. He hath a brother liveth thereabouts, a very sick man, but he is a highwayman.

John South of London. He liveth somewhere about Holborn. He was formerly a groom and now a highwayman.

Thomas Freeman of London somewhere about Ratliffe Highway he uses to lodge. He is a highwayman.

Samuel Rowles otherways called Doctor Lambe. He lodgeth in Goodmans Yard in Little Minories, London. He is a highwayman.

Cornelius Fullam is about London, but where I cannot tell. He is a highwayman.

One Ashbeham. He came out of Holland, is now about London, a highwayman . . .

Robert Goodden, and Morris More, and Jeames More, and William Cussens. All these come out of Holland once or twice every year and commit several robberies and so return again . . .

Richard Downes.

38. THE STATE OF INTERNAL TRADE, 1681

[*The Trade of England Revived* . . ., London, 1681,
pp. 1–2, 10–13, 21–3, 28–31, 33–5, 42–5, 50–54]

The Introduction

FORASMUCH as there is a very great complaint in most of the market towns in this kingdom of the *Great Decay of Trade*, both by many working, and especially by all ancient shopkeeping tradesmen, as the woollen draper, the linen draper, the mercer, the grocer, and others, whose trades were formerly the most flourishing in this kingdom, that now are become so mean and ordinary, that many interested therein cannot live upon them. This may afford matter of admiration to many persons, whilst considering withal that there are as many goods imported into this kingdom as ever there were, if not abundantly more; and so, consequently, there is as much sold as ever there were, if not much more. Now the end of this treatise is to shew that the reason is not from the total defect or want of trade, but from the irregularity or disorder thereof, it being quite out of the channel in which it was wont formerly to run. And this hath happened through a neglect of a due execution of those laws that are in force concerning trade; as likewise for want of additional laws to be made to keep it in its due bounds. (For a law not executed is almost as little significant as no law at all.) Now the ground of this grievance is because many do believe that all men promiscuously ought to have liberty to set up any trade for a livelihood, and especially the shopkeeping trade, and that a restraint hereof doth much impeach ingenuity. Whence it is that tradesmen can seldom be redressed herein, although they have often attempted it to their great cost and charge. But certainly in former ages people were of another opinion, as appeareth by that statute of 5 Queen Eliz. which prohibiteth the taking of any artificer's son to be an apprentice to many shopkeeping trades that are mentioned in that statute. And likewise the son of anyone, unless his parent had forty shillings per annum, a freehold estate; which was to be certified under the hands and seals of three justices of the peace.

And for this reason, a long time there hath been little or no inspection made into trade in the cities and market towns in England; that all things in trade are come to a wonderful confusion, as will appear by the sequel of this treatise. Nay, there is scarce anything of affairs in a kingdom or a state, but in time will be out of order, if it be not prevented by reviving old, or constituting new laws, additional thereunto. For humane laws are such, that in time there will be reason, either to add something to, or take something from them. And whilst that anything is out of order, all men that are therein concerned are prejudiced by it. And so it is at this time with trade, which rendereth it unprofitable to all men, and so doth rather hinder ingenuity than further it and promote it; profit being a chief and more immediate encouragement thereof, which puts men upon all praiseworthy and commendable undertakings. Now to the end that I may discover what it is that hath so much impaired the trade of this kingdom, I shall faithfully relate (as to matter of fact) what is the practice in most places in England, and shall in each particular suggest what may be necessary for the repairing thereof . . .

Concerning the Damage and Loss, too often Accruing to the Clothier, in the Sale of his Cloth

After the clothier hath taken all the care and pains that possibly he can to make his cloth both cheap and good, yet when he cometh to sell it, he cannot do it himself, the factor having gotten this business wholly into his hands; for formerly, when the clothiers left their cloth with them to sell, allotting them a certain price, yet notwithstanding they would many times abate two-pence or threepence in a yard, which the clothier would not have done, had he sold it himself. Now so soon as the buyers perceived this, they would buy of none but the factor. And, hence it is, they have usurped the sole power of selling the clothier's cloth, both for what price, and for what time, and to whom they please; in neither of which particulars they will be limited.

Now by this means the clothier's cloth is not only sold for less many times than can be afforded (that so the factor might have his salary), but they are also put to an unnecessary charge, for formerly the buyer always bought at Blackwell Hall, but now he doth buy at home; and the factor will at any time send him as many more pieces of cloth than he hath occasion to buy, and under pretence they are dis-heighted, will force the clothier to pay three or four shillings a piece for new pressing.

And so likewise they will sell for what time they please, detaining the clothier's money as long as they please; for he shall not know when his cloth is sold, nor to whom it is sold; yet a great space of time after, when the factor is in a good humour, then the clothier shall know the selling of his cloth. And after this also he must stay a considerable time before he hath his money. And then neither shall he know to whom his cloth is sold; because by this means, he can at any time put the clothier to have his money for his cloth of a person that is not solvent. So that should any clothier ever attempt, either to take their business out of the factor's hands, or to give off their trade (as many of them are desirous to do, being so abused by the factor), they can always by this means make the clothier truckle under them. And sometimes, when they are so kind to let the clothier have money for his occasions, they will enter it in their books as so much money lent to them. Besides, should they come to know the person to whom their cloth is sold, yet they would be not much the better for it, for without the factor's consent they will not pay the clothier one farthing, saying, they have had nothing to do with him, and so will not pay him any money at all; insomuch that the clothier in selling his cloth is as it were blindfolded, being always in the dark concerning it. And they have seldom any money to buy anything that they deal in beforehand, for the factor will let them have no more money than what will suffice to keep their trade going, and that on a slow and dull pace, by which means it is impossible that either wool or woollen cloth should rise much higher than now it is. As is evident in the late briskness of that trade, which had it not been for the factors (as was acknowledged by an eminent merchant) cloth would have risen at least eighteen pence or two shillings in a yard.

And hence it is there can be no poor clothiers follow the trade, that hath not a stock to lie in the factor's hands, which hath occasioned very great confusion in many other trades as well as this; for it hath put some upon retailing what they make, and others upon hawking their ware all about the country, until many of them are ruined by means of their great charge in travelling; but of both these particulars I shall treat hereafter in their proper place.

Neither hath this been any benefit to the merchant, for the factors having so great a stock of the west country clothiers in their hands, they can give what credit they please, and can, and do, make whomsoever they please merchants, or turn merchants themselves, by which means the old experienced merchants have been extremely prejudiced and wronged. Now to redress this great mischief to the clothing trade, these following particulars would be necessary to be offered.

1. That no clothier or serge maker, or anyone that makes any commodity with our English wool, be allowed, either they themselves or their factors, to sell the same anywhere in London, but in Blackwell Hall only.

2. That when the factor doth sell any clothier's cloth, that he be obliged to give the buyer a bill of the name of the person, and of the place where he liveth whose cloth he hath sold.

3. That notwithstanding the factor's selling of the clothier's cloth, yet the buyer should be debtor to the clothier, whose cloth it is, and not to the factor who sold the cloth, and in default of payment should be liable to be sued by the said clothier.

4. That if the factor do sell the cloth for less money then was set him by the clothier, or should trust any person without the clothier's particular consent to the trusting of that particular person, that in this case the factor should be debtor to the clothier for the full value of the cloth, which was allowed him by the clothier, in the same manner as if it were his proper debt.

5. To the end that the clothier might always know the time when his cloth is sold, and to whom, it would be necessary that there were a register in the Hall, wherein there might be entered the time when the cloth was sold, the factor's name that sold it, the clothier's name, and place of abode, whose cloth it is which is sold, and also the buyer's name and place of abode that hath bought the same. And in this and all other charges they observe a mediocrity . . .

Concerning Hawkers that do Proffer to sell Commodities by Wholesale

Of late years the whole trade of this kingdom is to proffer commodities to the buyer both by wholesale and retail, which hath much impaired all trades, because there is a vast difference between *What will you give?* and *What shall I give?* Now I shall first insist upon those that proffer their wares by wholesale, which are called hawkers, and which are not only the manufacturers themselves, but others besides them, viz. the women in London, in Exeter, and in Manchester, who do not only proffer commodities at the shops and warehouses, but also at inns to country chapmen. Likewise the Manchester men, the Sherborne men, and many others, that do travel from one market town to another, and there at some inn do proffer their wares to sell to the shopkeepers of the place.

That which did occasion men at first to retail those commodities which they made, did at first occasion this also, and is no less disadvantageous than that was, not only to the woollen manufacturers and silk weavers, but also to all the shopkeeping trades in England.

Now although at the first taking up of this hawking way, there were some who did get estates by it, there being then but few of them, by which means they took much more money, and stayed for less time in a place, than now they do; but it is quite otherwise at this day, the number of them being much augmented, by which means they take but little money, and are forced to tarry long in a place, because men do not mind their going away. For if one be gone, be sure another will quickly come. Whereupon some have stayed a fortnight in a country market town. Nay, some rugmakers have waited in London, absent from all their business at home, almost three months before they could vend their wares. And the charge of horsemeat and man's meat is no less than before. So that by reason of their long abode in a place, it doth cost these more now, than formerly it did them that took six times more money; whereby many of them are quite undone, and the rest that remain, who are sufficient men, are so extremely wearied with this way of dealing, that they would be heartily glad (as many of them have confessed) if there were a law to suppress them, that then trade might return into its old channel, where it hath run far better than ever since.

Moreover, this hawking trade doth utterly impair the wholesale trade in all the cities and market towns in England, but especially in the City of London, where are some trades in a manner come to nothing, because country chapmen do not buy of them now, scarce an eighth part of what they were wont to buy formerly.

And it is no less injurious to the retailing shopkeeping trade in all cities and market towns in England.

First, because they have been an occasion to many, that never served an apprenticeship to any shopkeeping trade, to set up the same, not only in cities and market towns, but also in every country village.

Secondly, because when they have been necessitated for money (as often they are by reason of their great expenses and their small trade), to sell their commodities by retail in the several market towns where they have been, and that at as low rates as they would sell by wholesale, have hereby greatly imposed upon their trades and themselves both. But hence may some raise these objections following.

Obj. 1. If this hawking trade be suppressed, what more convenient way can be found for the manufacturer to sell his wares, and also for the buyer to furnish himself with what he wants?

Sol. There is no better way both for the manufacturer to sell his wares, and also for the buyer to furnish himself with what he wants, than at a market. Of which conveniency I intend to treat hereafter.

Obj. 2. But if hawkers be suppressed, the shopkeepers will not have the convenience for the buying their commodities then, as they have now.

Sol. I answer that most of the shopkeepers in England are so sensible of the great wrong they have received from them, that they had rather ride a hundred miles to buy their commodities, than they should be tolerated.

Obj. 3. But if the hawkers be suppressed, it will not be much the better for the shopkeepers in country market towns; for then the Londoners and others will have warehouses in places in the country, which will be as injurious unto them as the hawkers have been.

Sol. For the prevention of this mischief to the trade of the country market towns, it would be necessary that all persons were prohibited by a law to have any warehouse, or to keep any factors or servants to sell commodities for them in any market town or city in England; save only there where they do live with their family . . .

Concerning the Shopkeeping Trades in this Kingdom

That which hath been the bane almost of all trades is the too great number of shopkeepers in this kingdom. For as it is related by Mr. Coke, in a treatise of his concerning trade, that there are ten thousand retailing shopkeepers more in London than are in Amsterdam.

Now the reason hereof is, first, because for many years there have been no other trades but these to receive the youth of this nation. Formerly, when the clothing trade did flourish with us, there were many sufficient men's sons put apprentices to this trade. Secondly, because the shopkeeping trade is an easy life, and thence many are induced to run into it, and there hath been no law to prevent it; or if there be any, it hath been very slackly executed, which maketh very many (like a mighty torrent) fall into it, which hath been verified for several years past by many husbandmen, labourers, and artificers, who have left off their working trades, and turned shopkeepers.

And of Quakers, great numbers of late years are become shopkeepers; for if a man that hath been very meanly bred, and was never worth much above a groat in all his life, do but turn Quaker, he is presently set up in one shopkeeping trade or other, and then many of them will compass sea and land to get this new Quaking shopkeeper a trade. And if he be of a trade that no other Quaker is of in the town or village, then he shall take all their money which they have occasion to lay out and expend in his way, their custom being to sell to all the world, but they will buy only of their own tribe. Insomuch that it is conceived by some wise men that they will in a short time engross the whole trade of the kingdom into their hands.

And then again, there are some of the silk weavers, but more of the clothiers, that deal in as many if not in far more commodities than any shopkeeper doth that hath been apprentice to his trade; for they sell not only the cloth that they make, but stuffs, linen, and many other things; and have such ways to put off their commodities which the shopkeeper hath not; for they will truck them off for shoes with the shoemaker, for candles with the chandler, and sometimes with the butcher for meat, and will make their workfolks to take the same for their work (although there be an express statute against it), and then these workfolk will sell the same again for money, to buy such necessaries which they want.

And it is not much better with them of the City of London, for there are many that do live in a chamber that do take twice as much money as many shopkeepers do, who pay four times the rent that they do, so that it cannot be imagined what an innumerable company of shopkeepers are in every place; and such practices as these have utterly impaired all shopkeeping trades in this kingdom, which are grievances never suffered in former times, being against the common good of the people of this nation. And it's desired they were speedily redressed for these following reasons.

First, because the shopkeeping trade is both a convenient and easy way for the gentry, clergy, and commonalty of this kingdom to provide for their younger sons, that so the bulk of their estates may go to the eldest. For there are few younger sons, who are tradesmen, that have much above one year's revenue of their father's estate for their patrimony. Now these, being kept close to business in the time of their youth, do many of them come to be sober and industrious men; and with this small portion to live a little answerable to the family from whence they descended, being serviceable in their generation both to their king and country, and many times keep up the name and grandeur of their family, when their eldest brother by his vicious and intemperate life hath lost it. And oftentimes it proveth advantageous to their daughters too; for it doth frequently happen, when the gentry die, that they leave but small portions to their daughters, scarce sufficient to prefer them to gentlemen of great revenues (paralleled to their families), yet nevertheless may be thought worthy and deserving of tradesmen who are the younger sons of gentlemen, and by their matching with such as these, do come to live a little suitably to their birth and breeding.

Indeed the Inns of Court and the universities must be acknowledged to be both of them places fit for the preferment of younger sons; but everyone hath not a genius capable of learning those noble (yet abstruse) sciences, there taught and professed, who notwithstanding are capable enough of a shop-keeping trade. Besides, if everyone were fit for either of these, yet they would not suffice to receive a third part even of this sort of youth, and then what should be done with the rest? Should they be brought up to no employment, but be left to the extravagancy of their youthful lusts, to commit such impieties and debaucheries which may justly entitle them to the compellations given by Augustus Caesar to his lewd children, viz. to be called the botches and biles of their family? As it is observable in those countries where the gentry disdain to place forth their children to trades, who therefore turn very dissolute and vicious, and no way serviceable (in times of peace) in their generation, either to their king or country where they live.

Secondly, because shopkeepers by reason of their education were never used to labour, and should their trades be destroyed by these means, they will not know how to maintain themselves and their families. But they that have been bred to work may labour in any other employment, if that to which they have been bred will not maintain them.

Thirdly, because this hath rendered the shopkeeping trade to be unprofitable, like unto many unstinted commons that nobody is the better for. Now where there is no order or rule there must be confusion; as it is in trades at this time. And yet there is order and rule observed in other vocations, and why not so in this? The minister must not preach until he is ordained; the lawyer must not plead before he is called to the Bar; the chirurgeon must not practise before he hath his licence; neither can the midwife practise before she hath her licence too: and therefore why should any set up a shopkeeping trade, before they have been made free of the same?

This is one reason why so few apprentices, after they come out of their time, do get into the world, or can make any benefit of their trades. Wherefore it concerneth all whatsoever, whether gentlemen or clergymen, to be very solicitous for the preservation of this way of life, which is so conducing to the preferment of their children.

Fourthly, because it will cost a round sum of money before a child can be settled in any shopkeeping trade. First, to breed him at school and to make him fit for the same. Secondly, to place him forth to the said trade when he is fit; which will cost in a country market town not less than fifty or sixty pounds, but in London upwards of an hundred; so that these trades do seem to be purchased, and that not only with money by the parents, but with a servitude also by the son.

Therefore, as I conceive, they ought to have the properties of their trades confirmed unto them, even as other men have the properties of their lands confirmed unto them. That is, that no person do set up any shopkeeping trade, unless they be made free of the same. And if any should plead that it might be lawful for one man to use another's land as his own for a livelihood, he would presently be accounted a Leveller and a ridiculous fellow. And certainly no less can he be accounted that should argue it might be lawful for one man to use another's trade. For this trade is bought with the parent's money, and the son's servitude, and intended for a future livelihood for the son in the same manner as land is bought by the father, and settled upon the child for his future livelihood and comfortable subsistence . . .

Now to this end I shall suggest some particulars that may be esteemed necessary: first for the settling of a right order herein, and afterwards for continuing the same when once established. For the settling of the shopkeeping trade: . . . That in all the cities and market towns in England, the shopkeepers do all they can at the first settling of trades to distinguish the same, as much as may be, one from another. It is true, custom formeth trades, and in some few places they are hereby very well distinguished already; yet in many places they are not. And although every trade cannot be distinguished as they are in London, yet in many places they may come near it, especially in some eminent cities and market towns, as Oxford, Salisbury, Northampton, and the like; and we may instance farther in Marlborough, a little town (in comparison of these), where they almost have this distinction, and live better upon their trades than they do in more noted places where their trades are not so distinct; for in these latter, many shopkeepers do not get so much by their trades, as some workmen do by their labour. The reason is clear: for if a man hath not a very great stock, he cannot be sufficiently furnished with the commodities belonging to so many trades. Yet there are few places of eminency, but may admit of these trades as several and distinct, viz. a woollen draper, a linen draper, a mercer that may also sell all sorts of silver and gold lace, and silks and buttons, and all other silken wares that are for trimming either to men's or women's clothes; a milliner, who should not be suffered to cut any wrought silks as the mercers do, but only to sell them in hoods and scarves ready made; the semsterer, who should also sell linen only in things ready made; the upholsterer, the ironmonger, the bookseller, the apothecary, the grocer, and the chandler, who might sell bacon and eggs, butter and cheese, oatmeal, and salt, fish and fowl, poultry, and rabbits, mustard, and verjuice, hops, brooms, maps, and brushes. I have named all the commodities that may belong to this trade, because I find it in no place distinguished, and which would in most places be a good trade. The tallow chandler, who might not only make and sell tallow candles, but wax candles also and torches, who might sell all sorts of glasses, and bottles, crockery, and earthenware. The haberdasher of hats, in regard that women of late years do not so commonly wear hats as they were wont formerly, may be allowed to make their hats, and so may their trade be as good as most shopkeeping working trades. The baker's trade would be much bettered, if none but they were permitted to retail meal, and that they did retail also all sorts of grain. And when trade is once distinguished, it would be necessary to preserve it so; which must be by hindering others to deal in such commodities that do properly appertain to another trade. This would be a very great advantage to young men that have but stock enough to compass one trade, and none can in reason be against it; save only some overgrown tradesmen, that have stock enough to engross many trades . . .

Concerning Petty Shopkeepers living in Country Villages

This is another thing that (as well as pedlars) doth greatly increase and add to the number of shopkeepers, and doth likewise contribute towards the ruining of the cities and market towns in England, and which was never wont to be formerly; for now in every country village where is (it may be) not above ten houses, there is a shopkeeper, and one that never served any apprenticeship to any shopkeeping trade whatsoever; and many of those are not such that do deal only in pins or such small wares, but such that deal in as many substantial commodities as any do that live in cities and market towns, who have not less than 1,000*l.* worth of goods in their shops, for which they pay not one farthing of any tax at all, either parochial or national.

Certainly all men must needs apprehend that if this, and pedlars, be suffered that cities and market towns must needs be impoverished, because then there will be little occasion (I say) to bring the country people to them, the which hath happened in a very great measure already. For in some places there is not a fifth part of the money taken by the shopkeepers as was formerly, and in many places not half, and in some particular trades there is (as may be made appear) 25,000*l.* stock made use of less than there was heretofore. And there are these several reasons following, why it is necessary that market towns and cities should be encouraged and upheld in their trades.

1. Because the people that do live in cities and market towns do depend wholly upon a trade for the maintenance both of themselves and their families. And if their trade be taken from them by such ways as these are, they will be at a very great loss to know what to do, because they were never bred to anything else. Yet so it is not with those that deal in villages, who have been bred in some other way. And they have, or may have, some other way of living besides the shopkeeping trade.

2. Because if cities and market towns be impoverished, then the general part of the people of this kingdom will lose that necessary conveniency before mentioned for the preferment of their children. And this is one reason that when many parents have been at great charge in placing forth their children to trades in cities and market towns, and the children have faithfully served out their full time, that, after all, they are but little the better for it, because pedlars, and shopkeepers in villages, such that never served any apprenticeship to any shopkeeping trade, do intercept a very great part of the trade from coming to them.

3. This will be a great means to depopulate not only the cities and market towns, but also the whole kingdom; for when men can find little or no encouragement in their trades, then they will endeavour to transplant themselves into other countries, where they may have better encouragement, by which means we shall lose our people; whereas (in the opinion of many wise men) we do already want more people in England than now we have, there being very great numbers that have gone, not only into our own plantations, but into Holland, and settled there.

4. If cities and market towns be impoverished and depopulated, then there will not be raised out of them that proportion of all manner of taxes as now there is; so that the burthen hereof will be the heavier upon lands and revenues in the country. And it will be a very great diminution of all those standing taxes that the cities and market towns do bear the only, or at least the greatest, proportion as they do in the excise of beer and ale, for little is gathered anywhere else. And the farmers of the excise are always sensible of the ebbing and flowing of trade, whose excise doth ebb and flow accordingly. And then if cities and market towns grow poor, the chimney money will never increase thereby. The gatherers of this tax are able to give an account what multitudes of paupers are exempted by certificates in cities and market

owns in England; and yet notwithstanding there be many do pay who had need also be exempted.

5. If cities and market towns be impoverished and depopulated of their wealthy and rich inhabitants for want of trade, the great and numerous poor that are in most of them will want to be relieved, which is a burthen that doth lie very heavy upon them already. For in some market towns there are many that are not worth much above a hundred pound stock, which do not pay less than ten shillings a year towards the relief of the poor; which is such a burthen that, if it lay upon the country farmer, it would much weaken him in the paying of his rent. Now if the poor should not be relieved, what can be expected, but that swarms of them would go into the country for relief, as already they do in many places? And when the ruder sort cannot get enough by begging, they will by pilfering and stealing. So that the consideration of these poor, and the many younger brothers that will be out of any way of living, with the like contingencies, will administer just occasion to any wise and intelligent person, easily to presage the misfortunes and miseries that will hereupon necessarily ensue throughout this kingdom.

6. If cities and market towns be impoverished and depopulated for want of a trade, then what will the country man do to have money for all his commodities, as his butter, his cheese, his cattle, his wool, his corn, and his fruit? The shopkeepers in the country villages will yield but little help in this case, and the pedlars much less. It is manifest that the people living in cities and market towns consume all these commodities of the farmers, and do help them to ready money for the same; by which means they have wherewith to pay their rent, and serve their other occasions; and it is impossible for them to subsist but by this way. So that in all reason this kindness ought to be reciprocal, and when it is so, it is the better for both; for it cannot be supposed that tradesmen in cities and market towns should ever hold out, to buy the farmers' commodities, and help them constantly to money for them, if they should always go home, and lay out little or no part thereof again with them.

7. If cities and market towns be impoverished and depopulated for want of trade, the kingdom may then be obnoxious to its enemies upon all occasions. For these use to be the fences and bulwarks of a country, insomuch that in some other countries they are so far from admitting of tradesmen to live in villages, that their gentry do not live there, but in the great cities and towns; by which means they have greater towns than we generally have; and most of their towns are walled, and so are not only able to resist an enemy, but also upon all occasions to succour and save those that shall fly unto them . . .

Now to the end that trade might be promoted in this kingdom, and that it may be regulated and set in such order that it might run in its right current, and that we might be able to balance either the Dutch or French herein, I shall humbly suggest these three necessary particulars, that in all probability will effect the same.

If there were a council for trade made up of some eminent tradesmen of the City of London, mixed with some of the country, and some eminent clothiers, who might consider what might be necessary for the promotion of trade, and for the right settling thereof, and who might suggest the same to the Parliament when they do meet, that so they may have the less to do herein; for the whole structure of trade is very much out of frame at present, which would require much time to set it right again; and the Parliament do seldom sit above two or three months or thereabouts at a time, and then they have such a throng of other business obtruding them, that they have little or no leisure to mind the concerns of trade.

Concerning all Trades being in Companies

If all those of a trade were of one and the same company, and had power to make some bylaws for the good of their trade, it would extremely conduce not only to the promotion of the same, but to the keeping of it in a right and good order, preserving (at least) a *temperamentum ad justitiam*, if not *ad pondus* in our trades and negotiations.

And doubtless *ab origine* it was so in London, as appears by the several denominations of their several companies; the defect whereof, I judge, is the reason that the trade of that City is declining, and grown so consumptive, and (unless suitable and timely means be used in order to its recovery) will certainly and suddenly expire. For if none were of a company but those only that were of the same trade, they would be frequently whetting one another to do something that might be for the advancement thereof; and everyone would refrain the doing of anything that might give a wound to the same, for fear of being reprehended by the company.

But now if any person's trade do differ from the trade of his company, of which he is free, he doth then mind but little the trade of that company, because he hath a small benefit by it; but if his trade be the same with the company of which he is free, then he is very often mindful of what may be necessary to promote the same, because he doth expect a benefit by it.

Now (I conceive) this might easily be reduced to what it was at first; for it would be no prejudice to any of the companies, for everyone to have the liberty to come into that company that his trade is of, and to be in the same state and degree therein, as he was in, in that company that he came out of, without paying anything more for it; because, as they shall hereby lose some of their members out of every company, so will there be received some more into them.

Obj. Now there are two companies in London, viz. the girdlers and fletchers, that the trades thereof are quite lost and gone, there being none of either of them; and if this device should take place, the rents belonging to those two halls will be lost, because there will be nobody to look after them.

Sol. That the linen drapers have no hall, and is no company, which now is the most flourishing trade of the City. Therefore it would be very convenient to join these two halls together, and to make them belong to the Linen Drapers' Company.

And then to the end that this order might continue, it would be necessary that no person be suffered to set up the trade of any particular company, unless he be first made free of the same.

Obj. But if this be so, then the privilege of the City will be lost; which is, that he that is free of any trade, may set up any other whatsoever, that he can best live upon.

Sol. My meaning is, that he that hath been apprentice to a working trade should not have the privilege of setting up the shopkeeping trade, and that for the reasons that have been already given. Yet I deny not but that it might be convenient enough for any shopkeeper (that is only of buying and selling) to have that privilege to leave his own trade, and to take up another shopkeeping trade, that he may live better upon. But then it would be necessary that he should be enjoined to leave his own trade altogether, and to quit his freedom of his company, and that within a certain time, that may be thought convenient; and that he be also further enjoined to take his freedom of that company as the trade is of that he intends to set up, and that within such a convenient time.

And as this being in companies is necessary for shopkeepers, and all other trades, even so it is for merchants too, that all they that do traffic to any particular country, which should exceedingly encourage all foreign trade; for there would be then such an order in the trade of every particular country that men would gain thereby, whereas now it doth too often happen that they do lose.

I know there are very wise men that are very much against merchants being in companies, but I cannot find that any merchandising trade is managed so well as those that are managed by companies; and this appeareth by the Dutch, who do trade altogether in companies, and who is it that hath such success in trade as they have?; likewise our Hamburg trade was never carried on better than when they were in a company, and it was then better for clothiers too than ever it hath been since. And I cannot but believe that if the fishing trade, that is so advantageous to the Dutch, were committed to a company, it would in a short time turn to a very good account.

But I suppose that the reason that many are against merchants being in companies is because hereby many men would be barred from adventuring to any country, unless they were free of that same particular company. Now to help this, it would be necessary that any one should have the liberty to be of any company of merchants that he hath a mind unto, always provided that every such person do engage to submit to the laws and orders of the said company. And if it be so, it can be no prejudice to any man, for he that hath an estate enough, may be free of many companies, and so may adventure into many countries.

Obj. But now every particular trade cannot be a particular company in few other places but in London, by reason of the paucity of the traders there.

But yet, nevertheless, they may be in companies in the country towns, for there may be many trades that may conveniently be of one company; as all these shopkeeping trades, viz. the woollen and linen draper, the mercer, the milliner, the apothecary, the grocer, the chandler, the ironmonger, and the bookseller; even so many shopkeeping working trades may be of another company, and many other working trades that are not shopkeeping trades may be of another, and those that employ the poor may be a distinct company likewise.

39. MARKET TOWNS IN 1681

['Thomas Baskerville's Journeys in England, *temp*. Car. II',
Hist. MSS. Commission, XXIX, *Portland*, II, pp. 269-70, 289-91]

[The market at Norwich]

A little way from this castle on the opposite side of a hill is the chief market place of this city, and this being the only place where all things are brought to be sold for the food of this great city, they not as in London allowing markets in several places, make it vastly full of provisions, especially on Saturdays, where I saw the greatest shambles for butchers' meat I had ever yet seen, and the like also for poultry and dairy meats, which dairy people also bring many quarters of veal with their butter and cheese, and I believe also in their seasons pork and hog-meats. These people fill a square of ground on the side of a hill twice as big [as] Abingdon market place. They setting their goods in ranges as near as may be one above another, only allowing room for single persons to pass between; and above these the butchers have their shambles and such kind of people as sell fish, of which there was plenty of such kinds as the seas hereabouts afford, viz. crabs, flounders, mackerel, very cheap, but lobster for sea fish and pike or jack for river fish were dear enough. They asked me for one pike under 2 foot, 2*s*. 6*d*., and for a pot of pickled oysters they would have a shilling. Here I saw excellent oatmeal which being curiously hulled looked like French barley, with great store of gingerbread and other edible things. And for grain in the corn market, which is on the other side the market house, as large for space of ground as that on which the dairy people stand, I saw wheat, rye, oats, malt ground and not ground, French wheat, and but little barley, because the season for malting was over.

Their chief market house stands in the midst of this great market place, now very full of people and provisions, being circular or round in form, having chained to the several pillars thereof bushels, pecks, scales, and other things for the measuring and weighing of such goods as are brought to the market. And over against this declivity where the market people stand is a fair walk before the prime inns and houses of the market place, called the gentlemen's walk or walking place, which is kept free for that purpose from the encumbrance of stalls, tradesmen, and their goods. About the middle of this walk is the sign of the 'King's Head' where we lay, Mrs. Berne, a widow, then landlady, who keeps a good ordinary on Saturdays for 12 pence meat, where we dined in the company of many gentlemen. The names of those I remember and was most intimate with were Captain Springhall of Reedham, Mr. Elwin, and Mr. Wharton, gentlemen of Yarmouth. Here is also in the compass of this market place a fair town hall, where the mayor and his brethren with the livery men of this city keep a great feast, presenting the ladies that come thither with marchpanes to carry away. They have also fine shows in the streets, in some measure like that of the Lord Mayor's Day of London, and, as Mr. Burton told me, one of the eminent scholars of his school does usually make an elegant speech to the mayor and his brethren as they pass by, richly clad in their scarlet robes.

The chief trade of this famous town mostly consists in making stuffs and worsted stockings, they in these sorts of manufactures excelling all other places. As to the river it is not so broad as the Thames below Oxon, yet the boats that trade between this and Yarmouth usually carry between 20 and 30 tons. Taking a boat for pleasure to view this city by water, the boatman brought us to a fair garden belonging to the Duke of Norfolk, having handsome stairs leading to the water by which we ascended into the garden and saw a good bowling-green, and many fine walks; the gardener now keeping good liquors and fruits to entertain such as come there to see it. From this garden for the rest of the city down stream, and about a furlong up stream, there are no houses built on the other side the river to hinder that prospect into the country; but after, as we went further up the stream, the city is built on both sides the river, here being divers parishes and a tolerable big town for houses on the right hand side. In this passage where the city encloses both sides of the river we rowed under five or six bridges and then landed at the Duke of Norfolk's palace, a sumptuous new built house, not yet finished within, but seated in a dung-hole place, though it has cost the Duke already 30 thousand pounds in building, as the gentleman that shewed it told us, for it hath but little room for gardens, and is pent up on all sides, both on this and the other side the river, with tradesmen's and dyers' houses, who foul the water by their constant washing and cleaning their cloth, whereas had it been built adjoining to the aforesaid garden, it had stood in a delicate place. Above this house there are more bridges upon the river which I cannot give account of.

Here is in this city an order the like is nowhere else to be found in any town in England, and that is, the butchers are obliged to sell the meat they kill the fore part of the week by Thursday night, for on a Friday night, speaking to our landlady for a joint of mutton to be roasted for our suppers, she told us it was not to be had. And this they do to oblige the fishermen to bring plenty of fish from the sea, as also to make good the sale of that kind of food, so that, as some gentlemen of Yarmouth told me, they many times there for that reason have but bare or scanty markets of fish . . .

[Northampton]

Hampton [= Northampton] is about six or seven miles from Tortester [= Towcester]. We went through a village called Milton, and being come within two miles of Northampton, we had a fair prospect of the town seated by a river, on ground gently rising on the other side the stream, to which the way leads over a stone bridge. And about a mile on the right hand in another road stands a fair cross with the effigies of some kings and queens cut in stone work. The town seems to be not much less than Oxford, having fair streets and strong built houses of freestone of an ochre colour in many places, with fair inns and very spacious market place. It hath likewise to adorn it four churches, viz. St. Peter's, St. Sepulchre's, Allhallows, and St. Giles'; and at the end of the town which leads towards Daintree [= Daventry] an old castle. This town some years since this journey hath suffered under a dreadful conflagration, three parts or more of it being totally ruined by that furious element, but 'tis since, phœnix-like risen out of her ashes in a far more noble and beauteous form, the houses of the streets being now built in very good order with excellent freestone and 'bellconies', and some of the inns are such gallant and stately structures the like is scarcely elsewhere to be seen.

Some weeks after the fire I went thither to see this ruinous heap, when I found about the middle of the town an indifferent house standing, and all the other houses for a good distance round about it burnt down, and yet the upper stories of it were only studded with lath and plaster work; 'twas a small inn and had for the sign a shoemaker's last with this motto 'I have sought after good ale over the town and here I have found it at last'. The strangeness of the preservation made me alight to discover of the innkeeper how it could possibly be effected, who told me by the help of some friends hoisting some hogsheads of beer out of the cellar, and being very diligent to cool those parts of the house which were very hot, they did preserve it.

Sir William Farmer, before spoken of, having a fair house at the lower end of the town, it was turned into an inn immediately after the fire, and so were some other gentlemen's houses in the outward borders of the town. Here is kept on St. James's day a great fair where many good horses are bought and sold, as also at other fairs held in this town when the days come . . .

[Worcester]

From Oster [= Alcester] it is twelve miles to Worcester. We had a fair prospect of it from a hill in the way a mile or more before we came to it. The way to this city is a reddish earth and very bad for travellers in winter, so that for the benefit of horsemen in dirty weather they have made a causeway extending some miles from the town. As touching the city of Worcester, I think 'tis bigger than Oxford, and very full of people, but the streets, excepting that running through the city to the bridge, and another thwarting the upper end of this street, are narrow, and old decayed buildings. Here are twelve or thirteen churches, with that on the other side Severn, to which a fair bridge with six large arches big enough for hoys to pass under, gives the passage. This river is navigable for these kind of vessels to Shrewsbury and further, and from those parts they bring down abundance of coal to serve the city and other places beneath it, and from Bristol they bring merchantable goods up stream again to serve these parts. Along the banks of Severn here, which is well nigh a bow-shot over, running with a nimble clear current, are large fertile meadows, but that which is most remarkable as touching ingenuity on the shore of the town side is a waterwork, which the stream of the river, without the help of horses, having a wheel which gives motion to suckers and forcers, it pumps the water so high into a leaden cistern that it serves any part of the city. Nevertheless, that water may be more plentiful they have horses also at work to force up water, and here also, which I have nowhere else seen, save in the city of Ely, they fetch water from the river upon horses in leathern bags, to sell . . .

40. ON THE DECAYING TRADE OF TOWNS, AND ITS CAUSES, 1681

[University of London, Goldsmith's Library Pamphlet, Cat. No. 2416]

CONSIDERATIONS
Offered to all the
CORPORATIONS
of
ENGLAND

Well worth their Observation, containing seasonable Advice to them in their future Elections of Burgesses to serve in Parliament, merely in relation to, and so far forth only, as such Elections affect Trade, and are, as will appear hereby, the main Cause of its present Decay.

EXPERIENCE does sufficiently assure every trading man in this kingdom, that there is a great and general decay of trade, but the true reason of this decay is known to few, and they very likely who do perceive it, having little or no interest by it, are little or not all concerned to remedy it; divers causes are assigned by divers men, according to their different interest and principles; the divine charges it upon the sinful lives of men, for which God has brought this, and threatens other yet severer judgements, and he is not altogether mistaken, it being on all hands confessed, that for the sins of a nation are God's judgements upon it, but as the design of these sheets is to enquire into second and causes merely humane, I shall pass over this first, with this observation only, that if that were the only reason, as the sins of the nation are general and common to all orders and degrees of men, the judgements for those sins would be so too; but here is a heavier portion upon one part of the land than upon the rest, and they who are most afflicted are not perhaps the greatest offenders.

To keep therefore within my bounds and to my first purpose of humane causes: that your factious schismatics (those enemies of God and the king) who hate and mislike the government only because they have no share in it (and who, fearing the pretence of religion to stale a cheat, are glad to lay hold on any), are they who most cry out for the decay of trade, though they have least reason so to do, since I shall make it appear anon they are the main cause of it, is visible to all men, these impute that decay to the miscarriages in government; and whilst their restless spirits (which still long for the fleshpots of their old Egypt in which the true Israel was by them enslaved) are afraid too openly to declare against the government, they do the utmost to undermine what they dare not directly assault, in commending and slyly insinuating the good days of the late times, the plenty, power, riches, and reputation of their dear Commonwealth. Thus labouring to create some disturbance, that in the troubled waters they may fish for themselves, and catch once more some share in the government which God and nature have not formed, the king called, nor their own abilities qualified them for.

I come now to the true cause, which as I have already said is chiefly in and from them who most complain; if trade have not run in its old current; if manufactors of all sorts are brought so low that workmen can scarce be paid so as to live, and their masters get bread at the same time; if through this abatement of the value of manufactures, men are so far discouraged from making them that thousands of men are thereby without employ; men become averse to the breeding up of their children to trades, by which they are not likely to get a livelihood, and tradesmen as backward in taking youth into their service, when they have not a prospect of work enough to answer the charges of their servants and their own pains. The great reason of all this decay is that trade is not in that esteem it was formerly, and the cause of the decrease of that esteem is plain, because it has not of late years had the advantages and encouragements it once had, and which without doubt by the laws and constitutions of the kingdom it ought still to have.

These discourages and disadvantages of trade, the true causes of its decay, are no less truly the effects of the undue elections of Members to serve in Parliament, in which these ill affected gentlemen have for these last fifty years had a far greater interest than the rest of men who had voices in elections; I call the elections undue, because I find them directly against the plain words and sense of such statutes as direct elections.

'Tis well known of late years, the House of Commons has been filled with gentlemen, whose ignorance of and unconcern for trade has by degrees brought it to the condition it is now in; and the end I propose to myself in this, is to convince all corporations that it is their duty and interest in the elections hereafter to choose such men who live and subsist by trade, and whose interests are of necessity to rise and fall as that does; that it is their duty will appear from the Acts of Parliament, and that it is their interest also will, I hope, be made pretty plain from what I shall hereafter set down.

There are several statutes concerning elections, as you will find them set down in the margent, the first of these directs the time and manner of giving notice in the county of an election to be; the second confirms the first, fines the sheriff who shall act contrary to it in one hundred pounds; the third I shall speak of last; the fourth appoints every knight of the shire that shall be chosen to have forty shillings a year at least of freehold in the county where he shall be chosen, and to be resident and dwelling in the same county; the fifth obliges every man who shall have a voice in the election of a knight of the shire, to have likewise forty shillings a year, and to be dwelling in the same county; the sixth provides against false returns, and appoints penalties on the sheriffs in that case. The third which is most to the present purpose, confirming former statutes, appoints what men shall be chosen burgesses, and how qualified for the election, which being so material and necessary for all men to know, I have thought good to set it down in its own words, the rather for that it is very short.

First that the statutes of the election of knights of the shires to come to the Parliament be holden and kept in all points adjoining to the same, that the knights of the shires, which from henceforth shall be chosen in every shire, be not chosen unless they be resident within the shire where they shall be chosen, the day of the date of the writ of the summons of the Parliament. And that the knights and esquires, and other which shall be choosers of those knights of the shires be also resident within the same shires in manner and form as is aforesaid. And moreover it is ordained and established that the citizens and burgesses of the cities and boroughs be chosen men, citizens, and burgesses, resident, dwelling, and free in the same cities and boroughs, and no other in any wise.

Thus far the statute which is very short and very plain. Here the King with his Parliament, observing now at their time gentlemen freeholders were sometimes returned for boroughs who had interests of their own to manage, and these being opposite to those of tradesmen, whose burgesses they were, they were not like to favour these against themselves, nor to take that care of trade as was requisite for the public good, of which, and of the ways and means of improving it, they were wholly ignorant.

These things considered by King and Parliament, to prevent the growing mischief, they did very seasonably apply that early remedy of this Act of Parliament, obliging thereby corporations to choose representatives among themselves of their own cities and boroughs, inhabiting and dwelling among them, and sure this was done with as great wisdom as justice; for since the design of burgesses from every corporation was (and still is) that each city and borough might have somebody on their behalfs present in Parliament well versed in their ways and means of dealing, best acquainted with their grievances, and consequently best able to represent them; that so through the

7 H. 4. Ch. 15,
11 H. 4. Ch. 1,
1 H. 5. Ch. 1,
8 H. 6. Ch. 7, 10,
H. 6. Ch. 2, 23,
H. 6, Ch. 16.

1 H. 5. Ch. 1.

endeavours of every burgess in particular, the mischiefs and grievances of every part being made known by those who best knew them, the whole nation might be preserved and its interests advanced; I do not see nor can conceive how any man can be presumed better qualified to answer these ends, than such men as the statute directs, viz. citizens and burgesses resident, dwelling, and free in the same cities and boroughs and in no other wise; . . . and indeed I should be glad that any man would shew me how according to this statute most of our late elections be made out: how by your statute is a gentleman of the Temple a fit Member for Worcester or Taunton? Or how a very worthy knight resident and dwelling in Southampton Square (though otherwise of very great abilities) sufficiently qualified for a burgess of Plymouth? How these gentlemen, I say (though never so learned in all other things), can be supposed to understand perfectly the particular interest of cities and towns, in which perhaps they were set foot but at elections? Or what reason tradesmen have to hope or promise themselves that strangers (being gentlemen, whose interests, if they run not directly counter to, are yet very different from theirs who choose them) should be more concerned for their good (though in opposition to their own) than men of their own body, obliged by the same interests, and therefore moved by the same considerations, is not within my understanding . . .

I. What has the House of Commons, being full of gentlemen, done, as for instance (not to run back into times, which it were to be wished were as absolutely forgot as the guilt of them is forgiven) in 1660? It was necessary to improve the revenue of the Crown, they did it by easing themselves and laying the burthen upon the trading part of the people.

The Court of Wards and Liveries, tenures *in capite* and by knight's service were one of the goodliest jewels in the Crown, a high and vast prerogative it was, and such a one by means whereof the kings of England had a strange hand over all the gentry, by the great interest they had in all their houses as well over the persons of their children as their estates; yet this prerogative extended but to them, tradesmen were not at all concerned; this therefore they thought fit to remove, but that the Crown might be no loser (as there was no reason it should) something was to be found out equivalent, the excise, which just before had been given for the King's life, was thought fittest, and was accordingly settled upon the Crown in fee.

12. Ca. 2di.
Ch. 24.

II. The taking away these Courts has been as prejudicial to the yeomanry, as it has been useful to the gentry, who before of interest were obliged to make their farms less, and to let long leases at reasonable rates; but now they erect great farms which few are able to rent, and rack the poor tenants.

III. All the assessments and revenues of the Crown are chiefly paid by the middle sort of people, as tenths and first fruits from the clergy, customs by merchants, excise by brewers, chimney money by tenants, freeholders paying nothing certain to the Crown, which is a great disadvantage to the trading people that freeholders are not obliged to some proportion, at least in payments with them.

IV. Upon a presumption of raising the product of England, many laws have been neglected, which would be highly for the interest of the trading sort of people, and some laws have been made directly contrary to their interest, which is no wonder when amongst the lawgivers there are so few (if any) that either understand what may prejudice or advance trade, or if they do, through self interest, politicly dissemble that knowledge. Of this sort are all those laws which give leave for the exportation of the growth of England without manufacturing. Secondly, most of those laws prohibit the growth of other countries, which if trading were free, we might with great advantage purchase with our own manufactures. Of this kind there is a very late one, the Irish Bill, which enriching only a few in the west of England, is out of every housekeeper's way in London and most counties twenty shillings a year for every person in his family, besides the disadvantage of our artificers in exchange of manufacture, and our Irish merchant in exchange of money.

Before I pass further, I must needs here mention one great damage the Crown itself sustains by this bill. For the victualling the Navy stands his Majesty each pound of beef once as much again as his neighbours, the French and Dutch, to whom the Irish (being forbidden England) are forced to sell their cattle at a very low rate; thus the King loses, the City loses, all Ireland or a good part of it suffers, when besides the French and Dutch, a few west country gentlemen and their tenants only gain by it.

V. There are many laws which would be of very great use for the public interest, which upon the same account are neglected and laid aside; as first the most excellent Statute of the fifth of the Queen, Ch. 5, the very title of which were sufficient to recommend it. It is an Act touching politic constitutions for the maintenance of the Navy. In this statute amongst other things, that great and wise princess, and as true a Protestant as the best of them that distinguish themselves by the name, makes several provisions for the increase of shipping and sailors, appointing them certain fish days, by which means they might be encouraged through the certainty of a market for fish to build vessels, bring up and employ seamen, and for want of which, those few that do now use fishing, carry it into other countries, where they are sure of a market, so that we find by experience that fish is cheaper in other countries of Europe than it is here in England, though that fish be taken upon our coast and by our countrymen. Secondly, flesh would be at a more reasonable rate, if that prodigious quantity were not each day devoured, and for which we are looked upon as such gluttons by the world, even to become a byword among the nations, for who has not heard it said that London must needs be a strange beast that in six months consumes more flesh than all Spain in seven years, and this was another end of that statute.

VI. The laws ought to be revived which preserves the property of the trading corporation, and those which regard aliens, not that at this time, when the wisdom of King and Council think fit in so extraordinary an occasion to receive and encourage them to use their trades, I presume to offer anything further than that the statute, whereby they cannot work but as retained by English, nor take other apprentices than English, saving their own children, be at that time looked well after; for that by such means, these aliens might freely trade, and the profit be shared between them and the English.

VII. The laws against hawkers ought to be revived, by whom great abuses are committed. Wares are ill made and trade brought low, all which matters now so heavy on tradesmen would be remedied, if so in their elections they pursued the Act of Parliament, and made choice of such men as were sensible of such grievances, and were obliged as well of interest as in justice to redress them.

There are likewise many things very advantageous and beneficial that might be passed into laws, if such elections were,

1. As first, that freeholders should constantly bear an equal share in payments to the Crown with the trading people; that would enable the King to force a trade abroad, and encourage manufactures at home.

2. That a register might be established to prevent cheats, which fall most on tradesmen, and the many trivial suits in law, upon several and inconsiderable accounts, a blessing not to be hoped for as long as lawyers fill the House.

3. That all linen cloth under the value of 3*s.* an ell might be prohibited, and a valuable tax set upon our own manufactured cloth, to make up the loss the Crown will receive by that prohibition. This would employ a million of people, and if the work were carried on by a public stock, it would in three years' time abate as much in the poor's book, as the first advanced stock would amount to.

4. That many persons having little or no estate (who live at a rate much above their ranks and fortunes, whereby the tradesmen of whom they take up must needs be losers) may be obliged to take to some honest employment.

5. That money lent upon land security should not receive above 4*l.* 10*s.* per cent, and money upon personal security be at 8*l.* per cent. The present equality of interest money, without respect to the difference of the security, having this disadvantage, that 6*l.* per cent. being more profitable than the land itself at 20 years' purchase, men choose rather to lend upon land, than purchase it; hence arise mortgages, whereby so many have been cheated; where, if this remedy were had, men would choose to buy outright, and fraud prevented.

From these considerations I presume it is by this time pretty plain that it is the interest of all the corporations in England to make choice in their elections hereafter of tradesmen of their own respective corporations; it being as absurd as injurious to trust all the trade of England in the hands of men, who neither truly understand it, nor are concerned to improve and advance it, it being clearly the interest of freeholders that the number of tradesmen increase, though not their fortunes, that tradesmen be many and poor.

There is no doubt but after the making of the Statute of H. 5th citizens and tradesmen were returned to serve in Parliament; and 'tis very clear that the reason why that custom has been discontinued was by reason of the charges each city and borough was at in paying their Members, which made them give ear to those who voluntarily proffered their service, though they have dearly paid for it since. Surely there is scarce any corporation so poor, but amongst them may be found two men of such fortunes as does enable them to bear the expense of that service, though otherwise the paying of members is by far the less evil, considering what burthens have been laid upon them by a House of Commons made up of gentlemen and lawyers.

The greatest strength and riches of England were formerly in the hands of the middle sort of people, and is not yet so far alienated but that it may be retrieved, if care be taken to make due elections; without which the wealth of the nation will quickly be engrossed into a few hands, and what ways or means men then shall have to raise their fortunes by diligence and industry, every ordinary judgement can satisfy itself.

From these late elections it has followed that the interests of corporations have been neglected, their grievances unregarded, whilst so many learned gentlemen, have thought everything less than the whole kingdom at a lump, too mean for their consideration.

The bare name of a statesman, or stickler, has of late preferred many men to elections, and they have held themselves obliged to make good the opinion their electors had entertained of them; so that one may say every single burgess has of late been not so much the representative of a corporation, as of the whole kingdom.

The reason men give to excuse the great neglect of the interest of corporations is very plausible. Corporations, say they, are but little members of the body politic, of which the state is the head. If that be diseased and its humours not purged, the several members will be affected, and that I allow. But whether the ways and measures lately pursued with so much zeal and passion be the properest means to purge what ill humours are in the head, so as to restore health and vigour to every member, is a question. May we not reasonably think that if every Member would study the particular advantages of that county, city, borough he serves for, make it his business to enquire well into their interests, and represent their real grievances, and each in their turns get the concurrence of the whole House to the remedying thereof; may we not think, I say, that this way of curing and comforting every Member severally (which would produce in the end ease and safety to all) might do the business every whit as well? Yet this is not to be expected whilst by a monstrous mistrust of the honesty or ability of our own fellow citizens (not like London, who has wisely at all times preserved that great and important right of sending Members of her own) we accept of gentlemen, whom (if but for their eager desire of the employment, being strangers to us) we might very reasonably suspect to have some other and further ends and designs by the election than our interests and concerns. For I cannot be brought to believe that a gentleman, one whom I have never obliged, of different interests from me, will spend a thousand pounds to carry an election, merely to serve mine. How unlikely this is, and unreasonable soever it be to believe it, yet we swallow the pill, and are as fond of choosing them, as they are glad to be chosen. Thus whilst we cry out liberty and property, full of needless and imaginary fears and apprehensions from higher powers, we ourselves are the greatest betrayers of our rights and liberties, whilst we, rashly and un-advisedly, trust them and our religion in the hands of men whose principles in religion, maxims of state, secret grudges, and distastes at the government upon private accounts, we as little understand as they do our true interests.

And now whilst we may lawfully do ourselves justice, to neglect it, and promise it to ourselves from other men, is surely great indiscretion. The mischiefs and inconveniences of undue elections are, I hope, made out, the burthen that lies so heavy on tradesmen most plain. What is wanting to perfect the happiness of the nation, and the means to arrive at it set down; and all this to be done with much ease and security. If therefore the con-siderations of duty cannot move men to stand their own friends, at least let the dear argument of self interest be as prevalent in this, as it usually is upon all other occasions.

41. CARRIERS AND PEDLARS SUSPECTED OF CARRYING SEDITIOUS LITERATURE, 1684

[P.R.O., SP 44/338, ff. 349–50. State Papers Domestic, Warrant Book]

Charles Earl of Shrewsbury.

Whereas credible information hath been given that diverse treasonable and seditious printed libels, books, and papers have been and are carried and dispersed by carriers, wagoners, packhorsemen, higglers, and others, to the great disturbance and danger of the public peace; for the discovery and prevention of the same, these are in his Majesty's name to authorize and require you, taking a constable or other legal officer to your assistance, to make diligent search for all such printed libels, books, and papers upon or about the persons in all and every the chambers and warehouses of all and every the said carriers, wagoners, and packhorse men, and higglers now on the western roads, and such libels, books, and papers as shall be found to seize and secure and bring and deliver the same, to the end that the offenders therein may be proceeded against according to law. And in the due execution thereof, all sheriffs, mayors, bailiffs, justices of the peace, constables, head-boroughs, and others whom it may concern are hereby required to be aiding and assisting as they will answer the contrary at their utmost peril; and for so etc.

Given etc. Whitehall, 25th May, 1684.

To Arthur Clunn, servant to his Majesty's General Letter Office.

42. PARISHIONERS IN ST. CLEMENTS PARISH SEEK INCORPORATION IN THE CITY OF OXFORD, 1684

[*Oxford Council Acts, 1665–1701*, ed. M. G. Hobson,
Oxford Hist. Soc., Second Ser. II, 1939, pp. 162–3]

28 January

WHEREAS the parishioners of Bridgett, alias St. Clements, lately petitioned his Majesty that their parish might be incorporated with the City of Oxford and since several of the inhabitants have signed the said petition, the house agrees that all those who signed shall have the city freedom provided that the petition take effect and the said parish be incorporated in the city and the said persons take up their freedom within a month after the said parish be incorporated.

A true copy of St. Clements petition:

To the King's most excellent Majesty
    The humble petition of the parishioners and inhabitants of the parish of Brigett, alias St. Clements, near the City of Oxon.

Humbly sheweth that whereas the said parish lies adjoining to the said city of Oxon and may conveniently be incorporated to and with the said city and being informed your Majesty is now graciously pleased to add to the said city several new privileges and franchises, our petitioners therefore most humbly pray that your Majesty will be pleased to incorporate your petitioners' said parish to and with the said city, which will be of great advantage to the said city as well as your petitioners, and your petitioners shall ever pray, etc.

William White [and 39 other signatories].

43. AN OPPOSITION GROUP IN ST. CLEMENTS ASSERTS ITSELF, 1684

[P.R.O., SP 29/436, no. 79]

[January 31, 1684]

To the king's most excellent Majesty,
the petition of all the landholders and owners of houses and lands and tenements in the parish of St. Clements in the county of Oxford

HUMBLY sheweth that the parish of St. Clements aforesaid is and time out of mind hath been a parish of itself distinct and in a place remote from the city of Oxford, and never was subject to any of the jurisdiction nor within the liberties of the said city.

That your Majesty's petitioners having several tenements in the said parish, the said tenants with several inmates there, some of them for their own private ends, some by fraud, and others by threatening, have lately been induced to subscribe a petition to your Majesty for a grant to incorporate or bring in the said parish with the said city or within the liberties thereof, contrary to the minds and desires not only of your Majesty's petitioners who are the sole landlords and owners of the said parish but of many of the tenants who were so subtly induced to petition your Majesty as aforesaid.

That such a grant if obtained will make your Majesty's petitioners liable to such burdens, taxes, and charges as will be a great wrong to your Majesty's petitioners. And will tend to the utter ruin of many of them, their family, and posterity.

Therefore, your petitioners humbly pray that considering the premises and that your petitioners and their predecessors were great sufferers in the late rebellion (many of their houses being demolished and their orchards and gardens destroyed by the raising of fortifications for the service of your Majesty's royal father of blessed memory), your most gracious Majesty will not be pleased to make any such grant to incorporate the said parish with the said city or to bring it within the liberties or the jurisdiction thereof.

And your Majesty's petitioners as in duty bound shall ever pray, etc.

Rob. Harsnett, rector of St. Clements [and 14 other signatories.]

[Endorsed:] The petition of the parish of St. Clements against their being incorporated with the city of Oxford.

44. JOHN AUBREY'S LIST OF WILTSHIRE FAIRS, 1684-5

[Bodleian Library, Oxford, MS. Aubrey 2 (John Aubrey's MS. of the *Natural History of Wiltshire*), ff. 147v-8]

Fairs

TO ADJUST these two following chapters, I should consult with our farmers, graziers, and butchers; but not having that opportunity (here in London), I will set down concerning them what occurs to my memory, and touch only at the principal ones.

The most celebrated fair in Wiltshire for sheep is at Castle Combe on St. George's Day (23 April) whither sheepmasters do come as far as from Northamptonshire. Here is a good cross and market house; and heretofore was a staple of wool as John Scrope, lord of this manor, affirms to me. The market here is now very inconsiderable.

At Wilton is a very noted fair for sheep on St. George's Day also; and another on St. Giles's Day, *sc.* September the first. Graziers etc. from Buckinghamshire come hither to buy sheep.

At Chilmark is a good fair for sheep on St. Margaret's Day, *sc.* 20 July.

Bulford (near Salisbury) a fair on Lammas Day. 'Tis an eminent fair for wool and sheep. The eve is for wool and cheese.

At the city of New Sarum is a very great fair for cloth at Twelftyde called Twelfe market.

In the parish of All Cannings is St. Anne's Hill (vulgarly called Tann Hill) where every year on St. Anne's Day (26 of July) is kept a great fair within an old camp called Oldbury. The chief commodities are sheep, oxen, and fineries. This fair would be more considerable but that Bristow fair happens at the same time.

At Devizes several fairs but the greatest is the green cheese at Michaelmas. It continues about a week.

Wilton was the head town of the county till Bishop Bingham built the bridge at Harnham, *anno* —— which turned away the old Roman way . . . and brought the trade to New Sarum, where it hath ever since continued.

Weyhill Fair is in Hants. adjoining Wiltshire. It is an extraordinary great one and lasts ——. Here is a mean old church where St. Thomas Becket was sometime a priest, and they say did some miracle. After his canonization hitherto were made frequent pilgrimages at this time of the year (which is his ——). The concourse of people was so great that hucksters brought walnuts and other fruits and accommodation (here are not above half a dozen houses); and this was the occasion and rise of this famous fair which (I believe) is held only by prescription.

Magdalen Hill Fair, near Winchester, is also a great fair. They send cheese thither from Gloucestershire and from north Wiltshire.

45. A YOUNG MAN SETS UP AS A SHOPKEEPER IN LANCASTER, 1687–8

[J. D. Marshall, *The Autobiography of William Stout of Lancaster, 1665–1752*, Chetham Soc., 3rd Ser., XIV, 1967, pp. 89–90]

In 1687

SO SOON as I had taken a shop, I applied to my mother and brother in order to get what money I could of what was due by my father's will, which was fifty pound, let by my father upon bond to John Hodgson, merchant, designed for me, and 3*l*. 10*s*. interest. And I sold 3 acres of land in Kellet Intacks to Henry Batson for 33*l*.; and some land my father bought of George Gardner I sold to my brother Josias for 33*l*.; left me by my father's will, in all, 119*l*. 10*s*. and I borrowed twelve pound which I repaid the 2nd of 12 mo: following, so that the said 119*l*. 10*s*. was all that I could command as due by my father's will. And I borrowed of my sister 10*l*. which I kept many years.

All this money was got ready, and I bought deals and boards and employed a joiner to make chests and draw boxes to fit the shop. The time of my apprenticeship was not out till the first of the third month next, but there was several of our neighbours, shopkeepers, determined to go to London the end of Lent Assizes. Upon application to my master he discharged me from my apprenticeship in order to have the opportunity of going with them. And my brother Josias offering to lend me a horse, I made ready for the journey and took with me 120*l.* of the aforesaid sum. I set forward the beginning of the 2nd month, 1688, in company of Thomas Green and other neighbours, and one Manser of Borwick and William Clarkson of Halton, two youths who went for preferment. And we all got well to London in five days, and lodged at the Swan with Two Necks in Lad Lane.[1] And as soon as I got there I applied to such tradesmen as I was recommended to, and bought of sundry persons goods to the value of two hundred pounds or upwards, and paid each of them about half ready money, as was then usual to do by any young man beginning trade.

And the *Edward and Jane* ketch, James Myers master, being then taking in lading for Lancaster, I got all my goods on board him in a week, and was then ready to return; which I did with my neighbours so far as Stony Stratford, and then left them and came along by way of Northampton, Leicester, and Nottingham to Sheffield.

In 1688

I brought down with me from London to Sheffield about twenty pounds, which I laid out there in Sheffield and Birmingham manufactories and got well home the end of that week. And the next week forwarded the finishing the shop, and laid out the remaining twenty pound in that and in buying nails and other things of this country's manufactories. And that day a week after I got home, the ship got to Lancaster in seven days' passage from London hither; got the goods landed and the shop and cellar fixed and furnished with about three hundreds worth of goods against the summer fair.

And I took of the shop a small room, for a bed, table, and a small light, where I lodged. And upon the 28th day of the 3rd month, 1688, I went to board with Alderman Thomas Baynes at the price of five pounds a year, victuals and washing. But lodged in the shop, so was seldom in the house, which was adjoining to my shop, but at victuals, summer or winter; for in my apprenticeship, and some time after, we were frequently called up at all times of the night to serve customers, [which] obliged us to have a bed in the shop.

At Midsummer Fair I had good encouragement, without inviting any of my master's or neighbour's customers, which was a practice much then used, but by me always detested as being contrary to the golden rule to do to others as I would they should do to me. My sister Elin came to the fair to assist me—and on the market days—and was as ready in serving retail customers as a young apprentice could have done. And I always detested

---

[1] This was an inn, booking, and parcel office from which wagons started to the north of England. The name is a corruption of 'Swan with Two Nicks'.

that [which] is common, to ask more for goods than the market price, or what they may be afforded for; but usually set the price at one word, which seemed offensive to many who think they never buy cheap except they get abatement of the first price set upon them—and it's common for the buyer to ask the lowest price. Which, if answered, the wilful insist of abatement; to whom I answered they should not tempt any to break their word. And I observed that such plain dealing obliged worthy customers and made business go forward with few words . . .

46. REASONS FOR SUPPRESSING PEDLARS AND HAWKERS, 1691

[P.R.O., SP 32/3, no. 96]

REASONS humbly offered to the consideration of the High Court of Parliament by the drapers, mercers, haberdashers, grocers, hosiers, glass sellers, cutlers, and other trading house and shopkeepers of this nation of the great decay of their trades. That there are a sort of people called by the name of pedlars, hawkers, and petty chapfolks who, contrary to law, do carry about, dispose, and sell in all cities and towns of this kingdom very great quantities of several sorts of goods and commodities belonging to the said trades, to the ruin and destruction of the said tradesmen, and to the great inconvenience and danger of the whole nation in general, in these particulars following: viz.

I. That the said hawkers and pedlars are computed and boast themselves to be a great number, who are most of them single, lusty, and able of body either to serve his Majesty or to get their livings by lawful ways, and do notwithstanding trade in all places and go about to all noblemen's and gentlemen's houses to vend their commodities, to the destruction of the shopkeepers in the adjoining towns, who are made hereby incapable to discharge their debts and obligations to the merchants and others that trust them.

II. That in vain will it be for gentlemen or others to breed up any of their sons to trades, giving great sums of money and long service, if every vagrant and pedlar shall have this permission.

III. That 'tis impossible for persons so chargeably educated, liable to all taxes, paying great rents, having families and children, to support a livelihood, if these be permitted their employ.

IV. That most of them pay neither scot nor lot, taxes, rent, or any other charge; so that of an unavoidable necessity, they must be destructive to those that lie under those performances.

V. That they multiply daily and have within few years trebled their number, arriving to that unsufferable practice as to take servants, contract for years, some retaining three or four apiece, which must of necessity be as a canker to eat out the life of trade.

VI. That 'tis the earnest desire of the tradesmen of this nation, the legal putting down these men, as groaning under the burden caused by them; there being many families ruined, their wives and children begging in a deplorable condition, having had their bread taken out of their mouths.

VII. That supposing but 10,000, a number far less than they boast themselves to be, and everyone selling but £100 worth of goods in the year, a sum much too moderate, will amount in the whole to £100,000, the moderate profit of which will maintain 2,530 families, allowing £40 per annum to the maintenance of every family.

VIII. That the greatest part of these people are no real natives but most of another nation whose great encouragements are such that they daily flock from their own country into ours only to follow this trade.

IX. That this growing enormity was in its bud seen, so that in the reigns of Queen Mary, Queen Elizabeth, and King James, were three acts made for the suppressing them; and by law looked on as vagrants, but since our unhappy domestic war they have arrived to this prodigious number.

X. That 'tis really destructive to the interest and government of this land as well as trade to suffer such a number who under all disguises may take this employ as knowing every place, strength, and ways thereof; so as several inconveniences may accrue to the disturbance of this nation; some of them wearing swords already in defiance of authority, as also the increase of robbers, breaking open of houses, or any other mischief whatsoever.

XI. That in some by-ports of this nation several persons are induced to bring in many prohibited commodities, to the ruining of many handicraftsmen, as having an opportunity of selling them by these men; as also in these places stealing his Majesty's customs by which clandestine ways they many times have great advantage above the shopkeepers who are regulated by his Majesty's laws.

XII. That it is very infamous as well as detrimental to have the trade of so eminent a nation as ours carried and bandied at the backs of a loose and vagrant sort of people most of them without house or being, and begging, if not stealing, in most places where they come.

XIII. That under pretence of selling Scotch cloth, a linen so inconsiderable that, 'tis rationally supposed, not £20,000 worth is made in the year, there is near 2 millions of other foreign goods sold; so that by the same argument might Dutch, Germans, and French dispose of their commodities in the same manner to the utter destruction of all trading natives whatsoever.

XIV. That no true conveniencies can be proposed for the tolerating these men, either to state or trade; the one receiving daily a great detriment by the irregular addition of so great a number; the other no convenience at all but the contrary; their wandering lives fixing them in no payments which very consideration doth daily make them increase, and will in time bring the most considerable part of the taxes on the gentry. There being in most corporations tradesmen breaking, rents failing; so that 'tis very difficult for gentlemen or others to place their sons to any trade or employ that is not invaded by them.

XV. That whereas 'tis supposed they sell cheaper than tradesmen, 'tis at best but a vulgar error, unless some things that sinisterly comes to their hands by way of defrauding his Majesty's customs; otherwise taking all opportunities by false measures, as a yard when it should be an ell, by altering and false naming their commodities, do to the utmost of their power fraudulently deceive his Majesty's honest and well-meaning subjects.

XVI. That as by a very moderate computation 3,740 families are every year disfurnished of a maintenance, they all paying scot and lot; what sad inconveniency will accrue in some farther race of time, there being already a want of people in most towns and villages of this kingdom.

XVII. That 'tis to be highly feared such a number of young, lusty, vagrant people, increasing as they do, knowing once their strength, who can meet in any part of this nation in three weeks time (may at last grow like the banditties of Italy) outlaws, bidding defiance to law and government (it being against all safety and rules of policy) to indulge those who are no way beneficial to king nor country.

XVIII. That they very often corrupt men's servants where they come, and tempt them to steal their masters' provisions or goods to truck with them for such things as they have a mind to or occasion for. And for glasses, being a light commodity, if wandering glassmen are not suppressed, they will and may carry any other commodities in the straw in which glasses and earthenwares are always packed.

XIX. That this nation doth abound with a multitude of poor who by parish duties are maintained; so that 'tis conceived no less than 100,000 persons are thereby kept, a burden no way contributed to by pedlars, hawkers, wanderers, etc. But wholly lies on the gentry, tradesmen, and corporations; so that without some redress, they will not be able any longer to support the poor's necessities; which will be to the ruin and perishing of many thousand souls, who are now relieved by them.

London: printed for Charles Palmer, 1691.

47. BARGE TRAFFIC ON THE RIVER SEVERN, 1692

[P.R.O., E134, 4 W. & M., Mich. 50]

[Deposition of a witness taken at Gloucester in a suit concerning tolls and customs paid by vessels on the River Severn passing under the bridge at Gloucester, 1692]

ARNOLD ARAM of the city of Gloucester, gent., 50 years or thereabouts, sworn and examined, deposeth as followeth:

To the first interrogatory this deponent saith that he doth know the defendants, John Chance, the elder, and John Chance, the younger, who both live in the city of Worcester and have both of them followed the vocation or employment of troughmen and been owners of one trough or barge apiece, and usually passed and repassed upon the river of Severn with their said boats or vessels to and from the cities of Worcester and Bristol for the space of ten years last past or thereabouts.

2, 3, 4. To the 2nd, 3rd, and 4th interrogatory this deponent saith that the defendants for the space of ten years last past or thereabouts have usually about sixteen or eighteen times in a year conveyed in their said boat from the city of Worcester wheat and malt, Manchester packs, and iron ware, and linen, amounting as this deponent believeth to the burthen of 20 tons or thereabouts; and back again from the city of Bristol to the city of Worcester they have usually carried upon the said river of Severn in their said boat the like burden of 20 tons of wine, tobacco, grocery wares, coals, lead, and wool, and other merchandise . . .

48. THE COMMONS DEBATE ON A BILL AGAINST HAWKERS AND PEDLARS, 1693

[All Soul's College, Oxford, Parliamentary Diary of N. Luttrell, pp. 21, 82, 315-7, 429]

12 November 1691

Mr. Tredenham moved and was seconded by Mr. Boscawen to bring in a bill for suppressing of hawkers and pedlars, and ordered accordingly.

24 November 1692

Mr. Nicholas presented the bill against hawkers and pedlars entitled for preventing decay of trade in cities, corporations, and market towns.

2 February 1692/3

Upon the report of the bill against hawkers and pedlars.

Sir J. Dorrel spoke against it for that it was to take away the living of several thousand people which consequently would tend to dispeople the nation, which he thought not our interest. Then this bill puts it into the inhabitants of corporations to exact upon the country gentlemen as they please as it tends to spoil and ruin your servants whom you must [send] to a town if you want never so small a thing, whereas before they were brought home to your door.

Mr. Hambden was against it. Mr. Neal against it, for it takes away a conveniency gentlemen have by buying things at home and will have this inconvenience to hinder the expense of several commodities. Mr. Boscawen thought it a very good bill because it would encourage the corporations who send you hither and make them better able to bear their share of taxes for support of this government.

Sir Edward Seymor was against it and not for passing it now which had been travelling in this House ever since he sat here, that he was sorry to see that we were always taking care to sell cheap and buy dear which would effectually be provided for in this bill by putting it in shopkeepers' hands to put their own prices upon you.

Sir Ralph Carr, Lord Castleton, and Mr. Goldwel were for it being a sort of people that pay no taxes to the government nor contribute to any parish charges, that carry about libels against the government and tend to corrupt your children and others by carrying letters and helping on other intrigues; besides it is but a temporary law for five years; and if it be not found good it will not be continued.

Mr. Blofield was for it, he computed these pedlars (who are generally Scotchmen) go away with a third part of the trade of the nation.

Sir John Morton was also for the bill, but Sir Joseph Tredenham was against it.

Mr. Freke, the younger, tendered a clause to give leave to any person who is an inhabitant or has a dwelling in any town or corporation to send goods abroad to sell by himself or his servant.

They who were for the bill were against the clause and said it would elude the whole bill. It was received and read twice and upon the question to be made part of the bill, the House divided.

$$\text{Tellers For} \begin{cases} \text{Yeas} & \left.\begin{array}{l}\text{Mr. Arnold} \\ \text{Mr. Freke}\end{array}\right\} \quad 138 \\ \text{Noes} & \left.\begin{array}{l}\text{Mr. Goldwel} \\ \text{Mr. Fenwick}\end{array}\right\} \quad 199 \end{cases}$$

Mr. Harley was against the bill being engrossed and to enter it as the reason thereof for that great sums of money had been collected for the carrying it. Sir Thomas Clarges against it also for that reason and also for that this would establish monopolies by Act of Parliament. Mr. Arnold against it, also Mr. Jeffryes, and Dr. Barbone, and Col. Titus. Sir Walter Young for the bill.

So at last the question for engrossing the bill with the amendments was put.

House divided.

$$\begin{array}{ll} \text{Yeas} & \left.\begin{array}{l}\text{Sir Walter Young} \\ \text{Sir Ralph Carr}\end{array}\right\} \quad 230 \\ \text{Noes} & \left.\begin{array}{l}\text{Sir Samuel Barnardiston} \\ \text{Sir Robert Cotton}\end{array}\right\} \quad 130 \end{array}$$

9 March 1692/3

Sir John Bolles presented a petition from several tradesmen to desire this House to address to his Majesty to issue his proclamation for putting the laws in execution against hawkers and pedlars.

But upon the question for receiving it, carried in the negative, the House not thinking it proper and nothing but what justices of peace might do if they pleased.

49. THE CHARTING OF THE ENGLISH COAST,
1693

[*Great Britain's Coasting Pilot: being a Survey of the Sea Coast
of England from the River Thames to the westward* . . . by
Captain Grenvile Collins, Hydrographer in Ordinary to the
King and Queen's most Excellent Majesties, London, 1693]

The Preface to the Reader

To my fellow mariners of Great Britain,
Gentlemen,

His most excellent Majesty, King Charles II, who was a great lover of the
noble art of navigation, finding that there were no sea charts or maps of these
kingdoms but what were Dutch, and copies from them, and those very
erroneous, his Majesty out of his great zeal for the better improvement of
navigation was pleased in the year 1681 to give me command of a yacht for
the making this survey in which service I spent seven years' time.

The intent of this survey is only to give directions to mariners to sail along
the coast of Great Britain, and how to carry a ship into any harbour, river,
port, road, bay, or creek with safety, and how to avoid all dangers known.

It sometimes happens, and that too frequently, that when ships have made
long and dangerous voyages, and are come home richly laden, [they] have been
shipwrecked on their native coast whereby both merchants, owners, and
mariners have been impoverished . . . As many ships are lost by ignorance
and negligence as by stress of weather, so a master of a ship hath a very great
charge, and ought to be a sober man as well as a skilful mariner. All helps
of art, care, and circumspection are to be used by him that the lives of
mariners (the most useful of his Majesty's subjects at this juncture) and the
fortunes of honest merchants under his care, may be preserved. To supply
the defects of which, I have been employed by their Majesties' predecessors
and encouraged by ingenious and noble benefactors. And as I have hitherto
made it my business to make these true figures of our coasts and harbours so
to serve my country, I shall not be wanting to give them such additions and
amendments as I shall find hereafter needful. Wishing you always happy and
successful voyages, with prosperity to the nation and its forces by sea and
land, that as we have been hitherto so we may even be at home, sovereigns of
seas and umpires of the differences betwixt our neighbours abroad . . .

50. AN ACT TO LICENSE HAWKERS AND PEDLARS, 1696-7

[Statutes of the Realm, VII, pp. 266-9]

An Act for licensing Hawkers and Pedlars for a further provision for the Payment of the Interest of the Transport Debt for the reducing of Ireland.

8 and 9 Gul. III, Chapter XXV.

I. WHEREAS an Act of Parliament was made in the sixth and seventh years of his Majesty's reign entitled an act for granting to his Majesty several additional duties upon coffee, tea, chocolate, and spices towards satisfaction of the debts due for transport service for the reduction of Ireland, in which provision was made for the payment of interest at five pounds per centum for three years for the principal sum of three hundred and thirty thousand seven hundred and sixty nine pounds ten shillings seven pence then allowed to be due for the said transport service for the reducing of Ireland, which duties have proved very deficient to answer such interest; we your Majesty's most dutiful and loyal subjects the Commons in Parliament assembled, being willing that a further provision may be made and fund raised for making good to your Majesty's said subjects the deficiency of that provision, do hereby give and grant unto your Majesty the duties herein after mentioned, and do humbly beseech your Majesty that it may be enacted; and be it enacted by the King's most excellent Majesty by and with the advice and consent of the Lords Spiritual and Temporal and Commons in this present Parliament assembled, and by the authority of the same, that from and after the four and twentieth day of June one thousand six hundred ninety seven until the five and twentieth day of June which shall be in the year of our Lord one thousand six hundred ninety eight there shall be answered and paid to his Majesty, his heirs, and successors by every hawker, pedlar, petty chapman, or any other trading person or persons going from town to town or to other men's houses and travelling either on foot or with horse, horses, or otherwise within the kingdom of England, dominion of Wales, or town of Berwick upon Tweed (except as hereinafter is excepted) carrying to sell, or exposing to sale, any goods, wares, or merchandises a duty of four pounds, and that every person so travelling with a horse, ass, or mule, or other beast bearing or drawing burthen shall pay the sum of four pounds from the said four and twentieth day of June, one thousand six hundred ninety seven, to the five and twentieth day of June, one thousand six hundred ninety eight, for each horse, ass, or mule, or other beast bearing or drawing burthen he or she shall so travel with over and above the said first mentioned duty of four pounds.

II. And be it further enacted by the authority aforesaid that every pedlar, hawker, petty chapman, and other trading person or persons, so travelling as aforesaid, shall before the four and twentieth day of June, one thousand six hundred ninety seven, deliver or cause to be delivered unto the commissioners for transportation, or any person or persons authorized or deputed by them or the major part of them in writing under their hands and seals, a note in writing under his or her hand or under the hand of some person by her or them authorized in that behalf, how and in what manner he or she will travel and trade, whether on foot or with one or more horse or horses, ass or asses, mule or mules, or other beast or beasts of burthen for her or his so travelling and trading, for which he or she shall thereupon pay or cause to be paid unto the said commissioners for transportation or any person or persons authorized or deputed by them or the major part of them in writing under their hands and seals, one moiety of the duty by this act payable for the same, and give security by bond with one or more sufficient sureties to be taken in his Majesty's name for the true payment of the other moiety of the said duties at the end of six calendar months, unless the party shall choose to pay down the other moiety of the said duty, in which case he or she shall be allowed after the rate of two shillings in the pound for prompt payment of the same, and thereupon a licence shall be granted unto him or her so to travel or trade by the said commissioners for transportation or any two or more of them.

III. And be it further enacted that if any such hawker, pedlar, or petty chapman, from and after the said four and twentieth day of June, one thousand six hundred ninety seven, be found trading as aforesaid without or contrary to such licence, such person shall for each and every such offence forfeit the sum of twelve pounds, the one moiety thereof to the informer and the other moiety to the poor of the parish wherein such offender shall be discovered, and that every person so trading who, upon demand made by any justice of the peace, mayor, constable, or other officer of the peace of any town corporate or borough where he or she shall so trade, shall refuse to produce and show unto such justice of peace, mayor, constable, or other officer of the peace, his or her licence for so trading to be granted as aforesaid that then the person so refusing shall forfeit five pounds to be paid to the churchwardens of the parish where such demand shall be made to the use of the poor of the same, and for non-payment thereof shall suffer as a common vagrant and be committed to the house of correction.

IV. And be it enacted by the authority aforesaid that it shall and may be lawful for the said commissioners for transportation or any two or more of them, and they are hereby directed appointed and required upon the terms aforesaid and upon the receipt and security given as aforesaid, to grant a licence to be by them subscribed to every hawker, pedlar, petty chapman, or any other trading person for him or herself, or for him or herself with one or more horses, asses, mules, or other beasts which he or she shall travel with as the case shall require, for which licence there shall be taken only one shilling unless such hawker, pedlar, or petty chapman, shall travel with horse, ass, or mule, or other beast of burthen, and in that case there shall be paid for such licence two shillings only over and above the duties aforesaid and no more, and that the said commissioners shall keep a separate and distinct account of the duties granted by this Act and pay the money arising thereby into his Majesty's Exchequer . . .

VIII. And it is further enacted by the authority aforesaid that it shall and may be lawful for any person and persons whatsoever to seize and detain any such hawker, pedlar, petty chapman, or other trading person or persons as aforesaid till such time as he, she, or they shall produce a licence in that behalf if he, she, or they have any, and if he, she, or they shall be found trading without a licence contrary to this Act for such reasonable time as he, she, or they may give notice to the constable, headborough, tithingman, churchwarden, overseer of the poor, or some other parish officer or officers, who are hereby required to carry such person so seized before some one of his Majesty's justices of the peace of the county or place where such offence or offences shall be committed, which said justice of the peace is hereby authorized and strictly required either upon the confession of the party offending or due proof by witness upon oath (which he is hereby empowered to administer) that the person so brought before him had so traded as aforesaid, and that no such licence shall be produced by such offender before the said justice by warrant under his hand and seal to cause the said sum of twelve pounds to be forthwith levied by distress and sale of the offender or offenders' goods, wares, or merchandises, rendering the overplus if any be to the owner or owners thereof after true deduction of the reasonable charge for taking the said distress, and out of the said sale to pay the said respective penalties and forfeitures aforesaid.

IX. Provided always and be it enacted that this act or anything herein contained shall not extend to prohibit any person from selling of any Acts of Parliament, forms of prayer, proclamations, gazettes, licensed almanacs or other printed papers licensed by authority, or any fish, fruit, or victuals, nor to hinder any person or persons who are the real workers or makers of any goods or wares within the kingdom of England, dominion of Wales, or town of Berwick upon Tweed, or his, her, or their children, apprentices, servants, or agents from carrying abroad, exposing to sale, and selling any of the said goods and wares of his, her, or their own making in any public mart, fairs, markets, or elsewhere, nor any tinker, cooper, glazier, plumbers, harness-menders, or other persons usually trading in mending kettles, tubs, household goods, or harness whatsoever from going about and carrying with him or them proper materials for mending the same . . .

XII. Provided always and it is hereby further enacted that nothing herein contained shall extend or be construed to extend to hinder any person or persons from selling or exposing to sale any sorts of goods or merchandises in any public mart, market, or fair, within the kingdom of England, dominion of Wales, or town of Berwick upon Tweed, but that such person and persons may do therein as they lawfully might have done before the making of this act, anything herein contained to the contrary notwithstanding . . .

XVII. Provided always and be it further enacted by the authority aforesaid

that this Act or anything therein contained shall not extend or be construed
to give any power for the licensing of any hawker, pedlar, or petty chapman
to sell or expose to sale any wares or merchandises in any city, borough, town
corporate, or market town within this realm any otherwise than might have
been done before the making of this Act, anything therein contained to the
contrary in any wise notwithstanding.

51. MEANS OF TRADE AND TRAVEL AT LANCASTER, 1698

[J. D. Marshall, *The Autobiography of William Stout of
Lancaster, 1665–1752*, Chetham Soc., 3rd Ser., XIV, 1967,
pp. 122–3]

In 1698

I, HAVING an intention to go to the yearly meeting at London this year,
had a horse offered by my brother Leonard and well kept in my stable. He
was well in the evening and found dead in the morning, a few days before my
intended journey. But about the same time a man came down from London
in order to be a preacher to a Presbyterian or Independent congregation
here, who had a horse lent there; and, to return him again, and hearing of my
going, offered me the horse to ride upon, trusting to my care of him, and to
deliver him in London as directed—which I accepted. Which I thought
would save the charge of keeping a horse in London, and I then thought of
hiring one down. The horse carried me well and was well received at London.
I went from here the beginning of the third month, and accidentally met with
James Penny of Penny Bridge going to London [with his sister] in order to
collect the effects of their brother, lately dead there, who were good and
agreeable company. And at Warrington we met with several Friends, men
and women, going to that meeting, and also agreeable company, that I never
went to London at so little charge as at that time, or so good entertainment.
James Penny, his sister, and I took up our lodgings at the Swan with Two
Necks in Lad Lane whilst they stayed in London.

I duly attended the general yearly meeting, which was large, unanimous,
peaceable, and edifying; and afterwards, at the desire of the owners of the ship,
building at Wharton aforesaid, I bought for her masts, sails, rigging, anchors,
and cables, etc., and got them put on board the *Edward and Jane* ketch,
Thomas Thorn, master (but when I was first at London, James Myers was
master of her). She was now full and ready to sail for Liverpool. And I
resolved to come in her by sea to Liverpool; and we had a very ready passage
to Gravesend, where we stopped a tide to clear out, and then had a fair wind
to the Downs, but did not come to an anchor there. And the wind being
south-west, we proceeded with a great many ships, who made but little
progress; but ours being a good sailer, we got ahead of them, except a Dutch

dogger. We kept the sea along the coast of Kent and Sussex, but were obliged to go within the Isle of Wight near Portsmouth and through the King's fleet at Spithead, and came to an anchor at Jack in the Basket, near Lymington, whither we went in our boat to buy some provisions. We were at anchor there some days, the wind being strong westward. We came out at the Needles, but the wind not favourable and turning to the west till we came near Plymouth, most of the ships in company put in there; but ours stood to the southwards and tacked into Mount's Bay and afterwards to the south, the wind being west, till at the next tack we weathered the Land's End and came betwixt [that] and the Isles of Scilly. And now the westerly wind favoured us so that we got from the Land's End to Holly Head [=Holyhead] in two days, and went within the Skerries, and next night, in the night, to Liverpool town side all well and in good health.

52. OPPOSITION TO A PROPOSAL TO MAKE THE RIVER WEAVER NAVIGABLE, 1699[?]

[T. S. Willan, *The Navigation of the River Weaver in the Eighteenth Century*, Chetham Soc., 3rd Ser , III, p. 142]

Sir George Warburton, Lord Gerard, Sir Richard Brooke, Sir Willoughby Aston, Thomas Cholmondeley, and Richard Legh to the gentlemen and other inhabitants of Bucklow and Macclesfield Hundreds. 1699[?][1]

Gentlemen,

By intelligence from London and some practices in the country, we find that the projectors, concerning whom we have formerly troubled you, have renewed their design and prepared a bill now ready to be presented in Parliament for making the River Weaver navigable from Frodsham Bridge towards Northwich. We think it needless to represent to you how injurious this bill would prove to those who have lands lying near the river and destructive to the trade of this county, especially of Middlewich and Nantwich and all the adjacent salt works, since the easy import of coals from Lancashire to Northwich and export of their salt would certainly enable the proprietors there to undersell and ruin all the other salt works which are supplied with coals from Staffordshire or Wales, whereby about four thousand families, now subsisting by the land carriage of those coals, salt, and malt, would be utterly ruined and left to be maintained at the charges of their respective parishes, and the rents of those lands where they inhabit and

---

[1] This letter is printed in Hughes, *Studies in Administration and Finance*, p. 257, where it is ascribed to 1709, but the signatures show that it must belong to the earlier struggle of 1699. Of the signatories, Sir Willoughby Aston died in December 1702, Thomas Cholmondeley in February 1702, and Lord Gerard, who must have been Charles, sixth lord Gerard of Gerards Bromley, died in April 1707.

of those near their roads would be impaired. After which some few proprietors of rock salt and brine in and near to Northwich (who alone can be
enriched by this project), having engrossed the trade, would impose the price
of salt at their own pleasure and raise their fortunes on the ruin of the
country. We have prepared a petition to be heard by our counsel against the
said bill and if ye approve it, we desire your concurrence with us, believing
your subscription will be as serviceable to the country as obliging to, gentlemen, your humble servants.

P.S. We send the like petition to other hundreds for expedition, intending
to unite them all in one roll.

53. TRAVEL IN ENGLAND, 1699

[Guy Miège, *The New State of England under our present Monarch,*
King William III, London, 1699, part II, p. 22]

Of the English way of travelling by land either horseback
or in coaches

BESIDES the conveniency of travelling by water either by sea or here and
there upon rivers, I may say the English nation is the best provided of any
for land travel as to horses and coaches. The truth is there is not perhaps a
country so proper for 'tis generally so open and level.

Travelling on horseback is so common a thing in England that the meanest
sort of people use it as well as the rest. Which sometimes fills the roads with
riders not without frays now and then about giving the way. And as English
horses are the best for expedition, so 'tis rare upon the road to see an Englishman but upon the gallop.

But for persons that are tender or disabled, England excels all other
nations in the conveniency of stage coaches going at certain times to all
parts of England, at least to the most noted places. Which is done with so
much speed that some will reach 50 miles in a summer day; and at so easy
rates that it is in some places less than a shilling for every five miles.

54. A DEFENCE OF HAWKERS AS SELLERS
OF PERISHABLE GOODS, 1700

[John Houghton, *A Collection for the Improvement of Husbandry*
and Trade, ed. Richard Bradley, 1727, III, p. 7]

A Defence of Hawkers

15 March 1700

I DO presume that the cause of vending so many as are consumed[1] is, in a
great measure, their being hawked about the streets; for without doubt
importunity and opportunity do great things. And if such people buy them

---

[1] These remarks follow upon a reference to figs and their consumption in London.

of the shopkeepers, as I believe they generally do, I cannot see where the damage is to corporations. I do think that a great trade is far better for any country than a little one; and I never yet met with the man that could pretend with any colour of reason that such doings caused a lesser consumption. I would fain have those that are against them consider what would become of our milk and mackerel, our other fish, oranges, and lemons, etc. if nobody could buy a single pennyworth unless they went to a market or a shop for them. Besides there are vast quantities of damaged goods that would never be sold if 'twere not for carrying to the mob in this manner.

V. OVERSEAS TRADE

---

1. THE FISHING INDUSTRY IN 1601

[John Keymer's Observations made upon the Dutch Fishing about the Year 1601, London, 1664, pp. 8–12]

I HAVE seen of English, Scottish, French, Hollanders, Emdeners, Bremeners, Hamburgers and others, near 3,000 sail fishing at one time, upon the coast of Scotland, Shetland, Orkney, Cattney, Northfarrel, Fowl Isle, and divers other places.

All the busses of Holland, France, Emden, and Hamborough have their first lading of herrings near Baughawanes, and above 1,000 sail of pinks, welboats, doggerboats take cod, ling, and other fish there. Furthermore, all the great staple ling called Holland ling, taken only by the Hollanders, are gotten about these isles, wherewith they serve all Christendom.

From the staple near Berwick all along the coast of England to the Thames mouth, are innumerable shoals and variety of fish; besides the multitude of cods, lings, and herrings, as mackerels, whitings, haddock, soles, thorneback, floith, skate, brett, gurnet, turbot, plaice, congers, butts, and others innumerable.

From the Thames mouth all over the coasts of Kent, Sussex, Hampshire, Wiltshire, and Dorsetshire, not such store of cod, ling, and herrings; yet the like variety of other fish (and more) as the eyes of the fishermongers of London, the country, and their fishermen can testify.

All over the coasts of Devonshire and Cornwall, exceeding great shoals and variety of fish, with pilchards and herrings; the last year in June, such multitudes of herrings came so near the shore of Claverly Key, and all over those places, that the people went with that small provision of nets they had, and took and drew them up the land in such plenty that they were sold for 4s. the thousand, the number of a barrel, and were such store that they gave them to their hogs to eat, and buried the rest in the ground, for lack of salt and barrels to preserve them.

Also about 20 miles from thence, there was abundance of herrings spread the seas, but the people took no more than they could spend presently, for lack of provision to take and preserve them, of which there is great want about England.

From the mouth of Severn round about the coast of Wales, Holyhead, Westchester, Liverpool, and so along the coasts of England to Scotland, there is store and variety of fish.

All over the coast of Ireland, Galloway, Sligo, and the coasts of Cannaugh to Ballishanon, the Band, and the north of Ireland, Longford, Karickfargus, and Strengford, there is store and variety of fish; besides the multitude of cods, lings, herrings, salmons, seals, porpoises, wherpool, and dogfish.

In the mouth of Ireland, not far from Donegal, there are such multitudes of herrings, that it is hardly to be believed, so big and large that 3 herrings make a yard in length: from Carlingford to Dundalk, the Bay of Dublin, and Wexford, Waterford, Bearhaven, Crookehaven, and so round about the coast of Ireland the like variety, and fish in abundance.

The French, Hollanders, Emdeners, Bremeners, Hamburgers, and others fish upon the coast of England, Scotland, and Ireland; and this is the difference between them and us, they go forth in June to seek the shoals of herrings, and having found them, do dwell amongst them, coming along with them until November, taking them in great abundance; and we stay till the herrings come home to our own coast, and some time suffer them to pass by us before we look out, and so lose God's blessing.

All these nations do beat upon all his Majesty's coasts for fish, with great ships take and carry away innumerable riches, when our little boats, crayers, and cobles, dare not look out at sea but in fair weather (for in foul weather the sea swalloweth them up) neither dare they fish far from the shore in fair weather, their boats are so slender and slight.

The people of Ireland, and round about the coasts of England, after they have been at sea and brought home their vessels full of fish, will not go to sea again for more till those be spent and they in debt, till necessity compels them, unless it be some few, and they prosper, yet they are loath to take too much, lest it should be too cheap, for they never seek other markets but their own; and our fishermen go to sea overnight to take fish to serve the markets the next day, and some at 3 o'clock in the morning go to fetch fish, and yet return home at 9 o'clock in the same morning to serve their market with their boats full, laden with cod and ling and other fish, and then to the alehouse, drinking day and night, till all be spent, and they in debt, and can be no longer trusted, and then to sea again for more. This is the life of these people where great riches is to be gotten.

Such an excellent benefit hath God sent his Majesty and his kingdoms, as, let all the kingdoms in Christendom be put together, they are not able to compare with the fishing upon these coasts, nor yet the Spanish Indies: I speak it knowingly.

And further, let all the mines of these kingdoms, as lead, tin, iron, copper, alum, yea, cloth and wool be put together, yet, the fishing will do more good to his Majesty's kingdoms than all these, in these four points.

First, for the augmentation, maintenance, and increase of navigation and mariners, which hath ever been held a special jewel for England.

Secondly, in bringing in to his Majesty and kingdoms great riches of all kinds, and making such strength of ships and mariners, as will make all nations of the world to veil the bonnet to England.

Thirdly, for the bringing in, and making employment for all people, both young and old, for the keeping of them from begging and stealing, and other disorders; and hereby his Majesty shall make exceeding great trade and traffic within this land, upon the seas, as the like hath never been effected by any king of England for the general good.

Fourthly, for the bringing in, and making all things plenty, and causing many storehouses in England to be erected and filled full of fish, to serve ourselves and transport into other kingdoms; like as Blackwell Hall in London and other places in England are with cloth, which continually are emptied and yet always filled.

It is most evident true (God be thanked) that there is fish and herrings enough, and vent enough for us all, if we had as many busses as they; for the 20 hundred great busses belonging to Holland, France, Emden, and Hamborough, and above 200 new busses which they build and increase yearly (all not able to serve Christendom with fish and herrings) they are scarce and dear in most foreign kingdoms in Lent; and afterwards few or none to be had until August. For in the east and north-east regions, and so in most foreign kingdoms and dukedoms, the herrings are every day's meat winter and summer, as well to make them drink as to suffice their appetites; in such exceeding request are the herrings that there is great utterance for them in all parts through Christendom, and in the heathen countries; so that if we had 20 score busses, and increase them to 20 hundred, yet is there vent enough and herrings enough for us all to take upon his Majesty's coasts, God continue it.

And for as much as God hath sent this excellent blessing to his Majesty above all other kings, and that this huge quantity of fish and herrings do offer themselves to his Majesty's kingdoms beyond all nations, and that it is manifest that the trade of fishing is work master to all other trades, and by that means the Dutch increase their farthings to pounds, and their pounds to thousands, and what fruitfulness is in their country, and not a beggar there, everyone getting his own living, is admirable to behold, that the poor man though he be blind, and have but one hand, will get his own living by turning the wheel for making cables and cordage; and others, that have not one leg, will get his own living sitting on a seat with knitting and making of nets and hooks; every boy and wench from ten and twelve years and upwards will get their own living by winding hemp, spinning yarn, making twine and thread for nets, so idleness, beggary, and penury will be driven out of this land by commodious constitutions, as in other places they do, which never any statute heretofore made could bring to pass, to the great glory of God and comfort of his Majesty's subjects.

2. EXETER MERCHANT ADVENTURERS AND THE FRENCH TRADE, 1601–2

[Exeter City Library, Minute Book of the Exeter
Merchant Adventurers' Company]

The Court kept and holden the 19th day of February in the 43rd year of the reign of our sovereign lady Elizabeth before the Governor, Consuls, and Company.

At this court it is presented that Roger Yeo late apprentice to Mr. Nicholas Martin, deceased, hath divers and sundry times heretofore adventured into France not having taken the oath of a freeman as an apprentice within his term, contrary to a certain act heretofore made, incurring the penalty of £20, whereupon the said Roger did submit himself to the whole house for his said fine and hath put in surety for answering thereof Jeffrey Waltham and John Sheere, whereupon Mr. Governor did move the whole company whether he should have abated of the xx*li*. the sum of xviii*li*. or xix*li*. and thereupon the whole company did agree that he should have abated xix*li*. and so is to pay Mr. Treasurer xx*s*. . . .

Also at this court it is agreed by the governor, consuls, and whole company that Mr. Governor and Mr. Hugh Crossinge shall ride to Dorchester Assizes of purpose to confer with Mr. Recorder of Exeter and the officers of Weymouth concerning a new custom of late raised upon woollen cloths transported for France outwards and for all other merchandises homewards. And further the whole company do agree to pay two-thirds towards their charges not only for a journey by them of late made to Weymouth, as also for this journey to Dorchester and Weymouth.

Also at this court licence is granted to William Skinner, apprentice to Mr. ——[1] to trade into the parts of France for his own use, any act heretofore made to the contrary notwithstanding, and paid the fees, viz. vi*s*. viii*d*. and x*d*. to the clerk and beadle . . .

*   *   *

The Court holden and kept xxiiii day of February in the xliiiith year of the reign of our sovereign lady Elizabeth etc., before the Governor, Consuls, and Company etc. . . .

At this court it is agreed by the governor, consuls, and whole company that letters shall be sent forthwith by a footman to Totnes, Barnstaple, Dartmouth, Tiverton, Taunton, Lyme, and Chard to this effect to have their opinions and consent that letters might be directed to the Lords of her Majesty's most honourable Privy Council for information of divers wrongs offered by the Dunkirks to the merchants of this western parts. And also to have their best opinions what course is fittest to be taken for the speedy

[1] MS torn.

reformation thereof and to have their answers here on Thursday, the iiiith of March next by eight of the clock in the forenoon. And that Mr. Dorchester, Mr. Germyn, Mr. Sampforde, Mr. Hugh Crossinge, John Sandey, and Henry Sweete or four of them shall pen and post the said letters.

3. A COMPARISON OF THE NAVY IN 1588 AND 1602/3

[Bodleian Library, Oxford, MS. North a2, f.1]

To the right worshipful Mr. Doctor Caesar, Master of her Highness's Court of Requests and Judge of the Admiralty

YOUR worship's most humble orators, the master, wardens, assistants, and company, seamen of the Trinity House of Deptford Strand in Kent, do humbly beseech your worship to prefer to her Majesty this our demonstration of the present state of the navigation of this realm with a comparison of the time present with the state of the navy and mariners in the year 1588.

The navy of England hath been always held and accompted to be the bulwark and strength of the land and did well appear in the year 1588, her Majesty then having on the seas for men of war 150 sail of good ships whereof 40 only were her own and the rest, 110 sail, of her subjects, belonging to all the ports of this land.

And at that time also there were ships trading from hence to all parts and countries whereunto her Majesty by her subjects hath trade, viz. to Barbary, to all places within the Straits, France, Holland, Hamburg, Stade, Denmark, Melving, Spruse land, Muscovy, besides the fishing and trade to Newcastle continued, and many small men of war then also at the West Indies and on other parts of the King of Spain his dominions.

The number of the ships at that time thus employed in trading we judge to be 150 sail being in burden the one with the other 150 tons, so that the shipping in '88 in this land were 300 sail and the number of men at that time employed in those 300 ships were 30,000, viz.

In the 40 ships of her Majesty's	12,000 men
In the 110 sail of her subjects, being men of war	12,000 men
In the 150 sail of merchants employed in trading were	6,000 men
	30,000 men

But if it would please her Highness at this present to take knowledge by some honourable course of the estate now of our navigation in the land, together with the ships and men, her Highness shall find the decay thereof to be such as would be most grievous to her Majesty to hear, and no less lamentable to us to declare. Namely, that her Majesty hath a hundred sail of shipping less in the land now than in the year 1588. The mariners decayed, being her Majesty's loving subjects, not less than one third part, yea, we fear greatly, the one half is not that then were. The great want of whom God grant her Majesty may never find. But if at any time her Majesty shall need to make forth the like navy or fleet of ships to encounter with the enemy and to defend this land, her Majesty shall then find the want and decay both of ships and men to be such as we aver upon serious and mature deliberation.

Yea, the decay will yearly and daily increase both of ships and men without some speedy and special redress from her Majesty, to the great grief and sorrow of her Majesty's loyal and loving subjects, and to the great joy of all her Majesty's enemies. And as our bounden duty hath caused us to declare the one, namely, our minds in the great decay of ships and mariners, so we hold ourselves by duty no less bound to show our judgement for the restoration and preservation of the same again.

First, therefore, that it would please her Majesty to provide that the merchants may not for their private profit as they do employ the ships of strangers, setting both their ships and men on work, and suffering our ships and men to lie still, preferring their particular gain before the common good of this land, daily setting strangers on work for Bordeaux and other parts of France, also for Denmark, Danzig, Melving, and the Sound, to the great good and increase of the navigation of the stranger and to the great hurt and decay both of our ships and men.

Secondly, the Bordeaux merchants were wont to employ 70 or 80 sail of ships yearly, their freight 40 and 50 years past 30s. per ton, and 8 and 10 years past 36s. and 38s. per ton. But now they freight not here at home 10 ships in a year. Yet men that have shipping willing to set them on work do go to Bordeaux to seek their freight where the merchants, having the advantage, give them but 20s. and 24s. per ton, which freight is not enough to pay the proper charge of the ship for her voyage.

Thirdly, the ships that are freighted by our merchants for all other ports and places have such small and slender freights that the owners are not able to maintain their ships, much less able to give unto poor mariners a convenient pay or salary for their service fit to defray their necessaries, especially if they be married. The evil hereof is not the least cause of the decay of our navigation, for hereby ships decrease and poor men for want go to the enemy for pay.

Fourthly, that it would please her Majesty to appoint commissioners that may in this time of troubles set down what freight the merchants shall pay upon every ton to every port or place now traded unto, and what wage each man shall have for his voyage, so that the poor mariners may have convenient maintenance and the owners encouraged to maintain and increase their shipping.

Fifthly, fishing which hath been a great increase of mariners as a special nursery to it is now almost wholly decayed, witness all the fishing towns upon the coast (both to the northward and westward) partly by means of too much liberty which all men have to eat flesh, and partly by the quantity of fish brought into this land by the strangers, whereof they make no small gain making thereof a staple in the City of London.

That it would therefore please her Majesty in tender commiseration of the premises to take knowledge of these evils and by such honourable courses as her Highness shall think meetest to provide some present relief, that so the navigation of this land may flourish again to the safety of her Majesty's royal person, the great good and increase of wealth to this her Highness's realm and dominions, with increase of joy to all her loving subjects, and to the great fear and terror of all her Majesty's enemies.

Amen

[Endorsed:] Remonstrances of the decay of English ships and mariners and means to help it. Penult. Januar. 1602.

4. SIR EDWIN SANDYS'S REPORT FROM THE COMMITTEE ON FREE TRADE, 1604

[Commons Journals, I, pp. 218–21]

Die Lunae, 21 Maii 1604

S ir Edwyn Sandys maketh a large report of the travel and proceeding of the committee in the two bills for free trade; viz.

B. For all merchants to have free liberty of trade into all countries, as is used in all other nations.

B. For the enlargement of trade for his Majesty's subjects into foreign countries.

The effect of this report, together with the further proceeding of the bill, I received afterwards, penned by himself, and entitled, 'Instructions touching the Bill for Free Trade,' as followeth:

The committees from the House of the Commons sat five whole afternoons upon these bills; there was a great concourse of clothiers and merchants of all parts of the realm, and especially of London, who were so divided, as that all the clothiers, and, in effect, all the merchants of England, complained grievously of the engrossing and restraint of trade by the rich merchants of London as being to the undoing, or great hindrance, of all the rest; and of London merchants, three parts joined in the same complaint against a fourth part; and of that fourth part, some standing stiffly for their own company, yet repined at other companies. Divers writings and informations were exhibited on both parts; learned counsel was heard for the bill, and divers of the principal aldermen of London against it; all reasons exactly weighed and examined; the bill, together with the reasons on both sides, was returned and reported by the committees to the House; where, at the third reading, it was three several days debated,[1] and in the end passed with great consent and

---

[1] In the margin, against these words, is written *Quaere.*

applause of the House (as being for the exceeding benefit of all the land) scarce forty voices dissenting from it.

The most weighty reasons for the enlargement of trade were these:

All free subjects are born inheritable, as to their land, so also to the free _Natural right._ exercise of their industry, in those trades whereto they apply themselves, and whereby they are to live. Merchandise, being the chief and richest of all other, and of greater extent and importance than all the rest, it is against the natural right and liberty of the subjects of England to restrain it into the hands of some few, as now it is; for although there may be now some five or six thousand persons, counting children and prentices, free of the several companies of the merchants, in the whole; yet apparent it is, that the governors of these companies, by their monopolizing orders, have so handled the matter, as that the mass of the whole trade of all the realm is in the hands of some two hundred persons at the most, the rest serving for a show only, and reaping small benefit.

The law stands for it; and a law made 12th of Henry the seventh, never _Judgement of_ repealed by Parliament, only restrained sithence by charters, unduly, or by _Parliament._ untrue suggestions, procured (by which means all other monopolies have had their original) and the first of those charters since the making of that statute (which was purchased in the end of the reign of Henry the seventh, at what time Empson and Dudley were instruments of so much wronging and oppressing the people) yet doth in no wise restrain this liberty of free trade, but expressly allow it (with reverence unto that very Act in the 12th of his reign) and so continued till the reign of Queen Elizabeth.

The example of all other nations generally in the world, who avoid in _Examples of_ themselves and hate in us this monopolizing way of traffic; for it cannot be _nations._ otherwise counted than a monopoly, when so large a commodity is restrained into the hands of so few, in proportion, to the prejudice of all other, who, by law and natural right, might have interest therein. And whereas some allege, that there are like companies in other countries; as of the East Indies in Lisbon, the House of Contraction there, the Fontego at Venice, the Travesana at Nuremberg; these allegations are either untrue, or unproper. There are places of assembly for merchants, and to consult for good orders in all other countries, but without restraint of trading from any man; and how traffic, by this freedom, doth flourish in other countries, and principally in the Low Countries, far more than in ours, is apparent to all the world.

The increase of the wealth generally of all the land, by the ready vent of _Wealth._ all the commodities to the merchants at higher rate; for where many buyers are, ware grows dearer; and they that buy dear at home, must sell dear abroad. This also will make our people more industrious.

The more equal distribution of the wealth of the land, which is a great _Equal_ stability and strength to the realm, even as the equal distributing of the _distribution._ nourishment in a man's body; the contrary whereof is inconvenient in all estates, and oftentimes breaks out into mischief; when too much fulness doth puff up some by presumption, and too much emptiness leaves the rest in perpetual discontent, the mother of desire of innovations and troubles; and this is the proper fruit of monopolies. Example may be in London, and the rest of the realm: the custom and impost of London come to a hundred and ten thousand pound a year, and of the rest of the whole realm but to seventeen thousand pound.

Strength. The increase of shipping, and especially of mariners, in all ports in England. How greatly the mariners of the realm have decayed in all places of latter times, and with how great danger of the state in these late wars, is known to them who have been employed in that kind of service; who do also attribute the cause thereof to this restraint of trade; free traffic being the breeder and maintainer of ships and mariners, as by memorable example in the Low Countries may be seen.

Profit of the Crown. The increase of custom and subsidy to the king, which doth necessarily follow the increase of foreign traffic and wealth. And they which say otherwise, will dare to say anything. These reasons are in great part set down in the Act of the 12th of Henry VIIth; other particular reasons there are, which this present time doth not yield.

Opportunity abroad. Under our gracious Solomon, a prince of wisdom and peace, we are like to be in league or amity with all nations; whereby, as there will be greater freedom abroad to trade to all places, so fit to have greater at home for all persons to trade. This alteration of times may make that fit now, which in times of hostility might have seemed unfit.

Necessity at home. And as there will be greater opportunity abroad, so also much greater necessity at home; for what else shall become of gentlemen's younger sons, who cannot live by arms, when there is no wars, and learning preferments are common to all, and mean? So that nothing remains fit for them, save only merchandise (and such is the use of other politic nations) unless they turn serving men, which is a poor inheritance.

The general reasons to continue the restraint of trade, and the answer to them, were these:

Imputation of the state. It is a taint to the king and state that these restrained companies should be called or counted monopolies; and by this Act we insist and strengthen the complaint of the haven towns and other nations against the state, for suffering such companies.

Answer. The same reason doth justify all the monopolies that ever were. It is no touch to the state, if abuses creep in; but if reformation, desired by Parliament, be denied. But surely this taint doth no ways attaint his Majesty, who hath declared himself a just enemy to all these unjust monopolies.

Not monopolies. These companies are not monopolies; for a monopoly is when liberty of selling, due to all men by right, is restrained to one, with prejudice of all others.

Answer. The name of monopoly, though taken originally for personal unity, yet is fitly extended to all improportionable paucity of the sellers in regard of the ware which is sold. If ten men had the only sale of all the horses in England this were a monopoly; much more the Company of Merchant Adventurers, which, in effect not above two hundred, have the managing of the two third parts of the clothing of this realm, which might well maintain many thousands merchants more. And with how great prejudice this is, sundry ways, to all the land, let example suffice; let the crue of all the clothiers of England testify; and the utter overthrow of infinite poor persons, which live by them and their works. For the clothiers, having no utterance of their cloth but to the Merchant Adventurers, they, by a complot among themselves, will buy but at what time, what quantity, and what price themselves list; whereby the clothiers are fain often to return with loss, to lay their cloths to pawn, to slack their trade, to the utter ruin of their poor workmen, with their wives and children.

These companies keep up the price of our commodities abroad by avoiding *Keeping up our commodities.* an over glut of our commodities in places whereto they trade. And this experience doth witness; for our cloth is of late years much dearer than in former times; whereas contrariwise, when trade is free, many sellers will make ware cheap, and of less estimation.

It is true that all monopolies keep up their commodities for their own *Answer.* private lucre; but they do it unjustly, and to the discontent of all other men; which hath been the cause of so many edicts of the empire against the Company of Merchant Adventurers, which hath driven them so often to shift their marts; and is the cause that our merchants are so generally hated, no other nation Christian either using or enduring such restrained companies in matter of merchandises. Howbeit both by reason and experience we may conjecture, that there is no greater —— that if trade be made free, our commodities will much abate their price abroad; for the merchants must first buy their commodities at home; and where many buyers are, wares will grow dearer; and buying dear at home, he must sell dear abroad. For it is not true that there will be greater glut of our commodities in foreign parts. The sellers will be more, but the wares sold will be much the same, especially in those principal commodities which grow out of the land. It is the store of the merchandise, not the multitude of merchants, which doth make things cheaper. Besides, when trade is free, it is likely that many young men will seek out new places, and trade further for great benefit, whereby the glut in the former places will be less. The weakness of their argument of experience is plain; for not cloth only, but all other things in the world are risen greatly in price; and in France, where there is no companies, our kerseys are sold at exceeding good price, and as dear, in proportion, as broad cloths by the Merchant Adventurers. But if it were so, that they kept up our commodities abroad; so do they, by the same skill, foreign commodities at home. So a few rich men do gain by their outgoing, and the whole land doth lose much more by their return. They say that they gain little by return of foreign commodities. There lieth a mystery, for it is true, and will be avowed upon certain knowledge, that upon the arrival of the Merchant Adventurers' fleet, the commodities, on the other side, are ordinarily raised at least twenty in the hundred; for so do they quit one wrong with another. But hereby the loss still falls heavy on the subject, who is damnified now again in the commodities returned, as he was before in the engrossing of those which were issued.

Venting all now. The companies that now are do vent all the commodities of the land, and yet are they hardly able to live one by another.

Answer. It is not all vented, which the land might spare; and that by reason of the courses held by these companies, to their own excessive gain, and certain loss of all other men. Besides, when traffic shall flourish with us, as doth in other countries, where trade is free, and namely in the Low Countries, who thereby have supported the huge charge of their long wars, things merchantable will increase daily by this encouragement to the subject's industry, even as there they do; for natural commodities are more than trebled by access of art and industry. And howsoever, yet the division of wealth will be more equal; for now, by the plotting of the governor of these companies, some few overgrown men devour the wealth, and make merry, whilst the rest, even of their own companies, do want and weep.

Prenticeship necessary. This Act makes it lawful to become merchants without prenticeship; which is an injury to them which have served, and hurt to them that serve not; who, venturing unskilfully, shall be sure of loss.

Answer. The loss of new merchants, it may be, is as much the desire as fear of the objectors; but they that have served, have their skill for their labour; and they that serve not, must be at charge of a factor, or join with their friends, and learn skill by them; or at leastwise men adventure their stocks with other men, after the fashion of the Low Countries and other places, where trade doth flourish. By the same reason young gentlemen might be kept from their lands for want of skill to govern them.

Dissolving companies. This Act, by enlarging the companies, and giving free access to all men doth in effect dissolve them; for hardly are they able to govern those that are in already; and where government faileth, there will be certain confusion.

Answer. This Act dissolveth no company, taketh away no good government. Those orders in companies, which tend to monopoly, it abrogateth. Orders for necessary contribution to public charges it establisheth. The rest it leaves as it found them, neither in worse state, nor better. It is weakness to say that a greater multitude cannot be governed; for so neither kings in their dominions, and subjects, nor cities in their amplitude should increase. If for matter of merchandise there were no such government at all, nor more than there is for our merchants in France, or hath been at Stade for divers years past, or than there is in the Low Countries, where are the best merchants in the world; yet provident men would consult and join together in that which were for their common benefit, ease, and safety. Such companies there are in other countries, but no such monopolies as ours are.

Joint stock necessary. This Act is against trading in a joint stock together, which in long and dangerous voyages (as to Musco, and especially the East Indies) is necessary;

for in that voyage one alone will not adventure; besides the merchants must keep some port there amongst the infidels.

It is true, that it is fit to trade to the East Indies with a joint stock, and so *Answer.* do the Hollanders; this Act therefore doth not forbid men to trade in a joint stock, if they list, and see it fit; only forbiddeth to constrain men to trade so against their wills; which heretofore in other trades, and, at this day in the Muscovy trade doth turn to the great damage both of the commonwealth and of the particular persons so constrained to trade. The Muscovy Company, consisting of eightscore, or thereabouts, have fifteen directors, who manage the whole trade; these limit to every man the proportion of stock, which he shall trade for, make one purse and stock of all, and consign it into the hands of one agent at Musco, and so again, at their return, to one agent at London, who sell all, and give such account as they please. This is a strong and a shameful monopoly; a monopoly in a monopoly; both abroad and at home; a whole company by this means is become as one man, who alone hath the uttering of all the commodities of so great a country. The inconveniences, which have ensued thereof, are three apparent:

First, by this means they vent less of our commodities; for, by reason of the one agent, they vent all through his hands; by which means the Hollanders have come in between us; who, trading thither in several with our own English commodities (which are most proper for that country) utter much more than our own merchants, and make quicker return; which hath occasioned many Englishmen to join in trade with the Hollanders, to the detriment of the King's Majesty in his customs. And by this means that trade is like utterly to decay; for the Hollanders have grown in short time from two ships to above twenty. This spring they are gone to Muscovy with near thirty ships, and our men but with seven. The like fell out in the Turkey Company, when they constrained men to a joint stock; since the breaking of which combination, there go four ships for one.

Secondly, in their return with Muscovy commodities, they greatly prejudice the commonwealth and state. Example in cordage, which they bring home in such scarcity, and sell so dearly, as that they have raised it in short time from twenty to thirty shillings; yea, to sell their ware dear, they have contracted with the buyer not to bring any more of that commodity within three years after.

Thirdly, this is hurtful to all the young merchants of their own company, who cannot forbear their stock so long as now they do, and desire to employ their own industry in managing it, and having oftentimes been all damnified by the breaking of that general factor.

In divers places, as namely in Turkey and Muscovy, the merchants are *Public charges.* at charge of sending presents, maintaining ambassadors, consuls, and agents, which are otherwise also necessary for the service of his Majesty, and of the state; these charges are now defrayed by these companies.

This matter is expressly provided for by this Act, that all that trade to *Answer.* those places shall be contributory to those charges.

The now merchants will give over. The like attempt for free trade was *in anno* 1588, at what time, liberty being given to all men to buy cloths at Westminster, the Merchant Adventurers gave over to trade at all; whereby the cloth of the land lying on the clothiers' hands, they were forced, by petition, to get the former restraint restored.

Answer. This is true; and the same mischief were likely to ensue again; for it is said that the same policy is now in speech in their company. But the times being well altered from war to peace, this mischief would be but short, and other merchants soon grow to take their places, if they should, as (being rich) they may, forsake them. But it were to be trusted, that this stomachness, being to their own loss, would not long continue; howsoever it doth not stand with the dignity of Parliament, either to fear or favour the forwardness of any subject.

The rich will eat out the poor If poor merchants should trade together with the rich, the rich beyond the seas would buy out the poor, being not able to sell at the instant, to make themselves savers; and so there would grow a monopoly *ex facto*. This reason sheweth thus much, that a crafty head with a greedy heart, and a rich purse, is able to take advantage of the need of his neighbour (which no man doubteth of) but if the difficulties and dishonesties should deter men from action, and not rather increase their diligence and wariness, then should there be no trading at all in any sort.

Strangers will eat out the English. If all men may be merchants, the sons of strangers denized will, in time, eat out the natural merchants of this kingdom.

Answer. If the sons of strangers become natural English, why should they not reap a subject's part? And more they cannot reap. If any further mischief should grow, it might at all times, by a new Act, be easily remedied.

All men may go out of the realm. If trade be free for all men, then all may become merchants, and under that pretext any man may go out of the realm; which will be good news for the Papists.

Answer. This conceit is weak; for so it may be said that all men may become mariners, and so quit the kingdom; and it is provided by express words of the bill that they may not go out of the realm, but for their present traffic.

Against London. This Act is against London, and the wealth thereof, which is necessary to be upheld being the head city of the kingdom.

Answer. Nay, it is for London, unless we will confine London into some two hundred men's purses; the rest of the City of London, together with the whole realm, sue mainly for this bill; and they cry, they are undone if it should be crossed.

Hurt to the king's customs. It will be prejudicial to the king's customs who, in other parts, will easier be deceived than here in London.

Answer. Nothing can be more clear, than that if transport and return of merchandise will increase by this Act, also the king's customs, which depend thereon, must withal increase. And if this bill may pass if the king be pleased to let his customs to farm, to give 5,000*l.* a year more than, *communibus annis*, hath been made these last years. The deceiving of the king is now when, for want of this freedom, men are enforced to purchase the vent of their commodities out of creeks, because they cannot be admitted to public trade, whereas otherwise they should have no reason to hazard their whole estate, for the saving of so reasonable a duty. As for faults in officers, they may as well happen in London, as in any other place.

During freedom of trade small ships would be employed to vent our commodities, and so our great ships, being the guard of the land would decay. It is war, more than traffic, that maintaineth great ships; and therefore, if any decay grow, it will be chiefly by peace, which the wisdom of the state will have a regard of; but for as much as depends of traffic, no doubt the number of smaller ships will grow by this freedom, and especially mariners, whereof the want is greatest, and of whom the smallest vessels are the proper nurseries. But that the great ships will decay doth not necessarily follow; for the main trade of all the white cloth, and much of other kind, is shipped from the port of London, and will be still, it being the fittest port of the kingdom for Germany and the Low Countries, where the Merchants Adventurers' trade only lieth; who shall have little cause to alter their shipping. Then for the Levant sea, Muscovy, and East Indies, whither we trade with great ships, the employing of them will be still requisite in the merchant's discretion; for otherwise both the commodity of the returned will be less, and the adventure too great in so rich lading, not to provide for more than ordinary assurance against the common hazard at sea. *[margin: Decay of great ships.]*

Other particular reasons there are for restraint of trade in favour of certain company.

The Company of Merchants Adventurers is very ancient, and they have heretofore been great credit to the kings, for borrowing money in the Low Countries and Germany. *[margin: Merchants Adventurers.]*

The Company indeed is as ancient as Thomas of Becket, their founder, and may still continue. Their restraining of others, which this bill doth seek to redress, is not so ancient, and was disallowed by Parliament in the twelfth year of Henry the seventh; which Act stands impeached by particular charter, but never by consent of the realm repealed. But in truth this company, being the spring of all monopolies, and engrossing the grand staple commodities of cloth into so few men's hands, deserves least favour. The credit of the king hath been in the cloth (not in their persons) which will be as much hereafter, as heretofore. *[margin: Answer.]*

The Muscovy Company, by reason of the chargeable invention of that trade two and fifty years since, and their often great loss, was established by Act of Parliament in the eighth year of Queen Elizabeth. *[margin: Muscovy Company.]*

The chargeable invention hath been a reason worthy of respect thirty or forty years ago when the inventors were living, and their charge not recompensed by countervailable gain; which, sithence it hath been their loss, hath been their own fault, in employing one factor, who hath abused them all. Private Acts for favour, when the cause thereof is ceased, are often revoked. *[margin: Answer.]*

Howbeit this bill dissolveth no company, only enlargeth them, and abrogateth their unjust orders for monopolies.

Another argument there is, not to be answered by reason, but by their integrity, and love of their country, who shall be assaulted with it. In sum, the bill is a good bill, though not in all points, perhaps, so perfect as it might be; which defects may be soon remedied and supplied in future Parliament.

In the midst of this report (which by that occasion was stayed) came down from the Lords Sir John Crook and Mr. D. Stanhope, with this message:

That, upon consideration of the message from this House for a conference touching their lordships joining in petition to his Majesty, for leave to treat of wardship, respite of homage, primer seisin, etc., they have, for that purpose, appointed thirty to meet with some proportionable number of this House; and desire that the committees named may come furnished with the grounds and reasons to induce the king, as they also mean to do; and do wish the time may be on Friday in the afternoon; the place, the painted chamber.

That they will be ready to meet with the number of thirty of this House.

Answer.
After this message, Sir Edwyn Sandys proceeded in the report, and delivered in the two bills for free trade; the first (being the principal bill) with amendments; which were twice read; and the bill, upon question, ordered to be engrossed.

5. TRADE WITH FRANCE, *c.* 1604
[B.M., Stowe MS. 132, ff. 148–51]

SEVERAL sorts of merchandise carried out of England into France as followeth:

In primis all sorts of northern kersies; —— [?] dozens, long cloths, and penistons; Kendal cottons; Welsh cottons; bays of all sorts; Devonshire dozens; Totnes kersies; Reading kersies; kersies made now of late years in Dorset and Somerset shires great quantity; pin whites made in Devonshire; Hampton serges or cloth rash; Suffolk and Kentish cloths for the south parts of France; Bridgwater reds; all sorts of Norwich stuffs; fustians; herrings from Yarmouth in great quantity; pilchards from the west parts; lead in great quantity; tin; iron; sea coals great quantity; wool by the staplers; calf skins and sheep skins in great quantity; India hides; Beare; copperas; saffron; wax; dry fish out of Newfoundland; worsted stockings great quantity; Muscovy tallow; flax and hemp that comes out of the East parts; pitch and tar; soap in great quantity; ox horns and deer's horns; old shoes and many bones; glovers' sheads and old linen cloth to make paper of, and other commodities which no money could be made off but in France; ashes.

Several sorts of merchandise brought out of France into England:

In primis Normandy canvas, brown and whited paper of all sorts; buckerams; prunes; teasels for dressing of cloth; silk grograms; tuft taffaties; velvets;

mill stones; plaster of Paris; wool cards; tennis balls; combs, pins, and divers sorts of haberdash wares; lockerams and dowlas; vittery canvas; Poldavis and middrick; rape oil; Province oils; Rochelle salt; Gascony wines; Bordeaux feathers; rozen [=rosin]; woad; whale fins; liquorice; hops; Paris silver and gold both fine and false in thread and as much bawlion of gold and silver as hath come out of Spain, as that may be proved; girdles and hangers and saddles for great horse; attires for ladies besides divers rich commodities from Paris as cloth of silver and gold; ollifants' teeth for cutlers; apples and walnuts store; kids' skins great store.

A note of the clothing towns in Yorkshire which cloth is uttered in no place beyond the seas but in France: [The names of 100 towns follow, beginning Wakefield, Leeds.] There are in number one hundred and one towns besides other villages near to those towns and that clothing doth maintain above three score and ten thousand people that live by the cloth-making only for France with making of kersies and dozens.

A note of the clothing towns and villages within the Barony of Kendal and near thereunto adjoining: [The names of 57 places follow.] There are three score towns and villages which do only make Kendal cloth, called northern cottons, which be carried over into France, and there is above 15,000 people maintained by the same.

A note of the clothing town[s] in Lancashire for the most part: [The names of 31 places follow.] In all thirty towns and villages which do only make friezes and cotton called Manchester cottons which is only carried into France, and there is maintained by that means 10,000 people which live by that trade.

A note of the shires in Wales that make cloth: [The names of 13 counties including Shropshire follow.] These thirteen shires are maintained by the making of Welsh cottons and only sold in France. There be above 100,000 people that do live by the making of these cottons.

There be three shires wholly maintained in the west country by making of western kersies and pin whites which only live by sending of their kersies and pin whites into France, besides many other towns and villages which live by that trade, and doth maintain above 100,000 people at least in all that country.

There be many poor maintained by making of bays the which is carried into France in a great quantity as into any other places beyond the seas.

There be many poor maintained by carrying of Kentish and Suffolk cloths into France.

There are as many goods ships maintained by the trade in France as for Bordeaux for wines and for bowraise and Rochelle for salt and other places for other commodities; in no other foreign kingdoms where trade is used by English merchants so many ships employed as be for France, and great store of ships maintained by carrying of sea coal into France.

The number and the value of cloth kersies, cottons, and bays carried into

all the parts of France every year doth come to by estimation above ——,
besides other commodities carried out of England for France only, for the
great custom paid to his Majesty throughout England is to be seen at the pipe
office, and there your Honours may be certified of the truth how much of all
sorts of cloth and other commodities is carried out of England into France.

There is as much dyed and dressed cloth of all sorts counting kersies and
cottons carried to Bordeaux, Rochelle, Bayonne, St. Malo, Nantes, and other
places in Brittany as is carried into Spain.

6. THE DISADVANTAGES OF MERCHANTS TRADING TO FRANCE WITHOUT ORGANIZATION IN A COMPANY, 1605

[Historical MSS. Commission, *Salisbury MSS.*, XX, pp. 161–2]

[Lord Treasurer Dorset, to the Customs Officers at the Ports]

I HAVE received letters from the Council to the effect following, that whereas
upon the suit of the chiefest of merchants that trade into France, in respect
they have no authority by corporation or otherwise to levy any sum of money
amongst themselves for the defraying those necessary charges which concern
the good of the whole company and their trade, it was found necessary to
lay a small imposition or tax upon all kind of cloths and woollen commodities that are transported by them out of his Majesty's realm into the French
dominions for this purpose only, to bear the charges that had been sustained
and were necessary to be employed for the freeing of them from a hard edict
made by the French king in the year 1600, for the confiscation of our English
cloths for divers defects pretended to be in them; whereupon divers letters
were written unto me by which I was required to give direction unto all the
officers of all the ports and customs for the levying and gathering of that
imposition. And for that there is now a commission granted by his Majesty
unto Sir Thomas Parry, his Majesty's ambassador there, to treat about the
revoking or qualifying of that edict, whereby his Majesty's subjects receive
so great prejudice as unless they may be freed from the same, they shall not
be able to continue their trade and intercourse; for the prosecution whereof
they have chosen merchants, clothiers, and other persons of experience in
these matters, to go over expressly to attend the ambassador and to follow
that business: which charges, besides the former disbursements not yet
satisfied, cannot be supported and borne by the small impositions and rates
formerly set down without some further order taken. Forsomuch as upon
conference lately had with the chiefest French merchants, a new rate and
imposition has been set down doubling the former to the which all the chiefest of them have given their allowance and consent, as a thing most necessary
to be done for the following of these causes importing the whole trade; I am
required by their Lordships' said letters to direct my letters newly to the

several officers of all ports and customs, requiring them for causes above specified to cause this imposition and tax of increase hereunder written to be collected according to their former direction, and in such measure and form, and for the space of four years from the date hereof, as is contained in those letters which their Lordships did then send unto me, and with which by mine you have been formerly acquainted. In regard whereof these are straitly to will and require you from henceforth to be very diligent to collect this new imposition and tax of increase of these several commodities hereunder written according to the effect of their Lordships' said letters. And in so doing, this shall be your warrant.—From Dorset House, this 10th of July, 1605.

[Endorsed:] Whereas the receipt of the French imposition has been much impaired of that it would have grown unto, by reason that some masters of ships have entered for Spain, Barbey Islands, or some other places, when they have been bound for France or Brittany; these are to will and require you that as you have already authority, so to take the oath of every English master of any ship that enters not for France, that he is neither bound nor will lay on land in any part of France or dominions of the French king any of those commodities which by the merchants were entered upon him and are in his ship.

7. AN OPINION ON TRADING COMPANIES TO FRANCE AND SPAIN, 1605

[Historical MSS. Commission, IX, *Salisbury MSS.*, XVII, pp. 418–19]

[Chief Justice Popham to the Earl of Salisbury]

1605, Sept. 11.—I have received your letters of 9 Sept., wherein I find questions moved of greater difficulty than I would anyway of myself have entered into. But upon your letters, they are for some of them, both for the law of such difficulty, and for matters of state of such moment, as would require very exact and sound considerations before they were resolved on. Nevertheless in that you require it, as so short a time and as the state of my body (which lately was such as I thought I should never see London again) will permit, I will acquaint you with some points I have heretofore conceived concerning these matters. First, for the trade into the territories of the Grand Seignior, I hold it no question but that his Majesty may by law incorporate a company for it, with such conditions as shall be fitting. But for that of France and Spain I would ask to be further advised before I set down my conceit therein. But this much I must say that I have always found (what pretences soever the merchants make to draw themselves into companies) they ever have in it their private ends, and all those take their ground from the Merchant Adventurers, and yet their cases may haply differ. I dare affirm, if that company should be permitted to do that which they pretend to have power to do by their charter, and have often attempted to put in practice (but have been put from it chiefly by your father's means in his lifetime), they might within few years have enriched themselves infinitely, and impoverished the state and whole commonweal extremely; and what may grow of this in after ages I know not, but I may fear. This I hold as a principle, that it is not convenient that merchants have such power passed over unto them that they may govern the estate of things both at home and abroad as they list, and they not to be curbed therein by the state, but that if they should be they might say, as myself have heard them in time past, they have been wronged. But for the matter of drawing the trades of France and Spain into companies, I fear me it will overthrow all the towns, shipping, and mariners of the west parts, because the young merchants of those parts begin with very small stocks, and cannot deal here upon such credit as young merchants may do in London, and their stocks and wealths have increased by their often returns; and by that means they make more of 100*l.* in the year than the merchants of London do of 200*l.* Now if they be barred of their often returns, they can hardly raise benefit sufficient to support their estates, much less to increase it, and then must both their shipping and mariners decay in those parts. Haply it will be answered that those shall trade as they have done. But when their patent is once passed, and the trade somewhat settled, then must those men be complained of as interlopers and overthrowers of the merchant-like trading into those parts, and either it must be taken away or the chief of this new company fail of their purpose. Some of the principal merchants westward may be drawn to like of this course, for so were some when the first corporation for Spain was passed in the late Queen's time; but it was no sooner put in practice, but both they and all the rest of the western merchants found out the drift of the merchants of London that followed it; whereupon they so much repined at it, that they were resolved to petition against it, but that the breach fell out presently between England and Spain, which interrupted it. I know you have well observed the general course of merchants heretofore in matters concerning their trades, wherein they aim still at their own present good, without respect unto the state. The event of this in my opinion concerns the state, all men that live on their revenue or husbandry, and a multitude of artisans so deeply as will appear when it shall come in dispute, that I doubt not but there will be very good considerations had both before it pass and in passing of it.—At Lytlecott, 11 Sept. 1605.

P.S. [in Popham's hand]. I know your lordship both will and can look farther into matters of this kind than myself, and therefore do submit what I have said to your better judgement. I doubt not but that France would if they might upon any correspondence with their neighbours' countries shake off foreign manufactures, and thereof it grows the French king takes such hold of the falsity used in the making of our clothes traded that ways; which firstly surely must be reformed, otherwise I see not how the inconveniences (which by that means we draw on ourselves) can be avoided. No doubt but upon just occasion, as this now in question, the king may for a time forbid his subjects to trade to any country, and who that breaks that injunction is to be punished by the state. And to discern the true purpose of those which design these companies, it may please you to will them to set down the manner how they would have the trades ordered, and thereby it will soon be discerned what they earned in it. My paper will give me leave to write no more.

8. THE SPANISH COMPANY RESUMES ACTIVITY AFTER THE WAR, 1605

[B.M., Add. MS. 9365, ff. 61–2, 65–70. Register of the Courts of the Spanish Merchants, 1603–5]

A COURT of Assistants holden at Pewterers Hall upon Wednesday, the xvith day of October, 1605.

24th Article in the last treaty of peace hath these words: Item that the grant and privilege given by the princes to merchants of either of the kingdoms coming to their said kingdoms, and which privileges through the wars have ceased, shall from henceforth wholly be revived and have their full force and strength.

And whereas the English merchants have lately elected these five consuls for these five several places: St. Lucar and Seville, Hugh Bourman; Lisbon, Hugh Lea; Biscay, James Wich; Bayon [=Bayona] in Galicia, Francis Lambert; Malaga, Humphrey Wotton; they most humbly pray his Majesty's gracious letters to the King of Spain to the intent that all such consuls as the company have or shall elect may enjoy all the said privileges and authorities granted as aforesaid. And that the King of Spain would write to the Duke of Medina in that behalf [There follows the copy of the king's letters to the English ambassador in Spain.] . . .

A General Court holden at Pewterers Hall upon Wednesday the 6th day of November, 1605.

. . . To this court resorted Henry Waade of Topsham in the county of Devon making claim to the freedom by ancient trade by virtue of a clause included in the charter of *decimo nono* Elizabeth because his father was a trader into Spain before 1568. But upon examination it appeared that his father was dead at the time of the granting of the same charter, whereupon the company perused over an order taken at a general court holden the 8th day of November, 1577, at which time question was moved and entreated upon the admitting of such ancient merchants' children and servants, whose fathers or masters were usual traders into Spain or Portugal before *anno* 1568, and nevertheless dead before the grant of the said Letters Patent. And then it was agreed, concluded, and adjudged by the whole court that it was not necessary that any such should be received or admitted for that they be without the compass of the express words of the said grant, as by the said order may appear, which order is also lately confirmed the xxxth day of August last. Nevertheless, forasmuch as it is affirmed that the company cannot make and order to bar any man of his right granted by charter, it is agreed that the opinion of Mr. Dodderidge, his Majesty's Solicitor General, shall be used upon that point of the charter. And that Mr. Dorrington, Mr. Harrison, and the secretary together with the said Henry Waade shall all resort unto him to understand his resolution therein. And the fee to be paid indifferently by the company and Mr. Waade. And upon relation made of his opinion, the company will do that which to right and equity shall appertain . . .

At this court these four persons following making claim to their freedom by ancient trade, viz. Humphrey Hanford, grocer, by service with Mr. Henry Colthurst, Humphrey Walweyne, grocer, by service with Mr. Nicholas Style, Gregory Guybon, mercer, by service with Mr. Nicholas Heath, and Zachery Parke, by service with Mr. William Parkyn of King's Lynn, being all ancient traders whose several claims being examined were found capable by ancient trade, and paid their several fines of vi*s*. viii*d*. apiece and were admitted and sworn accordingly.

Also William Fisher, the son of John Fisher of Ipswich, claiming the freedom by patrimony in the right of his father, and allowed at a former general court holden xiii August last, did at this court pay his fine of vi*s*. viii*d*., took the oath of a freeman by ancient trade, and was admitted accordingly . . .

Upon consideration had to a letter lately received from Totnes shewing how far distant and inconvenient Totnes and the other towns following lie from Exeter, it is therefore ordered that Totnes and the said towns shall be clearly exempted from the government of Exeter. And that a deputy shall be elected for Totnes and the same several towns and they to govern of themselves. And the several towns to be under the jurisdiction of Totnes, viz. Dartmouth, Tynemouth [=Teignmouth], Newton Bushel, Kingswear, Kingsbridge, Salcombe, Asperton [=Ashprington], Staffarton [=Staverton], Broadhempston, and Toore, and no allowance to be made either to Deputy or Assistants.

To this court resorted William Greenewell, a mere merchant and free of the Eastland Company, desiring the freedom of this society and (according to our charter) did offer to procure a like freedom for one of this society to be free of the Eastland Company, unto whom answer was made that he should have shortly delivered unto him by Mr. President and four of the Assistants the name of one of this company, and upon procuring of the freedom of the Eastland Company for such person so to be named, the said William Greenewell should be received and admitted into the freedom of this society accordingly . . .

A general court holden at Pewterers Hall upon Friday, the viiith day of November, 1605.

... Whereas the first day of the Parliament some exceptions were taken in the lower House of Parliament to the charter lately granted to this society, and a committee appointed to consider of the same and to draw a bill to be tendered to the house against our charter; whereof the company, taking notice, Mr. President, Mr. Deputy, and the Secretary resorted to the Middle Temple Hall where the committee sat, desiring to understand of them in what points they did except against our charter, whereupon they delivered two propositions to this or the like effect, viz. first, whether if merchants incorporated to trade [to] Spain and Portugal will permit and suffer that all manner of persons that shall adventure to the sea to take fish may carry their fish freely for those countries and there sell it at their will and pleasure and return from thence all sorts of merchandises at their will and pleasure; the second, whether the company will permit and suffer all gentlemen, yeomen, farmers, and all others of what quality soever to carry corn into Spain and Portugal and to make their return in merchandise from thence at their will and pleasure.

And did require Mr. President to confer with the company and return their answers before Wednesday after, which was the chief and special matter that moved him to call this court, upon full and deliberate consideration whereunto had, it is resolved and agreed that the company shall depend and stand upon the validity of their charter, and not to give any consent or agreement to the proposition required.

9. THE SPANISH COMPANY VIEWED FROM ANOTHER ANGLE, 1605

[B.M., Harleian MS. 1875, ff. 228–31. Sir Charles Cornwallis's Correspondence etc. as Ambassador to Spain, 1605, 1606]

A Letter written [by Sir Charles Cornwallis, English ambassador in Spain, from Valladolid] to the Merchants and Factors of Lisbon in answer of one of theirs [1605]

THE mutability and little consideration I have found in you that be merchants and factors in the city is very strange unto me.

At my first coming to this court, there was a letter shewed unto me signed with 20 or 30 of your hands to desire the confirmation of Rowland Maylard (now deceased) in consulship there. Within few days after another letter was presented unto me directly contradicting the former, disallowing Maylard and commending Edward Baynes for the place. For mine own particular the said Maylard having formerly possessed the place and recommended with so many hands I was contented to allow of him, but with caution that if he should be misliked by the company when he should be established, then he should presently relinquish to Baynes (after his death). I denied my assent for the office, only was content that in the interim, till a consul should be appointed by the merchants, he might supply the place.

It now seemeth unto me that holding your former changing and uncertain courses you would prefer a third, one Rowles.

Against Baynes you make two exceptions, one, the neediness of his estate, the other his contrary affection in religion. What the estates of either Baynes or Rowles are I well understand not, neither am much inclined to build my belief upon your reports wherein you have been so variable. I suppose that neither of their estates could breed much benefit or prejudice to your business in this short time until the company do send a consul.

And as for religion I certainly understand that Rowles is as settled and obstinate a Papist as the other and therefore in that regard neither of them fit if any other of our nation being a good Christian would be received by the king and state here.

For the other matters of your complaints I hope by such letters and dispatches as I have formerly sent thither, you have good proof of my cares and endeavours, though unsolicited by any of you to have dealt in the same.

You received from me orders for avoiding your trouble by visiting of your ships by inquisitors and others for the reasonable valuation of your goods and good usage of the same in the Custom House, for the quiet possession of the goods of such our nation as should there die by the heirs or assigns of them, and that you shall be no worse entreated than those that are his Majesty's own subjects. Of these you were never pleased by any letter to give significa-tion either of your receipt of them or thanks to me for my travails.

I much fear you are led there by some brother that walks inordinately. If so it be, you shall do well to become more soundly and better advised. He that could not content himself within bounds in his own profession is not likely to teach much temper and good orders in yours.

For my poor countrymen in the galleys, before I heard from [you] I had begun to use the best as also for diverse others that are in Andolazia for the poor man of Bastable [= Barnstaple?] whose barque and fish was taken,[1] although neither himself nor any of you (in that due regard of him that would well have become you) either sent unto me his name or any writings to enable me to undertake his cause. Yet out of that duty and love that I have and will always bear to my country (to whom it shall be within my power to procure relief) I have of myself by means of mine honourable friends by extraordinary course obtained his Majesty's letters for free visitation to [be] made unto him.

I have also procured another general letter to the viceroy for all manner of favours to be done unto my countrymen that either do or shall traffic

---

[1] This case is referred to in a letter to the Duke of Lerma from Sir Charles Cornwallis, c. 15 Sept. 1605 (ff. 130v–131): 'Yesterday came a complaint to me of a fisherman taken upon the sea that came from the Newfoundland laden with fish (having in the vessel but four men and two boys). Though upon the sea he was taken, yet because he had not certi-ficate out of England and his fish sealed (which were a strange thing to be required upon that kind of merchandise) his barque, himself, and his men are, as I hear, embarked and some of them sent to the galleys. This was done by the galleys of Lisbon coming from Seville and the English barque in her way to port.'

there. Both which I will send by one Rivett, my servant, whom I hope this week to dispatch thither.

For the staying of your ships and making use of your boats contrary to your wills, I long since prayed redress from the king who answered that there was and should [be] straight order taken for the same. So as if any such wrong be offered you are to complain to the viceroy who, not seeing present remedy therein, if you signify it unto me I doubt not to procure punishment to them that shall do it and amends unto you that shall suffer it.

And so having given you an account of what I have done, I commend me heartily unto you and desire I may hear of some more settled and stayed good orders amongst you.

> Your loving friend,
> Ch. Co.

10. EXETER'S SHIPPING TRADE FOR TWO MONTHS, 1609

[Exeter City Library, Customs Rolls, 6–8 Jas. I, 1608–11]

A BRIEF Note of all such Entry of Ships as have been entered in the King's Majesty's Custom House of Exon as have come from beyond the seas since Crispinmas 1608 until the 24th of April in the year of our Lord, 1610 . . . [The book starts with December 29, 1608.]

27th March, 1609: Le William of Pettinwinne 40 tons from Dundee with barley; Le Sunne of Flushing 70 tons from Flushing with rye and cordage; Le Primrose of Jarzy [= Jersey] 55 tons from Garnzy [= Guernsey] with rye and wheat; Le Elizabeth of Beere 10 tons from Sherbrooke with canvas; Le James of Mountweare 40 tons from Croisicke with salt; 29th [March]: Le Lion of Topsham 20 tons from St. Malo with canvas.

8th April: Le Susan of Topsham 20 tons from St. Malo with canvas.

12th: Le Elizabeth of Jarzy 15 tons from Jarzy with canvas and treg.[1]

15th: Le Garland of Topsham 30 tons from Murles with white wares.

19th: Le Phenix of Lime 20 tons from Murles with white wares; Le Margarett of Ushant 23 tons from Croisicke with salt.

20th: Le William and John of Exmouth 30 tons from St. Michaels with oade [= woad]; Le Francis of Mountweare 30 tons from Rochelle with salt.

22nd: Le Grace of God of Powderham 18 tons from Rochelle with canvas and salt.

24th: Le Ladonesa of Nuelle 24 tons from Nuelle with salt.

26th: Le Michael of Exmouth 40 tons from Tenerife with sugar and wines.

30th: Le Jane of Croisicke 25 tons from Croisicke with salt:

3rd of May: Le Philip and Mary of Weymouth 20 tons from Bilbao with iron, wools, and oil.

---

[1] Treg. signifies treager, a linen cloth. See also p. 303.

5th: Le Gift of God of Croisicke 15 tons from Rochelle with salt, vinegar, and raisins; Le Drunkard of Deepe [=Dieppe] 18 tons from Deepe with glasses and wheat.

8th: Le Margaret and John of Aldborough 160 tons from Quinborough with rye.

16th: Le Angel of Middleborough 40 tons from Flushing with rye; Le Pernina of Penmarse 35 tons from St. Sebastian with iron, feathers, and rozen; Le Robert of Dartmouth 10 tons from Murles with white wares.

19th: Le Diamond of Topsham 40 tons from St. Lucar with oil and sacks.

22nd: Le Jane of Oldron 17 tons from Rochelle with salt and vinegar.

23rd: Le Pellican of Dart 20 tons from Avero with oil, wools, salt, and deals.

24th: Le Bludone of Harlinge 100 tons from Danske with deals, ores, rye, sturgeon, clapboards, glasses.

11. AN ATTEMPT AT A BALANCE OF TRADE BY SIR LIONEL CRANFIELD AND OTHERS, 1612–14[1]

[B.M., Lansdowne MS. 152, ff. 180–3. Caesar Papers]

Merchandises exported

	li.	*s.*	*d.*
From Christmas 1612 to Christmas 1613			
Custom *Portu* London is	61,322	16	7
Custom of the outports is	25,471	19	7
Wrappers being the tenth cloth bay and cotton	7,000		
Fish of our own fishing and by statute freed from custom may be estimated to be per annum	7,000		
Foreign goods imported and exported again free of custom by Privy Seal	3,737	4	5
	104,532	0	7
The which is the 20th part of goods exported and being so multiplied produceth the value to be the sum of	2,090,640	11	8
unto which is to be added the custom paid outwards which is	86,794	16	2
unto which is also to be added the imposts which is	10,000		
unto which is likewise to be added the merchants' gain, fraught of ships, and other petty charges paid both here and in foreign countries, which may be estimated to be	300,000		
Then the total value of goods exported, these particulars being added, is	2,487,435	7	10

[1] This document is indexed at the beginning of the volume under the title 'Balances of trade by Sir Lionel Cranfield, Mr. John Wostenholme, and others'. It is clearly the work of more than one hand. The asterisks towards the end of each year's account indicate where one hand ends and another begins.

Merchandises imported

	li.	s.	d.
From Christmas 1612 to Christmas 1613			
Custom *Portu* London is	4,825	1	9
Custom of the outports is	13,030	9	9
Custom of the silks is	15,477		
Custom of Venice gold and silver	700		
French wines	2,000		
Spanish wines, etc.	1,200		
Allowance of 5 per cent is	4,000		
Whereunto to be added the underrating of silks ⅓ part after 12,000*li.* per annum	4,000		
To be added also the underrating of all wines ⅔ of that they cost	6,400		
To be added likewise the underrating of linen and many other kinds of merchandises ⅓ after 36,000*li.* per annum	12,000		
Then the total of the custom is	107,057	11	6
The which is the 20th part of goods imported and being so multiplied produceth the value to be	2,141,151	10	0
The which being defaulted from the exportation, it doth appear that the importation is overbalanced this present year	346,283	17	10
	2,487,435	7	10

*   *   *

	li.	s.	d.
But admit his own form of account to be good and the custom outwards to be 104,532*li.* 0*s.* 7*d.* and one fifth part to be added hereunto for the merchants' gains and other petty charges, then would it produce the sum of	125,438	8	8
And admit that the customs inwards were this year 84,657*li.* 11*s.* 7*d.* and that one third part was to be added thereunto in regard of the underrating thereof, then would it produce the sum of	112,876	15	5
Yet the receipt outwards is more than inwards this year	12,561	13	3
And so by his own account the exportation doth overbalance the importation in the value of goods exported	251,233	5	0

*   *   *

Merchandises exported

	li.	s.	d.
From Christmas 1613 to Christmas 1614			
Custom *Portu* London is	64,324	16	1
Custom of the outports is	24,650	6	3
Wrappers being the tenth cloth bay and cotton	7,000		

li. s. d.

Fish of our own fishing and by statute freed from custom
  may be estimated to be per annum   7,000

Foreign goods imported and exported again freed from
  custom by Privy Seal per annum   7,815

The total of the custom is   110,790 2 4

The which is the 20th part of goods exported and being
  so multiplied doth produce the value to be the sum of   2,215,802 6 8
whereunto is to be added the custom paid outwards
  which is   88,975 2 5
unto which is also to be added the imposts paid outwards
  which is   10,000
unto which is also to be added the merchants' gains, fraught
  of ships, and other petty charges paid both here and in
  foreign countries, which may be estimated to be per
  annum   300,000

Then the total value of the goods exported, these
  particulars being added is   2,614,777 9 1

Merchandises imported

From Christmas 1613 to Christmas 1614   *li. s. d.*
Custom *Portu* London is   48,464 13 6
Custom of the outports is   15,729 19 1
Custom of the silks is   15,562
Custom of Venice gold and silver is   7,000
French wines   200
Spanish wines, etc.   1,200
Allowance of 5 per cent is   4,000
To be added hereunto the underrating of linen and many
  other kinds of merchandises $\frac{1}{3}$ after 36,000*li.* per annum   12,000
To be added hereunto the underrating of silks $\frac{1}{3}$ part of
  that they cost after 12,000*li.* per annum is   4,000
To be added hereunto the underrating of all wines $\frac{2}{3}$ of
  that they cost   6,400

Then the total of the custom is   110,056 12 7

The which is the 20th part of goods imported, and being
  so multiplied doth produce the value to be   2,220,132 11 8
The which being defaulted from the exportation, it
  doth appear that the importation is overbalanced this
  year   413,644 17 5

                2,614,777 9 1

*   *   *

	li.	*s.*	*d.*

But admit his own form of account to be good and the
   customs outwards to be 110,790*li.* 2*s.* 4*d.* and ⅕ to be
   added for the merchants' gains, fraught of ships, and
   other petty charges, then would it produce the sum of   132,948   2   9
And admit that the customs inwards were this year
   87,656*li.* 12*s.* 7*d.* and ⅓ were to be added in regard
   of the underrating thereof, then the same would produce
   this year's custom to be the sum of   116,875   10   1
Yet the receipt outwards is more than inwards this year   16,072   12   8

And so by his own form of account the exportation doth
   this year overbalance the importation in the value of the
   goods exported   321,452   13   4

               *   *   *

According to his form of account the exportation
   exceedeth the importation for the first year by   251,233   5   0
      and for the second year by   321,452   13   4
So that the exportation for these two years exceedeth
   importation by   572,685   18   4

               *   *   *

The conclusion for both according to my form of account
The exportation exceedeth the importation for the first
   year by   346,283   17   10
And for the second year by   413,644   17   5
So that the exportation for these two years exceedeth the
   importation by   759,928   15   3

[Endorsed:] A computation of the value of all merchandises exported and imported out and into the realm of England shewing the difference betwixt the value of the exportation and importation for two years successively.

    A computation of all merchandises exported out and imported into England in one year by Mr. Wostenholme, 21 May, 1615.

12. ENGLISH TRADE IN JAPAN, 1615

[Diary of Richard Cocks, Cape Merchant in the English Factory in Japan, 1615–22, ed. E. M. Thompson, Vol. I, Hakluyt Soc., LXVI, 1883, pp. 29, 33–4, 41–3, 45–6]

August 1 [1615] . . . And I thought good to note down that the China Capt., Andrea Dittis, came and told me how his brother Whaw at Langasaque desired to have it under my handwriting touching procuring trade into China. For, as he sayeth, they have laid out 3,000 *taies*[1] already to make way, and make reckoning it will cost them 5,000 *taies* more, in all 8,000 *taies* (I say

---

[1] A *tayle* equalled 10 *mas*; 1 *mas* equalled 6*d.* sterling.

eight thousand *taies*); which, if in case they procure us free trade into China, we are to pay them the said eight thousand *taies* back, with what else shall be thought fitting. But if they do not procure us free trade into China, the loss to stand upon themselves.

I forgot to note down how Jorge Durois wrote me how a great Holland ship was cast away on the coast of Lucan in the Phillippinas, out of the which the country people saved 5 great pieces of ordnance, and that most part of the men were cast away in the ship, and those which escaped per swimming were taken prisoners and sent to Manila . . .

August 6 . . . Capt. Speck[1] came late to the English house and Sir Matias with him and desired my company to go and see a piece of ordnance cast; which I did, but marvelled at their workmanship. For they carried the metal in ladles above 20 yards from the place where the mould stood, and so put it in ladleful after ladle; and yet made as formal ordinance as we do in Christendom, both of brass and iron. Captain Speck told me neither workmanship nor stuff did not stand him in half the price it cost them in Christendom.

Captain Speck told me he received a bark's lading of copper this day from Sackay and that his bark departed from thence three days after Mr. Eaton was departed from thence. God send him hither in safety . . .

August 18. I went to Cochi to visit Capt. Adams and see our junk work. Went forward and carried him a bottle Spanish wine, two hens, one duck, a piece of pork, eight loaves bread and six millans and returned to Firando to dinner, having invited Albaro Monues who told me the Dutch mariners used him ill yesterday in words, calling him Cornudo, he being a married man. Whereupon grew some quarrel, for which 4 or 5 Dutch mariners were ducked at yard arm and each one 40 strips at capstan.

Also the China Capt. returned in our bark, the wind being still contrary, and, having given order along the coast to send our pilots if our ship came in sight, he went to Langasaque and stayed half a day, and bringeth word that his brother told him that the common report amongst both Spaniards and Portingals was that now they took the English to be their enemies, as well as the Hollanders, and therefore would take all our ships which traded into these parts of the world, etc. But I remember the old proverb, that 'God sends a cursed cow short horns'.

I find on a sudden that Mr. Wickham grows very sullen humorous and, as I am informed, giveth out that he is not the Company's servant, but at will, and therefore will rather seek out for his return for England in some shipping from Langasaque to Siam or Pattania. I think the reason is that he hath fingered 5 or 6 *cattis* of good ambergris in the Liqueas, and thinketh to make an India voyage for himself, and to return Capt. or General for the Company at his pleasure. Once truly I, and I think all the rest of the English in these parts, desire rather his room than company. He is turbulent.

August 19.—Taccamon Dono sent me a present of 8 hens. And I wrote a letter to Capt. Adams how the China Capt.'s brother had lent us 325 *gantes*

---

[1] Capt. Speck was head of the Dutch factory.

of shark oil, and therefore wished him to send a man to Andrea, our host, to buy 400 or 500 *gantes* oil at 10 *tais* per hundred *gantes*, as he informed us there was enough to be had, to the intent we may pay what we owe and have to serve our turn. And I delivered fifty *taies* plate bars to Mr. Nealson to lay out about charge of junk.

And Mr. Nealson paid Yaiemon Dono, our junk carpenter, forty 8 *taies* in plate of bars, and is in full payment for 170 planks for the junk at 4 *mas* per piece; the rest, being 20 *taies*, was paid per him before.

August 20.—I received a letter from Capt. Adams from Cochi, dated this day, how a bark with Spaniards from Langasaque put into that road and came from Mallia[1] in shipping. The[y] say Don Lues de Fashardo did fight with 20 sail of Hollanders bound for the East Indies, and hath sunk or taken 12 of them, and the rest escaped by flight. Also the[y] say the King of Spain hath wars with the Turk, and that this news is come from Madrid in 6 months per way of New Spain.

And, after all, the Spaniards came to the English house, viz., Miguel de Salinas, Captain Medina, and a German called Marcus, with Alferis Tuerto and Lues Martin, and Albaro Monues accompanied them. They used many complementos and told me of Don Lues Fachardos discomfiting the Holland fleet going for the East Indies, but after such a divers sort that I can scarce believe it to be true; as also that 4 sail of English ships were passed the Straits of Magilanus into the South Sea . . .

August 25.—I delivered one hundred rials of eight to Mr. Nealson to employ in stuffs with Dutch mariners who, as it should seem, have met with some prize per way; otherways they could not afford to sell so good cheap . . .

August 29.—I wrote a letter to Capt. Adams how his scrivano told me our carpenters said they would not work a stroke on the junk except I gave them a bill of my hand to pay them as they were paid the last year: which I think is a trampo [= trap] of the Dutch to get our carpenters from us to serve their own turns, they now pretending to set out their rotten junk for to carry provision to the Moluccas. So I willed Capt. Adams to content them with a bill or what else so our business may go forward . . .

13. THE PRIVY COUNCIL CONSIDERS THE BALANCE OF TRADE, 1616

[Acts of the Privy Council, 1615–16, pp. 477–81]

At Whitehall, on Tuesday morning, the 9 of April, 1616.

Present: The Lord Archbishop of Canterbury, Lord Chancellor [etc.]

Upon consideration heretofore had of the inequality of trade, and the importation of foreign commodities by merchant strangers to an exceeding great value, more than is exported by them of the native commodities of this

---

[1] Probably a slip for Manila.

realm, by means whereof the money and coin of this kingdom is exported; which, in a short time, will wholly exhaust the treasure of this realm, and produce many other extremities, to the prejudice and danger of the state; it was thought meet that consideration should be taken of the statutes of employment, which the wisdom of former times had provided, as well for the avoiding of that inconvenience, as for the advancement of the native commodities of the realm, and many other public benefits. And to the end the said laws might be the better known and executed, the same being diligently weighed and maturely considered of, were summarily collected into certain plain and short articles, expressed in an Act of Council, and entered into this Register the 19 of December last, as by the said Act will at large appear.

And to the end so good a work might proceed and take effect, as is requisite and expedient for the public, their lordships did this day call before them Mr. Alderman Cockain with divers of the Company of the King's Merchant Adventurers; to whom they propounded the unsufferable inconveniences arising by the inequality of trade, and the means of reformation thereof, by putting in execution the statutes of employment, collected into the foresaid articles. Which being distinctly and plainly read unto them, their lordships demanded how they conceived the same might stand with the great work of dyeing, dressing, and ample venting of cloth, and whether they knew any cause why the said articles should not be put in execution. To which they answered, that the putting in execution of those articles would, in their opinion, redound to the exceeding benefit and good of the realm, and particularly to the advancement of the trade of cloth, so far as they themselves heretofore did make bold, in some of their petitions exhibited to this Board, to intimate their desire for putting in execution the statutes of employment.

This being done, and the chamber voided, their lordships called in Sir William Garroway, Mr. Alderman Jones, Mr. Wolstenham, and Mr. Salter, farmers of the Customs; and after the like proposition made unto them, and the foresaid articles distinctly read in their hearing, demanded of them what they conceived thereof, and how the same would stand with his Majesty's Customs. To which they made answer *una voce*, that doubtless it would prove generally profitable for the state, and that they themselves, finding the inconvenience and disorders in the trade of strangers, had a purpose to have been suitors to their lordships, that the statutes of employment might be put in execution.

A brief computation of the value of all goods imported and exported into and out of the port of London by merchant strangers, according to the printed *Book of Rates*, excepting the wines inwards and cloth outwards, both of them rated by a medium, being not valued in the said *Book of Rates*, viz. for one whole year begun from the feast of the birth of our Lord God, 1610, and ended at the same feast 1611, being by the space of one whole year as followeth:

IMPORTATION

	£ s. d.	£ s. d.
The value of the goods inwards according to the *Book of Rates*	348,252 9 4	
More for the allowance of five in the hundredth to the merchants..	17,000 0 0	
		365,252 9 4
The trade of strangers, consisting for the most part of the finest commodities, the same by estimate are underrated in the printed book to one third part, which cometh to		121,750 16 4
The French wines, besides 65s. for custom, butlerage, and impost upon the ton, thirty shillings the freight, thirty shillings the leakage, and fifteen shillings for petty charges, in all seven pounds for the charges of the ton, six hundred and twelve tons one hogshead, rated at 12l. the ton clear above charges for that year		7,347 0 0
Rhenish wines, 1,033 awnes and a half, at 40 shillings the awne..		3,100 10 0
Muskadells, two hundred fourscore fifteen and a half butts, besides 43 shillings and sixpence for impost, and 50 shillings for freight, at 13l. the butt above charges		3,841 10 0
Corsica wine, two hundred and seventy-seven butts and a half, besides charges, at eight pounds the butt..		2,228 0 0
Spanish wines, eight hundred and fifty-four butts and pipes, besides charges, at ten pounds the butt		8,540 0 0
		£512,060 5 8

EXPORTATION

	£ s. d.
The goods exported according to the *Book of Rates*, besides wrappers	64,372 11 0
Allowance for wrappers of three hundred and thirty double bays at four pounds, and ninety-two single bays at forty shillings the piece	1,504 0 0
Allowance for cottons one thousand six hundred and thirty-nine godes, at six pounds the hundred	88 0 0
Cloth of all sorts reduced in short cloths four thousand five hundred and ninety-six, rated one with another at 8l. the cloth..	36,768 0 0
Allowance for wrappers four hundred and fifty-nine cloths, at like rate of eight pounds the cloth	3,672 0 0
Goods brought in and shipped forth by certificate	3,883 8 2
Allowance for foaring bear	2,000 0 0
Allowances for wine shipped out	2,099 10 0
Goods shipped by warrant free of custom	1,915 5 0
The custom subsidy and impost paid here by strangers ..	8,914 19 0
	£125,227 13 2

And so the importation exceedeth the exportation the sum of .. £386,832 12 6

14. A COMPARISON BETWEEN THE PROCLAMATIONS OF THE LEVANT AND EASTLAND COMPANIES RESERVING THEIR TRADING MONOPOLIES, 1615 and 1622

[R. W. K. Hinton, *The Eastland Trade and the Commonweal in the Seventeenth Century*, Cambridge, 1959, pp. 175–6]

[The Proclamation of the Levant Company, 1615, with the variant text of the Eastland Company's Proclamation, 1622, shown in brackets]

By the King

A PROCLAMATION, prohibiting the bringing in of any commodities *traded from the Levant* [1622: traded by the Eastland merchants] into this kingdom; as well by subjects as strangers, not free of that company; also containing a publication of certain statutes, for the restraint of all his Majesty's subjects, from shipping any commodities in strangers' bottoms, either into this kingdom, or out of the same.

It is a great part of our princely care, to maintain and increase the trade of our merchants, and the strength of our navy, the one being as the veins whereby wealth is imported into our estate, and the other as principal sinews for the strength and service of our crown and kingdom:

Whereas therefore the society and company *of our merchants trading the Levant seas* [1622: of our Eastland merchants, trading the Baltic seas], have by the space *of thirty years past* [1622: of forty years past], at the least, had a settled, and constant possession of trade in those parts and have had the sole bringing in of the commodities of those countries, *as namely currants, cotton wools, wines of Candy, galls, etc.* [1622: as namely hemp, flax, potashes, soap ashes, Polonia wool, cordage, yarn, Eastland linen cloth, pitch, tar, and wood] whereby our kingdom hath been much enriched, *our great ships* [1622: our ships] and mariners set on work, and the honour and fame of our nation and kingdom spread and enlarged *in those remote parts* [1622: in those parts]:

And whereas, for their further encouragement, the said company have had, and enjoyed by Letters Patents under the great seal of England, *as well in the time of the late Queen, as in our own time* [1622: in the time of the late Queen Elizabeth] privilege for the sole bringing in of the said commodities, *with general prohibitions and restraints, as well of natural subjects, being not free of that society, as of all strangers and aliens whatsoever, to bring in any of the said commodities, contrary to the privilege of the said company* [1622: with general prohibitions and restraints of others not licensed and authorized by the said Letters Patents, to traffic or trade contrary to the tenor of the same Letters Patents]:

We minding the upholding and continuance of the said trade, and not to suffer that the said society shall sustain any violation or diminution of their liberties and privileges, have thought good to ratify and publish unto all persons, as well subjects as strangers, the said *privilege* [1622: privileges] and restraints, to the end that none of them presume to attempt anything against the same; and do hereby straitly charge and command all our customers, comptrollers, and all other our officers at the ports, and also the farmers of our customs and their deputies and waiters that they suffer not *any currants, cotton wool, wines of Candy, galls* [1622: any hemp, flax, potashes, soap ashes, Polonia wool, cordage, yarn, Eastland linen cloth, pitch, tar, or wood] nor any other commodities whatsoever, brought from any the foreign parts or regions, wherein the said company have used to trade, to be landed, except only such as shall be brought in by such as are free of the said company. [1622: Provided always that the importation of corn and grain be left free and without restraint; anything herein contained to the contrary notwithstanding.]

Furthermore, whereas there hath been in ancient time divers good and politic laws made against the shipping of merchandises in strangers' bottoms, either inward or outward, as namely the statutes of 5 Richard II, 4 Henry VII, 32 Henry VIII, etc. which laws have of later years been much neglected, to the great prejudice of the navigation of our kingdom: we do straitly charge and command, that the said laws be from henceforth duly put in execution *upon the great and grievous pains* [1622: upon the pains] therein contained, and upon pain of our high indignation and displeasure towards all our officers and ministers, which shall be found slack and remiss in procuring and assisting the due execution of the said laws.

Given at Whitehall, the seventeenth day of April, in the thirteenth year of our reign of England, France, and Ireland, and of Scotland the eight and fortieth. [1622: Given at our Court at Theobalds, the one and twentieth day of July, in the twentieth year of our reign of England, France, and Ireland, and of Scotland the five and fiftieth.]

God save the King.

15. LOSSES ON THREE VOYAGES OF THE GUINEA COMPANY, 1618-20

[P.R.O., SP 14/124, no. 115]

An Account of three several Voyages set forth for River Gambra upon a Trade there and upon the Discovery, viz.

Debitor

	£	s.	d.
1618. For so much adventured by 32 adventurers in the Katharine, Samuel Lambert master, the charges and cargason setting to sea..	1,856	19	2
1619. For so much paid out by the said adventurers in a new ship, the former being lost, the new ship called the St. John, Tho. Coxe master, cost, cargason, and charges paid by Capt. Love..	876	2	0
More the said cost paid by Mr. Abr. Williams ..	1,112	4	0

£   s.   d.

1620. For so much adventured by the said [Adventurers] in the
Syon, Robert Melhugget master, and the St. John, Hugh Mus-
grave master, the cargason, and charges setting forth 1,920 16   8
More paid wages and freight at return 1,300 18   9

7,067   0   7

[Creditor]
£   s.   d.

1619. The whole adventure lost, the ship being taken and most of
the men slain..   0   0   0
1620. The returns made of this voyage was hides sold for   ..   80   0   0
1621. The returns made of this voyage was hides, teeth, wax, etc.
and amount to 1,386 12   3
So the total loss by 3 voyages   5,600   8   4

7,067   0   7

[Endorsed:] A Balance of the Gambrai's Voyages.

16. JOHN KEYMER'S OBSERVATIONS TOUCHING TRADE AND COMMERCE, 1618–20[1]

[I. D., *A Clear and Evident Way for Enriching the Nations of England and Ireland and for setting very great Numbers of Poore on Work*, London, 1650, pp. 2–6, 8–11]

THOSE who have travelled the United Provinces have observed those countries grow potent, and abound in all things to serve themselves and other nations, where little groweth, raising their estate to such an admirable height, as they are at this day even a wonder to the world. Which, well weighed, will appear to come from these seas and this land; out of which they drain and still covet to exhaust our wealth and coin, and with our own commodities weaken us, and finally beat us quite out of trading in other countries. Which experience tells, they more fully obtain by their convenient privileges and settled constitutions, than England with all the laws and super-abundance of homebred commodities which God hath vouchsafed these seas and this land. By these privileges they draw multitudes of merchants to trade with them, and many other nations to inhabit amongst them, which makes them populous. They make storehouses of all foreign commodities; where-with, upon every occasion of scarcity and dearth, they are able to furnish

---

[1] This pamphlet was printed in the *The Works of Sir Walter Raleigh*, Oxford, 1829, as *Observations touching Trade and Commerce with the Hollander and other Nations; presented to King James* by W. Raleigh. The version printed here is that re-published in 1650 under another title, and attributed to I. D. It is dated 1620 in Bodleian MS., Tanner 103, f. 207v., but John Houghton in *A Collection for the Improvement of Husbandry and Trade* (ed. R. Bradley, London, 1727, III, p. 328) dates it 1618.

foreign countries with plenty of those commodities, which before in time of plenty they engrossed, and brought home from the same places; which doth greatly augment power and treasure to their state, besides the common good in setting their people and poor on work.

To these privileges they add smallness of custom and liberty of trade, which makes them flourish; and their countries plentiful of all kind of coin and commodities, and their merchants so rich, that when a loss cometh they scarce feel it.

They have also at present many advantages of us; one is by their fashioned ships, called boyers, hoybarks, hoys, and others, that are made to hold great bulk of merchandise, and to sail with a few men for profit. For example: though an English ship of 200 tons, and a Holland ship or any other of the petty states of the same burthen, be at Dansk or any other place beyond the seas, or in England; they do serve the merchant better cheap by 40*l.* in the 100 in his freight, than we can, by reason he hath but nine or ten mariners, and we near thirty. Thus he saveth twenty men's meat and wages in a voyage, and so in all other their ships accordingly to their burthen; by which means they are freighted wheresoever they come to great profit, whilst our ships lie still and decay, or go to Newcastle for coals.

Add to this their smallness of custom inwards and outwards, whereof we have daily experience: for if 2 English ships, or 2 of any other nation be at Bordeaux, both laden with wines of 300 tuns apiece, the one bound for Holland or any other petty state, the other for England; the merchant shall pay about 900*l.* custom here, and other duties, when the other in Holland or any other petty states shall be cleared for less than 50*l.*, and so in all other wares and merchandises accordingly, which draweth all nations to traffic with them. And although it seems but small duties which they receive; yet the multitudes of all kind of commodities and coin is so great that is brought in by themselves and others, and carried out by themselves and others, that they receive more customs and duties to the state (by the greatness of their commerce) in one year, than England doth in two; for the hundredth part of commodities are not spent in Holland, but vented into other countries; which maketh all the country merchants to buy and sell, and increase ships and mariners to transport them.

Notwithstanding their excises brings them great revenues; yet whosoever will adventure to Bordeaux but for six tuns of wines, shall be free of excise in his own house all the year long. And this is done (of purpose) to animate and increase merchants in their country.

And if it happen that a trade be stopped by any foreign nation (which they heretofore usually had) or hear of any good trading (which they never had) they will hinder others, and seek either by favour, money, or force, to open the gap of traffic for advancement of themselves, and employment of their people.

And when there is a new trade or course erected, they give free customs inwards and outwards, for the better maintenance of navigation, and encouragement of the people to that business . . . And this is not in the Netherlands only, but all nations may buy and sell freely in France, and there is free custom outwards twice or thrice in a year; at which times our merchants themselves do make their great sales of English commodities, and do buy and lade their great bulk of French commodities to serve for the whole year. In Rochelle and in Britain [=Brittany], free custom all the year long (except some small toll) which maketh great traffic, and maketh them flourish.

In Denmark, to encourage and enrich their merchants, and to increase ships and mariners, free custom all the year long for their own merchants (except one month between Bartholomewtide and Michaelmas).

The Hanse towns have likewise advantage of us, and in most things imitate the Hollanders, which maketh them exceeding rich and plentiful of all kinds of commodities and coin, and so strong in ships and mariners that some of their towns have near 1,000 sail of ships.

The merchandises of France, Portugal, Spain, Italy, Turkey, East and West Indies are transported most by the Hollanders and other petty states into the east and north-east kingdoms of Pomerland, Spruceland, Poland, Denmark, Swethen, Leifland, and Germany; and the merchandise brought from the last mentioned kingdoms (being wonderfully many) are likewise by the Hollanders and other petty states transported into the southern and western dominions; and yet the situation of England lieth far better for a storehouse to serve the southern, east, and north-east regions than they, and hath far better means to do it, if we will bend our course for it.

No sooner a dearth of fish, wine, or corn here, or other merchandise, but forthwith the Emdeners, Hamburgers, and Hollanders, out of their storehouses lade 50, 100, or more ships, dispersing themselves round about this kingdom, and carry away great store of coin and wealth for little commodities, in those times of dearth; by which means they suck our Commonwealth of their riches, cut down our merchants, and decay our navigation, not with their natural commodities which groweth in their own country, but the merchandises of other countries and kingdoms. Therefore, it is far more easy for us to serve ourselves, hold up our merchants, increase our ships and mariners, strengthen the kingdom, and not only keep our money in our own realm (which other nations still rob us of), but bring in theirs who carry ours away, and make the bank of coin and storehouse to serve other nations as well and far better cheap than they in England.

Amsterdam is never without 700,000 quarters of corn, besides the plenty they daily vent, and none of this groweth in their own country. A dearth in England, France, Spain, Italy, Portugal, or other places, is truly observed to enrich Holland seven years after, and likewise the petty states.

For example: the dearth, November 1614, the Hamburgers, Emdeners, and Hollanders, out of their storehouses furnished this kingdom, and from Southampton, Exeter, and Bristol, only in a year and a half, carried away near two hundred thousand pounds; which being true, then what great quantity of coin was transported from all ports of this nation? It cannot be esteemed so little as two millions, to the great decay of this realm, impoverishing the people, discredit to the company of merchants, and dishonour to the land, that any nation that have not corn in their own country growing, should serve this famous kingdom which God hath so enabled within itself. And if so much in 1614, five times as much between 1648 and 1649.[1]

These have a continual trade into this kingdom with 500 or 600 ships yearly, with merchandises of other countries and kingdoms, and store them up, until the prices rise to their minds. And we trade not with 50 ships into their country in a year; their number are about this realm every easterly wind for the most part, to lade coals and other merchandise. Again, unless there be a scarcity, dearth, or high prices, merchants do forbear that place, where great impositions are laid upon the merchandise. And those places slenderly shipped, ill served, and at dear rates, and oftentimes in scarcity, and want of employment for the people . . .

There was an intercourse of traffic in Genoa, and in that city was the flower of commerce, as appeareth by their ancient records and sumptuous buildings; all nations traded with merchandises to them, and there was the storehouse of all Italy and other places. But after they had set a great custom of XVI per cent all nations left trading with them, which made them give themselves wholly to usury; and at this day we have not 3 ships go thither in a year. On the contrary, the Duke of Florence builded Ligorn, and set small customs upon merchandise, gave them great and pleasing privileges; which hath made that a rich and strong city, with a flourishing state and trade . . .

The abundance of corn groweth in the east kingdoms. But the great storehouses for grain, to serve Christendom and the heathen countries (in the time of dearth), is in the Low Countries, wherewith, upon every occasion of scarcity and dearth, they enrich themselves seven years after, and employ their people, and get great freight for their ships in other countries; and we not one in that course.

The mighty vineyards, and store of salt, is in France and Spain. But the great vintage, and staple of salt, is in the Low Countries; and they send near 1,000 sail of ships with salt and wine only into the east kingdoms yearly, besides many other places; and we not one in that course.

The exceeding groves of wood are in the east kingdoms. But the huge piles of wainscot, clapboards, fir deal, masts, and timber is in the Low Countries, where none groweth; wherewith they serve themselves and other parts and this kingdom with those commodities. They have 500 or 600 great long ships continually using that trade; and we not one in that course.

The wool, cloth, lead, and tin, with divers commodities, are in England. But by means of our wool and cloth going out rough, undressed, and undyed, there is an exceeding manufactory in the Low Countries, wherewith they serve themselves and other nations; which advanceth greatly the employ-ment of their people at home and traffic abroad, and putteth down ours in

---

[1] This sentence is an interpolation for the 1650 edition.

foreign parts where our merchants trade unto with our own commodities, we dressing and dyeing it basely; they to that perfection, that they will not fail colour, or be threadbare in seven years' wearing.

We send into the east kingdoms yearly but 100 ships; and our trade chiefly dependeth upon three towns, Elbing, Kingsborough, and Dantzick, for making our sales, and buying their commodities sent into this realm at dear rates, which this kingdom beareth the burthen of.

The Low Countries send into the east kingdoms yearly about 3,000 ships, trading into every city and port town, taking the advantage and vending their commodities to exceeding profit, buying and lading their ships with plenty of those commodities which they have from every of those towns 20 per cent better cheap than we, by reason of the difference of their coin; and their fish yieldeth ready money; which greatly advanceth their traffic, and decayeth ours.

They send into France, Spain, Portugal, and Italy from the east kingdoms (that passeth through the Sound, and through our narrow seas) yearly of the east country commodities about 2,000 ships, and we none in that course.

They trade into all cities and port towns in France. We chiefly to five or six.

They traffic into every city and port town round about this land, with 500 or 600 ships yearly. And we chiefly but to three towns in their country, and but with 40 ships.

Notwithstanding the Low Countries have as many ships and vessels as all the kingdoms of Christendom have (let England be one), and build every year near 1,000 ships, and not a timber tree growing in their own country; also all their homebred commodities that grow in their land in a year, less than 100 good ships are able to carry away at one time. Yet they handle the matter so (for setting them all on work) that their traffic with the Hanse towns exceedeth in shipping all Christendom.

We have all things of our own in superabundance to increase traffic, and timber to build ships, and commodities of our own to load about 1,000 ships and vessels at one time (besides the great fishing), and as fast as they have made their voyages might lade, and so year after year, all the year long to continue. Yet our ships and mariners decline, and traffic and merchants daily decay.

The main bulk and mass of herrings, from whence they raise so many millions yearly, that enricheth other kingdoms', kings', and states' coffers, and likewise their own people, proceedeth from our sea and land. And the return of the commodities and coin they bring home in exchange of fish and other commodities are so huge, as would declare a large discourse apart. All the amends they make us is, they beat us out of trade in all parts with our own commodities.

For instance: we had a great trade in Russia 70 years; and about fourteen years past, we sent store of goodly ships to trade in those parts, and three years past we set out but four, and this last year two or three. But to the contrary, the Hollanders about 20 years since traded thither with two ships only, yet now they are increased to about thirty or forty, and one of their ships is as great as two of ours; and the same time (in their troubles there) that we decreased, they increased; and the chiefest commodities they carry thither with them is English cloth, herrings taken on our coast, English lead and pewter made of our tin, besides other commodities. All which we may do better than they. And although it be a cheap country, and the trade very gainful, yet we have almost brought it to nought by disorderly trading, joint stock, and the merchants bandying themselves one against another.

We used to have 8 or 9 great ships to go continually a fishing to Wardhouse, and this year but one; and so *pro rato* they outgo us in all kind of fishing and merchandising in all countries, by reason they spare no cost, nor deny no privileges that may encourage advancement of trade and manufactory.

If it stand with the good liking of the States to take notice of these things conceived to be fit for their consideration, which is tendered unto them out of unfained zeal to the advancement of the general good of all subjects; it being apparent that no three kingdoms in Christendom can compare with this for support of traffic, and continual employment of the people within themselves, having so many great means both by sea and land to enrich, multiply the navy, enlarge traffic, make the nation powerful, and people rich, who through idleness are poor, wanting employment; many land and coast towns much ruinated; need of coin; shipping, traffic, and mariners decayed; whilst neighbour princes (without these means) abound in wealth, enlarge their towns, increase their shipping, traffic, and mariners, and find out such employment for their people that are all advantages to their Commonwealth; only by ordaining commodious constitutions in merchandising, and fulness of trade to all their people in manufactory.

God hath blessed this nation with incomparable benefits; as with copper, lead, iron, tin, alum, copperas, saffron, fells, and divers other native commodities, to the number of an hundred, and other manufactories vendible to the number of a thousand (as shall appear), besides corn, whereof great quantity or beer is made, and most transported by strangers; as also wool, whereof much is shipped forth unwrought into cloth or stuffs, and cloth transported undyed, which doth employ and maintain near 50,000 people in foreign parts, our own people wanting that employment in England, many of them being enforced to live in great want, and seek it beyond the seas.

Coals, which doth employ near 600 strangers' ships yearly to transport them out of this kingdom, whilst we do not employ twenty ships in that course.

Iron ordnance, which is a jewel of great value far more than it is accounted, by reason that no other country could ever attain unto it, although they have essayed it with great charge.

Timber for building of ships, and commodities plenty to lade them, which commodities other nations want; yet we decline in shipping, traffic, and mariners.

These inconveniences happen by three causes especially:
1. The unprofitable course of merchandising.
2. Want of the true course of full manufactory of our homebred commodities.
3. Undervaluing our coins contrary to the rules of other nations.

For instance: the Merchant Adventurers by overtrading upon credit, or with money taken up upon exchange, whereby they lose usually 10, or 12, and sometimes 15, or 16 per cent are enforced to make sale of their cloths at under-rates to keep their credit; whereby cloth (being the jewel of the land) is undervalued, and the merchant in short time eaten out.

The merchants of Ipswich, whose trade for Elbing is chiefly for fine cloths, and some few sorting cloths (all dyed and dressed within this land), do for the most part buy their fine cloths upon time, and by reason they go so much upon credit, they are enforced (not being able to stand upon their markets) to sell, giving 15 or 18 months day of payment for their cloths. And having sold them, they then presently sell their bills (so taken for cloth) allowing after the rate of 14 or 15, and sometimes 20 per cent, which money they employ forthwith in wares at excessive prices, and lose as much more that way, by that time their wares be sold at home. Thus by over-running themselves upon credit, they disable themselves and others, enhancing the price of foreign commodities, and pulling down the rates of their own.

The west country merchants, that trade with cloths into France or Spain, do usually employ their servants; young men of small experience (and doth not London do likewise?), who by cunning combining of the French and Spanish merchants are so entrapped, that when all customs and charges be accounted, their masters shall hardly receive their principal money. As for returns out of France, their silver and gold is so high rated, that our merchants cannot bring it home, but to great loss. Therefore, the French merchants set higher rates of their commodities, which we must either buy dear, or let our money lie dead there a long time, until we may conveniently employ the same.

The northern merchants of York, Hull, and Newcastle trade only in white kersies and coloured dozens; and every merchant (be his adventure never so small) doth for the most part send over an unexperienced youth, unfit for merchandising; which bringeth to the stranger great advantage, but to his master and commonweal great hindrance. For they, before their goods be landed, go to the stranger, and buy such quantities of iron, flax, corn, and other commodities as they are bound to lade their ships withal, which ships they engage themselves to relade within three weeks or a month, and do give the price the merchant stranger asketh, because he giveth them credit, and lets them ship away their iron, flax, and other commodities, before they have sold their kersies and other cloths; by which means extraordinary dear commodities are returned into the realm, and the servant also enforced to sell his cloths underfoot, and oftentimes to loss, to keep his credit, and to make payment for the goods before shipped home, having some 20 days or a month's respite to sell the cloths and to give the merchant satisfaction for his iron, flax, and other wares; by which extremities our homebred commodities are abased . . .

17. CAUSES OF THE DECAY OF TRADE, 1621

[Bodleian Library, Oxford, MS. North a2, ff. 241–2]

28 February, 1620

A THREEFOLD ASSERTION that the pretermitted custom is not the cause of the decay of trade:

1. The pretermitted custom is by God's law warranted to be taken and paid.
2. It is warranted to be taken and paid by the laws of the land.
3. It was given to his Majesty as well by the merchants themselves as others in the first year of his Majesty's reign towards his Highness's great charge in keeping the narrow seas for preservation of the realm and for intercourse of merchandise . . .

The Causes of the Decay of Trade:

1. The untimely project of dyeing and dressing of cloths before transportation.
2. The bad making of cloths in the reign of Ed. 4 caused foreign nations to burn our cloths and of latter times caused the French king to burn them.
3. The sending of our wools out of England, Wales, Scotland, and Ireland into foreign parts.
4. The wars in Christendom.
5. The merchant strangers calling in their money and desisting from trade upon their censure in the Star Chamber for transporting coin.
6. The small fellowship of the Hamburg merchants in comparison they were in former years, whereby they are less able to vent our home commodities.
7. The goodness of our coin whereby it is transported by stealth and made over by exchange.
8. The plague of pestilence in the Eastland country which continues to the great loss of all merchants trading thither especially the merchants of the northern parts . . .

Special Observations

. . . For there is made 360,000 cloths in a year whereof about 140,000 are yearly transported, and the residue being 220,000 cloths are worn in the realm, whereby his Majesty loseth of the ancient due which divers of his noble progenitors had when wool was transported in kind 110,000*l.* a year, which the commons gain for all that charge they were at when the cloths worn in the realm were made beyond the seas and afterward imported. Besides they paid 14*d.* a cloth custom upon the importation which comes unto 23,000*l.* a year, and these two sums of 110,000*l.* and 23,000*l.* of ancient coin results unto 399,000 pounds of our coin. All which his Majesty loseth, the subjects save it. Moreover, the merchant strangers gain of those cloths by them imported after the rate of 15*l.* per annum which is far less than merchants usually gain and that for 220,000 cloths comes to about 160,000*l.* per annum of ancient coin which is four hundred and four score thousand pounds of our money. All which, viz. 399,000*l.* and 480,000*l.* amounting in the whole unto 879,000*l.* sterling of our money, is saved by the inhabitants of this realm, and hereunto add the care and singular benefit which the inhabitants of the realm have obtained by the improvement of their wool and of the manufacture thereof into cloth, which in the improvement of the wool that goes to the making of 360,000 cloths, which being reckoned but at 40*s.* the 3 tod and ¼ of wool for a cloth and 3*l.* 10*s.* for the manufacture thereof, and it results unto 1,980,000 pounds a year . . .

[Endorsed:] Concerning pretermitted customs.

18. THE NEW MUSCOVY COMPANY APPEALS FOR RELIEF FROM THE DEBTS OF THE OLD COMPANY, 1621

[P.R.O., SP 14/123, no. 41]

19 October [1621]

THIS day upon a report from the Lord President of the Council and the Master of the Rolls unto whom, with Sir Richard Weston, kt. or to any two of them, their lordships had referred the petition of the merchants now trading to Russia, by which they desire that such goods as are lately arrived from thence may not be liable to the debts of the old Company. Forasmuch as it appeareth unto their lordships that the last year's adventure was raised at what time the merchants were [?] so much discouraged with former losses that, without special order and encouragement from the state, that trade had been utterly discontinued and overthrown. And that divers new adventurers that joined in the last year's stock would not have adventured but upon assurance that their goods should not be seized for the former debts of the Company, to which some of them were no way liable as not being of that society, whereunto their lordships did then yield (as much as in them was) for the reviving of that trade, which otherwise would have been lost to the unspeakable prejudice of the public. Their lordships, having now again taken into their due consideration as well the importance of the foresaid trade as a former order of the Board of the last of March 1620, have thought fit and accordingly ordered that the product of the last year's adventure into

Russia shall in no sort be liable to any former debts of the Company. Of which their lordships order all those whom it concerns hereby to take notice.

19. EDWARD MISSELDEN COMPILES A BALANCE OF TRADE, 1621–2

[E. Misselden, *The Circle of Commerce or the Balance of Trade, in Defence of Free Trade: opposed to Malynes Little Fish and his Great Whale, and poized against them in the Scale, wherein also Exchanges in General are considered; and therein the whole Trade of this Kingdom with Foreign Countries is digested into a Balance of Trade for the Benefit of the Publique necessary for the Present and Future Times*, London, 1623, pp. 127–30]

AND now we will come to the positive constitution of our own form, to bring to the balance the state of the present time and trade; wherein I will give you a taste of one year's collections of the kingdom's trade, in this form following, viz.

The Balance of the Trade of the Kingdom is Debitor, for all the Exportations of the Merchandise thereof, for one whole year, from Christmas *anno* 1621 to Christmas *anno* 1622 as followeth:

	li.	s.	d.
Custom of the Port of London	50,406	6	4
Custom of the outports	26,756	18	0
The custom of wrappers of cloths, bays, and cottons, free of custom, being the tenth part of 50,000 pounds, which is the custom of them all	5,000	0	0
The custom of the fish of our own fishing, and which is freed from custom by statute, by computation	7,000	0	0
The custom of goods shipped out by certificate, viz. of foreign goods brought in, and for want of vent in the kingdom, shipped out again, which are freed of custom by his Majesty's gracious grant of Privy Seal	8,050	0	0
The total of all the custom is	97,213	4	4

	li.	s.	d.
Which total being multiplied by twenty, because the custom is valued by twelve pence in the pound, produceth the value of all the goods exported to amount unto	1,944,264	7	1
The net custom of which value, at twelve pence in the pound, the wrappers, fish, and goods shipped out by certificate deducted, is the 2 sums first before mentioned, and is	77,163	4	4
The impost of bays, tin, lead, and pewter, which only are imposed outwards, amounteth to	7,370	1	5

li. s. d.

The merchants' gain, freight, and petty charges upon
1,944,264*li.* being the whole value of the exportations as
above appeareth, at 15 per cent, is 291,639 0 0

The total exportations, with charges, amount to 2,320,436 12 10

The Balance of the Trade of the Kingdom is Creditor, for all the Importations of the Merchandise thereof, for one whole year, from Christmas *anno* 1621 to Christmas *anno* 1622 as followeth:

li. s. d.

The custom of the Port of London	68,280	9	1
The custom of the outports	19,579	2	6
The custom of wines of all sorts, all other merchandise being included in the former, is	3,200	0	0
The custom amounts to	91,059	11	7
One third part thereof to be added, for the underrating of goods in custom to that they are worth, or cost, is	30,353	3	10
Also the allowance of 5 per cent upon £91,059 11*s.* 7*d.* is	4,552	19	7
The total sum amounts to	125,965	15	0
Which total, being multiplied by 20 produceth the value of all the goods imported, to amount unto	2,519,315	0	0
Fine goods secretly conveyed inwards, more than outwards	100,000	0	0
The total importations amount to	2,619,315	0	0
The total exportations	2,320,436	12	10
The remainder sheweth that there is more imported this year than was exported, by the sum of	298,878	7	2

So then we see it to our grief that we are fallen into a great underbalance of trade with other nations. We felt it before in sense; but now we know it by science. We found it before in operation; but now we see it in speculation. Trade alas fails and faints, and we in it.

20. REASONS FOR THE DECAY OF THE CLOTH TRADE, 1622[?]

[B.M., Add. MS. 34217, f. 10. Book of Fane, first Earl of Westmorland]

The Causes of the Decay of the Trade of Clothing, etc., with Remedies

1. Of the first, the price of wools in the hands of the wool grower is no cause, for that wools are fallen the third or fourth part in price.

2. Neither is the clothier any cause for that they sell their cloth unto the merchant under the price of former times and yet they cannot sell the whole manufacture for the merchant will not take the cloth at the same low prices which the clothier is able to afford, although he sell his cloth now 30*li.* in the hundred cheaper than in former times.

3. Therefore the cause resteth in the buying and ventage of the cloth into and out of the merchants' hands by the privilege granted unto certain of the Adventurers inhibiting all others to buy cloths to be exported, but the merchants of their own company.

4. This privilege is divided into many petty companies for several countries where cloth may be vented insomuch that to transport cloth into Muscovia none do buy cloth but one —— Freeman.

5. Out of this privilege are also derived contracts with certain towns and companies of strangers in foreign nations to deliver the English white cloths at those towns only.

6. Thence is also derived the inhibition that some countries or places cannot buy immediately but that cloth must first be sold (for example) to the Hollanders before it can come to the subjects of the Archduchess receiving a great imposition for licence money to pass to the prejudice of the English.

7. Out of this privilege is derived a power of imposing upon every cloth sold in Blackwell Hall to be exported (since the treaty with Sir William Cocken did end) to the value of 7*s.* 6*d.* upon long cloths amounting unto (if vent were as it hath been) above 20,000*li.* per annum.

8. Thence is also derived a power to restrain any of their own company in buying to a small number of cloths whereby the clothier being disappointed of sale is driven of necessity to undersell others for buying (not of the company) having been kept in prison till they have taken oath or entered into bonds to forbear.

9. Proof is offered in particular cases that none will buy John a Stiles cloth but he shall be driven to sell to John a Downe, his old chapman, at his price and pleasure by combination.

10. And also the cloths of such a country shall not be bought as for instance from the 21 of April until the 17 of May not one Woster [= Worcester] cloth hath been bought in Blackwell Hall, although confessed as seasonable as any, and the clothier, seeking to sell to the Adventurer, receiveth answer that he may do well to sell to their new company, so little compassion is shewed by them in this time of so great necessity, and so great presumption of the advantage by this privilege, having the clothiers in their mercy.

11. Other privileges have been obtained for drawing into one hand necessary materials to be used in clothing, in so much that red wood wherewith it will be undertaken, the kingdom may be served at xviii or xx*s.* the hundred is raised to iiii*li.* x*s.* the hundred.

12. The impositions and customs were never in any time so great nor these all at once in use and likewise in Holland and other places, whereby hath been proved that a cloth sold by the clothier at 5*li.* price hath before it be cut in

Holland for use had 4*li*. 13*s*. 4*d*. more laid upon it (admitting what is laid by the Hollanders for licence money 5*li*. 1*s*. 0*d*.).

13. The making of cloth in Holland by the help of wools, fells, and yarn from Ireland, Scotland, and England with the fullers earth and other materials.

Since no merchant will buy cloths to vent them out of England but for gain, no clothier continue the making of cloth but for his own benefit, all these burdens of impositions, privileges, and combinations do finally fall upon the wool growers, which bringeth great loss to the poor subject, which upon a careful and judicious computation by Sir John Popham, late lord chief justice of England, and divers others well experienced persons, was demonstrated in that the abatement of xii*d*. in a tod of wool throughout the kingdom of England in one year would amount to the sum of 80,000*li*.

The Help and Means of Relief in the Trade of Clothing

1. It is humbly desired that there may be free trade of buying and selling, leaving only order for government that the credit of cloths truly made may be maintained without power in any company to be continued either of imposing or exacting any valuable sum for admission into the company, clearing the monopoly of red wood and other monopolies laying burthens upon clothing.

2. That what cloth the Merchant Adventurer will not buy off upon the Thursday, it may be lawful for any person, denizen or stranger (paying the king's duties), on the Friday or Saturday to buy as well as he and to export without restraint whither they please.

3. That transportation of cloth may be made oftener viz. once a month, and his Majesty's shipping may (at the charge of the merchant) for their sureties waft over the merchandises as need shall require.

4. That endeavour be used that the imposition for licence in foreign countries may be moderated and that free passage may be had wheresoever best sale with least burden may be gotten, stirring up foreign nations to strive for the trade of English cloths with the best conditions a nation may gain.

5. That his Majesty will take into his princely consideration the present necessity of his clothiers and many thousands depending upon them and what the several charges are laid upon cloths all now in use, submitting to his singular and deep judgement that if all new and late charges were taken off, yet a reparation might be made of all dues to his Majesty if all the wools of England and Ireland be manufactured and so cheap afforded into other countries (with the employment of infinite people) that no other country could be able to gain by the making of cloth.

6 That no wools, wool fells, yarn, or fullers earth be conveyed beyond the seas to any place out of England, Scotland, Ireland, and the Isles.

7. That foreign commodities be brought into this land either by sale of our cloth there first made or by bartering for our English cloth.

8. The reasons and proofs of benefit that will come by free trade are confirmed by the experience made about the year '87 when, for the remedying of a like inconvenience, a staple of cloths was kept at Westminster and likewise when the new company was set up, upon the project of Sir William Cockin, which presently took of cloth to the benefit of all sorts of people.

Lastly, that the liberty of trade is no new thing they may be pleased to see the statutes of 12 of Hen. 7 and 27 Edw. 3 which shew the true government of a staple.

21. REASONS FOR THE DECAY OF THE TRADE OF THE OUTPORTS, 1624

[BM, Hargrave MS. 321, ff. 80–2, 133–4, 136–7]

Reason of the Decay of Trade of Merchants in the Port of Chester

1. The imposition of pretermitted customs upon all sorts of cloths exported taken in the port.

2. Great quantity of Spanish iron formerly imported by the merchants of this port to the number of 300 tons yearly. And now in regard of the store of the English iron made near unto those parts, that there is not vented here above 60 tons of Spanish iron in this whole port by the merchants.

3. Merchants coming out of Ireland, tradesmen dwelling in divers parts of Wales adjoining to this city, petty chapmen, and pedlars accustomed to buy all sorts of commodities here in this city of our merchants and other tradesmen now furnish themselves at London to the great decay of trade here.

4. Londoners of fairs [sic] as at other times bringing in such store of all commodities here both by sea as by land that they do overcloy this place with all sorts of commodities so that our merchants and retailers cannot have vent for those commodities they import and have.

5. The merchants of the Eastland company of London and other places seem to debar our merchants from trading unto Danzig as unto other places within the Sound.

6. A greater imposition of Irish yarn heretofore imposed in this place by the farmers of the customs of the said yarn than is at Liverpool being but a member of this port, so that little cometh unto this place, the which is a great hindrance of trade to this city.

7. A restraint in Ireland for the importing of sheep fells as wools, which some Londoners (as we are informed) have a grant of, so that this city as the places near adjoining is much hindered. And this hath been the hindrance of a great trade here.

8 The undervalue of all sorts of cloths and other English commodities exported into all places.

9. Lack of vent of wools here in respect of former times.

Reason of the Want of Coin

1. Irish commodities imported into this place, as hides, tallow, yarn, beef, and divers other sorts of commodities sold here for money, but most part or all of the money exported by them and not employed here.

2. Irish cattle great store brought over and the money most or all carried back and not employed.

3. Scottish men coming forth of Scotland with great quantity of linen cloths and sold here and the monies carried to Scotland to the value 3,000*li.* per annum.

4. The exportation of coin by the East India Company of London (as we conceive) is the especiallest and chiefest reason we can allege for the want of coin . . .

Reasons of the Decay of Trade

PLYMOUTH

1. Restraint of trade to certain companies of merchants of London.

2. The overburthening of trade with impositions discourageth and disableth merchants.

3. The store of cloth made in parts beyond the seas which if we undersell not, as by reason of the many charges upon our cloths we cannot, will in time banish most of our cloth.

4. The great damage and fear of loss by pirates.

5. The Hollanders out-trading us in our own commodities as in Muscovy and other places and this is by reason of our trading in company and they at large.

TOTNES, DARTMOUTH, BRIDGWATER

The decay of the western trade as the false making of the New Draperies which were wont to be the commodities sent for Spain and the Levant seas. And in France the[y] make the coarse cloths there as good cheap as we can send them thither. And the Levant commodities they return not for which they were wont to carry fish and other commodities.

POOLE

And into the eastern parts they may not go whence they were wont to fetch masts, deal, hemp, tar, and pitch. And there New[found]land voyages for fishing are much defeated of late. The trade of the west country for coarse cloth is utterly decayed. This was wont to supply the kingdom with lockerams and canvas, for the coarse cloths are there better made than here.

EXON [= EXETER]

Merchants do generally undersell the commodities of England in Spain and France hoping to make great gain by the exchange of monies, which is, it may be, after 15 per cent. By reason of the trade to the East Indies the trade to Lisbon in Portingale is decayed. Thither was wont to be vented great store of our coarse cloth with yield of spices better cheap than we have them from the East Indian merchants, and this is a great hindrance to the vent of cloths.

The west country cannot vent their coarse cloths but for France and Spain. When these fail them, all trade is taken from them.

The false making and false dyeing of our cloth and manufactures makes great stand of our cloths and stuffs . . .

HULL

The Eastland was wont to be the great vent for northern cloths, kerseys, and dozens but now in Danse, Prussia, and Silesia great store of kerseys are made, so ours vent not by reason of the great tolls they pay to the king of Denmark, Duke of Prussia, and King of Pole. With the burthens at home upon the cloths there is little profit to be made, for any of the kerseys and dozens that are here worth 30s. are sold there for 33s. 9d. Defalk 7s. 9d. for charges, there remains but 26s. 9d. So in loss to them kerseys are now sold 3s. a piece cheaper than in Prussia[? ?] and yet not a third part so many vented; also the merchants are tied there to employ upon country commodities.

CARLISLE

Carlisle complains that all the revenue of their country goeth southward to pay rents to great landlords whose land is there, and now having there all is desolate with them. And that Scotland, who were wont to buy their corn and cattle, now bring cattle and corn to their markets and leave all their commodities upon their hands. Also that Berwick, having licence for transportation of fells, wools, hides, tallow, and other prohibited commodities makes all those things dear unto them . . .

22. LONDON MERCHANTS OPPOSE INTERLOPERS IN THE GREENLAND TRADE, 1627
[P.R.O., SP 16/58, no. 56]

To the Rt. Hon. the Lords and others of his Majesty's most honourable Privy Council, the humble petition of the English merchants for discovery of new trades called the Muscovia Company.

SHEWING that in the business touching the right of fishing in Greenland belonging to the petitioners, and the interloping of York and Hull, after a reference thereof by this honourable Board to twelve of the same to report, and after a sub-reference from them to his Majesty's Council learned and a certificate from them, it pleased six of the committees the 12th of January last to direct an accommodation for this year to the intent the accommodation of the fishings might be upheld appointing 3,000 tons of shipping to be sent forth, whereof York and Hull to have a fifth part.

How far this act may bind, your petitioners presume not to resolve albeit (under favour) they conceive the same to be but of the nature of a report. But forasmuch as they are not willing to incur the least opinion of contempt or refractoriness, and do find that that intended course of accommodation is attended with great inconveniences and like to breed dangerous events even to the utter subversion and loss not only of that country and trade but also of the trade of Moscow so necessary and important to this realm.

Your petitioners are therefore induced out of their care of the public good and for the preservation of the honour and commerce of this kingdom, besides their own particular interests, to make offer and overture to your grace's consideration of the evil consequences already arisen and the great dangers like to ensue to the end, if those trades and that country be lost, your petitioners to whom the sole managing of both stands committed may be innocent of so great an evil.

First, the admission of York and Hull will not add strength to the defence of that country as is supposed but rather weaken it and enforce your petitioners (who have ever yet defended it against all nations) to desert the same.

Secondly, by precedent of this accommodation, one Nathaniel Edwards by pretext of a void Scottish patent as also one Andrew Hawes, a cheesemonger of London, by no warrant is now setting out certain shipping for Greenland and making preparation here and hath inveigled the best of your petitioners' harpooners into his service to the managing of their present intended voyage.

Thirdly, the towns of Yarmouth and Lynn are attempting the like, and those examples admitted may invite others so that your petitioners must leave the trade or spill the blood of their own countrymen or send out their forces for mere preservation of the country for other men's private benefits and without hope of anything but assured loss to themselves.

Fourthly, if they continue not the trade with great strength of men and ships the country will be quickly lost, for no force but London's can defend it except his Majesty will undertake it.

Their humble suit therefore is that your lordships for the public cause will take these things to consideration and if it shall stand with your pleasures that your petitioners shall continue the trade, that then you will vouchsafe to call before you the said Edwards and Hawes to answer the premises and in the interim to make stay of their preparation, as also the design of Yarmouth and Lynn. And for those of York and Hull, if your lordships shall approve of an accommodation for this year that yet it may be with a salvo of your petitioners' right, and so limited that it may not prejudice nor overthrow your petitioners' voyage nor impeach their privileges, and that they may give good bonds to perform such articles as themselves agreed in former years, when by mediation and articles they were admitted of consideration of your petitioners' rights.

And they shall ever pray etc.

[Endorsed:] 30 March, 1627.

23. AN ENQUIRY INTO ILLEGAL IMPORTS AND EXPORTS AT BRISTOL, 1627

[P.R.O., E178/5319]

Miscellaneous depositions in connection with an enquiry into the import and export of prohibited commodities at Bristol, 3 Chas. I.

JOHN HAYLES of Bewdley in the county of Worcester, tanner, aged 52 years or thereabouts, sworn and examined, deposeth as followeth: To the first interrogatory this deponent saith that Richard Vickris in the interrogatory named did about St. James's Fair in the year of our Lord God 1636 buy of William Wildy, a tanner, three score hides or thereabouts which this deponent knoweth to be true for that this deponent lying in an inn together in Bristol and having some dealing with the said Richard Vickris, the said Wildy desired this deponent to help him to sell the said hides to the said Richard Vickris, wherewith this deponent acquainted the said Richard Vickris, whereupon the said Richard Vickris told this deponent that he would not meddle with them unless the said Wildy would take his oath that they were Irish hides. And this deponent saith that he was present with the said Wildy when he did take his oath before some magistrate or officer of Bristol that the same hides were Irish hides, and thereupon the said Richard Vickris did buy the said hides as aforesaid. And this deponent also saith that he doth verily believe that the same hides were Irish hides and tanned by the said Wildy or his servants at Bewdley for that the said Wildy hath used to trade into Ireland for the space of six years past or thereabouts and doth usually buy hides there and bring them over and cause them to be tanned in Bewdley aforesaid.

*   *   *

Philip Dickenson of the City of Bristol, merchant and deputy searcher of the said port of Bristol, aged 63 years or thereabouts, sworn and examined, deposeth as followeth: To the fourth and sixth interrogatories he saith that he doth know that in the year of our Lord 1636 Mr. Hugh Lewes did seize certain quantities of hides which were shipped to be transported . . . [and] hath been at great charges and expense of money by reason of the said seizure for boatmen, hauliers, porters, and other labourers. And the reason induceth this deponent so to believe is for that he knoweth that such labourers in such kind are unwilling to be employed in seizure of the merchants' goods except they be doubly, or trebly, paid.[1] And saith further that he doth verily believe that it hath cost the said searcher in charges for the said labourers and

---

[1] This attitude is further explained by another deponent thus: 'they affirmed that unless such extraordinary pay should be given them they would not do it, affirming that they did thereby go against their masters the merchants and that they should thereby lose their usual employment by the said merchants.'

prosecution of the said suit above £100 more or less for that he (to this deponent's knowledge) the said searcher hath been driven to ride several journeys to London about the said suit, and besides this deponent himself hath been experienced in business of the like nature. And further saith that the searcher of the said port of Bristol and other king's officers there are now more disheartened than heretofore in making of seizures for that the farmers' deputies are willing to put down and suppress the said searcher and for that, as he thinketh, the merchants do join together in the charge in prosecution of such cases against the said searcher.

*　　　*　　　*

[In connection with enquiries into exports of butter, 14 Chas. I.]

Elizabeth Browne, the wife of James Browne of the City of Bristol, blacksmith, aged 40 years or thereabouts, sworn and examined, deposeth as followeth:

To the second interrogatory this deponent saith that she did at that time in that year when the said Mr. Tomlinson was mayor usually pay in the markets at Bristol for salt butter $4\frac{1}{2}d.$ or $5d.$ a pound and bought none under. And this deponent further saith that she knoweth no reason why it should be so dear but that, as it was commonly reported amongst the poor people, that it was because the merchants carried it away beyond the seas.

24. GOVERNMENT ENCOURAGEMENT TO THE GREENLAND FISHERY, 1628

[P.R.O., SP 16/91, no. 53]

At Whitehall the 25th of January, 1627.

Present: the King's Majesty, Lord Keeper . . . [etc., members of the Privy Council].

Upon notice this day read to the Board by the Muscovia merchants trading to Greenland, showing that the petitioners were the first discoverers of that place and have for many years together maintained thither the trade of fishing for whales, which trade hath been a special means for breeding of seamen and setting great ships on work. But this last year they have made a very hard voyage of it, and are much discouraged in that trade, by reason that the commodities returned from that place which is the King's own land is imported by strangers, so that the petitioners do not now vent in this land above the one half of the whale oil and fins which formerly they did, but the kingdom is furnished from them, whereas in like cases, both for the Levant and Eastland, the commodities of those countries have not been suffered to be imported neither by strangers nor those of our own nation not free of those companies. The benefit of which restraints have well appeared by the number of great ships it hath increased. Nor hath the said company as yet received satisfaction for the great losses they had sustained by the Netherlanders in that country. Their lordships taking the same into their considerations have thought fit and ordered that no oil or whale fins shall hereafter be imported into this kingdom out of the parts of the Netherlands or any other foreign parts. And the company are admonished not to make this restraint the occasion of selling their commodities at too dear a rate. And the Lord Treasurer is hereby prayed and required to take effectual order with the officers of the several ports to prevent the importation of the said oil and fins by the Dutch or any others accordingly.

Extr. Will Belper

[Endorsed:] 25 January, 1627. Order of the Lords for prohibiting the bringing in of whale oil and fins from foreign parts by Greenland fishery.

25. CUSTOMS FRAUDS AT THE PORT OF COLCHESTER, 1629

[P.R.O., E178/5301]

Depositions taken at Colchester in December 1629
concerning customs frauds.

WILLIAM HARVEY of Wivenhoe aforesaid, mariner, aged 42 years or thereabouts, sworn upon the holy evangelists, deposeth and saith:
To the 26th article he saith that he knoweth of four firkins of butter which were transported from Colchester unto Rotterdam in Holland in April last past with his Majesty's licence in the ketch of this examinate called the Hawk of Wivenhoe whereof this examinate was then master. And more to this article he deposeth not.

John Gisling of Camphere in Zealand, mariner, aged four and twenty years or thereabouts, sworn upon the holy evangelists, deposeth and saith:
To the fourth article he saith that divers times within two years and a half last past he hath paid to Abraham Johns and Anthony Bland, searchers of the port of Colchester, sometimes five shillings, sometimes less, over and above the usual customs, for transporting wheat, rye, barley, and malt beyond the seas. To the 6th article he denieth that he hath transported (to his knowledge) within the time in the article specified any wheat, rye, barley, or malt without payment of custom.
To the 7th article he saith that he hath transported beyond the seas within the space of two years last past at several times many firkins of butter but the number he remembereth not for which he hath paid custom, but denieth that he hath paid any sum or sums of money to any officer for transporting any without licence. But he saith that Mr. Nuttall hath often given him liberty to carry over four or five firkins at a time without paying any custom for the same.[1]

---

[1] Other depositions suggest that butter for victualling ships was allowed without paying custom.

To the 24th article he saith that in June A.D. 1628 he, this examinate, did carry in the ship in the article mentioned unto Camphere in Zealand by the appointment of Mr. Nuttall between four score and five score firkins of butter from the port of Colchester. And he saith that he knoweth not for whose accompt the same was or who was the owner of them but he saith that Mr. Nuttall told him that they were for one Mr. Leman of London. And he saith that the same was corrupt butter. But he knoweth not whether any money was paid for suffering of the said butter to pass without his Majesty's licence but saith that he had a cocket for the said butter from the said Mr. Nuttall, Customer of the said port of Colchester.

To the 28th article he saith that he paid the customs at Colchester to Mr. Nuttall for the corn which he carried from thence when this examinate's ship was seized at Gravesend in April last past. And that all his said corn was entered before his departure from the port of Colchester by the said Mr. Nuttall, Customer of the said port. And he denieth that he paid anything for the amending of the entry. And he confesseth that William Munt of Colchester, mariner, did bring the five lasts of corrupt malt mentioned in the article aboard this examinate's ship lying below Wivenhoe.

Nathaniel Strickson of Colchester, merchant, being re-examined, deposeth:

To the 13th article that about the time in the article mentioned a certain quantity of wheat was brought from France into the port of Colchester in a barque or vessel of Wivenhoe whereof William Eastward was master, which corn was left with this deponent to dispose of at his pleasure. And he saith that some of the said corn this deponent did sell at Colchester and some other part thereof was transported into Holland. And further answers to this article he refuseth to make for that he thinketh his answer already made is sufficient answer to the article . . .

To the 30th article he saith that within the time in the article mentioned he hath not landed any wines at all at the port of Colchester.

Christopher Austen alias Galloway of Colchester aforesaid, mariner, aged three score and four years or thereabouts, sworn and examined, produced only to the 38th article, deposeth and saith that he hath been a master of a ship or ships of Colchester by the space of forty years together last past. And he saith that Jonas Legg, Surveyor of the port of Colchester, hath not at any time given leave or liberty to this deponent or to any other person or persons whatsoever to this deponent's knowledge for the transporting of butter or other prohibited goods whatsoever.

Philip Allen of Colchester aforesaid, merchant, aged 38 years or thereabouts, sworn and examined, deposeth and saith:

To the 16th article he saith that Daniel Sherman and Gilbert Tyall have told this deponent that they are part owners of the ship called the Speedwell of Colchester mentioned in the article. And he hath also heard that Mr. Edward Nuttall is owner of part of the said ship.

To the 26th article he saith that he hath seen at several times within the time in the article mentioned three or four firkins of butter at a time and sometimes more aboard of divers ships and vessels, as namely aboard the ship of John de Lewe and of John Gisling and of divers other vessels which he now remembereth not, which were by them transported beyond the seas from Colchester without his Majesty's licence.

To the 30th article he saith that he this deponent hath within a year past landed about 30 tuns of wine at the port of Colchester. And that he hath paid to Mr. Nuttall, Customer of the said port, for landing the same 53s. 4d. upon every tun. And this deponent, demanding of the said Mr. Nuttall by what authority he did demand and receive so much money upon every tun, he the said Mr. Nuttall told him that he had order for the same by letters either from the Lords of the Council or the wine farmers but from which of them this deponent remembereth not. And he further saith that the said Mr. Nuttall did promise this deponent that if other outports did not pay the like imposition, he would repay him again so much as he received over and above the usual customs.

To the 31st article he saith that he hath paid unto Mr. Nuttall, Customer of the port of Colchester, for custom and imposition from 20 March, 1627, to 20 March, 1629, the sum of £500 or thereabouts. And he saith that he cannot get an accompt from the said Mr. Nuttall as he hath formerly had from Mr. Jonas Legg and others who have been collectors of the customs there. And what the reason is why the said Mr. Nuttall will not give him accompt he knoweth not, neither will the said Mr. Nuttall render any reason for the same.

26. COMPLAINTS FROM ENGLISH MERCHANTS IN THE FRENCH TRADE, 1629[?]

[P.R.O., SP 16/155, no. 57]

Complaints of the English merchants trafficking in Bordeaux, 1629[?]

THAT whereas heretofore they paid but 3½ per cent custom and that with some moderation, they are now since the last peace constrained to pay 6 per cent and that with all rigour contrary to the treaty of commerce and the articles agreed upon between his late Majesty of famous memory and Henry the 4th.

Whereas formerly upon arrival they enjoyed their goods and so had the benefit (by present sales) of making their best markets, now they are compelled to bring them into the customs warehouse to be visited which tendeth to their extreme loss and prejudice not only in the abusing and spoiling of their said goods by the officers' careless tossing and tumbling of them in the opening, but by the unjust delay used by the said customers in the visitation of their goods in so much that the Frenchmen's goods of the same nature with the Englishmen's being first visited, and these latter being forced to stay four or five days for theirs, the first have the benefit of the first markets and so sell their wares to advantage, the latter come to the latter end and must sell as they can many times to loss, or else must keep their goods in their hands, which doth prove a very great discouragement, disadvantage, and disgrace to the English nation.

Whereas all other nations have the liberty of coming up the river of Garonne to Bordeaux without being forced to unlade their cannon at Blaye, the English only are compelled to unship theirs there, which is an extraordinary disadvantage and injury unto them for, first, besides the disgrace to the nation, the merchant thereby loseth so much time that not only the French but even strangers, as the Dutch, etc., which are in company, get the start of them, and selling their commodities before the English can arrive, their goods coming late, are looked on but as refuse ware, and the market being as were glutted with the former wares of the French and strangers, the goods of the English are either altogether neglected or little respected, to their extreme loss and very great discouragement.

Secondly, the masters of our ships are so frighted with the thought of the unshipping and reshipping of their cannon at Blaye that they are with much difficulty and great wages hardly drawn to that employment, and many times none can be procured to go, insomuch that the merchants are every year compelled to hire and employ French, which tends to the great decay of mariners and shipping at home, and to the enriching of the French who peradventure do continue that grievance to enjoy the said fruits thereof.

All these things appear to be the greater unkindnesses from the French unto the English nation, in regard the subjects of France trafficking in these parts are no way molested with any of the said incumbrances, whereas if his sacred Majesty's princely pleasure were suitable to his royal power he might with as much justice charge the French every way with as many burthens as they lay now upon the English, but seeing that his gracious clemency is such that he seeks and desires to overcome evil with good, their ingratitude is the greater that do not requite him.

A fourth complaint there is but of that we cannot accuse the French, but wherein our merchants themselves are to be complained of, and that is the employing of the French as factors for their affairs in France, from whence ariseth diverse inconveniences and prejudices. First to the state, for by reason of this, whensoever his Majesty shall have any design upon any part of France where their men negotiate, they presently to save their goods there dispatch letters of advice to their French factors with order to draw in debts, clear accounts, and to freeze their estates, which letters the factors (not daring to keep secret for fear of being held an intelligencer in case it should be known that they had any such letter) doth straightways carry them to the chief president, who suddenly posteth them to the King or Chief Secretary of State, so the design comes to be discovered before it be put in execution, as it fell out in the last barinet[?] of Retz[?] at what time the plot was by that means discovered long before at Bordeaux and thence sent to the King.

The second inconvenience redounds to the merchants themselves for by this means the French do discover the secrets and mystery of their trade which cannot choose but be an extraordinary wrong to themselves, at least-wise will be in time, but likewise to the other merchants not guilty of that disorder and to those shall trade thither in succeeding ages. The third inconvenience toucheth the education of youth, whose friends, seeing that so many French are employed, are utterly discouraged to bring up their youth that way for fear that when they have spent much time and means in learning that mystery they shall find no employment.

The fourth is that it is an evil example, and may for the future (as we see for the time past it hath done) make others to follow the same evil custom, and so in process of time the French only, and no English, shall have that employment which will prove a prejudice to this nation of no small consequence.

A fifth thing there is that is an extraordinary grievance and that is the using of brokers, which though long custom hath made almost a law, yet I know no reason why a remedy may not be found thereunto, nor wherefore we should be more enchained to that thraldom than the Dutch who, scorning both the use of the broker and the employing of any French factor, do live among themselves in unity, reserving to themselves the secrets and mysteries of their trade, and by employing their own nation only do thrive and prosper by many degrees better than the English nation.

Complaints of the English merchants at Rochelle

That whereas they never paid anything heretofore for anchorage, they are now taxed with 5 sols upon every ton of all vessels[?] that come in.

That whereas they never paid anything towards the maintenance of the French poor, they are now forced to contribute thereunto, and that not at certain rates, but at such as please the magistrates of the old town.

Thirdly, that they are threatened by the officers of the town not to have hereafter liberty of remaining there above three months together, and not to be annual residents as they used to be heretofore, which is likewise an innovation proceeding from an unnecessary and false jealousy, and will prove a very great trouble to the factors to remove so often and much hinder the younger sort who in so short a time cannot possibly get the language or learn the nature of the French trade and commodities.

Complaints of the merchants at Morlaix in Bretagne

That whereas heretofore time out of mind they have enjoyed the freedom of freighting their own ships with their own goods to be exported out of

France as the French in like manner have the same privilege in England according to the 6th article agreed upon between our late sovereign of blessed memory and Henry the 4th of France, now the French do begin to cavil with the English, and contrary to the treaty of commerce and the said article, the seneschal of Morlaix hath lately made an order that no English vessel whatsoever shall ever hereafter be freighted with any goods soever so long as there shall be found any French barque in port. By virtue of which unjust sentence never verified in Parliament nor published by authority and therefore of no authority, one Blanchard, a merchant of that town came violently upon the barque of one Henry Gaudy, called the Elinor of Weymouth, which the English had new freighted with goods to the value of above 20,000*li*., and caused the said goods to be taken forth of the said Elinor which was strong with cannon, men, muskets, and munition, fit to resist pirates of which those coasts were then very full, and put them into his feeble barque which was small, had no arms, and was of no resistance against pirates, and not only so, but cut the cordage of the Elinor and degreed her. Whereof, when the English complained, instead of receiving justice, upon pretence of having disobeyed the aforesaid order, the said seneschal imprisoned the master of the barque, some of his men, and some of the factors the space of 8 or 10 days, and condemned them in divers ammaundes as by the copy of the sentence answered more at large appeareth.

That whereas in times past they have been accustomed for their mutual comforts to live together in one house (as the English in other parts of France do) some 20 or 30 of them, now there [is] an order made (as by the copy annexed appeareth) and for what cause they know not, but such as are trivial, that no man shall presume to lodge hereafter above 5 or 6 at the most together, which will prove an extraordinary discomfort and inconvenience to the said factors as might be instanced in divers particulars, which would be too tedious to rehearse and are fitter to be related by word of mouth.

Lastly, they are much sensible of the employment of French factors by the English merchants and would be as glad of the reformation thereof as the former merchants in other places.

[Endorsed:] Complaints of the Merchants in France.

27. A THREAT TO THE MONOPOLY OF THE GUINEA COMPANY, 1637

[P.R.O., CO 1/9, no. 75]

AFTER our hearty commendations: whereas we are informed by Humphrey Slany, Nicholas Crisp, William Clobery and others of the Guinea Company to whom his Majesty hath granted a patent for the sole trading into Guinea, Binney, and Angola in the parts of Africa that John Crisp and others have fitted and set out a ship called the Talbot of the burthen of about 150 tons with men and goods, only fit for Guinea trade, resolving under pretence of going to Barbary to trade upon the coasts of Guinea and to take nigers, and to carry them to other foreign parts whereby to defeat his Majesty of his customs and to the great prejudice of the said company being contrary to his Majesty's said patent and proclamation.

These are therefore to pray and require you to make present stay of the said ships and goods until you shall receive our further directions and order therein; for which this shall be your warrant

And so we rest
Your very loving friends

London

J. Pany, J. Coke, Fran. Windebank.

Whitehall, 11 November, 1637

[Endorsed:] To our very loving friend, Sir John Pennington, kt., admiral, or to any the captains of his Majesty's ships or castles or other his Majesty's officers to whom it may appertain where the said ship is. A warrant from the Lord's Committee[?] for the staying the Talbot of the 12th of November, 1637.

28. CUSTOMS FRAUDS AT THE PORT OF SANDWICH, 1637
[P.R.O., E 178/6027]

Depositions taken at Sandwich in May, 13 Chas. I,
concerning customs frauds at Sandwich, Kent.

JOHN WAADE of Dover in the county of Kent, gentleman, aged 78 years or thereabouts, deposeth and answereth as followeth:
To the third article this deponent saith that Jacob Brames, his Majesty's Customer of Kent, hath a house standing upon the quay in Dover with divers private storehouses therein, wherein are laid in and shipped out divers sorts of goods, and that Arnold Brames, merchant, brother of the said Jacob Brames, hath dwelt together in the said house with the said Jacob for eight years or thereabouts last past which said Arnold is a great merchant and an owner of shipping and likewise a factor for strangers, but whether his brother or any other of his Majesty's officers be partners with him in shipping, this deponent knoweth not.

John Reston of Dover, gentleman, aged 34 years or thereabouts, sworn and examined, saith as followeth:
To the third article this deponent saith ... that the said Arnold Brames is a great owner of shipping, a great merchant, and a great factor, as well for the English as strangers ...

To the fourth article this deponent saith that about three years since or upward he did know a pack of goods was shipped out of Jacob Brames, his storehouse, into a barque of Callice whereof Cloud Curdeere was master about noon or presently after, but whose the goods were or what they were this deponent knoweth not, and that he did see the searchers' deputies go aboard the said ship to seize the said pack of goods, and this deponent heard someone belonging to the ship tell Jacob Brames standing upon the pier head at Dover that the said pack was seized by the searchers' deputies, namely Anthony Keylocke and James Frost, for that they had no cocket for the said pack; to whom the said Jacob Brames answered to let them not have it but carry it away. I will bear you out of it. Upon that the said searchers came out of the said ship into a boat thinking to come ashore, but hearing what Jacob Brames had said, considered better of it and went aboard again the said ship, which, being under sail, the said deputy searchers were carried into the road by the said ship; and this deponent then standing upon the pier head heard the said searcher and the mariners at high words, and did see the said mariners give many blows and thrusts to the said searchers, whereby they forced them overboard into their boat, and some of the townsmen, standing upon the pier head with him, this deponent, they cried shame to see how the Frenchmen did so abuse the said searchers; whereupon the said Jacob Brames answered it was no matter, what did they make there, or words to that effect. Afterwards the said Curdeere returning to Dover was there arrested at the suit of one of the said searchers' deputies, namely James Frost, which said Curdeere being in the custody of one of the water bailiffs was bailed by the said Jacob Brames and forthwith conveyed himself away and never seen in Dover since . . .

To the seventh article this deponent saith that about the latter end of October last one Edward Ranger, the Dover Post, came down from London on horseback to Dover and this deponent going into his house for a letter saw the said Ranger take three or four bags out of his portmantile and called his man and commanded him to carry a bag of gold to Mr. Brames, his house; whereupon this deponent went forth of the said Dover post house and watched his said servant and saw him go into the said Mr. Brames, his house. Presently after this deponent went towards the pier head and there saw two French shallops lying on the north side of the pier head, and supposing that those shallops lay there to receive and carry away some gold or other prohibited commodities, this deponent watched about the said Mr. Brames, his house, till about ten of the clock at night in which time he this deponent saw a light in one of the storehouses of the said Mr. Brames near adjoining to his house and heard company in the same storehouse, and mistrusting they did intend to carry some prohibited goods into the said shallops that night, this deponent went from the said storehouse to lie in wait for their coming that way; and between eleven or twelve of the clock at night he this deponent saw four persons which came from the said Brames, his store house, and going towards the said shallops and passing by him, he this deponent knew John Robers a porter belonging to Mr. Brames, the Customer or the merchant one, Jacob Garrison, and two other of the said Brameses, their servants, whose names this deponent knoweth not, and this deponent, rising up from the ground, overtook the said Garrison being the last of them and closing with him, took hold of a bag of gold under his arm, but he this deponent seeing the other three cast down their burdens and coming towards him he this deponent drew his knife and cut the said bag whereupon a great quantity of gold fell upon the ground as this deponent did perfectly perceive it to be gold for that it was bright starlight.

29. TRADE TO AMSTERDAM AND SMYRNA, 1638

[Lewes Roberts, *The Merchants Mapp of Commerce*, London, 1638, II, pp. 110–13; I, pp. 118–19]

Of Amsterdam and the Trade thereof

THE trade of this city is much enlarged since the passage of Antwerp was stopped, and the trade of the inhabitants to the East and West Indies, occasioned by their industry, their love to navigation, and not the least by a great plenty of monies which they deliver out at easy rates at interest as wanting land or other means to put out the same to better benefit, nothing being left them but commerce and navigation to employ the same, and of late days England and other neighbouring countries are found to have their estate going at interest according to the custom of the place, which is 8 per cent, whereas in their own countries 4 and 5 per cent is as much as the same will yield them.

But for the coins, weights, and measures, as I observed them, I shall here insert, and refer the rest to the better experienced.

They keep their account as in Antwerp, by which all these parts were regulated in former time for what concerned traffic.

Their monies have also a correspondency with Antwerp coins, but enhanced or debased as they see occasion by reason of their great yearly disbursements, and ordinarily the same is found to be as in the account of Antwerp, so as that their liver or pound, which is twenty shillings Flemish, may be accounted twelve shillings sterling.

Florins 6 makes that pound of 20 *stivers* per florin.

Stivers 120 makes a pound of grosse.

6 stivers a Flemish shilling.

Stivers 5 is accounted as much as 6*d.* sterling or 5 *sold turnois.*

Stiver 1 is a *sold turnois.*

A grosse is 6 *deniers turnois.*

Catolus *gulden* is 20 *stivers*, 2 shillings sterling, or 20 *sols turnois.*

Besides these as the current monies of the country, all coins of Europe do pass here currently for their value, and are received and paid in payments for merchandise accordingly.

Their weight is the pound, 100 whereof makes their *Quintall*, which 100 or *Quintar* is held in London to be *incirca* 111 English, yet some allege that the same truly calculated will not produce above 108*li. sutle*, and for the concordancy see further.

Their measures is the *ell*, which reduced to yards English is found to be 134 *elles* for 100 yards of London, and the 100 *elles* of London are here 167½ *elles*, so that the 100 *elles* here makes in London about 74 yards, or 60½ *elles incirca*, and 40 *Flemish elles* make in England 24 *elles*.

In the exchanges this place is governed by Antwerp, rising and falling according to their present occasions and the value current of their monies, which is often enhanced and debased, it being very frequently observed in this city and the rest subject to the Netherlands or to the United Provinces, that when they have occasions of great receipts, they are decried in value, and raised again where they have occasions by their wars, or otherwise of great disbursement, according to which diversity of needful occasions, the exchange of the place is observed to alter, therefore therein cannot be prescribed any direct rules, though the most part it is found by common difference to be about 3 per cent worse than the exchanges practised in Antwerp.

Now for the 100 *lib.* weight here in use, I find the same thus by observation of some friends to answer and agree with these places, as in Antwerp: 107*li*; Königsberg: 132; Constantinople: 93 *Rot*; Copenhagen: 102*lib.*; Danzig: 126; Flanders in general: 117; Florence: 133; Hamburg: 102; London: 110; Lyons ordinary: 118; Mantua: 155; Marseilles: 119; Melvin: 131; Milan of 12 ounce: 151; Stockholm: 127; Venice *sutle*: 167; Venice *grosse*: 103; Vienna: 90; Naples: 128; Nuremberg: 99; Paris: 98; Portugal: 113; Prague: 93; Ragusa: 140; Revel: 126; Rouen by Viconte: 97; Rochelle small: 118; Rome: 139; Saint Omer: 117; Saragossa: 119; Seville small weight: 113; Sicily 12 ounce: 161; Stralsund: 98; Toulouse: 118; Verona: 95; Urbino: 144.

And thus much shall serve for the concordancy of the weights here practised.

The measure of length here in use is an *ell*, which thus is found to make with other places, I say, the 100 *elles* doth yield in Aleppo: 106 *pico*; Argiere: 135 *covad*; Alexandria: 122 *pico*; Antwerp: 99 *elles*; Königsberg: 123; Constantinople: 111½ *pico*; Florence for silk: 101 *brac*; Genoa: 120 *brac*; Granada: 82 *vares*; Hamburg: 121 *elles*; Lisbon short: 82 *vares*; Rome: 33 *canes*; Valencia: 72 *can*; London: 59 *elles*; London woollen: 73½ *yards*; Lyons linen: 59 *alnes*; Marseilles woollen: 33 *can*; Middelburg: 99 *elles*; Milan linen: 118 *bra*; Nuremberg: 118 *elles*; Paris: 58 *alns*; Prague cloth: 109 *elles*; Ragusa: 118 *bra*; Rouen: 57 *alns*; Seville: 82 *vares*; Stockholm: 123 *elles*.

Besides these measures of length, the concave measures are in use.

Corn is here sold by the *last*, which contains 24 small barrels, each barrel 1½ *Muydens* or *Muys*, each *Muyden* contains 1²⁄₂₄ sacks, each sack being three *archetelings*, which is 3¹¹⁄₂₉ *shepels*, so that the *last* of corn contains 108 *shepels*, and this *last* is observed to make in Antwerp: 37½ *vertules*; Bordeaux: 38

boiseaux; Bruges: 17½ *bootes*; Cyprus: 40 *medinos*; Emden: 55 *werps*; Hamburg: 83 *shepels*; Lisbon: 225 *alquiers*; London: 10 *quarters* . . .

Of Smyrna and the trade thereof

The principal trade of this city was within these few years transported hither from the island Scio where the consuls abovesaid had their residence, and from thence are entitled consuls of Scio and Smyrna, but by reason that scale both for sales and investments had then a dependency upon this, it was found more proper and less chargeable to remove their abode and warehouses hither, and by that means this became the principal port, the goodness of the harbour much furthering the same, being both under the command of the *Grand Signior*, and within these later years much enriched by the trade of English, French, and Venetians.

The commodities that are found here to abound, and that are hence transported into other countries of Christendom, are cotton wools, which in great plenty grow in the adjoining plains of this city; also Galles for dyers, aniseeds, cordovants, wax, cotton and grogram yarn, cute, carpets, grograms, mohers, chamblets, and some fruits and drugs; raw Persia silk is likewise hither brought by land from Persia; and all other commodities found in Turkey or of that growth is here to be had, and the commodities here vented from England are cloths of Suffolk and Gloucester, kersies of Yorkshire and Hampshire, lead, tin, calicoes, pepper, indigo, and other spices which within these late years we had formerly from this and other places of Turkey, and which now by the commodity of the East India trade and navigation, we carry to them; and from Venice is brought some cloth paper, silks, velvets, etc. and from France some few cloths and paper, etc.

The coins current of Smyrna are those of Constantinople, and generally those of all that empire, which I shall shew when I treat of that city, and for that cause here omit it, and their accounts they also keep here in the same nature with them, and therefore refer you to that place in both these particulars.

The weights of Smyrna and Scio, for they agree both in one, is the *quintar*, which contains 100 *rotolos*, or 42 *oakes*, and every *oake* being 400 *drams*, and every *lodoro* being 176 *drams*, and the pound *haberdepois* hath been found to be 148 *drams*, and the *quintal* of 42 *oakes* abovesaid, which produceth 119 *li. English*, but in many commodities it is found to answer but 117 *li*. so that *incirca* 9¼ *drams* is 1 ounce English *haberdepois*.

They have here in use two measures, one for linen and another for woollen, but because they nearly agree with Constantinople I will refer the same to that place.

The customs paid by the English here and throughout all Turkey, by virtue of their capitulations with the great Turk, is only three *per centum*; and oftentimes the Custom House of Scio and of Smyrna is in one man's hands, and though by their capitulations it is so agreed, that those goods that have once paid custom in one port, should not pay any more being thence exported to any place of his dominions, and that commands have been granted to that end by the *grand Signior* at several times; yet the justice of that country is so defective in this particular, that the commodities landed in Smyrna, and paying there three *per centum*, and afterward transported to Constantinople, pay there again another three *per centum*, or compound with the customer, which sometimes is done at 1½ *per centum*, and sometimes at less; note that here as in all parts of Turkey the Venetians, French, and Dutch pay five *per cent*, two *per cent* more than the English, which is grounded upon their capitulations with the Emperor.

The port charges of clearing a ship in Smyrna is paid in commodities of our country, and was to that end thus at first regulated; but since converted into payment by money, as to the *cadie* who is to have five *pico* of Venice cloth, and a bundle of cony skins for a vest, which in the infancy of our English trade was here found to be much requested.

The *cadies* servant to have 3½ *pico* English cloth. The *cadies* caya to have 3 *pico* of *ditto*. The *cadies* scrivan to have a *chicquine in gold*. The cadies *pages* to have 2½ *dollers*. The *Mosur Bashaw* to have 1½ *pico cloth*. The *cadies janisaries* to have a *chicquine*. All which charges amount *incirca* to 68 *dollers*.

To conclude, the trade of this port it is most noted for the abundance of cottons which hence is transported to England, France, Holland, and Italy, estimated yearly to be about 20,000 *quintal*, and is found here to grow in the adjoining plains, which they do sow as we do corn, the stalk being no bigger than that of wheat, but stronger and tougher, bearing a head, round and bearded and hard as a stone, which when it is ripe it breaketh and is delivered of a soft white bombast or cotton, mixed with seed, which they separate with an instrument, selling the wool, but reserving the seed for the next harvest; see more of this trade in Cyprus and Constantinople, to which I refer the inquirer.

30. REASONS FOR THE DECAY OF TRADE
TO FRANCE, 1641
[B.M., Stowe MS. 132, ff. 298–9]

ACCORDING to an order of the honourable committee of all the members of the Commons House of Parliament of the fifth of this present, January 1640 [1641], the merchants of London trading into France do humbly present the reasons which are (as they conceive) the decay of trade into that kingdom together with the remedies.[1]

1. The excessive charges laid upon the English cloth and stuffs of all sorts

---

[1] The numbering of the items in this document is erratic and no attempt has been made here to rationalize it.

by custom, pretermitted customs, subsidy, and impost together with extraordinary fees of officers, clerks, searchers, wayters and other ministers in
his Majesty's Custom House for entries, cockets, certificates, and such like
hath so raised the price thereof that it hath made way for the vent and sale of
cloth and stuffs made in France which otherwise could not have been
effected.

REMEDIES

i. That all unnecessary charges may be taken off the English cloth and stuffs.
ii. That the customs which shall be imposed upon the manufactures of this
kingdom which are exported be small and the greater charge laid upon the
returns of the proceeds of those goods and of all others which shall be
imported. The importation of goods from France is at present five times as
much as the exportation of goods from hence thither which chiefly ariseth
from the great trade drawn of late years by strangers who heretofore imported
no considerable quantity of wines or other goods but contented themselves
with the sale of them in France. And did usually take off from the English
merchants the manufactures of this kingdom for their wines and other goods,
whereby merchants were maintained, great quantities of English manufactures
vented, and much shipping employed, no foreign trade employing more
shipping and breeding more mariners than it formerly did for that in the
winter season when English shipping is not employed into the Baltic seas and
other eastern parts, by reason those seas are then frozen, they were employed
into France for wines and salt, whereas now, by reason of the great encouragement which the French have from the state there and the quick sales
they find here, being able to undersell the English merchants, for that they
pay small or no duties in France and do pay here but 3s. the ton more than
his Majesty's own subjects, and live here privately as lodgers paying no
duties to his Majesty nor house rent nor any such like charge, and making
small or no return of the proceed of their goods in English manufactures (as
by the laws of kingdom they ought to do), they have almost gained the whole
trade into their own hands.

REMEDIES

[i.] That the statute of employment may be put in execution which will not
only be a means of the vent of the English manufactures but will increase
his Majesty's revenue in his customs.
ii. Whereas wine is rated but at 3s. subsidy and is raised by impost and composition for purveyance to 4li. so that the stranger paying double subsidy
payeth only 3s. per tun more than the English merchant, if the subsidy be
raised to some equal value as it is on other commodities and the impost taken
off, the strangers' charge would in some equalize the English, by which means
they would not be so well enabled to undersell the English as now they do.
iii. The restoring the free importation of salt, the restraint thereof having of

late much hindered the employment of the English navigation and their fishing.

REMEDY

1. That the transportation of wools into those parts may be prohibited.

4. The false and ill-making of English cloth, perpetuanas, Norwich stuffs, and other New Draperies.

REMEDY

That the laws concerning the true making of cloth may be revived with such alterations, additions, and explanations as to the great wisdom of this honourable assembly shall be thought meet.

The great difference in value between the English and French coins being above 40*li*. in the 100*li*. doth not only lessen the vent of the English manufactures but doth occasion the exportation of gold and the enhancing of the exchange. The remedy whereof is humbly left to the grave consideration of this honourable assembly.

6. The ill managing of trade by men that are not bred merchants who, being brought up in other trades and professions, not contenting themselves to live within their own calling, become merchants and through their ignorance and want of experience have brought much hurt and confusion to trade which would be remedied by a settled government.

The great number of bankrupts and the long and tedious suits in law arising upon differences of accounts between merchants and tradesmen, both which would be remedied by settling the law merchant in this kingdom whereof the merchants trading into France have happy experience in Normandy and other parts of that kingdom.

31. SOME CORRESPONDENCE FROM FACTORS IN EUROPE CONCERNING CLOTH SALES, 1641–2

[P.R.O., SP 46/84, nos. 92, 93, 94, 104, 154, 188, 103]

George Warner   Rotterdam, 15th July, 1641

Loving friend,

I salute you, etc. Yours of the 25th June past I have received, with the enclosed to the Company which I have delivered; and your excuse was so authentic that it was generally allowed of, and you are excused till they shall call you again. Yesterday was our first show day, and generally found very good sales for whites, but for colours never worse. I could not sell any of your cloths but have promise of a merchant to come tomorrow, who, if we can agree, will buy the whole parcel. For patterns I cannot get any, and also they are so various that they never hold long by one colour. Last shipping the[y] looked for light greys and now they desire most sad musk colour, low priced, and if you could send such, the lower priced the better, they will go off. I sold yesterday within 50 whites as many as I did receive per the ship. This being all at present that I have to enlarge upon, I take leave and rest

Yours to command,
Brian Ball.

Exc° 38s. 10d. do vz°[1]

Postscript: ——[2] cannot meet with so small a bill otherwise I had made home so much money as I have of yours. I shall do it per Frost. Mr. Whitmore is come from Hamburg, stays here for a fair wind. Idem B.B.

*   *   *

Mr. George Warner   Hamburg ad 10th August, 1641

Sir,

In my last I certified you of the balks or spars which stand at Souther Kopfen in Sweden being 4,800 which have formerly been a good commodity for this town and Lübeck, being transported for Spain in great abundance. But now they are fallen so much in price as scarce producing the freight and charges they will cost to bring hither as not less than 5s. the piece for freight; and above 6s. 8d. they will not yield; that adding the tolls and other charges it will be more than they will yield, and freight must be present money which I have not, that of necessity they must remain there still, though as my friend relateth the greater part doth begin to grow black with standing. What to do therein, I know not, which may give you content. But these and all other debts standing out and produceth no money which doth not a little grieve me. My friend which receiveth them there bringeth me in for charges 98 n s the which I have been forced to pay him, and now I know your occasions call also for money, the which I protest I have not, there being nothing but my stipend to live on, the which is so small that it will hardly bring both ends together, and yet nevertheless though I cannot do what I should, nor what I would, yet I must do what I can; and wait upon future times in hope to do more, the which I doubt not of.

Sir, you have a servant now come over as I do understand, the which hath that liberty to eat out of the English house for six months or a year. If you think it convenient to let him lie and diet with me, you may shorten what he should pay another way. He shall have that is sufficient though I should want myself and what I can help him either in learning the Dutch tongue or other ways, I shall not be wanting. And thus not doubting of your accustomed favour, I rest

Yours to command to the utmost of his power,
Peter Clerkes

[Endorsed:] To Mr. George Warner, merchant in London. Port a Antwerpe.

*   *   *

[1] Double usance.   [2] MS torn away.

Mr. George Warner   Rotterdam, 14 October, 1641

Sir,

My last to you was the 23rd past advising you of sale of 3 clo. to which I refer you. Since which I have not received any from you. These to advise you of two cloths sold, viz. the 8th present to Jemant Municke of Ziericksee: 1 Spa. clo. no. 913: yards 23½ at 15s. per *ell* Brabants; the 13th to Jacob Casteell of Rotterdam 1 Spa. clo. no. 923: yards 24 at 14s. 4d. per ell.

2 clo. sold which you may please to accept of. Here is at present little to do: low prices; colours musk, colours castanias and such most requested. This being all at present that I have to enlarge, I take leave and rest

Yours to command
Brian Ball

Exc° 38s. 10d. do vzo

[Endorsed:] Mr. Ball 14 October, 1641. To Mr. George Warner, merchant in London. P[er] post

*   *   *

Mr. George Warner   Rotterdam, 10th March, 1641

Loving friend,

Yours of the 21st January I have received taking notice what you write concerning your business that if it were trouble to me you would quit me of it; which I should be well contented, for I find that colours require a whole man's labour to look after them; and that whites and colours agree not together and I desire not to keep cloth that I cannot vent. I have of late foreborne to write you because I desired to have made some ample sales before I wrote you, and have endeavoured what I can, but it will not be. Your cloths are much overrated or dearer bought in than others, for Mr. Kenricke can afford better cloth for cheaper. Besides your cloths hold not out their measure for of those I have sold I have abatement for shortness.

I have lately sold for you 3 cloths viz.
the 2nd of Feb. to Lodowick Sack of Rotterdam 1 Spa. clo. no. 22 cost S K[1] at 16s. 8d. Flemish per ell.
4th ditto to Nicholas Duchemin 1 Spa. clo. no. 25 cost n½[1] at 15s. per ell.
14   „   to Cornelis van Roie of Utrick 1 Spa. clo. fine no. 852 sold by the cloth at 54s. Flemish.

3 clo. sold if you shall please to dispose of them to any other, I shall be willing to resign them. Your two bills I have paid Mr. Gore.

This being in some haste I take leave and rest,

Yours to command,
Brian Ball

Exc°. 37s. 9d. do vzo.

*   *   *

[1] These symbols record the price in a private code.

Mr. George Warner   Rotterdam, 12th August, 1641

Loving friend,

I salute you. My last to you was the 15th past in answer to of yours of the 25th June. I wrote you that you were excused for appearing for assistant to which said letter I refer you, etc. Since which I have received none from you, and not having sold anything for you although I have one uttered, I was bid money lately by an Amsterdamer for all your cloths but at so poor a price that there would have been much loss by them. They are much too fine for this place. Coarse cloths are most desired. I would have before this made home that little money I had of yours in cash but could not get so small a bill, but have now got one near so much, which I send here enclosed being 36*li*. 5*s*. sterling delivered John Quarles at 38*s*. 8*d*. do vzo. pbl. [=payable] in London per Mr. Samuel Charles. If you could send some coarse musk colour [to] be offered here at 13*s*. or 14*s*. Flemish the ell, I should hope to sell them better and to help of those. That being all I have to enlarge of at present, I take leave and rest,

Yours to command,

Brian Ball

Exc°. 38*s*. 9*d*. and 10*d*. do vzo.

[Endorsed:] Mr. Lee 1641. To Mr. George Warriner, merchant in London. Quis Lynn Warriner.

*   *   *

Mr. George Warner   Adi the 10 of May, 1642. Livorno

Sir,

Hence copy have yours of the pd. last with bill of lading and invoice for what goods you have laden on the Exeter merchant where [I] may presume your most benefit shall be agined [=gained], etc. I conceive you find no encouragement for Spanish cloths so could wish you for the future to forbear. Bays well bought from 15*d*. to 20*d*. a yard. Certes to be in September in request, and for the Spring good elbroads, to be here in February in broad tillets[1] for woollen goods. These be the chief and their true season which may serve you for your government. As yet Mr. Ellam cannot dispose of the indigo and yours very little looked after. Pray God send you better success hereafter. What possible may be done you may depend of. Your last draft of 1,000 is accepted, and the usual punctuality shall follow. Presuming your favoured letters in the like kind for the which we shall rest grateful, will ever remain

Sir, we have to answer yours of the 8th post. The account of your Spa. cloths is gone but whether it will be to your liking or no cannot tell. There is no marvel why the worm breeds in cloths for, since the planting of rapeseed in

---

[1] Tillet: a wrapper of cloth.

England, the clothiers have got a trick to mix that oil with olive oil and the first will never scour out, which, lying long packed, breeds a worm. The worms were the least tare in these, for there was one piece much stained with a white stuff which we could conjecture to be nothing else but lime. For the three barrels of indigo at Genoa, Mr. Ellam adviseth us that it will not yield now above 34 Fl. [=Flemish] so shall write for it hither and seek to put it off the best we may to clear a bad business. By the Peter and Andrew you shall have the satins for the last sold. That draft made on Retano for account of Mr. Jordan Fairfax is accepted and shall be paid in due time p. traviso. Lead none in town to sell. Pepper p. 8s. is what have to say do rest.

At your command,
John Fairfax and Thos. Barnsley.

[Endorsed:] to Mr. George Warner, merchant in London

*   *   *

Laus Deo in Amsterdam, 7th October, 1642

Loving friend, Mr. Warner, my hearty commendations.

I have five days past received yours of 24th September, and for your 3 barrels of Lahore indigo as yet here is no conveniency of shipping them as formerly I wrote you for Leghorn until the return of the Muscovy ships which are not yet arrived but now daily expected. At their return the Straits ships will begin to lade and not before then; so it will be yet a month or six weeks before any shipping can be ready to go that way, and then your three barrels shall be shipped for Leghorn, if in the interim you do not recall your former order which, if you should not, I pray write me their names a little plainer, for in your former letter I cannot well read the names to whom you gave order to consign them unto. Indigo remaineth here a drug and no vent for the English sort of Lahore. It will not here ——[1] for above 12s. Fl. [=Flemish] per lb. yet I hear it is worth in —— 7s. 6d. or 8s. sterling per lb. which is at least 15s. 6d. or 16s. Fl. —— at and can be sent no time shall be neglected —— and many other commodities are as drugs here —— being too much over laid so until further —— do cease and commit you to God's protection, resting

Your loving friend,
Henry Whitaker.

---

[1] MS. torn at edge.

32. INSTRUCTIONS TO THE COUNCIL OF TRADE, 1650[1]

[C. M. Andrews, *British Committees, Commissions, and Councils of Trade and Plantations, 1622–75*, Johns Hopkins University Studies, XXVI, 1908, pp. 115–16]

First.—They are to take notice of all the native commodities of this land, or what time and industry may hereafter make native and advise how they may not only be fully manufactured, but well and truly wrought, to the honour and profit of the Commonwealth.

Secondly.—They are to consider how the trades and manufactures of this nation may most fitly and equally be distributed to every part thereof; to the end that one part may not abound with trade, and another remain poor and desolate for the want of the same.

Thirdly.—They are to consult how the trade may most conveniently be driven from one part of this land to another. To which purpose they are to consider how the rivers may be made more navigable and the ports more capable of shipping.

Fourthly.—They are to consider how the commodities of this land may be vented, to the best advantage thereof, into foreign countries, and not under-valued by the evil management of trade; and that they advise how obstructions of trade into foreign parts may be removed; and devise by all means, how new ways and places may be found out, for the better venting of the native commodities of this land.

Fifthly.—They are to advise how free ports or landing places for foreign commodities imported (without paying of custom if again exported) may be appointed in several parts of this land, and in what manner the same is best to be effected.

Sixthly.—They are to consider of some way that a most exact account be kept of all commodities imported and exported through the land, to the end that a perfect balance of trade may be taken, whereby the Commonwealth may not be impoverished, by receiving of commodities yearly from foreign parts of a greater value than what was carried out.

Seventhly.—They are duly to consider the value of the English coins, and the par thereof, in relation to the intrinsic value which it bears in weight and fineness with the coins of other nations. Also to consider of the state of the exchange, and of the gain or loss that comes to the Commonwealth by the exchange now used by the merchants.

Eighthly.—They are (in order to the regulating and benefit of trade) seriously to consider what customs, imposts, and excise is fit to be laid upon all goods and commodities, either native or imported, and how the said

---

[1] These instructions form part of the Act of 1 August 1650 'for the advancing and regulating of the trade of this Commonwealth.'—C. H. Firth and R. S. Rait, *Acts and Ordinances of the Interregnum, 1642–1660*, pp. 403–6.

customs, imposts, and excise may be best ordered and regulated, and so equally laid and evenly managed, as neither trade may thereby be hindered, nor the state made incapable to defray the public charges of the Commonwealth.

Ninthly.—They are to take into their consideration whether it be necessary to give way to a more open or free trade than that of companies and societies, and in what manner it is fittest to be done; wherein, notwithstanding, they are to take care that government and order in trade may be preserved and confusion avoided.

Tenthly.—They are to inform themselves of the particular ordinances, orders, grants, patents, and constitutions of the several companies of merchants and handicraftsmen, to the end that if any of them tend to the hurt of the public, they may be laid down in such manner as the Parliament shall think fit.

Eleventhly.—They are to consider the great trade of fishing, and that not only upon the coasts of England and Ireland but likewise of Iceland, Greenland, Newfoundland, and New England, or elsewhere, and to take care that the fishermen may be encouraged to go on in their labours, to the increase of shipping and mariners.

Twelfthly.—They are to take into their consideration the English plantations in America or elsewhere, and to advise how those plantations may be best managed, and made most useful for this Commonwealth, and how the commodities thereof may be so multiplied and improved, as (if it be possible) those plantations alone may supply the Commonwealth of England with whatsoever it necessarily wants.

33. THE NAVIGATION ACT, 1651

[S. R. Gardiner, *Constitutional Documents of the Puritan Revolution, 1625–1660*, Oxford, 1906, pp. 468–71]

Goods from Foreign Parts by whom to be imported

FOR the increase of the shipping and the encouragement of the navigation of this nation, which under the good providence and protection of God is so great a means of the welfare and safety of this Commonwealth: be it enacted by this present Parliament, and the authority thereof, that from and after the first day of December, one thousand six hundred fifty and one, and from thence forwards, no goods or commodities whatsoever of the growth, production or manufacture of Asia, Africa, or America, or of any part thereof; or of any islands belonging to them, or which are described or laid down in the usual maps or cards of those places, as well of the English plantations as others, shall be imported or brought into this Commonwealth of England, or into Ireland, or any other lands, islands, plantations, or territories to this Commonwealth belonging, or in their possession, in any other ship or ships, vessel or vessels whatsoever, but only in such as do truly and without fraud belong only to the people of this Commonwealth, or the plantations thereof, as the proprietors or right owners thereof; and whereof the master and mariners are also for the most part of them of the people of this Commonwealth, under the penalty of the forfeiture and loss of all the goods that shall be imported contrary to this Act; as also of the ship (with all her tackle, guns, and apparel) in which the said goods or commodities shall be so brought in and imported; the one moiety to the use of the Commonwealth, and the other moiety to the use and behoof of any person or persons who shall seize the goods or commodities, and shall prosecute the same in any court of record within this Commonwealth.

And it is further enacted by the authority aforesaid, that no goods or commodities of the growth, production, or manufacture of Europe, or of any part thereof, shall after the first day of December, one thousand six hundred fifty and one, be imported or brought into this Commonwealth of England, or into Ireland, or any other lands, islands, plantations, or territories to this Commonwealth belonging, or in their possession, in any ship or ships, vessel or vessels whatsoever, but in such as do truly and without fraud belong only to the people of this Commonwealth, as the true owners and proprietors thereof, and in no other, except only such foreign ships and vessels as do truly and properly belong to the people of that country or place, of which the said goods are the growth, production, or manufacture; or to such ports where the said goods can only be, or most usually are first shipped for transportation; and that under the same penalty of forfeiture and loss expressed in the former branch of this Act, the said forfeitures to be recovered and employed as is therein expressed.

And it is further enacted by the authority aforesaid, that no goods or commodities that are of foreign growth, production, or manufacture, and which are to be brought into this Commonwealth in shipping belonging to the people thereof, shall be by them shipped or brought from any other place or places, country or countries, but only from those of their said growth, production, or manufacture, or from those ports where the said goods and commodities can only, or are, or usually have been first shipped for transportation; and from none other places or countries, under the same penalty of forfeiture and loss expressed in the first branch of this Act, the said forfeitures to be recovered and employed as is therein expressed.

And it is further enacted by the authority aforesaid, that no sort of cod fish, ling, herring, pilchard, or any other kind of salted fish, usually fished for and caught by the people of this nation; nor any oil made, or that shall be made of any kind of fish whatsoever, nor any whale fins, or whale bones, shall from henceforth be imported into this Commonwealth or into Ireland, or any other lands, islands, plantations, or territories thereto belonging, or in their possession, but only such as shall be caught in vessels that do or shall truly and properly belong to the people of this nation, as proprietors and right owners thereof; and the said fish to be cured, and the oil aforesaid made by the people of this Commonwealth, under the penalty and loss expressed in the first branch of this present Act; the said forfeit to be recovered and employed as is there expressed.

And it is further enacted by the authority aforesaid, that no sort of cod, ling, herring, or pilchard, or any other kind of salted fish whatsoever, which shall be caught and cured by the people of this Commonwealth, shall be from and after the first of February, one thousand six hundred fifty three, exported from any place or places belonging to this Commonwealth, in any other ship or ships, vessel or vessels, save only in such as do truly and properly appertain to the people of this Commonwealth, as right owners; and whereof the master and mariners are for the most part of them English, under the penalty and loss expressed in the said first branch of this present Act; the said forfeit to be recovered and employed as is there expressed.

Provided always, that this Act, nor anything therein contained, extend not, or be meant to restrain the importation of any of the commodities of the Straits[1] or Levant seas, laden in the shipping of this nation as aforesaid, at the usual ports or places for lading of them heretofore, within the said Straits or Levant seas, though the said commodities be not of the very growth of the said places.

Provided also, that this Act nor anything therein contained, extend not, nor be meant to restrain the importing of any East India commodities laden in the shipping of this nation, at the usual port or places for lading of them heretofore in any part of those seas, to the southward and eastward of Cabo Bona Esperanza,[2] although the said ports be not the very places of their growth.

Provided also, that it shall and may be lawful to and for any of the people of this Commonwealth, in vessels or ships to them belonging, and whereof the master and mariners are of this nation as aforesaid, to load and bring in from any of the ports of Spain and Portugal all sorts of goods or commodities that have come from, or any way belonged unto, the plantations or dominions or either of them respectively.

Be it also further enacted by the authority aforesaid, that from henceforth it shall not be lawful to any person or persons whatsoever to load or cause to be laden and carried in any bottom or bottoms, ship or ships, vessel or vessels whatsoever, whereof any stranger or strangers born (unless such be denizens or naturalized) be owners, or masters, any fish, victual, wares, or things of what kind or nature soever the same shall be, from one port or creek of this Commonwealth, to another port or creek of the same, under penalty to every one that shall offend contrary to the true meaning of this branch of this present Act, to forfeit all the goods that shall be so laden or carried, as also the ship upon which they shall be so laden or carried, the same forfeit to be recovered and employed as directed in the first branch of this present Act.

---

[1] 'The Straits' are the Straits of Gibraltar, but the term includes the Mediterranean, or, as here, the western part of it.

[2] The Cape of Good Hope.

Lastly, that this Act, nor anything therein contained, extend not to bullion, nor yet to any goods taken, or that shall be taken by way of reprisal by any ship or ships, having commission from this Commonwealth.

Provided, that this Act, or anything therein contained, shall not extend, nor be construed to extend to any silk or silk wares which shall be brought by land from any part of Italy, and there bought with the proceed of English commodities, sold either for money or in barter; but that it shall and may be lawful for any of the people of this Commonwealth to ship the same in English vessels from Ostend, Nieuport, Rotterdam, Middelburg, Amsterdam, or any ports thereabouts, the owners and proprietors first making oath by themselves, or other credible witnesses, before the Commissioners of the Customs for the time being or their deputies, or one of the Barons of the Exchequer, that the goods aforesaid were so bought for his or their own proper account in Italy.

34. THE STATE OF TRADE BETWEEN ENGLAND AND HOLLAND, 1651

[R. W. K. Hinton, *The Eastland Trade and the Commonweal in the Seventeenth Century*, Cambridge, 1959, pp. 205–11]

The Advocate: or, a Narrative of the State and Condition of Things between the English and Dutch Nation, in relation to Trade, and the consequences depending thereupon, to either Commonwealth; as it was presented in August 1651.

by Benjamin Worsley

IT HATH been a thing for many years generally received, that the design of Spain (and which, to this day, he still in his Councils carries on) is to get the universal Monarchy of Christendom. Nor is it a thing less true (how little soever observed) that our neighbours [the Dutch] (after they had settled their liberty, and been a while encouraged by prosperity) have, likewise, for some years, aimed to lay a foundation to themselves for engrossing the universal trade not only of Christendom, but, indeed, of the greater part of the known world; that so they might poiz the affairs of any other state about them, and make their own considerable, if not by the largeness of their country; yet, however, by the greatness of their wealth; and by their potency at sea, in strength and multitude of shipping.

For the clear and certain carrying on of which, there being none (that was) like to be so great a bar to them, in this their aim, as the English nation; nor any that lay so conveniently to keep up a proportion of trade with them; it concerned them, therefore, by all means and ways possible to discourage and beat out the English in all places of trade, as far (at least) as was discreet for them, without too much alarming them; of having too early or hasty a breach with them.

Their particular practices to which purpose in the East Indies, at Guinea, Greenland, Russia, with the several unfair carriages (of some among them) to us, in those places; and even in our own seas, is not intended to be here mentioned. It sufficeth, that these following advantages they had clearly gotten above us:

1. In the great trade they did drive to Eastland, and to the Baltic Sea; for masts, timber, hemp, pitch, tar, copper, iron, saltpetre, all sorts of grain, potashes, etc. the like most necessary commodities.

2. In their herring-fishing; employing yearly upon the coast of this land only above 2,000 sail of great vessels or shipping.

3. In the preserving and advancing their manufactures; their clothing trade of late arising and increasing (as it is judged) to above 60,000 cloths yearly.

4. In their East India trade; and by it, monopolizing three sorts of spices almost to the whole world; as, cloves, nuts, and mace, and lately much cinnamon.

The means whereby they have pursued and upheld these advantages were by the great number of shipping they have constantly built; and by the manner of managing their trade and shipping, in a conformity and direction to their grand end. For:

1. Few merchants' ships among the Hollanders were ships of much defence, unless these going to India; and so they were neither at so great a charge of guns in building them; nor did carry a proportion of men or victual (in setting them out) near, or answerable to, English shipping of the same burthen.

2. Several trades they did drive in fleets, with great flutes or vessels, having never a gun at all in them, nor more men than would possibly sail them, as most of their Eastland trade, their herring buss trade, and their salt trade, which were driven after this manner.

3. Those their fleets were, and have been always carefully and constantly attended with a convoy at the public charge; and which was alway ready beforehand, and had their directions given them not from the State, but from the several admiralties; whereby they were held to their duty, and strictly tied up to that service.

4. Much of the trade which they did drive to the southward (not in fleets, nor with convoy, but in single shipping) they would often insure in England; so that when loss came, it was we sometimes that bare it, and our stock that was lessened and diminished by it.

By all which means:

1. They did engross the whole trade of all bulky commodities (to themselves singly), as timber, clapboard, masts, grain, salt, etc.

2. And were, in some commodities, able to go as cheap again for freight, as we: in some, half as cheap; and near in all, a full third penny cheaper than we.

Which cheapness of freight produced again other great advantages to themselves. For:

1. In some commodities it was above 20 in the hundred gain; in some 15; in others 10; and near 4 or 5 per cent in most (which was a year's interest with them). And by which:

2. They were sure to get the preference of the market of us in other countries and if occasion were, to undersell us also as much per cent in all places, and upon all trades; yea, sometimes in our own commodities. And this together with an easy pretence of the unsafety of our English shipping through our late troubles.

3. Compelled our nation (that we might maintain a stock going with them) to hire and freight the Holland shipping, without which, indeed, we could not well have held up a trade here with them, either out or home; which being once begun by some, was immediately (by reason of the advantage of it) followed by as many others as could. But this (though a good and beneficial expedient for the particular merchant) begat notwithstanding several very great mischiefs to this nation in general. For:

1. By this we encouraged the building more and more of our neighbour's shipping, and discouraged our own; which hereupon were laid up by the walls in great numbers.

2. We increased (by this) their great trade for the Baltic Sea and Eastland, and gave them still the greater opportunity to make themselves the mart and masters over us, of all commodities belonging to the building or furnishing of shipping, whereby their trade still came home in a circle; they (like wise men) laying such a course, as one part of it strengthened another.

3. We disobliged and discontented our own people and seamen, and insensibly weakened the strength and defence of this nation. For by this course, we must at length have been reduced to have hired their mariners, when we come to set out our men of war: nor was it possible (had it held) to have prevented it.

4. They, by this means, carried away much unnecessary treasure out of this nation, taken for freights; and so insensibly impoverished also this country; our money occasioning a luxe to their people, while our own seamen starved at home for mere want, and through lack of employment.

5. And as the cheapness of their freight enabled them to undersell us abroad, in many commodities carried to foreign markets by them, and by us, to sell; so it enabled them equally to overbid us abroad for the foreign commodities, which they and we bought, and to raise the price of them upon us, which while they had liberty to bring in hither, they either prevented our merchant of the first of the market, and then made us pay sauce for them; or, if not, they carried them into their country: or here watched the opportunity of another seasonable vent of them. And thus they served us, as for all our Norway, Eastland, and Russia commodities; so also lately in our wines, fruits, oils, currants, etc. which were the commodities of Spain, Canaries, and the Straits. By both these means (viz. by discouraging and beating us

down abroad in the selling of some commodities; and by raising and enhancing us abroad in the price, or buying up of others) concluding with themselves, to weary us out at length from all trade, and to have the sole buying and selling of all commodities for us.

For this method and manner of managing their affairs, daily adding to their stock, and answerably diminishing the stock and treasure of this nation; and by laying it so, as it run thus in a circle, each part of it (as we said) strengthening another part, it would unavoidably have tended to a greater and greater disenabling us to hold any trade with them; and to have made themselves, for wealth and shipping, the masters over us; a sufficient testimony of which (over and above what we have said also) we might further see in the actual progress that they had gained upon us in our shipping. For:

1. In our trade of Eastland, whereas we did use formerly to send thither 200 sail of shipping in a year, we now did not send 16 sail. The Hollanders in the mean time employing not less then 600 sail thither; and whereby (had not a good providence crossed or hindered a strict alliance and conjunction between some of those eastern states and them) we must soon have given them their price, and been at their disposing for all commodities belonging to shipping. And then it had been too great an hazard for us (by any law made here) to have recovered our trade from them.

2. In our plantations they had three, if not four sail of ships, for our one; whereas they never suffered us so much as to trade at all in any place or plantation settled by them.

3. In India they have 20 sail, and above, for our one.

4. At Spain, Canaries, Zant, with several other places in the Straits, where they formerly rarely laded hither one ship of goods, they now lately laded hither more than we.

And thus, in the way and manner of the managing the trade in their shipping, lay much of their vigilance to gain their advantage and design upon us.

A second course (therefore), whereby they do and have upheld their advantages above us, is the greatness of the stock they employ, which (as we now intimated) was more and more increased by the wisdom of this their method in shipping. And which, on the other side, as it did increase and grow great, did enable them the more to give the laws of trade to us, both in the government of the exchange, and of the markets abroad for foreign commodities.

A third course for the gaining and upholding their advantages of us, was the singular and prudent care they took in preserving the credit of most of those commodities which are their own proper manufactures; by which they keep up the repute and sale of them abroad; taking hereby a very great advantage of the contrary neglect in us; and by this means, likewise, very much damnifying and spoiling us.

Which that we may clearly see of what import this one thing alone is to us, we shall here set down certain general canons or rules, belonging to manufactures.

1. That although Divine Providence, in the greatness of his wisdom, hath placed natural commodities, some here, some there; yet no manufacture or artificial commodity but may possibly be had or transplanted into any country.

2. That all manufactures (especially such as are of necessity) if they are of a certain goodness, they are (like coin) of a certain value and price also; and so on the contrary. If of an uncertain goodness, they, etc.

3. That two persons selling or making commodities of a like goodness, he shall have the preference of the market, that will sell them the cheapest. And so two nations likewise.

4. That the cheapness of manufactures and artificial commodities doth altogether depend upon the plenty and cheapness of the matter, and upon the like cheapness of price, for handy labour.

And these (though few) being unalterable laws in all manufactures, it cannot but be acknowledged that it is through our want of the like care, as our neighbours, and only through that, that the Hollander hath any kind of woollen manufacture. For:

1. The matter of no woollen manufacture groweth in his country at all; but he is forced to fetch it from other places; whereas we have it here, within this nation, plenty.

2. The price of labour depending much upon the price of victuals, house-rent, and other things necessary, it is certain (especially to any that know both countries) that all this is much cheaper with us, than with our neighbours, and are like so to be.

3. Our nation, as they were heretofore the only workmen of these commodities; so none can excel them for art, skill, or goodness, were but encouragement given them, and an order, regulation, and government of the manufactures settled among them. And therefore it is not our neighbour's singular industry above us, or a power they have to work cheaper than us; so much as it is the carelessness of this nation, in keeping our manufactures to their due contents, weight, and goodness. Their neglect in settling a regulation, government, and superspection over them, and in inflicting due and just punishments for the false-making of them. That is (humbly conceived to be) the cause of the so great thriving of our neighbour's clothing, and of the so great ruin and decay (on the contrary) of our own woollen manufactures, and of the people depending upon them.

A fourth course taken by our neighbours is the improvements of trade that they have made by their treaties or articles of confederations with other princes; and by making this their care and protection of trade abroad in all places their interest of state. Thus taking hold of the juncture of circumstances, and making use of the necessity of the King of Denmark, they have farmed the Sound of him. Thus also at the Treaty of Münster have they reserved a power of shutting us out of the Scheldt; and have carefully in that peace concluded on several other articles and provisions in order to the securing and promoting of their traffic. And thus—etc.

A fifth course (and not the least means for the upholding and increasing their trade) is the smallness of their custom or port duties; also their prudent laying on and taking off impositions, for the furtherance of their own manufactures, and for the encouragement of bringing in some, and discouragement of bringing in other commodities; and of which they have given us two ill instances: the one in laying on a great tax upon our English cloths and manufactures; the other in forbidding our cloths wholly to be imported, if dressed or dyed in the cloth; of both which we have had some cause to complain long, as being plainly an inhibition of commerce, and, if not strictly against the laws of nations, yet at least against the course of amity, alliance, and friendship.

A sixth way hath been the constant reward and encouragement given to persons bringing in inventions; making of new discoveries, and propounding things profitable for public and common interest: which (how little a thing soever it may seem to some), yet it hath ever been, and is constantly, a very great spur to industry.

And these are humbly asserted to be the principal causes of their so much greatness and flourishing in trade above us.

Other causes that have been less principal and accessary to these, are:

1. The easiness or lowness of interest in that country.
2. The great facilitating of their trade by a bank.
3. And last of all (the only thing proper to them) the dearness and scarcity of land; and the dividing their estates equally to their children; whereby trade is (as it were) continued in a line without interruption; the contrary being customary with us.

Animadversion

All which discourse being only an evidence given in from matter of known fact; it will (as is humbly conceived) manifest itself:

I. That our neighbours have no such extraordinary advantage in matter of trade, either through their country, its situation, or otherwise, as is proper or peculiar to them only, beyond all other nations (as hath been long the opinion of some), but it is the manner of their care, and of the government that is among them, and the mere vigilance over trade, that is observed by them. For if the nature of those courses, which they have taken and pursued for the encouragement of trade, be looked into and considered (as they are obvious to any other that will please to heed them), it cannot be imagined but they shall make any people great, rich, and flourishing in trade, that useth them; and therefore that they will do the like in any other place as well as in Holland, if put in execution, especially if it be a place, as this of ours is, seated for trade, and the people of the country apt for it . . .

35. INSTRUCTIONS FOR A JOURNEY
TO AFRICA, 1651

[E. Donnan, *Documents illustrative of the History of the Slave Trade to America, I, 1441–1700*, New York, 1965, pp. 126–8]

[The Guinea Company to James Pope]

London, the 17 September, 1651

Mr. James Pope.

Loving friend,

We desire you in the first place to perform your duty unto Almighty God that so we may expect a blessing from him upon your endeavours which God grant. You are to embark yourself upon the ship *Friendship*, Captain John Blake commander, and being dispatched from Gravesend you are to desire the said Captain Blake to hasten into the Downs and from thence with the first opportunity of wind and weather that God shall send to sail directly for the river of Gambra [= Gambia] in Guinea taking into your company the *James*, bound for Sierra Leone, and any other good ships that you shall there find; and when it pleaseth God you arrive in the river of Gambra, in the first place you are to set up your two barges with the two pinnaces, and having manned, victualled, and fitted the barges, you are immediately to send them away up the river with one or both of the small boats as you shall see occasion, to find out Mr. Langley with our letter directed unto him, leaving one factor at Baraconda by the way.

Upon this ship we have laden a cargo of goods and provisions as per invoice and bill of lading amounting unto £—— consigned unto you or your assigns, which we desire may be put off to our most advantage, for hides, wax, and teeth, gold, ambergris, or any other merchantable commodity you shall meet withal, disposing of our factors at several places as you shall see occasion, viz. Mr. Benjamin Clark, whom we conceive will be fitting to be our accountant for the receiving in or delivering out of the *Friendship* any goods, Richard Swan, who hath had experience for many years of the trade with negers and Portugals at Sierra Leone, him you may employ at any of your factories as you shall see convenient, Richard Dobb and Nicholas Bowles, all which factors you are to settle there except Mr. Clark who is to return for England upon the *Friendship* . . .

At your arrival upon the Coast you may stop at Refisco (= Rufisque or Rio Fresco) to give those people notice that you are coming upon the coast to trade and bound for Gambra, that if they will provide any goods you will deal with them. The like word you may send thence to Porto Dally and Joally[1] giving them notice of your arrival. The French aquavitae and most part of the crystal is not yet come. You may expect it by the pinnace *John*

---

[1] Portudal and Joal; i.e. the English had evidently settled factors both up the river and at the trading posts on the coast.

which we stay here to carry it after you, by whom we will write you and send you the invoice and bill of lading. For your trade in the river for wax, hides, and elephants' teeth, we desire you to cut the price at as low rate as you can to ease us what you may of the Also's[?] desiring you to procure as many hides, teeth, and wax as you can that the ship may be full laden, whereby to countervail our great charge of freight, victual, and wages, having a special regard that the hides be well cured and that they be well dried and beaten before you lade them aboard.

The two barges, etc. we desire may be dispatched with all expedition up to Mr. Langley as aforesaid, fitted and victualled with all things necessary, which, arriving with him, they are to be at his order and direction; and when it pleaseth God that Mr. Langley shall return in the *Friendship* we desire that he may have all due accommodation and respect from Captain Blake and yourself, taking a particular account of what gold he returneth, and to be safe put up in the iron chest which he hath with him, and if he bring down any mineral ore, sand, or earth in barrels, that they be also safely stowed in the ship until their arrival here, consigned here in London by bill of lading to us that sign your commission for the use of ourselves and the rest of the Adventurers in this new discovery, and in like manner for the hides, teeth, and wax, etc. that you shall lade aboard the *Friendship*. When God shall send Mr. Langley aboard the *Friendship* and bring us a comfortable return, our order is that you do with all expedition dispatch away the pinnace *John* for London with large advice that we may prepare against the next year timely both for the discovery and trade, and if anything be omitted in this our commission which you think may be for the good and benefit of our voyage, we leave it to your discretion to do therein as you shall see cause.

We desire you to settle a factory for us at the most convenient place to have command of that river. For what debts we have owing in the river of the last voyage by Francisco Vaz de Franca and Andreas Perdegon, etc. we desire may be recovered in and that you trust as little of our goods for the future as you can . . .

We pray you prohibit all private trade of the seamen or others what you can, forbidding all men the buying of hides, for we will have none laden aboard the *Friendship* but what is for our accompt. We pray you buy for us 15 or 20 young lusty negers of about 15 years of age, bring them home with you for London, laying in that country provisions for them as you shall see needful. Also bring a certificate home with you that the four butts of wine laden the last voyage in the *Dolphin* and the three pipes of wine now laden in the *Friendship* were all sold to Portugal merchants and others in the river of Gambra, putting your own name and some other of your men there unto the said certificate, which we pray you fail not to do . . .

We have not further to enlarge only praying the Almighty to bless you with life and health for a prosperous success upon our affairs, we rest

Your loving friends,

Row. Wilson; Maurice Thomson; John Woods.

36. INSTRUCTIONS TO THE EAST INDIA COMPANY'S AGENT VOYAGING VIA AFRICA TO INDIA, 1652

[Bodleian Library, Oxford, MS. Eng. Hist. c. 63,ff. 73–4. Correspondence of Nicholas Buckridge, agent for the East India Company at Gombroon, relating chiefly to Persian affairs, 1659–60]

COMMISSION and instructions given by us, the President and Council of India, Persia, etc. unto Mr. Nicholas Buckridge, bound to Cape Corinthes, coast of Suffola, Mozambique, or Millinda.

Our loving friend, Mr. Nicholas Buckridge,

By the encouragement we have received from you by what you relate unto us of a hopeful and beneficial trade that is to be procured about Cape Corinthes and other places upon the coast of Suffola [= Sofala], Mozambique, and Millinda, which being once thoroughly discovered may with the assistance of the Almighty prove very advantageous unto our honourable employers, we are induced once more to make trial of what it shall please the Lord to make you instrumental in the discovery of those parts, to the glory of his name, the honour of our nation, and benefit of our said employers, and for that purpose we have caused their pinnace Assada to be trimmed, victualled, and manned, and laden aboard her a cargo of goods to the import according to invoice delivered you, on which ship we would have you take your passage and as wind and weather shall permit sail unto the Cape Corinthes or any port or place thereabouts or to any port of place upon the coast of Suffola, Millinda, or Mozambique and there to discover, sell, barter, or exchange what goods soever you have on board for account of the honourable company with what people soever you shall encounter, and for what commodity you shall find amongst them, as gold, elephants' teeth, etc. which you know may be for their advantage, and with the same, with what convenient speed you may, return to this port of Surat to render an account to us, the president and council, of what you have effected in this same voyage.

And because we would not have your hopeful design in any way to be prejudiced by our strict injunction, we have left you free to go to what port or place in the above named parts you think good, and to trade with what kind of people soever you shall there find, and have likewise ordered the master of the said pinnace, Assada, to follow your order in sailing to such port as you shall advise, and there to stay until you shall order his departure; and so from port to port as you shall have occasion to direct and the ship may safely come, but withal we advise you not to come under command of any Portugal fortification, or trust yourselves with them more than necessity requires, neither part with any of your goods till you have satisfaction for it, or well secured to have it at such a time as you agree—as within four or five days or the like—but we would not have you in any place p[ut?] off goods to be paid the next year or when you shall return thither again or dispose of anything other than for present satisfaction, but rather return the goods again upon the ships with you . . .

Yet for your more security as the state of affairs now stand between us and the Dutch, we would have you to order your business that you may come to Augustine Bay before the arrival of any of the Europe ships, that by them you may be informed whether we have war or peace with the Dutch, and accordingly order yourself. If you find we have peace and they come so timely that you may gain the Cape of Guardefen by the 5th or 10th August, then you are to hasten thither and berth[?] yourselves to pass in the month of the Gulph that you may be ready to surprise any vessel belonging to Decan that hath not our pass. We send by you a letter to the commander of such ships as shall come out of Europe to that purpose, and for what money treasure or rich commodities they have on board, let it be seized on for your company's use, and let the vessel go again, giving them a receipt for what money you take from them. And take a note from them how much it is also, not suffering anything to be taken from them but what you shall register. But in case you should meet with no Europe ships either there or at Johanna before the 20th August, nor by other means be advised that we have peace with the Dutch, then endeavour to gain the coast of India and go into Bone Bay and there remain in case of war with the Dutch till further order from us. You have for your assistant one John Mudfatt, a servant of the company; as you find him capable and diligent, you may employ him, but we would have you instruct and advise him in what you see him wanting in that he may be the better able to do the company good service hereafter.

There is also Mr. Porter that came upon the Assada desiring to accompany you in this voyage, to which we have condescended and given him licence to carry with him two small bales of paupes[?] with this proviso that he deliver them into your hands to dispose of, and not to make sales of them until such goods as you have of the company be first put off. You will find him a rational man, and one that will stand you in some stead upon occasion, the consideration whereof induceth us to license him to voyage with you.

The like care you are to take of any other goods that are upon the ships to whomsoever they belong, that you suffer not any man to dispose of aught until you have first made sale of that belongeth to the company, and then if they have any small matter amongst them, let them in the name of God make the best of it, but see you so order the sale of it for them that they spoil not the trade we hope to have in the future, so hoping your endeavour will be in no way wanting in the improvement of this design to the most advantage. We commit you to the protection of the Almighty, praying for his blessing upon these your undertakings and a safe return unto

Your loving friends,

Jerr. Blackman; Edw. Pearce; Geo. Oxinden; Tho. Breton. Swally Marratte, the 12th December, 1652.

[Endorsed:] Commission to be observed by Mr. Nicholas Buckridge, dated the 12th December, 1652.

37. BENJAMIN WORSLEY ON FREE PORTS AS A MEANS TO IMPROVE TRADE, 1652

[R. W. K. Hinton, *The Eastland Trade and the Commonweal in the Seventeenth Century*, Cambridge, 1959, pp. 213, 215-18]

Free Ports,
The Nature and Necessity of them Stated
by Benjamin Worsley

... Arguments tendered to move this Nation to undertake the like general Mart, as hath the Hollander; drawn, first, from expectation of like benefit to us, that our neighbours have upon this accompt certainly gained to themselves, seeing this kind of trade would effectually conduce both to the increasing, and to the better distributing riches to this nation, than by that we now have; that is, if ports for landing and storing up foreign commodities, and exporting them again upon such easy duties, as we may hold the market in all other countries with our neighbours the Hollanders, may in all the fittest places of this Commonwealth be opened.

Secondly, it would tend as much also to the increasing the power and strength of this nation, both by land and by sea; as well in guarding and plentifully planting and peopling those maritime or frontier towns, and the countries thereabouts, which shall be appointed and allowed for free ports; as in multiplying the shipping of our country. A proof of which we have already had in Dover, which, after the composition trade was settled there (that made it in some kind a free port) did within ten years time arise from nothing to have near two hundred sail of pretty great shipping; with an increase of stock, houses, and all things answerable, although, having lost it now but near as long, it is quite decayed in all again.

More particularly, opening of free ports will conduce to the quickening of trade; to the employment of the poor throughout the whole Commonwealth: to the making of all foreign commodities more cheap, and more plentiful; seeing every man will bring in, when he knows he may (if he find no market here) freely carry it out again. It will likewise serve to the preventing of famine, and scarcity of corn; to the raising the exchange, and bringing in of bullion; to the augmenting of the revenue of the state: and to the making other nations more dependent upon this.

As a further inducement to all which, is offered to consideration the many advantages that this Commonwealth hath above our neighbours, the Hollanders (how much soever they have raised themselves by this art), for the putting in practice such an universal intercourse of traffic as is desired. As first, from the largeness of this Commonwealth's dominions, and number of our ports and harbours, above those of our neighbours.

Secondly, from the plenty of commodity we have from within ourselves, and from our own plantations; which alone, being now restrained to our own shipping, will afford a stock very great to begin with.

Thirdly, from the freedom and independency that our shipping have upon the ports of any other state, or nation; and the sovereignty we keep and maintain in our own channel. Whereas it is well known that our neighbours the Hollanders' ships, have not only a great, but a necessary relying upon the ports and protection of this Commonwealth; great fleets of their shipping continually being forced to put in, and for the most part to winter in our harbours, we in the mean time very seldom or rarely bearing into any foreign port for shelter.

Fourthly, from the privileges many of our ports have for being fitter outlets on any winds than those of our neighbours, and better situated for most trades, either southerly or northerly.

Lastly, from the boldness of our coast's safe and excellent roadsteads; and for being at all seasons free from being frozen in and stopped; whereas our neighbours have on the other side a flat and dangerous coast, barred and inconvenient harbours, and such as are, by reason of ice, shut up and useless for almost a third or fourth part of the year; which singular conveniencies or privileges coming to this nation so immediately from providence, are not altogether to be neglected.

The third consideration (although in some regard most principal to be weighed) is the inconveniencies we at present lie under from the trade we have; and the damages that will unavoidably grow upon us, if this trade only continue; for, first, the trade we now drive tends, or is only for consumption; it being very little of foreign commodities that is re-transported upon the present encouragement or settled rate of half custom.

For, though it may be objected, that look what tonnage, subsidy, or custom is paid upon foreign goods inwards, which are spent in the nation, is only disbursed for a while by the merchant, and at length really accompted for to the immediate buyer or spender; and that therefore this custom inwards, though it should be great, cannot destroy the merchant. Yet the case is, however, very different, and altogether otherwise in a tax or rate of half that custom set upon all the same unconsumed goods when carried outwards, specially if there was an overvaluing (as in many there is) of those goods inwards.

Seeing although it be said the other was paid by the nation (that is the custom inwards) upon all goods here spent; yet this custom outwards is solely taken from the purse of the merchant, and cannot be reimbursed to him again in other countries, especially when another foreign merchant shall carry the same commodity thither, and by paying less custom shall afford it cheaper; for then this tax outward must eat our merchant up by little and little, and put a discouragement upon him.

For example, the Hollander and we deal for spice, for wines, for sugar, indigo, silk, cotton, and for the manufacture of Spanish wool: all which (with other commodities) we fetch from the places of their growth or first production, in the respective shipping of each nation; for some of which commodities our merchants at coming in pay in custom, in impost, and by over-rating the commodity 10, 15, and in some things near 20 per cent which, if those goods were sold here, and spent in the Commonwealth, the merchant perhaps could not so much feel it (unless in a perishable and uncertain commodity, where he oft suffers) for he then rates his goods accordingly when he sells them.

But if he shall desire to transport again those goods into the Eastlands, into the Straits, or into any other places or countries where he knows they are wanted; though of this great custom he do receive the one half back again, yet if the Hollanders shall upon the same goods pay but 2 per cent custom, they have the advantage by this means before our merchant of 5, 6, or 8 per cent in their market (beyond sea), being clean so much loss as to our merchant, so to the nation, and to the employment of its shipping; this kind of outward trade being by this means at length wholly left off and deserted.

These two wholly differing in kind one from another; for a nation to deal or traffic in wares and merchandises for its own expense and consumption, as country gentlemen, or ordinary tradesmen; and for a nation to make itself a shop, and to buy and sell for the furnishing and provision of other nations; as a man that keeps a warehouse, or storehouse; which latter trade is that we speak of.

In regard that a nation, that only buys and trades to furnish itself, is confined to a stock, and such a stock as must not exceed its own expense or consumption; and the employment of shipping and returns of foreign goods must be still as confined, and limited answerably; and neither trade, nor shipping, nor stock are at utmost able to exceed the value of our native commodity exported. For if the liberty here of the merchant and people for trading and buying of foreign commodity should exceed our exportation, or the value thereof, and not rather be less than otherwise, it doth but tend more and more to the loss of our wealth, and to our decay and ruin.

Wherefore all consultations whatsoever about trade, if free ports be not opened, and this wholesale or general trade be not encouraged, do still but terminate in some advice or other about regulating our consumption; and have no other good at farthest, but preventional, that our balance of import exceed not our export: which to confine ourselves to alone, is, on the other side, a course so short, as it will neither serve to raise the strength of this nation in shipping, or to govern the exchange abroad; nor yet to avoid the damage and mischief the subtilty of the foreign merchant will hereby bring upon us.

Whereas if free ports be opened, and exportation of foreign goods encouraged, not only the mischief of the consumption and carrying out of our treasure, and of lowness of exchange, will most effectually be prevented, but both our stock and shipping will be indefinitely or proportionably increased.

Lastly, a great part of the revenue of the state is for want of this general trade clearly lost; for supposing free ports to be opened, we must grant there will be an access of wealth to the nation, and an increase to this Commonwealth by strangers.

And consequently, our consumption of foreign commodities will not be at all less, but more, and therefore the income or custom paid upon it. Over and above which, the state may have a custom or duty in a very short time of one per cent, upon the value of some millions of goods yearly, which now (by reason of the discouragements aforesaid) are carried into other parts, and for which they yet receive not one farthing.

38. THE ACCOUNT OF A MERCHANT IN THE SPICE TRADE, 1652

[Herefordshire County Record Office, Foley Collection, F/IV/AD/1. John Foley's Account Book, 1650–4[1]]

Tunis, July 1652

ACCOMPT of 301 sacks of seeds, viz. 180 sacks of annis, and 121 sacks of cummin seed, which were bought at Algier as per contra and now sold to Capt. Nicholas Terricke for account of the Interressents as per contra may appear the charges with cost as follows:

To prime cost of 301 sacks seeds qt. 659,88 at 5S per lb.	S3,299 20[2]	
To the contador @ 19½ per sack	112 45	
To canvas, pack, and thread	28 0	
To the Hamals 3 @ per sack	17 19	
To average 26 @ p vy°	27 0	
To consolage at Algier 2 per cwt.	65 50	
To provision and brokerage 4 per cwt.	142 11	
	3,692 30	
To freight from Algier to Tunis $1 per qt.	660	
To charges at Tunis for warehouse room	30	
Whole costs and charges which was received of Capt. Terricke per Mr. John Sandys	4,382 30	

Mr. Henry Hunt 12/32 parts of S4,382 30 is	S1,643	24	3
Mr. Hugh Norris 8/32 parts of S4,382 30 is	1,095	33	6
Mr. Jeffrey Howland 4/32 parts of S4,382 30 is	547	42	9
Mr. Roger Browne 2/32 parts of S4,382 30 is	273	47	4
Capt. Thomas Harman 5/32 parts of S4,382 30 is	684	40	6
Mr. Thomas Hughs 1/32 part of S4,382 30 is	136	49	8
	4,382	30	0

[1] John Foley was a member of the Levant Company.

[2] The *quintar* contained 42 *oakes* which was equivalent to 119 lbs avoirdupois. The account appears to be in piastres, aspers, and burburs: 1 piastre = 52 aspers; 1 asper = 12 burburs; S = piastre; @ = asper.

39. REFLECTIONS ON THE FREE PORT AGITATION, 1653

[Thomas Violet, *Mysteries and Secrets of Trade and Mint Affairs . . .*, London, 1653, pp. 5–6. University of London, Goldsmiths' Library Pamphlet, Cat. No. 1307.]

The Advancement of Merchandise

. . . If you will have trade flourish, give the same encouragements to merchants strangers here, as they have in Amsterdam, and other parts of Christendom; they have found that course to be thriving to them for many years, and themselves and the strangers that have planted amongst them to be both equally advantaged by it. And in France, Spain, Leghorn, Genoa, Poland, and many other places, where all strangers of what nation soever pay no more custom than the natives themselves; and this business had not been now to do, had it not been for the old farmers in the Custom House. About fourteen years ago I was employed by the late king to have settled it (when the business of silver, to be brought up to be coined from Dover, was concluded of). But I found my Lord Cottington and the old farmers against free ports, out of an opinion that Cottington ever had to be averse against any model of the Dutch, it savouring of a Commonwealth too much, and not being suitable to his designs, which was always for monarchy and the Spanish greatness. The old farmers I do verily believe were not against it out of any averseness or envy to the wealth of this nation's increase by a free trade, but for some other reasons, and some as I am confident were that upon letting in of a free trade, you would draw a great many merchants strangers in here, which are very prying and subtle men, men acquainted with managing the excise and customs in Holland, and they would presently discover that which they (the farmers) above all other things laboured to keep as a secret, which was the excessive gain every one of them made by the farm. Secondly, that upon new alteration in the model of the farm, there might come new undertakers, and so they might be disappointed of their money that they had advanced, which after upon another occasion fell out heavily upon them.

But sure I am, divers of the best merchants in London, and true lovers of this nation, have told me, and will justify it to be true, had I effected it to make free ports all over the nation fourteen years ago, the Commonwealth had got millions of money by it before this time; then you would have had many score of rich merchants up and down the ports of this nation, which would have managed trade, not as it hath been (the miscarriage, I fear me, hath in part been willingly, and requires a strict examination). But if you had made trade free, they would have kept stout men of war at sea, gone with convoys, being readier to offend than to take affronts at sea; which would have been highly for the honour of the nation, whose sad losses, most coming by disorder and the covetousness of some merchants, might have been all avoided, the losses, amounting within this twenty months to more than would have kept a convoy sufficient to defend all the trade of this nation for thirty years. If it be examined, I do verily believe, it is not the French that take these ships, but our own seamen, that serves them, and goes in by connivance . . .

40. THE NAVIGATION ACT, 1660

[Statutes of the Realm, V, pp. 246–50]

An Act for the Encouraging and Increasing of Shipping and Navigation

12 Car. II, cap. 18

F OR the increase of shipping and encouragement of the navigation of this nation, wherein under the good providence and protection of God the wealth, safety, and strength of this kingdom is so much concerned, be it enacted . . . that from and after the first day of December one thousand six hundred and sixty and from thence forward no goods or commodities whatsoever shall be imported into or exported out of any lands, islands, plantations, or territories to his Majesty belonging or in his possession, or which may hereafter belong unto or be in the possession of his Majesty, his heirs, and successors, in Asia, Africa, or America, in any other ships or ships, vessel or vessels whatsoever, but in such ships or vessels as do truly and without fraud belong only to the people of England or Ireland, dominion of Wales, or town of Berwick upon Tweed, or are of the built of and belonging to any of the said lands, islands, plantations, or territories as the proprietors and right owners thereof, and whereof the master and three-fourths of the mariners at least are English, under the penalty of the forfeiture and loss of all the goods and commodities which shall be imported into, or exported out of, any the aforesaid places in any other ship or vessel, as also of the ship or vessel with all its guns, furniture, tackle, ammunition, and apparel, one third part thereof to his Majesty, his heirs, and successors, one third part to the governor of such land, plantation, island, or territory where such default shall be committed, in case the said ship or goods be there seized, or otherwise that third part also to his Majesty, his heirs, and successors, and the other third part to him or them who shall seize, inform, or sue for the same . . . And all admirals and other commanders at sea of any the ships of war or other ship having commission from his Majesty, or from his heirs or successors, are hereby authorized and strictly required to seize and bring in as prize all such ships or vessels as shall have offended contrary hereunto, and deliver them to the Court of Admiralty, there to be proceeded against; and in case of condemnation, one moiety of such forfeitures shall be to the use of such admirals or commanders and their companies, to be divided and proportioned amongst them according to the

rules and orders of the sea in cases of ships taken prize, and the other moiety
to the use of his Majesty, his heirs, and successors.

II. And be it enacted, that no alien or person not born within the allegiance
of our sovereign lord the king, his heirs, and successors, or naturalized or
made a free denizen, shall from and after the first day of February which
shall be in the year of our Lord one thousand six hundred sixty-one[1] exercise
the trade or occupation of a merchant or factor in any the said places, upon
pain of the forfeiture and loss of all his goods and chattels, or which are in his
possession, one third to his Majesty, his heirs, and successors, one third to the
governor of the plantation where such person shall so offend, and the other
third to him or them that shall inform or sue for the same in any of his
Majesty's courts in the plantation where such offence shall be committed . . .

III. And it is further enacted . . . that no goods or commodities whatsoever
of the growth, production, or manufacture of Africa, Asia, or America, or of
any part thereof, . . . be imported into England, Ireland, or Wales, islands of
Guernsey or Jersey or town of Berwick upon Tweed, in any other ship or
ships . . .[2] under the penalty of the forfeiture of all such goods and commodities, and of the ship or vessel in which they were imported . . .

IV. And it is further enacted . . . that no goods or commodities that are of
foreign growth, production, or manufacture, and which are to be brought into
England, Ireland, Wales, the islands of Guernsey and Jersey or town of
Berwick upon Tweed in English-built shipping, or other shipping belonging
to some of the aforesaid places, and navigated by English mariners as abovesaid, shall be shipped or brought from any other place or places, country or
countries, but only from those of their said growth, production, or manufacture, or from those ports where the said goods and commodities can only
or are or usually have been first shipped for transportation, . . . under the
penalty of the forfeiture of all such of the aforesaid goods as shall be imported
from any other place or country contrary to the true intent and meaning
hereof, as also of the ship in which they were imported . . .

V. And it is further enacted . . . that any sort of ling, stockfish, pilchard, or
any other kind of dried or salted fish usually fished for and caught by the
people of England, Ireland, Wales, or town of Berwick upon Tweed, or any
sort of codfish or herring, or any oil or blubber made or that shall be made
of any kind of fish whatsoever, or any whale fins or whale bones which shall
be imported into England, Ireland, Wales, or town of Berwick upon Tweed,
not having been caught in vessels truly and properly belonging thereunto as
proprietors and right owners thereof, and the said fish cured, saved, or dried,
and the oil and blubber aforesaid (which shall be accounted and pay as oil)
not made by the people thereof, and shall be imported into England, Ireland
or Wales, or town of Berwick upon Tweed, shall pay double aliens' custom.

VI. And be it further enacted . . . that from henceforth it shall not be
lawful to any person or persons whatsoever to load or cause to be loaden and
carried in any bottom or bottoms, ship or ships, vessel or vessels whatsoever,

[1] 1661/2.   [2] As in section 1.

whereof any stranger or strangers born (unless such as shall be denizens or naturalized) be owners, part owners, or master, and whereof three-fourths of the mariners at least shall not be English, any fish, victual, wares, goods, commodities, or things of what kind or nature soever the same shall be, from one port or creek of England, Ireland, Wales, islands of Guernsey or Jersey, or town of Berwick upon Tweed to another port or creek of the same or of any of them, under penalty for everyone that shall offend contrary to the true meaning of this branch of this present Act to forfeit all such goods as shall be loaden and carried in any such ship or vessel, together with the ship or vessel . . .

VII. And it is further enacted . . . that where any ease, abatement, or privilege is given in the Book of Rates to goods or commodities imported or exported in English-built shipping, that is to say shipping built in England, Ireland, Wales, islands of Guernsey or Jersey, or town of Berwick upon Tweed, or in any the lands, islands, dominions, or territories to his Majesty in Africa, Asia, or America belonging or in his possession, that it is always to be understood and provided that the master and three-fourths of the mariners of the said ships at least be also English . . .

VIII. And it is further enacted . . . that no goods or commodities of the growth, production, or manufacture of Muscovy, or of any the countries, dominions, or territories to the great duke or emperor of Muscovy or Russia belonging, as also that no sorts of masts, timber or boards, no foreign salt, pitch, tar, rosin, hemp or flax, raisins, figs, prunes, olive oils, no sort of corn or grain, sugar, potashes, wines, vinegar, or spirits called aqua vitae, or brandy wine, shall from and after the first day of April which shall be in the year of our Lord one thousand six hundred sixty-one be imported into England, Ireland, Wales, or town of Berwick upon Tweed in any ship or ships, vessel or vessels whatsoever, but in such as do truly and without fraud belong to the people thereof or of some of them as the true owners and proprietors thereof, and whereof the master and three-fourths of the mariners at least are English; and that no currants nor commodities of the growth, production, or manufacture of any the countries, islands, dominions, or territories of the Ottoman or Turkish Empire belonging shall from and after the first day of September which shall be in the year of our Lord one thousand six hundred sixty-one be imported into any the forementioned places in any ship or vessel but which is of English built and navigated as aforesaid and in no other, except only such foreign ships and vessels as are of the built of that country or place of which the said goods are the growth, production, or manufacture respectively, or of such port where the said goods can only be, or most usually are, first shipped for transportation and whereof the master and three-fourths of the mariners at least are of the said country or place, under the penalty and forfeiture of ship and goods . . .

XIV. Provided also, that it shall and may be lawful to and for any of the people of England, Ireland, Wales, islands of Guernsey or Jersey, or town of Berwick upon Tweed, in vessels or ships to them belonging and whereof the master and three-fourths of the mariners at least are English, to load and bring in from any of the ports of Spain or Portugal or western islands, commonly called Azores or Madeira or Canary Islands, all sorts of goods or commodities of the growth, production, or manufacture of the plantations or dominions of either of them respectively.

XV. Provided that this Act or anything therein contained extend not to bullion, nor yet to any goods taken, or that shall be bona fide taken, by way of reprisal by any ship or ships belonging to England, Ireland, or Wales, islands of Guernsey or Jersey, or town of Berwick upon Tweed, and whereof the master and three-fourths of the mariners at least are English, having commission from his Majesty, his heirs, and successors . . .

XVIII. And it is further enacted . . . that from and after the first day of April which shall be in the year of our Lord one thousand six hundred sixty-one no sugars, tobacco, cotton wool, indigos, ginger, fustic, or other dyeing wood of the growth, production, or manufacture of any English plantations in America, Asia, or Africa shall be shipped, carried, conveyed, or transported from any of the said English plantations to any land, island, territory, dominion, port, or place whatsoever than to such other English plantations as do belong to his Majesty, his heirs, and successors, or to the kingdom of England or Ireland or principality of Wales or town of Berwick upon Tweed, there to be laid on shore, under the penalty of the forfeiture of the said goods or the full value thereof, as also of the ship . . .

XIX. And be it further enacted . . . that for every ship or vessel which from and after the five and twentieth day of December in the year of our Lord one thousand six hundred and sixty shall set sail out of or from England, Ireland, Wales, or town of Berwick upon Tweed for any English plantation in America, Asia, or Africa, sufficient bond shall be given with one surety to the chief officers of the custom house of such port or place from whence the said ship shall set sail, to the value of one thousand pounds if the ship be of less burthen than one hundred tons, and of the sum of two thousand pounds if the ship shall be of greater burthen; that in case the said ship or vessel shall load any of the said commodities at any of the said English plantations, that the same commodities shall be by the said ship brought to some port of England, Ireland, Wales, or to the port or town of Berwick upon Tweed, and shall there unload and put on shore the same, the danger of the seas only excepted; and for all ships coming from any other port or place to any of the aforesaid plantations who by this Act are permitted to trade there, that the governor of such English plantation shall before the said ship or vessel be permitted to load on board any of the said commodities take bond in manner and to the value aforesaid for each respective ship or vessel, that such ship or vessel shall carry all the aforesaid goods that shall be laden on board in the said ship to some other of his Majesty's English plantations, or to England, Ireland, Wales, or town of Berwick upon Tweed; and that every ship or vessel which shall load or take on board any of the aforesaid goods until such bond given to the said governor or certificate produced from the officers of any custom house of England, Ireland, Wales, or of the town of Berwick, that such bond have been there duly given, shall be forfeited; . . . and the said governors and every of them shall twice in every year after the first day of January one thousand six hundred and sixty[1] return true copies of all such bonds by him so taken to the chief officers of the custom in London.

41. INSTRUCTIONS TO THE COUNCIL FOR TRADE, SEPTEMBER, 1668

[P.R.O., SP 29/247, no. 15]

INSTRUCTIONS to our most dear and entirely beloved brother, James, Duke of York, our High Admiral of England, our right trusty and entirely beloved cousin, Prince Rupert, our right trusty and right well beloved counsellors, Sir Orlando Bridgman, knight and baronet, Lord Keeper of our Great Seal of England . . . [etc.], commissioners appointed by the commission annexed for the keeping of a control and superinspection upon the whole trade and commerce of this nation.

You are to take notice of the several advantages belonging to these three nations with respect to their improvement in manufacture. And to consider not only what manufactures are wanting in this nation and what means may most conduce to the invitation of them, but how the manufactures we already have and are possessed of may be best improved and may be truest, fullest, and most perfectly wrought according to the statutes in that case provided for the better honour and credit of this nation, and for the recovery again of the repute of the trade of it abroad in foreign countries.

And to this end you are also to consider of the said several statutes and of the directions therein contained and how the said statutes are executed and observed at present and rightly to inform yourselves of the several powers and trusts committed by the said statutes or by any of our grants to such officers as are by the law of this land to take the care and oversight of any part of the said manufactures in any respect and in what manner they discharge their respective duties therein. That if any abuse or inconveniences have grown to the public through the neglect, fraud, or corruption of the said officers, their ministers, servants, or deputies, a stop may speedily be put to it and the said inconveniencies arising to the public may be removed.

You are to consider as far as you may how the trade and manufacture of this nation may most fitly and equally be distributed to all and every the parts of it, to the end that if possible one part may not abound with trade and another remain poor and distressed for want of it.

You are to consult of the most convenient ways for expediting and facilitating the carriage of all manner of commodities by land or by water, either within any part of this his Majesty's dominions, or from beyond the seas, and

---

[1] 1660/1.

to advise how the said respective commodities may be conveyed with least expense and with the greatest profit and advantage to this nation.

To which end you are to consider what sort of vessels may be most fit for the management of each trade, and especially for the import or transport of the most gross and bulky commodities, and where the said vessels may be easiest and cheapest built; as also to consider what rivers would most conduce to the promotion of trade if made more navigable, and what havens or ports are decayed, that, being restored, would render them and the trade of them more useful to us and to the nation.

You are to consider how the several manufactures and commodities of these kingdoms may be uttered to their best advantage abroad in foreign countries, and how the abatement and undervaluing of their price may be best prevented, and how any imprudence or disorderliness that hath been practised among the merchants or their factors herein may most effectually be suppressed and remedied.

You are likewise thoroughly to weigh and consider the ends, grounds, and motives for erecting the several companies and societies of merchants that are now standing, or for the abolishing and neglecting of such others as have been heretofore thought fit to be laid aside. And how the ends and pretences for the making and incorporating any of the said societies have been really pursued, what the inconveniencies are that you manifestly find our experience declares to attend a free trade without the said societies, or what complaints tending to the encroachments of the privileges of the said societies upon the just liberties and rights of others do appear before you, with the proofs on either side, that, upon a due and mature consideration of the whole, every trade be so distinctly settled that nothing to the general detriment and harm of the nation may, either under the colour of companies or pretence of free trade, be really permitted or countenanced.

You are in like manner as oft as occasion shall require to consider of the powers and constitutions granted by statute or otherwise to the several corporations of handicraftsmen within this nation, together with the bylaws and customs made by the said corporations, under pretence of the said powers, to the end that if any of the said powers, customs, or bylaws be found manifestly inconvenient to the public they may be redressed, and such other order taken therein as may be most convenient.

You are very strictly to enquire and diligently to inform yourselves what ways and by what usual methods, practices, or sleights the wool of this nation comes to be stolen, embezzled, and sent abroad into foreign parts, raw and unmanufactured, contrary to the law and statutes in that case provided; what places, ports, havens, or creeks, are most suspected for, or most propable [sic] to give an opportunity to the said fraud in England or elsewhere, and who they are that, dwelling near the said places or creeks, are observed most to trade in or buy up the said wools, to the end that nothing of care or watch may be omitted but all such strict and severe courses may be taken, that an evil so mischievous and inconvenient to this nation may be totally prevented.

You are to consider of the great craft of fishing, not only upon this coast and the coast of Ireland, but upon the coasts of Scotland, Jutland, Iceland, Greenland, Newfoundland, and New England, with what other places or countries you are informed may be fit and convenient for the same. And you are particularly to examine what decay hath been observed of the said fishing for this last twenty years in any of the said places, with the reasons, grounds, or occasions of it, and to deliberate upon all such ways and means as shall be offered to you or shall be conceived most effectual by you for encouraging and restoring the said craft and increasing the number of seamen through it.

You are to take into your consideration the several plantations of this nation in America, as well those upon the Continent as those upon the Islands of the Chariblees or elsewhere, and to inform yourselves of the value of the trade of them and how far they have of late years increased or decreased in the said trade. You are likewise to advise how the said plantations may be further promoted and how the commodities of them may be best improved and regulated and advanced, so as that this kingdom may from the said plantations alone, if possible, be supplied with all those commodities (whatsoever they be) that other countries lying in the same climate do afford.

You are to enquire and inform yourselves what foreign trades this nation hath formerly had, which are now lost, as also to satisfy yourselves as far as you may of the grounds and means whereby the same came to be occasioned and what may be the most probable ways for the gaining and restoring of them.

You are to examine the several articles of peace and commerce that are at present in force between us and any other foreign prince or state whatever, to the end that all such privileges as have been granted to the benefit, freedom, and advantage of our merchants in any country may not only be the more carefully upheld and better performed, but as far as is possible drawn into precedent for other countries. And that all such clauses, restrictions, or provisions as tend to the manifest injury or any other way to the prejudice and obstruction of our trade may be represented to us for our princely care and cognizance to it.

You are to consider and advise how and where free ports for landing and storing up of all foreign commodities imported without paying more than some small duty or acknowledgement to us (provided they be within competent time again exported and in the mean time no way embezzled, altered, or diminished) may be best erected or appointed within any port of this our kingdom. And how the said privileges may be so carefully effected and so cautiously limited as that all merchants, strangers and foreigners as well as natives, may be encouraged, and yet no damage or prejudice may accrue to us in the revenue that is settled.

You are therefore prudently to consider and deliberate what extraordinary customs, impost, taxes, or excise may best and most for the advantage of this nation be put upon some, or eased on other commodities, for the better preventing either the excess of superfluity and expense of the nation, or for the greater encouragement of our own manufactures.

You are also carefully to enquire and inform yourselves what new and extraordinary imposts, duties, or taxes are by the vigilance of any of our neighbours or by any other prince or state in enmity with us, put upon any of our manufactures and native commodities within their respective dominions to the prejudice, hindrance, or discouragement of the sale and export of them. And whether the said duties, taxes, or imposts are not contrary to the articles of peace or commerce respectively in force between them and us. And what course you shall upon the whole judge most expedient either to remove the said taxes again or to provide against the evil and inconvenience of them.

You are, as there shall be occasion, to take into consideration the coin of this nation with the advantage or disadvantage coming of the exchange into or from other foreign parts. You are also to consider the consequences of the commutation of our gold into the bullion or plate of other countries or of our bullion or plate into gold, with the causes and grounds of the plenty of either of those species at some times above the other, and the methods usually practised by the goldsmiths or others to effect the said plenty or scarcity of either of the said species respectively, with the rates that are most fit, that the said species of coin should from time to time hold proportionably the one to the other, a due, careful, and circumspect respect being had to the mints and valuations of our neighbours about the same matter.

You are likewise prudently to consult and deliberate what the conveniencies or inconveniencies may be to us or to the nation by a free permission of the export of all manner of coin and bullion or by a yet more strict and severe prohibition of it, with what ways or courses shall upon the whole appear most advisable to you both for the preservation and increase of the coin of this nation.

You are seriously to consider of the interest of money both in these and in our several neighbouring countries, with the difference respectively of it in each state or kingdom about us, what influences or consequences the same may have upon trade, or how or which way appearing, to the end all circumstances being daily weighed and compared together, you may be able to propound what rate of interest may be best and most practical as well as most advisable for the nation, as also what courses by erecting of banks or otherwise may be most effectual for the easiest, cheapest, and readiest of furnishing of money.

You are to consider how a due and exact account may be kept of all the commodities exported from or imported into any of the ports or custom houses of this nation to the end that a perfect balance of trade may be taken, and that we may have a thorough inspection how the commodity or consumption of this nation increaseth or decreaseth, and that we may give such orders thereupon as to us in our princely wisdom shall be thought meet.

You are further yearly to take account from all parts what shipping or vessels belong to each port or haven within this kingdom and of what burden and force each vessel or ship is and for what places generally employed. And are likewise to examine whether the said vessels or ships are fewer or more in any of the said respective harbours or ports than they have been within the last thirty or forty years, with the cause of their respective increase or decay, to the end that the method being also for the future observed, we may have a perfect and exact account not only of the strength of the nation by sea but of the increase or decay of our navigation.

You are to give all possible encouragement to all such persons as shall offer anything about any of the aforesaid particulars that shall tend to the public benefit, good, and advantage of this nation. And you are from time [to time] to deliver your opinions and conclusions concerning the matters contained in these present instructions in writing under your respective hands with the reasons or grounds moving you to the said opinion or conclusion. And you are to present the same to us to do thereupon as in our royal wisdom shall seem fit.

You shall pursue such further instructions concerning the premises as shall from time to time be given you by us under our sign manual.

42. THE HAMBURG COMPANY LEGISLATES AGAINST UNFREEMEN, 1669

[University of London, Goldsmiths' Library, MS. 402.]

Hamburg the 26th Januarii, 1668.

For the remedying the great disorders which the company at Dordrecht have certified us they find amongst several of our members both at London and in the north in employing unfreemen to buy and ship off woollen manufactures for them, and also in buying all sorts of cloth for strangers and interlopers, we have found it necessary to pass these following orders:

First that all woollen manufactures which shall be found to have been shipped off from any parts of England into the parts of the company's privileges by any person or persons but such as are members of the company shall be looked upon as mis-shipped and proceeded against accordingly.

Secondly, that no member of the company shall buy in England any woollen commodities for unfreemen, natives or foreigners, to be sent into the company's privileges beyond the seas, upon the penalty of £50 sterling for the first offence, £100 sterling for the second offence, and so *toties quoties* they shall be found to have offended. And in case any member of the company shall entertain commissions to buy in those woollen manufactures for unfreemen, they are to take care and security that those woollen commodities shall not be transported into the parts of the company's privileges beyond the seas, for that we have now resolved and ordered that for all goods so bought, which shall be found to have been sent into the company's privileges, the members of the company who shall be discovered to have bought in those goods shall be in the Broke for mis-shipping.

Lastly, we have ordered that no member of the company shall in the future presume to employ unfreemen to buy in woollen manufactures for them in England for that we have resolved to be very strict in levying the penalties of 15 per £100 according to the ancient order in that case made and provided.

Endorsed:] Orders made by the company at Hamburg the 26th January 1668 besides the order at same time for taking the martly oath.

43. WOOL SMUGGLING ON THE KENT COAST, 1669

[House of Lords Record Office, Main Papers H.L., 19 October, 1669]

EXPERIENCE of the officers of Dover of the difficulties in prosecuting the transporters of wool.[1]

1. That they cannot resist the force that is used in conveying it aboard for there are such numbers that accompany it with clubs and weapons that they are not able to resist them.

2. That the troops of horse are of little or no use as quartered about Canterbury nor indeed anywhere else unless they were divided into small parties in every village along the coast and kept constant watch and patrols every night.

3. That boats by sea are as ineffectual for these wool stealers are so guided by lights and signs from the shore that they will defeat the industry of the most diligent persons that can be set to catch them.

4. If they be in danger to be taken they throw out all the wool into the sea and then no proof can be made that they had wool in them to punish the men or forfeit the boat.

5. If the wool be taken on land with all imaginable circumstances of transportation, the owners will bring some persons to swear that positively it was designed for another place and use and defeat the informer, a plain instance whereof was yesterday in the Exchequer Court and at several other times, which the officers can make out in particulars, showing how they are totally discouraged to prosecute any further in this matter.

6. The Act of Parliament is defective in the forfeiture of the boats, that it is a most difficult and almost impossible thing to forfeit any boat though known to be a common wool carrier.

(The officers present will speak to particulars if required.)

[Endorsed:] Information of the officers of Dover concerning transporting of wools etc., Dec. 1669.

---

[1] This document accompanies the draft of an Act to prevent frauds in exporting wool, wool fells, etc.

44. A LOAN TO A YOUNG BRISTOL
MERCHANT, 1669

[Patrick McGrath, *Merchants and Merchandise in Seventeenth-
Century Bristol*, Bristol Rec. Soc., XIX, 1955, p. 23]

12 March 1669

Whereas I Humphry Creswicke of the City of Bristol, merchant, am
now bound beyond the seas, and wanting conveniences for my setting forth,
viz: apparel, diet, etc. did desire my brother, Francis Creswicke, to furnish
me with the sum of sixty pounds, and for the better securing my said brother,
I do now promise to give him a discharge, if required, when come to the age
of twenty and one years, and the receipt of the said sixty pounds I do hereby
acknowledge, and that as part of the legacy left me by my grandmother,
Cicely Hooke, in witness whereof, I have hereto put my hand and seal this
twelfth day of March 1668/9.

Humphry Creswicke[1]

In the presence of Nath. Haggatt, Dan. Pym.

45. A CRITIQUE OF THE NAVIGATION
ACTS, 1668–71[?][2]

[Bodleian Library, Oxford, MS. Rawlinson A 478, ff. 88–9]

THE Act of Navigation which was made by the Long Parliament forbids any
but English ships sailed by English masters and mariners to trade to the
plantations, and left such ships at liberty to transport their sugars, etc. to
what market they pleased, so that the ships were usually fraught with the
commodities of the growth of England or some other part of Europe, the
which they carried to the plantations and sold, and some of these ships took
in a lading of sugar and went into the Straits, or France, Holland, or Hamburg and there sold it and then invested their effects in the growth of those
countries and brought it home for England so that the Straits, France,
Hamburg, and Holland, were furnished with sugars at as cheap a rate as the
English, who are the best planters in the world, could make it and live by it,
by which Brasil who had great impositions upon its sugar was reduced from
sending 70,000 chests of sugar annually unto Europe unto less than 20,000,
for many planters there gave over making of sugar, finding the charge to
exceed the profit and France and Holland finding their markets supplied at a

---

[1] Seals attached.

[2] An inscription on the flyleaf of this volume describes it as the manuscript of William
Bridgeman, esq., clerk of the Privy Council in the reign of James II. This document,
however, is one of a group concerned with the profits from sugar gained by English, French,
and other planters and merchants during the years 1668–71. See, for example, f. 63, 'The
State of the Case of the Sugar Plantations in America', endorsed 1670.

cheap rate by the English had no thoughts of increasing or making new sugar plantations in the West Indies for, there being a great charge and stock required in the settling of a new plantation, no man could find profit in the doing of it so that the English nation was in a very fair way of becoming sole masters of the manufacture of sugar which would have been to the very great advantage of the trade and navigation of this kingdom.

The Act of Navigation that was made since his Majesty's restoration commands the bringing the growths of all the plantations directly for England and there to unload and land them. A great part of this sugar, etc. is transported into the Straits, France, Holland, and Germany. The usual price of Muscovados sugar at London is 30s. per hundred which clears not above 16 or 17 to the importer or planter, and that rate do the merchants give for it that transport it so that considering the charge in shipping, fraught, the new hazard, and the time a man is out of his money, added to 30s. the first cost, it must yield 40s. in the market to which it is transported, or the transporter will have no consideration for his adventure, so that it plainly appears that a 100lb. of sugar, which yields the English planter 16 or 17s., will yield 40s. to the Dutch planter, and by reason of 2 livres custom in France more upon foreign sugar than upon French, 43s. 6d. to the French planter, which considering that sugar is the money of the plantations and is of more or less value in exchange against the necessaries for life and planting at the price it yields in the market to which it is transported, makes sugar-making above three times as profitable to the French and Dutch planter as it is to the English, which hath very much encouraged their planting of sugar in the West Indies, for when this last Act of Navigation was made, the French made sugar only on half of St. Christophers and the Dutch none at all. Since the making of this Act the French have increased their making of sugar upon St. Christophers and filled Martinico and Guadeloupa with sugar works, and have begun to plant in Granados, St. Crus, and Marigallent and Cayan, and the Dutch that had none before have now Barbitias, de Sa Cube, and Barouma upon the main planted with sugar and had Statia, Satia, and Tobago Islands, that were in a very flourishing condition of making sugar when they were taken and destroyed by the English, and now have the addition of Surinam, which was formerly a hopeful English colony, so that it is by all men, who have inspected the West India affairs, believed that the French who have liberty to transport their sugars to any market will within these three or four years not only supply France with all the sugar it wants but supply other markets also that formerly bought of the English, and in a few years the Dutch will do the same. So that it plainly appears that without the enlargement of the Act of Navigation the Dutch and French will wholly beat the English out of the sugar trade in the Straits, Holland, France, and Germany, by underselling them, and being of late, as well by this Act as through the imprudent management or misfortunes of the late governors of the English, increased treble in their proportion of number and strength in these parts and like to increase more daily by the coming of their colonies, not only of more men from France and Holland, but also from the English plantations, many of whose inhabitants are already gone to live amongst them and many more induced by profit and forced by uneasiness about to do the same, so that if some sudden and effectual remedy be not applied, it will be in a short time in the power of the French and Dutch, who are increasing, to turn the English, who are daily decreasing in the number of their defendants, out of their possessions to the utter loss of the plantations and the sugar trade to this nation.

Now let us consider what advantage the confirming all the growth of the plantations to be brought to England is to this nation. It decreaseth the employment of our shipping and increaseth that of our neighbours, for the commodities which foreigners have out of England are tin, lead, woollen manufacture, sugar, and tobacco. The three first are stored in a little room, sugar and tobacco are bulky and these in the time of the first Act of Navigation were, in English ships, sailed by English masters and mariners, carried from the plantations directly into Holland, France, and Germany, and those ships took in the growths of those countries and brought them into England at cheaper rates than their own ships could do, considering they could have no freight back, the bulky commodities being as aforesaid carried to them. But now the ships of Holland and Hamburg bring their own commodities to us and go back again laden with sugar and tobacco all which was formerly performed by English ships.

The only advantage that is brought to the nation by the confirming the growth of the plantations to be brought into England is that for the present it adds about 10,000*l.* per annum to the customs; the growth of the plantations have formerly amounted to in yearly value about 800,000*l.* whereof the value of 400,000*l.* may be spent in the nation, the other 400,000*l.* is transported to foreign markets; that which is transported hath one half of the custom paid back, the remainder amounts to 6*d.* in the lb. which of 400,000*l.* is 10,000 exactly, and for this inconsiderable sum if continued are apparently to be lost the advantages following which the plantations bring to this nation:

1. By the goods exported for their supply and their growths imported for the use of the nation they bring a considerable revenue to his Majesty's custom house.

2. They have formerly employed 400 ships annually; the Barbados alone in the seven preceding years before the arrival of Francis Lord Willoughby have employed 2,257 sail of ships as the records of that island will make appear.

3. That which is more than all the rest the plantations do furnish this nation with 800,000*l.* per annum value of native commodities produced from the earth by the labour of its people, without costing one penny of this nation's bullion, and a very inconsiderable quantity of those commodities that are vendible to the people of other nations, and this treasure keeps the great wheel of trade going which without it must stop and decay. For it is the opinion of the most experienced and ingenious merchants of this nation that

the exportation and importation of this nation are by the decay of our woollen manufactures upon a balance. So that if England have three millions of native commodity to export, she wants three millions of the growths of other countries, but if this 800,000*l.* per annum the plantations furnish should be lopped off, it is apparent she must export some of her bullion annually to fetch in those commodities she wants or not import so much by 800,000*l.* per annum as formerly, whereby his Majesty by the present saving of 6*d.* in the pound of 400,000*l.* in value of the growths of the plantations exported will by the continuance not only lose that but by the total loss of the plantations will come to lose the customs of 800,000*l.* per annum, that pays it may be 18*d.* in the pound, which amounts to 60,000*l.* per annum, and by the loss of an employment of 400 sail of ships and 8,000 seamen annually take off so much of the number of English ships and seamen and add them to the Dutch and French or to which of those two nations into whose hands the sugar trade shall fall, which will make them 800 sail of ships and 16,000 seamen stronger upon the balance than they were formerly.

[Endorsed:] The last Act of Navigation, how destructive to the plantations and they how beneficial to this nation.

46. AN OPINION OFFERED TO THE COUNCIL OF TRADE ON THE ADVANTAGES OF TRADE WITH THE PLANTATIONS, 1671[?]

[Bodleian Library, Oxford, MS. Rawlinson A 478, ff. 65–8.]

My Lord,

In order to acquit my engagement to your lordship to propound something for the reforming of our trade that might be acceptable to the nation as to his Majesty, and to confirm the opinion I made bold to deliver your lordship that there was nothing in trade now left us that was either so valuable or so capable of being improved by us as that of our plantations, I shall with all humbleness submit the considerations following to your lordship's most accurate judgement . . . and shall in the first place crave leave to reflect upon the peculiar advantages which this nation hath by the trade of our plantations above any other.

Not only in common with all other trades as by the increasing this trade we do necessarily increase the customs of the nation and the number and strength of our shipping, which we may be said to do equally by all trades even by our Newcastle or coal trade, but as our plantations have several things besides of extraordinary convenience attending them, which no other trade else hath and which therefore makes the concern of them to be far more highly considerable to this nation, seeing no trade can be had with any other countries but both the trader and the trade itself is subject necessarily to all such laws, rules, impositions, and restrictions in the said trade as the government of that country . . . shall for its own interest think fit to lay upon it, whereas in our own plantations, the trade being wholly in his Majesty's dominions, it is subject to no other law or imposition than what shall upon due deliberation be thought best for the public weal of the nation, nor can any that are foreigners trade at all in them without leave first had from his Majesty which his Majesty, having prudently thought fit to debar them of by this means, by how much the greater his trade is and by how much the more employment it affords, by so much the more benefit appropriated to ourselves exclusive to others; for none being capable of having any commerce in the said plantations beside ourselves, the freight both outward and homeward of all the whole trade, be it never so great, is still within ourselves which is evident.

2ndly. In all other trades we carry but little of our manufacture out beside our drapery, and but rarely much of foreign commodity, whereas in our trade to the plantations we carry not only all sorts of iron, brass, tin, and leaden manufactures with several others of leather, silk, and woollen, but all sorts of provisions and drink and all other necessaries, which we cannot with any profit carry into other countries, nor do we carry much less of foreign commodity than of our own, and all with equal encouragement to the merchants, so that though our own consumption at home tends indeed to the impoverishing of us, yet the consumption of our plantations abroad, by how much the greater and more prodigal they are, serves not only to the enriching of our merchants and seamen but the enriching generally of all sorts of our tradesmen in England, which is manifest no other trade whatsoever besides doth.

3rdly. In all other trades by how much the more valuable the commodities are that we return, and by how much the more we do import of them, by so much the more we do usually consume of our own wealth, and by over-balancing our trade do lessen and decrease the stock and treasure of the nation, whereas in the trade of our plantations, by how much the more valuable the commodities are which are produced there, and by how much the greater quantity it is that we import of them, by so much the more we do not only ease of our bullion and expense at home, but by exporting the commodities abroad into foreign parts again, we do further increase the balance of our trade, and make a recompense for that consumption of foreign commodity which, being so great as it is, would unavoidably otherwise be a ruin to us. And this, my Lord, is yet the more considerable because, if an account be taken of the customs of all our foreign import for this last twenty years, and this be compared with our export (excluding our plantation trade) the latter will be found so much short of the former that it will evidently appear to your lordship and to any that will examine it that this nation must long since have totally sunk (the decay of our drapery for this last twenty or thirty years considered) had not the providence of God by supplying about the same time a new trade and acquisition from our plantations

most remarkably preserved it. And this I . . . the more particularly mention
. . . not only because what is here asserted is capable of being easily examined,
but because, if found to be true, it discovers an affair of very great consequence
to the government: viz. that the plantations considered in their present state
do not more, if so much, depend upon the interest of England as the interest
of England doth now depend upon them. For if the balance of our trade can
now no way possibly be preserved or kept up without them, it is not only
manifest how much we stand in need of them and how incapable we are at
present to subsist without the trade of them, but equally manifest the very
interest of this nation and of the trade of it is now changed and vastly different
from what it was forty years since.

For whereas then our woollen manufactures were so great that we supplied
not only by Hamburg with other of the Hanse towns thereabouts, and by
these furnished Saxony with other parts of Germany lying upon the Elbe
as far as Silesia, but further accommodated all the eastern countries of Denmark, Sweden, Prussia, Poland, Russia, etc. and, besides all these, furnished
yearly Holland itself who then traded up into the Rhine and other parts
chiefly with our own manufactures, and whereas during the war between
Holland and Spain we had the trades of Spain and Portugal wholly and the
trade of Italy and Turkey also near entire ourselves, few of the Dutch then
comparatively trading in these parts, unless under the convoy of the English,
and that by both these advantages which we had above any other nation, we
had not only a stock and revenue suitable, but such a surplus as did greatly
overbalance our expense.

Since that time so it is, my Lord, that the decay of our manufactures hath
been on the other hand so extreme, as that we now do not furnish a third part
so much of cloth into any of the countries above named with respect to what
we then did; and our trade into Spain and the Straits since the general peace
of Münster and our breach with that country coming now to be common and
the Dutch by both these advantages and carrying a great share of the foreign
freight from us being grown into a stock of money and trade above us, and
being able, through the greatness of this stock, to bring down the interest of
money much beneath us as they are by these steps manifestly risen in their
trade, and we sensibly grown to a decay in our stock and our trade; so speaking
rationally of things, nothing offers itself to view by which we may recover our
trade again, if we shall pursue the same methods of trade now that we have
formerly been accustomed to.

For as we cannot propound to ourselves now so much as a probable way
ever to regain our manufactures (at least not within the compass of an age), so
this being so much lost as it is, we cannot without sumptuary laws (which
generally alarm other nations that are about us and, by minding them to
follow the same precedent, do in the end hurt us) ever hope our manufactures
and native commodities should balance the greatness of our consumption and
expense, and consequently must of necessity think of some way how elsewhere we may be able to supply it; wherefore if to supply the defect of our

manufactures there cannot in a way of trade anything visibly be propounded, unless by the acquisitions which we now have through the trade and benefit our plantations as it must cast the consideration of your lordship the more fixtly and intently upon them, and upon the improvement of the trade of them, so the absolute necessity that we have now to do this will easily demonstrate that the interest of England in the trade of it is changed and that we cannot pursue it aright by the same measures and methods which we have formerly taken of it.

[4thly.] In other trades as some parts of England do live more conveniently than the rest for driving them, so doth the stock also, for the said trades lie in a few hands in comparison of others inasmuch as little or no trade to the Baltic sea from Bristol, Plymouth, or other parts of the west; little fishing is in some parts of England in comparison of what is in some other parts; little or no trade in Guinea, Barbary, Italy, Turkey, or the East Indies but what is driven in companies only.

None of which inconveniencies are properly in the trade of our plantations, seeing shipping doth not only go thither from London but from Weymouth, Dartmouth, Plymouth, Bristol, and all other parts of the west country. Neither is their trade stinted to any company but all his Majesty's subjects, whether in England or Ireland, may without any special licence trade thither if they will, so that the trade of our plantations doth not as some other trades swell one part of the kingdom and make all the rest feeble and lean, but is a trade that far more equally distributes itse[lf] into all the parts of these nations, than any or all the trade we have besides.

5ly. And this is done the easier also because in all other trades we are forced to seek out such men as have been abroad and as have acquired the knowledge of other foreign languages to be factors [to] us because such only as are so acquainted are capable of being employed in those places by us, whereas in the trade of our plantations, there being no such need, every man is left in greater latitude to send whom he will so he be fit for the business that he trusts him in, and though he have no other language than his own which is a great advantage . . .

Whereas the trade of all other countries, how many so ever we trade among, can at most but increase our shipping or our treasure, this trade of our plantations doth not only increase both these equally, but with the increase of itself increaseth also the limits of our dwelling; adding as it increaseth not only the trade of one climate after another to us, but joining the countries themselves and the inheritance of them as well as their trades to these his Majesty's territories and dominions; and by adding the inheritance of them, laying a just foundation for the making them in every age an affair of state and of far greater care, weight, and import, therefore, to the Crown than others and now much more than they were in their infancy when they first began.

And indeed, my lord, if no nation were ever observed to compass any great thing in trade that did not make it an affair essential to their government, it is much the more to be feared we shall scarce ever do anything effectually for the regaining our trade and strength by sea through our plantations, if having so many reasons to mind them above any other trade that is now left us, we shall notwithstanding relinquish the care of them to chance or suffer the trade of them to be managed as it will manage itself, without taking any steady or formed councils for the governing and regulating of it . . .

47. THE MONOPOLY OF THE EASTLAND COMPANY THREATENED, 1673

[House of Lords Record Office, Main Papers H.L., 28 March, 1673]

To the Right Honourable the Lords Spiritual and Temporal assembled in Parliament, the humble petition of the governor, assistants and fellowship of Eastland merchants.

SHEWETH that the petitioners are informed that a bill is brought up from the honourable House of Commons touching the fishing and plantation trade, in the close whereof without any dependence on the rest of the bill it is expressed that for encouragement of the Eastland trade liberty is granted to all persons, natives, and foreigners, to trade to Sweden, Denmark, and Norway, which, instead of promoting that trade (at first gained out of the hands of strangers by a regulation), will be a means to deprive the English totally both of that trade and shipping.

That the interest of the Eastland Company is also greatly concerned in the said clause, the same having a tendency to the infringement of their rights and privileges granted by his Majesty and his royal progenitors. And the petitioners, humbly hoping they have sufficient reasons to offer to your lordships against the said clause and for preserving the trade under the present regulation, they therefore humbly pray that before the said clause be passed the petitioners may be heard by their counsel at the bar of this honourable House and admitted to shew their reasons for laying aside the said clause.

And they shall every pray, etc.

Ri: Chiverton, governor.

[Endorsed:] The humble petition of the Company of Eastland merchants, 28 March, 1673

48. A BILL OF ADVENTURE IN A VOYAGE TO THE EAST INDIES, 1674

T. Blount, *The Several Forms of Instruments relating to the Affairs of Merchants and Traders, very useful for Scriveners in London and other Maritim Towns and Places of Trade*, London, 1674, pp. 210–11]

A Bill for Money in a Voyage to the East Indies

To ALL, etc. I A.B. of London, etc. do send greeting. Whereas I the said A.B. do intend by God's grace to make a voyage unto the East Indies in the good ship called the Pearl of London, being now thither bound, whereof is master under God C.D. And whereas E.F. of, etc. the day of the date hereof hath paid and delivered unto me the said A.B. the sum of fifty pound of lawful monies of England, whereof I do hereby acknowledge the receipt, the adventure of which said fifty pound, the said E.F. is content and agreed to bear and stand to out and home.

Now know ye, that I the said A.B. do covenant and grant, for me, mine executors, and administrators to and with the said E.F., his executors, administrators, and assigns, by these presents, that I the said A.B., my executors, administrators, or assigns, shall and will dispose, convert, and employ, the said fifty pound to and for the best and most benefit and advantage of the said E.F., his executors, administrators, or assigns, according to the best of my skill and knowledge in the said voyage.

And also that I the said A.B., mine executors, administrators, or assigns, within thirty days after my return from the said voyage, or the arrival and discharge of the said ship within the port of London, which shall first happen, shall not only give and deliver unto the said E.F., his executors, administrators, or assigns, a just and true accompt of the disposition and management of the said adventure; but also truly pay and deliver, or cause to be paid and delivered unto the said E.F., his executors, administrators, or assigns, all such money and proceed as shall by the foot of the said accompt appear to be due and coming to him the said A.B., his executors, administrators, or assigns.

In witness, etc.

49. THE FORM OF A BILL OF BOTTOMRY, 1674

[Ibid., pp. 214–16]

The Form of a Bill of Bottomry

To ALL, etc. I A.B., owner and master of the good ship, called the I. of London, of the burthen of one hundred tons, or thereabouts, now riding at anchor on the river of Thames, within the port of London, and bound for a voyage to St. Mallowes in France, and from thence to return back to London to make her discharge, do send greeting in our Lord God everlasting.

And whereas I the said A.B. at the ensealing and delivery hereof am necessitated to take up, upon the adventure of the said ship, the sum of fifty pounds of lawful money of England, for setting forth the said ship to sea, and for furnishing of her with provision and necessaries for the said voyage, which said sum of fifty pound, C.D. of London, merchant, hath at my request supplied, and lent unto me, at ten pound for the said fifty pound during the said voyage.

Now know ye, that I the said A.B. do for me, mine executors, and administrators, covenant, grant, and agree, to and with the said C.D., his executors, and administrators by these presents: that the said ship shall with the first good wind and weather that God shall send, after the tenth day of this present month of May, depart from the said river of Thames, and shall by God's blessing directly, as wind and weather shall serve, proceed and sail unto St. Mallowes in France, and having there tarried until, etc. and the opportunity of a convoy, or being sooner dispatched (which shall first happen) shall depart from thence, and shall by God's blessing, as wind and weather serve, from thence directly sail, return, and come back, to the river of Thames to finish and end her voyage.

And I the said A.B. do for the consideration aforesaid bind myself, mine heirs, executors, administrators, goods, and chattels, and namely the said ship with the freight, tackle, and apparel of the same, to pay unto the said C.D., his executors, administrators, or assigns, the sum of sixty pound of lawful monies of England, within one and twenty days next after the return and safe arrival of the said ship in the said river of Thames from the said intended voyage.

And I the said A.B. do for me, mine executors, and administrators covenant and grant to and with the said C.D., his executors, and administrators by these presents: that I the said A.B., at the ensealing and executing of these presents, am true and lawful owner and master of the said ship, and have power and authority to charge and engage the said ship, as aforesaid, and that the said ship shall at all times after be liable and chargeable for the payment of the said sixty pound, according to the true intent and meaning of these presents.

And finally it is hereby declared and agreed that, in case the said ship shall be lost, miscarry, or cast away, which God forbid, before her next arrival on the said river of Thames, from the said intended voyage, that then the said payment of the said sixty pound shall cease and determine, and the loss thereof be wholly born and sustained by the said C.D., his executors, and administrators, and that then, and from thenceforth, every matter and thing herein before contained on the part and behalf of the said A.B. shall determine and be utterly void, anything herein before contained to the contrary thereof in any wise notwithstanding. In witness, etc.

And for the consideration aforesaid, and for the better performance of all and singular the premises, on my part to be done and performed, according to the true intent and meaning of these presents: I the said A.B. have bargained and sold, and by these presents do bargain and sell unto the said C.D., his executors, and administrators, all the said ship, and the tackle amunition, ordnance, apparel, and furniture thereunto belonging.

And the said A.B. for himself, his executors, and administrators doth covenant and agree to and with the said C.D., his executors, and administrators by these presents: that he the said A.B., at the time of the ensealing hereof, is the true and lawful owner of the said ship and premises, and that the same and every part thereof now are and be, and so in case any default of payment of the said sixty pound, or any part thereof, contrary to the agreement aforesaid, shall from henceforth for ever be free and clear, and freely and clearly discharged of and from all and all manner of former, and other bargain and sales, titles, troubles, charges, and encumbrances whatsoever.

Provided nevertheless and upon condition that if the said A.B., his executors, or administrators, shall well and truly pay, or cause to be paid unto the said C.D., his executors, administrators, or assigns the said sixty pound, and every part thereof according to the intent and true meaning of these presents, and likewise perform the covenants herein before contained on his and their part to be done and performed; that then this present bargain and sale of the said ship and premises, and every matter and thing therein contained shall cease and be void and of none effect to all intents and purposes; anything herein before contained, to the contrary thereof, in anywise notwithstanding, etc.

50. A NEWCASTLE LEAD MERCHANT'S TRADE TO THE LOW COUNTRIES, 1675

[Cambridge University Library, MS. Add. 91. Blackett Correspondence]

Newcastle, September 6, 1675

Mr. Walter Chaytor.

Sir,

I have shipped in the *John and Henry* of Newcastle, Barth. Kirkhouse master, 400 ps [=pigs] lead for Amsterdam as per the enclosed bill of lading, with whom I have prevailed to come to Rotterdam, which he hath promised me he will do if the wind presents for his purpose, so that if he do come, you are desired to receive the said 400 ps lead and dispose thereof for my most advantage, paying the master freight as if he went for Amsterdam. My advice is to keep it awhile for I have observed that good markets most commonly present in the winter time, but you being in the place is more able to judge than I. So I leave all to your discretion, and note this as my own concern. The master hath 400 ps more which likewise receive and dispose thereof for my father's most advantage. Note this as his concern and for future look upon us as two different persons.[1]

I have before me yours of this date. Do thank you for your advice, so shall send you no more of that lead marked I.M. Your exchange is high; no remedy but patience, for I know not how to help myself seeing you think I might make better advantage by returns. Pray tell me in what, for I do assure you I know not of any commodity of which I can make 2p. of a gil. besides the

---

[1] This refers to the dissolution of a partnership between Blackett and his father. See below, p. 541.

venter, retailing of it, and hazard of bad debts. I shall write you my further mind per next. In the mean time, remain

M. B[lackett].

* * *

Newcastle, September 7, 1675

Mr. Robert Jackson.

Sir,

I have before me yours of the 6th which before I answer pray take notice that the company is separated and that for future I am to act for myself, occasioned by my father's marrying again. So direct your letters to each of us accordingly as you shall have occasion. What is vii [sic] past is my father's concern but for future look upon us as two several persons.

Your account is right and booked accordingly; and shall give you credit for the 1d. a gallon which you scruple. I have received the £30 upon John Conscit's bill. Pray let me have an account of the beans at your leisure. At present no money to be procured in this place upon return. I do not say none at all, but 'tis very scarce, which some perceiving will not part with their monies without advance. I have met with one that hath £200 or £300 which you may command, provided you will allow 1% and make your bill at 10 or 15/ds date, so that you see the world is turned, when advance must be given for bills. Your answer pray afford per first for the party can dispose of his money upon the above expressed terms. But for you I have prevailed with him to keep it by him till Saturday next.

Rye 3s. 9d.   Beans 2s. 7d.   Oats 18d.   Butter 17s.   Lead £12

My respects to all friends about you,

I am

M.B.

* * *

Newcastle, September 7, 1675

Mr. Edmond Herrison.

Sir,

I have before me yours of the 2nd present. For answer, no lead in town that I know of is sold under £12 per fodder, under which price I cannot buy a pig, nor will I do any business for any man living under 1½% commission, for I do assure [you] I am not at all concerned with Sir William nor my brother neither, the company being separated. So for future am to act for myself *solii*. No vessels going for Rouen to which place seldom any goes from this port.

I am,

M.B.

* * *

Newcastle, September 17, 1675
Mr. Nicholas Verlaan.

Sir,

My last was of the 14 present to which refer you. Since none from you, the less at present to enlarge upon, this being chiefly to advise you that I have shipped and consigned unto you by the *Welcome* of London, Richard Streeter master, 400 ps lead which, after good arrival, you are desired to receive and dispose thereof for my most advantage, paying the master 10 stuyvers per piece freight with a stuyver upon a gilder for primage and average. My father consigns unto you 400 ps more by said vessel but they are easily distinguished the one from the other, though neither have any particular mark, for all mine are round at both ends and at bottom, whereas my father's have all one broad end and almost flat at bottom, which pray mind and take care that the one be not mixed with the other, and to cellar them so that each be laid by themselves. I hope Bartho. Kirkhouse is arrived ere this and that Richard Streeter who sailed this morning will be with you as soon as this, good news of which would be very acceptable unto

M.B.

51. THE SLAVE TRADE IN 1676

[E. Donnan, *Documents illustrative of the History of the Slave Trade to America*, I, *1441–1700*, New York, 1965, pp. 215–6]

[Answer of the Royal African Company to the Privy Council]
October 26, 1676.

After which was read the answer of the Royal Company received the 6th July, 1676. That it is therein alleged the company very scantily supply Barbados with negro servants and those at excessive prices; to which the company reply that they have been settled little above four years; in the two first, navigation was obstructed by the Dutch war and general embargoes laid on all ships. Yet the company sent forty-seven ships to carry soldiers and ammunition etc. to preserve the forts and factories in Guinea whence they proceeded with negroes to the plantations and four of the ships to Barbados. The third year, the war being ended, the company most vigorously prosecuted their trade and thence sent out fifteen ships to the coast of Africa, and ordered six of them to Barbados with about 2,000 negroes which their factors disposed of at a much lower price than was usual before this company was established. Last year they sent twenty ships to Africa and appointed eight of them with about 3,000 negroes to Barbados. It is alleged that the company have sold their negroes at 20*l*. and 30*l*. per head, but an examination of the company's books shows the price to have been about 15*l*. per head. By the company's last letters there remained owing to them about 25,000*l*. besides the 3,000 negroes sent last year which may swell the debt to 70,000*l*.

sterling or more. This present year the company have already sent ships and intend more by which the company hope their lordships may be satisfied what little reason they have to complain, which the company believe they would not have done but to prevent the company's complaint against them.

Andrew King, sub-governor; Gabriel Roberts, deputy governor.

52. INSURANCE AND OTHER CHARGES ON MERCHANT SHIPS, 1676

[K. Molloy, *De Jure Maritimo et Navali: or a Treatise of Affaires Maritime and of Commerce*, London, 1676, pp. 241–3, 255–6]

Of Policies of Assurance

FEW or scarce any insure the whole ship but the subscriptions being for sums certain as 50*l*. or 500*l*. at the *Premio* then current, which when the adventure is born they receive. But if a loss happens, the *Premio* is deducted together with the usual abatemate so that the insured receive much about 8 per cent if a loss happens.

[Marginal note adds:] The subscription mentions as if the *Premio* had been actually received, but it is seldom done till the adventure is born.

The policies nowadays are so large that almost all those curious questions that former ages and the civilians according to the law maritime, nay, and the common lawyers too, have controverted are now out of debate; scarce any misfortune that can happen or provision to be made but the same is taken care for in the policies that are now used; for they insure against heaven and earth, stress of weather, storms, enemies, pirates, rovers, etc. or whatsoever detriment shall happen or come to the thing insured, etc. is provided for . . .

If a ship be insured from London to ——, and blank being so left of purpose by the lader to prevent her surprise by the enemy, in her voyage she happens to be cast away, though there be private instructions for her port, yet the insured sit down by the loss by reason of the uncertainty.

[Marginal note adds:] Case of Monsieur Gourdan, governor of Calais, *anno* 1589 . . .

Of Wharfage, Primage, and Average

Wharfage is money paid for landing wares at a wharf or for shipping or taking in goods into a boat or barge. They commonly keep boats or lighters of their own for the carrying out and bringing in of goods in which, if a loss or detriment happens, they may in some cases be made liable . . .

Primage and *petilodmanage* is likewise due to the master and mariners for the use of his cables and ropes to discharge the goods; and to the mariners for loading and unloading of the ship or vessel. It is commonly about 12*d*. per tun . . .

Petty average is another little small duty which merchants pay to the master when they only take tonnage over and above the freight, the which is a small recompense or gratuity for the master's care over the lading; and in the bills of lading they are expressed after freight, together with *primage* and *average* accustomed.

The French ships commonly term the gratuity *Hatt-money* and our English merchants pay it our masters over the freight. It is sometimes more, sometimes less: 2 or 3 pieces.

53. LETTERS FROM A SUGAR PLANTER IN THE WEST INDIES, 1676–81

[*A Young Squire of the Seventeenth Century from the Papers* (*A.D. 1676–86*) *of Christopher Jeaffreson*, ed. J. C. Jeaffreson, I, London, 1878, pp. 183–6, 190–3, 204–6, 210–17, 255–60]

St. Christophers, June 5, 1676

Dear Cousin,[1]

I am now, thanks be to God, arrived safe at St. Christopher where I have exposed your goods to sale together with my own; but I find the island in a much poorer condition than I expected. Insomuch so, that there is little hope of vending anything, but what necessity enforces people to become our chapmen for; and that I must give credit for to the rich as well as the poor, which I find to be altogether the custom of these isles. Nor have I received a pound of sugar nor of indigo (except of two or three persons) for all the sales which I have made, which have been pretty considerable . . . Your goods came by very little damage, and some of them will I hope prove a good commodity; but the trade being prohibited between the English and the French upon this island hinders the sale of dry commodities very much. But yet what does sell turns to indifferent good accompt; insomuch that I should be sorry to be forced to buy anything here that I could be furnished with from Old England.

I promised to inform you what are the best commodities in these parts. I must begin with Madeira wine, as the most profitable; for the merchant sends to that island baizes, serges, that is perpetuanes, hats, cheese, butter, white and red herrings, pilchards, and beef, all which, if they come to a bad market there, are good commodities here, but being trucked there for wines makes a double profit of the voyage. And there is no living here without those wines. Therefore, when any ships are bound for those parts, and from thence hither I desire you would make a small venture for me, though it be but for three or four pipes. If you consign the goods to Mr. Pickford and Mr. Obediah Allen, I doubt not they will be just in shipping the value for my use. It is

---

[1] Most of the letters were addressed to Christopher Jeaffreson's cousin, Mr. Poyntz, an upholsterer of Cornhill, London.

worth sometimes five or seven pounds a pipe. If you can do this with conveniency, it would save me the charge of buying it here. And if there be more than enough for my own drinking I fear not to dispose of it well.

Whatsoever other goods you send me, I desire you would ship them if possible on vessels bound for this island; if not, directing to Nevis which is near; but if she be bound to several ports 'tis dangerous. At Michaelmas there will set out another fleet for these ports, amongst which, if there be any bound for this island, or if not, one that is bound for Nevis, I desire you would send a box of Castill soap, a chest of candles, two grey hats fit for my own wearing (well wrought, or else the sun will make them flap), four more of an ordinary sort, half a dozen barrels of beef, and a small case of drinking glasses. Provisions are scarce here, and I was not well advised in not bringing with me all that I write for now . . . If you can procure me a carpenter or two, and one or two masons, they will be very serviceable, if they bring their tools with them. I pray you hearken out for such, and for a joiner, such servants are as gold in these parts. I desire you would act for me at home, as I do for you here, and I hope to give you satisfaction in what you have trusted me with; and let not this letter from a young merchant or rather poor planter (for so I intend to be) now disencourage you . . .

Your affectionate kinsman,

Christopher Jeaffreson

*   *   *

St. Christopher's, 22 June, 1676.

Dear Cousin,

I writ to you by the *Jacob and Mary*, by which I give you an accompt that your goods are safe in a storehouse, and have received but little damage, but the poverty of this island makes the market bad, and requires time to vend commodities. But I shall act for you as if it were for myself; and I find in this season, while the ships are here, a glut of merchandise, which makes the sales more slow than I hope they will be hereafter. I promised to send you word what is most vendible in these parts. First, I shall give you as good advice as I can concerning those things you deal in, as your chairs that do not fold, your bed ticks, serges of cloth colours, your striped curtains and valances, your carpets of low prices. But too many of these things would soon cloy the country, because they are not but for the better sort. The most part here lie in hammakers, sit upon benches, clothe themselves in camies or some finer linen, and never cover the table but at meals. For your buckrams, printed stuffs, white serges, hangings, or cushions, I would counsel you never to send any more, till you hear I have sold these. The other commodities are sometimes asked after, which makes me think they will sell in time . . . There is no commodity better in these parts than Madeira wines. They are so generally and so plentifully drunk; being the only strong drink that is natural here, except brandy and rum, which are too hot. I have no more to request of you at present, but that you would, if possible, procure me a carpenter and a mason. They would be very useful to me, now that I am about to settle my plantation myself. For I intend to turn planter, and to set up a sugar work, which will cost me some pence, but much the less if I could have such servants . . .

I am, Sir,

Your most hearty loving kinsman and servant,

Christopher Jeaffreson.

Postscript.—There is a parcel of books in an old trunk at your house, amongst which there is one in folio, called 'Coke upon Littleton'. Pray send it me, and some of the other little law books, as *The Compleat Solicitor*, for everyone is his own lawyer in these parts.

*   *   *

To the writer's father-in-law, Colonel George Gamiell, London.]

St. Christopher's Island, 22 June, 1676.

Honoured Sir,

. . . To undertake sugar making, I have great convenience for a work; and I intend, God willing, to try my fortune in planting canes, notwithstanding the great discouragement I meet with, upon the accompt of the French, who are twice as strong as we. But the island being allowed by all that know it to be, without exception, the best in these parts, if under the power of one prince only, I have great confidence that our king will make such provisions for the defence of his interest here, that the French will never have cause to boast of such an advantage, as would be the entire enjoyment of so pleasant and fruitful an island; which encourages me to go on to improve my concerns, as well as I can . . .

*   *   *

St. Christopher's, 14 November, 1676.

Dear Cousin,

I thank you for your kind letter. It was a cargo of loving expressions and came to no bad market; but in a particular manner I acknowledge your courtesy in giving me so early advice of those clouds that threaten us from the French horizon; though I hope they will all be dispersed. But it may be a great advantage to us here, upon some accounts, if we could be sure to have timely notice of an approaching war; for, as we look upon it, the victory in these parts is gained more by striking the first blow, than by a multitude of blows. We had a rumour of the same before I received yours, but now that report is quelled; and we now talk of a particular amity between us and our neighbours in this island, which has been formerly treated of and almost concluded:—that the French and we should maintain our peace between ourselves, whatsoever happen between our princes at home. It would be the only way to make this island flourish, but I doubt it will never come to that. Which if it did, it would be worth while to send the commodities hither; whereas now the French, who are richer by far than we, hardly dare trade with us, lest their goods should be seized, nor dare the English trust them, who have not the liberty of bringing in their sugar:—but that, indeed, is chiefly occasioned by the rigidness of their West India Company . . . You forgot to give me advice what prices sugar and indigo bear at home. But I desire you would by your next tell me what the clear profits of this 484 pounds eight ounces of indigo comes to in London, for it goes current here at 2s. the pound, that is every ounce is worth a pound of sugar, which is valued here at 1½d.; 16 pounds of sugar for one pound of indigo . . . Madeira wine is now a drug by reason of a glut which seldom happens. But it is no sure commodity . . .

*   *   *

[To the writer's father-in-law, Colonel George Gamiell, London.]

St. Christopher's Island, 12 May, 1677.

Honoured Sir,

. . . I go on expending money upon my plantation, in hopes it will repay me with interest; but I must have patience, for it will require time, as well as a large expense, before the sugar work can be perfected. It is now esteemed here a great folly for a man to expose his time or goods to the hazard of indigo or tobacco, sugar being now the only thriving and valuable commodity. I have had some offers for the renting of my land; but I have not thought them considerable, after so much has been laid out upon it, though I am something cautious of running too hastily into debt, considering our condition in this island, where we have scarce five hundred able English men, comprehending the two thin companies his Majesty is pleased to maintain here. The French are three or four times the number (if not more), though they lost two hundred of their old soldiers and best men (if not more) with their deputy governor (under Monsieur D'Estrées) at Tobago; where, according to relation, there was the hottest service that many ages can tell of; it being very easy with the help of wind and current to enter the harbour, but very difficult to get out . . .

There is at present a very good understanding between the two nations upon this island; and it hath been (according to outward appearance) the desire of both parties to establish so firm a league between us (and to get it ratified by the two kings), that whatsoever difference happen in Europe, a perpetual amity may be retained and preserved here. But in the meantime, the French are erecting two land forts, contrary to what has been formerly practised in this island. But I think they only took example by us; who are endeavouring to raise such a fortification as may serve both for sea and land; but the great taxes, requisite to the carrying on so great a work, seems so intolerable to the poor inhabitants, that several leave the island. Insomuch that, whilst we acquire some strength by fortifications, we grow weak by depopulation; though the work be very necessary, in case of a sudden rupture, for a retreat till some succours arrive from Nevis, upon which this island hath some dependence. But those hopes would be frustrated; if our General were not (as we hope he will be) furnished with a frigate or two upon such an occasion, for the transporting of himself and men, who otherwise would run a great risk of being taken by any French man of war or privateer, that may lie at Basse Terre.

Nor could this island well subsist in a time of war, without two or three of his Majesty's ships to secure the coast and trade; for it has been found of late that both Dutch and French have made great preparations, and have carried on the war very vigorously in these parts . . .

The wars here are more destructive than in any other parts of the world; for twenty years' peace will hardly resettle the devastation of one years' war. As appears by this island, where the sad works of the last unhappy difference, in the year sixty-six, are not half worn out; nor is the island a quarter so well peopled as it then was. Nor is there any great hope of the contrary; seeing so few white servants are sent hither, and those that do come are most of them Irish. Yet even in the poor condition this island is now in, it is far more considerable to his Majesty, and the interest of England, than in former times, when it was in the most flourishing condition, while the Hollanders managed the trade here, who kept their storehouses mostly amongst the French, so that the produce of the English plantations was carried either into the French grounds, or shipped for Holland, whilst their commodities were vended here. 'Tis true the planter found the sweet of this, for they sold cheap, and allowed a year or two for payment. But now the growth and goods of our own nation are taken off by the inhabitants; and their sugar or indigo, etc., are shipped in English bottoms for England, to the increase of his Majesty's customs, and the encouragement of navigation. And more, since the wars between Holland and France, the French are forced to deal with our merchants, insomuch that a great part of their sugar is likewise shipped for England. I believe there are no less than forty or fifty sail of ships that come to this island and Nevis every year; but few of them to this island as yet, it being not so well settled. The most part of the goods are brought hither in shallops, in which the sugars are returned to the ships. . . There are a great many French and Dutch inhabitants in the English ground. A Hamburger bought part of my plantation of Delve, and hath enjoyed it till now as his own. But I obtained a verdict against him for it, and am now in possession of it myself, and have planted part of it with sugar canes.

I rest, Sir, your obedient son,

Christopher Jeaffreson.

*   *   *

St. Christopher's Island, 6 May 1681.

Dear Cousin,

... It is long since my request to you to send me some white servants, especially a mason, carpenter, tailor, smith, cooper, or any handy craftsman; and now I am necessitated to reiterate my said request to you, not only for a clerk or tradesman, but for any sort of men, and one or two women, if they can be found. They are generally wanted in this island; and all my bond servants are gone free. The last of them was Joseph Demure, formerly one of the porter's men belonging to the lodge at Whitehall. He is married and lives very well; though his father imagines him dead and writ to me for his wages, which I have paid him to the value of near forty pounds sterling. Yet I was no loser by him, for he is a tailor and a good workman. I question not but that, if I were in London, I could take my choice. I remember the objection you returned, in answer to my said request, was that people would make their conditions before they would transport themselves. Which I acknowledged to be prudence in them. But usually such persons as are volunteers for the West Indies are under such circumstances as may reasonably induce them to oblige themselves to an apprenticeship, at least for four years, in hopes of the advantages they may probably make for themselves at the end of the term, during which they are instructed in the nature and customs of the place.

It is seldom seen that the ingenious or industrious men fail of raising their fortunes in any part of the Indies, especially here, or where the land is not thoroughly settled. There are now several examples of it to my knowledge—men raised from little or nothing to vast estates. And I can assure you our slaves live as well now as the servants did formerly. The white servants are so respected that, if they will not be too refractory, they may live much better than thousands of the poor people in England during their very servitude, or at least as well.

For a tailor, a cooper, a carpenter, a joiner, a mason, a smith—which are the trades most necessary here—I would allow to such an one, when a good workman, a thousand pounds of sugar wages, for each year that he should serve me, with what must be paid for their passages, tools, or instruments. For one that can handle his pen—he may deserve as much, but we seldom give it, because such men are more plenty, and have other advantages. As for labourers and menial servants, their passages being paid, they must expect only food, raiment, and lodging, until their term (which is never less than four years) be expired, and then by the laws and customs of the island they are to have four hundred pounds of sugar, to begin the world with. Thus I have told you the conditions I would willingly make. But I do not tie you up just to what I have proposed. A little more may be added, as you see convenient, and as much less as you please. Only the four hundred pounds of sugar will admit of no abatement. For if Newgate and Bridewell should spew out their spawn into these islands, it would meet with no less encouragement; for no gaol bird can be so incorrigible, but there is hope of his conformity here, as well as of his preferment, which some have happily experimented;

insomuch that all sorts of men are welcome to the public, as well as the private, interests of the island. Therefore, if you could send me some of any sort of the aforementioned people, you would do me a singular kindness; and though I were intended for England, they would meet with good entertainment by those I should leave behind me; for which purpose I have convenanted with Edward Thorn for a certain time, in case I had left the island, of which I am not at all resolved for the present.

Scotchmen and Welshmen we esteem the best servants; and the Irish the worst, many of them being even good for nothing but mischief. I believe, if you will endeavour it, you may find Scotch and English, that would willingly change their climate upon the aforementioned terms, and much more when they are directed to a certain place and person, of whose character they may be well informed. How many broken traders, miserable debtors, penniless spendthrifts, discontented persons, travelling heads and scatterbrains would joyfully embrace such offers!—the first, to shun their greedy creditors and loathsome gaols; . . .; the third, to fill their bellies though with the bread of affliction; the fourth, to leave an unkind mistress or dishonest wife, or something worse; the fifth, to satify fond curiosity; sixth, he knows not why, unless to cross his friends, and seek his fortune. These and the like humours first peopled the Indies, and made them a kind of Bedlam for a short time. But from such brain-sick humours have come many solid and sober men as these modern times testify . . .

Dear Cousin, etc. etc.

Christopher Jeaffreson

54. SIR HENRY COVENTRY'S MEMORIAL CONCERNING PIRACY ON THE HIGH SEAS, 1678

[Bodleian Library, Oxford, MS. Fr.c.28, f. 221]

The Paquet Boat robbed by an Ostender coming from Calais to Dover

Il y a quelques tems que Sa Majesté fut informée que le paquet boat passant de Calais à Douvre le 18me de febvrier avoit esté pille par un Capre dont on ignoroit le nom et le port, sur quoy ell ordonna que recherche exacte seroit incessament faite de cette violence, que l'on a depuis peu decouvert avoir esté commise par une barque ostendoise armée en cours et commandée par le nommé Pierre Mansfeldt, porteur d'une commission d'Espagne, qui aiant bordé le paquet boat y entra avec quinze hommes de son equipage, les armes à la main et après avoir blessé plusieurs des passagers, dont la plus part estoient subjets de sa Majesté et en avoir mêmes jetté un dans la mer, ils les devalisèrent entièrement et emportèrent toutes les marchandises qui estoient dans le dt. paquet boat. C'est pourquoi, Monsieur, je vous envoye ce mémoire par ordre de sa Majesté tant pour vous faire plainte de cette action si inhumaine et si prejudicielle à la bonne correspondance entre les deux nations, que pour vous prier de tenir la main à ce qu'elle ne demeure pas impunie, en sorte que le dt. Mansfeldt et ses complices soient chastiés exemplairement, afin de prévenir par ce moyen de semblables insultes à l'advenir.

Fait à Whitehall, le 17me de Mars 1677/8

H.C.

55. THE ROYAL AFRICAN COMPANY IN FINANCIAL DIFFICULTIES, 1679

[Historical MSS. Commission, *Seventh Report*, pp. 476–7. Papers of Sir Harry Verney, bart.]

1679, Oct. 30, London.—John Verney to Sir R. Verney

If the King should want money I'm sure he cannot borrow any of the R. African Company for that's as poor as a courtier, the last Parliament having done their business for 'em, so that we cannot have a penny dividend this year; but we go on paying off our debts, that if the company be broke nobody may be sufferers but those that are of it . . .

56. A BILL OF LADING, 1679

[Herefordshire County Record Office, Foley Collection, F/IV/BJ/5]

SHIPPED by the Grace of God in good order and well conditioned by *Richard Foley*[1] in and upon the good ship called the *Hannah Pinke of London* whereof is master under God for this present voyage *George Churchey*, and now riding at anchor in the *River of Theame* [= Thames] and by God's grace bound for *Guinea*, to say *4 cask nails and 2 fardles* being marked and numbered as in the margent (*Caske R F No. 1; 2; 3; 4. Fard. No. 1; 2*) and are to be delivered in the like good order and well conditioned at the aforesaid Port of *Guinea* (the danger of the seas only excepted) into *George Churchey's command* or to *his* assigns, he or they paying freight for the said goods *accustomary* with primage and average accustomed. In witness whereof the master or purser of the said ship hath affirmed to three bills of lading all of this tenor and date, the one of which three bills being accomplished, the other two to stand void. And so God send the good ship to her desired port in safety.

Amen, dated in *London the —— day of September, 1679*

George Churchey.

---

[1] This is a printed certificate on which the italicized words were inserted in ink.

57. A LONDON MERCHANT'S SUGGESTIONS FOR REMEDYING LOW WOOL PRICES, 1685

[Bodleian Library, Oxford, MS. Aubrey 2, f. 140.: Aubrey's
MS. of *The Natural History of Wiltshire*]

Sir,

The discourse[1] you sent me sheweth the fall of the rents of lands for some years past and supposeth the cause thereof to have been the importation of cattle and the fall of the price of wool and insisteth on the last and as a remedy proposeth:

1. The raising a duty on Spanish wool imported.
2. To enjoin the wearing of garments only made of English wool to all under such a degree both at home and in our plantations.
3. To consider the decay of the Hamburg Company and the causes thereof.
4. To enjoin the strict making of all cloth true according to the statutes.
5. To reform the Blackwell Hall factors.

Before I consider these particulars I shall consider whether it doth consist with the welfare of our trade in wool at home or abroad to raise the same, for if England be not the alone country affording wool, but the other countries do also the same as Ireland, the Low Countries, Germany, France, etc., and if England outdo the rest at the common markets, it must be in the cheapness thereof, and if also in our manufactures thereof, it must be in the cheapness of working the same, equal if not exceeding other countries. For the commodity at the commodity market which is equal with others of the same kind in goodness, etc. can be afforded at a lower price than the rest, will outsell them in quantity and so gain the advantage in trade; there can therefore be no way of raising our wools at home without the general prejudice of the nation. There are two ways indeed of raising the price therein which I shall but need to name to show the unpracticableness of them. The first is by destroying the $\frac{1}{2}$ or $\frac{1}{3}$ of our sheep, or the like quantity of our wools which, without the concord of the other nations concerned also in the same trade to do the same, would be indeed their advantage but our great prejudice. The second is to permit the exportation of our wools which if we can all manufacture at home at as cheap rates as can be done abroad, we shall by such exportation give so much labour out of our hands into the hands of strangers to our great prejudice, which also our parliaments have wisely foreseen and therefore so strictly forbid the exportation of all wools and encouraged the importation of all other commodities that assist to the making and completing of the manufactures, by low duties at their entrance, and permitting Spanish wool to enter duty free, because useful with our wools to make fine cloth.

As to the enjoining of all people under a certain degree both at home and in our plantations to wear only cloth made of English wool, I suppose under

---

[1] This refers to George Clark, *A Treatise of Wool* . . ., 1685, see Section III, pp. 304–5.

cloth he meaneth all other stuffs made of wool. Will that not discourage the silk manufactures of late so much increased among [us], and whether the proportion of people more employed about the increase of the wool trade thereby would be more than what are now employed in that proportion of the silk trade which thereby would be diminished.

Concerning the Hamburg Company if what the gentlemen affirm be true that more wool manufactures have been vended in the limits of their trade for the time that the trade was free than during any like time that they enjoyed the sole trade, then will the concerns of the company not come in consideration to the advance of the wool trade.

The strict and true making of all our wool manufactures to certain rules for truth and goodness would be doubtless a great furtherance of our trade.

As to a duty to be raised on Spanish wool at importation, if the manufactures made with the mixture thereof are or can only be made in England, it might raise these manufactures without much prejudice, but if they are or can be made elsewhere and they impose not a like duty thereon in their countries, it must for the former reasons prejudice our trade therein.

Lastly, concerning the Blackwell Hall factors, since their trade as such is not settled by any law or limited to any certain number, but that either the clothier himself or any other whom he please may sell the [same] for him. If any of them deal not honestly with him he may choose another among their number whom he judgeth more honest or settle a new man to do the same for him.

Therefore, I see not how our wools at present can be raised by any artificial devise without discouraging our manufactory trade and encouraging that of others abroad, except other countries concerned with us in the same trade concur to use the same devise with us.

Did all our wools manufactured at home but serve our own use without need of exportation and the importation of foreign wool manufactures forbid, we might then without prejudice raise our own wools, but if our wools manufactured exceed our expense then must we accommodate the price thereof to the general market.

This letter was sent to me by Mr. Francis Lodwyck, merchant of London and Fellow of the Royal Society, 1685.

58. A BROKEN COVENANT OF APPRENTICESHIP, 1688

[Patrick McGrath, *Merchants and Merchandise in Seventeenth-Century Bristol*, Bristol Rec. Soc., XIX, 1955, pp. 23–4]

Civitas Bristol. 7 May 1688.
COMPLAINT having been this day made unto us whose names are hereunto subscribed, his Majesty's justices of the peace of and for this city and county

on behalf of Josiah Cook,[1] who by indentures of apprenticeship made and registered in the Tolzey according to custom bearing date the thirteenth day of March which was in the second year of his now Majesty's reign, was put apprentice to Sir Thomas Earle, knight, and Dame Elienor his wife, to serve them in the art of a mariner for seven years; that the said Sir Thomas Earle hath turned away the said apprentice and doth suffer him to wander about the country and refuses to find him necessaries as by the covenants in the said indenture he ought to do, so that the said apprentice is destitute of habitation which (if continued) will in probability tend to his utter ruin. It is therefore by us hereby ordered that notice be given to the said Sir Thomas Earle that unless he or some other on his behalf appear and shew good cause to the contrary, the justices here will on Wednesday the sixteenth day of May instant proceed to hear and examine the said matter of complaint and will thereupon take order either for discharging the said apprentice from future service by force of the said indentures or otherwise for providing him necessaries as by the said indenture and law ought to be. Given under our hands and seals this seventh day of May *anno Regni Regis Jacobi Anglie etc. quarto annoque Domini* 1688.[2]

Thomas Day Maior
Io.ⁿ Lawford

59. A DEBATE ON THE CLOTH TRADE, 1693

[Parliamentary Diary of N. Luttrell, All Souls College MS. 158b, pp. 365–9]

February 17, 1692/3

THE engrossed bill for reviving a part of the Act for preventing the exportation of wool and encouraging the woollen manufactures was read the third time. Sir J. Guise offered a rider to raise the same duties for payment of the Hamburg Company's debts as they paid before. But rejected because to raise money, which ought not to be but in a committee of the whole House.

Mr. Sandford. I am against this bill because it is to give our woollen trade to foreigners; then it will ruin and destroy your trade at last though at present it seems to be greater, and it sets aside the Hamburg Company who first brought this trade into the nation and hath hitherto preserved it and will, if this bill do not pass.

Sir Walter Young was for it, because it seemed highly reasonable to encourage the free exportation of every manufacture, for the more hands our cloth is carried out by the better; it raises your wool and is for the benefit of the country.

---

[1] Josias, son of William Cooke, merchant, was apprenticed to Sir Thomas Earle and his wife on 13 March 1684 (Bristol Apprenticeship Book, 1684–9, f. 19ᵛ).

[2] There is no further record of proceedings.

Sir J. Knight was against the bill and urged that the price of wool, though it was somewhat better at present, did not arise from this bill; the true reason is Ireland, which used to send over a great deal of wool, has afforded you none lately. They made serges there formerly so that a want there must occasion a greater consumption of it here. Besides can any imagine if there be a vent for the commodity abroad that the company will not export cloth enough for their own advantage, but this trade as it is now managed is carried on by foreigners who will not be very forward to maintain the credit of your manufacture, for all they mind is their own profit and the advantage that arises to them thereby; is carried out of the nation who are so much the poorer for it, whereas if this trade be carried on in the regular channel by the Hamburg Company the benefit will redound to the nation; this company consists of your own natives, have great privileges granted to them at Hamburg, and have a bank there for carrying on this trade, which if you break, your bullion must be exported to carry on the trade; therefore, I am against the bill.

Sir J. Dorrel was for the bill for that he thought it against the interest of the nation to limit and confine trade to companies who will set the dice upon others and sell at their own price.

Mr. Smith was against the bill for that this was a joint in a company [sic], those I agree are mischievous and circumscribe trade, but when it is a well regulated company, it is otherwise, they will sell for a reasonable profit, then here is no mischief for any native of this kingdom may be free of it for £13 6s. 8d., and if you will reduce the price thereof the Company are very willing.

Sir Edw. Hussey was for the bill; the more exporters of a manufacture the better.

Sir Samuel Dashwood was against the bill; the only argument for it is that there hath been more exported for three years past. I agree it in some measure to be true, but he did not think it arose from the exportation thereof that had been for the three years last past, but from other causes.

Mr. Boscawen was for it because the more exporters the cheaper it would go out, and the cheaper it is, the more you will send abroad, and the better able to undersell your neighbours.

Sir Edwd. Seymour. The woollen manufacture is a specious thing, but I am afraid that in this matter contending only for the name, if the bill were really for the benefit thereof, I doubt not but I should have heard from my corporation in the matter, but I take the bill before you to be a door to let in foreigners, and when they have got their trade into their hands, they will beat you out of it, or make their own terms with you and set their own prices; the true reason of the exporting more of the woollen trade to Hamburg and Holland is because of the war. The sea in some measure to Italy is now shut up, and therefore you export it to Hamburg and Holland in greater quantities, and thence it is carried by land, etc. to those places so that I do not think this bill is for the interest of the nation.

Mr. Clark. It is very strange that an open trade and a free exportation of any commodity should not be for the interest of this nation; the truth of which appears in comparing the custom house books of the port of London for the three last years with the three precedings; in the last there has been 160,000*l.* worth in the woollen manufacture exported more than before.

Sir Chris. Musgrave. The reasons of your greater exportations more than formerly are such as these: Ireland hath made no woollen cloths for three years past; the prohibition of trade with France by the German princes who used to supply them with great quantities; then there have been several ships exported with this manufacture, who being taken by the French privateers, the merchant has been forced to send the like quantity to supply the loss thereof . . . then they are foreigners who run away with this trade and not the English, to encourage whom is against the policy of this nation before our merchants who are not concerned in it, only one at Exeter, Mr. Elwell, who is the factor for the foreigners, so though there be many exporters of it, yet there is in a manner but one buyer; but in the Hamburg Company 'tis otherwise, every man buys for himself so the company is not confined; for those reasons he was against the bill.

Mr. Papillon and Mr. Perry were against the bill. Mr. Blowfield also and affirmed that though there had been more exported for the three years past, viz. 89, 90, 91 than for the years before, viz. 86, 87, 88 in the port of London; yet out of England in general from the several ports there had been less exported in the three last years than before as had been undeniably made to appear to him by the farmers of the aulnage duty; and it stands with reason that more should be exported from the port of London during the war because of the danger of the seas from privateers, etc. whom to avoid they send up their goods to London and export them hence, because of the conveniency of convoys which go from hence.

Mr. Bowyer, Sir Chas. Sedley were against the bill for it would prejudice our navigation, for as it is always the policy of this nation to lay high duties on commodities brought in foreign bottoms, so by this foreigners' goods will be excused by going in English bottoms. Dr. Barbon was for the bill. The question was put that the bill do pass.

Tellers for	Yeas	Sir Walter Young Mr. Clark	88
	Noes	Sir J. Guise Mr. Smith	155

60. INSTRUCTIONS FROM THE HUDSON BAY COMPANY TO THE GOVERNOR OF YORK FORT, 1693

[*Hudson's Bay Copy Booke of Letters, Commissions, Instructions Outward, 1688–96*, ed. E. E. Rich *et al.*, Hudson's Bay Record Soc., XX, 1957, pp. 185–7, 190, 192–7, 200]

Governor and Council,

Your letter of the 9th September 1692 per Capt. Edgcomb came safe to our hands the latter end of October following which was in answer to ours of the 17th June foregoing, by which we were informed the French had made no attempt upon you last year, which gave you opportunity to complete your fortifications, and at the arrival of our ships you write 'twas completed, a draught of which we have received, and as far as we understand it's regular and strong, doubt not in case of any onset you may defend it. We take notice that you have made no alteration in the standard of trade which we earnestly expected, for, all considered, it ought to be done, everything standing us in double what it did in time of peace; and that must be reason to all men of understanding to consider the arguments and reasons that have been writ you in this very affair. Nay, you know if we would force the Indians, they must give double the price or starve. Therefore we do again recommend to you that you get two skins more per gun and so proportionable in all other commodities that vend there. For inducement to the Indians to give you more for our goods, you may make a larger present than usual to the chief Capt. of Rivers and leading men; and not expect more in return from them than formerly, so that they may be induced to advance the standard which will make the rest to follow their example the more willingly. So that by a little more than ordinary given away you will bring a considerable advance. In the whole with them this may be done privately, the common Indians not knowing of it, which yet notwithstanding we refer to your discretion... We must again and more earnestly than ever recommend to you the greatest frugality imaginable in all manner of provisions which are excessive dear all over Europe, especially all sorts of grain which are double the price they were last year and for beef and pork the half dearer than before, and such unseasonable weather we have had and like to continue that we are in great fear of a dearth all over Europe.[1] Yet notwithstanding the dearness at present we have completed your indent in all things this voyage. We are glad that Henery Kelsey is safe returned and brought a good fleet of Indians down with him, and hope he has effected that which he was sent about in keeping the Indians

---

[1] The year 1692 began a series of bad seasons traditionally referred to as the barren years at the close of the seventeenth century. Wheat, according to one authority, was 46s. 8d. per quarter of nine bushels, and in the following year the price rose to 67s. 8d. See Baker, *Records of the Seasons, Prices of Agricultural Produce, and Phenomena observed in the British Isles* (1883 and 1912), pp. 165–6.

from warring one with another, that they may have the more time to look after their trade and bring larger quantity of furs and other trade with them to the factory, which you may also dissuade them from when they are with you by telling them what advantages they may make, that the more furs they bring, the more goods they will be able to purchase of us; which will enable them to live more comfortably and keep them from want in time of scarcity, and that you inculcate into them better morals than they yet understand; that it doth advantage them nothing to kill and destroy one another, that thereby they may so weaken themselves that the wild ravenous beasts may grow too numerous for them and destroy those that survive. Besides if fair means will not prevail, you may tell them if they war and destroy one another, those that are the occasion of it, whoever they are, you will not sell them any more guns, powder, or shot which will expose them to their enemies who will have the master of them and quite destroy them from the earth, them and their wives and children, which must work some terror in them, and that you are sent thither to keep peace amongst them; and that on the other side, if they do live peaceably and quietly without war, you will let them have anything you have for their support and be kind to them all, and supply them with all necessaries, let their number be never so great. These and other arguments you may use to them as they occur to your mind and memory. We are very sorry you have not sent out and made some further trial in the whale fishing, and think you need not send out such a number of men as you mention in your letter: 20 men, which is a third part of your number, but that if you had spared 12 at most to have navigated the *Albemarle* to Churchill river after she was come within the rocks, you might have laid her safe, and gone out with ten hands, leaving only 2 hands to have looked after her. She being still in sight, no danger could have happened and with the rest there mightabeen a considerable quantity of fish taken that would have helped in this extremity of time, for their wages, whether fishing or sleeping, is the same ... Though there grows no turpentine about the factory, the ground being low and swampy, yet we are of opinion that upon higher ground especially upon the hills there are large trees that do afford it, which might easily be discovered without much trouble or hazard, if two or three good travellers would undertake it in summer time when fowl and deer come your way, with what provisions they can carry with them from the factory, might travel a month right out one way one year and another way another year, and they might have directions from the Indians where such trees grow and so easily discover that and probably other things too. We will not suffer any trade with the Indians but what is for the company's account, and therefore pray make a strict scrutiny therein, and return their names whomsoever they are. As for French brandy there is none to be had in England nor suffered to be brought in. Nay, if it were suffered, there's such scarcity of it in France that they will neither suffer that or wine to be exported thence. Therefore, pray make much of that you have, for we know not when we shall send you more. It's privately sold here for 10 or 12s. p. gallon. Some spirits are distilled in England, but the materials wherewith it's made are so scarce and the high impositions upon it makes it excessive dear. Some of it was sent you two years agone, but we heard no commendations from you of it. We are afraid it will not keep a year about, though the distillers affirm 'twill keep 7 years . . .

It is not our desires that the ship's stores should be mixed with those for the factory; they are mark with different marks and those for the factory are entered in the invoices.

Halfstead whom you sent home is a stout fellow and hardy lad, else would not have grown so much since he went hence. Such persons you ought not to suffer to depart the country till their times be expired, but those that are sickly and weak you may send home.

The Indian we return you, and if you find him not serviceable in travelling, working, etc. pray send him to the bottom of the bay where he will be out of the acquaintance Port Nelson Indians.

The iron stoves are now sent you and everything according to your directions, with all the appurtenances. But our deputy governor[1] who hath lived 20 years in cold countries is of an opinion you had better have them smaller than bigger than the first, except you have very large rooms indeed, for the heat of them if too hot made will affect the head and cause some distempers among you, except you have a casement of 3 inches broad and 4 long made in the top of one window to open in case of any bad smell or too much heat, which may often happen, and one quarter of a hour will purify the room again if left open; and that you take care you do not scutt the scutt too soon which, if you do before the wood be wholly burnt to a coal without any smoke, it will suffocate and much damage the brain. We recommend to your great care that no damage by fire happen by the stoves, for if there be any timber work near them it will soon take fire. Therefore, pray be very careful that you heat them moderately, and open the door before they make to much flame.

There might be some defect in some meal last year. In the greatest care there may happen some misfortunes, but you may be assured that we will take all the care imaginable and 'tis our interest so to do for we pay as much for it as for the sweetest.

Without your advice we had sent no brass pans. Indeed, for Guinea there go from hence many, but we never heard that they went to any cold countries before. Therefore, the fault is your own if they vend not. We take notice what guns you have mentioned, and the works you have made for your defence which is very well, but except the men within do use them with courage and prudence, they will not defend themselves. But we hope and rest assured you will not be wanting in any respect to defend the fort if occasion should offer.

We wonder that much that amongst all the seamen that have stayed with you there some two, some three years, and more that you should not have a person fit to command the *Albemarle*, and more especially now she is not gone

---

[1] Samuel Clarke, first elected deputy governor in November 1692.

ten miles from the factory. We apprehend there needs no great artifice to sail her so far and back to the fort. Nay, we think you should have experience seamen several might sail her to Churchill river and back, because we understand they need not be out of sight of land.

The two geese you sent, we thank you for them, and this far in answer to your letter.

We found at the opening of some bundles of parchment beaver several skins wanting, there being but twenty-six skins in them. For the future be exact in the tale of them, for we do not know whom to charge with them but your remissness in telling of them, when they were packed; and hereafter pack fifty skins instead of thirty. Let the skins of each bundle be as sizeable as you can, or else the smallest may be easily plucked out; but if you must be forced to pack small and great together, then let the smaller be in the middle. There has been many mistakes made by the last year bills of exchange, drawn upon by our servants in not having the governor's hand by them, notwithstanding former orders to the contrary. Therefore, we again give you in charge to acquaint our people that we will pay no bill which shall not have the governor's hand to it. We also order you to be very cautious in suffering any to run in our debts above their wages due to them.

We are yearly at vast charges for casks. Therefore, for the future we expect you send home all such casks as can be spared, as also those broken, binding up the staves and heads together, loading in every ship a proportion as they are in bigness . . .

We would have you, when any ship is with you bound to the bottom of the bay, to send thither some of those goods that you are over stored with and cannot sell, and let us know the quantities, as also the qualities you do send, that you may have credit for them.

We find few of our gun chests returned which cost us considerably every year. Therefore, the future as they are emptied, send them home filled with coat beaver.

If you have many wolves or ravenous beasts that will destroy cattle about the factory, we recommend to you to destroy them totally; as also to encourage the Indians to do the like, for we are resolved by God's help to send some cows, goats, and swine the next year, not doubting but they may be maintained and fed there very well; and, therefore, desire that a convenient house in some dry warm place may be built to put them in against they arrive, provided you do not find upon mature deliberation the climate altogether impossible for their subsistence; and that one or two with dogs and guns may attend them in the day time as long as they can feed abroad, and housed every night, and watched by one or two for their better security; and that food may be provided for them as soon as they arrive next year. We have sent you scythes, forks, etc. to cut and make hay with, whereof we understand there is enough not far from the factory for one hundred head of cattle and more, and therefore we expect you to make provision accordingly for sixteen or eighteen cows for the whole winter till spring comes on again. And we know if we can keep great cattle, swine and goats may easily be kept, which if we can bring to pass as we are morally assured, for Finland and Lapland are as cold and colder, and more barren and unfruitful, and much longer nights than at York fort, and yet at those places cattle are maintained, and it would be of great advantage both to the factory and us to have cattle maintained at York fort, in case of any miscarriage of our ships, as also the benefit you will have of fresh provisions.

We desire a bottle or two of that juice that you tap out of the trees which you mixed with your drink when any one is troubled with the scurvy,[1] or if you have plenty of it, that you would send more with directions how you use it there.

We have sent you all manner of seeds for a garden which we doubt not but you will improve now you see the conveniency of roots and gardening herbs, with a book giving the best directions how to use them. You must sow them in sundry sorts of ground that you may see which will prove best to bring them to perfection. And to raise a height of ground or hedge of reeds or some fence to keep the norwest wind from them, and then there is no doubt of their coming to perfection as well as in any part of Sweden and Norway, you having already had great benefit by what you have sowed.

And likewise we recommend to you the sowing corn we have sent you of all grains. Some as for wheat you may sow a gallon in one place and a gallon in another. As soon as the ships come, it must be sowed under furrow as termed in England that it may be at least 4 or 5 inches under the earth when dug and laid hollow. Let the event be what it will, it matters not; you will see in April whether it comes up or not, if it doth come up and proves too rank when you see it, so you may mow the top of it off; if it be not rank, then let it grow on in God's name.

Then in the Spring as soon as you can get the spade into the ground, sow again of wheat, barley, oats, beans, and peas, but must not be so deep in the earth, not above 2 inches and $\frac{1}{2}$ and sow them in several places, and when you see them come up, you must break the clods and make them lie fine; but the beans and peas you need not be so curious in; let the event be what it will, let it be done.

If all be lost, the loss is to us and nobody else. But if it should take, what comfort will it be to those that inhabit there, as you find by the turnips already, for such rich mould as has lain fallow, it may be from the Creation, cannot choose but bring forth strongly, especially where such plenty of snow is all the winter, which keep everything warm and is as we say in England the poor man's dung.

We must put you in mind of one general fault, that is in omitting to give us the dimension of things you write for, nor for what use they are, which

---

[1] When wintering 1535–6 on the site of the present city of Quebec, Jacques Cartier's men were beset by scurvy. On the advice of an Indian he treated them successfully with a decoction of the leaves and bark of the tree 'Annedda', which, according to Dr. Jacques Rousseau, *Jacques Cartier et 'La Grosse Maladie'*, was the 'annedda' tree of Jacques Cartier.

may occasion us to heap up a great quantity of goods to no purpose. For it is ten to one whether we hit the right sort; as, for instance, you write now for two rings of iron wire, one small, and another great. Whether you know it not, there are twenty and more sizes of iron wire. What shall we do in this case? If we send none, you will say you are neglected. If we send, they may not be the right sort, and so worth nothing to you, and then so much is lost. And it is in many other commodities that you give us no advice neither in size, sort, quality, or quantity, which is a grand fault and pray let it be amended. You mention perpetuanes[1] but say not what colour, so that we can but guess whether we send the right or not. If we know the use, we might come nearer to your desires. But consider what a confusion you put us in when things are not duly expressed. And this has been always your defect though often put in mind of it; yet you neglect it.

If, when you come to want anything, you put it forthwith into a memorand. book, the commodity, quality, and quantity of it, and for what use, and then put it into your indent at last, it would make everything easy to us and you too. And that you do not defer the writing of your general letter so long and so late as you do; which makes things done in a hurry, and then there is nothing done well or else something is forgotten. We would know what you do with the shot bags. We find not that any one Indian buys the quantity of a bag, so they cannot need them, and if they are used to any other use in the factory, will rather send you linen cloth. But we will have the bags returned us every year and put into a chest or box, and the number mentioned in the invoice, and so of all casks whether broken or whole returned, and the like for gun chests. We have sent you some flax and hemp seeds which we will also have sowed upon ground most suitable to it, and for directions we refer you to the printed book now sent you.

Mr. Knight we find will have occasion for two or more carpenters at the bottom of the bay which we fear we shall not be able to send him this voyage. Therefore desire you to send two or what you can possibly spare. We conclude your works is done is there, and hope you may spare all you have for one year. The next year he may return them to you again if occasion require it . . .

We desire a particular account of the disposal of that large supply of brandy and leaf tobacco, etc., sent you last year, our intentions and resolutions being to send over sufficient quantities of brandy, sugar, clothes, etc. that so the company may wholly supply the factory, instead of others, hoping thereby to lessen the extravagant wages of our servants, which is practised in all companies' factories whatsoever. In order, pray advise what quantities of each may be proper to send next shipping.

We had sent you a far greater supply of Barrill [= Brazil] tobacco, had not the ship in which it was consigned to us come to a mischance, which occasioned its not arriving before the departure of our ships, as also the same by the Irish Brouges.

We would have the company's packet made up for the future in double

---

[1] Perpetuana was a durable wool fabric.

paper covers, and not in a trunk as formerly, the postage being 2*s.* an ounce which occasioned the last poststage to amount to twelve pounds for that packet only. Let the contents of the packet for the time to come be only the general letter, invoice, bills of loading, and signal, all the letters, books, etc. in a packet distinct. We remain wishing you all health and prosperity.

Your Lo. friends

Samuell Clarke, deputy governor, Tho. Pitts, Robt. Lancashire, John Smith, Robt. Nicholas.

London, 17 June 1693

61. BRISTOL MERCHANTS INTERVENE TO CURB THE INFLUENCE OF LONDON ON THE PROPOSED COUNCIL OF TRADE, 1695

[R. M. Lees, 'Parliament and the Proposal for a Council of Trade, 1695–6', *English Historical Review*, LIV, 1939, pp. 57–9]

[Correspondence of John Cary of Bristol]

Bristol, December 16th 1695.

Sr. Thomas Day and Major Yate.[1]

Having notice from different hands that the House of Commons had voted a council or committee of trade, we think it a constitution which will tend very much to the interest of England if well settled in the beginning, and we cannot think this can be, except the trading cities are represented therein by able men such as they shall think fit to recommend who are acquainted with their several interests. If it be made up of courtiers inexperienced in trade, 'twill become only a matter of charge to the nation; if of Londoners, they will endeavour to overrule things so as they shall best conduce to the bringing all trade to that great city, without respect to the other ports. Now we recommend it to you as our judgement, that such a committee cannot be formed to the advantage of the trade of England in general so well, as when made up of persons sent up from all the parts thereof, as well the counties, as some particular trading cities and ports. We desire that you give us a true light of this affair that, when we better understand the meaning of it, we may be more able to make you such proposals as we shall think best agreeable to the interest of this city; but if the members thereof are to be named out of hand by the king (as some this day advise) we desire you will please to take care that we may have the favour of recommending one or more to represent this city therein. . . .

Honoured Sirs,

Your Honours' most humble servants,

William Swimmer, Michael Pope, John Cary, William Andrews, George Mason, etc.

* * *

[1] Members for Bristol.

London,
December 19th 1695

Gentlemen,

We have yours of the 16th instant wherein you take notice of some debates of the committee of the whole House in reference to a council of trade, which we think a business of great consequence, and may be of no small advantage to the nation, and we find his Majesty hath thought fit and it's said a commission is come forth accordingly and the persons nominated, and some of the greatest quality and others of lesser rank, and acquainted with trade; on which head the committee will be tomorrow, and then this matter will be better understood. But we did not find that the House were inclinable to nominate any out of the House, and then the House of Lords would have joined in some of their number. So that affair is at a great uncertainty and whether will prove advantageous to trade or not very doubtful . . .

We are, Sirs, your humble servants,
Thomas Day and R. Yate.

*   *   *

December 21st 1695

. . . we are apprehensive you mistook our design in what we then wrote you, for it had been all one to us whom you recommended, whether a member of the House, or anyone else, provided he would have undertaken the fatigue and made it his business to promote the interest of this city. For as we then wrote you, London would swallow up the trade of England if the members of that society being in that interest should bend their endeavours to promote its advantage, and this they will do if made up of merchants chosen from that city. Nor do you advise us what methods you either had or designed to take to prevent it, or that you had made any applications on our behalf. We humbly make bold to offer to you our opinions that it would be very necessary you stir in this affair, and if you find your own interest will not be strong enough, that you endeavour to get the members of Bridgwater and those other western ports to join with you, who are on the same footing with us, and equally obliged to secure themselves against the growing greatness of London, and by this means you may at least effect what is desired for this city, being in itself a very reasonable request. . . . Please to pardon our importunity in this business of the council of trade, because we look upon it to be a thing of great consequence to this city.

[Signed as above with the addition of William Davies and John Swimmer]

*   *   *

December 23rd 1695

We have yours of 21st, and take notice that we mistook what you intended when you wrote about the commissioners of trade. We can say no more of it now, that matter being referred to Thursday seven-night, and whether the

House will on that day (which is appointed for the House to be in a committee for trade) then consider of commissioners we cannot talk now. But as any proceeding is made therein you shall have notice. His Majesty hath appointed ten or more commissioners of trade but whether the Commons will rest satisfied with that commission is not yet determined.

There is no doubt but the Londoners will endeavour their own interest; and the other parts of the kingdom must be as careful of theirs. And we shall join with the members of the western and other parts to do what we can to secure ourselves against the growing greatness of London . . .

*   *   *

December 28th 1695

We have the honour of yours 23rd instant, as also the enclosed print, with the names of the commissioners pitched on by the king to make up a council of trade, men according to our judgement altogether improper for such an undertaking, and we hope the House will be of the same opinion. . . . Enclosed we send you a petition from the merchants and other traders of this city setting forth our thoughts on that subject, which we desire you will please to get read, and to strengthen it with what interest you can make, and perhaps it may be followed from other places, if the members like of this for a precedent. We cannot think that the king will refuse to receive advice from his Parliament in this weighty affair, which will be only a charge to the nation, if put in the hands of men unskilful in trade. . . .

William Swimmer, William Davies, Michael Pope, John Cary, Edward Halket, Richard Bayly, etc.

62. THE ROYAL AFRICAN COMPANY DEFENDS ITS MONOPOLY AGAINST ITS OPPONENTS, 1696

[*Commons Journals*, XI, pp. 592, 622]

24 November 1696

A PETITION of the Royal African Company of England was presented to the House, and read: setting forth, that the trade to Guinea cannot be maintained without forts and castles, for the preservation of the Europeans against the natives there, in the way of a joint stock, by companies, who are only able to defray the charge; and therefore, other nations, who trade thither, trade in societies; that the said trade ought to be supported by England being of greatest advantage to it, by exporting the woollen, and other English manufactures; and in supplying his Majesty's plantations with negroes; that the petitioners have been very great losers by the war; and did, the last session, represent to the House, that unless they should be supported and encouraged, they could not longer maintain their forts and factories; and, consequently, that trade would be lost to this nation; many potent rivals lying in wait to supplant the petitioners, who are informed that the Scotch East India Company are sending five ships to trade to Africa, that, last session, this House gave leave that a bill should be brought in; and such proceedings were had thereon that the petitioners hoped it would pass; but, in coming in late, the same could not be completed; and praying leave to bring in a bill for preserving and establishing the trade to Africa, according to the charter granted to the said company; or with such alterations, as may be thought necessary.

Ordered, that leave be given to bring in a bill for preserving and establishing the trade to Africa. And that Mr. Blowfield and Mr. Culliford do prepare and bring in the bill.

* * *

1 December 1696

A petition of sundry merchants and others of the City of London relating to the trade to Africa and the plantations was presented to the House and read, setting forth: that the trade to Africa is of great importance to England and might be much enlarged if all persons had free liberty to trade thither without molestation; that they conceive by a company under such regulations as that to Turkey all necessary public charge might be maintained better than by a company with a joint stock, and the trade thereby be best improved; and praying that they may be heard before any bill do pass to confine the said trade to a company with a joint stock exclusive of others.

Ordered that the consideration of the said petition be referred to the committee of the whole House to whom the bill for setting and regulating the trade to Africa is committed.

63. THE APPOINTMENT OF AN INSPECTOR-GENERAL OF EXPORTS AND IMPORTS, 1696

[G. N. Clark, *Guide to English Commercial Statistics, 1696–1782*, Royal Hist. Soc. Guides and Handbooks, I, London, 1938, pp. 3–4]

Custom House, London, 15 July 1696
To the Right Honourable the Lords Commissioners of his Majesty's Treasury, Presentment by the Commissioners for managing and causing to be levied and collected his Majesty's Customs, Subsidies, and other Duties.

THE Commissioners taking into consideration the great usefulness of keeping a distinct accompt of the importation and exportation of all commodities into and out of this kingdom; and to and from what places the same are exported or imported; in order to make a balance of the trade between this kingdom and any other part of the world, and finding the great difficulty there is to come at such an accompt, when at any time called upon for the same, for want of such a method; and particularly being required by the House of Lords in the last session of Parliament to lay before that House an accompt of three years' exportations and importations, they were forced to return answer from the officers of the Customs that they were not able during the session to prepare such an accompt. And although several officers both inwards and outwards have been ever since employed in collecting the same; they have not hitherto been able to go through half that work. The Commissioners being also required by that House, that for the future such an accompt should be kept of the importations and exportations as may answer the ends aforesaid. And having also received an order from his Majesty's Commissioners of Trade and Plantations to send an accompt of the importations and exportations to and from Sweden and Denmark for 14 years past, which for want of such a method is not without great difficulty to be done, and probably the like accompt may be called for, for the trades to and from other parts; the commissioners are humbly of opinion that, as well in obedience to the commands of the House of Lords, as for the public utility, and that they may be able to answer all exigencies of this kind upon demand, it may be necessary to have an officer of skill and experience in the customs to collect from every day entries in the Custom House such a distributive accompt as may answer the end aforesaid, and also to digest the books of the outports into the same distribution and *method*.[1] And the Commissioners, having lately received their Lordships' commands to have it in their thoughts to find some suitable employment for Mr. Culliford, whose long experience and skill in the business of the customs may render him properly qualified for such an undertaking, they humbly propose Mr. Culliford for the said employment, under the character of Inspector General of the Exports and Imports,[2] to be assisted with such a number of clerks, as may enable him to perform that work, which must be done with great exactness and care, with such allowance of salary as their Lordships shall think his merit, and the nature of so laborious and exact a work may require.

Robert Clayton, Robert Southwell, Walter Yonge, Ja. Chadwicke, Ben Overton, Sam Clarke.

[1] In the margin is the signature of Charles Godolphin, who presumably underlined the word 'method'.
[2] Culliford was in fact appointed to this office.

64. THE COMMISSIONERS OF TRADE AND PLANTATIONS REPORT ON THE STATE OF TRADE, 1697[1]

[*House of Lords MSS.*, N.S., X, 1712–14, no. 3018, pp. 153–62]

State of the Trade of the Kingdom in 1697

Preface relating to the Commission

YOUR Majesty by your commission having required us amongst other things to enquire, examine, and take an account of the state and condition of the general trade of England, and also of the several particular trades to all foreign parts and how the same respectively are advanced or decayed, and the causes and occasions thereof, and to enquire into and examine what trades are or may prove hurtful, or are or may be made beneficial, and how advantageous trades may be improved and extended and such as are hurtful and prejudicial rectified or discouraged, and to enquire into the several obstructions of trade and the means of removing the same, and also in what manner and by what proper methods trade may be most effectually protected and secured in all the parts thereof, and to consider by what means the several useful and profitable manufactures already settled may be further improved, and how and in what manner new and profitable manufactures may be introduced.

Trade in general

We have made enquiries into the state of trade in general from the year 1670 to the present time, and upon the best calculations we can make by the duties paid at the Custom House, we are of opinion that trade in general did considerably increase from the end of the Dutch War in 1673 to *anno* 1688, when the late war began. But trade being subject to many accidents and variations, and all accounts and informations relating thereunto being liable to objections, it does not appear in what proportion nor how much each trade hath increased from year to year. But finding that we have imported from some countries goods to a greater original value than we have exported thither, and it being certain that some private persons may enrich themselves by trading in commodities which may at the same time diminish the wealth and treasure of the nation, to which no addition can be made by trade but what is gained from foreigners and foreign countries, and that such an overbalance has not been made good by any circulation in trade or exchange so as to make such trades advantageous for this nation as they have of late been carried on, we have in our enquiries particularly distinguished the same from others that have a better foundation, conceiving that such trades have occasioned the exportation of coin or bullion or hindered the importation thereof.

---

[1] This report was laid before the Commons on 18 January 1699.—*Commons Journals*, XII, pp. 432–5. On 10 June 1713, the Commissioners of Trade and Plantations were ordered to lay it before the Lords, and this was done on 15 June 1713.

Trade with Sweden and the Baltic

The iron, hemp, pitch, tar, wire, masts, and deals imported from Sweden and south side of the Baltic Sea, we find hath much increased upon us, and that the first cost of late years amounts to above £200,000 per annum, viz.:

Iron..	£70,000
Hemp	90,000
Wire	10,000
Pitch and tar	15,000
Copper, masts, deals, furs, and other goods	20,000
	£205,000

and that the ships employed of late in that trade are not above one half English bottoms; and that the King of Sweden did about the year 1680 lay a duty of above 50 per cent upon our woollen goods imported there, and encouraged woollen manufactures in his own dominions, carried on by the help of wool from England (as we are informed) but exported thither by way of Scotland, and encouraged the expense of such by the example of the Court. And also having *anno* 1696 laid such difficulties on the English merchants as have constrained them to leave the country, did by these means so discourage the importation of English goods that we have not exported thither the value of £40,000 per annum since the laying of those duties, by which we are overbalanced about £200,000 per annum in goods and freights.

Denmark and Norway

From Norway and other parts belonging to the King of Denmark, we find the importation of timber and deals much augmented since the fire of London and increase of buildings, and so much thereof in foreign bottoms that from Michaelmas 1691 to Michaelmas 1696 there were entered in the Custom House at London 1,070 foreign ships from those parts and but 39 English, our ships being charged there with some duties more than Danes, and our exportation of goods thither not £10,000 per annum (those people supplying themselves with what they want chiefly from Holland and Hamburg), and therefore were overbalanced in that trade by goods and freights at least £150,000 per annum.

France

From France the importations have gradually increased from *anno* 1670 to the beginning of the late war in wines, brandies, silks, linen, and many sorts of other goods, for though there was a prohibition of French wine during some of those years, yet it was brought in under other names and in the same years our exportations thither have decreased. The first computation that we find of that trade stands in the books we have in our custody in a report made by Sir George Downing, then one of the Commissioners of the Customs, to the Lords of the Privy Council, then a Committee for Trade, dated the 9th of March 1675, where 'tis calculated that in one year there were imported from France as many silks as amounted to £300,000, linens £500,700, wines 11,000 tuns, brandies 4,000 tuns, computed together at £217,000 which with salt, paper, prunes, vinegar, and other commodities upon the first cost in France amounted in all to £1,136,150 4s. 0d., sterling besides point laces and what was brought in privately, and that our exports to France the same year amounted to but £171,021 6s. 8d. And although we believe that the silks and linens are overvalued in the said report, yet we suppose that the goods then brought in privately (not there estimated) and the increase of the importation of wine and brandy after that time, are equivalent to that overvaluation, for by other computations we are informed that *anno* 1685 the wines imported thence amounted to above 20,000 tuns and the brandies 6,000 tuns. And by the receipt of the excise it appears that, in the year ending at Midsummer 1689, the imports of brandies amounted to near 8,000 tuns, of which we suppose very little came then from any place but France, and we are informed that the wines that year exceeded 20,000 tuns. And the French King having *anno* 1654, 1660, 1664, and 1667 increased the duties on our woollen goods and on our lead, tin, coals, tobacco, sugar, fish, and other commodities, which we usually imported into his dominions, and also laid an imposition of 50 sols Tournois per tun on all English ships, and restrained the importation of woollen manufactures to the ports of Calais and Dieppe, and other goods to some other inconvenient ports, and *in anno* 1686 laid great duties on all East India goods and restrained their importation also to select ports, and at the same time, by example and otherwise encouraging the consumption of the cloth, stuffs, silks, and other goods made by his own people, all which amounted to a prohibition in many cases in receiving goods from England, we are of opinion that we have been overbalanced in that trade, in most of the said years, about one million per annum.

East India

From the East India our importations from the year 1670 to the year 1688 have amounted upon the sales here to about one million per annum, as we are informed, of which we suppose about one half is usually re-exported; and our exportations in goods for those parts did not exceed £70,000 per annum, and in bullion entered by the company from the year 1675 to 1685 about £400,000 per annum; but what was more exported in bullion for the carrying on of that trade from England and Spain by private traders to those parts, we have no certain information.

Spain, Portugal, Italy, Turkey, Barbary, and Guinea

From Spain, Portugal, Italy, Turkey, Barbary, and Guinea, we humbly conceive the importation of goods have not exceeded the exportation, and that there came from those parts many goods that are improvable by a further manufacture here, and the said trades being chiefly carried on by the exportation of our products and manufactures, and very advantageous by the re-exportations of goods received from thence, we humbly conceive they deserve all encouragement.

Plantations

From your Majesty's plantations in America great quantities of tobacco, sugar, and other goods are usually imported, exceeding much in value the goods exported thither. But the better half of such goods being sent from hence to markets abroad having paid considerable duties here, although the more southern colonies are much more beneficial to England than the northern, yet seeing all contribute to the taking off great quantities of our woollen goods, other products, and handicraft wares, and to maintain and increase our navigation, and the inhabitants being your Majesty's subjects, we humbly conceive the trade to and from those colonies deserve the greatest encouragement and will be very advantageous, as long as the Acts of Navigation and Trade be duly observed; and whereas the planting and curing of tobacco, sugar, cotton, indigo, and ginger, the chief commodities of those plantations to make them most advantageous for this nation and beneficial to the planters is best carried on by the labour of negroes, we humbly conceive it is convenient that all encouragement should be given that the said colonies be supplied plentifully with negroes and at the cheapest rates.

Hamburg

The trade to Hamburg is very advantageous, for from that great mart most part of Germany is supplied with our woollen manufactures and other commodities of the growth of these kingdoms or of your Majesty's plantations, which pay at Hamburg but small duties by reason of the privileges which your Majesty's subjects enjoy there preferably to all others. And our returns thence are in goods for necessary use and not such as feed luxury. We therefore are humbly of opinion that this trade have all encouragement as being very beneficial to this nation and to your Majesty's subjects established there.

Holland and Flanders

From Flanders and Holland our trades have been much enlarged during the late war from what they were before, and we do not foresee how they can hereafter have the advantage of an overbalance over us if the Acts of Navigation prohibiting the importation of goods from any country but such as are of their own growth and manufacture, and the laws for prohibiting lace from Flanders, etc., be duly observed and executed.

Russia

From Russia our importations, computed upon the first cost there, have not exceeded our exportations, and it is a trade which we suppose may be improved as well by the expense of tobacco, as of our woollen and other goods, but the present Company, who have the sole management of that trade, being reduced to 13 persons, are so small a number that it should not be so narrowly confined. Therefore, we are humbly of opinion that if more of your Majesty's subjects were admitted into that Company under small fines (as is appointed in the case of the Eastland Company by the Act of 25 Charles II, cap. 7) it would be a means to enlarge the said trade and make the benefits more extensive to your Majesty's subjects.

Fisheries

During the said course of years, our fishing trades to Newfoundland, Greenland and the Northern Seas, as likewise on our own coast for pilchards and herrings, have decreased, occasioned (as we presume) by the increase of other trades which have been found more beneficial to the traders and easy to the seamen which has drawn off our people from those trades and given opportunity to foreigners more used to hard labour and diet to get a great share of them.

Remedies relating to Sweden and the Baltic

To remedy the inconveniency this nation suffers by the trade to Swedeland and the south side of the Baltic, being your Majesty's kingdom of Ireland is capable to afford hemp and flax which may be brought thence in English ships and probably within a short time may be improved and increased to be as good and as cheap as what comes from those places, we humbly conceive if (besides the encouragements given by an Act made in the 7th and 8th years of your Majesty's reign entitled an Act for encouraging the linen manufacture of Ireland and bringing flax and hemp into and the making of sail cloth in this kingdom. And what we humbly represented upon that subject the 31st of August last) a further inducement could be given by your Majesty's Commissioners of the Navy by settling a fund in Ireland to take from thence what hemp they may want for your Majesty's navy at such rates paid there in ready money as may be thought sufficient to encourage the sowing and cultivating of that commodity there, it may be so far promoted that in a short time that kingdom may produce hemp and flax sufficient not only to furnish themselves for carrying on the linen manufacture, but this kingdom also with what may be necessary for all occasions. And if the agents lately sent by your Majesty's directions to New England in order to have pitch, tar, and copper from thence, have the success designed, and the use of English iron and what comes from Bilboa be promoted in all cases where the advantage the Swedish iron hath by toughness doth not make it absolutely necessary, it may be hoped this trade may be brought to near a balance in a short time. But if the King of Sweden could be prevailed with to revoke his order made in 1680, by which he laid great duties on English goods, and to grant a permission to the English merchants that they may reside in Stockholm and other parts of his dominions, with an exemption from high duties, and with such privileges as may enable them to trade freely as usually granted to your Majesty's subjects by other princes in amity with your Majesty, it would also contribute to make this trade more easy and beneficial.

Remedies relating to Denmark and Norway

To remedy the inconveniences this nation suffers by the trade to Denmark, being the carriage of bulky goods, which employ most shipping, amounts to near as much as the first cost, and the ships only proper for that trade are those commonly called Cals, not convenient for any other trade but for that and the Swedish, being we have not any number of them of English build, nor can build any of them but with double the cost of what are built in foreign parts, and that we can't build a sufficient number for the carrying on of that trade without probably losing more by the carriage of such goods in the meantime than the ships may cost. And being also they will be useful to balance the trade with Swedeland, we humbly conceive it may be convenient it be enacted that all ships that may be employed in the trade to Denmark or Sweden, bought within the term of 5 years and constantly owned and sailed by the natives of this kingdom, may be naturalized and have the privilege of English-built ships; and for promoting the consumption of our goods there, a privilege obtained for our merchants to reside and trade freely, paying small duties on all goods from England, and nothing extraordinary imposed on English ships, would be a means to consume more goods there and employ more of our ships and alter the balance of that trade.

Remedies relating to France

To remedy the inconveniences that may be apprehended by a trade with France, being the goods formerly imported from thence did so much exceed our exports, and may again if that trade be laid open and this nation should run into the like fond expense of commodities from thence before your Majesty be assured of a relaxation of the edicts there, and such freedom allowed to your subjects as may afford a mutual conveniency by the consumption of our goods there, being the French King did by several arrets and tariffs before the late war impose such duties and restraints upon many and the goods usually exported hence as amounted to a prohibition, and hath (as we are informed) since the peace by an edict of the 19th October last in general words referring to all nations confirmed the same with some additional severities, and expressly prohibited the importation of the most valuable

East India goods, we humbly conceive that the duties and impositions now charged on French goods can't be taken off without laying this nation open to great disadvantage by that trade, till by a Treaty of Commerce matters relating to trade can be settled on such conditions as may prevent the like overbalance for the future.

And whereas trade depends on sale and consumption and that nothing but a lessening of the expense of French goods can probably reduce that trade to a balance, we humbly propose that the wearing and using of our home made silks, cloths, stuffs, and other useful goods may be encouraged by your Majesty's royal example and the example of your Court, and that the manufacture in this kingdom of lustrings and alamodes and of all other silks and of linen and paper may be promoted, which may be a means not only to lessen the importations from France but to give a large employment to your people here.

And whereas brandy before the year 1660 was imported in so small quantities that we do not find any mention of it in the Book of Rates then made, and the expense of it hath since increased to near 8,000 tuns per annum, which reckoning one sort with another at £20 per tun may cost in France near £160,000 annually, being it hath been found by experience to have occasioned debauchery prejudicial to the health of your Majesty's subjects and loss of many of their lives, and proved a great hindrance to the consumption of malt, if it could be totally prohibited, we humbly conceive it would be for the good of your people and ease of the nation in the carrying on of this trade.

Remedies relating to East India

To remedy in some manner the inconvenience which may arise from the exportation of bullion to the East Indies, we humbly conceive that, unless the East India Company shall make it appear that their constant re-exportations of goods brought from the East Indies do occasion the bringing in of as much bullion as they first carried out, it may be requisite that the wearing or consumption of the manufactured goods of India, Persia, or China, made of silk or herb mixed with either of those materials, as also of painted or stained calicoes and of all handicraft wares imported from those parts, be discouraged and lessened in these kingdoms and your Majesty's plantations in America. And whereas a great trade may be carried on from one part of the East Indies to another in English shipping, by which so much gain may be made as will procure a great part of the goods we received from thence, we therefore humbly conceive that trade ought to be much encouraged.

Remedies relating to fisheries

To remove the difficulties under which our fisheries of Greenland and upon our own coasts and the coasts of Ireland now labour, we humbly conceive that the Greenland Company and the Royal Fishery of England, being (as we are informed) now intent upon the exerting some new endeavours in pursuance of each of their respective powers, the said companies do deserve all possible encouragement as occasioned from time to time shall require [sic]. And for the Newfoundland fishery after the care your Majesty has already taken in the recovery of that country and fortifying St. Johns, the principal harbour there, for the security thereof we can at present add nothing farther than that there be a due execution of the Western Charter and that your Majesty will be pleased from time to time to allow proper convoys for the security of those ships from Salee men and other sea robbers that are used to molest that trade.

Manufactures

We have also in pursuance of your Majesty's said commission made enquiries into the state and condition of our manufactures and how they may be improved.

Woollen manufacture

We are of opinion that the woollen manufacture, which we take to be the most valuable, hath very much increased since the year 1670 and that our weavers and makers are improved in making several useful sorts with great variety; but we find that it is in danger to be much prejudiced by the growth of the like manufactures made in other countries, much promoted by wool carried from England, Scotland, and Ireland. We are informed that great quantities are frequently landed in Holland from Scotland, which we suppose is most carried there out of England or Ireland; particularly there was landed at Rotterdam from Scotland in the beginning of October last 982 bags; and that from Romney Marsh and other places on the coast of Kent and Sussex there hath been imported into Calais and other parts in France, according to the best computations we can get, near 2,000 sacks per annum ever since this war, each sack containing 240 pounds weight, which wool unwrought thus carried out is so great a help to the working up the wool of foreign growth that other nations do now make great quantities of woollen manufactures, to the great hindrance of those made in England and detriment of this nation.

Woollen manufacture in Ireland

We also find that the woollen manufacture in Ireland hath increased since the year 1665 as follows:—

Anno	New Draperies pieces	Old Draperies pieces	Frieze yards
1665	224	32	444,381
1687	11,360	103	1,129,716
1696	4,413	34¾	104,167

Upon consideration of all which we humbly conceive that it is also absolutely necessary for the preservation of this manufacture that the laws against the carrying of wool out of England into Scotland, and out of Ireland to any place but England, and those against carrying it out of England unwrought, may be strictly put in execution. And in order to divert your Majesty's subjects in Ireland from their application to the woollen manufacture, that all possible encouragement be given them towards carrying on that of linen, that having a full employment therein the woollen may be entirely reserved to England.

Silk manufacture

We also find that the manufacture of silk hath much increased since the year 1670, and that our English weavers do make several sorts as good as any made in foreign parts; but that the weavers are under a great discouragement to make them and the shopkeepers to store their shops with them, lest the sale of them should be hindered by silks from France, especially such as depend upon figures and fashions, those coming from thence being generally preferred by the consumer before what is invented by our weavers here.

Linen manufacture

We don't find that the linen manufacture in this kingdom hath made any great progress of late. The stock subscribed for that purpose was soon diverted by a stock jobbing trade, and thereby all the Corporation disabled to promote it, and though that Corporation do still subsist, yet they have not any looms; but what linens they sell at their sale are only such as they buy of weavers in Yorkshire, Durham, and Lancashire. But we find not only those but other counties are capable to afford great quantities of hemp and flax, and therefore as good linen for all ordinary uses may be made in England as any that comes from abroad, and that 'tis a manufacture that would be of great use for the employment of both sexes, from 5 years old and upwards, and that in remote counties wages are cheap and the people inclined to carry on the said manufacture, which if it could be increased would give a great employment to the poor, and prevent the importation of great quantities of linen now imported on us from France and other foreign countries. Wherefore we are humbly of opinion that encouragement be given to the said manufacture by keeping on a considerable duty on all linens imported except from Ireland, and by such other ways as may be thought convenient.

Paper manufacture

We find that the paper manufacture hath also been hindered by the perversion of the stock subscribed for that purpose into a stock jobbing trade, the corporation, now in being, having but 8 mills of their own, they make, as we are informed, of all sorts about 100,000 reams per annum of white paper. We humbly conceive it is also a very useful manufacture, deserving all encouragement, and that we may improve to make as good as what comes from abroad, but the want of white rags, which are the chief material for that commodity, hath proved a great hindrance to the progress of it; but for the encouragement of it we humbly conceive that all paper imported ought to pay a higher duty than paper made at home.

Obstructions to trade: Book of Rates

We have also enquired into the obstructions in trade and how such may be removed to render it more beneficial, and are humbly of opinion that by the great changes and variations which have happened in trade since the making the Book of Rates *anno* 1660, and some impositions since laid on commodities, the duties collected have proved great obstructions to some trades and given advantage to our neighbour nations, as the duties on coarse sugars, and materials for dyeing, and on some other goods, by what is repaid by debentures when re-exported being made cheaper to be manufactured in foreign parts than here at home, which hath occasioned the loss of a great part of our dyeing trade, and of that of refining sugars, and of some others, and by the falling price of some commodities and advance of others since the making of that Book, the duties now collected are unequal. And being that of 1,400 commodities there enumerated, we do not find above 400 useful for a further manufacture or for naval stores nor often re-exported except to the plantations, the rest being most goods and handicraft wares and perfectly manufactured abroad or commodities only useful to increase luxury consumed at home, and under the title of customs outward some of the manufactures and products of this nation charged with considerable duties which we suppose hath proved the hindrance to their exportation; wherefore for a general relief to trade and for preventing all advantages taken by our neighbouring nations, we humbly offer that a new Book of Rates be made, wherein due care may be taken in settling of the several rates and duties by easing those commodities that are for a further manufacture or otherwise necessary or convenient, and by loading such other commodities as may appear hurtful to England, which without diminishing your Majesty's revenue, may remove most obstructions that are now obvious in the carrying on of such trades as are good, and be a hindrance or final discouragement to such as are bad.

Transferring of bonds, etc.

And whereas a great part of trade is carried on by credit and trust in dealing, we humbly conceive if it were enacted that it shall not hereafter be in the power of any person that hath by any writing under his hand, testified by two witnesses, assigned or transferred any bond, bill, or note, made to him by any other person to make void, release, or discharge the said bond, bill, or note, or any of the money due on such bond, bill, or note, or any part thereof, after such assignment made on the said bond, bill, or note; but that such assignee shall have the same right, power, and authority to sue such person indebted by such bond, bill, or note in his own name and to recover the money so due as if such bond, bill, or note had been made originally to himself, that then traders would more frequently take bonds, notes, or bills for such goods as they may sell, to be paid at time, and would transfer and assign the same to others as their occasions may require and thereby make such bonds, bills, and notes very useful and subservient for the carrying on and increasing of trade.

Bylaws of Corporations

And having observed that among the several statutes formerly made relating to trade and the many bylaws of particular corporations, there are some which prove obstructions to the general good of trade. We are humbly of opinion that if a new Book of Rates be made, that may be a proper time to consider of those laws and to propose necessary remedies.

Scotch East India Company; Pirates; Act of Navigation

And whereas we have upon several occasions represented to your Majesty the dangers which threaten our trade from the Scotch East India Company and from the increase of pirates in the East and West Indies, as also from the breaches made upon the Act of Navigation and other matters referring to the plantations, in which your Majesty hath been graciously pleased to signify your Royal pleasure, we humbly conceive it may not be necessary at present to repeat the same.

All which nevertheless is most humbly submitted. [Signed:] J. Bridgewater, Tankerville, Ph. Meadows, Wm. Blathwayt, Jno. Pollexfen, Abr. Hill, George Stepney. Dated Whitehall, December 23rd 1697. [Endorsed:] as delivered by the Lord Guilford from the Commissioners Trade and Plantations, 15 June 1713.

65. A PLEA FOR A SMALL ENTRY FEE INTO THE RUSSIA COMPANY, 1698

[Bodleian Library, Oxford, MS. Don c. 68]

THE
Charge of Companies of Merchants
More equally born
By Impositions on Trade than Fines for Admissions

THE government's design in giving companies of merchants (not trading with joint stocks) a power in their charters to take fines of other merchants, their fellow subjects, for admission into the freedom of their companies, and the companies pretence for taking them, were that those fines might help to bear the charge of those companies; but neither was, nor could be intended as a bar to keep other English merchants out of those trades; for that would destroy the end and design of erecting those societies, which was for the enlarging and improvement of trade, not to cramp, restrain, and clog it.

But companies, and more especially that of Russia, the better to engross trade into a few hands, and to manage it more for their own advantage, have always endeavoured to keep as many out of them, and consequently out of their trades, as possibly they could; nay, so far did the Russia Company proceed, as to make a bylaw, not to admit any person to their freedom by purchase on any terms whatsoever; knowing that a few could better combine together, and agree upon rates to put upon their commodities than greater numbers; or however a few were not so likely to overdrive a trade as many. Therefore their care was to make the door of entrance strait and difficult; and they found by experience (which is beyond all arguments) that the most certain way to effect their purpose of keeping men out of their trades, was to exact great fines for their admission into the freedom of it.

This, and no other good reason, has been the cause that companies have insisted upon large fines for freedom to trade.

The Parliament, *in anno* 1673, being sensible that trade was hindered by great fines, did enact that every English merchant should be admitted into the freedom of the Eastland Company for forty shillings; indeed, before that Act, that company took only a fine of 20*l*. yet that was thought so much that it kept almost all merchants out of that trade, and the reason the Parliament had to make that law was afterward evident; for in seven years before that Act, viz. from *anno* 1666 to 1673, while they kept their fine at 20*l*. and had by their charter all the trade of Norway, Denmark, Sweden, Pomerania, Prussia, Poland, Coorland and Leisland, there were only eight persons, besides their apprentices, purchased their freedom of that company.

Whereas in the next seven years, after the fine was by Act of Parliament reduced to 40*s*. though the trade of Norway, Denmark, and Sweden, were by the same Act left free, by which means the company's trade was reduced to one half of what it was before, yet there were no less than fifty-six persons purchased their freedom, which was seven times as many as had purchased their freedom the seven years before.

The Hamburg Company, by a voluntary reduction of their fine, from 13*l*. 6*s*. 8*d*. to 40*s*. found likewise the same effect by increasing the number of freemen.

And since it is manifest by what has been observed above that a fine of 20*l*. and 13*l*. 6*s*. 8*d*. did prove sufficient bars to keep men out of the Eastland and Hamburg Companies; no man can imagine that a fine of fifty pounds hath not proved a much stronger bar to keep men out of the Russia trade; when it will appear that in 12 or 15 years past, there have not three men purchased their freedom of the company, besides their apprentices, who are not reckoned in the number of those that took their freedoms of the Eastland Company.

And yet the trade of Russia is capable of such improvement, as might (if the admission into it was easy) employ as many ships, seamen, and money, as all the trade the Eastland Company have in all the places within their present privileges; and consequently as many persons would be concerned in it.

When men can be admitted into a company for a very small sum, they will take their freedoms and make a trial of the trade, though they have but small stocks to trade with, no knowledge of the trade, nor any great inclination to it. But a large fine, as it hath been, so will ever be a certain bar to all such; and 'tis an undoubted maxim, that many hands, and much stock, always make the greatest improvement of trade, and advantage to any kingdom.

Now if it can be clearly demonstrated, that by another method the charge of the company may be defrayed, by a way more equal upon all the traders, and more beneficial to trade with respect to the nation, by bringing more hands and stock into trade, it's hoped such a new method will be made use of instead of the old one.

It's evident beyond all controversy that the necessary charge, or a convenient stock to support the company, can be always more equally raised out of men's trade by imposition, proportionable to every man's concern in that trade, than by great fines; for by imposition, there would be ever an exact and perfect equality observed. Because he that traded for much, would pay much; and he that traded for little, would pay little; so every man would bear his due proportion and no more.

Whereas great fines bears hard upon those that have but small stocks to employ, and utterly discourages such, and others that are unacquainted with the trade, from entering into those companies; which as it hinders the increase of hands and stock, is so far prejudicial to the trade of the kingdom; and only an advantage to a few private persons, which to promote, to the prejudice of the nation, can never be thought the care of a Parliament.

If what has been said do make it evident that the charge of the Russia Company may be maintained, and that trade better improved with very small fines, or none at all, but only by impositions laid equally upon the whole trade; it is humbly hoped the Parliament will reduce the fine for admission into that company, so as will encourage all merchants to enter into it.

[Endorsed:] My husband wrote this paper in the year 1698.[1]

---

[1] The volume in which this printed pamphlet appears came from the library of the Heathcotes of Hursley. Most of the other manuscripts were by Samuel Heathcote, the 'husband' referred to in the endorsement above; one was by Sir Gilbert Heathcote.

66. A LANCASTER MERCHANT'S EXPERIENCE OF TRADE TO VIRGINIA, 1698–9

[J. D. Marshall, *The Autobiography of William Stout of Lancaster, 1665–1752*, 1967, pp. 123–4, 129–30]

In 1698

AT MY coming home,[1] I went to board and lodge with Joshua Lawson, where I remained till the 3rd of 3rd month next, in which time I was employed in about the building the ship and fitting her out for a voyage for Virginia, and providing a cargo. All which was completed about the eight[h] month. She was named the *Imployment*, and James Myers, master. Her cargo was in goods, cost three hundred and sixty pound, which we thought sufficient to purchase her loading of tobacco, about 150 hogsheads; and was consigned to the management of the said James Myers, who sailed in the 9th month, and called at Dublin to take in provisions.

In this year, Robert Haydock of Liverpool freighted a ship for Philadelphia, to take in such passengers as were disposed to go to settle in Pennsylvania. Upon which there were more than twenty persons, old and young of our meeting of Lancaster, took this opportunity, sold their estates, and took their families. Amongst them was George Godsalve, a young man was brought up in a grocer and draper's shop, and was disposed to go there with his substance as a merchant. And for his encouragement I adventured with him a parcel of woollen, linen, and other goods suitable for that country, to the value of one hundred and ten pounds, and consigned them wholly to his care and management for me . . .

In 1699

In the fifth month this year, our ship the *Imployment* arrived from Virginia —but not much more than half laden with tobacco, so made a losing voyage. My part of the cargo outward was 61*l*. 8*s*. 0*d*., and the freight of my share 49*l*.; and my part of the tobacco received was 5,697 [lb], which at 3*d*. a pound on board, as the market price then was, came to 71*l*. 4*s*. 0*d*., so that I lost by this voyage 39*l*. 4*s*. 0*d*. And in the ninth month this year we fit out the said ship again upon a voyage to Barbados, and placed in her John Gardner as master, took in her sundry dry goods, and took in provisions at Dublin to make up her load. My part of the cargo was one hundred and ten pounds, and was consigned to William Heysam in Barbados, where she arrived, and returned in due time. And I had returned in goods one hundred and forty two pounds, freight and duty thirty pounds, so that I had in return only the value I sent. So the profit remained there, in debts outstanding and goods unsold, about twenty three pounds, to be accounted for the next voyage thither.

---

[1] To Lancaster from a Quaker meeting in London.

In this year we had advice of the ship *Britannia*'s arrival at Philadelphia, but in a lamentable condition. She was a large ship and a dull sailer, and had above one hundred passengers on board, and a hot and dry season in which an infectious distemper seized them, of which at least one half of the passengers died. And many of them heads [of] families, particularly Christopher and John Atkinson and Thomas Willson from this town, who left three widows and above ten fatherless children, and also George Godsalve, to whom I assigned over my aforesaid adventure of one hundred and ten pound, died at sea as they were going. So that there was none living, at the ship's arrival that was capable to undertake the management of his concerns, so that the goods laid a long time undisposed of, and much damaged, before we could authorize any to take care of them. But after a year we got John Coward, who was William Godsalve's wife's brother, who was then a factor in Virginia for some merchants in London, to go to Philadelphia to look after and dispose of them; who sold them and brought the produce of them into Virginia and purchased tobacco with the same, in all sixty-two hogsheads, which was shipped for London in thirteen ships, of which 33 hogsheads in 7 ships came safe to London. And cleared, after freight and duty paid, forty nine pounds; and 15 hogsheads in two ships was lost at sea, and 14 hogsheads in five ships which came to London safe, but upon sale after freight and duty paid lost four pounds, which was deducted from what the rest was sold for above freight and duty. Also we had some bread and flour sent to Barbados, and returns made to London in sugar and ginger produced about 20*l*. But never got account of [the] sale of our goods at Philadelphia, or any account current from John Coward or any other person, nor what the whole of George Godsalve's own effects were. But as my adventure was one hundred and ten pounds, and I suppose his own was the like sum, but the returns we got was not above eighty pounds, so that I lost by this adventure at least seventy pounds, after at least four years' delay, before we got what was to be had as aforesaid.

At this time, many people were disposed to sell their estates and go to Pennsylvania to dwell. That country, which eighteen years ago was a wilderness, was now become well inhabited, and the city Philadelphia[1] now improved to two miles square and at least one thousand houses. But the misfortune of this ship discouraged many from removing. . . .

---

[1] William Penn obtained a grant from the Crown of the territory that became known as Pennsylvania in 1681. The next twenty years was the great period of Quaker migration.

67. THE COMMISSIONERS OF TRADE AND PLANTATIONS REPORT ON THE STATE OF TRADE, 1702

[*House of Lords MSS.*, N.S., V, 1702–4, pp. 66–73]

Nov. 20. Trade.—Account of the trade of this Kingdom, since the last Session of Parliament. Laid before the House this day. [*Lords Journals*, vol. XVII, p. 169]

To the Right Hon. the Lords Spiritual and Temporal, in Parliament assembled, May it please your Lordships,

IN obedience to your Lordships' order of the 7th inst., requiring us to lay before your Lordships an account of the state of the trade of this kingdom since the last session of Parliament, we humbly represent, that the war against France and Spain being proclaimed a little before the end of the last session, it soon made a great alteration in the state and current of trade, and put a stop to that which was carried on with those countries and the Mediterranean. And as we had some time before, in prospect of such a breach, directed the several governors of her Majesty's plantations to send to us a speedy account of the state of defence of each government, and of what might be wanting to put them in a better posture against an enemy, and having accordingly received such accounts, we did according to our duty lay the same before her Majesty with our humble opinion in relation to ships of war, soldiers, guns, and ammunition to be sent from hence, and to the fortifications there. Whereupon, her Majesty has been pleased to give the necessary directions, and several stores of war have been sent to the plantations, and other suitable provisions made, which has tended very much to the security and encouragement of the trade of those parts. That Col. Codrington, Governor-in-Chief of the Leeward Islands, upon notification of the war and instructions from hence, having possessed himself of the French part of the island of St. Christopher, so that the whole island is now brought under her Majesty's subjection, there does by that means accrue a very great advantage to our sugar trade. That upon representations made of the great importance of the tobacco trade from Virginia and Maryland, her Majesty was pleased to appoint five men-of-war, under whose convoy the shipping from those provinces, consisting of about 150 sail, have arrived safe in England. And, as we find by accounts from Virginia, there were exported from that province from 10 Nov. 1701 to the 10 July 1702, 37,205 hogsheads of tobacco, being the last crop. And from Maryland for the same time, 32,000 hogsheads, or thereabouts, which exceeds the exports of former years.

That the colonies under proprietary and charter governments continuing to be nurseries of illegal trade and guilty of other irregular practices, to the great prejudice of her Majesty's revenue and of fair traders and otherwise, we have from time to time laid before her Majesty the several complaints that have been brought to us relating thereto, and represented upon the whole, as the only means of preventing illegal trade and rendering those provinces useful to England, that they may by the legislative power of this kingdom be brought under the immediate government of the Crown. And, having interposed our best endeavours with the several proprietors, we have prevailed with those of East and West Jersey to resign their pretended right to government into her Majesty's hands. And, for the better support of regular trade, we have moved her Majesty that, until an Act be made for re-uniting those colonies, security be given for the Lieutenant-Governors of those proprietaries that they shall duly observe the Acts of trade; which has been complied with accordingly for the Lieutenant-Governors of Carolina and the Bahama Islands, and we are expecting the like for Pennsylvania. To which we add that Col. Dudley, her Majesty's Governor of Massachusetts Bay, having been empowered by a commission from her Majesty to command the militia of Rhode Island and the adjacent county, did thereupon transport himself thither, but was refused to be obeyed by the Council and those in government there. The said Col. Dudley further informs us that he found the island in great disorder and confusion, as it has long been a receptacle for pirates and illegal traders; that the Quakers and their friends had got the sole power into their hands, and would admit none other into any place of trust; that though there are men of good estate and abilities in that colony, they were excluded from any share of the government, nor could act to any good purpose, if they had been admitted during the present disorders. To remedy which mischief, as well in this island which is of no small importance to the English trade and navigation, as in the neighbouring charter government of Connecticut, and to regulate the general state of trade in those parts, we can propose no other effectual means than that the legislative power of the kingdom, as has been before mentioned, do bring those and other proprietaries and charter governments under an immediate dependance on the Crown. That we have offered our opinion for establishing a settled course of correspondence by packet boats, to sail frequently for Barbados, the Leeward Islands, and Jamaica, from whence opportunities do ordinarily present of sending to the continent; and that method of conveyance having been undertaken by Mr. Dummer, and already begun to be put in practice under his direction, we humbly conceive it will not only be a convenience to merchants and our plantation trade, but may otherwise in this time of war be of great use to the government. That it being requisite for the general security and trade of her Majesty's plantations, and more especially of those on the continent of America, that they should upon occasion assist each other in proportion to their respective abilities; and a quota of assistance to be given by several of them towards the security and defence of New York, which lies the most exposed to the French, having been directed by his late Majesty, as we have formerly represented to your Lordships, we have renewed our directions to the respective Governors that they be very punctual in the execution of those orders. That, in relation to trade with foreign nations, we have upon occasion offered our thoughts upon such treaties as have been communicated to us; in particular upon the project of a marine treaty between England and Sweden, transmitted by Mr. Robinson, her Majesty's Minister at Stockholm, we have made several observations of such heads to be insisted upon as we conceive might tend to the advantage of the trade of England in those parts. We have, likewise, by her Majesty's direction, considered the treaties between the Crown of England and the States General of the United Provinces, with particular regard to what concerns trade, and have thereupon offered what appears to us reasonable to be demanded from them, and suitable to the interest of England. That the trade and fishery of Newfoundland requiring a constant care to prevent the irregularities that are frequently practised by the inhabitants, or those that yearly resort thither, to secure their fishery, and as much as possible in this time of war to annoy the enemy, we did accordingly prepare instructions for the commodore of the squadron sent thither this summer, with heads of enquiries to be made by him into the state of that trade, also relating to the soldiers there in pay, and to the fortifications necessary for the defence and security of our principal harbours, and further directed him to enquire into the abuses committed there, and not only to regulate the same during his stay in those parts, but to report to us at his return what remedies he conceives may be fitly applied to those evils, in order to such further directions as shall be necessary against the next season. To all which having now received his answers, we thereby find that the state of that trade and fishery has this last season been as follows, viz.:

Abstract of an Account of the Fishery of Newfoundland
for the year 1702.

Number of ships	
Fishing ships	16
Sack ships	25
	41
Burden of fishing ships	1,330 tons
Number of men belonging to the said ships	411
Number of boats	
Fishing ships boats	35
By-boats	9
Inhabitants' boats	371
	415
Number of by-boatmen	
Masters	11
Servants	81
	92

Quantity of fish made
By fishing ships	8,100
By inhabitants and by-boats	74,040
	82,140 cwt

Quantity of fish carried to market	56,590 cwt
Quantity of train made by	
Fishing ships	175
Inhabitants and by-boats	1,290
	1,465 hogsheads
Number of stages	266
Number of inhabitants	
Men	259
Women	208
Children	441
Servants	1,494
	2,402

And though it does hereby appear that our fishery has not been so considerable this year as other preceding years, which must be imputed chiefly to the interruptions and difficulties occasioned by the war and the want of a vent for our fish in the dominions of Spain and other parts of the Mediterranean, yet the success that her Majesty's ships of war have had in taking and destroying the French ships employed in that trade has been so great, that besides the present advantage, we cannot but expect it will very much discourage them and tend to the increase and better improvement of our trade and fishery there the next year.

That we have by her Majesty's command made particular enquiries into the state of the woollen manufacture as the most considerable branch of the trade of this kingdom, and have humbly represented the same to her Majesty, together with our observations and proposals thereupon, as follow, viz.:

From Michaelmas 1662 to Michaelmas 1663, our general exports amounted to £2,022,812.

From Michaelmas 1668 to Michaelmas 1669, they amounted to £2,063,274.

Whereof we judge that near two-thirds were of woollen manufacture. And by the late accounts of the Inspector General of the Customs, since the establishment of that office, we find our general exports:

	£
From Michaelmas 1697 to Michaelmas 1698, amounted to	6,361,105
From Xmas 1698 to Xmas 1699	6,788,166
From Xmas 1699 to Xmas 1700	7,302,716

And our exports in woollen manufactures alone for the same years, viz.:

£

From Xmas 1697 to Michaelmas 1698, amounted to 3,120,615
From Xmas 1699 to Xmas 1700 2,989,163
From Xmas 1700 to Xmas 1701 3,128,366

The particular sorts and quantities whereof we find also by his accounts are as follows, viz.:

From Michaelmas 1697 to Michaelmas 1698

Bays of all sorts	88,693 pieces
Cloths of all sorts	80,700 pieces
Cottons	423,278 goads
Flannels and friezes	402,240 yards
Hats	184,650 doz.
Stockings	143,823 doz.
Kerseys	66,938 pieces
Stuffs, serges, says	5,727,929 lbs.

From Xmas 1699 to Xmas 1700

Bays of all sorts	81,584 pieces
Cloths of all sorts	58,500 pieces
Cottons	443,406 goads
Flannels and friezes	443,139 yards
Hats	
Stockings	94,665 doz.
Kerseys	58,017 pieces
Stuffs, serges, says	6,660,983 lbs.

From Xmas 1700 to Xmas 1701

Bays of all sorts	86,912 pieces
Cloths of all sorts	68,188 pieces
Cottons	438,354 goads
Flannels and friezes	462,888 yards
Hats	129,622 doz.
Stockings	94,183 doz.
Kerseys	60,133 pieces
Stuffs, serges, says	6,159,767 lbs.

and some small quantities of other sorts of no great value, by which it appears that there has of late years been a considerable increase in our exports of the woollen manufactures, the value thereof in the year 1701, exceeding that of the year 1662, by more than a million. We are likewise informed by the Turkey Company, that from the end of the late war to the beginning of the present war, they have exported more draperies than they did for the like number of years formerly. But we observe that the general increase of these exports has chiefly consisted in the new draperies, viz. stuffs, says, serges, etc., and we humbly conceive that the complaints which may have been made by the proprietors of wool and by the clothiers of a fall in the price of the goods have been occasioned by several extraordinary causes: as the interruption that trade in general has met with by war, the improvements of land in

England, and the great additions that have been made to our stock of wool by importations from Ireland, which together have sunk the price of wool and of other woollen goods. The importations of wool from Ireland in the years 1693, 1694, and 1695 have amounted to 140,000 stone, but in the years 1699, 1700, and 1701, to 936,808 stone. The lands in England have been very much improved since the year 1670, by clover and other grass seeds, by which they feed a greater number of sheep than formerly, and our stock of wool is thereby augmented. We have also of late years increased our manufacture of superfine cloths (made of Spanish wool only), which has occasioned for some years past a greater importation of Spanish wool than heretofore.

We do likewise find that the woollen manufactures in Ireland are of late years increased, and that in divers foreign countries, as in France, Holland, Flanders, Spain, Portugal, Sweden, Silesia, Lüneburg, and other parts of Germany, new manufactures have been set up, which we take to be another reason why our trade in woollen goods has not been further enlarged. We also observe of later years, great numbers of people are enticed over to her Majesty's northern colonies in America, and particularly to those under proprietary and charter governments, which persons, while they were in England, did contribute to the consumption of our woollen manufacture, but, being entertained there, do with the rest of the inhabitants clothe themselves, children, and servants with the woollen manufacture of the product of those countries. And not only so, but divers manufacturers and workmen also are carried over upon specious pretences of a more easy livelihood in those parts. And in this manner those proprietaries do not only clothe themselves with woollen goods, but furnish the same commodity to the more southern plantations, notwithstanding the prohibition in the Act of 10 and 11 of his late Majesty. And by their application to this sort of trade, instead of confining themselves to the production of such commodities as are agreeable to the true design and intention of their settlements, they have improved their skill to such a degree, that we have been particularly informed by persons employed by us to make enquiries, that as good druggets are made in those countries as any in England, and sold there for 4s. and 4s. 6d. per yard that country money. To which we also crave leave to add, that those plantations having several dyeing wares, either of their own product or in their neighbourhood, much cheaper than the same can be procured in England, they are able to afford those manufactures much cheaper than they can be sent thither from hence.

We think ourselves further obliged to take notice, that the importation from India into this kingdom of those sorts of manufactured goods proper for the same uses as our stuffs, serges, says, druggets, etc., having very much increased of late years, and the same not being brought over in return of our woollen manufactures exported, but purchased chiefly by bullion carried thither, they do intend to obstruct the consumption of our woollen manufactures made at home. It is likewise observable that since the Act which prohibits the wearing of several sorts of East India goods, great quantities thereof (as appears by the entries of the Custom House) are now shipped off to her Majesty's colonies in the West Indies, by which and the manufacture of wool carried on in those parts, the consumption of those goods usually sent thither is greatly obstructed, and the intended effect of that Act defeated thereby. We are informed by several merchants concerned in the woollen trade, that the prohibiting of painted calicoes from India to be consumed in England has not had the desired success; for though it was hoped that this prohibition would have discouraged the consumption of those goods, we find that the allowing calicoes unstained to be brought in has occasioned such an increase of the printing and staining calicoes here, and the printers and painters have brought that art to such perfection, that it is more prejudicial to us than it was before the passing that Act. For whereas then the calicoes painted in India were most used by the better sort of people, whilst the poor continued to wear and use our woollen goods, the calicoes now painted in England are so very cheap and so much in fashion, that persons of all qualities and degrees clothe themselves and furnish their houses in a great measure with them.

The Turkey Company have also continued their complaints to us, that their trade is obstructed by the East India Company, who do not vend in India those draperies which they export from hence, but send them to Ispahan and from thence to Tauris and other northern parts of Persia, which is a mischief not to be prevented, otherwise than by the East India Company being enjoined to send such woollen goods as they cannot sell in India to China, Japan, and other Eastern countries, where their vent may not be an obstruction to the Turkey Company's trade, which, we conceive, was intended by the preamble of their charter, as we humbly represented to his late Majesty by our report dated 19 January 1697/8. The said Turkey Company having further acquainted us with the difficulties they lie under to carry on their trade in this time of war, and thereupon desired that a convoy may be granted them for the ships they might speedily send out; we have laid that matter before her Majesty for her royal determination. We further observe that the nature of trade is such, that it depends upon the mutual conveniency which every nation finds in the barter and exchange of the commodities of their own growth, for those of the growth of other countries, according to which rule it is apparent that the consumption of the English woollen goods abroad, particularly in Turkey and Italy, is supported by our taking off the raw silks of those countries; and we are, therefore, humbly of opinion that the importation of raw silk, in such quantities as they are returned for our woollen goods, ought not to be discouraged, as well because the vent of our goods in those parts is carried on thereby, as also that a great number of her Majesty's subjects are supported by manufacturing those silks here, and the nation supplied with wrought silks at the cheapest rates. Upon discourse with persons most knowing in the winding and making up of our wool, it appears that the clothiers' trade may be further improved, if the wool were more carefully and faithfully wound up in the fleece (according to the several

Acts of Parliament) without loose locks, hair, and dirt, to the great prejudice of the clothiers who buy the same; which ill practice we find has much increased of late.

The deceit used by those who fabric and finish our cloths, in the stretching and ill making them, as well as in the giving them false lengths and breadths—which abuses were designed to be prevented by the aulnage duty—we conceive to be other obstructions to our woollen manufacture. And, in relation to the better improvement of our trade in woollen goods, we are humbly of opinion that the high duties laid here upon dyeing wares hinder the dyeing and finishing of those goods here, by which the dyers, pressers, and other traders are much prejudiced; great quantities of our woollen goods are sent out white and dyed in Holland, Hamburg, and other parts, the customs, which are drawn back upon the exportation of our dyeing wares, rendering those wares so cheap to foreigners as to afford them the means of dyeing our woollen goods abroad cheaper than can be done in England, and consequently gives them a greater advantage in carrying out such goods white than after being dyed and finished.

As to the particular improvement of the exportation of the woollen manufacture, great care has been taken, for some years past, in those counties (viz. Kent and Sussex) where the running of wool has been chiefly carried on. New officers were appointed in the year 1697 to prevent the same; and the management of that service was committed to Mr. Henry Baker. The Commissioners of her Majesty's Customs were ordered to give special direction to their several under-officers on the coasts of those counties to be aiding to him. He has likewise from time to time made his application to this Board, and has received our best assistance, and such has been the success of the methods taken for the prevention of this evil, by putting the laws in execution against such offenders, and by the impeachment in Parliament of the French smugglers, whose trade was carried on by these illegal practices and correspondence, that the several convictions appear to amount to no less than the sum of 68,249*l.* And by these methods and prosecutions this unlawful trade is almost destroyed in those counties. But whereas the like abuses are carried on and will probably increase in other maritime counties, unless the like care be taken to prevent it; and whereas several of those unlawful traders, who have been disturbed in the counties of Kent and Sussex before mentioned, have betaken themselves to other parts upon the coasts, we humbly propose it as expedient, that a guard of civil officers, under a regular establishment and with proper instructions, be likewise appointed in such other maritime counties of this kingdom where these ill courses shall appear to be carried on, and particularly in the northern counties adjacent to Scotland, which guard, we judge, will be able to bear their own charge with considerable advantage to her Majesty's revenue, and may procure the great benefit aimed at, of keeping our wool at home. Upon this head we have only to add that every pound of wool thus exported has, in the return, usually produced above ten times the value of its prime cost here. And we conceive that the temptation to such excessive profit can only be opposed by an extraordinary care; and that the most vigorous putting the laws against these abuses in execution, without favour or remission, together with the assistance of the officers aforementioned, under a strict discipline, will prove the most effectual means of curing this evil.

Whitehall, 18 Nov. 1702.

Dartmouth, Ph. Meadows, Wm. Blathwayt, John Pollexfen,
Mat. Prior, Robert Cecil.

68. PROBLEMS IN OBTAINING ACCURATE TRADE FIGURES FROM THE CUSTOMS ACCOUNTS, 1712

[G. N. Clark, *Guide to English Commercial Statistics, 1696–1782*,
Royal Hist. Soc. Guides and Handbooks, I, London, 1938,
pp. 57–9, 80–1]

[A Letter from Mr. D'Avenant to Lowndes]

April 4th 1712.

Sir,

In a report[1] to the commissioners appointed to state the public accompts, which by their precept, dated the 17th July 1711, I was directed to make, concerning the present condition of trade, and which was delivered the 10th of December following, I have among other things taken notice that from the time the outward duties upon the woollen goods exported were taken off, the merchants have made their entries of those commodities at pleasure, as well in the outports as London; but generally they have entered greater quantities than were really exported, to carry on some mystery of trade, which though it might prove of advantage to a few persons here and there, could never be profitable to the public, in regard it must beget uncertainties in foreign markets and sometimes an overplus of those goods and result at last in a trick of the exporters to deceive one another, at which they would not venture when the commodities had such a duty upon 'em as the merchant could not afford to play with; but to what value those over-entries might amount, I could not compute, for the proper officers, receiving no duties from thence, keep no perfect register as I can find; and large entries are frequently made when perhaps less quantities are shipped off, which indeed are marked in the body of the cockets by the queen's searchers, but no distinct accompt thereof is kept, so that in free goods 'tis impossible for me to check, or correct by the searchers' books, the entries brought up to my office.

You know, sir, I have often complained to you of this practice, and of what

---

[1] Printed in D'Avenant's *Works*, vol. v (1771), pp. 347 ff.

ill consequence it may be to remain in the dark in so material a branch of our exportation as the woollen manufacture has always been, and upon which the trade of England turns so much, nor have you been wanting in your endeavours to prevent this mischief, by offering some time since a clause to compel the exporters under a penalty to just and true entries, which clause, for some private interest, met with opposition in the House of Commons and was rejected.

I have observed few laws are effectual but such as execute themselves and am afraid, that though a clause could be obtained obliging the merchant to true entries, and compelling the officers to keep a true register thereof, yet if no advantage is thereby to accrue, either to the Crown or to the officers, such entries will continue to be made at random and the government will be still uncertain as to the increase or decrease of the woollen trade.

I did therefore lay before the Parliament commissioners, that it was difficult to find a good reason why this small duty of 5 per cent upon the said exports was taken off, at a season when there was such a necessity of loading all the importations to England. That it would be well worth the consideration of the wisest heads whether this free export of the woollen goods and the bounty upon corn exported be not rather a profit to our neighbours than to the body of this kingdom, and that the duties upon the woollen goods, for the three last (while they paid subsidy) by a medium of the said three years amounted to £43,213 per annum. I likewise laid before the said commissioners a distinct accompt, showing the quantities of the woollen manufactures exported in three years, with the amount of the subsidy duties paid thereupon, as also the quantities of the said goods entered for exportation in three years after the said duties were taken off by an Act passed in the 11 and 12 of his late Majesty King William, with a computation of what the subsidy duties would have amounted to if the same had been continued.

I farther hinted, that if these duties were laid afresh upon outward goods (which duties did not appear such a burthen as the debts of the nation might not render tolerable) they would either be a good present fund for money, or might come in aid and ease of some branch of our importation which is overtaxed and that though but two and a half per cent should be laid, it would be a means to prevent the merchant from over-entries and bring upwards of £20,000 per annum to the public.

I find by my books, that the exportation of woollen goods is every year larger and larger, but at the same time 'tis obvious, that there is a general complaint all over England of wool being a drug, so that upon the whole I am inclined to believe there may be over-entries made of those commodities, not so much in the fine draperies as in the perpetuanas, serges, says, and stuffs.

If 'tis thought of any consequence to the government to have a yearly view before 'em how the woollen manufacture stands, I cannot see how 'tis to be compassed, unless by some law the merchant be obliged to a regular and true entry, under a penalty, and unless at the same time the proper officer by the said Act shall be directed to keep an accompt of the true quantities exported, to which the Inspector General of exports and imports may have recourse, in order to check the entries when they are to be posted in his ledgers.

Such a clause in some Act would in a great measure prevent this ill practice, which will render all accompts of free goods exported uncertain and our trade for woollen manufacture may slip out of our hands before we are sensible of the mischief.

But the true way to render these accompts certain would be to lay afresh some outward duty upon 'em, which in this scarcity of funds, the House of Commons perhaps may hearken to.

If you judge this paper contains anything material, and fit to be communicated to my Lord Treasurer, I desire you would lay it before his lordship from

Sir,

Your most humble and most obedient servant,

Charles d'Avenant.

*   *   *

[John Oxenford writing in *An Essay on the Balance of Trade, Christmas 1698–Christmas 1719*]

To come at the value of exports sold by England to foreign countries, deduct from the total value of exports as it stands in the Inspector's books . . .

If greater quantities of goods are overvalued among the exports than are exported, it must be either:

First, by means of double entries;

Secondly, by the merchant's entering outwards, to make ostentation of his trade in the printed bills of entry, greater quantities of goods than he after exported.

In both these cases greater quantities of goods may be valued among the exports than are really exported, for the quantities in the port of London are valued as they are found in the bills of entry. The Inspector General has no other rule to guide him; neither can he distinguish by the bills what quantity of goods are twice entered and not exported, but values the whole quantities in every bill as if they were exported, and therefore, in the case of double entries, values the same goods twice over, once more than he ought to do; in the case of entries for ostentation he values goods that never were exported; in both cases greater quantities than were exported.

Double entries happen chiefly, if not altogether, in the port of London, where the merchant has sometimes choice of several ships in which to export his goods, and therefore when he has entered out his goods in one ship he may alter his mind and make a new entry of the same goods in another; and entries for ostentations in the printed bills, if there is any such thing, can be only in the port of London, for no bills of entry are printed for the outports. Besides no part of this charge can be against the outports, for the officers return from thence to the Inspector General, not the bills of entry, but the very quantity of goods that are exported, and even in the port of London these entries are chiefly to be said of woollen manufactures, and the few other goods that are exported free.

But now who can believe that the double entries or the entries for ostentation amount to very great quantities? The merchant will hardly put himself to the trouble or even the charge of a new cocket for a second entry for the same goods without apparent necessity, and the pretender would soon expose himself to the whole exchange, and instead of gaining the reputation of a great trader would be thought a bankrupt or little better.

But lastly, to bring this matter to some certainty, the lords commissioners of trade as I have been informed caused the searchers' books of the port of London (from whence it seems the Inspector General ought rather to be supplied with the quantities of goods exported than from the bills of entry) to be examined, and the quantities of three or four of our woollen manufactures exported to be extracted for two years since the peace; and upon comparing the quantities of the Inspector General with those of the searchers' officer, the former were found not to exceed 4 per cent in the whole.

Now if the woollen manufactures and the few other goods that are exported free are the chief, if not the only, goods over entered, whether by double entries or entries for ostentation, and if these are not half the whole from the port of London, as indeed they are not, then 4 per cent over-entered of the former will not amount to 2 per cent on our whole exports from the port of London; and as the very quantity of goods exported from the outports are returned to the Inspector General, and nothing is to be deducted from the value of the latter on account of over-entries, over-entries at the port of London may probably not exceed one per cent, to be deducted on that account from the value of exports from all England . . .

69. THE MERCHANT ADVENTURERS' VIEWS ON FREE TRADE, 1716

[P.R.O., CO 389/25, pp. 356v, 359–69]

January 20, 1715/16

MEMORANDUM from the Hamburg Company relating to the state of their trade to the Right Honourable the Lords Commissioners for Trade and Plantations . . . [relates the history of the Merchant Adventurers in the Middle Ages, under the Tudors and early Stuarts, and up to the Restoration of Charles II when the Merchant Adventurers' charter was renewed] . . .

However, soon after several interlopers and clothiers, hoping to obtain some favour from the new restored government, petitioned the Parliament for a free trade upon the specious pretence that great quantities of cloth were lying upon the hands of poor clothiers, which they could dispose of in case such a free exportation were granted. The opinion of his Majesty in Council was that the experiment would not have the promised effect, but rather tend to the prejudice of the trade, and make the cure afterwards more difficult. However, after several deliberations, their importunity prevailed so far upon the desire of the House of Commons, that a proclamation for a free trade for six months was by the king ordered to be published, with the free consent of the Company of Merchants Adventurers of England (as the very words of the proclamation, dated the 14th May, 1662 do express it). This time being expired but having not produced the promised effect of increasing the trade, the Company was again restored to their ancient right of the sole exportation of the woollen manufactures to the parts of their privileges by a proclamation dated the 8th April, 1663, containing among other things in favour of the Company that his Majesty, being certified by the petition of the clothiers themselves, as also the general complaint in all clothing counties, that the late liberty hath not produced the promised and expected effect, had with the advice of his Privy Council thought fit for the restoration and conservation of the trade of the woollen manufactures to restore the Merchants Adventurers to their ancient right of sole exportation, and to the end that this trade may be the better improved, ordered the said Company to receive into the freedom of their fellowship all subjects that shall desire it, paying £13 6s. 8d. at their admittance, all of London to be mere merchants, but of the outports to be bred merchants though shopkeepers.

Upon this as many subjects as desired it were admitted and the trade of the woollen manufacture was carried on under order and regulation to the great benefit and increase of the vent of our woollen manufactures abroad. But the effect and consequences of the forementioned dispensation for a free trade, and another granted in 1666 during the war with Holland very much obstructed their good intention, for the interlopers and chiefly foreigners of Germany as well as Holland, having now found an inlet into the trade of the woollen manufacture, still contrived ways to continue their irregular trade with intention to ruin the Company and to get the trade of our woollen manufactures into their own hands.

In these mischievous practices the said interlopers and foreigners went on until the year 1683 when it was discovered that several persons, principally aliens and foreigners, endeavoured to destroy the Company. And being under no rule and regulation, did take upon them to ship woollen manufactures out of this kingdom, and by several deceitful practices of the said foreigners in counterfeiting the marks, seals, and tillets of persons free of the Company, the said trade will be in great danger of being much impaired if not totally lost to the natives of England. His Majesty by his royal proclamation, dated the 13th June, 1683, confirmed the Merchants Adventurers in their ancient right of solely exporting the woollen manufactures to the parts of their privileges, but withal to admit all subjects to the freedom of the Company that shall desire it within a year for £13 6s. 8d. sterling as a fine, in the same manner as was ordered in 1663 above mentioned.

After this settlement of the Company the trade of the woollen manufactures was very successfully carried on by them, and the vent thereof increased very much in Germany, the Company constantly keeping a great number of large warehouses always filled with our woollen manufactures to a very great value, from £5,000 to £20,000 sterling of all sorts proper for the markets in Germany, and much more than sufficient to supply the same. And the Germans constantly resorted to Hamburg from several parts for the buying of all sorts of English woollen manufactures, and when they could not come thither to see and buy goods themselves, the English merchants residing in Hamburg furnished them according to their patterns as effectually as they possibly could have been directly from England.

In this manner the trade of the woollen manufactures was successfully managed by English subjects only, to the great advantage of our kingdom until the first year of King William and Queen Mary, when a clause was inserted in a bill prohibiting the exportation of wool, that for three years it shall be lawful for any person or persons whatsoever to buy cloth stuffs, stockings, or any other manufacture of wool made in England, and freely to export the same into any parts beyond the seas, paying the usual custom. The effect of which liberty proved very prejudicial and destructive to the Company, and brings them in the next place to shew what decrease the Company's trade has since met with, and the causes and occasions thereof.

Since the above mentioned freedom of trade, the Company has from time to time declined, and at present is reduced to such a sinking condition that they must of necessity be soon totally ruined, if not relieved and countenanced by the authority of his Majesty and the Parliament.

The forementioned clause making it lawful for all persons freely to export the woollen manufactures of England into any parts beyond the seas was limited to three years, which time being expired, a bill was again brought into the House contrived chiefly by foreigners for the continuing of it. But the Company and several clothiers being heard against that bill, it was rejected. Yet nothing was done for the Company, but the freedom of exportation by all persons is still continued as much as if the former grant were yet in force, although in the years 1693 and 1694 the Company proved to the satisfaction of the Committee of Parliament that the exportation during the three years of liberty had not been greater than in three years before. And if it could have been proved that it was greater, yet that was not to be attributed to the freedom granted but unto other accidents, viz. a great consumption by our armies abroad; vast quantities sent through Hamburg into Italy and other parts; the supplying of very considerable quantities taken by the French; and other temporary reasons, which subsist still. Nay, since the duty of woollen goods has been taken off, it has been several times found at Hamburg that foreigners have entered a considerable number of packs to be exported both from London and Hull. But when they arrived at Hamburg, it appeared by the contents of the lading that not half the number of packs had been shipped which were entered by the cockets, so that this trick was made use of to make the exportation seem very considerable, and to conceal the decay of trade, which for this and the reasons beforesaid is at present not so apparent to the public as it is to traders themselves.

Before the last liberty of exportation was granted to all persons, the Company had many large warehouses in Hamburg, stocked with all sorts of woollen goods to the value of many thousand pounds. These since the liberty of trade are reduced to a very small number and in a little time will come to none at all, for now most of the foreign merchants in the several parts of Germany, as well as those of Hamburg, who formerly used to buy of the Company, bring their goods from England themselves, nay, even shopkeepers do the same, and for the supply of their occasions employ Dutch factors in England, so that when all persons who used formerly to buy of the Company get the woollen goods from England directly themselves, there will be nobody left to sell to and then the trade of the Company must needs be at an end.

Since the trade of the woollen manufactures was given free and foreigners let into it, they have found means almost totally to exclude the English merchants from the trade to Holland, Zealand, Brabant, and Flanders, for the Company's trade into those parts is quite lost, the residency which they had at Dordrecht, where they enjoyed great privileges, and carried on a most considerable trade is altogether ruined, and not an English merchant left there. And now these foreigners are endeavouring to beat the Company out of their trade at Hamburg also, which, if this liberty of trade be continued, will unavoidably be accomplished.

As soon as the foreigners by the free liberty of trade became principal in our market in buying, he presently and ever since has endeavoured to beat down the price of goods, which forced the maker to make his goods worse for to secure a profit, and then by extraordinary measure which they have exacted, extraordinary stretching and straining has been occasioned. Whereas before, when this trade was carried on by English merchants only, cloth was kept up to a true and good making. This sinister practice of straining and falsifying goods answers the end of private profit, which is all that foreigners aim at, who care not what the consequences will be.

The foreigners since the liberty of trade employ English factors in England no longer than to bring their own countrymen and relations into credit, who they send into England and recommend to English factors. And when those have got acquaintance and knowledge in the way of buying, the English factors are turned off, and this is practised by them not only in London but all England over, to the great prejudice of his Majesty's subjects. And experience has shewed that several of them being crept into credit with clothiers and factors and by them largely trusted, have, after they were run deeply into debt for woollen goods bought, taken an opportunity to fly the land, to the ruin of the clothiers and others both in the north and west, which proves destructive to the trade abroad, those goods being often sold there for two-thirds of the first cost.

The many and great privileges which the Company has enjoyed in
Hamburg both to the honour and great advantage of our nation, for above
one hundred years, are grounded upon bringing trade thither and making
that the staple and mart for the trade into the north part of Germany, which,
when foreigners supply the market and when the Company has nothing of
the trade left, but is quite beat out of it by foreigners, those great and honourable privileges, the like of which no other nation has nor will ever be able to
obtain, must needs be lost, and cease of themselves . . .

70. FOREIGN TRADE VERSUS FUNDHOLDING, 1716
[P.R.O., CO 389/25, pp. 401, 410–13]

March 24, 1715/16

Representation relating to the woollen manufactures, particularly
the decrease of the exportation of cloth
[to the Lords Commissioners for Trade and Plantations]

. . . From the whole [i.e. the reports from various groups of merchants] we
must observe in general that the clothing trade of this kingdom is manifestly exposed by the increase of the woollen manufactures in other countries.
And therefore we most humbly propose in order to secure the consumption
of our own and to discourage foreign manufactures that our woollen manufactures may be so carefully indulged and encouraged at home that the
merchants may be enabled to transport them as cheap as possible abroad . . .
   But upon the several memorials of the merchants we must further observe
1. with respect to the trade with Germany that although the restraining of
the exportation of the woollen manufactures to the Company of Merchants
Adventurers might formerly square with the interest of the kingdom, yet
since this trade, as it is now carried on without such restriction, has been
increasing for several years past and is still very considerable, viz.
   Woollen manufactures exported to Germany amounted to: in the last
Peace, £330,683; during the war, £488,011; in 1713 and 1714, £388,751
per annum. We cannot think it reasonable that the course thereof should be
interrupted, nor can see how the aforesaid decrease since the present peace
could be remedied by such a regulation.
   However, it must be allowed that foreign merchants have a very considerable share in this, and a much larger in the Holland and Flanders trade.
And we apprehend it cannot be otherwise so long as the Funds and stocks
settled in the late wars render a more certain and greater gain than any
foreign trade whatsoever . . .

VI. FINANCE AND THE COINAGE

1. DRAFT OF A PROCLAMATION ANNOUNCING COPPER COINS FOR SMALL CHANGE, *c.* 1600

[B.M., Harl. MS.698, F.54]

WHEREAS in the beginning of our reign, to the great honour and profit of us and all our people, we did restore and reduce the monies of our realm from dross and base matter unto fine gold and fine silver[1] (which by God's favour we intend to continue and maintain), yet because the rate and division of our silver monies is such, and as the present time requireth cannot well be altered, as that with any conveniency any smaller money may be made thereof than a penny or three farthings; nevertheless we have been often informed and do perceive what great necessity our loving subjects have of smaller monies as of halfpence and farthings, and chiefly what loss and hindrance the poor sort do sustain by lack thereof (whereof we have pitiful consideration); and bending ourself to the remedy of the same, divers devices have been tendered to us and our Privy Council, as well showing means how the said small monies might be made both fair in shew and sufficient in quantity as also complaining of a long continued and yet a very intolerable and arrogant disorder used by private persons in making of tokens of lead and tin generally coined and put out instead of such small monies by grocers, vintners, chandlers, and alehouse keepers, and divers other persons, therein manifestly derogating from our princely honour and royal dignity, which complaint we have considered of as very just and reasonable; but because the devices offered therewith have all tended to the breach of the fine standard of our coin in such small monies so required and would have a mixture for the same of coarse and base alloy, to the slander and discredit of our fine silver monies now being, we have clearly rejected all the same devices; and yet weighing with ourself the great disorder used in the said tokens, and how that our said subjects have great loss and no manner of profitable ease thereby whilst they serve not in any wise to be uttered or paid again but only at that shop or place where they were first received:

Therefore we do by these presents straightly forbid and command that none of the said former tokens or any such like of what device or invention soever, at any time from or after the Feast of All Saints next coming, shall

---

[1] See P. L. Hughes and J. F. Larkin, *Tudor Royal Proclamations*, II, *The Later Tudors, 1558–1603* (1969), nos. 471, 475, 478. This draft proclamation is printed in volume III (1969), pp. 222–4.

be made or used without our special warrant and commission in that behalf; upon pain that the person and persons making or using the same shall suffer imprisonment of their bodies by the space of one whole year, and shall moreover pay such fine to our use as shall be assessed by our Privy Council in our Star Chamber at Westminster.

And forasmuch as upon great deliberation we well perceive that of necessity our said subjects must either have halfpence and farthings, or else tokens to supply the stead thereof; and because that such small monies cannot be made of the fine silver of our monies whilst the same are at 5s. the ounce, but that they will be so small as that they can neither be well kept or used in payment:

Therefore, for the ease of our said subjects and to serve their necessity in this case, we have taken order that by our authority there shall be pledges or tokens made of pure and fine copper of halfpence and farthings, whereof every pledge of an halfpenny shall weigh 24 grams, and that of the farthing 12 grams; in the making whereof we intend to employ such costs and charges as that any so evil disposed shall hardly attain to counterfeit the same.

And yet more surely to avoid such counterfeiting, we, only in that respect and not otherwise, do as well rate and value by authority hereof every of the said pledges of 24 grams in weight to pass and be current as aforesaid in place and stead of an halfpenny throughout all our realms [and] dominions, to and amongst all persons whatsoever; and likewise every of the said pledges of 12 grams in weight to pass and be current as aforesaid in place and stead of a farthing; as also do privilege all and every the same pledges so by our authority and commission to be made by the name of our coin, and so to pass and be current from one to another amongst all persons throughout all our said realms and dominions from and after the said Feast of All Saints next coming; and do straightly charge and command all our loving subjects and all other person and persons whatsoever from thenceforth to take and receive the said several pledges for their several values set as aforesaid; upon pain of our high displeasure and such further punishment as we by the laws of our realm may impose upon them if they offend in that behalf. Provided always, and yet our pleasure is and by these presents we do expressly command, that after the first delivery of the said pledges any of the same shall not be used in any payment whereas the same payment shall exceed 20s. of our current money; and that in any such payment being 20s. as aforesaid or under, there shall not be paid above one groat in value of the pledges aforesaid.

And for the further ease and use of our said loving subjects and for the preservation of all our monies of gold and silver truly and uprightly to their standard, whereof they are now appointed to be by the ordinances by us made in our mint, and to remove all occasions which might in any wise be to the alteration thereof, we will presently take order that there shall be coined such a competent number of pence of the fine standard of our said silver monies as to us shall seem meet. And we will also before the said Feast of

All Saints appoint a special workman which shall make so many only of the said pledges as we shall think necessary to the ease of our people; and will also appoint our special officer to be resident in some notorious place to be assigned to that purpose in our city of London, which there shall be ready at all times, from and after the said Feast of All Saints, to make exchange to all our loving subjects for other money, delivering to every man which shall have need thereof two parts of his payment in the said silver pence, and a third part of the pledges aforesaid according to such sum as any person or persons shall be disposed to exchange in that behalf.

For we will take such present order herein that no greater quantity shall be made of the pledges aforesaid than shall be barely necessary for the ease and use of our said loving subjects. Neither have we devised the same for any other intent but that whilst we do abandon and take away those former tokens which without prejudice of our regal estate and dignity we may not longer endure, that our loving subjects, by our warrant and commission for the common ease and much more benefit of them all, might instead thereof have far more convenient pledges, universally payable in all petty payments and receipts, as specially in changing of three pence, three halfpence, and pence, and such like, in all places throughout all our realms and dominions.

2. AN OPINION ON THE CORRUPT ASSESSMENT OF TAXES, c. 1600

[Francis Tate, 'An Explanation of the Court of Star Chamber' (c. 1600), *A Collection of Curious Discourses*, ed. T. Hearne, 2nd. ed., 1771, II, pp. 288–9]

THESE be the pains that law hath provided; and these be the evils that former times have espied concerning the matter of retainments.

But yet there is in time a further mischief begotten; the which, if those laws had foreseen, they would have whetted a sharp edge against it. For seeing that in former ages the payment of subsidies, the service of musters, and other common charges of this our time were not usual, the harm of retainments was not then so thoroughly seen and discovered as now it is. There is nothing more usual at this day than to retain the wealthiest yeomanry and others, by forbearing them wholly, or charging them lightly to make recompense of their service, by robbing of the king's coffers, or defrauding him and the realm of that help which they might bring, if they were equally burdened as their neighbours are, and not favoured by them that manage those services, in respect that they belong unto them. Which things considered, it is to be wished that either sharp laws were provided, or at the least that former laws were more severely executed against unlawful retainments.

3. AN ATTEMPT BY PROCLAMATION TO ARREST THE DRAIN OF MONEY INTO IRELAND, 1601

[Paul L. Hughes and James F. Larkin, *Tudor Royal Proclamations*, New Haven, 1969, III, pp. 234–5]

[Greenwich, 3 July 1601, Elizabeth I]

THE Queen's most excellent majesty having found by experience of late years, since the time that she hath had cause to send extraordinary sums of monies into her realm of Ireland for the payment of the great forces[1] which there she maintaineth, that infinite discommodities and loss doth arise to this her realm of England by transporting of the sterling monies of this realm into Ireland, for that the same do for the most part either come into the hands of the rebels whereby they are enabled to continue their wicked and detestable rebellion and treasons, providing themselves by the help of those monies of arms and munitions of wars from foreign parts, or else are transported from thence into other countries by merchants for lack of commodities whereon to employ them, and hereby this realm exhausted of the treasure which should be kept within the same; her Majesty also finding by the laws of this realm in the times of her progenitors made, and specially by one Act of Parliament[2] made in the 19th year of her Highness's grandfather of famous memory, King Henry VII, yet continuing in force and effect, that, for like inconveniences then felt, the transportation of monies out of this realm into Ireland was expressly and severely forbidden under great penalties:

Her Highness hath thought good, for remedy of the like inconveniences in time to come, to put in execution those former laws restraining the transportation of monies into Ireland.

Wherefore her Majesty doth straightly charge and command all judges, justices, magistrates, and officers to whom it shall appertain to see severe and due execution of such laws as do prohibit the transportation of her coins of England into Ireland, and namely the said statute made in the 19th year of the reign of her Majesty's grandfather, and doth also by this proclamation admonish all her loving subjects of both her realms, and all others trading in her realm of Ireland, that they shall from henceforth forbear all transportation

---

[1] On 3 March 1600 the Council had notified officials in Ireland of the decision against further shipping of silver money to that country and of the Queen's plan for future payment of the royal forces there in brass coin (*Acts of the Privy Council*, p. 197). The minting of this base coin was ordered on 17 April 1601 (ibid., vol. 31, p. 286). On 28 April Thomas Knevett, Warden of the Mint, was ordered by the Council to deliver to George Carey, Treasurer at War in Ireland, the sum of £50,000 in the newly minted coin: £49,000 to be in shilling, sixpence, and threepence pieces, and £1,000 in pence and halfpence pieces (ibid. 303). A Council letter of 30 November 1601 directed issuance of £5,200 of seized Spanish gold from the Exchequer to Knevett for further coinage of coins 'of the Irish standard' (ibid., vol. 32, p. 409).

[2] 19 Henry VII, c. 5, 1504.

of monies of England into Ireland contrary to the said laws and statutes, for that her Majesty will cause the former laws and statutes prohibiting the said transportation of money to be so straightly looked unto and executed as the penalties thereof shall fall heavily upon the offenders against the same, without any hope of remission.

4. THE METHOD OF ASSESSING TAXES IN MOULTON, LINCOLNSHIRE, 1603

[P.R.O., E 134, 1 Jas. I, Mich. 4]

DEPOSITIONS taken at Spalding before Sir William Rigdon, kt., and John Butcher, gent., by virtue of a commission to them and others directed out of the King's Majesty's High Court of Exchequer for the examining of witnesses as well on the part and behalf of William Brooke and William Butcher, plaintiffs, as also on the part and behalf of Thomas Welby, Downhall Burgess, and others, defendants, the 5th day of October in the first year of the reign of our sovereign Lord James by the grace of God king of England, Scotland, France, and Ireland, defender of the faith, etc. 1603 . . .

Nicholas Scarlet of Moulton in the county of Lincolnshire, husbandman, of the age of 50 years or thereabouts sworn and examined, and saith as followeth:

To the third interrogatory he this deponent saith that about xiiii years ago he was both an assessor for the tax in Moulton and also hath written the books for the same.

To the fourth interrogatory he this deponent saith that the townsmen of Moulton did usually at the time when he was amongst them assess the strangers and foreigners to the fifteenth and taxes for her Majesty before they assessed themselves. And what they wanted in the sum of the said tax in their said imposition upon the strangers, the townsmen of Moulton supplied and made up. And further this deponent saith that when he was an assessor or writ their books for the tax they assessed strangers and foreigners having land or cattle within the parish of Moulton sometime at threepence the acre and sometime at 3d. the beast and eight pence the score of sheep for a single tax at their choice.

5. JAMES I RAISES A LOAN, 1608

[*Cal. S.P. Venetian, 1607–10*, no. 176; In Italian, from the Venetian archives]

Feb. 21, 1608
[Zorzi Giustinian, Venetian Ambassador in England, to the Doge and Senate]

THE King, finding that he may require money at this juncture, has issued strict orders to his Council to devise means for raising it. After discussing the question for many days they have come to the conclusion that the best way would be the usual way of a loan not only from the City but from a large part of the country. The amount is to be a million of gold and it will all be raised in a few days, owing to the wealth of private individuals and to the diligence employed by Council, which, without putting pressure on anyone, succeeds in inducing them all to contribute in proportion to their wealth. The King pledges himself to pay ten per cent, which is the usual rate of interest in this kingdom [*s'aggionge a questo l'obligo del Rè di pagare dieci per cento, ch'è l'ordinario interesse del Regno*], and each contributor receives a bond under the great seal guaranteeing repayment, that is to say the very highest security they can possibly desire, and one which is very seldom given by the sovereign. Foreigners are not exempt unless they show repugnance. The object for which this money is required, though not specifically stated, is for Ireland, where matters though quiet are still a cause for suspicion, especially as the peace in Flanders will leave Spain the freer . . .

6. THE METHOD OF ASSESSING TAXES IN LITTLE HALE, LINCOLNSHIRE, 1609

[P.R.O., C2 Jas. I, T 11/32]

Ult. October, 1609

THE Rt. Hon. Thomas Lord Ellesmere, Lord Chancellor of England

In most humble wise complaining shew unto your hon. good lordship your suppliants, Michael Thompson, Robert Callis, and George Ording, of Little Hale in the county of Lincoln, yeomen, that whereas your suppliants are severally and respectively owners and possessors of several and respective farms and tenancies in Little Hale aforesaid, to which farms the farmers thereof from time whence the memory of man is not to the contrary have had and respectively used, as belonging and appertaining thereto, common of pasture in a fen or great waste in Hale aforesaid and in Bicker in the said county of Lincoln for all and all manner of cattle as belonging unto their said farms, which were either the own proper cattle of such farms or which the said farmers had and did agist, and of which for the time they had and took the profit of to their own uses and for no other nor in other manner. And whereas also one Robert Carr of Little Hale aforesaid, shoemaker, is and hath been for these five or six years last past possessed of a certain messuage and of certain lands, meadows, and pastures thereunto belonging and appertaining in Little Hale aforesaid for the term of certain years, some whereof be yet to come, to which said messuage, lands, and premises in the possession of the said Carr the owners thereof have time out of memory used and had as belonging and appertaining thereunto common of pasture in the said fen and great waste in Hale and Bicker aforesaid for all and all manner of their cattle which were for the time the proper cattle of the farmers and possessors of the said grounds or of the which the owners and possessors thereof had in demise and lease, and received the use and profit thereof coming to their own uses and for no other nor in other manner, which said fen or great waste is all and the only place and grounds your said suppliants and others their neighbours and townsmen have for the depasturing of their cattle in as aforesaid, which custom of commoning is for the better memory thereof set down and registered in certain ancient books of the town of Little Hale, remaining most commonly in the custody of some one of the commoners for and to the use of all the rest for the approving of their said customs and use of commoning when as occasion should serve, for which commonable cattle the owners and possessors thereof be and have time out of memory used to be assessed, rated, and taxed by the polls and numbers thereof in all lays and sessments made or to be made either for and towards the payment of his Majesty's taxes and payments of the wages and salaries of the common soldiers of the town as also for all other common affairs and businesses of the said town. And every commoner have time out of memory used and accustomed to pay towards such sessments according to the rate and number of such his commonable cattle and for none other.

Now so it is, if it may please your good lordship, the said Robert Carr, being a very sleight and cunning fellow and such a one as seeks to oppress his poor neighbours by his nimble and subtle shifts and conveyances, hath for the space of these five years or more last past entertained at sundry and several times divers and sundry horses, mares, oxen, dry kine, sheep, and other cattle, the properties whereof did appertain to divers people and persons, foreigners not inhabiting in the said town or village of Little Hale aforesaid nor which had any common therein nor were in any sort interested in the soil of the said fen or great marsh, some of which cattle, to the number of 20 horses and mares or thereabouts, 5 dry kine, 10 young cattle, and 200 sheep or thereabouts, appertained and the properties of them were and did belong unto Henry Carr and Edward Carr, brethren of the said Robert Carr as your suppliants are verily persuaded, who had not any right of common there or interest in the said soil. And the residence of the said cattle to the number of 40 old sheep or thereabouts, 10 horses and mares, and divers young cattle did belong, and the properties of them were and did appertain, unto divers and sundry persons unknown unto your suppliants which had not any right of common or pasture in the said fen or great marsh nor had not any interest in the soil there and yet all of them were protected under the name of the said Robert Carr and by his practice entertained and sometimes by him craftily challenged and claimed as his own proper cattle and goods. But when as any sums of money were intended to be rated, sessed, and levied by the inhabitants of Little Hale aforesaid and commoners in the said fen or marsh by the number of their cattle, then the said Robert Carr utterly disclaimed to have any property in the said cattle or anything to do therewithal, and then alleged that the same cattle did belong unto other men whose names notwithstanding he concealed and kept and keepeth from the knowledge of your suppliants to the intent they should not have any course in law to redress their wrongs and injuries. And some small whiles before such rates, taxations, and sessments were to be concluded and agreed upon, he used some subtle shift or other either to put out of the way into some private place or cover the said strangers' cattle or else gave to the owners thereof notice to the end they might fetch and convey them out of the said fen and great marshes, by means whereof for the said cattle his Majesty was defrauded of his taxes or other duties due to be paid therefore, as also your suppliants and the rest of the inhabitants of Hale aforesaid, and commoners in the said fen and great marsh were thereby sessed and taxed at higher and greater rates by much than they should have been if the said cattle entertained by the said Carr should be duly and honestly paid for as they ought for to have been if the owners thereof could have been known. And also your suppliants by the foresaid undue means and practice of the said Robert Carr have their commons in the said fen and great marsh eaten up and wrongfully devoured by the cattle of such strangers and foreigners as the said Robert Carr bringeth in and entertaineth, to the exceeding great loss and damage and hindrance of the commoners in the said fen and great marsh. But in especial to the intolerable and insupportable loss and damage of your suppliants who be for the most part farmers and tenants and pay great rents to their landlords for such their farms and commons as aforesaid, and have given and paid and do give and pay the greater rents, fines, and incomes for their said farms by reason and in respect of their commons in the said fen and great marsh. And the said Carr is the more harkened and emboldened to attempt and put in practice his said unlawful actions because he hath by subtle means got and procured into his hands and custody the ancient town books which do mention and plainly declare the manner and use of common aforesaid which he refuseth to restore to your suppliants or to any of them. The said town books to whom the custody thereof do belong to the use of all the rest of the commoners there by reason of their farms, the owners whereof, or some of them, have always had the custody thereof to the use of the rest. And threateneth to cancel and deface the same without the which the true and right use of commons in the said fen and great marsh cannot be certainly declared. And also in respect the said Robert Carr well knoweth that your suppliants nor any of them cannot come to the knowledge whose cattle those were which the said Robert Carr entertaineth as aforesaid and be remedyless at and by the commons laws of this realm for to bring any action for the redressing of their wrongs and injuries dealing as also for ——[1] the said Robert Carr from continuing in his former practices and shifts which he as yet useth and continueth . . .

[Your suppliants] are wholly destitute of aid and succour in the premises at and by the common laws of this kingdom and are altogether remedyless unless your lordship in your wonted clemency do lend and give them relief in this honourable Court of Chancery in course of equity. To which end may it please your good lordship the premises being tenderly considered to grant

[1] Parchment torn away.

unto your suppliants his Majesty's most gracious writ of subpoena to be directed to the said Robert Carr commanding him thereby at a certain day and under a certain pain therein to be limited personally to be and appear before your lordship in this honourable Court of Chancery to answer the premises and further to abide and stand to such further order therein as to your lordship shall seem best to stand with equity and good conscience. And your suppliants shall be bound to pray for your lordship in health and prosperity long to continue.

Robert Callis.

7. SUGGESTIONS FOR IMPROVING ROYAL REVENUES, 1621 [?]
[P.R.O., SP 14/123, no. 80]

Heads for Relief of the King's Estate [October 1621?]

To make a stay of all pensions. Which being put in practice by my Lord Treasurer Suffolk and myself was found full of clamour and therefore laid asleep by the Lords.

1. To raise the price of foreign coin and enhance our home silver in proportion to our gold. This carries a fair show of [wealth][1] at the first sight but in the end impoverisheth the King, etc. and kingdom and in that respect hath long been demurred upon and suspended by the Lords.

2. To improve the Irish revenue and diminish the charge out of England. This hath been thrice sitten upon and is still before the Lords.

3. To sell the King's lands. Whereof the best being already culled out and that which is left stated for many years [it will diminish the revenue][2] and perchance make the people afraid that the Crown will be enforced to levy upon tax and imposing when the lands are gone.

4. To grant them in fee farm the lands, etc., trebling the rents. This will change lands into rents and, as it is true that it takes away some unnecessary officers, so I doubt it may impair the honour of the Crown in part.

5. To disafforest of forests of the King's own soil and sale of the woods thereof. A safe enriching of the Crown and a welcome act to the people.

6. To make profit of encroachments upon the King's manors and lands. Which besides will be a precedent for his Majesty to enclose and improve his own wastes; notwithstanding is to be tenderly handled.

9. To abate the charge and number of foreign ambassadors. By the precedent of Hen. 7.

With many other petty heads collected between my late Lord Treasurer Mandeville and myself.

[1] This word is omitted from the text but appears in another copy of the same document, SP14/123, no. 79.
[2] As in note 1.

8. A cutting of all bounty and magnificence for a time which will not diminish the honour of a Crown but rather raise it by order and expectation.

[Endorsed:] Draft of Heads for Relief of the King's estate.[1]
[In another hand] Sec. Winwood's hand.

8. THE BURDEN OF THE SUBSIDY
IN LINCOLNSHIRE, 1621
[P.R.O., SP 14/123, no. 77]

Right Honourable

After the receipt of your lordships' letters expressing the great care your honours have of our good service in the taxation of the first payment of the second subsidy granted to his Majesty, we took order that notice should be given to all the commissioners generally through the whole county to meet this day at Lincoln to consider of some course for your lordships' better satisfaction therein. And being divers of us assembled upon that occasion we have thought good to acquaint your lordships, first, that whereas we perceive it is observed that this last subsidy doth not equal the former in proportion, we did generally use our best endeavours to advance it as much as lay in our power, but knowing and feeling the strange alteration and decay both of our rents, commodities, and estates which have generally befallen us within these two or three years, we were very hardly censured by the country for insisting so much as we did upon the continuance of the former rates, and were very glad that we could uphold it so much as we did, especially considering how many of our manors, lordships, and lands have been lately aliened unto Londoners and other strangers, which make no abode amongst us. But for that which was taxed we had then as hereafter (God willing we will have) as great care as may be to appoint such collectors as shall be both able and willing readily to pay that to his Majesty's use which shall be committed to their charge to collect. And touching the justices of the peace, all whom your lordships desire to have rated at xx*l.* lands per annum, and us to assess one another the more highly to give others the better contentment to be taxed more largely, we have had due consideration thereof and thereupon have spoken with divers of them who think it too burthensome for their small estates to be so rated, considering the daily charge they undergo by their pains in his Majesty's several services. And therefore submit themselves to your lordships' pleasure for the continuance of their places. For ourselves who have subscribed hereunto, we do all undergo that rate or a greater already, and some of us rather for example than otherwise, were it not that we are both very desirous to advance his Majesty's service and to

---

[1] Another copy of this document is in the hand of Richard Willis, secretary to Lord Treasurer Cranfield with corrections by the Lord Treasurer.

give your lordships the best contentment in our small powers. And so humbly taking our leaves we rest always

Your lordships' ready to do you service

G. Manners, Richard Amcotts, Tho. Grantham, Jo. Thorold, Hammond Whichcot, Ro. Willoughby, J. Wray, Nic. Saunderson, William Lelham, Francis South, Will. Hansarde, Rich. Southbro, Rich. Kinge.

[Endorsed:] Oct. 1621, from the commissioners of subsidies for Lincoln.

9. THE EAST INDIA COMPANY NEGOTIATES WITH THE MINT CONCERNING THE IMPORT OF FOREIGN GOLD AND SILVER, 1628

[Acts of the Privy Council, September 1627–June 1628, p. 466]

30 May

WHEREAS his Majesty by his Letters Patents bearing date the 18th day of February in the 3rd year of his reign hath given licence under the great seal of England to the Governor and Company of Merchants of London trading into the East Indies to transport the quantity of 60,000*li.* in foreign gold, and if they cannot procure so much foreign gold, that then it shall be lawful for them to transport 40,000*li.* in English gold to make up the said 60,000*li.*, so that they bring in in lieu thereof 40,000*li.* either in foreign gold or silver into his Majesty's Mint within 6 months, as in the said Letters Patents more at large is expressed; forasmuch as it appeareth by endorsement upon the said Letters Patents, by the officers of the Custom House, London, that the said company hath transported this year by virtue of the said Letters Patents only 25,000*li.* of the said 40,000*li.* in English gold, of which they have already brought into his Majesty's Mint the sum of 8,000*li.*, or thereabouts, and promiseth within the time limited by the said Letters Patents to bring in so much more as shall make up the full sum of 25,000*li.*, and in that respect humbly desire that they may be freed from their covenant in the said Letters Patents, whereby they are enjoined to bring into his Majesty's Mint to be there coined within the time aforesaid the sum of 40,000*li.*, their Lordships upon consideration of the said Company's humble request, conceiving the same to be just and reasonable, and agreeable to the true intent and meaning of the said Letters Patents, do upon the certificate aforesaid order and declare that it is his Majesty's pleasure, that no advantage shall be taken against the said Company in respect of the said covenant for not bringing into his Majesty's Mint the said 40,000*li.* in foreign gold, but that they shall be absolutely freed and discharged thereof, provided that they bring into his Majesty's Mint within the time limited by the said Letters Patents so much more foreign gold as, together with that which they have already brought in and coined, shall make up the said sum of 15,000*li.* so transported by them, as aforesaid. Whereof all persons whom it may concern are hereby required to take notice and to govern themselves accordingly.

10. SIR FRANCIS COTTINGTON'S PEACE TREATY WITH SPAIN BRINGS SPANISH SILVER TO THE MINT, 1631

[Cal. S.P. Venetian, XXII, 1629–32, pp. 490–1; in Italian, from the Venetian archives]

[Giovanni Soranzo, Venetian Ambassador in England, to the Doge and Senate 28 March, 1631]

COTTINGTON has returned from Spain. For state affairs he brings the greatest protestations of the Catholics' good will to satisfy the king here; and for private affairs he also comes laden with advantages, with the bargain arranged for Flanders for 200,000 crowns, with goods exported free of duty, so that for his own profit, in various kinds of negotiation he will have quite 50,000 ducats. He has established a course of exchange for Flanders, so that all the money which the Spaniards used to provide by way of Genoa they will now arrange for with the merchants here. On the other hand, they afford every convenience to the Spaniards for sea trade, *while they constantly keep restricting the privileges of the Dutch. These can no longer enter the ports here with their booty, because it is immediately sequestrated, partly under the title of interested parties, in consideration of the Spaniards, and partly owing to the king claiming the right to a large portion of what comes in of this character. Accordingly, they are greatly incommoded, and I gather that they are so disturbed in Holland that they propose to send a solemn embassy of seven ambassadors, one for each province, in order to show the king how things have changed and the harm done to his best friends. The Spaniards wish for nothing better than to foment distrust and excite quarrels, so that the Dutch may altogether lose the convenience of these ports, which are useful and necessary to them; indeed, the ambassador himself told me that without them they cannot make war on the Spaniards . . .*[1]

11. A DEFENCE OF THE COURT OF WARDS, 1630s

[E. Coke, The Fourth Part of the Institutes of the Laws of England concerning the Jurisdiction of the Courts, London, 1644, pp. 193–4]

AND where some have objected that wardship is a badge of servitude, for that in the writ of *Nativo habendo*, one of the explees (amongst others) is

---

[1] The part in italics was in cipher.

capiendo redemptionem ab eo pro filiis et filiabus maritandis et aliis villanis serviciis; that is, taking ransom of him for the marriage of his sons and daughters and other villain services. To this it is answered that the king for marriage of his wards taketh no ransoms but such moderate sums of money as in respect of the quality and state of the ward, he or she, all circumstances considered, is able to pay, and in regard thereof, he hath the protection of the Court of Wards during minority. But if ransoms should be taken, it should not only be against the right institution of wardships before remembered, but also a badge of servitude; and, therefore, by the Statute of Magna Carta of H.3, cap. 4, 5, 6 (seeing the crown had a long possession of the wardship of the body and lands of the king's tenant by knight's service) it was provided, first, that the king or his grantee or committee should not take of the lands of the heir[1] but reasonable issues, reasonable customs, and reasonable services without destruction etc. (and all unreasonable and excessive things are against the common law: *excessivum omne in jure reprobatur*). Secondly, shall keep up the houses and other inheritance of the heir and deliver to the heir all his lands stored with ploughs and all other things (woods and all) at least as he received them; whereby it appeareth that the value of the marriage should be so reasonable as the heir should not at his full age be enforced for payment thereof to sell either lands or goods. Thirdly, that if the heir be married, that he be advanced thereby and not disparaged.

John, Earl of Oxford, being the king's ward, married without the king's licence for the which, both for the contempt and for the duty to the king for so marrying, he was fined at three thousand pounds, which was not the value of his lands by one year. And yet he petitioned in Parliament to be pardoned of part thereof, which was thought reasonable. And certainly the reasonable rating of wardships of the body and lands is both according to the laws of the realm and a mean[s] of increase of the king's revenue.

12. NICHOLAS BRIOT ON COINAGE PROBLEMS, 1634

[P.R.O., SP 16/275, no. 44]

October 13, 1634

To the King's most excellent Majesty, the humble remonstrance of Nicholas Briot touching the regulating of the matter of the coin

FOR attaining unto a good and profitable information of the coin it is requisite to have a perfect knowledge of the proportion of gold to silver used in the neighbouring kingdoms like unto this, as in France, Spain, and without consideration of other estates which commonly depend and draw out of greater dominions the matter for the coinage of their monies.

---

[1] Marginal note says: note, *reasonable* thrice repeated that it might be observed.

That which is to be reformed for the present doth consist in three principal points, the first is to hinder the transporting, raising of the price, clipping, and counterfeiting of the said monies. The second to proportionate the silver and gold to one another in such manner that they may be brought again into this land by the subjects and strangers that trade therein indifferently without making any advantage more upon the one than the other as they do nowadays. The third that by the means of the said reformation all the rights belonging to his Majesty upon the coinage and dependencies thereof may come duly to his Majesty's use.

It is to be observed that the proportion of gold to silver is at this present in use and practice now to wit: the ounce of gold is worth in England $13\frac{1}{5}$ of silver; in France $12\frac{7}{8}$; in Spain $13\frac{1}{3}$; Flanders $12\frac{1}{2}$; Millaine and Germany 12, or thereabouts, which proportions stand in force in the said kingdoms, to wit, in England by virtue of the last proclamation, 1611, and that of France by the Edict, 1615, and that of Spain by the Ordinance, 1609.

By the comparing of the proportions abovesaid and by the computation and reduction of the several weights of the said kingdoms one with the other, which may be made either severally or jointly, it will be verified that gold is dear in comparison of silver in this kingdom of England by $2\frac{1}{2}$ in the hundred than in Spain, and by 3 in the hundred than in France in comparison of the proportion of the silver to the gold of the said kingdoms, and from those differences of proportions do proceed the transporting thereof.

It is to be noted that in the reign of Queen Elizabeth the proportion of gold to silver in this kingdom was 10, in Spain 12, and in France 11, from which differences it doth ensue that the proportions between gold and silver they now are, or have been heretofore, cannot be permanent, but subject to alteration, and hereafter cannot be constant without prejudice and inconvenience for two reasons. First, in regard of other neighbouring kingdoms, it cannot be unless all should generally agree upon one and the same price of gold and silver, which is not possible to be expected. Secondly, by reason of domestic occasions in any commonwealth or kingdom when either for want of good intelligence, inadvertence in the officers, practice of merchants for private ends, or other such like accidents, the gold or silver grows to be scant, then it must needs follow that the one becomes cheap and of small esteem and the other is raised to a higher price by reason of the want and scarceness thereof.

As now, for example, in France either by a particular toleration or through the necessity of public affairs, the gold coined after the coin of the said kingdom, and likewise some other foreign coins, have course at the rate of 15 in proportion to silver.

But it doth follow by the aforesaid examples of the differences of the said proportions observed by the neighbours of this state that we should therefore not imitate them in their disorders, but in business of this nature everyone ought to look to their own conservation by the establishing a proportion advantageous for themselves.

And because only gold and silver amongst all metals receive proportion and correspondence one with the other, though they differ in excellency, nevertheless, in the tradings grounded upon the universal consent of nations, he that is bound to pay in gold is admitted to pay in silver, provided it be a just and limited quantity.

Wherefore the coins which are made of the said two metals, their prices, and value ought to be answerable in all sorts of payments, negotiation, and traffic, which depend upon the orderly regulating of the coin. For it is of great importance that in all payments one should have his sums in sums in solid quantity of gold and silver, which can no ways be diminished in their intrinsical fineness, for by lessening their weights or raising of their prices without defrauding and impoverishing the creditor, which thing all wise tradesmen and bankers do look narrowly unto that they may be sure to receive the same quantity of gold and silver which they expect in exchange for their commodities, which they will be sure to hold at a dearer rate when they see others seek to defraud them by raising the price, or lessening the weight of their coins, which causeth a dearth of all things, as, for example, the disorders which at this time are in Scotland in the course of foreign coins hath raised not only the rate of exchange, but also of all kinds of commodities and manufactures brought thither either from England or any other neighbouring countries.

May it therefore please his sacred Majesty (for establishing the said regular equality in the coins) that the coinage of gold may be continued upon the same fineness and remedy as it is now, so doing, the *richesses* and wealth of this kingdom will be preserved and kept at home, and the revenues as well in general as particular will be free from losses and incommodities which ordinarily do ensue upon raising or abasing of the said coins. As likewise to continue the coinage of silver upon the same fineness as it is now but that the price may be raised 2s. in the pound weight ready coined and that the said pound of weight hereafter shall be cut after the rate of 64s. whereas now it is but at 62s. As also that there may be coinage of small pieces of silver of such weight and price as shall be thought convenient to be current at the rate of 66s. the pound ready coined.

This small augmentation of the said 2s. upon the said pound weight of silver cannot be termed an abatement of the coin but rather a conformity of proportion of the silver unto gold. So that his Majesty may justly appropriate to himself the whole benefit of the said augmentation without allowing any higher price for silver to the merchant, for three particular reasons:

First, because if the price of silver were increased to the merchant, that would be an occasion of separating the heavy pieces from the light and of melting or transporting thereof without benefit to the King. Besides that the increasing of the price to the merchants would make them negligent to bring in gold to the mint, finding more advantage by silver.

Secondly, because there is no necessity of a greater augmentation of the price of silver to the merchant as long as the Edict of France, and especially the Ordinance of Spain, stand in force, out of which places the greatest part of the silver doth come, which may be brought into this land ready coined, in regard of the price thereof mentioned in the Ordinance of Spain with profit upon the silver at the rate of 3¾ per centum, besides what they gain upon their commodities, which is a sufficient and reasonable gain for the merchant. Thirdly, because also of the price of the silver be increased to the merchants that might give occasion likewise to the King of Spain to raise the price of silver, though since the introduction of the coinage of ryals which was *anno* 1497 136 years ago the said King of Spain hath had no occasion to raise the price of his silver but rather of his gold three several times, having been thereunto compelled by the example of the kings of England and France as doth appear by the edicts and ordinances of the said kingdom.

Moreover, it is in the power of the sovereign prince to take what rights he thinks good, and to lay such prizes and impositions as he list upon the coinage as well of gold as of silver, stamped with their image, names, or arms, as is used by the King of Spain, who levy and draw more impositions from their subjects upon coinage of gold and silver than the kings of England and France both together.

Besides the abovesaid reasons his Majesty reserving to himself the benefit arising by the said augmentation as well upon great as small coins will by that means redress and prevent many abuses which are practised about his coins. First of all, it will be a means to hinder the goldsmiths that they cannot with so much advantage melt the current coins of silver to put in works as they have done heretofore. Secondly, the said augmentation will bar and hinder the transporting and sale of silver for gold in the Low Countries, which transporting and carrying over they have heretofore and do still use because of the proportion of 12½ of silver to gold which they observe. Thirdly, by means of the augmentation of 2s. in the pound of silver upon the small coin more than upon the great, his Majesty may give an increase of allowance upon the workmanship of the said small money, that a greater quantity thereof may be coined for the use of his subjects, which cannot be done now, because there is but a small quantity conditioned by the indenture of the mint to be coined, as also the allowance upon the workmanship is not sufficient of itself. Besides the said small coin being inferior and less in value by 2s. in the pound weight than the great, this abatement will hinder it from being melted and transported, as it is at this present, with more benefit than the great coin, by the separating of the strong and heavy piece from the work and light [sic]. By this means it will remain in the country for the use of the people.

And for prevention of abuses the proportion of the small coin of 66s. in the pound weight may be limited to such a quantity as his Majesty shall think sufficient for the use of the country and that not to be exceeded. But all the rest of the silver to be at 64s. in the pound weight which is the greatest augmentation of proportion that I conceive the silver can bear without danger of exporting the gold and melting of the silver now current without any benefit to his Majesty.

13. A PROSECUTION FOR CURRENCY OFFENCES, 1636

[John Rushworth, *Historical Collections*, London, 1721 ed., I, part ii, pp. 350–2]

In Camera Stellat' coram Concilio ibidem Decimo Septimo Februarii, Anno Domini Caroli Regis 12

THIS day came to be heard the matter of complaint exhibited into this Court by Sir John Bankes, knight, his Majesty's Attorney General, plaintiff against Henry Futter, Henry Sweeting, Peter Hern, John Terry, Arnold Brames, Isaac Gold, Randal Crew, Francis Brogden, Luke Lee, Timothy Eman, John Perryn, and Edward Vaughan, for transporting of gold and silver out of this kingdom into foreign parts, and for culling out the weightiest money, and for melting down his Majesty's coin into bullion, and giving above the prices of his Majesty's Mint for gold and silver (as by the said information more at large, it doth and may appear). In the opening and prosecution of which cause, his Majesty's said Attorney informed the Court, that in pursuance of their Lordship's order at Council Board, he did before issue joined in this cause, enter a rule, that he would not at this time proceed in the examination of any witnesses, touching the buying of gold and silver above the price appointed to be given at his Majesty's Mint, but reserve that part of the cause to be examined, heard, and considered of hereafter, if their Lordships should think fit. Thereunto their Lordships again consented, holding it most meet so to be done. And upon full and deliberate hearing of the other matters complained of against all the before named defendants, except Francis Brogden whom his Majesty's said Attorney did not now proceed against by direction of this court, in respect he was gone beyond the seas before his cause was set down to be heard, and was not yet returned as was verified by oath. It appeared that notwithstanding his Majesty out of his princely care for the good of his subjects, foreseeing the dangerous consequences, which would ensue the transportation of gold and silver out of this kingdom, did by his proclamation and articles *vicessimo quinto Maii tertio Caroli* [1627], prohibit and command that no person should then after without his Majesty's licence, transport, carry, and convey out of this realm any gold or silver, either in coin, plate, vessels, jewels, goldsmiths' work, bullion or other mass, or otherwise whatsoever. And that no person should aid, assist, counsel, or any ways partake, or consent with any other person, purposing or attempting to transport, carry, or convey out of this realm any gold or silver, in any species or kind as aforesaid, either by gathering or getting together such gold or silver, or by packing up the same fit for transportation, or conveying the same to or towards any port, haven, or other place of exportation, or by any other way or colour. And that no goldsmith, finer, or parter, or other person whatsoever, of what mystery, trade, or quality soever, should melt, or cause to be molten any gold or silver coins, which were then, or hereafter should be the current monies of any his Majesty's realms or dominions, either to make plate, vessel, or for any other manufacture or use, or should cull or sort from the rest any the weightier monies, to the intent to convey the same out of this realm, or to otherwise alter it from coin, the same being also contrary to divers laws and other proclamations.

Yet the said defendant, Henry Sweeting, between the month of April 1629, and the month of June, *undecimo Caroli*, did send the sum of fifteen hundred pounds to Dover by a footpost, and willed him to send the same over to Callis [= Calais], to one John Lovell, a merchant there; which he did according to the said Sweeting his directions. And the said defendant Peter Hern, within the space of two or three years last past, sent by the said footpost to Dover about 3,000*l.* to one Nathaniel Pringall, who as himself confessed, sent the same over to Callis in France; and the said Hern (as himself also confessed to one of the witnesses whose testimony was now read) at another time sent 500*l.* to Callis to one Isaac Lamews. And the said defendant John Terry sent up one Rainger, a footpost, 200*l.* to one John Wallopp of Dover, who at that time shewed the said Rainger a letter from the said Terry, to him the said Wallopp, to send the said two hundred pounds to one Peter Pool at Callis, which the said Wallopp did, and accordingly as he afterwards told the said Rainger and the said Terry about three or four years since, sent one hundred and fifteen pound more to the said Wallopp to Dover, who sent the same to Callis to the said Peter Pool, as he was directed. And the said Arnold Brames (as himself confesseth) hath within seven years last past sent divers quantities of foreign coin and bullion into France, Flanders, and other foreign parts to coin in bags, and the bullion which came from Spain.

It likewise plainly appeared to this Honourable Court, the defendant Timothy Eman's constant course, from the year of our Lord God 1621, until the year of 1631, was to receive merchants' money, and then to employ his servants to cull and sort out by the balance, the heaviest shillings and sixpences, and afterward sold them by the ounce, and thereby made three pound in the hundred profit, it being usual to find 14, 15, 16*l.* or more heavy in 100*l.*, and in the year 1628, 1629, 1630, 1631, the said defendant caused his servants to cull 500,000*l.* a year, which did produce 7, or 8,000*l.* yearly heavy money, which in part he melted down into ingots, and so sold them, and the greatest part he sold unmelted to the value of 20,000*l.* and the said defendant was also furnished by divers several persons with heavy culled English money, to whom he gave sometimes two shillings and sometimes three shillings in a hundred pound to have the culling thereof; and the said defendant Eman, from the year 1621 or 1622, to the year 1626, did melt down 5,000*l.* and from 1626 to the year 1631 he did melt down 15,000*l.* and had profit out of the said money so melted down amounting to above 1,000*l.*, and the defendant

Henry Futter did buy and gather together light gold, and did furnish one Violet with 1,000*l.* of light gold, beyond the allowance of great rates, knowing he either bought it either to transport himself, or to furnish transporters therewithal. And the defendant John Perryn (as himself confesseth, and is proved against him), bought certain quantities of heavy English coin, and melted the same into bullion.

Upon grave and deliberate consideration of all which matters, the Court did declare and adjudge the said defendants, Henry Sweeting, Peter Hern and John Terry guilty of transportation of English gold, and the defendant Arnold Brames of transportation of foreign coin and bullion into such several parts beyond the seas, the defendant Timothy Eman of culling out and melting down the heavy coin of this kingdom for his own particular end and private gain, the defendant Henry Futter of buying light gold and selling the same again to furnish transporters, and the defendant John Perryn of melting down his Majesty's heavy coin; all which offences their Lordships held to be of a very great and dangerous consequence, and very prejudicial to the good and flourishing estate of this kingdom, and therefore to deserve a sharp and severe censure. In respect whereof their Lordships, having well and gravely weighed the nature and quality of each particular man's offence, have ordered, adjudged, and decreed, that the said defendants, Henry Futter, Henry Sweeting, Peter Hern, John Terry, Arnold Brames, Timothy Eman and John Perryn, shall all of them stand to be committed to the prison of the Fleet, and pay for their several fines to his Majesty's use as followeth; viz. Peter Hern, John Terry, and Timothy Eman 2,000*l.* apiece, Arnold Brames 1,000*l.*, Henry Futter and Henry Sweeting 500*l.* apiece, and John Perryn 100*l.* And as touching the defendants, Isaac Gold, Randal Crew, and Luke Lee, albeit it did appear that they being East Country merchants, had transported out of the kingdom, and carried over in their ships several small sums and quantities of Rix-Dollers which the Court holds and declares to be an offence punishable in that Court, if it be done without his Majesty's licence; yet in respect it did not clearly appear that they had transported any great quantities, and for that the necessity of the trade requires the exportation and carrying with them of some monies, to defray customs and other necessary occasions in their voyages to Norway, the Court did forbear at this time to censure them, and did dismiss and discharge them of and from any other attendance thereabouts hereafter. And for the defendant, Edward Vaughan, it was ordered he be dismissed and discharged of and from any further attendance thereabouts hereafter.

14. SHIP MONEY: TOTALS FOR
THE COUNTIES, 1636-7
[P.R.O., SP 16/376, no. 104]

Sums charged upon each county for the shipping business, this year 1636
and 1637

	li.		li.
Berkshire	4,000	Northamptonshire	6,000
Buckinghamshire	4,500	Nottinghamshire	3,500
Bedfordshire	3,000	Northumberland	3,100
Bristol	1,000	N. Wales	4,000
Cornwall	5,500	Norfolk	7,800
Cambridge	3,500	Oxfordshire	3,500
Cumberland ⎫ Westmorland ⎭	1,400	Rutlandshire	800
		Somersetshire	8,000
Cheshire	3,000	Surrey	3,500
Devonshire	9,000	Sussex	5,000
Derbyshire	3,500	Suffolk	8,000
Durham	2,000	Staffordshire	3,000
Essex	8,000	S. Wales	5,000
Gloucestershire	5,500	Shropshire	4,500
Hampshire	6,000	Warwickshire	4,000
Herefordshire	3,500	Westmorland ⎫ Cumberland ⎭	700 *ut supra*
Hertfordshire	4,000		
Huntingdonshire	2,000	Worcestershire	3,500
Kent and the		Wiltshire	7,000
Cinque ports	8,000	Yorkshire	12,000
Lancashire	4,000		
Lincolnshire	8,000	*Summa totalis*	£210,600
Leicestershire	4,500		
London	1,400		
Middlesex	5,000		
Monmouth	1,500		

15. A PLAN TO REMEDY ABUSES IN THE
ASSESSMENT OF SHIP MONEY, 1637
[P.R.O., SP 16/381, no. 37]

The way to remedy this abuse by which neither sheriff nor high constable
shall be left to their discretion. There is in every county a rate which is
called the great composition of his Majesty's most honourable household.
And this is yearly gathered by the high constables in money and paid in to
the hands of some one gentleman nominated for treasurer in that service
for one year. This was imposed upon every parish by themselves, two of

every parish being summoned in the behalf of the parish, and hath continued without either murmuring or alteration in most counties about sixty years.

This composition therefore is the best guide for the imposing of the ship money. For example, the great composition in the county of Kent is somewhat above 2,000*li.* per annum. This sum four times raiseth 8,000*li.* the sum charged on the county with an overplus. But in all places about the Ch.[1] of Axtane there is five or six times the said sum charged. So that in probability there is 10,000*li.* charged at least, or, if less in other places, it is extreme partiality. And dishonesty and partiality are the same to those that suffer, only partiality is the worst and breed [sic] more discontent.

The only objection can be made against this is that at the first settling the composition great men favoured their parishes. The answer: that it is impossible to have anything so exact but something may be said against it. But sixty years' continuance without either murmuring or alteration pleads sufficiently for it. And better any rule than the discretion of one man. And yet I daresay who ever make this objection, if his payment be looked upon, shall find the sheriff hath been favourable to him.

But this must be a guide only to the Chs., not parishes, but when it comes to be rated by every several parish, then the poor's cess is the best guide in which every man is charged by ability as well as land. And if any great man in a parish do favour himself, it is the fault of the parish who by the law may have remedy either at Quarter Sessions or by the judge of assize. But I hope no gentleman is so unworthy to spare himself to lay it upon his poor neighbours.

And this I conceive the best way to take away the abuse and discontent and to ease the sheriff of much trouble (unless he desire to fish in troubled waters). All which I humbly offer, but leave it to more honourable and better judgements to approve or condemn.

To shew that the abuse of imposing the ship money by the sheriff upon the Chs. and by the high constable upon the parishes make the discontent and burden much greater than the charge itself.

In the first year there was charged upon the Ch. of Axtane in Kent but 160*li.* and then was there an overcharge upon the county of between 200 and 300*li.* by the sheriff's confession, but I believe, if well examined, much more. The second year was charged upon the same Ch. an 170*li.* This year is charged upon the same Ch. an 180*li.* By which is manifest there is no rule of imposing but as the sheriff's favour or malice lead him, take off and imposeth at his pleasure.

Or if all part[s] be raised in proportion then of necessity this year there is above a 1,000*li.* overcharged upon the county. But partiality is much more grievous to be patient than dishonesty.

The very same liberty taken by the sheriff of imposing upon the Chs. is used by the high constables upon the several parishes within his division. So that the sheriff and high constables do trample upon all men and their estate

---

[1] 'Ch.' is the author's idiosyncratic way of denoting 'Hundred'.

[sic] which causeth much murmuring. And the reason gentlemen do not complain to the Lords of his Majesty's most honourable Privy Council is that they are unwilling to stand in competition with so mean fellows as high constables now are, for it is not in their powers to be dishonest, but only partial.

For what is imposed by superiors we take patiently but if by equals or inferiors it cannot be so well digested. And this is easily to be remedied, if please authority to command.

[Endorsed:] 5 Feb. 1637. Sir Anthony Weldon concerning the collecting of ship money.

16. UNFAIR ASSESSMENTS FOR SHIP MONEY IN SHELTON, BEDFORDSHIRE, 1636–7

[P.R.O., SP 16/376, no. 98]

1636. A taxation made by Mr. Manning, Mr. Lea, and Edward Woodley of Shelton for the king's ship money, who, taxing themselves with the lords of the manor not at 2*d.* an acre and one Mr. Peter Mallory, heir to the lord of the manor, who hath a personal estate, beside an office which is reported to be worth 100*li.* a year, is taxed at nothing.

And other poor tenants which are farmers, whose lands are taxed some at 2*s.* 4*d.* an acre and some cottagers at 2*s.* 4*d.* an acre, and divers others in the same kind, is oppressed.

William Chapman, John Michell, Peter Rofe, Thomas Mee, George Sheppard, William Russell.

1637. A taxation made by John Ivorye and Mr. Lea for the ship money who taxed themselves not at 2½*d.* an acre and other farmers which they favoured who are not taxed at 1½*d.* an acre.

And other poor farmers which are tenants which are taxed at 4*d.* the acre. And some poor cottagers at 1*s.* the acre and divers others in the same kind is oppressed.

William Chapman, John Michell, John Allingham, Peter Rofe, Thomas Mee, George Sheppard, William Russell.

[Endorsed:] Shelton tax for the ship money

17. AN UNFAIR RATING ASSESSMENT AT BISHOPS STORTFORD, HERTS., 1637

[Herts. County Record Office, Quarter Sessions Book, 2a, f. 201d]

THE Bench being this present Session [9 and 10 Jan. 1636/7] informed by the petition of Dame Margaret Denny, Thomas Archer, George Hawkins,

John Miller, and divers other of the inhabitants of Stortford within this county in manner following, viz. that the parishioners there have used from time to time to make a rate called the forty shillings rate (or the constable's rate) being a rate for all manner of town charges, and thereby to tax every man by ability, not by land (in regard the town consisteth most of tradesmen who hold little or no lands in their hand) until of late some of the parishioners rather out of spleen and malice than of any just cause or ground have endeavoured to break the ancient custom and usage, and have set on foot a new manner of rating both by lands and ability too. And to that end some of the parishioners (who hold little or no land) have met together and made a rate, and thereby have not only eased themselves, but have highly taxed landholders for their land and for their ability and stock all three, contrary to all law and justice (as the petitioners conceive), and contrary to the old custom and manner of rating. Notwithstanding it is well known that many other taxes and charges, as namely composition, wheat, oats, hay, straw, veal, and bacon, the king's carriages, and other taxes, are laid upon landholders which are not comprehended within the said forty shilling rate. So that the greatest burthen and charge of the whole town will lie upon landholders and poor farmers if this manner of rating be suffered. And thereupon the petitioners humbly prayed the Bench that the old custom and manner of rating might be still continued, or at leastwise that all the parishioners may be enjoined to make a rate by ability only and not by land, and that without partiality, as by the said petition remaining on the file of the present Session may appear.

This court taking the premises into consideration declareth that no person ought to be rated twice; that all persons living in the parish ought to be rated by their abilities within the parish including the land they hold and occupy in the parish; that those that hold land lying within the parish and live out of the parish ought to be rated for the lands only that they hold in the parish; and that no person ought to be rated for rents coming in for that their tenants are rated for the land. And therefore this court doth order that from hence-forth the forty shilling rate or constable's rate of Stortford aforesaid shall be made according to the declaration aforesaid and in no other manner.

18. ECONOMIC CHANGE AND ITS EFFECT ON RATING ASSESSMENTS IN CHESHUNT, HERTS., 1637

[Herts. County Record Office, Quarter Sessions Book 2a, f. 203d]

WHEREAS the Court was informed this present Session by the petition of the inhabitants of Cheshunt within this county in form following, viz. that the said parish did heretofore consist of divers good farms and freeholders of good abilities and men of trades as maltsters, mealmen, and the like, who were well able to support all the charges of the parish and county; but for the space of twenty years past and upwards there having been enclosed into his Majesty's parks of Theobalds and Cheshunt above two thousand acres of good ground, many of those farmers and freeholders are turned cottagers, and have nothing to live upon but a small house and two or three acres of ground. And by reason of his late Majesty's residence at Theobalds the trades are altogether laid aside and turned into innkeepers and victuallers, so as by the access of foreigners attending about the court and depopulation of ancient farms turned into cottages, the charge of the parish is much increased, and the means of supply exceedingly decreased. And yet the said parish though much impoverished standeth still charged with all rates to the country in as full a proportion as when it was in greatest prosperity, it being conceived that it is more replenished with gentry than ever it was, who by all probabilities are better able to undergo the burthen of the country than inferior persons; whereas in truth (except some four or five gentlemen) all the rest are either servants to his Majesty or citizens of London, the first of them freed sometimes by his Majesty's express command as now in the rate of ship money and other things, and sometimes freeing themselves by their resolutions and overawing of poor officers that they dare not enter into their houses to distrain for any rates. And the other the citizens cometh a month or two in the summer time, and are gone when any charge or burthen should rest upon them. So as almost the whole burthen rests upon some few yeomen, very few of which have twenty pounds per annum to live upon. And the petitioners therefore have besought this Bench to refer the consideration of the premises to some of his Majesty's justices of the peace of this county, to the end that if the said inhabitants should make the truth thereof appear before them, such order might be taken for their relief in bringing down the former rates of the said parish to such proportion as, considering the allegations aforesaid, shall be consonant to justice and equity and suitable to the numbers of acres in other parishes. This court referreth the consideration of the premises to the Right Honourable Henry Earl of Dover, Sir Richard Lucy, and Sir John Garrard, knights and baronets, Sir John Boteler, Sir Thomas Fanshawe, Sir William Litton and Sir John Watts, knights, and William Preistley, esquire, justices of the peace of this county or to any four of them, desiring them with all convenient speed to meet thereabout and take such order for the relief of the said inhabitants in the premises as to them the said justices or to any four of them shall seem fitting.

19. DIFFICULTIES IN COLLECTING SHIP MONEY IN NORFOLK, 1638
[P.R.O., SP 16/389, no. 9]

Norfolk

MATHEW STEVENSON and Roger Reynolds, two chief constables of Blofield Hundred within the said county have not collected and paid unto me one penny of the ship rate imposed upon that hundred. And I am informed and do believe that they have been very backward and cold in calling upon the petty constables to demand or gather the same within their several parishes, albeit I have by frequent and most pressing letters and warrants urged upon them (even as I have upon others) the levying of ship money, and have appointed them divers several days for the payment thereof unto me at all which days and times they have failed to pay anything.

William Meek one of the chief constables of Clavering Hundred within the said county hath not gathered and paid any part of the ship rate imposed upon the said hundred, whereas his partner, chief constable of that hundred, hath paid a good part of that which was to be gathered up within his division, whereby I am assured that the said William Meek have neglected his duty in levying the same.

Thomas Dawson, one of the chief constables of Depewade Hundred in the said county hath collected and paid but £28 within his division of that hundred, whereas his partner, chief constable for his division, hath paid almost all his part of the ship rate. And further I have found good cause to suspect the said Dawson to be very negligent of his duty in levying and collecting that part of ship money within his charge.

I am informed that Edmond Holt of Hemblington in Walsham Hundred and Edward Hilton of Lingwood in Blofield Hundred, being attorneys at the law, have not paid their ship rates and that many others are by them encouraged to stand out . . .

There be many more in the county to be complained of. I have thought it best to certify these few, not desiring to draw up multitudes before their lordships. And I have not hitherto troubled their lordships with any. If their lordships be pleased to afford some assistance to my work, I have good hope that all or very near all the shipping monies of that county will be paid in. But by that power which is only in my own hands, I cannot presume upon the levying of much more in the county. I affirm the truth of all the premises by subscribing my hand.

1 May, 1638   Fran. Asteley

I pray move their lordships to be pleased to write to all the corporations of that county (except Thetford) to make speedy payment of their assessments of ship money for I do observe that the parts of the county adjacent to them have an eye at them and upon their delay and slackness are not so forward as otherwise I think they would be.

                                                             Fran. Asteley
[Endorsed:] 2 May, 1638. The high sheriff of Norfolk. Complaint against Mathew Stevenson, Roger Reynolds and other high constables in that county for neglect of gathering the ship money.

20. CLIPPED MONEY PAID AS SHIP MONEY, 1639
[P.R.O., SP 16/421, no. 73]

[Nicholas More, sheriff of Co. Monmouth, to Secretary Nicholas]

SINCE my last letter I have paid unto the Treasurer of the Navy 400*l.* of the ship money, but 7*l.* thereof was returned again for light gold, and some monies besides for allowances were disbursed by my servant, which was strange unto me for I weighed the gold myself, and as I remember the worst piece was standing [=standard] weight with the allowance. I used much diligence and entreaty to procure gold for silver, both for the ease of carriage and his Majesty's use and service. Since which time with much ado I have lately received the rest of the money, lacking 20*l.* or thereabouts, the which I expect every hour, but it is in such ragged pieces as broken groats, quarter pieces of thirteenpence halfpennies, ten pence halfpennies, harpers, and fourpence halfpennies, that I have had much labour to number the same, the which I intend, God willing, to change into good money or gold, and to send up the same very speedily into the office. In the meantime, with remembrance of my love I commit you to God and will ever remain,

Your truly loving friend,

to be commanded by you,

Nicho. More

Crick, 18 May, 1639

[Endorsed:] To the wo[rshipful] my very loving friend Edward Nicholas, esq., one of his Majesty's clerks of the Council, present these with speed.

21. THE STOP OF THE MINT, 1640
[P.R.O., SP 16/459, no. 36]

[Part of a newsletter from Edmund Rossingham to Edward, Viscount Conway, July 4, 1640]

. . . on Saturday last, by a warrant under the King's hand, all the money in the Mint brought in by merchants to the value of about £100,000 was seized upon for the King's present necessity. And those merchants are to repair to my Lord Treasurer to receive security for their principal, and 8*l.* per cent interest. This stop hath put the merchants into great disorder, wherefore they join all together to petition his Majesty and to set down the ill consequences that this stop will beget. The merchants knew nothing till Sunday night after the King was gone from Whitehall to Oatlands.

22. THE STOP OF THE MINT: A FOREIGNER'S ACCOUNT, 1640

[*Cal. S.P. Venetian XXV, 1640–2*, pp. 58–9; Italian, from the Venetian Archives]

[Giovanni Giustinian, Venetian Ambassador in England, to the Doge and Senate]

THIS week the king has come more than once from Oatlands to this city to take part in long consultations with the ministers which have all turned upon the ways of providing a certain amount of money to meet the present expenses, which have reduced the treasures of the crown to the last extreme. After many conferences they decided to avail themselves of the third part of the silver at present in the mint, brought there by individuals to be coined into money, granting them in compensation 8 per cent per annum, with a promise on the customs as security for the capital and the king's word to pay it off within six months, which is not believed.

This new plan, which does not receive general approval is deeply resented by the interested parties, who have represented in writing the very serious prejudice which will result to the mart here, pointing out specially that on the arrival of the news in Spain the further dispatch of silver will be suspended, and this kingdom will lose those advantages which have brought so much wealth in the past, not less to the state than to the individual. But the necessity under which his Majesty's affairs labour has not left any room for the consideration of such matters, although it is with regret, and the decree has been issued. As it strikes a severe blow at the Genoese merchants of Madrid, proprietors of this silver, it has also aroused the serious apprehensions of the Spanish ambassadors, who fear that if they continue to send specie from that Court for the requirements of Flanders, the king, when still harder pressed, may decide to seize it, as Queen Elizabeth did before. Accordingly they have sent a courier in haste to their master with special news of this event. If it compels the Spaniards to abstain from sending the money here, it will prove very hurtful to the interests of that crown.

Besides this measure they have decided to coin 500,000 of their pounds with three parts of copper and only one of silver, to be of the same value as those which are all silver. They are now devoting their ingenuity to find a way to put this in practice. Everyone recognizes the harmful consequences and those who are most skilled believe that it will involve insuperable difficulties, for as the people here are not accustomed to use such base money, it will be difficult to oblige them to take it. The merchants of the India and Levant Companies oppose the decision strongly, more than others interested in trade, and are making vigorous efforts to have it rescinded . . .

London, the 27th July, 1640.

23. THE KING'S EXPEDIENT
FOR RAISING MONEY, 1640
[P.R.O., SP 16/460, no. 56]

[Part of a letter from Edmund Rossingham to
Edward, viscount Conway, July 21, 1640]

... concerning the brass money thus the last week the merchants of London,
the several companies, namely, the East India Company, the Merchant
Adventurers, the Turkey Company, they all preferred their several petitions
to his Majesty to show the mischief which would accompany the introducing
of the brass money. The king read only the Merchant Adventurers' petition,
but finding no other way to relieve his present necessity his Majesty resolved
to go on with the coining of brass money, whereupon Mr. Attorney was
ordered to make haste to perfect the proclamation and Mr. Sergeant Heath
was joined with Mr. Attorney to draw this proclamation. The stamps are
made, which are the king's arms on the one side and the portcullis on the
other side of the coin. And I hear the king does promise in his proclamation
to call in all that money again when his necessity is over. Yet his Majesty did
not so resolve to coin brass money but he would waive that way of supplying
himself if so be the City would lend him 200,000*l.* upon interest and good
security and also to let fall the ship money for this year in the City. But the
citizens pretend to great poverty as they know not how to spare and supply
his Majesty with that sum of money, wherefore the brass money is like to go
on. But more of this hereafter ...

24. THE VENETIAN AMBASSADOR REPORTS
ON THE CROWN'S FINANCIAL EXPEDIENTS,
1640
[*Cal. S.P. Venetian*, XXV, 1640–2, nos. 89, 95, 107;
Italian, from the Venetian archives]

[Giovanni Giustinian, Venetian Ambassador in England,
to the Doge and Senate]

Aug. 3, 1640

HIS Majesty remains at Oatlands with the majority of the ministers. Their
most anxious concern is to facilitate the success of the decision to introduce
copper money into this kingdom. But the difficulties in the way, which
constantly increase, retard the execution. In addition to the keen remonstrances of the merchants, this city has expressed in a very open manner its
own dissatisfaction and the disorder that this decree will produce. If it is put
in force it will certainly affect the trade of this mart, and for this reason every

one is waiting with curiosity to see what will happen. Those who are best informed believe that the king will be compelled to change his mind, or, if he persists, he will run the risk of not being obeyed, with consequent loss of reputation . . .

* * *

August 17, 1640

. . . After careful enquiry into the disadvantages that might follow the introduction of copper money, and hearing the determined statements of the merchants that they will not take it, the execution of the order has been postponed. With the ever pressing need of money the king has taken the step of asking this city, for the third time, for a loan of 200,000*l.* promising, in order to make the way easier, that it shall not be used for warlike purposes, but to establish a beneficial peace in this kingdom. All the same the Council met and by a unanimous vote answered frankly that they could not satisfy the demands of his Majesty, as the grant of money ought to depend on the judgement of Parliament alone and not on this city only and a small member of that body. From these last experiences all hopes of obtaining succour without a fresh convocation of Parliament, which is universally longed for, have fallen to the ground . . .

* * *

September 7, 1640. London

. . . Fresh requests for loans have been made of this city, but have met with no better response than before, and they have definitely refused to contribute without a vote of Parliament. Not knowing where else to go they have tried to obtain on credit from the India Company all the pepper brought by the ships, which have recently arrived, amounting to 70,000*l.* with the idea of selling it afterwards to the merchants at a loss, who will readily supply the money. But when negotiations were opened with the interested parties and the heads of the Company, they showed no inclination to entrust their capital to the king, and unless they take it by force, as was done before with the money which lay in the Tower, it seems likely that this last expedient will fail also, involving as it does most hurtful consequences to the traders of this mart.

His Majesty has unexpectedly issued a proclamation to the sheriffs whose duty it is to collect the last tax known as ship money, which the people have been unwilling to pay in the past, although under pressure, informing them that they must satisfy the Treasury within a month, under pain of severe penalties, as he is determined to have prompt obedience and full payment. These, on the contrary, claim that the royal authority does not extend to the imposition of the greater charges, and they refuse to pay. Dissatisfaction constantly increases and without any advantage they keep preparing material for the most serious outbreak. It is feared that this is very near, much to the alarm of good men and of foreigners in particular. Owing to this fear the custody of the Tower has been committed to Cottington,[1] one of the most capable of the ministers, with orders from the king that in case of a rising he is to raise platforms of earthworks in the Tower and take steps to command the city with guns. May God avert the need for such service to his Majesty and for the safety of private individuals . . .

London, the 7th September, 1640.

25. PURVEYANCE IN LINCOLNSHIRE, 1640

[P.R.O., Exchequer Depositions, E134, 16 Chas. I, Trin. 2]

DEPOSITIONS of witnesses[2] taken by us, Thomas Trollope, esq., Samuel Cust, esq., Thomas Love, gent., and Phillip Jolly, gent., 27 May, 1640, by virtue of his Majesty's commission out of his Highness's Court of Exchequer issuing, to us directed, between his Majesty's Attorney General, plaintiff, and William Turlington and Robert Banand, defendants, as followeth:

Richard Fynn of Leake in Holland in the county of Lincoln, gent., aged 50 years or thereabouts, sworn and examined, saith as followeth:

To the first interrogatory he saith that he knoweth William Porey and Henry Pratt but no other in the interrogatory named.

To the second interrogatory he saith that he knoweth that the inhabitants of the parts of Holland in the county of Lincoln are yearly chargeable and charged with the providing of twenty fat oxen and 200 sheep for composition provisions of beeves and muttons for his Majesty's household. And further to this interrogatory he cannot depose.

To the third interrogatory this deponent saith that he doth verily believe that the inhabitants of the parts of Holland about the time in the interrogatory mentioned [i.e. end July, 1637] did contract and agree with the said William Porey for the delivery of the composition provision of beeves and muttons for his Majesty's service for the year following, to begin from the first of May in the thirteenth year of his Majesty's reign, for he being one of the chief constables in the said parts of Holland had a warrant from the justices of the peace there for the levying of his part of the said composition.

To the fourth interrogatory this deponent saith that about the time in the last deposition mentioned he, this deponent, did pay the sum of four score one pound thirteen shillings and fourpence unto the said William Porey or his assigns being part of the £350 in the interrogatory mentioned.

To the sixth interrogatory[3] he saith that the said William Porey was a great grazier and a great dealer for cattle in the county of Lincoln.

---

[1] Appointed Constable on Aug. 25–Sep. 24.—*Cal. S.P. Dom.*, *1640*, p. 629.

[2] This is the evidence of one only of several witnesses in the case. It is preceded in the document by a list of interrogatories.

[3] The fifth interrogatory is omitted in the document.

To the seventh interrogatory he saith that he doth verily believe that the said William Porey did fail to serve in the composition and provision of beeves and muttons according to his said agreement. And that the said inhabitants of the said parts of Holland were enforced to make a new composition with his Majesty's officers for that year's provision. And that he, this deponent, being one of the chief constables there, paid the sum of four score eighteen pounds eighteen shillings and threepence halfpenny in monies and one pound eight shillings and fourpence in return for that year's provision unto Dymock Walpole, esq., one of his Majesty's justices of the peace in the aforesaid parts for his Highness's use over and above the aforesaid sum of £81 13s. 4d. formerly paid to the said William Porey, as is in the fourth interrogatory formerly mentioned.

26. A PLAN TO IMPROVE THE KING'S FINANCES, 1641

[P.R.O., SP 16/479, no. 89]

[April?] 1641

THE first thing your lordship is to take care of is to have the present state of the whole revenue clearly set down, that it may appear in what condition your lordship doth receive it, whereof some remonstrance is to be made to his Majesty and the lords of the Privy Council. And for your better satisfaction therein, first a balance of the revenue is to be made whereby it may appear what his Majesty's estate doth annually amount unto and what his Majesty's annual charge is, the casual revenue being computed by a medium of seven or ten years, and the casual expenses in the like manner. This balance is to be made by Sir Robert Pye and —— Bingley, one of the auditors of the imprests, some other auditor being added to their assistance; and I take auditor Philips to be the fittest man; or rather by a commission to be issued to these and some others. Secondly, your lordship must be particularly informed by Sir Robert Pye and Sir Edward Wardour of all the anticipations upon his Majesty's revenue, and of all his Majesty's debts by Great Seal and Privy Seal, for which there are no assignations made. Thirdly, your lordship must have a brief information, from some officers of the customs, how the great and petty farms are for the present disposed and for how long they are leased or contracted for, and under what rents; what collections of impositions or other duties there are which are in danger to be totally lost by the present Parliament, or to be impaired by any alteration of state or of trade at home or abroad. By these informations your lordships will be enabled in some measure to understand the present state of the revenue, so as to represent the same to his Majesty and the Council; which being done, the next care may be to reduce things to some better order than you received them, which cannot be well done but by the Parliament, nor by them neither unless things be prepared for them.

The first thing may be to reduce all pensions and other payments into the receipt of the Exchequer, whereof divers are at this time assigned upon other revenues. The reducing of them to the Exchequer is both legal and regular and will bring all the revenues and all payments under one survey and account, and make your lordships have the true power of the king's payments which otherwise you have not. The second thing is what may be saved, and what charges may be retrenched in his Majesty's estate, wherein I believe, upon a careful examination of the king's estate, very much may be done in these particulars and some others, viz. in his Majesty's and the Prince's house, in pensions bought and transacted from man to man, and some others likewise in the wardrobe and the stables, in superfluous and unuseful officers in the castles and forts, in ordering the customs and some other revenues and in divers other particulars. It will be very difficult (by reason of the great anticipations) to make the king subsist upon his own revenue without supply from his people in Parliament. But if subsidies were given I conceive it very easy: first, because the subsidies would give the king credit; secondly, some anticipations upon present and immediate revenues might be removed, and the king make use thereof for his present subsistence, and appoint the same anticipations to be paid out of the subsidies. It will be a matter of very great importance to forbear anticipations for the future as much as possible may be; and I think it very possible to forbear them if the revenue be once balanced, settled, and regulated, some annual provision being made for the king's just debts. There are several monthly payments into the Exchequer from the great farm, and divers other collections of the customs, impositions, and other duties, which are for the monthly supply of the King and Queen's household charge, for the works, for the Treasurer of the Chamber, for the Guard, and divers other necessary payments.

Your lordship must be particularly informed by Sir Robert Pye of these monthly payments, what and how much they are, and out of what revenues particularly, and to what uses they are issued. And there must be especial care to establish these payments, and to settle as many monthly payments as possibly may be because this will be a means of much security and quiet to your lordship and will keep much clamour and complaint from the king.

The government of the revenue of Ireland and all the affairs of that kingdom hath formerly depended principally upon the Lord Treasurer until my Lord Lieutenant's time, who procured such instructions and powers as made him independent of all but the king and himself. Your lordship must therefore take some care that the instructions of the next Deputy be conformed to ancient precedents, and not to that of my Lord Lieutenant; and that a correspondence and dependence be settled between your lordship and the Lord Deputy and other officers of that kingdom as the Vice Treasurer, who is likewise Treasurer for the army, the Masters of the Wards and Rolls.

[Endorsed:] Revenue. This was intended for my Lord of Bedford.

27. A LOAN TO A LABOURER, 1642

[P.R.O., SP 46/88, no. 159. Papers of Sir Thomas Hyde
of Albury, Herts.]

RECEIVED by me Thomas Allen of Aylesbury in the county of Buckinghamshire, labourer, of Sir Thomas Hide of Albury in the county of Hertford,
baronet, the sum of 40s. of lawful money of England to be paid at Chesters
Inn, London, to the said Sir Thomas Hide the 20th day of June next ensuing,
and hereunto I the said Thomas Allen have set my hand dated the xiiiith day
of March, A.D. 1641.

The mark of Thomas Allen

[Witness]: Jo. Hall.

28. THE INTRODUCTION OF EXCISE, 1643

[C. H. Firth and R. S. Rait, *Acts and Ordinances of the
Interregnum, 1642–1660*, I, pp. 202–7]

An Ordinance for the speedy Raising and Levying of Moneys, set by way of
Charge or new Impost, on the several Commodities mentioned in the
Schedule hereunto annexed; as well for the better securing of Trade, as for
the maintenance of the Forces raised for the Defence of the King and
Parliament, both by Sea and Land, as for and towards the Payment of the
Debts of the Commonwealth, for which the Public Faith is, or shall be given.
[22 July, 1643.]

THE Lords and Commons now assembled in Parliament, taking into their
serious consideration the great danger that this kingdom lyeth under, through
the implacable malice and treachery of Papists and other malignant persons,
who have, and daily do wickedly practise and endeavour the utter ruin and
extirpation of the Protestant religion, the privilege of Parliament, and the
liberty of the subject; insomuch, that there is no probable way left them for
the preservation of this nation how to prevent the said malicious practices,
but by raising of monies for the purposes first above mentioned, until it
shall please Almighty God in his mercy to move the King's Majesty's heart
to confide in, and concur with both his Houses of Parliament, for the
establishing of a blessed and happy peace, which by both Houses is much
desired and prayed for. And forasmuch as many great levies have been already
made for the purposes first above mentioned, which the well-affected party
to the Protestant religion have hitherto willingly paid, to their great charge;
and the malignants of this kingdom have hitherto practised by all cunning
ways and means how to evade and elude the payment of any part thereof. By
reason whereof the Lords and Commons do hold it fit, that some constant
and equal way for the levying of monies for the future maintenance of the

Parliament forces, and other great affairs of the commonwealth may be had and established, whereby the said malignants and neutrals may be brought to and compelled to pay their proportionable parts of the aforesaid charge, and that the levies hereafter to be made for the purposes aforesaid, may be borne with as much indifferency to the subject in general as may be.

I. Be it therefore ordered, ordained, and declared by the said Lords and

Commons: that the several rates and charges in a schedule hereunto annexed[1] and contained; shall be set and laid, and are hereby laid, charged, and imposed upon all and every the commodities in the said schedule particularly expressed, as the same are particularly therein taxed and rated, as well upon those that are already brought into this realm, or the dominion of Wales, and town of Berwick, and every of them; and are remaining in the hands of any merchant, buyer, or seller, or other owner thereof respectively, as upon any of the commodities in the schedule mentioned, which hereafter shall be imported into this kingdom of England, dominion of Wales, and town of Berwick, or any of them.

II. And be it further ordained by the said Lords and Commons, that for the better levying of the monies hereby to be raised, that an office from henceforth, by force and virtue of these presents shall be, and is hereby erected, made, and appointed in the City of London, called or known by the name of the Office of Excise or New Impost, whereof there shall be eight commissioners to govern the same, and one of them to be treasurer, with several registers, collectors, clerks, and other subordinate officers, as the eight commissioners (or the major part of them) for the time being, shall with the approbation of the Committee of Lords and Commons, appointed for the advance of money, and making of other provisions for the army, (sitting at Haberdashers' Hall, London) nominate and appoint. And it shall and may be lawful to and for the said eight commissioners, or the major part of them, with the consent of the said committee, to displace any of the said subordinate officers from time to time, if they see cause so to do . . .

VI. That the said commissioners and treasurer shall quarterly make their accompt of all their receipts and disbursements, unto one or more auditors that shall from the said Houses be appointed to receive the same; which said auditor or auditors shall take the like oath and in such manner as is appointed for the said other officers, and shall keep a duplicate of all accompts and entries in the said severall offices; the same to be presented to the said Houses, when, and as often as, it shall be required: And that it shall be lawful to and for every of the said commissioners to make a deputy for whom he will answer . . .

VIII. That for all such goods as are already bought from the merchant or importer, which is to pay excise; the said treasurer shall have power to give

---

[1] The schedule of articles to be charged with excise includes tobacco, wine, cider, perry, beer, ale, imported groceries, viz. raisins, figs, currants, sugar, and pepper, imported silks and wrought silks, furs, hats, imported lace, imported leather, imported linens, imported thread, and imported wire.

eight months' time for the payment of the excise, so that the parties pay one eight part of the excise every month, until he hath paid the full. And if the party chargeable with the excise desire to rebate for the time so allowed him for the payment of the excise, then it shall be lawful for the said treasurer to abate for six months, after the rate of twelve *per centum*.

Rebate.

IX. That for all inland commodities upon which there is any excise set, which upon the passing of this ordinance shall be found in the hands or custody of any person or persons whatsoever, it shall and may be lawful to and for the said treasurer for the time being, to give eight months' time of payment for the excise, so as the party who is to pay the same do during the said eight months pay one eight part thereof every month. And if the party chargeable with the excise desire to rebate for the time so allowed him for the payment of the excise, then it shall be lawful for the said treasurer to abate for six months after the rate of twelve *per centum per annum* provided always that if upon the search of any inland commodities mentioned in the schedule hereunto annexed to pay excise, there be found in the hands of any person or persons but two hogsheads of wine, or four barrels of beer, and no more, that when the party which by the said schedule is to pay the excise, shall pay but half the excise due for the same, so that he pay ready money for it.

X. That all and every the merchants and importers of any of the several foreign commodities in the schedule mentioned, and all ale and common beer brewers shall weekly cause to be entered into the said office a true and perfect list or account, as well of all and every the several commodities by them respectively and weekly sold, as of the names of the buyers thereof, and of those to whose use the same is bought, and that they shall not deliver any of the said commodities unto any of the buyers thereof, or other person or persons, until the same shall be so entered, and that the buyer have procured a ticket, under the hand of the treasurer for the time being, signifying that he hath paid the rates set upon the said commodities, or given security for the same . . .

Merchants, importers, and brewers to render weekly accounts.

XIII. That all and every person and persons whatsoever, that keep or shall keep private houses and families, as well in the City of London, and suburbs thereof, as in all other parts of the kingdom, dominion of Wales, and town of Berwick, which brew, or shall cause to be brewed, their own ale and beer for the sustenance of their families, or do make, or cause to be made, any cider and perry, for the purposes aforesaid, shall monthly cause the like entries to be made of all such quantities of ale and beer, cider and perry, so by them brewed, or caused to be brewed or made, on the like penalties to be levied on the offenders herein, and disposed of as aforesaid . . .

Persons brewing for private use to make like entries.

XV. That this Ordinance shall begin to take place and effect from the 25 of July, 1643, and from thence to continue only for three years, then next ensuing, unless both Houses of Parliament, during that time, shall declare that it shall continue for any longer time, and then this ordinance to continue for such further or longer time as shall be so appointed . . .

Commencement and continuance of this ordinance.

XXI. That the said commissioners, or the major part of them, shall from

time to time appoint any officer or officers belonging to the said office, to
enter into the cellars, shops, warehouses, storehouses, or other places of
every person or persons that selleth, buyeth, or spendeth any of the said
commodities, to search and see what quantities of any of the said commodities
every such hath on his hands, or any other person or persons to his
use . . .

XXIII. That all justices of peace, mayors, bailiffs, sheriffs, constables, and
all other officers, be from time to time aiding and assisting to the said commissioners
and other officers, and to every of them appointed by this ordinance,
in the execution of any the ordinances herein mentioned . . .

Margin note: Enter cellars, etc.

Margin note: Justices, etc. to be aiding.

29. LONDON'S FINANCIAL STRAITS, 1643

[*The Parliamentary or Constitutional History of England . . .
by several Hands*, vol. XII, 2nd ed., 1762, pp. 443–7]

An. 19. Car. I, 1643. November

THE House being informed that divers of the Committee of the Militia of
London were at the door, and desired to propound something to the House,
they were called in. And Mr. Speaker, by command of the House, acquainted
them that they had liberty to speak: whereupon Alderman Gibbs spoke as
follows:

That they are of the Militia of London, and are sent by them to make
known to this House, that the City of London is, at this time, under two
great wants, and desire leave to express them.

1. They are in great want of money, and desire you should know the causes
of it.

It is not unknown that we have advanced great sums, at several times,
being thereto solicited by several members of this House, both for this
kingdom and the kingdom of Ireland; and have received several securities for
repayment of them; as the royal subsidy, the twentieth part, the weekly
assessments, and other engagements; but, of all these, nor of any one of
these, have we received any benefit.

We humbly recommend unto you the remedy, that the members of this
honourable House may be encouraged to make use of their interests, in their
several counties, for the collecting and bringing up those monies, that we
may be the better able to do you service. The want of it doth admit of great
inconvenience, for where the king's party break in, they get the money; and
the state, in the mean time, pays use for it; and we are disenabled for the
want of it.

Another occasion of our great wants is those many disbursements, at
several times, for our several services, that we have made; and the many
provisions we have issued for arms, ammunition, and victuals, upon extreme
exigents, for my Lord General's army. We have likewise issued out great

engagements to our army that went twice into Kent and Gloucester, and done those great services. We have issued out great sums of money, to raise forces under Sir William Waller, when he was broken all to pieces; and some to those forces now abroad.

When our accounts are settled, we shall then crave leave to tender them unto you; whereupon, we hope, we shall receive satisfaction; for, since we bear the charge of the kingdom, we should be repaid out of the kingdom.

Our forces, now abroad, want money; two regiments of horse, consisting of 14 troops, and three regiments of foot, under the command of my Lord General, have been abroad above a month; besides three regiments with Sir William Waller: ten thousand pounds for those with my Lord General; and four or five thousand to those with Sir William Waller. They are citizens, civilly bred, and cannot make use of those means for their supply, as other common soldiers do that are used to the war; and now are brought to those necessities that they must come home. We have used our utmost endeavour to supply them; but, at present, we cannot help them. We have addressed ourselves to my Lord General, hoping to have had some of the monies that was going to my Lord General, for the payment of our forces. My Lord General declared he was not able to spare it, unless it be the three thousand pounds allotted him for the recruiting his army; and what ill consequence this may produce, I am sorry to mention.

2. You are not ignorant that, for these many months past, my Lord General hath wanted recruiting; and so weak, that he hath not been able to do the service of the kingdom, or restrain the enemy from enlarging his quarters. Consider, our city forces were raised for the guard of the city, and are tradesmen, and when they are abroad their plough lieth still at home; and, besides, they lose their employment; and you cannot be ignorant that, if the course be continued, it will be a great wasting of men.

For preventing whereof this remedy is offered, that my Lord General's army be speedily recruited; and that the City of London may be considered of as a place that hath much advanced, and is drawn dry. Our rich men are gone, because the city is the place of taxes and burdens; trade is decayed, and our shops shut up in a great measure; our poor do much increase. We desire you, for future taxes, that they may bear but their proportion, and not be overburdened. I should be loath to be misunderstood, that any that hear me should think we begin to be discouraged in the service of the Parliament. Though our difficulties be great, nay, if far greater, we shall no ways alter our resolutions; but, according to our Covenant, do our endeavours. We are not able, neither are we willing, to bear those reproaches cast upon us, who do allege that we are a turbulent and factious people, and seditious; all for war, and will admit of no peace on any terms. These are bitter aspersions out of black mouths and bitter pens. We are not willing to anticipate, but wait upon the Great Council, so we are not willing to bear such aspersions; for it is peace we pray for and fight for; but such a peace as is for the glory of God, and safety of religion. And this we desire to live to see, and to die rather than to outlive it; and do wait your time to take such opportunity in these things as may stand with your great occasions; and, till then, we remain your humble servants. This one word more we desire to leave with you, to supply us with monies as may lead us out of these difficulties.

The Aldermen and citizens were again called in, and Mr. Speaker, by the command of the House, acquainted them, 'That the House had considered of what they had propounded unto them, and found it to be full of weight, and to deserve a sadder and further consideration, than to give a sudden and particular answer unto. They had and would distribute it into such way of proceedings, as might give them the speediest and clearest satisfaction. The House hath likewise taken notice, how, upon all occasions, they have expressed their affections to the public; and how, at this time, they have assured them of their constant resolution to continue in the defence of religion, liberty, and privileges of Parliament. He is commanded to return them, and by them the whole Committee of the Militia and city, hearty thanks for their true love and zeal to the public; and to assure them, that neither in the desires that they have now propounded, nor in anything else that may advance the public security, shall they want the encouragement and assistance of this House.'

30. A ROYALIST ACCOUNT OF DESPERATE SHIFTS FOR MONEY BY KING AND PARLIAMENT, 1643-4

[The History of the Rebellion and Civil Wars in England by Edward, Earl of Clarendon, Oxford, 1839, pp. 413, 502-3]

1643. ... after all those mountains of promises and undertakings, the wants [of Parliament] were greater, and the city more importuned for money, and the Parliament visibly more necessitated for want of it, than they had been before; and instead of dispersing the king's army and bringing the king back to his Parliament, a sudden direction was given and a vigorous execution of that direction was begun, to draw a line about the City of London and Westminster and to fortify it; lest the king's forces might break in upon them; which made the people suspect the state of their affairs to be worse than in truth it was; and so far were they from any thoughts of peace and accommodation that the House of Commons raged more furiously than ever; and every day engaged themselves in conclusions more monstrous than they had yet entered upon. For the supply of the charge of the war, they proposed settling and imposing an excise upon such commodities as might best bear it; which was a burden the people of England had hitherto reproached other nations with as a mark of slavery, and as never feared by themselves; and for the exercise of the sovereign power, they resolved it fit to make a new great seal, to be always resident with the Houses. But the Lords were not yet arrived at that presumption, but plainly refused to concur with them in either . . .

1644. The hope of peace . . . did not in any degree make the counsels remiss for the providing of money to supply the army, upon which they had more hope than for a treaty. But the expedients for money were not easily thought upon; though there was a considerable part of the kingdom within the king's quarters, the inhabitants were frequently robbed and plundered by the incursions of the enemy, and not very well secured against the royal troops, who began to practise all the licence of war. The nobility and gentry, who were not officers of the army, lived for the most part in Oxford; and all that they could draw from their estates was but enough for their own subsistence; they durst not enter upon charging the people in general lest they should be thought to take upon them to be a Parliament; and their care was that the common people might be preserved from burdens; and they were as careful not to expose the king's honour or name to affronts and refusals, but were willing that the envy and clamour, if there should be any, should fall upon themselves.

They appointed all the members of the Commons 'to bring in the names of all the gentlemen of estate and other persons who were reputed to be rich within their several precincts; and what sum of money everybody might be well able to supply the king with, in this exigent of the public state.' And then a form of a letter was conceived which should be sent to everyone of them for such a sum, 'the letter to be subscribed by the two Speakers of the Houses to the end that the people might know that it was by the advice of the members of Parliament assembled there; which was as much the advice of Parliament as could be delivered at that time in the kingdom'.

When the way and method of this was approved by the Lords, and his Majesty likewise consented to it, they began the better to encourage others with themselves and caused letters to be signed and delivered to the several members of both Houses 'for such sums as they were well disposed to furnish', which were to that proportion as gave good encouragement to others; and the like letters to all persons of condition who were in the town. And by this means there was a sum raised in ready money and credit that did supply many necessary occasions, near the sum of one hundred thousand pounds, whereof some came in every day to enable the king to provide for the next campania; which, the spring coming on, was to be expected early; the Parliament having raised vast sums of money and being like to bring many armies into the field. All who were to furnish money upon these letters had liberty to bring or send it in plate, if that was for their convenience; the king having called the officers and workmen of his mint to Oxford, who coined such plate as was brought in. His Majesty likewise made a grant of some forests, parks, and other lands to certain persons in trust for the securing of such money as should be borrowed, or those persons who should be bound for the payment of such money; and by this means likewise many considerable sums of money were procured, and cloth, and shoes, and shirts were provided for the army.

The two Houses at Westminster who called themselves, and they are often called in this discourse, the Parliament, had at this time by an ordinance, that is an order of both Houses, laid an imposition, which they called an excise, upon wine, beer, ale, and many other commodities, to be paid in the manner very punctually and methodically set down by them, for the carrying on the war. And this was the first time that ever the name of payment of excise was heard of, or practised in England; laid on by those who pretended to be most jealous of any exaction upon the people. And this pattern being then printed and published at London was thought by the members at Oxford as a good expedient to be followed by the king; and thereupon it was settled and to be governed and regulated by commissioners, in the same method it was done at London. And in Oxford, Bristol, and other garrisons it did yield a reasonable supply for the provision of arms and ammunition, which for the most part it was assigned to, both sides making ample declarations with bitter reproaches upon the necessity that drew on this imposition, 'that it should be continued no longer than to the end of the war, and then laid down and utterly abolished'; which few wise men believed it would ever be.

31. THE FINANCIAL BURDEN OF WAR IN NOTTINGHAMSHIRE, 1646

[*Lords' Journals*, IX, p. 72]

11 March, 1646

For the Right honourable Edward, Earl of Manchester, Speaker of the Honourable House of Peers *pro tempore*.

My Lords,

Having yesterday, on my way hither, received your Lordships' orders for the preventing or removing the quarters of the army out of the Eastern Association, I then gave your Lordships an account why I could not give immediate observance to your commands; and have now thought fit to give your Lordships the reason of the army's removal thither: that provisions in the quarters about Nottingham, where the army last lay, were so far spent, that I was necessitated to remove thence; and, upon a serious consideration had with my Council of War, finding that the whole kingdom being in a like settled posture, and upon foot of accompt in point of taxes and assessments; and that there was a necessity of my removal either into those parts which have been like burthened with those where I then quartered, and where I had formerly been, which have been oppressed as well by plunder as free quarter of the enemy, or into the Eastern Association; the latter was judged most reasonable. And I resolved to remove the army accordingly, that I might thereby give ease to those parts that have so long groaned under the burthen of this war. I have acquainted the House of Commons with the same; and if it shall please the Houses to give any other orders in the quartering of the army, it shall be most carefully observed by

Your Lordships' most humble servant,

T. FAIRFAX.

Saffron Walden,
March 9, 1646.

32. THE SOLDIERS PETITION FOR THEIR ARREARS, 1647

[Lords' Journals, IX, p. 528]

16 November, 1647

To his Excellency Sir Thomas Fairfax, our noble general,
the humble petition of many officers and soldiers
under his command.

SHEWETH that, in judgement and conscience, we engaged in the war against the king, under your excellency's command, to preserve and vindicate the freedoms of our native country, and of the Parliament in order thereunto.

That, by the blessing of God, all those our enemies are fallen or fled before us.

That, for the same ends, and for our own rights, for our service, we were forced to hazard ourselves in disputing the Parliament's commands; and those our opposers have been likewise subdued.

That the countries have petitioned your Excellency to procure the long-expected settlement of their freedoms.

That we have waited many months for the securing to us and all the free-born people their native rights, and for our indemnity and arrears as soldiers; and our hearts bleed to see our country consume under continued distractions and heavy oppressions.

That we see no hope of indemnity for us and our assistants, nor of settling the foundations of freedom, but by entering into this agreement; which we herewith offer to your Excellency, desiring your concurrence therein.

That we have seen and felt the sad consequences of being divided and scattered, before our native freedoms were settled, and our arrears secured, and such a way established for constant pay that we may know where to receive it monthly without fail.

That we are bound in conscience, from the sense of our duty to our native country, and in mercy to ourselves, to keep together, with our swords in our hands, to maintain these our freedoms, for which the Parliament first invited us to take arms, to see our arrears and pay secured, and our dear country freed from its intolerable burthens.

May it therefore please your Excellency, to go on in owning and leading us, in maintenance of this our cause, to the righteousness whereof God hath borne such clear witness. And in the prosecution of these things, we humbly desire to live and die under your Excellency's conduct.

The *People's Engagement* was annexed to this petition, with these words printed on the back side, in great letters, ENGLAND'S FREEDOM, SOLDIERS' RIGHTS.

33. A PROTEST FROM THE ARMY AGAINST THE SALE OF DEBENTURES, 1649

[B.M., E575/17 Thomason Tracts. The Perfect Weekly Account, October 3–October 10, 1649, pp. 628–9]

THIS day a letter was presented to the House from his Excellency the Lord Fairfax and a petition of the officers of the army, in these words:

Mr. Speaker,

This enclosed in the humble desires of the Council of War, in prevention of the disorderly buying of debentures of the soldiers at inconsiderable rates, as it more fully declares. My desire unto you is, that you will please to present it to the Parliament, that they may take such course for restraint and prevention thereof, as they in their wisdom shall think fit.

Kensington, 3 October   Sir, I am your very humble servant,

T. Fairfax.

For the honourable William Lenthall, esq., Speaker to the Right Honourable the Parliament of England.

To the Right Honourable the Commons of England
assembled in Parliament,
the humble petition of the Council of Officers of the Army
under the Command of the Lord Fairfax.

Sheweth that although you have, by your late gracious Act, made sufficient provision for satisfying the arrears of the officers and soldiers of the army by the sale of the manors, lands, parks, and chases belonging to the late King, to the satisfaction of all who understand your honourable and equal intention therein; nevertheless, some persons, having more respect to their own profit than either the honour of the Parliament or due satisfaction of the soldier, have so far prevailed upon the present necessity and ignorance of them that they have purchased their debentures at such inconsiderable rates, at 3*s.* 6*d.*

and 4*s.* per *l.* to the utter frustrating the soldier of his hardly-earned, long-expected, and by you fully intended reward, rendering them, their wives, and children into a necessitous condition, and thereby giving advantage unto such persons as wait for such opportunities to raise discontents amongst them to the great hazard, if not ruin of the army.

Your petitioners therefore humbly pray, that you will take the premises into your serious consideration, and not only give relief to those soldiers who through their own folly are deprived of the recompenses of their former services, and brought into present want and necessities by such indirect courses, which in all times have been provided against, but also strictly to prohibit all further proceedings of this kind for the future, according as you in your grave wisdoms shall think meet.

34. ARMY ARREARS OF PAY, 1651-4

[J. Y. Akerman, *Letters from Roundhead Officers written from Scotland and chiefly addressed to Captain Adam Baynes,
July MDCL—June MDCLX*, Edinburgh, 1856, p. 29, no. 52;
p. 104, no. 188; p. 105, no. 191]

[Captain Fitzwilliam to Captain Adam Baynes]

Sir,

I received a bill of ninety pounds of my Major to be paid by you, which I sent to my brother Robert, and desired him to receive the money of you, which he saith you cannot pay. Sir, my request to you is that you will do me the favour to pay it, or give it me under your hand that you cannot, or that you have not so much money of the Regiment's or my Major's in your hands, for the officers and soldiers are very importunate with me for it; and as for that hundred pounds that you say is not paid, it concerns me no more than the rest of the Regiment, for at my coming from London I acquainted my Collo. and Major what I had done, they was satisfied. Sir, I desire you let me have two or three words in answer that I may be able to satisfy both the officers and soldiers, in which doing you will much oblige, Sir,

Your humble servant,
Jo. Fitzwilliam.

Leith, June the 22nd, 1651.

*   *   *

[From Cornet J. Baynes]

Cousin,

I am glad the bills are comed safe to you. I thought to have paid you some money by Mr. Gerrard, and I understand by him that there is some stop made to our pay in England because of the money being all to be brought into the Exchange, so that we are three months in arrear, and must have a little patience. I have written to him about my 2*s.* a day augmentation. I would not lose it, if to be gotten. I fear the 60*li.* for my 400*li.* loss is also lost. I would fain have had it towards making Betty a little portion, but I cannot much grudge to want that I never looked for . . .

I remain your truly lo. Cousin,

J. Baynes.

Dalk[eith], October 31, 1654

*   *   *

[From Cornet Baynes]
Cousin,

I am glad the stop is removed as to our pay . . .

Your affectionate Cousin,

J. Baynes.

Dalkeith, November 14th, 1654.

35. PROPOSALS FOR REFORM OF THE MINT, 1652
[P.R.O., SP 18/24, no. 16]

At the Committee for the Council for the Mint, May the 14, 1652.
Propositions for the Debate of the Committee for the Mint for the Setting the Mint on Work, agreed to be reported to the Council for their further Consideration.

1. That the Council be pleased to move the Parliament to pass the Act for hindering the carrying out of our coin, the cutting, melting down of our coin by goldsmiths, and the giving more for bullion than the price of the mint.
2. That the book of essays [=assays] of coin domestic and foreign, and the par that foreign coin beareth as to our English, be reported to the House with the law for obliging our merchants to be regulated thereby, and that they be printed and published, whereby the exchange in other countries will be brought to right.
3ly. That the trade of being exchangers and buying up of foreign bullion by goldsmiths may be prohibited, and that, as formerly and in other states, an exchange office for the Commonwealth be speedily set up in the Tower of London to whom all bullion is to be sold at the price of the mint and for ready money, and from whom at the same price all artificers in the manufacture of gold and silver may have it for the nation's use.
4ly. That our gold be raised to what it is valued at by all other states of Christendom, the omission of which having drawn away all the English gold.
5ly. That for encouragement of merchants to bring bullion to the mint,

there be no more taken for coining for one year than doth defray the charge the state is at.

6ly. That the Parliament be moved to make current in England such merchantable coins as are now needed for and received by our merchants in foreign parts, except only such of pieces others as are base and adulterated, and that weights be provided to be sold by the state for receiving only such in payment as are of a new weight according to the published order.

7ly. That the Spaniard be treated with to bring his bullion hither as formerly to be coined for his soldiery in Flanders.

8ly. That some better way of coining be found out whereby the counterfeiting, clipping, unequalling of our coin may be prevented and reformed.

9ly. That an able officer may be appointed to give intelligence by search or other ways, and to keep a private book of all bullion imported into the nation custom free, and to see that it be brought into the mint, and not carried out again and other ways disposed of, as also to take care that the East India Company and others that have licences carry not out more than their allowance as they have done in years past.

May the 14, 1652.

Ordered by the Committee for the Mint that Sir James Harrington report to the Council the above written propositions as expedient to set the mint on work, rendering the same to the further consideration of the Council.

36. AN OPINION FROM AMSTERDAM ON THE PROBLEMS OF THE ENGLISH MINT, 1652
[P.R.O., SP 18/24, no. 21]

Amsterdam, 26 of May, 1652.

Noble Sir,

According to your desire by your letter dated 20 April last I have sent you my opinion about the causes of the obstruction of the mint in the Tower of London and also have made enquiry of others here that are well acquainted with the mystery of this business, and the true reason, as we conceive, that hindereth the State of England from coining of money. I have sent you herein this letter so you may be pleased to communicate it to any if you think it may do my country any service. I am assured if it be enquired after the State will find this I say to be true and my opinion may be something more than ordinary in this point for I ever had my mind bent to understand the mystery of mint and exchanges, having read great volumes put out by the Court of Moneyers in France; for they have a constant Court and Council for regulating for their monies and bullion of their nation and this court do constantly sit as any court of justice in Westminster to discover and punish all clippers and counterfeiters, and they have officers that hold intelligence about the preventing of all frauds in and upon the coins and discovering and punishing any that shall offend, and this is a sure way to keep their money from clipping now that they in France have restored them to their just weight and fineness; and such of a court ought to be put up in England, and strict laws made and men appointed to see those laws put in execution (for to make laws and not to put them in execution is to little or no purpose).

And truly my experience hath taught me those rules. That in any country that I have been in when the State doth not keep extraordinary watch on all such as are coiners and clippers and counterfeiters of money of their country, and the laws be not diligently put in execution against culling and sorting out the weightiest to be transported and the light and clipped left behind, it is a great imbasing of the current value of ——[1] England and all your silver money ——[?] daily is thus abused by goldsmiths and others. And when the State doth not employ such as do know how to make discovery of those offenders, but put into the mint upon recommendation of friends such persons as have no experience in such a mystery, I say it thereupon hath followed great damage to the State, for there are bankers and exchangers in Holland that know the ignorance of all your present mint men that have any place of trust and laugh at them. They say when the mint in the Tower flourished, there were in the office old Mr. Andrew Palmer, Mr. Rogers, and one Cogan. These men were all subtle mint men and held correspondence here and knew what to do to advance the mint in most parts of Christendom to fetch in monies and would always find one way or another to bring grist to their mill, but now your mint comes to be neglected, the monies adulterated and the State dishonoured, and I tell you the truth, I have been told here by people that come out of Ireland and I believe it to be true that there is a greater quantity of the state of England new coin counterfeited both of gold and silver than hath been coined in the mint at the Tower of London. And this I know. The States here took some English merchant men that had dispersed great quantity of the Parliament's gold as twenty shilling pieces and upon the trial they were not worth 4s. a piece; and they sent some of the gold to the Lord Mayor and Common Council of London and the examination of one Badland, an Englishman, who lay here as a factor for divers persons in London to vent and disperse this counterfeit gold for some merchants in London, but the business was by the merchants in London bribed and smothered; and it is very easy if the State please to find out the truth for the letter was sent to Alderman Andrews when he was mayor and to one Michell, the town clerk. They must know how this business came to be smothered for here we know it must be a gross abuse to the State in point of their monies to let such a business be neglected. And we hear—I pray enquire the truth of it—that your mint in the Tower of London is come to such contempt, where you were wont to coin forty thousand pounds a week and above twenty thousand pounds a week constantly in gold and silver, there is not so much coined in a year as was within this five year coined in a week, and that now your coin in your mint [is] nothing almost but counters

---

[1] Half a line faded and illegible.

and farthings. If it should be true, which I pray enquire the thing out, it is a high dishonour to the nation in so sacred a place as the mint is, to coin nothing but counters and farthings and in so famous a mint as the Tower of London. For the honour of the nation, use your interest to let their mint not be employed rather than suffer such trumpery as counters or farthings to be made within the walls. You at London little think that we at Amsterdam should take notice of these abuses, and say further that your mint is undervalued because your present officers have no skill or experience to find out the obstruction and abuses; for if they were not short-sighted men they would never suffer their mint to be abused with making counters, and, indeed, to cause your mint to be set on work, the master and wardens and chief officers must have a general knowledge of all the chief mints and mints masters and chief merchants in Christendom besides to know the mystery of exchange, a business not easily learned.

Sir, I pray mark what I say which is I know in Ireland at this very day that almost all the English money is clipped, and that it is not so weighty as when it was first coined by twenty pound in the 100*li.*, and that when the Dutch send them goods out of Holland, their shippers and factors always carry weights for to weigh all the money that they receive, and they will sell the commodities at 20 in the 100 more when they receive it in clipped monies than when they receive it in weighty money and I have weighed the English money here in Holland when they returned from Ireland and find 400*li.* of your culled and weighty money shall weigh 500*li.* light English money (I mean in tale) which clipped English money is transported back into England where it goes current at all sea ports, and there they will change it for a small matter in tale for weighty culled money, which heavy money they send for Holland. You must observe your clipped English money will make no more than to melt. I heard there are goldsmiths in London, Bristol, and several sea ports of the nation very guilty of clipping of money and false coiners, many in and about Lancashire and London, many of our bankers here have constantly a great trade with the goldsmiths and merchants in London for English gold and heavy English silver.

Your mint will never go till this be discovered that the bottom of it be examined, for their men are the sluices that drain all your money and destroy your mint. And upon a longer continuance of the stop of your mint great damage and mischief must necessarily follow, especially England who have no considerable mines to supply your treasure as Spain and other countries have. You cannot do as we do in Holland for we at the present are necessitated to make money a merchandise; we have so much I believe forty times more gold and silver there is at this day in the Low Countries than is in England. You have a compass of land and stock which they have not, besides they are so subtle in their banks which you have not, that they can bring in money and let it out again as they list. And when you have as much money as they, then do as they; but now you must recruit your mint and be very vigilant that no money comes into the nation but what shall be converted into coin. And by all ways and means find out the transporters of treasure for you must have money plentiful to pay your armies in England, Scotland, and Ireland and no small sums will serve your fleet; and as your business now stands, you have hardly money left to maintain the trade of the nation, the taxes will be collected with a great deal of difficulty and in a very short time impossible to be paid if you keep not strict laws and watchful officers to discover the transporters of gold and silver; for when your treasure comes to be exhausted it will breed a strong change in all parts of the State. Therefore, if you observe this rule that no person presume to cull and melt your current coins, nor to give for gold or silver above the price as settled by the State for the mint and to make enquiry and punish those that do or shall offend in the premises, and to hunt out all clippers and counterfeiters and transporters of treasure, with a great deal of difficulty you may restore your mint. In France about twelve years past the State was forced to decry and call in all their monies; they were so generally clipped both gold and silver, all their payments and commerce run into confusion because all their money was upon such uncertainty, no man could tell by tale the intrinsic value, and you have brought yourself almost to the point, for all your money you have in Ireland is clipped besides a world of counterfeit Spanish money, counterfeit English gold and silver, that your payments there are at no certainty for our factors; and we find it so in the returns, so that upon a medium we hold that since the war the whole stock in money there is not so good by twenty in the hundred as it is coined in the Tower, it hath fallen in such rogues' hands.

And you are little better for all your monies in England considering at what pass you are brought by some goldsmiths and merchants for almost all your gold is transported, and that little that is left in hucksters' hands that go to an exchanger in Lombard Street as we call him here, you must pay 6*li.*, 7*li.*, 8*li.*, 10*li.* and sometimes more to have one hundred pounds in gold for silver. And this hath been set on foot for the unlawful profit of a few, without any licence or law, to the destruction of your mint, for who will bring gold to be coined in the Tower to lose 2*s.* in twenty of what they can sometimes make to transport it? The like is for silver; it is a thing impossible to prevent this mischief but by giving life and vigour to old laws to make a strict enquiry of the offenders and to employ such as know the track to discover these abuses. The clipping of money was ordinarily done in France by gentlemen till they revived their court of monies, who by their vigilance discover the offenders, and they all die without mercy so that mischief is there prevented, and the wars of England hath almost put you to the same poster [=posture] for the last king went squirting up and down with his mints at Bristol, at Shrewsbury, at York, at Oxford, at Carlisle, and many other places; and when these garrisons were surrendered, these irons were carelessly neglected and come into knaves' hands and they fell first a-coining of great quantities of money in Lancashire and the materials they wrought on was only the clipping of English silver and pewter dishes. There hath some been there executed, but to this day the State knows not the hundred men in that county that are clippers and counterfeiters of money. The like is done at London and continues to ——[1] should employ in their mint such as would hunt dry foot to find these fellows; and the rest of transporters of gold and silver, there could not be a more or a better service to the State than to bring them all to justice.

But if you move this business to any person in power you must be sure to give them warning to have a care of believing or advising with the Guinea merchants, the East India merchants, or goldsmiths for these are the only offenders and without a joint confederation with each other these mischiefs of transporting money, diverting it from the mint when it is brought in bullion from beyond seas by giving for it 1*d.*, 2*d.*, in five shillings in silver, sixpence and 12*d.*, and sometimes 2*s.* in twenty for gold more than it will make in the mint, what doth the merchant care so he may be rich in his private how poor the public is, let the Commonwealth sink, let him, so he get profit. Send our gold and silver into foreign parts for cards, paper, pictures, glass, pearls, beads, and babyes [= baubles], Flanders laces, tobacco, or a hundred trifles, the nation buys all for ready money and good gold and silver is transported (we do esteem your expenses of foreign goods of a foreign growth is twice as much as your native goods you export), and this in a few years will drain all your stock and not leave you one penny.

I am confident and have others speak it that are knowing men. We have in Amsterdam more English gold than you have yourselves in all England. This gold hath been all sent within twenty years and could not come over without hands. I know myself great quantities of heavy English silver hath weekly come over in pinks and Dutch men o' war within these few years to the value of many hundred thousand pounds in the return of one commodity which was corn. I did wonder at the first how the merchant did transport out of London all weighty and culled English money into Holland till one of the bankers told me the way the merchants used which I would have you take notice and enquire after it, and you shall find it true to find out this business and to prevent it for future and punish the offenders. It will be a great service to the State for it is a most pernicious thing against a Commonwealth and ought to be prevented and punished with the greatest severity.

It is the goldsmiths especially those in Lombard Street are the great merchants' in London cashiers, and these goldsmiths will receive any man's money for nothing and pay it for them the next day or the same day, and this everybody that transports gold and silver and come over with it say to be true; but in the mean time the goldsmiths keep people in their houses that in their upper rooms cull and weigh all the English money they receive, and melt down the weighty, and transport it to foreign parts sometimes without melting. These keep banks of all the principal coins in Christendom in their shops where any may be furnished to transport what coins they will, and I hear there are a sort of them that clip and counterfeit gold and silver, both English coins and all other nations', and these and none but these are the

---

[1] Several words faded and illegible.

only men that destroy your mint and are the only instruments to transport your treasure; and till you can get a perfect discovery of these people and some of them are severely punished, it is in vain for you or any other to expect your mint to be set on work. And this I writ to you I know if it be carefully examined will all prove true to give a stop to this mischief, and to make a discovery of all those abuses upon examination of witnesses. It must be by a sharp law to discover what is past, to prevent for the time to come, and to employ such persons to find out this business as have been guilty themselves; and if the State make use of such a dark lanthorn, they will discover the bottom of this mischief which can never be truly searched and found out but by one that knows the trade. If you could light on such a fellow, he would do this business rarely and indeed he would deserve a very great reward if he be his true aftermaster and undo it. By this vigilant man you may prevent a scarcity of money which as your affair now stands may be one hundred times a greater mischief than a dearth of corn. I pray, Sir, remember my kind presents to your good lady and to all my friends. Sir, I take leave and remain

Your obliged and humble servant,
James Yard [?]

You have in England a great waste of silver in wearing gold lace and silver lace. I am informed there is made three hundred thousand pounds a year and that half of it is wasted. Inquire the truth if it be so it ought to be put down especially at this time till you recruit the nation with treasure and your mint flourish.

[Endorsed:] To the honourable Sir Robert Stone, knight, these, in London.

37. PROBLEMS OF MONEY SUPPLY, 1652

[Henry Robinson, Certain Proposals in Order to the People's Freedom and Accommodation in some Particulars with the Advancement of Trade and Navigation of this Commonwealth in General, 1652, pp. 15–19]

... Monies are likely carried out of England:

I. Either because there is more profit to be got by our monies abroad, than by remitting them by exchange, or employing them in commodities. Or,
II. Because it may be most commodious for travellers, or other passengers to carry them. Or,
III. Because such passengers are ignorant both in employing them, and remitting or returning them by exchange. But,
IV. And especially, because all the corn which is brought by strangers, and all the fish which the Hollanders take upon our coast or elsewhere, and sell in England, as at Yarmouth, Plymouth, etc. are sold for ready monies, and those monies in likelihood all exported, etc.

The gain on transporting monies may proceed:

1. Either because our commodities are grown dearer here in England to be bought. Or,
2. Grown cheaper abroad in foreign parts to be sold. Or,
3. Because that they give more for our monies than the intrinsical value, to melt them in foreign mints, or make them current in payments above their value.

And all these three respects will vanquish if we can but keep our trade in balance, or rather enlarge our exportation of commodities above our importation, and establish the exchange between us and other nations according to the par.

The undervaluing our monies by exchange, the accommodating passengers with monies wherever they go, who desire not to be troubled with commodities though they might get somewhat by them, and the supplying their ignorance both in employing and returning them may be done by engaging all merchants to observe the par in their exchanging according to certain tables wherein the intrinsical value of foreign coins in relation to ours is to be published; and if this fail, it may infallibly be effected, by constituting a Public Exchanger, or an Agent of the Commonwealth, who may be obliged to furnish all passengers with the full value of their monies in most principal places where they go, as likewise all merchants with whatsoever sums they desire; in which case men will not hazard the danger of exporting their monies, and, if they do and be discovered, must be made to pay for it without remission.

And when this course is settled, then it is propounded, that all persons be again prohibited exportation of monies; and that if the captain or master, master's mate, purser, master gunner, or gunner's mate, or boatswain do contrive or assist the exportation of monies, or but know thereof, and do not discover it, it shall be confiscation of the ship, besides double penalty to each of the parties so assisting, or concealing; and that the accuser or discoverer have one half of what is recovered, provided it be within five years after the fact was done. Within which time if any of the parties shall accuse the other, and make it appear by one or two witnesses, or otherwise, the accuser for the first time shall not only free himself from any penalty, but enjoy one half as discoverer. And the having above such a sum of money aboard any ship or vessel so long time together, and in such places, shall be understood a guiltiness of an exportation thereof. And if any other mariner or person belonging to the ship or vessel shall assist, or conceal the exportation as abovesaid, such mariners or person shall forfeit all his wages then due to him, and if he have none due, be liable to a fine, etc.

Now for enabling the Public Exchanger, or furnishing the Commonwealth's Agent with a stock of money and credit, whereby he may furnish all men's occasions by exchange, according to the par, as aforesaid: it is necessary that he have a stock, and how that may be raised gratis hath been made out to several worthy Members, and shall be further demonstrated when required.

Then, if the Commonwealth keep a correspondent, or banker in Paris, Antwerp, Amsterdam, Rotterdam, and in such like principal places of trade, and have a stock of money, or credit with each of them, their Public Exchanger may either return monies upon them, or receive charges from them according to the par or intrinsical value, which will hinder transportation, and this can be no damage or loss unto the Parliament, because their agents deal only according to the true worth of the coins in themselves at the mint, whatever the denominations be, or however they be lightened or imbased: and besides

1. If all monies delivered or received by exchange pass through this Public Exchanger or Banker's hands, or be ordered to be paid in bank, you may see who are deliverers, and who takers, and to and from what parts monies are remitted, and received, and by whom; and by this balance of exchanges you may see how the pulse of the balance of trade beats, by whom, and from whence the mischiefs concerning the same proceed, and be enabled to redress them.

2. As by an exact rule in the Custom House you may know what goods each foreigner imports and exports; so here you may see what monies he remits or receives, and make a balance; for strangers may be thought to be the greatest exporters of our monies, and those seamen, chiefly dealing likewise much in merchandise. Now till this be more fully made out by practise, it is humbly moved,

First, that no goldsmith or other person upon great penalties be suffered to melt any of the Commonwealth's coin.

Secondly, that no gold and silver lace be made in England, but of such silver and gold thread or plate, as is imported, until we see the bullion begin again to be imported into England.

Thirdly, that no monies be permitted to be sent into Ireland, New England, Barbados, Newfoundland, or any of our other plantations, until bullion begin to come in again.

Fourthly, that all gold and silver mines, formerly discovered within this land, may be now further searched into, and others more nearly sought after, for supplying us with a money stock of our own, until we can bring in one from abroad.

Fifthly, that there be no pence nor halfpence made of silver, because so subject to be worn out, broken, and quite lost.

Sixthly, that it be afresh declared what quantity of the Commonwealth's coin, and how much foreign coin every ship may carry for her own store or provision, against all wants or accidents, etc., and how they are to be furnished, etc. against all emergent occasions.

Be pleased to erect a Court of Merchants for the speedy determining all controversies about buying and selling, or any other emergencies relating to trade and navigation.

That bonds, bills of exchange, or other bills of debt, be made irrevocably assignable from one man to another, as often as the last assign shall please, together with the delivery of the said bonds or bills of debt, which will virtually multiply the stock of this nation as to trading to all intents and purposes, especially if you can induce the people by advantages to a voluntary registering thereof, for which purpose only there is a short proposal ready prepared to be produced upon command.

But above all other engines or instruments, the greatest preeminence is due unto a bank, which hath a capacity of infallible preventing the exportation of our own monies, and necessitating the importation of bullion and foreign coins. It will prevent the passing of false or clipped money, with the wear and waste of money by telling it; save all the time now spent in telling money; overrule the merchandising exchange, whereby the merchants of this nation have been merely cheated in all parts of the world, where exchanging by bills of exchange is practised. It is this only that can reduce and keep the grand balance of trade in favour of this nation, by preventing the importation of a greater quantity of foreign commodities, than we export of native. It is capable of multiplying the stock of the nation, for as much as concerns trading *in infinitum*. In brief, it is the Elixir or Philosopher's Stone, to which all nations, and everything within those nations must be subservient, either by fair means or by foul.

Be pleased to let the Bill for a County Register at last to pass, which hath been so many years preparing, and yet retarded, no doubt by some private respects or interests; I mean to pass in such a manner, as that a man, being to make a purchase of lands or houses, may in a quarter of an hour, and for a twelve-penny matter or thereabouts, see who is the true proprietor thereof, and what judgements, mortgages, and other incumbrances there are upon them; which with the voluntary registering of bonds and bills of debt, as aforesaid, will prevent three-fourth parts of all lawsuits, that otherwise will happen, and shorten such as shall be begun hereafter . . .

38. INVESTIGATIONS INTO FORGED
DEBENTURES, 1652–3
[P.R.O., SP 18/37, no. 16, I, II]

Whitehall, June 10, 1653.

In reference to an order of the Council, 4 June 1653, to me to state the matter of fact concerning Capt. Lovell and Ellen, his wife, and to certify the same to the Council, I humbly certify:

That in the beginning of July 1652, having the discovery of diverse that had and did counterfeit debentures and public faith bills, by order of the Council of State and afterwards of the Parliament, several of the chief of them were apprehended to the number of twelve and committed to prison, amongst whom Capt. Lovell was one, upon the informations (an abstract of which is hereunto annexed), wherein his wife seems to be chiefly concerned, and besides those twelve about thirty more, upon the examinations taken, appeared to have to do in the counterfeiting or putting off such debentures and bills, for the apprehension of most of which warrants were issued out by the Council.

Some of the chief were Fugill, Quick, and Bayly who, after many examinations, acknowledged the whole business and confessed that for seventeen months before that time they had to do in such forgeries, and Fugill said that he believed four parts in six of the bills put off at Worcester House on fee farms were counterfeits, which bills were sold at 6*d*., 8*d*., 10*d*., 12*d*., 14*d*. in the pound, and they were so exquisite in those forgeries that they could counterfeit any man's hand so that he should not know it from his own hand, and had made the whole such a mystery that scriveners, and citizens, and brokers were of their number, who drew and became bound at Drury House for those forged ones and some of the clerk's they had got into the bargain; and something they mentioned also of counterfeit leases upon examination; and after forty days' travail in this business, I found in Fugill's, Quick, Bayly, and Lovell's papers the names and sums of 115,045*li*. generally counterfeits.

Upon report hereof to the Council they ordered a report of the whole to be prepared for the Parliament, which I drew, and it was by the Council ordered to be reported to the Parliament by Col. Downes who, it seems, found no opportunity to make it.

The expectation the Council had of what orders the Parliament would give for the trial of these counterfeits and for further pursuance of the forgeries (the Council having only power to secure and examine) was the reason wherefore nothing hath been done further to this day, and that the forgers secured are yet under bail and their papers seized on by the warrant of the Council in my custody.

I have the copy of the said report by me and all the particulars in case the Council shall think fit to pursue it. Upon perusal whereof a way may be thought on to discover many hundred thousands of pounds in which the State hath been thus cheated, and after this rate neither will all the lands in England, Scotland, or Ireland satisfy public faith bills and debentures. And of this, out of duty to the Commonwealth, I should have given the Council an account, had not your commands in this case of Mrs. Lovell prevented me.

Geo. Bishop.

[Endorsed:] The State of the Case of Capt. Charles Lovell and Ellen, his wife, in reference to an Order of the Council of State for the preparing thereof by Capt. Geo. Bishop. 12 June, 1653.

*   *   *

Whitehall, July 19, 1652.

Information against Capt. Lovell and Mrs. Lovell, his wife.

Fugill's information, July 1, 1652: Fugill saith that Lovell was a confederate and dealer with Huet, Keies, Jackson, Thompson, Cannon, Spink in counterfeit debentures; that Mrs. Lovell desired Fursman (as he informed Fugill) to enter into partnership with them; that Huet and Lovell upon the return of their surveys have advised all their friends to take debentures of Mrs. Lovell or her compliants, as Bateson informed Fugill, Keies also, and Jackson informed Fugill that the parties aforesaid were confederates together for the end aforesaid. And Fugill saith he is confident that he is more guilty than himself.

Fugill's information, June 25, 1652: Fugill saith that Lovell's wife hath been one of the greatest dealers in false bills about London, and that Fursman said to him he had a false bill of her and that she desired him to deal with her, that he and she are suit about the bill, that if she will she can discover more than any for she hath been by him suspected to deal in false bills much longer than himself, but he could never perfectly perceive it. Her husband and Huet being surveyors, when they returned any survey, they recommended it to some friend and he that purchased they would recommend rather to her or them that dealt for her, that he is sure she dealt much in false bills, though prove it he cannot; that there were at least seven or eight that dealt thus together by way of truck for cloth.

Nonnally's information, June 26, 1652: Nonnally saith that Mrs. Lovell had many false debentures, some of which she put off and some were stayed at the Committee of the Army, and that she pretended that at the trial of John Lilburne she lost 3,000*li*. bills, but afterwards she had them in bonds, the said Nonnally's bill being one of them . . .

39. SOLDIERS' DEBENTURES AND THE PURCHASE OF CROWN LAND, 1653

[J. Y. Akerman, *Letters from Roundhead Officers written from Scotland and chiefly addressed to Captain Adam Baynes, July MDCL–June MDCLX*, Edinburgh, 1856, p. 58, nos. 105, 107]

[Cornet J. Baynes to Capt. A. Baynes]

Cousin,

Yours I received. I hope at length the Dutch and all enemies will be satisfied of their folly and madness in quarrelling with us. The cause in hand is and will be a burdensome stone to all that lift at it: blows may convince men, when words and reason will not. But why must John Lilburne be secured?

Mr. Talbot salutes you and all friends with you. Lieut. Wheatley (Major Smithson's Lieut.) hath arrears of about 1,200*li*. paid in upon Nonsuch and Holme Cultram. If my Lord have a mind to buy them (having his Majors) the Lieutenant is inclining to sell his also. Let me know my Lord's pleasure in it, that I may return answer to the Lieutenant, and what he will give, and when he will pay. No more now but my dear respects to my she cousin and all other friends, Mrs. Dawson, Mrs. Mary, etc.

I remain,

Your endeared cousin,

J. Baynes.

Dalk[eith], June 18, 1653.

*　　　*　　　*

[Thomas Lilburn and Francis Wilkinson to Capt. A. Baynes]

Sir,

Yours dated 11th instant we received, wherein you desire the several prices of the house, land, and wood apart, which indeed we wanting the survey, and none of us minding the place of Nonsuch so much as to enable us to set rates upon them asunder, we think it convenient if that we sell to let it go altogether: those that buy may agree better among themselves if that it fall not into one main hand. Truly we shall be very glad Major General Lambert have it, hoping it will prove a good pennyworth. We formerly writ to you we would abate Ma. Gen. somewhat of 9,500*li*. We desire to know what he will give for it, and then we shall resolve what to abate. I believe you know that 9,000*li*. was refused for it. And whereas you desire to know what is the lowest rates of soldiers' debentures, we think they will be about 12*s*. or 12 —— per *li*., and those of our —— troops are jointly upon —— and Abbeyholme. If that you please to give notice what you will give, we can give you a more positive answer in that particular. We believe you may have many about that rate. We expect your answer within twenty days, remaining Sir

Your very humble servants,

Tho. Lilburne, Francis Wilkinson.

Dalkeith, 28 June, 1653

40. ON THE WORKINGS OF THE EXCHANGE, 1655

[John Marius, *Advice concerning Bills of Exchange*,
2nd ed., London, 1655, pp. 1-11, 16-17, 60-1, 136-8]

Exchange excellent and necessary

EXCHANGE is by some held to be the most mysterious part of the art of merchandising and traffic, being grounded upon custom and experience. And the necessity and commodiousness of exchanges is seen in that it hath found a general allowance in all countries time out of mind, and yet is maintained with the general consent of all, for it prevents the danger and adventure of carriage of monies from one city or country to another.

And this is done only by two or three lines written on a small piece of paper, termed, a bill of exchange; which is so noble and excellent, that though it cannot properly (as I conceive) be called a specialty, because it wanteth those formalities which by the common law of England are thereunto required, as seal, and delivery, and witnesses; yet it is equivalent thereunto, if not beyond, or exceeding any specialty or bond, in its punctuality and precise payment, carrying with it a commanding power, though directed from the servant to the master; for if by him accepted, it concerneth him every whit as much to see it be paid with honour at the time, as the servant can desire, or the party to whom it is payable can expect, in regard the acceptor's credit lieth at stake. And if he fail of payment at the precise day, presently there will issue forth a protest, which may tell tales, and soon make a dilemma in his commerce; for he must not expect to continue his credit long that doth not pay his accepted bills at the time appointed, and besides his own, his servant or friend, the drawer's credit will also be wounded; besides the charges which are incident thereunto, and unavoidable payment of principal and charges at the end, if the party or parties are able, for both acceptor and drawer are bound until payment, as shall be more particularly shewed in this ensuing treatise. Thus much in general, for I love not to spend more words than need, or to tell a large story to little or no purpose.

Exchange what it is

Real exchange is nothing else, but to give or take up money in one city or town, to the end to have again, or to restore the just value thereof in money in another town, according to the price which shall be agreed upon between the taker and the deliverer, to allow or pay for the exchange of the money, and the loss of time which will be from the time the money is taken up or delivered until it be restored or received again.

Inland and Outland Bills all alike

And by this it appeareth, that a bill of exchange which shall be made for monies taken up at Edinburgh, York, Bristol, Exon, Plymouth, Dover, or any other part of England or Scotland, and payable at London, is in all things as effectual and binding as any bill of exchange made beyond the seas, and payable here in England, which we use to call an outland bill, and the other an inland bill, both the inland and the outland being made for monies taken up by exchange. And exchange of monies being a thing which may be done as well from one town to another, as from one country, kingdom, or nation to another, it must needs be that the bills of exchange which shall be made as well at one part as at another (I mean inland and outland) ought to be esteemed of equal worth, and the custom of merchants on both equally observed.

Four Persons to make an Exchange, and how called

Ordinarily there are four persons requisite to be employed in the taking up or remitting any parcel of money by exchange, (besides the broker which doth procure the parcel) as namely, two at the place where the money is taken up, and two at the place where the money is payable. 1. The party which doth deliver the money by exchange, whom we use to call the deliverer, or the giver, (and the French *le banquier*) because there are which do keep a stock of money only to negotiate by exchange, (as our usurers do money to deliver at interest) although these bankers will as well take up as deliver monies by exchange, according as they see it most advantageous unto them, by the rise or fall of the price of monies by exchange. 2. The taker or party which doth receive or take up money by exchange, and this party we usually call the drawer, because he may be said to be the chief occasion of the draft of those monies from one place to another by virtue of his bill of exchange. 3. The party which is to repay the money, or he upon whom the bill is drawn, or to whom the bill of exchange is directed. And fourthly, the party to whom the money is made payable, or he to whom the bill is sent to get accepted, and to receive the money when due according to the bill. So that by setting down these four parties and what use there is of them in exchange of monies, it is apparent that there must be a correspondency and familiar acquaintance held between the party which doth deliver monies by exchange, and he to whom the same is made payable, and the party which doth take up monies by exchange, and he on whom the bill is drawn.

Three Persons to make an Exchange

But sometimes there are but three persons needful in the doing a parcel of money by exchange, as first, the taker; secondly, the deliverer; and thirdly, the party on whom the bill is drawn. First, the taker, he makes and subscribes a bill of exchange for so much money by him received of the deliverer; secondly, the deliverer, he orders the bill to be made payable to himself or assigns for the value of himself; and thirdly, the party that is to pay the bill, for the taker he directs the bill to his friend or servant to pay the same. Now this way of exchange is very useful, according as occasion may be: for suppose I were to go from London to Plymouth, there to employ some monies in the buying of some commodity, I deliver my monies here in London to somebody who giveth me his bill of exchange on his friend, factor, or servant at Plymouth payable to myself, so I carry the bill along with me, and receive my money myself by virtue thereof at Plymouth.

Another way wherein only three persons are needful in the negotiation of monies by exchange; namely, 1. the drawer; 2. the party on whom it is drawn; 3. the party to whom it is payable. 1. The drawer, having monies in his hands belonging to the party to whom he orders the bill to be paid, doth make a bill of exchange himself, confessing the value received in his own hands, 2. charging it on his friend or factor, 3. payable to the party to whom he was indebted. There is yet one way more, wherein monies may be remitted by exchange only with the help of three persons. 1. the taker; 2. the deliverer; 3. the party to whom payable; as thus: if I were at Dartmouth, or

Exon, and intended to come to London, I would take up monies by exchange at Dartmouth or Exon, and subscribe bills of exchange for the same, confessing the value received of the deliverer, directed or drawn on myself, payable to whom the deliverer should appoint in London.

Two persons to make an exchange

Likewise a parcel of money may be done by exchange between two persons. First, the drawer, and secondly, the party on whom it is drawn. The drawer he makes a bill of exchange payable to himself, or order for the value in himself, and subscribes the bill, and directs it to the party that oweth him money, and is to pay it by exchange, by which bill (when the party on whom it is drawn hath accepted it) he becometh debtor to the drawer, and he, before the bill falls due, doth negotiate the parcel with another man, and so draws in the money at the place where he liveth, and makes only an assignment on the bill, payable to him of whom he hath received the value. The usefulness of framing bills of exchange after these several forms before mentioned will be found out according as each man's occasion shall present in his trade and commerce by exchange, which is so necessary, as that there is scarce a merchant but at sometime or other, one way or other, doth either receive or pay monies by bill of exchange.

Upon what the Exchange is valued

Now most countries using several kinds of monies, different in value one from another, the exchange is valued or rated upon some one certain, most considerable species or sort of money for each country or town, as followeth: The exchange of monies from London to Antwerp, Amsterdam, Middelburg, Lille, and Rotterdam, is usually accounted and valued on the pound sterling of 20s. English money, that is to say, to pay after the rate of so many shillings, and so many pence Flemish money for every pound sterling. The exchange from London to Hamburg is on the pound sterling to pay so many shillings, and so many pence Hamburg money per pound sterling, which differeth something from the Flemish money. The exchange from London for Paris and Rouen is valued on the French Crown, that is, to pay so many pence, and so many parts of a penny sterling for every French Crown. The exchange from London to Venice is made on the ducat, so many pence and parts of a penny sterling for every ducat. And the exchange from London to Leghorn is made on the doller or piece of eight, to pay so many pence and parts of a penny sterling for every doller. And these are the most usual places, for which there is a price current of exchange at London at present . . .

Usance for Venice, Hamburg, etc.

Note also, that usance from Venice to London is three months from the date of the bill of exchange, and from Hamburg to London, and so from

London to Hamburg bills of exchange are usually made payable at two months after the date of the bills, and accordingly the price current of exchange from London to Hamburg is valued and set down at two months from the date; the price current from London to Venice and Leghorn at three months, and for Antwerp, Amsterdam, Middelburg, Lille, Rotterdam, Paris, and Rouen at one month, or single usance; and so we call one month usance, two months double usance, three months treble usance.

No three days for acceptance

When any bill of exchange is sent unto you from beyond the seas, or from any inland town, to cause to be accepted, I would advise you presently to present the bill, so soon as possibly you can, to the party to whom it is directed, and request him to accept the same. If he refuse to accept it, you may presently cause a protest to be made for non-acceptance, and send it away with the next conveyance; for (according to the custom of merchants in London) there is not any three days respite to be allowed for acceptance before you can protest, but so soon as the bill hath been presented and acceptance refused, presently you may protest the very same day . . .

No such man to be found

If your bill of exchange be directed (suppose) to Nathaniel Q., merchant in London, and that you shall have enquired on the Royal Exchange, and other parts of the city for such a merchant, and shall not be able to find him out, or anybody that knoweth him, or that indeed there be not any such man of that name in London, then you must carry your bill to a notary public, and he must protest thereupon in due form.

Nobody at home

If when a bill of exchange is sent you to get accepted, and there be nobody at home at the house or place of abode of the party on whom the bill is drawn. Or if when your bill is due you cannot meet with the party at home, nor anybody else on his behalf to pay the money, you must cause protest to be made, either for non-acceptance, or for non-payment, at his dwelling house, or lodging, in his absence, which is as effectual, according to the known law of merchants, and the rules of equity, (being made in seasonable time) as if the same had been made speaking to him in person, for you cannot be bound (it being beyond your power) to make the party on whom the bill is drawn to abide at home, but in reason he is bound to attend his own business at seasonable hours, and it concerns him to keep a good correspondency with his own friends, especially in matters of bills of exchange, whereof he cannot be ignorant.

41. THE USE OF BILLS OF EXCHANGE, 1656

[J. Y. Akerman, *Letters from Roundhead Officers written from
Scotland and chiefly addressed to Captain Adam Baynes,
July MDCL–June MDCLX*, Edinburgh, 1856,
p. 126, no. 241; p. 139, no. 265]

[From Cornet J. Baynes]
Cousin,

I delivered your letter to Gen. Monck who will take it kindly if you can
befriend Dr. Clargis. I have drawn a bill of 200*li.* upon you, payable to Lt.
Colo. Ponnall or his assigns at 7 ds [= days] sight. If he make use of it, I
pray pay to content. If in anything you scruple the account between you and
myself, either first or last, I can now clear it for I have my old accounts with
me now. I remember something was disputable between us last time the
account was drawn up, but it may now be cleared if you desire it. I am glad
Mr. Dawson is in a public employment. Capt. Robert is not yet comed this
length: this week I expect him here. We have no news. I pray salute all
friends.

Your very lo. Cousin,

J. Baynes.

Leith, Jan. 8th, 1655/6
I pray cause your servant to deliver the enclosed.

*   *   *

[From Cornet J. Baynes]
Cousin,

I have by bill of exchange of this date drawn upon you the sum of sixteen
pounds payable at sight, for my uncle Livesay, which I pray answer out of
the 70*li.* I lately returned to you by the Treasurers at War. 50*li.* more of it I
intend my Lord Lambert but because I cannot get the amount cleared to send
to him, I forbear to write, and also to send a bill for the payment of it; but it
will not be long ere I do it. However, in the mean time, if my Lord have
occasion for the money, you may let him have it . . .

Your endeared Cousin,

J. Baynes.

Leith, May 3, 1659.

42. THE USE OF BILLS OF EXCHANGE AND BONDS IN OVERSEAS TRADE, 1656–86

[Patrick McGrath, *Merchants and Merchandise in Seventeenth-Century Bristol*, Bristol Record Soc., XIX, 1955, pp. 183, 189, 200–2]

[Bill of Exchange]

8 September 1656

These etc., that the 8th of September 1656 Francis Good, wife of John Good of Clifton in Comitate of Gloucester, gentleman, came, etc. and did depose etc. that the bill of exchange now produced and shewed to her drawn by John Bowen was never brought by her late husband, Thomas Chamber,[1] on whom it was drawn nor by her, this deponent, to the account of the said John Bowen. But by this deponent was paid and now stands unsatisfied and due to this deponent, witness my hand the day and year above written.

Richard Balman mayor.

*   *   *

[Loans repayable on return of a ship]

8 December 1660.

William Crabb[2] of the said city, merchant, maketh oath that before the ship Hare of Bristol, burden fifty tons or thereabouts, set sail last from the port of Bristol in her last voyage, he the deponent did let out at interest unto several persons certain sums of money payable again unto him at the return of the said ship to the port of Bristol that voyage with interest therefore, and the deponent had bonds of them for the same to the value of near forty pounds, and by reason of the loss of the said ship in Ireland the same principal money and interest remain all unsatisfied to this deponent.

All which, etc.   Aldworth

*   *   *

---

[1] Thomas Chamber(s) became free of the Merchant Venturers in 1631 (P. McGrath (ed.), *Records relating to the Society of Merchant Venturers of the City of Bristol in the Seventeenth Century*, Bristol Record Soc., XVII, 1952, p. 28). In 1645 he was about 76 years of age and was half-owner of a ship bound for the West Indies which was captured by the Parliamentary forces on its homeward voyage (Bristol Record Society, VI, p. 86). John Bowen had been his apprentice and became a freeman, 18 October 1649.

[2] Sheriff, 1665–6; mayor, 1676–7; died 14 October 1702, aged 87 (Beaven, *Bristol Lists, Municipal and Miscellaneous* (Bristol, 1899)). Does not appear to have become free as a merchant.

Miscellaneous Bills of Exchange recorded in James Twyford's Memorandum Book

Livorno [Leghorn], Ca: the 2nd October 1684

At usance pay this our first bill of exchange, our second and third not being paid, pay unto Mr. James Twyford or order the sum of dollers[1] one hundred at 55*d*. per doller for value received here of Captain William Fisher and place it to account as per advice, 23*l*. 2*s*. 6*d*. accepted John Brokinge

Broking Parker Holditch

Maryland, the 2nd March 1685/6

Thirty days after sight of this my first bill of exchange, my second not paid, pay to James Twyford or order the sum of two hundred and ten pounds current money of England value received here which place [=please] to accept of thy friend

Rich[d] Johns

To Samuell Groome, merchant in London.

A Morlaix, 17th September 1672

For 400 crown at 57*d*.

At double usance pay this our first of exchange unto the order of Monsieur Loues Masnade in the house of Mr. Thomas Kirwood, goldsmith in London, four hundred crowns at fifty seven pence per crown, the value received of him here by your humble servants

Tanner and Allen

To Mr. James Twyford, merchant on the bridge in Bristol
    7th November due 95*li*.

A Saint Malo, 28th Sept. 1672

At double usance of this our first bill of exchange, our second not paid, pay unto Mr. Barnerd Mitchell or order in Mr. Samuell Allen's house, London, sixty five crowns two thirds at fifty six pence five eighths per crown value of ourselves and place it to accompt as per advice from

Christ[r] Harewell and Company

To Mr. James Twyford in Bristol
    due 15th November 72*li*. 9*s*. 11*d*.

Waterford, November 22 1673

At twenty one days sight of this my sole bill of exchange pay or cause to be paid unto Mr. William French sum of seven pounds for value received of Mr. Robert Emmatt at the time make good payment and place it to accompt as by advice from your friend

Elias King

To Mr. James Twyford, merchant in Bristol

[1] Rix dollers.

Rotterdam, 4th November 1679

At usance pay this my first of exchange to Mr. Thomas Willett or order in the house of Mr. William Bard in Cheapside, London, one hundred pound sterling value of himself as per advise.

Your humble servant
Franc. Brome

To Mr. John Appleton
Mr. John Knight and Company,
merchants, Bristol
Accepted Jno Knight, Jno Appleton
Endorsed to Mr. James Hulbert or order.

Amsterdam, the 9th November *Anno* 1686 for 38*li*. 4*s*.

At double usance pay this my sole bill of exchange at the house of Mr. Thomas Morgan in London unto Mr. George Clifford or order thirty eight pounds four shillings sterling value of himself and place it to accompt as per advice.

Your humble servant
Wm Burgh

To Mr. James Twyford
and Company merchants
in Bristol.

Cadiz, 7th Feb. 1684 for 212*li*. 10*s*. at 51*d*. *per diem*.

At two months after date of this our second bill of exchange, first nor third being paid, pay unto Captain Edward Dowding or his order two hundred and twelve pounds sterling for the value received of himself and place it to account as per advice from

Cha. Russell, Peter Powny,
Tho. Slocombe

To the Right worshipful Sir Benjamin Newland in London
[Endorsed] Cadiz 7 Feb. 1684. Pay the contents hereof to Mr. James Twyford or order all mine Edw. Dowling.

43. COMMONS DEBATE ON THE PAYMENT OF DEBTS ON THE PUBLIC FAITH, 1657

[*Diary of Thomas Burton Esquire, member in the Parliaments of Oliver and Richard Cromwell from 1656 to 1659 ... with an introduction containing an Account of the Parliament of 1654*, ed. J. T. Rutt, London, 1828, II, pp. 238–44]

June 13, 1657.

Sir William Strickland. The Public Faith of the nation is now become a public despair, and rather than that faith should be violated, I would give a great part of what I have.

A great debate was here upon the fifth and twentieth parts, whether they ought to be included.

Captain Lilburn. I move, that 28,000*l*. lent for the Scotch army by Newcastle and Durham, and 10,000*l*. by Northumberland, in 1641, be comprehended in your provision.

Colonel Castle and *Mr. Godfrey* moved, that those that had security by the 400,000*l*. subsidy, that security being taken away, and arrears of 140,000*l*. discharged by the Act of Oblivion, it is but just that, if you will not give them an equivalent security, at least they should have the faith of the nation.

Major-General Disbrowe. This motion is against the orders of the House; and, it relating nothing to the report, you are now to go on with the report to agree with the Committee; and for new motions, they may come in more properly at another time.

The first part of the report, touching the stating of the accounts of Public Faith, and what debts shall be allowed being passed, the latter part of it was read, as to the way of satisfaction, by sale 'of the forest lands', and the lands in 'the four excepted counties in Ireland'.[1]

Major-General Disbrowe and *Major Aston.* If you sell your forests, you will destroy your navigation.[2] The counties in Ireland may go far beyond the satisfaction. Do not engage your security till you know what your debts are. It will not be honourable for you to retract your security.

Colonel Shapcott. I am confident there may be as much discovered of lands purchased by false bills, as will satisfy all those debts. I know where, for a 1,000*l*., they have got many 1,000*l*. a year; and will undertake to discover it.

Mr. Highland. This satisfaction is as empty as was the remainder of the 400,000*l*. offered yesterday. If you intend them a real satisfaction, it must be as propounded. As to the forests, there is not wood upon half or a third of the forests. Those counties in Ireland are not yet disposed of.

As to discoveries, you will hardly make so much of them as is pretended. I have heard that gentleman speak often of that. But this will shake the foundation of all men's estates, that have been sold over and over, and you ought to have discovered those fraudulent estates within a year. When you borrowed this money, you promised that those that lent you money freely should be paid out of the estates of delinquents, and those that fought against you; out of the estate of the king, that traitor.

Colonel Gorges. You have given the counties in Ireland in security to the

---

[1] The counties of Wicklow, Donegal, Longford, and Leitrim, with the *Myle-Lyne*, within the Shannon and the sea, within the province of Connaught, and county of Clare. In these, the forfeited lands had been set apart, for the satisfaction 'of the officers and soldiers who served the Commonwealth in Ireland before the 5th of June, 1649.'

[2] In this Parliament (25 Sept., 1656) Lord Whitelocke had brought in a Bill 'for increase and preservation of timber.' The Long Parliament had appointed a Committee (21 Nov., 1651) 'to consider how the mischiefs from felling of timber might be prevented.' See *Commons Journals.*

poor retired officers and soldiers who have ventured lives and all for you; which is more than the lending a sum of money. Though that way of discoveries be so much slighted, I know it may be considerable. In two months we drew out 200,000*l.* and, in as much time, we, or any you should employ, would get as much more.

Mr. Fowell. There may be great sums made out of fraudulent debentures, upon these discoveries; and though there be a great debt due to me, yet I have no hopes of being satisfied by the ways propounded. You have no other way to make up your revenue, but by improving of the forests and those four counties. As to reserving the timber, who will buy the land, if you reserve the timber?

Major-General Kelsey. These lands are all your refuge upon any occasion or strait. The best way to make up your revenue is to improve them at a rent. I would have you take some speedier course. This will not be done in seven years. I am confident the nation will never grudge to pay a tax of six or three months, for satisfaction of this debt.

Major Beake. I hope you will never sell the forests, but reserve them for the revenue, and that they may be improved at good rents, and so in time take off much of your charge. My motion is, that they may have their security transferred upon the four counties in Ireland.

The Lord Deputy. I think that none of the propositions will answer your end. The people to whom now you owe money are poor, and not able to go over into Ireland. The forests must make up the revenue.

Mr. Cary. I incline rather that a tax be laid for this. Nothing lies harder upon me than this business of the poor people that did so freely contribute. It is the most righteous thing that fraudulent debentures should satisfy these, that are true debts; or rather leave it generally that you will take care to give speedy satisfaction.

Captain Baynes. If you have your debts stated, you have done half your work. The way of satisfaction will be easy. But, if you publish it abroad, that you will satisfy them by lands or taxes, you will encourage men to counterfeit debentures. I would have you put a check upon disposing of any of the lands in Ireland, till the public debts be satisfied. Your best way will be to dispose of the forests by sale, reserving a fee farm rent. There is no care at all now taken of the forests. The wood and deer are destroyed, and the people, so they could but have their enclosures free from deer, would quit all their interest in the forest. Now they fully enjoy and claim the whole. So that, in time, you will have nothing at all. If you should sell them for ready money, it would not give you above two or three years' purchase; but I would have none disposed of, till all debts be stated.

Colonel Sydenham. You are now upon a work that will give you the greatest reputation that ever Parliament had. You are now about to satisfy your best friends, that came out to your help, upon principles of honesty and religion. They are poor, and if you assign lands to them, they must sell again. It may be, that which you give them for 20*s.* they may sell for 12*d.* it may be 4*d.*;

and people watch such opportunities, and have money, will prey upon their necessities.

As to the forests, I doubt by the time that all commoners, claimers, and other rights be set out, the forests will not yield so much. However, I would have that improved for a public revenue. I wish there were a way of revenue in view, that the people might see how that, in time, they may be eased of taxes. I hope there may be a great revenue made out of the four counties in Ireland. If the poor people see that their hopes are raised out of the dust, it will raise your reputation higher than anything you can do. I am confident, when your debts appear what they are, no good man will grudge to contribute his share to the satisfaction.

Major-General Goffe. I am sorry to hear that your faith is grown so despicable that poor people, after all this attendance, should take 4*s.* or 5*s.* per pound. I would have you make it your care that no man should sell his debentures under 20*s.* per pound, but would have all fully satisfied. God has much taken away that objection that you are not able. The nation is in a good condition, and we are able to pay. I would have it done by a general tax, after you know how it is stated.

Mr. Butler. I am glad to see that you are about so good a work. It is just that men should be satisfied that have lent you money, and also the poor soldiers that have bled for you. I have been none of those that have gained by the times. I am likely to be no gainer.

Four ways propounded to you.

1. Fraudulent sales. I think it is but just that those that have cheated you should be brought to justice.

2. Lands in Ireland. If you dispose not of them they will be gone, piece after piece, and those persons would people those counties, or the forest lands, anywhere, where you would assign them. You might reserve a fee farm rent upon them.

3. The forests, and they would be well content with them.

4. By a tax, I should as freely pay my share as any man; but some way or other must be taken to let the people see that you are in good earnest to satisfy them.

Colonel Cooper. I see no better way to satisfy this debt than by the way that is propounded. As to fraudulent debentures, it is hard to pay the public debts by public cheats. You did appoint some test to those debentures, and they passed that. Now if, after all this time, you come to discoveries of that kind, you will bring a flaw upon every man's estate. Those that sold the debentures are now turned informers, and those that would cheat one way may cheat another way, and then they may inform against all debentures, and cast a disgrace upon them all.

I cannot say what reputation a tax will have abroad, having now a tax upon them already. I doubt this would savour ill. I would have you put the question to agree with the Committee; and the House by this time are so possessed of the debate, that they know how to give their vote.

There are delinquents' estates unsold to 200,000*l*., and under the notion of giving small sums, I fear me they will slip away from you insensibly. Here is one Bill for the Earl of Derby, which will give away that from you, that for mending three words in one Act, will yield you 10,000*l*., to be paid in six days.

Colonel Jones. I move to re-commit this report. Those people before you are of the poorer sort, and lands will not satisfy their needs. It will be a long time before you can put the forests into a way of sale. Besides, those lands and the lands in Ireland are not in that condition as to be sold at any considerable rate. You will be puzzled to make up your revenue; and if it be laid in the balance, whether you will continue a tax to perpetuity for the revenue, or raise a present tax to pay those debts, the latter will be taken. I would have your Committee consider how a way may be found for ready money, to pay the poorer sort; and for the richer it is not just to propound a satisfaction till you understand your debt. That is not natural; and where wit and wickedness meet together, it will be a great temptation to counterfeit bills.

Colonel Sankey. You will do no good by re-committing this. I think it is well propounded to you to sell the forest lands, reserving a rent, which will answer your end, as to making up your revenue. I know no reason but you should revive the motion of the other day of that 200,000*l*. if so much remain out of the new buildings over and above 200,000*l*. to make up the 400,000*l*.

Captain Hatsel. I move to re-commit it. I would not have those lands sold at this time. You cannot sell them at any rates, so as to give suitable satisfaction to those poor people. Those that live in the west, what shall they do with lands in Ireland, or in those forests? A land tax will not be so pleasing at this time to raise this money.

Dr. Clarges. I move to agree with the Committee as to the last part, that the lands shall not be disposed of till this debt be satisfied.

Colonel Matthews. I move strongly to agree with the Committee, that the poor people may have a real satisfaction.

Mr. Waller. I have as much commiseration for those people as those that have expressed it with the greatest resentment; but I doubt that what was propounded will not do your work. As to the forests, I wonder men should forget that there is a chief magistrate, who must have a revenue. If we dispose of this, that must raise it, we shall entail a tax upon the people that posterity will not be able to cut off. As to reserving the timber, it is a strange proceeding for me to sell a wood, and reserve the timber. You will have but few chapmen. As to sending them amongst the wild beasts and birds in Ireland for satisfaction, it is but to add misery to affliction. Besides, you have debts in Ireland to which lands there are most properly applicable.

Major-General Whalley. I move to re-commit this report, that a speedy way may be propounded for satisfaction after the debts shall be stated; and that a declaration may be published to this purpose. But, indeed, for you to propound a security before you know what is your debt, is most unnatural.

Mr. Bampfield. The generality of the honest, good men of the nation are concerned in this. For my part, I should freely agree with the Committee that those lands be disposed of. But if this relish not, I shall move that the votes already passed, in order to this, be put into a bill for the stating of the debt, and calling officers to account.

Mr. Bond seconded that motion.

Mr. Godfrey. This is short of satisfaction, and will but put people to a greater loss than before, unless you propound also a way of satisfaction; that at least a stop may be made to the disposition of the lands, until this debt be satisfied.

Colonel Matthews seconded this motion.

The question being put for sale of the lands,[1] it passed in the negative.

Major-General Disbrowe. I move, that they shall not be disposed of by sale or gift, until those debts be satisfied; otherwise you exclude all disposition to improvement.

Mr. Pedley and Mr. Godfrey. If you put it, that these lands shall not be disposed of till these debts be satisfied, you exclude all satisfaction by those lands. These words should be added to the question—'by the sale of those lands or otherwise'.

These words being excepted against, these words were added—'until some provision be made for satisfaction, etc.'; and the question thus penned passed.[2]

44. COMMONWEALTH DEBTS AND REVENUES, 1658

[P.R.O., SP 18/181, no. 131]

[June?] 1658.

The debts on the Commonwealth with arrears to the armies and fleets to the beginning of October 1656, as it was given into the Parliament, was between 800,000*l.* and 900,000*l.* Besides that debt it was made out to the Parliament that the charge for one year insuring and ending October last would amount unto 2,400,000*l.* The provision propound[ed] for that was the Excise and Customs and the Exchequer revenue, estimated at 1,300,000*l.*, and 50,000*l.* a month taxes, which came to 1,900,000*l.*, and they ordered the raising of three months' taxes over again at 60,000*l.* per month in England and in Ireland in lieu of the three months' 20,000*l.*, and in Scotland 15,000*l.*, which in all come unto 215,000*l.* And the new buildings not valued to make up the rest, which was thought to have come to near 300,000*l.*, which would have completed the sum of 2,400,000*l.* But there is not above 3,000*l.* come in by the new buildings, and the Exchequer revenue is fallen short 200,000*l.*, which causeth the armies in the three nations to be in arrears 300,000*l.* or

---

[1] 'That all the forest lands in England and Wales, not yet disposed of, and all the lands within the four counties, not yet disposed of, be put into a speedy way of sale, for satisfaction of the Public Faith debts.'—*Commons Journals.*

[2] 'Resolved, that no further disposition, by sale or gift of the forest lands, etc. be made, until some provision be made for satisfaction of the said debt of the public faith.'—Ibid.

thereabouts, and the navy to be in arrears 540,000*l.* beside the former debts on the Excise and other debts on the Exchequer. Besides all this there is a year and almost half a year salary due to all the militia forces in England. By this rude account you cannot but understand the condition of your affairs and necessities of a speedy consideration. And if you please to put it into a way you may have an exact account of all monies received and how paid out.

45. THE EXPORT OF BULLION MADE LEGAL, 1663

[Statutes of the Realm, V, p. 451]

An Act for the Encouragement of Trade

15 Car. II, c. 7

CLAUSE IX. And forasmuch as several considerable and advantageous trades cannot be conveniently driven and carried on without the species of money or bullion, and that it is found by experience that they are carried in greatest abundance (as to a common market) to such places as give free liberty for exporting the same and the better to keep in and increase the current coins of this kingdom. Be it enacted and it is hereby enacted that from and after the first day of August one thousand six hundred sixty and three it shall and may be lawful to and for any person or persons whatsoever to export out of any port of England or Wales in which there is a customer or collector or out of the town of Berwick all sorts of foreign coin or bullion of gold or silver first making entry thereof in such custom house respectively without paying any duty, custom, poundage, or fee for the same, any law, statute, or usage to the contrary notwithstanding.

46. HEARTH TAX EXEMPTIONS, 1663

[P.R.O., Surrey Hearth Tax Papers, E179/257/30]

June the third 1663.

Whereas John Clarke of the same parish [i.e. St. Nicholas in the town of Guildford] is returned for two fire hearths, we hereby certify that the said John Clarke hath lately had (as he was digging chalk in a chalk pit) certain chalk fallen down upon him, which broke divers of his bones so that he is now made uncapable of working. And (being but poor before) is now so far from paying to hearth or poor that he hath relief from the parish. In witness whereof we have hereunto set our hands.

The mark of John Cot, George Jennings, Constables of the said town of Guildford for the half year ending at Lady Day last past.

*   *   *

Surrey. In the prince's liberty in the parish of Lambeth. These are to certify all whom it doth or may concern that Henry Early of Lambeth aforesaid, waterman, is a poor man not worth ten pounds, his debts being paid, having four small children, being all of them at this time sick, his wife also.

We therefore do humbly conceive that he is very fit to be excused from paying for hearths and stoves. Witness our hands this second day of July, 1663.

Rich. Peare, cur.; Gilburd Smith, John Burgin, churchwardens.

47. THE STATE OF THE MINT, 1664[?]

[P.R.O., SP 29/109, no. 88]

[1664?] The state of the mint as now it standeth is in such a low condition that there is nothing at all to set its men on work, for although the merchants and the goldsmiths here have had, and now have, great store of foreign coin and bullion, yet hitherto to the expectation of some alteration to be made by the laborious agitation of the merchants at his Majesty's Council for Trade and such others as have received their influence of siding with them and from them and so led by them to crave a free exportation of gold and silver being brought into England, hath hindered and stopped all passage of gold and silver to the mint, so as there hath not as yet been brought to be coined upon either their accounts the sum of one hundred pounds in silver since his Majesty's most happy arrival in this nation, partly caused by the expectation aforesaid, but now more especially by buying and selling gold and silver at far higher rates contrary to the established laws than is allowed in his Majesty's mint, which can never be employed until such thoughts and actions of liberty be restrained . . .

48. PROBLEMS IN COLLECTING TAXES, 1667

[P.R.O., Treasury Books T51/34, pp. 53-4]

Sir William D'Oyly, etc.

After our hearty commendations, finding by experience that divers of his Majesty's Receivers have turned to his Majesty's loss and prejudice what we had ordered in the matter of exchanging money by yourself and others employed to that purpose for his Majesty's advantage, and that instead of bringing in his Majesty's money sooner than by the wagons, the Receivers of the counties of most trade, where returns might be had quickest and with greatest facility, do, under pretence of returning the money, detain it from his Majesty's occasions longer than if the same stayed for the wagons. For prevention thereof for the future, we have thought fit to direct you that you strictly in our names require all the Receivers under your inspection and correspondence that, whensoever they return any of his Majesty's money, they make the bill payable to yourselves or one of you, that so their private correspondents here may not detain the king's money in their hands, and that at the time of the drawing the bill they send you advice of it, and upon what payment to place it, so that either with it or the next post they send you the bill itself, that they draw no bills but what shall be payable within twenty days after signing thereof, and that where any Receiver shall neglect to follow these and such other instructions as you shall give him in this matter, that you reckon the money in his hands and draw bills on him accordingly, which, if he shall fail to pay, you are then to acquaint us with his neglect, to the end we may cause such example to be made of his neglect or refusal to observe your directions as may deter others for the future from the like, and so we bid you heartily farewell and remain

Your very loving friend

Ashley; Clifford; J. Duncombe; W. Coventry

3rd of December, 1667.

49. THE DEBATE ON A LAND TAX, 1670

[*Debates of the House of Commons from the Year 1667 to the Year 1694, collected by Hon. Anchitel Grey Esq., who was thirty years member for the town of Derby . . . ,* 10 vols., London, 1769, I, pp. 314–17]

Debate on Land Taxes

Thursday, December 1.

Sir Thomas Clifford. We struggled with a debt, after the war, between two and three millions, though it might be thought there was not such a debt, because they were ashamed to bring it out. Though they gave 10 per cent yet every office was supplied, and by it they had credit. In all these straits the king spent not above half his revenue; whatever wanted, the king kept his navy in repair. The king was sensible how lands fell everywhere, and was unwilling to press you. The king was willing to part with his fee farm rents, and has and will place 700,000 or 800,000*l.* upon them; exposed his chimney-revenue, and his Wine Act; every year he spends 500,000*l.* more than his revenue. The death of one banker has spoiled all the rest, and gentlemen withdraw their money, and that trade is gone. Now, with all the credit of that vote, 6,000*l.* cannot be taken up, and two ships lie for want of the money. For beer, ale, and foreign commodities, on which you would transfer the king's debts, he will tell you the impossibility of that. If you pass your law, it is more convenient to begin at Midsummer, because it suits with the Law of Excise. The Customs at Michaelmas; commodities then come in; the anticipation and debt is to be paid in fourteen months time. If four or five bankers were to advance the money, the matter was not great; who knows what the money will do, and who will lend? But it is unanswerable, since you can never put it upon these funds. Most of the farmers are the bankers, and they will have a visible security. This is practicable, and will make it good of three millions yet unpaid; Wine Act, Chimney, Fee farm rents go towards it. We can put the house, stables, and all but the navy, without interest, but let there be 800,000 or 900,000*l*. for six years. The banker is gone, and this will enable the king never to take up, which certainly will do the king's work better than 1,200,000*l*. This will break the back of the bankers. After this, will be an undertaker, that you shall never be haunted with land tax, or home excise.

Sir William Coventry. Seconds the motion of taking off land tax. Whoever would make a difference between the king and kingdom, such is he that moves for land tax. Sometimes we fear the King of France, and sometimes all people fear us. Would have an account of the king's money, and though we are not Privy Counsellors, we are Counsellors, and hopes we shall be heard.

Lord *Hawley.* Moves for a land tax at 70,000*l*. per month, to begin at Christmas next.

Sir Robert Carr. Knows no way to secure us from a home excise but a land tax, which he hopes may be easy. Seconds the motion for 70,000*l*. per month, to begin at Christmas next.

Sir William Hickman. Has long feared this motion; he looks upon it as hazardous to the Crown. It is not only from gentlemen that have suffered, but upon tenants, who cannot keep on their market trade. Would raise the money, but would be secured from this.

Sir Thomas Hanmer. Thinks this is not so black as it is painted, and thirds the motion for a land tax.

Sir Nicholas Carew. The last land tax was brought up in waggons. The poor woman turned her purse strings wrong side outwards. Clifford puts you in mind of 30,000*l*. but not a word of 80,000*l*. given for no fleet. Must we now come to the thing which must be our support in invasion? As much money [has been] given to this king, as since the Conquest. The cost and charge is not the king's; but such as were not born to scarce a pad nag have a coach and six horses. That has consumed the king.

Mr. Garroway. Does not except against number of men or time. He has heard say, if we must give money, we shall have no fleet. When they asked 800,000*l*. he would have given a million to have heard no more of them. This land tax is a mark of our chains. If you will take the tenth beef, lamb, or bullock, or part of the land, take it; but would have a question, that no part of this be raised by land tax.

Sir William d'Oyly. We have no *Hannibal ad portas*, but we have a debt that eats like a canker. We are proposed uncertain things, that the experience of none of them will give you anything.

Sir Richard Temple. You have great rocks on all hands; yet nothing of money, by reason of our great poverty, can come acceptable to us. Cannot be of the mind of that gentleman, 'that he that moves for land tax is an enemy to king and kingdom;' but he must needs be that would have this debt unpaid, and advise what will not do it, an enemy to both king and kingdom. This does not only deliver you from a present evil, but prevents you of invasion spoken of. *Sir Robert Howard*. If the lands have no respite, the consumption must cease, and you consume not foreign commodities; therefore let it be one way or other; both ways will destroy one another. Moves to proceed some other way for the money than by land tax.

Colonel Birch. When you have pawned your land, what have you left to help yourself? That day you give land tax, you will sink land two years' value. The land of England will not come to itself these twenty years, for the wounds you have given it already.

Sir Thomas Clifford. Does verily believe that the zeal, which transports gentlemen to be against land tax, will put them upon finding out other ways.

Mr. Attorney Finch. What are we a doing, or whither are we a going? When you hear of three millions debt, and the king charges his own lands, and other duties towards the paying it, you will have this effect, that the monarchy shall be at ease, and no farther need of help. Would not any man purchase the safety of the kingdom with his blood? Will he not do it with his money? We may talk great words of being the balance of Christendom, and when our debts are always paying, and never paid, we shall lose that same. Every man says, it shall be the last; but why, by this question, you shall throw away the last remedy. Lay this to heart; if you put a negative upon the main question, you put a thorn into your own foot, which you can never pull out.

The question being put, that towards the king's supply there be a land tax, it passed in the negative.

50. THE DEBATE ON A LAND OR OFFICE TAX, 1670

[*Debates of the House of Commons from the Year 1667 to
the Year 1694, collected by Hon. Anchitel Grey Esq., who was
thirty years member for the town of Derby . . .*,
10 vols., London, 1769, I, pp. 323–7]

Wednesday, December 14 [1670].

In a Grand Committee on the Supply. Subsidy Debate resumed.

Mr. Spry. There are twenty-four millions of acres in England; at 1*d*. per acre, never so high by any calculation; 9,000 parishes. At 1*d*. per pound it will not do it; would have it at 12*d*. per pound.

Sir Charles Harbord. In England, seventy-six millions of acres the surface; he judged it in the ship money business, by the map, ten millions and a half *per annum* fallen in twenty years a million. Would bring the value to an equal burden, so as best to be borne; and as you would have it justly valued, so the calculation must not be a snare to any man; as if the land be worth 20*l*. to value it at 15*l.* so there will remain but nine parts of twelve, or seven of ten, whether at two-thirds or three-fourths.

Sir Thomas Gower. Would have the militia rate considered; that the king may make commissioners, and have power to give an oath, and to take one themselves. 8 *Henry* VIII, etc.

Sir Richard Temple. Thinks the calculation made a romance. If you had a calculation of acres, thinks you may be deceived in it. Land tax at 120,000*l.* a month, if you reckon 2*s.* per pound. Generally, one with another, all England comes to but 14,000,000*l.*—20 millions, 400,000*l.* at 1*d.* per pound. If England was then so much, he fears you cannot find now above ten or seven millions. Under three halfpence the pound, he fears it will never be raised. Would have commissioners named by the King, if in this House, fears we shall not raise half, by partiality, and hopes this way may never be altered, you will find it so easy a method.

Mr. Swynfin. The great point, and what deserves our first consideration, is the laying it upon intrinsic value of land; by so laying it, you put the whole kingdom to make a new levy; it will be found a vast work, and impossible; you must come to a consideration of every man's estate, high and low. In sessions, it is a hard matter to get a constable in a great parish, where apparently they are unequal, to give in a true value. The rich feeding and meadow lands are known. Of west and north, that are upon old rents, you never know, and never can, the true value; and lands vary in value every year. That strangers be put in Commissioners, will never do, for you will have strange values brought you in every country, who will think it their interest to give in the lowest value, and hide it from strangers, because it will be a standing value. Land tax was unequal, and yet the tax by law was to be levied by pound rent. Therefore would have it well weighed, whether by intrinsic value, or a subsidiary way. This discourse was all against order.

Sir Francis Goodrick. 29,140,000 acres, 1*d.* per acre, 100,000*l.* per annum. Every acre 2*s.* per acre, one with another.

Sir Charles Harbord. This monthly tax-way was unequal, 500*l.* as much as 1,000*l.* in many places. No man under 10*l.* per annum a subsidy man for land; 20*l.* per annum was the rate; two-thirds or three-fourths will be a safe rate; and formerly, when that rate was transgressed, they paid treble damages. Thinks two-thirds the most equal.

Mr. Garroway. Would have goods and money valued before land, to see what they will reach unto.

Sir Thomas Meres. Would have the bankers rated at 18*d.* per pound for the interest.

Sir Richard Temple. The gentlemen get some of this gain that lend, and the bankers the rest; therefore lands being fallen one-third, would have lands at 12*d.* and goods at 8*d.*

Sir Charles Harbord. Would not load all men because of the bankers. Would have all goods and trade at 4*d.*

Sir Richard Temple. The 24th part is 10*s.* in the 100*l.* Too high.

Mr. Boscawen. Land worth 1,000*l.* per annum does not yield 40*l.*

Resolved, that every 100*l.* shall pay 10*s.* Agreed to by the House on the 17th.

Sir Thomas Littleton. Would not have money in the banker's hand taxed on a different foot from other money particularly.

Thursday, December 15 [1670].

In a Grand Committee on the Supply.

Resolved, that personal estates and stock (excepting stock upon the ground, and household stuff) be taxed at 6*s.* per pound, having respect to debts, offices, etc. Agreed to by the House on the 17th.

Offices

Sir Thomas Lee. Moves that you will lay no more weight upon offices than upon land.

Sir Anthony Irby. Thinks they ought to pay more, because they pay no taxes to church nor poor.

Sir John Birkenhead. They are taxed in all places. Sees no reason they should be 12*d.* if land that is inheritable should not be more; it is unreasonable.

Sir Thomas Higgins. Tenants break, and lands fall; offices are constant profit, and would have them higher rated.

Sir Charles Harbord. A tenant for life pays as much as he that has the inheritance, because he takes it *cum onere.* Would have it 12*d.* in the pound, and that they may bear.

Sir John Knight. In the Poll Bill salaries out of offices did escape. Would have that considered.

Mr. Boscawen. You must allow for his time, and under-officers that attend, and would not have them rated higher than land.

Sir John Birkenhead. No man can value an office for life at above five years value; it is unreasonable to raise it to the height of land.

Sir Thomas Clifford. He that has an office of 400*l.* per annum it is better to him than land at 600*l.* per annum, being not charged with bridges, highways, poor, and many other things. Would have it at 2*s.* per pound.

Sir John Bramstone. Some offices are by deputy, others take up a man's whole time; he would have a difference.

Mr. Waller. We have long had a land tax, would now have an office tax.

Colonel Titus. Is for taxing them, but not for punishing them as criminal, because they are but for life. If he had an office of 400*l.* per annum would willingly change with any man of 600*l.* per annum. Would not have it higher than land.

Colonel Birch. He pays in London as much for his office as for his house. Would not have them punished more than malefactors, who are by one law only.

Resolved, That 2*s.* per pound be charged on offices.

Agreed to by the House on the 17th.

On Land rated in Subsidy

Sir Thomas Osborne. 12 millions come to 600,000*l.* a year; 720,000 at 2*s.* by the monthly tax. Yorkshire is easy, and the least that comes to is 18*d.* per pound. Would have 12*d.* at least.

Mr. Garroway. Never made his estimate of 800,000*l.* for the setting out this fleet, for it is much more than will do it. He gives it because the king demands it. 60,000 knights' fees, and the four northern counties and clergy left out; 8,000,000 of acres; this is some men's estimate.

Sir Robert Howard. Looks upon it as the most fatal thing in the world if this sum should fall short, and our being called to supply it again, will be a fatal thing. Would rather give somewhat more. If the 12*d.* should come up to the 800,000*l.* put that ever on the right hand; it would be much the safer, and no fatality in it.

Resolved, That 1*s.* per pound be charged on land. Agreed to by the House on the 17th

51. THE DEBATE ON A TAX ON GOODS AND STOCK IN TRADE, 1671

[*Debates of the House of Commons from the Year 1667 to the Year 1694, collected by Hon. Anchitel Grey Esq., who was thirty years member for the town of Derby* . . . , 10 vols, London, 1769, I, pp. 357–9]

Friday, January 20 [1670/71].

In a Grand Committee, on the Subsidy Bill.

Mr. Gould. If you rate a man at his goods, it may be he is worth 20,000*l.* and he has not half by him, and so you cannot tax above half. 75,000*l.* will come upon a poll.

Sir Thomas Meres. Upon the whole, let the raters rate every man according to his personal estate, debts comprised, and you will raise more money than upon the whole.

Sir William Coventry. Would have stock in trade left out; you have excepted it in other acts. Fears that it will be in this as in ill times, rather trust God with their souls, than men with their estates. Money I can hide, my goods I cannot, and so less will be found. 'Till the tax be over, I shall have as few goods in my shop as I can. The gentleman shall buy dearer, and that merchant shall have it in his warehouse by him; and so your woollen manufacture be put a stop to, and wool not sold, which will come home to the gentleman. Barley will not enable him to set up his farm; and says the maltster, 'I will have no stock by me', which in his hands is ware of trade, and so it must rest in the farmer's hand. Thinks that the nation will lose in manufacture, and the husbandman in tillage; therefore would have stock in trade excepted.

Mr. Garroway. You tax money at interest. The merchant brings wares in, and is taxed; the mercer that sells is taxed, and the salesman, when made up into cloths, and tailor; in all these hands it is taxed, and you pay it four times over. The last buyer pays for all, and it recoils back upon you.

Mr. Secretary Trevor. If a clothier have 100*l.* of his own, he is taxed, but his debt considered; but if a man have a moving stock, it must be left to the commissioners for taxing of trades. The sum is not great; 6*s.* per cent not so great as to change trade. You, by the clause, clearly intend stock, and only stock, not in part but in whole.

Sir Thomas Littleton. Intrinsic value is not taxed; only chattels personal, not chattels real, as in leases.

Colonel Birch. In subsidy tax one column is for land, and the other for personal estate; but for a man to discover all he owes is a most destructive thing to trade.

Sir Tho. Lee. 'Over and above debts'. Thinks it a most ruinous thing for every trader to discover his debts. Poor men will pay for an imaginary credit. Trade will be more easily discovered than money. Tax what you will here, the merchant cannot raise it abroad. Wool is taxed, and corn, and that will have an effect upon the farmer. We think to meet with the citizens, but we meet with ourselves in it. Is not clear, but that the husbandman's corn in his barn is again to be taxed, and will not be thought stock upon land. Trade abroad is driven much upon barter. Would have English growth excepted.

Sir Gilbert Talbot. Wool and corn were never taxed. It is not 6*s.* per cent at the worst, at four quarterly payments, and no man will, for that small sum, let his money lie dead.

Sir Thomas Meres. It will cause much disturbance, and will bring little in. It is the gentlemen's interest to throw out this clause.

Colonel Birch. The question is, whether the personal estates shall pay, and it is the gentlemen's interest to keep it in. This is intended for a precedent for the time to come, and if you will walk in this way, it is the gentleman's interest to make it as equal as he can. Men's shops must not be inventoried. Exempt this, and you will lay all the burden on the land. If this be for a precedent, you have gone too far; for a mercer, with 100*l.* stock, lives better than a man of 10*l.* a year. Lay a greater burden on land, and you sink the value two years' purchase more.

Sir William Coventry. 6*s.* per cent is no great sum; but he does not consider that he that buys stock of barley has many accidents attend it of charge, together with the interest of his money. Why should I do all this hoarding for? After the tax I will buy, and in the mean time put my money to interest, which I may conceal; for if he lends it to a man to stock with, he will take but 6 per cent but covenant against taxes.

52. SIR EDWARD DERING'S RECORD
OF THE DEBATES ON THE REVENUES, 1670-1

[The Parliamentary Diary of Sir Edward Dering, 1670–73,
B.M., Add. MS. 22467, ff. 45-48^v, 87-87^v, 97^v-98]

Wednesday, December 14 [1670].

... Then we went upon completing the king's supply, and for a long time
the discourse went upon the quantity of acres or of values of England, some
saying it was 18, some 12, some but 9 millions yearly; some that it was 50,
some 36, some 30, some but 24 millions of acres.

Some computed that since 2*s.* per pound did raise 70,000 *per mensem*,
which is 840,000 in one year, then 12*d.* per pound would raise 420,000.

Others saying that to the tax of 70,000 *per mensem* Cheshire and some other
counties did not pay above 5*d.* per pound, and therefore 12*d.* per pound at
the true full value would raise the whole sum of 80,000.

The most probable calculation I could hear was that the revenue of the
kingdom was about 12 millions per annum, the consequence whereof is that
12*d.* per pound of the true yearly value is 600,000.

Much was said that a subsidy of a penny per pound would raise 100,000,
and therefore we might give eight subsidies, to have them paid at four payments.

But at last Mr. Garroway moved that we were out of the way, and that it
was necessary to consider first what to lay upon money, goods, and offices,
before we came to lay anything at all upon lands, which had borne the burthen
all along; and the measure of lands, and the estimate we can make of them
being something more probable than any accompt we yet have of the rest, it is
fit to examine first what the rest will bear, that so we may supply it by a
charge upon the land.

Upon this we fell into a debate concerning charging of money, and it was
moved that all money should pay ten shillings for every hundred pounds. It
was desired by myself and others that the word 'at interest' should be added
to the question, for it may seem very reasonable that money which produceth
profit should also pay towards the king's supply, but for money which made
no profit and peradventure never should, there was no reason to charge it;
and how unfitting is it if a man, when this Act shall take effect, shall have a
100*l.* by him for his necessary expense, or if a gentleman have then received
500*l.* for his half year's rent, nay, if his tenant have but provided it and be to
pay it to his landlord within a week following, or a merchant who is going
with it in his hand to pay for wares, all this money must yet pay to the king.
And at last, how shall this money which is concealed and buried, be ever
found out to be taxed?

However, after all, the sense of the House was to tax all money whether at
interest or not at interest, and so it passed: to pay 10*s.* every 100*l.* to the king.
It was then moved that all in the bankers' hands might pay 15*s.* per cent.

Much was said in their defence, some that it would ruin them absolutely; some that what we should get from them was an inconsiderable sum and not worth the taking notice of, and so perhaps it is, but the House were so incensed against their rating interest at 10 per cent of the king that they resolved to put some discountenance upon them, and resolved, the committee being divided upon it, that 15s. per cent should be paid out of all money in the hands of the bankers.

Then they proceeded to vote that money may be lent to the king upon the security of this Act at 7 per cent interest and that also such money as should so be lent to his Majesty should not be taxed towards his supply but discharged of the 10s. per cent other money is liable to. This is done in hope to draw all the money out of the bankers' hands, supposing that all people will rather lend the king at 7 per cent than the banker at 6; and if the bankers will transfer their debts which they have upon the other branches of the revenue, and place them upon this to save the 15s. per cent, then the king's revenue shall presently be cleared, and he will immediately save 3 per cent.

Then we proceeded to tax all stock employed in trade and this was much opposed by the merchants, but there were two reasons offered which they did not answer:

1. That we had resolved this already, since we had voted goods should be taxed, for the word 'money' would not comprehend it, and if it did, then they must pay as money, which would be too much.

2. That in all taxes formerly used, and in all subsidies, goods were ever taxed, and when lands were taxed at four shillings the pound, goods were always taxed at 8 groats.

So we proceeded to the vote, and resolved that all stock in trade should pay at the rate of 6s. the hundred pound. We resolved that stock upon land and household stuff shall not be taxed.

Then the Speaker took the chair, and Mr. Seymour asked leave for this committee to sit again tomorrow morning upon the same business . . .

Thursday [December] 15 [1670].

The House began with reading a bill brought in by Colonel Birch for making one standing measure for corn and salt throughout the kingdoms, by which it is enacted they should be all measured by a sealed brass measure, which sealed measure should be had here in London, and bought by all corporations and market towns; and it enacts that nobody should shake their corn or salt, and some other unreasonable things; but the bill was committed to be amended.

Then we proceeded in a grand committee to complete the king's supply, and the first question was concerning stock in trade, and therein it was resolved that allowance and deductions be made for so much as was owing by the tradesman, for that no more was truly his own than what remained when his debt was paid.

Then we proceeded to tax officers, and it was moved by Sir Jonathan

Trelawny, and seconded by Sir Thomas Clifford, that all officers should pay 2*s.* per pound of the yearly values or income.

It was urged that there was no reason to tax offices higher than lands, no office being for more than a man's life, most of them being indeed but during the king's pleasure and therefore in no sort equal to an inheritance; that all offices had been taxed ever since the king's coming in equal with lands and so had their share of the burden, and had beside one tax particular upon them, which was not upon lands, which was that for the supply of the indigent loyal officers. Sir Jonathan Trelawny, Sir Thomas Clifford, Mr. Lawrence Hyde, Mr. Garroway, Mr. Weld spoke for it; Sir John Ernle, Sir Charles Harbord, Mr. Boscawen, Sir John Bramstone, and others spoke against it as highly unequal. The committee divided upon it, and it was carried they should be taxed at 2*s.* the pound.

Then we proceeded upon what remained to complete the king's supply, which was a pound rate upon the lands according to the full value. Much controversy was between the rates of 8*d.* per pound and 12*d.* per pound, and truly by computation 8*d.* per pound could not probably make up the sum voted of 800,000, for the account is stated several ways, and many had taken pains therein, but their calculations were very different.

At half an hour past two the question was put for 12*d.* per pound, and the affirmatives were 103, the negatives 97, in all 200.

The most probable estimate:

1. That the current money of the nation is not above 12 millions, which at 10*s.* every 100*l.* will make but 60,000.

2. That the stock in trade, deducting for debts and household stuffs, and stock upon land, which are not to be taxed, is not above 25 millions of pounds, which at 6*s.* the hundred pound will produce but 75,000.

3. That the officers at 2*s.* every hundred pound revenue will not produce above 25,000.

4. That the full yearly value of all the rent of lands and houses in England is not above 12 millions, which at twelve pence in the pound doth produce just 600,000 . . .

Saturday [March] 4, 1670/71.

The House turned into a grand committee to proceed upon the bill of excise upon foreign commodities, having first resolved to alter the method of collecting the duty from the first buyer, as now it stands, and make it payable by the merchant importer which will save all the charge of collecting it, for it will thus be done at the Custom House and by the same officers, and will save also half the bill, in length, at least, which consisteth in clauses adapted to the collection of it from the first buyer, and for preventing frauds of that nature.

Memo: All the merchants of the House seemed to be well content to have it payable by themselves, which may seem a paradox at first, since now they must lay down a great deal more money than otherwise they needed to have done, and that even before they sell their commodity. To which I think the true answer is this, that the merchants of the House are all rich men and of great stock, and will not suffer by laying out a little more money upon their first return, for they will find their advantage in it:

1. Because they shall have ten per cent discounted for what part of the duty they shall pay down in ready money before the time the duty is payable, which will be 9 months.

2. Because this will beat out all the young traders of small stock, who will not be able to advance money as the others can do, and so in a great measure keep the trade in the hands of those men who now have it.

Saturday [March] 18 [1671].

We sat forenoon and afternoon and went through the bill of foreign commodities. Safflower we excused from the payment of any new duty because it was very necessary for dyeing, and so, consequently, for our clothing trade. And then we had a third dispute upon iron wire, but at last again excluded iron wire and brass wire from any new duty. Then we had a long debate upon the corn clause; whether the allowance to be given to the king should be to all corn exported or only to corn exported in English bottoms; and it was by vote restrained to English bottoms, in favour to our navigation.

I did agree with the votes for wire and safflower, but I differed in this because this was not intended for navigation properly, but for encouragement of tillage, and benefit of the much decayed farmers, and no doubt but this will hinder one half, at least, of the benefit of this clause, for the east country ships which bring timber hither, and are ships made fit for carrying bulky commodities, and now return home empty, would doubtless have carried away much corn if they had had the encouragement of this Act.

53. A PROCLAMATION ANNOUNCING COPPER COINS AND PROHIBITING PRIVATE CURRENCIES, 1672

[B.M., C21, f.1 (50g)]

By the King a Proclamation for making current his Majesty's
Farthings and Halfpence of Copper and forbidding
all others to be used

CHARLES R.

Whereas of late years several persons and corporations upon pretence that there wanted small monies to be current in low and ordinary payments amongst the poorer sort, have presumed to cause certain pieces of brass, copper, and other base metals to be stamped with their private stamps, and then imposed those pieces upon our poor subjects for pence, halfpence, or farthings as the makers thereof were pleased to call them; whereby our subjects have been greatly defrauded and our royal authority and the laws of our kingdom violated. And whereas we, for prevention of the like abuses for the time to come did not only direct a severe prosecution of the offenders but did likewise command the officers of our mint to cause many thousands of pound of good sterling silver to be coined into single pence and twopences that so there might be good money current amongst the poorest of our subjects and fitted for their smaller traffic and commerce, hoping by one or both these means to have totally suppressed the unlawful practices of these offenders. Since which time we have found by experience that the mischief hath still increased partly by having our small silver monies bought in and hoarded up that so there might be a scarcity thereof in common payments, but chiefly by the vast gain and profit which these stampers make to themselves and for which they choose to run any hazards of law rather than quit the hopes of their private lucre.

We therefore taking the premises into our princely consideration and believing that our subjects would not easily be wrought upon to accept the farthings and halfpence of these private stampers if there were not some kind of necessity for such small coins to be made for public use, which cannot well be done in silver nor safely in any other metal, unless the intrinsic value of the coin be equal or near to that value for which it is made current, have thought fit by advice of our Privy Council to cause certain farthings and half-pence of copper to be stamped at our mint according to such form and with such impression as we have direction. And we have given special charge to our officers there that they cause such halfpence and farthings so to be coined to contain as much copper in weight as shall be of the true intrinsic value and worth of an halfpenny or farthing respectively, the charges of coining and uttering being only deducted. And we do further by this our royal proclamation declare, publish, and authorize the said halfpence and farthings of copper so coined and to be coined to be current money; and that the same from and after this instant 16th day of August shall pass and be received in all payments, bargains, and exchanges, to be had or made between our subjects which shall be under the value of sixpence and not otherwise nor in any other manner. And if any person or persons, bodies politic or corporate, shall after the 1st day of September next presume to make, vend, or utter any pence, halfpence, farthings, or other pieces of brass, copper, or other base metal other than the halfpence and farthings by this our royal proclamation authorized and allowed, or shall offer to counterfeit any of our halfpence or farthings, we shall hold all such offenders utterly inexcusable and shall cause their contempt of our laws and government to be chastised with exemplary severity.

Given at our Court at Whitehall the 16th day of August in the 24th year of our reign, 1672.

54. PETITION OF PRISONERS FOR DEBT, 1673

[House of Lords Record Office, Main Papers, H.L.,
7 March, 1672/3]

To the Right Honourable the Lords Spiritual and Temporal assembled
in Parliament, the humble petition of the prisoners in the King's
Bench Prison on the behalf of themselves and other prisoners in the
City of London, and in the counties of Middlesex and Surrey,
who have taken and are capable of taking the oath mentioned
in the late gracious Act of Parliament for the relief and release
of poor distressed prisoners for debt.[1]

SHEWETH that the late gracious Act hath not had those effects of mercy,
charity, and compassion for the relief and release of the persons of the
prisoners in this prison of the King's Bench and other prisons that were and
are imprisoned for debt and damages before the 14th of April 1671, as is
most humbly conceived was intended by his most gracious Majesty and the
honourable Houses of Parliament as other prisoners have had in most of the
counties of England, there having been no prisoners released out of this
prison of the King's Bench but such as were charged in execution before the
said 14th of April, 1671, though judgements for debts and damages were
entered upon record against them before the said 14th of April 1671, it
being, as is said, the opinion of the learned judges that the Act did not nor
doth extend to discharge any prisoner but such as were and are charged in
execution before that time. Other prisoners in the said prisons who have had
the allowance of eighteen pence or less for their weekly maintenance according to the Act appointed by the justices in their sessions have been kept in
prison upon their weekly maintenance, some for more than a year, when
neither estate, fraud, or false swearing did or hath appeared or hath been
proved against them, but merely upon the malice of the creditors to keep
and destroy the person of the prisoners in prison. The said Act having been
construed strictly against the prisoners as to the keeping their persons in
prison (the Clerk of the Peace of the county of Surrey saying to several
prisoners their persons must remain in prison until the Parliament make a
better or wiser Act) and favourably as to the creditors whose debts are secured
by a special proviso in the Act if ever the prisoners have estate or lands to
pay, as also favourably to and for the prison keepers as to their fees, chamber
rents, etc., for that none have been settled and established by the judges and
justices as appointed by the Act. The prisoners petitioners most humbly
pray your honours' gracious, charitable, and compassionate explanations
and constructions of and in the doubtful clauses and expressions of and in
the said Act for the relief and release of their persons out of the misery of a

---

[1] 22 and 23 Car. II, c. 20.

prison and the settling of the fees, chamber rents, etc., and a further Act for the relief of others whose persons are and may be in their like capacities and conditions, and that the fees may be settled and an Act passed for the relief of others in a like position. And your petitioners, etc.

Henry Duncome, Gilbert Standish, John Bridges, Peter Gale, Nicholas Bell, Job Palmer, William Powell, William Lord, on the behalf of themselves and many other prisoners.

55. AN OPINION ON THE LAW OF DEBTORS, 1674

[Carew Reynel, *The True English Interest*, 1674, pp. 80-3]

Laws, and easing of Debtors

CARE ought to be had, that the property, liberty, and advantage of the subject be the especial grounds of laws; and such laws extremely promoted that make for a general good and profit to the public. As for establishing unity in a nation, encouraging trade, giving employment to the people, and increasing populacy, and settling estates, the Register's office to be erected, might be beneficial if well managed.

And if usury were abated it would promote trade, advance lands, make men abler to give security, increase common charity, and generally make men more industrious.

Taking of [f] arrests on men's persons, would also be beneficial to the nation. And if all debts under fifty pounds were ended in the parish where the debt was, by the chief of the parishioners, it were very well.

And all debts under a hundred pound were concluded by three the next justices of peace, it would prove of good consequence.

Also care ought to be had, that men should not be imprisoned at all for small debts, nor long for any debt, men's persons being not an equal pawn for so vile a thing as money. And for great debts, if the law and goods would not satisfy, the person should be free, for by imprisoning he is undone, that should maintain his family; then all come to beggary. So the nation is prejudiced by the malice of ill creditors. And if men are more in debt than they are worth, they should yet have some small matter, as a fourth part unto themselves and family, uncapable to be seized on; otherwise the commonwealth suffers more by the absolute undoing of a man, than is countervailed by so exact justice; besides, religion, and the laws of nature, bind us to more charity, and the creditor that imprisons, and undoeth a man, ought to maintain him and his family; if not, the law ought to take care he may, without being beholding to the creditor; for 'tis better a rich creditor should lose something, than a poor subject be lost or rot in a prison.

Also it would be a great advantage to the public, and trade one with another, and foreign parts also, if bills of credit were made to be good in law, and answer debts; which should without ready money, maintain, and advance trade infinitely; for these bills would pass current as well as money, and save also very much the telling and luggage of carrying money up and down, and hinder the loss received by bad or clipped coin, and manage a vast trade with the tenth part of the silver now used, which would make money abound everywhere for the common uses and the ordinary conveniences of life. Many excellent improvements might be made by several new laws.

56. THE ORIGINS OF BANKING, 1676

[J. B. Martin, *The Grasshopper in Lombard Street*,
London, 1892, pp. 287–90, 92]

The Mystery of the New Fashioned
Goldsmiths, etc.

Sir,

Since you are pleased to demand my advice in the disposal of your son to the goldsmith's trade, and my opinion of the trade itself; I must trouble you more than I was willing to set down what I have observed of the goldsmiths since I have traded, and the steps of their rise and progress, and leave the judgement of the whole to yourself; 'tis but fit that a son should owe the good choice of his employment and way to his fortunes to the prudence and love of his father.

If I could now discourse you, I ought to be satisfied whether you have thoughts to put your son to a goldsmith of the old or new fashion, those of that profession having of late years wholly changed their way of trading. In my time their whole employment was to make and sell plate, to buy foreign coins and gold and silver imported to melt and cull them, and cause some to be coined at the Mint, and with the rest to furnish the refiners, plate makers, and merchants, as they found the price of gold and silver to vary, and as the merchants had occasion for foreign coins.

But about thirty years since, the civil wars giving opportunity to apprentices to leave their masters at will, and the old way having been for merchants to trust their cash in one of their servant's custody, many such cashiers left their masters in the lurch and went to the army, and merchants knew not how to confide in their apprentices; then did some merchants begin to put their cash into goldsmiths' hands to receive and pay for them (thinking it more secure), and the trade of plate being then but little worth, most of the nobility and gentry, and others melting down their old plate rather than buying new, and few daring to use or own plate, the goldsmiths sought to be the merchants' cash-keepers to receive and pay for nothing, few observing or conjecturing their profit they had for their pains.

It happened about that time that the then Parliament had coined out of plate and otherwise seven millions in half-crowns, and no mills being then used in the Mint, the money was of a very unequal weight, sometimes two-pence or threepence in an ounce difference, and the French and others then changing the value of their coins often, which made silver and gold of much greater value abroad than at our English Mint. The goldsmiths found a new mischievous trade to send all the money trusted in their hands into their cocklofts, where they had scales and various weights adapted for their pur-pose, and servants constantly weighed every half-crown (at least) and sorted them to melt for twopence or threepence, or sometimes less gain by the ounce, and sometimes their advantage being greater by the accidents of the rise or fall of the exchange, those heaviest coins were sent away in specie, several Frenchmen and other merchants making it their whole and only business weekly to transport the gold and silver so culled, either melted down or in specie; and from hence the goldsmiths set up another new trade of buying the old English gold coin at a rate much above its lawful coined value, buying and selling it at five, seven, eight, and ten pounds in the hundred more than it was coined for, still sending it away so fast, or supplying those with it whose business was to transport it, that by a modest computation eight parts of ten of the coined gold was suddenly consumed, and two shil-lings a piece was commonly given for gold, when a penny a piece was often given before to exchange gold into silver. The seven millions also of silver new coined, was apparently reduced to less than one million, and the people so abused in their money, that there was little coin passed in trade but overworn, washed, and clipped, to the great vexation and loss of the traders.

These unlawful practices and profits of the goldsmiths made them greedy to engross all the cash they could, and to combine with all men's servants who continued to keep any cash, to bring their monies to them to be culled, and to remain with them at fourpence the day interest *per centum* without the masters' privity. And having thus got money into their hands, they presumed upon some to come as fast as others was paid away; and upon that confidence of a running cash (as they call it) they begun to accommodate men with monies for weeks and months upon extraordinary gratuities, and supply all necessitous merchants that over traded their stock with present money for their bills of exchange, discounting sometimes double, perhaps treble interest for the time as they found the merchant more or less pinched.

Profit arising by this trade, some of them who had the highest credit undertook to receive gentlemen's rents as they were returned to town, and indeed any man's money, and to allow them some interest for it though it lay for a month only, or less, the owners calling for it by a hundred or fifty pounds at a time as their occasions and expenses wanted it; this new practice giving hopes to everybody to make profit of their money until the hour they spent it, and the conveniency, as they thought, to command their money when they pleased, which they could not do when lent at interest upon personal or real security; these hopes I say, drew a great cash into these new goldsmiths' hands, and some of them stuck to their old trade, but every of them that had friends and credit, aspired to this new mystery to become bankers or cashiers, and when Cromwell usurped the government, the greatest of them began to deal with him to supply his wants of money upon great advantages especially after they had bought those dollers whereof he robbed the Spaniards to about the value of 300,000*l.*

After the King's return, he wanting money, some of these bankers undertook to lend him not their own but other men's money, taking barefaced of him ten pound for the hundred, and by private contracts many bills, orders, tallies, and debts of the King's, above twenty, and sometimes thirty in the hundred, to the great dishonour of the government.

This prodigious unlawful gain induced all of them that could be credited with monies at interest to become lenders to the King to anticipate all the revenue, to take every grant of the Parliament into pawn as soon as it was given, I had almost said, before the Act was passed for it, and to outvie each other in buying and taking to pawn, bills, orders, and tallies, in effect, all the King's revenue passed their hands, and if Solomon be in the right, *that the borrower is a slave to the lender*, the king and kingdom became slaves to these bankers, and the kingdom gave no small share of their taxes to them, paying double and treble interest, as if they had not been able to raise money for the public service at the times it was requisite . . .

Sir,

I have given you my remarks upon the rise and growth of these new kind of goldsmiths, and I take them to have been in their highest ascendant or state about the time that our ships were burnt at Chatham by the Dutch: that cold storm of the people's fears that their money was not safe in the banker's hands blighted them, and since being in their declension, the famous stop upon the Exchequer almost blasted their very root, men being unwilling to trust money in their hands to lend his Majesty, so long as they hear the deplorable cries of the widow and the fatherless, whose money they say at feasts, they lent the King, and cannot repay them, no not their interest to buy them bread . . .

I leave it then to yourself to judge whether banking be like to continue half your son's apprenticeship, and whether all the arts that they can teach him can be worth one of the 200*l.* you design to give with him. I presume upon your pardon for my plainness and tediousness; yet I am prompted to say something more in point of conscience, doubting whether it be lawful to exercise any trade in a constant avowed breach of the laws of the kingdom, as all bankers do, these laws being made for the good of the society, to which the scripture commands obedience for conscience sake, where they are met contrary to the laws of God.

Perhaps it is worth the enquiry upon that account, whether any man that hath exercised the mystery of banking hath, living or dying, gone off the stage with a clear good estate, all his creditors being paid, fully paid. But I judge no man. I submit these thoughts and myself to your prudent censure, and remain,

Sir,

Your Humble Servant

J.R.

57. AN INLAND BILL OF EXCHANGE, 1677

[Herefordshire County Record Office, Foley Collection,
F/IV/AD/21, Correspondence, 1671–84]

Stourbridge, July the 14, 1677.

Sir,

Yours of the 10th this instant I received. And according to your grant and order, I have received £55 of Mr. John Sparry of Stourbridge, which money I have given him a bill for, which will be presented to you within a few days. It is to be paid to his brother, Mr. Joseph Sparry, an apprentice to Mr. Nicholas Ashton, woollen draper at the Sign of the Star on Ludgate Hill[1] . . .

Your humble servant,

Richard Wood.

Sir, I humbly thank you for the supply of money which I hope, with getting in Mr. Gibbons's money as fast as I can, will do our business till your rents[?][2] in the country come in, and against Michaelmas you shall[?] have a full account for this half year.

[Endorsed:] To his honoured master, Mr. John Foley, merchant, at Mrs. Brittins in Broad Street, London. Stourbridge, July 14, 1677. Richard Wood. Received 16 *die*, answered the 17 *die*.

58. THE DEBATE ON THE TAX ON NEW BUILDINGS, 1677

[*Debates of the House of Commons from the Year 1667 to
the Year 1694, collected by Hon. Anchitel Grey Esq., who was
thirty years member for the town of Derby* . . . , 10 vols,
London, 1769, V, 184–9]

Tuesday, February 19 [1677]

Sir Thomas Clarges. 'Tis not reasonable that those houses which have been nuisances two or three years should be taxed like those that have been forty

---

[1] Marginal note says 'bill paid'.   [2] Manuscript torn away.

years. In the borough a man may build by law, and 'tis no offence, for the
verdict upon these new buildings was passed upon that statute. When the
Lords find their inheritances equally taxed with the nation, they may pass
the bill; but when this tax is upon a number of Lords, will they not be heard
at their Bar? Which will occasion conferences, and hinder the progress of
affairs. Lord Chief Justice Vaughan, when here, said, 'That the law of
Parliament was the law of the land; and no man ought to be taxed but for
the spareable part of his revenue.' And is one half year's rent the spareable
part? I desire these gentlemen of the Long Robe would tell us whether it be
illegal to erect new houses.

Mr. Solicitor Winnington. It seems, there is some difference of opinion in
this matter amongst those of the Long Robe. I stand up, in the main, to
ease land. But I think there is a mistake in this of new buildings, etc. 'Tis
the interest of the House to establish the durable interest of the nation, the
freeholder. This debate is charging new buildings, and the reason in the
debate is, 'That they are a common nuisance'. Though I am not of the Coif,
yet I will presume to offer my reasons. A common nuisance is not dispensible
but by Act of Parliament, and is 'a detriment to all the king's subjects'.
27 Eliz. 'No buildings were to be within such a distance of London whatsoever.' But that was but for a number of years. I never knew a nuisance
enacted perpetual, but that of exportation of leather, and importation of
Irish Cattle. When the act was expired, notice was taken of the contempt of
it, against a proclamation. When Essex House was to be pulled down, the
Society of the Middle Temple thought it an inconvenience. They had the
best counsel they could get but were forced to sit down with as good a
composition as they could get. The first cause I ever was of was that between
Lord Clare, and Clement's Inn. Now they are not a nuisance. Yet there is
reason why they should be charged. I think, a very young man may remember
the increase of buildings about London. Nothing decays rents in the country
like new buildings about London. Labourers in the country, at sixpence and
eightpence a day, come here, and turn coachmen and footmen, and get a
little house, and live lazily; and in the country the farmer is constrained to
pay sixteen or eighteen pence a day, through the fewness of workmen, and
therefore can pay less rent. They will leave the country for better wages.
Sumptuous houses are a great invitation to gentlemen of quality, and their
wives, to come to London, where they live better, and more at their ease and
content, than with a greater number of servants and expense in the country.
I know not how Clarges finds it that the builders get but 4*l.* per cent, but I
know that if their houses are not in bad places, they get 15*l.* per cent. I would
have this charge on the landlord, to stop the increase here, for the landholder
must support the nation. The law takes notice of the freeholder, for trials
upon juries. The rest are but servants to them, and they, having greater
advantage, ought to bear the burden. 'Tis an easy matter then to propose a
charge upon them. I suppose you intend to charge some on land for certainty,
and that may be a certainty on the buildings also. They live better, and in more

plenty and profit than the freeholder, and they are but supernumeraries to serve them, and they ought to bear a part of this charge.

Mr. Williams. If this of new building be a project, I am against it; if not, I am for it. Therefore, in the first place, ascertain a proportion upon them towards this million you have voted. As to the nuisance, 'tis said only as an argument to induce you to tax them, not that we declare it so. Some things in themselves, and some things by accident, are nuisances, and you may consider your own condition of nuisance. Some will say 'A long Parliament is a nuisance', and for us to declare that a nuisance, may draw the people to think us so; and I would have these new buildings nuisances by accident. To run into all the circumstance of these buildings, whether the landlord or tenant shall pay this tax. There is also a mean proprietor. This will create a hundred questions. I would lay it therefore on the value; but if you lay sums upon them, you must have a calculation of their number 'since 1656', for the oldest must pay, they having had greater profit, and 'tis fit a general estimate of their number should be made. There are said to be about 20,000 houses, then you may lay an estimate, whether 400,000*l.* etc. Then I will go along with you, or else 'tis an improbable thing to raise any money on them.

Mr. Swynfin. The only strong reason I hear for this charge is, 'That 'twill ease your land', and that reason is grounded, 'because they draw common people and labourers hither'. Suppose you lay half a year's rent upon them, will that hinder gentlemen, and poor people and loose tenants from coming hither? So that these reasons work not with me. But is this that which turns the country up to London? Then you should make an Act to erect no more, and that will stop them. I am against this charge, till I know how much this will keep off the tax from land. To give my negative, or affirmative, I would value them before you put the question. It may come to this, that the receivers may not receive half what you rate them at, and the king not have half, and therefore some think this may raise 400,000*l.* and others not 40,000*l.* so that we shall lay an unusual tax, supposing to keep the burden off from land, and at last return to land again. I would agree how much shall be accepted to keep off tax from land. When the Chimney Act was computed ['twas] uncertainly, and we charge the subject we know not how. Let some gentlemen bring a clear estimate what these buildings will bear; else I cannot give my consent at all.

Sir Thomas Meres. If you will go back to the year 1630, it will raise you something. In 1654, it did not raise above 40,000*l.* and consider they must pay tax also. It will be four or five shillings in the pound upon them, and this is concurrent upon them besides the half year's rent, which is ten shillings in the pound. As Williams told you, if you lay it upon the original landlord that built it, he perhaps has not two shillings in the pound, and then there is a tenant, and a tenant under him. (And now you are in earnest, as I did not believe you were before). If you circle in the Bills of Mortality upon new foundations, from 1630, if that question pass, it will come to something. But for those just out of the Bills of Mortality, and they are not [to be] taxed, [to] pay nothing, that will be unjust. I would have the question 'from 1630, all the buildings within the weekly Bills of Mortality, upon new foundations'; and the other question, by degrees, step by step, till we know how much they will bear.

Mr. Sec. Coventry. There is scarce a year but three or four houses either fall down or are new built in Covent Garden, and they [to be] rated as you do old ones, that will be very hard and unequal.

Sir John Talbot. Moneyed men may be met with here. They are the builders, and send money abroad for foreign timber, where our crown pieces go for 5*s.* and 6*d.* and 6*s.* I would tax them.

Mr. Garroway. I look upon this tax as unjust, and therefore I am against it. I am taxed to the utmost in the country. If you will say, 'Tax them at the rate of the City of London by reason of their trade, but if for their monies because they have built houses', I know not, but by the same reason, you will tax all men that have raised estates since the King came in and had nothing before, as if they were Rosicrucian Knights that had got the powder of projection.

Mr. Secretary Coventry. If you put building as crime, 'tis a greater crime to build near the time of making the Statute than to have built farther off.

Sir John Talbot. From 1630 to 1640, the builder paid a fine to the King, by censure in the Star Chamber, and from 1640 to 1656 they paid likewise. Consider how great a proportion those paid that were then built; but I find my old house is not a jot eased by the new buildings in St. Margaret's Fields.

Sir Thomas Clarges. The Statute of Q. Elizabeth, spoken of, does not extend to such a distance from navigable rivers. But people may build on new foundations. Cottages are to have four acres. Boroughs and corporations are excepted out of that Act.

The first question was put, whether one half of the full yearly value should be charged upon all the buildings erected upon new foundations, without the City of London, and within the weekly Bills of Mortality, since 1630 (except such as were demolished by the late fire); which passed in the negative.

The second question, whether upon buildings, etc. since 1640, passed also in the negative.

The third question, whether upon buildings, etc. since 1656, passed in the affirmative, and was agreed to by the House.

Mr. Sacheverell. I would have an addition to the question. I look upon this tax, to be laid upon the new buildings towards the million you have voted, to be as a fine little sugar plum to quiet us for yesterday's vote of a million, etc. which will never be made much of. I believe this war intended with the French is such a war as that of Henry VII with France. We shall find that an Act of Re-assumption of lands granted from the crown will give more ease to the subject, and I move for an Act of Re-assumption, etc. since 1656.

Mr. Williams. I believe the thing very good, but not seasonable now, and very well worth your consideration in its time.

Sir Thomas Meres. These things relating to houses may be doubtful; but as for the crown lands, and those that have them, they were valued at 300,000*l*. etc. and they may raise something. If you vote a re-assumption, I am for it.

59. THE DEBATE ON A POLL TAX, 1677

[Debates of the House of Commons from the Year 1667 to the Year 1694, collected by Hon. Anchitel Grey Esq., who was thirty years member for the town of Derby . . . , 10 vols., London, 1769, V, pp. 198–9]

Thursday, February 21 [1677]

In a Grand Committee. On the Supply.

Col. Birch. I moved, the other day, to bring in a Poll Bill; that people may be registered in the parishes that walk about the streets in good clothes, and may pay something towards this charge, who spend more in a week, than a farmer can afford to do in a year. Not two of thirty of them are taxed by land tax. All the money coming up to London, to the head, I would take some blood from it by a tax upon new buildings, and that is but an ounce. I would poll this sort of people.

Sir Thomas Lee. Pray do not say, 'Here I can have you, and there I can have you'. I would not tax every man in every capacity, as was moved by Wheeler, to have this poll, after the other taxes.

Mr. Swynfin. This Poll Bill was offered you with great assurance, to leave all your lands untouched. I would have gentlemen consider that you are to raise a sum certain, but those that bring these things in tell us not how much they will ease lands; they tell you with no manner of certainty what sum this will discharge. Let us go step by step, and know first what this will amount to; some think half the money, and some more, and thereby we shall lay still as much upon land, upon this uncertainty. You have one instance of that of the new buildings. I would have the certainty stated, how much this will ease your lands.

Mr. Secretary Williamson. What I move you, must be the result of your debate. Before that be, can any man tell you precisely what this will amount to in the estimate, and what falls short to lay it upon your land. I wonder, by this way of reasoning, that you lay it so hard upon land first. I know not how the gentleman comes by that proposition, 'That there is no haste of the money', by this way of projecting. In the mean time, whilst that report of the buildings is coming from the committee, 'twill be plain and certain that it will not make the whole. I take it for granted that we must see what these things will bear first, for land must but bear what it can. The method I move for is a short way. And the poll is a more ready way than you can lay any-thing upon lands, and I move that *****[1] may be raised on the Poll Bill.

---

[1] Thus in MS.

60. AN EARLY INSURANCE POLICY, 1682

[B.M., Add. MS. 34,175, f. 18]

Number 1400[1]

THIS present instrument or policy of insurance witnesseth that *Dr. Nicholas Barbon and Samuel Tookie, gent.* in consideration of the sum of *seven pounds six shillings and eight pence* in hand paid by *Sir Wm. Twisden, baronet* for the insuring of an house situate on *the west side of Redcross Street now in the possession of Ralph Thompson, soapboiler, and distant southward from Barbican to the middle of the said house about seventy nine foot* for the term of *thirty one* years from the date hereof, do desire, direct, and appoint, that the Trustees for the time being for houses and lands settled for the insuring of houses against fire shall pay or satisfy unto the said *Sir William Twisden his* executors or administrators (or *his* or their assigns by endorsement on this present policy) the sum of *one hundred and sixty* pounds at the end of two months after the said house shall be burnt down, demolished, or damnified by or by reason or means of fire, and so often as any new house to be built in the place thereof shall be burnt down, demolished, or damnified by or by reason or means of fire within the said term of *thirty one* years the like sum of *one hundred and sixty* pounds if the said *Dr. Nicholas Barbon and Samuel Tookie* and their participants or some or one of them, his, or their heirs, executors, administrators, agents, or assigns shall not within the said two months pay unto the said *Sir William Twisden his* executors or administrators (or such his or their assigns) the said sum of *one hundred and sixty* pounds, or in case the said house or such new house be only damnified; then if such house be not repaired and put in so good condition as the same was before at the charge of the said *Dr. Nicholas Barbon and Samuel Tookie* and their participants or some or one of them, his or their heirs, executors, administrators, agents, or assigns within two months next after such damnification shall happen. Witness our hands and seals the *seventh day of August*, Anno Dom. *1682* annoqz. regni regis *Caroli 2di Angl. etc. tricesimo quarto*

Nicholas Barbon [seal]
Saml. Tookie [seal]

Sealed and delivered in the presence of Jno. Bland, Saml. Edmond, Will. Dalton.

---

[1] The original policy is in a copperplate hand into which the particular details, italicized here, were later inserted.

61. HOW TO REMEDY THE SHORTAGE
OF SMALL CHANGE, 1683

[John Houghton, *A Collection for the Improvement of Husbandry and Trade*, revised and re-issued by Richard Bradley, London, 1727, IV, pp. 238–40. [May] 1683]

A proposal to supply the defect of small money, from the great encourager of trade, Mr. Thomas Firmin of London

WHEREAS there are great inconveniencies in commerce and traffic, arising from the want of a ready exchange of money, occasioned by the non-coinage of small pieces of silver, and the failure of a sufficient supply of copper farthings, to the interruption of trading, hindrance of business, and loss of time in seeking exchange, and frequent trouble and vexation to tradesmen and shopkeepers, when haste and business are pressing and urgent upon them.

It is therefore humbly offered to the consideration of such as have the honour and opportunity of address to the king's most excellent Majesty, whether they might not do a very great piece of service to their country, if they would represent this grievance to his royal wisdom for redress, which would redound to the benefit and advantage of so great number of his subjects.

The coining of groats, twopences, and single pence having been, not without cause, disused, because the trouble and charge thereof doth outbalance the advantage; and they are inconvenient and troublesome for the payment of great sums. If there may be found out such a piece as will both serve for the payment of greater sums, and for exchange in lesser, it must needs be very beneficial and advantageous to all.

Now it is humbly offered to consideration, whether the coining of ten pence in silver, would not be useful to relieve his Majesty's subjects in great part from the former inconvenience, and serve excellently to both these ends, viz.

For exchange in small sums, and payment in greater

1. This piece will serve for exchange, and supply the want of groats and twopences, as appears by what follows.

If 2*d.*	must be paid.	Give one of these pieces for a shilling.
4*d.*		Receive a six pence for one piece.
8*d.*		Give two of these for a shilling.
14*d.*		Two shillings for one of these do it.
16*d.*		One of these with a sixpence does it.
20*d.*		Two pieces pay it.
22*d.*		A shilling with one of these does it.
2*s.* 2*d.*		Two of these and a sixpence do it.

2*s*. 4*d*.	This with a shilling and sixpence do it.
3*s*. 4*d*.	Four of these pieces do it.

It will serve also in the exchange of odd money, not only by the help of nine pences, but also when a trader hath but four farthings (which often falls out when he hath not eight) this piece may do him a great pleasure for the payment of these odd sums, viz. 11*d*. 17*d*. 21*d*. etc.

Victuallers and retailers, from whom a great part of the duty of excise belonging to his Majesty doth arise, will receive much benefit and ease hereby.

2. This piece will also be of good use for the payment of greater sums, which will be sooner told than in sixpences. For 24 of these will make 20*s*.; 18 of these will make 15*s*.; 12 of these will make 10*s*.; 6 of these will make 5*s*.; 3 of these will make 2*s*. 6*d*.

Thus will it serve to the payment of all sums, jointly, or severally, alone, or mixed with others; so that it will run aptly into sums of all denominations, while 24 make a pound, 16 a mark, 8 a noble.

What ease and convenience this will afford to his Majesty's trading subjects (which are a multitude) is not hard to be understood.

62. ANOTHER DEBATE ON THE LAND TAX, 1690

*[Debates of the House of Commons from the Year 1667 to
the Year 1694, collected by Hon. Anchitel Grey Esq., who was
thirty years member for the town of Derby . . . , 10 vols,
London, 1769, X, pp. 35–8]*

Wednesday, April 2 [1690].

On the Supply.

Sir William Strickland. Moves for instructions to the committees, 'That the supply be not raised upon land tax.'

Col. Austen, on Mr. Hampden's setting forth the necessity of supply. You have now two necessities, money and land; and give me leave to offer a third, the people's living. He that does not faithfully advise the king, is not a good subject.

Sir Henry Goodrick. I am of opinion, and do not doubt, but what has been said is true. All new experiments are uncertain. This only I desire, before we enter into a hasty resolution, to propose some ways to raise this money. The gentleman that moved it, I believe, can tell you ways; therefore I beseech you, at least, to weigh this, and not, by a vote, to expose the nation to ruin. Before you put such a question, pray let us debate it.

Sir Thomas Lee. I take it, the debate is upon 'Instructions to the committee, that no part of the supply shall be upon land.' I think it irregular in the House; but, if moved at the committee, it will be as strong as in the House.

In the House you are confined to debate, not as in a committee. I remember, in the Long Parliament, a great sum was to be raised, and home excise was proposed; those against land tax would have had a negative. You have so much money to raise; you have said you will do it. I know no way considerable but home excise. I assure you, I am not for land tax, which is absolutely destructive to you. You must keep yourselves in a condition to raise it upon land hereafter. I am neither for a land tax, nor a twelve penny subsidy. I speak plainly; if you bring this course of a negative into Parliament, the practice will be extremely inconvenient.

Sir Henry Goodrick. I have declared myself all along; I will deal fairly: I think the revenue ought to bear a great share of this; but to lay a negative upon land, customs, or excise, there is an equal latitude upon all these to put a negative. You were told of 'Three Necessities' from the Bar; perhaps the same necessity may be on other things; and, at last, necessity upon nothing. If this pass once in the negative, you lay such a baffle upon the committee, that they cannot get through it . . .

Sir Robert Cotton. Nothing but great necessity yesterday brought us to vote so great a sum of money, but have a care lest we put ourselves on greater necessity. We have an army in England, as well as in Ireland, and I know not whether we are safe without such a guard, and home excise to maintain that army. These things, so natural, we may expect may follow. I doubt not but the kingdom of England may raise money without burdening land. I hope gentlemen are so disposed, as not to be willing to bring the nation into necessity of such fatal consequences. Pray put the question. Let us keep England, whatever becomes of Ireland.

Sir Robert Rich. I was yesterday for the least sum. Whatever my opinion was yesterday, I will tell it you today, and I fear none tomorrow. You have been upon a long debate, upon a negative upon land tax. I would willingly go into a committee freely, but I own I am against all home excises.

Mr. Foley. If a land tax commence not till after Christmas, how must the king have any security to take up money for the present occasion? It is no such strange thing to put negatives.

Mr. Swynfin. As to the arguments against land tax, I have been here the best part of twenty years, and all the projects would never do. The way of our ancestors has always been upon land, and they abhorred excise, and all other projects. I wish we prove wiser than they. We had a war with the Dutch, as now we have with the French, and it was carried on no other way but by land tax. I am not for saving our lands to enslave our persons by excise. You have pitched upon a fund, and must have a security to raise it. If there should be a miscarriage in Ireland, it will be laid upon the House by the managers of that war. Let them have no pretence to lay the blame upon this House. I would fain see the tax laid upon something less vexatious, and that will not, in the end, come upon land. If you find other proposals less grievous to the people, you will deal best with yourselves, and the business is to leave it to the committee.

Mr. Harcourt. If you give the tax on land now, I fear you will lose as many men as you give pounds. The goodness of the prince, and his greatness too, is shown by the easiness of the government.

Resolved, That it be an instruction to the committee, that the Supply to be given to their Majesties be not laid upon land, without leave from the House.

63. A DEBATE ON THE LOWERING OF INTEREST RATES, 1691-2

[All Souls College, Oxford, MS. 158a. Parliamentary Diary of N. Luttrell, pp. 20, 201-2, 225, 258-9]

November 12, 1691.

Mr. Freke moved and was seconded by Sir Edw. Hussey for leave to bring in a bill for lowering of interest from 6 to 4 per cent.

Yeas { Sir Rob. Cotton / Sir Jos. Sredenham } 131

Noes { Mr. Palmer / Mr. Ash } 105

January 8, 1691/2.

A Bill for the lessening the interest of money read the second time.

Several spoke against it as Sir Christopher Musgrave, Sir George Hutchins, Sir Samuel Barnardiston, Sir John Knight, Sir Henry Gough, Sir Robt. Sawyer, Mr. Clark, Sir John Brownlow, Sir Wm. Strickland, Sir Peter Colleton, and Mr. Smith; for that it was a dangerous experiment to be tried at this time, it was taking away a sixth part of the moneyed man's estate, that it would ruin daughters and younger children, that money was a commodity and would rise or fall in interest according to the plenty or scarcity of money and was not to be restrained.

Several spoke for it, as Sir Robert Henly, Mr. Brockman, Lord Castleton, Sir Edward Hussey, Sir John Lowther of Lowther, Sir Charles Sedley, Mr. Howe, Mr. Papillon, Mr. Bowyer, Mr. Hambden and Sir Thomas Littleton and urged that the passing this law would be very advantageous to the kingdom, it would raise up the value of land and the rent thereof, and make the poor farmer better able to live and bring money to a nearer proportion with land, which bore all the charges of the government; it would mightily encourage trade for tho' plenty of money 'tis true will make interest low, yet 'tis trade makes plenty of money and the lowness of interest will increase trade, for 'tis observed that in Spain and Ireland where interest is high at 10 per cent, yet they have little money, trade being not great, but in Holland where interest is low there is a great trade. So at last the question was put for committing the Bill . . .

Tellers for	Yeas	Mr. Bickerstaffe Sir Rob. Henley	169
	Noes	Sir Sam. Barnardiston Col. Granville	153

So the Bill was committed . . .

January 15, 1691/2.

The Interest Bill was reported with amendments agreed to, and upon the question for engrossing it, 'twas opposed by Sir Christopher Musgrove, Mr. Pollexfen, Mr. Bathurst, Col. Sackvill, and Mr. Clark, but Sir Edw. Hussey and Sir John Dorrel were for it.

But on the question it was ordered to be engrossed.

January 23, 1691/2.

Engrossed Bill for reducing Interest was read the last time.

Several spoke against as the Solicitor General, Sir Christopher Musgrove, Mr. Jeffryes, Mr. Finch, Sir J. Knight, Mr. Loyd, Sir Peter Colleton, etc., and urged it to be a hard law to take away a fifth of those men's estates whose concerns lie in money; that this bill would have little effect being great sums were now to be had at 5 per cent, some at 4 per cent; that this would be prejudicial to such men who had small sums of money; then the time of this bill is unseasonable for interest is in Holland at 5 per cent and 'twill not be very proper to lower it now when money is so scarce; then this will discourage people to bring money into this kingdom, and as to the pretence it will advance the price of land: what you advance in your land you will lose in the interest of the money. Then this will render it difficult for all merchants to take up money on personal security to carry on his trade and to allege that where interest is low there is plenty of money, 'tis taking the effect for the cause, for 'tis plenty of money that lowers the interest of money and 'tis trade that makes plenty of money.

Others urged for the Bill, as Sir Joseph Tredenham, Mr. Papillon, Sir Rd. Temple, Sir Charles Sedley, Mr. Holt, Sir Robt. Henley, etc. and said that this would mightily encourage trade which was become now so dead and little profitable that, since more profit was to be made by money at interest than could be cleared by trade, few persons would employ their money in trade; then said it will discourage persons to bring their money in here to let it at interest. I like it not for such do more hurt and carry out of the nation both interest and principle; then low interest will benefit trade and much advance the same for where that is low you may be better able to trade with

your neighbours and they cannot then undersell you . . . the question was put
for passing the Bill

$$
\text{Tellers for}
\begin{cases}
\text{Yeas} & \begin{cases}\text{Sir Ed. Hussey} \\ \text{Mr. Methwin}\end{cases} \Big\} \quad 150 \\
\text{Noes} & \begin{cases}\text{Sir Rob. Danvers} \\ \text{Mr. Goldwell}\end{cases} \Big\} \quad 101
\end{cases}
$$

Sir Edward Hendred ordered to carry it to the Lords.

64. A LANCASTER GROCER'S COMMENTS
ON THE STATE OF THE COINAGE, 1693–6

The Autobiography of William Stout of Lancaster, 1665–1752,
ed. J. D. Marshall, 1967, pp. 108–10, 113–17]

In 1693

I laid out about 40s. in Samuel Fisher, Francis Hougill, and other Friends'
books, and earthenware and other household goods, which I paid for in
silver money, which at this time was much diminished by clipping. So that
where I was a stranger, they enquired where I came from and whether we
had such large money, and not diminished, in our country. The old money
which was coined before the Restoration of King Charles II was called
'hammered money', which had the King's reign and year of coining, etc.
stamped in a ring on each side on the outward. But in much of that money
the ring was cut away, which at least was one third of the weight of the sixpence, shilling, or half or whole crown it was cut from. This was taken notice
of by the government as a growing evil [which], if not remedied, would be
more fatal than a war with France. And to prevent the further diminishing
our coin, it was enacted that where any person received any hammered
money not diminished, they should punch a hole in the centre of it; and if
that piece afterwards was offered in payment, the person offering it was to be
deemed, and prosecuted as, the diminisher. Notwithstanding this, not much
of this holed money appeared; but the large money was either concealed or
melted down, and little but diminished money appeared. And as to the money
coined after the Restoration of King Charles II, called milled money, which
was lettered on the edge, there was scarce any of it to be seen, and [it was]
supposed to be melted down or counterfeited into the old coin clipped.

In 1693 and 1694

There was at that time very little silver coined, and what was coined was
hoarded, but abundance of gold was coined into guineas, which most payments were made in about this time . . .

The diminishing our old silver coin increased, and made great confusion
in trade, people being cautious in setting a price of their goods without
knowing in what money they should be paid. And although taxes were

multiplied upon account of the war, yet it was feared the distraction about
the coin would be more fatal than the war with France. And the king of
France fully expected the same would bring us into confusion.

In 1695

The old silver coin of this nation continued to be more and more diminished, which made great distraction in trade. And although the King encouraged the collectors of his revenue to take all pieces of the old silver coin
in payment that was not impaired within the inward ring, yet people did not
look upon that as a warrant in payment to each other. And as there was not
then any milled money, guineas began to advance in value in payment here to
22 or 23s. apiece, and all goods in the market advanced accordingly. And in
the third month this year, I being determined to go to London, got what
money I could exchanged for guineas or other gold coin. And in the beginning of this month I set forward for London, accompanied by Richard Green
and his sister Elin, William Godsalve, and Sarah Snow. We went by Manchester and Sheffield, where we stayed two nights, whilst I had time to
settle my accounts there, and buy and order what goods I had occasion for;
and left money with Thomas Ward to pay for them, and then set forward to
London by way of Nottingham, Northampton, and Newport Pagnell. And
got safe there, and first set Sarah Snow to her father's house, and then inned
at the Swan [with Two Necks] in Lad Laine, where we had hitherto always
lodged. At our coming to London, we found the old silver coin much more
diminished and counterfeited than in the country, and guineas were advanced
to 28 or 30s. apiece, which put the trade of the nation into great confusion,
and in particular with foreign nations, in respect to the price of exchange.
And as to the guineas we had, they advanced to us about 5s. apiece more than
we took them for in the country; and what I brought advanced to me about
14l. . . .

In the 6th month this year I went with Richard Green to Liverpool, where
we bought betwixt 2 and 300l. worth of tobacco, most of it [in] bulk, being
the last that was suffered to be imported loose or in small parcels, and an Act
of Parliament passed that no tobacco should be imported but in casks or
hogsheads, to weigh two hundred weight each neat, to prevent the running
it in bundles or small parcels to defraud the King of his customs. We bought
a good quantity now, to have the opportunity to pay for it in short money, as
it was now called. For in the later end of this year, the distraction was so
great that Parliament were convinced that there was no remedy but to call
in all the old money to be recoined; and that the King in his revenues should
take all the diminished [currency], either sterling or of a coarser alloy, in full
count, and recoin it into milled money; and to keep an account of the
deficiency, which should be made good by Parliament. And for the more
expedition, mints were erected at York, Norwich, Exeter, Bristol, and Chester,
to be there coined, and the letters Y, N, E, B, C, stamped on each piece
coined there to distinguish them. And a limited time set, in what time the

old money should be brought in to be recoined; and after that time a further time was limited for any person who had old money to be recoined, or plate. If they brought it into any of the said mints, it should be taken in at 5*s*. 8*d*. an ounce to be coined, and milled money given out for it in course, by which method most of the old money was recoined in a year. The last time to bring it in was the 4th of May 1697 [sic=error for 1696]. This gave great ease and satisfaction to all people and brought trade into order.

In 1695

I was collector of the land tax for Lancaster this year. It was 4*s*. in the pound and amounted to above 120*l*., and we were obliged by the Act to take any of the diminished money, either sterling or of a coarser alloy, which put us upon difficulties, [there] being people [who] would put upon us to take such as were brass or copper covered over with silver, which we took on condition, if not paid, to return it. But all then passed, and by my best observation, in new coining it must lose at least half. I was assisting the general receiver for the county, in taking one quarter for Lonsdale Hundred, about 300*l*., which must lose at least half, and in the south the loss must be greater. To make good this loss, the duty on windows was imposed,[1] which was continued many years for that use ...

In 1696

In this year, much of the old silver money was brought in to the mints by the collectors of the revenues of the Crown, as enacted, and [was] recoined and began to circulate. And as it came out, also the milled money coined in King Charles and King James's reign began to appear—which was supposed to have been melted down and coined in imitation of the diminished old coin. And for some years after this, there was as much of that money in all payments, as of the old money new coined, by which it appeared that vast sums of that money was concealed, and [showed] the opulency of this nation. And as the new money increased, guineas declined in value, and all goods advanced in price[2] [as the public began] to put off their old money and guineas; and a great trade in the nation, and public credit with all nations advanced. Which, being particularly [observed] by the king of France, he said if England could maintain a war, and at the same time remedy the ill

[1] In fact, the Window Tax was intended to defray the cost of recoinage.

[2] J. D. Marshall, the editor, adds the following note:
This no doubt was Stout's experience; but it does not follow that the rise was simply a result of the recoinage. Indeed, a reformed coinage should be expected to reflect the improvement in lower prices, stated in terms of silver coins. It is true that the government, to offset the temporary shortage of coin, issued exchequer bills (D. Macpherson, *Annals of Commerce* (London and Edinburgh, 1805), II, pp. 680–1), and the volume in circulation being thus increased, prices would tend to be maintained or to rise. What Stout thought had happened, perhaps, was that when, in addition to the new minted money, some of the better sorts of old coin came out of hoards, the resulting increase in the amount circulating sent prices up.

state of their coin, it was in vain to contend with them longer. And upon that he inclined to peace. After the time was out for the king's taking old money in count, and limited to 5s. 8d. an ounce, and new money appearing, all who had old money brought it out and paid their debts and bought goods for it. At this time I and Richard Greene went to Poulton, and there bought of James Baynes thirty hogsheads of tobacco at 9d. a pound, to pay all in old money, part by count and the rest at 5s. 8d. an ounce, which cleared us of the old silver money; and guineas came down to 22s.

65. WILLIAM LOWNDES'S VIEWS ON THE PROJECTED RECOINAGE, 1695

[W. Lowndes, *A Report containing an Essay for the Amendment of the Silver Coins*, London, 1695, pp. 115–16, 118–21, 125–6, 154]

To the Right Honourable the Lords Commissioners
of his Majesty's Treasury

. . . in consequence of the vitiating, diminishing, and counterfeiting of the current monies, it is come to pass, that great contentions do daily arise amongst the king's subjects, in fairs, markets, shops, and other places throughout the kingdom, about the passing or refusing of the same, to the disturbance of the public peace; many bargains, doings, and dealings are totally prevented and laid aside; which lessens trade in general; persons, before they conclude in any bargains, are necessitated first to settle the price or value of the very money they are to receive for their goods; and if it be in guineas at a high rate, or in clipped or bad monies, they set the price of their goods accordingly, which I think has been one great cause of raising the price not only of merchandises, but even of edibles, and other necessaries for the sustenance of the common people, to their great grievance. The receipt and collection of the public taxes, revenues, and debts (as well as of private men's incomes) are extremely retarded, to the damage of his Majesty, and to the prejudice of a vigorous prosecution of the war; so that there were never (at least since I had the honour to serve the crown) so many bonds given, and lying unsatisfied at the Custom Houses, or so vast an arrear of excises. And as for the land tax, your Lordships know how far 'tis affected with the bad monies, by the many complaints transmitted daily from the commissioners, receivers, and collectors thereof, and by comparing the sum brought into the Exchequer this year, with the timely payments of the like tax in preceding years. In fine, the mischiefs of the bad money (too many to enumerate) are so sensibly felt, that (I humbly conceive) they are sufficient to confute all the arguments against the recoining the same in this time of war, and even the objections against raising the silver in our coin to the proposed value . . .

The Means that must be Obtained, and the proper
Methods to be used in and for the Re-establishment
of the Silver Coins

In case his Majesty (taking into his princely consideration the great inconveniencies which the nation labours under by the badness of the monies)
shall be pleased to direct, that all such silver coins called crowns, half-
crowns, shillings, or testers, as have been formerly coined in the Royal Mint
or mints of England with the hammer, and are more or less diminished by
clipping, rounding, filing, or any other artifice, shall be melted and recoined,
my humble opinion is, that the general cautions following are to be observed:

First, that the work ought to be performed and finished in as little time as
may be, not only to obviate a further damage by clipping in the interim, but
also that the needful advantages of the new money may be the sooner obtained
for the service of the nation.

Secondly, that the loss, or the greatest part of it ought to be born by the
public, and not by particulars, who being very numerous will be prejudiced
against a reformation for the public benefit, if it is to be effected at the cost of
particular men, and who have great hopes of being indemnified by the votes
passed in their favour in the last session of Parliament.

Thirdly, this whole affair must be rendered easy, and very intelligible to
the common people, so that they must not be compelled to travel very far
when they part with their clipped money, or when they receive back the
value of it in the new coins, and in the mean time they must be furnished
with a useful and transferable credit that must take place in course of repayment, as fast as the new coins can be made.

Fourthly, that no room must be left for jealousy. And therefore all the
clipped monies in the several counties, far or near, are not to be brought
entirely to London, to be minted there, which would leave all the countries
very bare, and create great suspicions till its return.

Fifthly, that as soon as the king's officers begin to take in the clipped
monies, or presently after, the course for repaying the stated value thereof in
new monies ought to begin also, and to be carried on by the new monies,
which shall be coined from the silver of the old, so far as it will extend. And
that an Aid be given in Parliament to supply the residue in such time and
manner, as that there be no interruption or intervals in the course of repayment, till such times as the registers for the clipped monies to be brought in
shall be fully satisfied.

According to these general propositions, and some other requisites which
have occurred to me, I have employed my thoughts to reduce this whole
affair into practice, and do humbly offer to your lordships' consideration the
particulars following, as the scope and design of my report: that is to say,

First, that an Aid be granted in Parliament, and strictly appropriated for
or towards the making good of the loss by the said clipped monies, or so
much thereof as shall be thought reasonable to be defrayed by the public,

and the incident charges which shall be necessary in the performance of this service. Which aid, if it be commensurate to the whole loss, will by estimation, as above, amount to fifteen hundred thousand pounds; and if it be resolved that the public shall bear but half the loss, or any other part of it, then the Aid (in the grant thereof) may be proportioned accordingly. And the said Aid is humbly proposed to be either by a land tax of twelve pence in the pound, or by a yearly sum to be answered out of the continued impositions upon goods imported, or some other certain fond, to take effect within a year to come at the farthest . . .

Ninthly, that besides the principal mint within the Tower of London (where six presses can be wrought at the same time) there be settled and established nine other mints within England and Wales, to work with two presses in each, namely, one at Newcastle upon Tyne, to serve principally for the counties of Durham, Northumberland, Cumberland, and Westmorland; one at York to serve for the counties of York and Lancaster; one at Nottingham to serve for the counties of Nottingham, Lincoln, Derby, and Leicester; one at Chester to serve for Cheshire, Staffordshire, Salop, and North Wales; one at Hereford to serve for the counties of Hereford, Gloucester, Worcester, and South Wales; one at Exeter to serve for Cornwall, Devon, and Somerset: one at Salisbury to serve for the counties of Wilts., Dorset, and Hampshire; one at Oxon. to serve for the counties of Oxon., Bucks., Warwick, and Berks.; and one at Cambridge to serve for Norfolk, Suffolk, Huntingdon, Cambridge, and Bedfordshire; and that at London will serve for the rest. Nevertheless, these several mints are not intended to be so restrained but that a man may carry his money to any of them that lies most in his way; whereby there may be coined weekly (as I am informed) about fifty or sixty thousand pounds easily, which will finish the whole work in much less than a year's time. And that the dyes, presses, and other implements may be providing with as much haste as is possible, so as to be all fit for use by or before Christmas next . . .

I cannot forbear (before I end) to allege, that if the coins are to be amended and established according to these propositions (which may be rectified and improved by men of greater judgement and skill), I cannot foresee that even whilst the work is carrying on, there will accrue such public disorder, damage, or distress, as the nation labours under before the work is put in hand.

All which is most humbly submitted to your lordships' great wisdom and judgement.

12 September, 1695   William Lowndes

66. SUBSCRIPTIONS TO JOHN BRISCOE'S LAND BANK, 1695

[B.M., Printed Book 8223 e 7]

John Briscoe's Land Bank Scheme, 1695

An account of the value of the estates in the several counties subscribed towards the fund for a national land bank from Thursday, the 11th of June, to Saturday, the 27th of July, 1695.[1]

THE books of subscription for a Fund for a National Land Bank being laid open, the 11th of June at night, and the proposals mentioning that an account shall be published every month of the yearly value of the estates subscribed; it is thought fit to print and publish the same the first and third Mondays in every month until one hundred thousand pounds per annum or two millions in value shall be subscribed, of which there are subscriptions for £51,438 per annum to the value of about one million in the several counties following, viz.

	l. per annum		*l. per annum*
Bedfordshire	575	Monmouthshire	686
Berkshire	118	Norfolk	2,642
Buckinghamshire	590	Northamptonshire	1,400
Cambridge	850	Nottinghamshire	240
Cheshire	1,800	Northumberland	1,180
Cornwall	850	Oxfordshire	550
Cumberland		Rutland	
Derbyshire	155	Shropshire	600
Devon	2,030	Somerset	300
Dorset		Staffordshire	1,530
Durham	1,171	Suffolk	300
Essex	4,755	Sussex	515
Gloucestershire	793	Surrey	1,275
Hampshire	850	Warwickshire	
Herefordshire	1,021	Westmorland	22
Hertfordshire	490	Wiltshire	240
Huntingdonshire	1,065	Worcestershire	210
Kent	3,911	Yorkshire	4,001
Lancashire	50	Anglesey	
Leicestershire	420	Breconshire	1,000
Lincolnshire	2,335	Cardiganshire	
London and Middlesex	10,173	Carmarthenshire	

[1] This is the last page of a pamphlet which begins thus: The following proposals for and accounts of a national land bank having been printed at London, it's proveable many gentlemen who would have subscribed thereto by reason of the distance of their dwelling from thence have heard nothing or had but an imperfect account of it; for informing whom true copies of several of Mr. Briscoe's papers are herewith reprinted in order to be dispersed in several counties. *The freehold estates of England or England itself the best fund or security.*

	l. per annum		*l. per annum*
Caernarvonshire	15	Pembrokeshire	20
Denbighshire	686	Radnorshire	
Flintshire	24		
Glamorganshire			51,438
Merionethshire			
Montgomeryshire			

Note that any gentleman though never so remote may, pursuant to the proposals, authorize another to subscribe his estate.

John Briscoe

The subscription books continue to lie open at Thomas Gooding, sergeant at law, his chambers in Gray's Inn; at Philip Neave, esq., his chambers, the second staircase, Paper Buildings, in the Inner Temple; at Lawrence Braddon, esq., his chambers, no. 4, the second staircase at the New Square at Lincoln's Inn . . . [etc.]¹

67. THE CRISIS OF CREDIT, 1696

[P.R.O., State Paper Entry Book, SP 44/274, pp. 255–6]

Minutes of the Proceedings of the Lords Justices of England,
Whitehall, August 5, 1696

. . . Lords of the Treasury called in, viz. Mr. Montagu, Mr. Smith, and Sir Thomas Littleton. Declared that the expectations from the Land Bank were over, their subscription not amounting to above 36,000*l.* and none of that like to be paid, since it was upon conditions to be yet agreed upon; that their demands amounted to above 30 per cent, viz. 12 by way of discount, the exporting of 200,000*l.*, as the law allows, which is worth 10 per cent, and the interest upon the tallies they were to have, being 6 per cent more. So that the matter stood just as it was ten days before, when my Lord Portland arrived, only they had found remittances for 30,000*l.* which they should be in a worse condition if they were not able to satisfy at the time of repayment.

Considerations had whether they should propose a loan to the City. Great difficulties foreseen in it, that the matter would be much worse in case of a refusal or a mean subscription, and that they had no fund to propose to them but the credit of the Exchequer in general. Discourses had about a general subscription. The difficulty foreseen that some would subscribe without any premium only in consideration of the public, others would expect a recompense for the advance of any considerable sum, and it was questioned how that could be adjusted.

---

¹ At these addresses, according to the text of the pamphlet, 'any persons by themselves or others may subscribe lands, tenements, or hereditaments, whether freehold, copyhold, or leasehold to what yearly value they please to be settled upon such trustees as shall be chosen by the subscribers for funds to issue out bills of credit upon the security of such estates.'

Resolved that some of the Bank of England be spoke to and that it be seen what assistance they can give, and that the governor, deputy governor, and some of the directors have notice to attend their Excellencies tomorrow...

68. PETITIONS FOR A MINT AT EXETER AND YORK, 1696

[P.R.O., State Paper Entry Book, SP 44/238, p. 50; 44/237, pp. 153–4]

Petition of the Mayor and of the City of Exeter

UPON the petition of the mayor, aldermen, and common council, divers merchants, tradesmen, and other principal inhabitants of the city of Exeter, setting forth that, having enjoyed a considerable trade for several years past under the happy influence of his Majesty's government, and being at present sensible of the great mischiefs occasioned by the abasing the coin of this his Majesty's kingdom, there being almost a total obstruction to that trade they so lately enjoyed, and thereby many thousands of the poor inhabitants of this city reduced to the greatest extremities, and it being now under his Majesty's consideration by the advice of the Parliament to apply a suitable remedy to those great mischiefs by erecting several mints in several parts of this kingdom for new coining the money thereof, and praying that a mint may be settled in this city.

Whitehall, 22nd January, 1695/6

His Majesty is graciously pleased to refer this petition to the Rt. Hon. the Lords Commissioners of the Treasury who are to consider of the same and report to his Majesty what may fitly be done therein for the petitioners' gratification, whereupon he will declare his further pleasure.

Will. Trumbull

* * *

The Parliament men for the northern counties
To the king's most excellent Majesty,
the humble petition of the knights, citizens, and burgesses
in Parliament serving for the northern counties.

Sheweth that whereas by the late act of Parliament entitled an act for remedying the ill state of the coin of this kingdom it is amongst other things enacted that for the ease and benefit of your Majesty's subjects who live in the remote parts of the kingdom your Majesty will be graciously pleased to erect mints in such convenient places of the kingdom as in your great wisdom you shall think fit, being not less than four. And whereas there hath been heretofore a mint at the city of York and it being very convenient for the advantage of your Majesty and your subjects in the northern parts of the kingdom.

Your petitioners therefore humbly pray that your Majesty will be graciously pleased to take the premises into your royal consideration, and, if your Majesty think fit to settle any mints in the remote parts, that your city of York may be appointed as one for the ease and advantage of your subjects in the north of England.

And your petitioners shall ever pray etc.

Signed by 36 members of Parliament

Whitehall, 27th January, 1695/6.

*   *   *

Lords and Commissioners of the Treasury

My Lords,

The king being moved upon the enclosed petition of the members of Parliament serving for the northern counties for setting up a mint at York, his Majesty directs that it be transmitted to your lordships in order to be laid before his Majesty when you next attend him.

I am, my Lords, your lordships' most humble servant,

Shrewsbury.

69. THE RECOINAGE OF 1696 AND THREATS OF DISORDER

[P.R.O., State Paper Entry Book, SP 44/274, pp. 133–4, 169–70, 227–9]
Minutes of the Proceedings of the Lords Justices of England, Whitehall, May 24, 1696

. . . My Lord Steward produced a letter from Mr. Bagshaw setting forth the danger there was of an insurrection amongst the miners in Derbyshire upon their clipped money being refused, when they had nothing else to supply it. An evil without remedy, but the best care should be taken that could be for suppressing tumults.

*   *   *

June 16, 1696

. . . Letters read from the Lord Lonsdale about the riot at Kendal, from an exciseman about the riot at Halifax, from the Duke of Norfolk, that the gentlemen about Sheffield were for representing against the refusal of clipped money that was near punchable. Letter from Plymouth read about the difficulty to pay the soldiers their subsistence in money.

Ordered that Mr. Clark attend on Thursday about directions that the soldiers do not exact their subsistence in money but take it in provisions.

Considered that the disorders may in great part be remedied if people would submit to the putting of their narrow money by weight. Resolved that it be proposed on Thursday at Council to have a proclamation issue to that purpose . . .

Considerations had about the immediate coining of plate, and that a fund of 4,000*l*. or 5,000*l*. be provided for exchanging it as fast as it shall be brought in and assayed, and that the recompense of 6*d*. per ounce be given at the same time, which may be a means to prevent its being hoarded by goldsmiths.

*   *   *

21 July, 1696

A representation read of the 14th inst. from the Grand Jury and justices of the peace of Staffordshire concerning the apprehensions they are in of disturbances by reason of the present condition of the coin.

Ordered that an answer be returned them that if they could propose any remedy, their excellencies would willingly put it in practice being sensible of the difficulties the whole kingdom lies under, that those of them who are [of] Parliament know what hath been resolved in Parliament in order to amend the coin and that what hath been so settled cannot be altered but by the same authority and to recommend to them to be vigilant in preserving the public peace.

70. GODFREY'S TRACT ON THE BANK OF ENGLAND, *c.* 1696
[*Somers Tracts*, 1814 edn., XI, pp. 3–7]

A Short Account of the Bank of England, heretofore published by Michael Godfrey, esq., deceased

CONSIDERING the variety of opinions concerning the Bank, it may be thought a service to the public to give the following account of it, whereby 'twill appear, that the Bank, notwithstanding all the cavils which the wit and malice of its opponents have raised, is one of the best establishments that ever was made for the good of the kingdom. For how plausible soever their objections may seem, 'tis manifest they proceed in some from aversion to the government, in others from prejudice, false insinuations, or mistaken notions, but in most from self-interest.

The Bank is a society consisting of about 1300 persons, who, having subscribed 1,200,000*l*. pursuant to an Act of Parliament, are incorporated by the name of The Governor and Company of the Bank of England, and have a fund of 100,000*l*. per annum granted them, redeemable after eleven years, upon one year's notice; which 1,200,000*l*. they have paid into the Exchequer, by such payments as the public occasions required, and most of it long before the money could have been demanded.[1]

The subscriptions to the Bank were made by virtue of a commission under the great seal of England, grounded upon the said Act of Parliament, of which

---

[1] The bank's original charter was dated 27 July 1694.

public notice was given, and the commissioners were appointed to take all such voluntary subscriptions as should be made on or before the first day of August last, by any person or persons, natives or foreigners, bodies politic or corporate, towards the raising the said 1,200,000*l.*; and there was a proviso in the said Act, that if 600,000*l.* or more of the said 1,200,000*l.* should not be subscribed on or before the first day of August then next coming, that the power of making a corporation should cease, and the money be paid into the Exchequer by the respective subscribers and contributors. And notwithstanding all the endeavours of its adversaries, the whole 1,200,000*l.* was subscribed in ten days' time, though, if the subscriptions had not amounted to 600,000*l.*, the subscribers would have had but a bad bargain, and such as nobody would have taken off their hands for 20 per cent loss of their principal, and yet they would have received 8*l.* per cent per annum for their money; nor would the 1,200,000*l.* have been any thing near subscribed, but upon the prospect of their being incorporated to be the Bank of England.

It's observable, that the promoters of the Bank have proposed no advantage thereby to themselves above any of the other subscribers, all the profit being only *pro rata*, according to their stock; and though it cannot be imagined but that they intended to be largely concerned, yet it is so settled, that those who have but 500*l.* have one vote, and those who have never so much can have no more; and the directors have no salary fixed for their pains and attendance, but submit themselves wholly to what a general court will think fit to allow them; and any nine members, having each 500*l.* stock, may call a general court, and turn out the governor, deputy governor, and all or any of the directors, and choose others in their places; which are provisions so wise and effectual to prevent fraud in some, to the prejudice of the rest, that it hardly leaves room for any doubt of that nature.

I shall not attempt to enumerate all the advantages which the nation will receive by the Bank; however, I will mention some few, which alone are sufficient to recommend it, viz.

The Bank, besides the raising 1,200,000*l.* towards the charge of the war, cheaper than it could otherwise have been done, (and like the other public funds, tying the people faster to the government), will infallibly lower the interest of money, as well on public as private securities, which all other funds have advanced, and which hath been raised to an exorbitant rate, as to the public, by those who have made use of its necessities, and are now angry at the Bank because that will reduce it. And the lowering of interest, besides the encouragement it will be to industry and improvements, will, by a natural consequence, raise the value of land and increase trade, both which depend upon it; but it cannot be expected that land shall rise much whilst such high taxes continue upon it, and whilst there are so great advantages to be made by lending money to the public.

The Bank gives money for tallies on funds, having a credit of loan by Act of Parliament, and which are payable in two years' time, for the growing interest only, without any other allowance, on which there was used to be paid for the change, as much or more than the public interest. For even on the land tax, which is counted the best of all funds, there has been frequently given on tallies payable in three or four months' time, $1l.$, $1\frac{1}{3}$, $1\frac{3}{4}$, and two per cent premio, over and above the public interest, and tallies on some funds on which but 12 or 18 months past there was 25$l.$ and 30 per cent given over and above the public interest, are now taken by the Bank for nothing, and instead of allowing money to change them, there is now money given to procure them; so that tallies are become better than money, because there is 7 or 8 per cent per annum benefit whilst they are kept; and they are paid by the Bank, upon demand, to all those who desire to have money for them, which is in effect so much quick stock which the Bank has already increased to the nation, besides what it will farther add to its own credit.

Thus by a regular course, and without any violence, the Bank has made tallies current in payment, which is what has been so long wished for, but could not have been effected without the Bank (although there had been a law to compel it), and this has given such a reputation to all tallies, even those which are the most remote, that they are now currently taken by private persons at 6, 8, 10, 15, and 20$l.$ per cent less allowance than what was given but some few months before the Bank was established, all which losses on tallies was paid by the public; for it cannot be supposed, but that those who are to allow 15 or 20 per cent for discount of their tallies, make provision accordingly in the price they are to have for their commodities.

The Bank will likewise facilitate the future supplies, by making the funds which are to be given more useful and ready to answer the public occasions, and upon easier terms than what has been done during the war. For 'tis said they will lend money on the land tax at 6 per cent per annum, nay, some say at 5 per cent per annum; which will save the nation a great sum of money in interest, as well as what was usually paid for gratuities and other charges to procure loans; a method that some of the opposers of the Bank have been well acquainted with.

But now the Bank is established, and that all who want money, and have securities, know where to be supplied, and the terms, there cannot be such advantages made on the public or private men's necessities for the future.

The more credit the Bank has, and the more money is lodged in it, the more it will lessen interest, for want of occasions to improve it; and those who lodge their money in the Bank have it as much at their disposal as if it were in the hands of the goldsmiths, or in their own cash chest; and there is a greater value than the money which is deposited in the Bank that circulates by their credit, as much as if it were stirring in specie. And the bank bills serve already for returns and exchange to and from the remotest parts of the kingdom, and will in a little time do the like in foreign parts, which will lessen the exporting of bullion for the paying and maintaining our armies abroad during this war; and if the bulk of the money of the nation, which has been lodged with the goldsmiths, had been deposited in the Bank four or five years past, it had prevented its being so scandalously clipped, which one day or other must cost the nation a million and a half, or two millions, to repair . . .

The Bank being thus useful to the public extends itself likewise to accommodate all private men's occasions; for they lend money on mortgages, and real securities, at 5*l.* per cent per annum; and their very publishing they would do it has given a check to the raising the interest on them, from 5 to 6*l.* per cent per annum, as was attempted. And if the titles of land were made more secure, money would be lent thereon at 4*l.* per cent per annum, and in time of peace at 3*l.* per cent per annum. Foreign bills of exchange are discounted at 4½ per cent per annum, and inland bills and notes for debts at 6*l.* per cent per annum; and those who keep their cash in the Bank have the one discounted at 3*l.* per cent per annum, and the other at 4½ per cent per annum, for which most goldsmiths used to take 9 or 10 per cent per annum. And money is lent on pawns of commodities which are not perishable at 5*l.* per cent per annum; for which some in their necessities have paid more than double as much, to the ruin of many great traders.

Money is likewise lent on the fund of the orphans of the city of London, at 5*l.* per cent per annum, which will hinder several, who are necessitous, from being forced to sell their interest at under-rates.

And 'tis said they have agreed to set up a Lumbard to lend money on small pawns, for the relief of the poor, at one penny per month for 20 shillings, for which they now pay sixpence or twelvepence every week. And 'tis probable, if the Bank was not restrained by Act of Parliament, they might take into consideration the exchanging seamen's tickets for money, for a very small allowance, for which they have oftentimes paid 7 or 8 shillings in the pound.

The Bank will reduce the interest of money in England to 3*l.* per cent per annum in a few years, without any law to enforce it, in like manner as it is in all other countries where banks are established, whereby the trade of the nation may be driven upon more equal terms with the rest of our neighbours, where money is to be had at so much lower rates than what we in England have hitherto paid. And as the lessening the interest of money will infallibly raise the value of land, it had been worth while for the nobility and gentry, who are the proprietors of the real estates in England, to have given a land tax for the Bank of double the sum which was raised by it, if they could not otherwise have obtained it; for the falling the interest of money to 3*l.* per cent per annum, to which rate the Bank will reduce it, will unavoidably advance the price of land to above thirty years' purchase, which will raise the value of the lands of England at least 100 millions, and thereby abundantly reimburse the nation all the charges of the war; and will not only enable the gentry to make better provision for their younger children, but those who now owe money on their lands to pay off their debts, by the increase of the value of their estates.

The ease and security of the great receipts and payments of money which are made by the Bank (where people's cash is kept as it is at the goldsmiths) together with the safe depositing of it, are such advantages to recommend it, that they ought not to be passed over without some observation; especially considering how much money has been lost in England by the goldsmiths and scriveners breaking, which, in about 30 years past, cannot amount to so little as betwixt two and three millions, all which might have been prevented, had a Bank been sooner established. For none can lose by the Bank, they having a fund of 100,000*l.* per annum, and money or good securities besides, for as much as they owe, wherewith to pay all that trust them.

These are such services to the nation in general, which have been (and will be) done by the Bank, as could not have been done without it; and such arguments as these, arising from fact, are better demonstrations, and more convincing of the usefulness of it, than mere speculative notions urged by its opposers, can be to prejudice others against it; and therefore it would be an unaccountable sort of policy, to endeavour to deprive the nation of those vast advantages which it now does and will receive by it . . .

VII. ALIENS

1. ALIENS IN ENGLAND IN 1616
[P.R.O., SP 14/88, no. 112]

In the Statutes at large in the small print in the title of aliens, for retaining of apprentices and servants ready, Anno 1 Ric. 3, page 403, Anno 14 & 15 Hen. 8, page 530, 21 Hen. 8, 1a 16, page 557 and 815.
Against aliens taking of leases, vide page 816.[1]

The chronicles make mention of sundry punishments of them by the State, one in the reign of Hen. 2 by Thomas Beckett, Chancellor, who caused their houses to be pulled down and expelled them the realm. Also of divers outrages done against them, one on ill May day in the reign of Hen. 8.

By his Majesty two principal reformations have been made against them: 1. the forbidding of transportation by English merchants in strange bottoms to the increase of our navy 100 sail, the 2. the enhancing of gold which hath much restrained them from transporting the same, although it be yet very plentiful there.

Their chiefest cause of entertainment here of late was in charity to shroud them from persecution for religion; and, being here, their necessity became the mother of their ingenuity in devising many trades, before to us unknown.

The State, noting their diligence, and yet preventing the future inconvenience, enacted two special laws:

That they should entertain English apprentices and servants to learn these trades, the neglect whereof giveth them advantage to keep their mysteries to themselves, which hath made them bold of late to devise engines for working of tape, lace, ribbon and such, wherein one man doth more among them than seven Englishmen can do; so as their cheap sale of those commodities beggareth all our English artificers of that trade and enricheth them.

Since the making of the last Statute they are thought to be increased ten for one, so as no tenement is left to an English artificer to inhabit in divers parts of the city and suburbs, but they take them over their heads at a great rate.

So their numbers causeth the enhancing of the prices of victuals and house rents, and much furthereth the late disorderly new buildings, which is so burdenous to the subject that his Majesty hath not any work to perform for the good of his commons (especially in cities and towns) than by the taking

---

[1] These are page references to the writer's own notes.

of the benefit of the law upon them, a thing which is done against his own subjects by common informers. But their daily flocking hither without such remedy is like to grow scarce tolerable.

2. A FRENCH ALIEN SEEKS TO JOIN THE ENGLISH COMMUNITY IN NORWICH, 1621

[P.R.O., SP 14/122, no. 144. 25 September 1621]

[Letter from the Mayor and Aldermen of Norwich to the Privy Council.]

Our duties most humbly remembered, it pleased your lordships by your honourable letters of the tenth of July last to mention that your Honours had addressed unto us former letters touching the maintenance of the English ministers who had formerly complained that a great part of the allowance which by the strangers at their first coming hither had been voluntarily condescended unto, were of late years detained from them, and that Dennis Lermitt being then specially complained of in that behalf and sent for by your Honours' warrant, had submitted to what your Honours should prescribe therein.[1] And that since that time the said Dennis Lermitt hath complained unto your Honours that he, being a freeman and one of the livery of his company, and frequenting the English church in the parish where he dwelleth, where he is ready and willing to pay all church duties, is forced by those of the French congregation to resort to their church as formerly to his infinite vexation. And withal to refer the consideration of his complaint unto us to the end we might order such a course therein as should be most reasonable and meet.

It may now please your Honours to be informed that we upon receipt of your honourable letters brought unto us by the said Lermitt did call before us the said Lermitt and the minister and elders of that congregation, and upon full hearing of the said cause we found no just cause of the said Lermitt's complaint, nor any grievance or vexation to have been offered unto him, but only in this that he having been always a member of that church ever since his coming into this kingdom, it had pleased the city to make him a freeman and one of the livery of his company, and they of his own congregation had lately elected him to be one of the elders of that church. We knowing that to be the case of a great number of the strangers of like condition admitted to the freedom of this city, born in this kingdom and made denizens here, who do notwithstanding such their freedom, nativity, and denization, continue to be of their own congregation and to bear ordinary charges there in respect of their estates in wealth, and also to pay to the ministers and poor in the English parish where they dwell only according to the yearly value of their houses.

---

[1] Denis l'Hermite had been in trouble since 1612 for refusing to pay towards the maintenance of the parish minister, the Reverend F. Roberts. He was now refusing to worship in the Walloon church.

And considering withal how dangerous an innovation the said Dennis Lermitt had attempted by this his complaint, whereby he endeavoureth to gain liberty to depart from that church, we persuaded and required him to desist from that his intention. And he at our request was contented and did willingly submit to resort to the said French church as formerly he had done and to bear the said office of eldership there, whereunto he was elected, and to pay duties both there and in the parish of St Saviour's where he dwelleth according to orders from the Council Board formerly established, and now lately by your honourable letters of the 30th of May last commanded to be observed. Since which submission and consent of the said Dennis Lermitt he still refuseth to pay to Mr. Foulke Robarts, minister of St. Saviour's parish, the yearly sum of xx*s.* by us reasonably and advisedly assessed and set according to the yearly value of his house, and hath also associated himself unto Joell Desormeaux and Samuel Camby, two principal men of that French congregation who, being rich in means and refractory in condition, have upon some displeasure misconceived against Mr Peter De Lawne their minister whom we know to be a learned, grave, and discreet preacher, not only withheld from him their usual contribution but also have withdrawn themselves from that their congregation and church wherein they had formerly borne several offices and continued members thereof ever since their baptism. Albeit those personal differences have been heard and discussed by their own synods more than two years since and the same have been often particularly ripped up and heard before the now Lord Bishop of Norwich, and at other times before diverse justices of peace of this city, at which hearings they have been worthily blamed for their unjust calumnies concerning their minister and no just cause found of their separation. Yet do they still persist in their slanderous aspersions and resolution of departure from their church and will not be reformed therein. By reason of which their departure many other of the wealthier sort of the said congregation being likewise English born and denizens and freemen of the said city do threaten the like departure, which, if it should be permitted, the congregation will in short time be utterly dissolved, the employment of their poor who are profitably exercised in mechanical manufactures will be neglected, the charge of maintenance of their minister and of their aged and impotent people will be left upon a few indigent and unable persons, by means whereof many great and unavoidable inconveniences will befall this city and the government thereof.

Now forasmuch as that French or Walloon company hath been continued by the gracious favour of the late Queen Elizabeth and of the King's most excellent Majesty as a congregation apart from the English by the space of five and fifty years or more now past, and hath been all that time governed in respect of their church discipline by their minister and elders, and in respect of civil government by the Mayor and Aldermen of the said city. And for that the said Joel Desormeaux, Samuel Camby, and Dennis Lermitt and their adherents do now trouble, impugn, and withstand that government, endeavouring a dangerous innovation therein whose wilful and perverse practice without authority from your Honours cannot by us be timely prevented, we therefore humbly desire that the said Joel Desormeaux, Samuel Camby, and Dennis Lermitt and all others successively of that Walloon congregation, although born in this kingdom, may by your Honours be ordered to continue and be of that church and society so long as his Majesty shall be graciously pleased to permit the same, and that all persons so ordered to be of that congregation may be subject to such discipline as hath been by all the time aforesaid most usually practised amongst them, and that such of them as shall not conform themselves thereunto and shall not in case of their church discipline submit themselves to be ordered therein by the bishop of Norwich for the time being, and in case of civil government by the mayor and justices of peace of the said city, may by order from your honours be bound over to appear before your Honours to answer such their contempt and disobedience. So humbly offering the consideration hereof unto your honours as a cause much concerning the peaceable estate of this city and the companies therein, we most humbly take our leave this 25th of September 1621.

3. THE GOLDSMITHS' COMPLAINTS AGAINST THE ALIENS, 1622
[P.R.O., SP 14/127, no. 12]

To the right worshipful Sir Robert Heath, knight, his Majesty's Solicitor, the answer of the Wardens of the Company of Goldsmiths, London.

ACCORDING to your worships' direction we do hereby deliver the number and names of the aliens and strangers (besides many others not yet discovered) using and abusing the goldsmith's profession with sundry grievances that this company of goldsmiths have long suffered and endured by aliens and strangers within and near this city, together with our opinions what we conceive to be the fittest course for reformation.

And first the names of the said aliens and strangers: [179 names follow]. By reason of their great and increasing number in buying, selling, and making of gold and silver wares, jewels, precious stones, and other employments within this city and suburbs solely and properly belonging to the goldsmith's profession free of this city, the said aliens and strangers do take away a great part of the living and maintenance of the free goldsmiths of this city who are thereby exceedingly impoverished and disabled in their estates to bear public charges.

That the said aliens and strangers in their habitations are dispersed into many lanes and remote places of this city and suburbs, working in chambers, garrets, and other secret places where the wardens of this company may not have convenient access and recourse to search, by which means besides the unlimited number of servants and apprentices aliens kept by the said aliens and strangers (in which particular they usurp and enjoy more privilege than the freemen of this city) they make and sell many deceitful jewels, pearls, counterfeit stones, and other goldsmith's wares of gold and silver to the great deceit of the nobility and people of this kingdom, it being partly the means that the use and exercise of other mean trades are crept into the goldsmiths' row in Cheap and Lombard Street to the great disgrace of this city.

For reformation of which inconveniences we conceive it to be the fittest course by the wisdom of the state to provide that the great multitude of such aliens and strangers may be reduced to a far less number. And that they may not take any servants or apprentices but by the approbation and allowance of the wardens of the company of goldsmiths of this city and be subject unto them and their ordinances in all matters of government concerning their mystery, as in former ancient times they have been accustomed and in all other well governed cities in foreign parts is used.

Secondly, that all such aliens and strangers may be strictly tied not to sell any jewels, plate, pearls, precious stones, or other goldsmiths' works of gold or silver, but to mere goldsmiths dwelling in Cheapside and Lombard Street, because it hath been often found by experience that aliens and strangers, having made or imported and here uttered such deceitful jewels, precious stones and pearls, and other goldsmiths' wares, have afterwards absented themselves into foreign parts to the great deceit and prejudice of the nobility and gentry of this nation; and many of the said aliens and strangers having bought jewels, pearls, and precious stones here of the nobility and others do secretly transport them into foreign parts by which practices his Majesty is greatly defrauded in his customs inward and outward.

Thirdly, that none of the said aliens or strangers be permitted to work in the goldsmith's profession for any other person but the goldsmiths aforesaid by which means we conceive that his Majesty's subjects shall receive better satisfaction and not be deceived as by often experience hath plainly appeared.

Fourthly, that for the avoiding of that daily great mischief in selling of stolen plate and other goldsmiths' wares in lanes and secret places and corners of this city and suburbs, which hath been and is prejudicial to many of his Majesty's good subjects and to continue the ancient beauty and ornament of this city, namely the goldsmiths' row in Cheap and Lombard Street, at this time so much changed by the mixture of inferior trades and occupations, that some speedy course be taken by the state to redress these mischiefs so apparently increasing.

Lastly, we conceive it will be very material and necessary in these times that the statute laws of this realm and common council of this city now in force concerning aliens and strangers be duly and strictly put in execution. All which premises we humbly leave to better judgement and consideration.

James Feke, John Braye, John Gravett, William Cawdell, Wardens of the Goldsmiths.

7 January, 1621

4. THE COOPERS' COMPLAINT AGAINST THE ALIENS, 1622
[P.R.O., SP 14/127, no. 14]

To the right worshipful Sir Robert Heath, knight, his Majesty's Solicitor, etc.

MAY it please your worship to be informed by us the Master and Wardens of the Company of Cowpers, London, that these parties hereunder named do employ and set on work in the art of cowpers these aliens hereunder also named, that is to say:

Mr. James Demetrius, a brewer in East Smithfield, an alien born, but as we are informed, naturalized, doth keep and employ in the same trade of cowpers John Lemans, Nicholas Stephens, Mathew Garnedg and another, cowpers' aliens. Mr. Peter Leonard, a brewer in East Smithfield, an alien born, keepeth also Peter Vandelore, Hance Coliner, Leonard Shoppas alias Sheepe, Harman Rowleff, cowpers' aliens.

Mr. Hayward, a brewer at Limehouse, keepeth also Derick Ornson, cowper's alien. Mr. ——, a brewer, at the Hermitage in St Katherine's keepeth John Jellicoe alias Jeninge, cowper's alien.

Mr. Paggen, a brewer at Dowgate keepeth Cornelius Husdell.

Also there are housekeepers aliens using the cowper's trade, viz. Albert. Cone alias Johnson, Widow Tibballs, Gyles de Grove, dwelling in East Smithfield, beside many others whom we cannot name.

And under favour we conceive if these aliens were not so employed, that then many poor cowpers, natural English, which are charged with wives, children, and families, and are not able to maintain them for want of work might be there employed and thereby the better enabled to maintain their charge. Beside the English coopers do bear and pay many assessments and duties which the aliens do not. And so we humbly take leave of your worship

Your worship's in all duty
The Master and Wardens of the Cowpers, London.

5. THE CLOCKMAKERS' PROTEST AGAINST THE ALIENS, 1622
[P.R.O., SP 14/127, no. 15]

The aggrievances of the clockmakers, citizens and inhabitants in London.

FIRST, they find themselves much aggrieved both in their estates, credits, and trading through the multiplicity of foreigners using their profession in London, for that the complainants, being housekeepers and charged and chargeable to all payments, taxes, and tallages for his Majesty and the city of London, they are interrupted and discredited in the use of their trade by the interposition of many strangers invading this realm; whereby their art is not only by the bad workmanship of strangers disgraced, but they disenabled to make sale of their commodities at such rates as they may reasonably live by.

Secondly, for that divers strangers inhabiting in and about London do usually go to gentlemen's and noblemen's chambers and other places to offer their works to sale, which (for the most part) being not serviceable (the parties buying the same for the outward show only, which commonly is beautiful), are much deceived in the true value, which rests in the inwork only, and cannot be amended or by the buyers perceived.

Thirdly, for that divers of the said art here have been so much abused by the said strangers, as that if any gentleman of worth have been in their shops, divers of them hereunder named strangers, born out of this kingdom, observing the same, have watched the gentleman going out of the complainants' shops, and not only disenabled the complainants' works, but have told them that the complainants bought their work of them, and that if those gentlemen would go with them, they would not only sell them the like but better cheap by much, whereby through the buyer's unskilfulness and the fugitiveness of the sellers, divers persons of worth have been utterly deceived of their money by strangers under colour of fair words and promises.

Fourthly, for that divers of the said strangers do not only inhabit privately in chambers in or near the city of London, and there live at easy and small rates and rents, not taxed as others, but grow so bold to intrude upon the privileges of this kingdom, that is not only to take apprentices with money for few years, but also to keep open shop, and those apprentices never being able to be made good workmen by them, the said strangers either (as commonly they do) departing this kingdom, leave those apprentices to make most unserviceable work, whereby the said art is not only disgraced but the buyers much abused and deceived.

Wherefore the said clockmakers, citizens and inhabitants in London, most humbly pray that forasmuch as the company of the said art are of themselves well able to serve this kingdom with good and serviceable work, and that strangers do much superabound them in number as by the names of both hereunder subscribed may appear, that you will be pleased (and the rather for that the laws of all foreign parts being that no Englishman or other stranger shall work there except under a master of the same nation where he shall be then resident) that the like course may be here taken; and that for the avoiding of the said deceits no foreign work may be imported of that nature upon such penalty as shall be fit. And your suppliants as in duty bound pray for your eternal prosperity.

Names of all the clockmakers householders in London. [16 names follow.]

The names of the known strangers of the same art dwelling in and about London. [32 names follow including 2 servants and 4 apprentices. 13 other apprentices are mentioned but not named.]

6. ALIEN BROKERS IN LONDON, 1622
[P.R.O., SP 14/127, no. 17]

The Names of all the Stranger Brokers in the City of London with the Places of their Habitation.

MARTIN GHERAERT in Lime Street; David Stanier in St Hellens; Paul Desmaistres in Lime Street; Charles Hugobart in Broad Street; David Derkin in Lothbury; Cornelius Mandervert in the Steelyard Manternach; Barnard Lutichius in Coleman Street; Peter van Dale in Lime Street; John Sion in Pudding Lane; John van Benden without Cripplegate; —— Lucutella the elder in Mark Lane; Augustine Lucutella in Fenchurch Street; Maure Barto in Lothbury; Esay Duce in Crutched Friars; John Clant upon Fresh Wharf; John de Lange in St Hellens; Walter Artfen in Buttolph Lane; John Blomer in Love Lane; William Byard in Love Lane; Vincent Syon on the Bankside; Abraham Villyers in Pudding Lane.

The Dutch brokers or leadgers, which do much wrong the commonwealth by engrossing all or most part of the seafish brought unto this city by water, as also for oil, madder, hops, and many other foreign commodities brought to this city to be sold, viz. Peter van Penan in St Buttolph's parish, Giles de Butt, and Francis Peneteare in Buttolph Lane.

7. THE COMPLAINT OF THE LEATHER DRESSERS AGAINST THE ALIENS, 1622[?]
[P.R.O., SP 14/127, no. 21]

To the right worshipful Sir Edmund Bowyer, knight lieutenant of this county of Surrey and to the rest of his Majesty's justices in Surrey, etc., the humble supplication and complaint of the leather dressers in and about the borough of Southwark in this county of Surrey.

MAY it please your worships to be advertised that we being many of us of our trade that have great charge of wife and children to maintain and by reason of some abuses amongst us are put out of work and have not wherewith to supply our necessities, but specially we find ourselves to be most wronged by one Peeter de Vons, a Dutchman, and therefore we beseech your worships to peruse these articles following, not doubting then but that you will take such order with him as others shall be thereby admonished how they do offend in the like nature.

First, the said Peeter de Vonse, being now a master workman, did never serve but three years at the said trade himself as an apprentice.[1] Secondly,

---

[1] A marginal note against this item says 'he will prove his [sic] served his time.'

the said Peeter doth set at work divers journeymen who never did serve their apprenticeships according to the statute in that case provided.[1] Thirdly, the said Peter doth say that he will maintain, uphold, and set at work such journeymen in despite of any man that shall say to the contrary.[2] Also the said Peeter hath set such offenders, being aliens and strangers, at work and put away ancient workmen that did serve their apprenticeships well and honestly and do pay all duties to them appertaining in the parishes where they do dwell.

Also certain of these offenders (which were strangers) being retained and set at work by the said Peeter have abused divers maids and gotten them with child, and when they have so done, they ran away, namely Henry de Vonse, brother to the said Peeter and one Henrick, his servant also. Moreover, the said Peeter doth besides the trade of a leatherdresser use the mystery or trade of a distiller of *aqua vitae* and the trade of a fuller which we think he cannot do, neither hath any Englishman amongst us the like privilege so to do.[3]

And whereas the said Peeter doth allege that the dressing of oil leather is no trade of Englishmen but a trade brought into England lately by the Dutchmen, but to that we answer that the Dutchmen did bring in the dressing of buff hides into oil leather here, but for buckskins, stag skins, goats, sheep skins, and lamb skins and the like, they were dressed here before any Dutchman dressed leather in England and doth belong to the trade of the glovers or leather dressers.

Moreover, whereas your worships did give order that one John Barkman, a Dutchman, should bring you a certificate that he had served his father three years, and then to be bound for four years more or else to serve seven years, this Peeter de Vonse hath reported that he will come and fetch this fellow from the house where he works and will set him at work in despite of any man.[4] Further, whereas the said Peeter saith that he is a free denizen, our request to your worships is that you would examine this point whether he be a lawful free denizen or no, and then he being one whether he be not subject to the same laws of this realm as we are or no.[5]

8. SIR WILLIAM COURTEN OBTAINS THE TRADING PRIVILEGES OF AN ENGLISHMAN, 1628

[*Acts of the Privy Council, September 1627–June 1628*, pp. 466–7]

30 May

WHEREAS by an order made the 26th of October last (for reasons therein expressed, and according to ancient usage) the sons of strangers till the

---

[1] Marginal note: 'if they be strangers, they must be subject.'
[2] Marginal note: 'He must have such as will do his work.'
[3] Marginal note: 'confesseth.'   [4] Marginal note: 'denyeth'.
[5] Marginal note: 'is a free denizen'.

second descent are to pay strangers' customs, which order is fit to be duly
kept for the advancement of his Majesty's customs, and whereas Sir William
Courten, knight, holding his case to be differing from others, exhibited a
petition this day to the Board, wherein he sheweth, that he was born in the
city of London, and that his father before him had been a long inhabitant
here in London, paying scot and lot in the city and all other duties (insomuch
as he was reputed as an Englishman), and at the time of the birth of the said
Sir William Courten (and before that) his father was a free denizen, and the
said Sir William ever since he traded hath enjoyed the privilege of an Englishman and paid his Majesty's customs accordingly, and hath settled himself
and laid out the most part of his estate within this kingdom, and planted
himself and his posterity here; for all which respects, but specially for divers
good offices and extraordinary services the said Sir William hath performed
to this state, therefore it is thought fit and so ordered that the said Sir William
shall from henceforth be suffered to trade freely (paying only his customs)
as an Englishman doth, and as formerly he hath done, we being well assured
that he will not make use of this liberty any way to his Majesty's disprofit (by
colouring any strangers' goods), but rather make it an encouragement to him
to trade more amply for the king's profit and his own. The premises therefore
considered, we do hereby declare that the said Sir William Courten, notwithstanding the former order of the 26th of October, is to enjoy this liberty
without interruption or molestation of any the officers towards the Custom
House. Whereof we pray and require the Lord Treasurer to take notice and
to give speedy and effectual order to the officers and farmers of the Customs
and others, whom it may concern, that they proceed accordingly. Dated etc.
[Signed:] Lord Keeper, Lord President, . . . [etc.].

9. ALIENS IN HATFIELD CHASE, 1636
[P.R.O., SP 16/327, no. 47]

[Archbishop Neile of York to Archbishop Laud]

Salutem in Christo

May it please your Grace to pardon me, if I trouble you with a longer
letter than perhaps you would expect. And to begin with those thanks which
I owe you, for your great love and favour which you showed to our church of
York, at the hearing of the cause betwixt the church and the city; and I
humbly pray your Grace to do me this favour, to present my most humble
and bounden service to his sacred Majesty, and dutiful acknowledgement of
his exceeding great goodness manifested to our church at his loyal hearing
and gracious ordering of that cause.

I make bold to acquaint your Grace with a business of importance (as I
think) much concerning both the state and the church, which I knew not of
till this my coming into the country, which is this. I find that the drainers

of the Level of Hatfield Chase do not employ any Englishmen (that I can hear of) in the husbanding of those grounds, but altogether employ Frenchmen, and a few Dutchmen, who come into the kingdom daily in great numbers, and are already become a plantation of some two hundred families (as I am informed), and more are daily expected to come by ships' fulls. I hear there is at this present a ship full at Hull yet unlanded, and another ship full is said to be at Harwich of the same kind. This new plantation hath been on foot for some years past, and they have set up among themselves the form and discipline of the French church. A barn of Sir Phillibert Vernatty is the place which they use for their church, whither the whole company have resort on Sundays; where they baptize in a dish, after their own manner, and administer the sacrament after their homely fashion of sitting. For their government, they have their consistory of the minister, three lay elders, and three deacons. The place or barn, wherein they perform their divine service, is on the very edge of Lincolnshire, adjoining upon Yorkshire; by advantage whereof, they pretend licence given them by the bishop of Lincoln, *non in scriptis, sed verbo tenus*, to have their exercises of religion according to the form of the French church, as it is permitted to French and Dutch in other parts of the realm. Their minister, who hath been with them these two years, is one Peter Bontemps, admitted into the ministry (as he saith) by the French ministers at Leyden. I have spoken with him, and from his mouth I have the effect of that I have here before written. I make bold to send your Grace a letter of his which he wrote to the Sharers in the Level whereby your Grace will see how it is endeavoured to bring the form of the French church into England, which I shall ever to the uttermost of my power oppose, and I trust his sacred Majesty will uphold me therein, and enable me to bring them to the practice of our book of Common Prayer and none other, they being permitted to have the use thereof in the French tongue; whereof they may have as many books already printed as they can desire.

I think your Grace can remember, how that one day I made known to the Lords of the Council, that Sir Phillibert Vernatty had moved me for my favour that the strangers, that dwelt upon this Level, might build a chapel for the exercise of divine service: whereto I answered I would afford them all lawful favour so as they would conform themselves to the Church of England; otherwise not. At which time I also moved their Lordships for their favour, that if Sir Phillibert Vernatty should at any time move their Lordships to any other purpose, their Lordships would second me in my resolution and answer given to him in this business: of which my motion their Lordships well allowed. And I beseech your Grace to move his Majesty to uphold me therein, that neither Sir Phillibert Vernatty nor any other may obtain anything of his Majesty to the contrary.

It seemeth, that upon the answer that I gave to Sir Phillibert Vernatty, he, finding how near Lincoln diocese bordered upon Yorkshire, made his recourse to my Lord of Lincoln, hoping to find that favour of him, which I had denied, and perhaps obtained as much as is aforesaid. I hear they have burned bricks, and are preparing materials to build a chapel there in Lincoln diocese, to which all the inhabitants of the Level, though dwelling in my diocese, might repair. But I shall (by the Grace of God) prohibit those that live in my diocese to go thither. I am very confident that your Grace doth favour me in this my resolution, and will assist me in constraining them to conform themselves to the Church of England. And I leave the politic part of this business to his Majesty's great wisdom and consideration, with what conveniency and safety to this state such a plantation should be permitted to be of strangers, men of very mean condition, that upon advantage may become as vipers nourished in our bosoms, that take the bread out of the mouths of English subjects by overbidding them in the rents of the land that they hold, and doing more work for a groat than an Englishman can do for sixpence. And if your Grace did know in what cottages these people live, and how they fare for food, you would wonder at it . . .

Your Grace's very loving friend and brother
B. Ebor.

From Southwell. 23 *Junii*, 1636

10. A DEFENCE OF ALIENS BY THOMAS VIOLET, 1653

[Thomas Violet, *Mysteries and Secrets of Trade and Mint Affairs* . . ., London, 1653, pp. 17–18. University of London, Goldsmiths' Library Pamphlet, Cat. No. 1307]

. . . If these merchant strangers, such as abide here with their families, were all naturalized, some men say they would buy up all our land, and in time supplant the nation. Truly the contrary hath been seen and known, for those that are here merchant strangers, but especially the Dutch, that have all turned into English; what wealth they have gotten, hath all been bestowed on the English nation: as first, Sir Peter Vanlore, Sir Thomas Curtel, Sir Moses Trian, Lucas Lucey, Vandeput, Fortrees, Lamot, Francis Sion, Jacob Oils, De Boise, Ganes, Matthew Godscale, Bultel Derrick Host, Hermes Dolens, Vanbrough, Littler Rousiot, Vandecouter, De Fisher, Terance, Lodick, Cross Corsellioos, Vanackers, De Labars, Chamberlain, Sir William Courten, Antonie, Sir Peter Ricot, Adam Lawrence, Lucas Jacobs, James Stenirs, Demestrias, Sass, Depester, and many more that abide and plant amongst us in London, and other parts of the nation, most of them are married into English families, and are English.

And it cannot be denied that most of these men have originally, by their forefathers, brought many industrious manufactures into this land; by which means, this nation hath equally been enriched with the merchant strangers; witness Colchester, Norwich, Canterbury, and the sea port towns wherein they live, the people being willing to pay all duties, and helpful to their neighbours, an industrious nation, and by their frugality, and long continuance in following their trade, attain the reward of their vigilance, being riches. And when that they have it, do they not disperse it amongst us, marrying our daughters, our sons marrying their daughters, and so we become one nation? I have ever esteemed a good Dutch merchant as beneficial to us and our nation, as they in Holland esteem of their Dutch cows; one brings a great deal of milk to the pail, and these men a great advantage to the commonwealth by planting amongst us. And put the case the state should, by privileges given them, invite many merchant strangers to come and plant amongst us, I say, merchants, and disperse themselves into several parts of this nation, and that these men would, and should be admitted to buy our lands, and bring over their banks of money, you would quickly find money to be here at five in the hundred, and your lands at double and treble the price. For in Holland, they will give three-score years' purchase for land; would not this, that they object as an argument against their coming hither, be the most advantageous to this nation, both to the gentry and tradesmen? The gentry should double and treble his stock in land, the tradesman would have money at five per cent whereas he pays now eight and can hardly get it. Besides, they give with their daughters great portions; a ton, and two tons of gold with one of them, is ordinary there. These men come to manure our lands, and improve our nation by their draining and other husbandry, to teach our nation the fishing trade, and make our harbours their storehouses, and what we have been so long labouring to get, which is their fishing trade, a great part will be brought to our harbours, and will invite and stir up our seamen by their example to be as industrious as they. And when all is done, this wealth wholly falls into this nation; for they are English in two ages, and by former experience, we know what great advantage we have had by their planting amongst us . . .

11. LONDON CRAFTSMEN PETITION AGAINST THE ALIENS, 1654

[P.R.O., SP 18/71, nos. 20 and 20, I]

To His Highness the Lord Protector of England, Scotland, and Ireland, and the Dominions thereunto belonging, the humble petition of the Masters and Wardens of the several handicraft companies of the city of London.

SHEWETH that your petitioners, hearing of a petition exhibited to the Parliament by the French and Walloon strangers residing in and about the city of London praying not only the exercise of their religion, but likewise the free use of their several trades; . . . your petitioners thereupon exhibited their petition to the honourable the Council of State praying a copy of the aliens' petition and to be heard, both which were granted by the Council of State . . .

Now forasmuch as your petitioners have observed the late Parliament and Council of State very ready to accelerate and answer the desires of the said aliens (a people no way beneficial or advantageous to this nation or to the cause asserted against the enemies thereof but rather affected to them) . . .

Your petitioners therefore most humbly desire your Highness would be pleased, according to your accustomed clemency and pious disposition for the administering of justice and that in a speedy manner (if it may stand with your Highness's wisdom and conveniency), to peruse your petitioners' grievances and reasons . . .

And your petitioners, as in duty bound, shall ever pray, etc.

John Parker, William Symonds, Henry White [and 22 other signatures, 4 of merchant tailors, six of weavers, 3 of comb makers, 3 of hatband makers, 3 of cutlers, and 3 of cardmakers].

[Endorsed:] 4 May, 1654. His Highness doth refer the consideration of this petition to the Council.—Jo. Thurloe.

*   *   *

Reasons humbly offered by the native manufactory tradesmen to this honourable Committee why aliens should not be permitted freely to use manufactory trades in or near London. And the mischiefs and inconveniences which will follow if they should be permitted so to do.

1. There is a sufficient number of natives of such artificers to supply this Commonwealth with all sorts of manufactories used in England and more now than can well live one by another.
2. These artificers are as able and skilful in their several trades as strangers, and so the less use of strangers.
3. By the Statute of 5 Eliz. cap. 4 all are restrained from working other than as apprentices until they have served full seven years at the least, which is a fair time to learn, and a long and difficult time to serve, and it with patience must be endured before they are permitted by the said statute to use any manufactory trade for themselves under great penalties. The reasons of making which statute were these two: first, that men should be skilful in such trades as they profess that the Commonwealth might be well served. Secondly, that some men might not presently leap into trade to the prejudice of others who have served a tedious apprenticeship for it, and many times, having better purses, might entertain servants and so engross work into their own hands to the enriching of themselves and impoverishing of others and that in relation of natives among themselves [sic].
4. There are none of these artificers natives but are of one corporation or other subject not only to view and search but also to punishment for their offence if any be found either of the badness and deceitfulness of their manufactories or for their working contrary to the law, and that not only by

the statute laws but by several ordinances and constitutions made in their several corporations for the better ordering and governing of their trades, to none of which strangers are liable.

5. And as they are all cast into one company or other, so they are subject and liable to all charges and offices in their companies for the supporting and upholding of their companies in credit and reputation, as also the managing and executing of those ordinances or bylaws searching and viewing the manufactory of their respective corporations, besides the offices that they are to bear and do bear in the Commonwealth from the scavenger to the Lord Mayor, together with their services in juries, assessors, and collectors of the monthly assessment, and all other ordinary and extraordinary employments through the whole course of their lives, to a very vast expense of their time, labour, and estates, to none of which any strangers are subject or liable.

6. So that reckon and accompt all these things together, and deduct these charges out of the gains of their several trades which must bear all, the strangers may well undersell them and so by an inevitable consequence will utterly ruin and undo them in short time which, they being a very considerable part of this nation for number and serviceable employments in the Commonwealth, cannot but produce very great mischiefs and inconveniences to the Commonwealth in general and to the said manufactory tradesmen in particular, trade by such means being so unequally balanced that the strangers will soon eat out the natives.

7. These strangers have engrossed a great part of the trade to themselves and invite over their own countrymen and employ them in their several trades when as the natives are enforced for want of employment in their trades to turn tankard bearers, porters, and to use other mean and servile employments for a miserable subsistence or to live idly or do worse, which cannot but be of very sad consequence in short time.

8. These strangers take great houses, and divide them into several habitations and take inmates and so pester all places where they come to the great danger of infection and noisome diseases which is found to be too true by too often experience.

9. It is believed that very few if any of these strangers which now use manufactory trades in and about London have been persecuted hither out of their own country for the Protestant religion. But if any such should be, it is humbly hoped that such persons shall not presently be in a better capacity than the natives here by setting up trades and being presently masters and taking what servants of their own countrymen they please, the law allowing them only to work as servants to the natives.

10. It is manifestly clear that whatsoever these strangers get in their trade is gotten from us who are not for the most part the richest men in this Commonwealth, and yet these strangers and their families are maintained altogether by getting what we should get in our trades for the maintenance of us and our families, so that the burden of keeping these men is by such means laid upon our shoulders who are most of us scarce able to sustain our burdens.

And if pretence of persecution for religion must serve the turn, it will soon occasion an inlet of strangers in such numbers as in short time would grow numberless if not prevented in time.

11. Divers Parliaments have been so sensible of the premises that they have made divers statutes directly to countenance and encourage the natives in their manufactory trades and utterly to suppress or qualify the using of the said trade by strangers or importing of manufactories made and wrought beyond the seas (a thing in these days very frequent and usual) as the statute of 7 Ed. 4, cap. 3; 1 R. 3, cap. 9 and 10, 1 Hen. 7, cap. 10, 21 H. 8, cap. 16, 22 Hen. 8, cap. 13, 32 Hen. 8, cap. 16. The reasons and causes of making the which said statutes are mentioned and expressed in the statutes themselves and are as follows: to restrain the excessive number and unreasonable behaviour of strangers; secondly, because of the great detriment which did arise thereby to the subjects in general; thirdly, because it occasioned the natives for lack of work to fall into idleness; fourthly, because of the great falsehood and deceit practised by strangers in the making of their wares and their uttering the same at unreasonable prices, and their cunning and deceitful avoiding the governors of trade when searched for unlawful and unserviceable wares; fifthly, because they subtly convey and send over sea divers prohibited commodities; sixthly, because when they have gathered much riches and money, they conveyed the same over sea; seventhly, because many times they converted the same to the supply of the enemies of the nation; eighthly, because many times through the occasion of want of work, the native artificers fell to theft, murder, and other great offences, and so were put to death by the law to the great dishonour of the English nation; ninthly, for that the great number and continual recourse of strangers caused an extreme scarcity of grain and victual throughout the Commonwealth.

Further Reasons presented by the Petitioners against the Strangers

1. Because the handicrafts have been the very nursery out of whom the greatest part of the soldiery since the beginning of the war hath been replenished.
2. Because the greatest part of the army consisteth of handicraftsmen.
3. Because they have engrossed the principal part of all handicraft trades into their own hands, and by reason thereof all those in the army, if they should be disbanded, would want employment.
4. Because they are persons generally disaffected to the Commonwealth and by reason thereof at the beginning of the late wars, whilst the petitioners engaged for the Parliament and declined their trades, the aliens stayed at home keeping servants of their own country and so by degrees got all trading into their own hands. So that the war being ended, the natives which hazarded their lives could get no work in their trades, by means whereof they were forced to fall to very dishonourable employments and into miserable inconveniences, viz. some to turn porters, labourers, chimney sweepers, and small coalmen, others to beg their bread for themselves and families, and others to leave their wives and children and go into remote and obscure places.

5. Inasmuch as the statute appoints every man that is to have benefit by any trade to serve seven years at the least and prohibits everyone that doth not, and inasmuch as it is by virtue of the law only that we enjoy whether lands or goods, which assigns and marks out to everyone his proper part, and declares what he may call his own and what not. Therefore, by the same reason that strangers shall be permitted to come and take away from the natives the benefit of their trade having not served for the same; by the same may they come and share with any man in his inheritance, the native having acquired as great an interest and profit in his trade by his service, undergone many times with unspeakable hardship and tediousness of time, as the purchaser hath in his lands by his money.

If it be objected they are Protestants and fly hither because of persecution, to this we answer: first, that if being a Protestant be a good argument for strangers to use a trade, then would it be far better argument for the natives who ought much more to be admitted, not only because they are Protestants but because they had the happiness to be born within the Commonwealth of England. But if strangers shall be permitted and Englishmen denied, certainly they might accompt it a nursery to be born in England. Secondly, admit they fly hither for persecution, it doth not therefore follow they should be masters as soon as they come over. But the law hath provided as well for the preservation of strangers by allowing them to work to English masters as servants and thereby to get a maintenance, as also for the good of Englishmen by giving them the precedency, wherein the law more regarded the setting of the affections of the natives than the praise of the aliens; for it cannot be judged prudence so to gratify the one and discontent the other. Thirdly, because it is the practice of all other nations to prefer their natives before strangers. And hence it is if an Englishman goeth into France or Germany he shall not be permitted to work but as a servant although they are of the same religion or profession with themselves. Lastly, we desire these intrusions and usurpations of strangers may be suppressed, not only for the reasons aforesaid but also because of the near relations between the Commonwealth and the governors thereof, who are as it were the fathers, guardians, and protectors of their people and so have been accounted in all ages.

12. THE ALIEN COMMUNITY IN NORWICH, 1655
[P.R.O., SP 18/101, nos. 6; 6, I, and 6, II]

To His Highness the Lord Protector of the Commonwealth of England, Scotland, and Ireland, and the Dominions thereunto belonging, the humble petition of the strangers of the Walloon congregation of the City of Norwich.

MOST humbly sheweth that your petitioners for their religion deserted their native countries and are Protestants of the reformed religion professed in

England and in times of persecution have always found this country their sanctuary and refuge, and this nation their defence; and by the Letters Patents of King Edward the sixth, Queen Elizabeth, and their successors have constantly been warranted and upheld, under whose shelter they have not only enjoyed the free use and exercise of their religion in their native language, but were also freely permitted to use their several trades and thereby maintained their ministers and poor, and, moreover, upon all occasions have voluntarily lent and contributed their monies, diligently paid their assessments both lot and scot in their several parishes for the ministry and poor of the same.

Now forasmuch as your petitioners are a congregation consisting most of handicraftsmen are and have been of late years hindered from the setting awork of strangers that have repaired hither for the free exercise of their religion, whereby their said congregation is already extremely diminished, and without some speedy remedy will undoubtedly be ruined. And divers Protestants beyond the sea living in persecution will be totally disencouraged to come and shelter themselves in these countries, by reason whereof your petitioners will no ways be able to maintain their poor, whose only subsistence is the voluntary contributions of the members of the said congregation.

Your petitioners may to the honour of their city with all humility declare that Norwich was the first place that friendly received Protestant strangers, and those strangers were the first that learned the English divers and sundry manufactures made of wool which formerly were exported, tending much to the enriching of this nation and increasing of trade in this Commonwealth, and have always since been upheld by former princes and countenanced by the mayor and aldermen of the said city, as your petitioners can by divers acts make it appear.

Wherefore your petitioners most humbly pray that your Highness would be graciously pleased to confirm the privileges granted them by King Edward and his successors, as well for the free exercise of their religion in their own language, as for the use and exercise of their trades, and that such liberty may be granted to Protestant strangers as shall repair hither as your Highness in your grave wisdom shall think fitting, that so your petitioners may peaceably enjoy the benefit thereof by maintaining their charge and also paying of other duties and taxes as formerly they have done.

And your petitioners as by duty bound shall ever pray, etc.

*   *   *

To all right honourable right worshipful and others of what estate or degree soever to whom these presents shall appertain or the same shall see or read, Thomas Anguish, mayor of the City of Norwich and others the justices of the peace of our sovereign lord the King for the county of the said city and the rest of the aldermen in the same, greeting in our Lord God.

Know ye that in the 17th year of the reign of our late sovereign Lady Queen Elizabeth many aliens strangers born out of the realm of England were by

her Majesty's Letters Patents of toleration under her great seal of England
licensed and admitted to dwell and inhabit within the city for the exercising
the faculties of making many and sundry outlandish commodities of new
denise [=design?] which had not been used or seen made within the said
realm of England; and who were means to convert wools of all sorts growing
in this realm into their several stuffs of new denise and to set no small numbers
of the poorer sort of people to work whereby great numbers of the said poor
were kept from idleness and begging. Since which time many of those strangers have departed out of the said realm and some are dead, others have come
and succeeded and do inhabit, dwell, and abide in the said city by virtue of
the said Letters Patents, and do use and exercise the making and working of
sundry sorts of cloths and stuffs of new denise; and at their first entrance to
dwell in the said city did willingly submit themselves to be ordered and
governed by many good and profitable constitutions and orders denised and
made, part by the governors of the city and part by themselves, ratified,
allowed, and confirmed by the magistrates of the same city as well for their
quiet and peaceable government as for the true and workmanly making of
their said stuffs and commodities not formerly made within this realm, as the
subjects and people that should buy, sell, and merchandise the same should
not be deceived or defrauded either breadth, length, and number of threads
which every sort of their cloths should be of and contain; for which purpose
and better performance of those services, and to continue their stuffs in
credit both with the merchant and retailer, the said strangers had, ever since
their coming to the said city, and yet have officers yearly sworn before the
mayor of the said city to view, search, and so continually those orders and
constitutions to be truly observed and kept, and the offenders in any sort or
kind to be duly punished; among which alien strangers many of the Walloon
country did and yet do inhabit and dwell within the said city, and are of the
French congregation in the same; and have been there resident by the space
of six and forty years together, who have exercised, made, and wrought
sundry cloths and stuffs called buffins, mockadoes, velours all of linen,
velours, linen, and cruell carletts, damask, says of dry cruell after the fashion
Lile Ameens and Monydry, grograins, double mockadoes, ollyets, bumbasins
of silk and sciet [sic], silk burrato bumbasins alias rash, with the ground of
linen, silk, says, tuft, taffety all silk, striped says, broad lyles, Spanish satins,
cross billetts of silk and sciet fustinado, fustian of linen, and catton filizetis of
cruel serge de Boice of cruell, silk filizetis, silk serge de Boice, silk say, striped
tobines, silk tufted and striped great waled satins, catalownes trepodelis,
tufted buffins, catalowne says, striped and plain serges de boice in catalowne
figuratoes brato pearled and striped tufted says and such like of new denise,
having duly observed and kept those ordinances and constitutions so made
and allowed as aforesaid. And do in all dutiful obedience submit themselves
to be ordered and governed according to the first meaning and intention of
their receiving and allowance to inhabit within the said city; and so continue
true and faithful as well in the workmanship and goodness of their stuffs as

in the length, breadth, and numbers of threads, which in their several works are to be observed and kept, which are from time to time viewed and searched by the sworn officers who give them seals by which is discerned in all points their goodness and their defects, if any be either in length, breadth, workmanship, or number of threads, so as the simplest cannot be deceived in them. And by their endeavours and labours do so exercise themselves and families according to their callings as they continue both profitable to the commonweal and maintenance of themselves, their wives, and children and in such sort as they have not one begging person among them to their great commendation. All which as well in regard of their long continuance amongst us, their dutiful and lowly behaviour to governors and government, as at the humble suit of the said Walloons, we have caused this our certificate and testimonial to be made in form aforesaid.

Given under the Seal of Mayoralty of the said City of Norwich; and to the which the justices of peace and the rest of the aldermen in the said city have fixed their seals and subscribed their names, the 10th day of December in the 9th year of the reign of our sovereign Lord James by the grace of God, king of England, France, and Ireland, Defender of the Faith, and of Scotland the five and fortieth, 1611.

And subscribed [22 signatures including that of Thomas Anguish, mayor]. And sealed with two and twenty seals on red wax thereunder imprinted. This present copy agreeth word for word with the original *Quod attestatur Wyatus.*

Daniel Scot, public notary[?].

1655

*   *   *

Copy

Whereas a petition hath been lately exhibited unto His Majesty by certain Walloon weavers within the City of Norwich on the behalf of themselves and the rest of their nation and company humbly representing that notwithstanding sundry gracious and extraordinary privileges and liberties granted unto them by the late Queen of famous memory under the Great Seal of England concerning the free exercise of their trade and mystery in making stuffs of New Drapery and other manufactures within that city, certain busy promoters have lately called them into question by information in the Crown Office, pretending the breach of a statute for bringing up their children and servants in the foresaid mystery without binding them to serve apprenticeships for seven years as his Majesty's natural born subjects in such cases are enjoined to do, forasmuch as his Majesty is given to understand that the said company of Walloons are a peculiar society under the government of the Mayor, Justices, and Aldermen of that city of Norwich, who are appointed to oversee their works and manufactures and accordingly to give allowance thereof, and that by ancient custom, privilege, and toleration they have been always exempted from the yoke of the statute aforementioned, and therefore the proceedings which have been used against them in that respect to be sinister and not warrantable, savouring rather of corruption than intent of reformation. As well for these just considerations as also in respect of the extraordinary merit of that people who by their commendable skill and industry have so singularly deserved of that city and of the Commonwealth in general and, which is not to be forgotten, by that free and voluntary contribution wherewith they have lately charged themselves towards the present loan, have particularly testified their humble duty, zeal, and affection to his Majesty, as by the right honourable the Earl of Northampton, Lord Lieutenant of that county unto his Majesty is reported. It is therefore this day ordered and determined (his Majesty's express pleasure signified) that the petitioners and generally all the Walloon congregation in the City of Norwich shall freely enjoy such benefit of toleration in the exercise of their religion and course of their trades as hitherto they have done, and that no information shall be accepted of against the said company of Walloons for not having served their apprenticeships according to the statute aforementioned, and that in the mean time all informations already preferred against them be discharged; and the names of such informers or other persons as shall presume hereafter to molest them to be presented to this Board. Whereof the Mayor, Justices, and Aldermen of the city of Norwich are to take notice, and to see the order precisely and carefully performed accordingly forasmuch as concerneth them and every of them in their several places and authority. Given at the Court at Whitehall, the xxixth of March, 1612.

Was subscribed [10 signatures including that of the Earl of Northampton], and was sealed with a seal on red wax at the beginning in the main entry. The present copy agreeth word for word with the original. *Quod attestatur Wyatus*

Daniel Scot, public notary[?]

[Endorsed:] A Petition of the Walloon Church at Norwich. Rec. 30 Oct. 1655.

13. AN ALIEN FELTMAKER OF MAIDSTONE COMPLAINS OF INTERFERENCE IN HIS TRADE, 1658

[P.R.O., SP 18/183, nos. 58 and 58, I]

To his Highness the Lord Protector of England, Scotland, and Ireland, etc., the humble petition of Salomon Gravett of Maidstone in Kent.

HUMBLY sheweth that your petitioner, being born in the dominions of the King of Spain near Flanders and being a Protestant, hath been forced to shelter himself in England these twenty years to enjoy the liberty of his religion, where he hath married to an English wife, whom, together with children he hath of her, he hath for some years maintained peaceably by a lawful calling, being a feltmaker of his trade. But the Company of Hatmakers of London and the Haberdashers about the place of his residence have of late, to his utter undoing and of his family's, disturbed him in the exercise of his said trade, upon pretence that being a stranger he is forbidden by the laws of the land to exercise any calling.

He therefore humbly prayeth that your Highness in the tender respects of the Protestant religion and charity to a poor stranger driven out of his own country for the same, and who hath all the time he hath lived in England behaved himself according to that profession and in all submissive obedience to the present government, will graciously be pleased to grant him the liberty of maintaining his family as he hath done by his poor calling or trade.

And your poor petitioner as in duty bound shall ever pray, etc.

Solomon Gravett

Rec. 26 October, 1658

*　　*　　*

Right Honourable,

I am bold to trouble your Lordship on the behalf of this bearer, one Solomon Gravett, a poor Protestant stranger, born in Hainault in High Flanders, and now for divers years past inhabiting in this town of Maidstone, who from his youth together with his father about twenty years since were forced to forsake their country and come for shelter for religion's sake into England, where he hath ever since continued and hath exercised the trade of a felt-maker to which he was brought up; and did enjoy the use of several years in London as other Protestant strangers in like condition according to the several grants unto them by Letters Patents in the times of Queen Elizabeth, King James, and the late King Charles; the continuance of which liberties, as I am informed, was by the Parliament in the time of the late Lord Protector recommended to the care of the Council. In pursuance whereof the Lord President of the Council directed his letters to the Lord Mayor, of some of which particulars he hath copies to shew your Lordship for further satisfaction. But so it is that of late he hath been several times prosecuted by indictments here in this town upon the statute of the first of King James, chapter 17, for using that trade, not having served therein seven years as an apprentice. But upon consideration of the general importance of the case hath been dismissed the court. But he is now prosecuted by information against him for the same cause in the Exchequer Court, where he is to appear to answer upon this first return of this term the 20th day of this instant October. I knew not to whom better to recommend his case, being of so general a concernment to all Protestant strangers, than to yourself whom I know to be tenderly apprehensive of cases of this nature. You will perceive by his copies of the Council's letters what resentment the like case hath formerly found with the Parliament, the Lord Protector, and Council, besides what hath been under former governments, as the copies of the Letters Patents will make appear, which doth the more embolden me to give your Lordship this present trouble of promoting his address unto you, craving your Lordship's furtherance to the poor man in his humble petition so far as it shall appear unto you to be just and honourable. The person, so far as I could observe of him during his abode here in this town, doth carry himself diligently and industriously in his calling and soberly and orderly in his conversation. I shall not add further to your trouble at present but craving pardon I rest

Your Lordship's most humble servant.

Lambarde Godfrey

Maidstone, 9th
October, 1658

[Endorsed:] Solomon Gravet. To the Right Honourable the Lord Philip Jones, one of the lords of His Highness's Privy Council, these humbly present.

14. A PETITION BY LONDON CRAFTSMEN AGAINST THE ALIENS, 1660

[P.R.O., SP 29/21, no. 108]

To the King's most excellent Majesty,
the humble petition of divers shopkeepers, tradesmen, and artificers,
as well in behalf of themselves as of several thousands of others
inhabiting in and about your Majesty's City of London.

MOST humbly sheweth that your petitioners have heretofore by means of those good laws made obtained a livelihood for themselves and families and been enabled with freedom and cheerfulness to contribute towards your Majesty's subsidies and other public charge, strict provision having been made by the statute of the 3rd of Edward IV and the 19th of Henry VII against the importing of several commodities of your petitioners' trades, as woollen cloth, laces, corses, ribbons, fringes of silk and of thread, laces of thread silk, twined silk in any wise embroidered, laces of gold, of silk or gold points, girdles, calls, and divers other commodities in the said statutes particularly mentioned. By reason of which laws the natives were well provided for and the English trade exceedingly encouraged and so abundantly increased that it brought not only a great advantage to the kingdom in respect of customs but many thousand persons in and about London have had their absolute subsistence and dependence thereupon.

But now so it is, may it please your Majesty, that of late years all sorts of manufactures contrary to those laws have been imported in great quantities by occasion of the confederacy with the French by the late usurper Cromwell, not only in violation of the laws of the kingdom but to the ruin of thousands of your petitioners and the English trade. And your petitioners do further show unto your gracious Majesty that divers aliens and others under them do daily import from France and other parts several sorts of commodities into your Majesty's kingdom of England besides the goods prohibited above mentioned, as all sorts of rich French silks and stuffs, all sorts of gold and silver laces, buttons, and all kinds of embroidery, and divers other wares and merchandises, which they offer here to sell by retail to all manner of persons, especially to the gentry and others of great quality in their families, inns, chambers, and other private places, contrary to the statutes made in the 16 of Richard II and the 1st. of Richard III and to divers other wholesome laws and statutes made in the reign of several kings and queens of England, your Majesty's royal progenitors, and against the charter and privileges of your great city of London, and is an exceeding damage to your royal Majesty's revenue by defrauding you of your customs, the persons that thus sell having no certain habitations nor bear any charges in this your kingdom.

And besides the offences above mentioned under which your petitioners have a long time so sadly groaned, your petitioners do humbly shew unto your Majesty that multitudes of aliens have also taken upon them to exercise their several vocations within this city and liberties thereof and places adjacent contrary to the several statutes of the 1st of Richard III, the 1st of Henry VII, and the 5th of Elizabeth in that behalf made and against the right and customs of the city of London, being encouraged thereunto by pretence of certain letters of grace pretended to be granted by the aforesaid usurper Cromwell.

By means of all which premises if some timely remedy be not applied your petitioners do with much sorrow of heart conceive that the utter ruin of the trade of this your city of London is approaching, and that the manufacture of your liege people in general all through this your Majesty's kingdom will be utterly overthrown thereby and your petitioners with many other corporations impoverished and undone.

And forasmuch as your Majesty's laws could not be put in execution against those offenders by reason of the late troubles and the usurped power over your Majesty's liege people, whereby the offenders are grown to so great a number and carry their business with so much subtlety and privacy that it is impossible for your petitioners to discover their practices or to bring informations against them according to law, such liberty not being endured by other nations, many of your petitioners having felt the grievous rigour of their laws for exercising their trades amongst them.

In tender consideration whereof we your Majesty's most loyal and obedient subjects being encouraged by your Majesty's gracious letter from Breda testifying your princely and zealous affection for the good of this city in particular and of your kingdom in general do humbly implore your Majesty to take the premises into your grave and serious consideration, and that your Majesty will be graciously pleased to grant your royal proclamation strictly prohibiting the importation of the commodities before mentioned to be prohibited and forbidding of aliens from exercising their several vocations in this your kingdom. And that the several statutes and laws in force may be speedily executed against the said several offenders in such manner as to your royal Majesty's wisdom shall seem expedient. And your petitioners as in all duty bound shall ever pray for your Majesty's long reign and happiness.

Wm. Bolton; Charles Doyley; Francis Manby; Jo. Turner [and four more pages of signatures].

[Endorsed:] At the Court at Whitehall this 24th of November, 1660.

His Majesty is graciously pleased to refer this petition to the lords his Majesty's most honourable Privy Council to consider thereof and advise his Majesty what they conceive fit to be done therein and then his Majesty will declare his further pleasure.

Edw. Nicholas

15. THE COUNCIL OF TRADE DELIBERATES ON THE PETITION AGAINST THE ALIENS, 1661

[P.R.O., SP 29/21, no. 110]

Opinion of the Council of Trade upon shopkeepers' petition.

Thursday, 14th of March, 1660
At the Council for Trade

Mercers' Hall, London.

May it please your Majesty,

In obedience to your Majesty's order, sitting in your royal Council dated the 28th of November last, upon the petition of the shopkeepers, tradesmen, and artificers [of] London annexed, this Council have seriously considered the contents thereof at several meetings. And having conferred with the petitioners thereupon, have examined the statutes cited in the petition, and had several affidavits produced to prove the matter of fact complained of. And do humbly certify that they do find the whole, as it is therein stated, to be true. But as to the remedy propounded by the petitioners, this Council humbly offer as followeth:

1. It is true that there are multitudes of foreigners who do employ themselves in the manufactures specified in the petition about the City of London; but

i. The number of them are very great, amounting to very many thousands and to hinder them from exercising their crafts were to expose them to very great misery.

ii. Very many or the most part of them have planted themselves here for their religion and conscience sake.

iii. The Hollanders do invite all sorts of strangers to come and dwell among them, especially handicraft men, and it is certain that in the multitude of a people consists the strength of a kingdom.

iv. If these people should remove, they would plant their manufactures elsewhere to the prejudice of the kingdom; as, on the contrary, by strangers coming hither, they have from time to time brought into this kingdom the most considerable manufactures of wools, as the baymaking of Colchester, the stuffs of Norwich and Sandwich etc., and all other old and new Drapery, as also of silks, as the silks-making of London, Canterbury, etc.

v. These are a poor sort of people who do not remove their habitations and so carry not the wealth of the land out of the kingdom, but marry and incorporate here and bring their children up in the same crafts and occupations, who become native English.

So as for these reasons, this Council cannot think fit to offer at any new thing for restraining of them. But as to the laws in force the petitioners may take their course.

2. As to the importation of foreign manufactures also complained of in the said petition, this Council find it too true that great quantities of those and other such manufactures are daily imported to the great prejudice of this kingdom, whose poor are thereby defrauded of the subsistence they might have by the making thereof at home, and vast quantities of money and bullion are exported for the purchasing these foreign fancies, and they find that this evil doth daily increase. But as to the remedy propounded by the petitioners, viz. a proclamation prohibiting the importation thereof, this Council humbly conceive that this will not do the work, in regard:

i. The statutes against their importation are very express and in force, and the law open.

ii. The customs to be paid for them are so great as that if they were duly paid the importers could not be able to sell them to any profit.

iii. But these being fine goods of small bulk and of great value are stolen in and do avoid both the statutes and the custom house, and consequently will also avoid his Majesty's proclamation.

But this Council is of opinion that if it shall be thought fit by example to encourage the wearing of English manufactures and to discountenance the wearing and wearers of foreign manufactures, as it would take off the opinion of foreign, so it would bring into fashion and esteem the home-made manufacture. And in the issue would both produce all those good effects which the laws intended, and also with better success attain the end aimed at by the petitioners than the proclamation propounded and desired.

16. AN ACT TO ATTRACT ALIEN WORKERS IN LINEN AND TAPESTRY, 1663

[Statutes of the Realm, V, p. 498]

An Act for Encouraging the Manufactures of Making Linen Cloth and Tapestry (15 Car. II, c. 15)

Recital that manufactures of foreign hemp, etc. is imported, to the detriment of the kingdom. WHEREAS vast quantities of linen cloth and other manufactures of hemp and flax and of tapestry hangings are daily imported into this kingdom from foreign parts to the great detriment and impoverishment thereof, the monies and quick stock of this kingdom being thereby daily greatly exhausted and diminished and the poor thereof unemployed while the materials for the Reasons for passing this Act. making of such hangings are here more plentiful and better and cheaper than those places from whence they are imported, and flax and hemp might be had here in great abundance and very good if by setting up the manufacture of such commodities as are made thereof it would be taken off the hands of such as sow and plant the same; for the encouragement therefore of those manufactures be it enacted and it is hereby enacted by the King's most excellent Majesty by and with the advice and consent of the Lords Spiritual and Temporal and Commons in this present Parliament assembled and by the All persons, natives or foreigners, may without fee set up and use the dressing and other trades of hemp trades herein mentioned. authority thereof that from and after the first day of October next ensuing it shall and may be lawful for any person or persons whatsoever, native or foreigner, freely and without paying any acknowledgement fee or other gratuity for the same in any place of England or Wales privileged or unprivileged, corporate or not corporate, to set up and exercise the trade, occupation, or mystery of breaking, hickling, or dressing of hemp or flax as also for making and whitening of thread, as also of spinning, weaving, making, whitening, or bleaching of any sort of cloth whatsoever made of hemp or flax only, as also the trade, occupation, or mystery of making of twine or nets for fishery or of stoving of cordage, as also the trade, occupation, or mystery of making any sort of tapestry hangings; any law, statute, or usage to the contrary in any wise notwithstanding.

And all foreigners that shall really and bona fide set up and use any of the II. Foreigners using any of the said trades for three years, and taking the oaths of allegiance and supremacy, to be considered as natural born subjects. trades and manufactures aforesaid by the space of three years in this kingdom of England, dominion of Wales, and town of Berwick upon Tweed shall from thenceforth, taking the oaths of allegiance and supremacy before two justices of the peace near unto their dwellings who are hereby authorized to administer the same, enjoy all privileges whatsoever as the natural born subjects of this kingdom.

And it is hereby enacted and declared that such foreigners as shall exercise III. Not to be liable to greater taxes, etc. Exception. any of the trades aforesaid by virtue of this Act shall not any time be liable to any other or greater taxes, payments, or impositions than such as are or shall be paid by his Majesty's natural born subjects unless in case they shall use and exercise merchandise into and from foreign parts, in which case they shall be liable to pay such customs as have usually been paid by aliens during the space of five years next ensuing and no longer.

17. A PLEA ON BEHALF OF ALIEN IMMIGRANTS,
c. 1668–9[?]
[Bodleian Library, Oxford, MS. Rawlinson A 478, ff. 28, 97][1]

For the right honourable the Lords of the Committee of Trade. Reasons humbly offered by the ministers and others of the French and Dutch churches, London, to back the petition wherein we beg from his Majesty a liberty for the artificers of other countries that come to settle here.

1. It is evident that thereby the manufactures which hitherto have been and still are made in France, Flanders, and Holland might be made here.
2. We humbly conceive that the same reasons which moved the Parliament to make an act for the improvement of the manufactures of linning, etc., may move his sacred Majesty to grant the same liberty and privilege to all weavers of silk, hair, or worsted stuff, for the quantities of these commodities that are made beyond the seas and daily imported into this kingdom are as considerable as those that are made of flax and hemp. It is true indeed that silk and hair do not grow here as flax and hemp. But if those kinds of manufactures were encouraged here, whereas vast quantities of raw silks, mohairs, yarn, and wools are constantly fetch[ed] by the French and others from Turkey and Italy wherewith they make silks and hair stuffs, which are afterwards imported into this realm, the English merchants might be encouraged to send for greater quantities of the said commodities and thereby should be sold so much the more of the ancient wool manufactures of this kingdom.
3. We humbly conceive that the granting of such a liberty is the best way to attain the end which the Parliament aimed at in making the Act before mentioned, for there would come from beyond the seas more linning weavers if they were sure that in case they find no employment in that kind of weaving, they shall be suffered to work in silk and hair stuffs for to get a present subsistence.

These reasons we should not have been so bold as to offer had we not had your honours' command to do it, so we humbly entreat your lordships to represent our humble desires to his sacred Majesty by such ways and reasons as to your honours shall seem best that so by your honours' means we may obtain from his Majesty some favours in the behalf of the strangers who come here to enjoy more freely the liberty of their consciences.

[1] An inscription on the flyleaf of this volume describes it as the 'MS. of William Bridgeman, esq., clerk of the Council in the reign of King James II'. But the argument of this document is closely linked with the debate on the decay of trade, 1669. See above, pp. 68–78. Moreover, the proposals of the French congregation in the second document seem to be linked with the remarks of Thomas Papillon of London, merchant, to the Committee of the House of Lords on the Decay of Rents and Trade. His own version of what he said to that committee included the following: 'I gave them an account of some French weavers that were now imprisoned by the Weavers Company for working here, which practice was to drive away trade and not the way to increase it.'—A. F. W. Papillon, *Memoirs of Thomas Papillon of London, Merchant, 1623–1702*, 1887, pp. 71–2.

We do humbly conceive that the reasons which moved the Parliament to make an act for linning weavers and others might also move his Majesty to give liberty to the silk weavers and several other handicraftmen. So we humbly beseech his Majesty to grant us such a gracious letter as did his glorious predecessors and to declare to the Companies that his royal will and pleasure is that they should not molest or disturb those that come over from beyond the seas nor them that set them at work or else to find another way in his great wisdom he shall think convenient.

* * *

Proposals made by the French congregation in London to the bailiffs, wardens, and assistants of the Worshipful Company of Weavers of London.

First that it may please the said bailiffs, wardens, and assistants to cause the four prisoners now in the new prison at Clerkenwell upon the indictments of certain of the yeomanry of the said Company to be set at liberty.

Secondly, that the said bailiffs, wardens, assistants, and company of weavers will be pleased to permit and suffer the said four prisoners and other Protestant strangers now in this kingdom, and those that shall come hither to make profession of the Protestant religion, to work and to be set at work, and to employ others to work of the weaving trade without trouble or molestation to them or those that shall employ them; provided the said persons have served to the trade of weaving according to the custom of the several places from whence they came or shall come, and that they make it appear by indentures, letters of mastership, certificate, or other testimony, or else that they are sons of master weavers or have sufficient skill in the said mystery, they paying to the Company of Weavers the usual rates for their admittance to work and do as aforesaid.

Thirdly, that the above mentioned persons may be permitted to use the abovesaid trade six months before such their admission.

Which proposals contain no greater liberty than those strangers that now are here and their predecessors have had and enjoyed for one hundred years last past or more.

And these proposals are made with humble submission to his sacred Majesty and his most honourable Privy Council for their approbation.

18. ARGUMENTS IN FAVOUR OF NATURALIZING ALIENS, 1673

[*The Grand Concern of England explained, in several Proposals offered to the Consideration of Parliament . . . by a lover of his Country and Well-wisher to the Prosperity both of the King and Kingdoms*, London, 1673, *Harleian Miscellany*, VIII, London, 1746, pp. 532–4]

. . . The fourth thing proposed is, that an Act be passed for a general naturalization of all foreign Protestants, and for granting liberty of conscience to such of them as shall come over and inhabit amongst us, and that the like liberty be given to his Majesty's subjects at home. There is nothing so much wanting in England as people; and, of all sorts of people, the industrious and laborious sort, and handicraftmen, are wanted to till and improve our land, and help to manufacture the staple commodities of the kingdom; which would add greatly to the riches thereof.

The two last great plagues, the Civil Wars at home, and the several wars with Holland, Spain, and France, have destroyed several hundred thousands of men, which lived amongst us; besides, vast numbers have transported themselves, or been transported into Ireland and other our foreign plantations; who, when they were living amongst us, did eat our provisions, wore off our manufactures; employed themselves in some calling or other, beneficial to the nation; the want of which calls for a supply of people from some place or other; and it is, in my judgement, worthy our observation, that the men, thus lost from amongst us, are of greater consideration, and the loss more mischievous to the kingdom than merely the death or removal of so many persons, considering that they were men in the prime of their years in perfect strength; such, who had they not died, or been killed, or removed, might every year have begotten children, and thereby increased the world; so that three times the number of children might have been better spared than they. For instance: say there be but one hundred thousand men, by these means, gone from amongst us; and, instead of them three hundred thousand children had been taken away, and the men left, it would have been much better; for they in two years and a half, or three years' time, might have gotten so many children again; but the men dying or being gone, and the children living, it may be ten or twenty years before they come to marry and beget children. And, notwithstanding the great mischief this nation hath sustained by the loss of these men, yet so inconsiderate are the inhabitants thereof, concerning their own interest (which, if possible, is to have the kingdom full of people) that they are taking up another way to prevent the peopling thereof for the future, there being, almost all over England, a spirit of madness running abroad, and possessing men against marrying, rather choosing to have mistresses, by whom very few ever have any children. And many married women, by their lewd conversations, prevent the bringing forth many children, which otherwise they might have had. These humours and practices, if continued, will prove so mischievous, that, unless foreigners come in amongst us, in few years there will not be people to manure our lands, eat our provisions, wear our manufactures, or manufacture the staple commodities that are of the growth of the kingdom; without which, it is no wonder if lands yield little rent, or sell not for above fourteen or fifteen years' purchase.

And if foreigners must come over, or our estates here grow worse, there must then encouragement be given them so to do; else they will think themselves well seated where they are, following their trades, increasing their estates, enjoying all the liberties and privileges of free-born subjects, know how, and have liberty and encouragement, to improve their estates; and, when they have got them, can keep them; therefore will never come themselves, nor bring over their families or estates amongst us here, to be accounted of as aliens or strangers, such as may not purchase estates amongst us; and, if they do, shall not enjoy the same, nor their children after them. That sort of people which we most want are such, who, though they would come over and dwell amongst us, yet cannot spare fifty or sixty pounds out of their stock to procure themselves naturalized by Act of Parliament; especially if they bring over wife and children with them, which would be more advantageous for us, than for them to come over alone. Or, if they should spare money to naturalize themselves, yet, perhaps, they may not have so much as to pay for the naturalizing of their wives and children; who, as our laws are, cannot be permitted to inherit what their fathers purchase, unless they be naturalized also. So that an Act for a general naturalization is absolutely necessary, if we will be supplied with people from foreign parts. But the passing such an Act alone will not be sufficient to encourage foreigners to come and dwell amongst us; there must be liberty of conscience also granted unto them; and they must be assured that they shall not be imprisoned, banished, or have their estates seized, and taken from them and sold, only for differing from the Church of England, in the way of their discipline, whilst they agree in the fundamentals of religion, live peaceably under the civil government, and disturb not the government of the church established. For they, having such liberty abroad where they are, will not, without assurance of the same here, be induced to come amongst us. How many thousands have left England, and gone to seek shelter in foreign parts, for the persecution they were under, for their consciences, who otherwise, with their families, would have continued amongst us? How many have been forced to leave their trades, by being kept in prison, and having their goods and estates taken from them? How many, for fear of being undone, not knowing, but that, as soon as their goods come into their shops, they may be seized, for their having been at conventicles, have left their trades, drawn off their stocks, and keep up their money, not knowing how soon they may have occasion to make use of it in the time of their distresses, which, otherwise, would have been employed in trade, to the benefit of the kingdom? How many thousands of farmers have been necessitated to leave their farms, and come to dwell in London, or to live obscurely in the country, for fear, lest, when they should have employed their stocks, ploughed and sowed their land, reaped their corn, and stocked their pasture land, all should be taken from them, and they imprisoned, and forced from their families, for their religion? Are not these great mischiefs to the kingdom, and great reasons of the decay of trade, and of gentlemen their wanting tenants for their land? A thing so generally complained of all over England, that men are not suffered to live as they would do quietly, and employ and improve their stocks, as they might do, to the advantage of trade, and the kingdom in general; which, if they were permitted, would occasion the consumption of more of the provisions and manufactures of the kingdom, employ more poor people at work, and thereby improve the rent of lands, and would send many of the gentry and farmers, who left the country for the reasons aforesaid, and now live obscure in London, and some other places, back to their country houses, or to their farms again; it would remove their fears, quiet their minds, and cause their purses again to be opened, and every one would be putting himself upon some way of improving his estate, and not live upon the main stock, as now they are forced to do. It were greatly to be wished that there were more love and charity amongst us; and that all men would consider seriously what they do, when they take upon themselves thus to impose their own principles upon all others, as such that are only right, and condemn all others, as erroneous. This is to magnify themselves as infallible, and despise all others.

Upon all these reasons, I humbly submit to judgement, whether an Act for a general Naturalization and Liberty of Conscience be not absolutely necessary at this time; and whether the passing thereof may not be of great advantage to the kingdom, since it would increase trade, promote a vast consumption of the manufactures and provisions of the kingdom; make us more industrious, employ more of our poor, increase his Majesty's revenue of customs, and bring our lands to let for greater rents, and to sell more years purchase than ever heretofore they would have done.

19. AN UNSUCCESSFUL BILL TO NATURALIZE ALIENS, 1673

[House of Lords Record Office, Main Papers, H.L., February 4, 1672/3]

An Act for Naturalization[1]

FORASMUCH as nothing doth contribute more to the strength and wealth of a nation than the abundance of industrious people inhabiting therein. And forasmuch as it is most certain that several nations may receive as great mutual benefit by learning the inventions of each other as by the exchange of their native commodities, which the people of this your Majesty's kingdom have with great advantage found during the reign of some of your Majesty's royal predecessors by the manufactures which, having been taught by foreigners, have since been practised to the great and visible improvement of the riches of this your Majesty's kingdom. To the end therefore that all opportunities of the like advantages may be embraced for the future, either for introducing new or improving the present manufactures of this your Majesty's kingdom. Be it enacted by the king's most excellent Majesty by and with the advice and consent of the Lords Spiritual and Temporal and Commons in this present Parliament assembled, and by the authority of the same, that from henceforth any person or persons being Christians (though born beyond the seas under the jurisdiction of any foreign prince or state)

---

[1] This bill was dropped in the Commons with the end of the Session.

who shall take this oath following: I A.B. do swear that I will bear faith and true allegiance to our sovereign lord the King, his heirs, and successors; and shall likewise subscribe this declaration: I A.B. do declare that I do not believe that there is any transubstantiation in the elements of bread and wine in the sacrament of the Lord's supper upon or after the consecration thereof by any person whatsoever; before the mayor or chief magistrate of any city or town corporate or before any two or more justices of the peace within this realm (which mayor, chief magistrate, or justices of the peace is and are hereby authorized to administer the same and receive the said subscription in all such cases) and shall bring or cause to be brought a certificate thereof under the seal of the said city or town corporate or under the hands and seals of the said justices to be entered in a book to be kept on record for that purpose by the clerk of the Parliaments for the time being (who or his deputy is hereby authorized and required to enter the same and sign the said certificate so entered) shall and may (from and after the time of such taking the said oath and subscribing the said declaration and entering him, her, or themselves a subject or subjects to your Majesty by recording his, her, or their respective certificates as aforesaid) purchase and hold lands or houses, sue and plead in any of your Majesty's courts, and enjoy all benefits, privileges, and advantages of naturalization as fully to all intents and purposes as if he, she, or they were by name naturalized by Act of Parliament, and shall be deemed and taken as your Majesty's natural born subjects in all respects and to all intents and purposes. And be it further enacted by the authority aforesaid that all justices of the peace before whom the said oaths shall be taken and declaration subscribed by any such person or persons as aforesaid are hereby required to cause the name or names of the said person or persons to be registered by the clerk of the peace at the next general Quarter Sessions to be held in their respective counties.[1] Provided nevertheless and it is hereby further declared that nothing herein contained shall be construed to extend in any wise to the avoiding a certain clause in an Act made in the 12th year of your Majesty's reign entitled an Act for the encouraging and increasing of Shipping and Navigation, by which clause it is declared that no ship shall be esteemed an English ship unless she be navigated by a master and three-fourth parts of the mariners English, but that the same shall still be understood of persons born within your Majesty's allegiance and not of persons naturalized by virtue of this or any other Act.

[Endorsed:] An Act of Naturalization. *Prima vice lecta*: 4° Feb. 1672

2do vice lecta: 7mo Feb. 1672

At the end of the bill add: Provided also that no person shall have the benefit provided by this Act who shall not come into this kingdom and be naturalized before the end of five years to be accounted from March 25 in the year of our Lord, 1673.[1]

---

[1] This clause was added in committee on March 27.

20. DEBATE ON THE NATURALIZATION OF ALIENS, 1677

[*Debates of the House of Commons from the Year 1667 to the Year 1694, collected by Hon. Anchitel Grey Esq., who was thirty years member for the town of Derby* . . . ,10 vols., London, 1769, I, p. 56]

Tuesday, December 3, 1677

[The Bill of general Naturalization was read a second time in the House of Commons.]

Pro. Col. Birch and others said, we want people to consume our provisions. Other countries have worked us out of all trade by doing it. An encouragement to the Protestant religion, which we ever have been the protectors of. The destruction of trade is by naturalizing a few people, who draw away our trade by dealing with the French and other foreigners, whose families reside not amongst us.

Contra. It was urged, that it would draw on the pretence of a standing army to keep so many strangers quiet, and would endanger the religion established, by introducing liberty of conscience.

Mr. Solicitor. A fortunate and a prosperous people will be ever a populous people. But the fairest morning that ever was, we see, is set under a cloud. Till we are an established people, we must never think of this Bill but as a mockery. In 1637, we were looked upon as an established and flourishing people; then land and trade were at the height. At that time several foreign nations delighted to settle amongst us, whose posterity still remain. This Bill of naturalization seems to forbid and deny foreigners, for it provides not for freedom in corporations, to set up a trade without being free, which he must buy. Merchants we want not, nor they stock, but we want handicraft people to make up our commodities.

21. MORE ARGUMENTS AGAINST ALIENS, 1685

[University of London, Goldsmiths' Library Broadsides, Cat. No. 2620]

Reasons humbly offered by the inhabitants of the City and Liberty of Westminster and of other places within the weekly bills of mortality to the knights, citizens, and burgesses in this present Parliament assembled against the passing of a bill entitled An Act for the enabling of Protestant strangers to exercise their trades in the places in the said Act mentioned.

1. If this bill should pass, aliens would in time engross all the trade of these places into their own hands to the great grievance of his Majesty's natural born subjects.

2. If they come to be once established here by a law, his Majesty cannot then remove them upon any occasion whatsoever.

3. This would give any neighbouring nation a great opportunity of correspondence with them, and so make an interest in case of a war or of an invasion or a rebellion, and 'tis much feared that the late great confluence of strangers hither was in order to no good end for that these people were invited over and encouraged here by them only that were the conspirators in the late plot and were observed to crowd the Lord Russell's and Shaftesbury's door; and that that faction were the only patrons is apparent in that Papillon and Dubois, both Walloons, were the greatest sticklers in this affair and both members of the French Protestant church, yet took the sacrament to serve a turn.

4. This would make all foreigners promote the sale of foreign manufacture in which their trade will mostly consist, in greater measure than now they do, to the decay of our own manufacture which is your worthy care to preserve.

5. It will discourage Englishmen from breeding their children to trades and consequently the gentry will want opportunity of disposing of their younger children.

6. That no Englishman of what religion soever (be he never so good an artificer) is suffered in Paris under the severest of penalties, viz. seizing and loss of his goods, to work or sell any, except under a Frenchman, in the nature of a servant.

7. That if by trading here they get money, they return rich into their respective countries and purchase estates there; if poor, they run away and leave their children to be maintained by the parish.

All which is most humbly submitted to your honours' great prudence and consideration.

22. STILL MORE ARGUMENT AGAINST NATURALIZING ALIENS, 1699

[University of London, Goldsmiths' Library Broadsides, Cat. No. 3612]

An Humble Address to the honourable House of Commons on the behalf of the Traders of England against naturalizing Aliens.

THE naturalization of aliens is unreasonable and unjust in betraying the right of the younger brothers, and is of dangerous consequence to the government. For if any king should design to set up arbitrary power, he may hire an army of aliens, and these taking the oath, he may bring them in and there can be no opposition because they are free by your own act. And what Papist in the world (being in necessity) but will take the oath and test to come into England? Examples also tell us how pernicious it hath been to several nations to suffer aliens to inhabit in this kingdom. Were not the Jews destructive to the Egyptians? The Romans invited by this nation afterwards became hard task masters, and the Saxons were the ruin of the natives. And I pray God to open our eyes to consider of what dangerous consequence this extravagant charity of ours to the French may prove if not our ruin at last, for the French king is our inveterate enemy and above all people the French hate us; and now by his craft he hath got an army in our bowels. For Mr. Renew, a French merchant, owns that there is but five and forty thousand seven hundred Protestants of French in this city, and that was the account he gave to the king the Sessions of Parliament before Christmas was a twelve month, and bragged of the designed liberty to give them £20,000 by Act of Parliament for the relief of their poor. At the same time he owns that there is above an hundred thousand French Papists in this city, and these Papists are consequently enemies to this government. And any man that will but consider may soon determine the event of such proceedings; for no man knows the mutability of fortune, and if the French king should have an opportunity to land upon us, and when your armies are gone out to fight him, persuade these to rise and fire your city and massacre your wives and children, your hand would soon grow feeble in the field. And especially at this time they are more dangerous because the kingdom is in parties. Here are Jacobites and Papists to join with them. It is great imprudence in us to let the French live here for they undermine the merchants in their trade, betraying the ships to the enemy, going out and coming in, and they set up shops and follow manual occupations more free than the native born; so that the rights of the younger brothers of the nation are betrayed. By the same laws made our ancestors that gave the elder brother the estate, they also made several statute laws against aliens for security of the younger brothers in their trades and manual occupations. Therefore, the naturalizing or permitting aliens to trade in this nation is unreasonable and unjust. What was the reason that true blue Protestant Dupée's case was never examined into in his sending four ships laden with lead to the French king? And what is the reason that several French merchants (pretended Protestants) refuse the oaths? But I have been informed before these pretended Protestants came out of France they had sworn to be true to the French king. And how came it to pass that Dupée and partners durst venture four ships to come from Leghorn laden with 600 tun of Florence wine without a convoy when the French fleet was out and our Straits fleet was in such danger? They would never have ventured if they had not had the king of France's pass. The French king is a great politian[sic] that he would never have let these merchants come out of his country with so great wealths as they pretend to but to serve him here. In my judgement it will be the security of the nation and to weaken our enemy the French king to command all these French Papists to depart the kingdom by midsummer day, and to seize their effects they have got here to be employed for the carrying on the ——, and for the Protestants, send them into Ireland which wants people, for we that are younger brothers in trade have borne the burthen long enough, to the utter ruin of several thousand of us, circumventing us in our trades by the bigoted fancy of the gentry to their commodities; when in a true examination the French do but bubble and cheat them. For in the whole earth there is nothing so substantial as the English workmanship.

If these aliens be disposed, we will with a free mind contribute to all the extremities of taxes or any burthen whatsoever and expose our estates and lives for the defence of our king and kingdom; for a nation's security is unanimity amongst themselves. Let all these *varlets de chambre* and *Madam de Gouvernants* that dispossess the younger gentlemen and gentlewomen of their places and persons of quality together with the French cooks and the merchants be sent away lest they become one day a thorn in your side and insulting masters over you. This I humbly beg for the necessity of my poor countrymen traders whose poverty every day grows more and more; and that we may have unanimity amongst ourselves which will be a discouragement to our foreign and domestic enemies.

Gentlemen, you that are chosen by the Corporations ought to defend their rights. Sirs, there's never a Corporation (though insensibly) but suffers by these aliens, but it is more severe upon us in this city of London, and I hope you will discharge the trust reposed in you. We had more traders than trade before these aliens came in; if you want countrymen to till your ground, you will be mistaken in your measures in bringing in aliens, for the French had rather beg than work at hard labour; for one Englishman will do more in one day at hard labour than a Frenchman in three.

Gentlemen, you have had of late too sad experience of petitioning for your right and not being answered. You was put to the necessity to defend them then by force and it hath cost you very dear. Therefore, I humbly pray you to endeavour to prevent the putting that extreme necessity upon your younger brothers.

London, Printed in the year 1699.

23. THE ACT NATURALIZING ALIEN PROTESTANTS, 1708[1]

[Statutes of the Realm, IX, p. 63]

An Act for Naturalizing Foreign Protestants[1]
7° Annae, C.5

WHEREAS the increase of people is a means of advancing the wealth and strength of a nation; and whereas many strangers of the Protestant or Reformed religion out of a due consideration of the happy constitution of the government of this realm would be induced to transport themselves and their estates into this kingdom if they might be made partakers of the advantages and privileges which the natural born subjects thereof do enjoy; be it enacted by the Queen's most excellent Majesty by and with the advice and consent of the Lords Spiritual and Temporal and Commons in Parliament assembled and by the authority of the same that all persons born out of the ligeance of her Majesty, her heirs, or successors who shall take and subscribe the oaths

Reasons for passing this Act.

Stat. 6 Ann. c. 78, § 3.

---

[1] This statute was repealed in 1711.

and make, repeat, and subscribe the Declaration appointed by an Act made in the sixth year of her present Majesty's reign entitled An Act to make further provision for electing and summoning sixteen peers of Scotland to sit in the House of Peers in the Parliament of Great Britain, and for trying peers for offences committed in Scotland, and for the further regulating of voters in elections of members to serve in Parliament, which said oaths shall be taken and subscribed and declaration made, repeated, and subscribed in the Courts of Chancery, Queen's Bench, Common Pleas, or Exchequer in term time in England or in any of them in open court or before the Lords of Council and Session or Lords of Justiciary or Barons of the Exchequer in open court in Scotland, or at some General Quarter Sessions of the Peace to be held for the county where he or they do or shall inhabit, reside, or settle between the hours of nine and twelve in the forenoon, the taking and subscribing of which oaths and the making, repeating, and subscribing such declaration shall be entered on record in the same Courts, for the doing whereof only one shilling shall be paid, all and every such persons shall be deemed, adjudged, and taken to be her Majesty's natural born subjects of this kingdom to all intents, constructions, and purposes as if they and every of them had been or were born within this kingdom.

I. In what manner and where the oaths to be taken.

Provided always and be it enacted by the authority aforesaid that no person or persons of what quality condition or place soever shall be naturalized by virtue of this Act unless the said person or persons shall have received the sacrament of the Lord's Supper in some Protestant or reformed Congregation within this kingdom of Great Britain within three months before their taking the oaths in this Act mentioned, and shall at the time and place of taking and subscribing the said oaths and of the making, repeating, and subscribing the said declaration produce a certificate signed by the person administering the said sacrament and attested by two credible witnesses whereof an entry shall be made of record in the said court without any fee or reward.

II. Persons naturalized, first to take the sacrament, and produce certificate thereof.

And be it further enacted by the authority aforesaid that the children of all natural born subjects born out of the ligeance of her Majesty, her heirs, and successors shall be deemed, adjudged, and taken to be natural born subjects of this kingdom to all intents, constructions, and purposes whatsoever.

III. Children of naturalized persons, born out of England, deemed natural born subjects.

And be it further enacted by the authority aforesaid that all persons born out of the ligeance of her Majesty, her heirs, or successors who shall qualify themselves in the Courts of Chancery, Queen's Bench, Common Pleas, or Exchequer within the kingdom of Ireland or at some General Quarter Sessions of the Peace to be held for the county where he or they do or shall inhabit, reside, or settle within the said kingdom in like manner as persons are by this Act required to do within the kingdom of Great Britain, all and every such persons shall be deemed, adjudged, and taken to be her Majesty's natural born subjects of the said kingdom of Ireland to all intents, constructions, and purposes as if they and every of them had been or were born within the said kingdom of Ireland.

IV. Persons born out of liegance, to qualify themselves.

VIII. WEALTH, POPULATION, AND LAND: SOME CONTEMPORARY STATISTICS

1. POPULATION AND INCOMES, 1600

[*The State of England, 1600, by Sir Thomas Wilson*, ed. F. J. Fisher, Camden Soc., 3rd Ser., LII, 1936, pp. 16–25]

The number of subjects and division

I T were too impossible a matter to go about to observe the method in this to tell how many subjects these kingdoms contain, albeit I could make a reasonable conjecture knowing the number of parishes and, for the most part, how each province is peopled; but it shall not be necessary to rove at this matter as Botero, a stranger, hath done who never came within 1,000 mile of these countries and yet doth talk [sic] upon him to set down how many souls there be in this kingdom, as he doth of many others, by hearsay.

But whereas Botero[1] confesseth in his first relation, about 30 years since, that for soldiers England was able to make 2 millions of armed men besides horsemen, I cannot be induced to believe that; but this I know that *anno* 1588, when the mountain's mouse, the invincible Spanish armada, was so fearfully expected, there was commission to bring into the field to the musters in every part of the realm all men that were of perfect sense and limb from 16 to 60, except noblemen, gentlemen, clergymen, scholars, and lawyers, officers, and such as had public charges, leaving of the countrymen only sufficient to till the ground, and then in all those musters there were numbered 300,000, which is half as many more [sic] as Botero speaks of, but to say that the half or third part of them were fit to be *hommes d'armes*, as he termeth them, I can neither affirm nor believe. So much for the people which make the strength of the realm; for boys, women, children and impotent and unfit persons for war I leave to their conjectures which can guess according to this proportion. . . .

Quintuplex est divisio subitorum Angliae : Nobiles, Cives, Yeemani, Artisani, Opifices rusticorum.

Nobilitas duplex est per prima divisione : laica, clera. Subdividitur etiam in nobilitatem maiorem que continet : marchiones, comites, vicecomites, barones, et

---

[1] Giovanni Botero (1544–1617), Italian economist and political theorist. This reference to him is somewhat puzzling, as his famous *Relationi Universali* did not appear until 1591 and do not contain the statement here quoted. In any case, the following sentences suggest that two millions is a slip for 200,000.

episcopos; minorum [que continet]: equites, armigeros, generosos, ministros, literatos omnes qui gradus aliquos in Academiis acceperunt.

Marchiones 2 sunt Wincestriae et Northamptoniae, hodie autem non est Marchio Northamptoniae sed Marchionissa solummodo obijt enim ultimus sine prole masculo.

Comites sunt 18—Oxford, Northumberland, Shrewsbury, Kant, Derb', Worcester, Rutland, Comberland', et Sussex, Huntington', Bath', Southampton', Bedford', Penbroch', Hartford', Essex, Lincoln', Nottingham' noviter anno hoc creatus pro servitio apud Cales ob quam rem Comes Essex iure potest cantare hos ego versiculos.[1]

Vicecomites 2 sunt Vicecomes de Monteacuto Montague et Bindoniae.

Barones sunt 39 qui tenent ordinem sequentem—D. Audleyns, Zouch, Willoughby de Ersby, Berkely, Morley, Dacre, Cobham, Stafford, Grey, Scroope, Dudley, Sturton, Lomley, Montjoy, Ogle, Darcey, Sandes, Vaulx, Windsor, Burgh, Wentworth, Cromwell, Mordant, Wharton, Eures, Willoughby of Parham, Rich, Darcy, Sheffield, North, Howerd, Honsdon, Chaundos, Buckhurst, Saint John, Burghley, de la Ware, Compton, Noreys.

The ability and state of the common people of England

It cannot de denied but the common people are very rich, albeit they be much decayed from the states they were wont to have, for the gentlemen, which were wont to addict themselves to the wars, are now for the most part grown to become good husbands and know as well how to improve their lands to the uttermost as the farmer or countryman, so that they take their farms into their hands as the leases expire, and either till themselves or else let them out to those who will give most; whereby the yeomanry of England is decayed and become servants to gentlemen, which were wont to be the glory of the country and good neighbourhood and hospitality; notwith-standing there are yet some store of those yeomen left who have long leases of such lands and lordships as they hold, yea, I know many yeomen in divers provinces in England which are able yearly to dispend betwixt three or five hundred pound yearly by their lands and leases and some twice and some thrice as much; but my young masters the sons of such, not contented with their states of their fathers to be counted yeoman and called John or Robert (such an one), but must skip into his velvet breeches and silken doublet and, getting to be admitted into some Inn of Court or Chancery, must ever after think scorn to be called any other than gentlemen; which gentlemen indeed, perceiving them unfit to do them that service that their fathers did, when their leases do expire, turn them out of their lands, which was never wont to be done, the farmer accounting his state as good as inheritance in times past, and let them to such as are not by their bad pennyworths able to gentleman it as others have done.

---

[1] The earls are given '*secundum ordinem eorum antiquitates et antecedentia*'.

Commonalty

Notwithstanding this that the great yeomanry is decayed, yet by this means the commonalty is increased 20 now perhaps with their labour and diligence, living well and wealthily of that land which our great yeoman held before, who did no other good but maintain beef and brews for such idle persons as would come and eat it, a fine daughter or 2 to be married after with 10,000*l.* to some covetous mongrel gentleman. Of these yeomen of the richest sort which are able to lend the Queen money (as they do ordinarily upon her letters called privy seals whensover she hath any wars defensive or offensive or any other enterprise) there are accounted to be about 10,000 in country villages besides citizens.

There are, moreover, of yeomen of meaner ability which are called freeholders, for that they are owners of lands which hold by no base service of any lord or superior, such as are able to keep 10 or 11 or 8 or 6 milch kine, 5 or 6 horses to till their ground, besides young beasts and sheep and are accounted to be worth each of them in all their substance and stock betwixt 3 and 5 hundred pounds sterling more or less, of these, I say, there are reckoned to be in England and Wales about the number of 80,000, as I have seen in sheriffs' books.

The rest are copyholders and cottagers, as they call them, who hold some land and tenements of some other lord which is parcel of the demesne of his seignory or manor at the will of the lord, and these are, some of them, men of as great ability as any of the rest; and some poor, and live chiefly upon country labour working by the day for meat and drink and some small wages; these last are they which are thrust out to service in war, the richer sort of yeomen and their sons being trained but not sent out of the land, but kept to defend against invasion at home unless they will go voluntary as many do. Notwithstanding, the captain will sometimes press them to the end to get a bribe to release them.

The number of this latter sort is uncertain because there is no books or records kept of them, unless it be in private stewards' hands which is impossible to be gathered altogether, but I can give a reasonable guess by reason of an office which for 7 years together I exercised, wherein I had occasion to take the names of all the inhabitants of 5 shires.

The state of citizens

These, by reason of the great privileges they enjoy, every city being, as it were, a commonwealth among themselves, no other officer of the Queen nor other having authority to intermeddle amongst them, must needs be exceeding well to pass. They are not taxed but by their own officers of the[ir] own brotherhood, every art having one or two of his own which are continually of the council of the city in all affairs to see that nothing pass contrary to their profit; besides they are not suffered to be idle in their cities as they be in other parts of Christendom, but every child of 6 or 7 years old is forced to some art whereby he gaineth his own living and some thing besides to help to enrich his parents or master. I have known in one city, viz. Norwich, where the accounts having been made yearly what children from 6 to 10 years have earned towards their keeping in a year, and it hath been accounted that it hath risen to 12,000 pounds sterling which they have gained, besides other keeping, and that chiefly by knitting of fine jersey stockings, every child being able at or soon after 7 years to earn 4 shillings a week at that trade, which the merchants uttered at London; and some trading therewith with France and other parts. And in that city I have known in my time 24 aldermen which were esteemed to be worth 20,000*l.* apiece, some much more, and the better sort of citizens the half; but if we should speak of London and some other maritime places we should find it much exceeding this rate, it is well known that at this time there are in London some merchants worth 100,000*l.* and he is not accounted rich that cannot reach to 50,000 or near it ...

The state of the nobility and the number

I have seen divers books which have been collected by secretaries and counsellors of estate which did exactly show the several revenues of every nobleman, knights, and gentlemen through the realm, and curiously collected by an uncle of mine[1] which not long since was principal secretary to the Queen ...

[Of] earls some daily decay, some increase according to the course of the world, but that which I have noted by perusing many of the said books, and of the later sort, is that still the total sum groweth much to one reckoning and that is to 100,000*l.* rent yearly, accounting them all in gross to avoid prolixity. If a man would proportion this amongst 19 earls and a marquis it would be no great matter, to every one 5,000*l.* rent, but as some exceed that much, so many come short of it.

The 39 barons and 2 viscounts do not much exceed that sum, their revenue is reckoned together to amount to 120,000*l.* yearly.

The bishops' revenues amount to about 22,500*l.* yearly altogether whereof 3 of them, viz. Canterbury, Winchester, and Ely, receive rent per annum betwixt 2,000*l.* and 3,000*l.*, the rest betwixt 1,000*l.* and 500*l.* and some less.

The deans are the chief ecclesiastical persons of every cathedral church next unto the bishops whose command over the prebends and canons is more than the bishops, and their commodities in letting the church lands and bestowing the places and offices is very great, otherwise their revenue is not much, the best not exceeding 300*l.* yearly, and the rest some 200, some 100, and many less, their whole revenue accounted through England amounted to the sum of 4,500*l.* yearly or thereabouts.

But this must be understood, that the state of the clergy is not altogether

---

[1] In the margin:—'Dr. Wilson', i.e. Dr. Thomas Wilson (1525?–1581), Secretary of State from 1577, and a noted scholar and author.

so bare as may perhaps be conjectured by the smallness of their revenue, for that they never raise nor rack their rents nor put out tenants as the noblemen and gentlemen do to the uttermost penny; but do let their lands as they were let 100 years since, reserving to themselves and their successors some commodities besides the bare rent, as corn, muttons, beef, poultry, or such like; but to say the truth, their wings are well clipped of late by courtiers and noblemen and some quite cut away, both feather, flesh, and bone.

These are the states of the nobility, both clergy and lay, which are called *nobilitas maior*; there rests to touch those of the meaner nobility, which are termed *nobilitas minor* and are either knights, esquires, gentlemen, lawyers, professors, and ministers, archdeacons, prebends, and vicars.

The state and number of knights

There are accounted to be in England about the number of 500 knights as I have reckoned them, both by divers commissions of every several shire remaining in the Chancery Office for making of justices of peace, of which commission all knights to be unless they be put by for religion or some particular disfavour. I reckon not among these my Lord of Essex knights (whose father living or many of them hardly good gentlemen and which for a difference of their knighthood are scornfully called Cales, Roan[1], or Irish knights) but such as are chief men in their countries both for living and reputations, though many of them know scarcely that knighthood means, but are made knights for the credit of their country and to induce them to live in a more honourable manner, both for their own credit and the service of their prince and country, than otherwise perhaps they would do; these for the most part are men for living betwixt 1,000 and 2,000*l.* yearly, and many of them equal the best barons and come not much behind many earls as I have divers, viz. Sir John Peeter, Sir John Harington, Sir Nicholas Bacon, and others, who are thought to be able to dispend yearly betwixt 5,000*l.* and 7,000*l.* of good land.

The number and state of gentlemen

Those which we call esquires are gentlemen whose ancestors are or have been knights, or else they are the heirs and eldest of their houses and of some competent quantity of revenue fit to be called to office and authority in their country where they live; of these there are esteemed to be in England, as I have seen by the book of musters of every several shire, to the number of 16,000 or thereabout, whereof there are of them in commissions of the peace about 1,400 in every province—in some 40, in some 50, some 30, more or less; these are men in living betwixt 1,000*l.* and 500*l.* rent. Especially about London and the counties adjoining, where their lands are set to the highest,

[1] i.e. Rouen.

he is not counted of any great reckoning unless he be betwixt 1,000 marks or 1,000*l.*, but northward and far off a gentleman of good reputation may be content with 300*l.* and 400*l.* yearly. These are the elder brothers.

The state of great younger brethren

I cannot speak of the number of younger brothers, albeit I be one of the number myself, but for their estate there is no man hath better cause to know it, nor less cause to praise it; their state is of all stations for gentlemen most miserable, for if our fathers possess 1,000 or 2,000*l.* yearly at his death, he cannot give a foot of land to his younger children in inheritance, unless it be by lease for 21 years or for 3 lives (or unless his land be socage tenure whereof there is little, or gavelkind, such as is only in one province, in Kent), or else be purchased by himself and not descended. Then he may demise as much as he thinks good to his younger children, but such a fever hectic hath custom brought in and inured amongst fathers, and such fond desire they have to leave a great shew of the stock of their house, though the branches be withered, that they will not do it, but my elder brother forsooth must be my master. He must have all, and all the rest, that which the cat left on the malt heap, perhaps some small annuity during his life or what please our elder brother's worship to bestow upon us if we please him, and my mistress his wife. This I must confess doth us good someways, for it makes us industrious to apply ourselves to letters or to arms, whereby many times we become my master elder brothers' masters, or at least their betters in honour and reputation, while he lives at home like a mome and knows the sound of no other bell but his own.

The estate of common lawyers

This sort and order of people within these 40 or 50 years, since the practice of civil law hath been as it were wholly banished and abrogated, and since the clergy hath been trodden down by the taking away of church livings, and since the long continuance of peace hath bred an inward canker and rest in men's minds, the people doing nothing but jar and wrangle one with another, these lawyers by the ruins of neighbours' contentions are grown so great, so rich, and so proud, that no other sort dare meddle with them; their number is so great now that, to say the truth, they can scarcely live one by another, the practice being drawn into a few hands of those which are most renowned, and all the rest live by pettifogging, seeking means to set their neighbours at variance whereby they may gain on both sides. This is one of the greatest inconveniences in the land, that the number of the lawyers are so great they undo the country people and buy up all the lands that are to be sold, so that young gentlemen or others newly coming to their livings, some of them prying into his evidence will find the means to set him at variance with some other, or some other with him, by some pretence or quiddity, and when they have half consumed themselves in suit they are fain to sell their land to follow the process and pay their debts, and then that becomes a prey to lawyers.

For the greatness of some of them it is incredible not to speak of the 12 chief judges and the multitude of sergeants, which are most of them counted men of 20,000 or 30,000*l.* yearly, there is one at this day of a meaner degree, viz. the Queen's attorney,[1] who, within this 10 years in my knowledge was not able to dispend above 100*l.* a year and now by his own lands, his coins, and his office he may dispend betwixt 12 and 14 thousand.

There are in number of sergeants about 30, counsellers about 2,000, and as many attorneys, besides solicitors, and pettifoggers an infinite number, there being no province, city, town, nor scarce village free from them, unless the Isle of Anglesey, which boast they never had lawyers nor foxes.

The state of civil lawyers

This state of all others is the weakest, they having no means but by practice in the Arches and other the Bishops of Canterbury's Courts, and some small practice in some other consistories. There are of them some 24 belonging to the Arches which gain well, and every bishop hath a chancellor that liveth in some good credit, the rest, God wot, are fain to become poor commissaries and officials of deans and archdeacons, which ride up and down the country to keep courts for correcting of bawdy matters, etc. and take great pains for small gains.

2. PROBLEMS OF OVERPOPULATION, 1609

[Robert Gray, *A Good Speed to Virginia*, London, 1609, pages not numbered]

THERE is nothing more dangerous for the estate of commonwealths than when the people do increase to a greater multitude and number than may justly parallel with the largeness of the place and country. For hereupon comes oppression and diverse kind of wrongs, mutinies, sedition, commotion, and rebellion, scarcity, dearth, poverty, and sundry sorts of calamities, which either breed the conversion or eversion of cities and commonwealths. For even as blood though it be the best humour in the body yet, if it abound in greater quantity than the state of the body will bear, doth endanger the body and oftentimes destroys it. So although the honour of the king be in the multitude of people, Pro. 14.28, yet when this multitude of people increaseth to overgreat a number, the commonwealth stands subject to many perilous inconveniences, for which cause many nations, perceiving their people to

---

[1] In margin: 'Sir Ed. Coke.' For the eighteenth-century traditions of Coke's earnings, see Daines Barrington, *Observations on the more Ancient Statutes*, 4th ed., London, 1775, p. 508.

increase above a due and proportionable number, they have sent their over-flowing multitudes abroad into other countries and provinces, to the end they might preserve their own in greater peace and prosperity. So we see the husbandman deal with his grounds when they are overcharged with cattle: he removes them from one ground to another, and so he provideth well both for his cattle and for his grounds; and so doth the master of the bee garden, when he sees a hive pestered with multitudes of bees, he drives the hive and so reapeth a greater gain by his ware and honey.

And hereupon many statesmen have thought nothing more profitable for populous commonwealths than to have foreign and extern wars to the end that thereby the superfluous branches might be cut off. This was the cause why Scipio when he had conquered Carthage would not have it utterly ruina-ted, lest, saith he, the Romans having no wars abroad, move civil wars amongst themselves at home. Others, seeing the multitude of their people increase, have planted colonies with them; others have banished them into remote countries; and the children of Joseph here being pestered with multitude come to Joshua to be directed and relieved. This should teach us of this kingdom and country prudence and providence, the Lord hath blessed us, and we are grown to be a great people, so that one lot is not sufficient for us. Our multitudes, like too much blood in the body, do infect our country with plague and poverty. Our land hath brought forth but it hath not milk sufficient in the breast thereof to nourish all those children which it hath brought forth. It affordeth neither employment nor preferment for those that depend upon it. And hereupon it is that many serviceable men give themselves to lewd courses, as to robbing by the highway, theft, and cozening, sharking upon the land, piracy upon the sea, and so are cut off by shameful and untimely death. Others live prophanely, riotously, and idly, to the great dishonour of Almighty God, the detriment of the commonwealth. Now our case standing thus, it behoveth everyone to devise a remedy for this misery . . .

3. PROBLEMS OF UNDERPOPULATION, 1674

[Carew Reynel, *The True English Interest*, 1674, pp. 59–67]

Of Marriage and Populacy

THE country complains of small vend of commodities, which proceeds especially from want of people; for our people were consumed mightily in these late years, some three hundred thousand were killed in the last Civil Wars; and about two hundred thousand more have been wasted in re-peopling Ireland; and two hundred thousand lost in the great sickness, and as many more gone to plantations. So that these things must bring us low of people, whereas did we establish the fishery manufactures, and enclosure, it would quickly recruit us. For we are able to contain twice the number of people we are, merely by enclosures. Though if we had but a million more of people than now, we should quickly see how trade and the vend of things would alter for the better. And this would hinder people from going out of the nation, when they may have land, preferment, or employment here.

Another way for increasing populacy is by encouraging all sorts of trading people to come and inhabit here, which is done by making all nations free denizens, that will live here. And why should not we, as the Hollanders do at Amsterdam, declare all the world to have freedom in our nation, as their own? It would make us thrive infinitely, and bring in all the arts, manufactures, and ingenuity of Europe. Some object, they would breed a mixed nation. As for that they would signify nothing, as to the number of our own. If it did, why may not several nations live under one government, as they do in Holland?; trading people value not that; they love to live where they are most secure. Besides, coming in by degrees they would not be considerable. And generally they that come over are men that would marry English women, so are English presently; and are good preferment to ordinary women, being generally tradesmen, and manufacturing men, as we see in many French and Dutch already, that are perfectly English. However in half an age they would be as much English as ourselves, the old stock going off, and the children being born in England, supplying their places; and however at present live as quietly, and are good subjects, and as great lovers of us and the kingdom as others; or else they would never leave their own nation, so formally to inhabit here. For all that do so leave their country shew an extraordinary affection unto this place, and so are by all means to be received and countenanced. Whatever they are before, when once they come here, to be under our laws, customs, and government, they are soon all one with us. By this means also we should draw back our own English from Holland and all Europe besides, and many of our plantations also . . .

Another way of being populous is countenancing marriage and a settled life, giving it many privileges more than either single or debauched persons, and that none but married persons be capable of any profitable office or preferment. This is the very original of the well being and continuance of nations. Upon this property, families, and civil government depends, also trade, riches, populacy; and without this a nation crumbles to nothing. Besides, married people are more honest, economical, and industrious. By the laws of Lycurgus, elderly bachelors were banished the company of all civil and honest people. Where a nation is given to be licentious, they breed but few children. Lewd women make away their children, or order it so they never have many. And it is an ill custom in many country parishes, where they, as much as they can, hinder poor people from marrying; for at present they are the very stock and seminary of the kingdom, they marry apace, and get a laborious hardy generation, which is best for a nation. They value not portions, so they are able to serve, work, or any way earn their living, which is a brave humour. For we ought to increase the world for the public good; and to be contented in a mean, and not sacrifice our thoughts to ambition.

And were it not for these poor honest people, we should be almost desolate. Strictness of matrimonial laws, and penalties against lewdness breeds constancy and pleasure in lawful ties, and hinders the very thoughts of loose designs, making people follow their callings quietly and soberly, when the pain of the penalty spoils the sweet of luxury, and every honest man would be glad, that by this means himself is also kept from such vices, otherwise he would be apt to commit.

There is a great complaint of many people flocking out beyond sea to plantations. Why is it not prevented? It cannot be done by force, for who can keep in such that are ready to starve for want of bread, wherefore it must be done by raising of employments, professions, and trade for young persons, and children, which would encourage people to get them. For by that means we may employ twice the number of people that we have. What makes New England, Jamaica, and the plantations abroad, increase so fast but because they have employments and estates for all people, and no poor among them, which encourages people to come from abroad, and their own people to marry, and get children? When they know, as soon as they are grown up, they can give every child an estate, by setting them out so many acres in a fresh plantation, so they increase *ad infinitum*, till they have stocked the islands and country full; as they have in Barbadoes, which island being not above twenty eight miles long, and fourteen miles broad, yet by relation contains fifty thousand English besides twice as many blacks. And if we did set up manufactures, and enclose the forests, we should populate as much; we having several forests bigger than the Barbadoes. And great estates should not be desired to leave children but so much as to help industry. Why should not ingenious persons, by public establishment, be allowed forty or fifty acres to a family, out of these lands, which are now more charges than benefit? How brave a provision this would be for ruined families, and improvement to the riches, populacy, and grandeur of the nation. Who can blame people to go beyond seas, when they cannot live here? It is mere need and force that drives them out of the kingdom. And it is a sign of great ingenuity that they will go, and strive to live anywhere. England is not half peopled, and yet we find not employment for those we have. Therefore judge you how it would increase people and employments, if the forests were enclosed, and how many people lie wanting now, that this would help and relieve.

4. SIR WILLIAM PETTY ON THE POPULATION OF LONDON, 1686

[Sir William Petty, *An Essay concerning the Multiplication of Mankind together with another Essay in Political Arithmetick concerning the Growth of the City of London . . .*, London, 1686, pp. 5–16]

Of the Growth of the City of London: and of the Measures, Periods, Causes, and Consequences thereof

What is meant by London

B Y the City of London, we mean the housing within the walls of the old city, with the liberties thereof, Westminster, the Borough of Southwark, and so much of the built ground in Middlesex and Surrey, whose houses are contiguous unto, or within call of those aforementioned. Or else we mean the housing which stand upon the ninety seven parishes within the walls of London; upon the sixteen parishes next, without them; the ten parishes of Westminster, and the seven parishes without them all; all which one hundred and thirty parishes are comprehended within the weekly *Bills of Mortality*.

What is meant by the growth of London

The growth of this city is measured . . . by the number of inhabitants; according to which latter sense only, we make our computations in this essay.

Till a better rule can be obtained, we conceive that the proportion of the people may be sufficiently measured by the proportion of the burials in such years as were neither remarkable for extraordinary healthfulness or sickliness.

In what measures the city hath increased

That the city hath increased in this latter sense appears from the *Bills of Mortality*, represented in the two following tables, viz. one whereof is a continuation for eighteen years, ending 1682, of that table which was published in the 117th page of the *Book of the Observations upon the London Bills of Mortality*, printed in the year 1676. The other sheweth what number of people died at a medium of two years, indifferently taken, at about twenty years' distance from each other.

The First of the said two tables

An. Dom.	97 Parishes	16 Parishes	Out Parishes	Buried in all	Besides of the Plague	Christened
1665	5,320	12,463	10,925	28,708	68,596	9,967
1666	1,689	3,969	5,082	10,740	1,998	8,997
1667	7,761	6,405	8,641	15,807	35	10,938
1668	796	6,865	9,603	17,267	14	11,633

The First of the said two tables—*cont.*

An. Dom.	97 Parishes	16 Parishes	Out Parishes	Buried in all	Besides of the Plague	Christened
1669	1,323	7,500	10,440	19,263	3	12,335
1670	1,890	7,808	10,500	20,198		11,997
1671	1,723	5,938	8,063	15,724	5	12,510
1672	2,237	6,788	9,200	18,225	5	12,593
1673	2,307	6,302	8,890	17,499	5	11,895
1674	2,801	7,522	10,875	21,198	3	11,851
1675	2,555	5,986	8,702	17,243	1	11,775
1676	2,756	6,508	9,466	18,730	2	12,399
1677	2,817	6,632	9,616	19,065	2	12,626
1678	3,060	6,705	10,908	20,673	5	12,601
1679	3,074	7,481	11,173	21,728	2	12,288
1680	3,076	7,066	10,911	21,053		12,747
1681	3,669	8,136	12,166	23,971		13,355
1682	2,975	7,009	10,707	20,691		12,653

According to which latter table there died as followeth.

The Latter of the said two Tables.
There died in London,
At a medium between the years.

1604 and 1605—5,135. *A* [5185][1]
1621 and 1622—8,527. *B*
1641 and 1642—11,883. *C*
1661 and 1662—15,148. *D*
1681 and 1682—22,331. *E*

Wherein observe, that the number *C* is double to *A* and 806 over. That *D* is double to *B* within 1906. That *C* and *D* is double to *A B* within 293. That *E* is double to *C* within 1,435. That *D* and *E* is double to *B* and *C* within 3,341. And that *C* and *D* and *E* are double to *A* and *B* and *C* within 1,736 [1738]. And that *E* is above quadruple to *A*. All which differences (every way considered) do allow the doubling of the people of London in forty years, to be a sufficient estimate thereof in round numbers, and without the trouble of fractions. We also say, that 669,930 is near the number of people now in London, because the burials are 22,331 which multiplied by 30, (on dying yearly out of 30, as appears in the 94 page of the aforementioned *Observations*) maketh the said number; and because there are 84,000 tenanted houses (as we are credibly informed) which at 8 in each, makes 672,000 souls; the said two accounts differing inconsiderably from each other.

We have thus pretty well found out in what number of years (viz. in about 40) that the City of London hath doubled; and the present number of inhabitants to be about 670,000. We must now also endeavour the same for the whole territory of England and Wales. In order whereunto we first say,

[1] The bracketed corrections are from C. H. Hull, ed., *The Economic Writings of Sir William Petty*, 1899, II, pp. 458–9.

that the assessment of London is about an eleventh part of the whole territory and therefore that the people of the whole may well be eleven times that of London, viz. about 7,369,000 souls; with which account that of the poll money, hearth money, and the bishops' later numbering of the communicants, do pretty well agree; wherefore although the said number of 7,369,000 be not (as it cannot be) a demonstrated truth, yet it will serve for a good supposition, which is as much as we want at present.

As for the time in which the people double, it is yet more hard to be found. For we have good experience (in the said 94 page of that aforementioned *Observations*) that in the country, but one of fifty die per annum; and, by other late accounts, that there have been sometimes but 24 births for 23 burials, the which two points, if they were universally and constantly true, there would be colour enough to say, that the people doubled but in about 1,200 years. As for example: suppose there be 600 people, of which let a fiftieth part die per annum, then there shall die 12 per annum; and if the births be as 24 to 23, then the increase of the people shall be somewhat above half a man per annum, and consequently the supposed number of 600, cannot be doubled but in 1,126 years, which to reckon in round numbers, and for that the aforementioned fractions were not exact, we had rather call 1,200.

There are also other good observations, that even in the country, one in about 30 or 32 per annum hath died, and that there have been five births for four burials. Now according to this doctrine, 20 will die per annum out of the above 600, and 25 will be born, so as the increase will be 5, which is a hundred and twentieth part of the said 600. So as we have two fair computations, differing from each other as one to ten; and there are also several other good observations for other measures.

I might here insert, that although the births in this last computation be 25 of 600, or a twenty-fourth part of the people; yet that in natural possibility, they may be near thrice as many, and near 75. For that by some late observations, the teeming females between 15 and 44 are about 180 of the said 600, and the males of between 18 and 59 are about 180 also, and that every teeming woman can bear a child once in two years; from all which it is plain, that the births may be 90, and abating 15 for sickness, young abortions, and natural barrenness, there may remain 75 births, which is an eighth of the people; which by some observations we found to be but a two and thirtieth part, or but a quarter of what is thus shewn to be naturally possible. Now, according to this reckoning, if the births may be 75 of 600, and the burials but 15, then the annual increase of the people will be 60; and so the said 600 people may double in 10 years, which differs yet more from 1,200 above mentioned. Now, to get out of this difficulty, and to temper those vast disagreements, I took the medium of 50 and 30 dying per annum, and pitched upon 40; and I also took the medium between 24 births and 23 burials, and 5 births for 4 burials, viz. allowing about 10 births for 9 burials; upon which supposition, there must die 15 per annum out of the above mentioned 600, and the births must be 16 and two-thirds, and the increase 1 and two-thirds, or five thirds of a man, which number compared with 1,800 thirds, or 600 men, gives 360 years for the time of doubling (including some allowance for wars, plagues, and famine, the effects whereof, though they be terrible at the times and places where they happen, yet, in a period of 360 years, is no great matter in the whole nation. For the plagues of England in 20 years hath carried away scarce an eightieth part of the people of the whole nation; and the late 10 years' Civil Wars, (the like whereof hath not been in several ages before) did not take away above a fortieth part of the whole people.)

According to which account or measure of doubling, if there be now in England and Wales 7 millions 400 thousand people, there were about 5 millions 526 thousand in the beginning of Queen Elizabeth's reign, *anno* 1560 and about two millions at the Norman conquest, of which consult the Doomsday Book and my Lord Hale's *Origination of Mankind*.

5. THE EXPECTATION OF LIFE IN 1693

[John Lowthorp, *The Philosophical Transactions and Collections to the End of the Year 1700 Abridg'd* . . . , vol. III, pp. 677–8]

[Edmund Halley contributed to the *Philosophical Transactions* of the Royal Society in 1693 a calculation of mortality rates in Breslau with the intention of valuing annuities upon lives thereon. He chose Breslau, the capital of Silesia, on the grounds that it was a 'standard' place, far from the sea, and with few strangers. It was a small town, whose poor were employed in the manufacture of linen, the only merchandise of the place. 'For these reasons', he concluded, 'the degrees of mortality in this city seem most proper for a standard.' There followed elaborate calculations on the expectation of life, the age structure of the population, and the value of annuities for lives, followed by these general observations:]

IT MAY not perhaps be unacceptable to observe farther from these tables how unjustly we repine at the shortness of our lives and think ourselves wronged if we attain not old age; whereas it appears hereby that the one half of those that are born are dead in 17 years' time, 1,238 being in that time reduced to 619. So that instead of murmuring at what we call an untimely death, we ought to account it as a blessing that we have survived, perhaps by many years, that period of life whereat the one half of the whole race of mankind does not arrive. I shall also observe that the growth and increase of mankind is not so much stinted by anything in the nature of the species, as it is from the cautious difficulty most people make to adventure on the state of marriage, from the prospect of the trouble and charge of providing for a family. For, by computation from the Table, I find that there are nearly 15,000 persons above 16 and under 45, of which at least 7,000 are women capable to bear children. Of these notwithstanding there are but 1,238 born yearly, which is but little more than a 6th part. So that about one in 6, of these women, do breed yearly; whereas were they all married, it would not appear strange or unlikely that 4 of 6 should bring a child every year. The political consequences hereof I shall not insist on; only the strength and glory of a king being in the multitude of his subjects, I shall hint that above all things celibacy ought to be discouraged; as by extraordinary taxing and military service; and those who have numerous families of children to be countenanced and encouraged, by such laws as the *Jus Trium Liberorum* among the Romans; but especially by an effectual care to provide for the subsistence of the poor, by finding them employments, whereby they may earn their bread, without being chargeable to the public.

6. A FIRST DRAFT OF GREGORY KING'S 'OBSERVATIONS' FROM HIS NOTEBOOK, 1695, AND JOURNAL, 1696[1]

[J. P. Cooper, 'The Social Distribution of Land and Men in England, 1436–1700', *Econ. Hist. Rev.*, 2nd Ser., XX, no. 3, 1967, Appendices I & II]

[Extracts from Gregory King's Notebook]

SUPPOSE England to contain 30,000,000 of Acres[2] [*39 million*][3] And the Rents thereof 8,000,000 of Pounds [*10 million*] Then one acre with another is worth about 5s. per acre. [*6s. 2d.*]
The 30 Millions of Acres may be thus apportioned

	acres		
Arable[4]	9,000,000	at 3s. 4d. per[5] acre	1,500,000*li.*
	[*11*]	[*5s. 10d.*]	
Pasture[6]	13,000,000	at 6s. per acre[7]	3,900,000

---

[1] The Notebook (P.R.O., T 64/302) was written in 1695, shortly before *The Natural and Political Observations* (see p. 770 below). The Journal (now in G.L.C. Record Office) appears to belong to early 1696. They contain drafts and calculations which are the basis of many statements in the finished tract.

[2] Acreage is just under 32·5 million.

[3] Figures in square brackets and italics are from *Natural and Political Observations* . . .; unless otherwise stated they refer to England and Wales.

[4] The 'Kashnor' MS. of the *Observations* in the National Library of Australia, Canberra, shows that in 1697, in reply to criticisms by Robert Harley, King reduced his estimate of the arable to 9 million acres and the rent per acre to 5s. 6d. He also reduced the rent of meadow and pasture to 8s. 6d., and increased his estimate of the yield of grain 'I agree the seed corn in general to be about one seventh of the Produce.' See p. 796 below.

[5] 4s. struck out.

[6] '10,000,000 acres Grazing, 3,000,000 acres Hay.'

[7] [*Pasture and Meadow 10 million at 9s. an acre.*]

Meadow for Hay	4,000,000	at 10s. per acre	2,000,000
Heaths and Barren grounds	3,000,000	at 2s. per acre	300,000
	[10]	[1s.]	
Roads Rivers and Lakes	1,000,000[1]	at 6d. per acre	25,000
	30,000,000[2]		7,725,000
			acres

at 3s. 4d. per acre	The Crown Lands	3,000,000[3] [?]	300,000li.
at [?] 4s. per[4] acre	150 [160] Temporal Lords at 2000li. per annum each [2800]	1,500,000	300,000
5s. per acre	26 Spiritual Lords at 1,200li. [£1300] per annum	124,800	31,200
5s. per acre	4,000 Dean and Chapters Lands, Colleges and Corporations	400,000	100,000
5s. per acre	10,000[5] Glebe Lands of the Clergy	80,000	20,000
5s. per acre	1,400 [800] Baronets and [600] Knights at 600li. per annum[6]	3,360,000	840,000
5s. per acre	4,000 [3,000] Esquires at 300li. [£450] per annum	4,800,000	1,200,000
5s. 6d. per acre	12,000 [12,000] Gentlemen at 100li. per annum [280]	4,363,636	1,200,000
6s.[7] per acre	40,000 [40,000] Freeholders at 50li. per annum or upwards [£84]	6,666,666	2,000,000
6s. per acre	400,000 [140,000] Freeholders at 5li. per annum or under 50li. per annum [£50]	6,666,666	2,000,000
		30,561,768[8] [sic]	7,991,200

Acres	of the Arable land
1,000,000	Wheat at 20 bushels per acre . . .[9]
2,500,000[10]	Rye at 20 bushels per acre . . .
1,500,000	Oats at 15 bushels per acre . . .
2,000,000	Barley at 16 bushels per acre . . .[11]

[1] [*Rivers, Lakes 500,000 acres at 2s.; Roads and Waste Land 500,000 acres.*]

[2] Gregory King's journal [called the Burns Journal because it belonged to John Burns (G.L.C. Record Office)], p. 169, gives the following acreages for 1695: Arable 9 million, 'Pasture and Profitable Land' 19 million, 'Woods and Waste' 11 million.

[3] If the number of acres is correct, the rent should be £500,000. It is difficult to believe that King could have meant this, so perhaps the number of acres should be 1,800,000.

[4] This is probably a slip for 5s. in view of the figure for the clergy.

[5] [*8,000 clergymen.*]

[6] [*Baronets' income £880, knights' £600.*]

[7] Possibly originally 6s. 8d.

[8] The original total reading 32,864,800 has been struck out. The acreages for the baronets, esquires, gentlemen, and both sorts of freeholders were all apparently altered in order to achieve the new total, which should be 30,961,768.

[9] [*12 million bushels, exclusive of seed corn, and quarter or a fifth of the produce.*]

[10] The first figure seems to have been altered, perhaps in error for the one above.

[11] [*25 million net.*] This is the only instance where both estimates agree.

1,000,000 Peas and Beans at 10 bushels per acre . . .
2,000,000 Fallow
———————
9,000,000[1] [sic]

Pasture land may winter Summer each acre 1[2] Beeve besides Calves and 5 sheep besides lambs to another acre Which would make the Stock of Cattle to be 6,000,000 of Beeves, Whereof 3 millions consumed annually and 30,000,000 of muttons whereof 15 millions consumed. . . This quantity will answer to 7 oz. and ½ of Mutton and Beef together including swine's flesh and Goat's flesh for each Head *per diem* for 2 millions of People[3] which is not much above what may reasonably be allowed. So the Pasture ground at 13,000,000 of Acres seems a good Computation or at least not much over.

Hay ground

Pasture 3,000,000 of acres at 1 Load per acre—	3,000,000	
Loads at 20 C per load 60,000,000 C worth		1,000,000*li*.[4]
Meadow 4,000,000 of acres at 2 Load per acre—	8,000,000	
—at 20 C per Load 160,000,000 cwt.—		3,000,000*li*.

Which for near 4 millions of Cattle is 3 Load per Head per annum or 55 or 60 C.
And allowing 2 C per week for each Head, in a maintenance for 30 weeks and the other 22 weeks to be allowed for grazing.
[Estimates of the total consumption of foodstuffs which follow are very much higher than those in *Two Tracts by Gregory King*, ed. G. E. Barnett, Baltimore, 1936, pp. 37–40.][5]

Which for 6 millions of People is 4*li*. per head per annum		
Whereof the Diet for 1,000,000 of Infants or children at 20s.		1,000,000
3 Of 2 millions of Paupers and Day Labourers at 40s. per annum[6]		4,000,000
1 Of 2 millions of Farmers and Freeholders at 5*li*.		10,000,000
Of ½ million of Tradesmen at 6*li*. per annum		3,000,000
Of 400,000 Freeholders of 50*li*. per annum or upwards at 6*li*.		2,400,000
Of 150,000 or 250,000 Retainers to Noblemen and Gentlemen at 8*li*.		1,400,000
[or]		1,600,000
Of 100,000 Noblemen and Gentlemen and their Children at 20*li*.[7]		2,800,000
		———————
		22,600,000 [sic]
which wants 2 or 3 million[8]		24,000,000

—

[1] P.R.O. T64/302, fo. 14. The total should be 10,000,000.

[2] Originally 2.

[3] [*2·7 million eat flesh constantly average* 6⅗ *oz. per head per day*, p. 38.]

[4] The first figure is not clearly legible.

[5] e.g. 3 million beeves and calves against 800,000; sheep and lambs 11 million and 3·2 million; swine 6 million and 3·2 million; only the 24 millions of bushels of malt are the same.

[6] The figures in the margin are interesting examples of King's uncertainty about the number of paupers.

[7] 50,000 has been crossed out.

[8] The last two figures were increased in order to reach the required total of £24 million. The adjustments have not been completed successfully in the estimate of retainers. The expense of noblemen and gentlemen was originally a figure less than £20, probably £16.

So the Expenses of the Nation are

	Diet	24,000,000
	Clothes	24,000,000
Incident Charges and Expenses.		12,000,000
		60,000,000

So that if the Rents are 12 millions The Product of the Land is five times as much. So the greatest Taxes are to be raised upon the Product of the Land and of Trades, Employments, and Offices, and not upon the Rents.

Families			
	200	Lords Spiritual and Temporal	at 40 per Family
	1,500	Knights and Baronets	at 24 per Family
	3,000	[or] 3,800 Esquires	at 16 per Family [*10*]
	15,000	Gentlemen	at 10 per Family [*8*]
	80,000	Freeholders at 50 *li.* per annum	at 8 per Family [*7*]
	200,000[1]	Freeholders at 10*li.* per annum	at 6 per Family [*5*]
	400,000[2]	Farmers	at 5 per Family [*5*]
	100,000	Cottagers and day labourers and paupers	at 4 per Family[3]
	300,000	Tradesmen and professions	at 5 per Family[4]
	1,100,000	[sic] [*1,360,586*]	

[Extracts from Gregory King's Journal[5]]

That the Lords Spiritual and Temporal and Peers of Scotland and Ireland commonly residing in England	are about		200
their eldest and younger Sons of all ages	,,	,,	160
Baronets of this Kingdom	,,	,,	780
Knights of this Kingdom	,,	,,	620
Sergeants at Law and Deans of Cathedral and Collegiate Churches	,,	,,	70
Esquires and reputed Esquires including such as are or have been Parliament men, Sheriffs of counties, Justices of Peace, Deputy Lieutenants, Mayors and Sheriffs of London and some of the principal Cities, Commission Officers, Barristers at Law, etc.	,,	,,	3,500
	or		3,000
Gentlemen or reputed Gentlemen paying as such[6]	,,	,,	20,000
[12,000]	or		13,000
Canons and Prebendaries	are about		400
the Clergy of England charged as Gentlemen or having a living of 50*li.* or 60*li.* per annum	,,	,,	2,000
the Dissenting Ministers and Teachers	,,	,,	500
the Widows of all Degrees and qualities and the Widows of 100*li.* per annum or 1000*li.* personal estate [1200]	,,	,,	3,000
the Drs. of Divinity, Law, and Physic	,,	,,	400
the Double Beneficed clergymen of 120*li.* per annum	,,	,,	200

[1] The first figure was altered to what looks like a 2.

[2] The first figure is not clearly legible, it could be a 5.

[3] [*Labouring People and outservants* 3½ *; paupers and cottagers* 3¼.]

[4] P.R.O., T64/302, fos. 18, 18v.

[5] This is the Burns Journal, 1696, pp. 280-1. Figures in [ ] from p. 74.

[6] In the margin: 'That the Gentlemen and those who are above Gentlemen and under a peer having 300*li.* p.a. or upwards are about 6,000 [3,500].'

merchants of London living in or within 10 miles of London and not free of London	are about			60
Tradesmen, Shopkeepers, and Vintners worth 300*li.*	,,	,,		10,000
Merchants, Tradesmen, or Artificers living in a house of 30*li.* per annum in London or within 20 miles of London,	,,	,,		10,000
whereof the merchants and brokers to merchants are about 500 [400]				500
. . . ¹the Merchants Strangers				60
Merchants Jews				30
Jews Brokers				8
Jews of 16 years old				250

		rather	
. . . ²the Servants having about 3*li.* per annum or upwards	150,000	[or]	200,000
the Servants having under 3*li.* per annum	350,000	[or]	400,000

³the Cursiters, Philazers, Attorneys, Solicitors, Clerks in
Chancery, or Exchequer, or other Courts in Law or Equity,
Scriveners, Chancellors, Commissaries, Advocates,

Proctors, public notaries, and other officers are about			2,000
unmarried women worth 100*li.* are about [500]			1,000
the persons finding a horse to the Militia are about			4,000
the persons keeping a Coach, Chariot or Calash not finding a Horse are about 2,000 or one moiety of the Coaches			2,000
the persons keeping Hackney and Stage Coaches are about			1,500
the Gentlemen of 300*li.* and 16 years of age and not taking the Oaths are about			300
the Men and Women in the Kingdom who receive Alms [700,000]	800, [or]	750, [or]	700,000
their children under 16 are [300,000] 500,	540, 440,		300,000
poor Housekeeping Men and Women not paying to Church and Poor [740,000]	700, 650,		700,000
their children under 16 [460,000]	500		450,000
the Day Labourers and their Wives are about 400,000 and their children under 16 [250,000 + 150,000 Servants in Husbandry]	300		250,000
Servants in Husbandry and their wives are about 300,000 and their children under 16	160,		150,000
the Parents who have 4 Children or more and are not worth 50*li.* are about 150,000 [200,000] and their children under 16			150,000

3,900,000	2,850,000
3,060,000	2,700,000
	[sic]

That those 3,060,000 Poor People usually exempt from Taxes in all Polls
are equal to the Inhabitants of 860,000 houses at above $3\frac{1}{2}$ to a House; and
that the remaining 2,400,000 [or] 2,340,000 upon whom the Poll Tax is

---

¹ In the margin: 'Stock of East India, Guinea, and Hudson Bay is now but £600,000;
Shares in the New River, Thames, Hyde Park and Marylebone Waters and King's Printing
House about 10,000.'

² Persons taxed for personal estate not taxed for above £2 million; profits of offices, places,
and public employments taxed for about £80,000; pensions and annuities out the king's
revenue for £30,000; the article judges and judicial officers in 1 Wm. and Mary for £30,000.

³ In the margin.

raised, are equal to the Inhabitants of 540,000 [or] 450,000 Houses at 5½ to a House.[1]

So that in Round Numbers the Insolvent Persons in a Poll Tax, where the non-contributors to Church and Poor are Exempted, as well as their Children under 16, are 3 millions or 2,850,000;

and the Solvent are 2,400,000 or 2,550,000

7. GREGORY KING ON THE STATE OF ENGLAND IN 1695

[*Two Tracts by Gregory King*, ed. George E. Barnett, Baltimore, 1936, pp. 16–18, 21–32, 35–49]

Natural and Political Observations upon the State and Condition of England

WHEREAS the ensuing treatise depends chiefly upon the knowledge of the true number of people in England, and such other circumstances relating thereunto, as have been collected from the assessments on marriages, births, and burials, parish registers, and other public accounts; we shall first exhibit the calculation of the number of people, as they appear by the said assessments.

1. As to the number of the people of England.

In this calculation, we shall consider.
1. The number of inhabited houses.
2. The number of people to each house.
3. The number of transitory people, and vagrants.

The number of houses in the kingdom, as charged in the books of the Hearth Office at Lady Day 1690 were 1,319,215.

The kingdom increasing at this time about 9,000 people per annum as will appear in the ensuing discourse.

The increase of houses should be about 2,000 per annum. But by reason of the present war with France not much above 1,000 per annum. So that by the year 1695 the increase cannot have been above 6 or 7,000; which makes

---

[1] In the margin: '2,850,000 Insolvent, 805,000 houses at 3½ per House; 2,550,000 Solvent, 485,000 houses at 5¼ per House; Houses insolvent 800,000, solvent 500,000.'

These estimates are related to those on pp. 74–5 of the Journal and all give higher figures for those receiving alms and not paying rates than in *Two Tracts*, p. 42, and below, p. 785. They show that these are attempts to relate the estimates of population and social groups to the quarterly poll tax of 1691, knowing only its total yield and assuming (p. 74) that 150,000 were omitted by neglect and that the yield of the special rates on various groups was £122,700, which was too high for the estimates of those excused or paying at ordinary rates.

the present number of houses, that is to say such as were so charged in the books of the Hearth Office to be about 1,326,000.

But whereas the chimney money being charged on the tenant or inhabitant, the divided houses stand as so many distinct dwellings in the accounts of the said Hearth Office; and whereas the empty houses, smiths' shops, etc. are included in the said account, all which may very well amount to 1 in 36 or 37 (or near 3 per cent) which in the whole may be about 36,000 houses, it follows:

That the true number of inhabited houses in England, is not above	1,290,000
Which however in a round number, we shall call	1,300,000
And shall thus apportion,	
	Houses
London and the bills of mortality	105,000
The other cities and market towns	195,000
The villages and hamlets	1,000,000
In all,	1,300,000

Having thus adjusted the number of inhabited houses, we come to proportion the number of souls to each house according to what we have observed from the said assessments on marriages, births, and burials, in several parts of the kingdom, viz.

That London within the walls produced at a medium almost		5½ souls per house
The 16 parishes without the walls	Full	4½ souls per house
And the rest of the said bills	almost	4½ souls per house
That the other cities and market towns produced at a medium		4⅓ souls per house
And the villages and hamlets at a medium	about	4 souls per house
Accordingly the number of people computed from the said assessments amounts to		5,318,100 souls

As by the following scheme:

	Inhabited Houses	Souls per House	Number of Souls
The 97 parishes within the walls	13,500	at 5·4	72,900
The 16 parishes without the walls	32,500	at 4·6	149,500
The 15 out parishes in Middlesex and Surrey	35,000	at 4·4	154,000
The 7 parishes in the city and liberties of Westminster	24,000	at 4·3	103,200
So London and the bills of mortality contain	105,000	at 4·57	479,600
The other cities and market towns	195,000	at 4·3	838,500
The villages and hamlets	1,000,000	at 4	4,000,000
In all	1,300,000	at 4·9	5,318,100

But considering that the omissions in the said assessments may well be:

In London and the bills of mortality	10 per cent or	47,960 souls
In the cities and towns	2 per cent or	16,500 souls
In the villages and hamlets	1 per cent or	40,000 souls
	In all	104,460 souls

It follows that the true number of people dwelling in the 1,300,000 inhabited houses should be 5,422,560 souls.

According to the following scheme:

	People by the Assessments	Omissions in the Assessments	Number of People in all		
The 97 parishes	72,900	7,290	80,190 at almost 6	heads per house
The 16 parishes	149,500	14,950	164,450 at above 5	heads per house
The 15 parishes	154,000	15,400	169,400 at above 4·8	heads per house
The 7 parishes	103,200	10,320	113,520 at almost 4¾	heads per house
The bills of mortality	479,600	47,960	527,560 at above 5	heads per house
The cities and towns	838,500	16,500	855,000 at almost 4·4	heads per house
The villages	4,000,000	40,000	4,040,000 at 4·4	heads per house
Total	5,318,100	104,460	5,422,560 at above 4·17	heads per house

Lastly, whereas the number of transitory people, as seamen and soldiers, may be accounted 140,000, whereof near one half or 60,000 have no place in the said assessments, and that the number of vagrants, viz. hawkers, pedlars, crate carriers, gypsies, thieves, and beggars may be reckoned 30,000; whereof above one half or 20,000 may not be taken notice of in the said assessments, making in all 80,000 persons: it follows that the whole number of the people of England is much about 5,500,000 souls.

viz. London and the bills of mortality	530,000 souls
The other cities and market towns	870,000 souls
The villages and hamlets	4,100,000 souls
In all	5,500,000 souls

. . . .

3. The Several Distinctions of the People, as to Males, and Females, Married, and Unmarried, Children, Servants, and Sojourners.

That the 5 millions and a half of souls in England, including the transitory people and vagrants, appear by the assessments on marriages, births, and burials, to bear the following proportions in relation to males and females, viz.

	Males		Females	Males	Females	Both
In London and the bills of mortality	10	to	13	230,000	300,000	530,000
In the other cities and market towns	8	to	9	410,000	460,000	870,000
In the villages and hamlets	100	to	99	2,060,000	2,040,000	4,100,000
	27	to	28	2,700,000	2,800,000	5,500,000

That as to other distinctions, they appear by the said assessments to bear these proportions:

		People	Males	Females
Husbands and wives at above	34½ per cent	1,900,000	950,000	950,000
Widowers at above	1½ per cent	90,000	90,000	
Widows at almost	4½ per cent	240,000		240,000
Children at above	45 per cent	2,500,000	1,300,000	1,200,000
Servants at almost	10½ per cent	560,000	260,000	300,000
Sojourners and single persons	4 per cent	210,000	100,000	110,000
	100	5,500,000	2,700,000	2,800,000

And that the different proportions in each of the said articles between London, the great towns, and the villages may the better appear, we have exhibited the following scheme.

	London and Bills of Mortality Souls		The other Cities and great Towns Souls		The Villages and Hamlets Souls	
Husbands and wives	37 per cent	196,000	36 per cent	313,200	34 per cent	1,394,000
Widowers	2 per cent	10,600	2 per cent	17,400	1½ per cent	61,500
Widows	7 per cent	37,100	6 per cent	52,200	4½ per cent	184,500
Children	33 per cent	174,900	40 per cent	348,000	47 per cent	1,927,000
Servants	13 per cent	68,900	11 per cent	95,700	10 per cent	410,000
Sojourners, etc.	8 per cent	42,400	5 per cent	43,500	3 per cent	123,000
	100	930,000	100	870,000	100	4,100,000

4. The Several Ages of the People.

That the yearly births of the kingdom being 190,000 souls

	In all	Males	Females
Those under 1 year old are	170,000	90,000	80,000
Those under 5 years old are	820,000	415,000	405,000
Those under 10 years old are	1,520,000	764,000	756,000
Those under 16 years old are	2,240,000	1,122,000	1,118,000
Those above 16 years old are	3,260,000	1,578,000	1,682,000
Those above 21 years old are	2,700,000	1,300,000	1,400,000
Those above 25 years old are	2,400,000	1,150,000	1,250,000
Those above 60 years old are	600,000	270,000	330,000

So that the number of communicants is in all 3,260,000 souls.

And the number of fighting men between 16 and 60 is 1,310,000.

That the bachelors are about 28 per cent of the whole.

Whereof those under 25 years are $25\frac{1}{2}$ per cent.

And those above 25 years are $2\frac{1}{2}$ per cent.

That the maidens are about $28\frac{1}{2}$ per cent of the whole.

Whereof those under 25 years are $26\frac{1}{2}$ per cent.

And those above 25 years are 2 per cent.

That the males and females in the kingdom in general are aged one with another $27\frac{1}{2}$ years.

That in the kingdom in general there is near as many people living under 20 years of age, as there is above 20.

Whereof, one half of the males is under 19 years, and one half of the females is under 21 years.

	At a medium		Years
That the husbands are aged	43 years apiece which at	$17\frac{1}{4}$ per cent makes	742
The wives	40 years apiece	$17\frac{1}{4}$	690
The widowers	56 years apiece	$1\frac{1}{2}$	84
The widows	60 years apiece	$4\frac{1}{2}$	270
The children	12 years apiece	45	540
The servants	27 years apiece	$10\frac{1}{2}$	284
The sojourners	35 years apiece	4	140
At a medium $27\frac{1}{2}$		100 persons	2,750 years

5. The Origination and Increase of the People of England.

That if the world was repeopled from 8 persons after the Flood, and that England was peopled originally by two persons, or by a number not exceeding 20 persons; such first peopling was about the year of the world 2200 or 2300, viz. 600 years after the Flood; and 1,600 or 1,700 years before the birth of our Saviour, at which time the world had between one and two millions of people only.

But if the first peopling of England was by a colony or colonies consisting of a number between 100 and 1,000 people (which is most probable), such colony or colonies were brought over between the year of the world 2400 and 2600, viz. about 800 or 900 years after the Flood, and 1,400 or 1,500 years before the birth of our Saviour at which time the world had about a million of families, and 4 or 5 millions of people.

From which hypothesis it will follow by an orderly series of increase:

That when the Romans invaded England 53 years before our Saviour's time, the kingdom had about 360,000 people, and at our Saviour's birth about 400,000 people.

That at the Norman conquest *anno* Christi 1066 the kingdom had somewhat above two millions of people.

That *anno* 1260 or about 200 years after the Norman conquest the kingdom had 2,750,000 people, or half the present number; so that the people of England have doubled in about 435 years last past.

That in probability the next doubling of the people of England will be in about 600 years to come, or by the year of our Lord 2300. At which time it will have 11 millions of people; but that the next doubling after that will not be (in all probability) in less than 1,200 or 1,300 years more, or by the year of our Lord 3500 or 3600; at which time the kingdom will have 22 millions of souls, or 4 times its present number in case the world should last so long. Now the kingdom containing but 39 millions of acres, it will then have less than 2 acres to each head, and consequently will not then be capable of any further increase.

That the increase of the kingdom for every 100 years of the last preceding term of doubling, and the subsequent term of doubling, has been, and in probability will be according to the following scheme.

Anno Christi	Number of People	Increase every 100 years
1300	2,860,000	440,000
1400	3,300,000	540,000
1500	3,840,000	780,000
1600	4,620,000	880,000
1700	5,500,000	920,000
1800	6,420,000	930,000
1900	7,350,000	930,000
2000	8,280,000	925,000
2100	9,205,000	910,000
2200	10,115,000	885,000
2300	11,000,000	

Whereby it appears that the increase of the kingdom, being 880,000 people in the last 100 years, and 920,000 in the next succeeding 100 years, the annual increase at this time is about 9,000 souls per annum. But whereas the yearly burials of the kingdom are about 1 in 32 or 170,000 souls; and the yearly births 1 in 28 or 190,000 souls, whereby the yearly increase should be 20,000 souls.

It is to be noted,

1. That the allowance for plagues, and great mortalities comes to at a medium	4,000 per annum
2. Foreign or civil wars at a medium	3,500 per annum
3. The sea constantly employing about 40,000 precipitates the death of about	2,500 per annum
4. The plantations (over and above the accession of foreigners) carry away	1,000 per annum
In all	11,000 per annum
Whereby the net annual increase is but	9,000
In all	20,000

That of these 20,000 souls which would be the annual increase of the kingdom by procreation, were it not for the forementioned abatements.

The country increases annually by procreation   20,000 souls
The cities and towns (exclusive of London)   2,000 souls
But London and the bills of mortality decrease annually   2,000 souls

So that London requires a supply of 2,000 per annum to keep it from decreasing, besides a further supply of about 3,000 per annum for its increase at this time. In all 5,000 or a moiety of the kingdom's neat increase.

That allowing London and the bills of mortality to have contained in Julius Cæsar's time between 4 and 5,000 souls; and at the Norman conquest about 24,000 souls, and at this time about 530,000 souls, the increase thereof hath been, and in probability will be according to the following scheme of the duplication of its inhabitants:

Number of Souls	Anno Christi	Number of years in which the people of London have doubled
8,280	330	—— 500
16,560	830	—— 400
33,120	1230	—— 270
66,240	1500	—— 85
132,480	1585	—— 36
264,960	1621	—— 74
529,920	1695	—— 205
1,059,840	1900	—— 1,100
2,119,680	3000	

Whereby it appears that London has doubled 3 times since the year 1500. So that it is now 8 times as big as it was then. And the present yearly increase of London and the bills of mortality would have been (had it not been for the present war) 3,000 souls per annum.

But in relation to the present war we are to consider,

That if the nation do at this time contain   5,500,000 souls
It did contain *anno* 1688 about 50,000 more or   5,550,000 souls
For that instead of a decrease of 11,000 per annum out of the yearly increase by procreation of 20,000, the said decrease has been at a medium 19,000 per annum. In all for 7 years   133,000
And that instead of an increase of 20,000 per annum by procreation, the said increase has been at a medium but 12,000 per annum. In all for 7 years   84,000

So that the kingdom has decreased in 7 years   49,000

Observations about Procreation

Accounting the People to be 5,500,000 Souls

By the forementioned assessments on marriages, births, and burials, and the collectors' returns thereupon, and by the parish registers, it appears that the proportions of marriages, births, and burials, is according to the following scheme:

	People	Annual Marriages		
London and bills of mortality	530,000	1 in 106	In all 5,000	producing 4 children each
The cities and market towns	870,000	1 in 128	In all 6,800	producing 4·5 children each
The villages and hamlets	4,100,000	1 in 141	In all 29,200	producing 4·8 children each
	5,500,000	1 in 134	41,000	4·64

	Annual Births		Annual Burials	
London and bills of mortality	1 in 26½	In all 20,000	1 in 14·1	In all 22,000
The cities and market towns	1 in 28½	In all 30 000	1 in 30·4	In all 28,600
The villages and hamlets	1 in 29·4	In all 139,400	1 in 34·4	In all 119,400
	1 in 28·85	190,000	1 in 32·35	170,000

Whence we may observe that in 1,000 coexisting persons,

there are 71 or 72 marriages in the country producing 34·3 children; 78 marriages in towns producing 35·2 children; 94 marriages in London producing 37·6 children.

Whereby it follows:

1. That though each marriage in London produceth fewer people than in the country, yet London in general having a greater proportion of breeders is more prolific than the other great towns, and the great towns are more prolific than the country.
2. That if the people of London of all ages were as long lived as those in the country, London would increase in people much faster *pro rato* than the country.
3. That the reason why each marriage in London produces fewer children than the country marriages seems to be,
1. From the more frequent fornications and adulteries.
2. From a greater luxury and intemperance.
3. From a greater intenseness or business.
4. From the unhealthfulness of the coal smoke.
5. From a greater inequality of age between the husbands and wives.

And that it may appear what the effect is of the inequality of ages in married couples, I have collected the following observations from a certain great town (Lichfield), in the middle of the kingdom, consisting of near 3,000 souls.

1. That there is no child of any parents now living in the said town where the wife is 17 years older than the husband, or the husband 19 years older than the wife.
2. That the whole number of children being 1,060, the number of those where the mother was older than the father is 228, and where the husband was older than the wife 832
3. That one moiety of the whole number of children in the said town are the product of such parents, where the husband is 4 or more years older than the wife.

4. That the greatest number of children with respect to any one number of years of difference in age between the husband and wife, is where the husband is two years older than the wife, the product whereof is 147 or a 7th part of the whole.

5. That an equality in age in the husband and wife is not so prolific as an inequality, provided that inequality exceed not a superiority of 4 years in the wife, or 10 years in the husband; for the equality of years produced but 23 children, whereas one year's inequality in the age of the parents either way produced above 60.

6. That of the said 1,060 children in the whole town near 3 quarters of them are the product of coalitions from 2 years' superiority of age in the wife inclusive to 6 years' superiority of age in the husband inclusive.

7. That the highest powers in men and women for procreation is in that town at 31 years of age in the husband and 28 in the wife, the produce of the former being 86 children, and of the latter 83.

8. That one moiety of the said 1,060 children are the product of fathers from 28 to 35 years of age inclusive and of mothers from 25 to 32.

Whence it follows that a just equality or too great an inequality of age in marriages are prejudicial to the increase of mankind, and that the early or late marriages in men and women do tend little to the propagation of human race.

Lastly, from a consideration of the male and female children in the said town, and the ages of their parents at the time when such children were respectively conceived, a scheme may be established of the powers of generation, and the inclination of the several coalitions towards the producing the one or the other sex, according to the superiority of power in either sex, at the time of such respective coalitions.

6. The annual income, and expense of the nation as it stood *anno* 1688.

	Sterling
That the yearly income of the nation *anno* 1688 was	43,500,000
That the yearly expense of the nation was	41,700,000
That then the yearly increase of wealth was	1,800,000
That the yearly rent of the lands were about	10,000,000
of the burgage or housing about	2,000,000
of all other hereditaments about	1,000,000
In all	13,000,000
That the yearly produce of trade, arts, and labour was about	30,500,000
In all	43,500,000

That the number of inhabited houses being about   1,300,000
The number of families about   1,360,000
And the number of people about   5,500,000
The people answer to 4¼ per house, and 4 per family
That the yearly estates or income of the several families answer

	£	s.	d.	
In common to about	32	0	0	per family
And about	7	18	0	per head
That the yearly expense of the nation is about	7	11	4	per head
And the yearly increase about		6	8	per head

That the whole value of the kingdom in general is
about   £650,000,000 sterling

	sterling
The 13 millions of yearly rents, at about 18 years' purchase	234,000,000
The 30 millions and a half per annum by trade, arts, labour, etc., at near 11 years' purchase (which being the value of the 5 millions and a half of people at £60 per head) come to	330,000,000
The stock of the kingdom in money, plate, jewels, and household goods about	28,000,000
The stock of the kingdom in shipping, forts, ammunition, stores, foreign or home goods, wares, and provisions for trade abroad, or consumption at home, and all instruments and materials relating thereunto	33,000,000
The livestock of the kingdom in cattle, beasts, fowl, etc.	25,000,000

In all £650,000,000

[The Table on pp. 780–81 comes here in the MS.]

7. The Several Sorts of Land in England, with the Value and Product thereof

England and Wales contains 39 millions of acres, viz.

	Acres	Value	Rent
Arable land	11,000,000 at 5s. 10d. per acre		£3,200,000
Pasture and meadow	10,000,000 at 9s. per acre		4,500,000
Woods and coppices	3,000,000 at 5s. per acre		750,000
Forests, parks, and commons	3,000,000 at 3s. 6d. per acre		550,000
Heaths, moors, mountains, and barren land	10,000,000 at 1s. per acre		500,000
Houses and homesteads, gardens and orchards, churches and churchyards	1,000,000 {	The land	450,000
	{	The buildings	2,000,000
Rivers, lakes, meres, and ponds	500,000 at 2s. per acre		50,000
Roads, ways, and waste land	500,000 at 2s. per acre		

In all 39,000,000 at 6s. 2d. per acre   £12,000,000

A Scheme of the Income and Expense of the several Families of England Calculated for the Year 1688.

Number of Families	Ranks, Degrees, Titles, and Qualifications	Heads per Family	Number of Persons	Yearly Income per Family £	s.	Total of the Estates or Income £	Yearly Income per Head £	s.	Expense per Head £	s.	d.	Increase per Head £	s.	d.	Total Increase per annum £
160	Temporal Lords	40	6,400	2800	0	448,000	70	0	60	0	0	10	0	0	£64,000
26	Spiritual Lords	20	520	1300	0	33,800	65	0	55	0	0	10	0	0	5,200
800	Baronets	16	12,800	880	0	704,000	55	0	51	0	0	4	0	0	51,200
600	Knights	13	7,800	650	0	390,000	50	0	46	0	0	4	0	0	31,200
3,000	Esquires	10	30,000	450	0	1,200,000	45	0	42	0	0	3	0	0	90,000
12,000	Gentlemen	8	96,000	280	0	2,880,000	35	0	32	10	0	2	10	0	240,000
5,000	Persons in offices	8	40,000	240	0	1,200,000	30	0	27	0	0	3	0	0	120,000
5,000	Persons in offices	6	30,000	120	0	600,000	20	0	18	0	0	2	0	0	60,000
2,000	Merchants and traders by sea	8	16,000	400	0	800,000	50	0	40	0	0	10	0	0	160,000
8,000	Merchants and traders by sea	6	48,000	200	0	1,600,000	33	0	28	0	0	5	0	0	240,000
10,000	Persons in the law	7	70,000	140	0	1,400,000	20	0	17	0	0	3	0	0	210,000
2,000	Clergymen	6	12,000	60	0	120,000	10	0	9	0	0	1	0	0	12,000
8,000	Clergymen	5	40,000	45	0	360,000	9	0	8	0	0	1	0	0	40,000
40,000	Freeholders	7	280,000	84	0	3,360,000	12	0	11	0	0	1	0	0	280,000
140,000	Freeholders	5	700,000	50	0	7,000,000	10	0	9	10	0		10	0	350,000
150,000	Farmers	5	750,000	44	0	6,600,000	8	15	8	10	0		5	0	187,000
16,000	Persons in sciences and liberal arts	5	80,000	60	0	960,000	12	0	11	10	0		10	0	40,000
40,000	Shopkeepers and tradesmen	4½	180,000	45	0	1,800,000	10	0	9	10	0		10	0	90,000
60,000	Artisans and handicrafts	4	240,000	40	0	2,400,000	10	0	9	10	0		10	0	120,000
5,000	Naval officers	4	20,000	80	0	400,000	20	0	18	0	0	2	0	0	40,000
4,000	Military officers	4	16,000	60	0	240,000	15	0	14	0	0	1	0	0	16,000
511,586 Fam.		5¼	2,675,520	67	0	34,495,800	12	18	12	0	0		18	0	£2,447,100

Number	Rank	Decrease		£ s.	£	£ s.	£ s. d.	£ s. d.	£ s. d.
50,000	Common seamen	150,000	3	20 0	1,000,000	7 0	7 10 0	10 0	£75,000
364,000	Labouring people and outservants	1,275,000	$3\frac{1}{2}$	15 0	5,460,000	4 10	4 12 0	2 0	127,500
400,000	Cottagers and paupers	1,300,000	$3\frac{1}{4}$	6 10	2,000,000	2 0	2 5 0	5 0	325,000
35,000	Common soldiers	70,000	2	14 0	490,000	7 0	7 10 0	10 0	35,000
849,000 Fams.	Vagrants	2,795,000	$3\frac{1}{4}$	10 10	8,950,000	3 5	3 9 0	4 0	£562,000
		30,000			60,000	3 2	3 0 0	1 0 0	60,000
849,000		2,825,000	$3\frac{1}{4}$	10 10	9,010,000	3 3	3 7 6	4 6	£622,000

So the General Account is.

Number	Rank	Decrease		£ s.	£	£ s.	£ s. d.	£ s. d.	£ s. d.
511,586 Fam.	increasing the wealth of the kingdom	2,675,520	$5\frac{1}{4}$	67 0	34,495,800	12 18	12 0 0	18 6	£2,447,100
849,000 Fam.	decreasing the wealth of the kingdom	2,825,000	$3\frac{1}{4}$	10 10	9,010,000	3 3	3 7 6	4 6	622,000
1,360,586 Fam.	Neat totals	5,500,520	$4\frac{1}{20}$	32 0	43,505,800	7 18	7 11 3	6 9	£1,825,100

	True yearly value	Value as rated to the 4s. Tax	Produce of the 4s. Tax
So the yearly rents or value of the land is	10 millions	6,500,000	1,300,000
The houses and buildings	2 millions	1,500,000	300,000
All other hereditaments	1 million	500,000	100,000
Personal estates, etc.	1 million	550,000	100,000
In all	14 millions	9,050,000	1,800,000

So that whereas the tax of 4s. per pound produces but

It should produce (if duly assessed)

£1,800,000

£2,800,000

The produce of the arable land I thus estimate:

	of Bushels	per Bushel	Value
Wheat	12 millions	at 3s. 6d.	£2,100,000
Rye	8 millions	at 2s. 6d.	1,000,000
Barley	25 millions	at 2s.	2,500,000
Oats	16 millions	at 1s. 6d.	1,200,000
Peas	7 millions	at 2s. 6d.	875,000
Beans	4 millions	at 2s. 6d.	500,000
Vetches, etc.	1 million	at 2s.	100,000
	73 millions	at 2s. 3d.	£8,275,000

This is only the neat produce exclusive of the seed corn which in some sorts of grain being near a 4th of the produce, in others a 5th, may in general be reckoned about 17 millions of bushels more, which makes the whole produce to be 90 millions of bushels which at 2s. 3d. per bushel in common is full 10 millions sterling.

These 73 millions of bushels of grain are the product of 10 of the 11 millions of acres of arable land, the other million of acres producing hemp, flax, woad, saffron, dyeing weeds, etc. The value of the product whereof is about 1 million sterling.

So that the rent of the corn land being under £3,000,000 per annum and the neat produce thereof above 8 millions, the produce is near treble to the rent.

Now the rents or yearly value of the pasture and meadow, woods, coppices, forests, parks, commons, heaths, and moors, mountains, and barren land being £6,250,000 sterling, the produce can scarce make above two rents or 12 millions. There being little charge either in cultivating the land or gathering the produce thereof, comparatively to what there is in the arable land. This produce is principally in and by cattle, hay, timber, and firewood.

The produce by cattle in butter, cheese, and milk is about	£2,500,000
The value of the wool yearly shorn is about	2,000,000
The value of the horses yearly bred is about	250,000

The value of the flesh yearly spent as food is about   3,350,000
The value of the tallow and hides of the cattle   600,000
The value of hay yearly consumed by horses about   1,300,000
The hay yearly consumed by other cattle   1,000,000
The timber yearly felled for building and such uses   500,000
The wood yearly spent in firing and petty uses   500,000

So the produce (including 1 million sterling in hay spent by
cattle) is in all   £12,000,000

An estimate of the livestock of the nation:

	Yearly breed or Increase	The whole Stock	Value of each besides the Skin £ s. d.	Value of the Stock £
Beeves, Stirks, and Calves	800,000	4,500,000	2 0 0	9,000,000
Sheep and Lambs	3,200,000	11,000,000	8 0	4,400,000
Swine and Pigs	1,300,000	2,000,000	16 0	1,600,000
Deer and Fawns	20,000	100,000	2 0 0	200,000
Goats and Kids	10,000	50,000	10 0	25,000
Hares and Leverets	12,000	24,000	1 6	1,800
Rabbits and Conies	2,000,000	1,000,000	5	21,100
	7,342,000	18,074,000		£15,247,900

So the value of the livestock for food is   £15,247,900
The value of the horses (and asses), being 1,200,000 at £2 10s. each, breed-
ing annually 100,000 is   3,000,000
The value of the pelts & skins (over & above the wool)   2,400,000

                                                                     £20,647,900

The value of the wool yearly shorn (or pelted) 10,000,000 fleeces, 2,000,000 lb.
at 4s. per fleece or 28s. per tod at 12d. per lb.   2,000,000
The value of the whole stock of tame fowl as geese, turkeys, hens, ducks,
pigeons, swans, and peacocks   460,000
The whole stock of wild fowl about   12,000

                                                     In all   £23,119,900

An estimate of the yearly consumption of flesh in the nation:

	Number of the Yearly Consumption	Weight of each Carcase	Price of a pound Weight	Price of each Beast	Value of the Yearly Consumption	Weight of the Yearly Consumption
Beeves and calves	800,000	260 lb. wt.	1d. 3f.	1 18 0	1,520,000	208,000,000 lb. wt.
Sheep and lambs	3,200,000	32	2 1	6 0	960,000	102,400,000
Swine and pigs	1,300,000	46	3 0	11 6	750,000	59,800,000
Deer and fawns	20,000	70	6 0	1 15 0	35,000	1,400,000
Goats and kids	10,000	36	2 2	7 6	4,000	360,000
Hares and leverets	12,000	2½	7 0	1 6	900	30,000
Rabbits and conies	2,000,000	¾–½	6 0	5	42,100	1,700,000
	7,342,000				3,302,000	373,690,000
Tame fowl			at 6d. per pound		600,000	24,000,000
Wild fowl			at 12d. per pound		20,000	400,000
			In all		£3,922,000	398,090,000 lb wt.

Which for 5½ millions of people is in value, 14s. 3d. per annum, ½d. *per diem fere*; in weight, 72 lb. 6 oz. per annum, 3⅙ oz. *per diem*. But for 2,700,000 persons being the value of those who eat flesh constantly, the foresaid proportion of 398,090,000 pound weight of flesh yearly spent as food comes to 6⅖ ounces per head *per diem* and 147½ pound weight per head per annum; besides Dutch beef, Westphalia bacon, etc.

The remaining 2,800,000 persons not eating of flesh being these:

infants under 13 months old	200,000
sick persons	40,000
Part of 700,000 persons, who feed on fish at least 2 days in 7	260,000
Part of 1,760,000 persons contained in 440,000 families who by reason of their poverty do not contribute to church or poor, and consequently eat not flesh above 2 days in 7	1,280,000
Part of 1,200,000 persons contained in 400,000 families who receive alms and consequently eat not flesh above once a week	1,020,000
	2,800,000

8. The Beer, Ale, and Malt annually consumed in England, and the Revenue of Excise arising thereby

That the arable land of England is near 11 millions of acres, of which the barley land is almost a third, or 3,200,000 acres. Whereof somewhat above two-thirds being yearly sowed, and the other third fallow, the land yearly sowed with barley is about 2,200,000 acres. Which at 15 bushels per acre is 33 millions of bushels of barley, viz. malted and brewed into ale and beer, 21½ millions of bushels; malted and made into spirits and for other uses, 1 million of bushels, [making] 22½ millions malted; seed corn at near 4 bushels per acre, 8½ millions of bushels; barley for bread, feeding of poultry, etc., 2 millions of bushels, [making] 10½ [millions] unmalted. In all 33 millions of bushels.

Which 22½ millions of bushels of malted barley may well produce 24 millions of bushels of malt. That malt brewed into ale and beer is 23 millions of bushels, whereof the malt brewed for sale is much about 13,500,000 bushels, and for private use 9,500,000 bushels. And that the difference between the years 1688 and 1695 is according to the following scheme:

	Bushels of malt	Barrels strong			Barrels	
Anno 1688	15,900,000 producing	5,300,000	Excised	4,800,000 at 2s. 6d. per barrel	£600,000
			Not excised	500,000	
	7,100,000 producing	Barrels small 7,100,000	Excised	2,400,000 at 6d. per barrel	60,000
			Not excised	4,700,000	
	23,000,000	12,400,000			£660,000
Anno 1695	14,500,000 producing	Barrels strong 3,850,000	Excised	3,200,000 at 4s. 9d. per barrel	£766,100
			Not excised	620,000	
	7,500,000 producing	Barrels small 7,500,000	Excised	2,200,000 at 1s. 3d. per barrel	137,500
			Not excised	5,300,000	
	22,000,000	11,350,000			£903,600

Whence it follows that if the drink brewed for private use *anno* 1688 had paid the then duty of excise, it had come to £180,000, and in the whole £840,000.

That if the drink brewed for private use *anno* 1695 should pay the present duty it would come to £408,250, and in the whole £1,311,850.

That raising the excise has reduced the consumption of malt from 23 millions of bushels to 22 millions.

That it has reduced the quantity of drink brewed from 12,400,000 barrels to 11,350,000 barrels.

That it has decreased public brewing from 4,800,000 barrels of strong drink to 3,233,000 barrels, and from 2,400,000 barrels of small to 2,200,000 barrels. And that it hath increased private brewing from 500,000 barrels of strong to 620,000 barrels, and from 4,700,000 barrels of small to 5,300,000 barrels.

Lastly that 9*d.* per bushel on malt at the kiln is much about equivalent to the present excise, and that 18*d.* per bushel on malt at the mashfatt would come to one million sterling.

9. A Calculation of the Poll Bills and some other Taxes and what may be raised by some Commodities not yet taxed

That the produce of the 12*d.* Poll 1st William and Mary being £288,300, and of the quarterly poll 3rd William and Mary £597,500, the people of England do not appear by the 1st poll bills to be above 5,400,000 souls, though in the consumption and expense of the nation they answer to near 5,500,000 souls.

As by the following scheme:

	12*d.* Poll First Wm. and Mary	Quarterly Poll 3*d.* Wm. and Mary
The number of people as they answered in the Poll Tax	5,400,000	5,390,000
viz.		
Persons receiving alms	600,000	620,000
Their children under 16 years	300,000	310,000
Persons not paying to church and poor (660,000)		670,000
Their children under 16 years	600,000	610,000
Children under 16 of day labourers	240,000	260,000
Children under 16 of servants in husbandry	140,000	160,000
Children under 16 of such as have 4 children or more, and are not worth £50 (150,000 parents)	180,000	200,000
Omitted by neglect or otherwise deficient	100,000	120,000
So the number of those that were excused or insolvent is	2,150,000	2,950,000
The number of the solvent people	3,250,000	2,440,000
In all	5,400,000	5,390,000

	At 12*d.* per head	At 4*s.* per Head
So the common duty of the solvent people amounted to	£162,500	£488,000
And all other parts of the said polls.	125,800	109,500
In all	£288,300	£597,500

Note: That the quarterly poll excused all such as by reason of their poverty did not contribute to church and poor, whereas the 12 penny poll excused only their children under 16 years, but not the parents themselves. Whereby the quarterly poll excused 600,000 persons, more than the 12 penny poll by that single article.

That if all persons had paid the common duty only upon the 12 penny poll, without anything for degrees, titles, or qualifications it would have raised near as much as it did, or £275,000, and that if all persons had paid only the common duty of 4*s.* upon the quarterly poll, it would have raised near twice as much as it did, or £1,100,000.

Of the Present Duty on Marriages, Births, and Burials,
Accounting the People to be 5,400,000 souls

As a Medium in times of Peace		In all		Common duty	But *anno* 1695	Thus	
Yearly Burials	1 in 32	170,000 at 4*s.*	each	£34,000	1 in 29½	183,000	£36,600
Births	1 in 28	190,000 at 2*s.*	each	19,000	1 in 30½	177,000	17,700
Marriages	1 in 132	41,000 at 2*s.*	6*d.*	5,125	1 in 140	39,000	4,875
Bachelors	1 in 40	140,000 at 1*s.*		7,000	1 in 40	140,000	7,000
Widowers	1 in 200	27,000 at 1*s.*		1,350	1 in 200	27,000	1,850
			In all	66,475			67,525

Omissions, Frauds, and Insolvent

In					
Burials	6	per cent	10,000 at 4*s.* each.	£2,000
Births	3	per cent	6,000 at 2*s.*	600
Marriages	2½	per cent	1,000 at 2*s.* 6*d.*	125
Bachelors	10	per cent	14,000 at 1*s.*	700
Widowers	5	per cent	1,500 at 1*s.*	75
			In all	3,500

Excused by Receiving Alms

In					
Burials			nil	nil
Births	30	per cent	60,000 at 2*s.* each.	6,000
Marriages	10	per cent	4,000 at 2*d.* 6*d.*	500
Bachelors	5	per cent	7,000 at 1*s.*	350
Widowers	20	per cent	6,000 at 1*s.*	250
			In all	£7,100

So the common duty comes to   66,475
And the deductions   10,600

Whereby the neat produce of the common duty is   £55,875

The persons charged for quality are about 1 in 10 of the whole.

viz.

Burials	17,000	at 14s. each	£11,900
Births	19,000	at 8s. each	7,600
Marriages	4,000	at 10s. each	2,000
Bachelors	14,000	at 5s. each	3,500
Widowers	3,000	at 5s. each	1,500

In all for quality   £26,500

Omissions, frauds, and insolvents in
quality a 20th part, or   £1,325

Whereby the neat produce for quality
is   25,175
And the neat produce of the common
duty   55,875

So the neat produce in all should be   81,050
Whereas it is given for   £130,000

Of the Present Duty on Houses and Windows for Supplying the Deficiency of the Clipped Money

The number of inhabited houses is near 1,300,000, the number of windows under 9,000,000

Whereof 980,000 under 10 windows at 2s. per house	£98,000
270,000 under 20 windows at 6s. per house	81,000
50,000 above 20 windows at 10s. per house	25,000
1,300,000	£204,000

Out of which deducting:

	Houses	
For those who receive alms	330,000 at 2s. per house	£33,000
Those who do not pay to church and poor	380,000 at 2s. 4d.	44,000
Omissions, frauds, and defaulters	40,000 at 4s.	8,000

Insolvent in all	750,000	£85,000
Solvent in all	550,000	119,000

So that the neat produce is but   £119,000 per annum
Whereas it being granted for 7 years and valued at £1,200,000
it is given for above   £170,000 per annum

But whereas the premium and interest money upon advancing such part of the sum (which the act hath given credit for) as the fund will bear, may be estimated at 12 or 13 per cent, and the collecting and other charges 5 or 6 per cent, in all 18 or 19 per cent, it follows that the neat produce to the Exchequer will be but £100,000 per annum applicable to the discharge of principal and interest. But if one half of the £1,200,000 be advanced the first year upon the credit of the Act, and that a 4th part of the said £119,000 should be paid in the first year in light hammered money worth only ¾th of the tale, the produce of the first year applicable to discharge of principal money will not be above £50,000.

So that if the whole deficiency of the clipped money should instead of £1,200,000 amount to £2,400,000, it will be about 24 years before the said duty will discharge the principal and interest, though there should be no further anticipations thereon than £500,000 or £600,000 at the first; and though the said duty should produce by the end of the said 24 years £114,000 per annum clear, applicable to the discharge of the principal.

As to some commodities not yet taxed:

	£ per annum
That a half penny per lb. weight on common soap and a penny per lb. weight on Castile soap will raise near	50,000
That a half penny per lb. on candles will raise about	70,000
That 3 half pence in the shilling on leather parchment and vellum will be	100,000
That 1d. per bushel on malt will raise £100,000 per annum. Consequently 3d. per bushel will raise 300,000 per annum	300,000
That 3d. per bushel on wheat will raise	150,000
That 2d. per bushel on rye will raise	67,000
That 1d. per bushel on all barley and oats brought to the mill, will raise	13,000
In all	750,000
That 1d. in the crown of the value of all live cattle will raise	400,000
That 1d. in the shilling on all flesh spent as food will raise	300,000
That 3d. per fleece for each fleece of wool shorn will raise	100,000
In all	800,000
That 2s. per lb. on all material for building or repairs will raise	300,000
That 10 per cent upon all wool consumed or manufactured will raise	500,000

10. The state of the Nation *anno* 1695

	Millions Sterling
That the present income of the nation is a million less than it was *anno* 1688 and is now but about	42½
That the yearly expense is about 40½ millions and the taxes 5 millions in all	45½
That the kingdom does now yearly decrease	3
That if the war continue to *anno* 1698 inclusive the yearly income will in probability be but	38½
The Expense 38½ millions ⎫ In all Taxes 4 millions ⎭	42½
The yearly decrease	4

Anno	Annual Income of the Nation	Annual expense of the Nation	Ordinary Revenue of the Crown	Extraordinary Taxes actually raised	Annual Expense In all	Increase or Decrease of the Nation
1688	43,500	41,700 m.	2,000,000		41,700,000	Incr. 1,800,000
1689	43,600	41,500 m.	1,800,000	3,000,000	44,500,000	Decr. 900,000
1690	43,700	41,500 m.	1,800,000	4,000,000	45,500,000	Decr. 1,800,000
1691	43,800	41,400 m.	1,700,000	4,000,000	45,400,000	Decr. 1,600,000
1692	43,800	41,200 m.	1,700,000	4,000,000	45,200,000	Decr. 1,400,000
1693	43,600	41,000 m.	1,600,000	4,000,000	45,000,000	Decr. 1,400,000
1694	43,100	40,800 m.	1,600,000	5,000,000	45,800,000	Decr. 2,700,000
1695	42,500	40,500 m.	1,500,000	5,000,000	45,500,000	Decr. 3,000,000
1696	41,600	40,100 m.	1,500,000	4,500,000	44,600,000	Decr. 3,000,000
1697	40,200	39,300 m.	1,400,000	4,500,000	43,800,000	Decr. 3,600,000
1698	38,500	38,500 m.	1,400,000	4,000,000	42,500,000	Decr. 4,000,000

Hence we may infer:

Millions sterling

That in 7 years from 1688 to 1695 inclusive the taxes have amounted
to effectually   29
But that the kingdom is scarce actually decreased   13
So that by industry and frugality there has been saved full   16
That by the year 1698 inclusive the taxes will in 10 years have amounted
to in all probability effectually   42
And the kingdom will be actually decreased 23½ millions. That after the year 1695 the taxes actually raised will fall short every year more and more to that degree, that the war cannot well be sustained beyond the year 1698 upon the foot it now stands, unless

1. The yearly income of the nation can be increased.
2. Or the yearly expense diminished.
3. Or a foreign or home credit be obtained or established.
4. Or the confederacy be enlarged.
5. Or the state of the war altered.
6. Or a general excise in effect introduced.

Now whereas by the foregoing scheme, the wealth of the kingdom seems to be actually decreased almost 13 millions sterling between 1688 and 1695 inclusive, and will probably decrease by 1698 inclusive above 10 millions and a half more, in all about 23 millions and a half in 10 years, the said decrease seems to be thus chargeable.

	The Stock of the Kingdom 1688	Decrease by the year 1695	Remaining Stock anno 1695	Decrease by the year 1698	Remaining Stock anno 1698
Coined silver	8,500,000	4,000,000	4,500,000	1,500,000	3,000,000
Coined gold	3,000,000		3,000,000	1,500,000	1,500,000
Uncoined silver and gold	500,000	400,000	100,000	100,000	
Wrought plate, rings, etc.	4,000,000	1,600,000	2,400,000	1,200,000	1,200,000
Jewels	1,500,000	500,000	1,000,000	200,000	800,000
Furniture, apparel, etc.	10,500,000	2,500,000	8,000,000	1,500,000	6,500,000
	28,000 000	9,000,000	19,000,000	6,000,000	13,000,000
Stock for trade, consumption, etc.	33,000,000	3,000,000	30,000,000	3,500,000	26,500,000
The livestock in cattle, etc.	25,000,000	1,000,000	24,000,000	1,000,000	23,000,000
	86,000,000	13,000,000	73,000,000	10,500,000	62,500,000

Hence it follows that, if the stock of the nation, which was 86 millions sterling *anno* 1688 viz. about double to the yearly income and expense, shall be decreased to 62 millions and a half by *anno* 1698, the war cannot well be sustained longer than that year for these reasons:

1. For that the money of the kingdom will then be but $4\frac{1}{2}$ millions, viz. but one tenth of the annual expense, less than which cannot circulate the whole.

2. That the wrought plate will be little above a million, consequently nothing to be spared further than that article.

3. That 7 millions in jewels, household stuff, furniture, apparel, etc., is the least quantity we can imagine that article reduceable unto, the bedding of the kingdom amounting to one half of that sum.

4. That if the stock of the kingdom, in shipping, forts, and castles, and in naval and military stores and appointments, and for foreign trade, and home consumption, and all the branches of that article, be reduced from 33 to 26 millions; if it should be further lessened, the nation cannot be secure, trade cannot be carried on, nor a sufficient stock of provisions left to supply us in times of difficulty.

5. That if the livestock of the nation, which will then be diminished a 12th part, should be further diminished, it may occasion an excessive rise of the price of wool, leather, flesh, butter, and cheese, not much short of a famine; unless the number of people decrease proportionately; the effect whereof will be equally pernicious.

8. GREGORY KING ELABORATES ON HIS CALCULATIONS IN REPLY TO CRITICISMS BY ROBERT HARLEY, 1697

[National Library of Australia, Canberra, 'Kashnor' MS. of *Natural and Political Observations upon the State and Condition of England* by Gregory King[1]]

[The other cities and market towns 195,000. See above, pp. 771–2.[2]]
Ro. Harley: Are these estimated or numbered from the Hearth Tax? If estimated by what rates are the proportions made?
Gregory King: Mr. Adams did about 18 years ago collect the number of houses in the cities and great towns as well as in the villages from the hearth books ... and the general housing of the kingdom amounted upon his totting them but to 1,120,000 or thereabouts. The increase since that time is not 40,000 and the new discoveries for which there was particular encouragements, including all the cottages and paupers, could not by the year

---

[1] Professor D. V. Glass gives a description and the provenance of this manuscript in 'Two Papers on Gregory King', in *Population in History*, ed. D. V. Glass and D. E. C. Eversley (1965), p. 184 and n. 7, with a detailed discussion of its demographic data (pp. 163–5, 182–214). Its relationship to the *Natural and Political Observations* is explained by its title page: 'Observations and Conclusions Natural and Political Upon the State and Condition of England, etc., by G. K. Esq., Lancaster Herald of Arms, anno Domini 1696, with Notes, Observations, and Enquiries, upon the same by R. H. Esqr., anno Domini 1697, With Mr. K's Further Observations in Answer to Mr. H's Inquiries anno 1697'. King's comments end with section 9 and are there dated 31 May 1697.

[2] Items in brackets thus [   ] refer to headings in the *Natural and Political Observations*, reprinted in this volume on the pages indicated.

1690 be above 60 or 80,000 more; whereby the general account of the kingdom will not rise to above 1,220 or 1,240,000 houses.

I was privy to the account and this previous knowledge with my own observations from the assessments on marriages, births, and burials returned me from several cities and market towns was a foundation for me to compute the number of the houses in the cities and market towns (exclusive of the bills of mortality) thus:

4 cities of between 5 and 6,000 houses each one with another	22,000
10 other cities or great towns of 1,800 houses each	18,000
30 other cities and great towns of 500 houses each	15,000
100 other cities and great towns of 300 houses each	30,000
250 other cities and great towns of 200 houses each	50,000
400 other cities and great towns of 150 houses each	60,000
	195,000

[In the Villages and Hamlets . . . See above, pp. 771–2.]

Harley: In many counties especially remote from London, some from superstition of numbering the people, others for other reasons were less exact than in London.

King: As to the country assessments I am certain that where they were anything regular they were more exact than those in London. For the parishes in England, having at a medium 130 houses to each parish, containing about 550 souls, there is scarce an assessor but knows every man, woman, and child in the parish, but it is much otherwise in London, where the parishes have one with another 800 houses and 4,000 souls and where an assessor shall scarce know 5 families on each side of him. So that I am of opinion my allowance for the omissions in those regular assessments (for it was such only I could make any use of) is very near the matter . . .

(1) [Yearly rent of the Lands £10 million. See above, p. 778.]

Harley: Is not this too high?

(2) [Rent of Housing £2 million.]

Harley: This cannot be 1/5 of the land rents.

(3) [Rent of all other Hereditaments £1 million.]

Harley: What can they be distinct from the last heads to amount to that value?

King: (1) The yearly rents of the lands 10 millions, I cannot think it too high upon this consideration:

1. That the 1s. and 2s. Aids *Anno* 1° Wm. Ma. produced 1,566,000 pounds even when there was a concurrent Poll, consequently the four shillings should produce 2,088,000 pounds.

2. The 4s. Aid *Anno* 4 Wm. Ma. did actually produce 1,977,000 pounds. But there being no Poll current that year, there must be a deduction of about 100,000*l.* for such articles as used to be charged in the Poll Bills, but were now charged in the Pound rate. So that the 4s. upon hereditaments only

produced about 1,900,000 and I think is not yet fallen lower than 1,800,000 pounds. Consequently the rents of lands, tenements, and hereditaments as answered in taxes is upwards of 9 millions. But the author of *Ways and Means* (page 102) reckons if that tax were strictly executed it would raise 3 millions. And then the whole rents with all the other articles of the 4*s*. Aid would be equivalent to 15 million in rents, whereof those articles that are not properly hereditaments, having raised about 100,000*li.* in the Aids and Polls, etc., possibly being well executed, ought to raise 200,000*li.* which is equal to a million in rents. The rest of the land, tenements, and hereditaments by that author's computation should be 14,000,000*li.* which I reckon but 13 millions viz.

	The Land	10 millions
	The Buildings	2 millions
	Other Hereditaments	1 million
		13 millions
Besides	Personal Estates	1 million
	In All	14 millions

Now if the whole has produced very near 2 millions in taxes to the 4*s*. Aid and consequently answered to near 10 millions in rents, etc., and yet would not amount to the value of 14 millions in all or 2,800,000*li.* in taxes being strictly executed, then the omissions, the fraud, the favour, and the great underrating complained of in the North and West is nothing so considerable as we are apt to believe. For we must suppose some favour even in London and the 11 Home Counties; so that to advance the 4*s*. Aid to 14 millions in rents, etc., we may (considering that London, the 11 Home Counties, and the rest of the kingdom bear these proportions following in the money actually raised) make a further charge upon 'em as follows to complete the tax full at 4*s*. per *lib*.

	Produce	To be charged	Deficiency
Rated at 3*s*. 6*d*. London, Westm., Midsx.	310,000	a 7th part more	6*d*. per £ 44,500
at 3*s*. 2*d*. the 11 Home Counties	630,000	a 4th part more	9*d*. per £ 157,000
at 2*s*. 6*d*. the rest of the kingdom	1,040,000	6/10 parts more	1*s*. 6*d*. per £ 624,000
			826,000
Produce	1,980,000		
Deficiency	826,000		
Total	2,806,000		

But the rents of houses being not so valuable as land rents, I do not see but that London raised a full proportion when it came to near a sixth part of the actual produce of the whole kingdom or a 9th part of what the kingdom ought to have produced to the 4*s*. Aid.

(2) As to the value of the housing I estimate it thus:

Real value		in taxes
105,000 houses in the bills of mortality at £11	1,160,000 @ £9	945,000
195,000 houses in towns at £2-5-0	440,000 @ £1-15-0	340,000
20,000 houses of the nobility, bishops, barts., knights, esquires, gentlemen, clergy at £8	160,000 @ £6	120,000
380,000 houses of freeholders, farmers, and others paying above 20s. per annum at £1-10-0	570,000 @ £1-2-6	427,500
590,000 poor houses and cottages under 20s. per annum at 6s. 8d.	196,000	
	£2,526,000	£1,832,500

Within the Bills of Mortality:

Houses	Rent	Total Rent
5,000 at	£40	£200,000
10,000 at	£23	£230,000
20,000 at	£15	£300,000
30,000 at	£9	£270,000
40,000 at	£4	£160,000
105,000 at	£11	£1,160,000

But deducting out of the 4th article 180,000 houses going along with the land,

	Real Value	Value in Taxes
at £2-0-0	£360,000	
at £1-10-0		£270,000
and the 590,000 poor houses or cottages	£200,000	
	£560,000	£270,000
there remains for the rentable houses	£1,966,000	£1,562,000

Now whereas by this calculation the houses within the bills of mortality are near one half of the rents of the whole housing of England, but in the produce of the tax are three-fifths of the produce of the housing of the kingdom, we are to observe:

1. That London, Westminster, and Middlesex produced to the 4s. Aid *Anno* 4 Wm. Ma. about £313,000. Consequently the rents, hereditaments, etc., were in value £1,565,000
2. That the Houses in Middlesex out of the bills of mortality are equal to the houses in Surrey within the said bills.
3. That the neat land in Middlesex (besides houses and gardens) is 180,000 acres, whereupon we say

	Rent	Total	Produce in the 4s. Tax
1. That the 105,000 inhabited houses in London, Middlesex, Westminster, and besides 5 or 6,000 not inhabited; in all 111,000 at	£9-0-0	999,000	200,000
2. That the 180,000 acres of neat land in Middlesex at per acre	£0-12-6	112,000	22,000

3. That personal estates at a 9th of the rents and 24s. per £100	2,000,000	24,000
4. That the East India and other comp. stocks at 24s. per £100	1,200,000	14,400
5. That the Waters and the King's Printing House comes to		4,000
6. The Custom House and the Navy Office		8,300
7. The offices at Westminster Hall, the Exchequer, and King's Servants		20,000
8. All other offices, employments, church livings, and other hereditaments		20,000
		312,700

(3) Other hereditaments in the kingdom in general are such as are particularly mentioned in the acts distinct from land rents, as quarries, mines of coal, tin, lead, copper, mundial iron or other mines, ironworks, saltsprings, and saltworks, alum mines or works, woods, underwoods, coppices, fishings, tithes, and tolls whatsoever. To which I may add the mills themselves (not being included among the houses), prisons, schools, offices, and employments in the country, and many other yearly profits which may well amount to a million sterling per annum in a round number.

[That the yearly produce of trade, arts, and labour was. See above, pp. 778, 781.]

Harley: By what rule is the product of trade, etc., estimated?

King: In calculating the product of trade, arts, and labour, I considered the computations of trade made by others, the natural product of the land and its improvement by manufacture and how consumed at home or sent abroad and what was imported from other countries to us. But especially I considered these 3 heads:

1. The number of the people.

2. The expense of the kingdom in diet, apparel, and such incident charges as tend only to the consumption of things.

3. The state of the kingdom and the value thereof at present and at such time as it had but half the present number of people, that thereby I might ascertain the annual increase of its wealth at a medium. I confess I did not rely on such former calculations of this kind as I had then met with, because they had but a loose notion of the true number of the people; and I have that assuredness in my numbering them, that I make it the touchstone to all other calculations. Sir Wm. Petty assigns 7*li.* per head as the common expense of mankind (which I take to be too little for England and too great for the world in general); this with his number of people, viz. 7,400,000 would make the annual expense 51,800,000*li.*, but with my number of 5½ millions of souls is but 38,500,000*li.* at most. 'Tis true in his *Verbum Sapienti*, page 3, he comes nearer the true number of people in calling 'em about 6 millions. But his allowance of £6 13s. 4d. for their annual expense or 4½d. per diem for food, housing, clothes, and all other necessaries is certainly too little unless he confines it to personal necessaries only; though it would be more than

enough in proportion to Mons. Souligne's allowance for the people of France ... I then considered the principal article, diet, according to the several degrees living; and I found the poorest sort, whose general expense was but 3*li*. per annum or 2*d*. per diem, spent ⅔ or somewhat above 5 farthings per diem in diet; the middle sort whose general expense was 7*li*. per head spent 4*li*., per annum in diet; and the better sort whose general expense was above 50*li*. per head per annum spent less than a third in diet. I distributed my people into classes, I proportioned their food and raiment and other expenses, I considered how this answered the general product of the land. The revenue of the excise gave me a light into the quantity of malt and drink; others had given account of the wine imported, a due allowance of bread corn was to be made; the milk, butter, and cheese depended upon the stock of kine, and that stock upon the proportion of pasture and of other cattle; the allowance of flesh depended on the stock of cattle for food in general; fish, fowl, eggs, fruit and garden stuff, salt, oil, pickles, spices, grocery, confectionery wares, and the like required a due consideration. Upon the whole I reckoned that diet came to about 21 millions; apparel to about half that sum; and incident expenses relating to consumption, much the same as apparel in time of peace. Though possibly upon second thoughts I may be inclined to think the diet not much above 20 millions and the other articles proportionable to it; in all 39 millions or 40 at most. I then considered that when the kingdom had but half the people, it was not above a 4th part of the present value; and that if it should have double the number, it would be worth 5 times the present value ... computed ... at 650 millions ... I framed the following scheme:

Anno Domini	People	Value of the Nation	
660	1,350,000	60 millions	
			100 millions or 166,000*li*. per annum
1260	2,700,000	160 millions	
			490 millions or 1,120,000*li*. per annum
1695	5,400,000	650 millions	
			2,350 millions or 3,800,000*li*. per annum
2300	10,800,000	3,000 millions	

By which I concluded that if the kingdom increased in value of the capital stock, the last term of doubling its people, above a million sterling per annum, it may at this time be reckoned to increase *communibus annis* near 2 millions sterling or 1,800,000*li*. Consequently if the expense was near 42 millions and the increase 1,800,000, the whole income was 43½ millions and that if the rents of the land, tenements, and hereditaments was above 13 millions, the superlucration by trade, arts, and labour was 30¼ millions sterling.

And that the yearly expense of the kingdom at £7 11*s*. 4*d*. per head is   41,617,000*li*.

The yearly increase at 6*s*. 8*d*. per head is   1,833,000*li*.

So that the total is not 45,450,000 but   43,450,000*li*.

But if the whole expense be but little above 39 millions, the improvement by trade, arts, and labour will be but 28 millions which at 12 years' purchase is 336 millions sterling.

... Now the value of man's labour in England answers to 60 or 70*li.* per head, yet the superlucration over and above diet, apparel, and necessary incidents not being above 2 millions per annum, or a 15th part of 30 million, the value of the men, women, and children to be sold as slaves is not above 22 million at 4*li.* per head at a medium; viz. the children under 10 years old at 12 million worse than nothing; those between 10 and 16 and those between 60 and 100 at nothing; and those between 16 and 60 at 34 million or 14*li.* per head; viz. the females at 9 or 10*li.*, the males at 18 or 20*li.* per head ... since the labour of man is subject to more accidents than houses which Sir William Petty does value at 12 years' purchase, I do not see but that 11 years may be sufficient for man's labour considering all contingencies.

[The several sorts of land ... See above, p. 977.]

Harley: Arable land at 5*s.* 10*d.* too high a medium; so is pasture and meadow at 9*s.*

King: I have since reduced 'em to 5*s.* 6*d.* for arable and 8*s.* 6*d.* for pasture by making some small alterations in the several species of land, and lower than this they will not bear.

[Produce of the Arable Land ... See above, p. 782.]

Harley: None of the grain enumerated require more than 1/5 for seed, others from 1/6 to 1/10 if the husband be good. Rape seed omitted which is now m[uch] sown with great advantage.

King: I agree the seed corn in general to be about 1/7 of the produce.

Harley: It can be made to appear by a particular of charge that the produce must be more or the ground could not be tilled by anyone though rent free.

King: Produce of corn land treble to the rent, this (being exclusive of the seed corn) is the common way of reckoning and will certainly do well enough for land of 7*s.* or 8*s.* per acre or upwards, but for poor or low priced land I allow it may require to produce 4 rents (tithe included) over and above the seed corn. For in computing the charge of barley ground for three years (whereof one year fallow) at 3*s.* per acre rent and at 5*s.* 6*d.* per acre rent and at 8*s.* per acre rent, I find that the charge exclusive of the rent and the seed corn is as follows:

Charge of 3 years
£. s. d.

at 3*s.*	the charge 3 rents	1-7-0
at 5*s.* 6*d.*	the charge 2⅛ rents	1-15-0
at 8*s.*	the charge 1⅔ rents	2-0-0

And that the produce to equal the charge, including the rent and seed corn and tithe must be

	bushels	
For the 3*s.* land	27	per acre the 2 crops
For the 5*s.* 6*d.* land	29	} at 2*s.* per bushel
For the 8*s.* land	32	

But to raise a profit equal to the rent 30⅓, 37, and 44 bushels of the two crops And exclusive of seed corn 11¾, 15½, 19$\frac{1}{32}$

	Seed corn	Produce exclusive of seed
Seed in 2 years	7 bushels	23½
	6 bushels	31 }both crops
	5 bushels	39

So that upon reconsidering that article, having reduced the arable land from 10 to 9 millions of acres, and the price per acre from 5s. 10d. to 5s. 6d.; the neat produce of the arable land in general (tithe included) is 4 rents. But allowing a 12th part for tithes, the neat produce will be 3 rents and 3/4 or somewhat better.

I should be glad to see your particular by which the charge of arable land amounts to 4 rents.

[An Estimate of the yearly consumption of Flesh . . . See above, p. 783.]

Harley: The exact number slaughtered in the bills of mortality is kept and may be had. Is not 260lb. weight too high, because little cattle are more bred now than formerly?

King: If the precise number slaughtered within the bills of mortality with their weight may be had, which I doubt it cannot, it would give a great light into the matter; there being by my computation full a 5th in weight of the beeves and calves spent or slain therein of what is spent in the whole kingdom, and in value about 3 tenths of the whole. But surely 260lb. weight for a beef's carcase and a calf's together (including the tallow and offal) cannot be too high at a medium. For the calves killed as veal being not above a 16th part of the co-existing stock of black cattle, or about a 3rd part of the animal breed or consumption; and the beasts killed as beef about an 8th part of the co-existing stock or two-thirds of the animal increase or breed; it follows that there are about 267,000 calves killed yearly in the kingdom as veal and about 533,000 beeves. The carcase of each calf (reckoning the offal to a 5th part of the whole) at 50lb. weight, or the neat carcase at 40lb. weight, and the tallow and offal at about a 4th or 5th part more, i.e. 70 or 65lb. weight, in all 365lb. weight; the veal at 2 farthing a pound or 9s. 4d. each calf; the beef at almost 7 farthings per lb. or 52s. 4d. each beef. Now 40s. being a very low price for a beef and 8 or 10li. not an extraordinary price especially in the London markets, I cannot think of a juster weight at a medium than 50lb. weight for calves and 360 or 370lb. weight for beeves, which answers in common to 260lb. weight; and for the London butcheries 62lb. weight for calves [at] 3½d. [per lb.] or 18s. per calf and about 400lb. weight for beeves at about 2¾d. per lb. or 4li. 10s., or 4li. 11s. per beef.

Harley: Are not more sheep, etc., killed than the quadruple of beeves?

King: There are by my table more sheep killed in England than the quadruple of beeves, viz. beeves and calves 800,000, sheep and lambs 3,600,000, which is as 1 to 4½, and perchance 1 to 5 might be yet a better proportion by increasing the number of the yearly consumption of sheep and lambs to 4 millions. For I reckon in muttons the yearly increase (which I all along suppose equal to the yearly consumption) is a third part of the co-existing stock. But out of that yearly increase, if a tenth part be deducted for sheep dying of the rot *communibus annis*, then the number slain for food will be, as I have already stated it, only 3,600,000. But surely Sir Wm. Petty's calculation of 3 million of black cattle and but 4 million of sheep in Ireland is not well proportioned.

9. CHARLES DAVENANT'S CALCULATIONS ON THE REVENUES OF THE KINGDOM, 1695

[*The Political and Commercial Works of Charles d'Avenant relating to the Trade and Revenue of England*, ed. Sir. C. Whitworth, London, 1771, I, pp. 26–9, 32–5, 37–48, 53, 57–61]

An Essay upon Ways and Means

Of poll money

THERE is nothing can make it better apparent how displeasing poll money is to the people, than the observation how ill it is brought in, and answered to the king. For where taxes seem hard and oppressive, in particular to the poor, the country gentlemen proceed in the levying of them with no zeal nor affection.

The first single poll that was given in this reign amounted to 288,310*l.* 19*s.* 6½*d.*; with which the quarterly poll holds no manner of proportion. It is true, the qualifications are taxed differently in the two Acts. Money is charged in the first, and not in the second, and titles are put higher in one than the other. But considering how many were brought in by the second Act, and at high rates, which were not reached by the first, the quadruple poll might reasonably have produced near four times as much as the single, and it yielded little more than half.

Quarterly poll.

			l.	*s.*	*d.*
London, Middlesex, and Westminster	——	——	97,622	5	11
Rest of England	——	——	499,896	7	1¼
		Total	597,518	13	0¼

Single poll.

			l.	*s.*	*d.*
London, Middlesex, and Westminster	——	——	80,280	9	4½
Rest of England	——	——	208,030	10	2
		Total	288,310	19	6½
Total of the quarterly poll			597,518	13	0¼
		Difference	309,207	13	5¾

The houses in England, as appears by the books of hearth money, are about 1,300,000, of which 500,000 are cottages, inhabited by the poorer sort; so that we may reckon there are not above 800,000 families liable to the payment of poll money; and though, in the common computation of the whole people, there may not be above 6 persons to a house, one with another, yet, in computing the 800,000 richer families, we may very well allow them to contain, one with another, 7 persons, which would be 5,600,000 heads; and reckon but a third part of these qualified within the Act to pay 4s. per head, the poll bill on that single article ought to have produced 373,333*li*.

What the 1*l*. per quarter upon gentlemen and merchants worth 300*l*. and such as belong to the law; and what the 10s. per quarter upon tradesmen, shopkeepers, and vintners, worth 300*l*. might have yielded, is difficult to compute; but, perhaps, the commissioners names in the Act of Parliament for the monthly assessment, 4to and 5to Gul. and Mar. may be no ill guide in the matter. The commissioners then were about ten thousand, and we may reasonably suppose (and any gentleman may compute for his own country, and he will find) that, one country with another, not an eighth part are named commissioners of those persons who, in estate, real or personal, are worth 300*l*. and if so, we may reckon there are in England 80,000 persons liable to the payment of one pound per quarter; by which account, the king should have received on that article 320,000*l*.

When we reflect upon the great number of tradesmen, shopkeepers, and vintners that are in England, it cannot seem any extravagant computation to reckon there are 40,000 persons of that sort, worth 300*l*. and liable to the payment of ten shillings per quarter; upon which head the king should have received 80,000*l*. And allowing but 26,667*l*. for all other persons charged by that Act, the quarterly poll ought to have yielded the king,

	l.
For the common people at 4s. per head	373,333
For the gentlemen, etc. at 4*l*. per head	320,000
For tradesmen, etc. at 2*l*. per head	80,000
For other persons charged by the act	26,667
In all	800,000

	l.	*s.*	*d.*
But there was received only	597,518	13	0¼

The principal articles in this computation seem very much confirmed by what the first poll yielded; for if there had not been in England about 1,866,666 persons who paid 12*d*. per head, and about 80,000 of the sort who paid 1*l*. per head, that poll could not have produced in the country only 208,330*l*. 10s. 2*d*. for money and titles were generally charged in London.

In the poll now in being, such are charged who are worth in estate, real or personal, 600*l*. which may make some difference in the 2*d*. article; but the 3*d*. article should now increase, considering all persons, by this Act, are to pay 10s. per quarter that are worth 300*l*. in estate, real or personal, which seems to take in stock of all kinds; whereas, in the former Act, only tradesmen, shopkeepers, and vintners were comprehended; so that if the present poll were strictly collected, it would produce about 800,000*l*. and yet as far as can be judged by the accounts hitherto come up, it is not like to yield so much money as the former.

When a tax yields no more than half what in reason might be expected from it, we may plainly see it grates upon all sorts of people, and such ways and means of raising money should be rarely made use of by any government.

Of the new customs and duty upon tonnage

Of the Monthly Assessment and Aids upon a Pound rate

Subsidies, fifteenths, and tenths were the ancient ways and means in this kingdom of supplying the government.

But what estates, and in what manner land was thereby rated, is a matter very perplexed in our records, and would ask more time to explain than the brevity designed in this essay will admit of.

Lord Coke, *Institutes*, 4, pp. 33 and 34, values a subsidy at 70,000*l*. and tenths and fifteenths at 20,000*l*. and says they were 4*s*. in the pound upon land, and 2*s*. 8*d*. upon personal estates . . .

How ancient the inequality is between the taxes in the north and west, and the home counties, so much complained of, cannot easily be traced; for in an assessment of 400,000*l*. (17 and 18 Car. 1) we find the rates upon the northern and western counties to lie just as they do in our present assessment; and though there might be some reason to ease the north in that tax, because those parts had been great sufferers by the Scotch army, yet in 1642, when that Act passed, the sword of civil war was not as yet drawn; and the west and other counties had not yet at all been harassed; so that the favour, which the north and west have met with in land taxes, is a little older than the civil war, and may be attributed to that care, which the great number of members they send up have always had, of their concerns in Parliament.

When the civil war broke out, the commonwealth chiefly subsisted by excises, for they could gather land taxes only where they were strongest.

In 1647, their authority was generally owned over all the nation, and then they began to raise land taxes regularly by a monthly assessment.

When the war was over, there was real reason to ease the north and west, and accordingly the Parliament considered what counties had least felt the war, those in their assessments they rated highest, and they spared such places as had been most harassed by the armies of either side; and this was the distinction they made (and not as is vulgarly thought) that of associated or non-associated counties; for most counties of England, during that war, had been some time or other associated, and by ordinance of Parliament.

But still perhaps it had not fared so well with the north and west, notwithstanding their sufferings, if their cause had not been maintained in the House of Commons by a sufficient number of friends and advocates.

The places which had been least sensible of those calamities, or were soonest rid of them, and that had been under the wings of the Parliament, and their army, were London and Middlesex, Surrey and Southwark,

Hertfordshire, Bedfordshire, Cambridgeshire, Kent, Essex, Norfolk, Suffolk, Berks, Bucks, and Oxfordshire.

And they kept to the same measure of favouring the distant counties, and laying the chief burthen upon those nearest London, as long as the authority of the Commonwealth lasted.

When King Charles the Second was restored, the northern and western gentlemen were strong enough in the House of Commons to get continued the method of assessment then in practice, which was so favourable to them; and in the Act 12 Car. 2. for raising 70,000*l.* for 1 month, it is particularly provided, that it shall be raised in such proportion as the last 70,000*l.* per month was raised by ordinance of state; since which time till now, the counties distant from London have continued in the constant possession of being favourably handled in all assessments.

The first attempt of reducing assessments to some equality, was made in the year 1660 . . .

Ship money was an arbitrary and illegal tax, therefore it concerned the contrivers of it to lay it as equally upon the nation as possible; for it would have been a double grievance to the people, if it had been imposed both against law and also with partiality. On the contrary, it imported the ministers of that time to give their new invention all the fair colours imaginable, and to make that, which was unjust in its nature, at least just and equal in its manner; and no doubt in the rating of it, they had duly weighed and considered the strength and weakness, riches and poverty, trade and fertility, and every circumstance of each particular county; with some regard also to the proportion it bore in the ancient subsidies.

And, upon these grounds, it is more than probable the committee of the House of Commons proceeded in 1660, when they made the ship money their model and pattern of a fair and equal assessment.

Since the late war with France, land has been taxed in different manners, by an assessment, and by a pound rate; but both ways it will perhaps appear, that the north and west have not borne their due share and proportion of the common burthen.

The 1st aid given to their Majesties upon land was by a monthly assessment of 68,820*l.* 19*s.* 1*d.* per month, 1 Gul. and Mar.

The 2nd aid upon land was of 12*d.* per pound. In this Act their Majesties had power to nominate the commissioners under the great seal of England, but were advised to put in all the same persons again, who had been commissioners in the monthly assessment; the assessors in this Act were upon oath, 1 Gul. and Mar.

The 3rd aid upon land was of 2*s.* in the pound. In this Act the assessors were upon oath, 1 Gul. and Mar.

The 4th aid upon land was by a monthly assessment of 137,641*l.* 18*s.* 2*d.* per month, 2 Gul. and Mar.

The 5th aid upon land was by the same monthly assessment, 3 Gul. and Mar.

	1		2			3			4			5		
A TABLE of the	Produce of each County in the monthly Assessment of 137,641*l.* 18*s.* 2*d.* per Month.		Produce of each County in the Poll Money, 1 *Guil. and Mariae.*			Produce of each County in the Aid of 1*s.* 2*d.* per Pound 1 *Guil. and Mariae.*			Produce of each County in the quarterly Poll, 3 and 4 *Guil. and Mariae.*			Produce of each County in the Aid of 4*s.* in the Pound, 4 *Guil. and Mariae.*		
	l.	*s.*	*l.*	*s.*	*d.*	*l.*	*s.*	*d.*	*l.*	*s.*	*d.*	*l.*	*s.*	*d.*
Bedfordshire	21,525	6	2,618	17	4	21,872	19	2	6,400	11	9¾	28,554	15	1¼
Berkshire	27,175	18	4,420	3	6	31,708	2	9	10,353	3	5	41,054	0	9½
Buckinghamshire	31,567	14	4,640	5	11	36,670	7	6¼	9,550	6	2	47,661	1	1
Cambridgeshire and Isle of Ely	32,877	10	4,113	4	10	25,535	6	1	9,612	15	2	32,844	16	3½
Cheshire and Chester	19,230	12	4,542	3	5	23,634	11	5¾	8,791	10	0	28,596	14	0¼
Cornwall	36,981	18	4,622	0	7	24,566	2	9½	9,613	19	10	31,976	0	0
Cumberland	4,039	6	1,114	12	6	2,673	4	7½	2,116	11	6	3,713	18	4
Derbyshire	20,698	0	3,556	3	3	18,198	10	7¼	7,883	4	6	24,093	19	10¼
Devonshire and Exon	80,311	16	12,519	6	7	65,867	19	4	28,821	9	3	82,086	6	2
Dorsetshire and Poole	32,532	2	3,900	12	0	24,878	17	0¾	9,737	3	10	33,116	7	9
Durham, Northumberland, and Berwick	16,718	18	6,244	17	6	22,344	0	7	13,028	19	9	25,146	11	11
Essex	74,362	12	8,156	8	2	71,642	13	9½	20,820	10	2	90,895	14	7
Gloucestershire and Gloucester	44,349	18	5,755	0	8	35,030	9	8¼	13,508	17	9	47,523	13	2
Herefordshire	27,160	0	3,070	3	10	14,947	4	1	6,480	12	10	20,409	2	6
Hertfordshire	32,299	10	4,346	2	2	33,415	14	4	11,054	1	1½	42,973	5	4¼
Huntingdonshire	15,209	0	1,605	0	10	11,598	3	0¾	4,238	16	4	15,497	5	1
Kent	79,846	8	10,115	17	1	66,912	13	1½	24,275	2	5	83,450	3	5
Lancashire	24,160	4	5,938	16	1	17,214	11	2¾	12,732	15	2	21,300	0	0
Leicestershire	26,033	2	3,738	5	4	26,708	5	11¼	10,002	8	7½	35,088	9	7
Lincolnshire and Lincoln	61,802	8	7,683	11	8	58,447	5	4	19,248	1	10	72,265	11	10¼
Northamptonshire	33,933	16	5,551	14	0	36,673	7	3½	12,348	1	8	48,111	12	10
Nottinghamshire	20,961	12	3,137	17	11	21,690	0	6¾	7,085	9	8	27,276	2	6¼
Norfolk and Norwich	85,214	8	9,491	9	10	64,077	13	10¾	24,521	18	8	84,729	14	10¼
Oxfordshire	27,252	16	5,328	0	10	30,903	10	5¾	10,728	13	4	39,038	12	8½
Rutland	5,770	14	797	16	8	3,971	13	10¾	1,785	7	4	5,555	3	11
Salop	28,889	0	4,886	12	10	22,088	0	10	10,783	12	8	29,035	15	0
Staffordshire and Lichfield	20,774	0	4,210	12	10	20,934	5	8½	8,725	3	2	27,082	10	5
Somersetshire and Bristol	71,302	16	8,776	19	10	57,443	19	1	22,295	14	3½	73,728	18	7¼
Southamptonshire	52,546	8	6,209	14	7	42,063	3	7¾	14,083	6	2	55,188	5	2
Suffolk	79,164	16	7,756	3	9	57,667	14	0	19,865	3	10	74,201	18	3¾
Surrey and Southwark	38,328	4	8,442	3	2	52,858	5	0	20,444	12	10	66,984	17	0
Sussex	43,713	6	6,302	15	4	48,142	6	3	12,924	16	11½	60,819	12	0
Warwickshire and Coventry	28,618	10	4,365	7	10	30,478	7	7¼	10,441	17	5	39,864	12	9
Worcestershire and Worcester	26,626	4	3,713	15	1	25,824	0	5½	9,763	18	3	33,144	0	0
Wiltshire	47,205	2	5,952	19	0	39,327	2	2¼	13,771	2	3½	51,672	7	11½
Westmorland	2,784	0	806	5	2	2,269	4	0	1,737	7	0	3,014	7	4
Yorkshire, with York and Hull	83,262	4	17,441	18	7	69,201	11	8½	39,289	9	1	91,620	13	8¾
Wales, North and South	70,503	6	12,156	9	8	39,854	4	9¾	21,029	11	0	51,256	6	8
London, Middlesex, and Westminster	175,969	12	80,280	9	4½	267,311	16	9½	97,622	5	11	307,140	8	5¾
Grand Totals	1,651,702	16	288,310	19	6½	1,566,627	10	9½	597,518	13	0¼	1,977,713	17	1¼
Of the 11 home Counties, viz. Surrey and Southwark, Hertford, Bedford, Cambridge, Kent, Essex, Norfolk, Suffolk, Berks, Bucks, and Oxon, Total is	529,615	2	69,428	16	7	493,265	0	1¾	167,626	18	11¼	632,388	19	6½
Of the rest of England, excluding London, Middlesex, and Westminster, Total is	946,118	2	138,601	13	7	806,050	13	10¼	332,269	8	2	1,038,184	9	1

6	7	8	9	10	11	12
Produce of each County for two Millions, according to the Apportionment of 1660.	Produce of each County according to the Assessment of the Ship Money.	Produce of each County for Excise on Beer and Ale in the Year 1689.	Number of Houses in each County according to the Hearth Books of Lady-day 1690.	Number of Hearths in each County according to the Books of Lady-day 1690.	Produce of each County according to the Assessment of 400,000*l.* 17 and 18 Car. 1.	An Estimate of the Poor Rate for one Year, made in the latter End of King Charles the Second's Reign.
l.	*l.*	*l.* *s.* *d.*			*l.* *s.* *d.*	*l.*
28,000	3,000	5,549 7 3	12,170	21,280	4,372 1 0	6,911
34,000	4,000	9,105 12 9½	16,996	37,550	5,628 14 2	9,800
38,000	4,500	7,261 16 5½	18,688	35,337	6,712 2 6	14,800
36,000	3,500	10,442 7 1	18,629	36,478	8,496 11 1	9,128
28,000	3,000	9,836 10 4½	25,592	40,865	3,168 13 9	5,796
48,000	5,500	10,595 12 3½	26,613	54,588	10,110 15 9	9,257
8,000	800	5,746 10 4	15,279	20,863	633 18 0	4,988
28,000	3,500	11,960 12 4¼	24,944	36,901	2,819 1 7½	7,953
100,000	9,000	34,525 7 11	56,202	135,230	30,084 16 6	34,764
40,000	5,000	7,568 11 7½	17,859	42,951	7,782 0 9	13,885
28,000	2,300	21,216 8 3	53,345	66,169	2,385 9 4½	13,620
96,000	8,000	21,676 4 5	40,545	85,700	18,048 9 9	37,348
50,000	5,500	14,704 8 3	34,476	61,909	11,086 19 5	19,600
32,000	3,500	6,256 5 9½	16,744	27,998	7,146 4 6	8,687
36,000	4,000	13,264 2 11½	17,488	39,064	7,525 10 0	10,760
18,000	2,000	4,437 7 4½	8,713	14,323	3,533 8 9	5,850
96,000	8,000	24,647 15 10½	46,674	107,576	21,100 10 4½	29,875
32,000	1,000	14,501 4 4½	46,961	68,923	4,353 11 3	7,200
36,000	4,500	8,258 18 9½	20,448	31,606	3,848 5 0	11,600
80,000	8,000	15,949 4 5½	45,019	66,119	13,483 17 7½	31,500
50,000	6,000	9,845 17 8½	26,904	43,504	4,869 16 6	21,516
28,000	3,500	5,837 10 4¼	17,818	30,695	3,010 4 9	11,760
96,000	7,800	26,899 11 6¼	56,579	102,467	24,452 10 7½	46,200
34,000	3,500	11,804 9 6	19,627	42,016	6,418 4 9	7,950
7,600	800	1,435 8 8	3,661	5,998	1,053 14 3	3,730
38,000	4,500	9,874 9 3	27,471	45,586	4,560 5 3	13,375
28,000	3,000	10,927 7 0	26,278	42,120	3,831 17 3	7,150
85,000	9,000	31,133 9 2	45,900	106,462	17,806 17 6	30,263
60,000	6,000	11,160 18 7½	28,557	60,419	14,691 15 0	13,173
96,000	8,000	19,635 9 8½	47,537	88,797	20,609 17 0	25,750
36,000	3,500	34,234 1 10½	40,610	88,685	10,808 1 3	15,600
52,000	5,000	7,730 10 1½	23,451	52,617	10,914 15 9	18,720
36,000	4,000	11,639 3 10	22,700	38,148	5,771 8 9	9,800
36,000	3,500	12,793 10 1½	24,440	39,455	6,158 15 3	10,640
54,000	7,000	10,679 8 8½	27,418	57,542	11,704 19 0	18,240
6,000	600	2,322 16 1	6,691	20,065	547 1 4½	1,890
116,000	12,000	52,286 19 8½	121,052	174,202	19,030 16 0	26,150
109,800	10,500	26,431 18 4	77,921	127,751	9,766 7 0	33,753
140,000	20,180	140,358 13 2	111,215	365,568	54,831 9 0	56,380
2,000,400	206,980	694,476 2 5¾	1,319,215	2,563,527	403,159 17 5	665,362
626,000	57,800	184,520 19 5¼	335,543	684,950	134,172 12 6	214,122
1,234,400	129,000	369,596 9 10½	872,457	1,513,009	214,155 15 11	394,860

The 6th aid upon land was by a pound rate of 4*s.* in the pound. In this Act the assessors are not upon oath, 4 Gul. and Mar.

The 7th aid upon land is by the same pound rate and the assessors are upon oath, 5 Gul. and Mar.

In order to shew what proportion each part of the kingdom bears in the assessment, and in the pound rate, here is framed a table (No. I.) of 12 columns.

. . . The excise, and number of houses and hearths, are no ill measures to form a judgement by, of the trade, wealth, and abilities of a country.

Particularly Sir William Petty, who was esteemed the best computer we ever had, in all his political arithmetic, both for England and Ireland, did very much govern himself by the hearth money.

Some light may be also had in this matter from the late polls which have been in the kingdom.

The article of ship money shews how persons unconcerned did think each county ought to be rated.

The apportionment of 1660 makes it appear what was the opinion of a very able committee of the House of Commons upon this subject.

The aid of 1*s.* and 2*s.* in the pound, set down in the table, shews that a pound rate has raised more, in proportion, than it does at present; for if 3*s.* in the pound did raise 1,566,627*l.* 10*s.* 9½*d.*, 4*s.* in the pound ought to raise 2,088,836*l.* 14*s.* 4½*d.*

The poor rates, set down in the table, may be very useful to such as love computations, and who are inquisitive into the common business of the nation, and desirous to know its strength and weakness. It was collected with great labour and expense, by Mr. Ar. Mo. a very knowing person.

He had not the account of Wales, but according to the proportion Wales bears to the rest of the kingdom in other taxes, the poor rate there must have been about 33,753*l.* So that the poor rate, at that time, through the whole nation, was about 665,362*l.*

By the comparison of all these particulars, some light, peradventure, may be given, and computations made, that will a little help to the forming a right judgement, how all parts of the kingdom may be rated in a land tax, with somewhat more of equality.

But the observations and inferences, which shall be made from this table, are humbly submitted to such as take delight in calculations of this kind; and it is hoped such a scheme will set better judgements, and abler heads, to work upon a matter that deserves so well to be effectually considered.

All substantial merchants will acknowledge that stealing customs, and running goods, is against their common interest, because such as have that art are not upon an equal foot of trade with the rest.

In the same manner, where a tax is unequally levied, the gentlemen are not upon the same foot of maintaining their part, and providing for their families, which cannot consist with the public good.

From the table here set down, there may be made these observations:

1st, That it evidently appears several ways that the north and west, or the counties that lie towards the north and west, are at least two-thirds of England, reckoned without London, Westminster, and Middlesex.

2dly, That there is good ground to conjecture that the north and west, or the counties that lie towards the north and west, are near three-quarters of the kingdom, reckoned without London, Westminster, and Middlesex.

3dly, That from a general calculation of the whole, there seems good reason to believe that London, Middlesex, and Westminster, are not above one-tenth part of the kingdom.

In the excise on beer and ale, the north and west, compared with the 11 home counties, are as 554,117*l.* is to 184,520*l.* which is full two-thirds.

In the number of houses, the north and west, compared with the 11 home counties, are as 1,208,000 are to 335,543 houses, which is about three-fourths.

In the number of hearths, the north and west, compared with the 11 home counties, are as 2,197,959 to 684,950 hearths, which is much above two-thirds.

In the single poll, the north and west, compared with the 11 home counties, are as 208,030*l.* is to 69,428*l.* which is about two-thirds.

In the quarterly poll, the north and west, compared with the 11 home counties, are as 499,896*l.* is to 167,626*l.* which is about two-thirds.

In the assessment of ship money, the north and west, compared with the 11 home counties, are as 186,800*l.* is to 57,800*l.* which is full two-thirds.

In an assessment of two millions, according to the apportionment of 1660, the north and west, compared with the 11 home counties, would be as 1,860,400*l.* is to 626,000*l.* which is about two-thirds.

In the poor rates, the north and west, compared with the 11 home counties, are as 608,982*l.* is to 214,122*l.* which is near two-thirds.

So that it appears here plainly, by 8 different instances, the north and west are at least two-thirds of the kingdom, reckoned without London, Westminster, and Middlesex. According to which calculation, the monthly assessment, which runs thus:

The monthly assessment

	l.
North and western counties —— —— ——	946,118
The 11 home counties —— —— ——	529,615
London, Westminster, and Middlesex —— ——	175,969
Total	1,651,702

should run thus:

	l.
North and western counties —— —— ——	983,822
The 11 home counties —— —— ——	491,911
London, Westminster, and Middlesex —— ——	175,969
Total	1,651,702

So in the pound rate of 4*s.* in the pound, according to this calculation, if the 11 home counties, which are but one-third, raise 632,388*l.* the other two-thirds should raise 1,264,776*l.* And the pound rate, which runs thus:

				l.
North and western counties	——	——	——	1,038,184
The 11 home counties	——	——	——	632,388
London, Westminster, and Middlesex		——		307,140
	Total			1,977,712

should run thus:

				l.
North and western counties	——	——	——	1,264,776
The 11 home counties	——	——	——	632,388
London, Westminster, and Middlesex		——		307,140
	Total			2,204,304

But, all things duly considered, there seem very probable reasons to believe the north and west are three-fourths of the kingdom, reckoned without London, Middlesex, and Westminster.

For, as to the excise, all who know that revenue must grant that, in the north and west, the country in many parts is so wild, and the houses lie so dispersed, that the retailers cannot be so well watched as in the home counties, where the dealers are in a narrower compass, and have less opportunities to deceive the king's officers. More private families take their drink of the common brewers in the counties near London, than at a distance, which swells the excise of the home counties. Setting that aside, and if the revenue could possibly be as well watched in the distant parts as it is near London, the excise of the north and west would, probably, answer near three-fourths of the whole, without London, etc.

As to the polls, it is notoriously known that the payment for degrees and qualities of persons is by no means so narrowly looked after and exacted in the north and west, as in the home counties; and if it were, the poll money in the north and west would in all likelihood answer three-fourths of the whole, reckoned without London, etc.

As to the north and west bearing no higher a proportion in the poor rate than scarce two-thirds with the rest of England, there is, perhaps, this to be said, that in the distant parts provisions are cheaper; so they maintain their poor at an easier rate than in the counties near London.

In the north and west their manufactures afford employment to the poorer sort; and there are not so many there who live upon the charity of others, as near London, where luxury and idleness abound . . .

But the various ways of improving land are now of late years got into the northern and western counties; clover, sainfoin, trefoil, marl, and lime are particularly beneficial to countries that have great store of barren ground.

The north and west of late years have had a greater proportion of foreign trade than the home counties.

The use of sea coal in London has more than trebled of late years, which is a great advantage to the north.

The prohibition of Irish cattle is wholly beneficial to the northern and western counties, and has improved their land, and is hurtful to the rest of England.

Land seems to have been almost at the height of its improvement, and near the rack rent, about the year 1636, in the 11 home counties.

And in the north and west, it has been ever since improving; so that, in all probability, those counties, which were formerly rated as two-thirds, may now be esteemed and valued as three-fourths of the kingdom.

Upon the whole matter, the hearth money seems the best measure to form a judgement by, of the wealth of each country; and, by consequence, what proportion it ought to bear in any land tax.

For, from the number of houses, we may compute the people.

Where the numbers of people are, generally speaking, there are the manufactures, and consumption of home commodities; there is the wealth and trade; and there land improves, and rents are highest.

In the number of houses, the north and west are about three-fourths of the kingdom.

From whence, upon probable grounds, may be inferred that the north and west are three-fourths of the rents and value of England, still reckoning without London, etc.

And if so, and if the 11 home counties are but one-fourth part, the monthly assessment should run thus:

			l.	*s.*
North and western counties	——	——	1,106,799	18
The 11 home counties	——	——	368,933	6
London, Westminster, and Middlesex	——	175,969	12
		Total	1,651,702	16

And it likewise follows, that if in the pound rate of 4*s.* per pound, the 11 home counties, which are here reckoned but at one-fourth part of the kingdom, produced 632,388*l.*, then the north and west, which are three-fourths, should produce 1,897,164*l.*

And a pound rate of 4*s.* in the pound, throughout the whole kingdom, would be:

			l.
North and western counties	——	——	1,897,164
The 11 home counties	——	——	632,388
London, Westminster, and Middlesex	——	307,140
		Total	2,836,692

It may be seen, in the accounts of the Exchequer, that, in the ancient subsidies, the north and western counties have been all along favoured, and the reasons for it may be easily assigned. Worcestershire, Gloucestershire, Herefordshire, Shropshire, and Cheshire, were subject to the incursions of the Welsh. The 4 northern counties, and Yorkshire, were always to be upon their guard, against the inroads of the Scots. The western parts lay exposed to descents, and invasions of the French; so that the private and particular charge in their defence, which lay upon those counties more than others, might be a sufficient cause to give them ease in all public burthens.

The Parliament, 17 and 18 Car. 1 in their assessment of 400,000*l*., plainly took their measures from the ancient subsidies.

And with that assessment, Car. 1, agree the rates laid upon each county by the Commonwealth.

And what the north and west pay in the pound rate, and what is laid upon them in our present monthly assessment, seem to answer it exactly; all which may be seen by comparing the rates in the table upon each county.

But the equity and reason ceasing, which made our ancestors so favourable to them, and they enjoying the same common protection, and the public necessities requiring great sums of money; it seems but just and fair that they should neither favour themselves, nor oppose the being, in all taxes, upon an equal foot with the rest of the nation.

The last observation offered from the table is that London, Westminster, and Middlesex, are not above one-tenth part of the kingdom, which, if plainly made out, will clear a great many points, and very much confirm the calculation that has been made of what the north and west might raise in the pound rate ...

If 111,215 houses in and about London, with no more ground than what they stand upon, are, in rent, 1 million and a half per annum, it is hardly possible but that the 1,208,000 houses in the country, with all the land about them and all the benefits that attend land, must be in rent 13,500,000 per ann.

And whoever considers this seriously, will perhaps be inclined to think, that the 4*s*. aid would raise at least 3,000,000, if it were levied in other parts of England with the same care and exactness as it is in London, Westminster, and Middlesex, which are under the eye and influence of the government.

And if the aid could be brought to raise such a sum, the war would almost be maintained by the charge upon land only.

It is notoriously known that a great many persons, both in the assessment and aids, pay full one-fifth part of their estates; if the rest did so, all would be upon an equal foot; which, in justice and reason, the subjects of the same prince should be in every good government.

But this will be very hard to compass in that long possession many countries are in, of being favourably handled in all taxes ...

... What a pound rate of 4*s*. in the pound upon money might produce is very hard to compute because in that matter there is scarce any rule or measure to go by; but supposing money at interest to be one-sixteenth part (as some think) of the annual value and income of England, there is then 20,000,000 of money at interest (which may be and yet not one-third part of that sum in specie in the kingdom) and if there are 20,000,000, at interest at 5 per cent a pound rate of 4*s*. in the pound, upon money, would raise 200,000*l*.

That which has made quarterly polls so distasteful, is charging the poorer

sort; but if they were all exempted, a quarterly poll well levied might raise
500,000*l.*

And here it may not be amiss to take notice that if, in the pound rate upon
land, 1*s.* were taken off from the landlord, and placed upon the tenant, it
would ease those who have borne all the weight; nor can it seem oppressive
to the tenants, considering how well they have fared hitherto.

So that a mixed aid, by a pound rate upon land and money, and by a
quarterly poll, all carefully levied, might raise,

				l.
By 4*s.* pound rate upon land	—	—	3,000,000
By 4*s.* pound rate upon money	—	—	200,000
By a quarterly poll ——	——	——	——	500,000
		Total	3,700,000

Which, without any new ways and means, would come very near raising that
sum to which the expense of the war has hitherto amounted.

If in a war that is so expensive, and is thought so necessary for our preservation, all people would agree to promote equality, no doubt great sums
might be raised in this nation, and the country, in all aids, would be found to
answer as well as London.

That London, Westminster, and Middlesex, pay about one-sixth part in
the aid, is very plain; and that they are not above one-tenth part of the
kingdom's general rental, is very probable.

What proportion in other wealth and substance London bears to the rest of
England, is very hard to determine.

But some landed men will start up and say, it is true, London bears one-
sixth, it ought to bear one half, it has all the wealth; and the immoderate
growth of that city undoes and ruins all the country.

It may therefore be well worth the enquiry of thinking men, what truth
there is in this common and received notion, that the growth of London is
pernicious to England; that the kingdom is like a rickety body, with a head
too big for the other members.

For some people, who have thought much upon this subject, are inclined to
believe that the growth of that city is advantageous to the nation, and they
seem to ground their opinion upon the following reasons:

That no empire was ever great, without having a great and populous city.

That the Romans drew all the conquered cities of Italy into Rome.

That the people of Attica were no better than a crew of rude herdsmen;
and neither flourished in war, nor in civil arts, till Theseus persuaded them to
inhabit Athens.

That the greatness of London will best preserve our constitution, because,
where there is a great and powerful city, the prince will hardly enterprise
upon the liberties of that people; in the same manner, a rich and powerful
city seldom rebels upon vain and slight occasions.

On these grounds, and many others, some people are led to think the growth of London not hurtful to the nation; but, on the contrary, to believe that there is not an acre of land in the country, be it never so distant, that is not in some degree bettered by the growth, trade, and riches of that city.

Perhaps, if all the wealth and substance of London could be truly rated in a tax of 4,000,000, that city would pay one-fourth part without any hardship to it.

But, probably, there is nothing but excises that will truly and equally rate all sort of wealth and substance, and bring in all sort of persons, chiefly those in great cities, to contribute in the public burthens.

We have now gone through the chief ways and means, hitherto made use of, for carrying on the present war, in which an impartial land tax is chiefly recommended, as most agreeable to the ancient constitution of this kingdom.

If it shall be thought expedient to go by the way of a monthly assessment, the apportionment of 1660 seems a more equal distribution of the common burthen, than has been as yet made use of; according to which, the home counties would pay as they do now; London, Westminster, and Middlesex, may be rated at the sum they have paid in the aid of 4s. in the pound.

And the assessment would run thus:

	l.	*s.*	*d.*
Northern and western counties —— ——	1,234,400		
The 11 home counties—— —— ——	626,000		
London, Westminster, and Middlesex ——	307,140	8	5¼
Total	2,167,540	8	5¼

A far larger sum might indeed be produced by a pound rate, equally and impartially levied through the whole kingdom.

But some will object that to levy a pound rate strictly, by commissioners of the king's naming, may occasion oppression and discontents in the country; and that such a method of raising taxes may create so many officers among the best of the gentry dependent upon the court, as may be dangerous to liberty.

Besides, the northern and western counties, especially such as lie most distant, will affirm that, out of the same value in estates, they are not able to pay the same pound rate, because their rents are not so well paid; their returns and markets are not so quick; and they taste not that benefit of trade, and greatness of London, in the same degree as the home counties.

It may be likewise objected that land taxes in general (and chiefly if strictly levied) must be very ruinous to the gentry, if the war should continue for any long time.

And since, to a wise and virtuous prince, no sum of money can be desirable that is levied with the oppression and discontent of his people, it may not be amiss to enquire, what other ways there are of supplying the war, which may be more easy to the nation.

Excises have had an ill repute with such as have not thoroughly weighed and compared them with other taxes; but however, it may not be improper to examine a little into the nature of such a fund of revenue, to what degree it would supply the war, and how far it may be consistent with the safety of our constitution.

10. SOME AGRICULTURAL STATISTICS
BY GREGORY KING, 1697
[Bodleian Library, Oxford, MS. Rawlinson D, 924, no. 73, f. 430]

MISCELLANEA

As to ploughing I observed that 26 furrows made 8 yards in breadth. $8 \times 36 = 288$ inches which divided by 26 is near 11 inches each furrow, and they drove at about a mile and a $\frac{1}{2}$ or a mile and $\frac{3}{4}$ per hour.

At about 11 inches furrow, 3 yards and $\frac{1}{4}$ in length, makes a yard square. $4840 \times 3\frac{1}{4} = 15,730$ yards and so many yards in length makes an acre, or near 9 mile, which at 1 mile and a $\frac{1}{2}$ per hour is near 6 hours ploughing each acre, but at 1 mile $\times \frac{3}{4}$ per hour is about 5 hours per acre, and ploughing 7 hours, viz. from 7 to 2 or from 8 to 3 is an acre and a $\frac{1}{4}$ or an acre and a half per diem.

Thus 9 millions of arable acres having *communibus annis* 2 ploughings each including the fallow year makes each year 18 millions of acres of ploughing and 12 or 14 millions of days work, or at a medium 13 millions of days work. And allowing that each plough may work 80 days per annum, then the number of ploughs for tillage is 162,500 ploughs or at 85 or 86 days each 150,000 ploughs. Each plough ploughing 120 acres per annum singly or 60 acres per annum at 2 ploughings each. But supposing one-fifth part of three ploughings besides be performed by hired ploughs, then the number of plough teams is but 120,000 which at 3 horses to each team is 360,000 horses. And allowing 1 draught ox to 6 horses is, moreover, 60,000 oxen employed in draught, whereof 100,000 living upon their own estates. And that the farmers are about 60,000. In all 160,000. If then there be in England 140,000 freeholders, each freeholder one with another may have in his own hands about 50 acres of arable or 5 millions of acres, and each farmer about 66 acres, or 4 millions of acres, and one with another somewhat above 56 acres. That the lands may be thus occupied: 100,000 freeholders and farmers using their own teams at 75 acres in common: 7,500,000 [acres]; 60,000 freeholders and farmers hiring their teams at 25 acres in common: 1,500,000; [total] 9,000,000 [acres].

Gloucester City contains about 1,120 houses and about 4,750 souls and is in proportion to Lichfield as 19 to 12. And is somewhat more than the hundredth part of London in houses and somewhat less than the 100th part of London in people.

1697, July 21. Informed on the road that 9 pecks of wheat will sow a statute acre and 8 of rye.

That 4 bushels or $4\frac{1}{2}$ of barley will sow a like acre.

That the best land takes up the most seed corn.

That 20 bushels or three quarters of winter corn is a good crop on good land.
That there is common field land about Wallingford of 20*s*. per acre neat.
But that ordinarily common field land in those parts is about 5*s*. or 5*s*. 6*d*.
per acre.
That they ordinarily plough about an acre and a ¼ per diem, it being hard land
when they plough but an acre.
That barley yields a greater increase than winter corn by about a 4th.
That there has been (but it was prodigious) 7 quarters of wheat produced
from an acre.
That it was extraordinary to have 4 quarters per acre yet that has been
produced in a field of several acres *puta* 20.
[July] 22. Informed at the Lamb at Abingdon by Mrs. Ely, where the
Collectors of the Excise keep their sitting, that a neighbour, one Hodgkins
or Potkins or such a name, a great maltster, paid 500*l*. for his stock of malt at
6*d*. per bushel and gave security to pay 200*l*. more. He is an Anabaptist but
a very rich man. Formerly he used to preach. He was at first only a leather
bottlemaker, and once as he was preaching, some Oxford scholars came into
his Congregational barn and began the song—I wish in heaven his soul may
dwell that first invented the leather bottle.

11. CHARLES DAVENANT DRAWS CONCLUSIONS FROM GREGORY KING'S FIGURES ON THE PRODUCE OF AGRICULTURE, 1699

[The Political and Commercial Works of Charles d'Avenant
relating to the Trade and Revenue of England, ed. Sir
C. Whitworth, London, 1771, II, pp. 220–9]

An Essay upon the probable methods of making a people gainers in the balance of trade

[In the preceding pages of this essay, Charles Davenant enumerated Gregory
King's figures on the use of land in the kingdom, and the produce and value
of arable and livestock. See above, pp. 779, 782–3.]
FROM these schemes we shall make such observations as we think may relate
to our present subject.

Of the 39 millions of acres in territory belonging to England, he lays down
that there may be above a fourth part, viz. 10 millions of acres in heaths,
moors, mountains, and barren land; three millions of acres in woods and
coppices, and three millions in forests, parks, and commons. This division
of the land seems to be made with great judgement: first, because it agrees
very well with the consumption of several commodities, of which we can
come at a near knowledge by the exercises now in being. Secondly, it corre-
sponds exactly with that increase in the kingdom's general rental, which, for
these last hundred years, may have been observed from the produce of divers
land taxes, and from several other particulars.

And there are undeniable reasons to be given, that this general rental, *anno* 1600, did not exceed six millions per annum but through the help of that wealth which has flowed in to us by our foreign trade, it has advanced in several periods of time from six to eight, from eight to ten, and from 10 to 14 millions per annum. When the general rental was but six millions per annum there was a great deal more barren land; of that which was cultivated, very much was capable of melioration; and there were more forests, woods, coppices, commons, and waste ground, than there is now, which our wealth did enable us from time to time to enclose, cultivate, and improve.

And for the future, as we grow in riches, and as our people increase, those many millions of acres which now are barren, will by degrees most of them be improved and cultivated; for there is hardly any sort of ground which numbers of men will not render fertile . . .

As to our quantity of land, in relation to its inhabitants, as the case stands, we seem now to have about $7\frac{1}{4}$ acres per head; but there are many reasons to think that England is capable of nourishing double its present number of people, which supposing them now to be 5,500,000, would be 11 millions, and even then there will be as many acres per head as they have in Holland. And when we have this complement of men, either in the natural course of time, or sooner, by the help of good conduct, we shall be in a state of power to deal with any strength in Europe. In the natural course of time this cannot happen in a great while, but the common progression of things may be hastened by art, so that if we are studious to preserve and increase our people, peradventure in not many years, we may have hands enough, not only to make us safe from the insults of others, but to render us formidable to all our neighbours . . .

The value of the wheat, barley, and rye, necessary for the sustenance of England, amounts at least to six millions of pounds per annum at the common rate; from whence it is apparent, that if a long dearth should happen here, such as they lately had in France, though we may be supplied upon more easy terms than France was, and though we might still keep our people alive, yet that a disaster of this kind would exhaust more of our money than a war of ten years' continuance. Suppose (which God forbid) that, for two or three years successively, the season should prove so bad as to deprive us of half our usual crop; to supply such a want, what immense sums must be carried out of the kingdom? And it may be made evident, that such a scarcity did very much drain the French.

To provide against a calamity of the like nature, is no doubt of the highest consequence. That we have been deficient in this point of polity is too notorious, though providence has taken more care of us than a negligent people deserve. However, we have had outrageous famines in England, and in Edward III's reign, corn did once rise to 13 times the common value; this, indeed, can hardly happen again, because there are more different sorts of soils improved and manured now than in that age; but at several times we have suffered wants of this kind very afflicting, and some time or other our negligence in a matter of such concern to the people's welfare may come to be more severely punished.

By the best accounts we are able to procure, from such as have looked into these things, we find that in England, in a plentiful year, there is not above five months' stock of grain at the time of the succeeding harvest, and not above four months' stock in an indifferent year, which is but a slender provision against any evil accident. We enjoy the benefit of such different soils, viz. high lands and low lands, where one hits when the other fails, and nowadays we seldom see corn above treble its common rate, which however would be fatal, if it should at any time continue so long as to make large supplies from abroad necessary to us. It is observed, that but $\frac{1}{10}$ defect in the harvest may raise the price $\frac{3}{10}$ths, and when we have but half our crop of wheat, which now and then happens, the remainder is spun out by thrift and good management, and eked out by the use of other grain; but this will not do for above one year, and would be a small help in the succession of two or three unseasonable harvests; for the scarcity even of one year is very destructive, in which many of the poorest sort perish, either for want of sufficient food, or by unwholesome diet.

We take it, that a defect in the harvest may raise the price of corn in the following proportions:

Defect raises the price above the common rate.

1 tenth	3 tenths
2 tenths	8 tenths
3 tenths	1·6 tenths
4 tenths	2·8 tenths.
5 tenths	4·5 tenths.

So that when corn rises to treble the common rate, it may be presumed that we want above $\frac{1}{3}$rd of the common produce; and if we should want $\frac{5}{10}$ths, or half the common produce, the price would rise to near five times the common rate.

We dwell the longer upon this subject, being convinced in judgement that nothing in the world can more impoverish a country, nor tend more to set it back with other people in the balance of trade for a long while, than such a calamity; it is indeed the scourge of God; but improvident states are more liable to it than wiser nations.

The Hollanders cannot nourish their people from their territory, and must always seek for assistance from abroad; but in prospect that the harvest may be bad now and then, in some, and even in all those places from whence they fetch their corn, whereby in scarce times they would be imposed upon, they take care to have granaries and storehouses, where in plenty years they lay up vast quantities of all sorts of grain against a dearer season; by which good and prudent economy, those dearths which in their turn have afflicted most other countries, fall but lightly upon their common people . . .

It may therefore be worth the consideration of such as study the good of England, whether it would not be advisable, and for the public welfare, to settle a fund for erecting in every county granaries capable of containing such a quantity of corn as may nourish the people for a certain time, upon any emergent occasion, and as may hinder us at all times from purchasing at a dear rate our own product from our more wary neighbours . . .

It would likewise be very advisable to review the ancient laws concerning corn, for they no ways square with the present numbers of our people, nor with the growth of London, and indeed ought to be more adapted to many other circumstances of the times we now live in . . .

We have looked into Mr. King's computation of the corn, because it should be the fundamental care of a good government to provide that the people never want it, for two or three years' defect there pulls down whatever the merchant has been doing for a long time.

As to his estimate of our livestock in cattle, many conclusions perhaps useful may be formed from it, which we omit as fearing to be too voluminous. We shall only observe, that it seems more the national interest of England to employ its land to the breeding and feeding of cattle, than to the produce of corn; for, as Mr. Fortrey has well noted,[1] 'The profit of one acre of pasture in the flesh, hide, and tallow of an ox, or in the flesh, wool, and tallow of a sheep, or in the carcase of a horse, is of so much greater value abroad, than the like yield of the earth would be in corn; that the exportation of this nation might be at least double to what it is, if rightly disposed.'

It is true, in these matters men are apt to follow what they think their particular profit, but the influence of good laws would go a great way towards inclining them more to pursue what is for the general advantage; and indeed the private concerns of men should be always made subservient to the public interest.

[1] S. Fortrey, *England's Interest and Improvement* . . ., Cambridge, 1663, p. 15.

INDEX